HOLT

FLORIDA

Elements of LITERATURE

Introductory Course

Kylene Beers

Carol Jago

Deborah Appleman

Leila Christenbury

Sara Kajder

Linda Rief

HOLT, RINEHART AND WINSTON

Acknowledgments and other credits appear on pages 926-931, which are an extension of the copyright page.

Printed in the United States of America

ISBN 978-0-03-099303-9
ISBN 0-03-099303-2

1 2 3 4 5 048 10 09 08

Program Authors

Kylene Beers is the senior program author for *Elements of Literature*. A former middle school teacher, she is now Senior Reading Advisor to Secondary Schools for Teachers College Reading and Writing Project at Columbia University. She is the author of *When Kids Can't Read: What Teachers Can Do* and co-editor (with Linda Rief and Robert E. Probst) of *Adolescent Literacy: Turning Promise into Practice*. The former editor of the National Council of Teachers of English (NCTE) literacy journal *Voices from the Middle*, Dr. Beers is the NCTE vice-president and will assume the presidency in 2008. With articles in *English Journal, Journal of Adolescent and Adult Literacy, School Library Journal, Middle Matters,* and *Voices from the Middle,* she speaks both nationally and internationally as a recognized authority on struggling readers. Dr. Beers has served on the review boards of *English Journal, The ALAN Review,* the Special Interest Group on Adolescent Literature of the International Reading Association, and the Assembly on Literature for Adolescents of the NCTE. She is the 2001 recipient of the Richard W. Halley Award given by NCTE for outstanding contributions to middle school literacy.

Carol Jago is a teacher with thirty-two years of experience at Santa Monica High School in California. The author of nine books on education, she continues to share her experiences as a writer and as a speaker at conferences and seminars across the country. Her wide and varied experience in standards assessment and secondary education in general has made her a sought-after speaker. As an author, Ms. Jago also works closely with Heinemann Publishers and with the National Council of Teachers of English. Her long-time association with NCTE led to her June 2007 election to a four-year term on the council's board. During that term she will serve for one year as president of the council. She is also active with the California Association of Teachers of English (CATE) and has edited CATE's scholarly journal *California English* since 1996. Ms. Jago served on the planning committees for the 2009 NAEP Reading Framework and the 2011 NAEP Writing Framework.

Deborah Appleman is professor and chair of educational studies and director of the Summer Writing Program at Carleton College in Northfield, Minnesota. Dr. Appleman's primary research interests include adolescent response to literature, multicultural literature, and the teaching of literary theory in high school. With a team of classroom teachers, she co-edited *Braided Lives,* a multicultural literature anthology. In addition to many articles and book chapters, she is the author of

Linda Rief, Kylene Beers, Eric Cooper Patrick Schwarz, and Carol Jago

Critical Encounters in High School English: Teaching Critical Theory to Adolescents and co-author of *Teaching Literature to Adolescents*. Her most recent book, *Reading for Themselves*, explores the use of extracurricular book clubs to encourage adolescents to read for pleasure. Dr. Appleman was a high school English teacher, working in both urban and suburban schools. She is a frequent national speaker and consultant and continues to work weekly in high schools with students and teachers.

Leila Christenbury is a former high school English teacher and currently professor of English education at Virginia Commonwealth University, Richmond. The former editor of *English Journal*, she is the author of ten books, including *Writing on Demand, Making the Journey*, and *Retracing the Journey: Teaching and Learning in an American High School*. Past president of the National Council of Teachers of English, Dr. Christenbury is also a former member of the steering committee of the National Assessment of Educational Progress (NAEP). A recipient of the Rewey Belle Inglis Award for Outstanding Woman in English Teaching, Dr. Christenbury is a frequent speaker on issues of English teaching and learning and has been interviewed and quoted on CNN and in the *New York Times, USA Today, Washington Post, Chicago Tribune*, and *US News & World Report*.

Leila Christenbury, Héctor Rivera, Sara Kajder, Eric Cooper, and Deborah Appleman

Sara Kajder, author of *Bringing the Outside In: Visual Ways to Engage Reluctant Readers* and *The Tech-Savvy English Classroom*, is an assistant professor at Virginia Polytechnic Institute and State University (Virginia Tech). She has served as co-chair of NCTE's Conference on English Education (CEE) Technology Commission and of the Society for Information Technology and Teacher Education (SITE) English Education Committee. Dr. Kajder is the recipient of the first SITE National Technology Leadership Fellowship in English Education; she is a former English and language arts teacher for high school and middle school.

Linda Rief has been a classroom teacher for twenty-five years. She is author of *The Writer's-Reader's Notebook* and *Inside the Writer's-Reader's Notebook, Seeking Diversity, 100 Quickwrites*, and *Vision and Voice* as well as the co-author (with Kylene Beers and Robert E. Probst) of *Adolescent Literacy: Turning Promise into Practice*. Ms. Rief has written numerous chapters and journal articles, and she co-edited the first five years of *Voices from the Middle*. During the summer she teaches graduate courses at the University of New Hampshire and Northeastern University. She is a national and international consultant on adolescent literacy issues.

Program Consultants

Mabel Rivera, Harvey Daniels, Margaret McKeown, and Isabel Beck

Isabel L. Beck is professor of education and senior scientist at the University of Pittsburgh. Dr. Beck has conducted extensive research on vocabulary and comprehension and has published well over one hundred articles and several books, including *Improving Comprehension with Questioning the Author* (with Margaret McKeown) and *Bringing Words to Life: Robust Vocabulary Instruction* (with Margaret McKeown and Linda Kucan). Dr. Beck's numerous national awards include the Oscar S. Causey Award for outstanding research from the National Reading Conference and the William S. Gray Award from the International Reading Association for lifetime contributions to the field of reading research and practice.

Margaret G. McKeown is a senior scientist at the University of Pittsburgh's Learning Research and Development Center. Her research in reading comprehension and vocabulary has been published extensively in outlets for both research and practitioner audiences. Recognition of her work includes the International Reading Association's (IRA) Dissertation of the Year Award and a National Academy of Education Spencer Fellowship. Before her career in research, Dr. McKeown taught elementary school.

Amy Benjamin is a veteran teacher, literacy coach, consultant, and researcher in secondary-level literacy instruction. She has been recognized for excellence in teaching from the New York State English Council, Union College, and Tufts University. Ms. Benjamin is the author of several books about reading comprehension, writing instruction, grammar, and differentiation. Her most recent book (with Tom Oliva) is *Engaging Grammar: Practical Advice for Real Classrooms,* published by the National Council of Teachers of English. Ms. Benjamin has had a long association and leadership role with the NCTE's Assembly for the Teaching of English Grammar (ATEG).

Eric Cooper is the president of the National Urban Alliance for Effective Education (NUA) and co-founder of the Urban Partnership for Literacy with the IRA. He currently works with the NCTE to support improvements in urban education and collaborates with the Council of the Great City Schools. In line with his educational mission to support the improvement of education for urban and minority students, Dr. Cooper writes, lectures, and produces educational documentaries and talk shows to provide advocacy for children who live in disadvantaged circumstances.

Harvey Daniels is a former college professor and classroom teacher, working in urban and suburban Chicago schools. Known for his pioneering work on student book clubs, Dr. Daniels is author and co-author of many books, including *Literature Circles: Voice and Choice in Book Clubs and Reading Groups* and *Best Practice: Today's Standards for Teaching and Learning in America's Schools.*

Ben Garcia is associate director of education at the Skirball Cultural Center in Los Angeles, California, where he oversees school programs and teacher professional development. He is a board member of the Museum Educators of Southern California and presents regularly at conferences in the area of visual arts integration across curricula. Prior to the Skirball, he worked with classroom teachers for six years in the *Art and Language Arts* program at the J. Paul Getty Museum. Recent publications include *Art and Science: A Curriculum for K–12 Teachers* and *Neoclassicism and the*

PROGRAM CONSULTANTS continued

Enlightenment: A Curriculum for Middle and High School Teachers.

Judith L. Irvin taught middle school for several years before entering her career as a university professor. She now teaches courses in curriculum and instructional leadership and literacy at Florida State University. Dr. Irvin's many publications include *Reading and the High School Student: Strategies to Enhance Literacy* and *Integrating Literacy and Learning in the Content Area Classroom*. Her latest book, *Taking Action: A Leadership Model for Improving Adolescent Literacy,* is the result of a Carnegie-funded project and is published by the Association for Supervision and Curriculum Development.

Victoria Ramirez is the interim education director at the Museum of Fine Arts, Houston, Texas, where she plans and implements programs, resources, and publications for teachers and serves as liaison to local school districts and teacher organizations. She also chairs the Texas Art Education Association's museum division. Dr. Ramirez earned a doctoral degree in curriculum and instruction from the College of Education at the University of Houston and an M.A.T. in museum education from George Washington University. A former art history instructor at Houston Community College, Dr. Ramirez currently teaches education courses at the University of Houston.

Héctor H. Rivera is an assistant professor at Southern Methodist University, School of Education and Human Development. Dr. Rivera is also the director of the SMU Professional Development/ESL Supplemental Certification Program for Math and Science Teachers of At-Risk Middle and High School LEP Newcomer Adolescents. This federally funded program develops, delivers, and evaluates professional development for educators who work with at-risk newcomer adolescent students. Dr. Rivera is also collaborating on school reform projects in Guatemala and with the Institute of Arctic Education in Greenland.

Mabel Rivera is a research assistant professor at the Texas Institute for Measurement, Evaluation, and Statistics at the University of Houston. Her current research interests include the education of and prevention of reading difficulties in English-language learners. In addition, Dr. Rivera is involved in local and national service activities for preparing school personnel to teach students with special needs.

Amy Benjamin, Ben Garcia, Robin Scarcella, and Judith Irvin

Robin Scarcella is a professor at the University of California at Irvine, where she also directs the Program in Academic English/English as a Second Language. She has a Ph.D. in linguistics from the University of Southern California and an M.A. degree in education-second language acquisition from Stanford University. She has taught all grade levels. She has been active in shaping policies affecting language assessment, instruction, and teacher professional development. In the last four years, she has spoken to over ten thousand teachers and administrators. She has written over thirty scholarly articles that appear in such journals as the *TESOL Quarterly* and *Brain and Language*. Her most recent publication is *Accelerating Academic English: A Focus on the English Learner*.

Patrick Schwarz is professor of special education and chair of the Diversity in Learning and Development department for National-Louis University, Chicago, Illinois. He is author of *From Disability to Possibility* and *You're Welcome* (co-written with Paula Kluth), texts that have inspired teachers worldwide to reconceptualize inclusion to help all children. Other books co-written with Paula Kluth include *Just Give Him the Whale* and *Inclusion Bootcamp*. Dr. Schwarz also presents and consults worldwide through Creative Culture Consulting.

UNIT INTRODUCTION WRITERS ON WRITING

UNIT 1 FICTION

Cynthia Kadohata

"Sometimes I feel like I was born with an ache in my heart, and later I found that the only way to soothe the ache was to read and write."

UNIT 2 NONFICTION

Russell Freedman

"Nonfiction books allow us to glimpse worlds different from our own, yet much the same."

UNIT 3 POETRY

Janet Wong

"Poems will do that to you. They'll grab hold of loose memories like a cowboy roping cattle, and the next thing you know, you're all tied up."

UNIT 4 DRAMA

Willie Reale

"[Dramatic Writers] try to see and hear a world that an audience will accept and believe in and then to tell a story in that world."

Critical Reviewers

Lisa Archibald
Pasco Middle School
Dade City, Florida

Melinda Bogart
Switzerland Point Middle School
St. Augustine, Florida

Kathryn Abbey Chwalisz
Glenridge Middle School
Orlando, Florida

Parniece Crawford
Lockhart Middle School
Orlando, Florida

Chrissy Cuenca
Winston Park K-8 Center
Miami, Florida

Donna Dekersky
Jeaga Middle School
West Palm Beach, Florida

Lisa Anne Flowers
Olympia High School
Orlando, Florida

Lynne Rowan Harris
Augusta Raa Middle School
Tallahassee, Florida

Ikema Morris
Rays of Hope School
Sanford, Florida

Michael Mullan
Alice B. Landrum Middle School
Ponte Vedra Beach, Florida

Jennifer Nzeza
Booker Middle School
Sarasota, Florida

Dr. Jane N. White
Alice B. Landrum Middle School
Ponte Vedra Beach, Florida

Dee Ambrose-Stahl
Ligonier Valley High School
Ligonier, Pennsylvania

Abigayl Brown
Valley Stream Memorial
Junior High School
Valley Stream, New York

Kim Brown
Buckeye Valley Middle School
Delaware, Ohio

Heather Dick
Amherst Junior High School
Amherst, Ohio

Sabrina R. Dorsey
General Ray Davis Middle School
Stockbridge, Georgia

Gloria Feather
Independence Middle School
Pittsburgh, Pennsylvania

Sandi Green
Swanson Middle School
Arlington, Virginia

Bobbi Ann Hammill
Elderton High School
Elderton, Pennsylvania

Pat Harris
Bryant Middle School
Bryant, Arkansas

Clifford Hartline
Harrison Middle School
Grand Rapids, Michigan

Carolyn Matthews
Memphis City Schools
Memphis, Tennessee

Patricia Mentgen
John P. Freeman Optional School
Memphis, Tennessee

Marcia Rosen
Independence Middle School
Pittsburgh, Pennsylvania

Shahara M. Ruth
Tucker Middle School
Tucker, Georgia

Donna Scheidt
Highland Middle School
Highland, Indiana

Patricia Sherman
Baldwin Middle School
Baldwin, New York

Laura Jeannine Simon
Princeton Community
Middle School
Cincinnati, Ohio

Jennifer Warford
Boone County Schools
Florence, Kentucky

FIELD-TEST PARTICIPANTS

Brandi Anzaldua
North Richland Middle School
North Richland Hills, Texas

Julie Bruce-Magee
Kathleen & Tim Harney Middle School
Las Vegas, Nevada

Cheryl Carter
Murchison Middle School
Austin, Texas

Marcie Chesin
Lake Bluff Middle School
Lake Bluff, Illinois

Wendy Clancy
Dodson Middle School
Rancho Palos Verdes, California

Cynthia Colson
Forest Middle School
Forest, Virginia

Michelle Dobelbower
North Richland Middle School
North Richland Hills, Texas

Kathy Dubose
Murchison Middle School
Austin, Texas

Janice Heller
Eisenhower Middle School
Oregon, Ohio

Barbara Henry
Smith Middle School
Beaumont, Texas

Ashley Highsmith
Austin Middle School
Beaumont, Texas

Karen Houser
Marsteller Middle School
Bristow, Virginia

Janice Ingersoll
Portsmouth Middle School
Portland, Oregon

Katrina James-Barone
Francisco Middle School
San Francisco, California

Krista Johnson
Becker Middle School
Las Vegas, Nevada

Monica Jordan
Murchison Middle School
Austin, Texas

Mary Klein
Liberty Middle School
Powell, Ohio

Carol Kubaska
Lehi Elementary School
Mesa, Arizona

Patty Martinez
Murchison Middle School
Austin, Texas

Craig May
Walker Middle School
Salem, Oregon

Beth Morse
Fairbanks Middle School
Milford Center, Ohio

Marjean Nielsen
Hornell Junior High School
Hornell, New York

Alma Alvarez Salazar
Webster Middle School
Los Angeles, California

Michael Sedlak
Justice Myron E. Leavitt Middle School
Las Vegas, Nevada

Diana Snyder
Charles A. Mooney Middle School
Cleveland, Ohio

Sandra Thomason
Liberty Middle School
Powell, Ohio

Contents in Brief

Sunshine State Standards: Benchmarks for each collection can be found in the full Table of Contents on pages A4, A6, A8, A10, A12, A14, A16, A18, and A20.

UNIT 1 Fiction

COLLECTION 1 • Forms of Fiction

COLLECTION 2 • Short Story: Plot and Setting

COLLECTION 3 • Short Story: Character

COLLECTION 4 • Short Story: Theme

UNIT 2 Nonfiction

COLLECTION 5 • Elements of Nonfiction

UNIT 1

Fiction

COLLECTION 1 Forms of Fiction

"We need to travel that road of danger and laughter, of mystery and understanding, which has always been the road of stories."
—**Joseph Bruchac**

What Do You Think? Why do we tell, read, and listen to stories? In what ways are stories important in *your* life?

Sunshine State Standards: Benchmarks

LA.6.1.5.1; LA.6.1.6.1; LA.6.1.6.2; LA.6.1.6.3; LA.6.1.6.4; LA.6.1.6.5; LA.6.1.6.6; LA.6.1.6.7; LA.6.1.6.8; LA.6.1.6.9; LA.6.1.6.10; LA.6.1.7.1; LA.6.1.7.2; LA.6.1.7.3; LA.6.1.7.4; LA.6.1.7.5; LA.6.1.7.7; LA.6.1.7.8; LA.6.2.1.1; LA.6.2.1.2; LA.6.2.1.4; LA.6.2.1.7; LA.6.2.1.10; LA.6.2.2.1; LA.6.2.2.2; LA.6.2.2.4; LA.6.2.2.5; LA.6.3.2.1; LA.6.3.3.2; LA.6.3.4.2; LA.6.3.4.4; LA.6.3.5.3; LA.6.4.2.1; LA.6.4.2.2; LA.6.4.2.3; LA.6.4.2.4; LA.6.4.3.1; LA.6.5.2.2; LA.6.6.2.2; LA.6.6.4.1; LA.6.6.4.2

Literary Selections

Comparing Texts

Informational Text Focus

Fiction

COLLECTION 2 Short Story: Plot and Setting

"You never find yourself until you face the truth." —**Pearl Bailey**

What Do You Think? How can discovering a tough truth help you gain a better knowledge of who you are as a person?

Sunshine State Standards: Benchmarks

LA.6.1.6.1; LA.6.1.6.2; LA.6.1.6.3; LA.6.1.6.5; LA.6.1.6.7; LA.6.1.6.8; LA.6.1.6.9; LA.6.1.6.10; LA.6.1.7.1; LA.6.1.7.2; LA.6.1.7.3; LA.6.1.7.5; LA.6.1.7.7; LA.6.1.7.8; LA.6.2.1.2; LA.6.2.1.3; LA.6.2.1.4; LA.6.2.1.5; LA.6.2.1.6; LA.6.2.1.7; LA.6.2.1.9; LA.6.2.1.10; LA.6.2.2.1; LA.6.2.2.2; LA.6.2.2.3; LA.6.2.2.4; LA.6.2.2.5; LA.6.3.1.1; LA.6.3.1.2; LA.6.3.1.3; LA.6.3.2.1; LA.6.3.2.2; LA.6.3.4.4; LA.6.3.4.5; LA.6.4.1.1; LA.6.4.1.2; LA.6.4.3.1; LA.6.5.2.2; LA.6.6.2.2; LA.6.6.4.1

Literary Selections

UNIT 1

Fiction

COLLECTION 3 Short Story: Character

"Always do right; this will gratify some people and astonish the rest."
—**Mark Twain**

What Do You Think? How do you know what the right thing to do is? What do you think motivates people to "do right"?

Sunshine State Standards: Benchmarks

LA.6.1.6.1; LA.6.1.6.2; LA.6.1.6.4; LA.6.1.6.6; LA.6.1.6.7; LA.6.1.6.8; LA.6.1.6.9; LA.6.1.6.10; LA.6.1.7.1; LA.6.1.7.2; LA.6.1.7.3; LA.6.1.7.5; LA.6.1.7.6; LA.6.1.7.7; LA.6.1.7.8; LA.6.2.1.1; LA.6.2.1.2; LA.6.2.1.4; LA.6.2.1.5; LA.6.2.1.7; LA.6.2.1.10; LA.6.2.2.2; LA.6.2.2.5; LA.6.3.3.1; LA.6.3.3.2; LA.6.3.4.3; LA.6.3.4.4; LA.6.3.4.5; LA.6.3.5.2; LA.6.4.1.1; LA.6.4.1.2; LA.6.4.2.1; LA.6.4.2.2; LA.6.4.2.3; LA.6.4.2.4; LA.6.4.2.5; LA.6.4.3.1; LA.6.5.2.1; LA.6.6.1.3; LA.6.6.4.1

Literary Selections

UNIT 1

Fiction

COLLECTION 4 Short Story: Theme

"In every conceivable manner, the family is link to our past, bridge to our future."
—Alex Hailey

What Do You Think? How do the people you consider family help you find your place in the world?

Sunshine State Standards: Benchmarks

LA.6.1.5.1; LA.6.1.6.1; LA.6.1.6.3; LA.6.1.6.5; LA.6.1.6.7; LA.6.1.6.9; LA.6.1.6.10; LA.6.1.6.11; LA.6.1.7.1; LA.6.1.7.3; LA.6.1.7.4; LA.6.1.7.5; LA.6.1.7.6; LA.6.1.7.8; LA.6.2.1.2; LA.6.2.1.3; LA.6.2.1.4; LA.6.2.1.5: LA.6.2.1.7; LA.6.2.1.9; LA.6.2.1.10; LA.6.2.2.1; LA.6.2.2.2; LA.6.2.2.4; LA.6.2.2.5; LA.6.3.1.2; LA.6.3.1.3; LA.6.3.2.1; LA.6.3.2.2; LA.6.3.2.3; LA.6.3.3.1; LA.6.3.3.2; LA.6.3.3.4; LA.6.3.4.1; LA.6.3.4.2; LA.6.3.4.3; LA.6.3.4.4; LA.6.3.5.2; LA.6.3.5.3; LA.6.4.1.1; LA.6.4.1.2; LA.6.4.2.3; LA.6.5.1.1; LA.6.5.2.2; LA.6.6.1.1; LA.6.6.1.2; LA.6.6.2.1; LA.6.6.3.2; LA.6.6.4.1

Literary Selections

UNIT 2

Nonfiction

COLLECTION 5 Elements of Nonfiction

"The biggest adventure you can ever take is to live the life of your dreams." —**Oprah Winfrey**

What Do You Think? In what ways is life an adventure? How can you make your dreams come true in life?

Sunshine State Standards: Benchmarks

LA.6.1.6.1; LA.6.1.6.3; LA.6.1.6.4; LA.6.1.6.7; LA.6.1.6.8; LA.6.1.6.10; LA.6.1.7.2; LA.6.1.7.3; LA.6.1.7.8; LA.6.2.1.2; LA.6.2.1.5; LA.6.2.1.7; LA.6.2.1.10; LA.6.2.2.2; LA.6.2.2.3; LA.6.2.2.4; LA.6.2.2.5; LA.6.3.1.1; LA.6.3.1.2; LA.6.3.1.3; LA.6.3.2.1; LA.6.3.2.2; LA.6.3.2.3; LA.6.3.3.1; LA.6.3.3.2; LA.6.3.4.1; LA.6.3.4.2; LA.6.3.4.3; LA.6.3.4.4; LA.6.3.4.5; LA.6.3.5.2; LA.6.3.5.3; LA.6.4.1.1; LA.6.4.1.2; LA.6.4.2.1; LA.6.4.2.2; LA.6.4.2.3; LA.6.4.2.5; LA.6.4.3.1; LA.6.5.2.2; LA.6.6.2.1; LA.6.6.2.2; LA.6.6.2.3; LA.6.6.2.4; LA.6.6.3.2; LA.6.6.4.1; LA.6.6.4.2

Literary Selections

UNIT 2

Nonfiction

COLLECTION 6 Persuasive Texts and Media

"How wonderful it is that nobody need wait a single moment before starting to improve the world." —**Anne Frank**

What Do You Think? What actions can individuals take to improve the world?

Sunshine State Standards: Benchmarks

LA.6.1.6.1; LA.6.1.6.3; LA.6.1.6.4; LA.6.1.6.6; LA.6.1.6.9; LA.6.1.6.10; LA.6.1.7.2; LA.6.1.7.3; LA.6.1.7.5; LA.6.1.7.7; LA.6.1.7.8; LA.6.2.2.2; LA.6.2.2.3; LA.6.2.2.4; LA.6.2.2.5; LA.6.3.1.1; LA.6.3.1.2; LA.6.3.1.3; LA.6.3.2.1; LA.6.3.2.2; LA.6.3.3.1; LA.6.3.3.2; LA.6.3.3.3; LA.6.3.3.4; LA.6.3.4.1; LA.6.3.4.2; LA.6.3.4.4; LA.6.3.4.5; LA.6.4.2.3; LA.6.4.2.4; LA.6.4.3.1; LA.6.4.3.2; LA.6.5.2.1; LA.6.5.2.2; LA.6.6.3.1; LA.6.6.3.2

Comparing Texts

UNIT 3

Poetry

COLLECTION 7 Elements of Poetry

"The best and most beautiful things in the world cannot be seen or even touched—they must be felt with the heart." —**Helen Keller**

What Do You Think? How can poetry help us appreciate "the best and most beautiful things in the world"?

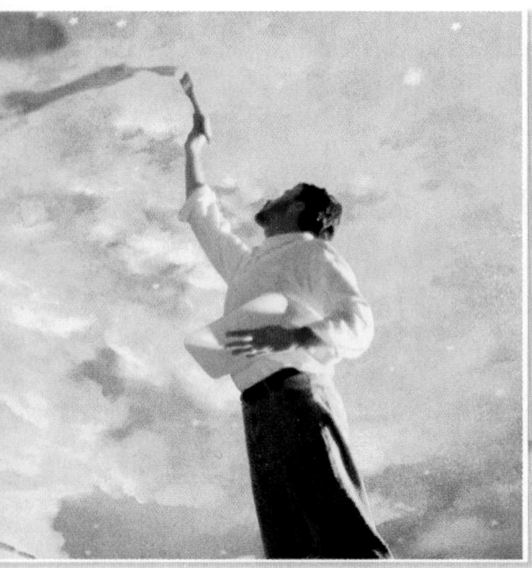

Sunshine State Standards: Benchmarks

LA.6.1.5.1; LA.6.1.6.1; LA.6.1.6.3; LA.6.1.6.4; LA.6.1.6.5; LA.6.1.6.6; LA.6.1.6.9; LA.6.1.6.10; LA.6.1.7.1; LA.6.1.7.2; LA.6.1.7.3; LA.6.1.7.7; LA.6.1.7.8; LA.6.2.1.1; LA.6.2.1.3; LA.6.2.1.4; LA.6.2.1.5; LA.6.2.1.7; LA.6.2.1.10; LA.6.2.2.3; LA.6.3.2.3; LA.6.3.3.1; LA.6.3.3.2; LA.6.3.3.3; LA.6.3.4.1; LA.6.3.5.2; LA.6.4.1.2; LA.6.4.2.3; LA.6.5.2.2

Literary Selections

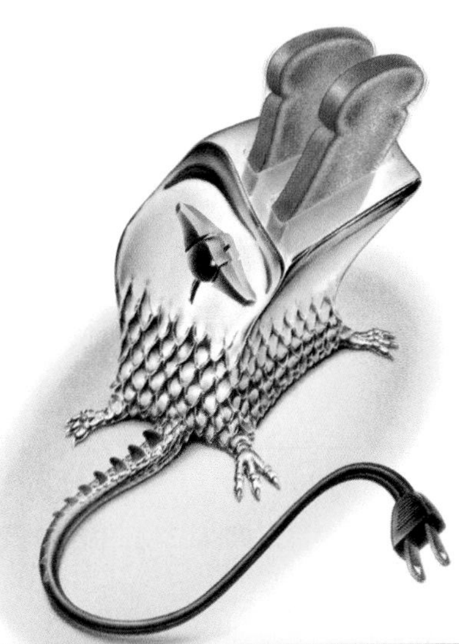

UNIT 4

Drama

COLLECTION 8 Elements of Drama

"Imagination is more important than knowledge. For knowledge is limited, whereas imagination embraces the entire world."

—Albert Einstein

What Do You Think? How can your imagination help you enter the fictional world of a play?

Sunshine State Standards: Benchmarks

LA.6.1.5.1; LA.6.1.6.1; LA.6.1.6.3; LA.6.1.6.4; LA.6.1.6.5; LA.6.1.6.7; LA.6.1.6.10; LA.6.1.6.11; LA.6.1.7.1; LA.6.1.7.3; LA.6.1.7.4; LA.6.1.7.5; LA.6.1.7.7; LA.6.1.7.8; LA.6.2.1.1; LA.6.2.1.2; LA.6.2.1.4; LA.6.2.1.5; LA.6.2.1.7; LA.6.2.1.8; LA.6.2.1.10; LA.6.2.2.4; LA.6.2.2.5; LA.6.3.1.1; LA.6.3.1.2; LA.6.3.1.3; LA.6.3.2.2; LA.6.3.2.3; LA.6.3.3.1; LA.6.3.3.2; LA.6.3.3.3; LA.6.3.3.4; LA.6.3.4.1; LA.6.3.4.3; LA.6.3.4.4; LA.6.3.5.1; LA.6.3.5.3; LA.6.4.1.1; LA.6.4.1.2; LA.6.4.2.3; LA.6.4.2.4; LA.6.5.2.1; LA.6.5.2.2; LA.6.6.2.1; LA.6.6.2.3; LA.6.6.3.1; LA.6.6.3.2

Selections by Alternative Themes

Selections are listed here in alternative theme groupings.

ANIMALS CAN TEACH US

DO THE RIGHT THING

FACING CHALLENGES, TAKING RISKS

FAMILY AND COMMUNITY

SELECTIONS BY ALTERNATIVE THEMES continued

FRIENDS, TOGETHER AND APART

GIFTS OF HERITAGE

LESSONS FROM THE PAST

THE LIGHTER SIDE OF LIFE

THE NATURAL WORLD

THE POWER OF LOVE

SELECTIONS BY ALTERNATIVE THEMES continued

WHAT IS A HERO?

THE WISDOM OF TRICKSTERS

WORLDS OF FANTASY

Skills, Workshops, and Features

SKILLS

LITERARY FOCUS ESSAYS BY LINDA RIEF

INFORMATIONAL TEXT FOCUS ESSAY BY LINDA RIEF

READING FOCUS ESSAYS BY KYLENE BEERS

LITERARY SKILLS

READING SKILLS FOR LITERARY TEXTS

READING SKILLS FOR INFORMATIONAL TEXTS

INFORMATIONAL TEXT SKILLS

VOCABULARY SKILLS

ACADEMIC VOCABULARY

LANGUAGE COACH

VOCABULARY DEVELOPMENT

WORKSHOPS

WRITING WORKSHOPS

PREPARING FOR FCAT WRITING+

LISTENING AND SPEAKING WORKSHOPS

FEATURES

ANALYZING VISUALS

CROSS-CURRICULAR LINKS

LITERARY PERSPECTIVES

GRAMMAR LINKS

STANDARDS REVIEW

LANGUAGE HANDBOOK

SPELLING HANDBOOK

COMMUNICATIONS HANDBOOK

MEDIA HANDBOOK

Why Be a Reader/Writer?

by **Kylene Beers**

ONCE UPON A TIME...

there were three bears—
Mama Bear... Papa Bear... and Baby Bear.
You've heard this story, right?

Goldilocks "visits" the Bear home while the family is out. She basically wrecks their place while searching for the food, chair, and bed that are *just right* for her. When the Bear family returns, Goldie runs off without even an "I'm-so-sorry" apology.

The Bears are left to clean up everything. End of story.

WHAT IS THE MESSAGE?

Isn't this an odd story to tell young children? What's it trying to teach them?

- Children can be more trouble than bears?
- Lock the door when we leave the house?
- Sometimes people might do things they know are wrong?

The message I like most is that we are all searching for the things that are just right for us. While I don't like the way Goldilocks went about getting those things, I do understand her need to find

the food,
the chair, and
the bed
that were ***just right***.

Goldilocks wanted things that fit her needs. Interestingly, as she grows and changes, those needs will change. She'll outgrow the ***just right*** chair. And the TOO BIG CHAIR will fit ***just right***.

You will find what is JUST RIGHT for you!

Puppies need special attention to the
You can't just feed a puppy anything

The Just Right! Reading/Writing Experience

When you read and write, you're often looking for the **just right** experience that fits your needs. This book gives you many opportunities to find out how a reading selection is **just right** for YOU. You'll read stories that make you say,

"I know exactly how that feels." OR

"That's just wrong. I don't agree with that." OR

"Wow! I'd never even thought about that!"

Finding how well a story fits YOU is what makes reading a **just right** experience for YOU.

If you look closely at all the writing assignments in this book—from the QuickWrites to Reader/Writer Notebook activities to essays—you'll see they have one thing in common:

They all help YOU explore
what YOU think and
how YOU feel
about what YOU read.

DISCOVER YOURSELF → DISCOVER YOUR THOUGHTS → DISCOVER YOUR FEELINGS → AND DISCOVER YOUR WORLD

All of these things are the **just right** part of being a reader/writer.

Sure, there are other good reasons to be a skillful reader and an effective writer—getting good grades, passing tests, getting into college. But the BEST reason—the **just right** reason—has to do with reading and writing to discover more about yourself and the world you live in.

So, let what you read and write this year act as a *mirror* that shows you more about yourself or a *window* that shows you worlds beyond where you live.

Whichever you do, you'll be discovering the reason that is **just right** for you.

Kylene Beers
Senior Author
Elements of Literature

How to Use Your Textbook

Getting to know a new textbook is like getting to know a new video game. In each case, you have to figure out how the game or book is structured and what the rules are. Knowing how your book is structured, you can be successful from the start.

UNIT 1

Fiction

Writers on Writing

Cynthia Kadohata

Japanese American author Cynthia Kadohata was born in Illinois and lived in several states as a child. In her books for adults and children, she often blends history, fiction, and her own memories to explore the lives of Asian Americans. Her children's book *Kira-Kira* was awarded the Newbery Medal in 2005.

Cynthia Kadohata on Fiction

"When I was a child I used to read everywhere: walking down the street, sitting in the bathtub, eating dinner. While I never thought I would become a writer, I think all the reading I did was training for the future. I believe nearly all writers are thus trained in childhood.

When I write fiction I have to "go into the zone," the way athletes do. Before I had a son, I could get into the zone by traveling through America by bus or train. Now that I have a son, I get into the zone by concentrating or by listening to music. Or I do light yoga to loosen up. Doing research for a novel also helps me a great deal when I'm stuck because interviewing people helps me go outside of myself and broadens my scope so I can keep writing. It's kind of a contradiction—I need to go outside of myself to reach deeper inside myself.

Sometimes I feel like I was born with an ache in my heart, and later I found that the only way to soothe the ache was to read and write. Other people may soothe the ache in other ways. I wanted to publish so badly I was like an animal in the intensity of the desire. To publish a book was to make a stand. My mother raised her kids to take a stand, to say what we believed, to develop the areas where we excelled, whether that was writing or understanding computers or raising kids. We could do anything we wanted, as long as we did our best. That may sound simple, but doing your best requires pushing yourself—pushing and pushing. Today my editor is the one who pushes me. I always think I can't do anything more with a manuscript, and she tells me not only that I can but also that I must. It's as if I'm running a marathon and get exhausted partway through, but she makes me go farther, faster, and better. It's a painful yet rewarding process, and I have no regrets."

Think as a Writer

Kadohata says she needs to "go into the zone" to write fiction. What does she mean? When—and how—do you "go into the zone"?

Writers on Writing 1

Writers on Writing

If you think about the authors of the selections in your book, you may think they are a rare breed, like astronauts or underwater explorers. **Writers on Writing** introduces you to authors whose stories, poems, plays, or articles began with experiences that were transformed by their words.

Collection Opener

What is the focus of each collection, or section of the book? What does the image suggest about what the collection will cover? On the right, you'll see a bold heading, that says "Plot and Setting" or "Character." These are the **literary skills** you will study in the collection. Also in bold type is the **Informational Text Focus** for the collection. These are the skills you might use when read a newspaper or web site. Keep the **What Do You Think?** question in mind as you go through the collection. Your answers may surprise even you.

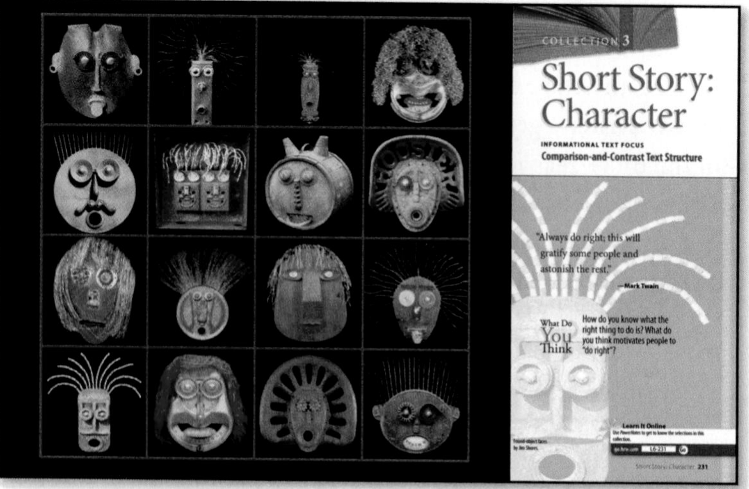

COLLECTION 3

Short Story: Character

INFORMATIONAL TEXT FOCUS

Comparison-and-Contrast Text Structure

"Always do right; this will gratify some people and astonish the rest."

—Mark Twain

What Do You Think

How do you know what the right thing to do is? What do you think motivates people to "do right"?

Learn It Online

go.hrw.com 16-231

Short Story: Character 231

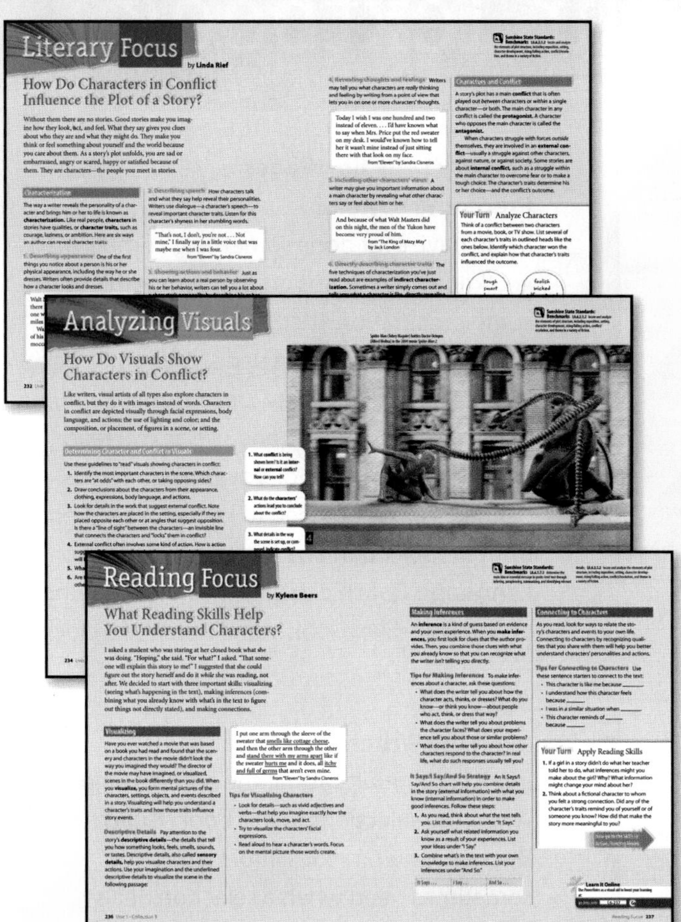

Literary Focus

Like a set of rules or a map, the **Literary Focus** shows you how literary elements work in stories and poems, helping you navigate through selections more easily. The Literary Focus will help you get to your destination—understanding and enjoying the selection.

Analyzing Visuals

Visuals are all around you: murals on buildings, magazine ads, or video-game graphics. Because you see images daily, you probably know quite a bit about analyzing them. **Analyzing Visuals** helps you apply these skills to understand the literary elements that drive the selections.

Reading Focus

Your mind is working all the time as you read, even if you're not aware of it. Still, all readers, even very good ones, sometimes don't understand what they've read. **Reading Focus** gives you the skills to help you improve your reading.

Reading Model

You tend to do things more quickly and easily if you have a model to follow. The **Reading Model** shows you the literary and reading skills that you will use in the collection so that you can learn them more quickly and easily.

Wrap Up

Think of **Wrap Up** as a bridge that gives you a chance to practice the skills on which the collection will focus. Wrap Up also introduces you to the collection's **Academic Vocabulary:** the language of school, business, and standardized tests. To be successful in school, you'll need to understand and use its language.

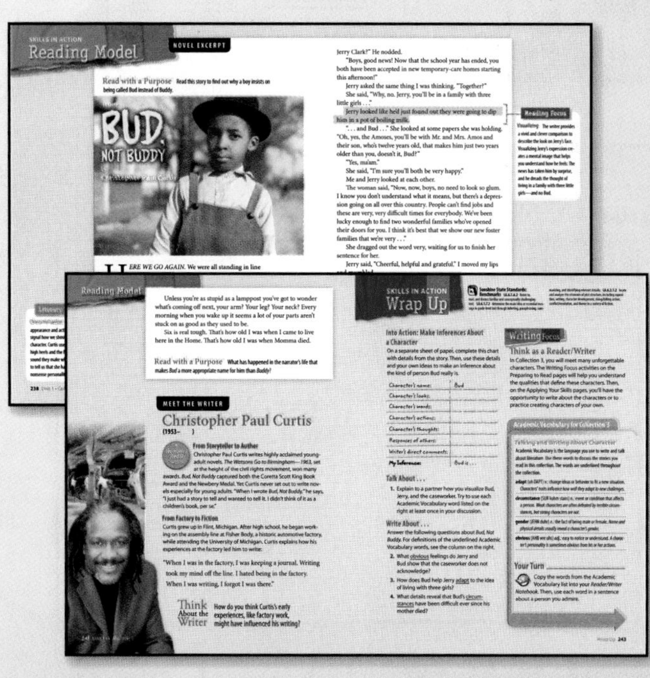

How to Use Your Textbook

Literary Selection Pages

Preparing to Read

If you have ever done something complicated, you know that things go more smoothly with some preparation. It's the same with reading. The **Preparing to Read** page gives you a boost by presenting the literary, reading, and writing skills you'll learn about and use as you read the selection. The list of **Vocabulary** words defines words you need to know for reading both the selection and beyond the selection. **Language Coach** explains the inner workings of English—like a look at the inside of a clock.

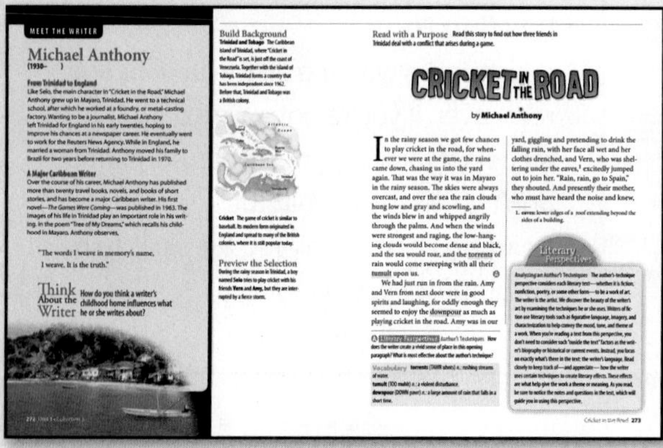

Selection

Meet the Writer gives you all kinds of interesting tidbits about the authors who wrote the selections in this book. **Build Background** provides information you sometimes need when a selection deals with unfamiliar times, places, or situations. **Preview the Selection** presents the selection's main character, like a movie trailer that hints at what is to come. **Read with a Purpose** helps you set a goal for your reading. It helps you answer the question, "What's the point of this selection?"

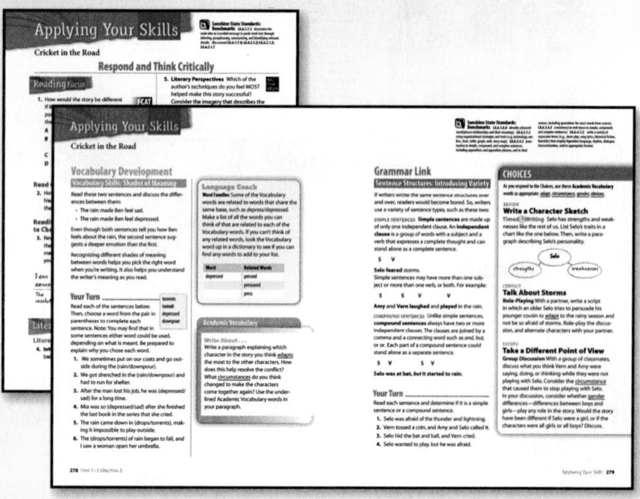

Applying Your Skills

If you have a special talent or hobby, you know that you have to practice to master it. In **Applying Your Skills,** you will apply the reading, literary, vocabulary, and language skills from the Preparing to Read page that you practiced as you read the selection. This gives you a chance to check on how you are mastering these skills.

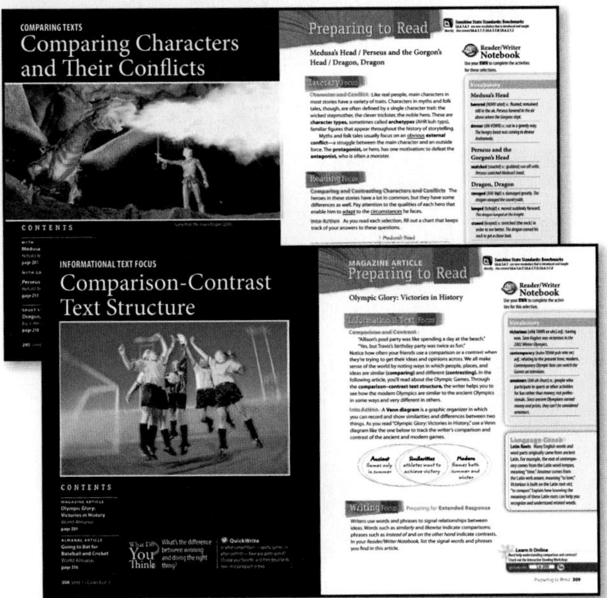
COMPARING TEXTS

Comparing Characters and Their Conflicts

Preparing to Read

Medusa's Head / Perseus and the Gorgon's Head / Dragon, Dragon

INFORMATIONAL TEXT FOCUS

Comparison-Contrast Text Structure

MAGAZINE ARTICLE

Preparing to Read

Olympic Glory: Victories in History

Comparing Texts

You probably compare people, places, and things all the time, such as a favorite singer's new songs with her previous album. In **Comparing Texts,** you will compare different works—sometimes by the same author, sometimes by different authors—that have something in common.

Informational Text Focus

If you've ever read a web site or followed a technical manual, you've been reading informational text. The skills you use in this type of reading are different than the ones you use for literary text. **Informational Text Focus** helps you gain the skills that will enable you to be a more successful reader in daily life and on standardized tests.

Practicing for FCAT

Do you dread test-taking time? Do you struggle over reading the passage and then choosing the correct answer? **Practicing for FCAT** can reduce your "guesses" and give you the practice you need to feel more confident during testing.

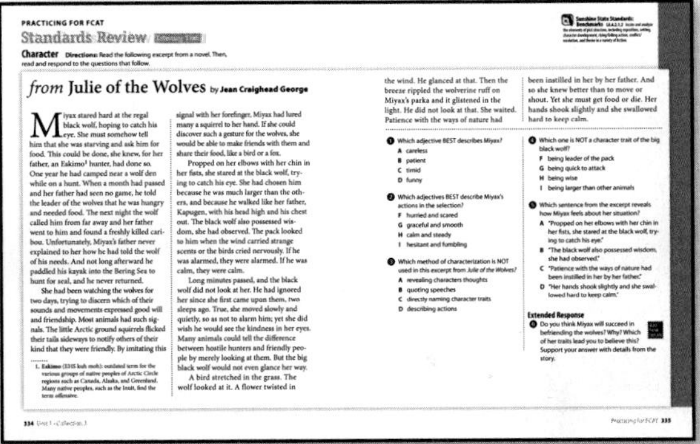
PRACTICING FOR FCAT

Standards Review

from Julie of the Wolves by Jean Craighead George

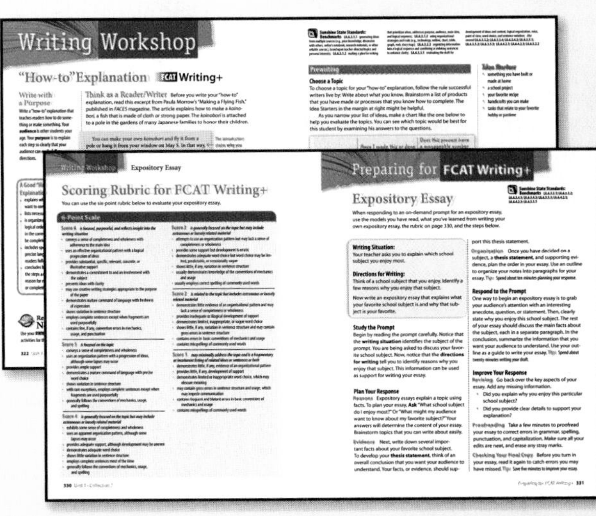
Writing Workshop

"How-to" Explanation

Scoring Rubric for FCAT Writing+

Preparing for FCAT Writing+

Expository Essay

Writing Workshop

Does a blank piece of paper send shivers up your spine? The **Writing Workshop** will help you tackle the page by showing you step-by-step through developing an effective piece of writing. Models, annotations, graphic organizers, and charts take the "What now?" out of writing for different purposes and audiences.

Preparing for FCAT Writing+

What's your idea of a nightmare? Maybe it's trying to respond to a writing prompt. **Preparing for FCAT+ Writing** helps you practice for on-demand, or timed, writing so that you can realize your dreams of success.

UNIT 1

Fiction

Writers on Writing

Cynthia Kadohata

Japanese American author Cynthia Kadohata was born in Illinois and lived in several states as a child. In her books for adults and children, she often blends history, fiction, and her own memories to explore the lives of Asian Americans. Her children's book *Kira-Kira* was awarded the Newbery Medal in 2005.

Cynthia Kadohata on Fiction

"When I was a child I used to read everywhere: walking down the street, sitting in the bathtub, eating dinner. While I never thought I would become a writer, I think all the reading I did was training for the future. I believe nearly all writers are thus trained in childhood.

When I write fiction I have to "go into the zone," the way athletes do. Before I had a son, I could get into the zone by traveling through America by bus or train. Now that I have a son, I get into the zone by concentrating or by listening to music. Or I do light yoga to loosen up. Doing research for a novel also helps me a great deal when I'm stuck because interviewing people helps me go outside of myself and broadens my scope so I can keep writing. It's kind of a contradiction—I need to go outside of myself to reach deeper inside myself.

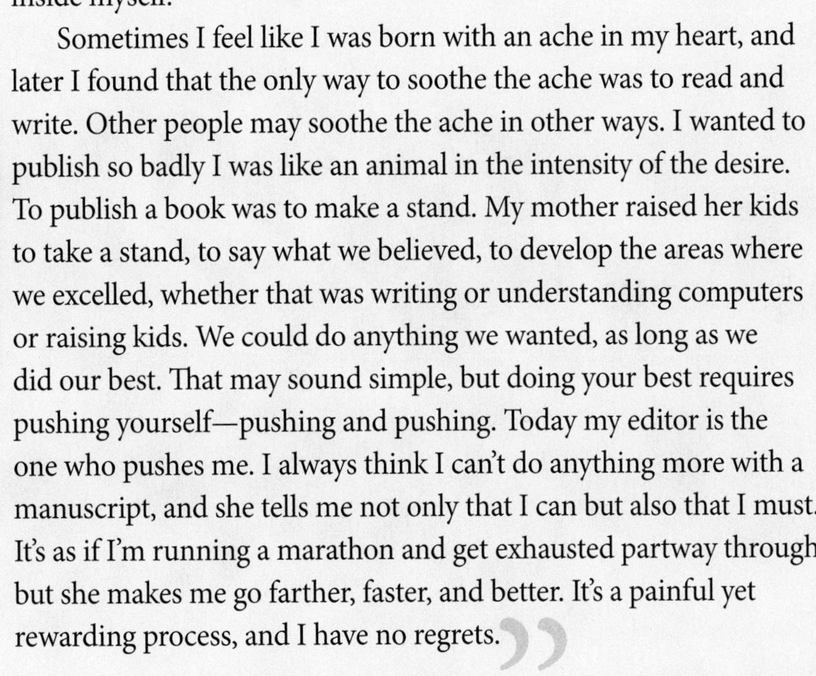

Sometimes I feel like I was born with an ache in my heart, and later I found that the only way to soothe the ache was to read and write. Other people may soothe the ache in other ways. I wanted to publish so badly I was like an animal in the intensity of the desire. To publish a book was to make a stand. My mother raised her kids to take a stand, to say what we believed, to develop the areas where we excelled, whether that was writing or understanding computers or raising kids. We could do anything we wanted, as long as we did our best. That may sound simple, but doing your best requires pushing yourself—pushing and pushing. Today my editor is the one who pushes me. I always think I can't do anything more with a manuscript, and she tells me not only that I can but also that I must. It's as if I'm running a marathon and get exhausted partway through, but she makes me go farther, faster, and better. It's a painful yet rewarding process, and I have no regrets."

Think as a Writer

Kadohata says she needs to "go into the zone" to write fiction. What does she mean? When—and how—do you "go into the zone"?

Collection 1

Forms of Fiction

INFORMATIONAL TEXT FOCUS

Structural Features of Media

"We need to travel that road of danger and laughter, of mystery and understanding, which has always been the road of stories."

—Joseph Bruchac

What Do You Think?

Why do we tell, read, and listen to stories? In what ways are stories important in *your* life?

Learn It Online

Learn more about fiction online at *NovelWise*:

go.hrw.com L6-3 Go 

Erosion (2000) by Jacek Yerka.

Literary Focus

by **Linda Rief**

What Are the Forms of Fiction?

Have you ever played the telephone game? The sentence that players start out with is usually not what the last person hears. Fiction writers play their own kind of telephone game. They start out with a "whisper in the ear"—an idea, image, feeling, or character. Then they ask the question "What if?"—and begin to play.

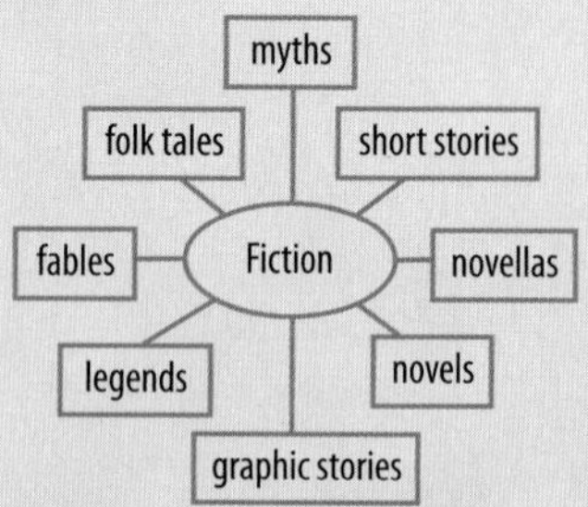

The Oldest Forms of Fiction

Why do people love **fiction—**made-up stories that are pure products of the imagination? Perhaps it's because fiction shows us something important about life. Fiction may not be factual, but what it reveals can be *true.*

The oldest forms of fiction come from forgotten or unknown storytellers who worked in the **oral tradition.** This body of cultural knowledge and wisdom has been passed down by word of mouth from generation to generation.

Myths and Epics Ancient peoples created stories called **myths** to explain their world, to answer such questions as these:

- Why is there day, and why is there night?
- What makes the seasons change?
- Why does death exist?

Characters in myths often appear in long stories called **epics—**tales about the deeds of heroes who possess qualities valued by their cultures.

> *"People of Uruk!"* cried Gilgamesh. "I go to the Forest of Cedar Trees. . . . There I shall do battle with Huwawa, the Evil One."
>
> from *Gilgamesh the Hero*
> by Geraldine McCaughrean

Fables A **fable** is a very brief "teaching tale" that presents a lesson about life, usually warning us about human weaknesses. Many fables end with a **moral,** a statement of the lesson they teach.

> If you let flattery go to your head, you'll pay the price.
>
> from "The Fox and the Crow" by Aesop

Folk Tales, Fairy Tales, Legends, and Tall Tales A **folk tale** is a fictional tale by an unknown, or anonymous (uh NAHN uh muhs), writer that has been passed down orally for generations. A special form of folk tale is the **fairy tale,** which often begins with the words "Once upon a time" and involves fantasy, a conflict between good and evil, and a happy ending. A **legend** is a folk tale or epic with some basis in historical fact, like tales of King Arthur. **Tall tales** are wild, exaggerated folk stories, often about legendary figures like Paul Bunyan. Most tales from the oral tradition have many different versions. There are hundreds of versions of "Cinderella" all over the world!

> "Better had let me tell you somethin," Bruh Rabbit said, "for I've seen Man, and I know him the real king of the forest."
>
> from "He Lion, Bruh Bear, and Bruh Rabbit"
> by Virginia Hamilton

Sunshine State Standards: Benchmarks LA.6.2.1.1 identify the characteristics of various genres (e.g., poetry, fiction, short story, dramatic literature) as forms with distinct characteristics and purposes.

Fiction Today

When people talk about fiction today, they are usually referring to short stories and novels. You can also experience fictional worlds in movies, TV shows, comic books, manga, video games, and other storytelling media. Readers often place fiction into specific categories, or **genres** (ZHAHN ruhz): mystery, romance, science fiction, historical fiction, adventure, fantasy, and so on.

Short Story A **short story** is just what it sounds like: a brief story about five to twenty pages long that you can read in one sitting. Short stories usually focus on one or two main characters, one main setting, and one main theme.

> Why did he raise his hand and volunteer? Why couldn't he have just sat there like the rest of the kids and not said anything?
>
> from "La Bamba" by Gary Soto

Novel A **novel** is a long fictional story, more than one hundred pages, that has more characters, settings, and themes than a short story. Because of a novel's length, its plot can be more complex, the characters and settings can be more detailed, and there can be more than one theme.

Novella Shorter than a novel but longer than a short story, a **novella** is often published with a collection of short stories or as a small book by itself.

> So my father slept. But that bothered me. I needed him awake. I was afraid of the dark and of the woods and of whatever lurked there.
>
> from *The Gold Cadillac* by Mildred D. Taylor

Other Forms of Fiction Fiction takes many other forms, too, and you'll find some of those forms in this book. **Plays** (or **dramas**), radio and television **scripts, narrative poems** (poems that tell a story), **graphic stories** and novels (illustrated stories told in comic-book style), and **comic strips** are all forms of fiction that writers use to entertain us—as well as give us new insights into our lives.

"Yo, novella!"

Your Turn Identify Forms of Fiction

1. Identify one myth, one folk tale, one short story, and one novel you are familiar with.
2. With a classmate, identify at least one example of each of these categories, or genres, of fiction: adventure, fantasy, romance, historical fiction, science fiction, mystery, horror. Explain your choices to the class.

Learn It Online
Explore forms of fiction with *PowerNotes* at:
go.hrw.com L6-5 Go

Analyzing Visuals

How Can Forms of Art Help You Understand Forms of Fiction?

Storytellers express themselves in many forms and for many purposes. Ancient storytellers presented their ideas in the form of myths, fables, folk tales, and epics. Modern storytellers use newer forms of fiction: the short story, novella, and novel. Just as all storytellers choose the form of fiction that best suits their purpose, visual artists also express themselves in different forms: drawings, paintings, photographs, mixed media, and sculptures.

Prehistoric horse painting in Lascaux Cave, France.

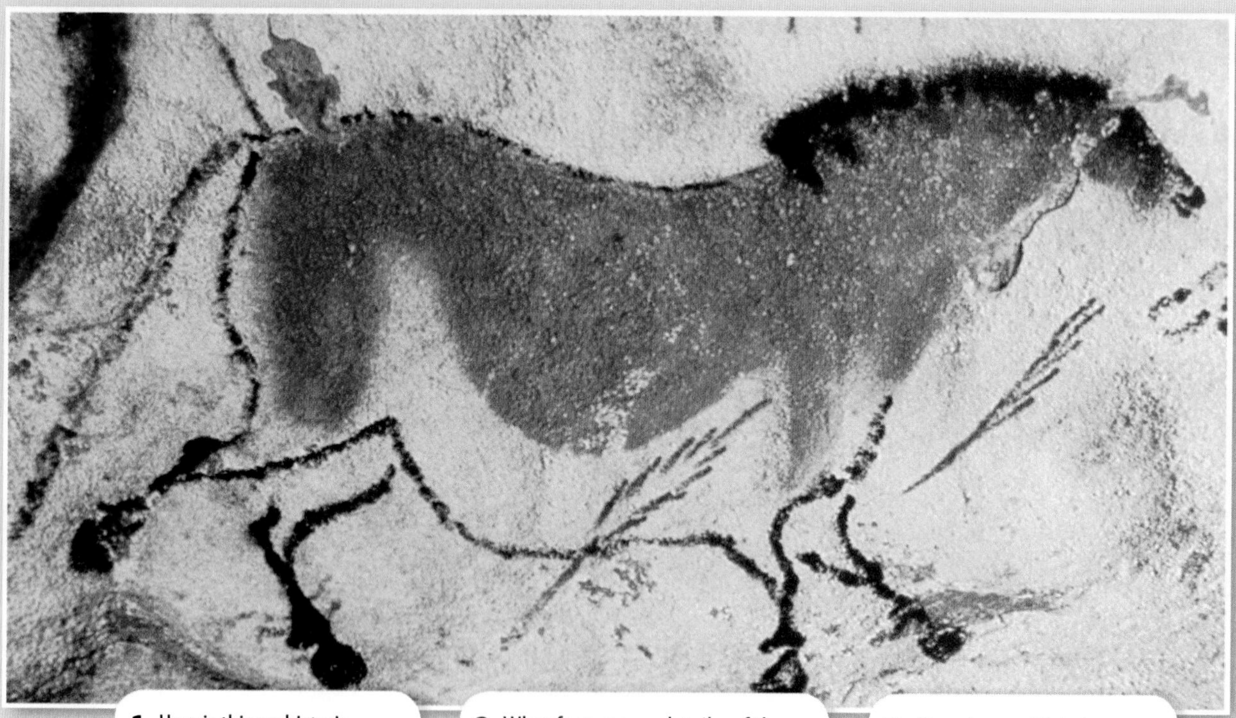

1. How is this prehistoric horse similar to or different from other images of horses you have seen?

2. What features, or details, of the horse seem especially important to this ancient artist? What might these features tell you about the purpose of the painting?

3. How do you think the artist felt about this horse?

Sunshine State Standards: Benchmarks LA.6.2.1.1 identify the characteristics of various genres (e.g., poetry, fiction, short story, dramatic literature) as forms with distinct characteristics and purposes.

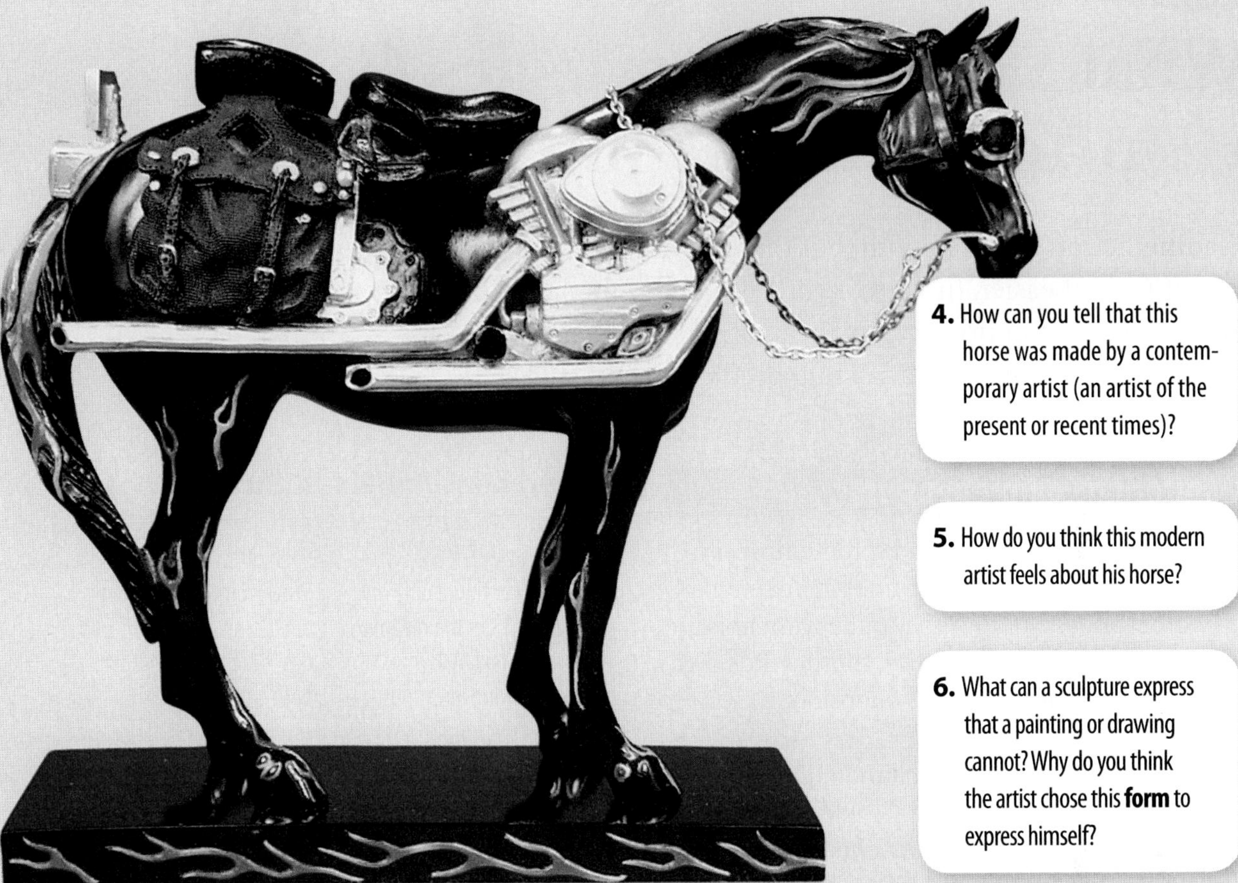

Motorcycle Mustang by David Losoya. The Trail of Painted Ponies, Inc.

4. How can you tell that this horse was made by a contemporary artist (an artist of the present or recent times)?

5. How do you think this modern artist feels about his horse?

6. What can a sculpture express that a painting or drawing cannot? Why do you think the artist chose this **form** to express himself?

Comparing Forms in Art

Use these guidelines to help you think about forms in art:

1. Ask yourself: Is the work a painting? a sculpture? something else?
2. Identify the subject of the art. How does the artist feel about the subject?
3. Try to determine the artist's purpose. Why do you think the artist chose this particular form to express his or her purpose?

Your Turn Write About Forms of Art

Write a paragraph about a work of art in this book that you especially like. Identify the form, state what you think the artist's purpose is, and explain why you think the artist chose that form to express his or her purpose.

Reading Focus

by **Kylene Beers**

What Skills and Strategies Can Help You Read Fiction?

Reading fiction should be fun, but that doesn't mean it's always easy. It can get easier, though, if you learn to apply these skills and strategies: monitoring comprehension, setting a purpose for reading, and making and adjusting predictions.

Monitoring Comprehension

Have you ever finished reading something, only to realize you can't say much about it? You read the words, but you didn't really get any meaning. The way to get meaning from all those words on a page is to monitor your comprehension.

Comprehension means "understanding." When you **monitor your comprehension,** you check to make sure you *really* understand what you're reading. The steps in the flowchart below show you how to stay focused and get meaning from a text:

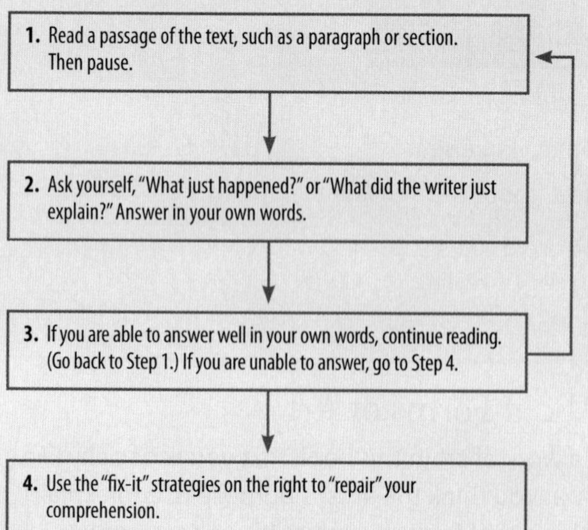

1. Read a passage of the text, such as a paragraph or section. Then pause.
2. Ask yourself, "What just happened?" or "What did the writer just explain?" Answer in your own words.
3. If you are able to answer well in your own words, continue reading. (Go back to Step 1.) If you are unable to answer, go to Step 4.
4. Use the "fix-it" strategies on the right to "repair" your comprehension.

Comprehension "Fix-It" Strategies

What Happened?	How Do I Fix It?
First, try to figure out why you didn't get the meaning from the text. Ask yourself the following questions:	When you've figured out what caused your difficulty, use these strategies to get back on track:
Did you **read too fast**?	**Read the passage again** more slowly and carefully.
Are there **unfamiliar words** in the passage?	Try to **figure out the meaning** of unfamiliar words. Use a dictionary if necessary.
Have **new ideas** been introduced?	Consult a **reference source,** such as an encyclopedia or trustworthy Web site, if there are ideas you don't understand.
Did you **forget key information** from earlier in the text?	**Re-read earlier passages** to refresh your memory about key details.

LA.6.1.7.1 use background knowledge of subject and related content areas, prereading strategies, graphic representations, and knowledge of text structure to make and confirm complex predictions of content, purpose, and organization of a reading selection; **LA.6.1.7.8** use strategies to repair comprehension of grade-appropriate text when self-monitoring indicates confusion, including but not limited to rereading, checking context clues, predicting, note-making, summarizing, using graphic and semantic organizers, questioning, and clarifying by checking other sources.

Setting a Purpose for Reading

When you read the latest book in your favorite fantasy series, you probably don't read it the same way you read your science textbook. Your main **purpose,** or reason, for reading the fantasy is to be entertained, so you will probably read it much more quickly than the textbook. The table below shows some general purposes for reading a few different types of texts.

Text	Purposes for Reading
Comic book	to be entertained
Science textbook	to gain information
Historical novel	to be entertained; to learn more about a historical period
Technical directions	to complete a task

When you **set a purpose** for reading, you're defining your specific reading goals and deciding what you, as a reader, need to do to meet those goals. Having a clear purpose in mind can help you choose texts to read and get the most out of them. Often, you will have multiple purposes for reading, and they may even change as you read.

Making and Adjusting Predictions

Have you ever figured out "whodunit" in a mystery novel before the truth was revealed? If so, you made a correct prediction. **Predictions** are educated guesses about what will happen next in a story. You make predictions based on a combination of prior knowledge (what you already know) and information in the text. When you get new information as you read, you may need to **adjust** the predictions you made earlier. Don't worry if your predictions aren't always correct—part of the fun of reading is being surprised, and a good writer will often surprise you.

A Model for Predicting Read the excerpt below from Gary Soto's story "La Bamba." Notice how a reader might make and later have to adjust a prediction. You'll have to read the selection yourself to see if this reader was correct.

> Manuel thought they had a great talent show. The entire school would be amazed. His mother and father would be proud, and his brothers and sisters would be jealous and pout. It would be a night to remember.

← Manuel just seems too confident here. He thinks everything will go perfectly in the talent show, but I think he may be in for a big surprise.

Your Turn Apply Reading Skills

1. You finish reading a paragraph and realize that there were several important words you didn't understand. What can you do?
2. What purpose might you set if you were going to read instructions for installing computer software? How would you read the instructions?
3. In a story about a lovable soccer team that keeps losing, the team gets a new coach who teaches them to believe in themselves. What do you predict will happen in the story?

Now go to the Skills in Action: Reading Model

Learn It Online
For tips on applying reading strategies to longer works, visit NovelWise at:
go.hrw.com
L6-9
Go

FOLK TALE

Build Background

"The Storytelling Stone" comes from the **oral tradition** of the Seneca people. The Seneca originally lived in the woodlands of what is now New York State. They were one of the five nations of the Iroquois League, which also included the Cayuga, Onondaga, Oneida, and Mohawk.

Literary Focus

Forms of Fiction: Folk Tale Tales from the oral tradition often begin with phrases like "In another time before this one" that tell you the story takes place a long time ago.

Reading Focus

Monitoring Comprehension Pause here to make sure you understand what just happened. (The boy discovered that the stone is speaking to him.) It's important to begin monitoring your comprehension early in your reading.

Read with a Purpose Read the following folk tale to discover the Seneca people's explanation of the origin, or beginning, of stories.

The Storytelling Stone

retold by **John Cech**

In another time before this one, there was a boy who hunted every day in the forest. Once, late in the afternoon, he stopped beside a large rock and sat down near it to fix his bow and make new points on his arrows.

A man's voice spoke to him. "I will tell you a story," it said.

The boy was startled and a little afraid, but he searched all around the stone to find the source of the voice. It could only be the rock, he thought. It must have *orenda,* the magic power the old men talk about. So he spoke to it.

"What did you say you wanted to tell me?"

"They are called stories; they are traditions. But first you must give me a present for telling it to you."

"Will this partridge do?" asked the boy, placing one of the birds he had hunted that day on the stone.

"Come back in the evening," the stone said, "and you will hear a legend about the world that was."

In the evening the boy sat on the stone again. The voice told him of the people who lived in the sky above, the "first people," the ones with great magic. Among them lived an old woman who dreamed that the large tree with the white blossoms that stood in the center of her village should be dug up by its roots. When she told her people about this, they followed the dream's instructions, uprooting the tree. They were frightened and angry over the hole it left and threw the old woman into it. She fell to earth, and the earth, which was completely under water then, had to be brought up from the depths by the animals and put upon the turtle's back and patted by the beavers' tails and allowed to grow before it could receive her who had fallen from the sky.

When he finished the tale, he noticed the boy had dozed off and so he said, "You must tell me if you become sleepy, and we can rest. If you sleep you will not hear. It is better that you come back tomorrow evening, and I will tell you more. Remember to bring my present."

Next day the boy hunted and in the evening returned to the rock with a string of birds. This time he did not miss a word. He came the next evening and the one after that.

"Where do you disappear to at night?" his friend asked him one day when they were out hunting together.

"I go to hear stories," he replied.

"What are they?"

"I don't know how to tell you about them, but come with me tonight and you will hear for yourself."

Reading Focus

Monitoring Comprehension Break down long sentences like this one. Identify who fell and how the animals prepared for the fall.

Reading Focus

Making and Adjusting Predictions Predictions are often based on prior knowledge. You know that folk tales are passed down by storytellers and that the boy loves hearing stories. You might predict that the boy will become a storyteller himself.

So he brought his friend to the stone, and its voice filled their ears with the tales of Genonsgwa and the stone coats, the Flying Heads, and the Porcupine people until the boys were sleepy and the stone sent them home to their beds.

Soon the whole village was buzzing with the news of the stone and the tales. The boys led the tribe to the place where the stone stood. The people carried fresh game with them which they left for the stone. They marveled over the things called tales that fell from its mouth. No one had ever heard about "The Master of Life" and "He Who Is Our Grandfather," or his enemy "He Who Is Clad in Ice." They did not know about such things as the songs of the corn or the prayer for harvest, and the wisest among them knew then that they had known nothing until the stone had begun to speak. It took four years for the stone to tell all the tales, but the nights passed quickly.

The rock called the boy one evening after the others had left and said to him, "One day you will become old and be unable to hunt. These tales will help you in your old age. Tell the legends to others, but make sure that they give you something in return for them." And after it had told the boy the last story, the stone was silent and never spoke again.

Reading Focus

Making and Adjusting Predictions As you get more information, you may have to adjust your predictions. At this point, though, the earlier prediction about the boy becoming a storyteller still seems likely.

The boy grew up and grew old. He did not forget the legends, and he told them to anyone who came to his lodge to listen. Many traveled from faraway tribes to hear the stories from the old man who had learned them from the stone when

Analyzing Visuals

Viewing and Interpreting How would hearing stories from this storyteller be different from hearing them from the storytelling stone?

he was a boy. They gladly gave him tobacco, meat, and pelts, for he knew the stories of their beginnings, too, and could tell them as well as the ones about his own tribe. There were few nights when his lodge did not have a crowd of listeners, enthralled[1] and intent, catching the tales to take home with them to their own hearths.

That is the way stories came to be and why there are many stories in the world where none had been before. The people from the other world before ours, the ones who had the strong and wonderful magic that the stone told about, are the ones we cannot stop telling stories about, even today.

1. **enthralled** (ehn THRAWLD): fascinated; held captive by interest.

Read with a Purpose According to this folk tale, how did stories come to be?

Literary Focus

Forms of Fiction: Folk Tale Characters in folk tales are often simple "types" rather than complicated individuals. The boy, whose name we never learn, is now an old man who passes down the stories he heard. That people pay him for his storytelling suggests how important stories are to the Seneca culture.

Reading Focus

Setting a Purpose for Reading By setting a purpose at the beginning, you were able to think about possible answers to this question as you read.

MEET THE WRITER

John Cech

(1944–)

A Born Storyteller

It's no wonder that John Cech is interested in the origin of stories—he's been telling them his whole life. When he was a child, he made up tales about the famous fictional detective Sherlock Holmes to entertain his friends. According to a teacher's note on his third-grade report card, however, he spent too much time telling stories and not enough working on class assignments! That teacher would probably be proud of Cech today. He successfully balances his classroom duties as an English professor with his ongoing love of storytelling.

Literature for Kids

In fact, stories—including Cech's recollections of his own childhood—have served him well in his profession. An award-winning writer and scholar, Cech serves as director of the University of Florida's Center for Children's Literature and Culture. The center is devoted to the study of literature and other media, both classic and modern, produced for young audiences. Cech himself has written several children's books, as well as books, articles, and reviews for adults.

Time for *Recess!*

One way that Cech shares his insights into childhood with interested adults is through *Recess!*—the daily three-minute radio show that he produces and hosts. The program airs on public radio stations across the country and explores topics in children's culture. It features book and movie reviews, historical notes, and original stories and essays.

"In the events and the literature of childhood lie the seeds . . . of the imagination."

Think About the Writer Cech often writes for and about young people. What qualities make a story interesting to a reader your age?

SKILLS IN ACTION

Wrap Up

Sunshine State Standards: Benchmarks **LA.6.1.6.1** use new vocabulary that is introduced and taught directly; **LA.6.1.6.2** listen to, read, and discuss familiar and conceptually challenging text; **LA.6.1.7.8** use strategies to repair comprehension of grade-appropriate text when self-monitoring indicates confusion, including but not limited to rereading, checking context clues, predicting, note-making, summarizing, using graphic and semantic organizers, questioning, and clarifying by checking other sources.

Into Action: Monitoring Comprehension

You should have stopped regularly to monitor your comprehension as you read "The Storytelling Stone." Using the question-and-answer chart below, make sure that you understood the main events of the story. If you can't answer a particular question, go back and re-read the passage.

What happened? Q and A

Q	A
Q: What does the stone want to tell the boy? What does it expect from him?	A:
Q: How do the villagers react to the stories they hear?	A:
Q: When the boy is an old man, to whom does he tell stories?	A:

Talk About . . .

1. "The Storytelling Stone" shows the power and importance of stories. With a partner, discuss why you think stories are so important to people. Try to use each Academic Vocabulary word listed on the right at least once in your discussion.

Write About . . .

Answer the following questions about "The Storytelling Stone." For definitions of the underlined Academic Vocabulary words, see the column on the right.

2. What are some of the special features of folk tales that you found in the story?
3. Explain the concept of an "oral tradition." How are you able to read "The Storytelling Stone" today even though it wasn't written down for generations and its original author is unknown?

Writing Focus

Think as a Reader/Writer

In Collection 1, you'll read different forms of fiction. The Writing Focus activities on the Preparing to Read pages show you how each writer makes his or her writing unique and interesting. On the Applying Your Skills pages, you'll practice these aspects of writer's craft in your own writing.

Academic Vocabulary for Collection 1

Talking and Writing About Forms of Fiction

Academic Vocabulary is the language you use to write and talk about literature. Use these words to discuss the fiction you read in this collection. They are underlined throughout the collection.

features (FEE chuhrz) *n.:* important, typical parts. *The different forms of fiction each have defining features.*

interpret (ihn TUR priht) *v.:* decide on the meaning of something. *When we interpret stories, we can learn lessons about life.*

concept (KAHN sehpt) *n.:* idea of how something is or could be. *The concept of storytelling exists in all cultures.*

indicate (IHN duh kayt) *v.:* show; express; suggest. *Parts of "The Storytelling Stone" indicate some of the Seneca's religious beliefs.*

Your Turn

Copy the words from the Academic Vocabulary list into your *Reader/Writer Notebook*. Then, use each word in a sentence about your favorite story. Practice using these Academic Vocabulary words as you talk and write about the selections in this collection.

SHORT STORY

Preparing to Read

La Bamba

by **Gary Soto**

What Do You Think?

How can reading stories about events in the life of a young person like yourself give you insights into your own life?

QuickWrite

Most lists of "Top Ten Things People Fear Most" include "public speaking" and "performance in front of an audience." Have you ever had to perform in front of an audience? What was it like? Jot down a few notes about the experience.

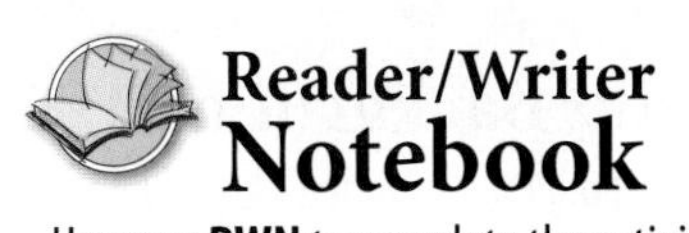

Reader/Writer Notebook

Use your **RWN** to complete the activities for this selection.

Sunshine State Standards: Benchmarks **LA.6.1.5.1** adjust reading rate based on purpose, text difficulty, form, and style; **LA.6.1.6.1** use new vocabulary that is introduced and taught directly; **LA.6.1.7.1** use background knowledge of subject and related content areas, prereading strategies, graphic representations, and knowledge of text structure to make and confirm complex predictions of content, purpose, and organization of a reading selection; *Also covered* **LA.6.1.7.8; LA.6.2.1.1**

Literary Focus

Forms of Fiction: Short Story A **short story** is a brief fictional narrative usually from five to twenty pages long. Short stories can be about anything. Whatever they are about, though, they are built in the same way: They have a character or characters dealing with a conflict (problem), main events that lead to a climax, and a resolution of the conflict. These building blocks are also found in novels and novellas, but the short story is, well, short. The typical short story has just one or two main characters and one conflict. Good short stories deliver an emotional punch, and they deliver it fast.

Reading Focus

Making Predictions As you read, you make **predictions,** or educated guesses about what will happen next. You base your guesses on **clues**—details in the story—that the writer gives you, combined with what you already know from your own experience.

Into Action As you read "La Bamba," use a prediction chart like the one below to keep track of the predictions you make about what will happen next. Identify the clues you have found, and then write down the predictions you made based on those clues.

Clue	Prediction
Mr. Roybal gets frustrated with the record player during rehearsal.	The record player might not work during the talent show.

Writing Focus

Think as a Reader/Writer

Find It in Your Reading As you read this short story, identify at least five details that help make the main character, Manuel, and his experiences come alive for you. Copy these details into your *Reader/Writer Notebook.*

Vocabulary

jammed (jamd) *v.:* got stuck and became unworkable. *When the lever jammed, Mr. Roybal almost lost it.*

maneuvered (muh NOO vuhrd) *v.:* moved, as a group, into position. *The cast maneuvered back onto the stage.*

groove (groov) *n.:* state of being comfortable. *Manuel got into the groove once he felt more comfortable on the stage.*

cast (kast) *n.:* group of performers in a play or event. *The audience appreciated the cast's efforts.*

Language Coach

Oral Fluency Two of the words above have the same vowel sound, but that vowel sound is spelled in a different way in each word. Identify the two words that have the same vowel sound but very different spellings.

Learn It Online

For a preview of this story, see the video introduction on:

go.hrw.com L6-17 Go

MEET THE WRITER

Learn It Online
Read more about Soto online at:
go.hrw.com L6-18 Go

Gary Soto
(1952–)

"My Friends . . . Jump Up and Down on the Page"

Gary Soto grew up in a Mexican American family in California's San Joaquin (SAN waw KEEN) Valley. He remembers himself as an active kid who liked the playground better than the classroom and loved to compete against others in games. He was not a very good student, he claims, until he went to college and discovered poetry—and an urge to become a writer himself. He won recognition by recapturing the world of his childhood in words.

> "When I first started writing recollections and short stories . . . I needed full-fledged stories and the patience of a monk. I needed to recall the narrative, characters, small moments, dates, places, etc. I was responsible for my writing, and, thus, it was tremendous work to keep it all in order. When I was writing *Living up the Street* . . . I wrote, rewrote, and rewrote the rewrite, so that my friends would jump up and down on the page."

Think About the Writer How can a writer many years older than you, like Soto, convey what it's like to be your age?

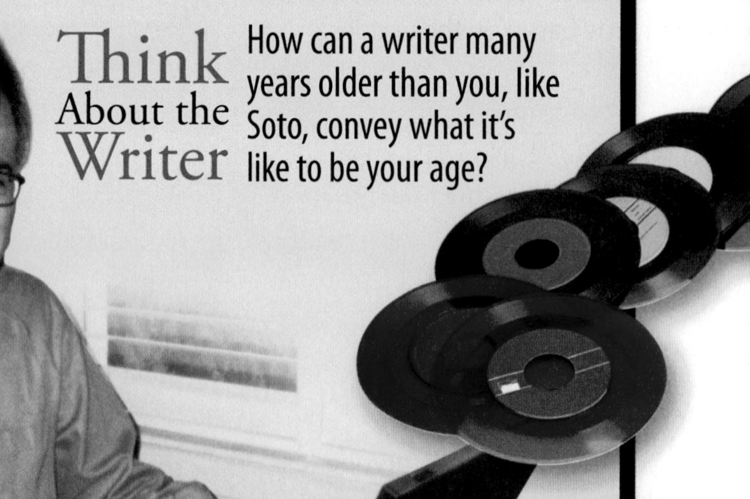

Build Background

The first digitally recorded music came on the market in the early 1980s in the form of audio CDs. The birth of the CD signaled the end of the long era of the vinyl record, which had been the primary audio format of the twentieth century.

Records are vinyl disks that contain cut grooves. These grooves correspond to sound waves. Putting a stylus, or needle, into the grooves and rotating the record on a turntable, or record player, made the stylus vibrate, which reproduced the recorded sounds.

Records got scratched easily by being dropped or mishandled—or even from a slip of the stylus that read the grooves. A scratch could ruin a record by making the needle get stuck, playing the same bit of music over and over.

Preview the Selection

Manuel is the story's main character, an average kid attending a typical school. As the story begins, he is regretting his decision to participate in his school's talent show.

Read with a Purpose Read the following short story to see how a boy close to your own age feels as he deals with being onstage in a school talent show.

La Bamba

by **Gary Soto**

Manuel was the fourth of seven children and looked like a lot of kids in his neighborhood: black hair, brown face, and skinny legs scuffed from summer play. But summer was giving way to fall: The trees were turning red, the lawns brown, and the pomegranate trees were heavy with fruit. Manuel walked to school in the frosty morning, kicking leaves and thinking of tomorrow's talent show. He was still amazed that he had volunteered. He was going to pretend to sing Ritchie Valens's[1] "La Bamba" before the entire school.

Why did I raise my hand? he asked himself, but in his heart he knew the answer. He yearned for the limelight. He wanted applause as loud as a thunderstorm and to hear his friends say, "Man, that was bad!" And he wanted to impress the girls, especially Petra Lopez, the second-prettiest girl in his class. The prettiest was already taken by his friend Ernie. Manuel knew he should be reasonable since he himself was not great-looking, just average. **A**

Manuel kicked through the fresh-fallen leaves. When he got to school, he realized he had forgotten his math workbook. If the teacher found out, he would have to stay after school and miss practice for the talent show. But fortunately for him, they did drills that morning.

During lunch Manuel hung around with Benny, who was also in the talent show. Benny was going to play the trumpet in spite of the fat lip he had gotten playing football.

"How do I look?" Manuel asked. He cleared his throat and started moving his lips in pantomime. No words came out, just a hiss that sounded like a snake. Manuel tried to look emotional, flailing his arms on the high notes and opening his eyes and mouth as wide as he could when he came to "Para bailar la baaaaammmba."[2]

After Manuel finished, Benny said it looked all right but suggested Manuel dance while he sang. Manuel thought for a moment and decided it was a good idea.

"Yeah, just think you're like Michael

1. **Ritchie Valens** (1941–1959), the professional singer mentioned in the story, was the first Mexican American rock star. In 1959, when he was only seventeen, Valens was killed in a plane crash.

2. **para bailar la bamba** (PAH rah BY lahr lah BAHM bah): Spanish for "to dance the bamba."

A **Read and Discuss** What is the author letting us know about Manuel?

Jackson or someone like that," Benny suggested. "But don't get carried away."

During rehearsal, Mr. Roybal, nervous about his debut as the school's talent co-ordinator, cursed under his breath when the lever that controlled the speed on the record player jammed.

"Darn," he growled, trying to force the lever. "What's wrong with you?"

"Is it broken?" Manuel asked, bending over for a closer look. It looked all right to him.

Mr. Roybal assured Manuel that he would have a good record player at the talent show, even if it meant bringing his own stereo from home. **B**

Manuel sat in a folding chair, twirling his record on his thumb. He watched a skit about personal hygiene, a mother-and-daughter violin duo, five first-grade girls jumping rope, a karate kid breaking boards, three girls singing "Like a Virgin," and a skit about the pilgrims. If the record player hadn't been broken, he would have gone after the karate kid, an easy act to follow, he told himself.

As he twirled his forty-five record, Manuel thought they had a great talent show. The entire school would be amazed. His mother and father would be proud, and his brothers and sisters would be jealous and pout. It would be a night to remember. **C**

Benny walked onto the stage, raised his trumpet to his mouth, and waited for his cue. Mr. Roybal raised his hand like a symphony conductor and let it fall dramatically. Benny inhaled and blew so loud that Manuel dropped his record, which rolled across the cafeteria floor until it hit a wall. Manuel raced after it, picked it up, and wiped it clean.

"Boy, I'm glad it didn't break," he said with a sigh.

That night Manuel had to do the dishes and a lot of homework, so he could only practice in the shower. In bed he prayed that he wouldn't mess up. He prayed that it wouldn't be like when he was a first-grader. For Science Week he had wired together a C battery and a bulb and told everyone he had discovered how a flashlight worked. He was so pleased with himself that he practiced for hours pressing the wire to the battery, making the bulb wink a dim, orangish light. He showed it to so many kids in his neighborhood that when it was time to show his class how a flashlight worked, the battery was dead. He pressed the wire to the battery, but the bulb didn't respond. He pressed until his thumb hurt and some kids in the back started snickering.

But Manuel fell asleep confident that nothing would go wrong this time.

The next morning his father and mother beamed at him. They were proud that he was going to be in the talent show.

"I wish you would tell us what you're doing," his mother said. His father, a

---

B **Reading Focus** **Making Predictions** Based on this conversation between Manuel and Mr. Roybal, what do you predict will happen at the talent show?

C **Read and Discuss** What do Manuel's thoughts about his family indicate about him?

Vocabulary **jammed** (jamd) *v.:* got stuck and became unworkable.

pharmacist who wore a blue smock with his name on a plastic rectangle, looked up from the newspaper and sided with his wife. "Yes, what are you doing in the talent show?" **D**

"You'll see," Manuel said, with his mouth full of Cheerios.

The day whizzed by, and so did his afternoon chores and dinner. Suddenly he was dressed in his best clothes and standing next to Benny backstage, listening to the commotion as the cafeteria filled with school kids and parents. The lights dimmed, and Mr. Roybal, sweaty in a tight suit and a necktie with a large knot, wet his lips and parted the stage curtains. **E**

"Good evening, everyone," the kids behind the curtain heard him say. "Good evening to you," some of the smart-alecky kids said back to him.

"Tonight we bring you the best John Burroughs Elementary has to offer, and I'm sure that you'll be both pleased and amazed that our little school houses so much talent. And now, without further ado, let's get on with the show." He turned and, with a swish of his hand, commanded, "Part the curtain." The curtains parted in jerks. A girl dressed as a toothbrush and a boy dressed as a dirty gray tooth walked onto the stage and sang:

Brush, brush, brush
Floss, floss, floss
Gargle the germs away—hey! hey! hey!

After they finished singing, they turned to Mr. Roybal, who dropped his hand. The toothbrush dashed around the stage after the dirty tooth, which was laughing and having a great time until it slipped and nearly rolled off the stage.

Analyzing Visuals **Viewing and Interpreting**
Why do you think Manuel chooses to pantomime a song by the 1950s Latino rock star Ritchie Valens, shown here?

Mr. Roybal jumped out and caught it just in time. "Are you OK?"

The dirty tooth answered, "Ask my dentist," which drew laughter and applause from the audience.

The violin duo played next, and except for one time when the girl got lost, they sounded fine. People applauded, and

---

D **Reading Focus** **Making Predictions** What do you think will happen next? What clues in the story helped you make that prediction?

E **Literary Focus** **Short Story** What are the main events of the story so far? Who is the main character, and what does he want? What might stand in his way?

some even stood up. Then the first-grade girls maneuvered onto the stage while jumping rope. They were all smiles and bouncing ponytails as a hundred cameras flashed at once. Mothers "awhed" and fathers sat up proudly.

The karate kid was next. He did a few kicks, yells, and chops, and finally, when his father held up a board, punched it in two. The audience clapped and looked at each other, wide-eyed with respect. The boy bowed to the audience, and father and son ran off the stage.

Manuel remained behind the stage, shivering with fear. He mouthed the words to "La Bamba" and swayed left to right. Why did he raise his hand and volunteer? Why couldn't he have just sat there like the rest of the kids and not said anything? While the karate kid was onstage, Mr. Roybal, more sweaty than before, took Manuel's forty-five record and placed it on a new record player. **F**

"You ready?" Mr. Roybal asked.

"Yeah . . ."

Mr. Roybal walked back on stage and announced that Manuel Gomez, a fifth-grader in Mrs. Knight's class, was going to pantomime Ritchie Valens's classic hit "La Bamba."

The cafeteria roared with applause. Manuel was nervous but loved the noisy crowd. He pictured his mother and father applauding loudly and his brothers and sisters also clapping, though not as energetically.

Manuel walked on stage and the song started immediately. Glassy-eyed from the shock of being in front of so many people, Manuel moved his lips and swayed in a made-up dance step. He couldn't see his parents, but he could see his brother Mario, who was a year younger, thumb-wrestling with a friend. Mario was wearing Manuel's favorite shirt; he would deal with Mario later. He saw some other kids get up and head for the drinking fountain, and a baby sitting in the middle of an aisle sucking her thumb and watching him intently.

What am I doing here? thought

F **Read and Discuss** How do you interpret what Manuel is feeling now?

Vocabulary **maneuvered** (muh NOO vuhrd) *v.:* moved, as a group, into position.

Manuel. This is no fun at all. Everyone was just sitting there. Some people were moving to the beat, but most were just watching him, like they would a monkey at the zoo. **G**

But when Manuel did a fancy dance step, there was a burst of applause and some girls screamed. Manuel tried another dance step. He heard more applause and screams and started getting into the groove as he shivered and snaked like Michael Jackson around the stage. But the record got stuck, and he had to sing

Para bailar la bamba
Para bailar la bamba
Para bailar la bamba
Para bailar la bamba

again and again. **H**

Manuel couldn't believe his bad luck. The audience began to laugh and stand up in their chairs. Manuel remembered how the forty-five record had dropped from his hand and rolled across the cafeteria floor. It probably got scratched, he thought, and now it was stuck, and he was stuck dancing and moving his lips to the same words over and over. He had never been so embarrassed. He would have to ask his parents to move the family out of town.

After Mr. Roybal ripped the needle across the record, Manuel slowed his dance steps to a halt. He didn't know what to do except bow to the audience, which applauded wildly, and scoot off the stage, on the verge of tears. This was worse than the homemade flashlight. At least no one laughed then; they just snickered.

Manuel stood alone, trying hard to hold back the tears as Benny, center stage, played his trumpet. Manuel was jealous because he sounded great, then mad as he recalled that it was Benny's loud trumpet playing that made the forty-five record fly out of his hands. But when the entire cast lined up for a curtain call, Manuel received a burst of applause that was so loud it shook the walls of the cafeteria. Later, as he mingled with the kids and parents, everyone patted him on the shoulder and told him, "Way to go. You were really funny." **I**

Funny? Manuel thought. Did he do something funny?

Funny. Crazy. Hilarious. These were the words people said to him. He was confused but beyond caring. All he knew was that people were paying attention to him, and his brothers and sisters looked at him with a mixture of jealousy and awe. He was going to pull Mario aside and punch him in the arm for wearing his shirt, but he cooled it. He was enjoying the limelight. A teacher brought him cookies and punch, and the popular kids who had never before given him the time of day now clustered around him. Ricardo, the editor of the school bulletin, asked him how he made the needle stick.

"It just happened," Manuel said, crunching on a star-shaped cookie.

At home that night his father, eager

G **Read and Discuss** What does Manuel mean when he says that people "were watching him, like they would a monkey at the zoo"? What is he feeling?

H **Reading Focus** **Making Predictions** What earlier clues indicated that something like this might happen?

I **Read and Discuss** What's the reaction to Manuel's performance? Explain whether this matches his concept of what happened.

Vocabulary **groove** (groov) *n.:* state of being comfortable.
cast (kast) *n.:* group of performers in a play or event.

Analyzing Visuals

Viewing and Interpreting Is this audience reacting the way you imagined Manuel's audience reacted? Why or why not?

to undo the buttons on his shirt and ease into his La-Z-Boy recliner, asked Manuel the same thing, how he managed to make the song stick on the words "Para bailar la bamba."

Manuel thought quickly and reached for scientific jargon he had read in magazines. "Easy, Dad. I used laser tracking with high optics and low functional decibels per channel." His proud but confused father told him to be quiet and go to bed. **J**

"Ah, que niños tan truchas,"[3] he said as he walked to the kitchen for a glass of milk. "I don't know how you kids nowadays get so smart."

Manuel, feeling happy, went to his bedroom, undressed, and slipped into his pajamas. He looked in the mirror and began to pantomime "La Bamba," but stopped because he was tired of the song. He crawled into bed. The sheets were as cold as the moon that stood over the peach tree in their backyard.

He was relieved that the day was over. Next year, when they asked for volunteers for the talent show, he wouldn't raise his hand. Probably. **K**

3. **que niños tan truchas** (kay NEEN yohs tahn TROO chahs): Spanish for "what smart kids."

J **Literary Focus** **Short Story** Interpret Manuel's answer to his father's question. Why does he give his father a different answer than he gave Ricardo?

K **Read and Discuss** What does it tell us about Manuel that he *probably* won't volunteer for the talent show next year?

Applying Your Skills

Sunshine State Standards: Benchmarks LA.6.1.7.1 use background knowledge of subject and related content areas, prereading strategies, graphic representations, and knowledge of text structure to make and confirm complex predictions of content, purpose, and organization of a reading selection; *Also covered* LA.6.1.7.4; LA.6.1.7.8; LA.6.2.1.2; LA.6.4.1.1

La Bamba

Respond and Think Critically

Reading Focus

1. What was the author's purpose for writing this story? FCAT
   - **A** to entertain readers through humor
   - **B** to describe his own childhood experience
   - **C** to inform readers about his favorite song
   - **D** to persuade readers to try out for talent shows

Read with a Purpose

2. How does Manuel feel about the talent show before, during, and after his performance? Support your answer with details from the story. READ THINK EXPLAIN

Reading Skills: Making Predictions

3. Look at the prediction chart you filled in as you read the story. Now, add a third column to the chart and fill it in with what actually happened. Did things turn out as expected?

Clue	Prediction	What Actually Happened
Mr. Roybal gets frustrated with the record player during rehearsal.	The record player might not work during the talent show.	

Literary Focus

Literary Analysis

4. **Compare** Compare Manuel's concept of what being in the talent show would be like to what actually happened. Why didn't the audience see Manuel's performance as a disaster?

5. **Infer** How likely is it that Manuel will volunteer for the talent show next year? Use examples from the story to support your answer. READ THINK EXPLAIN

6. **Extend** What does this story show us about how things don't always turn out the way we hope or expect them to? What lesson can readers draw from this clash of expectations and reality?

Literary Skills: Short Story

7. **Analyze** What is the major **conflict**, or problem, that Manuel must overcome in this story? How is the conflict finally resolved?

Literary Skills Review: Similes

8. **Interpret** A **simile** is a comparison between two unlike things using a word such as *like* or *as*. Identify the simile used to describe the audience as Manuel takes the stage. What does this comparison indicate about Manuel?

Writing Focus

Think as a Reader/Writer

Use It in Your Writing Write a short narrative about another talent show participant. Use descriptive details to bring the character to life.

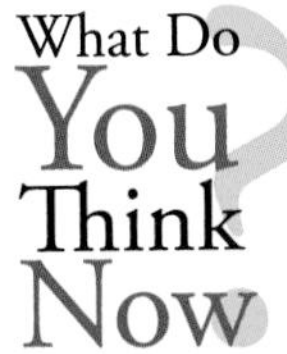

What Do You Think Now? How would you react to a potentially embarrassing situation like Manuel's talent show experience?

Applying Your Skills

La Bamba

Vocabulary Development

Words with Multiple Meanings

Multiple-meaning words have more than one meaning. Often, the different meanings are completely unrelated to one another. When you look up a multiple-meaning word in a dictionary, you'll find a numbered list of definitions, as in this example:

shower (SHOW uhr) *n.* **1.** a brief rainfall **2.** a party at which someone is honored and given gifts **3.** a bath in which water pours down on the body —*v.* **1.** to spray **2.** to pour forth like a shower **3.** to take a shower

If you see a multiple-meaning word and you're not sure which definition is intended, look at the word's **context,** or the meaning that surrounds it. If the word *shower* appears with words like *weather, rain, soaked,* or *umbrella,* you know that *shower* must refer to rainfall. If you're still confused, look at the definitions listed in a dictionary and choose the one that fits best in the sentence.

Here is a sentence from "La Bamba." Which definition of *shower* fits best in this context?

> "That night Manuel had to do the dishes and a lot of homework, so he could only practice in the shower."

The sentence below is not from the story. Which definition of *shower* fits best in this context?

> Manuel's family threw his older sister a shower before her wedding.

Your Turn

jammed
maneuvered
groove
cast

Choose two of the Vocabulary words to the right. For each, write *two* sentences that show *two* distinct meanings of the word. Use a dictionary for help.

Language Coach

new
boot

Oral Fluency Many words in English have the same vowel sound but different spellings. The examples at right have the same /oo/ sound, but each is spelled in a different way. A Vocabulary word above, *maneuvered,* shows you a third way to spell this /oo/ sound. Think of three word pairs that have the same vowel sound but different spellings.

Academic Vocabulary

Talk About . . .

Describe Manuel's concept of his family. What do his views indicate about his relationship with them? Interpret Manuel's ideas about his family, and write your ideas in your *Reader/Writer Notebook.*

Learn It Online
For vocabulary tutorials, visit WordSharp on:
go.hrw.com
L6-26
Go

Sunshine State Standards: Benchmarks **LA.6.1.5.1** adjust reading rate based on purpose, text difficulty, form, and style; **LA.6.1.6.1** use new vocabulary that is introduced and taught directly; **LA.6.1.6.9** determine the correct meaning of words with multiple meanings in context; **LA.6.3.4.4** the eight parts of speech (noun, pronoun, verb, adverb, adjective, conjunction, preposition, interjection); **LA.6.4.2.1** write in a variety of informational/expository forms (e.g., summaries, procedures, instructions, experiments, rubrics, how-to manuals, assembly instructions); **LA.6.6.4.1** use appropriate available technologies to enhance communication and achieve a purpose (e.g., video, online).

Grammar Link

Common and Proper Nouns

What is "La Bamba"? It's the name of a story—and the title of a song. It's a **noun**—a word used to name a person, place, thing, or idea.

Persons	Manuel, mother, Benny
Places	neighborhood, John Burroughs Elementary School, cafeteria
Things	stage, song, "La Bamba"
Ideas	limelight, talent, luck

A **common noun** is a general name for a person, place, thing, or idea, while a **proper noun** names a particular one. A proper noun begins with a capital letter, while a common noun is not capitalized.

Common Noun	Proper Noun
school	John Burroughs Elementary School
teacher	Mrs. Knight
brother	Mario
song	"La Bamba"

Your Turn

In the sentences that follow, underline the common nouns and circle the proper nouns.

1. Manuel decides to pantomime a song in the talent show.
2. The boy practices singing "La Bamba" in the shower.
3. Mario is thumb-wrestling with a friend.
4. Manuel will confront his brother later.
5. Ritchie Valens, a 1950s rock star, was killed in a plane crash.

CHOICES

As your respond to the Choices, use these **Academic Vocabulary** words as appropriate: features, interpret, concept, indicate.

REVIEW

Analyze the Story

Timed Writing In a brief essay, identify the main character of "La Bamba" and the **conflict**, or problem, he faces. Identify the **climax** of the story—the most exciting part—and describe how the conflict is resolved. Then, indicate whether the resolution is believable. Support your conclusion with details from the story.

CONNECT

Create a Brochure

Group Work With a small group, develop a concept for a brochure called "How to Deal with Stage Fright." Find articles and books on the topic and interview people who do a lot of performing or public speaking, such as musicians and business consultants. Write up the information you've collected in the form of a brochure.

EXTEND

Research Two Technologies

TechFocus Find information in a library or on the Internet that explains the way sound is recorded and played back in vinyl records and compact discs. Draw diagrams to help explain the process of recording sounds. Add captions that point out which features are similar and different between the two formats.

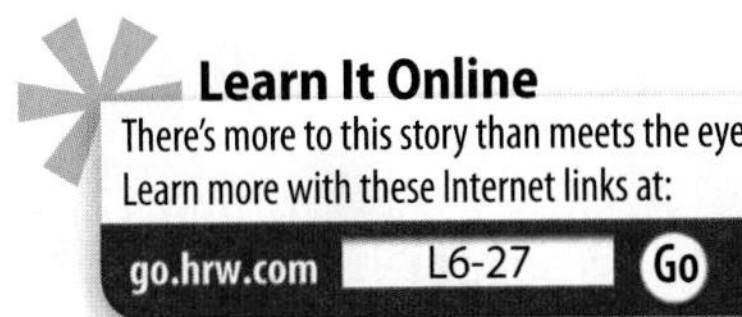

Learn It Online
There's more to this story than meets the eye.
Learn more with these Internet links at:
go.hrw.com
L6-27
Go

NOVELLA

Preparing to Read

The Gold Cadillac

by **Mildred D. Taylor**

What Do You Think?

How can a fictional story give us different insights into historical events than a nonfiction account can?

QuickWrite

Did you know that at one time in the United States, African Americans were not allowed to eat in "whites-only" restaurants? Write down your thoughts about this.

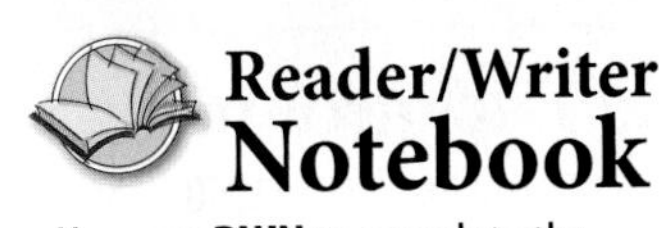

Reader/Writer Notebook

Use your **RWN** to complete the activities for this selection.

Sunshine State Standards: Benchmarks **LA.6.1.6.5** relate new vocabulary to familiar words; **LA.6.1.7.1** use background knowledge of subject and related content areas, prereading strategies, graphic representations, and knowledge of text structure to make and confirm complex predictions of content, purpose, and organization of a reading selection; **LA.6.2.1.1** identify the characteristics of various genres (e.g., poetry, fiction, short story, dramatic literature) as forms with distinct characteristics and purposes; **LA.6.2.1.9** explain how ideas, values, and themes of a literary work often reflect the historical period in which it was written.

Literary Focus

Forms of Fiction: Novella The novel, novella, and short story are all members of the family of fiction. They all have plot, characters, setting, and theme—elements you'll learn more about in Collections 2–4. A **novella** is short enough to be published with other stories yet long enough to be published by itself. *The Gold Cadillac* is a novella; it was first published as a short book.

Literary Perspectives Apply the literary perspective described on page 31 as you read this novella.

Reading Focus

Making and Adjusting Predictions When you read, you use clues from the text and your own experiences to **make predictions** about what will happen or be revealed next. As you continue reading, new information may cause you to interpret what is going on in a new way and **adjust your predictions.**

Into Action When you are prompted to make a prediction—or when one occurs to you—stop and use a chart like the one below to indicate what's happening in the story. Then, record your prediction and give a reason for it. Adjust your predictions as necessary.

In the story	I predict	Because
the narrator and her sister see the Cadillac	that the father bought it	the father drives up in it and is grinning and happy

Writing Focus

Think as a Reader/Writer

Find It in Your Reading As you read this novella, use your *Reader/Writer Notebook* to jot down details in the story that relate to concepts like beauty, richness, pride, and luxury. Identify where these details appear, and explain what they add to the story.

Vocabulary

evident (EHV uh duhnt) *adj.:* easily seen or understood; obvious. *It's evident to everyone that Dee is angry.*

rural (RUR uhl) *adj.:* having to do with country life. *The narrator's grandparents live on a big farm in a rural area.*

dusk (duhsk) *n.:* the period of time when the sky darkens as the sun goes down. *As dusk approached, 'lois became more frightened.*

ignorance (IHG nuhr uhns) *n.:* lack of knowledge. *Her father says that people sometimes pass unfair laws out of ignorance.*

Language Coach

Word Forms Some nouns have related adjective forms. To create an adjective from the noun form, you simply add to or change the ending of the noun.

For example:
hair (*n.*) + –*y* = hairy (*adj.*)

Which of the Vocabulary words above can you change to an adjective by adding –*y*?

Learn It Online
Check out the *PowerNotes* introduction to this story online at:

go.hrw.com L6-29 

MEET THE WRITER

Learn It Online
Read more about Taylor online at:
go.hrw.com L6-30 Go

Mildred D. Taylor

(1943–)

Weaving Memories into Fiction

Mildred D. Taylor was born in Mississippi, but her family moved to the North when she was only a few months old, escaping segregation, the enforced separation of white people and African Americans. Taylor has always drawn upon her memories of both the North and South in her work.

Road Trips

Even though Taylor's family relocated, they maintained their ties to Mississippi and the South. They made a yearly trek back to Mississippi to visit the relatives who remained. In fact, car trips became an important part of family life.

> "I loved those years. . . . Because my father, my uncles, and my older male cousins all loved cars, we often rode in caravan out to the park, where the men would park their cars in a long, impressive row and shine them in the shade of the trees. . . . And sometimes we took even longer trips, down country highways into the land called the South."

Nancy N. Jacobs

Think About the Writer If you were a writer, which of your own experiences would you draw on for *your* stories?

Build Background

This story takes place around 1950—a period between the end of the Civil War (1861–1865), when African Americans were freed from slavery, and the civil rights era (1955–1968), in which they were finally granted full and equal rights in American society. During this time, black Americans were segregated, or kept apart from white Americans in many ways. For example, African Americans often had to use separate bathrooms, sit in the backs of buses, or see movies in their own theaters. Segregation was especially widespread and severe in the South.

By 1950, the U.S. Army had already been desegregated. Therefore, black soldiers could serve and fight alongside white soldiers. Some of the characters in this story served in the military. Although they served their country honorably, at home they faced discrimination.

Preview the Selection

The narrator of this story goes by a somewhat unusual nickname—**'lois.** (The apostrophe means it's short for her full first name.) The other members of 'lois's immediate family are her older sister, **Wilma,** her mother, **Dee,** and her father, **Wilbert.**

Read with a Purpose Read this novella to discover how a gold Cadillac brings a family face to face with segregation in the South.

The Gold Cadillac

by **Mildred D. Taylor**

My sister and I were playing out on the front lawn when the gold Cadillac rolled up and my father stepped from behind the wheel. We ran to him, our eyes filled with wonder. "Daddy, whose Cadillac?" I asked.

And Wilma demanded, "Where's our Mercury?"

My father grinned. "Go get your mother and I'll tell you all about it."

"Is it ours?" I cried. "Daddy, is it ours?"

"Get your mother!" he laughed. "And tell her to hurry!"

Wilma and I ran off to obey, as Mr. Pondexter next door came from his house to see what this new Cadillac was all about. We threw open the front door, ran through the downstairs front parlor and straight through the house to the kitchen, where my mother was cooking and one of my aunts was helping her. "Come on, Mother-Dear!" we cried together. "Daddy say come on out and see this new car!"

"What?" said my mother, her face showing her surprise. "What're you talking about?" **A**

"A Cadillac!" I cried.

"He said hurry up!" relayed Wilma.

And then we took off again, up the back stairs to the second floor of the duplex. Running down the hall, we banged on all the apartment doors. My uncles and their wives stepped to the doors. It was good it was a Saturday morning. Everybody was home.

Literary Perspectives

The following perspective will help you think about the characters and events in *The Gold Cadillac.*

Analyzing Credibility in Literature All fiction asks us to "suspend disbelief"—to let ourselves be pulled into the world of a story even though we know it is not "real." In myths, fables, and folk tales, we expect magical occurrences and other "unrealistic" features. In realistic fiction, however, we expect the characters and plot to be more believable, or credible. For example, if a character doesn't talk and act the way a real person might, we find ourselves questioning the credibility of that character. Credibility is particularly important in historical fiction—fiction based on things that really happened. Consider the credibility of this novella, an example of historical fiction. As you read, pay attention to the notes and questions in the text, which will guide you in using this perspective.

A **Reading Focus** **Making Predictions** How do you predict 'lois's mother will react to the new car?

"We got us a Cadillac! We got us a Cadillac!" Wilma and I proclaimed in unison.[1] **B**

We had decided that the Cadillac had to be ours if our father was driving it and holding on to the keys. "Come on see!" Then we raced on, through the upstairs sunroom, down the front steps, through the downstairs sunroom, and out to the Cadillac. Mr. Pondexter was still there. Mr. LeRoy and Mr. Courtland from down the street were there too, and all were admiring the Cadillac as my father stood proudly by, pointing out the various features.

"Brand-new 1950 Coupe deVille!" I heard one of the men saying.

"Just off the showroom floor!" my father said. "I just couldn't resist it."

My sister and I eased up to the car and peeked in. It was all gold inside. Gold leather seats. Gold carpeting. Gold dashboard. It was like no car we had owned before. It looked like a car for rich folks.

"Daddy, are we rich?" I asked. My father laughed.

"Daddy, it's ours, isn't it?" asked Wilma, who was older and more practical than I. She didn't intend to give her heart too quickly to something that wasn't hers.

"You like it?"

"Oh, Daddy, yes!"

He looked at me. "What 'bout you, 'lois?" **C**

1. **in unison** (ihn YOO nuh suhn): in chorus; in the same words, spoken at the same time.

"Yes, sir!"

My father laughed again. "Then I expect I can't much disappoint my girls, can I? It's ours, all right!"

Wilma and I hugged our father with our joy. My uncles came from the house, and my aunts, carrying their babies, came out too. Everybody surrounded the car and owwed and ahhed. Nobody could believe it. **D**

Then my mother came out.

Everybody stood back grinning as she approached the car. There was no smile on her face. We all waited for her to speak. She stared at the car, then looked at my father, standing there as proud as he could be. Finally she said, "You didn't buy this car, did you, Wilbert?"

"Gotta admit I did. Couldn't resist it."

"But . . . but what about our Mercury? It was perfectly good!"

"Don't you like the Cadillac, Dee?"

"That Mercury wasn't even a year old!"

My father nodded. "And I'm sure whoever buys it is going to get themselves a good car. But we've got ourselves a better one. Now stop frowning, honey, and let's take ourselves a ride in our brand-new Cadillac!"

My mother shook her head. "I've got food on the stove," she said and, turning away, walked back to the house.

There was an awkward silence, and then my father said, "You know Dee never did much like surprises. Guess this here Cadillac was a bit too much for her. I best go smooth things out with her."

B **Read and Discuss** What has the author set up for us so far?

C **Literary Focus** **Novella** Who is the main character in this novella? How can you tell?

D **Read and Discuss** What does this scene show us about the relationship between the sisters and their father?

Elm and Cumberland View #3 by Connie Hayes.

Everybody watched as he went after my mother. But when he came back, he was alone.

"Well, what she say?" asked one of my uncles.

My father shrugged and smiled. "Told me I bought this Cadillac alone, I could just ride in it alone."

Another uncle laughed. "Uh-oh! Guess she told you!"

"Oh, she'll come around," said one of my aunts. "Any woman would be proud to ride in this car." **E**

"That's what I'm banking on," said my father as he went around to the street side of the car and opened the door. "All right! Who's for a ride?" **F**

"We are!" Wilma and I cried.

All three of my uncles and one of my aunts, still holding her baby, and Mr. Pondexter climbed in with us, and we took off for the first ride in the gold Cadillac. It was a glorious ride, and we drove all through the city of Toledo. We rode past the church and past the school. We rode through

E **Read and Discuss** What's been going on with Dee in this scene? How do you interpret her behavior?

F **Literary Perspectives** **Analyzing Credibility in Literature** Does the dialogue here (the character's spoken words) make these characters seem more credible or less credible? Explain.

Ottawa Hills, where the rich folks lived, and on into Walbridge Park and past the zoo, then along the Maumee River. But none of us had had enough of the car, so my father put the car on the road and we drove all the way to Detroit. We had plenty of family there, and everybody was just as pleased as could be about the Cadillac. My father told our Detroit relatives that he was in the doghouse with my mother about buying the Cadillac. My uncles told them she wouldn't ride in the car. All the Detroit family thought that was funny, and everybody, including my father, laughed about it and said my mother would come around. **G**

It was early evening by the time we got back home, and I could see from my mother's face she had not come around. She was angry now not only about the car, but that we had been gone so long. I didn't understand that, since my father had called her as soon as we reached Detroit to let her know where we were. I had heard him myself. I didn't understand either why she did not like that fine Cadillac and thought she was being terribly disagreeable with my father. That night, as she tucked Wilma and me in bed, I told her that too.

"Is this your business?" she asked.

"Well, I just think you ought to be nice to Daddy. I think you ought to ride in that car with him! It' d sure make him happy."

"I think you ought to go to sleep," she said and turned out the light.

Later I heard her arguing with my father. "We're supposed to be saving for a house!" she said.

"We've already got a house!" said my father.

"But you said you wanted a house in a better neighborhood. I thought that's what we both said!"

"I haven't changed my mind."

"Well, you have a mighty funny way of saving for it, then. Your brothers are saving for houses of their own, and you don't see them out buying new cars every year!"

"We'll still get the house, Dee. That's a promise!"

"Not with new Cadillacs we won't!" said my mother, and then she said a very loud good night, and all was quiet.

The next day was Sunday, and everybody figured that my mother would be sure to give in and ride in the Cadillac. After all, the family always went to church together on Sunday. But she didn't give in. What was worse, she wouldn't let Wilma and me ride in the Cadillac either. She took us each by the hand, walked past the Cadillac where my father stood waiting, and headed on toward the church three blocks away. I was really mad at her now. I had been looking forward to driving up to the church in that gold Cadillac and having everybody see. **H**

On most Sunday afternoons during the summertime, my mother, my father, Wilma, and I would go for a ride. Sometimes we just rode around the city and visited friends and family. Sometimes we made short trips over to Chicago or Peoria or Detroit to see relatives there or to Cleveland, where we had relatives too, but we could also see the Cleveland Indians play. Sometimes we

---

G **Literary Focus** **Novella** So far, where have the events of this novella taken place?

H **Read and Discuss** What does this segment indicate about Dee's anger regarding the Cadillac purchase?

joined our aunts and uncles and drove in a caravan[2] out to the park or to the beach. At the park or the beach, Wilma and I would run and play. My mother and my aunts would spread a picnic, and my father and my uncles would shine their cars.

But on this Sunday afternoon, my mother refused to ride anywhere. She told Wilma and me that we could go. So we left her alone in the big, empty house, and the family cars, led by the gold Cadillac, headed for the park. For a while I played and had a good time, but then I stopped playing and went to sit with my father. Despite his laughter he seemed sad to me. I think he was missing my mother as much as I was. **I**

That evening, my father took my mother to dinner down at the corner cafe. They walked. Wilma and I stayed at the house, chasing fireflies in the backyard. My aunts and uncles sat in the yard and on the porch, talking and laughing about the day and watching us. It was a soft summer's evening, the kind that came every day and was expected. The smell of charcoal and of barbecue drifting from up the block, the sound of laughter and music and talk drifting from yard to yard were all a part of it. Soon one of my uncles joined Wilma and me in our chase of fireflies, and when my mother and father came home, we were at it still. My mother and father watched us for a while, while everybody else watched them to see if my father would take out the Cadillac and if my mother would slide in beside him to take a ride. But it soon became evident that the dinner had not changed my mother's mind. She still refused to ride in the Cadillac. I just couldn't understand her objection to it. **J**

She still refused to ride in the Cadillac. I just couldn't understand her objection to it.

Though my mother didn't like the Cadillac, everybody else in the neighborhood certainly did. That meant quite a few folks too, since we lived on a very busy block. On one corner was a grocery store, a cleaner's, and a gas station. Across the street was a beauty shop and a fish market, and down the street was a bar, another grocery store, the Dixie Theater, the cafe, and a drugstore. There were always people strolling to or from one of these places, and because our house was right in the middle of the block, just about everybody had to pass our house and the gold Cadillac. Sometimes people took in the Cadillac as they walked, their heads turning for a lon-

2. **caravan** (KAR uh van): group of cars traveling together.

I **Literary Perspectives** **Analyzing Credibility in Literature** Nobody seems to agree with Dee's objection to the Cadillac purchase. Explain whether you think her reaction is believable or not.

J **Read and Discuss** How have these scenes added to what we know about 'lois's father and mother?

Vocabulary **evident** (EHV uh duhnt) *adj.:* easily seen or understood; obvious.

ger look as they passed. Then there were people who just outright stopped and took a good look before continuing on their way. I was proud to say that car belonged to my family. I felt mighty important as people called to me as I ran down the street. "'Ey, 'lois! How's that Cadillac, girl? Riding fine?" I told my mother how much everybody liked that car. She was not impressed and made no comment. **K**

Since just about everybody on the block knew everybody else, most folks knew that my mother wouldn't ride in the Cadillac. Because of that, my father took a lot of good-natured kidding from the men. My mother got kidded too, as the women said if she didn't ride in that car, maybe some other woman would. And everybody laughed about it and began to bet on who would give in first, my mother or my father. But then my father said he was going to drive the car south into Mississippi to visit my grandparents, and everybody stopped laughing.

My uncles stopped.

So did my aunts.

Everybody.

"Look here, Wilbert," said one of my uncles, "it's too dangerous. It's like putting a loaded gun to your head."

"I paid good money for that car," said my father. "That gives me a right to drive it where I please. Even down to Mississippi."

My uncles argued with him and tried to talk him out of driving the car south. So did my aunts, and so did the neighbors, Mr. LeRoy, Mr. Courtland, and Mr. Pondexter. They said it was a dangerous thing, a mighty dangerous thing, for a black man to drive an expensive car into the rural South.

Analyzing Visuals **Viewing and Interpreting** What character traits do you infer from this portrait that seem similar to 'lois's traits?

Harlem Girl 1 (1925) by Fritz Winold Reiss.

Museum of Art and Archaeology, University of Missouri-Columbia. Gift of Mr. W. Tjark Reiss.

K **Read and Discuss** What does this segment show us about 'lois?

Vocabulary **rural** (RUR uhl) *adj.:* having to do with country life.

"Not much those folks hate more'n to see a northern Negro coming down there in a fine car," said Mr. Pondexter. "They see those Ohio license plates, they'll figure you coming down uppity, trying to lord your fine car over them!"

I listened, but I didn't understand. I didn't understand why they didn't want my father to drive that car south. It was his.

"Listen to Pondexter, Wilbert!" cried another uncle. "We might've fought a war to free people overseas, but we're not free here! Man, those white folks down south'll lynch[3] you soon's look at you. You know that!" **L**

Wilma and I looked at each other. Neither one of us knew what *lynch* meant, but the word sent a shiver through us. We held each other's hand.

My father was silent, then he said: "All my life I've had to be heedful of what white folks thought. Well, I'm tired of that. I worked hard for everything I got. Got it honest, too. Now I got that Cadillac because I liked it and because it meant something to me that somebody like me from Mississippi could go and buy it. It's my car, I paid for it, and I'm driving it south." **M**

My mother, who had said nothing through all this, now stood. "Then the girls and I'll be going too," she said.

3. **lynch** (lihnch): kill a person without legal authority, usually by hanging. Lynchings are committed by violent mobs that have taken the law into their own hands.

"No!" said my father.

My mother only looked at him and went off to the kitchen.

My father shook his head. It seemed he didn't want us to go. My uncles looked at each other, then at my father. "You set on doing this, we'll all go," they said. "That way we can watch out for each other." My father took a moment and nodded. Then my aunts got up and went off to their kitchens too.

All the next day, my aunts and my mother cooked and the house was filled with delicious smells. They fried chicken and baked hams and cakes and sweet potato pies and mixed potato salad. They filled jugs with water and punch and coffee. Then they packed everything in huge picnic baskets, along with bread and boiled eggs, oranges and apples, plates and napkins, spoons and forks and cups. They placed all that food on the back seats of the cars. It was like a grand, grand picnic we were going on, and Wilma and I were mighty excited. We could hardly wait to start.

My father, my mother, Wilma, and I got into the Cadillac. My uncles, my aunts, my cousins got into the Ford, the Buick, and the Chevrolet, and we rolled off in our caravan headed south. Though my mother was finally riding in the Cadillac, she had no praise for it. In fact, she said nothing about it at all. She still seemed upset, and since she still seemed to feel the same about the car, I wondered why she had insisted upon making this trip with my father. **N**

L **Reading Focus** **Making Predictions** From Mr. Pondexter's and the uncles' warnings, what do you think will happen on the trip?

M **Literary Focus** **Novella** What is the main conflict, or problem, in this novella?

N **Read and Discuss** What is 'lois thinking about during the trip? What does this tell you about her?

We left the city of Toledo behind, drove through Bowling Green and down through the Ohio countryside of farms and small towns, through Dayton and Cincinnati, and across the Ohio River into Kentucky. On the other side of the river, my father stopped the car and looked back at Wilma and me and said, "Now from here on, whenever we stop and there're white people around, I don't want either one of you to say a word. *Not one word!* Your mother and I'll do the talking. That understood?"

"Yes, sir," Wilma and I both said, though we didn't truly understand why.

My father nodded, looked at my mother, and started the car again. We rolled on, down Highway 25 and through the bluegrass hills of Kentucky. Soon we began to see signs. Signs that read: "White Only, Colored Not Allowed." Hours later, we left the Bluegrass State and crossed into Tennessee. Now we saw even more of the signs saying: "White Only, Colored Not Allowed." We saw the signs above water fountains and in restaurant windows. We saw them in ice cream parlors and at hamburger stands. We saw them in front of hotels and motels, and on the restroom doors of filling stations. I didn't like the signs. I felt as if I were in a foreign land.

I couldn't understand why the signs were there, and I asked my father what the signs meant. He said they meant we couldn't drink from the water fountains. He said they meant we couldn't stop to sleep in the motels. He said they meant we couldn't stop to eat in the restaurants. I looked at the grand picnic basket I had been enjoying so much. Now I understood why my mother had packed it. Suddenly the picnic did not seem so grand. **O**

Finally we reached Memphis. We got there at a bad time. Traffic was heavy and we got separated from the rest of the family. We tried to find them but it was no use. We had to go on alone. We reached the Mississippi state line, and soon after, we heard a police siren. A police car came up behind us. My father slowed the Cadillac, then stopped. Two white policemen got out of their car. They eyeballed the Cadillac and told my father to get out. **P**

"Whose car is this, boy?" they asked.

I saw anger in my father's eyes. "It's mine," he said.

"You're a liar," said one of the policemen. "You stole this car."

"Turn around, put your hands on top of that car, and spread-eagle," said the other policeman.

My father did as he was told. They searched him and I didn't understand why.

I didn't understand either why they had called my father a liar and didn't believe that the Cadillac was his. I wanted to ask, but I remembered my father's warning not to say a word, and I obeyed that warning.

The policemen told my father to get in the back of the police car. My father did. One policeman got back into the police car. The other policeman slid behind the wheel of our Cadillac. The police car started off. The Cadillac followed. Wilma and I looked at each other and at our mother. We didn't know what to think. We were scared.

The Cadillac followed the police car into a small town and stopped in front of

---

O **Read and Discuss** What is 'lois thinking about the grand picnic now?

P **Reading Focus** **Making Predictions** What do you predict the police will do to 'lois's father? Why?

Mississippi postcard.

Analyzing Visuals **Viewing and Interpreting** What kind of greeting have 'lois and her family received so far on their visit to Mississippi?

the police station. The policeman stepped out of our Cadillac and took the keys. The other policeman took my father into the police station.

"Mother-Dear!" Wilma and I cried. "What're they going to do to our daddy? They going to hurt him?"

"He'll be all right," said my mother. "He'll be all right." But she didn't sound so sure of that. She seemed worried. Q

We waited. More than three hours we waited. Finally my father came out of the police station. We had lots of questions to ask him. He said the police had given him a ticket for speeding and locked him up. But then the judge had come. My father had paid the ticket and they had let him go.

He started the Cadillac and drove slowly out of the town, below the speed limit. The police car followed us. People standing on steps and sitting on porches and in front of stores stared at us as we passed. Finally we were out of the town. The police car still followed. Dusk was falling. The night

Q **Read and Discuss** How does 'lois handle the unfolding events with the police?

Vocabulary **dusk** (duhsk) *n.:* the period of time when the sky darkens as the sun goes down.

Black Mountain, U.S. 70 (1957) by Joseph Garlock, 29 x 37 inches, gouache on board.

grew black, and finally the police car turned around and left us.

We drove and drove. But my father was tired now and my grandparents' farm was still far away. My father said he had to get some sleep, and since my mother didn't drive, he pulled into a grove of trees at the side of the road and stopped.

"I'll keep watch," said my mother.

"Wake me if you see anybody," said my father.

"Just rest," said my mother.

So my father slept. But that bothered me. I needed him awake. I was afraid of the dark and of the woods and of whatever lurked there. My father was the one who kept us safe, he and my uncles. But already the police had taken my father away from us once today, and my uncles were lost.

"Go to sleep, baby," said my mother. "Go to sleep." Ⓡ

But I was afraid to sleep until my father woke. I had to help my mother keep watch. I figured I had to help protect us too, in case the police came back and tried to take my father away again. There was a long, sharp knife in the picnic basket, and I took hold of it, clutching it tightly in my hand. Ready to strike, I sat there in the back of the car, eyes wide, searching the blackness outside the Cadillac. Wilma, for a while, searched the night too, then she fell asleep. I didn't want to sleep, but soon I found I couldn't help myself as an unwelcome drowsiness came over me. I had an uneasy sleep, and when I woke, it was dawn and my father was gently shaking me. I woke with a start and my hand went up, but the knife wasn't there. My mother had it.

Ⓡ **Read and Discuss** What's going on now?

My father took my hand. "Why were you holding the knife, 'lois?" he asked.

I looked at him and at my mother. "I—I was scared," I said.

My father was thoughtful. "No need to be scared now, sugar," he said. "Daddy's here and so is Mother-Dear." **S**

Then after a glance at my mother, he got out of the car, walked to the road, looked down it one way, then the other. When he came back and started the motor, he turned the Cadillac north, not south.

"What're you doing?" asked my mother.

"Heading back to Memphis," said my father. "Cousin Halton's there. We'll leave the Cadillac and get his car. Driving this car any farther south with you and the girls in the car, it's just not worth the risk."

And so that's what we did. Instead of driving through Mississippi in golden splendor, we traveled its streets and roads and highways in Cousin Halton's solid, yet not so splendid, four-year-old Chevy. When we reached my grandparents' farm, my uncles and aunts were already there. Everybody was glad to see us. They had been worried. They asked about the Cadillac. My father told them what had happened, and they nodded and said he had done the best thing.

We stayed one week in Mississippi. During that week I often saw my father, looking deep in thought, walk off alone across the family land. I saw my mother watching him. One day I ran after my father, took his hand, and walked the land with him. I asked him all the questions that were on my mind. I asked him why the policemen had treated him the way they had and why people didn't want us to eat in the restaurants or drink from the water fountains or sleep in the hotels. I told him I just didn't understand all that.

My father looked at me and said that it all was a difficult thing to understand and he didn't really understand it himself. He said it all had to do with the fact that black people had once been forced to be slaves. He said it had to do with our skins being colored. He said it had to do with stupidity and ignorance. He said it had to do with the law, the law that said we could be treated like this here in the South. And for that matter, he added, any other place in these United States where folks thought the same as so many folks did here in the South. But he also said, "I'm hoping one day though we can drive that long road down here and there won't be any signs. I'm hoping one day the police won't stop us just because of the color of our skins and we're riding in a gold Cadillac with northern plates." **T**

When the week ended, we said a sad goodbye to my grandparents and all the Mississippi family and headed in a caravan back toward Memphis. In Memphis, we returned Cousin Halton's car and got our Cadillac. Once we were home, my father put the Cadillac in the garage and didn't drive it. I didn't hear my mother say any more about the Cadillac. I didn't hear my father speak of it either. **U**

S **Reading Focus** **Making Predictions** Will the family keep going south, or will they go back? What makes you think so?

T **Read and Discuss** What effect do you think 'lois's questions have on her father?

U **Reading Focus** **Making Predictions** What do you predict the family will do with the Cadillac?

Vocabulary **ignorance** (IHG nuhr uhns) *n.:* lack of knowledge.

Some days passed, and then on a bright Saturday afternoon while Wilma and I were playing in the backyard, I saw my father go into the garage. He opened the garage doors wide so the sunshine streamed in and began to shine the Cadillac. I saw my mother at the kitchen window staring out across the yard at my father. For a long time, she stood there watching my father shine his car. Then she came out and crossed the yard to the garage, and I heard her say, "Wilbert, you keep the car."

He looked at her as if he had not heard.

"You keep it," she repeated and turned and walked back to the house.

My father watched her until the back door had shut behind her. Then he went on shining the car and soon began to sing. About an hour later he got into the car and drove away. That evening when he came back, he was walking. The Cadillac was nowhere in sight.

"Daddy, where's our new Cadillac?" I demanded to know. So did Wilma.

He smiled and put his hand on my head. "Sold it," he said as my mother came into the room.

"But how come?" I asked. "We poor now?"

"No, sugar. We've got more money towards our new house now, and we're all together. I figure that makes us about the richest folks in the world." He smiled at my mother, and she smiled too and came into his arms. **V**

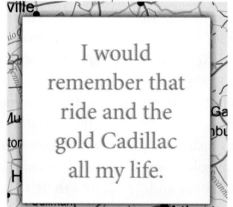

I would remember that ride and the gold Cadillac all my life.

After that, we drove around in an old 1930s Model A Ford my father had. He said he'd factory-ordered us another Mercury, this time with my mother's approval. Despite that, most folks on the block figured we had fallen on hard times after such a splashy showing of good times, and some folks even laughed at us as the Ford rattled around the city. I must admit that at first I was pretty much embarrassed to be riding around in that old Ford after the splendor of the Cadillac. But my father said to hold my head high. We and the family knew the truth. As fine as the Cadillac had been, he said, it had pulled us apart for a while. Now, as ragged and noisy as that old Ford was, we all rode in it together, and we were a family again. So I held my head high.

Still, though, I thought often of that Cadillac. We had had the Cadillac only a little more than a month, but I wouldn't soon forget its splendor or how I'd felt riding around inside it. I wouldn't soon forget either the ride we had taken south in it. I wouldn't soon forget the signs, the policemen, or my fear. I would remember that ride and the gold Cadillac all my life. **W**

V **Literary Perspectives** **Analyzing Credibility in Literature** How credible is this turn of events? Explain why it seems either believable or unbelievable to you.

W **Literary Focus** **Novella** What is the theme, or main message, of this novella?

Applying Your Skills

The Gold Cadillac

Sunshine State Standards: Benchmarks **LA.6.1.7.1** use background knowledge of subject and related content areas, prereading strategies, graphic representations, and knowledge of text structure to make and confirm complex predictions of content, purpose, and organization of a reading selection; *Also covered* **LA.6.1.7.8; LA.6.2.1.1; LA.6.2.1.2; LA.6.4.2.3**

Respond and Think Critically

Reading Focus

1. Which clue below helps you predict that the family will eventually get rid of the Cadillac? 
   A Everybody in the neighborhood likes it.
   B The family seems wealthy because of it.
   C The narrator's mother refuses to ride in it.
   D The narrator's father is very proud of it.

Read with a Purpose

2. What does 'lois learn from her trip to the South? What does her father learn?

Reading Skills: Making and Adjusting Predictions

3. Add a fourth column to the predictions chart you filled out, and note in it if your predictions were correct. Use a check mark (✓) for "yes" and an *X* for "no." What new information caused you to adjust the *X* predictions?

In the story	I predict	Because	
the narrator and her sister see the Cadillac	that the father bought it	the father drives up in it and is grinning and happy	✓
the girls go get their mother			

Literary Focus

Literary Analysis

4. **Analyze** What do you think the gold Cadillac stands for in the eyes of Wilbert and his neighbors? What details in the story <u>indicate</u> this? Support your response with details from the text. 

5. **Literary Perspectives** How is the credibility of *The Gold Cadillac*'s **plot** (the events that make up the story) dependent upon the **setting** (where and when the story takes place)?

Literary Skills: Novella

6. **Extend** If you were Mildred Taylor and had to edit down *The Gold Cadillac* to half its length, what would you have to change? Which <u>features</u> of the story would have to remain for the <u>concept</u> to stay the same?

Literary Skills Review: Point of View

7. **Analyze** From whose point of view are the story's events told? How might the story be different if it were told by a different character? Support your response with details from the text. READ THINK EXPLAIN

Writing Focus

Think as a Reader/Writer

Use It in Your Writing Look at the list you made of details about richness, beauty, and luxury. Think about something important to you, such as a possession, a place, or an activity. Write a descriptive paragraph about it, using details that show its importance to you and what it adds to your life.

What has this story shown you about the power of fiction to depict events based on historical fact?

The Gold Cadillac

Vocabulary Development

Semantic Mapping

Just as 'lois has many family relationships in *The Gold Cadillac,* words have relationships with other words. For example, words can be **synonyms** (have the same or similar meanings) or **antonyms** (have opposite or nearly opposite meanings). These are only two of the many relationships that can exist between words. A **semantic map,** like the one below, is a good way of showing certain word relationships.

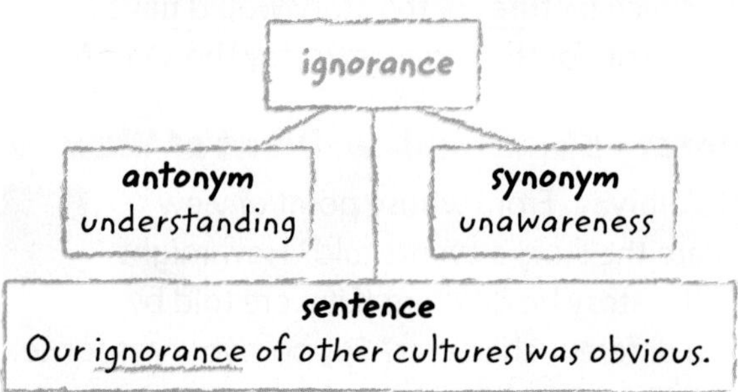

Your Turn

evident
rural
dusk
ignorance

Using the semantic map above as a model, map the three other Vocabulary words: *evident, rural,* and *dusk*. At the top of each map, write a Vocabulary word. Then, write a synonym and an antonym and a sentence using the word.

Language Coach

Word Forms You can often change one word to another, related word by adding to or changing the end of the word. For example, to change the noun *importance* to the adjective *important*, you change the ending, or suffix, like this:

import~~ance~~ (*n.*) + *–ant* = important (*adj.*)

Which of the Vocabulary words can you similarly change to an adjective by using the suffix *–ant*?

Academic Vocabulary

Write About . . .

Which details in *The Gold Cadillac* indicate that it is set in the past? In a paragraph, describe the features of the story that clearly distinguish it from life today. What concept of the past does this story present?

Learn It Online
Learn more about synonyms and antonyms online at:
go.hrw.com
L6-44
Go

Sunshine State Standards: Benchmarks **LA.6.1.6.5** relate new vocabulary to familiar words; **LA.6.1.6.8** identify advanced word/phrase relationships and their meanings; **LA.6.3.4.4** the eight parts of speech (noun, pronoun, verb, adverb, adjective, conjunction, preposition, interjection); **LA.6.6.2.2** collect, evaluate and summarize information using a variety of techniques from multiple sources (e.g., encyclopedias, websites, experts) that includes paraphrasing to convey ideas and details from the source, main idea(s) and relevant details; **LA.6.6.4.1** use appropriate available technologies to enhance communication and achieve a purpose (e.g., video, online).

Grammar Link

Pronouns Cut the Clutter

Have you ever listened to someone repeat the same thing over and over instead of getting to some new point? If so, you were probably bored and found it difficult to keep listening. You're lucky that English is full of **pronouns**—words that are used in place of nouns and, sometimes, other pronouns. Without pronouns, people would have to repeat themselves every time they spoke. For example, look at the following repetitive sentence:

> ***The father*** **told** ***the father's daughter*** **that** ***the father*** **wanted** ***the father's daughter*** **to ride in the car.**

Pronouns shorten this sentence, making it much easier to read (and listen to):

> **The father told** ***his*** **daughter that** ***he*** **wanted** ***her*** **to ride in the car.**

Your Turn

Rewrite each of the following sentences by replacing any repeated nouns with pronouns.

1. Wilma ran toward Wilma's father in the Cadillac.
2. The Cadillac was like no car we owned before because the Cadillac looked like a car for rich folks.
3. I could see from my mother's face that my father had not changed my mother's mind.
4. 'lois's father said that the police had given 'lois's father a ticket for speeding and locked 'lois's father up in jail.
5. We picked up Cousin Halton's Chevy in Memphis and drove Cousin Halton's Chevy into Mississippi.

CHOICES

As you respond to the Choices, use these **Academic Vocabulary** words as appropiate: features, interpret, concept, indicate.

REVIEW

Reflect on Forms of Fiction

Timed Writing Mildred Taylor based this novella on some of her own memories. Why didn't she just write a nonfiction piece about one of those memories instead of creating fictional characters and events? In a paragraph, discuss how this story would be different if it were written as nonfiction instead of fiction.

CONNECT

Draw a Map

Group Activity Using pencils or a computer drawing tool, create a map of the route that 'lois's family drives in their gold Cadillac. Use color and other methods to show such features as which states had segregation laws. Be sure to indicate where important story events occur.

EXTEND

Research the Facts

Before the Civil Rights Act of 1964, the South was a very different place than it is today. Make a list of some of the things 'lois sees on her trip that puzzle or disturb her. Then, in the library or on the Internet, research articles and photographs about the pre–civil rights South. Has the author accurately depicted what the South was like around 1950? Share your findings with the class.

Learn It Online
Take a deeper look at this story using these Internet links at:
go.hrw.com L6-45 Go

FOLK TALE AND FABLES

Preparing to Read

He Lion, Bruh Bear, and Bruh Rabbit

African American folk tale
retold by **Virginia Hamilton**

The Fox and the Crow *and* The Wolf and the House Dog

by **Aesop**

What Do You Think?

Why do we like stories about clever animals who outsmart their enemies?

QuickWrite

Write about the things trickster animals say and do in stories. Start with tricksters you may know from cartoons, such as Bugs Bunny and the Road Runner.

Little Red Riding Hood (1992) by William Wegman.

Reader/Writer Notebook

Use your **RWN** to complete the activities for these selections.

Sunshine State Standards: Benchmarks **LA.6.1.6.4** categorize key vocabulary and identify salient features; **LA.6.1.7.8** use strategies to repair comprehension of grade-appropriate text when self-monitoring indicates confusion, including but not limited to rereading, checking context clues, predicting, note-making, summarizing, using graphic and semantic organizers, questioning, and clarifying by checking other sources; **LA.6.2.1.1** identify the characteristics of various genres (e.g., poetry, fiction, short story, dramatic literature) as forms with distinct characteristics and purposes.

Literary Focus

Forms of Fiction: Folk Tales and Fables **Folk tales** and **fables** have been around for thousands of years—a much longer time than novels, novellas, and short stories. Traditional folk tales and fables were told aloud long before they were written down.

The Trickster The heroes of many folk tales are **tricksters**—characters who outsmart bigger, more powerful enemies. Most tricksters are underdogs—weak characters who seem unlikely to win. Tricksters triumph because they're clever, even if they seem silly or even stupid. Their tricks often teach important lessons.

TechFocus As you read these stories, think about how you might use a word-processing or drawing program to create an illustrated, graphic story version of a folk tale or fable.

Reading Focus

Monitoring Comprehension To check your understanding, pause regularly and ask yourself questions about the text.

Into Action Asking questions about what you've read is key to **monitoring your comprehension.** Stop at least twice—once in the middle and once at the end—as you read each of the tales.

The Big Questions	. . . and Answers
What just happened?	
Why did it happen?	
What characters were involved?	

Writing Focus

Think as a Reader/Writer

Find It in Your Reading As you read these folk tales and fables, keep lists of the strong characters and the weak characters in each story. Explain what makes each character weak or strong.

Vocabulary

He Lion, Bruh Bear, and Bruh Rabbit

lair (lair) *n.:* home of a wild animal; den. *He Lion had built his lair on the cliff.*

The Fox and the Crow

suspicion (suh SPIHSH uhn) *n.:* feeling that someone is guilty of something. *At first, Crow viewed Fox with suspicion.*

impressing (ihm PREHS ihng) *v.:* making someone feel admiration. *House Dog was impressing Wolf with descriptions of foods.*

flattery (FLAT uhr ee) *n.:* praise that is false or pretended. *The Crow makes the mistake of believing flattery.*

Language Coach

Homophones Have you ever heard words that sound the same but are spelled differently and mean different things? The word *bear,* for example, sounds like the word *bare.* These words are **homophones** (HAHM uh fohnz), the tricksters of the word world! Don't let them fool you; just remember what each word means.

1. If you were talking about an animal, which word would you use? (*bear/bare*)
2. If you were talking about a tree with no leaves, which word would you use? (*bear/bare*)

Learn It Online

Take a closer look at vocabulary on:

go.hrw.com L6-47 

Learn It Online
Read more on Hamilton's life at:
go.hrw.com L6-48 Go

Virginia Hamilton
(1936–2002)

For most of her life, Virginia Hamilton lived where she was born and raised: Yellow Springs, Ohio. Her grandfather settled there after escaping from slavery in pre–Civil War days. Hamilton recalls her family fondly:

"My mother's 'people' were warm-hearted, tight with money, generous to the sick and landless, close-mouthed, and fond of telling tales and gossip about one another and even their ancestors. They were a part of me from the time I understood that I belonged to all of them."

Aesop
(sixth century B.C.)

Not much is known about Aesop. According to an ancient historian, he came from Africa and was held in slavery in Greece. The fables he is said to have written may have originally come from ancient India. Aesop eventually won his freedom, but he met a violent death, perhaps because his fables made dangerous political points about concepts like liberty.

Think About the Writers

Why do you think people throughout time have used fictional tales to teach important lessons?

Build Background

Folk tales like "He Lion, Bruh Bear, and Bruh Rabbit" originally came from Africa. On the surface, the stories seem to be entertaining tales about mean big animals and crafty little ones. If you read between the lines, however, you might interpret these tales a little differently. Folk tales and fables usually present an idea or lesson to which we humans need to pay attention.

Preview the Selections

In the folk tale, **he Lion** thunders through the forest scaring the small animals, who go to **Bruh Bear** and **Bruh Rabbit** for help.

In the fables, **Fox** tries to get **Crow** to give up a chunk of cheese, and **House Dog** tries to persuade **Wolf** to try living in the village.

Read with a Purpose Read this fable, and decide if he Lion gets what he deserves.

He Lion, Bruh Bear, and Bruh Rabbit

African American folk tale retold by **Virginia Hamilton**

Say that he Lion would get up each and every mornin. Stretch and walk around. He'd roar, "ME AND MYSELF. ME AND MYSELF," like that. Scare all the little animals so they were afraid to come outside in the sunshine. Afraid to go huntin or fishin or whatever the little animals wanted to do.

"What we gone do about it?" they asked one another. Squirrel leapin from branch to branch, just scared. Possum playin dead, couldn't hardly move him.

He Lion just went on, stickin out his chest and roarin, "ME AND MYSELF. ME AND MYSELF."

The little animals held a sit-down talk, and one by one and two by two and all by all, they decide to go see Bruh Bear and Bruh Rabbit. For they know that Bruh Bear been around. And Bruh Rabbit say he has, too.

So they went to Bruh Bear and Bruh Rabbit. Said, "We have some trouble. Old he Lion, him scarin everybody, roarin every mornin and all day, 'ME AND MYSELF. ME AND MYSELF,' like that." **A**

"Why he Lion want to do that?" Bruh Bear said.

"Is that all he Lion have to say?" Bruh Rabbit asked.

"We don't know why, but that's all he Lion can tell us and we didn't ask him to tell us that," said the little animals. "And him scarin the children with it. And we wish him to stop it."

"Well, I'll go see him, talk to him. I've known he Lion a long kind of time," Bruh Bear said.

"I'll go with you," said Bruh Rabbit. "I've known he Lion most long as you." **B**

That bear and that rabbit went off through the forest. They kept hearin somethin. Mumble, mumble. Couldn't make it out. They got farther in the forest. They heard it plain now. "ME AND MYSELF. ME AND MYSELF."

"Well, well, well," said Bruh Bear. He wasn't scared. He'd been around the whole forest, seen a lot.

"My, my, my," said Bruh Rabbit. He'd

A **Reading Focus** **Monitoring Comprehension** Who are the characters so far, and what is their problem?

B **Read and Discuss** What have we learned so far?

seen enough to know not to be afraid of an old he lion. Now old he lions could be dangerous, but you had to know how to handle them.

The bear and the rabbit climbed up and up the cliff where he Lion had his lair. They found him. Kept their distance. He watchin them and they watchin him. Everybody actin cordial.[1]

"Hear tell you are scarin everybody, all the little animals, with your roarin all the time," Bruh Rabbit said.

"I roars when I pleases," he Lion said.

"Well, might could you leave off the noise first thing in the mornin, so the little animals can get what they want to eat and drink?" asked Bruh Bear.

"Listen," said he Lion, and then he roared: "ME AND MYSELF. ME AND MYSELF. Nobody tell me what not to do," he said. "I'm the king of the forest, *me and myself*."

"Better had let me tell you somethin," Bruh Rabbit said, "for I've seen Man, and I know him the real king of the forest." **C**

He Lion was quiet awhile. He looked straight through that scrawny lil Rabbit like he was nothin at all. He looked at Bruh Bear and figured he' d talk to him.

"You, Bear, you been around," he Lion said.

"That's true," said old Bruh Bear. "I been about everywhere. I've been around the whole forest."

"Then you must know somethin," he Lion said.

"I know lots," said Bruh Bear, slow and quiet-like.

"Tell me what you know about Man," he Lion said. "He think him the king of the forest?"

"Well, now, I'll tell you," said Bruh Bear,

1. **cordial** (KAWR juhl): warm and friendly.

C **Reading Focus** **Monitoring Comprehension** Why does Bruh Rabbit say this to he Lion?

Vocabulary **lair** (lair) *n.:* home of a wild animal; den.

"I been around, but I haven't ever come across Man that I know of. Couldn't tell you nothin about him."

So he Lion had to turn back to Bruh Rabbit. He didn't want to but he had to. "So what?" he said to that lil scrawny hare.

"Well, you got to come down from there if you want to see Man," Bruh Rabbit said. "Come down from there and I'll show you him." **D**

He Lion thought a minute, an hour, and a whole day. Then, the next day, he came on down.

He roared just once, "ME AND MYSELF. ME AND MYSELF. Now," he said, "come show me Man."

So they set out. He Lion, Bruh Bear, and Bruh Rabbit. They go along and they go along, rangin the forest. Pretty soon, they come to a clearin. And playin in it is a little fellow about nine years old.

"Is that there Man?" asked he Lion.

"Why no, that one is called Will Be, but it sure is not Man," said Bruh Rabbit.

So they went along and they went along. Pretty soon, they come upon a shade tree. And sleepin under it is an old, olden fellow, about ninety years olden.

"There must lie Man," spoke he Lion. "I knew him wasn't gone be much."

"That's not Man," said Bruh Rabbit. "That fellow is Was Once. You'll know it when you see Man." **E**

So they went on along. He Lion is gettin tired of strollin. So he roars, "ME AND MYSELF. ME AND MYSELF." Upsets Bear so that Bear doubles over and runs and climbs a tree.

"Come down from there," Bruh Rabbit tellin him. So after a while Bear comes down. He keepin his distance from he Lion, anyhow. And they set out some more. Goin along quiet and slow.

In a little while they come to a road. And comin on way down the road, Bruh Rabbit sees Man comin. Man about twenty-one years old. Big and strong, with a big gun over his shoulder.

"There!" Bruh Rabbit says. "See there, he Lion? There's Man. You better go meet him."

"I will," says he Lion. And he sticks out his chest and he roars, "ME AND MYSELF. ME AND MYSELF." All the way to Man he's roarin proud, "ME AND MYSELF, ME AND MYSELF!"

D **Literary Focus** **Folk Tale** In this folk tale, who's most likely the trickster, Bruh Bear or Bruh Rabbit? Why do you think so?

E **Read and Discuss** What happened? What is Bruh Rabbit talking about when he refers to *Man*, *Will Be*, and *Was Once*?

Analyzing Visuals **Viewing and Interpreting**

In what ways is this lion similar to or different from he Lion in this folk tale?

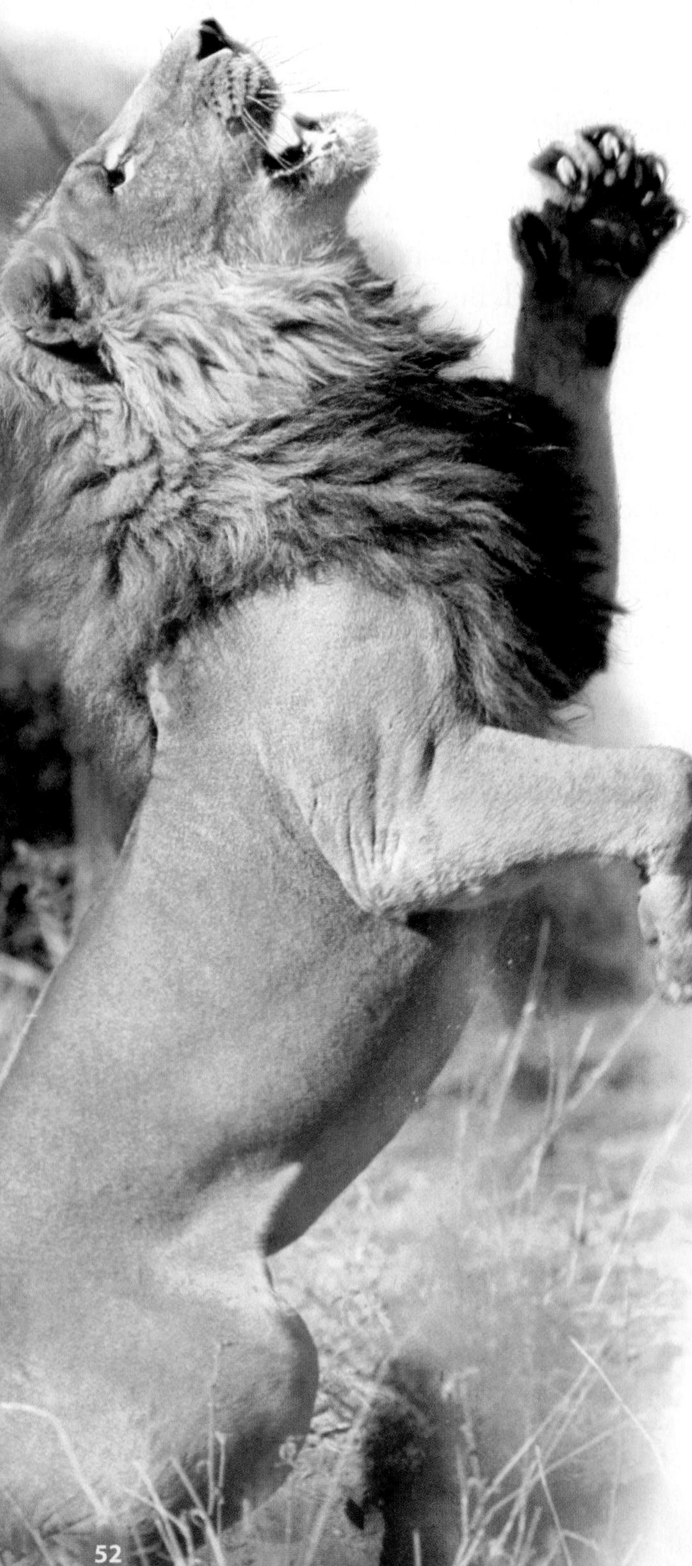

"Come on, Bruh Bear, let's go!" Bruh Rabbit says.

"What for?" Bruh Bear wants to know.

"You better come on!" And Bruh Rabbit takes ahold of Bruh Bear and half drags him to a thicket. And there he makin the Bear hide with him.

For here comes Man. He sees old he Lion real good now. He drops to one knee and he takes aim with his big gun.

Old he Lion is roarin his head off: "ME AND MYSELF! ME AND MYSELF!"

The big gun goes off: PA-LOOOM!

He Lion falls back hard on his tail.

The gun goes off again. PA-LOOOM!

He Lion is flyin through the air. He lands in the thicket.

"Well, did you see Man?" asked Bruh Bear. **F**

"I seen him," said he Lion. "Man spoken to me unkind, and got a great long stick him keepin on his shoulder. Then Man taken that stick down and him speakin real mean. Thunderin at me and lightnin comin from that stick, awful bad. Made me sick. I had to turn around. And Man pointin that stick again and thunderin at me some more. So I come in here, cause it seem like him throwed some stickers at me each time it thunder, too." **G**

F **Literary Focus** **Folk Tale** Humor is part of many folk tales. What humor do you find in this scene?

G **Reading Focus** **Monitoring Comprehension** What happened when he Lion met Man?

"So you've met Man, and you know zactly what that kind of him is," says Bruh Rabbit.

"I surely do know that," he Lion said back.

A while after he Lion met Man, things were some better in the forest. Bruh Bear knew what Man looked like so he could keep out of his way. That rabbit always did know to keep out of Man's way. The little animals could go out in the mornin because he Lion was more peaceable. He didn't walk around roarin at the top of his voice all the time. And when he Lion did lift that voice of his, it was like, "Me and Myself and Man. Me and Myself and Man." Like that. H

Wasn't too loud at all. 

H **Read and Discuss** How's the story tied up at the end?

I **Literary Focus** **Folk Tale** What concept of bullies and bullying does this folk tale present? What lesson does it teach?

Analyzing Visuals **Viewing and Interpreting** How do the bear and rabbit in this picture reflect the outcome of the story?

Read with a Purpose Read this fable to see if a fox can outsmart a crow.

The Fox and the Crow (A)

by **Aesop**

Greek fable, dramatized by **Mara Rockliff**

Narrator. One fine morning a Fox was wandering through the woods, enjoying the lovely spring weather.

Fox. Lovely spring weather is all very well, but a fox can't live on sunshine and fresh air. I could use some breakfast right about now.

Narrator. Suddenly he noticed a Crow sitting on the branch of a tree above him. The Fox didn't think much of crows as a rule, but this particular Crow had something very interesting in her beak.

Fox. Cheese. Mmm. A nice big yellow chunk of cheese. I would love that cheese. I deserve that cheese. But how can I get that cheese? (B)

Narrator. The Fox thought awhile, and then he called up to the Crow.

Fox. Good morning, you fabulous bird.

Narrator. The Crow looked at him suspiciously. But she kept her beak closed tightly on the cheese and said nothing.

Fox. What beautiful beady eyes you have! And you certainly look great in black feathers. I've seen a lot of birds in my time, but you outbird them all. A bird with your good looks must have a voice to match. Oh, if only I could hear you sing just one song. Then I would know you were truly the Greatest Bird on Earth. (C)

Narrator. Listening to all this flattery, the Crow forgot her suspicion of the Fox. She forgot her cheese, too. All she could think of was impressing the Fox with a song. So she opened her beak wide and let out a loud "Caw!" Down fell the cheese, right into the Fox's open mouth.

Fox. Thanks! That tasted every bit as good as it looked. Well, now I know you have a voice—and I hope I never have to hear it again. But where are your brains?

All Together. If you let flattery go to your head, you'll pay the price. (D)

(A) **Literary Focus Fable** What behaviors do you associate with foxes and with crows?

(B) **Read and Discuss** What problem does Fox have?

(C) **Literary Focus Fable** Who is the trickster in this fable, and how do you know?

(D) **Read and Discuss** What is the moral, or lesson, of this tale?

Vocabulary **suspicion** (suh SPIHSH uhn) *n.:* feeling that someone is guilty of something.

impressing (ihm PREHS ihng) *v.:* making someone feel admiration.

flattery (FLAT uhr ee) *n.:* praise that is false or pretended.

Read with a Purpose Read this fable to see if a hungry wolf would change places with a well-fed dog.

The Wolf and the House Dog

by **Aesop**

Greek fable, dramatized by **Mara Rockliff**

Narrator. Once there was a Wolf who never got enough to eat. Her mouth watered when she looked at the fat geese and chickens kept by the people of the village. But every time she tried to steal one, the watchful village dogs would bark and warn their owners. **A**

Wolf. Really, I'm nothing but skin and bones. It makes me sad just thinking about it.

Narrator. One night the Wolf met up with a House Dog who had wandered a little too far from home. The Wolf would gladly have eaten him right then and there.

A **Reading Focus** **Monitoring Comprehension** Why is the Wolf so hungry?

Wolf. Dog stew . . . cold dog pie . . . or maybe just dog on a bun, with plenty of mustard and ketchup . . .

Narrator. But the House Dog looked too big and strong for the Wolf, who was weak from hunger. So the Wolf spoke to him very humbly and politely.

Wolf. How handsome you are! You look so healthy and well fed and delicious—I mean, uh, terrific. You look terrific. Really.

House Dog. Well, you look terrible. I don't know why you live out here in these miserable woods, where you have to fight so hard for every crummy little scrap of food. You should come live in the village like me. You could eat like a king there.

Wolf. What do I have to do?

House Dog. Hardly anything. Chase kids on bicycles. Bark at the mailman every now and then. Lie around the house letting people pet you. Just for that they'll feed you till you burst—enormous steak bones with fat hanging off them, pizza crusts, bits of chicken, leftovers like you wouldn't believe. **B**

> How handsome you are! You look so healthy and well fed and delicious—I mean, uh, terrific. You look terrific.

Narrator. The Wolf nearly cried with happiness as she imagined how wonderful her new life was going to be. But then she noticed a strange ring around the Dog's neck where the hair had been rubbed off.

Wolf. What happened to your neck?

House Dog. Oh . . . ah . . . nothing. It's nothing, really. **C**

Wolf. I've never seen anything like it. Is it a disease?

House Dog. Don't be silly. It's just the mark of the collar that they fasten my chain to.

Wolf. A chain! You mean you can't go wherever you like?

House Dog. Well, not always. But what's the difference?

Wolf. What's the difference? Are you kidding? I wouldn't give up my freedom for the biggest, juiciest steak in the world. Never mind a few lousy bones.

Narrator. The Wolf ran away, back to the woods. She never went near the village again, no matter how hungry she got.

All Together. Nothing is worth more than freedom. **D**

B **Read and Discuss** What is the author setting up for us? What does the conversation between the Wolf and the House Dog reveal to us?

C **Reading Focus** **Monitoring Comprehension** How does House Dog feel when he says these words? How do you know?

D **Read and Discuss** What does the Wolf think of House Dog's idea? Why does the Wolf have a change of heart?

Applying Your Skills

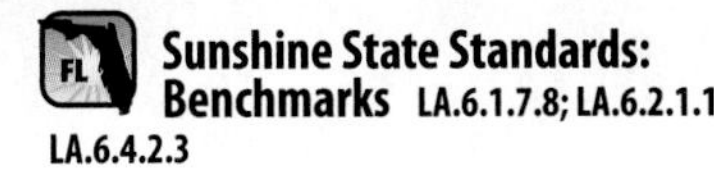

FL
Sunshine State Standards:
Benchmarks LA.6.1.7.8; LA.6.2.1.1;
LA.6.4.2.3

He Lion, Bruh Bear, and Bruh Rabbit / Aesop's Fables

Respond and Think Critically

Reading Focus

1. With which statement below would Aesop MOST likely agree? **FCAT**
   A The fox is a greedy and mean animal.
   B Freedom is more important than food.
   C House dogs are happier than foxes.
   D Flattery helps to make you feel good.

Read with a Purpose

2. In "He Lion, Bruh Bear, and Bruh Rabbit," do you think the punishment handed out by Bruh Bear and Bruh Rabbit was appropriate for he Lion's actions? Explain.
3. In "The Wolf and the House Dog," why does Wolf value freedom so much? What is she willing to give up for freedom?

Reading Skills: Monitoring Comprehension

4. Did your comprehension break down at any point as you read these selections? If so, how did pausing regularly and asking and answering questions about the text help you?

Literary Focus

Literary Analysis

5. **Analyze** What qualities do we associate with real rabbits and foxes that make people think they would be good tricksters? Would a lion or bear be a likely trickster? Why or why not? Support your answer with examples from the text. READ THINK EXPLAIN
6. **Interpret** What does the Lion mean when he roars, "ME AND MYSELF. ME AND MYSELF"?
7. **Infer** At the end of "He Lion . . . ," he Lion roars less loudly and less often. What does this change in his behavior indicate?
8. **Extend** What kind of people are like he Lion and the Crow? What do these tales tell you about such people?

Literary Skills: Folk Tales and Fables

9. **Analyze** Folk tales and fables present **morals,** or lessons about how to get along in the world. What lessons are taught in these stories? What do you think about each lesson? Support your response with details from the text. READ THINK EXPLAIN

Literary Skills Review: Character

10. **Analyze** A **character** is a person or animal in a literary work. In these three selections, the characters are animals who talk and act like people. What can animal characters show us about human nature?

Writing Focus

Think as a Reader/Writer

Use It in Your Writing Review your list of weak and powerful characters. Think about the lessons in these tales. Then, write two paragraphs in response to these questions: How can a character who seems powerful be outsmarted by a weaker character? Is it better to be clever, or strong?

Why are stories about small and weak characters cleverly outsmarting large and powerful characters still popular today?

Applying Your Skills

He Lion, Bruh Bear, and Bruh Rabbit / Aesop's Fables

Vocabulary Development

Vocabulary Skills: Multiple Meanings

Multiple-meaning words can be confusing. A multiple-meaning word is always spelled the same way, but it means different things in different **contexts.** To find the correct meaning of a word, look at its context—the words around it. Then, try out each meaning in the context of the sentence.

Your Turn

Choose the correct meaning of each italicized word.

1. Does a fox know the difference between *right* and wrong?
   - **a.** opposite of left
   - **b.** what is just and proper
2. He broke every *rule* in the forest.
   - **a.** law
   - **b.** line
3. He Lion went flying through the *air*.
   - **a.** tone
   - **b.** sky
4. "I surely do know that," he Lion answered *back*.
   - **a.** in return
   - **b.** part of a chair

Language Coach

Homophones *To, too,* and *two* are **homophones**—words that sound alike but are spelled differently and have different meanings. (The word *homophone* comes from the Greek words *homos*, meaning "same," and *phone*, meaning "sound.")

to: toward; in the direction of (*to* is also part of the infinitive form of a verb)
too: also; more than enough
two: a number—one plus one

Choose the correct word in the underlined pair in each sentence.

The little animals go to/two see Bruh Bear and Bruh Rabbit because he Lion is making too/to much noise. He Lion doesn't like talking too/to Bruh Rabbit. He Lion's roar is too/to loud for Bruh Bear. He Lion wants two/to see Man. After seeing Man, he Lion is no longer two/too loud.

Academic Vocabulary

Talk About . . .

With a partner, take turns sharing how you interpret the story. Discuss what the story says about a concept like freedom. Use the underlined Academic Vocabulary words in your discussion.

Learn It Online
Sharpen your word skills with *WordSharp* at:
go.hrw.com
L6-58
Go

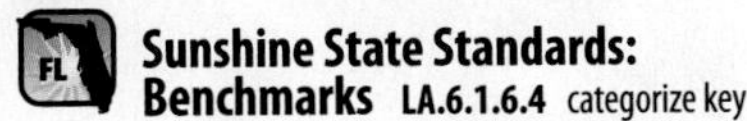

Sunshine State Standards: Benchmarks **LA.6.1.6.4** categorize key vocabulary and identify salient features; **LA.6.1.6.9** determine the correct meaning of words with multiple meanings in context; **LA.6.3.4.4** the eight parts of speech (noun, pronoun, verb, adverb, adjective, conjunction, preposition, interjection); **LA.6.3.5.3** share the writing with the intended audience; **LA.6.5.2.2** deliver narrative and informative presentations, including oral responses to literature, and adjust oral language, body language, eye contact, gestures, technology and supporting graphics appropriate to the situation; *Also covered* **LA.6.6.4.2**

Grammar Link

Describing with Adjectives

An **adjective** is a word that is used to modify a noun or a pronoun. To **modify** a word means to describe the word or to make its meaning more definite. An adjective modifies a noun or pronoun by adding information about *what kind, which one, how many,* or *how much.*

What Kind?	Which One or Ones?	How Many or How Much?
suspicious crow	**other** Lion	**two** gators
tasty cheese	**any** day	**no** water
spring morning	**these** woods	**most** children

Adjectives usually come before the words they modify. Sometimes, however, an adjective comes *after* the word it modifies.

> The bear is quiet. (The predicate adjective *quiet* modifies *bear.*)
>
> He Lion, tense and nervous, roared out, "ME AND MYSELF." (The adjectives *tense* and *nervous* modify the noun *He Lion.*)

Note: The words *a, an,* and *the* are a special kind of adjective called **articles.**

Your Turn

Identify the adjectives and words they modify in the sentences below. Do not include *a, an,* or *the.*

1. Bruh Rabbit is scrawny but clever.
2. The Fox enjoyed the lovely weather and fresh air.
3. What beautiful beady eyes the Crow has!
4. The House Dog told the Wolf about the plentiful, huge meals he eats.

CHOICES

As you respond to the Choices, use these **Academic Vocabulary** words as appropriate: features, interpret, concept, indicate.

REVIEW

Respond to a Moral

Timed Writing Write a personal response to one of the morals in the two Aesop's fables you have read. Explain whether you agree or disagree with the moral, using examples from your personal experience and your own knowledge.

CONNECT

Create a Graphic Fable

TechFocus Use software tools or other media to create an original fable in graphic story form that could teach one of these lessons: "Kindness is never wasted" or "The grass is always greener on the other side of the fence." Keep in mind the features of graphic stories: They are told in panels, and the words characters speak are put in word balloons.

EXTEND

Perform a Story

Group Activity Form a group, and present "He Lion, Bruh Bear, and Bruh Rabbit" or another folk tale of your choice in an oral reading. Break the story into scenes, and decide whether you need a narrator. Then, write out each character's lines, indicate how they should be spoken, and share them with your class.

Learn It Online
Expand your understanding of these stories at:
go.hrw.com
L6-59
Go

MYTH/EPIC

Preparing to Read

Do or Die from Gilgamesh the Hero

by **Geraldine McCaughrean**

What Do You Think?

In what ways might a hero in a story from five thousand years ago be similar to and different from a hero in a story written today?

QuickWrite

In the movie *Spider-Man 2*, Aunt May says, "I believe there's a hero in all of us who keeps us honest, gives us strength, makes us noble, and finally allows us to die with pride. . . ." Do you agree or disagree? Explain.

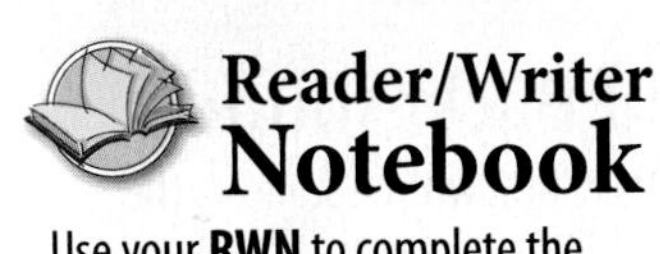

Reader/Writer Notebook

Use your **RWN** to complete the activities for this selection.

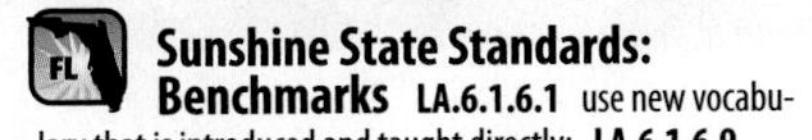

Sunshine State Standards: Benchmarks **LA.6.1.6.1** use new vocabulary that is introduced and taught directly; **LA.6.1.6.9** determine the correct meaning of words with multiple meanings in context; **LA.6.1.7.1** use background knowledge of subject and related content areas, prereading strategies, graphic representations, and knowledge of text structure to make and confirm complex predictions of content, purpose, and organization of a reading selection; *Also covered* **LA.6.1.7.8; LA.6.2.1.1; LA.6.4.2.2**

Literary Focus

Forms of Fiction: Myth and Epic **Myths** are probably the world's oldest stories. They deal with basic human issues such as love, war, and death. There are two main kinds of myth. The **origin myth** explains how something in the world began or was created. The **hero myth** describes the adventures of a superhuman hero who goes on a quest, or journey, to perform great deeds.

The story of Gilgamesh is a type of hero myth called an **epic**—a long story about the quest of a hero who is a leader of his culture.

Reading Focus

Setting a Purpose When you **set a purpose** for reading, you decide on your reading goals. Are you reading to be entertained, or are you looking for information? Reading with a purpose means that you will probably stop often, ask and answer questions, and re-read passages as you go along. You may start out with one purpose in mind and then switch to another.

Into Action Use a chart like the one below to set a purpose for reading. List any new purposes, and check off completed purposes.

What's Your Purpose?

Purpose 1	to read an exciting story about a hero with superhuman powers	☐
Purpose 2		☐

Writing Focus

Think as a Reader/Writer

Find It in Your Reading List examples of the most vivid descriptions, details, and images in "Do or Die." How do these features of the writing bring the characters and events to life?

TechFocus Many video games are quests. Could the story of Gilgamesh and Enkidu be the basis for a good video game?

Vocabulary

clenched (klehnchd) *v.:* closed tightly. *Gilgamesh clenched his fists as he spoke.*

splendor (SPLEHN duhr) *n.:* brightness; glory. *Gilgamesh praised Shamash's splendor.*

rash (rash) *adj.: reckless;* impatient. *Gilgamesh made a rash decision.*

invincible (ihn VIHN suh buhl) *adj.:* unable to be defeated. *The counselors warned that Huwawa was invincible.*

erupt (ih RUHPT) *v.:* release suddenly or violently. *Gilgamesh saw a volcano erupt in his dream.*

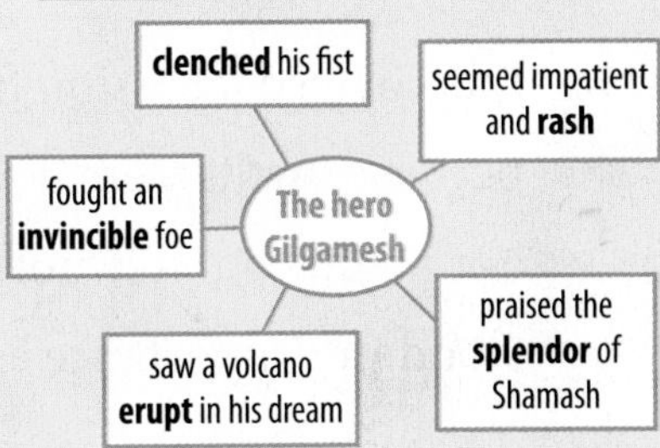

Language Coach

Multiple-Meaning Words If you saw the word *bat* by itself, how would you know if it meant a winged mammal, a piece of baseball equipment, or the action of hitting a ball? If you saw *bat* in a sentence, though, you'd be able to tell which meaning was intended. Which word above has two very different meanings?

Learn It Online
There's more to words than just definitions. Get the whole story on:

go.hrw.com L6-61 

MEET THE WRITER

Geraldine McCaughrean

(1951–)

Her Dream Job

A resident of Berkshire, England, Geraldine McCaughrean (ma KAWRK ruhn) has won some of the United Kingdom's highest honors for children's writers. Early in her career, though, she was happy just to consider herself a professional writer. Today, with more than 130 books to her credit, she continues to feel lucky: "It still seems almost wicked to do something so enjoyable for a living."

Old Stories Made New

One thing McCaughrean enjoys as much as writing new stories is "rewriting" old ones—that is, making up new versions of classic stories for today's readers. Many of her books are based on myths and legends first told countless years ago. Among these classics are some of the world's oldest stories—like Gilgamesh.

"I discovered a passion for myth. Perhaps it is because myths were never told 'for children' or 'for adults,' but to whole communities who understood the importance and magic of storytelling."

Think About the Writer Geraldine McCaughrean loves making her living from writing. What would be *your* ideal job?

Build Background

One of the oldest written stories is the *Epic of Gilgamesh,* from the part of the Middle East that today includes Iraq. Almost five thousand years old, the epic tells the story of a proud king with superhuman powers who battles monsters and goes on a quest to find the secret of eternal life. This episode from a retelling of the epic by a contemporary writer focuses on Gilgamesh's determination to make a name for himself by killing the greatest monster of all.

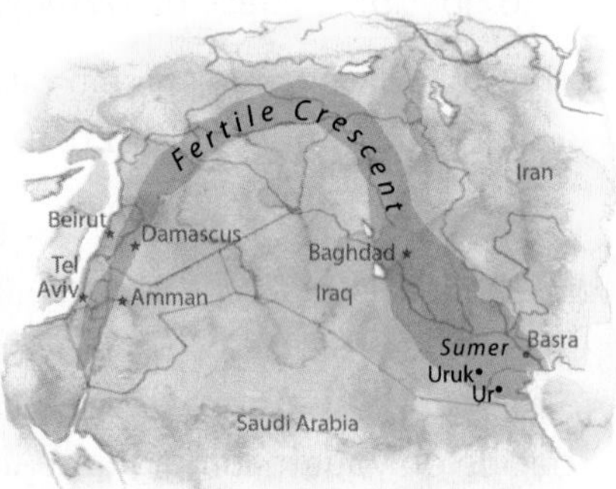

Preview the Selection

Use this list to help you keep the cast of characters straight.

Gilgamesh (GIHL guh mehsh)—part god and part man, possessing special powers, he is the king of the city of Uruk

Enkidu (EHN kee doo)—also called the Wild Man, he lived among wild animals before becoming Gilgamesh's best friend

Ishtar (IHSH tahr)—goddess of love and war

Huwawa (hoo WAH wah)—an enormous and powerful monster, also called Guardian or Protector of the Cedar Forests

Shamash (SHAW mush)—the Sun God

Ninsun (NIHN suhn)—Gilgamesh's mother, a goddess

Read with a Purpose Read this myth to discover the qualities of an ancient hero named Gilgamesh. How do his actions reveal what he truly values?

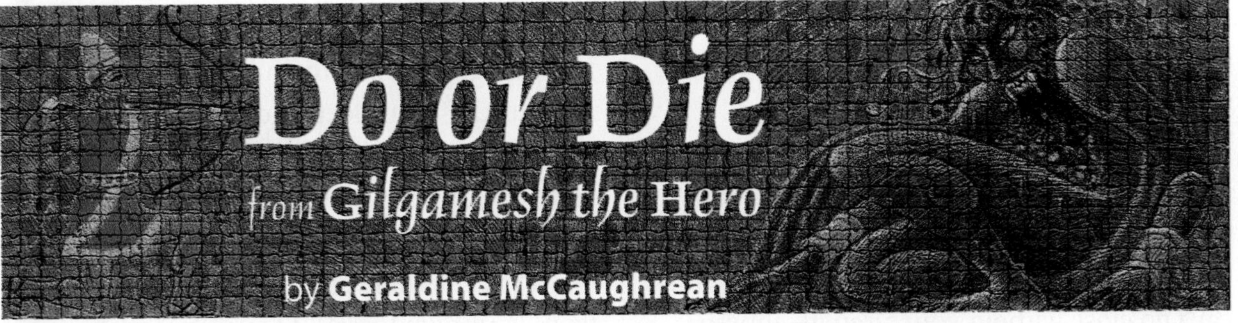

Do or Die

from Gilgamesh the Hero

by **Geraldine McCaughrean**

Like the axe in his dream, Gilgamesh wore Enkidu at his side and swore never to be parted from him. "I must have been mad to contemplate marriage," he told Enkidu, "especially to Ishtar!"

Gilgamesh schooled Enkidu in the ways of civilization, and then Enkidu taught him the way of the wild places: how the honey-ant gathers its winter food, how mistletoe grows without a root, how water can be mined out of the driest desert.

They wrestled and raced and hunted and talked, and the people of Uruk breathed a sigh of relief and gave thanks to the gods.

Enkidu had roamed far afield, into the wildest places. He had seen things which Gilgamesh had never seen. He had swum in both the Tigris and the Euphrates, had stood on the summit of Mount Nisir where the ark ran aground after the Great Flood; had seen the monstrous Huwawa, Protector of the Cedar Forests, and the Scorpionmen who guard the roadway to the Garden of the Gods. One day, as Gilgamesh showed Enkidu the sights of the city, he pointed out the carved stone friezes[1] recording the deeds of Uruk's great men. **A**

"Where are the deeds of Gilgamesh?" asked Enkidu.

"Here!" cried Gilgamesh, spread-eagling himself against the wall. "This blank. So far I've done nothing worth carving in stone. But soon! Soon, Enkidu! You and I are going on such an adventure that no wall will be large enough to record it!" **B**

"We are?" Enkidu too flattened himself against the wall, striking a grand pose. "Where? When? Now?" The very ends of his long hair crackled with energy.

"It was you who gave me the idea. Who's the most frightening foe in the whole world?"

Enkidu racked his brains. "Gilgamesh is. Ask his enemies."

Gilgamesh laughed. "Someone far more dangerous! We are going to fight Huwawa, Guardian of the Cedar Forests, and kill him and bring home cedarwood to build new gates for Uruk!"

1. **friezes** (FREEZ ehz): ornamental bands of decoration around a building.

A **Literary Focus** **Myth** What details in this paragraph indicate that this is a myth and not some other kind of story?

B **Read and Discuss** What is Gilgamesh planning? Why?

Enkidu stepped away from the wall. "Ah, now, listen. You're forgetting, I've *seen* Huwawa. He's a monster among monsters! The trees are small alongside him. His strength is the stuff of legends. He never sleeps. When a fox stamps its paw sixty leagues[2] away, Huwawa hears it. He lives for battle! He was made for no other purpose than to guard the forest. No one goes there, for fear of him . . . Besides, a kind of magic surrounds Him. You can't go close without your strength ebbing away. If you had seen Huwawa . . ."

"I would have killed him already!" declared Gilgamesh. "We have to make our mark! Don't we? What are you afraid of?"

"Of getting killed," said Enkidu candidly.

Gilgamesh spread his arms high above his head as if reaching up to clutch the hems of the gods. "Then we'll have died gloriously, won't we? And our names will be written in clouds of glory on the noonday sky! . . . Fame is everything, Enkidu, isn't it? Why live if not to make a mark on the world? To blaze a trail through it! To do deeds worthy of remembrance! Do or die!" Both his fists were clenched, his feet set square on to life, like a prize-fighter. **C**

A surge of love and pride thrilled through Enkidu. "Do or die!" he cried, and closed his own hand around the King's upraised fist. "Just do me one favor. The Cedar Forest belongs to Shamash the Sun. Don't fly in the face of the gods. Tell Shamash what you want to do. Ask his blessing." **D**

That is how Gilgamesh came to be standing, at high noon, in the full glare of the sun, a white kid[3] at his feet, and in his right hand a silver scepter[4] which caught the sunbeams as he spoke. "O Sun! O lord and master, who sees all! Only help me do this thing, and I shall build you a temple all of cedar wood—wood from your own forests. O Sun, you who are robed in fiery splendor, surely you understand a man's need to cloak himself in glory?"

Swaying as he prayed, Gilgamesh felt the tears on his cheeks dry to streaks of white salt. Then it was as if a red hot hand rested on the crown of his head. Shamash had given his blessing.

Crowds of curious onlookers had gathered, round-eyed, fearful, wondering. *"People of Uruk!"* cried Gilgamesh. "I go to the Forest of Cedar Trees, to cut cedar for new city gates and a temple to the god Shamash! There I shall do battle with Huwawa, the Evil One. Pray for me, and make offerings to the Sun. I shall bring back such glory to Uruk that the name of Uruk will live forever in the annals of the world!" **E**

The crowd gave a nervous laugh and burst out singing. A clumsy, shuffling dance carried them home to their houses.

---

2. **leagues** (leegz): units of distance, from about 2.4 to 4.6 miles.

3. **kid:** young goat.

4. **scepter** (SEHP tuhr): staff or baton carried by a ruler on ceremonial occasions. Often decorated and made of special materials, it is a symbol of authority.

C **Literary Focus** **Setting a Purpose** What details would you pay attention to here if your purpose in reading this story were to answer the question "What kind of hero is Gilgamesh?"

D **Read and Discuss** What is Gilgamesh's plan?

E **Literary Focus** **Myth and Epic** The hero of an epic usually tries to gain resources or glory for his people. What details in these last three paragraphs indicate that Gilgamesh is an epic hero?

Vocabulary **clenched** (klehnchd) *v.:* closed tightly.
splendor (SPLEHN duhr) *n.:* brightness; glory.

Gilgamesh and Enkidu went to the forges and gave orders for two axes and two swords. Armorers and craftsmen went out into the ancient groves and cut willow and box wood for axe handles and spear shafts. But they sent to Anshan in Persia for wood fine enough to make the King's bow. The axe of Gilgamesh was called, "Might of Heroes," his bow "Anshan." Every stage of the craftsmanship was watched over by Gilgamesh and Enkidu, for they knew that their lives would depend on these weapons. **F**

As the golden sparks flew up from the anvil, the elderly counselors of Uruk gathered in the doorway of the forge. Their old heads were white with the snow of wisdom. "You are young, Gilgamesh. Youth is rash. We beg you to reconsider. This Huwawa is a thing of spirit and magic—invincible!"

But Gilgamesh only laughed. "What do you want me to do, gentlemen? Sit at home for three score years? Wrap up warm in winter and keep cool in the summer, and stay safe here in Uruk?" The blacksmith passed a finished sword into his outstretched hands. It weighed as much as a grown man, but he handled it as delicately as a newborn baby.

The counselors shook their wise old heads. There is no telling young people anything they do not want to hear. They comforted themselves on the way home, saying, "If anyone can do this thing, it is Gilgamesh and his friend, the Wild Man." **G**

F **Read and Discuss** What are Gilgamesh and Enkidu doing?

G **Read and Discuss** What did we learn from the conversation between Gilgamesh and the counselors?

Vocabulary **rash** (rash) *adj.:* reckless; impatient.
invincible (ihn VIHN suh buhl) *adj.:* unable to be defeated.

Analyzing Visuals **Viewing and Interpreting**
What scene from the story does this illustration depict?

Ninsun, the King's mother, sent for Enkidu. "Remember to dig a well every evening, Enkidu, and offer up pure water to the Sun God every day . . . Oh, look after him, Enkidu! You are not my son: I did not give birth to you. But bring Gilgamesh safe home and I shall adopt you as my own. I'm relying on you, Enkidu!"

The Wild Man bowed his head. For the first time, he realized that there was someone else in the word who loved Gilgamesh as much as he did.

What a way it was to the land of the cedar forests! Even though the friends walked fifty leagues a day, and accomplished in three days what it would take others six weeks to do, they still had seven mountains to cross before they stood at the forest gate.

Carved in a dozen languages were warnings and prohibitions:[5]

"DO NOT ENTER"

"CUT NO TREES, ON PAIN OF DEATH"

"THIS FOREST IS PROTECTED BY HUWAWA, TERROR OF THE EARTH" **H**

And yet the woodlands beyond the gate were as greenly peaceful as the bottom of a lake. Birdsong rippled outwards from it in tinkling wavelets. Enkidu shoved open the gate.

His knees sagged. His head spun, His hands prickled as though stabbed by a thousand splinters. He jumped awkwardly backwards. "Gilgamesh! Don't go in there! The magic is too strong! The moment I touched the gate, my strength failed me!"

But Gilgamesh was already whistling his way along the broad green pathways of the wood. **I**

In the center of the forest stood a green mountain—a perfect cone rising up so high that its peak was hidden by cloud. Its peaceful slopes seemed a perfect place to sleep. Without even troubling to dig a well and refill their water skins, the friends stretched out on the ground. Still, they slept hand-in-hand, so as to wake one another at the first sign of danger.

At midnight, Enkidu woke to the feeling of his knuckles being crushed together. Gilgamesh was sitting bolt upright, his eyes glistening in the dark. "I had a dream!" he said. "I dreamt the top of the mountain melted, and the earth spewed out its blood—fire and molten rock, and so much smoke and ash that the sun turned black. What does it mean?"

Enkidu laughed and extricated his hand. "It means we've come to the land of volcanoes, friend," he said, "In this part of the world the mountains erupt like spots on a young man's cheek. What else did you dream?"

"I dreamt that the earth trembled under me, and clouds of dust flew up so that I couldn't breathe, couldn't see, and everything around me caught fire like kindling!

5. **prohibitions (proh uh BIHSH uhnz): orders forbidding something.**

6. **portent** (PAWR tehnt): omen; sign or warning of something, usually evil.

H Reading Focus Setting a Purpose Explain whether your purpose in reading this story has changed at all. If so, why has it changed?

I Literary Focus Myth and Epic Epic heroes often travel with companions who have personalities different from their own. How is Enkidu similar to and different from Gilgamesh?

Vocabulary **erupt** (ih RUHPT) *v.:* burst forth.

SOCIAL STUDIES **LINK**

Cuneiform and Sumerian Writing

Gilgamesh's story was written thousands of years ago on clay tablets that seem to be covered with scratch marks. These marks are cuneiform (kyoo NEE uh fawrm), the world's oldest writing. Cuneiform was etched into the surfaces of soft clay tablets with a pointed stick, or stylus. The tablets were then left in the sun to dry and harden.

The Sumerians, skilled traders who lived in Mesopotamia (part of modern-day Iraq) more than five thousand years ago, developed cuneiform to keep track of what they traded. Very few of the ancient tablets that have been discovered are literary works. Most of them are bookkeeping, inventory, and tax records!

Ask Yourself

Would you expect most cultures to use writing more for recording stories or for informational purposes—like business? Why?

What kind of portent[6] is that for the gods to send me? What does it mean?"

Again Enkidu laughed. "It means we are in the land of earthquakes! Do you know nothing? The world's skin is like the skin of a lizard—now and then the scales twitch, and the earth shakes. What else did you dream?"

"I dreamt a bull," said Gilgamesh, his teeth chattering at the memory of it. "Not just a bull, I mean: a giant of a bull—bigger than twenty bulls. It was head-down and charging right at you, and there was nothing I could do! Nothing! Nothing!"

Enkidu scratched his head. "Huwawa is nothing like a bull," he said, puzzled. "His face is like a lion and he has fangs like a dragon. I don't know why you should dream a . . . Gilgamesh?" **J**

But Gilgamesh had fallen asleep, his head on Enkidu's shoulder. When daylight came, he was still sound asleep. Enkidu touched him. Enkidu shook him. Enkidu took hold of him by the ears and banged his head on the ground, but he would not wake up. He was under the influence of Huwawa's magic. **K**

The whole day came and went, and still Gilgamesh slept. Enkidu was panic-stricken. "*Wake up!*" he bellowed in his friend's ear. "*Wake up!* Must I tell your mother that I let you die in your sleep? Do you want Huwawa to find you like this?"

He slapped Gilgamesh. He rolled him down the hill. He held their empty water skins over his friend—oh, why had he not heeded Ninsun's advice? Enkidu dug and dug, but found no water. He ran and ran,

---

J **Read and Discuss** What has Gilgamesh been telling Enkidu? How has Enkidu responded?

K **Literary Focus Myth** What features and details here tell you that you are reading a myth and not, for example, a regular adventure story?

Analyzing Visuals Viewing and Interpreting

In this illustration, which features of Huwawa's face express his personality and reputation?

until pebbles flew from under his feet as sparks had from the blacksmith's hammer. At last he heard the soft tinkle of trickling water. Splashing into the stream, he scooped the water skin through the cool, delicious water. Then back he ran and, upending the bag, emptied it in the King's face.

At last, the dark brown eyes opened. Stretching himself, Gilgamesh picked up his breast plate and put it on. He was perfectly calm. "Let us go and meet our enemy."

Enkidu kicked aside his bow in disgust. "You go if you like, but I'm going back to the city. You have no idea . . . You don't know what you are up against! Me, I'll go back and tell your mother how brave you are, how heroic, how glorious . . . how dead."

Gilgamesh calmly strung his bow. "Don't launch the funeral barge yet. What can go wrong with the two of us side by side?"

"Do you really want me to tell you?" said Enkidu. **L**

Inside his cedarwood house, the giant Huwawa cocked his giant head on one side and listened. A smile came to his lips which curled like the bark from a silver birch. He reached out and took down his first cloak of splendor. Six more hung alongside it, woven out of magic and the fibers of the forest. He opened his door, stuck out his head and bellowed.

"WHO HAS COME INTO THE FOREST? LET HIM DIE!"

All the acorns fell from the trees—all the nests of the previous spring. He looked, and as he looked, the beam of his looking

---

L **Read and Discuss** What is happening in this dialogue between Enkidu and Gilgamesh?

scythed[7] down trees. He nodded his head, and malign[8] magic rolled through the forest, bluer and deeper than drifts of bluebells. Then he stepped out of doors. The green forest was like grass around his feet. He blotted out the sun.

Gilgamesh, caught in the coal-black shadow, looked up. "Oh, Enkidu," he said. He had never thought anything could be so big.

Then Shamash the Sun looked down and saw Gilgamesh and his friend like two tiny ants in the path of an elephant's stampede.

The Sun breathed in, fetching the warm winds. He reached out to sea and grasped the north wind and the waterspouts, lightning and phosphorescent[9] fire. He turned about and about, and the elements were twisted into a single whiplash, its thongs sharp with hail and sleet.

But the Guardian only ran back into his house and grabbed his second cloak. He had been formed to protect the forests, and even the master of those forests could not call him to heel.

Gilgamesh was wielding his axe now, hacking at the outermost wall of the lodge to bring it down. Seven walls, one inside another, and inside the seventh the Guardian, bellowing flame and destruction. Huwawa put on the third of his seven cloaks.

But with every passing moment, more of the winds of Heaven piled up around the cedar wood lodge. They turned back Huwawa's powers like a mirror turns back light. The Guardian put on the fourth of his seven cloaks, and the wall of his lodge bowed outwards, so great was the magic within. Huwawa put on the fifth and sixth of his seven cloaks and for twenty thousand leagues, the cedar forests trembled. **M**

At last the seventh cedar wall fell, and Gilgamesh and Enkidu, axes in hand, came face to face with Huwawa. Seven cloaks billowed round him like the rays of a rainbow; magic shone from his open mouth, from the heels of his hands, from the fabric of his skin. Huwawa might be terrible, but he was also magnificent. **N**

Suddenly, a cyclone of twisted wind and heat bound him round: he was powerless to strike the heroes dead. "Let me go, Gilgamesh!" he said. "Spare me and I shall be your slave, and cut down the trees myself to build you a fitting palace."

Gilgamesh hesitated. He glanced sideways at Enkidu.

"Don't listen to him!" urged Enkidu. "It's a trick. Kill him!"

Gilgamesh swung back his axe over one shoulder. "But, Enkidu . . . if we kill him, all that glory will be lost to the world forever!"

"Don't let him fool you, Gilgamesh!" (He was not at all sure how long those ropes of wind binding Huwawa's arms would hold him, how long before the giant would squirm free.)

It took three blows to dispatch the Guardian of the Forests. He sprawled on his

7. **scythed** (sythd): cut with a tool that has a long, curved handle and a single-edged, curved blade.
8. **malign** (muh LYN): evil; showing strong ill will.
9. **phosphorescent** (fahs fuh REHS uhnt): glowing; giving off low light after exposure to a light source.

M **Literary Focus** **Myth** Gods and goddesses often show up in myths to help—or hinder—the hero. How is Shamash, the Sun, playing a role in Gilgamesh's quest?

N **Read and Discuss** What is going on with Huwawa? In what specific instances could a foe be both "terrible" and "magnificent"?

face, the trees falling flat for acres around. The phosphorescent glory which had hung about Huwawa went out like a blown candle. He was a mound of vegetable matter, a hummock in the landscape.

Dead. **O**

Gilgamesh, walking the length of the Guardian's dead body, felt the spark of life flare up inside his own. He had survived! He was alive—even more alive than before. All the colors of the forest were more bright, the birdsong sweeter, the smells more delectable. The touch of his friend's hand on his arm made him dizzy with joy.

They found the tallest cedar tree in the entire forest and hacked it down. It fell with a deafening hiss of leaves. From this the carpenters of Uruk would fashion a mighty gate to the city. **P**

Then, in reverence to the Sun, Gilgamesh washed himself in the river, put on clean robes and made an offering of cold water to Shamash, holding up the silver bowl while the noonday heat drank it up in steamy white sips.

And looking down, Ishtar, goddess of Love, saw the finest sight the world had to offer—a young man, covered in glory, triumphant, silhouetted against the sinking sun, a silver bowl upraised, face shining with pent-up happiness—King Gilgamesh. **Q**

O **Reading Focus** **Setting a Purpose** If your purpose in reading this story were to look out for details familiar to you from other stories in books or media, what would you notice here?

P **Literary Focus** **Myth and Epic** How is Gilgamesh living up to the role of an epic hero?

Q **Read and Discuss** How has the story ended for Gilgamesh? for Huwawa? Where do you suppose Enkidu is now?

Analyzing Visuals **Viewing and Interpreting**
How does this image match the description of Gilgamesh in the final paragraph?

Applying Your Skills

Sunshine State Standards: Benchmarks **LA.6.1.7.3** determine the main idea or essential message in grade-level text through inferring, paraphrasing, summarizing, and identifying relevant details; *Also covered* **LA.6.1.7.8; LA.6.2.1.1; LA.6.2.1.2; LA.6.4.2.3**

Do or Die

Respond and Think Critically

Reading Focus

1. With which statement would Gilgamesh MOST likely agree? **FCAT**
   A Friends are the most important thing of all.
   B All people can be heroic.
   C A dull life is not worth living.
   D Monsters should be treated with kindness.

Read with a Purpose

2. What are Gilgamesh's heroic qualities? What do his actions indicate about what he values?

Reading Skills: Setting a Purpose

3. Look back over the chart you made to track your purposes for reading. How many times did your purpose change, and why?

What's Your Purpose?

Purpose 1:	to read an exciting story about a hero with superhuman powers	☐
Purpose 2:		☐

Literary Focus

Literary Analysis

4. **Interpret** What qualities do Gilgamesh and Enkidu share? How are the two friends different? Support your response with details from the story.

5. **Infer** When Gilgamesh is so close to victory, why does he hesitate to kill Huwawa? What does this tell you about Gilgamesh?

Literary Skills: Myth and Epic

6. **Analyze** Gilgamesh is the hero of this epic. Explain how his actions reveal his qualities as a hero. Use details from the story to support your answer.

7. **Evaluate** This story is almost five thousand years old. What is it about the story's concept that makes it enjoyable for audiences today? What modern stories might be loved and remembered hundreds of years from now?

Literary Skills Review: Setting

8. **Evaluate** **Setting** is the location and time period of a work of fiction. Setting can be so important that a story could not happen in any other time or place. Could this story be set in a different time and place? Explain.

Writing Focus

Think as a Reader/Writer

Use It in Your Writing Choose one character from this story, and write your own description of him or her. Build on the author's descriptions you noted in your *Reader/Writer Notebook.*

What new thoughts do you have about heroes and people's need for them after reading about Gilgamesh?

Applying Your Skills

Do or Die

Vocabulary Development

Shades of Meaning: Connotations

The different shades of meaning connected with words are called **connotations.** Connotations, or suggested meanings, help us interpret what the words we read or hear *really* mean. If a friend told you that you were self-confident, you'd probably be flattered. How would you feel, though, if your friend said you were bossy, conceited, or pushy?

Self-confident has a neutral or even positive connotation, but *conceited* has the negative connotation of "thinking too much of oneself."

Consider the word in italics in this sentence:

"The counselors shook their *wise* old heads."

Smart, intelligent, and *knowledgeable* are all synonyms of *wise*, but *wise* has the most positive connotation of mature knowledge and experience.

Think about the connotations of words as you read. Be especially aware of words that have strong positive or negative connotations.

Your Turn

clenched
splendor
rash
invincible
erupt

Use a Vocabulary word from the list to the right to replace the word or words in italics in each sentence below. Then, next to each sentence, write *negative, neutral,* or *positive* to identify each Vocabulary word's connotation.

1. The elders worried that Gilgamesh was simply an *impatient* young man.
2. Gilgamesh *tightened* his fists and stood firm.
3. The monster Huwawa seemed *unbeatable*.
4. Did the mountains *burst up* from the earth?
5. The Sun God Shamash shone with *brightness*.

Language Coach

Multiple-Meaning Words Words that are spelled the same and sound the same can have completely different meanings. *Rash* can mean "reckless" or "hasty," but it can also refer to red spots on your skin! For each of the words to the right, write two sentences, each using different meanings of the same word. You may use a dictionary if needed.

deed
stamps
mark
blaze
score

Academic Vocabulary

Talk About . . .

With a small group, interpret this statement from Gilgamesh: "Fame is everything, Enkidu, isn't it?" What do you think is Gilgamesh's concept of fame? Include specific examples from the text that indicate what fame means to Gilgamesh and how it motivates his actions. Use the underlined Academic Vocabulary words in your discussion.

Learn It Online
Explore shades of meaning with WordSharp:
go.hrw.com
L6-72
Go

Sunshine State Standards: Benchmarks **LA.6.3.4.4** the eight parts of speech (noun, pronoun, verb, adverb, adjective, conjunction, preposition, interjection); **LA.6.4.2.4** write a variety of informal communications (e.g., friendly letters, thank-you notes, messages) and formal communications (e.g., conventional business letters, invitations) that follow a format and that have a clearly stated purpose and that include the date, proper salutation, body, closing and signature; **LA.6.6.4.1** use appropriate available technologies to enhance communication and achieve a purpose (e.g., video, online).

Grammar Link

Relative and Interrogative Pronouns

Words like *he, she, we,* or *they* are easy to recognize as pronouns, but words like *which, who,* and *whose* are also pronouns. In fact, they are special pronouns that do "double duty." Sometimes they are **relative pronouns**—pronouns used to introduce an adjective clause (a series of descriptive words that act like an adjective):

Gilgamesh, *who* is a hero, has a friend named Enkidu.

At other times they might be **interrogative pronouns**, used to introduce a question:

Who is Enkidu?

COMMON RELATIVE PRONOUNS

that which who whom whose

The mountain peak *that* rises above us is hidden.

INTERROGATIVE PRONOUNS

Who has come into the forest with Gilgamesh?

what which who whom whose

Your Turn

Identify the pronouns in italics in each of the following sentences as *relative* or *interrogative*.

1. *Who* found the tallest cedar tree in the forest?
2. To *whom* did Enkidu lend his sword?
3. The gates *that* protect Uruk must be replaced.
4. Enkidu is the one *whose* help is most needed.

Writing Application Using interrogative pronouns, write three questions about "Do or Die." Answer each question with a sentence that includes a relative pronoun.

CHOICES

As you respond to the Choices, use these **Academic Vocabulary** words as appropriate: features, interpret, concept, indicate.

REVIEW

Write a Letter to the Editor

Timed Writing As one of Gilgamesh's subjects, write a letter to the editor of the *Daily Tablet*. Express how you interpret Gilgamesh's actions. Was Gilgamesh being heroic or irresponsible? Do you think he acted to benefit his people, or was he motivated by selfish needs? Should he have killed Huwawa or let him live? Cite details from the story to support your views.

CONNECT

Design the Characters

TechFocus Review the author's descriptions of Gilgamesh, Enkidu, and Huwawa. Imagine how they might be designed as characters in a video game. Draw, paint, sculpt, adapt an action figure, or make a collage of your concept of these characters. Display your work in class.

EXTEND

Discussing a Modern Gilgamesh

Partner Talk With another student, describe a concept for a modern-day Gilgamesh. What kind of person would today's Gilgamesh be—a king, a politician, an athlete? What would be his goals, and how would he achieve them? What values would he fight for? Who would be his Enkidu, and who (or what) would be the Huwawa they fight against? Share your ideas with the class.

Learn It Online
There's more to this story than meets the eye. Expand your view at:

go.hrw.com L6-73 

COMPARING TEXTS

Comparing and Contrasting Short Stories

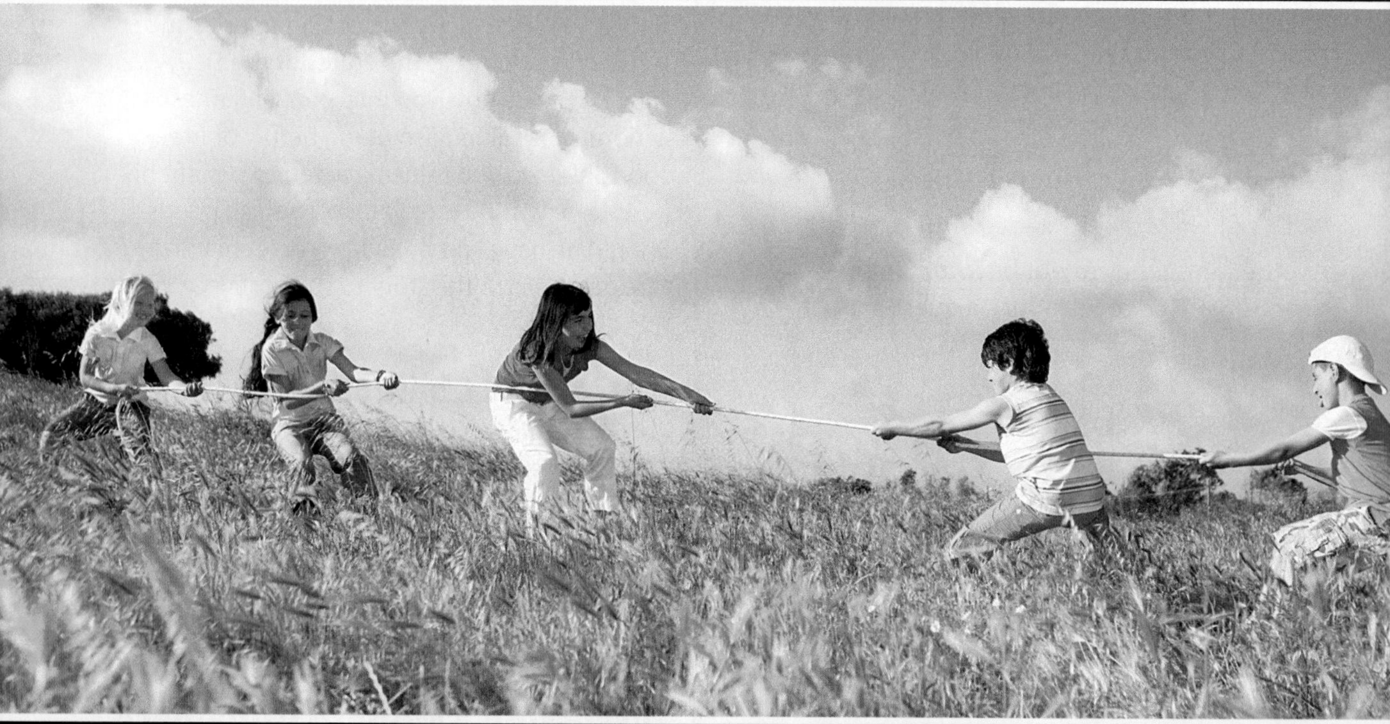

CONTENTS

What Do You Think?

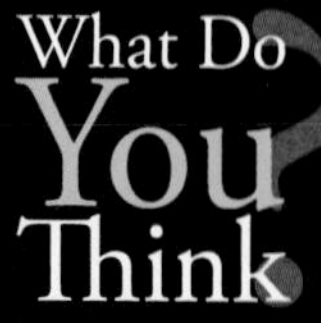

What's enjoyable about fiction that closely resembles real life?

QuickTalk
What kind of fiction do you prefer: fiction that "takes you away" to worlds of adventure, mystery, or the past; or fiction that resembles real life? Why?

Preparing to Read

Sunshine State Standards: Benchmarks
LA.6.1.6.4 categorize key vocabulary and identify salient features; **LA.6.1.7.7** compare and contrast elements in multiple texts; *Also covered* **LA.6.1.7.8; LA.6.2.1.1; LA.6.4.2.2**

The Southpaw / Concha

Literary Focus

Forms of Fiction: Short Story Short stories are short fictional prose narratives that usually present one or more characters in a **conflict,** or struggle, of some kind. The first story here is told in the form of notes a boy and a girl who have big issues send to each other. The second story is told by a **narrator** who is a character in the story. In both stories, the lively words of the characters—whether in the form of written words or dialogue—reveal their values, their personalities, and, of course, their conflicts.

Reading Focus

Comparing and Contrasting When you **compare** two things, you look for similarities. When you **contrast** two things, you look for differences. The two stories that follow have many features in common, and they have many differences.

Into Action As you read, take notes about these story features:

Story Features	"The Southpaw"	"Concha"
the form the story is told in		
the characters in the story		
the main conflict in the story		
how the conflict is resolved		

Writing Focus

Think as a Reader/Writer

Find It in Your Reading These stories use the kind of language real kids might use. As you read, write down in your *Reader/Writer Notebook* some words and phrases that seem very realistic to you.

Reader/Writer Notebook

Use your **RWN** to complete the activities for these selections.

Vocabulary

Concha

treacherous (TREHCH uhr uhs) *adj.:* dangerous. *The children played with the treacherous red ants.*

timid (TIHM ihd) *adj.:* shy; lacking self-confidence. *Concha was timid and avoided rough games.*

feat (feet) *n.:* accomplishment; daring act. *Concha's feat amazed most of the children.*

investigate (ihn VEHS tuh gayt) *v.:* look into; examine. *No adults came to investigate the cries.*

remedy (REHM uh dee) *n.:* cure; solution. *Mud was the best remedy for ant bites.*

Language Coach

Homophones Which word above is a **homophone**—a word that sounds like another word but has a different meaning? How do you spell the word it sounds like?

Learn It Online

Organize your thoughts! Use one of the interactive graphic organizers at:

go.hrw.com L6-75 

MEET THE WRITERS

Learn It Online
Get more on Viorst's life at:
go.hrw.com L6-76 Go

Courtesy of the author.

Judith Viorst
(1931–)

Laughing at the Ups and Downs

When she was only seven years old, Judith Viorst decided that she wanted to be a writer. At first she wrote about "deadly serious things." Later, she found success in writing humorously about the ups and downs of everyday life. Viorst once explained her approach to successfully writing about young people this way: "Kids need to encounter kids like themselves—kids who can sometimes be crabby and fresh and rebellious, kids who talk back and disobey, tell fibs and get into trouble, and are nonetheless still likable and redeemable."

Mary Helen Ponce
(1938–)

From a Latina Perspective

Like the characters in "Concha," Mary Helen Ponce grew up in Pacoima, California, in a Mexican American community. Many of her stories are based on her own life. "I chose to write of a loving family that, throughout the journey, is sustained by bonds of mutual love and respect," she says. Today, Ponce often speaks and writes of the problems of women, especially of Latina women whose contributions to the American Southwest have been forgotten by history.

Think About the Writers

Both writers use humor to tell their stories. Why might it be important to view life experiences with a sense of humor?

Preview the Selections

"The Southpaw" takes an unusual form. It's told completely through notes written back and forth between two friends—**Janet** and **Richard.**

In "Concha," the narrator is a character in the story. So is her brother **Joey** and several friends: **Mundo**, a boy; **Beto**, another boy; **Virgie,** a girl; and of course **Concha,** the girl whose name is the title of the story.

SHORT STORY

THE SOUTHPAW[1]

by **Judith Viorst**

Read with a Purpose

As you read, notice how this writer brings two characters and a situation to life just by reproducing notes that are passed back and forth.

Build Background

This story was written before the days of computer and wireless technology, so the characters communicate through handwritten notes on whatever scraps of paper are handy. The focus is a baseball team that Richard plays for and manages. When the story was written, it was almost unthinkable for a girl to play on a boy's team.

Dear Richard,

Don't invite me to your birthday party because I'm not coming. And give back the Disneyland sweatshirt I said you could wear. If I'm not good enough to play on your team, I'm not good enough to be friends with.

Your former friend,

Janet

P.S. I hope when you go to the dentist he finds 20 cavities.

Dear Janet,

Here is your stupid Disneyland sweatshirt, if that's how you're going to be. I want my comic books now—finished or not. No girl has ever played on the Mapes Street baseball team, and as long as I'm captain, no girl ever will.

Your former friend,

Richard

P.S. I hope when you go for your checkup you need a tetanus shot. **A**

1. **The Southpaw:** The title is a sports slang term for a left-handed person, especially a left-handed pitcher in baseball.

A **Read and Discuss** What has the author set up for us?

Dear Richard,

I'm changing my goldfish's name from Richard to Stanley. Don't count on my vote for class president next year. Just because I'm a member of the ballet club doesn't mean I'm not a terrific ballplayer.

Your former friend,

Janet

P.S. I see you lost your first game 28-0.

Dear Janet,

I'm not saving anymore seats for you on the bus. For all I care you can stand the whole way to school. Why don't you just forget about baseball and learn something nice like knitting?

Your former friend,

Richard

P.S. Wait until Wednesday.

Dear Richard,

My father said I could call someone to go with us for a ride and hot-fudge sundaes. In case you didn't notice, I didn't call you.

Your former friend,

Janet

P.S. I see you lost your second game, 34-0.

Dear Janet,

Remember when I took the laces out of my blue-and-white sneakers and gave them to you? I want them back.

Your former friend,

Richard

P.S. Wait until Friday. 

Dear Richard,

Congratulations on your unbroken record. Eight straight losses, wow: I understand you're the laughing stock of New Jersey.

Your former friend,

Janet

P.S. Why don't you and your team forget about baseball and learn something nice like knitting maybe? C

B **Literary Focus** **Short Story** What are you learning about Janet from the notes so far?

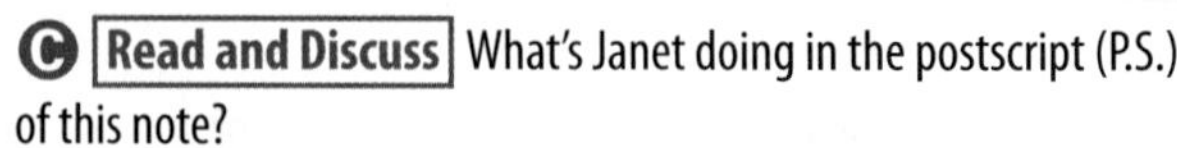

C **Read and Discuss** What's Janet doing in the postscript (P.S.) of this note?

Dear Janet,

Here's the silver horseback riding trophy that you gave me. I don't think I want to keep it anymore.

Your former friend,

Richard

P.S. I didn't think you'd be the kind who'd kick a man when he's down.

Dear Richard,

I wasn't kicking exactly. I was kicking back.

Your former friend,

Janet

P.S. In case you were wondering, my batting average is .345.

Dear Janet,

Alfie is having his tonsils out tomorrow. We might be able to let you catch next week.

Richard D

Dear Richard,

I pitch.

Janet

Dear Janet,

Joel is moving to Kansas and Danny sprained his wrist. How about a permanent place in the outfield?

Richard

D **Read and Discuss** What's going on here?

Dear Richard,
I pitch.
Janet **E**

Dear Janet,

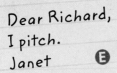

Ronnie caught the chicken pox and Leo broke his toe and Elwood has these stupid violin lessons. I'll give you first base, and that's my final offer.

Richard

Dear Richard,

Susan Reilly plays first base, Marilyn Jackson catches, Ethel Kahn plays center field, I pitch. It's a package deal.

Janet

P.S. Sorry about your 12-game losing streak.

Dear Janet,

Please! Not Marilyn Jackson.

Richard

Dear Richard,

Nobody ever said that I was unreasonable. How about Lizzie Martindale instead?

Janet

Dear Janet,

At least could you call your goldfish Richard again?

Your friend,

Richard **F**

Analyzing Visuals **Viewing and Interpreting** What about this girl's appearance reminds you of Janet?

E **Read and Discuss** What's Janet doing by sending the same note again?

F **Literary Focus** **Conflict** How is the conflict resolved finally? What has each side given up?

Applying Your Skills

Sunshine State Standards: Benchmarks **LA.6.1.7.5** analyze a variety of text structures (e.g., comparison/contrast, cause/effect, chronological order, argument/support, lists) and text features (main headings with subheadings) and explain their impact on meaning in text; *Also covered* **LA.6.2.1.1; LA.6.2.1.2; LA.6.4.2.4**

The Southpaw

Respond and Think Critically

Reading Focus

1. What is the main conflict in the story? **FCAT**
   - **A** Janet wants to play for Richard's team.
   - **B** Richard won't let Janet play on his baseball team.
   - **C** Janet won't return Richard's comic books.
   - **D** Richard killed Janet's pet goldfish.

Read with a Purpose

2. Describe how the author indicates each note writer's personality.

Reading Skills: Comparing and Contrasting

3. What is similar about the way Richard and Janet write to each other? Of the two, who do you think is better at reaching a way to work out their differences? Why?

Literary Focus

Literary Analysis

4. **Infer** What clues indicate what the relationship between Janet and Richard was like before they started writing these notes?
5. **Analyze** How do you interpret Richard and Janet's relationship? Explain what all this back-and-forth note writing tells you about how they really feel about each other. Support your answer with details from the story. READ THINK EXPLAIN
6. **Evaluate** Do you like the concept of using notes to tell a story? Why or why not?
7. **Make Judgments** How did you respond to Richard and Janet as characters? Complete these statements:

I think Janet is . . .	
I think Richard is . . .	
If I were Richard, I would . . .	
If I were Janet, I would . . .	

8. **Extend** Try reversing the situation in this story. What judgments do girls make against boys? How do those judgments, or prejudices, cause conflicts?
9. **Analyze** How does this story demonstrate the ways being stubborn and closed-minded can get in the way of a good friendship?

Literary Skills: Short Story

10. **Evaluate** If this story had been written in a typical short story format, would it have been more or less effective? Explain. In what ways would a more typical version be different from the form of this story?

Writing Focus

Think as a Reader/Writer

Use It in Your Writing Look back at your *Reader/Writer Notebook*. What were some of your favorite lines in these notes? Try writing the next two notes that Janet and Richard might send to each other. Be sure to capture their personalities.

SHORT STORY

Concha

by **Mary Helen Ponce**

Read with a Purpose

Read this story to see if you agree that Concha holds "first place for bravery."

Preparing to Read for this selection is on page 75.

Build Background

This writer is known for mixing Spanish and English in her stories, so you'll find many Spanish words in italic type here. If you read closely, you'll also find that most of the Spanish words are explained in context. For example, in the first sentence the narrator says that as children she and her brother Joey were left alone to find ways *para divertirnos*. If you do not know what this Spanish phrase means, you can find the meaning right away in the next part of the sentence: "to keep ourselves busy."

While growing up in the small barrio of Pacoima, my younger brother Joey and I were left alone to find ways *para divertirnos*, to keep ourselves busy—and out of our mother's way. One way in which we whiled away long summer days was by making pea shooters. These were made from a hollow reed which we first cleaned with a piece of wire. We then collected berries from *los pirules,* the pepper trees that lined our driveway. Once we amassed enough dry berries we put them in our mouths and spat them out at each other through the pea shooter.

The berries had a terrible taste—they were even said to be poison! I was most careful not to swallow them. We selected only the hard, firm peas. The soft ones, we knew, would get mushy, crumble in our mouths and force us to gag—and lose a fight. During an important battle a short pause could spell defeat. Oftentimes while playing with Joey I watched closely. When he appeared to gag I dashed back to the pepper tree to load up on ammunition. I pelted him without mercy until he begged me to stop. **A**

"No more. Ya no," Joey cried as he bent over to spit berries. "No more!"

"Ha, ha I got you now." I spat berries at Joey until, exhausted, we called a truce and slumped onto a wooden bench. **B**

In fall our game came to a halt—the trees dried up; the berries fell to the ground. This was a sign for us to begin other games.

A **Literary Focus** **Short Story/Conflict** What conflict have the children created for themselves? Why is it important not to lose a battle?

B **Read and Discuss** What situation is the author setting up for us?

Our games were seasonal. During early spring we made whistles from the long blades of grass that grew in the open field behind our house. In winter we made dams, forts, and canals from the soft mud that was our street. We tied burnt matchsticks together with string. These were our men. We positioned them along the forts (camouflaged with small branches). We also played kick the can, but our most challenging game was playing with red ants.

The ants were of the common variety: red, round and treacherous. They invaded our yard and the *llano* every summer. We always knew where ants could be found, *donde habia hormigas*. We liked to build mud and grass forts smack in the middle of ant territory. The ants were the enemy, the matchstickmen the heroes, or good guys.

Playing with ants was a real challenge! While placing our men in battle positions we timed it so as not to get bitten. We delighted in beating the ants at their own game. **C**

Sometimes we got really brave and picked up ants with a stick, then twirled the stick around until the ants got dizzy-drunk (or so we thought)—and fell to the ground. We made ridges of dirt and pushed the ants inside, covered them with dirt and made bets as to how long it would take them to dig their way out.

Concha, my best friend and neighbor, was quite timid at school. She avoided all rough games such as kickball and Red Rover. When it came to playing with ants, however, Concha held first place for bravery. She could stand with her feet atop an anthill for the longest time! We stood trembling as ants

C Reading Focus **Comparing and Contrasting** How is the game with ants different from the other games the narrator has described so far?

Vocabulary **treacherous** (TREHCH uhr uhs) *adj.:* dangerous.
timid (TIHM ihd) *adj.:* shy; lacking self-confidence.

Analyzing Visuals **Viewing and Interpreting**
What sort of game are these two boys playing? In what ways might it be similar to the games the kids in this story are playing?

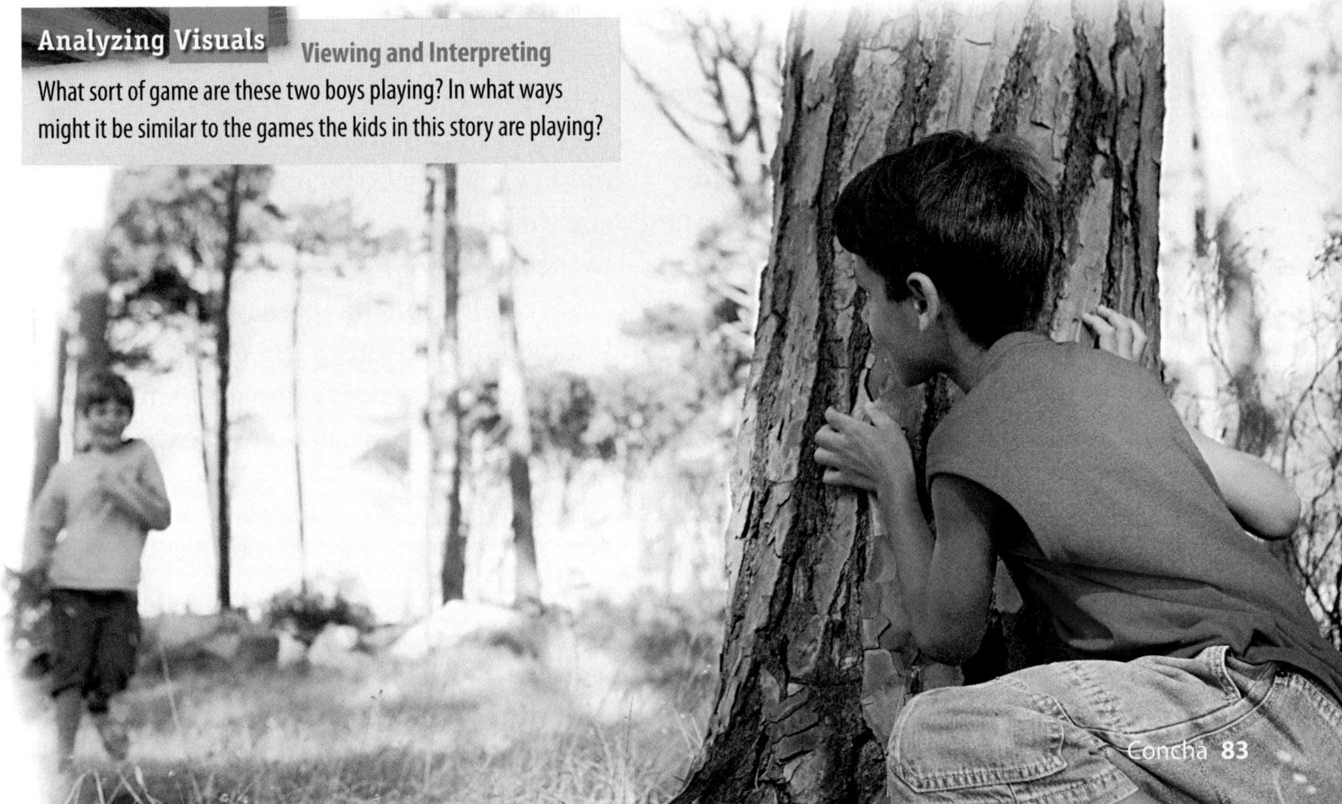

crawled up our shoes, then quickly stomped our feet to scare them off. But Concha never lost her nerve. D

One time we decided to have an ant contest. The prize was a candy bar—a Sugar Daddy sucker. We first found an anthill, lined up, then took turns standing beside the anthill while the juicy red ants climbed over our shoes. We dared not move—but when the first ant moved towards our ankles we stomped away, our Oxfords making swirls of dust that allowed us to retreat to the sidelines. But not Concha. She remained in place as big red ants crept up her shoes. One, five, ten! We stood and counted, holding our breath as the ants continued to climb. Fifteen, twenty! Twenty ants were crawling over Concha! E

We stood and counted, holding our breath as the ants continued to climb. Fifteen, twenty! Twenty ants were crawling over Concha!

"*Ujule*, she sure ain't scared," cried Mundo in a hushed voice. "*No le tiene miedo a las hormigas*."

"Uhhhhh," answered Beto, his eyes wide.

". . . I mean for a girl," added Mundo as he poked Beto in the ribs. We knew Beto liked Concha—and always came to her rescue.

We stood and counted ants. We were so caught up in this feat that we failed to notice the twenty-first ant that climbed up the back of Concha's sock . . . and bit her!

"Ay, ay, ay," screeched Concha.

"Gosh, she's gonna die," cried an alarmed Virgie as she helped stomp out ants. "She's gonna die!"

"She's too stupid to die," laughed Mundo, busy brushing ants off his feet. "She's too stupid."

"But sometimes people die when ants bite them," insisted Virgie, her face pale. "They gets real sick."

"The ants will probably die," Mundo snickered, holding his stomach and laughing loudly. "Ah, ha, ha."

"Gosh you're mean," said a shocked Virgie, hands on hips. "You are so mean."

"Yeah, but I ain't stupid."

"Come on you guys, let's get her to the *mangera*," Beto cried as he reached out to Concha who by now had decided she would live. "Come on, let's take her to the faucet." F

We held Concha by the waist as she hobbled to the water faucet. Her cries were now mere whimpers as no grownup had come out to investigate. From experience

---

D **Read and Discuss** What's Concha able to do?

E **Read and Discuss** What do you learn about Concha's personality from the way she plays the ant game?

F **Literary Focus Short Story/Conflict** What conflicts do you identify among the various characters? Who is for Concha, and who is against her?

Vocabulary **feat** (feet) *n.:* accomplishment; daring act.
investigate (ihn VEHS tuh gayt) *v.:* look into; examine.

we knew that if a first cry did not bring someone to our aid we should stop crying—or go home.

We helped Concha to the faucet, turned it on and began to mix water with dirt. We knew the best remedy for insect bites was *lodo*. We applied mud to all bug stings to stop the swelling. Mud was especially good for wasp stings, the yellowjackets we so feared—and from which we ran away at top speed. Whenever bees came close we stood still until they flew away, but there were no set rules on how to get rid of *avispas*. We hit out at them, and tried to scare them off but the yellowjackets were fierce! In desperation we flung dirt at them, screamed and ran home.

Not long after the ant incident Concha decided she was not about to run when a huge wasp broke up our game of jacks. She stood still, so still the wasp remained on her dark head for what seemed like hours. We stood and watched, thinking perhaps the wasp had mistaken Concha's curly hair for a bush! We watched—and waited.

"*Ujule,* she sure is brave," exclaimed Virgie as she sucked on a Popsicle. "She sure is brave."

"She's stupid," grunted Mundo, trying to be indifferent. "She's just a big show-off who thinks she's so big."

"So are you," began Virgie, backing off. "So are you."

"Yeah? Ya wanna make something outta it?"

"Let's go," interrupted Beto in his soft voice.

"*Ya vamonos.*" He smiled at Concha—who smiled back. **G**

In time the wasp flew away. Concha immediately began to brag about how a "real big wasp" sat on her hair for hours. She never mentioned the ant contest—nor the twenty-first ant that led her to *el lodo*. **H**

G **Literary Focus** **Short Story/Conflict** What conflict does Beto resolve? How does he do this?

H **Read and Discuss** What do the reactions of Beto and Mundo demonstrate about them?

Vocabulary **remedy** (REHM uh dee) *n.:* cure; solution.

Analyzing Visuals

Viewing and Interpreting How closely does this image match your concept of Concha? What aspects of Concha's personality do you see here?

Applying Your Skills

Sunshine State Standards: Benchmarks **LA.6.1.6.1** use new vocabulary that is introduced and taught directly; **LA.6.1.7.7** compare and contrast elements in multiple texts; *Also covered* **LA.6.1.7.8; LA.6.2.1.1; LA.6.2.1.2; LA.6.4.2.3**

Concha

Respond and Think Critically

Reading Focus

1. How does the setting influence the story? FCAT
   A The games change with the seasons.
   B The boys hate the wintertime.
   C Concha is very brave.
   D An ant bites Concha.

Read with a Purpose

2. Do you agree with the narrator that Concha is brave? Why or why not?

Reading Skills: Comparing and Contrasting

3. Use a Venn diagram like the one below to find the similarities and differences between "Concha" and "The Southpaw." The differences go in the outer circles. The similarities go in the space where the circles overlap.

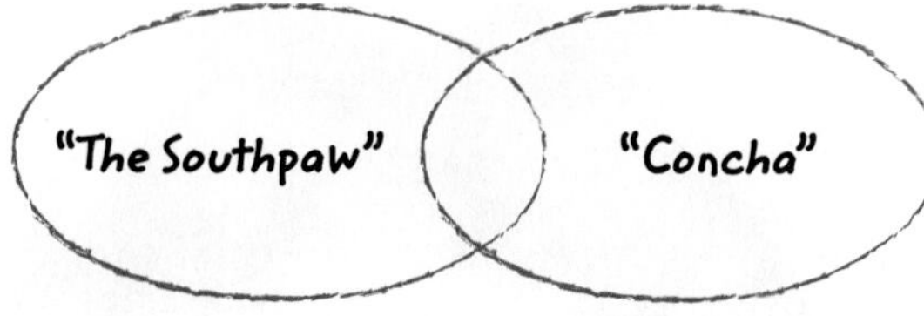

Vocabulary Check

Match the Vocabulary words in the first column with their definitions in the second column.

4. **remedy**	a. shy
5. **investigate**	b. cure
6. **treacherous**	c. accomplishment
7. **timid**	d. look into
8. **feat**	e. dangerous

Literary Focus

Literary Analysis

9. **Interpret** What do you think is Concha's motive, or reason, for standing on the anthill and later letting the wasp sit in her hair? Support your answer with details from the story. READ THINK EXPLAIN

10. **Analyze** All of the characters in this story have different attitudes toward Concha. Describe the concept of Concha each of these characters seems to have.

The Narrator	Virgie
Beto	Mundo

Literary Skills: Short Story

11. **Evaluate** Among the important features of short stories are characters, a main conflict, and a solution to the conflict. Indicate whether or not you think the conflict in "Concha" is interesting and whether it is resolved in a satisfying way.

Writing Focus

Think as a Reader/Writer

Use It in Your Writing Write a brief paragraph explaining whether you think the characters in "Concha" act and speak like real kids. Use examples from the notes you took in your *Reader/Writer Notebook*. Do some of the characters come across as more "real" than others? Explain.

COMPARING TEXTS

Wrap Up

Sunshine State Standards: Benchmarks LA.6.1.7.7 compare and contrast elements in multiple texts; **LA.6.4.1.2** write a variety of expressive forms (e.g., short play, song lyrics, historical fiction, limericks) that employ figurative language, rhythm, dialogue, characterization, and/or appropriate format; **LA.6.4.2.3** write informational/expository essays (e.g., process, description, explanation, comparison/ contrast, problem/solution) that include a thesis statement, supporting details, and introductory, body, and concluding paragraphs.

The Southpaw / Concha

Writing Focus

Write a Comparison-Contrast Essay

To help you write an essay comparing and contrasting "The Southpaw" and "Concha," start with the Venn diagram you filled in on page 86. You can organize your essay in one of two ways:

1. Write two paragraphs, one for each selection. In your first paragraph, write all about "The Southpaw," describing the characters, the conflict, and the resolution of the conflict. In your second paragraph, present the same information for "Concha." Then, wrap up your essay with a final paragraph in which you indicate the main ways the selections are alike and different and explain what you learned from reading them.
2. Write three paragraphs—one on the *characters* in both selections, one on the *conflict* of both selections, and one on the *resolution of the conflict* in both selections. Conclude your essay with a paragraph that sums up how the two selections are alike and different and what you learned from them.

Use the workshop on writing a Comparison-Contrast Essay, pages 106–113, for help with this assignment.

What Do You Think Now? Should fiction reflect our lives or take us to different worlds? How have these stories influenced your opinion on that question?

CHOICES

As you respond to the Choices, use these **Academic Vocabulary** words as appropriate: features, interpret, concept, indicate.

REVIEW

Compare Female Characters

Timed Writing Compare and contrast the characters of Janet and Concha, or Janet and the narrator of "Concha." In what ways are their personalities similar? different? What aspects of their personalities indicate that the girls handle conflict in different ways?

CONNECT

Write a Story in Letters

TechFocus Work with a partner to create a "collaborative story" (a story written with another person) in the form of e-mails or text messages sent back and forth between two characters. Indicate through the messages that your characters are having a conflict over something. Be sure you resolve the conflict by the end of your story.

EXTEND

Draw a Comic Strip

Create a comic strip of at least three panels showing an interaction between a boy and a girl in one of these stories. (You could also make up your own comic strip about a conflict between a boy and a girl.) Your comic strip should have a concept, or idea behind it, such as "Boys and girls don't always speak the same language."

INFORMATIONAL TEXT FOCUS

Structural Features of Popular Media

Tales (1988) by Jonathan Green. Oil on masonite (24" x 36")
From the collection of Kyung Riihimaki. Photography by Tim Stamm

CONTENTS

What can we learn from stories of times past?

QuickTalk
Name some popular stories fro
you and most of your classmat
these stories so memorable?

MAGAZINE ARTICLE

Preparing to Read

Sunshine State Standards: Benchmarks **LA.6.1.6.10** determine meanings of words, pronunciation, parts of speech, etymologies, and alternate word choices by using a dictionary, thesaurus, and digital tools; *Also covered* **LA.6.2.2.1; LA.6.2.2.4; LA.6.4.2.2**

Making It Up As We Go

Use your **RWN** to complete the activities for this selection.

Informational Text Focus

Structural Features of a Magazine Like most types of informational materials, **magazines** have special structural features that give you an overview of what is inside—the contents.

- **The cover** The cover's art and main headline usually announce the lead article and other feature articles.
- **The contents page** The contents page at the front of the magazine lists the articles and tells you what pages they are on. The contents page is sometimes titled simply "Inside This Issue."

Before you read your next magazine article, take a minute to notice the way it's structured.

- **The title** Most magazine articles have titles that are written to catch the reader's interest.
- **The subtitle** An article may have a **subtitle,** a secondary title that tells you more about the article's subject. Beneath the subtitle, the name of the writer of the article may be listed.
- **Headings** **Headings** are words or phrases used to break up the text of an article into sections. They are often printed in a size or color intended to stand out. You can sometimes outline the main points of an article by listing the headings.
- **Illustrations** Many articles are illustrated with drawings, photographs, maps, graphs, and tables. Illustrations are often used to help you picture something described in an article and to provide more information. They may be accompanied by brief printed explanations called **captions.**

Writing Focus Preparing for Extended Response

As you read, use your *Reader/Writer Notebook* to jot down the main points of "Making It Up As We Go." You'll use your notes to answer an extended-response question later.

Vocabulary

prehistoric (pree hihs TAWR ihk) *adj.*: relating to the time before written history. *The prehistoric cave art was skillfully done.*

permanent (PUR muh nuhnt) *adj.*: lasting; unchanging. *The art might have provided a permanent record of a story.*

intriguing (ihn TREE gihng) *adj.*: causing great interest. *Scientists have intriguing ideas about the purpose of the cave art.*

Language Coach

Word History The word *intriguing* comes from the Latin word *intricare*, which means "to tangle up." How do you think the meaning of the Latin term is related to the meaning of *intriguing*?

Learn It Online

Explore an interactive magazine article with the Reading Workshop online:

go.hrw.com L6-89 

MAGAZINE ARTICLE

Making It Up As We Go

The **title** is often a catchy phrase intended to grab your interest.

THE HISTORY OF STORYTELLING

The **subtitle** tells you more about the article.

by Jennifer Kroll

Read with a Purpose

Read the following article to learn about the very long history of storytelling.

On an autumn day in 1879, eight-year-old Maria Sanz de Sautuola explored a cave on her family's land in Altamira, Spain. As her candle lit up a large chamber, Maria was startled and called to her father. "Look, Papa! Oxen!" she cried. The chamber was filled with animal paintings. From where she stood, oxen seemed to be running across the ceiling.

Similar paintings have since been found in more than 200 caves in Spain and France. The artwork shows such animals as mammoths, reindeer, and horses. Sometimes, symbols have been drawn on or near the creatures. At a cave called Font-du-Gaume, these symbols include upside-down *T*s and side-by-side circles with arches above them.

What did these pictures and symbols mean to the people who made them? We cannot know. But it is reasonable to wonder whether the images were used as a way of preserving stories—or as an aid in telling them. **A**

Headings break up the text into sections.

STONE-AGE STORYTELLERS

Maria and her father, Marcelino, found stone tools, pieces of pottery, oyster shells, and animal bones nearby before uncovering the art. Marcelino figured the items, and therefore the artwork, were created by prehistoric people called Cro-Magnons. Cro-Magnons were

Marcelino Sanz de Sautuola and his daughter Maria discover the cave paintings at Altamira.

hunters and gatherers who lived from about 40,000 to 10,000 years ago. They did not have written language as we do. But surely they had stories.

Imagine a Cro-Magnon storyteller standing in the Altamira cave, lighting up pictures to show parts of a story. Perhaps he stood where Maria stood. Maybe the flicker of fire from his torch made the oxen seem to run. **B**

PASS IT ON, PASS IT DOWN

Writing is a recent invention, only about 5,000 to 6,000 years old. Among the first people to develop a writing system were the Sumerians. They lived in the region that is now Iraq. Their writing system, called

A **Read and Discuss** What has the author told us in this first section?

B **Read and Discuss** How does this new information add to what we have already learned?

Vocabulary **prehistoric** (pree hihs TAWR ihk) *adj.*: relating to the time before written history.

FROM DRAWING TO WRITING

The Sumerians first wrote by using pictures to represent things and ideas. Gradually, the pictures became more like abstract symbols and less like illustrations of what they represented. These examples show how Sumerian writing changed over time.

	3300 B.C.	2800 B.C.	2400 B.C.	1800 B.C.
Heaven				
Grain				
Fish				
Bird				
Water				

Illustrations help you picture things described in the article.

THE RARE AND WONDERFUL WRITTEN WORD

JUST HOW NEW AND NOVEL IS WRITING? CONSIDER THESE FACTS:

- Modern humans (*Homo sapiens*) have existed for between 100,000 and 150,000 years. The earliest written language, though, dates from only 5,000 to 6,000 years ago.
- Perhaps tens of thousands of different languages have existed in human history. Stories have been told orally in most of these languages. But ***written*** stories exist in only a small percentage of all languages—about 106!
- About 6,000 languages are spoken in the world today. Only about 78 of them have a written form that is used for recording and saving stories.
- Even today, hundreds of languages with no written form are being used all over the world. C

C **Read and Discuss** The author has given us a number of facts here. What's the point of this information?

cuneiform, dates back to before 3000 B.C. The Sumerians wrote by pressing marks into moist clay tablets with a sharp reed. The tablets would be baked, hardening the clay so that it would last. They kept detailed business and government records. The Sumerians also wrote down stories. The *Epic of Gilgamesh* is a Sumerian story that's still told today. It was written on clay tablets that have lasted thousands of years.

Before developing writing, the Sumerians kept stories alive in the way most groups have throughout time. They passed on tales by word of mouth. Many of these ancient stories were written into the *Epic of Gilgamesh*. But the tales were passed from person to person for years before being pressed into clay.

A culture that passes on stories by word of mouth is said to have an *oral tradition*. The stories of such a culture differ from those of a *chirographic* (ky ruh GRAF ihk), or writing, culture in some ways. For one thing, written stories remain the same with each reading. But unwritten stories change with every telling. Each storyteller cannot help but give each story his or her own twist.

PREHISTORIC BLOGGERS? Ⓓ

The idea that a story may never be told the same twice might seem to go against the belief that a story is a permanent creation. Then again, maybe not. After all, we're used to seeing stories change as they shift forms—when a novel is made into a film, for example, or a film into a comic book.

The **caption** explains what is shown in an illustration.

American tall tales, like those about Paul Bunyan and Babe the Blue Ox (the subjects of this California sculpture), are examples of stories spread by word of mouth.

We still pass on stories by word of mouth, just as our ancestors did. Think of campers telling scary stories around a fire or fishers swapping "biggest catch" stories. Most people like to give a story their own "spin." Think of news passed around the school cafeteria or by Internet bloggers. Most Web writers don't just tell you what happened; they tell you what they *think* about what happened. The journalists Gregory Curtis and Daniel Burnstein have (separately) suggested that the Cro-Magnons might have done something similar when they drew symbols around cave paintings. Could the symbols be comments added to a story by later viewers or tellers? It is an intriguing idea. What do you think? Ⓔ

Read with a Purpose

What's something that has stayed the same throughout the history of storytelling?

Ⓓ **Informational Focus** **Structural Features** How do headings like this one help you while you read the article?

Ⓔ **Read and Discuss** How does early storytelling relate to some of today's forms of storytelling?

Vocabulary **permanent** (PUR muh nuhnt) *adj.*: lasting; unchanging.

intriguing (ihn TREE gihng) *adj.*: causing great interest.

MAGAZINE ARTICLE

Applying Your Skills

Sunshine State Standards: Benchmarks **LA.6.1.6.3** use context clues to determine meanings of unfamiliar words; **LA.6.1.7.2** analyze the author's purpose (e.g., to persuade, inform, entertain, or explain) and perspective in a variety of texts and understand how they affect meaning; **LA.6.2.2.4** identify the characteristics of a variety of types of nonfiction text (e.g., reference works, newspapers, biographies, procedures, instructions, practical/functional texts).

Making It Up As We Go

Practicing for FCAT

Informational Text and Vocabulary

1. Which of the following points is NOT made by the article?
   - **A** Paintings have been found in more than two hundred caves in Spain and France.
   - **B** Symbols painted in caves were used primarily as decorative art.
   - **C** Writing has been in existence for about five thousand to six thousand years.
   - **D** Chirographic cultures write down some of their stories.

2. What is "Pass It On, Pass It Down"?
   - **F** the magazine title
   - **G** a caption
   - **H** a heading
   - **I** an illustration

3. What do the illustrations in this article do?
   - **A** depict the animals painted in Altamira cave
   - **B** tell a story in the chirographic tradition
   - **C** show the marks made next to cave paintings
   - **D** support points made in the article

4. Why has the writer written this article?
   - **F** to teach readers about prehistoric paintings in the Altamira cave
   - **G** to explain that Cro-Magnons lived in caves
   - **H** to show how Sumerian writing changed gradually over time
   - **I** to suggest that the long tradition of storytelling may go back to prehistoric times

5. Read this sentence from the article.

   [The items] . . . were created by prehistoric people called Cro-Magnons.

   What does the word *prehistoric* mean?
   - **A** before humans
   - **B** recorded in writing
   - **C** ancient
   - **D** before recorded history

6. Read this sentence from the article.

   It is an intriguing idea.

   What does the word *intriguing* mean?
   - **F** interesting
   - **G** toughened
   - **H** boring
   - **I** dreamy

Writing Focus Extended Response

Use the notes you took while reading this article to describe the features of storytelling from the oral tradition. Support your response with details from the article.

What Do You Think Now?

What might the most ancient storytellers have in common with storytellers today?

NEWSPAPER ARTICLE

Preparing to Read

Sunshine State Standards: Benchmarks **LA.6.1.6.1** use new vocabulary that is introduced and taught directly; **LA.6.1.6.5** relate new vocabulary to familiar words; *Also covered* **LA.6.2.2.1; LA.6.2.2.4**

Iraqi Treasures Hunted

Reader/Writer Notebook

Use your **RWN** to complete the activities for this selection.

Informational Text Focus

Structural Features of a Newspaper Like most types of informational materials, **newspapers** have special structural features that help you find and understand the information you are looking for. Follow these tips when you are reading a newspaper:

- Learn about your newspaper's **sections.** A newspaper may be divided into sections for world and national news, local news, sports, weather, comics, classified ads, and other subjects. Decide which section is most likely to have the information you want.
- Scan the **headlines.** Headlines usually appear in large, heavy type and are not complete sentences. Good headlines indicate what an article is about and usually grab your attention.
- Beneath a headline, you will sometimes find a **byline,** the name of the writer. The article itself may begin with a **dateline,** which includes the name of the place where the news event happened and often the date it happened.
- Check the **lead,** the beginning of the article. News articles usually answer most or all of the *5W-How?* questions—*who? what? where? when? why?* and *how?*—in the lead. The less important information usually comes at the end of the article. Having the most important information up front makes skimming and scanning a newspaper much easier for readers.
- Some newspaper articles have pictures or graphics with **captions,** or short explanations. Newspapers may also have special side features called **sidebars**—additional information that is related to the article but placed in a separate box. Sidebars often have their own headings, illustrations, and captions.

Vocabulary

recovered (rih KUHV uhrd) *v.:* got back something lost. *Many of the stolen items have been recovered by the museum.*

civilizations (sihv uh luh ZAY shuhnz) *n.:* advanced cultures that are characteristic of particular times and places. *Mesopotamia was home to some of the earliest civilizations.*

authorities (uh THAWR uh teez) *n.:* people with the official responsibility for something. *Many artifacts were returned to the authorities.*

Language Coach

Word Definitions You can often discover a word's meaning based on its similarity to another word. For instance, you have learned the meaning of *civilization.* What do you think the words *civilized, civility,* and *civilian* might mean?

Writing Focus

Preparing for **Extended Response**

As you read, observe how structural features help you find information. You'll answer an extended-response question about structural features later.

Learn It Online

Learn about the features of a newspaper through *PowerNotes* online:

go.hrw.com L6-95

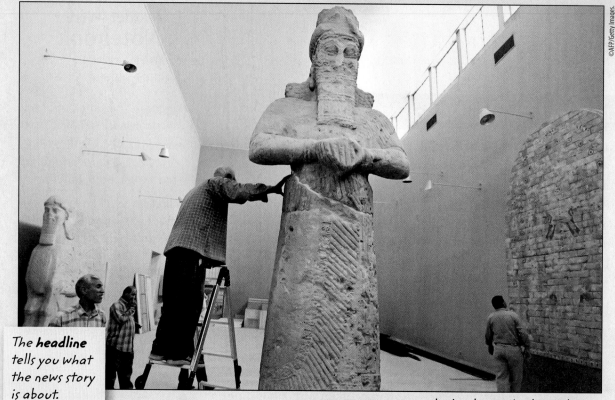

Iraqi workers repair a damaged statue.

*The **headline** tells you what the news story is about.*

IRAQI TREASURES HUNTED

Long after the looting of the National Museum, Iraq's treasures remain at risk.

*The **byline** tells you who wrote the article.*

by Barbara Bakowski

Read with a Purpose

Read the following article to find out about efforts to save Iraqi treasures of ancient art.

Build Background

In the days following the invasion of Iraq in 2003, U.S.-led military forces struggled to maintain order. As the city of Baghdad fell, it was easy for thieves, or looters, to take advantage of the confusion and disorder. Looters were even able to steal some of the nation's greatest treasures: ancient,

The **dateline** tells you where and (sometimes) when the news event happened.

STONY BROOK, N.Y., January 14 — Nearly four years have passed since looters removed thousands of items from Iraq's National Museum. Many of the missing pieces have been recovered. Historians and art experts, however, say Iraq's historical artifacts are still in danger.

After the robberies, museum director Donny George walled off much of the collection to protect the remains. George left Iraq in 2006 and is serving as a visiting professor at New York's Stony Brook University. Now looters are stealing items from throughout Iraq, says his Stony Brook colleague Dr. Elizabeth Stone, an expert in the archaeology of the Middle East. Dig sites are the new targets. Some of the objects being taken date back to the world's earliest civilizations.

"Mesopotamia had the world's first cities, first writing," Stone says. "All our ideas of how we live in cities came from there." (A)

The **lead** presents the most important information.

Birthplace of Civilization

Present-day Iraq occupies the land once called Mesopotamia. The name comes from a Greek word meaning "the land between rivers." In the plains between the Tigris and Euphrates rivers, some of the world's earliest settlements were founded: Sumer, Babylonia, and Assyria. "It was the cradle of civilization" more than 5,000 years ago, Stone says.

Early Mesopotamians were ahead of their time in many ways. They improved farming methods, created irrigation systems, learned how to measure time, wrote a set of laws, and invented the wheeled chariot. The Sumerians also invented cuneiform, one of the first writing systems in the world, before 3000 B.C. *The Epic of Gilgamesh*, a famous work of Sumerian literature, was recorded on clay tablets that still survive. It was written down in about 2000 B.C. (B)

Ancient Objects Stolen

Iraq's National Museum, founded in 1923, held the physical record of Mesopotamia's long history. The museum housed at least 500,000 valuable items. Then, in April 2003, U.S.-led troops moved into Baghdad. Looters used the resulting confusion as an opportunity to steal statues, coins, and more. In the final count, about 14,000 items from the museum were stolen, including the 5,000-year-old Warka mask and a copper sculpture known as the Bassetki statue.

Iraqi authorities, the United Nations, the U.S. government, and international law-enforcement officials began a search. Researchers at the Oriental Institute at the University of Chicago listed photographs and descriptions of the stolen objects on a Web site to aid in their recovery.

Relics Returned

Officials adopted a "no-questions-asked" policy to encourage the safe return of the missing

— Continued on Page 99 —

(A) **Read and Discuss** What has the author set up for us in these first three paragraphs?

(B) **Read and Discuss** What do all these inventions indicate about the early Mesopotamians?

Vocabulary **recovered** (rih KUHV uhrd) *v.:* got back something lost.
civilizations (sihv uh luh ZAY shuhnz) *n.:* advanced cultures that are characteristic of particular times and places.
authorities (uh THAWR uh teez) *n.:* people with the official responsibility for something.

The full-page **sidebar** goes into greater detail about a point in the article.

Riches from the Ruins

Ⓒ

Status: Found

Warka Mask—5,000-year-old marble mask from the Sumerian city of Uruk; one of the world's oldest realistic carvings and one of the world's oldest masks

Warka Vase—Stone (alabaster) vase from about 3000 B.C.; badly damaged during theft

Bassetki Statue—Copper sculpture from about 2300 B.C.

Nimrud Gold—Gold jewelry and precious stones dating from the eight and ninth centuries B.C.

Golden Harp of Ur—Gold and ivory harp from about 2600 B.C.; also badly damaged during looting

Clay Pot from Tall Hassuna—clay pot dating to the sixth millennium B.C., at least 1,500 years before the invention of the wheel

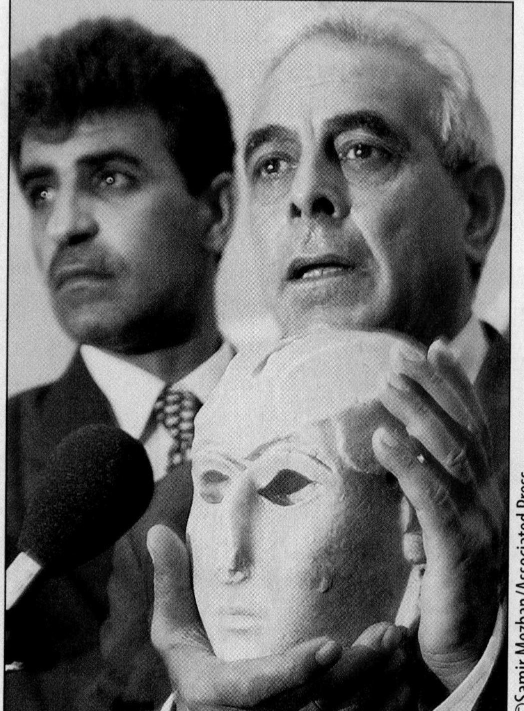

©Samir Mezban/Associated Press.

The 5,000-year-old "Warka mask," one of the most important artifacts stolen from Iraq's National Museum, is held up by Iraqi Minister of Culture Mufeed Muhammad Jawad Al Jazairee after it was found and returned to the police.

Status: Still Missing

Nimrud Lioness—Carved ivory and gold plaque dating to 800 B.C.

Hatra Goddess of Victory—Life-size head, made of copper, from the third century B.C.

Ninhursag Bull—One of two copper bulls from a temple built by the King of Ur around 2475 B.C.; the other has been recovered.

Lagash Statue—Headless inscribed limestone statue from about 2450 B.C.

Hatra Heads—Five statue heads from a city that thrived in the first century A.D.

Cuneiform Bricks—Nine bricks bearing royal inscriptions from the ancient Akkadian, Babylonian, and Sumerian empires.

Ⓒ **Informational Focus** **Structural Features** Why do you think the writer chose to put this information in a sidebar?

— Continued from Page 97 —

treasures. A few months after the looting, the Warka mask was returned to the museum. A police raid later in the year turned up the Bassetki statue. It had been hidden in a sewer in Iraq. A headless stone statue of a Sumerian king was recovered by American agents after it had been smuggled through Syria into the United States. Other treasures were found in the Netherlands, Britain, and Italy and were returned to Baghdad.

More than 5,000 of the stolen artifacts have been recovered. Experts say it may take decades to locate the rest. Some may never be found. Meanwhile, the National Museum remains closed to the public.

Looting Goes On

Experts in the United States and other countries say dig sites in Iraq are still being raided. "One of the many unfortunate consequences [of instability in Iraq is] widespread looting of archaeological sites," says Susan B. Downey. She is an art historian at the University of California, Los Angeles.

Iraqi law makes it illegal to remove artifacts from dig sites without government permission. But thieves digging at any of thousands of sites may be able to smuggle priceless goods out of the country. Those objects have not yet been recorded or photographed, and therefore will be easier for smugglers to sell. **D**

*The photographer's **credit** is usually printed along the side of the photo.*

*The **caption** explains what is shown in a picture.*

The head of a broken sculpture lies in a pile of rubble after looters plundered Iraq's National Museum for its treasures.

Read with a Purpose

What specific efforts have been made to save ancient Iraqi art?

Analyzing Visuals

Viewing and Interpreting What do you think happened here in the museum before this photograph was taken?

D **Read and Discuss** How do archaeological digs figure into the puzzle of stolen objects?

NEWSPAPER ARTICLE

Applying Your Skills

Sunshine State Standards: Benchmarks **LA.6.1.6.1** use new vocabulary that is introduced and taught directly; **LA.6.1.6.3** use context clues to determine meanings of unfamiliar words; **LA.6.1.7.3** determine the main idea or essential message in grade-level text through inferring, paraphrasing, summarizing, and identifying relevant details; **LA.6.2.1.1** identify the characteristics of various genres (e.g., poetry, fiction, short story, dramatic literature) as forms with distinct characteristics and purposes.

Iraqi Treasures Hunted

Practicing for FCAT

Informational Text and Vocabulary

1. In which section of the newspaper would you be MOST likely to find this article?
   - **A** Health
   - **B** Sports
   - **C** Entertainment
   - **D** World News

2. What does the byline tell you?
   - **F** the important information
   - **G** who wrote the article
   - **H** who is in charge of the museum
   - **I** what the article is about

3. According to the article, which artifact has NOT been returned to the museum?
   - **A** a Sumerian mask
   - **B** a copper sculpture
   - **C** a clay pot
   - **D** a carved ivory and gold plaque

4. Which statement BEST sums up the point of the news story?
   - **F** Thousands of artifacts were stolen from the Iraqi National Museum.
   - **G** Many stolen artifacts have been returned to the Iraqi museum.
   - **H** The Iraqi National Museum remains closed.
   - **I** Ancient Iraqi artifacts are still at risk of being stolen.

5. Read this sentence from the article.

   Iraqi authorities, the United Nations, the U.S. government, and international law-enforcement officials began a search.

   What does the word *authorities* mean?
   - **A** looters
   - **B** researchers
   - **C** officials
   - **D** journalists

6. Read this sentence from the article.

   Some of the objects being taken date back to the world's earliest civilizations.

   Which word is closest in meaning to the word *civilization*?
   - **F** society
   - **G** ancient city
   - **H** clay tablet
   - **I** artifact

Writing Focus Extended Response

Think as a Reader/Writer

How did the structural features of this article help you find information? Support your answer with details from the article.

In what sense can ancient artifacts be seen as stories from the past? What can these "stories" tell us?

WEB SITE

Preparing to Read

Sunshine State Standards: Benchmarks **LA.6.1.5.1** adjust reading rate based on purpose, text difficulty, form, and style; *Also covered* **LA.6.2.2.1; LA.6.2.2.4; LA.6.6.4.1**

CAVE Online

Reader/Writer Notebook

Use your **RWN** to complete the activities for this selection.

Informational Text Focus

Structural Features of a Web Site In the past, if a writer wanted to research a topic, he or she would probably look in a reference book or in a library. Today, we have another important source of information—the Internet.

There are several ways to find information on the Internet. You can go directly to a **Web site** if you know the URL (uniform resource locator), or address of the site. Sometimes you will want to use a **search engine** when you do research. A search will produce a list of Web sites relating to your topic. You can just click on the site name to go directly to the site. If you get too many results, you can refine your search by choosing more specific search terms. (Always keep in mind that not all Web sites contain reliable information. If you are doing research, you need to be sure that the Web site you are using has been created and is monitored by a trustworthy source.)

Getting Information Most Web sites share some basic structural features. Knowing them can help you find information online.

- Most of the features a site offers are shown on the site's **home page.** Start out by finding and reading basic information about the site, usually at the top or center of the home page.
- Look for a **table of contents,** a list of the site's other pages. This often appears on the side of the home page. You can generally reach the other pages of a site by clicking on the items listed in the table of contents.
- Look for **links,** Web sites related to the one you're exploring. You can often reach a link by clicking on its name. You can usually find a link in the table of contents or on the home page.

Vocabulary

techniques (tehk NEEKS) *n.:* ways of doing complex activities. *The new techniques will capture better images of the cave art.*

projection (pruh JEHKT shuhn) *n.:* display of an image made by shining light through a small version of the image. *The projection of the cave paintings made it seem as if I were in the actual cave.*

vivid (VIHV ihd) *adj.:* producing strong, clear images. *The vivid images of the cave drawings look like the real thing.*

Language Coach

Pronunciation and Fluency When you're learning how to pronounce unfamiliar words, it's important to pay attention to which syllable is stressed. In the word list above, look inside the parentheses for the syllable written in capital letters. That syllable is stressed. Practice pronouncing these words with a partner.

Writing Focus

Preparing for **Extended Response**

See how the structural features of a Web site can help you find information. You'll answer an extended-response question about structural features later.

Learn It Online

To learn more about analyzing Web sites, visit *MediaScope* on:

go.hrw.com L6-101 

WEB SITE

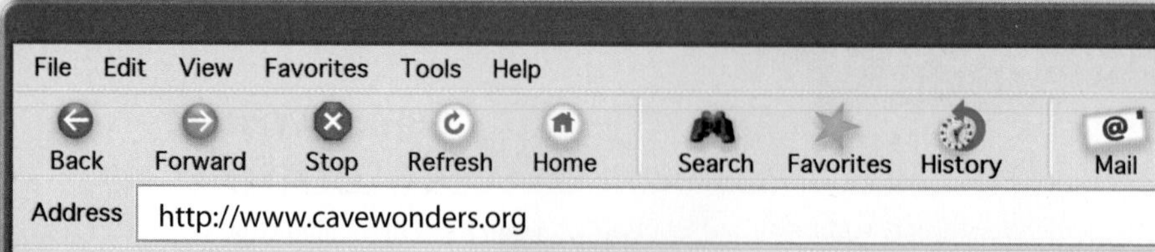

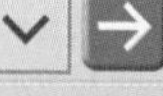

Read with a Purpose

Read this Web article to discover how technology will bring ancient art to a modern audience.

CAVE in cooperation with the Natural History Society

HOME | ABOUT | EXPLORER'S BLOG | SITE MAP | CONTACT **A**

FINDING YOUR WAY AROUND EARTH'S UNDERGROUND WONDERS

SEARCH | print e-mail fax

by THE WORLD ALMANAC

Home Page: These features at the top of the page outline the structure of the Web site.

INTRODUCTION

IN THIS ISSUE

Fungus Among Us: A Dangerous Intruder

News Board

Education

Ask the Digger

NEWS BOARD

PAST ISSUES

By Date

Contents: This list tells you what other topics the site covers.

NEWSBOARD

Copy That

Picture this: A team of artists is at work, creating a copy of prehistoric art from Lascaux cave in France. The tools being used are laser techniques and photographic projection. Therefore, the fake promises to be vivid and realistic. Team leader Renaud Sanson tells a Canadian newspaper that "advances in technology allow us to reproduce the tiniest detail." **B**

The replica will tour several cities around the world, carrying images of the famous

Detail of a painting showing a bull and horse in Lascaux cave. Click to enlarge.

A **Informational Focus** **Structural Features** Where would you click to get more information about CAVE?

B **Read and Discuss** What role does technology play in the world of prehistoric art?

Vocabulary **techniques** (tehk NEEKS) *n.:* ways of doing complex activities.
projection (pruh JEHKT shuhn) *n.:* display of an image made by shining light through a small version of the image.
vivid (VIHV ihd) *adj.:* producing strong, clear images.

Artists work to create a replica of the Lascaux cave art.

17,000-year-old cave art to a wide audience. If all goes as planned, the exhibit will be ready for showing in 2008. It will begin its tour near the Eiffel Tower in Paris.

Lascaux cave in southwestern France was an accidental discovery made by teens in 1940. It has astounded the art world and the public ever since. Rock paintings show bison, horses, stags, and other animals. The different stages of a hunt are clearly visible, as are the talents of those who did the artwork.

> FACTOID
>
> **“[The Lascaux cave] has been closed to the public since 1963 to protect the paintings.”**

The site has been closed to the public since 1963 to protect the paintings. It attracted so many people—over a thousand a day—that the paintings were being damaged by the carbon dioxide from visitors' breath! That's why a professor of fine arts, Benjamin Britton, decided to design software in 1990 that would allow people to go on "virtual visits" of Lascaux. Britton, who had to work from photographs, became a finalist for a 1995 Discover Award. Sanson has been able to go one better than Britton: He has been given special permission to enter the cave to complete this latest high-tech project. C

Not the First Replica

In 1983, long before Renaud Sanson began his painstaking reproduction of the Lascaux cave paintings, a replica of Lascaux opened not far from the

> C **Informational Focus** **Structural Features** How does Benjamin Britton's work connect to the great number of visitors who came and admired the work in Lascaux cave?

RELATED LINKS

Official Lascaux Cave Web Site

Discover Awards

Virtual Lascaux Software

Links: Clicking on an item in this list takes you to another Web site and more information.

A visitor to Lascaux II. This replica of two of the finest cave rooms opened in 1983. Click to enlarge. D

original site. This replica, called Lascaux II, is an accurate copy of two of the most famous sections of the cave: the Great Hall of the Bulls and the Painted Gallery. (Lascaux is really a system of caves. Other sections of the cave system have been given colorful names based on the type of art found in them: the Shaft of the Dead Man, the Chamber of Felines, and the Chamber of Engravings.) Visitors can go inside the Great Hall of the Bulls, where paintings covering a huge area of the cave walls show horses, bulls, stags, and a creature with twisted horns that is sometimes called "the unicorn." They can also see what is probably the largest single cave-art image in the world—a seventeen-foot-long bull. True to the original cave paintings, these animals are colorfully drawn in red, black, and a dark yellow-gold color called ocher (OH kuhr). Visitors to Lascaux II can also see the Painted Gallery, which features what many art historians see as the finest paintings. Wild oxen, horses, bison, ibexes, cows, and a stag cover nearly one hundred feet of wall space—including the ceiling.

And the replicas don't end there. Tourists can go to Le Thot, France, to see more reproductions of Lascaux cave paintings at the Center of Prehistoric Art.

Read with a Purpose

Why was technology needed to enable modern audiences to see this art?

D Informational Focus Structural Features How does this feature add to your understanding of what you're reading?

Internet

Applying Your Skills

Sunshine State Standards: Benchmarks **LA.6.1.6.1** use new vocabulary that is introduced and taught directly; **LA.6.1.7.2** analyze the author's purpose (e.g., to persuade, inform, entertain, or explain) and perspective in a variety of texts and understand how they affect meaning; *Also covered* **LA.6.1.7.3; LA.6.2.2.1**

CAVE Online

Practicing for FCAT

Informational Text and Vocabulary

1. What is the MAIN purpose of the article on this Web site?
   - **A** to criticize the work of Benjamin Britton
   - **B** to describe the paintings inside Lascaux cave
   - **C** to explain the importance of cave paintings
   - **D** to tell people about the cave paintings exhibit

2. What part of this Web site tells you that there are other topics discussed on it?
   - **F** the search field
   - **G** the table of contents
   - **H** the links section
   - **I** the photo captions

3. Where would you find information on the mission, or goals, of this Web site?
   - **A** the About section
   - **B** the captions
   - **C** the links
   - **D** the table of contents

4. Which statement BEST sums up the main idea of this Web site?
   - **F** The Natural History Society helps publish *CAVE* magazine.
   - **G** Lascaux cave is closed to tourists because their presence damages the artwork.
   - **H** Benjamin Britton was a finalist for a 1995 Discover Award.
   - **I** Scientists are recreating images in Lascaux for a traveling exhibit.

5. Read this sentence from the article.

   The tools being used are laser techniques and photographic projection.

   What does the word *projection* mean?
   - **A** drawing
   - **B** laser technique
   - **C** map
   - **D** display

6. Read this sentence from the article.

   Therefore, the fake promises to be vivid and realistic.

   What does the word *vivid* mean?
   - **F** bright
   - **G** blurry
   - **H** photographed
   - **I** enlarged

Writing Focus Extended Response

Describe the purpose of the CAVE Online Web site, and explain how its structural features reflect its purpose. Support your response with details from the text.

What stories of the past do you think the Lascaux cave paintings might tell?

Writing Workshop

Comparison-Contrast Essay **FCAT Writing+**

Write with a Purpose

Write a comparison-contrast essay that explores the similarities and differences between two literary works or two literary elements, such as characters, plot, or setting. The **purpose** of your essay is to inform your **audience**—in this case, your teacher or classmates.

A Good Comparison-Contrast Essay

- identifies the subjects being compared and states the main idea in the introduction
- includes at least two similarities and two differences
- uses consistent organization, such as the block method or point-by-point method
- supports statements with specific details and examples
- restates the main idea in the conclusion

Think as a Reader/Writer

You probably made comparisons as you read different forms of fiction and nonfiction in this collection. Before you write a comparison-contrast essay, read this excerpt from World Almanac's *Olympic Glory: Victories in History,* from page 311 of this book.

The ancient Games were summertime events. In the modern world, however, there are Winter Games as well. Like the ancient Games, the modern Summer and Winter Olympics are each held every four years, with the two alternating on even-numbered years.

← This specific **detail** illustrates a **similarity.**

When the Olympics began in 776 B.C., they consisted of one footrace—covering a distance of 600 feet. In contrast, twenty-eight summer sports were set for the year 2008, and seven sports were scheduled for the 2010 Winter Games. "The range of sports has expanded enormously," says [David] Potter [professor of Greek and Latin at the University of Michigan]. "The Olympians established a very small canon of sports initially. Now it appears to be an Olympian sport in itself to see what can be added each time."

← **Point-by-point organization** is used to **contrast** the number of sports included in the games.

Ancient Olympians battled the Mediterranean heat, so to toughen up, they practiced in the sun. At the events, according to historians, they wore little or no clothing. Such a dress code would be shocking to modern sensibilities and a blow to manufacturers of sportswear and accessories—who, like shoemakers, make certain to place their products in the public eye during the Olympic Games.

← Statements are supported with **examples,** including vivid images.

Think About the Professional Model

With a partner, discuss the following questions about the model.

1. What kind of evidence does the writer use to support this comparison-contrast?
2. What details illustrate the contrast between ancient and modern Olympic Games?

Use your **RWN** to complete the activities for this workshop.

Sunshine State Standards: Benchmarks **LA.6.3.1.1** generating ideas from multiple sources (e.g., prior knowledge, discussion with others, writer's notebook, research materials, or other reliable sources), based upon teacher-directed topics and personal interests; **LA.6.3.1.2** making a plan for writing that prioritizes ideas, addresses purpose, audience, main idea, and logical sequence; **LA.6.3.1.3** using organizational strategies and tools (e.g., technology, outline, chart, table, graph, web, story map); **LA.6.3.2.1** developing main ideas from the prewriting plan using primary and secondary sources appropriate to purpose and audience; **LA.6.3.3.1** evaluating the draft for development of ideas and content, logical organization, voice, point of view, word choice, and sentence variation; **LA.6.3.3.4** applying appropriate tools or strategies to evaluate and refine the draft (e.g., peer review, checklists, rubrics); *Also covered* **LA.6.3.4.1; LA.6.3.4.2; LA.6.3.4.3; LA.6.3.5.3; LA.6.4.2.3**

Prewriting

Choose Your Subjects

Select any two literary works that share at least one interesting point of comparison, such as similar characters, settings, subjects, or themes. You can begin by looking back through the selections in this collection and thinking about the Idea Starters at right.

Think About Your Subject, Purpose, and Audience

As you think about possible subjects for your essay, consider your purpose (why you are writing) and audience (your readers).

- Your main **purpose** is to give readers information about how two subjects are similar and how they are different.
- Your **audience** is a reader or readers who may—or may not—be familiar with the works you are comparing. If they are not familiar with the works, you must decide what kind of (and how much) background information you need to provide for them so that they can follow your ideas.

Find Similarities and Differences

Which features will you compare and contrast? If you choose to compare and contrast two short stories, discuss the same aspects of both works: plot elements, characters, or themes, for example. If you choose two characters, focus on each character's physical traits, actions, thoughts, and feelings. Describe the characters' main conflicts and how they resolve their conflicts.

A **Venn diagram** can help you brainstorm ideas about how your subjects are alike and different. Here's a Venn diagram based on the professional model on the previous page. The similarities are written where the circles overlap, and the differences are written where they don't overlap.

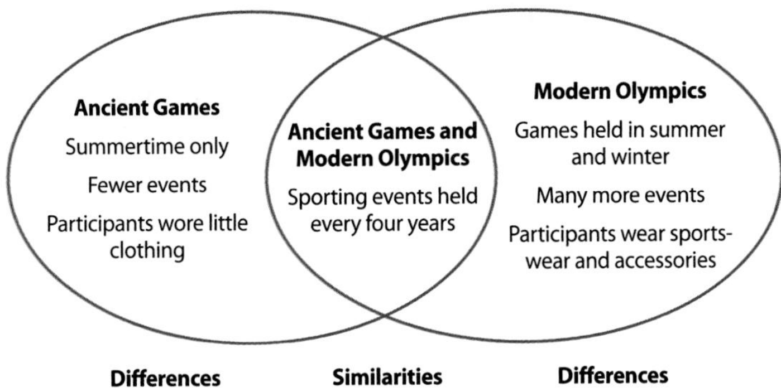

Idea Starters

- two characters with similar conflicts
- similar themes in two stories
- the role of setting in two works
- two myths, fables, or folk tales from different cultures

Peer Review

Survey your classmates to see how many of them are familiar with the works you plan to compare. You won't need to provide as much background for familiar works as you will for works that few others have read.

Your Turn

Get Started List some subjects for **comparison** in your **RWN.** Narrow your choices un til you have decided on the two that would make the most interesting comparison. Then, create a Venn diagram to list the **similarities** and **differences** you'll discuss in your essay.

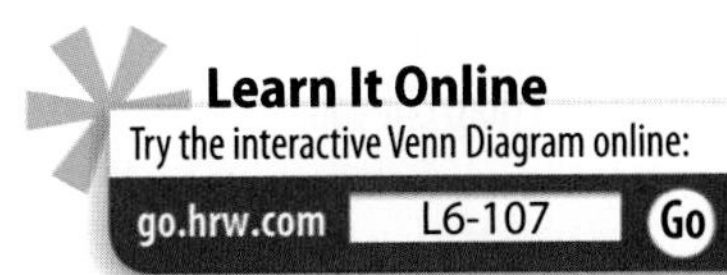

Learn It Online
Try the interactive Venn Diagram online:
go.hrw.com
L6-107
Go

Writing Tip

As you find specific details and supporting evidence from the texts that you might want to use in your essay, write them down. Don't forget to note the page number and paragraph where you found these examples so that you can go back to them later on if needed.

Gather Supporting Details

You may have a clear understanding of your subjects, but your audience will need more information. Look at the points of comparison you have listed in your Venn diagram. What specific examples would help your reader get the picture? If you say the settings of two stories are similar, support your statement with examples of *how* they're similar. For example, the two stories may both take place in a large city, or they may both take place in the same historical period.

Organize Your Ideas

The details in a comparison-contrast essay usually are organized in a particular pattern, using either the block method or the point-by-point method. Use a chart like one of those below to help you plan.

- **Block method:** In the block method, all points of comparison for a subject are presented at one time. For example, if you were comparing and contrasting two settings, you would present all the features of one setting in the first paragraph or section—where the setting is located, what time of day it is, what it looks like, and so on. Then, in the next paragraph or section, you would present all the same information about the features of the other setting.

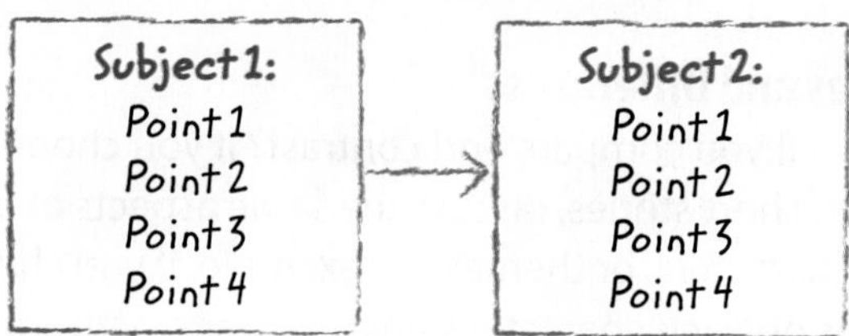

- **Point-by-point method:** In the point-by-point method, you present each point of comparison for both subjects before moving on to the next point of comparison. For example, you would compare both settings' geographical locations, then what time of year (or day) it is in each setting, then what the settings look like, and so on.

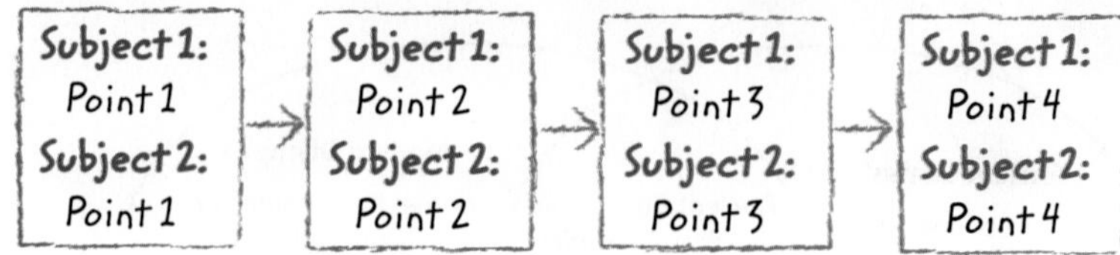

Your Turn

Choose Your Method of Organization Look at your subjects, your points of comparison, and the details you want to include. Which method of **organization** would work best for your comparison? Create a chart in your **RWN** like one of those shown on this page to help you map out your key points.

Drafting

Follow the Writer's Framework

Use the **Writer's Framework** at right to help you write your first draft. Once you have written your draft, compare it with the framework to make sure you haven't forgotten anything.

A Writer's Framework

Introduction
- Capture your reader's attention with a strong beginning.
- Identify your subject at the beginning of the essay.

Body
- Use the block method or point-by-point method.
- Explore at least two similarities and two differences between your subjects.
- Support your points of comparison with details and examples.

Conclusion
- Sum up the main points about your subjects.
- Restate your main idea.

Use Transitional Words and Phrases

Using words and phrases that signal **transitions,** or changes from one idea to another, can clarify your essay's organization, help paragraphs flow easily from one to the next, and enable your readers to follow your ideas. These words and phrases show similarities: *also, another, as well as, both, in addition, just as, like, neither, similarly, too.* These words and phrases show differences: *although, but, however, in contrast, instead, in spite of, nevertheless, on the other hand, unlike.* Use transitional words and phrases to shift from one point of comparison to the next or to introduce supporting examples.

Grammar Link Use Introductory Adverbial Phrases

Another useful kind of transition is the **adverbial phrase**—a prepositional phrase used as an adverb. Adverbial phrases answer the questions *when? where? how? why? how often? how long? to what extent?* An adverbial phrase may come before or after the word it modifies, but as a transition it is best used at the beginning of a sentence. Study these examples from the professional model on page 106:

"**In the modern world,** however, there are Winter Games as well."

"**At the events,** according to historians, they wore little or no clothing."

Writing Tip

Re-read your draft before you write your conclusion. A good conclusion should be more than just a summary. Elaborate on the main idea that you presented in your introduction. You might also extend the conclusion to cover related works or topics.

Your Turn

Write Your Draft Follow your plan and framework to write a draft of your essay. Be sure to consider the following:

- How can you capture your reader's interest?
- What **introductory adverbial phrases** can you use?

Peer Review

Working with a classmate, review each other's drafts and trade revision suggestions. Answer each question in the chart to identify where and how your drafts can be improved. As you discuss your papers, be sure to write down your classmate's suggestions. You can refer to your notes as you revise your draft.

Evaluating and Revising

After your draft is completed, it's time to go back through and smooth out the rough spots. You can improve your draft by using the evaluation questions and revision techniques shown below.

Comparison-Contrast Essay: Guidelines for Content and Organization

Evaluation Question	Tip	Revision Technique
1. Does your introduction state your main idea?	**Underline** the main idea.	**Add** a main idea statement if one is missing.
2. Do you discuss two or more similarities and two or more differences?	**Put a star** next to each example of comparison or contrast.	If necessary, **add** examples of comparison and contrast. **Delete** any statements that don't belong.
3. Is the body of your essay organized by either the block method or the point-by-point method?	**Label** the method of organization in the margin. **Write** ***A*** above each point about the first subject and ***B*** above each point about the second subject.	If necessary, **rearrange** statements into either block order or point-by-point order.
4. Do details and examples support points of comparison?	**Put a check mark** next to supporting details and examples.	**Add support** with details and examples, if necessary.
5. Do you use introductory phrases to transition from one point to the next?	**Highlight** introductory phrases used as transitions.	**Add** introductory adverbial phrases if transitions are needed.
6. Does your conclusion restate and expand on the main idea?	**Bracket** the main idea. **Underline** statements that expand your main idea.	**Summarize** the main idea. **Elaborate** on statements that may need to be expanded.

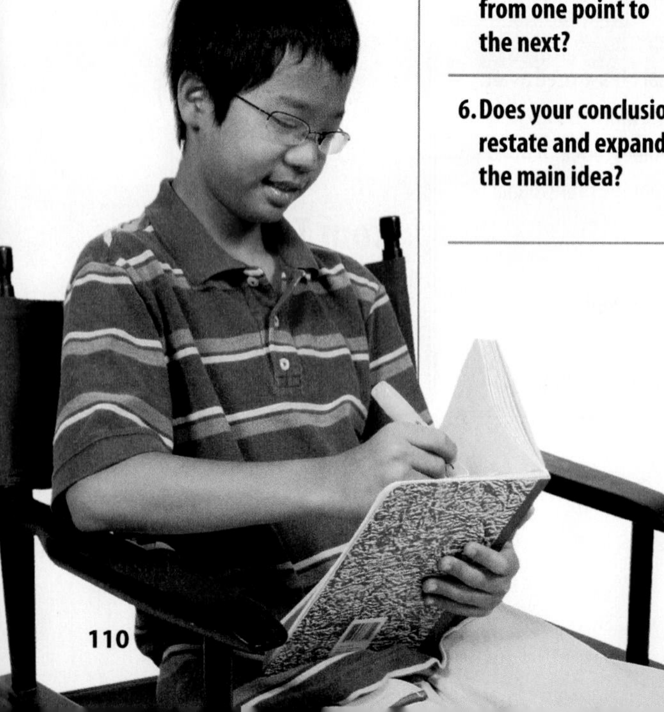

Read this student's draft along with the comments on its structure, its strengths, and how it could be made even better.

Student Draft

Oh No! The Earth Is Exploding!

by Erica Graham, Owasso Sixth-Grade Center

"Earth" by Oliver Herford and "Earth" by John Hall Wheelock are two poems about the destruction of Earth as viewed by a creature on another planet. Although the subjects are identical, the poems differ greatly in description and point of view.

In Herford's poem, the explosion of Earth is a beautiful sight to an innocent child who simply sees lights and color. Herford describes in great detail how the child from a planet far away witnesses the explosion as a beautiful shooting star rushing through the sky. Lines 6–12 paint a picture of what happens to the planet's creatures as Earth falls through space.

In Wheelock's poem, on the other hand, a Martian astronomer watches the destruction of Earth and states that it was bound to happen. His adult point of view is that the catastrophe means nothing to the Martians. The Martian astronomer dryly says the explosion proves that highly intelligent beings had been living there. He thinks that they are responsible for destroying their own planet.

← In the first sentence, Erica introduces the **subjects** she is going to compare and contrast. In the second sentence, her **main idea** statement includes both similarities and differences.

← Erica uses the **block** method, discussing each poem in a separate paragraph.

← Erica uses a **transitional phrase**, *on the other hand*, to link the paragraphs. She discusses the point of view of the Martian astronomer in Wheelock's poem.

MINI-LESSON How to Use the Block Method of Organization

Since Erica has chosen the block method of organization, she must address **both** points established in her main idea statement: description and point of view. Her third paragraph addresses only point of view, so Erica revises her draft to add a reference to the description—or lack of it—in the second poem.

Erica's Draft (end of third paragraph)

He thinks that they are responsible for destroying their own planet.

Erica's Revision (end of third paragraph)

He thinks that they are responsible for destroying their own planet. ^ *Even though the astronomer is watching the event, he does not describe it at all. The lack of description emphasizes how unimportant this event is to the Martian astronomer.*

Your Turn

Use an Organizational Method

Read your draft and ask yourself:

- Is my organizational method clear and consistent?
- Do I need to add support for any points of comparison?

Make any revisions that will strengthen the organization of your essay.

Student Draft *continues*

The **conclusion** restates the **main idea** from the introduction and makes a **connection to the reader.**

Both Oliver Herford's "Earth" and John Hall Wheelock's "Earth" are poems that view the Earth's destruction through the eyes of a creature on another planet. The child in Herford's poem may be easier to relate to than Wheelock's Martian astronomer, but their responses to Earth's destruction are equally surprising.

MINI-LESSON How to Expand the Main Idea in the Conclusion

In concluding your comparison-contrast essay, remember to restate your main points about the two subjects you are comparing. You may want to take your conclusion one step further and expand on your main points to give your reader something to consider. Can you make a connection to something beyond your topic that will make your comparison even more meaningful?

Erica revised her conclusion, summarizing her main points and making a connection to a deeper meaning. She shows how the two poems may deliver an important message about the planet Earth.

Erica's Revision

Both Oliver Herford's "Earth" and John Hall Wheelock's "Earth" are poems that view the Earth's destruction through the eyes of a creature on another planet. ^*Herford's poem provides a vivid description of the event, while Wheelock's is curiously lacking in description or emotion.*

The child in Herford's poem may be easier to relate to than Wheelock's Martian astronomer, but their responses to Earth's destruction are equally surprising. ^*Readers may be shocked that neither the child nor the astronomer views the Earth's destruction as such a bad thing. However, both poems force readers to consider that the Earth is fragile. These poems send the strong message that the Earth must be protected and cared for if it is to survive.*

Your Turn

Expand Your Conclusion

Review your conclusion. Have you summarized your main points? Is there anything you can add to show why these points are important?

Proofreading and Publishing

Proofreading

After you have revised your comparison-contrast essay, it's time to go back through it one more time to correct any errors in grammar, usage, or mechanics. It's easy to overlook your own errors, so you may want to have a classmate proofread, or edit, your essay as well.

Grammar Link Using Comparatives Correctly

A **comparative** is an adjective or adverb used to compare two things: *easier, better.* A **superlative** is an adjective or adverb used to compare three or more things: *easiest, best.* Erica looked closely at her work so that she could edit for two common mistakes people make when using comparatives:

- Use the comparative form, not the superlative, when you are comparing only two things.

"The child in Herford's poem may be ~~easiest~~ easier to relate to than Wheelock's Martian astronomer. . . ."

- Don't use *more* with *–er* to form a comparative.

"The child in Herford's poem may be ~~more~~ easier to relate to than Wheelock's Martian astronomer. . . ."

Publishing

Now it is time to publish your comparison-contrast essay, sharing it with a wider audience. Here are some ways to share your essay:

- Add photos or illustrations to your essay, and print the results in book form.
- Share your comparison-contrast essay orally. Practice reading it aloud, and then present it to your classmates.

Reflect on the Process In your *Reader/Writer Notebook,* write a short response to the following questions as you think about how you wrote your comparison-contrast essay.

1. How did you decide on your subjects for comparison? Were they easy to compare and contrast? Why or why not?
2. What strategies helped you select points of comparison?
3. Was the revision process helpful in improving your essay? What revision suggestions did you find most useful?

Proofreading Tip

Getting a "second pair of eyes"—having someone else edit your work— is a time-honored method of proofreading. Ask a classmate to proofread your essay, looking for misspellings, punctuation errors, and problems in sentence structure.

Your Turn

Proofred and Publish

Proofread your essay, paying special attention to your use of comparatives. Correct any errors you find, including errors in grammar, usage, and punctuation. Then, publish your essay for an audience.

Scoring Rubric for FCAT Writing+

You can use the six-point rubric below to evaluate your expository essay.

6-Point Scale

Score 6 ***is focused, purposeful, and reflects insight into the writing situation***

- conveys a sense of completeness and wholeness with adherence to the main idea
- uses an effective organizational pattern with a logical progression of ideas
- provides substantial, specific, relevant, concrete, or illustrative support
- demonstrates a commitment to and an involvement with the subject
- presents ideas with clarity
- may use creative writing strategies appropriate to the purpose of the paper
- demonstrates mature command of language with freshness of expression
- shows variation in sentence structure
- employs complete sentences except when fragments are used purposefully
- contains few, if any, convention errors in mechanics, usage, and punctuation

Score 5 ***is focused on the topic***

- conveys a sense of completeness and wholeness
- uses an organization pattern with a progression of ideas, although some lapses may occur
- provides ample support
- demonstrates a mature command of language with precise word choice
- shows variation in sentence structure
- with rare exceptions, employs complete sentences except when fragments are used purposefully
- generally follows the conventions of mechanics, usage, and spelling

Score 4 ***is generally focused on the topic but may include extraneous or loosely related material***

- exhibits some sense of completeness and wholeness
- uses an apparent organization pattern, although some lapses may occur
- provides adequate support, although development may be uneven
- demonstrates adequate word choice
- shows little variation in sentence structure
- employs complete sentences most of the time
- generally follows the conventions of mechanics, usage, and spelling

Score 3 ***is generally focused on the topic but may include extraneous or loosely related material***

- attempts to use an organization pattern but may lack a sense of completeness or wholeness
- provides some support but development is erratic
- demonstrates adequate word choice but word choice may be limited, predictable, or occasionally vague
- shows little, if any, variation in sentence structure
- usually demonstrates knowledge of the conventions of mechanics and usage
- usually employs correct spelling of commonly used words

Score 2 ***is related to the topic but includes extraneous or loosely related material***

- demonstrates little evidence of an organizational pattern and may lack a sense of completeness or wholeness
- provides inadequate or illogical development of support
- demonstrates limited, inappropriate, or vague word choice
- shows little, if any, variation in sentence structure and may contain gross errors in sentence structure
- contains errors in basic conventions of mechanics and usage
- contains misspellings of commonly used words

Score 1 ***may minimally address the topic and is a fragmentary or incoherent listing of related ideas or sentences or both***

- demonstrates little, if any, evidence of an organizational pattern
- provides little, if any, development of support
- demonstrates limited or inappropriate word choice, which may obscure meaning
- may contain gross errors in sentence structure and usage, which may impede communication
- contains frequent and blatant errors in basic conventions of mechanics and usage
- contains misspellings of commonly used words

Expository Essay

Sunshine State Standards: Benchmarks LA.6.3.1.2; LA.6.3.2.1; LA.6.3.3.1; LA.6.3.4.1; LA.6.3.4.2; LA.6.3.4.3; LA.6.3.5.3; LA.6.4.2.3

When responding to an on-demand writing task with an expository prompt, use what you've learned from the models you've read, the rubric on page 114, and from writing your own expository essays. Use the steps below to develop an expository essay.

Writing Situation:
Your history class is burying a time capsule to be opened by students at your school in 100 years. You have been asked to choose three objects to include in the time capsule.

Directions for Writing:
Be sure to explain why you have chosen these objects for the time capsule.

Now write an expository essay to your teacher identifying your three objects.

Study the Prompt

Begin by reading the prompt carefully. Note that the **writing situation** identifies the subject of the prompt. You are to choose three objects to include in the time capsule. Now, notice that the **directions for writing** identify the audience to whom the writing should be directed. Your audience is your teacher. **Tip:** Spend about five minutes studying the prompt.

Plan Your Response

Reasons Think about questions that will help you identify objects. **Ask,** "What is important to you in your school life?" Or "What do you think students would find interesting about clothes, music, or entertainment?" Your answers will become your reasons for writing and will help you determine the content of your essay.
Evidence What evidence can you use to support your choices? Include specific details that explain why the three objects are important to you.
Organization Next, plan the order of these details in your essay. Use an outline to organize your notes. **Tip:** Spend about ten minutes studying the prompt.

Respond to the Prompt

One way to begin an expository essay is to grab your audience's attention with an interesting anecdote or vivid description. Then, introduce your three objects to your readers. The rest of your essay should include supporting details that explain your three objects and why they are important to you. In the conclusion, summarize the information that you want your audience to understand. **Tip:** Spend about twenty minutes writing your essay.

Improve Your Response

Revising Go back over the key aspects of the prompt. Add any missing information.

- Did you explain why you chose your three objects?
- Did you provide clear details to support your explanation?

Proofreading Take a few minutes to proofread your essay to correct errors in grammar, spelling, punctuation, and capitalization. Make sure all your edits are neat and your paper is easy to read.

Checking Your Final Copy Before you turn in your paper, read it one more time to catch any errors you may have missed. **Tip:** Save five to ten minutes to improve your paper.

Presenting an Oral Narrative

Speak with a Purpose

Choose a story that you know well and would like to present orally. Practice delivering the story orally, and then present it to your class.

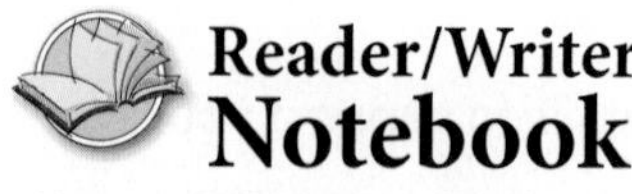

Reader/Writer Notebook

Use your **RWN** to complete the activities for this workshop.

Think as a Reader/Writer Many great stories, especially folk tales and myths, were first shared orally. When these stories were finally written down, the authors often tried to help readers "see" and "hear" the stories as they were originally told to listeners.

In the same way, as you tell a story, you try to make it as interesting and exciting for your audience as it was for you when you first read it.

Plan Your Presentation

Choose a Story

The best storytellers know that the secret of success lies in choosing the right story. First, the story must be one that you really enjoy or that means something to you. It might be a story that has been handed down from generation to generation in your family. It could be a trickster tale that made you laugh or a fable that conveys a profound moral truth. The story you choose to tell should be one that you think is worth sharing.

Here are some characteristics to look for as you choose a story to share orally:

- an exciting opening
- a theme or message that is very clear
- an easy-to-follow plot
- interesting characters
- vivid language, images, and dialogue
- an ending that surprises or "wows"

Adapt the Story

As a storyteller, remember that listeners are not the same as readers—they cannot go back and re-read parts of the story.

Keep It Simple Try to deliver the heart of the story without unnecessary details. Grab the listeners' attention from the beginning and never lose it. Present the key character descriptions, events, and details of time and place. Take your listeners through the plot in a clear way that they can easily follow. Begin with a hook that draws your listeners in, and end your story with a bang!

Sunshine State Standards: Benchmarks **LA.6.5.2.2** deliver narrative and informative presentations, including oral responses to literature, and adjust oral language, body language, eye contact, gestures, technology and supporting graphics appropriate to the situation.

Present Your Story

Practice Makes Perfect

The more you practice telling a story, the more comfortable you will get. It's a good idea to start by telling one person at a time before working up to groups. You will also want to practice by watching yourself in a mirror. This way you can work on both verbal and nonverbal parts of your storytelling. Each time you practice, remember to keep the whole flow of the story in mind. Your goal is to help listeners follow the story throughout your presentation.

Verbal Storytelling Skills

Verbal Storytelling Skills

Match your voice to what is happening in the story. Sound sad, tense, happy, angry—whatever fits. When you are speaking lines of dialogue, change your voice for each character.

Pace yourself. Change how loudly you speak and the speed at which you speak to match the story.

Exaggerate! How you say things can affect how well your audience listens. Speak more clearly and slowly than you think you need to.

Repeat as needed. Important ideas can be stated more than once so that listeners will be sure to hear them.

Nonverbal Storytelling Skills

- **Use body language.** Move your body in ways that reflect what you're saying.
- **Use facial expressions.** Your face should match the story's emotions.
- **Make eye contact.** Let your listeners know that you care about their response to the story.

A Good Oral Presentation

- begins and ends strongly
- is easy to follow from beginning to end
- brings characters, settings, and events to life
- keeps listeners interested through effective verbal and nonverbal strategies

Speaking Tip

Try to "become" your characters as you tell a story. Change your voice, posture, and body language as you change from one character to another. Taking on your characters' personalities can help you feel less self-conscious about presenting to a group of people.

Standards Review Literary Text

Forms of Fiction **Directions:** Read the following folk tale. Then, answer each question that follows.

Little Mangy One

Lebanese folk tale, retold by **Inea Bushnaq**

Once upon a time three little goats were grazing on the side of a stony hill. Their names were Siksik, Mikmik, and Jureybon, the Little Mangy One. Soon a hyena scented them and loped up. "Siksik!" called the hyena. "Yes sir!" answered the goat. "What are those points sticking out of your head?" "Those are my little horns, sir," said the goat. "What is that patch on your back?" continued the hyena. "That is my hair, sir," replied the goat. "Why are you shivering?" roared the hyena. "Because I am afraid of you, sir," said the goat. At this the hyena sprang and gobbled him right up. Next the hyena turned to Mikmik, who answered like his brother, and he too was quickly devoured.

Then the hyena approached Jureybon, the Little Mangy One. Before the hyena came within earshot, Jureybon began to snort. As the hyena drew nearer, Jureybon bellowed, "May a plague lay low your back, O cursed one! What have you come for?" "I wish to know what the two points on your head are," said the hyena. "Those? Why, those are my trusty sabers!" said the goat. "And the patch on your back, what is that?" said the hyena. "My sturdy shield, of course!" sneered the goat. "Then why are you shivering?" asked the hyena. "Shivering? I'm trembling with rage! I'm shaking with impatience, for I cannot wait to throttle you and squeeze your very soul till it starts out of your eye sockets!" snarled the goat, and began to advance on the hyena.

The hyena's heart stopped beating for an instant; then he turned and ran for his life. But Jureybon sprang after him over the rocks and gored him with his sharp little horns, slitting open his belly and freeing his two little brothers inside.

Sunshine State Standards: Benchmarks **LA.6.1.6.9** determine the correct meaning of words with multiple meanings in context; **LA.6.1.7.7** compare and contrast elements in multiple texts; **LA.6.2.1.1** identify the characteristics of various genres (e.g., poetry, fiction, short story, dramatic literature) as forms with distinct characteristics and purposes; **LA.6.2.1.4** identify and explain recurring themes across a variety of works (e.g., bravery, friendship, loyalty, good vs. evil).

1 Which characteristics of a folk tale does "Little Mangy One" have?

A It is about gods and heroes.

B It ends with a stated moral.

C It is a story based on a historical event.

D It has talking animals.

2 What important lesson about life does this folk tale give you?

F Scaring others is never a good idea.

G Cleverness can beat strength.

H You should run away from dangerous people.

I Brothers should take separate paths in life.

3 How was Jureybon's reaction to the hyena different from his brother's?

A He attacks the hyena.

B He is eaten by the hyena.

C He shakes with fear.

D He answers all of his questions.

4 Read this sentence from the selection.

Soon a hyena scented them and loped up.

Which sentence uses the word *scented* in the same way as it is used above?

F As soon as he entered the empty house, he scented trouble.

G Gardenias scented the warm summer air.

H The bloodhound scented the trail of the missing child.

I The scented candles smelled like cinnamon candy

Extended Response

5 Folk tales were passed along orally long before they were written down. What makes "Little Mangy One" a popular story to tell aloud? List at least three reasons. Support your answer with details from the selection.

READ THINK EXPLAIN

6 Describe how a folk tale, such as "He Lion, Bruh Bear, and Bruh Rabbit," differs from a longer story, such as *The Gold Cadillac*. Use examples from the selections to support your points.

READ THINK EXPLAIN

Standards Review Informational Text

Structural Features of Popular Media—Web Page

Directions: Read the Web page. Then, read and answer each question that follows.

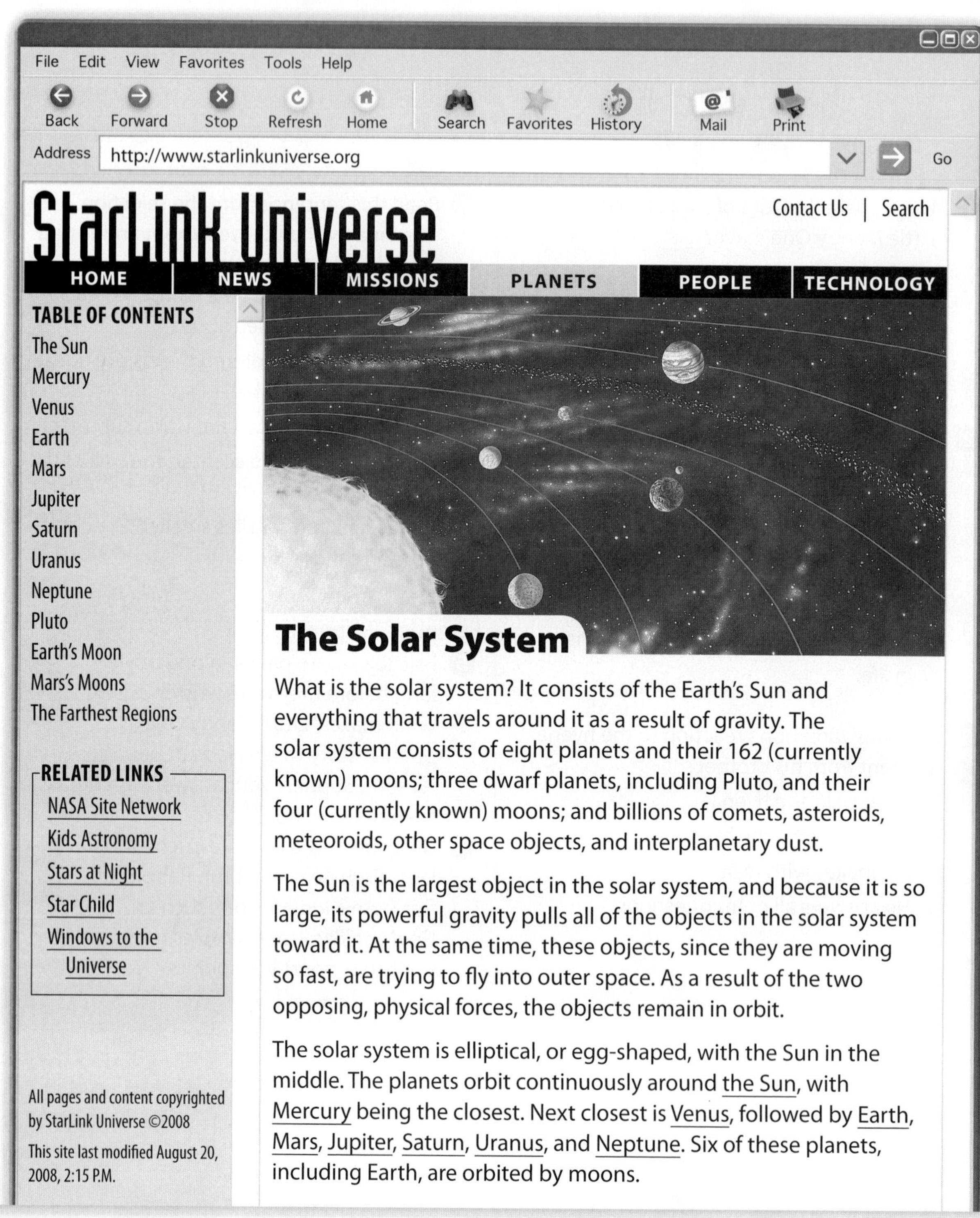

File Edit View Favorites Tools Help

Back Forward Stop Refresh Home Search Favorites History Mail Print

Address http://www.starlinkuniverse.org Go

StarLink Universe

Contact Us | Search

HOME | NEWS | MISSIONS | PLANETS | PEOPLE | TECHNOLOGY

TABLE OF CONTENTS

The Sun
Mercury
Venus
Earth
Mars
Jupiter
Saturn
Uranus
Neptune
Pluto
Earth's Moon
Mars's Moons
The Farthest Regions

RELATED LINKS

NASA Site Network
Kids Astronomy
Stars at Night
Star Child
Windows to the Universe

All pages and content copyrighted by StarLink Universe ©2008

This site last modified August 20, 2008, 2:15 P.M.

The Solar System

What is the solar system? It consists of the Earth's Sun and everything that travels around it as a result of gravity. The solar system consists of eight planets and their 162 (currently known) moons; three dwarf planets, including Pluto, and their four (currently known) moons; and billions of comets, asteroids, meteoroids, other space objects, and interplanetary dust.

The Sun is the largest object in the solar system, and because it is so large, its powerful gravity pulls all of the objects in the solar system toward it. At the same time, these objects, since they are moving so fast, are trying to fly into outer space. As a result of the two opposing, physical forces, the objects remain in orbit.

The solar system is elliptical, or egg-shaped, with the Sun in the middle. The planets orbit continuously around the Sun, with Mercury being the closest. Next closest is Venus, followed by Earth, Mars, Jupiter, Saturn, Uranus, and Neptune. Six of these planets, including Earth, are orbited by moons.

Sunshine State Standards: Benchmarks **LA.6.1.7.2** analyze the author's purpose (e.g., to persuade, inform, entertain, or explain) and perspective in a variety of texts and understand how they affect meaning; **LA.6.2.2.1** locate, use, and analyze specific information from organizational text features (e.g., table of contents, headings, captions, bold print, italics, glossaries, indices, key/guide words); **LA.6.2.2.2** use information from the text to answer questions related to the main idea or relevant details, maintaining chronological or logical order.

1. What is the main purpose of this Web page?
   - **A** to analyze scientific studies of Pluto
   - **B** to give information about the planets of the solar system
   - **C** to describe NASA's current missions
   - **D** to encourage space exploration

2. What is the Web page's source?
   - **F** the National Aeronautics and Space Administration (NASA)
   - **G** StarLink Universe
   - **H** the astronauts of the International Astronomical Union (IAU)
   - **I** a famous university's science department

3. Where would you go to find more information about NASA?
   - **A** Windows to the Universe
   - **B** Contact Us
   - **C** NASA Site Network
   - **D** Technology

4. When was this page last updated?
   - **F** August 20, 2008
   - **G** March 15, 2008
   - **H** December 3, 2007
   - **I** date not given

5. If you wanted to find out about the second closest planet to the Sun, which of these could you click on?
   - **A** "Mercury" in the table of contents
   - **B** "Neptune" at the bottom of the page
   - **C** "Venus" in the table of contents
   - **D** "Mars" at the bottom of the page

6. What in the table of contents might help you find out about faraway stars?
   - **F** the Sun
   - **G** Earth's Moon
   - **H** The Farthest Regions
   - **I** Mars's Moons

7. Which link would allow you to send a letter or e-mail to StarLink Universe?
   - **A** Contact Us
   - **B** Missions
   - **C** Search
   - **D** Windows to the Universe

Extended Response

8. Compare and contrast the information available in the table of contents with what's pictured in the main illustration. Support your answer with details from the text.

READ THINK EXPLAIN

Sunshine State Standards: Benchmarks LA.6.1.6.9 determine the correct meaning of words with multiple meanings in context.

Standards Review Vocabulary

Multiple-Meaning Words

Directions: Each of the sentences below is from a story in this collection. Read the sentence, and then choose the answer in which the italicized word is used in the same way.

Practicing For FCAT

1. Read this sentence from the story "La Bamba."

   "During rehearsal, Mr. Roybal, nervous about his debut as the school's talent co-ordinator, cursed under his breath when the lever that controlled the speed on the record player jammed."

   Which sentence uses the word *jammed* in the same way?

   A The musicians met in Mike's garage and jammed for hours.

   B I jammed my hand into the cookie jar only to find it empty.

   C We had to run the lawn mower at full speed after the throttle jammed.

   D Sarah jammed her thumb badly while playing basketball.

2. Read this sentence from "La Bamba."

   "He heard more applause and screams and started getting into the groove as he shivered and snaked like Michael Jackson around the stage."

   Which sentence uses the word *groove* in the same way?

   F My desk has a groove to hold pencils.

   G The school drill team got into a groove with the music, and their dance routine was flawless.

   H The old ax was so well used that it had a hand groove worn in its wooden handle.

   I My grandparents are stuck in a groove of eating the same breakfast at the café every Saturday.

3. Read this sentence from "La Bamba."

   "But when the entire cast lined up for a curtain call, Manuel received a burst of applause that was so loud it shook the walls of the cafeteria."

   Which sentence uses the word *cast* in the same way?

   A The cast was very strong except for the boy who played the jester; his acting was way too stiff.

   B After dinner on the beach, we walked to the water's edge and cast rocks into the surf.

   C Kelly's broken arm still hurt a little, but she allowed us to draw elaborate pictures all over her cast.

   D Fly fishing is very rewarding once you learn how to cast correctly.

Academic Vocabulary

Directions: Choose the best synonym for the Academic Vocabulary word in italics.

4. What is another word for *concept*?

   F structure

   G vision

   H feature

   I idea

Standards Review Writing

Sunshine State Standards: Benchmarks LA.6.1.7.5 analyze a variety of text structures (e.g., comparison/contrast, cause/effect, chronological order, argument/support, lists) and text features (main headings with subheadings) and explain their impact on meaning in text; *Also covered* **LA.6.3.3.2**

Comparison-Contrast Essay

Directions: Read the following paragraph from a comparison-contrast essay. Then, answer each question that follows.

[1] In Greek mythology the gods and goddesses live on Mount Olympus; in Norse mythology the deities live in Asgard. [2] Olympus and Asgard are very much alike. [3] On Olympus the family of gods enter and leave through a gate of clouds. [4] The palace of Zeus is a great hall where the gods and goddesses feast each day on ambrosia and nectar. [5] As they eat, Apollo plays his lyre. [6] When the sun sets, the gods return to their own homes to sleep. [7] Asgard is entered by crossing a rainbow bridge. [8] The great mansion of Odin is called Valhalla. [9] In Valhalla, Odin entertains the war heroes who have fallen in battle. [10] The Norse gods drink mead. [11] The flesh of the boar Schrimnir is cooked every day and then becomes whole again. [12] When not feasting, the warriors practice battle moves.

1. Which statement would follow sentence 2 the BEST?
   - **A** The gods and goddesses work very hard.
   - **B** Warriors are important in Norse mythology.
   - **C** However, they are different: Rules of Olympus ban mortals, whereas the Norse gods' laws welcome human heroes.
   - **D** All gods and goddesses live in splendid palaces.

2. What would be the BEST way to combine sentences 8 and 9?
   - **F** The great mansion of Odin is called Valhalla, and in Valhalla, Odin entertains the war heroes who have fallen in battle.
   - **G** The great mansion of Odin, Valhalla, is where Odin entertains the war heroes who have fallen in battle.
   - **H** In his great mansion of Valhalla, Odin entertains the war heroes who have fallen in battle.
   - **I** Valhalla is the great mansion of Odin, where the war heroes who have fallen in battle are entertained.

3. How could this passage be improved?
   - **A** by identifying Zeus, Apollo, and Odin
   - **B** by including a graphic organizer
   - **C** by renumbering the sentences
   - **D** by deleting sentences 1 and 2

Read On For Independent Reading

Fiction

Sounder

In his novel *Sounder,* William H. Armstrong tells the story of an African American sharecropper who is arrested for stealing food for his starving family. His son spends years searching for him; then one day the young man and Sounder, the family's hunting dog, hear footsteps approaching the house. This beloved story, winner of a Newbery Award in 1970, was made into a classic film in 1972.

Regarding the Sink

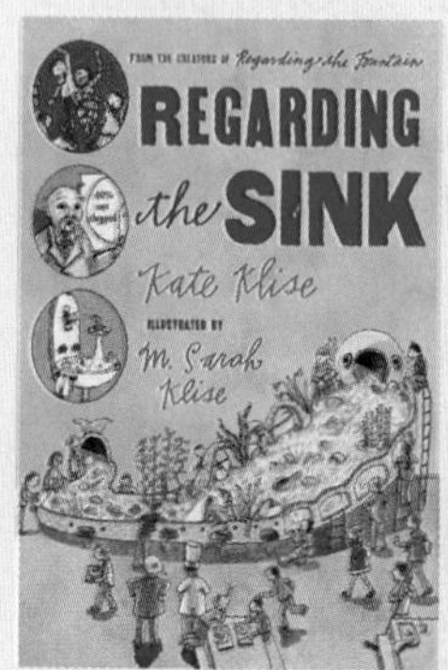

When a clogged cafeteria sink stinks up Geyser Creek Middle School, Sam N's sixth-grade class knows who can help—Florence Waters, the famous designer of the school's fountain. The problem is that Waters can't come to Geyser to create a new sink because she's gone missing. Kate Klise's *Regarding the Sink* leads the students on a quest to solve the mystery, a quest that takes them all the way to China.

World Myths and Folk Tales

For thousands of years people have been telling stories to better understand themselves, their communities, and their world. The enduring stories of many cultures appear together in *World Myths and Folk Tales.* From creation myths to Aesop's fables, these stories sometimes explain cultural beliefs, sometimes teach moral lessons, and almost always entertain. It's no wonder they have been told and retold for generations.

The Ch'i-Lin Purse

Linda Fang has collected her favorite ancient Chinese stories in *The Ch'i-Lin Purse.* Some of the stories come from ancient Chinese novels and operas, while others are inspired by actual historical events. All include twists and turns that will keep you on your toes. The stories are accompanied by lively illustrations.

Sunshine State Standards: Benchmarks LA.6.2.1.10 use interest and recommendation of others to select a balance of age and ability appropriate fiction materials to read (e.g., novels, historical fiction, mythology, poetry) to expand the core foundation of knowledge necessary to function as a fully literate member of a shared culture; *Also covered* **LA.6.2.2.5**

Nonfiction

The Mexican American Family Album

In *The Mexican American Family Album,* Dorothy and Thomas Hoobler detail some of the historical events that have shaped the lives of Mexican Americans. The book contains photographs and firsthand accounts of generations of Mexicans who immigrated to the United States.

Ashanti to Zulu: African Traditions

Margaret Musgrove introduces you to the cultures of twenty-six different African peoples in *Ashanti to Zulu: African Traditions.* Accompanying the text are Leo and Diane Dillon's highly detailed illustrations depicting life among these peoples. *Ashanti to Zulu* won the 1977 Caldecott Award for best illustrated book.

Ancient Mesopotamia: The Sumerians, Babylonians, and Assyrians

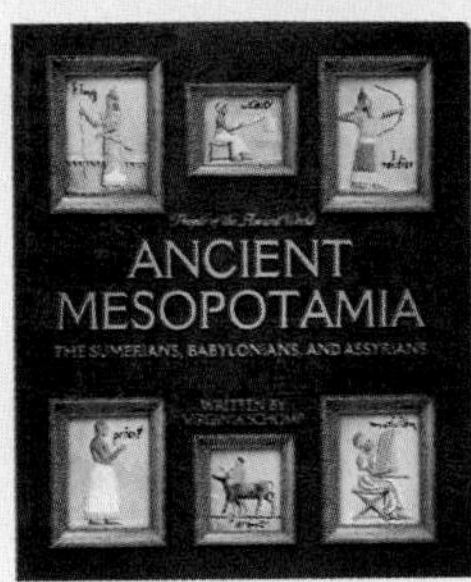

Three ancient civilizations thrived in the land of Mesopotamia. This colorful and inviting text by Virginia Schomp gives you the background of Gilgamesh's people, the Sumerians, who built the first cities. It also discusses the lawmaker Babylonians and the warrior Assyrians. Each culture is described by how its people lived, from the king to the peasants. You'll find a helpful time line and a biographical dictionary, which describes important historical figures.

But That's Another Story: Favorite Authors Introduce Popular Genres

Edited by Sandy Asher, *But That's Another Story: Famous Authors Introduce Popular Genres* explores different genres of fiction—suspense, humor, adventure, science fiction, and more. Each genre is represented by an original story from a well-known writer. The stories are sure to tempt you to dive deeper into your favorite genre.

Learn It Online
Explore other novels—and find tips for choosing, reading, and studying words—at:

go.hrw.com L6-125 

COLLECTION 2

Short Story: Plot and Setting

INFORMATIONAL TEXT FOCUS

Notes, Outlines, and Summaries

"You never find yourself until you face the truth."

—**Pearl Bailey**

What Do You Think

How can discovering a tough truth help you gain a better knowledge of who you are as a person?

Learn It Online

Use the interactive graphic organizers online to help you take notes:

go.hrw.com L6-127

Literary Focus

by **Linda Rief**

What Are Plot and Setting?

Everybody has stories: your great-grandfather's submarine struck by a torpedo during World War II; your best friend's mom rescuing three hikers stranded on a mountain in a blizzard; the most embarrassing thing that ever happened to you in school. The better a storyteller describes what happened—the plot—and where and when it happened—the setting—the more able the listeners or readers are to imagine and experience the story.

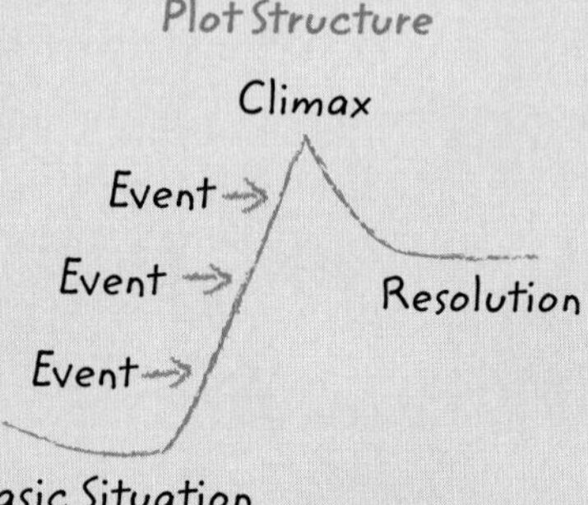

Plot

"What happened?" When you answer this question about a story, you're describing the **plot**—the series of related events that make up the story. A plot usually has four key parts:

1. Basic situation Most plots begin with a set-up of the story's **basic situation.** You learn what you need to know to follow the story as it unfolds. The basic situation answers these questions:

- Who is the main character?
- What does the main character want?
- What stands in the character's way? In other words, what is his or her problem, or conflict?

Conflict is the struggle that makes a story interesting and keeps you reading to see what happens next. There are two main types of conflict:

- **External conflict** puts the main character in a struggle with a force *outside* the character. The main character might clash with another character or with a situation, such as a dangerous ice storm or a badly damaged spaceship.
- **Internal conflict** takes place within a character. This kind of conflict comes from a struggle *inside* the character—to overcome fear, for example, or to exercise self-control.

Think about this story opener, which presents a character named Margot facing two conflicts—one with other characters and the other with her rain-soaked alien environment:

> It had been raining for seven years; thousands upon thousands of days compounded and filled from one end to the other with rain. . . .
>
> Margot stood apart from them, from these children who could never remember a time when there wasn't rain and rain and rain.
>
> from "All Summer in a Day"
> by Ray Bradbury

2. Complications If a story's conflict could be resolved easily, there wouldn't be much of a story. That's why writers introduce **complications** to the plot. Complications are additional problems that arise and prevent the main character from resolving the conflict. Complications, like the one depicted in the following example, help create **suspense,** the tension we feel about what's going to happen next. (Suspenseful stories are often called page turners, since readers can't wait to turn the page and see what happens next.)

> "Oh, but," Margot whispered, her eyes helpless. "But this is the day, the scientists predict, they say, they know, the sun . . ."
> "All a joke!" said the boy, and seized her roughly. "Hey everyone, let's put her in a closet before teacher comes!"
>
> from "All Summer in a Day"
> by Ray Bradbury

3. Climax A strong plot pulls you in and moves you along toward the **climax,** the most exciting part of the story. In the climax you find out how the conflict will be resolved, or worked out.

> The Moose took the ball and cradled it in his right hand. So far, so good. He hadn't fumbled. . . .
> He ran a couple of steps and looked out in front of him and said aloud, "Whoa!"
> Where had all those tacklers come from?
>
> from "Just Once"
> by Thomas J. Dygard

4. Resolution The final part of the plot, in which events are wrapped up and the story comes to a conclusion, is the **resolution.** Here the main character's problem is resolved—sometimes happily, sometimes not. What does the sentence below signal about the story's resolution?

> The Moose glanced at the coach, took another deep breath, and said, "Never again."
>
> from "Just Once"
> by Thomas J. Dygard

Setting

The **setting** is the place (where) and time (when) the action of a story takes place. Some stories could take place almost anywhere, but in most stories setting plays an important role. Sometimes setting is so essential to a plot that the story could not possibly take place anywhere else. The setting can influence a story in several ways:

Setting can create a sense of reality. Vivid **details** can make a setting seem very real to us, helping us imagine how people live, what they eat, how they dress, and where they work.

Setting can create atmosphere. Writers often use setting to create an **atmosphere,** or mood: creepy, peaceful, joyous, threatening.

Setting can provide conflict. In many stories the characters are in an **external conflict** with the setting. You see this kind of conflict often in movies, such as when a character is lost in a blizzard or struggles to survive on a deserted island. If the character is triumphant, the story has a happy resolution. If the setting is more powerful than the character, the story's resolution can be tragic.

Your Turn Analyze Plot and Setting

1. Trace the plot of a book, movie, or other story you know well by filling out a plot diagram like the one on page 128.
2. Identify a story you have read or viewed in which setting plays a crucial role. Explain how the setting influences the plot.

Learn It Online
Try the PowerNotes version of this lesson on:
go.hrw.com
L6-129
Go

Analyzing Visuals

How Do Artists Show Plot and Setting?

Many works of art tell a story or encourage you to imagine one. Because it's not possible to show all the events that make up a **plot,** an artist will choose one scene that shows an important moment in a story. The artist may include clues in the scene to suggest what has happened so far or what may happen next. The scene may also include details about the **setting,** or time and place of the scene. An artist uses color, line, and form to bring a setting to life, just as a writer uses descriptive details.

The title of Peter Hurd's painting *Eve of St. John* refers to midsummer's eve (June 23), close to the summer solstice—the longest day of the year. In many parts of the world, St. John's Eve is celebrated with bonfires and other symbols of light. The painting suggests a mysterious narrative as it freezes a moment in time.

Analyzing a Painting

Use these guidelines to help you analyze paintings:

1. What do you see in the painting? What seems to be happening?
2. If there are people, what can you tell about them from their appearance, clothing, expressions, and actions?
3. Find details that help you locate the scene in a particular time or place.
4. How do the shapes and colors in the painting help create a mood, or feeling?
5. Imagine yourself in the painting. What connections can you make between the subject of the painting and your own experiences?

Eve of Saint John (1960) by Peter Hurd.
Tempera on board (28 in. x 48 in. [71.12 cm x 121.92 cm]).
San Diego Museum of Art (Gift of Mr. and Mrs. Norton S. Walbridge).

1. Observe the details of the painting. Why might the girl be holding a candle?

2. Is there a story going on here? What do the horse and rider contribute to a suggested **plot**?

3. What do you learn from details of the **setting**? What time of day is it? How can you tell that it is summertime?

4. How does the artist use the **setting** to direct your attention to the most important parts of the painting?

Your Turn Write About Plot and Setting

Create your own story based on this painting. Where is this scene taking place? Who is the girl in the painting? In two paragraphs, describe why she is in the field, what she is doing, and what she is planning to do next. Who is the man on horseback? Who lives in the houses? If you wish, write a poem instead, using the painting's details as images in your poem.

Reading Focus

by **Kylene Beers**

What Skills Help You Understand Plot and Setting?

I asked a student what he thought of first when he thought about reading. "Finishing!" he replied. Then he got serious and said he worried that he didn't always understand what he was reading. I suggested that he use skills like sequencing, retelling, and summarizing to make sense of stories *during* and *after* his reading.

Sequencing

Sequence is the order of events in a story. Most stories are written in chronological order—logical time order, such as from morning to afternoon to evening. As you read, watch for words and phrases such as *later, the next morning,* and *earlier in the day.* They signal when events occur and are clues to help you in sequencing the plot.

Tips for Sequencing When you review a story, ask yourself these questions:

- What are the story's key events?
- When did each event happen?
- Did one event cause another event to happen? How do you know?

Using a Sequence Chart Show the order of events in a story with a chart like this:

Sequence
1. Describe the first important event.
2. Describe the second important event.
3. Describe the third important event.

Keep adding events in order until the story's end.

Retelling

Have you ever stopped after reading a difficult part of a story to think about what you just read? If you've tried to repeat what just happened in order to check your understanding, then you've used a strategy called **retelling.** Retelling helps you keep characters straight and understand the sequence of events in a story—and how those events are connected.

Tips for Retelling a Story

- As you read, pause for a moment when something important occurs or whenever you feel confused about what you just read.
- Then, review in your mind what just happened in the story, re-reading the passage if necessary.
- Finally, describe the information in your own words. You might jot down your retellings in your *Reader/Writer Notebook.*

Retelling to Understand Plot Keeping up with all the information in a story can be challenging. Retelling can help you identify the elements of a plot and keep all the information about a plot straight in your mind.

Sunshine State Standards: Benchmarks **LA.6.1.7.3** determine the main idea or essential message in grade-level text through inferring, paraphrasing, summarizing, and identifying relevant details; **LA.6.1.7.8** use strategies to repair comprehension of grade-appropriate text when self-monitoring indicates confusion, including but not limited to rereading, checking context clues, predicting, note-making, summarizing, using graphic and semantic organizers, questioning, and clarifying by checking other sources.

Use this **retelling sheet** to help you successfully retell the plot of any story:

Retelling Sheet

1. Basic situation

Begin with the **title** and **author** of the story. Then, tell where and when the story is set. Tell the **characters' names,** and explain how the characters are related or connected to one another. Explain what the main character wants to do.

2. Conflict

What is the main character's **conflict,** or problem? In other words, what is keeping the main character from getting what he or she wants?

3. Complications

Describe the **main events**—what happens as characters try to solve the conflict and roadblocks develop.

4. Climax

Describe the **climax,** the most suspenseful moment, when you discover how the main character will overcome the conflict—or be defeated.

5. Resolution

Tell what happens **after the climax.** How does the story end?

When you've finished a written retelling of a story, you can also add a personal response—your own thoughts and feelings about the story.

Using Time-Order Words A retelling should provide a clear and interesting presentation of a story. Avoid linking the events with a string of *and*'s. There is nothing as boring as an account of a story in which "and" and "and then" are repeated over and over. Here are some good **time-order words** to use instead:

then	*additionally*	*last*
after that	*following that*	*first*
next	*as a result*	*finally*

Summarizing

When you **summarize** a story, you tell about its main events in your own words. Summarizing is similar to retelling, but it involves identifying only the *most important* ideas and details. A good summary is shorter than a retelling and much, much shorter than the original story, since it includes only those key events that make up the plot.

Tips for Summarizing a Short Story

- Every few paragraphs, stop and try to restate in a sentence or two what the author wrote.
- When you're finished, go back and delete any details that don't seem crucial to the plot.
- Try to make your summary one page long at most. Sometimes you can summarize an entire short story in a single paragraph.

Your Turn Apply Reading Skills

1. Explain why recognizing the sequence of events in a plot is necessary to understanding the story.
2. Retell a favorite story that you know well. Then, summarize the story in a paragraph or two. Focus on the main events, not details.

Now go to the Skills in Action: Reading Model

Learn It Online

Find interactive graphic organizers to help you with sequencing and other reading skills at:

go.hrw.com 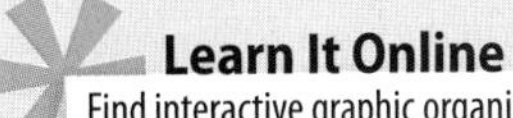 L6-133  Go

SHORT STORY

Read with a Purpose Read this story to see how Priscilla handles the bullies at her school.

Priscilla and the Wimps

by **Richard Peck**

Literary Focus

Setting The first sentence tells you that the story is set in a school. The time period is not as obvious, but as you read further, look for details that signal the story takes place before you were born. (It was written in the late 1970s.)

Listen, there was a time when you couldn't even go to the *rest room* in this school without a pass. And I'm not talking about those little pink tickets made out by some teacher. I'm talking about a pass that could cost anywhere up to a buck, sold by Monk Klutter.

Not that Mighty Monk ever touched money, not in public. The gang he ran, which ran the school for him, was his collection agency. They were Klutter's Kobras, a name spelled out in nailheads on six well-known black plastic windbreakers.

Monk's threads were more . . . subtle. A pile-lined suede battle jacket with lizard-skin flaps over tailored Levis and a pair of ostrich-skin boots, brassed-toed and suitable for kicking people around. One of his Kobras did nothing all day but walk a half step behind Monk, carrying a fitted bag with Monk's gym shoes, a roll of restroom passes, a cashbox, and a switchblade that Monk gave himself manicures with at lunch over at the Kobras' table.

Speaking of lunch, there were a few cases of advanced malnutrition among the newer kids. The ones who were a little slow in handing over a cut of their lunch money and were therefore barred from the cafeteria. Monk ran a tight ship.

I admit it. I'm five foot five, and when the Kobras slithered by, with or without Monk, I shrank. I admit this, too: I paid up on a regular basis. And I might add: so would you.

This school was old Monk's Garden of Eden.[1] Unfortunately for him, there was a serpent in it. The reason Monk didn't recognize trouble when it was staring him in the face is that the serpent in the Kobras' Eden was a girl.

Practically every guy in school could show you his scars. Fang marks from Kobras, you might say. And they were all highly visible in the shower room: lumps, lacerations,[2] blue bruises, you name it. But girls usually got off with a warning.

Except there was this one girl named Priscilla Roseberry. Picture a girl named Priscilla Roseberry, and you'll be light years off. Priscilla was, hands down, the largest student in our particular institution of learning. I'm not talking fat. I'm talking big. Even beautiful, in a bionic[3] way. Priscilla wasn't inclined toward organized crime. Otherwise, she could have put together a gang that would turn Klutter's Kobras into garter snakes.

Priscilla was basically a loner except she had one friend. A little guy named Melvin Detweiler. You talk about The Odd Couple. Melvin's one of the smallest guys above midget status ever seen. A really nice guy, but, you know—little. They even had lockers next to each other, in the same bank as mine. I don't know what they had going. I'm not saying this was a romance. After all, people deserve their privacy.

Literary Focus

Plot The writer provides an introduction to the basic situation of the story. Peck identifies the main characters and explains the central conflict: The school is being bullied by a gang. As you read, look for **complications**—new problems—that affect the main characters.

1. **Garden of Eden:** In the Bible, the paradise where Adam and Eve first lived.
2. **lacerations** (las uh RAY shuhnz): cuts.
3. **bionic** (by AHN ihk): having artificial body parts; in science fiction, bionic parts give people superhuman strength or other powers.

Priscilla was sort of above everything, if you'll pardon the pun.[4] And very calm, as only the very big can be. If there was anybody who didn't notice Klutter's Kobras, it was Priscilla.

Until one winter day after school when we were all grabbing our coats out of our lockers. And hurrying, since Klutter's Kobras made sweeps of the halls for after-school shakedowns.

Reading Focus

Sequencing Pay attention to the order of events in the story. Peck uses the phrase *Until one winter day* to signal the timing of a new event that changes the relationship between Priscilla and the Kobras. Watch for the sequence of events that follows.

Anyway, up to Melvin's locker swaggers one of the Kobras. Never mind his name. Gang members don't need names. They've got group identity. He reaches down and grabs little Melvin by the neck and slams his head against his locker door. The sound of skull against steel rippled all the way down the locker row, speeding the crowds on their way.

"Okay, let's see your pass," snarls the Kobra.

"A pass for what this time?" Melvin asks, probably still dazed.

"Let's call it a pass for very short people," says the Kobra, "a dwarf tax." He wheezes a little Kobra chuckle at his own wittiness. And already he's reaching for Melvin's wallet with the hand that isn't circling Melvin's windpipe. All this time, of course, Melvin and the Kobra are standing in Priscilla's big shadow.

She's taking her time shoving her books into her locker and pulling on a very large-size coat. Then, quicker than the eye, she brings the side of her enormous hand down in a chop that breaks the Kobra's hold on Melvin's throat. You could hear a pin drop in that hallway. Nobody'd ever laid a finger on a Kobra, let alone a hand the size of Priscilla's.

Reading Focus

Retelling This is an important event in the story. Retell important events in your own words to make sure you understand what happened. For example: "Priscilla puts her books away and then chops the Kobra's hand, breaking its grip on Melvin. Afterward, the hallway is really quiet because no one had ever hit a Kobra before."

Then Priscilla, who hardly ever says anything to anybody except Melvin, says to the Kobra, "Who's your leader, wimp?"

This practically blows the Kobra away. First he's chopped by a girl, and now she's acting like she doesn't know Monk Klutter, the Head Honcho of the World. He's so amazed, he tells her. "Monk Klutter."

"Never heard of him," Priscilla mentions. "Send him to see me." The Kobra just backs away from her like the whole situation is too big for him, which it is.

---

4. **pun:** humorous play on words, often involving two meanings of the same word or phrase.

Pretty soon Monk himself slides up. He jerks his head once, and his Kobras slither off down the hall. He's going to handle this interesting case personally. "Who is it around here doesn't know Monk Klutter?"

He's standing inches from Priscilla, but since he'd have to look up at her, he doesn't. "Never heard of him," says Priscilla.

Monk's not happy with this answer, but by now he's spotted Melvin, who's grown smaller in spite of himself. Monk breaks his own rule by reaching for Melvin with his own hands. "Kid," he says, "you're going to have to educate your girl friend."

His hands never quite make it to Melvin. In a move of pure poetry Priscilla has Monk in a hammerlock. His neck's popping like gunfire, and his head's bowed under the immense weight of her forearm. His suede jacket's peeling back, showing pile.

Priscilla's behind him in another easy motion. And with a single mighty thrust forward, frog-marches Monk into her own locker. It's incredible. His ostrich-skin boots click once in the air. And suddenly he's gone, neatly wedged into the locker, a perfect fit. Priscilla bangs the door shut, twirls the lock, and strolls out of school. Melvin goes with her, of course, trotting along below her shoulder. The last stragglers leave quietly.

Well, this is where fate, an even bigger force than Priscilla, steps in. It snows all that night, a blizzard. The whole town ices up. And school closes for a week.

Literary Focus

Plot The **climax** is the most suspenseful moment in the story. It occurs when we find out how the conflict will be resolved. This story's climax is a confrontation between Monk and Priscilla.

Reading Focus

Summarizing Remember that summarizing involves identifying only the key details. This paragraph can easily be summarized in one sentence: "Priscilla shoves Monk into her locker, locks him in, and then leaves with Melvin."

Read with a Purpose How does Priscilla deal with the bullies in this story? How else could she have handled them?

Analyzing Visuals

Viewing and Interpreting Which of Priscilla's character traits, as described in the story, do you see in this photograph?

MEET THE WRITER

Richard Peck

(1934–)

Taught by His Students

As a high school English teacher, Richard Peck became familiar with the reading habits of his teenage students: "It was my students who taught me to be a writer, though I had been hired to teach them. They taught me that a novel must entertain first before it can be anything else."

Although Peck liked his students and found their lives fascinating, he eventually decided the classroom wasn't the best place for him. He wanted to write young adult fiction—novels for readers around his students' ages. He has written more than thirty-two books to date, all of them on a typewriter. Before he left teaching, however, he learned about far more than his audience's taste in stories; he also learned about the problems that young people face both inside and outside of school. His books have been praised for dealing with such problems bravely and realistically.

Asking Honest Questions

Peck writes about tough topics, such as peer pressure, censorship, and death. He says that a goal of his writing is to "ask honest questions about serious issues." Although the answers to such questions aren't always pleasant, dealing with serious issues is a part of growing up. Peck hopes that his books help young people do just that. In his young adult novels he hopes that "the reader meets a worthy young character who takes one step nearer maturity, and he or she takes that step independently."

"A novel is never an answer; it's always a question."

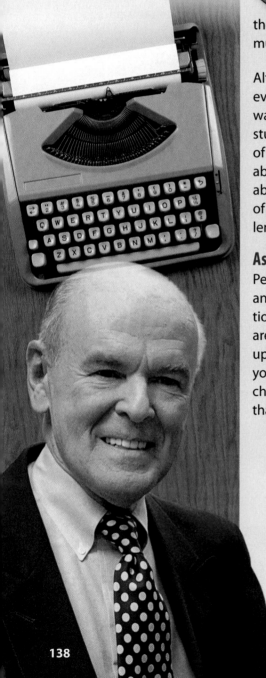

Think About the Writer Peck wants his writing to "ask honest questions about serious issues." What questions does he ask about bullying in "Priscilla and the Wimps"?

SKILLS IN ACTION Wrap Up

Sunshine State Standards: Benchmarks **LA.6.1.6.1** use new vocabulary that is introduced and taught directly; **LA.6.1.6.2** listen to, read, and discuss familiar and conceptually challenging text; **LA.6.1.7.3** determine the main idea or essential message in grade-level text through inferring, paraphrasing, summarizing, and identifying relevant details; **LA.6.1.7.8** use strategies to repair comprehension of grade-appropriate text when self-monitoring indicates confusion, including but not limited to rereading, checking context clues, predicting, note-making, summarizing, using graphic and semantic organizers, questioning, and clarifying by checking other sources; *Also covered* **LA.6.2.1.2**

Into Action: Summarizing the Plot

On a separate sheet of paper, draw and complete a diagram like this one to summarize the main events of "Priscilla and the Wimps":

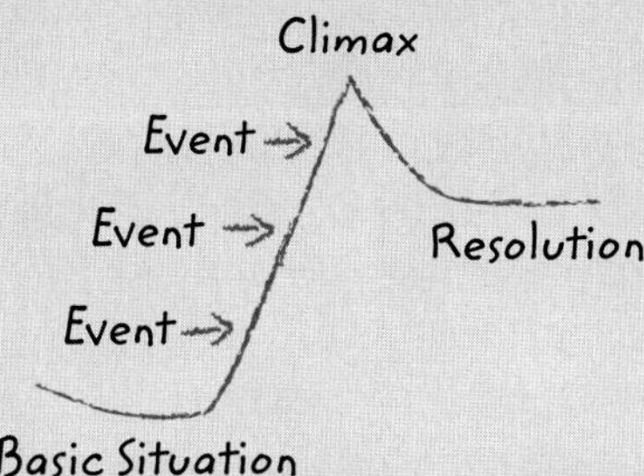

Talk About . . .

1. Retell your favorite part of "Priscilla and the Wimps" to a partner. Then, explain why you liked the story. In your explanation, try to use each Academic Vocabulary word listed on the right at least once.

Write About . . .

Answer the following questions about "Priscilla and the Wimps." For definitions of the underlined Academic Vocabulary words, see the column on the right.

2. What is the major conflict in the story?
3. How does Priscilla interact with Melvin, with other students who are not Kobras, and with the Kobras?
4. What does Priscilla achieve for all students when she defeats Monk?

Writing Focus

Think as a Reader/Writer

In Collection 2, the Writing Focus activities explain how writers create interesting plots and memorable settings. You'll have a chance to write about these methods and even practice them yourself.

Academic Vocabulary for Collection 2

Talking and Writing About Plot and Setting

Academic Vocabulary is the language you use to write and talk about literature. Use these words to discuss the stories you read in this collection. The words are underlined throughout the collection.

achieve (uh CHEEV) *v.:* succeed in getting a good result or in doing something you want. *The conflict in a story develops because of something the main character wants to achieve.*

create (kree AYT) *v.:* make something new exist or happen. *Writers use descriptive words to create a story setting.*

interact (ihn tuhr AKT) *v.:* talk to and deal with others. *Conflict can develop when characters interact and don't get along.*

major (MAY juhr) *adj.:* very large and important, especially compared with other things of a similar kind. *The major event in a story is the climax.*

Your Turn

Copy the Academic Vocabulary words into your *Reader/Writer Notebook*. Then, write a paragraph about the plot and setting of another story you've read. Use each Academic Vocabulary word at least once in the paragraph.

SHORT STORY

Preparing to Read

JUST ONCE

by **Thomas J. Dygard**

Black Shirts (1974) by Leroy Neiman.

What Do You Think? How can achieving something you think you want turn out unexpectedly?

QuickWrite

Write about some dreams or goals in your *Reader/Writer Notebook*. Choose one dream, and explain what would be the best thing about achieving it.

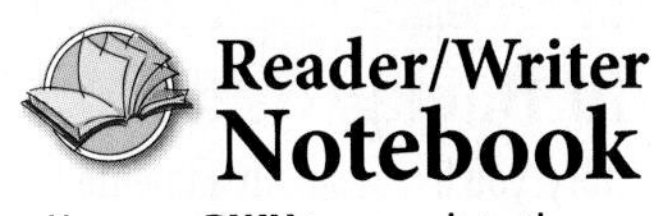

Reader/Writer Notebook

Use your **RWN** to complete the activities for this selection.

Sunshine State Standards: Benchmarks **LA.6.1.6.5** relate new vocabulary to familiar words; **LA.6.1.7.3** determine the main idea or essential message in grade-level text through inferring, paraphrasing, summarizing, and identifying relevant details; **LA.6.1.7.8** use strategies to repair comprehension of grade-appropriate text when self-monitoring indicates confusion, including but not limited to rereading, checking context clues, predicting, note-making, summarizing, using graphic and semantic organizers, questioning, and clarifying by checking other sources; **LA.6.2.1.2** locate and analyze the elements of plot structure, including exposition, setting, character development, rising/falling action, conflict/resolution, and theme in a variety of fiction.

Literary Focus

Plot and Conflict Most **plots** are built on these bare bones: The **basic situation** tells who the main characters are and what their conflict is. **Complications** arise as the characters interact, taking steps to overcome the conflict. As the story builds to a **climax,** the peak of the action, you see where the story is going. The **resolution** tells how the conflict is solved.

In this story a high school football player wants to achieve a dream. His campaign to make his dream come true creates **conflict**—a struggle between opposing characters or forces. Conflict pulls you into a story and won't let go until you find out who (or what) wins.

Reading Focus

Retelling You can use the **retelling** strategy to help you recall and understand the major events in a story. Retelling will help you organize the story's events better in your mind.

Into Action Use a **retelling** chart like this one to trace the main characters' conflicts in the story:

Who or what is in conflict?	Describe what's happening
The Moose has a conflict with his coach.	The Moose wants to carry the ball, but his coach won't let him because he's a lineman.

Writing Focus

Think as a Reader/Writer

Find It in Your Reading Much of what we know about the Moose, the main character in "Just Once," is provided by the narrator, the voice telling the story. As you read, record in your *Reader/Writer Notebook* what the narrator reveals about the Moose. How does this information help you fully understand the conflict?

Vocabulary

devastating (DEHV uh sTAY tihng) *adj:* causing great damage. *The Moose's devastating offensive move shocked the opposing team.*

nurturing (NUR chuhr ihng) *v.:* keeping alive. *The Moose's friends guessed that he had been nurturing his dream for a while.*

anonymous (uh NAHN uh muhs) *adj.:* unknown; unidentified. *The Moose was tired of being anonymous.*

tolerant (TAHL uhr uhnt) *adj.:* patient; accepting of others. *A less tolerant coach might have become angry.*

ponder (PAHN duhr) *v.:* think over carefully. *Coach Williams walked off to ponder the Moose's request.*

Language Coach

Word Families You can sometimes figure out an unfamiliar word's meaning if you notice that the word is similar to another word you know. For instance, if you know that the verb *tolerate* means "to put up with" or "be accepting of" something, you will probably recognize that the adjective *tolerant* refers to an attitude that is accepting, that can put up with things. List any words that relate to *devastating* or *nurturing* in your *Reader/Writer Notebook.*

Learn It Online
There's more to learn about words at:

go.hrw.com L6-141 

MEET THE WRITER

Thomas J. Dygard

(1931–1996)

"I'm Not a Writer. I'm a Rewriter."

For Thomas J. Dygard, writing and editing newspaper articles was a full-time job, but writing novels was what he loved most. Dygard wrote seventeen novels, all related to sports, for young people. Despite his years of working with words, he said he always considered writing a challenge.

Dygard worked as a reporter and bureau chief for the Associated Press, a news agency. He published his first novel, *Running Scared*, in 1977 and continued to publish one book a year until 1986.

> "My mistakes in my writing are so common that I'd bet I've thrown more pieces of paper in a wastebasket than any person alive. I'm not a writer. I'm a rewriter. As for having learned it all, I know that I haven't, and I also know that I never will."

Think About the Writer Dygard had to rewrite his stories repeatedly to get them right. How do you improve *your* writing?

Build Background

In this story, you'll read about a talented football player who is part of his team's offensive line. In football the offensive linemen block for other players and do not carry the ball themselves. Although the job they do is important, it isn't always a position that gets much attention. During running plays the offensive linemen try to clear the way for a running back to carry the ball and gain yards. The running back often gets the glory, while the linemen are the "unsung heroes."

Preview the Selection

In "Just Once" you'll meet **the Moose,** the nickname of the high school senior Bryan Jefferson Crawford. The Moose is a lineman on the Bedford City Bears high school football team. You'll also meet **Coach Buford Williams** and the Moose's teammates, **Jerry Dixon, Dan Blevins,** and **Larry Hinden**—all of whom have their own ideas about what the Moose's role on the team should be.

Read with a Purpose Read this selection to discover what a young football player learns when he finally gets something he has dreamed of.

JUST ONCE

by **Thomas J. Dygard**

Everybody liked the Moose. To his father and mother he was Bryan—as in Bryan Jefferson Crawford—but to everyone at Bedford City High he was the Moose. He was large and strong, as you might imagine from his nickname, and he was pretty fast on his feet—sort of nimble, you might say—considering his size. He didn't have a pretty face but he had a quick and easy smile—"sweet," some of the teachers called it; "nice," others said. But on the football field, the Moose was neither sweet nor nice. He was just strong and fast and a little bit devastating as the left tackle of the Bedford City Bears. When the Moose blocked somebody, he stayed blocked. When the Moose was called on to open a hole in the line for one of the Bears' runners, the hole more often than not resembled an open garage door.

Now in his senior season, the Moose had twice been named to the all-conference team and was considered a cinch for all-state. He spent a lot of his spare time, when he wasn't in a classroom or on the football field, reading letters from colleges eager to have the Moose pursue higher education—and football—at their institution.

But the Moose had a hang-up.

He didn't go public with his hang-up until the sixth game of the season. But, looking back, most of his teammates agreed that probably the Moose had been nurturing the hang-up secretly for two years or more.

The Moose wanted to carry the ball. **A**

For sure, the Moose was not the first interior lineman in the history of football, or even the history of Bedford City High, who banged heads up front and wore bruises like badges of honor—and dreamed of racing down the field with the ball to the end zone[1] while everybody in the bleachers screamed his name.

But most linemen, it seems, are able to stifle the urge. The idea may pop into

1. **end zone:** area between the goal line and the end line (the line marking the boundary of the playing area) at each end of a football field.

A Read and Discuss What has the writer told us about the Moose so far?

Vocabulary **devastating** (DEHV uh sTAY tihng) *adj:* causing great damage.
nurturing (NUR chuhr ihng) *v.:* keeping alive.

their minds from time to time, but in their hearts they know they can't run fast enough, they know they can't do that fancy dancing to elude tacklers, they know they aren't trained to read blocks. They know that their strengths and talents are best utilized in the line. Football is, after all, a team sport, and everyone plays the position where he most helps the team. And so these linemen, or most of them, go back to banging heads without saying the first word about the dream that flickered through their minds.

Not so with the Moose. **B**

That sixth game, when the Moose's hang-up first came into public view, had ended with the Moose truly in all his glory as the Bears' left tackle. Yes, glory—but uncheered and sort of anonymous. The Bears were trailing 21–17 and had the ball on Mitchell High's five-yard line, fourth down,[2] with time running out. The rule in such a situation is simple—the best back carries the ball behind the best blocker—and it is a rule seldom violated by those in control of their faculties.[3] The Bears, of course, followed the rule. That meant Jerry Dixon running behind the Moose's blocking. With the snap of the ball, the Moose knocked down one lineman, bumped another one aside, and charged forward to flatten an approaching linebacker. Jerry did a little jig behind the Moose and then ran into the end zone, virtually untouched, to win the game.

After circling in the end zone a moment while the cheers echoed through the night, Jerry did run across and hug the Moose, that's true. Jerry knew who had made the touchdown possible.

But it wasn't the Moose's name that everybody was shouting. The fans in the bleachers were cheering Jerry Dixon.

It was probably at that precise moment that the Moose decided to go public. **C**

In the dressing room, Coach Buford Williams was making his rounds among the cheering players and came to a halt in front of the Moose. "It was your great blocking that did it," he said.

"I want to carry the ball," the Moose said.

Coach Williams was already turning away and taking a step toward the next player due an accolade[4] when his brain registered the fact that the Moose had said something strange. He was expecting the Moose to say, "Aw, gee, thanks, Coach." That was what the Moose always said when the coach issued a compliment. But the Moose had said something else. The coach turned back to the Moose, a look of disbelief on his face. "What did you say?"

"I want to carry the ball."

2. **fourth down:** In football the team holding the ball is allowed four downs, or attempts to carry the ball forward at least ten yards.

3. **faculties:** mental powers.

4. **accolade** (AK uh layd): something said or done to express praise.

B **Read and Discuss** How is the Moose's dream of carrying the ball similar to and different from the thoughts of the other linemen?

C **Literary Focus** **Plot and Conflict** What is the main struggle, or conflict, in this story?

Vocabulary **anonymous** (uh NAHN uh muhs) *adj.:* unknown; unidentified.

Analyzing Visuals **Viewing and Interpreting** How does this photograph's point of view—seeing through the eyes of the main character—help you relate to the central conflict in this story?

Coach Williams was good at quick recoveries, as any high school football coach had better be. He gave a tolerant smile and a little nod and said, "You keep right on blocking, son." **D**

This time Coach Williams made good on his turn and moved away from the Moose.

The following week's practice and the next Friday's game passed without further incident. After all, the game was a road game over at Cartwright High, thirty-five miles away. The Moose wanted to carry the ball in front of the Bedford City fans.

Then the Moose went to work.

He caught up with the coach on the way to the practice field on Wednesday. "Remember," he said, leaning forward and down a little to get his face in the coach's face, "I said I want to carry the ball."

Coach Williams must have been thinking about something else because it took him a minute to look up into the Moose's face, and even then he didn't say anything.

"I meant it," the Moose said.

"Meant what?"

"I want to run the ball."

"Oh," Coach Williams said. Yes, he remembered. "Son, you're a great left tackle, a great blocker. Let's leave it that way." **E**

D **Read and Discuss** What does the coach think of the Moose's request? How can you tell?

Vocabulary **tolerant** (TAHL uhr uhnt) *adj.:* patient; accepting of others.

E **Reading Focus** **Retelling** What's going on between the Moose and his coach? Retell this part of the story in your own words.

The Moose let the remaining days of the practice week and then the game on Friday night against Edgewood High pass while he reviewed strategies. The review led him to Dan Blevins, the Bears' quarterback. If the signal caller would join in, maybe Coach Williams would listen.

"Yeah, I heard," Dan said. "But, look, what about Joe Wright at guard, Bill Slocum at right tackle, even Herbie Watson at center. They might all want to carry the ball. What are we going to do—take turns? It doesn't work that way."

So much for Dan Blevins.

The Moose found that most of the players in the backfield agreed with Dan. They couldn't see any reason why the Moose should carry the ball, especially in place of themselves. Even Jerry Dixon, who owed a lot of his glory to the Moose's blocking, gaped in disbelief at the Moose's idea. The Moose, however, got some support from his fellow linemen. Maybe they had dreams of their own, and saw value in a precedent.[5]

As the days went by, the word spread—not just on the practice field and in the corridors of Bedford City High, but all around town. The players by now were openly taking sides. Some thought it a jolly good idea that the Moose carry the ball. Others, like Dan Blevins, held to the purist[6] line—a left tackle plays left tackle, a ball carrier carries the ball, and that's it.

Around town, the vote wasn't even close. Everyone wanted the Moose to carry the ball. **F**

The players by now were openly taking sides. Some thought it a jolly good idea that the Moose carry the ball.

"Look, son," Coach Williams said to the Moose on the practice field the Thursday before the Benton Heights game, "this has gone far enough. Fun is fun. A joke is a joke. But let's drop it."

"Just once," the Moose pleaded.

Coach Williams looked at the Moose and didn't answer.

The Moose didn't know what that meant.

The Benton Heights Tigers were duck soup for the Bears, as everyone knew they would be. The Bears scored in their first three possessions and led 28–0 at the half. The hapless[7] Tigers had yet to cross the fifty-yard line under their own steam.

All the Bears, of course, were enjoying the way the game was going, as were the Bedford City fans jamming the bleachers.

Coach Williams looked irritated when the crowd on a couple of occasions broke into a chant: "Give the Moose the ball! Give the Moose the ball!" **G**

---

5. **precedent** (PREHS uh duhnt): action or statement that can serve as an example.

6. **purist** (PYUR ihst): someone who insists that rules be followed strictly.

7. **hapless:** unlucky.

F **Read and Discuss** What does the Moose's dream of carrying the ball have to do with the rest of the community?

G **Reading Focus** **Retelling** What's happening on the field and in the bleachers? Retell this section in your own words.

On the field, the Moose did not know whether to grin at hearing his name shouted by the crowd or to frown because the sound of his name was irritating the coach. Was the crowd going to talk Coach Williams into putting the Moose in the backfield? Probably not; Coach Williams didn't bow to that kind of pressure. Was the coach going to refuse to give the ball to the Moose just to show the crowd—and the Moose and the rest of the players—who was boss? The Moose feared so. **H**

In his time on the sideline, when the defensive unit was on the field, the Moose, of course, said nothing to Coach Williams. He knew better than to break the coach's concentration during a game—even a runaway victory—with a comment on any subject at all, much less his desire to carry the ball. As a matter of fact, the Moose was careful to stay out of the coach's line of vision, especially when the crowd was chanting "Give the Moose the ball!"

By the end of the third quarter the Bears were leading 42–0.

Coach Williams had been feeding substitutes into the game since halftime, but the Bears kept marching on. And now, in the opening minutes of the fourth quarter, the Moose and his teammates were standing on the Tigers' five-yard line, about to pile on another touchdown.

The Moose saw his substitute, Larry Hinden, getting a slap on the behind and then running onto the field. The Moose turned to leave.

Then he heard Larry tell the referee, "Hinden for Holbrook."

Holbrook? Chad Holbrook, the fullback?

Chad gave the coach a funny look and jogged off the field.

Larry joined the huddle and said, "Coach says the Moose at fullback and give him the ball." **I**

Dan Blevins said, "Really?"

"Really."

The Moose was giving his grin—"sweet," some of the teachers called it; "nice," others said.

"I want to do an end run," the Moose said. **J**

Dan looked at the sky a moment, then said, "What does it matter?"

The quarterback took the snap from center, moved back and to his right while turning, and extended the ball to the Moose.

The Moose took the ball and cradled it in his right hand. So far, so good. He hadn't fumbled. Probably both Coach Williams and Dan were surprised.

He ran a couple of steps and looked out in front and said aloud, "Whoa!"

Where had all those tacklers come from?

The whole world seemed to be peopled with players in red jerseys—the red of the Benton Heights Tigers. They all were looking straight at the Moose and advancing toward him. They looked very determined, and not

---

H **Read and Discuss** What's going on at the game? What does the Moose think about the crowd's actions?

I **Literary Focus** **Conflict** What part of his struggle has the Moose won?

J **Literary Focus** **Plot** How is the Moose complicating the situation here?

friendly at all. And there were so many of them. The Moose had faced tough guys in the line, but usually one at a time, or maybe two. But this—five or six. And all of them heading for him. K

The Moose screeched to a halt, whirled, and ran the other way.

Dan Blevins blocked somebody in a red jersey breaking through the middle of the line, and the Moose wanted to stop running and thank him. But he kept going.

His reverse had caught the Tigers' defenders going the wrong way, and the field in front of the Moose looked open. But his blockers were going the wrong way, too. Maybe that was why the field looked so open. What did it matter, though, with the field clear in front of him? This was going to be a cakewalk;[8] the Moose was going to score a touchdown.

Then, again—"Whoa!"

Players with red jerseys were beginning to fill the empty space—a lot of them. And they were all running toward the Moose. They were kind of low, with their arms spread, as if they wanted to hit him hard and then grab him. L

A picture of Jerry Dixon dancing his little jig and wriggling between tacklers flashed through the Moose's mind. How did Jerry do that? Well, no time to ponder that one right now.

The Moose lowered his shoulder and thundered ahead, into the cloud of red jerseys. Something hit his left thigh. It hurt. Then something pounded his hip, then his shoulder. They both hurt. Somebody was hanging on to him and was a terrible drag. How could he run with somebody hanging on to him? He knew he was going down, but maybe he was across the goal. He hit the ground hard, with somebody coming down on top of him, right on the small of his back.

The Moose couldn't move. They had him pinned. Wasn't the referee supposed to get these guys off?

Finally the load was gone and the Moose, still holding the ball, got to his knees and one hand, then stood.

He heard the screaming of the crowd, and he saw the scoreboard blinking.

He had scored.

His teammates were slapping him on the shoulder pads and laughing and shouting.

The Moose grinned, but he had a strange and distant look in his eyes.

He jogged to the sideline, the roars of the crowd still ringing in his ears.

"OK, son?" Coach Williams asked.

The Moose was puffing. He took a couple of deep breaths. He relived for a moment the first sight of a half dozen players in red jerseys, all with one target—him. He saw again the menacing horde of red jerseys that had risen up just when he'd thought he had clear sailing to the goal. They all zeroed in on him, the Moose, alone.

The Moose glanced at the coach, took another deep breath, and said, "Never again." M

8. cakewalk: easy job.

K **Read and Discuss** How are things looking for the Moose now?

L **Literary Focus** **Conflict** What complications have occurred that may prevent the Moose from reaching his goal?

M **Read and Discuss** The Moose finally realized his dream. Why does he tell the coach, "Never again"?

Vocabulary **ponder** (PAHN duhr) *v.:* think over carefully.

Applying Your Skills

Sunshine State Standards: Benchmarks LA.6.1.7.3 determine the main idea or essential message in grade-level text through inferring, paraphrasing, summarizing, and identifying relevant details; *Also covered* **LA.6.1.7.8; LA.6.2.1.2; LA.6.2.1.4**

Just Once

Respond and Think Critically

Reading Focus

1. How would this story change if it were not set on the football field? FCAT

A The Moose would not go to college.

B The Moose would have a different dream.

C The Moose would not have a great smile.

D The Moose would play football in his yard.

Read with a Purpose

2. What does the Moose learn after he achieves his dream? How does his dream turn out to be different from reality? Support your answer with details from the story.

Reading Skills: Retelling

3. Review the chart you filled in, and add a column showing how each conflict is resolved.

Who or what is in conflict?	Describe what's happening	How is the conflict resolved?
The Moose has a conflict with his coach.	The Moose wants to carry the ball, but his coach won't let him because he's a lineman.	The coach finally gives in, but running the ball isn't like the Moose thought it would be.

Literary Focus

Literary Analysis

4. **Connect** Besides athletes, who can appreciate or benefit from reading the story? Support your answer with details from the story.

Literary Skills: Plot and Conflict

5. **Infer** Describe the **conflict** the Moose faces when the crowd chants, "Give the Moose the ball!" What does he want to achieve? What prevents him from getting what he wants?

Literary Skills Review: Theme

6. **Evaluate** The **theme** is the major message a story reveals to us about life. What is the story's theme, or underlying message? Is it the same lesson that the Moose learns? Explain.

Writing Focus

Think as a Reader/Writer

Use It in Your Writing Review your notes about the description of the Moose. Then, develop a character who has a conflict. Without identifying the conflict, write a description of the character that provides insight into what drives him or her. Have the character interact with at least one other character. Ask classmates to guess what kind of conflict the main character has.

How do you think the Moose would feel about the expression "Be careful what you wish for—you may get it"?

Applying Your Skills

Just Once

Vocabulary Development

Vocabulary Skills: Context Clues

If you walked into class one day and there was someone other than your teacher at the desk, what would you assume? You'd probably assume that there was a substitute teacher that day. Even without knowing this person's name, you'd be able to infer, or make a guess about, who he or she was. You can do the same thing with words. You can look at what's around them—their **context**—and make an accurate guess about what they mean.

Your Turn

devastating
nurturing
anonymous
tolerant
ponder

In the following paragraph, each Vocabulary word appears in italics and has at least one **context clue** that will help you determine the its meaning**.** Copy the paragraph, and circle the clues that help you understand each word's meaning.

> The coach read aloud the *anonymous* note, wondering who had written it: "Please take some time to *ponder* our request carefully. You may think that it would have a *devastating* effect, but we're sure it won't ruin the sports program. It's time to be *tolerant* and fair. After all, we've been *nurturing* our dreams for months. Please let girls try out for the team."

Language Coach

Word Families Some words, like *tolerant* and *tolerate,* are related—that is, they come from the same word family. Write down two words that come from the same family as the Vocabulary word *devastating*. Then, write two words that come from the same family as *ponder*. Use a dictionary if necessary.

Academic Vocabulary

Write About . . .

Write a short paragraph explaining what the Moose did to achieve his goal. Provide examples of how the Moose chose to interact with Coach Williams. Was the Moose's approach effective, or should he have made a major change to the way he tried to persuade his coach? Use the underlined Academic Vocabulary words in your paragraph.

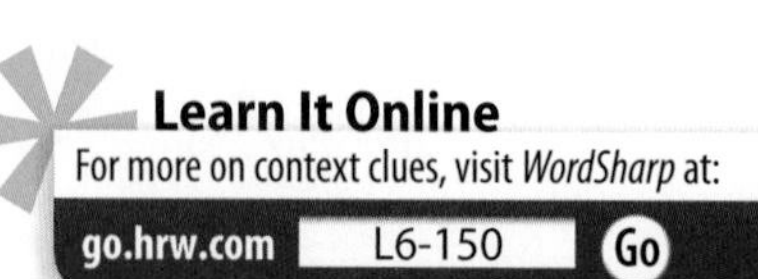

Learn It Online
For more on context clues, visit *WordSharp* at:
go.hrw.com
L6-150
Go

Sunshine State Standards: Benchmarks **LA.6.1.6.1** use new vocabulary that is introduced and taught directly; **LA.6.1.6.3** use context clues to determine meanings of unfamiliar words; **LA.6.1.6.5** relate new vocabulary to familiar words; **LA.6.1.7.3** determine the main idea or essential message in grade-level text through inferring, paraphrasing, summarizing, and identifying relevant details; **LA.6.2.2.3** organize information to show understanding (i.e., representing main ideas within text through charting, mapping, paraphrasing, summarizing, or comparing/contrasting); **LA.6.3.4.5** consistency in verb tense in simple, compound, and complex sentences; **LA.6.4.1.1** write narrative accounts with an engaging plot (including rising action, conflict, climax, falling action, and resolution) include a clearly described setting with figurative language and descriptive words or phrases to enhance style and tone.

Grammar Link

Verbs That Are Hard to Tackle

Some verbs are pretty predictable. They don't have tricky moves or zigzag back and forth. For that reason we call them **regular verbs**. The **past tense** and **past participle** of a regular verb are formed by adding *–d* or *–ed*. Some other verbs are more troublesome, though. Just as you think you might pin them down, they take a crazy turn and get away. These are **irregular verbs**. These verbs are unpredictable, so you just have to memorize their different forms.

Here are some irregular verbs from "Just Once":

Base Form	Past	Past Participle
rise	rose	(have) risen
say	said	(have) said
see	saw	(have) seen
think	thought	(have) thought

Your Turn

In the following sentences, find the incorrect verb forms, and replace them with the correct forms.

1. The Moose rised from the field and saw a cloud of red jerseys.
2. The Moose thinked he wanted to hear the fans cheer for him.
3. Yesterday the Moose sayed to the coach, "I want to carry the ball."
4. The number of red jerseys the Moose seed overwhelmed him.

CHOICES

As you respond to the Choices, use these **Academic Vocabulary** words as appropriate: achieve, create, interact, major.

REVIEW

Write a Summary

TechFocus Create a sportscast of the Bears-versus-Tigers game. First, write a **summary** of what happened. (Your retelling chart will help you do this.) Use details in the story to answer *who, what, when, where, why,* and *how* questions. Start with a snappy lead-in. Then, practice reading your report for a broadcast. Tape your reading, and play it for your classmates.

CONNECT

Write About a Conflict

Timed Writing Write about a time when you faced a conflict between doing what you wanted and doing what was best for a group or team, such as your family, friends, or an organization. Include important details, and end with some thoughts on what you learned.

EXTEND

Draw a Life Map

People want different things at different times in their lives. Draw a "life map" as a kind of road or journey, showing a person at one end and the person's goal at the other end. Draw some of the forces that person might have to overcome along the way. Then, write a paragraph explaining your map. (It does not have to be a map of the life *you* want.)

Learn It Online
Learn more about this story with these Internet links at:
go.hrw.com L6-151 Go

SHORT STORY

Preparing to Read

All Summer in a Day

by **Ray Bradbury**

What Do You Think?

What truths about ourselves can we learn in extreme, dangerous, or unusual situations?

QuickWrite

What kinds of environments or situations lift your spirits? What kinds of environments or situations bring out the worst in you? Write an explanation of how you think the settings we find ourselves in affect our moods, thoughts, and actions.

Reader/Writer Notebook

Use your **RWN** to complete the activities for this selection.

Sunshine State Standards: Benchmarks **LA.6.1.6.1** use new vocabulary that is introduced and taught directly; **LA.6.1.7.5** analyze a variety of text structures (e.g., comparison/contrast, cause/effect, chronological order, argument/support, lists) and text features (main headings with subheadings) and explain their impact on meaning in text; **LA.6.1.7.8** use strategies to repair comprehension of grade-appropriate text when self-monitoring indicates confusion, including but not limited to rereading, checking context clues, predicting, note-making, summarizing, using graphic and semantic organizers, questioning, and clarifying by checking other sources; *Also covered* **LA.6.2.1.2; LA.6.2.1.7; LA.6.6.2.2**

Literary Focus

Plot and Setting The **plot** is the series of events that make up a story, and the **setting** is the time and place in which the story occurs. In some stories the setting affects what the characters do and how the action unfolds. As you read this science fiction story, think about the role setting plays. How does the setting shape the action? If you changed any of the details of the setting, how would the story be affected?

Reading Focus

Sequencing The **sequence** is the order of events in a story. Placing the story events in the correct sequence is important for understanding how a story develops and what happens at key moments in the plot.

Into Action To keep track of the order of the main events in this story, use a sequence chart like the one below. Number each event, and describe it briefly. Add as many rows to the chart as you need to include all the key events. The first event is filled in for you.

Sequence Chart: "All Summer in a Day"
1. The children are watching for the rain to stop.
2.

TechFocus Research the atmosphere of a planet in our solar system other than Earth or Venus. What equipment and protection would be necessary for people to be able to live there?

Writing Focus

Think as a Reader/Writer

Find It in Your Reading Pay attention to unusual words and phrases Bradbury uses to describe the setting, such as "concussion of storms." List these descriptive images in your *Reader/Writer Notebook.*

Vocabulary

frail (frayl) *adj.:* not very strong; easily broken. *The girl was small and frail.*

vital (VY tuhl) *adj.:* necessary for life; very important. *It was vital that everyone see the sun.*

consequence (KAHN suh kwehns) *n.:* importance. *Their teacher realized the great consequence of the day.*

surged (surjd) *v.:* moved forward, as if in a wave. *The children surged toward the door, eager to escape.*

savored (SAY vuhrd) *v.:* delighted in. *The children savored the chance to play outside.*

Language Coach

Dialogue The words characters in a story speak is called **dialogue**. Bradbury brings this story to life with carefully crafted dialogue that moves events forward and reveals the feelings and motivations of the characters. There are no long conversations, but the dialogue is full of emotion. In your *Reader/Writer Notebook,* jot down examples of dialogue that powerfully reveals the feelings of the characters.

Learn It Online

For a preview of this story, see the video introduction at:

go.hrw.com L6-153 

MEET THE WRITER

Ray Bradbury
(1920–)

Space-Age Storyteller

Ray Bradbury has been called the world's greatest science fiction writer. He once described himself more simply: "I am a storyteller. That's all I've ever tried to be." Although Bradbury's stories are often set in outer space, his characters and their emotions are human and down-to-earth. Through this connection of the imagined and the real, Bradbury's fiction challenges the reader to question where we might be headed and what we might learn about ourselves now.

Imagine the Future

In his fiction, Bradbury encourages his readers to try to imagine the wonders the future will hold:

> "Everything confronting us in the next thirty years will be science-fictional, that is, impossible a few years ago. The things you are doing right now, if you had told anyone you'd be doing them when you were children, they would have laughed you out of school. . . ."

Think About the Writer What can imaginative tales like science fiction stories teach us about ourselves and our lives?

Build Background

"All Summer in a Day" takes place on the planet Venus in a future world where "rocket men and women," as Bradbury calls them, have come to live and set up a colony. Bradbury's description of Venus and its weather patterns is entirely fictional. As the second planet from the sun in our solar system, Venus is actually very hot and dry—and has no water.

Bradbury wrote his story in 1959, during a period (roughly 1957–1975) when the space race between the United States and the Soviet Union was in full swing. The two countries were in competition to see who would reach the moon first and who would go the farthest to make space travel a reality. Nine years after this story was written, the United States made the first moon landing, and many people thought it would not be long before spaceships made it to Mars and other planets.

Preview the Selection

On the planet Venus—as imagined by Bradbury—the sun appears for only two hours every seven years. A class of nine-year-olds eagerly awaits a brief glimpse of the sun, especially one student named **Margot.**

Read with a Purpose Read this story to see how a group of children on Venus react to a long-awaited event.

All Summer in a Day

by **Ray Bradbury**

"Ready."

"Ready."

"Now?"

"Soon."

"Do the scientists really know? Will it happen today, will it?"

"Look, look; see for yourself!"

The children pressed to each other like so many roses, so many weeds, intermixed, peering out for a look at the hidden sun.

It rained.

It had been raining for seven years; thousands upon thousands of days compounded and filled from one end to the other with rain, with the drum and gush of water, with the sweet crystal fall of showers and the concussion[1] of storms so heavy they were tidal waves come over the islands. A thousand forests had been crushed under the rain and grown up a thousand times to be crushed again. And this was the way life was forever on the planet Venus, and this was the schoolroom of the children of the rocket men and women who had come to a raining world to set up civilization and live out their lives. **A**

"It's stopping, it's stopping!"

"Yes, yes!"

Margot stood apart from them, from these children who could never remember a time when there wasn't rain and rain and rain. They were all nine years old, and if there had been a day, seven years ago, when the sun came out for an hour and showed its face to the stunned world, they could not recall. Sometimes, at night, she heard them stir, in remembrance, and she knew they were dreaming and remembering gold or a yellow crayon or a coin large enough to buy the world with. She knew they thought they remembered a warmness, like a blushing in the face, in the body, in the arms and legs and trembling hands. But then they always awoke to the tatting drum, the endless shaking down of clear bead necklaces upon the roof, the walk, the gardens, the forests, and their dreams were gone. **B**

1. **concussion** (kuhn KUHSH uhn): violent shaking or shock.

A **Literary Focus** **Setting** What is the major feature of this setting? Which details let you know this?

B **Literary Focus** **Plot** What past event does Margot think the other children might be remembering?

All day yesterday they had read in class about the sun. About how like a lemon it was, and how hot. And they had written small stories or essays or poems about it.

I think the sun is a flower
That blooms for just one hour.

That was Margot's poem, read in a quiet voice in the still classroom while the rain was falling outside.

"Aw, you didn't write that!" protested one of the boys.

"I did," said Margot. "*I did.*"

"William!" said the teacher.

But that was yesterday. Now the rain was slackening,[2] and the children were crushed in the great thick windows.

"Where's teacher?"

"She'll be back."

"She'd better hurry; we'll miss it!"

They turned on themselves like a feverish wheel, all tumbling spokes.

Margot stood alone. She was a very frail girl who looked as if she had been lost in the rain for years and the rain had washed out the blue from her eyes and the red from her mouth and the yellow from her hair. She was an old photograph dusted from an album, whitened away, and if she spoke at all her voice would be a ghost. Now she stood, separate, staring at the rain and the loud wet world beyond the huge glass.

"What're *you* looking at?" said William.

Margot said nothing.

"Speak when you're spoken to." He gave her a shove. But she did not move; rather she let herself be moved only by him and nothing else.

They edged away from her; they would not look at her. She felt them go away. And this was because she would play no games with them in the echoing tunnels of the underground city. If they tagged her and ran, she stood blinking after them and did not follow. When the class sang songs about happiness and life and games, her lips barely moved. Only when they sang about the sun and the summer did her lips move as she watched the drenched windows. **C**

And then, of course, the biggest crime of all was that she had come here only five years ago from Earth, and she remembered the sun and the way the sun was and the sky was when she was four in Ohio. And they, they had been on Venus all their lives, and they had been only two years old when last the sun came out and had long since forgotten the color and heat of it and the way it really was. But Margot remembered.

"It's like a penny," she said once, eyes closed.

"No, it's not!" the children cried.

"It's like a fire," she said, "in the stove."

"You're lying; you don't remember!" cried the children.

But she remembered and stood quietly apart from all of them and watched the patterning windows. And once, a month ago, she had refused to shower in the school shower rooms, had clutched her hands to her ears and over her head, screaming the water mustn't touch her head. So after that, dimly, dimly, she sensed it, she was

---

2. **slackening** (SLAK uh nihng): lessening; slowing.

C **Read and Discuss** What are we learning about how the other children view Margot?

Vocabulary **frail** (frayl) *adj.:* not very strong; easily broken.

different, and they knew her difference and kept away. **D**

There was talk that her father and mother were taking her back to Earth next year; it seemed vital to her that they do so, though it would mean the loss of thousands of dollars to her family. And so, the children hated her for all these reasons of big and little consequence. They hated her pale snow face, her waiting silence, her thinness, and her possible future. **E**

"Get away!" The boy gave her another push. "What're you waiting for?"

Then, for the first time, she turned and looked at him. And what she was waiting for was in her eyes.

"Well, don't wait around here!" cried the boy savagely. "You won't see nothing!"

Her lips moved.

"Nothing!" he cried. "It was all a joke, wasn't it?" He turned to the other children. "Nothing's happening today. Is it?"

They all blinked at him and then, understanding, laughed and shook their heads. "Nothing, nothing!"

"Oh, but," Margot whispered, her eyes helpless. "But this is the day, the scientists predict, they say, they know, the sun . . ."

"All a joke!" said the boy, and seized her roughly. "Hey everyone, let's put her in a closet before teacher comes!"

D **Literary Focus** **Setting** What kind of setting does Margot remember? How is it different from the setting of the story?

E **Read and Discuss** What is the author explaining to us here?

Vocabulary **vital** (VY tuhl) *adj.:* necessary for life; very important.
consequence (KAHN suh kwehns) *n.:* importance.

SCIENCE LINK

Life on Venus?

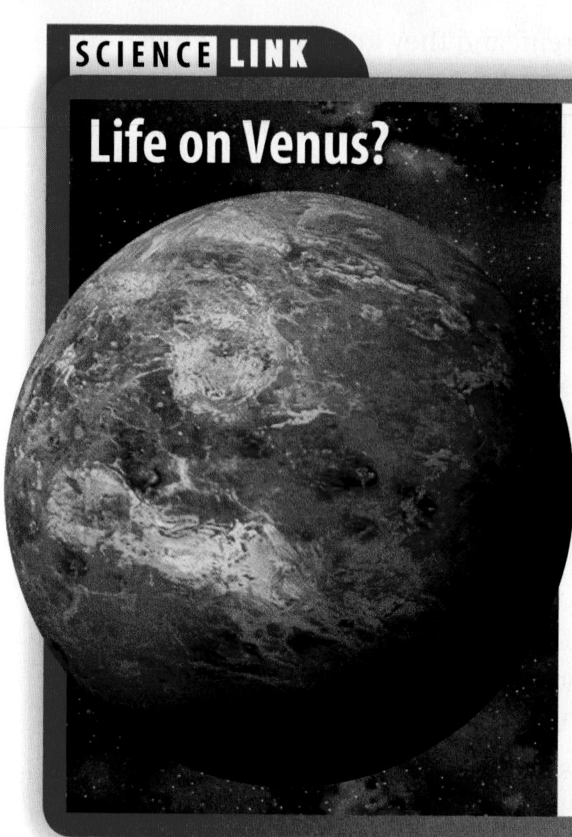

We don't know whether there's life on Venus. We can be pretty sure, though, that Ray Bradbury's science fiction vision of a rain-drenched Venus is more fiction than science.

Venus is the second planet from the Sun. Mercury is closer to the Sun, but Venus is hotter than Mercury because its atmosphere is full of thick clouds of sulfuric acid strong enough to etch metal and burn through your flesh. These clouds trap the sun's rays and increase the temperature to more than 800° (F).

It's too hot to rain on Venus, but scientists think its thick clouds might contain areas of lower temperatures where microscopic forms of life could exist. It's possible that small microbes are responsible for the types of gases in Venus's clouds. Could there be some form of life on Venus? Researchers will keep looking.

Ask Yourself

If life were found on Venus, how might people react?

"No," said Margot, falling back.

They surged about her, caught her up and bore her, protesting, and then pleading, and then crying, back into a tunnel, a room, a closet, where they slammed and locked the door. They stood looking at the door and saw it tremble from her beating and throwing herself against it. They heard her muffled cries. Then, smiling, they turned and went out and back down the tunnel, just as the teacher arrived. **F**

"Ready, children?" She glanced at her watch.

"Yes!" said everyone.

"Are we all here?"

"Yes!" **G**

The rain slackened still more.

They crowded to the huge door.

The rain stopped.

It was as if, in the midst of a film concerning an avalanche, a tornado, a hurricane, a volcanic eruption, something had, first, gone wrong with the sound apparatus, thus muffling and finally cutting off all noise, all of the blasts and repercussions and thunders, and then, second, ripped the film from the projector and inserted in its place a peaceful tropical slide which did not move or tremor. The world ground to a standstill. The silence was so immense and unbelievable that you felt your ears had been stuffed or you had lost your hearing altogether. The children put their

F Read and Discuss How do the children seem to feel about what they've done to Margot?

G Reading Focus **Sequence** Is everyone present at this point? Where is Margot now?

Vocabulary **surged** (surjd) *v.:* moved forward, as if in a wave.

hands to their ears. They stood apart. The door slid back and the smell of the silent, waiting world came in to them.

The sun came out.

It was the color of flaming bronze and it was very large. And the sky around it was a blazing blue tile color. And the jungle burned with sunlight as the children, released from their spell, rushed out, yelling, into the springtime.

"Now, don't go too far," called the teacher after them. "You've only two hours, you know. You wouldn't want to get caught out!"

But they were running and turning their faces up to the sky and feeling the sun on their cheeks like a warm iron; they were taking off their jackets and letting the sun burn their arms.

"Oh, it's better than the sun lamps, isn't it?"

"Much, much better!"

They stopped running and stood in the great jungle that covered Venus, that grew and never stopped growing, tumultuously,[3] even as you watched it. It was a nest of octopuses, clustering up great arms of fleshlike weed, wavering, flowering in this brief spring. It was the color of rubber and ash, this jungle, from the many years without sun. It was the color of stones and white cheeses and ink, and it was the color of the moon.

The children lay out, laughing, on the jungle mattress and heard it sigh and squeak under them, resilient[4] and alive. They ran among the trees, they slipped and fell, they pushed each other, they played hide-and-seek and tag, but most of all they squinted at the

3. **tumultuously** (too MUHL choo uhs lee): wildly; violently.

4. **resilient** (rih ZIHL yuhnt): springy, quick to recover.

Radiance by Simon Cook.

Analyzing Visuals **Viewing and Interpreting**

How does this image of the sun capture the scene in the story of the sun coming out?

sun until tears ran down their faces; they put their hands up to that yellowness and that amazing blueness and they breathed of the fresh, fresh air and listened and listened to the silence which suspended them in a blessed sea of no sound and no motion. They looked at everything and savored everything. Then, wildly, like animals escaped from their caves, they ran and ran in shouting circles. They ran for an hour and did not stop running. **H**

And then—

In the midst of their running, one of the girls wailed.

Everyone stopped.

The girl, standing in the open, held out her hand.

"Oh, look, look," she said, trembling.

They came slowly to look at her opened palm.

In the center of it, cupped and huge, was a single raindrop.

She began to cry, looking at it.

They glanced quietly at the sky.

"Oh. Oh."

A few cold drops fell on their noses and their cheeks and their mouths. The sun faded behind a stir of mist. A wind blew cool around them. They turned and started to walk back toward the underground house, their hands at their sides, their smiles vanishing away. **I**

A boom of thunder startled them, and like leaves before a new hurricane, they tumbled upon each other and ran. Lightning struck ten miles away, five miles away, a mile, a half-mile. The sky darkened into midnight in a flash.

They stood in the doorway of the underground for a moment until it was raining hard. Then they closed the door and heard the gigantic sound of the rain falling in tons and avalanches, everywhere and forever.

"Will it be seven more years?"

"Yes. Seven."

Then one of them gave a little cry.

"Margot!"

"What?"

"She's still in the closet where we locked her."

"Margot."

They stood as if someone had driven them, like so many stakes, into the floor. They looked at each other and then looked away. They glanced out at the world that was raining now and raining and raining steadily. They could not meet each other's glances. Their faces were solemn and pale. They looked at their hands and feet, their faces down.

"Margot."

One of the girls said, "Well . . . ?"

No one moved.

"Go on," whispered the girl.

They walked slowly down the hall in the sound of cold rain. They turned through the doorway to the room in the sound of the storm and thunder, lightning on their faces, blue and terrible. They walked over to the closet door slowly and stood by it.

Behind the closet door was only silence.

They unlocked the door, even more slowly, and let Margot out. **J**

H **Read and Discuss** What has happened here?

I **Reading Focus** **Sequence** How much time has passed since the children went outside? How do you know?

J **Read and Discuss** What does this say about the students?

Vocabulary **savored** (SAY vuhrd) *v.:* delighted in.

Applying Your Skills

Sunshine State Standards: Benchmarks LA.6.1.7.3 determine the main idea or essential message in grade-level text through inferring, paraphrasing, summarizing, and identifying relevant details; *Also covered* LA.6.1.7.5; LA.6.1.7.8; LA.6.2.1.2 LA.6.2.1.5

All Summer in a Day

Respond and Think Critically

Reading Focus

1. Which conflict from the story is an example of internal conflict?
   A the children vs. Margot
   B the children vs. their guilt
   C Margot vs. the rain
   D Margot vs. William

FCAT

Read with a Purpose

2. How do the children in this story react to the long-awaited event? Did their behavior surprise you? Explain. Support your answer with details from the story.

Reading Skills: Sequencing

3. Review the sequencing chart you made for "All Summer in a Day." Now, create a chart like the one below that focuses on the sequence of events from Margot's perspective. Compare and contrast the two charts. Mark with a star where the sequence of events begins to differ. How does this event change the "summer day" for Margot? for the other children?

Sequence Chart: Margot's Day
1. Margot is in the classroom with the other children waiting for the rain to stop.
2.

Literary Focus

Literary Analysis

4. **Analyze** How do you explain what the children did to Margot, knowing how much the sun means to her? How might this experience affect both Margot and the children who mistreated her?

Literary Skills: Plot and Setting

5. **Analyze** How does the setting of this story (including the weather) serve as a major plot element? Would there be a story if Bradbury's Venus had less extreme weather? Explain. Support your answer with details from the story.

READ THINK EXPLAIN

Literary Skills Review: Character

6. **Infer/Evaluate** From what you know of her character based on her behavior throughout the story, how do you think Margot will react when she is let out of the closet? Should Bradbury have described what happens next, or do you like the story as it is? Explain.

Writing Focus

Think as a Reader/Writer

Use It in Your Writing Use vivid language to describe a memorable weather experience.

If you were in the world of "All Summer in a Day," how might the setting affect you? What truths about yourself might you learn?

Applying Your Skills

All Summer in a Day

Vocabulary Development

Vocabulary Skills: Semantic Mapping

A strategy called **semantic mapping** can help you learn new words you come across in your reading. (The word *semantic* means "having to do with the meaning of words.") Semantic mapping involves studying a word in three different ways. Here is an example, using the Vocabulary word *surged* from the story:

- definition of *surged:* moved in a wave
- words with related meanings: *flooded, rushed*
- examples using the word or forms of it: Rivers *surge;* energy *surges.*

Now, put these parts together into a model of a semantic map, like this one, that is easy to follow:

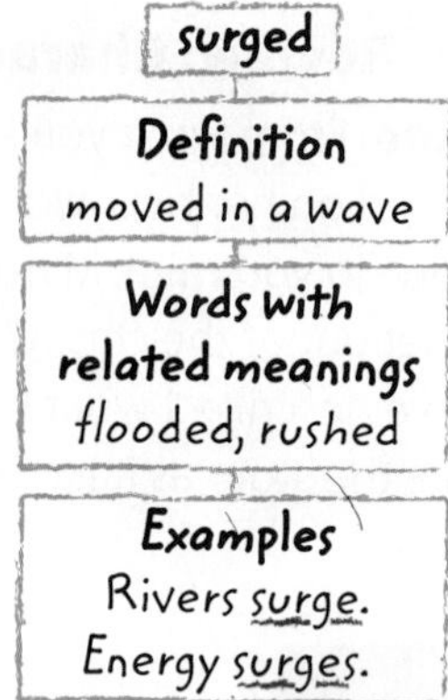

Your Turn

Using the semantic map for *surged* as a model, map the following Vocabulary words from the story: *frail, vital, consequence, savored.* Before you begin, find each word in the story and note how it is used. Look for related words in a dictionary or thesaurus.

Language Coach

Dialogue Bradbury does not always identify *who* is speaking in his dialogue. You know a different person is speaking when dialogue begins on a new line:

"Now?"

"Soon."

When Bradbury wants to be sure we know who is speaking, he includes a **speaker tag**—the name or description of the speaker:

"Aw, you didn't write that!" protested one of the boys.

"I did," said Margot. "I did."

Jot down passages of dialogue that you had a hard time following and add speaker tags. What clues do you look for so that you can know who is speaking?

Academic Vocabulary

Talk About . . .

With a partner, discuss the major event of "All Summer in a Day." Did the event likely create more conflict between Margot and the children, or do you think they will interact with her in more positive ways in the future? Use the underlined Academic Vocabulary words in your discussion.

Learn It Online
Sharpen your word skills with WordSharp at:
go.hrw.com
L6-162
Go

Sunshine State Standards: Benchmarks **LA.6.1.6.3** use context clues to determine meanings of unfamiliar words; **LA.6.3.4.4** the eight parts of speech (noun, pronoun, verb, adverb, adjective, conjunction, preposition, interjection); **LA.6.4.3.1** write persuasive text (e.g., advertisement, speech, essay, public service announcement) that establish and develop a controlling idea and supporting arguments for the validity of the proposed idea with detailed evidence; **LA.6.6.2.2** collect, evaluate and summarize information using a variety of techniques from multiple sources (e.g., encyclopedias, websites, experts) that includes paraphrasing to convey ideas and details from the source, main idea(s) and relevant details.

Grammar Link

Adverbs: Make It Specific

If you moved to a new town and it rained there for years, how would you tell your friends? "It rains constantly! I always dream about sunshine." Words like *constantly* and *always* are adverbs that help you describe the situation more clearly. Just as adjectives are words that make the meaning of a noun or a pronoun more specific, an adverb makes the meaning of a verb, adjective, or another adverb more specific.

Adverbs answer the following questions:

Where?	How often?	To what extent?
When?	*or*	*or*
How?	How long?	How much?

EXAMPLES: Please put Margot in **there.** (**There** modifies the verb put and tells where.)

William seized her **roughly**. (**Roughly** modifies the verb **seized** and tells **how.**)

Your Turn

Read each of the sentences below, and identify the adverb and the word or words each modifies.

EXAMPLE: Venus is a very interesting place.

Very—interesting

1. The students glanced quietly at the sky.
2. Nearby, another boy fell to the ground.
3. They ran quickly outside and laughed too much.
4. He slowly opened the door and let Margot out.

CHOICES

As you respond to the Choices, use these **Academic Vocabulary** words as appropriate: achieve, create, interact, major.

REVIEW

Diagram a Plot

Partner Work Fill out a diagram like this one, showing the plot of "All Summer in a Day":

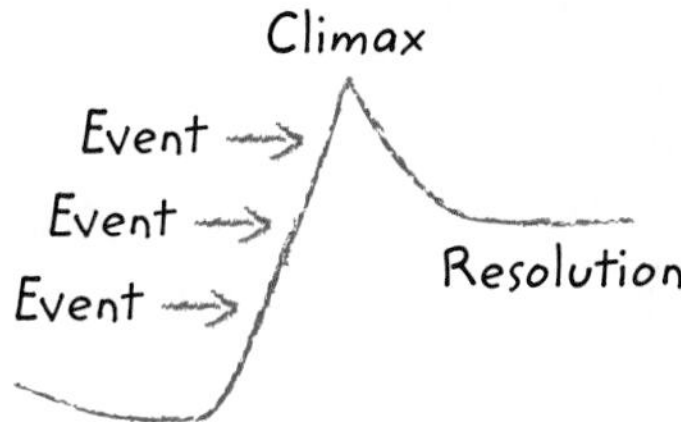

CONNECT

Write a Movie Proposal

TechFocus Create a proposal for a movie about people living in a colony on the *real* Venus. Go to the Web to learn what conditions on Venus are like. Describe the set designs and special effects that would be needed. What will be the story's major conflict?

EXTEND

Write a Persuasive Letter

Timed Writing Imagine that you're one of Margot's classmates and it's the day after the sun came out. Write a persuasive letter urging your classmates to change their attitudes toward Margot. End by suggesting what all of you should do to make up for your actions.

Learn It Online

Research background information on this stor y using these Internet links:

go.hrw.com L6-163 Go

SHORT STORY

Preparing to Read

The Bracelet

by **Yoshiko Uchida**

To School (1945) by Hisako Hibi.
Gift of Ibuki Hibi Lee, Japanese American National Museum (96.601.50).

What truths can we learn about ourselves when we can't control things changing in our lives?

QuickTalk

Can you think of a story or movie in which painful historical events are used to teach us never to repeat mistakes? With a partner, think of least two examples.

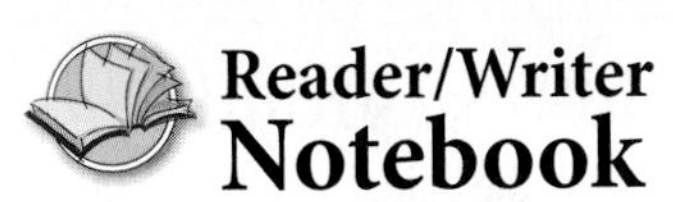

Reader/Writer **Notebook**

Use your **RWN** to complete the activities for this selection.

Sunshine State Standards: Benchmarks **LA.6.1.6.10** determine meanings of words, pronunciation, parts of speech, etymologies, and alternate word choices by using a dictionary, thesaurus, and digital tools; **LA.6.1.7.3** determine the main idea or essential message in grade-level text through inferring, paraphrasing, summarizing, and identifying relevant details; *Also covered* **LA.6.1.7.8; LA.6.2.1.2**

Literary Focus

Setting and Conflict Stories occur in a particular time and place—the story's **setting.** In some stories the setting is part of, or even the cause of, the main character's **conflict,** or struggle. This story starts out in one setting and moves to another, quite different, setting.

Literary Perspectives Use the literary perspective described on page 167 as you read this story.

Reading Focus

Summarizing When you **summarize** a story, you briefly retell the main ideas and important events in your own words.

Into Action As you read "The Bracelet," use an organizer like this one to list the ideas and events that a summary would include.

"The Bracelet"	Setting:
	Main Characters:
	Conflict:
Sequence of Main Events:	
1.	
2.	
Resolution (Ending):	

Writing Focus

Think as a Reader/Writer

Find It in Your Reading In each of the story's settings, the author uses contrast to show how the place has changed or is different than imagined. Create a "T" chart. On one side, record how each setting once was or how Ruri imagined it would be. On the other, note how each place has changed or how it looks in reality.

Vocabulary

evacuated (ih VAK yoo ayt uhd) *v.:* removed from an area. *In 1942, Japanese Americans were evacuated from the West Coast.*

interned (ihn TURND) *v.:* imprisoned or confined. *Ruri's father was interned in a prisoner-of-war camp.*

thrust (thruhst) *v.:* shoved; pushed. *Laurie thrust the bracelet into Ruri's hand.*

forsaken (fawr SAY kuhn) *adj.:* abandoned. *The garden looked as forsaken as Ruri felt when she had to leave home.*

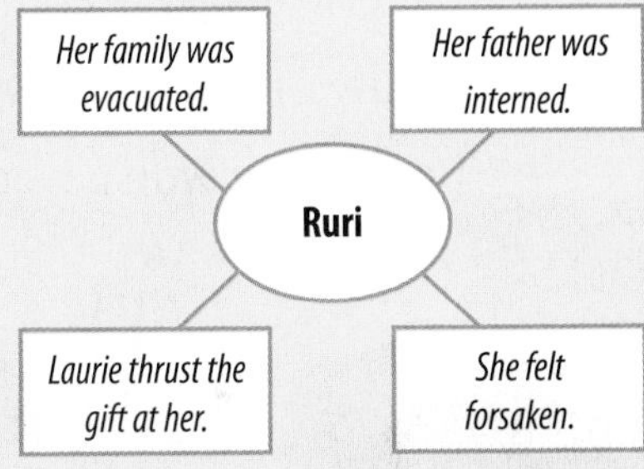

Language Coach

Words Borrowed from Other Languages

When people speaking different languages come into contact, they often borrow one another's words. American English has been borrowing words from other languages for centuries. Can you think of any words that have been borrowed from the Japanese language?

Learn It Online

Use the graphic organizers online to help you as you read:

go.hrw.com L6-165 

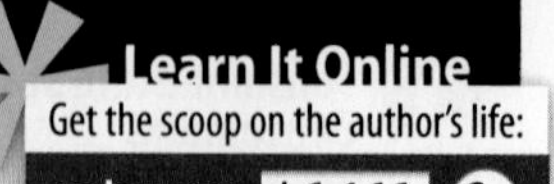
Learn It Online
Get the scoop on the author's life:
go.hrw.com L6-166 Go

MEET THE WRITER

Yoshiko Uchida

(1921–1992)

Writing to Keep It from Happening Again

Yoshiko Uchida was in her last year of college when the United States entered World War II. Like most people of Japanese descent on the West Coast, Uchida and her family were uprooted by the government and forced to go to an internment camp. She and her family lived at Tanforan Racetrack, in horse stall 40. Uchida later gave the same "address" to the fictional family in her short story "The Bracelet." Uchida said that in writing about the internment camps, she tried to give readers a sense of the courage and strength that enabled most Japanese Americans to endure this tragedy:

> "I always ask the children why they think I wrote *Journey to Topaz* and *Journey Home,* in which I tell of the wartime experiences of the Japanese Americans. . . . I continue the discussion until finally one of them will say, 'You wrote those books so it won't ever happen again.'"

Think About the Writer Why do you think Uchida feels it is important that people not forget the Japanese internment?

Build Background

Shortly after the United States entered World War II to fight against Japan after Pearl Harbor, more than 110,000 people of Japanese ancestry who were living in the United States were interned—forced to move to guarded camps. Most were American citizens who had been born here and had done nothing wrong. Nevertheless, the U.S. government feared that they might give support to Japan. When they were finally allowed to leave the internment camps after the war, many Japanese Americans found that other people had taken over their homes and businesses. In 1989, the U.S. government issued a formal apology to Japanese Americans for the injustice that had been done to them.

Preview the Selection

When **Ruri** and **her family** have to move to an internment camp simply because they are of Japanese descent, Ruri's best friend **Laurie** gives her a bracelet as a going-away gift.

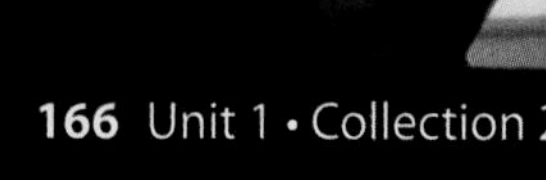

Read with a Purpose Read to learn how a young girl learns an important lesson when she is forced to move to an internment camp during World War II.

The Bracelet

by **Yoshiko Uchida**

"Mama, is it time to go?" I hadn't planned to cry, but the tears came suddenly, and I wiped them away with the back of my hand. I didn't want my older sister to see me crying.

"It's almost time, Ruri," my mother said gently. Her face was filled with a kind of sadness I had never seen before.

I looked around at my empty room. The clothes that Mama always told me to hang up in the closet, the junk piled on my dresser, the old rag doll I could never bear to part with—they were all gone. There was nothing left in my room, and there was nothing left in the rest of the house. The rugs and furniture were gone, the pictures and drapes were down, and the closets and cupboards were empty. The house was like a gift box after the nice thing inside was gone; just a lot of nothingness.

It was almost time to leave our home, but we weren't moving to a nicer house or to a new town. It was April 21, 1942. The United States and Japan were at war, and every Japanese person on the West Coast was being evacuated by the government to a concentration camp. Mama, my sister Keiko, and I were being sent from our home, and out of Berkeley, and eventually out of California. **A**

The doorbell rang, and I ran to answer it before my sister could. I thought maybe by some miracle a messenger from the government might be standing there, tall and proper and buttoned into a uniform, come to tell us it was all a terrible mistake, that we

Literary Perspectives

Historical Perspective We focus on the life of an author for a biographical perspective, but the historical perspective broadens our focus. It asks us to consider the world at the time the story was written. What important historical events shaped the author's thinking? What evidence of those events is in the text? How is the story tied to the historical period in which it is set? Could the story have happened in any other time or place?

A **Read and Discuss** What situation has the author described up to this point?

Vocabulary **evacuated** (ih VAK yoo ayt uhd) *v.:* removed from an area.

Analyzing Visuals

Viewing and Interpreting Why do people keep things like photographs, gifts, and other mementoes to remind them of past times?

wouldn't have to leave after all. Or maybe the messenger would have a telegram from Papa, who was interned in a prisoner-of-war camp in Montana because he had worked for a Japanese business firm. **B**

The FBI had come to pick up Papa and hundreds of other Japanese community leaders on the very day that Japanese planes had bombed Pearl Harbor. The government thought they were dangerous enemy aliens. If it weren't so sad, it would have been funny. Papa could no more be dangerous than the mayor of our city, and he was every bit as loyal to the United States. He had lived here since 1917. **C**

When I opened the door, it wasn't a messenger from anywhere. It was my best friend, Laurie Madison, from next door. She was

B **Reading Focus** **Summarize** What has happened so far? Who is the main character?

C **Read and Discuss** How does this information add to what we know about people going to internment camps?

Vocabulary **interned** (ihn TURND) *v.:* imprisoned or confined.

holding a package wrapped up like a birthday present, but she wasn't wearing her party dress, and her face drooped like a wilted tulip.

"Hi," she said. "I came to say goodbye."

She thrust the present at me and told me it was something to take to camp. "It's a bracelet," she said before I could open the package. "Put it on so you won't have to pack it." She knew I didn't have one inch of space left in my suitcase. We had been instructed to take only what we could carry into camp, and Mama had told us that we could each take only two suitcases.

"Then how are we ever going to pack the dishes and blankets and sheets they've told us to bring with us?" Keiko worried.

"I don't really know," Mama said, and she simply began packing those big impossible things into an enormous duffel bag—along with umbrellas, boots, a kettle, hot plate, and flashlight.

"Who's going to carry that huge sack?" I asked.

But Mama didn't worry about things like that. "Someone will help us," she said. "Don't worry." So I didn't.

Laurie wanted me to open her package and put on the bracelet before she left. It was a thin gold chain with a heart dangling on it. She helped me put it on, and I told her I'd never take it off, ever.

"Well, goodbye then," Laurie said awkwardly. "Come home soon."

"I will," I said, although I didn't know if I would ever get back to Berkeley again. **D**

I watched Laurie go down the block, her long blond pigtails bouncing as she walked. I wondered who would be sitting in my desk at Lincoln Junior High now that I was gone. Laurie kept turning and waving, even walking backward for a while, until she got to the corner. I didn't want to watch anymore, and I slammed the door shut. **E**

The next time the doorbell rang, it was Mrs. Simpson, our other neighbor. She was going to drive us to the Congregational Church, which was the Civil Control Station where all the Japanese of Berkeley were supposed to report.

It was time to go. "Come on, Ruri. Get your things," my sister called to me.

It was a warm day, but I put on a sweater and my coat so I wouldn't have to carry them, and I picked up my two suitcases. Each one had a tag with my name and our family number on it. Every Japanese family had to register and get a number. We were Family Number 13453.

Mama was taking one last look around our house. She was going from room to room, as though she were trying to take a mental picture of the house she had lived in for fifteen years, so she would never forget it. **F**

I saw her take a long last look at the garden that Papa loved. The irises beside the fish pond were just beginning to bloom. If

---

D **Reading Focus** **Summarize** In one or two sentences, tell what has happened since Laurie came to the door.

E **Read and Discuss** What is happening here between Laurie and Ruri?

F **Read and Discuss** What does Ruri think her mother is doing by looking at the empty rooms?

Vocabulary **thrust** (thruhst) *v.:* shoved; pushed.

Papa had been home, he would have cut the first iris blossom and brought it inside to Mama. "This one is for you," he would have said. And Mama would have smiled and said, "Thank you, Papa San"[1] and put it in her favorite cut-glass vase.

But the garden looked shabby and forsaken now that Papa was gone and Mama was too busy to take care of it. It looked the way I felt, sort of empty and lonely and abandoned. G

When Mrs. Simpson took us to the Civil Control Station, I felt even worse. I was scared, and for a minute I thought I was going to lose my breakfast right in front of everybody. There must have been over a thousand Japanese people gathered at the church. Some were old and some were young. Some were talking and laughing, and some were crying. I guess everybody else was scared too. No one knew exactly what was going to happen to us. We just knew we were being taken to the Tanforan Racetracks, which the army had turned into a camp for the Japanese. There were fourteen other camps like ours along the West Coast.

What scared me most were the soldiers standing at the doorway of the church hall. They were carrying guns with mounted bayonets. I wondered if they thought we would try to run away and whether they'd shoot us or come after us with their bayonets if we did. H

1. **San (sahn):** Japanese term added to names to indicate respect.

A long line of buses waited to take us to camp. There were trucks, too, for our baggage. And Mama was right; some men were there to help us load our duffel bag. When it was time to board the buses, I sat with Keiko, and Mama sat behind us. The bus went down Grove Street and passed the small Japanese food store where Mama used to order her bean-curd cakes and pickled radish. The windows were all boarded up, but there was a sign still hanging on the door that read, "We are loyal Americans."

The crazy thing about the whole evacuation was that we were all loyal Americans. Most of us were citizens because we had been born here. But our parents, who had come from Japan, couldn't become citizens because there was a law that prevented any Asian from becoming a citizen. Now everybody with a Japanese face was being shipped off to concentration camps.

"It's stupid," Keiko muttered as we saw the racetrack looming up beside the highway. "If there were any Japanese spies around, they'd have gone back to Japan long ago."

"I'll say," I agreed. My sister was in high school and she ought to know, I thought.

When the bus turned into Tanforan, there were more armed guards at the gate, and I saw barbed wire strung around the entire grounds. I felt as though I were going into a prison, but I hadn't done anything wrong. I

G **Literary Focus** **Setting** What mood does the author create with her description of the setting? Think of two adjectives that describe the feelings evoked by this scene.

H **Read and Discuss** What picture of events is the author describing for you now?

I **Read and Discuss** How does Ruri's sense that they are going to prison connect to the horse track and how the family is being treated?

Vocabulary **forsaken** (fawr SAY kuhn) *adj.:* abandoned.

August 20, 1942 by Yoshiko Uchida.

Analyzing Visuals **Viewing and Interpreting** How does this scene of an internment camp compare with the picture in your mind of the camp where Ruri and her family lived?

We streamed off the buses and poured into a huge room, where doctors looked down our throats and peeled back our eyelids to see if we had any diseases. Then we were given our housing assignments. The man in charge gave Mama a slip of paper. We were in Barrack 16, Apartment 40.

"Mama!" I said. "We're going to live in an apartment!" The only apartment I had ever seen was the one my piano teacher lived in. It was in an enormous building in San Francisco, with an elevator and thick-carpeted hallways. I thought how wonderful it would be to have our own elevator. A house was all right, but an apartment seemed elegant and special.

We walked down the racetrack, looking for Barrack 16. Mr. Noma, a friend of Papa's, helped us carry our bags. I was so busy looking around I slipped and almost fell on the muddy track. Army barracks had been built everywhere, all around the racetrack and even in the center oval.

Mr. Noma pointed beyond the track toward the horse stables. "I think your barrack is out there."

He was right. We came to a long stable that had once housed the horses of Tanforan, and we climbed up the wide ramp. Each stall had a number painted on it, and when we got to 40, Mr. Noma pushed open the door.

"Well, here it is," he said, "Apartment 40."

The stall was narrow and empty and dark. There were two small windows on each side of the door. Three folded army cots were on the dust-covered floor, and one light bulb dangled from the ceiling. That was all. This was our apartment, and it still smelled of horses.

Mama looked at my sister and then at me. "It won't be so bad when we fix it up," she began. "I'll ask Mrs. Simpson to send me some material for curtains. I could make some cushions too, and . . . well . . ." She stopped. She couldn't think of anything more to say. **J**

Mr. Noma said he'd go get some mattresses for us. "I'd better hurry before they're all gone." He rushed off. I think he wanted to leave so that he wouldn't have to see Mama cry. But he needn't have run off, because Mama didn't cry. She just went out to borrow a broom and began sweeping out the dust and dirt. "Will you girls set up the cots?" she asked.

It was only after we'd put up the last cot that I noticed my bracelet was gone. "I've lost Laurie's bracelet!" I screamed. "My bracelet's gone!"

"Those are things we can carry in our hearts and take with us no matter where we are sent."

We looked all over the stall and even down the ramp. I wanted to run back down the track and go over every inch of ground we'd walked on, but it was getting dark and Mama wouldn't let me.

I thought of what I'd promised Laurie. I wasn't ever going to take the bracelet off, not even when I went to take a shower. And now I had lost it on my very first day in camp. I wanted to cry.

I kept looking for it all the time we were in Tanforan. I didn't stop looking until the day we were sent to another camp, called Topaz, in the middle of a desert in Utah. And then I gave up. **K**

But Mama told me never mind. She said I didn't need a bracelet to remember Laurie, just as I didn't need anything to remember Papa or our home in Berkeley or all the people and things we loved and had left behind.

"Those are things we can carry in our hearts and take with us no matter where we are sent," she said. **L**

And I guess she was right. I've never forgotten Laurie, even now. **M**

J **Read and Discuss** How do the family's living arrangements connect to Ruri's idea of an apartment?

K **Reading Focus** **Summarize** In two or three sentences, tell what has happened since Ruri said goodbye to Laurie.

L **Literary Focus** **Conflict** Has Ruri's conflict been resolved? If so, how?

M **Read and Discuss** What does the conversation between Mama and Ruri teach Ruri?

Applying Your Skills

Sunshine State Standards: Benchmarks LA.6.1.7.3 determine the main idea or essential message in grade-level text through inferring, paraphrasing, summarizing, and identifying relevant details; *Also covered* **LA.6.2.1.2; LA.6.2.1.5**

The Bracelet

Respond and Think Critically

Reading Focus

1. How do you think the living arrangement for Ruri's family adds to the emotions the family is already experiencing? FCAT

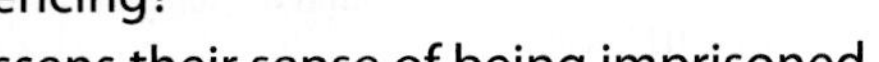

   A It lessens their sense of being imprisoned.
   B It gives them hope.
   C It eases their feeling of loss.
   D It makes their sorrow worse.

Read with a Purpose

2. What lesson does Ruri learn? Support your answer with details from the story.

Reading Skills: Summarizing

3. Review and revise the organizer that you filled in as you read the story. Be sure to add notes on the resolution, or ending. Now, use that chart to help you write a paragraph that summarizes the plot of this story.

Literary Focus

Literary Analysis

4. **Extend** Discuss the different ways experiences like Ruri's might affect the people involved. How might they deal with life in the future, and how might they interact with people who are different from them?

Literary Skills: Conflict and Setting

5. **Analyze** The plot centers on a major conflict that goes far beyond the characters in the story. Ruri's family is on one side of this conflict. Who or what is on the other side?
6. **Analyze** Identify the two settings in this story. Why are both so important to the plot? Support your answer with details from the story.

Literary Skills Review: Point of View

7. **Evaluate** In the **first-person point of view,** the narrator tells the story, using the personal pronoun *I*. Why do you think the writer chose to tell this story from Ruri's first-person point of view? What can Ruri tell you that no other character can tell you? What things does Ruri *not* know?

Writing Focus

Think as a Reader/Writer

Use It in Your Writing Review your "T" chart notes, observing how the author uses contrast in her descriptions of settings. Write a brief description of a place using contrasting details, such as *new/shabby* or *clean/messy*. Include a contrast between how you imagined the place to be and how it really appears.

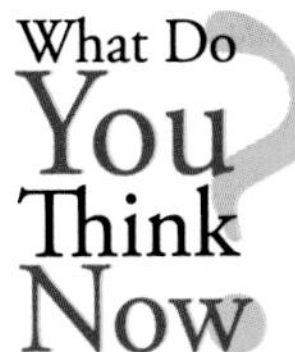

What truths do you think "The Bracelet" reveals about fairness and about a family enduring difficult and unexpected changes?

The Bracelet

Vocabulary Development

Word Origins

Many of the words we use today can be traced to Latin or Old English, the language used in England from the 400s until around the 1100s.

Your Turn

evacuated
interned
thrust
forsaken

From the Vocabulary words at right, choose the word that correctly completes each sentence below. Then, use each word in a sentence that shows you know its meaning.

1. The Old English word *forsacan,* meaning "to oppose," is related to the word ___________.
2. The Latin word *trudere,* meaning "push," is related to the word ___________.
3. The Latin word *internus,* meaning "inward," is related to the word ___________.
4. The Latin verb *vacuare,* meaning "to make empty," is the basis of the word ___________.

Academic Vocabulary

Talk About . . .

If you were Ruri, what would you do so that you could again interact in positive ways with non-Japanese people? How would you achieve peace of mind and get over resentment caused by how you and your family were treated?

Language Coach

kimono	(kih MOH noh)
futon	(FOO tahn)
karaoke	(kahr ee OH kee)
sayonara	(sah yoh NAH rah)
origami	(awr uh GAH mee)

Words Borrowed from Other Languages In the past century a number of Japanese words entered the English language. Use a dictionary to find out what each of the Japanese words in the box means. Then, fill in the blanks in the sentences that follow. Use context clues to find the words that fit best.

1. My cousin enjoyed sleeping on a ___________ so much, she said, "___________" to her mattress.
2. I brought my friend a beautiful silk ___________ for her birthday.
3. Flocks of ___________ cranes made from red paper decorated each table.
4. My grandfather sang ___________ at the party celebrating his ninetieth birthday.

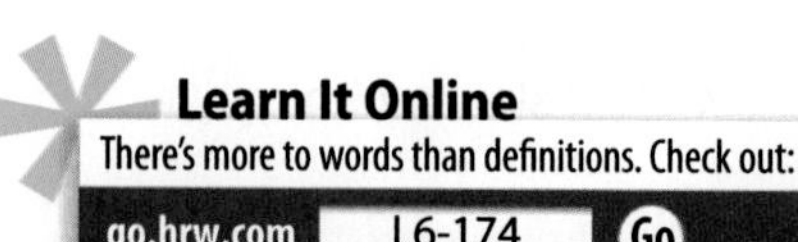

Learn It Online
There's more to words than definitions. Check out:
go.hrw.com
L6-174
Go

Sunshine State Standards: Benchmarks **LA.6.3.4.4** the eight parts of speech (noun, pronoun, verb, adverb, adjective, conjunction, preposition, interjection); **LA.6.4.1.1** write narrative accounts with an engaging plot (including rising action, conflict, climax, falling action, and resolution) include a clearly described setting with figurative language and descriptive words or phrases to enhance style and tone; **LA.6.4.3.1** write persuasive text (e.g., advertisement, speech, essay, public service announcement) that establish and develop a controlling idea and supporting arguments for the validity of the proposed idea with detailed evidence; *Also covered* **LA.6.6.4.1**

Grammar Link

Prepositional Phrases

A **prepositional phrase** is a word group that begins with a preposition and ends with a noun or pronoun. This noun or pronoun is called the **object of the preposition.** Look at the examples:

Preposition	Object of Preposition
I didn't have one inch of space left **in**	my **suitcase.**
I watched Laurie walk **down**	the **block.**

When a preposition has two objects, and one or more is a pronoun, use the **objective** form of the pronoun—the form used for the object of a preposition. To make sure you use the right pronoun form, take one pronoun at a time without the other object, like this:

Choices	The soldiers looked at my sister and **I/me.**
Incorrect	The soldiers looked at **I.**
Correct	The soldiers looked at **me.**
	The soldiers looked at my sister and **me.**

Your Turn

Identify the preposition and object or objects in each of the following sentences. If a pronoun is the object, choose the correct pronoun form.

Example	The bus drove toward Janice and I/me.
Answer	preposition: toward; objects: Janice, me

1. My dog ran from the cat.
2. The woman spoke with he/him and Michelle.
3. The ship disappeared beyond the horizon.
4. I walked slowly behind she/her.

CHOICES

As you respond to the Choices, use these **Academic Vocabulary** words as appropriate: achieve, create, interact, major.

REVIEW

Write a Blog Entry

TechFocus Imagine you are Ruri and you're writing a blog about your experiences in the camp so that your friend Laurie and your other friends from school can know about your life there. Describe what happens to you after you leave Berkeley, what the camp is like, and what happens to the bracelet Laurie gave you.

CONNECT

Write from Another Point of View

Ruri's mother tells her that we don't need things to remind us of people and places; we carry them in our hearts. Suppose that this story had been told from the point of view of Ruri's mother. Rewrite the scene between Ruri and Laurie near the beginning of the story, telling it from the persepective of Ruri's mother.

EXTEND

Write to Persuade Your Voters

Timed Writing Imagine that you are running for senator from your state shortly after World War II is over. Write a short persuasive speech that will convince voters that American citizens should never again be sent to internment camps if they have done nothing wrong. Be sure to explain your reasoning.

Learn It Online
Uncover more about the story with these Internet links:
go.hrw.com L6-175 Go

COMPARING TEXTS

Author Study: Walter Dean Myers

CONTENTS

What Do You Think?

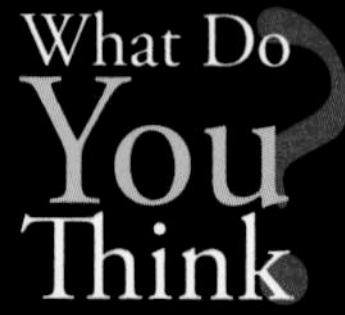

What truths about our own lives can a writer's messages teach us?

QuickWrite

Pretend you have an eager audience, ready to hear a message you would like to share about life. What is your message? What have you read or seen on television or in the movies that is similar to your message? Write your ideas.

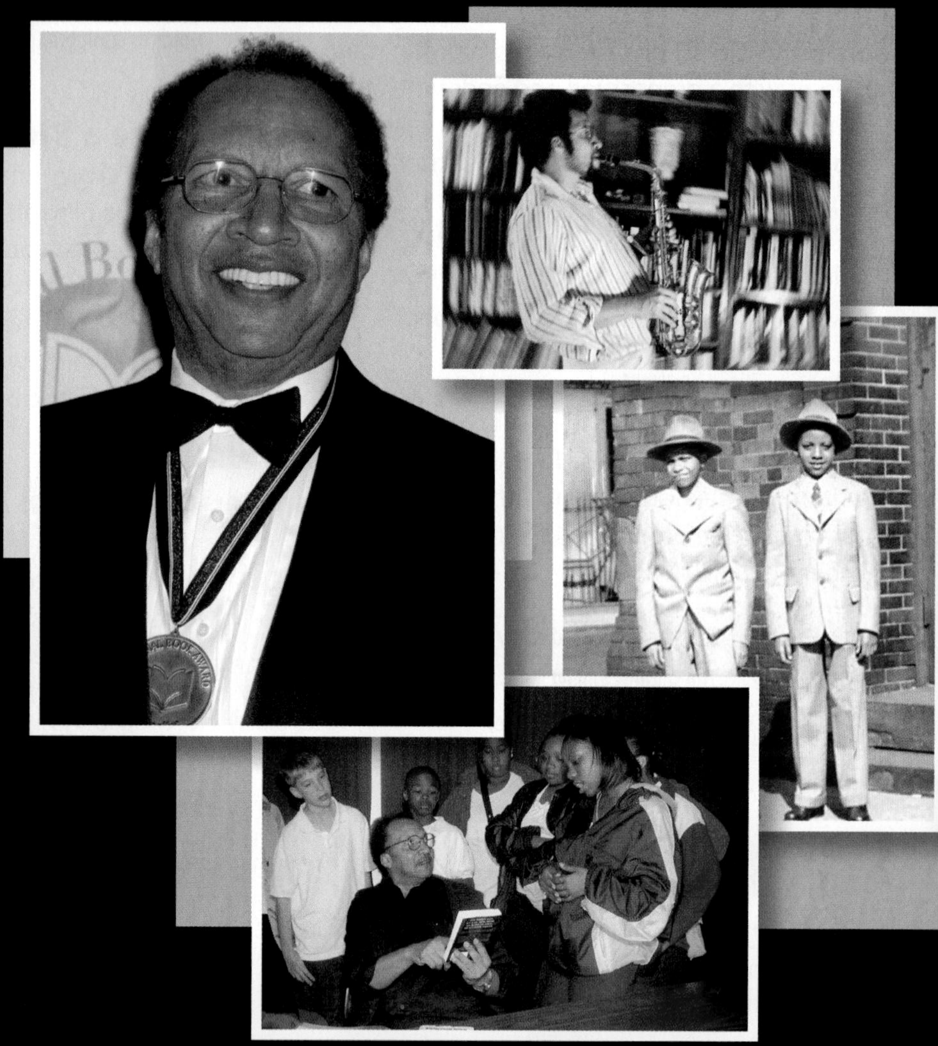

Preparing to Read

and taught directly; **LA.6.1.6.8** identify advanced word/phrase relationships and their meanings; *Also covered* **LA.6.1.7.2; LA.6.1.7.3; LA.6.1.7.8**

An Interview with Walter Dean Myers / The Game / The Golden Serpent / Love That Boy

Literary Focus

A Writer's Messages Walter Dean Myers's characters are often young, urban African Americans struggling to find their place in the world. One **message** you'll find throughout Myers's works is that we must accept responsibility for our own lives and try to understand the lives of others—especially those very different from us.

Reading Focus

Drawing Conclusions When you **draw conclusions,** you put together different pieces of information in order to see what they all have in common. You may find similar details and ideas in works by the same writer. These recurring ideas may be part of the messages that are most important to that writer.

Into Action For each selection, use a chart like the one below to gather evidence about what's important to Walter Dean Myers.

Evidence from the Text

"Interview"	"The Game"
Some important ideas in the interview with Walter Dean Myers are . . .	Some important ideas in "The Game" are . . .

My conclusion about Walter Dean Myers's work is . . .

Writing Focus

Think as a Reader/Writer

Find It in Your Reading In your *Reader/Writer Notebook,* jot down at least two details or ideas from each work that you really connect to—lines of dialogue or anything else that makes you think, "I like the way he said that" or "That's how I feel, too."

Use your **RWN** to complete the activities for these selections.

Vocabulary

Interview

montage (mahn TAHZH) *n.:* combination of pictures. *She arranged the pictures into a montage.*

The Game

defense (dih FEHNS) *n.:* team acting to keep the opposing team from scoring points. *Their team had a strong defense.*

The Golden Serpent

linen (LIHN uhn) *n.:* fine-quality writing paper, once made from linen rags. *The letter was written on the finest linen.*

fraud (frawd) *n.:* someone who pretends to be what he or she is not. *If the wise man could not solve the mystery, people would know he was a fraud.*

dismal (DIHZ muhl) *adj.:* cheerless; depressing. *The poor woman lived in a dismal place.*

Language Coach

Related Words The words *defend* and *defensive* are related to the word *defense.* Write a short paragraph in which you use each of these three words in its context.

Learn It Online

Increase your understanding of words at:

go.hrw.com L6-177 

Get more on the author's life and work at:
go.hrw.com L6-178 Go

Walter Dean Myers

(1937–)

Walter Dean Myers was born in West Virginia. His mother died when he was only eighteen months old, and his unemployed father was left to care for their large family. Poverty eventually forced his father to give Walter up to the Deans, a family who lived in New York City's Harlem.

Myers had a hard time in school. He had a severe speech problem and got into fights when kids teased him about it. In high school, he hung out with the "wrong crowd" and eventually dropped out to join the army. After leaving the army, he struggled to make a living.

Myers created a new life for himself through writing. Because of his speech problems, his fifth-grade teacher had encouraged him to express himself by writing. He started writing when he was nine and never stopped.

"It changed my life because I had no real education, and I needed something to validate myself. I needed to find value, and publishing gave me that value."

Key Elements of Myers's Writing

Different styles of language reflect the variety of genres (types of stories) he explores in his writing and the different subjects he writes about. Most often, his characters speak in **everyday language** that sounds the way people really speak.

Characters are often young African American men trying to achieve something in urban **settings** such as Harlem.

Interesting, suspenseful plots entertain readers, making them want to keep reading to find out what's going to happen.

Messages focus on exploring his characters' relationships to the world and their responsibilities to one another.

Think About the Writer

What qualities do you think help make Myers a successful writer?

A Myers Time Line

- **1937** Born on August 12 in West Virginia
- **1940** Adopted by Dean family
- **1954** Drops out of high school to join army
- **1969** Wins contest and publishes first book
- **1970** Takes job as editor
- **1975** Publishes first novel, *Fast Sam, Cool Clyde, and Stuff*
- **1977** Starts writing full time
- **1980** Wins Coretta Scott King Award for *The Young Landlords*
- **1989** *Scorpions* named Newbery Honor Book
- **2000** First winner of Michael L. Printz Award for *Monster*
- **2004** Publishes 80th book
- **2007** With son Christopher, publishes *Blues Journey and Jazz*

1940 1950 1960 1970 1980 1990 2000

AN INTERVIEW WITH Walter Dean Myers

from the New York Post

by Barbara Hoffman

Read with a Purpose

Read this interview to learn more about Myers's life and how he became a writer.

Build Background

Barbara Hoffman interviewed Walter Dean Myers in October 2004, just after his eightieth book, *Here in Harlem*, was published. She asked him questions that eighth-graders from Demarest School in New Jersey had put together, and Myers answered them. The interview first appeared in the newspaper the *New York Post*.

If you're anywhere near middle-school age, chances are you've read *Hoops*. Or *Monster* or *Scorpions*. Or any of the many other books by Walter Dean Myers.

His newest—and 80th—book came out this month. It's called *Here in Harlem,* and, unlike the gritty young-adult fiction he's famed for, it's a book of poems about his hometown, and the people—students, teachers, jazzmen—who made it tick.

"I have no memory of my mother at all," Myers told the *Post*. Born 67 years ago, in tiny Martinsburg, West Virginia, he was a year and a half old when she died. His father had seven children and was too poor to care for them, so the Dean family of Harlem adopted Walter when he was 3. (He later took their name by way of thanks.)

It was years before he saw his brothers and sisters and father again.

Still, said Myers, a father of three who lives in Jersey City, if he hadn't moved, he probably wouldn't have become writer:

"I had such a good experience with reading and books in the New York City school system," he says.

"I loved Yeats, Shakespeare, what have you. When I first began to write, I wrote odes[1] to everything," he says with laugh.

"Then I got older and discovered the fiction of James Baldwin. That gave me permission, so to speak, to write about African-American life, Harlem and the experiences of the poor." **A**

1. **odes:** formal, somewhat long poems, usually written in praise of someone or something.

A **Read and Discuss** What does Myers want to write about?

Walter Dean Myers and his brother George in front of Church of the Master at 122nd Street, Harlem, 1947.

He's been writing ever since. Recently, several dozen fans—Kathie Nolan's eighth-graders at the Demarest (N.J.) Middle School—had a bunch of questions for him. Here's how he answered them:

Barbara Hoffman: Are most of your books about your own life? Which ones?

Walter Dean Myers: Most of them are based on my own life or my own world view. *Somewhere in the Darkness* is about a boy who meets his father for the first time when he's a teenager. I met my father when he moved to my neighborhood. (B)

Hoffman: Who were your role models growing up?

Myers: I wanted to be an athlete—that's what I saw growing up. Sugar Ray Robinson[2] would come around our block and box with the kids; Willie Mays[3] would play stickball. I wanted to be a basketball player, but I left school at 17 to join the Army. When I got out, I just struggled to make a living. I worked at the post office, I worked tearing down buildings, I worked as a messenger—I was a twister in an electrical-cable factory. A big cable came out of the machine and I had to grab the cable and twist it.

Hoffman: What inspired your first book?

Myers: I saw a contest for children's books writers. I entered the picture book category, not knowing exactly what a picture book was. I did the text—about a father who takes a group of children to Central Park, and one child asked, "Where does the day go, at night?" And each child came up with an answer. The name of the book was *Where Does the Day Go?* It came out in 1969.

Hoffman: Did you take writing classes—and did they help?

Myers: I took a class with Lajos Egri, a Hungarian writer, in New York. He liked me very much and was very encouraging. I couldn't afford to take any more classes, and he let me stay for free. Years later, I took

2. **Sugar Ray Robinson:** an African American boxer in the 1940s and 1950s who is recognized as one of the greatest boxers of all time.
3. **Willie Mays:** an African American baseball player who played for the New York Giants in the 1950s and 1960s.

(B) **Literary Focus** **A Writer's Messages** When Myers says his books are based on his "own world view," what do you think he means?

a writing class at the New School[4] and was kicked out. The guy said I just didn't have the ability. He was very apologetic and said, "Some people have it and some don't." But I kept writing. **C**

Hoffman: How many revisions do you go through before you're finished?

Myers: Usually four or five. Before I begin a book, if it's a novel, I'll go through hip-hop magazines and pick out pictures of my characters; then my wife will put them on a large piece of oaktag and make a montage. Sometimes, she'll even create a scene I'll tell her about. That montage goes on my wall behind the computer. So whenever I sit down to work, I look up and there are all my characters, looking up at me.

4. **New School:** a well-known institution in New York City that offers courses for adults taught by scholars, artists, and professionals.

Hoffman: If you had one chance to change something about the world, what would you do?

Myers: Oy vey! [He laughs.] You know, I would give all children philosophy courses, because so many children don't understand that you have to make decisions early in life. We sort of let kids drift. When I go to places like Rikers Island[5] and see so many kids who've drifted into lives of crime, I wish someone had told them that education is a necessity—that how you conduct your life at 15 or 16 is going to affect you for as long as you live. There's no do-over. That's why, in my books, I write about the moral decisions kids have to make. Some people think I'm preachy—and I agree! **D**

5. **Rikers Island:** a jail complex run by the New York City Department of Correction.

C Reading Focus Drawing Conclusions What would make you keep writing after someone whose opinion you should respect said you don't have the ability?

D Read and Discuss How does Myers approach the writing process? How does he choose the topics he writes about?

Vocabulary **montage** (mahn TAHZH) *n.:* combination of pictures.

Analyzing Visuals

Viewing and Interpreting What sort of story could you write based on the pictures in this montage?

Handbook for Boys Mural
Constance Myers

Applying Your Skills

Sunshine State Standards: Benchmarks **LA.6.1.7.2** analyze the author's purpose (e.g., to persuade, inform, entertain, or explain) and perspective in a variety of texts and understand how they affect meaning; **LA.6.1.7.3** determine the main idea or essential message in grade-level text through inferring, paraphrasing, summarizing, and identifying relevant details; *Also covered* **LA.6.1.7.8; LA.6.2.1.5**

An Interview with Walter Dean Myers

Respond and Think Critically

Reading Focus

FCAT

1. Why does Walter Dean Myers think children should study philosophy?
   A to understand the consequences of their decisions
   B to use philosophical teachings later in their career
   C to have the background knowledge of different theories
   D to avoid running into lives of crime and danger

Read with a Purpose

2. How did Myers become a writer?

Reading Skills: Drawing Conclusions

3. Review the evidence you gathered about the author's ideas as you read the interview with Walter Dean Myers. What conclusions can you draw about him from this interview?

Evidence from the Text

Some important ideas in the interview with Walter Dean Myers are . . .

↓

My conclusions about Walter Dean Myers that I drew from the interview are . . .

Vocabulary Check

Answer the following question.

4. What does Myers's wife use to create a **montage**?

Literary Focus

Literary Analysis

READ THINK EXPLAIN

5. **Draw Conclusions** Myers talks about his good experience with reading in the New York City school system. Why is reading a major part of becoming a writer? Explain. Support your answer with details from the selection.
6. **Interpret** Why does Myers cut pictures out of magazines? Why does he keep these pictures in front of him as he works?
7. **Analyze** Myers says that growing up, his role models were athletes. Why do you think Myers joined the army instead of following his role models?

Literary Skills: A Writer's Messages

8. **Infer** Walter Dean Myers says, "How you conduct your life at 15 or 16 is going to affect you for as long as you live. There's no do-over." What message is Myers delivering here? What view of life does it express?

Writing Focus

Think as a Reader/Writer

Use It in Your Writing What did you like about Myers's responses? Did he say anything in this interview with which you especially agreed? Read through the details that you collected as you read. Choose one detail, and write a short paragraph to explain how his words connect to your own life.

NOVEL EXCERPT

THE GAME

by **Walter Dean Myers**

Read with a Purpose

Read this story to find out whether the narrator's team wins the championship.

Preparing to Read for this selection is on page 177.

Build Background

Although the word *basketball* doesn't appear until more than halfway through the story, "the game" refers to a basketball game—a championship basketball game. Walter Dean Myers writes about basketball often because basketball was a big part of his life as he grew up in Harlem. This story is an excerpt from Myers's first novel for young adults, *Fast Sam, Cool Clyde, and Stuff.*

We had practiced and practiced until it ran out of our ears. Every guy on the team knew every play. We were ready. It meant the championship. Everybody was there. I never saw so many people at the center at one time. We had never seen the other team play but Sam said that he knew some of the players and that they were good. Mr. Reese told us to go out and play as hard as we could every moment we were on the floor. We all shook hands in the locker room and then went out. Mostly we tried to ignore them warming up at the other end of the court but we couldn't help but look a few times. They were doing exactly what we were doing, just shooting a few lay-ups[1] and waiting for the game to begin. **A**

1. **lay-ups:** shots taken close to the basket, usually banked off the backboard.

They got the first tap and started passing the ball around. I mean they really started passing the ball around faster than anything I had ever seen. Zip! Zip! Zip! Two points! I didn't even know how they could *see* the ball, let alone get it inside to their big man.[2] We brought the ball down and one of their players stole the ball from Sam. We got back on defense but they weren't in a hurry. The same old thing. Zip! Zip! Zip! Two points! They could pass the ball better than anybody I ever saw. Then we brought the ball down again and Chalky missed a jump shot. He missed the backboard, the rim, everything. One of their players caught the ball and then brought it down and a few seconds later the score was 6–0. We couldn't even get

2. **their big man:** the center; this player is usually tall and plays close to the basket.

A **Reading Focus** **Drawing Conclusions** What is the setting of this story? What kind of center is this? Who are the teams competing for the championship?

Vocabulary **defense** (dih FEHNS) *n.:* team acting to keep the opposing team from scoring points.

close enough to foul[3] them. Chalky brought the ball down again, passed to Sam cutting across the lane,[4] and Sam walked. They brought the ball down and it was 8–0. **B**

They were really enjoying the game. You could see. Every time they scored they'd slap hands and carry on. Also, they had some cheerleaders. They had about five girls with little pink skirts on and white sweaters cheering for them. **C**

Clyde brought the ball down this time, passed into our center, a guy named Leon, and Leon turned and missed a hook. They got the rebound and came down, and Chalky missed a steal and fouled his man. That's when Mr. Reese called time out.

"Okay, now, just trade basket for basket. They make a basket, you take your time and you make a basket—don't rush it." Mr. Reese looked at his starting five. "Okay, now, every once in a while take a look over at me and I'll let you know when I want you to make your move. If I put my hands palm down, just keep on playing cool. If I stand up and put my hands up like this"—he put both hands up near his face—"that means to make your move. You understand that?" **D**

Everyone said that they understood. When the ball was back in play Chalky and Sam and Leon started setting picks[5] from the outside and then passed to Clyde for our first two points. They got the ball and started passing around again. Zip! Zip! Zip! But this time we were just waiting for that pass underneath and they knew it. Finally they tried a shot from outside and Chalky slapped it away to Sam on the break. We came down real quick and scored. On the way back Mr. Reese showed everybody that his palms were down. To keep playing cool.

They missed their next shot and fouled Chalky. They called time out and, much to my surprise, Mr. Reese put me in. My heart was beating so fast I thought I was going to have a heart attack. Chalky missed the foul shot but Leon slapped the ball out to Clyde, who passed it to me. I dribbled about two steps and threw it back to Leon in the bucket. Then I didn't know what to do so I did what Mr. Reese always told us. If you don't know what to do then, just move around. I started moving toward the corner and then I ran quickly toward the basket. I saw Sam coming at me from the other direction and it was a play. Two guards cutting past and one of the defensive men gets picked off. I ran as close as I could to Sam, and his man got picked off. Chalky threw the ball into him for an easy lay-up. They came down and missed again but one of

3. **foul:** making an illegal move on the court, such as grabbing a player.
4. **lane:** a section of the basketball court that players can't enter during a free throw.
5. **setting picks:** blocking defensive players to free up a teammate to make a shot.

B **Read and Discuss** How do occasional short sentences and phrases like "Zip! Zip! Zip!" help you visualize what's happening in this segment?

C **Reading Focus** **Drawing Conclusions** Who is the narrator of this story? How do you know?

D **Read and Discuss** What does Mr. Reese's advice show us about him and how he views his players?

their men got the rebound in. We brought the ball down and Sam went along the base line for a jump shot, but their center knocked the ball away. I caught it just before it went out at the corner and shot the ball. I remembered what Mr. Reese had said about following your shot in, and I started in after the ball but it went right in. It didn't touch the rim or anything. Swish! **E**

One of their players said to watch out for 17—that was me. I played about two minutes more, then Mr. Reese took me out. But I had scored another basket on a lay-up. We were coming back. Chalky and Sam were knocking away just about anything their guards were throwing up, and Leon, Chalky, and Sam controlled the defensive backboard. Mr. Reese brought in Cap, and Cap got fouled two times in two plays. At the end of the half, when I thought we were doing pretty well, I found out the score was 36–29. They were beating us by seven points. Mr. Reese didn't seem worried, though.

"Okay, everybody, stay cool. No sweat. Just keep it nice and easy." **F**

We came out in the second half and played it pretty cool. Once we came within one point, but then they ran it up to five again. We kept looking over to Mr. Reese to see what he wanted us to do and he would just put his palms down and nod his head for us to play cool. There were six minutes to go when Mr. Reese put me and another guy named Turk in. Now I didn't really understand why he did this because I know I'm not the best basketball player in the world, although I'm not bad, and I know Turk is worse than me. Also, he took out both Sam and Chalky, our two best players. We were still losing by five points, too. And they weren't doing anything wrong. There was a jump ball between Leon and their center when all of a sudden this big

Analyzing Visuals **Viewing and Interpreting**
Where was the photographer when this photo was taken?

E **Reading Focus** **Drawing Conclusions** The narrator says that he threw the ball to Leon "in the bucket." What does that mean? Where is Leon? What evidence did you use to figure that out?

F **Read and Discuss** How is Mr Reese's coaching paying off?

cheer goes up and everybody looks over to the sidelines. Well, there was Gloria, BB, Maria, Sharon, Kitty, and about four other girls, all dressed in white blouses and black skirts and with big T's on their blouses and they were our cheerleaders. One of their players said something stupid about them but I liked them. They looked real good to me. We controlled the jump and Turk drove right down the lane and made a lay-up. Turk actually made the lay-up. Turk once missed seven lay-ups in a row in practice and no one was even guarding him. But this one he made. Then one of their men double-dribbled and we got the ball and I passed it to Leon, who threw up a shot and got fouled. The shot went in and when he made the foul shot it added up to a three-point play. They started down court and Mr. Reese started yelling for us to give a foul. **G**

"Foul him! Foul him!" he yelled from the sidelines.

Now this was something we had worked on in practice and that Mr. Reese had told us would only work once in a game. Anybody who plays basketball knows that if you're fouled while shooting the ball you get two foul shots and if you're fouled while not shooting the ball you only get one. So when a guy knows you're going to foul him he'll try to get off a quick shot. At least that's what we hoped. When their guard came across the mid-court line, I ran at him as if I was going to foul him. Then, just as I was going to touch him, I stopped short and moved around him without touching him. Sure enough, he threw the ball wildly toward the basket. It went over the base line and it was our ball. Mr. Reese took me out and Turk and put Sam and Chalky back in. And the game was just about over. **H**

We hadn't realized it but in the two minutes that me and Turk played the score had been tied. When Sam and Chalky came back in they outscored the other team by four points in the last four minutes. We were the champs. We got the first-place trophies and we were so happy we were all jumping around and slapping each other on the back. Gloria and the other girls were just as happy as we were, and when we found that we had an extra trophy we gave it to them. Then Mr. Reese took us all in the locker room and shook each guy's hand and then went out and invited the parents and the girls in. He made a little speech about how he was proud of us and all, and not just because we won tonight but because we had worked so hard to win. When he finished everybody started clapping for us and, as usual, I started boo-hooing. But it wasn't so bad this time because Leon started boo-hooing worse than me.

You know what high is? We felt so good the next couple of days that it was ridiculous. We'd see someone in the street and we'd just walk up and be happy. Really. **I**

G **Read and Discuss** What do Mr. Reese's decisions to put the narrator and Turk into the game add to what we already know about the coach?

H **Read and Discuss** What's all this about fouling players?

I **Literary Focus** **A Writer's Messages** What do you think the message in this story is? Explain.

Applying Your Skills

The Game

Sunshine State Standards: Benchmarks **LA.6.1.6.9** determine the correct meaning of words with multiple meanings in context; **LA.6.1.7.2** analyze the author's purpose (e.g., to persuade, inform, entertain, or explain) and perspective in a variety of texts and understand how they affect meaning; *Also covered* **LA.6.1.7.3; LA.6.1.7.8; LA.6.2.1.5**

Respond and Think Critically

Reading Focus

1. How does the first-person point of view affect this story? FCAT

A We see how the crowd reacts during different parts of the game.

B We see how the entire team feels at the end of the game.

C We see how the narrator personally feels about the game.

D We see how the coach tells his players what to do.

Read with a Purpose

2. How does the narrator's team win the championship?

Reading Skills: Drawing Conclusions

3. Review the evidence you gathered as you read "The Game." What conclusions can you draw about Myers and his work?

Evidence from the Text

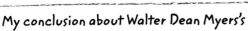

Some important ideas in "The Game" are...

↓

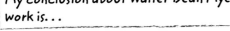

My conclusion about Walter Dean Myers's work is. . .

Vocabulary Check

Answer the following question.

4. What is an antonym for the **defense** on a team?

a. defenseless **c.** defenders

b. offense **d.** offenders

Literary Focus

Literary Analysis

5. Interpret By the time Mr. Reese calls the first timeout, what conclusion has the narrator already drawn about the other team? On what evidence does he abse this conclusion?

6. Evaluate The story is told from the first-person point of view of one of the players. How does this point of view affect the way Myers tells the story?

Literary Skills: A Writer's Messages

7. Analyze In the interview, Walter Dean Myers talks about decisions kids need to make early in life. What decisions have the kids in this story made? How do their decisions relate to the message of the story? Support your answer with details from the story. READ THINK EXPLAIN

Writing Focus

Think as a Reader/Writer

Use It in Your Writing Look at the sentences and lines of dialogue that you liked and jotted down in your *Reader/Writer Notebook.* Think of one of your experiences that you could write about. Write it as if you were talking to a friend.

FABLE
The Golden Serpent
retold by Walter Dean Myers

Read with a Purpose

Read this fable to learn how the wise man Pundabi solves the mystery of the Golden Serpent.

Preparing to Read for this selection is on page 177.

Build Background

Walter Dean Myers has written an amazing number of books in many different genres. He has written fiction, nonfiction, picture books, short stories, poems, and plays. He writes for young children as well as for teens. "The Golden Serpent" was first published as a picture book. Although many of his books are connected to his own background and to the life experience of African Americans, "The Golden Serpent" has characters, a plot, and a setting completely different from those of most of his other works. The story is based on an ancient fable from India.

There was once a very wise man. He lived on a high mountain and was called Pundabi. With him lived a young boy. The boy's name was Ali.

Each morning Ali would come down the mountain. He would sit in the shade of a fig tree. Many people would come to him. They brought him loaves of bread. In the bread were pieces of fine linen. There would be questions on the linen for the wise Pundabi to answer. They would be questions of life and death, or about the search for happiness.

Each evening Ali would climb the mountain and give the loaves of bread to Pundabi. Pundabi would answer all the questions. Then they would eat the bread.

Ali would take the answers down the mountain. He would give them to the waiting people. Pundabi and Ali lived well this way, and the people loved them dearly. **A**

One day a tall shadow fell across Ali. It was the shadow of the king himself.

"Are you Ali?" the king asked.

"I am he," Ali answered.

"And you live with the wise man Pundabi?"

"That is so," Ali replied.

A **Read and Discuss** What has the author told us so far about Pundabi and Ali?

Vocabulary **linen** (LIHN uhn) *n.:* fine-quality writing paper, once made from linen rags.

"And it is true that he is very wise?"

"Yes, it is true," said Ali.

"Then you must bring him to me," the king said.

So Ali went up the mountain. He told Pundabi of the king's request. Pundabi and Ali came down the mountain. They set out for the palace. They went past the river and through the marketplace. They went through the village. Finally they reached another high mountain. **B**

On top of this mountain was the palace.

"I want you to solve a mystery for me." The king spoke from his high throne. "But first we must have lunch." He clapped his hands twice.

Five men brought in five trays of food. There was a tray for Pundabi. There was a tray for Ali. And three trays for the king.

"I am very rich," the king said. "I have much gold and many rubies. And you, Pundabi, are very wise. I can pay you very well."

"What is the mystery?" asked Pundabi.

"I do not know," said the king. "That is for you to discover!"

"But how can Pundabi solve a mystery"—Ali wrung his hands—"if there is none to solve?"

"If you are truly wise, Pundabi, it will be done. If you do not solve it, then you are a fraud. I will put you in jail where you belong." Ali was very afraid. He began to shake.

But Pundabi said, "Let us take a walk. Perhaps our eyes will speak to us." **C**

B **Reading Focus** **Drawing Conclusions** Why does Pundabi, without question or hesitation, come down the mountain and make his way to the palace?

C **Read and Discuss** Now what is going on with Pundabi?

Vocabulary **fraud** (frawd) *n.:* someone who pretends to be what he or she is not

So they began to walk. They walked by the river.

They walked through the village. They stopped by the home of an old woman. They walked around the marketplace. Pundabi's eyes spoke to him.

Then Pundabi began to walk up the mountain toward the palace.

"We will surely go to jail," Ali said. "We cannot solve the mystery. We do not know what it is."

"But we do know what the mystery is." Pundabi spoke, a smile upon his face. "And perhaps we can solve it. Let us go and see the king."

"Have you solved the mystery yet?" the king asked.

"No," said Pundabi. "But we know what the mystery is! It is the mystery of the Golden Serpent."

"The Golden Serpent?" said the king.

"Yes," Pundabi said. "Where is your Golden Serpent?"

"I didn't know I had one," the king said.

"The thief must be very clever," Pundabi said.

"You must find it for me," said the king.

"Let us see," Pundabi said. "Someone must have taken it to sell. Let us go to the market."

So the king called his guards. And off they went to the market. **D**

In the market they came upon a young boy. The boy was turning wood.[1]

"Perhaps he has stolen the Golden Serpent." The king seized the boy by the arm.

"I have no Golden Serpent," the boy said. "I could not run away with it. My leg is bent from turning."

But the guards searched him well. They searched his blouse and the hay upon which he slept. They even looked at his bent leg.

"It is true," the guards said. "He has nothing. He can hardly walk."

Next they went to the village. They stopped at the house of a widow.

"We are searching for the Golden Serpent," said Pundabi, "which was stolen from the king."

"I do not have it," said the widow. "I have only this small cup of grain."

But the king did not trust her. So the guards searched her hut. They looked in the corners. They looked in the cupboard.

"It is true," said the guards. "She has nothing but this cup of grain."

"Let us go from this dismal place," the king said.

Outside they heard a strange cry. Three men walked together. They sang a sad song. The first had a stick. He swung it before him as he walked. The second walked behind the first. The third walked behind the second. Each had a hand on the other's shoulder.

"Perhaps," said Pundabi, "these are your thieves."

"These?" said the king. "Why, they

1. **turning wood:** shaping wood with a tool called a lathe. The lathe the boy is using is operated by a pedal, which accounts for the boy's bent leg.

D **Read and Discuss** How are things looking for Pundabi? What does the king think of Pundabi's discovery?

Vocabulary **dismal** (DIHZ muhl) *adj.:* cheerless; depressing.

cannot see!"

"How clever of them," said Pundabi. **E**

So they stopped the three blind men and asked of the king's Golden Serpent.

"No," said the first. "I have only this stick for comfort."

"No," said the second. "I have only the few coins I am given."

"No," said the third. "I have but these two friends."

But the king did not trust them. So the guards searched the three blind men.

"They have nothing," said the guards, "except a worm-eaten stick and a few coins. Nothing more." **F**

"Let us return to the palace," the king said.

"But we have not found the Golden Serpent," Pundabi said.

"I no longer want it," the king said bitterly. "I will pay you and you can leave." **G**

At the palace, the king had his counters pay Pundabi in gold coins.

"And what about your people?" Pundabi asked.

"My people?" asked the king.

"Yes. The crippled boy, the poor widow, and the blind beggars," said Ali.

"What about them, indeed!" said the king. "They did not find my Golden

---

E **Reading Focus** **Drawing Conclusions** What does Pundabi mean by this comment? Why does he say this to the king?

F **Reading Focus** **Drawing Conclusions** Why does Pundabi take the king to see all these unfortunate people and suggest to him that they have taken his Golden Serpent?

G **Read and Discuss** What are the king and Pundabi up to now? How is their search going?

Analyzing Visuals **Viewing and Interpreting** On which figure or figures is the main focus in this scene? Why do you think the artist illustrated the story in this way?

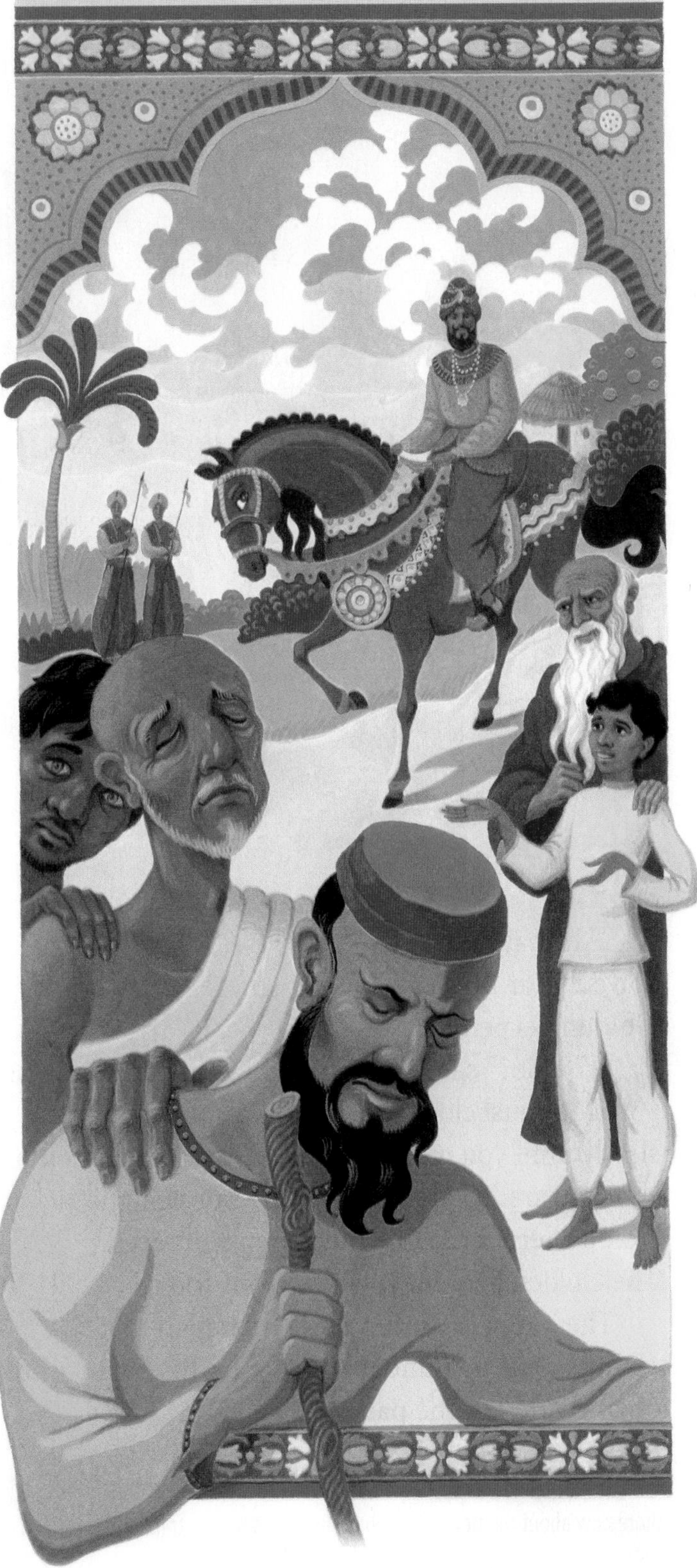

Analyzing Visuals **Viewing and Interpreting** How does the artist represent the Golden Serpent in this scene? Why is it called the Golden Serpent?

Serpent."

"Ah," said Pundabi, "I see. But I have solved your mystery. I know where the Golden Serpent is."

"You do?" said the king. "How splendid!"

"You must close your eyes and count slowly until you reach a hundred. But make sure you are alone so that no one can steal the Golden Serpent again. Then open your eyes. The Golden Serpent will be in your room."

The king closed his eyes and began to count slowly as Pundabi picked up his bag of gold and left the palace.

He went down the steep hill.

He gave some of the gold to the crippled boy.

He gave some to the widow. He gave some to the blind beggars.

"Pundabi," said Ali. "You are both wise and generous. But there is still one problem."

"And what is that?" asked Pundabi.

"When the king opens his eyes," said Ali, "he will still not find the Golden Serpent." **H**

"No," said Pundabi. "Some people never do. But that is another mystery." **I**

H **Reading Focus** **Drawing Conclusions** Do you know more now about the Golden Serpent? Now what do you think the Golden Serpent is?

I **Literary Focus** **A Writer's Messages** What is the message of this fable? Why do some people never find the Golden Serpent? Why is that a "mystery"?

Love That Boy

by **Walter Dean Myers**

Read with a Purpose

Read this poem to see how the speaker here cherishes his young son.

Preparing to Read for this selection is on page 177.

Build Background

Walter Dean Myers started out writing poems when he was in fifth grade. Almost fifty years later, he wrote "Love That Boy" for his book *Brown Angels*. The book is an album of turn-of-the-century photographs of African American children. Myers collected the photos from antique shops, flea markets, and auctions.

Love that boy,
like a rabbit loves to run
I said I love that boy
like a rabbit loves to run
Love to call him in the morning
love to call him
"Hey there, son!"

He walk like his grandpa
grins like his uncle Ben
I said he walk like his grandpa
and grins like his uncle Ben
Grins when he happy
when he sad he grins again **A**

His mama like to hold him
like to feed him cherry pie
I said his mama like to hold him
feed him that cherry pie
She can have him now
I'll get him by and by **B**

He got long roads to walk down
before the setting sun
I said he got a long, long road
to walk down,
before the setting sun
He'll be a long stride walker
and a good man before he done **C**

A **Reading Focus** **Drawing Conclusions** What is the speaker saying about his son?

B **Read and Discuss** What does the speaker mean when he says, "I'll get him by and by"?

C **Literary Focus** **A Writer's Messages** What is the author's message in this poem?

Applying Your Skills

Sunshine State Standards: Benchmarks **LA.6.1.6.1** use new vocabulary that is introduced and taught directly; **LA.6.1.7.2** analyze the author's purpose (e.g., to persuade, inform, entertain, or explain) and perspective in a variety of texts and understand how they affect meaning; *Also covered* **LA.6.1.7.3; LA.6.1.7.8; LA.6.2.1.2; LA.6.2.1.3; LA.6.2.1.5**

The Golden Serpent / Love That Boy

Respond and Think Critically

Reading Focus

1. What effect does the repetition in "Love That Boy" have on the poem? **FCAT**
   A It gives more information about the boy.
   B It reveals the boy's love of his parents.
   C It gives a better understanding of setting.
   D It makes the most important points clear.

Read with a Purpose

2. In "The Golden Serpent," how does Pundabi solve the mystery? In "Love That Boy," how does the speaker show his love for his son?

Reading Skills: Drawing Conclusions

3. Review the evidence of Myers's ideas and messages you gathered as you read "The Golden Serpent" and "Love That Boy." What conclusions can you draw about Walter Dean Myers and his work from this evidence?

Evidence from the Text

Some important ideas in "The Golden Serpent" are . . .	Some important ideas in "Love That Boy" are . . .

↓

My conclusion about Walter Dean Myers's work is . . .

Vocabulary Check

4. What would you be writing on if you wrote something on **linen**?
5. Why would Pundabi be a **fraud** if he could not solve the mystery?
6. Which is more likely to be a **dismal** place: a palace or a jail? Why?

Literary Focus

Literary Analysis

7. **Interpret** Who or what *is* the Golden Serpent?
8. **Evaluate** In the interview, Walter Dean Myers says he has no memory of his mother and didn't see his father again until long after his adoption. How does knowing this affect your appreciation of "Love That Boy"?

Literary Skills: A Writer's Messages

9. **Analysis** Walter Dean Myers believes that we fulfill our lives when we try to understand the lives of others. How does this message come across in "The Golden Serpent" and "Love That Boy"? Support your response with details from the texts. READ THINK EXPLAIN

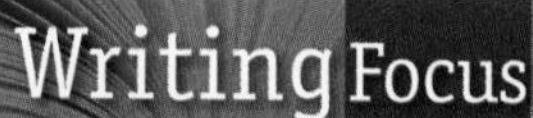

Writing Focus

Think as a Reader/Writer

Use It in Your Writing What did you most like—or dislike—about the way Myers wrote "The Golden Serpent" and "Love That Boy"? How did Myers help you connect to these works? Were you able to connect more to one than the other? Using the details that you collected in your *Reader/Writer Notebook*, respond to these questions in one or two paragraphs.

Sunshine State Standards: Benchmarks **LA.6.2.1.6** write a book report, review, or critique that compares two or more works by the same author; **LA.6.4.1.2** write a variety of expressive forms (e.g., short plays, song lyrics, historical fiction, limericks) that employ figurative language, rhythm, dialogue, characterization, and/or appropriate format; **LA.6.4.2.1** write in a variety of technical/informational forms (e.g., summaries, procedures, instructions, experiments, rubrics, how-to manuals, assembly instructions); **LA.6.6.4.1** use appropriate available technologies to enhance communication and achieve a purpose (e.g., video, online).

Author Study: Walter Dean Myers

Writing Focus

Think as a Reader/Writer

Making Connections to a Writer's Works Look back at the examples of Myers's writing that you wrote in your *Reader/Writer Notebook*. Did you like his straightforward descriptions, the way his characters talk, the way his characters interact, or the rhythm of his words? What sentences, descriptions, lines of dialogue, and even entire passages most helped you connect with Myers's different fictional "worlds"?

Use It in Your Writing Myers once said, "Ultimately, what I want to do with my writing is to make connections—to touch the lives of my characters and, through them, those of my readers." In a two-paragraph essay, explain whether you felt connections to Myers's characters and their situations. If you felt more connected to some works or characters than others, explain why. Use examples from your *Reader/Writer Notebook* to support your opinions.

What truths about life does Myers share in these works? How do these truths connect to your own life?

CHOICES

As you respond to the Choices, use these **Academic Vocabulary** words as appropriate: achieve, create, interact, major.

REVIEW

Write a "Do-Over"

Timed Writing In two or three paragraphs, describe an incident or decision (it can be an imaginary one) that you wish you could "do over." How has this incident or decision affected your life? How would you "do over" or fix the situation? What have you learned from it?

CONNECT

Write Your Own Tribute Poem

Myers's poem "Love That Boy" was the inspiration for Sharon Creech's book *Love That Dog,* which tells the story of a boy who discovers the power of words and poetry. Following the model of "Love That Boy," write your own tribute poem to someone or something you love.

EXTEND

Write a Screenplay

TechFocus With several others, choose "The Game" or "The Golden Serpent," and write all or part of it as a screenplay. Write dialogue and camera directions. To create a storyboard showing the sequence of events, see the storyboard template on the *Digital Storytelling* site.

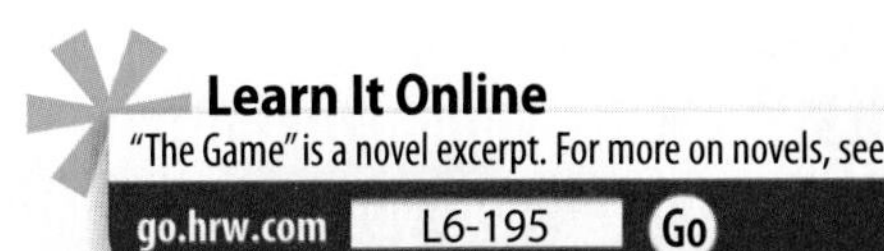

Learn It Online
"The Game" is a novel excerpt. For more on novels, see
go.hrw.com
L6-195
Go

INFORMATIONAL TEXT FOCUS

Notes, Outlines, and Summaries

CONTENTS

What Do You Think?

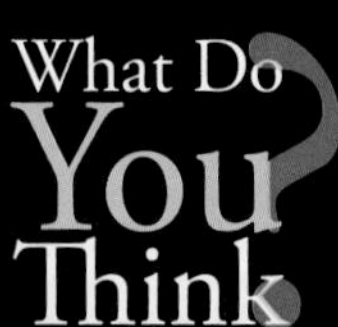

Facing the truth can mean admitting mistakes. How can coming to terms with mistakes help you overcome them?

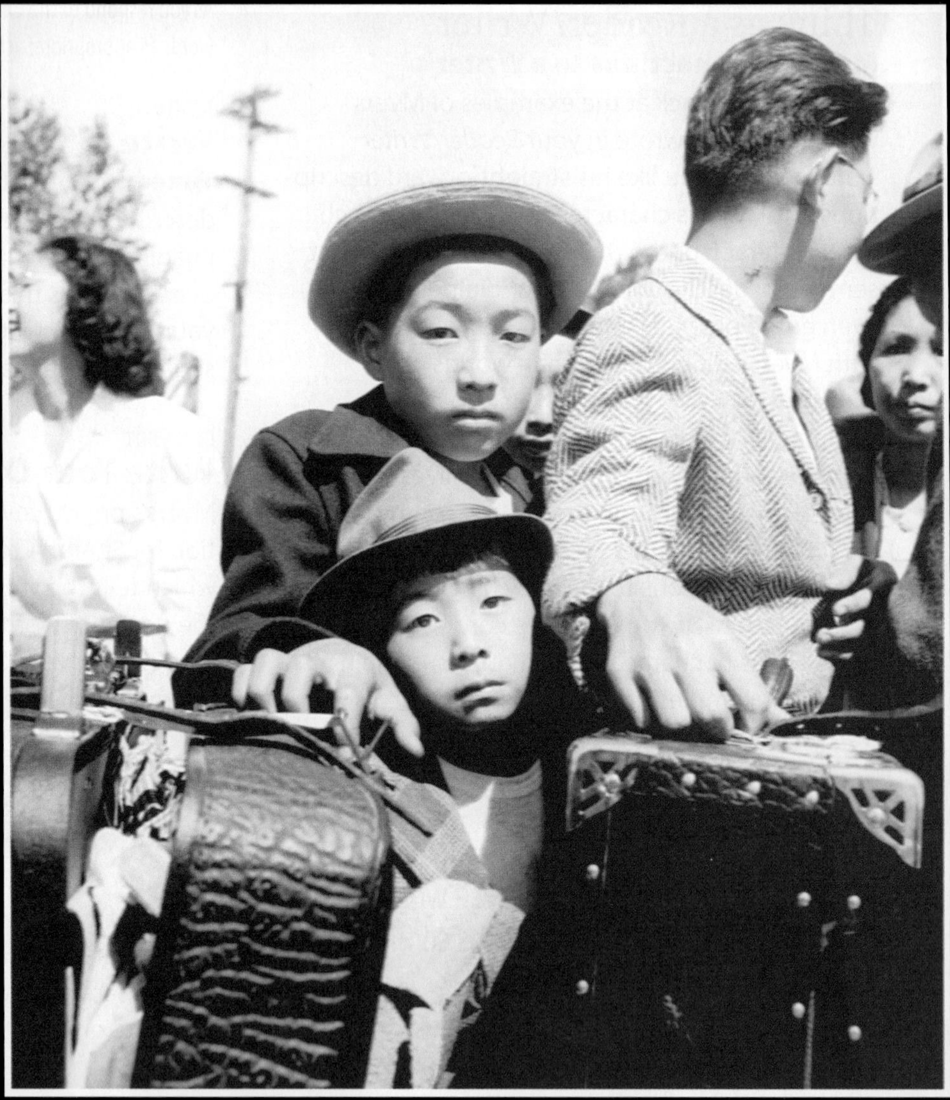

QuickWrite

Think of a time when you faced unfair treatment. Briefly describe the situation and what you found unfair about it. Were you offered an apology? If so, did it help? Explain how you dealt with your feelings of injustice.

Preparing to Read

Sunshine State Standards: Benchmarks **LA.6.1.6.1** use new vocabulary that is introduced and taught directly; *Also covered* **LA.6.1.6.7; LA.6.1.6.10; LA.6.2.2.3**

Wartime Mistakes, Peacetime Apologies

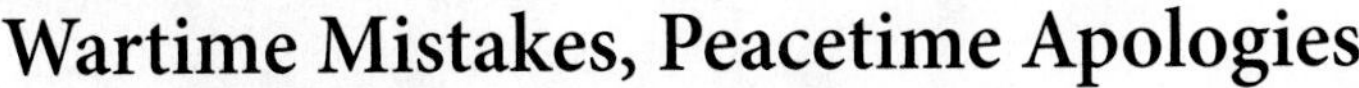

Reader/Writer Notebook

Use your **RWN** to complete the activities for this selection.

Informational Text Focus

Taking Notes "The Bracelet" (page 167) is fiction, but it is based on real historical events. Some of those events are explained in the following article. You'll learn the facts about Executive Order 9066 and how it affected one real-life Japanese American woman. As you read, you'll take **notes** on the information in the article.

Into Action To take logical, detailed notes, get some notecards and follow these steps:

1. Read through the selection once to find the main ideas, or most important points.
2. Make one card for each main idea.
3. Take notes about each main idea. List important details about it in your own words, or use quotation marks around the author's words. Your notecards will look like this:

Main Idea
- supporting detail
- supporting detail
- supporting detail
- supporting detail

The supporting details you choose to include should answer important questions about the main idea, such as *who? what? when? where? why?* and *how?*

Writing Focus

Preparing for **Extended Response**

As you read "Wartime Mistakes, Peacetime Apologies," look at the model cards that appear with the selection and write down the missing word or words in your *Reader/Writer Notebook*. Work with one idea at a time.

Vocabulary

prescribe (prih SKRYB) *v.:* define officially. *Governments often prescribe new laws during wartime.*

discretion (dihs KREHSH uhn) *n.:* authority to make decisions. *Executive orders are within the president's discretion.*

compensation (kahm puhn SAY shuhn) *n.:* payment given to make up for a loss or injury. *Internees received financial compensation in 1990.*

rectify (REHK tuh fy) *v.:* correct. *It is difficult to rectify the mistakes of the past.*

Language Coach

Word Parts A **suffix** is a word part attached to the end of a word or root. Knowing suffixes may help you determine a word's part of speech. For instance, the suffix *–fy* means "make or form into." It turns a word into an action word—a verb. Even if you didn't know the exact meaning of *rectify,* the suffix would tell you that the word is probably a verb. What two vocabulary words above share the same suffix? What is their part of speech? Look up the meaning of that suffix in a dictionary.

Learn It Online

Practice taking notes with the interactive Reading Workshop on:

go.hrw.com L6-197 Go

MAGAZINE ARTICLE

WARTIME MISTAKES, Peacetime Apologies

by Nancy Day, from *Cobblestone Magazine*

Read with a Purpose

Read the following article to discover what happened to many Japanese Americans during and after World War II—and who was responsible.

On March 13, 1942, Yoshiko Imamoto opened her door to face three FBI agents. They let her pack a nightgown and a Bible, then took her to jail while they "checked into a few things." Imamoto had lived in America for twenty-four years. She was a teacher and had done nothing wrong. But a month earlier, President Franklin D. Roosevelt had issued Executive Order 9066, which drastically changed the lives of Imamoto and more than 120,000 other people of Japanese ancestry living in the United States. **A**

When Japan bombed Pearl Harbor on December 7, 1941, Japanese Americans were caught in the middle. They felt like Americans but looked like the enemy. Neighbors and co-workers eyed them suspiciously. Then Executive Order 9066, issued on February 19, 1942, authorized the exclusion of "any or all persons" from any areas the military chose. The word "Japanese" was never used, but the order was designed to allow the military to force Japanese Americans living near the coast to leave their homes for the duration of the war. Some were allowed to move inland, but most, like Yoshiko Imamoto, were herded into prisonlike camps. **B**

A **Informational Focus** **Taking Notes** Which model notecard goes with the main idea of the first paragraph?

B **Informational Focus** **Taking Notes** Remember to answer important questions—such as *when?*—about the main ideas. What dates are given in this paragraph?

Yoshiko Imamoto

- On ______ (when?), the FBI arrested her with no warning.
- 24-year U.S. resident
- teacher
- had broken no laws

Pearl Harbor

- 12/7/1941
- Japan attacked U.S.
- Japanese Americans felt ______ (how?).
- They were treated ______ (how? by whom?).

Executive Order 9066

- issued by President Franklin D. Roosevelt
- affected ______ (how many?) people
- issued ______ (when?)
- allowed ______ (what?)
- never used ______ (what word?)
- Only ______ (who?) were moved.
- Most were moved ______ (where?).

Analyzing Visuals

Viewing and Interpreting How might this child reflect the sense of helplessness and confusion the Japanese Americans must have felt during the internment?

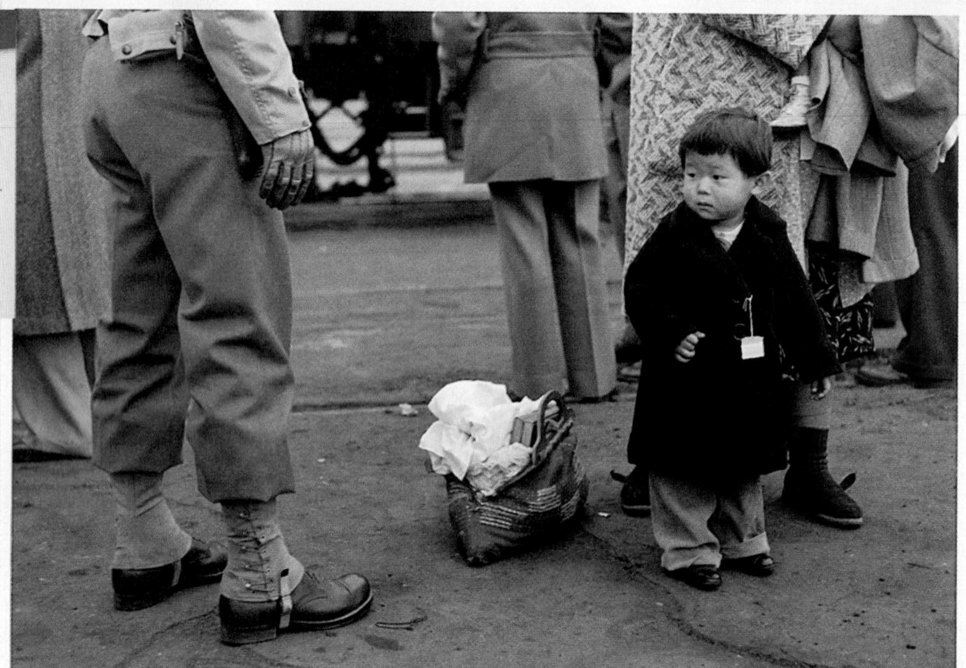

I hereby authorize and direct the Secretary of War, and the Military Commanders whom he may from time to time designate, whenever he or any designated Commander deems such action necessary or desirable, to prescribe military areas in such places and of such extent as he or the appropriate Military Commander may determine, from which any or all persons may be excluded, and with respect to which, the right of any person to enter, remain in, or leave shall be subject to whatever restrictions the Secretary of War or the appropriate Military Commander may impose in his discretion.

—**President Franklin D. Roosevelt,** excerpt from Executive Order 9066, 1942

Vocabulary **prescribe** (prih SKRYB) *v.:* define officially. **discretion** (dihs KREHSH uhn) *n.:* authority to make decisions.

After the war, Japanese Americans tried to start over. They had lost their jobs, their property, and their pride. Some used the Japanese American Evacuation Claims Act of 1948 to get compensation for property they had lost. But it was not until the late 1960s that cries for redress—compensation for all they had suffered—began to emerge.

In 1976, Executive Order 9066 was officially ended by President Gerald Ford. Four years later, President Jimmy Carter signed a bill that created the Commission on Wartime Relocation and Internment of Civilians (CWRIC) to investigate the relocation of Japanese Americans. The CWRIC concluded that Executive Order 9066 was "not justified by military necessity" but was the result of "race prejudice, war hysteria, and a failure of political leadership." In 1983, the commission recommended to Congress that each surviving Japanese American evacuee be given a payment of twenty thousand dollars and an apology. **C**

A bill to authorize the payments was introduced in the House of Representatives in 1983 but met resistance. Intensive lobbying[1] by Japanese Americans was met by arguments that the government had acted legally and appropriately at the time.

1. **lobbying** (LAHB ee ihng): activity aimed at influencing public officials.

C **Read and Discuss** What did we learn about Executive Order 9066?

Vocabulary **compensation** (kahm puhn SAY shuhn) *n.:* payment given to make up for a loss or injury.

After the War

- *Japanese Americans had lost ______ (what?).*
- *______ (what?) was used by some Japanese Americans to claim payment for lost property.*
- *______ (what?) began in the late 1960s.*

9066 Ended—Investigation Begun

- *______ (who?) ended 9066 in ______ (when?).*
- *______ (who?) authorized CWRIC ______ (to do what?).*
- *CWRIC recommended ______ (what?).*

Repayment

- *Bill introduced in House of Representatives in 1983.*
- *supported by Japanese Americans*
- *Opponents argued that ______ (what?).*

Analyzing Visuals

Viewing and Interpreting How do you think the people pictured here with President Reagan felt about the passing of the Civil Liberties Act? How do you know?

A monetary sum and words alone cannot restore lost years or erase painful memories; neither can they fully convey our Nation's resolve to rectify injustice and to uphold the rights of individuals. We can never fully right the wrongs of the past. But we can take a clear stand for justice and recognize that serious injustices were done to Japanese Americans during World War II.

—**President George H. W. Bush,** excerpt from letter accompanying redress checks, 1990

Vocabulary **rectify** (REHK tuh fy) *v.:* correct.

Meanwhile, three men who had long since served their jail sentences for refusing to comply with curfew[2] or relocation orders filed suit[3] to challenge the government's actions. The court ruled that the government had had no legal basis for detaining Japanese Americans.

The rulings increased pressure to provide redress. In 1988, Congress approved the final version of the redress bill, which became known as the Civil Liberties Act. It was signed by President Ronald Reagan on August 10, 1988. Two years later, Congress funded the payments. **D**

In 1990, at the age of ninety-three, Yoshiko Imamoto opened her door not to FBI agents, but to a small brown envelope containing a check for twenty thousand dollars and an apology from President George Bush. It had taken almost fifty years and the actions of four presidents, but the government had made redress and apologized for its mistakes. **E**

---

2. **curfew** (KUR fyoo): Shortly before the relocation began, the head of the Western Defense Command, Lt. Gen. John DeWitt, set a curfew. Between 8:00 P.M. and 6:00 A.M. each day, "all persons of Japanese ancestry" had to remain indoors, off the streets.
3. **filed suit:** went to court in an attempt to recover something.

Court Ruling

- ______ (who?) took the government to court.
- The court decided ______ (what?).
- This ruling helped build support for ______ (what?).

Add to Repayment card:

- Congress approved repayment bill in 1988.
- called Civil Liberties Act
- signed by ______ (whom?) ______ (when?)
- Payments were sent ______ (when?).

Add to Yoshiko Imamoto card:

- in 1990, received ______ (what?)
- She was 93 years old.
- It had taken ______ (how long?).
- It had taken the work of four presidents.

Read with a Purpose

How did the U.S. government recognize the injustices that Japanese Americans endured during World War II?

D Informational Focus **Taking Notes** Why should you add information to the Repayment card?

E Read and Discuss How does Yoshiko's story come full circle and connect to the beginning of the selection?

Applying Your Skills

Sunshine State Standards: Benchmarks **LA.6.1.6.1** use new vocabulary that is introduced and taught directly; **LA.6.2.2.2** use information from the text to answer questions related to the main idea or relevant details, maintaining chronological or logical order.

Wartime Mistakes, Peacetime Apologies

Practicing for FCAT

Informational Text and Vocabulary

1. When did Yoshiko Imamoto come to the United States?
   - **A** when she was a young woman
   - **B** when she was a mother with a young child
   - **C** when she was a baby
   - **D** when she was a child

2. Which two groups had a conflict after the discussion of a redress bill?
   - **F** Japanese Americans and people who felt that the government had done nothing wrong
   - **G** Japanese American members of Congress and other elected officials
   - **H** people who had been evacuated and those who were veterans of World War II
   - **I** the Supreme Court and Americans who felt that the government was wrong

3. Which sentence BEST summarizes the main ideas of the Executive Order 9066?
   - **A** Military commanders must follow instructions given by the secretary of war.
   - **B** When an area of any size is put under military control, all civilians in that area must be evacuated.
   - **C** The military may set aside certain areas and decide who enters, stays in, or leaves those areas.
   - **D** Japanese Americans must leave California.

4. What does President Franklin D. Roosevelt want to prescribe in the Executive Order 9066?
   - **F** a new rule
   - **G** less Japanese Americans
   - **H** a safer country
   - **I** a larger police force

5. Read the sentence from the passage.

   Some used the Japanese Americans Evacuation Claims Act of 1948 to get compensation for property they had lost.

   What does the word *compensation* mean?
   - **A** jobs
   - **B** payment
   - **C** bills
   - **D** laws

Writing Focus Extended Response

What was the Commission on Wartime Relocation and Internment of Citizens? What did its investigation achieve? Support your answer with details from the text.

What Do You Think Now

How do you think the survivors of internment reacted to the government's apology and repayment?

MAGAZINE ARTICLE

Preparing to Read

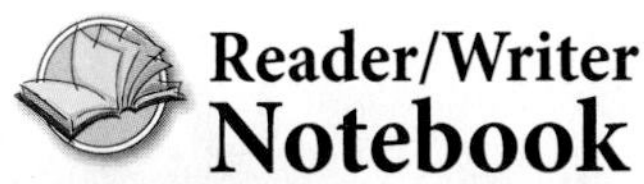

Sunshine State Standards: Benchmarks **LA.6.1.6.9** determine the correct meaning of words with multiple-meanings in context; *Also covered* **LA.6.1.7.3; LA.6.2.2.1; LA.6.2.2.3**

What a Character

Informational Text Focus

Outlining Preparing an **outline** is a good way to organize and better understand your notes about factual writing. Remember that when you take notes, you determine and record the **main ideas** and the **details** that support them. Once you've taken your notes, you can organize the main ideas in an outline like the one below. This is the beginning of an outline for "What a Character":

I. Takamoto's Internment (First Main Idea)
   A. Takamoto and his family sent to Manzanar Internment Camp (Detail supporting point I)
      1. After the bombing of Pearl Harbor, Japanese Americans were sent to internment camps (Detail supporting point A)

Summarizing A **summary** is a brief restatement of the main ideas or major events in a text. Creating summaries of informational materials is especially useful if you are doing research from a number of sources. Reviewing your summaries will help you recognize ways one source differs from another. Consider the following tips when you are summarizing a nonfiction text:

- A good summary is much shorter than the original text and includes only the most important points. In nonfiction, these are the **main ideas** and **key supporting details.**
- If you have already completed an outline, look at the first two levels of information (I, II, . . . and A, B, . . .). These are the main ideas and important details you'll probably want to include.

Writing Focus

Preparing for **Extended Response**

Writers of informational material know that an important idea needs to be obvious. They use headings that suggest main ideas and organize their writing so that supporting details flow from the main ideas. As you read "What a Character," pay attention to how it is organized.

Reader/Writer Notebook

Use your **RWN** to complete the activities for this selection.

Vocabulary

apprentice (uh PREHN tihs) *n.:* beginner; someone who is just starting to learn a craft or job. *Takamoto was an apprentice to Disney's animators.*

instrumental (ihn struh MEHN tuhl) *adj.:* helping to make something happen. *Takamoto was instrumental in Hanna-Barbera's success.*

legacy (LEHG uh see) *n.:* something handed down or left for others. *Takamoto's legacy for cartoon fans includes many memorable characters.*

Language Coach

Puns A pun (or play on words) often suggests more than one meaning of the same word. For example, the title of this article contains a pun. "What a Character" refers both to the subject of the article, Iwao Takamoto (a character is a memorable, unique, or funny person), and to his cartoon characters.

Identify and explain the pun in the following quotation about the animator Takamoto: "His admirers are still drawing lessons from his spirited ways."

Learn It Online

Do pictures and animation help you learn? Try the *PowerNotes* lesson on:

go.hrw.com L6-205 Go

MAGAZINE ARTICLE

What a Character: Iwao Takamoto and His Toons

by THE WORLD ALMANAC®

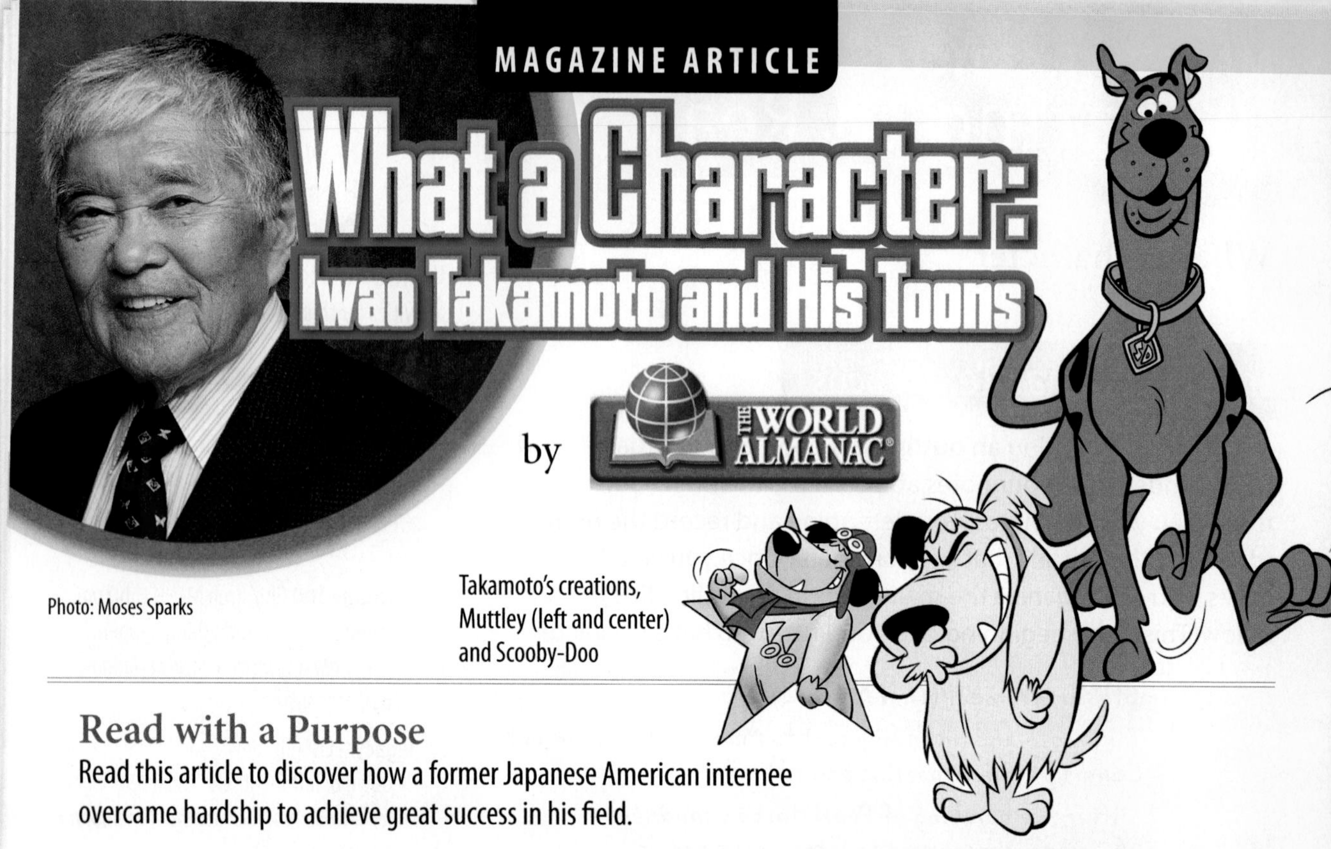

Photo: Moses Sparks

Takamoto's creations, Muttley (left and center) and Scooby-Doo

Read with a Purpose

Read this article to discover how a former Japanese American internee overcame hardship to achieve great success in his field.

Animated cartoons—or toons, as many call them today—aren't just for children any more. Books, magazines, and Web sites are devoted to cartoon trivia, and famous cartoon characters are everywhere in popular culture: on T-shirts, lunch boxes, toys, bedsheets, pajamas, fast foods, and practically any other kind of product you can name. Most of us know certain cartoon characters, but what do we know about the real people behind the toons—the writers, producers, directors, and, perhaps most importantly, the artists who bring these beloved characters to life? Here's the story of one of those artists, a name from the cartoon world everyone should know: Iwao Takamoto, the animator.

A Journey Begins in Manzanar

You'd never think that a Japanese internment camp near Los Angeles in the early 1940s and a cartoon canine by the name of Scooby-Doo could possibly have any connection to each other, but they do. The connection is animator Iwao Takamoto. His name may not be a household word, but many of his creations are. Takamoto's journey from an internment camp to the world of animation makes for a unique story of creative success. **A**

Takamoto, a Japanese American, was born in Los Angeles in 1925. By age 15, he had graduated ahead of his high school class. His promising future was put on hold when the Japanese bombed Pearl Harbor

A **Read and Discuss** What has the author set up for us here?

in 1941. He and his family were forced into Manzanar Internment Camp, in the desert outside Los Angeles.

Japan had been declared an enemy of war by the United States. Thousands of Japanese and Japanese Americans were shuttled into camps, supposedly for their and the country's protection. But out of bad situations, good sometimes comes, and this was true for Takamoto. While in Manzanar, the teenage Takamoto met some former Hollywood art directors who were interned with him. The men saw his sketches of scenes in the camp and encouraged him to draw. They gave him valuable informal training in illustration.

An Animated Life (B)

In order to escape the camp, Takamoto agreed to become a laborer, picking fruit in Idaho. But it was his drawing talent that freed him in the end. Just two months before the end of World War II, Takamoto contacted Disney Studios and landed an interview. He was not even fully aware of what Disney was or how large it was. Asked to bring his portfolio, he went to a corner store and bought sketchpads and pencils. He had no portfolio of work to show; he had been doing farm labor.

Over a weekend he filled two sketchpads with images, everything he liked to draw "from knights to cowboys." He got a job at Disney Studios on the spot. He became an apprentice, training under famous animators of the day during a Golden Age of animation.

At Disney, Takamoto had the chance to work on cartoon shorts and longer films. In the 1950s, he worked on popular Disney animated films such as *Cinderella, Peter Pan, Lady and the Tramp,* and *Sleeping Beauty.* He learned his craft at Disney but eventually realized that he could go no further there. In 1961, he took what he learned to Hanna-Barbera Studios, a company that was energizing TV cartoons with such creations as *Huckleberry Hound, Top Cat, The Yogi Bear Show,* and *The Flintstones.*

Takamoto at Disney

For the next 40 years, Takamoto designed for Hanna-Barbera, taking a hand in virtually everything, even licensed products and theme park rides. He brought such characters as Secret Squirrel and Atom Ant to life. Later, he was instrumental in launching *Josie and the Pussy Cats* and other successful cartoons. (C)

(B) **Informational Focus** **Outlining** What features of this article hint at its main ideas? How can they help you create an outline?

(C) **Informational Focus** **Summarizing** Summarize this short paragraph in one sentence.

Vocabulary **apprentice** (uh PREHN tihs) *n.:* beginner; someone who is just starting to learn a craft or job.
instrumental (ihn struh MEHN tuhl) *adj.:* helping to make something happen.

Crazy Canine Characters

Takamoto's legacy includes characters of all kinds. But his four-legged creations are his most memorable. There is Astro, the family dog on *The Jetsons;* the perpetually wheezing pooch Muttley of *The Wacky Races;* and the unforgettable Scooby-Doo of *Scooby-Doo, Where Are You?* a big dog who solves mysteries despite being afraid of practically everything.

By design, the animator made Scooby's appearance all wrong. Takamoto called Scooby-Doo a Great Dane, but most of the details of the cartoon dog's appearance were in fact the *opposite* of that breed's characteristics. "There was a lady that bred Great Danes," he said. "She showed me some pictures and talked about the important points of a Great Dane, like a straight back, straight legs, small chin and such. I decided to go the opposite and give him a hump back, bowed legs, big chin and such. Even his color was wrong."

Takamoto had an inventive sense of humor. Even nonsense inspired him. The name Scooby-Doo, for instance, came from a playful refrain[1] in the Frank Sinatra song "Strangers in the Night." Sinatra sings the phrase "scooby-dooby-do" as if it means something. **D**

Creative Recognition

For Scooby-Doo and other beloved and distinctive creations, Takamoto won the Windsor McKay Lifetime Achievement Award by the International Animated Film Association in 1996. The Japanese American National Museum honored him in 2001, and the Animation Guild gave him their Golden Award in 2005. **E**

Takamoto died in 2007 at age 81, but his admirers are still drawing lessons from his spirited ways. Imprisonment in a Japanese internment camp seemed to place his future in doubt, but it ended up putting him on the road to a lasting success. He went from a world of grim reality to a world of fantasy and imagination in a few short years. His death was a contradiction, too. He died of heart failure, but those who knew him say that, above all, he was full of heart. And that heart lives on in his beloved creations. **F**

1. **refrain** (rih FRAYN): phrase or verse repeated during a song.

Read with a Purpose

What did you find most surprising or inspiring about the story of Iwao Takamoto?

D **Read and Discuss** How did Takamoto approach the creation of cartoons, including Scooby-Doo?

E **Informational Focus** **Outlining** What main idea from this paragraph would you include as a main point in your outline?

F **Read and Discuss** How do the author's words "[the] Japanese internment camp seemed to place his future in doubt, but it ended up putting him on the road to a lasting success" sum up Takamoto's life as it was presented here?

Vocabulary **legacy** (LEHG uh see) *n.:* something handed down or left for others.

Applying Your Skills

Sunshine State Standards: Benchmarks **LA.6.1.6.1** use new vocabulary that is introduced and taught directly; **LA.6.1.7.2** analyze the author's purpose (e.g., to persuade, inform, entertain, or explain) and perspective in a variety of texts and understand how they affect meaning; *Also covered* **LA.6.2.2.3; LA.6.4.2.1**

What a Character

Practicing for FCAT

Informational Text and Vocabulary

1 Why do you think the writer lists the characters that Takamoto created?

A to show that cartoons are underappreciated
B to explain the process of animation
C to demonstrate Takamoto's importance
D to reveal facts about Takamoto's life

2 Which detail would NOT be a main heading in an outline for this passage?

F Takamoto picking fruit in Idaho
G Takamoto's internment
H Takamoto's animation career
I Takamoto's achievements

3 Which detail does NOT support the main heading, "Takamoto's animation career?"

A Takamoto landed an interview with Disney.
B At Disney, Takamoto worked on animated films.
C Takamoto was born in Los Angeles.
D Takamoto worked at Hanna-Barbera for forty years.

4 Read the sentence from the passage.

Later, he was instrumental in launching Josie and the Pussycats and other successful cartoons.

Which word is MOST similar in meaning to *instrumental*?

F brave
G useless
H worthless
I important

5 Read these sentences from the passage.

Takamoto's legacy includes characters of all kinds. But his four-legged creations are his most memorable.

What does the word *legacy* mean?

A something handed down to others
B something that is animated
C something kept for oneself
D something thrown away

6 Read the sentence from the passage.

He became an apprentice, training under famous animators of the day during a Golden Age of animation.

What does the word *apprentice* mean?

F an employer
G an animator
H a contestant
I a beginner

Writing Focus Extended Response

Write a brief summary of "What a Character." If you've completed an outline, use it to decide on the major points you want to include in the summary. Support your response with details from the story.

According to this article, Takamoto was "freed" by his talent. What does his success say about overcoming injustice?

Writing Workshop

Short Story

Write with a Purpose

Use your imagination to come up with a great idea for a short story. Your **purpose** is to entertain your readers. Your **audience** can be your friends, your classmates, or a larger group of people for whom you might publish your story.

A Good Short Story

- centers on a conflict or problem that a character has to solve
- includes a series of related events that keeps readers in suspense and leads to a climax
- provides a vividly detailed setting
- uses dialogue and action to develop the plot
- ends with a resolution of the conflict

Reader/Writer Notebook

Use your **RWN** to complete the activities for this workshop.

Think as a Reader/Writer

Reading the short stories in this collection introduced you to the techniques some writers use. Before you write your own short story, read this excerpt from "The Bracelet," (page 167) by Yoshiko Uchida. Notice how the writer introduces the main character and reveals the conflict.

"Mama, is it time to go?" I hadn't planned to cry, but the tears came suddenly, and I wiped them away with the back of my hand. I didn't want my older sister to see me crying.

← The writer establishes right away that the narrator, Ruri, is facing a difficult **conflict.**

"It's almost time, Ruri," my mother said gently. Her face was filled with a kind of sadness I had never seen before.

I looked around at my empty room. The clothes that Mama always told me to hang up in the closet, the junk piled on my dresser, the old rag doll I could never bear to part with—they were all gone. There was nothing left in my room, and there was nothing left in the rest of the house. The rugs and furniture were gone, the pictures and drapes were down, and the closets and cupboards were empty. The house was like a gift box after the nice thing inside was gone; just a lot of nothingness.

← Vivid **details** describe the **setting.**

It was almost time to leave our home, but we weren't moving to a nicer house or to a new town. It was April 21, 1942. The United States and Japan were at war, and every Japanese person on the West Coast was being evacuated by the government to a concentration camp. Mama, my sister Keiko, and I were being sent from our home, and out of Berkeley, and eventually out of California.

← Additional details further define the setting and describe an **external conflict,** war between the United States and Japan.

Think About the Professional Model

With a partner, discuss the following questions about the model.

1. How is Ruri's conflict linked to the external conflict of war?

2. How do details about the setting help you understand Ruri's feelings?

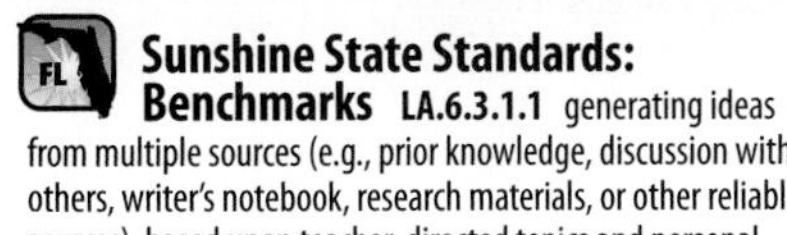

Sunshine State Standards: Benchmarks **LA.6.3.1.1** generating ideas from multiple sources (e.g., prior knowledge, discussion with others, writer's notebook, research materials, or other reliable sources), based upon teacher-directed topics and personal interests; **LA.6.3.1.2** making a plan for writing that prioritizes ideas, addresses purpose, audience, main idea, and logical sequence; **LA.6.3.1.3** using organizational strategies and tools (e.g., technology, outline, chart, table, graph, web, story map); **LA.6.3.2.1** developing main ideas from the prewriting plan using primary and secondary sources appropriate to purpose and audience; **LA.6.3.2.2** organizing information into a logical sequence and combining or deleting sentences to enhance clarity; *Also covered* **LA.6.3.3.1; LA.6.3.3.2; LA.6.3.3.4; LA.6.3.4.1; LA.6.3.4.2; LA.6.3.4.3; LA.6.3.5.1; LA.6.4.1.1**

Prewriting

Choose a Story Idea

When you write a short story, you can draw on your own experience, or you can let your imagination run wild. Ideas for short stories often begin with the question "What if?" What if your best friend won millions of dollars? What if you could read people's minds? Think about whether your story will center on characters, setting, or conflict. The Idea Starters in the margin might help you choose an idea for your story.

Identify Characters and Conflict

Once you have a basic story idea, define your **characters** and the problem, or **conflict,** they will face. What kinds of characters appeal to you? (Think of favorite characters from books, TV, and movies.) Perhaps you want to base your main character on a real historical figure. Make your characters and conflict believable so that readers will believe your character would face the kind of conflict you've chosen.

Plan Your Setting

In some stories, the **setting**—where and when the action takes place—plays as big a role as the characters or conflict. The chart below shows a plan for the setting of "Apples in the Snow," the Student Draft that begins on page 215. Create your own chart to brainstorm details about your story's setting.

Setting	Details
Place: Where does the story take place?	The story takes place in a small village in the southwestern United States.
Time: When does it take place, and how much time passes during the story?	The story takes place in modern times, and several days pass during the story.
Mood: How does the setting affect the conflict and characters?	A boy in a Native American village wants to become the tribe's medicine man. He is instructed by his elders to wander through the hills looking for apples in the snow.

Idea Starters

- a personal experience
- a news story that would make a good short story
- an interesting person who could be a model for your main character
- a particular problem that the characters have to overcome
- a "what if?" situation

Your Turn

Get Started Make notes in your **RWN** about your **story idea, conflict,** and **setting.** Then, write answers to these questions about your main character:

- How does the character act?
- How does the character look?
- What does the character think?
- What does the character say?
- How do other characters react to the main character?

Learn It Online
Try using an interactive graphic organizer at:

go.hrw.com  L6-211  Go

Think About Purpose and Audience

The **purpose** in writing a short story is usually to entertain. That doesn't mean the story has to be funny. It can be scary, thrilling, mysterious, tragic, or hilarious. Whichever direction your story takes, you want to keep your reader wondering what will happen next.

Who are your readers? Think about the **audience** you want to reach. Are they people you know? If so, what kind of plot would interest them? What types of characters would they relate to? What background information would you need to provide? If you want to reach a larger audience—people you don't know—what general assumptions can you make? What do most people find interesting, and why? Try to imagine the people you are writing for, and keep them in mind as you draft your story.

Writing Tip

Thinking about the problem, or **conflict,** in a story can help you develop your ideas. Will your story have an internal conflict to move the action of the plot, or will it have an external conflict?

Internal Conflict: A character struggles with an internal problem, such as insecurity, pride, or the desire to achieve a goal.

External Conflict: A character struggles with outside forces, such as another character or something in the environment.

Build the Plot

Your story's **plot**—the things that happen in the story—should have four main elements: the **conflict;** the **complications** that arise as characters deal with the conflict; the **climax,** or point of highest drama; and the **resolution,** which shows how the conflict is resolved. You can visualize these four elements in a diagram that shows the typical "shape" of a story.

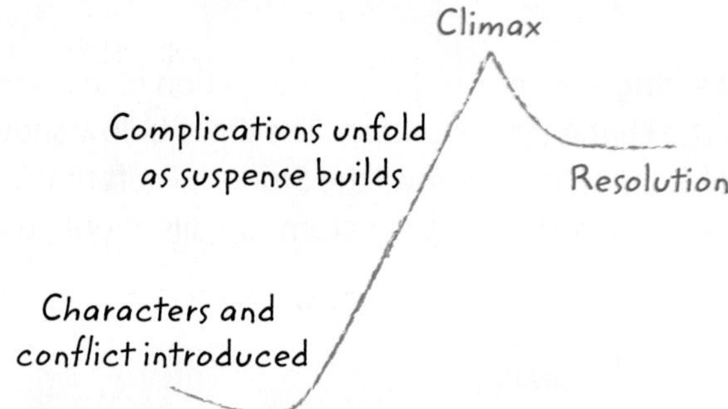

To map out your story, you may find it useful to fill out a story-planning model like this one:

My main character is ____________ (name of main character), *a* ____________ (identify character, such as "detective")

who ____________ (basic situation). *This character wants* ____________ (goal)

but ____________ (main conflict). *Eventually,* ____________ (climax).

In the end, ____________ (resolution).

Your Turn

Plan Your Plot Use your **RWN** to plan and record the **details** of your story's **plot.** Share your plan with a classmate, and consider any feedback you receive. Keep your **audience** in mind as you plan your story's plot details.

Drafting

Follow the Writer's Framework

To entertain your readers, you need to develop interesting characters, a vivid setting, and a believable story with a suspenseful plot. The **Writer's Framework** at right outlines how to plan your short story draft.

A Writer's Framework
Beginning
• Setting and main character
• Problem, or conflict
Middle
• Series of plot complications
• High point, or climax
End
• Outcome, or resolution of conflict

Determine Point of View and Use Dialogue

All short stories have a **narrator,** someone who tells the story. If the story is told by a character involved in the story's events, the story is told from a **first-person point of view.** In this point of view, the narrator refers to himself or herself with first-person pronouns *(I, me, my, mine),* and readers know only what that character sees, hears, and thinks. When the narrator is someone outside the story, the story is told from a **third-person point of view** using third-person pronouns *(he, she, they, them).* With this point of view, readers might be told the thoughts and feelings of all the characters **(omniscient point of view)** or those of only one character **(third-person-limited point of view).** Whichever point of view you choose, use it consistently throughout your story.

Use **dialogue** to develop characters, describe plot events, help create suspense or tension, describe setting, or explain the story's resolution. Be creative but realistic with your dialogue. Consider how your characters would really speak in a given situation.

Grammar Link **Punctuating Dialogue**

Read these rules for punctuating dialogue. Then, study the examples from "The Bracelet."

- Put quotation marks before and after a speaker's exact words. Place punctuation marks such as commas, question marks, and periods inside the closing quotation mark.

  "Mama, is it time to go**?"**

- Use a speaker tag, such as *she said,* to identify who is speaking. If a speaker tag comes *before* a quotation, put a comma after the tag. If a speaker tag comes in the *middle* of a quotation, put commas before and after the tag. If a speaker tag comes at the *end* of a sentence, put a comma or other appropriate punctuation at the end of the quotation, inside the quotation mark, and put a period at the end of the speaker tag.

  "It's almost time, Ruri**,"** **my mother said gently.**

Writing Tip

The way you introduce a character can be as imaginative as your plot. Look at how Yoshiko Uchida introduces Ruri through **dialogue** and the character's thoughts on page 167. Think about different ways to let your reader know what your characters are like.

Your Turn

Write Your Draft Use the Writer's Framework and the notes you made about your story's plot to write a draft of your story. Also think about the following:

- Who will be your **narrator**?
- What point of view will the narrator use?
- How will you use **dialogue** to move the story along?

Peer Review

Work with a peer to review each other's drafts. Answer each question in this chart to identify where and how your short stories can be improved. As you discuss your stories, be sure to take notes about each other's suggestions. You can refer to your notes as you revise your drafts.

Evaluating and Revising

Now that you've written your draft, you can go back and make improvements by answering the questions below. The tips in the middle column will help you evaluate your short story. The right column suggests techniques you can use to revise your draft.

Short Story: Guidelines for Content and Organization

Evaluation Question	Tip	Revision Technique
1. Will the reader be able to picture the setting?	**Put a check mark** next to details about the setting.	**Add** details about time and place, if needed.
2. Do the characters seem real?	**Highlight** character details, descriptions, and dialogue.	**Elaborate** as needed by adding sensory details, concrete language, and dialogue.
3. Is the problem, or conflict, of the story clear?	**Underline** the conflict.	If necessary, **add** sentences that describe the problem the characters face.
4. Are events arranged in order and clearly connected? Does the plot keep readers in suspense?	**Number** each event. Check that events are in correct order. **Bracket** words or sentences that help create suspense.	**Rearrange** events in order, if necessary. **Add** details to tie events together and to heighten suspense. **Cut or rearrange** details that reveal plot developments too soon.
5. Is the point of view clear and consistent?	**Circle** pronouns that establish the point of view in the opening paragraphs.	**Cut** pronouns or details that shift the point of view.
6. Is the conflict resolved? Does the story's resolution make sense?	**Draw a star** next to the story's climax and resolution.	**Add** a climax, or high point, if necessary. **Add** details to show how the conflict is resolved.

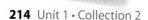

Use this student's draft and the comments about it as a model for revising your own short story.

Student Draft

Apples in the Snow

by Jane Caflisch, Kensington Intermediate

Little Bear longed to become the sacred medicine man of the tribe.

The elders thought it unwise for him to become the medicine man. They said that he was too wild and young. But Little Bear persisted. Finally, the elders said, "Go out into the hills. If you can find apples in the snow, it will be a sign that the Great Spirit wills you to become our medicine man."

Little Bear fasted all day. Then he set out into the hills. He climbed and searched to no avail for that day and the next. He stopped often to pray to Mon-o-La, the earth, and to the Great Spirit.

The opening sentence hints at the **conflict** the **main character** faces.

The second paragraph establishes the **conflict** and uses **dialogue** to reveal the elders' test for Little Bear.

The third paragraph outlines a **series of events** set in motion by the elders' test for Little Bear.

MINI-LESSON How to Use Dialogue for Characterization

Using dialogue is an excellent way to add information about characters and advance the action of the plot. Jane decides to revise her first paragraph to develop a dialogue between Little Bear and his father that tells us more about these characters and their relationship.

Jane's Draft of Paragraph One

Little Bear longed to become the sacred medicine man of the tribe.

Jane's Revision of Paragraph One

Little Bear longed to become the sacred medicine man of the tribe. ^ "Father, I have passed all tests for a young warrior in our tribe," Little Bear said humbly. "But I seek more challenge—more responsibility. I want to be our tribe's sacred medicine man."

"Little Bear," his father replied, "you have my permission to address the elders. Since you are only fourteen, they will surely reject your request."

Your Turn

Use Dialogue Read your draft and think about the following:

- Have you developed your characters thoroughly?
- Are there places where you can add dialogue to help develop the characters?

Student Draft *continues*

A **setting** within the main character's dream is described.

Then, on the third night, Little Bear had a dream. He dreamed that he was standing by a golden apple tree. Around it the snow had melted. Then from inside the tree came a musical voice. "Come pick my apples. I grow them for you, for you, for you. . . ." Little Bear awoke. He tried to think what the dream meant. While he thought, he walked up the hill.

The story reaches a **climax** as the main character achieves his goal.

Thinking and walking he soon reached the top. There he began to pray. When he opened his eyes, there were the golden apples of his dream. He waited for the voice to come, but when it did not, he decided that it had spoken in his dream and that was enough. So he picked the apples and started down the mountain, thanking the goodness of the spirits. When he turned to look at the tree, it was gone.

The conflict is **resolved.**

When he reached his village, there was great feasting. The elders told him that the golden tree was the tree of Mon-o-La. So Little Bear became Snow Child and assumed the role of the tribe's sacred medicine man.

MINI-LESSON How to Create an Effective Ending

In Jane's draft, the feasting occurs before the elders accept Little Bear as the tribe's medicine man. Jane decides to revise her ending to set the events in chronological order and give her story a more powerful ending. Rearranging the order of events and giving more details about the elders' decision will leave readers with a lasting image.

Jane's Draft of the Last Paragraph

When he reached his village, there was great feasting. The elders told him that the golden tree was the tree of Mon-o-La. So Little Bear became Snow Child and assumed the role of the tribe's sacred medicine man.

Jane's Revision of the Last Paragraph

When Little Bear reached the village, he humbly presented the golden apples to the elders. Smiling broadly, the chief elder raised the apples high above his head and proclaimed Little Bear the tribe's sacred medicine man: "You are now Snow Child." The entire village feasted in honor of Snow Child, their new sacred medicine man.

Your Turn

Add Drama to Your Ending

With a partner, review your ending. Does it wrap up the action of the story in a dramatic way? What could you add to your ending to make your story more powerful?

Proofreading and Publishing

Proofreading

After you have revised your short story, you want to make sure your final version is free of any errors in spelling, punctuation, and sentence structure. Proofread, or edit, your writing carefully, using proofreading marks to make the necessary corrections.

Grammar Link **Using Participial Phrases**

A **participle** is a verb form that is being used as an adjective to describe something. Because participial phrases provide action and movement in writing, they add variety to your sentences. When used at the beginning of a sentence, a participial phrase or series of phrases is separated from the main clause by a comma.

Jane used several participles in her story, but she forgot to separate the one below with a comma. She found the error when she was proofreading.

Jane's Draft	Thinking and walking he soon reached the top.
Jane's Revision	Thinking and walking, he soon reached the top.

Jane also used a participle at the end of a sentence and remembered her comma.

So he picked the apples and started down the mountain**,** thanking the goodness of the spirits.

Publishing

Think of creative ways to share your story. Consider the following:

- Record it as a dramatic presentation, and play it for your class.
- Turn it into a graphic novel, with illustrations and speech balloons.

Reflect on the Process In your *Reader/Writer Notebook,* write a short response to the following questions.

1. What was challenging about coming up with a story idea? Explain.
2. What techniques helped you plan your plot? What might you do differently next time?
3. How did you use dialogue to advance the plot? to describe setting? to develop characters?

Proofreading Tip

There are three main areas to focus on when proofreading: spelling, punctuation, and sentence structure. It makes sense to focus on just one area at a time while proofreading. Ask two peers to help you. Assign each person just one area to check.

Your Turn

Proofread and Publish As you proofread your short story, look for places you can add action with a participial phrase. Make sure you set all your phrases off correctly with commas. Publish your story for others to read.

Scoring Rubric

You can use one of the rubrics below to evaluate your short story from the Writing Workshop. Your teacher will tell you to use either the six-point or the four-point rubric.

6-Point Scale

Score 6 ***Demonstrates advanced success***
- focuses consistently on narrating a single incident or a unified sequence of incidents
- shows effective narrative sequence throughout, with smooth transitions
- offers a thoughtful, creative approach to the narration
- develops the story thoroughly, using precise and vivid descriptive and narrative details
- exhibits mature control of written language

Score 5 ***Demonstrates proficient success***
- focuses on narrating a single incident or a unified sequence of incidents
- shows effective narrative sequence, with transitions
- offers a thoughtful approach to the narration
- develops the story competently, using descriptive and narrative details
- exhibits sufficient control of written language

Score 4 ***Demonstrates competent success***
- focuses on a single incident or a unified sequence of incidents, with minor distractions
- shows effective narrative sequence, with minor lapses
- offers a mostly thoughtful approach to the narration
- develops the story adequately, with some descriptive and narrative details
- exhibits general control of written language

Score 3 ***Demonstrates limited success***
- includes some loosely related material that distracts from the writer's narrative focus
- shows some organization, with noticeable flaws in the narrative flow
- offers a routine, predictable approach to the narration
- develops the story with uneven use of descriptive and narrative detail
- exhibits limited control of written language

Score 2 ***Demonstrates basic success***
- includes loosely related material that seriously distracts from the writer's narrative focus
- shows minimal organization, with major gaps in the narrative flow
- offers a narrative that merely skims the surface
- develops the story with inadequate descriptive and narrative detail
- exhibits significant problems with control of written language

Score 1 ***Demonstrates emerging effort***
- shows little awareness of the topic and the narrative purpose
- lacks organization
- offers an unclear and confusing narrative
- develops the story with little or no detail
- exhibits major problems with control of written language

4-Point Scale

Score 4 ***Demonstrates advanced success***
- focuses consistently on narrating a single incident or a unified sequence of incidents
- shows effective narrative sequence throughout, with smooth transitions
- offers a thoughtful, creative approach to the narration
- develops the story thoroughly, using precise and vivid descriptive and narrative details
- exhibits mature control of written language

Score 3 ***Demonstrates competent success***
- focuses on narrating a single incident or a unified sequence of incidents, with minor distractions
- shows effective narrative sequence, with minor lapses
- offers a mostly thoughtful approach to the narration
- develops the story adequately, with some descriptive and narrative details
- exhibits general control of written language

Score 2 ***Demonstrates limited success***
- includes some loosely related material that distracts from the writer's narrative focus
- shows some organization, with noticeable flaws in the narrative flow
- offers a routine, predictable approach to the narration
- develops the story with uneven use of descriptive and narrative detail
- exhibits limited control of written language

Score 1 ***Demonstrates emerging effort***
- shows little awareness of the topic and the narrative purpose
- lacks organization
- offers an unclear and confusing narrative
- develops the story with little or no detail
- exhibits major problems with control of written language

Preparing for FCAT Writing+

Sunshine State Standards: Benchmarks LA.6.3.1.2 making a plan for writing that prioritizes ideas, addresses purpose, audience, main idea, and logical sequence; *Also covered* **LA.6.3.1.3**

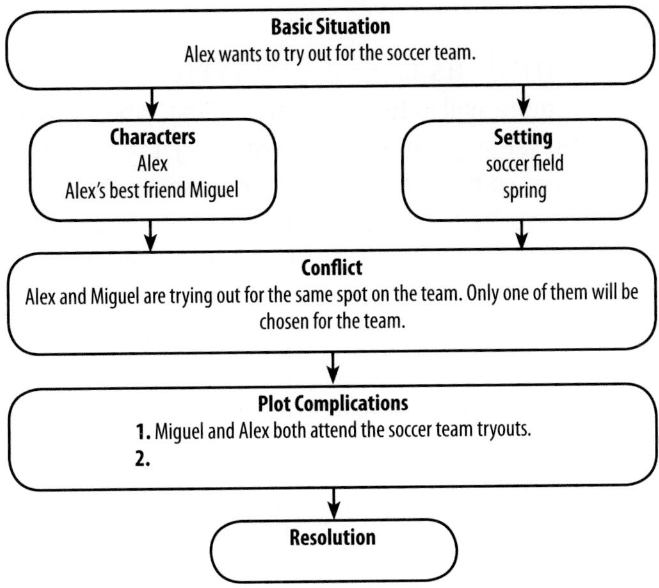

Basic Situation
Alex wants to try out for the soccer team.
Characters
Alex
Alex's best friend Miguel
Setting
soccer field
spring
Conflict
Alex and Miguel are trying out for the same spot on the team. Only one of them will be chosen for the team.
Plot Complications
1. Miguel and Alex both attend the soccer team tryouts.
2.
Resolution

1 Under which topic should details about other players on the soccer team be placed?

A characters

B setting

C conflict

D resolution

2 Which detail below should be added under the subtopic "Plot Complications"?

F Miguel and Alex have a friend named Shannon.

G Miguel is taller than Alex, and both boys have brown hair.

H Miguel plays better than Alex does at the soccer team tryouts.

I Miguel and Alex's school is called Hayside Middle School.

3 Which detail below should be added under the subtopic "Resolution"?

A Alex and Miguel have been best friends for five years.

B Alex and Miguel practice every day to prepare for the soccer team tryouts.

C Alex hurts his foot during the soccer team tryouts, and Miguel takes him to the doctor's office.

D Alex and Miguel decide not to join the team because their friendship is more important than soccer.

4 Based on the writing plan, what is Alanna planning to write?

F a biography of a famous soccer player

G an article persuading students to play soccer

H a set of instructions about how to play soccer

I a short story about friends who play soccer

Presenting a Short Story

Speak with a Purpose

Present your original short story as an oral fiction narrative. Practice telling the story, and then present it to your class.

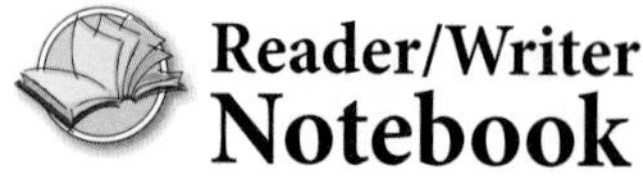

Use your **RWN** to complete the activities for this workshop.

Think as a Reader/Writer Writing and telling a short story require skill in two main areas. First, whether you are writing or orally presenting a story, you must bring it to life for the audience. Your details need to help readers or listeners see, hear, taste, smell, and feel what is going on. Second, you must hold your audience's attention by building suspense around a clearly defined problem that is solved at the end.

When you present a story orally, you have a few extra tools at your disposal. You can use your voice, face, and body to entertain your audience and get your point across. You can also see how your audience is responding and make adjustments when needed.

Adapt Your Short Story

Match the Story to the Audience

You may want to adapt your written short story for oral presentation. To figure out how much changing you want to do, consider your audience and purpose. The audience for your oral presentation will be your classmates. If you wrote your original story for a different audience, you might need to adapt or revise the story so your classmates get the most out of it. As for your story's purpose, ask yourself, "What effect do I want to have on my audience?" Short stories can scare people or make them laugh. They can be sad or lighthearted. They can even teach a lesson.

Set the Scene

Help your listeners understand right away the time and place in which your story is set. If your story has an unusual setting or one people might have trouble bringing to mind quickly, consider giving an introduction to the story, such as, "This story takes place in the Wild West, in the time of stagecoaches, pioneers, and plenty of land waiting to be claimed."

Present the Characters

Have fun with the dialogue. Change your voice for each character, and do what speaker tags can only tell readers to imagine. For example, laugh when the speaker tag says, "he said, laughing." Make sure your descriptions of the characters are as vivid as possible.

Sunshine State Standards: Benchmarks LA.6.5.2.2 deliver narrative and informative presentations, including oral responses to literature, and adjust oral language, body language, eye contact, gestures, technology and supporting graphics appropriate to the situation.

Deliver Your Short Story

It's Your Show!

Remember that your audience is not reading. They're watching and listening to you. Now is your chance to use the types of skills Hollywood stars have perfected. These skills fall into two categories: verbal and nonverbal. Verbal skills have to do with how you use your voice. Nonverbal skills involve your physical self.

Verbal Storytelling Skills

Use the right tone The tone of your voice is the overall feeling it communicates. To achieve the proper tone, first think about how the story makes you feel. Then, think about how you would share that feeling. If a story is funny, you might laugh often or show humor in your voice as you describe events or the details of setting.

Suggest a mood The mood of a character is how he or she is feeling. If a character's dialogue indicates that he or she is feeling sad, make sure your voice shows that mood.

Get into the rhythm The cadence (KAY duhns) of your voice, or the beat of the words as you speak them, can help create mood and build suspense. Think about speeding up and slowing down, stressing certain words or syllables, and varying the length of your sentences to match the story line.

Nonverbal Storytelling Skills

Use your body Just as you change your voice for each character, change your way of moving and standing as well. Use gestures to help support the meaning of what you are saying.

Use your face Think of the way facial expressions, such as a frown, a raised eyebrow, a wink, or a pout, can convey information about the story to your audience.

Make eye contact Let your listeners see that you know they are there. They are a part of the whole storytelling experience!

A Good Short Story Presentation

- has an appealing story line for the intended audience
- helps listeners recognize the setting right away
- brings characters to life through dialogue and vivid details
- presents a clear conflict and a well-developed plot
- keeps listeners interested through the use of effective verbal and nonverbal strategies

Speaking Tip

Using interesting verbal techniques does not mean you should forget to enunciate every word clearly. Always speak slowly, clearly, and loudly enough so that audience members in the back can hear and understand you.

Standards Review Literary Text

Plot and Setting

Directions: Read the following story. Then, answer each question that follows.

The Path Through the Cemetery

by **Leonard Q. Ross**

Ivan was a timid little man—so timid that the villagers called him "Pigeon" or mocked him with the title "Ivan the Terrible." Every night Ivan stopped in at the saloon which was on the edge of the village cemetery. Ivan never crossed the cemetery to get to his lonely shack on the other side. That path would save many minutes, but he had never taken it—not even in the full light of noon.

Late one winter's night, when bitter wind and snow beat against the saloon, the customers took up the familiar mockery. "Ivan's mother was scared by a canary when she carried him." "Ivan the Terrible—Ivan the Terribly Timid One."

Ivan's sickly protest only fed their taunts, and they jeered cruelly when the young Cossack lieutenant flung his horrid challenge at their quarry.

"You are a pigeon, Ivan. You'll walk all around the cemetery in this cold—but you dare not cross it."

Ivan murmured, "The cemetery is nothing to cross, Lieutenant. It is nothing but earth, like all the other earth."

The lieutenant cried, "A challenge, then! Cross the cemetery tonight, Ivan, and I'll give you five rubles—five gold rubles!"

Perhaps it was the vodka. Perhaps it was the temptation of the five gold rubles. No one ever knew why Ivan, moistening his lips, said suddenly: "Yes, Lieutenant, I'll cross the cemetery!"

The saloon echoed with their disbelief. The lieutenant winked to the men and unbuckled his saber. "Here, Ivan. When you get to the center of the cemetery, in front of the biggest tomb, stick the saber into the ground. In the morning we shall go there. And if the saber is in the ground—five gold rubles to you!"

Ivan took the saber. The men drank a toast: "To Ivan the Terrible!" They roared with laughter.

The wind howled around Ivan as he closed the door of the saloon behind him. The cold was knife-sharp. He buttoned his long coat and crossed the dirt road. He could hear the lieutenant's voice, louder than the rest, yelling after him, "Five rubles, pigeon! If you live!"

Ivan pushed the cemetery gate open. He walked fast. "Earth, just earth . . . like any other earth." But the darkness was a

Sunshine State Standards: Benchmarks LA.6.2.1.2 locate and analyze the elements of plot structure, including exposition, setting, character development, rising/falling action, conflict/resolution, and theme in a variety of fiction.

massive dread. "Five gold rubles . . ." The wind was cruel and the saber was like ice in his hands. Ivan shivered under the long, thick coat and broke into a limping run.

He recognized the large tomb. He must have sobbed—that was the sound that was drowned in the wind. And he knelt, cold and terrified, and drove the saber through the crust into the hard ground. With all his strength, he pushed it down to the hilt. It was done. The cemetery . . . the challenge . . . five gold rubles.

Ivan started to rise from his knees. But he could not move. Something held him. Something gripped him in an unyielding and implacable hold. Ivan tugged and lurched and pulled—gasping in his panic, shaken by a monstrous fear. But something held Ivan. He cried out in terror, then made senseless gurgling noises.

They found Ivan, next morning, on the ground in front of the tomb that was in the center of the cemetery. He was frozen to death. The look on his face was not that of a frozen man, but of a man killed by some nameless horror. And the lieutenant's saber was in the ground where Ivan had pounded it—through the dragging folds of his long coat.

---

1. Which word BEST describes Ivan?
   - **A** brave
   - **B** proud
   - **C** fearful
   - **D** sickly

2. What is Ivan's MAIN conflict in the story?
   - **F** that he must survive the cold
   - **G** that he must conquer his terror of the cemetery
   - **H** that he must fight the lieutenant
   - **I** that he must find the biggest tomb

3. What happens to Ivan when he drives the saber into the frozen ground?
   - **A** his heart gives out
   - **B** he overcomes his fear
   - **C** he sees a ghost
   - **D** he pins his coat to the ground

4. What has Ivan accomplished by the resolution of the story?
   - **F** claimed his five gold rubles
   - **G** frozen to death
   - **H** disappeared
   - **I** overcome his fear

Extended Response

5. What overall feeling does the setting of this story create? Support your answer with details from the story.

Standards Review Informational Text

Note Taking, Outlining, Summarizing

Directions: Read the following selection. Then, read and respond to the questions that follow.

Celebrating the Quinceañera by Mara Rockliff

You stand at the back of the church between your parents and godparents, your knees shaking. You feel special, and a bit awkward, in your first formal dress and your tiara. Your honor court has walked up the aisle ahead of you: fourteen girls in pastel dresses, fourteen boys in tuxedos. With you and your escort there are fifteen couples—one for each year of your life. The long months of planning and preparation have finally ended. Your quinceañera has begun.

The quinceañera (kee say ah NYEH ruh, from the Spanish words *quince,* "fifteen," and *años,* "years") is a rite of passage celebrated by Mexicans and Mexican Americans. People believe that the tradition can be traced back to the Aztec culture, in which girls commonly married at the age of fifteen. Today a girl's quinceañera marks her coming-of-age. It means she is ready to take on adult privileges and responsibilities.

The most important part of your quinceañera is the *misa de acción de gracias,* the thanksgiving Mass. You slowly walk up the aisle to the front of the church. You kneel, placing a bouquet of fifteen roses on the altar to thank the Virgin Mary for bringing you to this important day. A birthstone ring glitters on your finger, and a religious medal hangs from your neck, inscribed with your name and today's date—special gifts from adult relatives or friends of the family. The priest will bless your medal during the Mass.

Next comes a sermon, followed by prayers and readings from the Bible. You recite your speech, and the service ends. Then the photographer rushes over, and you pose for an endless series of photographs with your family and friends.

But the quinceañera celebration has just begun, for the fiesta is still to come. You enter to the sound of music, a traditional mariachi band or a DJ playing current hits. You dance in turn with your father, your grandfathers, your escort. You and your honor court perform a group dance that you have rehearsed. Then everyone joins in the dancing.

You're almost too excited to eat, but the food is wonderful. There's your favorite—chicken in mole sauce, made from chilies and unsweetened chocolate. The tables are covered with everything from tamales and corn soup to an elaborately decorated cake.

Later, as everyone watches, your father removes the flat shoes you have worn all day and replaces them with a pair of high

Sunshine State Standards: Benchmarks **LA.6.1.6.3** use context clues to determine meanings of unfamiliar words; **LA.6.1.7.3** determine the main idea or essential message in grade-level text through inferring, paraphrasing, summarizing, and identifying relevant details; **LA.6.3.1.2** making a plan for writing that prioritizes ideas, addresses purpose, audience, main idea, and logical sequence.

heels. In your parents' eyes you are no longer a child. They'll treat you differently from now on, and they'll expect you to act more like an adult as well.

Among your many gifts, one stands out: the last doll. It's not a toy for you to play with, of course; it's a symbol of the childhood you're leaving behind. If you have a younger sister, you might present it to her. You look around at the people who have watched you grow up. You see tears in many eyes. The quinceañera is a tradition many centuries old, but for you it will happen only once.

---

1 Which detail would NOT be used in an outline of this article under a main heading?

A girl dances with father and grandfathers

B honor court performs dance

C DJ or mariachi band plays music

D events that happen at the party

2 Which phrase BEST summarizes the author's description of a quinceañera celebration?

F a cherished cultural tradition

G a long, scary rite of passage

H an excuse for an expensive party

I a sad farewell to childhood

3 Which sentence BEST states the main idea of this article?

A The food is the best part of the quinceañera.

B The quinceañera happens only once in a girl's lifetime.

C The quinceañera is a girl's rite of passage into adulthood.

D Girls who celebrate their quinceañera usually do not appreciate what it represents.

4 Which one would you NOT include in a summary of this article?

F a definition of the word quinceañera

G a description of the parts of the quinceañera celebration

H a detailed list of the food, music, and gifts at a typical quinceañera

I an explanation of the significance of the quinceañera in a girl's life

Extended Response

5 Suppose you were taking notes on this article. Re-read the third and fourth paragraphs. Then, discuss four events from the quinceañera ceremony you would include in your notes. Discuss the events in the order they take place, and explain why each event is significant. Support your response with details from the text.

READ THINK EXPLAIN

Standards Review Vocabulary

Sunshine State Standards: Benchmarks LA.6.1.6.3 use context clues to determine meanings of unfamiliar words.

Context Clues

Directions: Use context clues to determine the meaning of the Vocabulary word in each of the following sentences.

Practicing For FCAT

1. Read the sentence from the story "Just Once."

   He was just strong and fast and a little bit devastating as the left tackle of the Bedford City Bears.

   What does *devastating* mean?

   A destructive
   B interesting
   C fulfilling
   D disappointing

2. Read the sentence from the story "All Summer in a Day."

   There was talk that her father and mother were taking her back to Earth next year; it seemed vital to her that they do so, thought it would mean the loss of thousands of dollars to her family.

   What does the word *vital* mean?

   F exciting
   G unfortunate
   H necessary
   I dangerous

3. Read the sentence from "Just Once."

   He gave a tolerant smile and a little nod and said, "You keep right on blocking..."

   What does *tolerant* mean?

   A tired
   B patient
   C confused
   D slow moving

4. Read the sentence from the story "The Bracelet."

   The United States and Japan were at war, and every Japanese person on the West Coast was being evacuated by the government to a concentration camp.

   What does the word *evacuated* mean?

   F cared for
   G forgotten
   H removed
   I misplaced

5. Read the sentences from "Just Once."

   How did Jerry do that? Well, no time to ponder that one right now.

   What does *ponder* mean?

   A think over
   B recover from
   C regret
   D shout

Academic Vocabulary

Directions: Use context clues to determine the meaning of the italicized Academic Vocabulary word in the sentence below.

6. Read this sentence.

   She had not made anything with paper before, so she was eager to *create* the origami flower.

   What does the word *create* mean?

   F destroy
   G include
   H produce
   I study

PRACTICING FOR FCAT

Standards Review 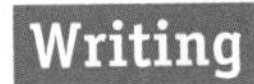

FL **Sunshine State Standards: Benchmarks** **LA.6.2.1.2** locate and analyze the elements of plot structure, including exposition, setting, character development, rising/falling action, conflict/resolution, and theme in a variety of fiction; *Also covered* **LA.6.2.1.7**

Short Story

Directions: Read this paragraph from a short story. Then, answer each question.

Flat Out of Luck

Mrs. Fiona McNulty was late. She smashed her wig onto her head, pulled up the suspenders on her overalls, crammed her feet into the openings of her oversized shoes, grabbed her bag of tricks, and raced out the door to her small car. "Oops," she thought to herself, "I should have had that tire checked. It looks low. I don't have time to check it now. I'll do it on the way home from the birthday party." Fifteen minutes later, in the middle of the five o'clock rush-hour traffic jam, Mrs. McNulty felt the tire go flat. She braced herself and moved as quickly as she could to the side of the road. She turned off the motor and climbed out of her car. "Great! What do I do now?" she thought. Mrs. McNulty was already late for her appearance at a child's birthday party as JoJo the Juggling Clown.

1 Which phrase does the writer use to establish the setting?

A "crammed her feet into the openings of her oversized shoes"

B "in the middle of the five o'clock rush-hour traffic jam"

C "braced herself and moved as quickly as she could"

D "should have had that tire checked"

2 Which sentence would be appropriate if the writer wanted to add sensory details to the story?

F The birthday party was at a house across town.

G She had to hurry if she wanted to be on time.

H She couldn't call anyone because she had left her cell phone at home.

I Passersby stared at the clown in a red wig and baggy overalls.

3 Why did the writer identify the character first as Mrs. Fiona McNulty and later as JoJo the Juggling Clown?

A to reveal that Mrs. McNulty is not a real person

B to clarify that the character changed her clothing in the car

C to create suspense by describing Mrs. McNulty's strange clothing before revealing that it is a clown's costume

D to cause the reader to feel sympathetic about Mrs. McNulty's situation

Read On

For Independent Reading

Fiction

Nothing but the Truth

Philip Molloy is suspended when he defies school policy by humming along to the national anthem. He *says* he is humming to be patriotic. But that's only part of the story: He really wants to irritate his English teacher, because Philip made a D in her class and it kept him off the track team. Philip's deception turns a minor infraction into a media circus in Avi's popular novel *Nothing but the Truth.*

Life As We Knew It

Imagine your life as the earth changes drastically overnight. An asteroid has knocked the moon from its orbit, causing gigantic tsunamis, worldwide earthquakes, and violent volcanoes, whose ashes blot out the sun. In Susan Beth Pfeffer's novel *Life As We Knew It,* fifteen-year-old Miranda keeps a journal as summer turns into arctic winter and her family survives on stockpiled supplies. Follow Miranda's story as she struggles to hold on to her most precious resource—hope.

Love That Dog

Do only girls write poetry? That's what the boy in *Love That Dog* thinks. As you follow the story of a boy and his dog, you'll see how encouragement, a pencil and some paper, and a great dog can help a guy find his voice. Sharon Creech's *Love That Dog* has won or been nominated for more than thirty awards.

Roughnecks

Once in a while you get a second chance. For Travis Cody, today is one of those times. His team, the Oil Camp Roughnecks, is facing the Pineview Pelicans for the state championship. Travis will have forty-eight minutes to redeem himself in a face-off with his rival, Jericho Grooms. In his debut novel set in southern Louisiana, Thomas Cochran takes us out on the gridiron and inside the mind of Travis Cody, who has one chance, one game, to prove he isn't a quitter.

Sunshine State Standards: **Benchmarks** **LA.6.2.1.10** use interest and recommendation of others to select a variety of age appropriate fiction materials (e.g., novels, historical fiction, mythology, poetry) to expand the core knowledge necessary to connect topics and function as a fully literate member of a shared culture; *Also covered* **LA.6.2.2.5**

Nonfiction

Through My Eyes

In *Through My Eyes,* Ruby Bridges tells what it was like to be the first African American student in an all-white elementary school. In this moving memoir, we see her confronting abuse and isolation with remarkable courage. Newspaper articles, photographs, and quotations from the time provide a deeper understanding of her struggle.

How We Lived: Invasion, War and Travel

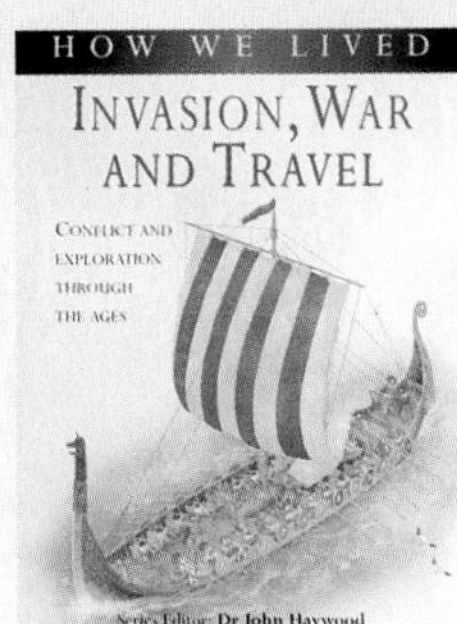

As early people found new methods of transportation, they saw new and distant lands. To expand their own civilization, they often had to fight for the new land. *Invasion, War and Travel* traces more than ten thousand years of the development of travel, empires, and weapons and the way each one influenced the other. John Haywood, editor of the How We Lived series, has included hundreds of maps, works of art, time lines, and photographs.

Here's Looking at Me: How Artists See Themselves

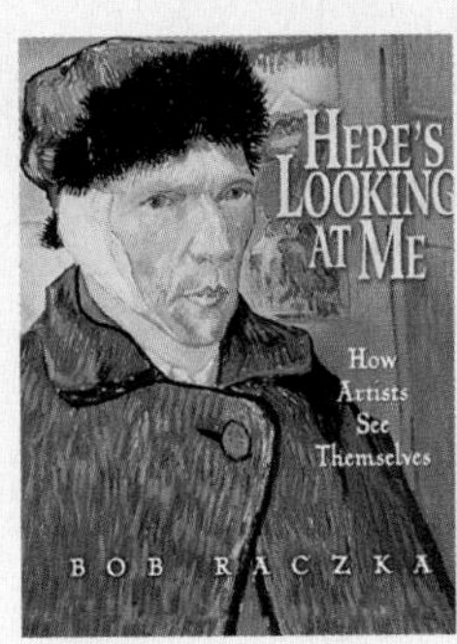

A self-portrait can sometimes tell you more about an artist than a detailed biography. In *Here's Looking at Me,* author Bob Raczka has chosen fourteen self-portraits by artists spanning more than five hundred years. The reproductions are clear and in color, and Razka's descriptions give you background into the artists' lives and history.

I Want to Be an Astronaut

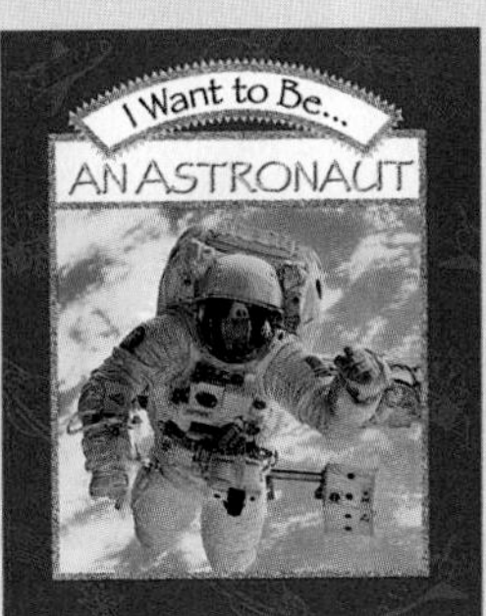

Filled with facts about the history and future of space exploration, *I Want to Be an Astronaut* by Stephanie Maze launches you toward a career as an astronaut. This book will help you take the first steps necessary to make your dreams of traveling to the moon and beyond come true.

Learn It Online

Find study guides for *Nothing but the Truth* and *Roughnecks* at *NovelWise* on:

go.hrw.com L6-229 

EXPIRED

COLLECTION 3

Short Story: Character

INFORMATIONAL TEXT FOCUS

Comparison-and-Contrast Text Structure

"Always do right; this will gratify some people and astonish the rest."

—Mark Twain

What Do You Think

How do you know what the right thing to do is? What do you think motivates people to "do right"?

Found-object faces by Jim Shores.

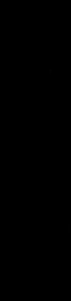

Learn It Online

Use *PowerNotes* to get to know the selections in this collection.

go.hrw.com L6-231 Go

Literary Focus

by **Linda Rief**

How Do Characters in Conflict Influence the Plot of a Story?

Without them there are no stories. Good stories make you imagine how they look, act, and feel. What they say gives you clues about who they are and what they might do. They make you think or feel something about yourself and the world because you care about them. As a story's plot unfolds, you are sad or embarrassed, angry or scared, happy or satisfied because of them. They are characters—the people you meet in stories.

Characterization

The way a writer reveals the personality of a character and brings him or her to life is known as **characterization.** Like real people, **characters** in stories have qualities, or **character traits,** such as courage, laziness, or ambition. Here are six ways an author can reveal character traits:

1. Describing appearance One of the first things you notice about a person is his or her physical appearance, including the way he or she dresses. Writers often provide details that describe how a character looks and dresses.

> Walt Masters is not a very large boy, but there is manliness in his make-up . . . the one white child in thousands of square miles of frozen wilderness.
>
> Walt has walked all the fourteen years of his life in sun-tanned, moose-hide moccasins.
>
> from "The King of Mazy May" by Jack London

2. Describing speech How characters talk and what they say help reveal their personalities. Writers use dialogue—a character's speech—to reveal important character traits. Listen for this character's shyness in her stumbling words.

> "That's not, I don't, you're not . . . Not mine," I finally say in a little voice that was maybe me when I was four.
>
> from "Eleven" by Sandra Cisneros

3. Showing actions and behavior Just as you can learn about a real person by observing his or her behavior, writers can tell you a lot about a character's personality by describing his or her actions and reactions.

> "I'm *not* playing!" I cried, stung. . . . I ran toward where I had put Vern's bat and ball and disappeared with them behind our house. Then I flung them with all my strength into the bushes.
>
> from "Cricket in the Road" by Michael Anthony

Sunshine State Standards: Benchmarks LA.6.2.1.2 locate and analyze the elements of plot structure, including exposition, setting, character development, rising/falling action, conflict/resolution, and theme in a variety of fiction.

4. Revealing thoughts and feelings Writers may tell you what characters are *really* thinking and feeling by writing from a point of view that lets you in on one or more characters' thoughts.

> Today I wish I was one hundred and two instead of eleven. . . . I'd have known what to say when Mrs. Price put the red sweater on my desk. I would've known how to tell her it wasn't mine instead of just sitting there with that look on my face.
>
> from "Eleven" by Sandra Cisneros

5. Including other characters' views A writer may give you important information about a main character by revealing what other characters say or feel about him or her.

> And because of what Walt Masters did on this night, the men of the Yukon have become very proud of him.
>
> from "The King of Mazy May" by Jack London

6. Directly describing character traits The five techniques of characterization you've just read about are examples of **indirect characterization.** Sometimes a writer simply comes out and tells you what a character is like, directly revealing his or her traits, emotions, and background. This sixth technique is called **direct characterization.**

> He has a good heart, and is not afraid of the darkness and loneliness, of man or beast or thing. His father is a good man, strong and brave, and Walt is growing up like him.
>
> from "The King of Mazy May" by Jack London

Characters and Conflict

A story's plot has a main **conflict** that is often played out *between* characters or *within* a single character—or both. The main character in any conflict is called the **protagonist.** A character who opposes the main character is called the **antagonist.**

When characters struggle with forces *outside* themselves, they are involved in an **external conflict**—usually a struggle against other characters, against nature, or against society. Some stories are about **internal conflict,** such as a struggle within the main character to overcome fear or to make a tough choice. The character's traits determine his or her choice—and the conflict's outcome.

Your Turn Analyze Characters

Think of a conflict between two characters from a movie, book, or TV show. List several of each character's traits in outlined heads like the ones below. Identify which character won the conflict, and explain how that character's traits influenced the outcome.

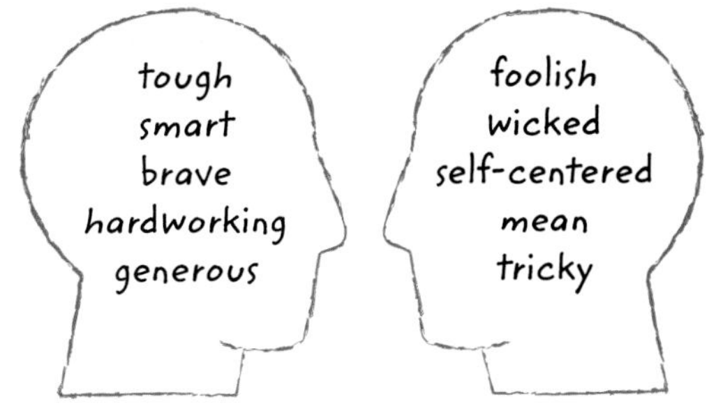

Learn It Online
To understand the role of characterization in novels, visit *NovelWise* at:
go.hrw.com
L6-233
Go

Analyzing Visuals

How Do Visuals Show Characters in Conflict?

Like writers, visual artists of all types also explore characters in conflict, but they do it with images instead of words. Characters in conflict are depicted visually through facial expressions, body language, and actions; the use of lighting and color; and the composition, or placement, of figures in a scene, or setting.

Determining Character and Conflict in Visuals

Use these guidelines to "read" visuals showing characters in conflict:

1. Identify the most important characters in the scene. Which characters are "at odds" with each other, or taking opposing sides?
2. Draw conclusions about the characters from their appearance, clothing, expressions, body language, and actions.
3. Look for details in the work that suggest external conflict. Note how the characters are placed in the setting, especially if they are placed opposite each other or at angles that suggest opposition. Is there a "line of sight" between the characters—an invisible line that connects the characters and "locks" them in conflict?
4. External conflict often involves some kind of action. How is action suggested? Can you predict what the next action in the sequence will be?
5. What mood is created by lighting and color?
6. Are there any clues that a character feels fear, indecision, or some other emotion that suggests some part of the conflict is internal?

1. What **conflict** is being shown here? Is it an **internal** or **external** conflict? How can you tell?

2. What do the **characters'** actions lead you to conclude about the conflict?

3. What details in the way the scene is set up, or composed, indicate conflict?

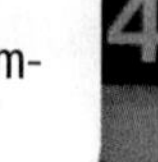

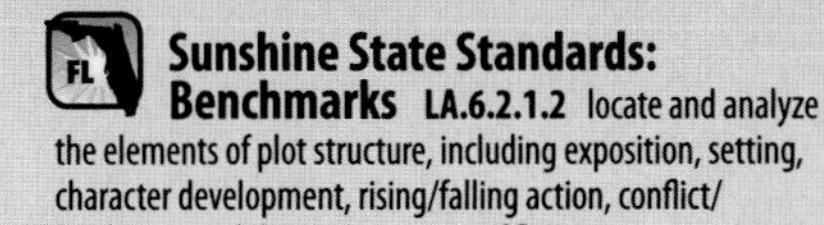

Sunshine State Standards: Benchmarks LA.6.2.1.2 locate and analyze the elements of plot structure, including exposition, setting, character development, rising/falling action, conflict/resolution, and theme in a variety of fiction.

Spider-Man (Tobey Maguire) battles Doctor Octopus (Alfred Molina) in the 2004 movie *Spider-Man 2*.

Your Turn Write About Character and Conflict

Find an image— a photograph, illustration, or other artwork—that shows a character or characters in an external conflict. Are there any clues that an internal conflict is taking place, too? Describe what seems to be going on in the picture and write an idea for a short story based on the image.

Reading Focus

by **Kylene Beers**

What Reading Skills Help You Understand Characters?

I asked a student who was staring at her closed book what she was doing. "Hoping," she said. "For what?" I asked. "That someone will explain this story to me!" I suggested that she could figure out the story herself and do it *while* she was reading, not after. We decided to start with three important skills: visualizing (seeing what's happening in the text), making inferences (combining what you already know with what's in the text to figure out things not directly stated), and making connections.

Visualizing

Have you ever watched a movie that was based on a book you had read and found that the scenery and characters in the movie didn't look the way you imagined they would? The director of the movie may have imagined, or visualized, scenes in the book differently than you did. When you **visualize,** you form mental pictures of the characters, settings, objects, and events described in a story. Visualizing will help you understand a character's traits and how those traits influence story events.

Descriptive Details Pay attention to the story's **descriptive details**—the details that tell you how something looks, feels, smells, sounds, or tastes. Descriptive details, also called **sensory details,** help you visualize characters and their actions. Use your imagination and the underlined descriptive details to visualize the scene in the following passage:

> I put one arm through the sleeve of the sweater that smells like cottage cheese, and then the other arm through the other and stand there with my arms apart like if the sweater hurts me and it does, all itchy and full of germs that aren't even mine.
>
> from "Eleven" by Sandra Cisneros

Tips for Visualizing Characters

- Look for details—such as vivid adjectives and verbs—that help you imagine exactly how the characters look, move, and act.
- Try to visualize the characters' facial expressions.
- Read aloud to hear a character's words. Focus on the mental picture those words create.

Sunshine State Standards: Benchmarks LA.6.1.7.3 determine the main idea or essential message in grade-level text through inferring, paraphrasing, summarizing, and identifying relevant details; LA.6.2.1.2 locate and analyze the elements of plot structure, including exposition, setting, character development, rising/falling action, conflict/resolution, and theme in a variety of fiction.

Making Inferences

An **inference** is a kind of guess based on evidence and your own experience. When you **make inferences,** you first look for clues that the author provides. Then, you combine those clues with what you already know so that you can recognize what the writer *isn't* telling you directly.

Tips for Making Inferences To make inferences about a character, ask these questions:

- What does the writer tell you about how the character acts, thinks, or dresses? What do you know—or think you know—about people who act, think, or dress that way?
- What does the writer tell you about problems the character faces? What does your experience tell you about those or similar problems?
- What does the writer tell you about how other characters respond to the character? In real life, what do such responses usually tell you?

It Says/I Say/And So Strategy An It Says/I Say/And So chart will help you combine details in the story (external information) with what you know (internal information) in order to make good inferences. Follow these steps:

1. As you read, think about what the text tells you. List that information under "It Says."
2. Ask yourself what related information you know as a result of your experiences. List your ideas under "I Say."
3. Combine what's in the text with your own knowledge to make inferences. List your inferences under "And So."

It Says . . .	I Say . . .	And So . . .

Connecting to Characters

As you read, look for ways to relate the story's characters and events to your own life. Connecting to characters by recognizing qualities that you share with them will help you better understand characters' personalities and actions.

Tips for Connecting to Characters Use these sentence starters to connect to the text:

- This character is like me because ________.
- I understand how this character feels because ______.
- I was in a similar situation when ________.
- This character reminds of ______ because ______.

Your Turn Apply Reading Skills

1. If a girl in a story didn't do what her teacher told her to do, what inferences might you make about the girl? Why? What information might change your mind about her?
2. Think about a fictional character to whom you felt a strong connection. Did any of the character's traits remind you of yourself or of someone you know? How did that make the story more meaningful to you?

Now go to the Skills in Action: Reading Model

Learn It Online
Use *PowerNotes* as a visual aid to boost your learning at:

go.hrw.com L6-237 Go

SKILLS IN ACTION

Reading Model

NOVEL EXCERPT

Read with a Purpose Read this story to find out why a boy insists on being called Bud instead of Buddy.

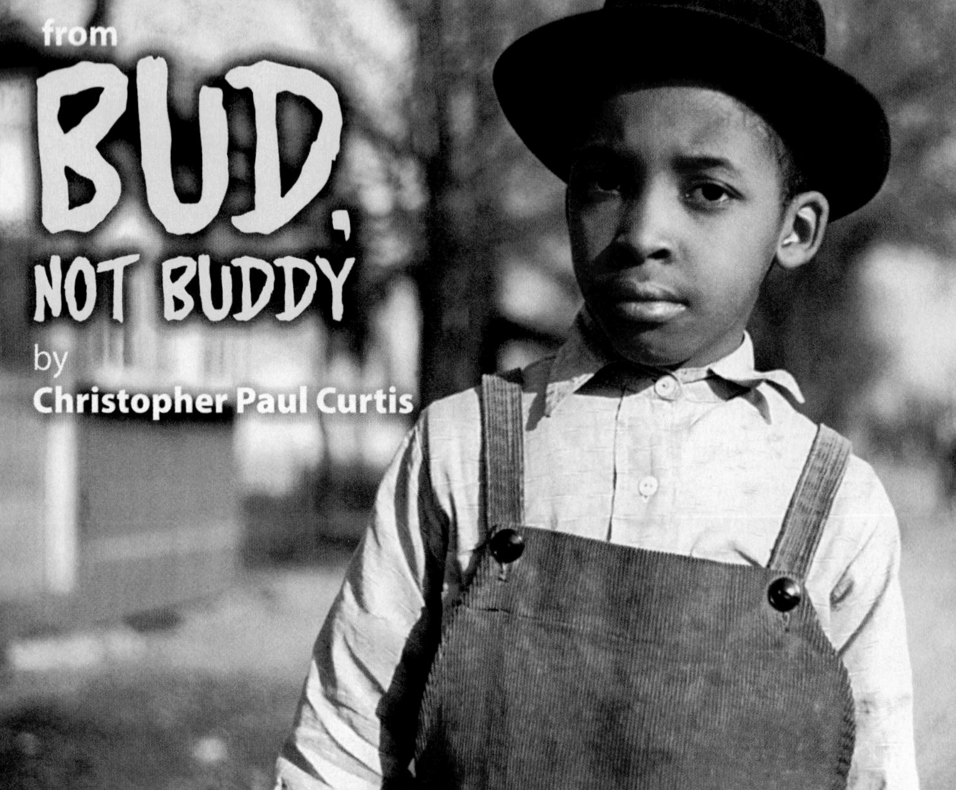

from

BUD, NOT BUDDY

by

Christopher Paul Curtis

HERE WE GO AGAIN. We were all standing in line waiting for breakfast when one of the caseworkers came in and *tap-tap-tap*ped down the line. Uh-oh, this meant bad news, either they'd found a foster home for somebody or somebody was about to get paddled. All the kids watched the woman as she moved along the line, her high-heeled shoes sounding like little firecrackers going off on the wooden floor.

Literary Focus

Characterization By describing appearance and actions, writers signal how we should feel about a character. Curtis uses the woman's high heels and the firecracker sound they make when she walks to tell us that she has a brisk, no-nonsense personality.

Shoot! She stopped at me and said, "Are you Buddy Caldwell?"

I said, "It's Bud, not Buddy, ma'am."

She put her hand on my shoulder and took me out of line. Then she pulled Jerry, one of the littler boys, over. "Aren't you

Jerry Clark?" He nodded.

"Boys, good news! Now that the school year has ended, you both have been accepted in new temporary-care homes starting this afternoon!"

Jerry asked the same thing I was thinking. "Together?"

She said, "Why, no. Jerry, you'll be in a family with three little girls . . ."

Jerry looked like he'd just found out they were going to dip him in a pot of boiling milk.

". . . and Bud . . ." She looked at some papers she was holding. "Oh, yes, the Amoses, you'll be with Mr. and Mrs. Amos and their son, who's twelve years old, that makes him just two years older than you, doesn't it, Bud?"

"Yes, ma'am."

She said, "I'm sure you'll both be very happy."

Me and Jerry looked at each other.

The woman said, "Now, now, boys, no need to look so glum. I know you don't understand what it means, but there's a depression going on all over this country. People can't find jobs and these are very, very difficult times for everybody. We've been lucky enough to find two wonderful families who've opened their doors for you. I think it's best that we show our new foster families that we're very . . ."

She dragged out the word very, waiting for us to finish her sentence for her.

Jerry said, "Cheerful, helpful and grateful." I moved my lips and mumbled.

She smiled and said, "Unfortunately, you won't have time for breakfast. I'll have a couple of pieces of fruit put in a bag. In the meantime go to the sleep room and strip your beds and gather all of your things."

Here we go again. I felt like I was walking in my sleep as I followed Jerry back to the room where all the boys' beds were jim-jammed together. This was the third foster home I was going to and I'm used to packing up and leaving, but it still surprises me that there are always a few seconds, right after they tell you you've got to go, when my nose gets all runny and my throat gets all choky and my eyes get all stingy. But the tears coming out doesn't happen to me anymore, I don't know when

Reading Focus

Visualizing The writer provides a vivid and clever comparison to describe the look on Jerry's face. Visualizing Jerry's expression creates a mental image that helps you understand how he feels: The news has taken him by surprise, and he dreads the thought of living in a family with three little girls—and no Bud.

Literary Focus

Characterization Writers also use a character's own thoughts and feelings to reveal personality. Bud shows here that he is sensitive and not as tough as the name *Bud* might imply.

it first happened, but it seems like my eyes don't cry no more.

Jerry sat on his bed and I could tell that he was losing the fight not to cry. Tears were popping out of his eyes and slipping down his cheeks.

Literary Focus

Characters and Conflict Jerry faces an internal conflict—his own sadness and his "fight not to cry." Jerry's feelings create a conflict for Bud, too, because Bud doesn't want Jerry to be upset. For Bud, the conflict is external as well as internal. Read on to see how this conflict is resolved.

I sat down next to him and said, "I know being in a house with three girls sounds terrible, Jerry, but it's a lot better than being with a boy who's a couple of years older than you. I'm the one who's going to have problems. A older boy is going to want to fight, but those little girls are going to treat you real good. They're going to treat you like some kind of special pet or something."

Jerry said, "You really think so?"

I said, "I'd trade you in a minute. The worst thing that's going to happen to you is that they're going to make you play house a lot. They'll probably make you be the baby and will hug you and do this kind of junk to you." I tickled Jerry under his chin and said, "Ga-ga goo-goo, baby-waby."

Jerry couldn't help but smile. I said, "You're going to be great."

Jerry looked like he wasn't so scared anymore so I went over to my bed and started getting ready.

Even though it was me who was in a lot of trouble I couldn't help but feel sorry for Jerry. Not only because he was going to have to live around three girls, but also because being six is a real rough age to be at. Most folks think you start to be a real adult when you're fifteen or sixteen years old, but that's not true, it really starts when you're around six.

It's at six that grown folks don't think you're a cute little kid anymore, they talk to you and expect that you understand everything they mean. And you'd best understand too, if you aren't looking for some real trouble, 'cause it's around six that grown folks stop giving you little swats and taps and jump clean up to giving you slugs that'll knock you right down and have you seeing stars in the middle of the day. The first foster home I was in taught me that real quick.

Reading Focus

Making Inferences The narrator does not tell you why he wants to be called Bud, but this statement is a clue. You can combine this clue with what you know about people and life to make an inference: Bud thinks of *Buddy* as a little kid's name and considers himself too grown up for it.

Six is a bad time too 'cause that's when some real scary things start to happen to your body, it's around then that your teeth start coming a-loose in your mouth.

You wake up one morning and it seems like your tongue is the first one to notice that something strange is going on, 'cause

Analyzing Visuals

Viewing and Interpreting How well do you think this photograph captures the internal conflict both Bud and Jerry are experiencing?

as soon as you get up there it is pushing and rubbing up against one of your front teeth and I'll be doggoned if that tooth isn't the littlest bit wiggly.

At first you think it's kind of funny, but the tooth keeps getting looser and looser and one day, in the middle of pushing the tooth back and forth and squinching your eyes shut, you pull it clean out. It's the scariest thing you can think of 'cause you lose control of your tongue at the same time and no matter how hard you try to stop it, it won't leave the new hole in your mouth alone, it keeps digging around in the spot where that tooth used to be.

You tell some adult about what's happening but all they do is say it's normal. You can't be too sure, though, 'cause it shakes you up a whole lot more than grown folks think it does when perfectly good parts of your body commence to loosening up and falling off of you.

Reading Focus

Connecting to Characters Relating to a character's traits, feelings, or situations can help you read for deeper meaning. Think about ways that you can connect with Bud. Did you have some of Bud's thoughts when you were losing your "baby teeth"? Have you ever been reassured by an adult who didn't really seem to understand how you felt? Writers often use common human experiences to make their characters come to life for readers.

Unless you're as stupid as a lamppost you've got to wonder what's coming off next, your arm? Your leg? Your neck? Every morning when you wake up it seems a lot of your parts aren't stuck on as good as they used to be.

Six is real tough. That's how old I was when I came to live here in the Home. That's how old I was when Momma died.

Read with a Purpose What has happened in the narrator's life that makes *Bud* a more appropriate name for him than *Buddy*?

MEET THE WRITER

Christopher Paul Curtis

(1953–)

From Storyteller to Author

Christopher Paul Curtis writes highly acclaimed young-adult novels. *The Watsons Go to Birmingham—1963,* set at the height of the civil rights movement, won many awards. *Bud, Not Buddy* captured both the Coretta Scott King Book Award and the Newbery Medal. Yet Curtis never set out to write novels especially for young adults. "When I wrote *Bud, Not Buddy,*" he says, "I just had a story to tell and wanted to tell it. I didn't think of it as a children's book, per se."

From Factory to Fiction

Curtis grew up in Flint, Michigan. After high school, he began working on the assembly line at Fisher Body, a historic automotive factory, while attending the University of Michigan. Curtis explains how his experiences at the factory led him to write:

"When I was in the factory, I was keeping a journal. Writing took my mind off the line. I hated being in the factory. When I was writing, I forgot I was there."

Think About the Writer How do you think Curtis's early experiences, like factory work, might have influenced his writing?

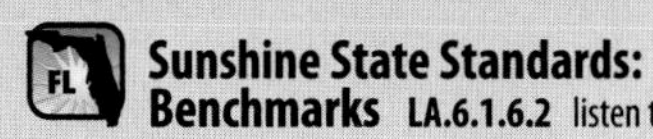

Sunshine State Standards: Benchmarks **LA.6.1.6.2** listen to, read, and discuss familiar and conceptually challenging text; **LA.6.1.7.3** determine the main idea or essential message in grade-level text through inferring, paraphrasing, summarizing, and identifying relevant details; **LA.6.2.1.2** locate and analyze the elements of plot structure, including exposition, setting, character development, rising/falling action, conflict/resolution, and theme in a variety of fiction.

Into Action: Make Inferences About a Character

On a separate sheet of paper, complete this chart with details from the story. Then, use these details and your own ideas to make an inference about the kind of person Bud really is.

Character's name:	Bud
Character's looks:	
Character's words:	
Character's actions:	
Character's thoughts:	
Responses of others:	
Writer's direct comments:	
My Inference:	Bud is . . .

Talk About . . .

1. Explain to a partner how you visualize Bud, Jerry, and the caseworker. Try to use each Academic Vocabulary word listed on the right at least once in your discussion.

Write About . . .

Answer the following questions about *Bud, Not Buddy.* For definitions of the underlined Academic Vocabulary words, see the column on the right.

2. What obvious feelings do Jerry and Bud show that the caseworker does not acknowledge?
3. How does Bud help Jerry adapt to the idea of living with three girls?
4. What details reveal that Bud's circumstances have been difficult ever since his mother died?

Writing Focus

Think as a Reader/Writer

In Collection 3, you will meet many unforgettable characters. The Writing Focus activities on the Preparing to Read pages will help you understand the qualities that define these characters. Then, on the Applying Your Skills pages, you'll have the opportunity to write about the characters or to practice creating characters of your own.

Academic Vocabulary for Collection 3

Talking and Writing About Character

Academic Vocabulary is the language you use to write and talk about literature. Use these words to discuss the stories you read in this collection. The words are underlined throughout the collection.

adapt (uh DAPT) *v.:* change ideas or behavior to fit a new situation. *Characters' traits influence how well they adapt to new challenges.*

circumstance (SUR kuhm stans) *n.:* event or condition that affects a person. *Weak characters are often defeated by terrible circumstances, but strong characters are not.*

gender (JEHN duhr) *n.:* the fact of being male or female. *Name and physical details usually reveal a character's gender.*

obvious (AHB vee uhs) *adj.:* easy to notice or understand. *A character's personality is sometimes obvious from his or her actions.*

Your Turn

Copy the words from the Academic Vocabulary list into your *Reader/Writer Notebook.* Then, use each word in a sentence about a person you admire.

SHORT STORY

Preparing to Read

Eleven

by **Sandra Cisneros**

Cumpleaños de Lala y Tudi (Lala and Tudi's Birthday Party) by Carmen Lomas Garza. Oil on canvas. 36" x 48".

What Do You Think? What can you learn about someone's character from how he or she acts in an embarrassing situation?

QuickWrite

What is your definition of an "embarrassing moment"? Describe a situation at school that might embarrass a student your age.

Reader/Writer Notebook

Use your **RWN** to complete the activities for this selection.

Sunshine State Standards: Benchmarks **LA.6.1.7.3** determine the main idea or essential message in grade-level text through inferring, paraphrasing, summarizing, and identifying relevant details; **LA.6.1.7.8** use strategies to repair comphrehension of grade-appropriate text when self-monitoring indicates confusion, including but not limited to rereading, checking context clues, predicting, note-making, summarizing, using graphic and semantic organizers, questioning, and clarifying by checking other sources; *Also covered* **LA.6.2.1.2; LA.6.2.1.7**

Literary Focus

Characterization The way a writer reveals a character's personality is called **characterization.** A writer may directly tell you that a character is shy or sad or may make it obvious by revealing a character's shy *actions* or sad *thoughts.* As you read "Eleven," notice how Rachel's character is revealed through her actions and thoughts.

Reading Focus

Making Inferences Writers seldom explain everything. You must figure out some things by making **inferences:** combining clues in the text with what you know to make an educated guess. Making inferences helps you uncover the story's full meaning.

Into Action Use a chart like this one to make at least two inferences about characters and events in "Eleven." An example is provided for you. Add rows to make inferences based on other details.

It Says . . . (in the story)	I Say . . . (what you know)	And So . . . (inference)
It's Rachel's birthday.	Birthdays are usually happy days that people look forward to.	Rachel must be excited about her birthday.

TechFocus As you read, imagine how Rachel would tell her story in a video diary. What would she say? How would she say it?

Writing Focus

Think as a Reader/Writer

Find It in Your Reading Cisneros creates word pictures that appeal to the senses: "My face all hot and spit coming out of my mouth because I can't stop the little animal noises coming out of me." This image connects to sight, touch, and hearing. List other sensory details from this story in your *Reader/Writer Notebook.*

Vocabulary

rattling (RAT lihng) *v.* used as *adj:* shaking and hitting together. *Rachel felt all the years of her life rattling inside her like coins in a metal box.*

raggedy (RAG uh dee) *adj.:* torn and in bad condition. *The sweater was worn and raggedy.*

itchy (IHCH ee) *adj.:* causing a feeling on the skin that makes you want to rub or scratch. *The red sweater was made of an itchy, uncomfortable material.*

invisible (ihn VIHZ uh buhl) *adj.:* not able to be seen. *Rachel wished that she could be invisible and disappear.*

Language Coach

Figurative Language In "Eleven," Rachel uses many interesting and vivid comparisons to describe how she feels on her birthday. When she says that growing older is "like an onion or like the rings inside a tree," she is using similes, a kind of figurative language. A **simile** is a comparison of unlike things that uses a word such as *like, as, than,* or *resembles.* Which of the Vocabulary example sentences above contains a simile?

Learn It Online

Strengthen your vocabulary with Word Watch at:

go.hrw.com L6-245 

Get more on the author's life at:

go.hrw.com L6-246 Go

MEET THE WRITER

Sandra Cisneros

(1954–)

Writing from Experience

Sandra Cisneros was born in Chicago, where she grew up speaking both Spanish and English. Although she sometimes had a hard time in school, she eventually became a teacher and a highly acclaimed writer. Today she lives in San Antonio, Texas. Her childhood experiences, her family, and her Mexican American heritage all find a place in her writing.

"Inside I'm Eleven"

In much of her writing, Cisneros explores the feeling of being shy and out-of-place. In this quotation, she describes what she sees when she looks back on her childhood:

> "When I think how I see myself, I would have to say at age eleven. I know I'm older on the outside, but inside I'm eleven. I'm the girl in the picture with the skinny arms and a crumpled shirt and crooked hair. I didn't like school because all they saw was the outside of me."

Think About the Writer What details convince you that Cisneros really *does* remember what being eleven is like?

Preview the Selection

On the day this story takes place, **Rachel,** the story's main character and narrator, is turning eleven years old. Rachel's birthday is complicated by a difficult circumstance at school.

Read with a Purpose Read this story to discover how a misunderstanding at school affects the eleventh birthday of a girl named Rachel.

Eleven

by **Sandra Cisneros**

What they don't understand about birthdays and what they never tell you is that when you're eleven, you're also ten, and nine, and eight, and seven, and six, and five, and four, and three, and two, and one. And when you wake up on your eleventh birthday you expect to feel eleven, but you don't. You open your eyes and everything's just like yesterday, only it's today. And you don't feel eleven at all. You feel like you're still ten. And you are—underneath the year that makes you eleven.

Like some days you might say something stupid, and that's the part of you that's still ten. Or maybe some days you might need to sit on your mama's lap because you're scared, and that's the part of you that's five. And maybe one day when you're all grown up maybe you will need to cry like if you're three, and that's okay. That's what I tell Mama when she's sad and needs to cry. Maybe she's feeling three. **A**

Because the way you grow old is kind of like an onion or like the rings inside a tree trunk or like my little wooden dolls that fit one inside the other, each year inside the next one. That's how being eleven years old is. **B**

You don't feel eleven. Not right away. It takes a few days, weeks even, sometimes even months before you say Eleven when they ask you. And you don't feel smart eleven, not until you're almost twelve. That's the way it is.

Only today I wish I didn't have only eleven years rattling inside me like pennies in a tin Band-Aid box. Today I wish I was one hundred and two instead of eleven because if I was one hundred and two I'd have known what to say when Mrs. Price put the red sweater on my desk. I would've known how to tell her it wasn't mine instead of just sitting there with that look on my face and nothing coming out of my mouth. **C**

A **Literary Focus** **Characterization** What do you learn about the narrator's personality from the thoughts and feelings she shares in this paragraph?

B **Read and Discuss** The author has given us a lot of information about what it means to be eleven. What point is she trying to make?

C **Read and Discuss** Why does the narrator wish she were 102 years old?

Vocabulary **rattling** (RAT lihng) *v.:* shaking and hitting together.

"Whose is this?" Mrs. Price says, and she holds the red sweater up in the air for all the class to see. "Whose? It's been sitting in the coatroom for a month."

"Not mine," says everybody. "Not me."

"It has to belong to somebody," Mrs. Price keeps saying, but nobody can remember. It's an ugly sweater with red plastic buttons and a collar and sleeves all stretched out like you could use it for a jump-rope. It's maybe a thousand years old and even if it belonged to me I wouldn't say so.

Maybe because I'm skinny, maybe because she doesn't like me, that stupid Sylvia Saldívar says, "I think it belongs to Rachel." An ugly sweater like that, all **raggedy** and old, but Mrs. Price believes her. Mrs. Price takes the sweater and puts it right on my desk, but when I open my mouth nothing comes out. **D**

"That's not, I don't, you're not . . . Not mine," I finally say in a little voice that was maybe me when I was four. **E**

"Of course it's yours," Mrs. Price says. "I remember you wearing it once." Because she's older and the teacher, she's right and I'm not.

Not mine, not mine, not mine, but Mrs. Price is already turning to page thirty-two, and math problem number four. I don't know why but all of a sudden I'm feeling sick inside, like the part of me that's three wants to come out of my eyes, only I squeeze them shut tight and bite down on my teeth real hard and try to remember today I am eleven, eleven. Mama is making a cake for me for tonight, and when Papa comes home everybody will sing Happy birthday, happy birthday to you. **F**

But when the sick feeling goes away and I open my eyes, the red sweater's still sitting there like a big red mountain. I move the red sweater to the corner of my desk with my ruler. I move my pencil and books and eraser as far from it as possible. I even move my chair a little to the right. Not mine, not mine, not mine.

But when the sick feeling goes away and I open my eyes, the red sweater's still sitting there like a big red mountain.

In my head I'm thinking how long till lunchtime, how long till I can take the red sweater and throw it over the schoolyard fence, or leave it hanging on a parking meter, or bunch it up into a little ball and toss it in the alley. Except when math period ends Mrs. Price says loud and in front of everybody, "Now, Rachel, that's enough," because she sees I've shoved the red sweater to the tippy-tip corner of my desk and it's hanging all over the edge like a waterfall, but I don't care.

"Rachel," Mrs. Price says. She says it like she's getting mad. "You put that sweater on right now and no more nonsense."

D Reading Focus **Making Inferences** What details in the story suggest why Rachel feels so strongly about the sweater?

E Literary Focus **Characterization** What do the narrator's self-description and speech in this and the previous paragraph tell you about her personality?

F Read and Discuss How do Rachel's thoughts here support the inference you made about her strong feelings?

Vocabulary **raggedy** (RAG uh dee) *adj.:* torn and in bad condition.

Portrait of a Girl by Rosa Ibarra.

Analyzing Visuals **Viewing and Interpreting** What characteristics does this girl seem to share with Rachel?

"But it's not—"

"Now!" Mrs. Price says.

This is when I wish I wasn't eleven, because all the years inside of me—ten, nine, eight, seven, six, five, four, three, two, and one—are pushing at the back of my eyes when I put one arm through one sleeve of the sweater that smells like cottage cheese, and then the other arm through the other and stand there with my arms apart like if the sweater hurts me and it does, all itchy and full of germs that aren't even mine.

That's when everything I've been holding in since this morning, since when Mrs. Price put the sweater on my desk, finally lets go, and all of a sudden I'm crying in front of everybody. I wish I was invisible but I'm not. I'm eleven and it's my birthday today and I'm crying like I'm three in front of everybody. I put my head down on the desk and bury my face in my stupid clown-sweater arms. My face all hot and spit coming out of my mouth because I can't stop the little animal noises from coming out of me, until there aren't any more tears left in my eyes, and it's just my body shaking like when you have the hiccups and my whole head hurts like when you drink milk too fast.

But the worst part is right before the bell rings for lunch. That stupid Phyllis Lopez, who is even dumber than Sylvia Saldívar, says she remembers the red sweater is hers! I take it off right away and give it to her, only Mrs. Price pretends like everything's okay. **G**

Today I'm eleven. There's a cake Mama's making for tonight, and when Papa comes home from work we'll eat it. There'll be candles and presents and everybody will sing Happy birthday, happy birthday to you, Rachel, only it's too late. **H**

I'm eleven today. I'm eleven, ten, nine, eight, seven, six, five, four, three, two, and one, but I wish I was one hundred and two. I wish I was anything but eleven, because I want today to be far away already, far away like a runaway balloon, like a tiny *o* in the sky, so tiny-tiny you have to close your eyes to see it. **I**

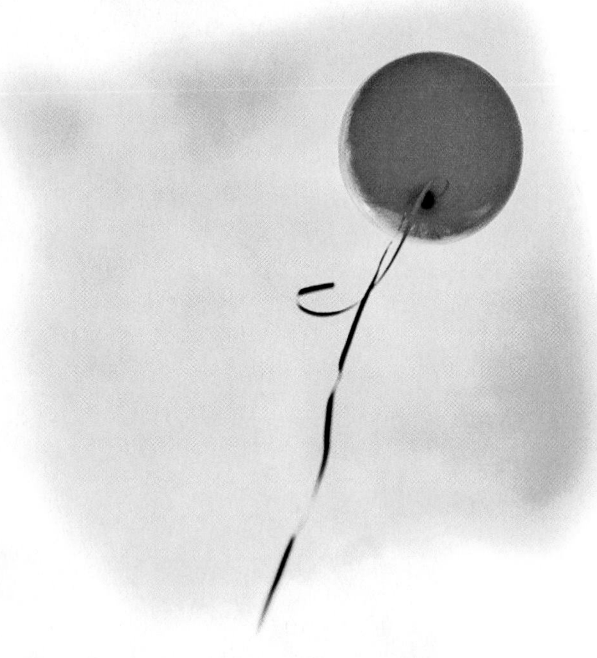

G **Read and Discuss** How does this situation connect with the inference you made about Rachel's feelings?

H **Reading Focus** **Making Inferences** What does Rachel mean by "it's too late"? Make an inference from clues in the story and your thoughts about how you might feel in a similar situation.

I **Read and Discuss** How has this birthday ended up for Rachel?

Vocabulary **itchy** (IHCH ee) *adj.:* causing a feeling on the skin that makes you want to rub or scratch.
invisible (ihn VIHZ uh buhl) *adj.:* not able to be seen.

Applying Your Skills

Sunshine State Standards: Benchmarks LA.6.1.7.3 determine the main idea or essential message in grade-level text through inferring, paraphrasing, summarizing, and identifying relevant details; *Also covered* LA.6.1.7.8; LA.6.2.1.2; LA.6.2.1.5; LA.6.4.1.1

Eleven

Respond and Think Critically

Reading Focus

1. Read this sentence from the story. FCAT
   I'm eleven, ten, nine, eight, seven, six, five, four, three, two, and one, but I wish I was one hundred and two.
   What point is the author making about age?
   A Aging changes the way you react to things.
   B Aging allows you to be more understanding.
   C Aging gives you more wisdom.
   D Aging still makes you the same person.

Read with a Purpose

2. What happens to Rachel that upsets her so much in class? How does this event affect her feelings about her eleventh birthday?

Reading Skills: Making Inferences

3. How do you think Rachel gets along with the other students? How does she feel about herself? Use the It Says/I Say/And So strategy to make inferences about both questions. (Look for other details to add under "It Says.")

It Says . . . In the story	I Say . . . What you know	And So . . . Inference
Rachel calls Sylvia "stupid."		
Rachel calls herself "skinny."		

Literary Focus

Literary Analysis

4. **Infer/Connect** What assumptions does Mrs. Price seem to make about Rachel? Support your response with details from the text.

5. **Make Judgments** Do you think Rachel makes her situation worse by how she acts over the sweater? Explain.
6. **Analyze/Infer** At the end of the story, Rachel says that "everybody will sing Happy birthday, . . . only it's too late." What is "too late"? What can you **infer** about Rachel and about how the situation has affected her?

Literary Skills: Characterization

7. **Analyze** What character traits does Rachel have? What methods of characterization does the author use to show these traits? Support your response with details from the text.

Writing Focus

Think as a Reader/Writer

Use It in Your Writing Using vivid sensory details, as Cisneros does, write a paragraph describing an imaginary embarrassing situation at school. Use your QuickWrite notes for ideas.

What Do You Think Now? Did Rachel do "the right thing" in an embarrassing situation? Did anyone? What could each character have done differently?

Applying Your Skills

Eleven

Vocabulary Development

Vocabulary Skills: Connotations

A word's **connotations** are the feelings and ideas that we associate, or connect, with the word. For example, Rachel calls the red sweater "ugly." Someone who didn't hate the sweater might just say it was "plain" or "unattractive." *Ugly* is a strong word that has very negative connotations.

Your Turn

rattling
raggedy
itchy
invisible

Think about *raggedy,* another word that Rachel uses to describe the sweater. Here are some words that mean more or less the same thing as *raggedy*.

• old	• torn
• tattered	• shabby
• worn out	• scruffy

None of the words has a truly positive connotation when applied to a sweater, but some of the words are more negative than others. Put the words in order, starting with the one whose connotations seem the least negative and ending with the one whose connotations seem the most negative. Include *raggedy* in the list.

For each remaining Vocabulary word (*rattling, itchy, invisible*), identify three or four synonyms—words with a similar meaning. Then, list the words in order of their connotations, from least negative to most negative. Use a thesaurus or a dictionary to help you find synonyms for each Vocabulary word.

Language Coach

Figurative Language Read this simile from "Eleven":

> "But when the sick feeling goes away and I open my eyes, the red sweater's still sitting there *like a big red mountain.*"

Remember that a **simile** is a comparison of unlike things that uses a comparing word such as *like, as, than,* or *resembles.* A **metaphor** is another example of figurative language, but unlike a simile, it compares unlike things without using any comparison words. A metaphor says that something *is* something else: The ugly red sweater *is a mountain, casting its shadow of disappointment over my birthday.* Come up with four of your own figurative descriptions of the sweater in "Eleven." Write two of them as similes and two as metaphors.

Academic Vocabulary

Talk About . . .

With a partner, discuss the circumstance that makes Rachel feel like her birthday is ruined. What makes it obvious that Mrs. Price has a particular view of Rachel? Use the underlined Academic Vocabulary words in your discussion.

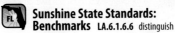

Sunshine State Standards: Benchmarks **LA.6.1.6.6** distinguish denotative and connotative meanings of words; **LA.6.2.1.2** locate and analyze the elements of plot structure, including exposition, setting, character development, rising/falling action, conflict/resolution, and theme in a variety of fiction; **LA.6.3.4.4** the eight parts of speech (noun, pronoun, verb, adverb, adjective, conjunction, preposition, interjection); **LA.6.4.1.1** write narrative accounts with an engaging plot (including rising action, conflict, climax, falling action, and resolution) include a clearly described setting with figurative language and descriptive words or phrases to enhance style and tone; **LA.6.6.4.1** use appropriate available technologies to enhance communication and achieve a purpose (e.g., video, online).

Grammar Link

Adjective Phrases: Adding Word Power

Just as one person working alone can accomplish only so much, one word working alone has its limitations. The adjective *large* can tell you that a cat is big, but what does *large* really mean? Adjectives like *large* or *small* don't pack a lot of power. They don't tell you *how* large or *how* small something is, or *what* it looks like. That's why we need adjective phrases. An **adjective phrase** is a group of words that, like an adjective, describes (or modifies) a noun or a pronoun. Adjective phrases add power to descriptions by answering questions like these.

What kind?	Which one?
How many?	How much?

An adjective phrase can tell you much more about the "large" cat:

EXAMPLE a large cat *with a fluffy striped tail as long as my arm*

Your Turn

Use your imagination, and add more details to the nouns below by joining an adjective phrase to each of the adjectives in italics.

1. *lonely* dog
2. *hungry* shark
3. *broken* chair
4. *tall* tree

Writing Application Go back to the work you did for the Writing Focus on page 251 and add adjective phrases to make your description of an embarrassing moment even more vivid.

CHOICES

As you respond to the Choices, use these **Academic Vocabulary** words as appropriate: adapt, circumstance, gender, obvious.

REVIEW

Write a Character Sketch

Partner Work With a partner, discuss how Cisneros reveals Rachel's personality. Consider obvious clues such as Rachel's physical appearance, words, actions, and thoughts. Also consider how the story's other characters respond to her. Use these details and your own ideas to make an inference about Rachel. Then, each of you should write your own short character sketch of Rachel. Compare your sketch with the one your partner wrote. Did you agree in your views of Rachel? If not, what were your points of difference, and why?

CONNECT

Describe a Birthday

Timed Writing What's *your* idea of a memorable birthday? Based on your own experiences or just on your imagination, describe your idea of the best, worst, most unusual, or funniest birthday. Use specific details as you describe this birthday.

EXTEND

Create a Video Diary

TechFocus Work with a partner to adapt this story as an entry in Rachel's video diary. Write a script, and film the diary entry in one take. Be sure to capture Rachel's personality and voice.

Learn It Online
Describe a birthday through a digital story. Find out how online:
go.hrw.com
L6-253
Go

SHORT STORY

Preparing to Read

THE KING OF MAZY MAY

by **Jack London**

What Do You Think?

How much would you risk to prevent a friend from being robbed or cheated?

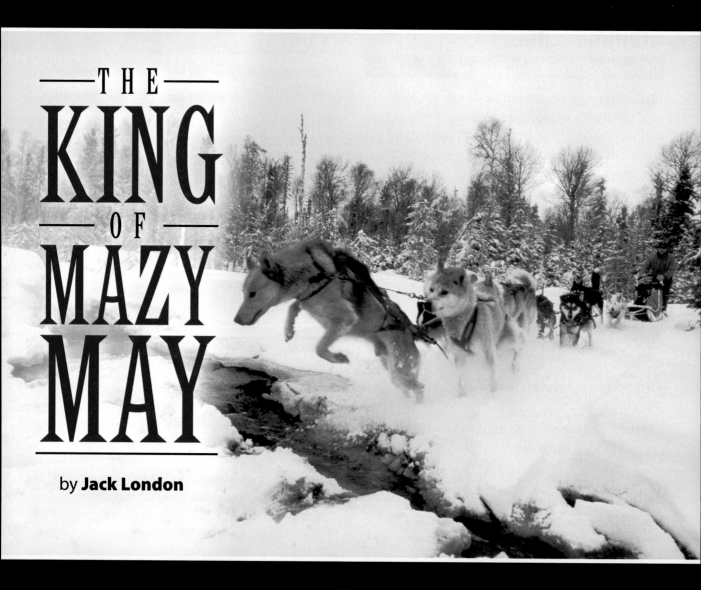

QuickWrite

How do you feel when you see people acting unfairly? What would you do to stop an obvious injustice? Jot down some of your ideas.

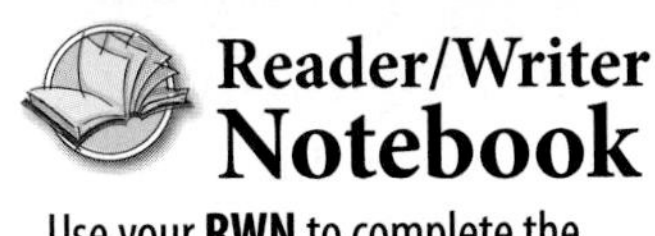

Reader/Writer Notebook

Use your **RWN** to complete the activities for this selection.

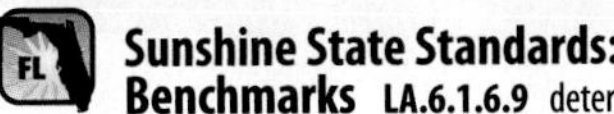

Sunshine State Standards: Benchmarks **LA.6.1.6.9** determine the correct meaning of words with multiple meanings in context; **LA.6.1.7.8** use strategies to repair comprehension of grade-appropriate text when self-monitoring indicates confusion, including but not limited to rereading, checking context clues, predicting, note-making, summarizing, using graphic and semantic organizers, questioning, and clarifying by checking other sources; **LA.6.2.1.2** locate and analyze the elements of plot structure, including exposition, setting, character development, rising/falling action, conflict/resolution, and theme in a variety of fiction.

Literary Focus

Characterization One of a writer's most important jobs is to make characters come alive. In this story, Walt is described as "not a very large boy, but there is manliness in his make-up." In those few words, London lets us know Walt is young, but mature for his age.

External Conflict Adventure stories usually focus on one or more **external conflicts** between the main character and an outside force, such as nature, a disaster, or other characters. In a conflict between people, the main character, or **protagonist,** struggles against another character, the **antagonist.**

Reading Focus

Visualizing Along with the author's words, you can rely on your "mind's eye" to create pictures of a story's setting, its characters, and the action that unfolds. **Visualizing** characters' actions can help you understand a story—and make it more exciting to read.

Into Action In your *Reader/Writer Notebook,* draw a concept map like this, and record descriptions that help you visualize events.

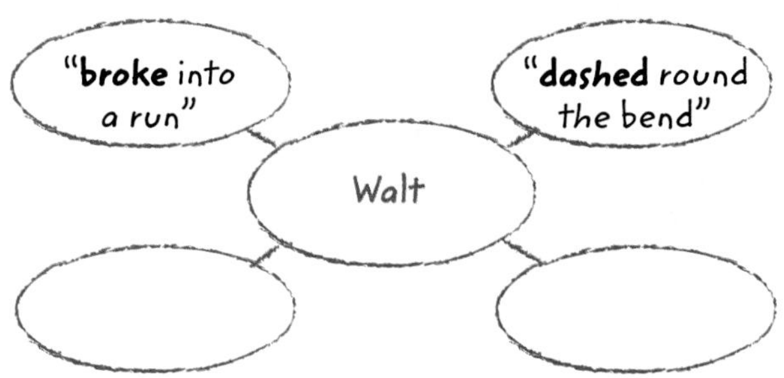

Writing Focus

Think as a Reader/Writer

Find It in Your Reading Writers can help us visualize a situation by using descriptive language. Verbs pack an especially strong punch. Record examples of this story's vivid verbs in your *Reader/Writer Notebook.*

Vocabulary

endured (ehn DURD) *v.:* withstood or held out under. *The dogs endured months of freezing weather.*

claim (klaym) *n.:* piece of land a prospector takes as his or her own. *Walt had to help the old man protect his claim.*

adjoining (uh JOY nihng) *adj.:* next to. *His claim was the one adjoining Walt's.*

stampede (stam PEED) *n.:* sudden rush. *A stampede of people arrived in search of gold.*

Language Coach

Multiple-Meaning Words Some words can have different meanings, depending on how they are used in a sentence. For example, the word *claim* means a piece of land in this story, but it can also be a verb meaning "to demand or ask for."

Learn It Online
Watch a video introduction to this story at:
go.hrw.com L6-255 Go

MEET THE WRITER

Jack London

(1876–1916)

Seeking Adventure

Jack London grew up very poor in Oakland, California, and worked in a factory as a young man. When he was 17, he worked on a seal-hunting ship, which gave him a taste for travel and adventure. Later, he tried a life of hitching rides on trains, which eventually landed him in jail for thirty days.

Determined to turn his life around, London studied hard, read a great deal, and began to write seriously.

The "Gold Mine" of Success

In 1897, London went to the Yukon Territory in Canada to witness the Gold Rush. This trip would turn out to be a "gold mine" of ideas he would draw on for the rest of his life. London became one of the most popular writers in the United States. As his stories were translated into many languages, his popularity expanded all over the world.

London died young, at forty. While his life was short, he had always expressed a desire to live his life to the fullest.

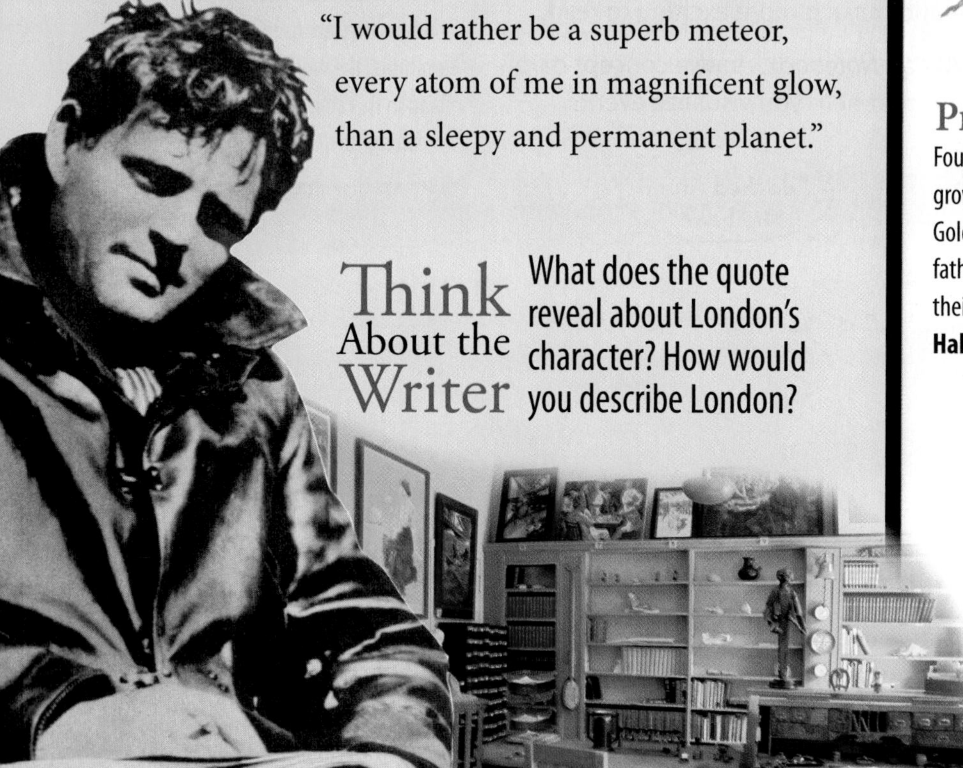

"I would rather be a superb meteor, every atom of me in magnificent glow, than a sleepy and permanent planet."

Think About the Writer What does the quote reveal about London's character? How would you describe London?

Build Background

Gold Rush This story is set on the Mazy May Creek in the Klondike, an area in the Yukon Territory of Canada. This is where the Yukon Gold Rush took place, starting at the very end of the nineteenth century. Thousands of people headed for this treacherous region of northern Canada to seek their fortune by "staking claims," or marking and claiming spots where they found gold. In this story, newcomers are trying to "jump claims," meaning they are trying to steal the rights to the gold in specific areas from those who have already claimed it.

Preview the Selection

Fourteen-year-old **Walt Masters** has grown up along the Yukon during the Gold Rush. Circumstances cause Walt's father to leave him alone to look after their claim and their neighbor **Loren Hall's** claim.

Read with a Purpose Read this story to learn how a young man risks his life to help out a friend during the Klondike Gold Rush.

THE KING OF MAZY MAY

by **Jack London**

Walt Masters is not a very large boy, but there is manliness in his make-up, and he himself, although he does not know a great deal that most boys know, knows much that other boys do not know. **A**

He has never seen a train of cars nor an elevator in his life, and for that matter he has never once looked upon a cornfield, a plow, a cow, or even a chicken. He has never had a pair of shoes on his feet, nor gone to a picnic or a party, nor talked to a girl. But he has seen the sun at midnight, watched the ice jams on one of the mightiest of rivers, and played beneath the northern lights, the one white child in thousands of square miles of frozen wilderness.

Walt has walked all the fourteen years of his life in sun-tanned, moose-hide moccasins, and he can go to the Indian camps and "talk big" with the men, and trade calico and beads with them for their precious furs.

A **Literary Focus** **Characterization** From the way London describes him at the beginning of the story, what kind of person would you say Walt is?

He can make bread without baking powder, yeast, or hops, shoot a moose at three hundred yards, and drive the wild wolf dogs fifty miles a day on the packed trail.

Last of all, he has a good heart, and is not afraid of the darkness and loneliness, of man or beast or thing. His father is a good man, strong and brave, and Walt is growing up like him. **B**

Walt was born a thousand miles or so down the Yukon, in a trading post below the Ramparts. After his mother died, his father and he came on up the river, step by step, from camp to camp, till now they are settled down on the Mazy May Creek in the Klondike country. Last year they and several others had spent much toil and time on the Mazy May, and endured great hardships; the creek, in turn, was just beginning to show up its richness and to reward them for their heavy labor. But with the news of their discoveries, strange men began to come and go through the short days and long nights, and many unjust things they did to the men who had worked so long upon the creek. **C**

Si Hartman had gone away on a moose hunt, to return and find new stakes driven and his claim jumped. George Lukens and his brother had lost their claims in a like manner, having delayed too long on the way to Dawson to record them. In short, it was the old story, and quite a number of the earnest, industrious prospectors had suffered similar losses.

But Walt Masters's father had recorded his claim at the start, so Walt had nothing to fear now that his father had gone on a short trip up the White River prospecting for quartz. Walt was well able to stay by himself in the cabin, cook his three meals a day, and look after things. Not only did he look after his father's claim, but he had agreed to keep an eye on the adjoining one of Loren Hall, who had started for Dawson to record it.

> Walt Masters's father had recorded his claim at the start, so Walt had nothing to fear.

Loren Hall was an old man, and he had no dogs, so he had to travel very slowly. After he had been gone some time, word came up the river that he had broken through the ice at Rosebud Creek, and frozen his feet so badly that he would not be able to travel for a couple of weeks. Then Walt Masters received the news that old Loren was nearly all right again, and about to move on afoot for Dawson as fast as a weakened man could.

Walt was worried, however; the claim was liable to be jumped at any moment

---

B **Reading Focus** **Visualizing** How do you picture Walt at this point in the story?

C **Read and Discuss** What is the author setting up for us? What seems to be the problem?

Vocabulary **endured** (ehn DURD) *v.:* withstood or held out under.
claim (klaym) *n.:* piece of land a prospector takes as his or her own.
adjoining (uh JOY nihng) *adj.:* next to.

because of this delay, and a fresh stampede had started in on the Mazy May. He did not like the looks of the newcomers, and one day, when five of them came by with crack dog teams and the lightest of camping outfits, he could see that they were prepared to make speed, and resolved to keep an eye on them. So he locked up the cabin and followed them, being at the same time careful to remain hidden.

Panning for gold.

He had not watched them long before he was sure that they were professional stampeders, bent on jumping all the claims in sight. Walt crept along the snow at the rim of the creek and saw them change many stakes, destroy old ones, and set up new ones. **D**

In the afternoon, with Walt always trailing on their heels, they came back down the creek, unharnessed their dogs, and went into camp within two claims of his cabin. When he saw them make preparations to cook, he hurried home to get something to eat himself, and then hurried back. He crept so close that he could hear them talking quite plainly, and by pushing the underbrush aside he could catch occasional glimpses of them. They had finished eating and were smoking around the fire.

"The creek is all right, boys," a large, black-bearded man, evidently the leader, said, "and I think the best thing we can do is to pull out tonight. The dogs can follow the trail; besides, it's going to be moonlight. What say you?"

"But it's going to be beastly cold," objected one of the party. "It's forty below zero now."

"An' sure, can't ye keep warm by jumpin' off the sleds an' runnin' after the dogs?" cried an Irishman. "An' who wouldn't? The creek's as rich as a United States mint! Faith, it's an ilegant chanst to be gettin' a run fer yer money! An' if ye don't run, it's mebbe you'll not get the money at all, at all."

"That's it," said the leader. "If we can get to Dawson and record, we're rich men; and there is no telling who's been sneaking along in our tracks, watching us, and perhaps now off to give the alarm. The thing for us to do is to rest the dogs a bit, and then hit the trail as hard as we can. What do you say?" **E**

D **Literary Focus** **External Conflict** With whom or what is Walt now in conflict? Explain why this conflict is external.

E **Literary Focus** **External Conflict** What external conflicts do the men around the campfire assume they will face?

Vocabulary **stampede** (stam PEED) *n.:* sudden rush.

Evidently the men had agreed with their leader, for Walt Masters could hear nothing but the rattle of the tin dishes which were being washed. Peering out cautiously, he could see the leader studying a piece of paper. Walt knew what it was at a glance—a list of all the unrecorded claims on Mazy May. Any man could get these lists by applying to the gold commissioner at Dawson.

"Thirty-two," the leader said lifting his face to the men. "Thirty-two isn't recorded, and this is thirty-three. Come on; let's take a look at it. I saw somebody had been working on it when we came up this morning."

Three of the men went with him, leaving one to remain in camp. Walt crept carefully after them till they came to Loren Hall's shaft. One of the men went down and built a fire on the bottom to thaw out the frozen gravel, while the others built another fire on the dump and melted water in a couple of gold pans. This they poured into a piece of canvas stretched between two logs, used by Loren Hall in which to wash his gold.

In a short time a couple of buckets of dirt were sent up by the man in the shaft, and Walt could see the others grouped anxiously about their leader as he proceeded to wash it. When this was finished, they stared at the broad streak of black sand and yellow gold grains on the bottom of the pan, and one of them called excitedly for the man who had remained in camp to come. Loren Hall had struck it rich and his claim was not yet recorded. It was plain that they were going to jump it. **F**

Walt lay in the snow, thinking rapidly. He was only a boy, but in the face of the threatened injustice to old lame Loren Hall he felt that he must do something. He waited and watched, with his mind made up, till he saw the men begin to square up new stakes. Then he crawled away till out of hearing, and broke into a run for the camp of the stampeders. Walt's father had taken their own dogs with him prospecting, and the boy knew how impossible it was for him to undertake the seventy miles to Dawson without the aid of dogs. **G**

> He was only a boy, but in the face of the threatened injustice to old lame Loren Hall he felt that he must do something.

Gaining the camp, he picked out, with an experienced eye, the easiest running sled and started to harness up the stampeders' dogs. There were three teams of six each, and from these he chose ten of the best. Realizing how necessary it was to have a good head dog, he strove to discover a leader amongst them; but he had little time in which to do it, for he could hear the voices of the returning men. By the time the team was in shape and everything ready, the claim-

F **Read and Discuss** What is happening with Walt here? Why doesn't Loren record his claim as Walt's dad did?

G **Literary Focus** **Characterization** How does the writer show us that Walt is not "only a boy"?

SOCIAL STUDIES LINK

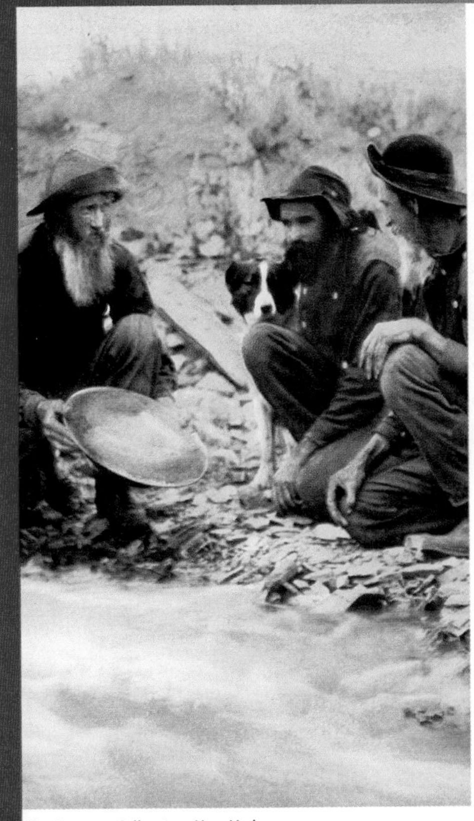
The Granger Collection, New York.

Yukon Gold Rush

Gold rush is the term used to describe a large number of people "rushing" to a place where gold is discovered. The greatest gold rush in American history began with the discovery of gold at Sutter's Mill, California, on January 24, 1848. Almost fifty years later, gold was discovered in the Klondike region of Canada's Yukon Territory. On August 17, 1896, George W. Carmack found a large amount of gold in a creek he named the Bonanza.

Word that gold was discovered in the Yukon did not reach the United States until July 1897. However, the news created a rush of thousands of people heading north on horseback. The thousands of unexpected visitors caused a famine in the region, and many of those hopeful for gold did not survive.

Some of the first people to the region were able to stake their claims and mine a rich vein of gold. Others could not find a claim or did not find gold in their claims. Some of these people continued on to find gold in Alaska. Others, unable to endure the difficulties, returned empty-handed to the United States.

By 1928, over $200 million worth of gold had been mined from the area. Several working mines continue to operate in the Yukon today.

Ask Yourself

Why do you think so many people risked their lives to find gold?

jumpers came into sight in an open place not more than a hundred yards from the trail, which ran down the bed of the creek. They cried out to Walt, but instead of giving heed to them, he grabbed up one of their fur sleeping robes, which lay loosely in the snow, and leaped upon the sled. (H)

"Mush! Hi! Mush on!" he cried to the animals, snapping the keen-lashed whip among them.

The dogs sprang against the yoke straps, and the sled jerked under way so suddenly as to almost throw him off. Then it curved into the creek, poising perilously on the runner. He was almost breathless with suspense, when it finally righted with a bound and sprang ahead again. The creek bank was high and he could not see the men, although he could hear the cries of the men and knew they were running to cut him off.

(H) **Read and Discuss** How does Walt's plan connect to what the author has revealed about Walt's character?

Analyzing Visuals

Viewing and Interpreting Why is this snow sculpture a fitting image for this story? What aspects of the story does it show?

He did not dare to think what would happen if they caught him; he just clung to the sled, his heart beating wildly, and watched the snow rim of the bank above him.

Suddenly, over this snow rim came the flying body of the Irishman, who had leaped straight for the sled in a desperate attempt to capture it; but he was an instant too late. Striking on the very rear of it, he was thrown from his feet, backward, into the snow. Yet, with the quickness of a cat, he had clutched the end of the sled with one hand, turned over, and was dragging behind on his breast, swearing at the boy and threatening all kinds of terrible things if he did not stop the dogs; but Walt cracked him sharply across the knuckles with the butt of the dog whip till he let go. **I**

It was eight miles from Walt's claim to the Yukon—eight very crooked miles, for the creek wound back and forth like a snake, "tying knots in itself," as George Lukens

---

I **Reading Focus** **Visualizing** How do you picture Walt and the Irishman at this point?

said. And because it was so crooked the dogs could not get up their best speed, while the sled ground heavily on its side against the curves, now to the right, now to the left. J

Travelers who had come up and down the Mazy May on foot, with packs on their backs, had declined to go round all the bends, and instead had made shortcuts across the narrow necks of creek bottom. Two of his pursuers had gone back to harness the remaining dogs, but the others took advantage of these shortcuts, running on foot, and before he knew it they had almost overtaken him.

"Halt!" they cried after him. "Stop, or we'll shoot!"

But Walt only yelled the harder at the dogs, and dashed round the bend with a couple of revolver bullets singing after him. At the next bend they had drawn up closer still, and the bullets struck uncomfortably near to him but at this point the Mazy May straightened out and ran for half a mile as the crow flies. Here the dogs stretched out in their long wolf swing, and the stampeders, quickly winded, slowed down and waited for their own sled to come up. K

Looking over his shoulder, Walt reasoned that they had not given up the chase for good, and that they would soon be after him again. So he wrapped the fur robe about him to shut out the stinging air, and lay flat on the empty sled, encouraging the dogs, as he well knew how.

At last, twisting abruptly between two river islands, he came upon the mighty Yukon sweeping grandly to the north. He could not see from bank to bank, and in the quick-falling twilight it loomed a great white sea of frozen stillness. There was not a sound, save the breathing of the dogs, and the churn of the steel-shod sled.

> There was not a sound, save the breathing of the dogs, and the churn of the steel-shod sled.

No snow had fallen for several weeks, and the traffic had packed the main river trail till it was hard and glassy as glare ice. Over this the sled flew along, and the dogs kept the trail fairly well, although Walt quickly discovered that he had made a mistake in choosing the leader. As they were driven in single file, without reins, he had to guide them by his voice, and it was evident the head dog had never learned the meaning of "gee" and "haw." He hugged the inside of the curves too closely, often forcing his comrades behind him into the soft snow, while several times he thus capsized the sled. L

There was no wind, but the speed at which he traveled created a bitter blast, and with the

---

J **Literary Focus** **External Conflict** What in this paragraph makes Walt's struggle more difficult?

K **Literary Focus** **Characterization** The stampeders threaten to shoot Walt. What does it say about him that he continues in spite of their threats?

L **Read and Discuss** What decision made by Walt is slowing him down and putting him in danger?

thermometer down to forty below, this bit through fur and flesh to the very bones. Aware that if he remained constantly upon the sled he would freeze to death, and knowing the practice of Arctic travelers, Walt shortened up one of the lashing thongs, and whenever he felt chilled, seized hold of it, jumped off, and ran behind till warmth was restored. Then he would climb on and rest till the process had to be repeated.

Looking back he could see the sled of his pursuers, drawn by eight dogs, rising and falling over the ice hummocks[1] like a boat in a seaway. The Irishman and the black-bearded leader were with it, taking turn in running and riding.

Night fell, and in the blackness of the first hour or so, Walt toiled desperately with his dogs. On account of the poor lead dog, they were constantly floundering off the beaten track into the soft snow, and the sled was as often riding on its side or top as it was in the proper way. This work and strain tried his strength sorely. Had he not been in such haste he could have avoided much of it, but he feared the stampeders would creep up in the darkness and overtake him. However, he could hear them yelling to their dogs, and knew from the sounds that they were coming up very slowly.

When the moon rose he was off Sixty Mile, and Dawson was only fifty miles away. He was almost exhausted, and breathed a sigh of relief as he climbed on the sled again. Looking back, he saw his enemies had crawled up within four hundred yards. At this space they remained, a black speck of motion on the white river breast. Strive as they would, they could not shorten this distance, and strive as he would, he could not increase it.

He had now discovered the proper lead dog, and he knew he could easily run away from them if he could only change the bad leader for the good one. But this was impossible, for a moment's delay, at the speed they were running, would bring the men behind upon him. (M)

When he got off the mouth of Rosebud Creek, just as he was topping a rise, the report of a gun and the ping of a bullet on

1. **ice hummocks** (YS HUHM uhks): small ice hills.

Analyzing Visuals

Viewing and Interpreting What role do dogs like these play in the success or failure of Walt's mission?

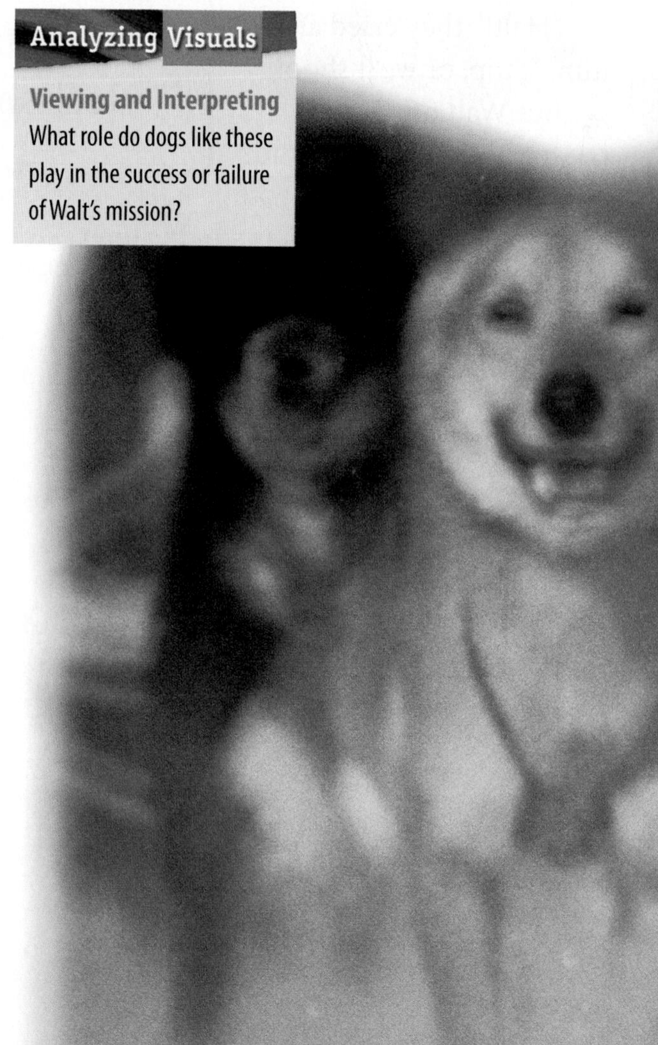

(M) **Read and Discuss** What are the positive and negative points of Walt's obvious need to stop and switch the lead dog?

the ice beside him told him that they were this time shooting at him with a rifle. And from then on, as he cleared the summit of each ice jam, he stretched flat on the leaping sled till the rifle shot from the rear warned him that he was safe till the next ice jam was reached.

Now it is very hard to lie on a moving sled, jumping and plunging and yawing[2] like a boat before the wind, and to shoot through the deceiving moonlight at an object four hundred yards away on another moving sled performing equally wild antics. So it is not to be wondered at that the black-bearded leader did not hit him. **N**

After several hours of this, during which, perhaps, a score of bullets had struck about him, their ammunition began to give out and their fire slackened. They took greater care, and shot at him at the

2. **yawing** (YAW ihng): turning from a straight course.

N **Reading Focus** **Visualizing** How does the author's language help you picture the situation and understand why the men could not hit Walt?

most favorable opportunities. He was also leaving them behind, the distance slowly increasing to six hundred yards.

Lifting clear on the crest of a great jam off Indian River, Walt Masters met with his first accident. A bullet sang past his ears, and struck the bad lead dog.

The poor brute plunged in a heap, with the rest of the team on top of him.

Like a flash Walt was by the leader. Cutting the traces with his hunting knife, he dragged the dying animal to one side and straightened out the team. **O**

He glanced back. The other sled was coming up like an express train. With half the dogs still over their traces, he cried "Mush on!" and leaped upon the sled just as the pursuers dashed abreast of him.

The other sled was coming up like an express train. With half the dogs still over their traces, he cried "Mush on!"

The Irishman was just preparing to spring for him—they were so sure they had him that they did not shoot—when Walt turned fiercely upon them with his whip.

He struck at their faces, and men must save their faces with their hands. So there was no shooting just then. Before they could recover from the hot rain of blows, Walt reached out from his sled, catching their wheel dog by the forelegs in mid spring, and throwing him heavily. This snarled the team, capsizing the sled and tangling his enemies up beautifully.

Away Walt flew, the runners of his sled fairly screaming as they bounded over the frozen surface. And what had seemed an accident proved to be a blessing in disguise. The proper lead dog was now to the fore, and he stretched low and whined with joy as he jerked his comrades along. **P**

By the time he reached Ainslie's Creek, seventeen miles from Dawson, Walt had left his pursuers, a tiny speck, far behind. At Monte Cristo Island he could no longer see them. And at Swede Creek, just as daylight was silvering the pines, he ran plump into the camp of old Loren Hall.

Almost as quick as it takes to tell it, Loren had his sleeping-furs rolled up, and had joined Walt on the sled. They permitted the dogs to travel more slowly, as there was no sign of the chase in the rear, and just as they pulled up at the gold commissioner's office in Dawson, Walt, who had kept his eyes open to the last, fell asleep. **Q**

And because of what Walt Masters did on this night, the men of the Yukon have become very proud of him, and always speak of him now as the King of Mazy May. **R**

O **Literary Focus** **External Conflict** Does Walt have any difficulty deciding to leave the wounded animal? Explain.

P **Read and Discuss** How does the dog team adapt to having a new leader?

Q **Literary Focus** **Characterization** Why does Walt wait until now to close his eyes? What do his actions say about him?

R **Read and Discuss** How does Jack London end the selection? What does the nickname "King of Mazy May" refer to?

Applying Your Skills

Sunshine State Standards: Benchmarks LA.6.1.7.3 determine the main idea or essential message in grade-level text through inferring, paraphrasing, summarizing, and identifying relevant details; *Also covered* LA.6.2.1.2; LA.6.2.1.5; LA.6.2.1.7; LA.6.4.1.1

The King of Mazy May

Respond and Think Critically

Reading Focus

1. Which adjective BEST characterizes Walt?
   A hesitant
   B courageous
   C athletic
   D proud

Read with a Purpose

2. What does Walt risk to help his neighbor?

Reading Skills: Visualizing

3. How well did the descriptions of Walt's actions that you recorded in your concept map as you read help you visualize Walt? Add a sketch of Walt to your concept map.

Literary Focus

Literary Analysis

4. **Interpret** Why do you think the "stampeders" try to stake other people's claims? Why don't they just find their own area to stake a claim?
5. **Evaluate** Explain whether you think Walt did the right thing by taking the newcomers' dogs. Are there any circumstances in which people might be justified in taking something that's not theirs? Discuss.

Literary Skills: Characterization

6. **Identify** Who is the protagonist in the story? Who are the antagonists?

7. **Analyze** How does the writer characterize Walt's pursuers? Support your answer with examples from the story.

Literary Skills Review: Suspense

READ THINK EXPLAIN

8. **Analyze** **Suspense** is the feeling that makes you worry about what might happen next. How does London create suspense in this adventure tale? Support your answer with details from the story.

Writing Focus

Think as a Reader/Writer

Use It in Your Writing Vivid, descriptive language helps you visualize the story better. What powerful verbs did you notice in the story? Write a paragraph describing an action that might take place in a short story of your own.

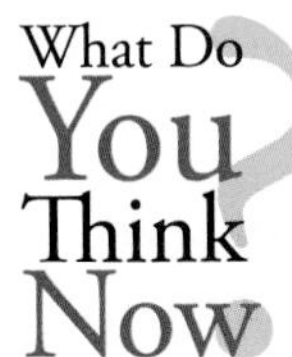

How did the story affect your ideas about injustice? Would you take action, as Walt did, to make sure justice was done? Explain.

Applying Your Skills

The King of Mazy May

Vocabulary Development

Words with Multiple Meanings

Multiple-meaning words are words with more than one meaning. When you look up a multiple-meaning word in a dictionary, you'll find a numbered list of definitions, as in this example.

alarm (uh LAHRM) *n.* **1.** a piece of equipment that makes a noise to warn people of danger **2.** a feeling of fear because something bad might happen **3.** a warning about something bad or dangerous that is happening

alarm (uh LAHRM) *v.* **1.** make someone feel very worried or frightened

If you come across a multiple-meaning word and you're not sure which meaning is the one intended, figure out what part of speech it is. Is it a noun, a verb, an adjective? Look at its **context,** the words around it, to see if you can determine the part of speech. If you're still confused, review the definitions listed in a dictionary. Then, choose the meaning that fits best in the sentence.

Here is a sentence from "The King of Mazy May." Which definitions of *record* and *alarm* fit best in this context?

> If we can get to Dawson and *record*, we're rich men; and there is no telling who's been sneaking along in our tracks, watching us, and perhaps now off to give the *alarm*.

Your Turn

- adjoining
- claim
- stampede
- endured

Two of the words in the list at right have alternate meanings and can be used as different parts of speech. Identify these words. For each word, write two sentences that show the two different meanings. Use a dictionary for help.

Language Coach

Multiple-Meaning Words To figure out a word's meaning, look for context clues. For example, read the following sentence from the story and look for context clues that tell you *which* meaning of the word is being used.

Walt climbed the hill until he was topping *the rise.*

Ask yourself: "Does the word *topping* describe an action or a thing?"

Academic Vocabulary

Talk About . . .

How does Walt's ability to adapt to a variety of circumstances help him survive? Use the underlined Academic Vocabulary words in your discussion.

Learn It Online
Focus on vocabulary. Visit *WordSharp* at:
go.hrw.com L6-268 Go

Sunshine State Standards: Benchmarks **LA.6.1.6.9** determine the correct meaning of words with multiple meanings in context; **LA.6.1.6.10** determine meanings of words, pronunciation, parts of speech, etymologies, and alternate word choices by using a dictionary, thesaurus, and digital tools; **LA.6.3.4.3** punctuation in simple, compound, and complex sentences, including appositives and appositive phrases, and in cited sources, including quotations for exact words from sources; **LA.6.4.2.3** write informational/ expository essays (e.g., process, description, explanation, comparison/ contrast, problem/solution) that include a thesis statement, supporting details, and introductory, body, and concluding paragraphs; **LA.6.4.2.4** write a variety of informal communications (e.g., friendly letters, thank-you notes, messages) and formal communications (e.g., conventional business letters, invitations) that follow a format and that have a clearly stated purpose and that include the date, proper salutation, body, closing and signature; **LA.6.4.3.1** write persuasive text (e.g., advertisement, speech, essay, public service announcement) that establishes and develops a controlling idea, using appropriate supporting arguments and detailed evidence; *Also covered* **LA.6.6.4.1**

Grammar Link

Understanding and Using Clauses

A **clause** is a group of words containing both a subject and a verb, but not all clauses are created equal. Some of them are called **independent clauses** because they have a subject and a verb and can stand alone as a complete sentence. Other types of clauses—called **subordinate clauses**—have a subject and a verb, but they don't make up a complete sentence. Here are some examples:

INDEPENDENT CLAUSE

S V

The **dogs can follow** the trail.

SUBORDINATE CLAUSE

S V

When **they came** by with crack dog teams

When an independent clause stands alone, it is called a sentence. (Usually the term *independent clause* is used only when such a clause is joined with another clause.) A subordinate clause must be joined with at least one independent clause to make a sentence and express a complete thought.

Your Turn

For each of the following items, decide if the italicized word group is an independent or subordinate clause.

1. *Where the dogs ran,* the snow was packed down.
2. As Walt looked up, *a bullet flew by him.*
3. *Loren Hall had struck it rich,* and his claim was not yet recorded.

CHOICES

As you respond to the Choices, use these **Academic Vocabulary** words as appropriate: adapt, circumstance, gender, obvious.

REVIEW

Write a Newspaper Article

Write an article that might have appeared in a newspaper after Walt made it to the commissioner's office in Dawson. Include the main events, unusual circumstances, and quotations from Walt, his father, and Loren Hall. Be sure to answer all the essential *Who? What? When? Where? Why?* and *How?* questions. Use vivid language and an attention-grabbing headline.

CONNECT

Write a Thank-You Letter

Timed Writing Imagine that you are Loren Hall. Write a letter in which you express your gratitude to Walt, mentioning key points of his character that helped him carry out his amazing deed under very dangerous circumstances.

EXTEND

Present a Story to an Audience

TechFocus Imagine that you are Walt and you are speaking to a local group about your experience. Write a speech explaining your actions and describing the things you had to do to adapt to difficult circumstances. Use visuals, such as slides of the area in winter or a videotape of dogsled racing, to illustrate your presentation. Deliver your presentation to your class, acting as Walt.

STORY

paring to Read

CRICKET IN THE ROAD

by **Michael Anthony**

Cricket, Sri Lanka (1998) by Andrew Macara

What Do You Think?

What's the best way to resolve a conflict with friends?

QuickWrite

Write about how you settle conflicts during a game that you play regularly with friends or family. How does

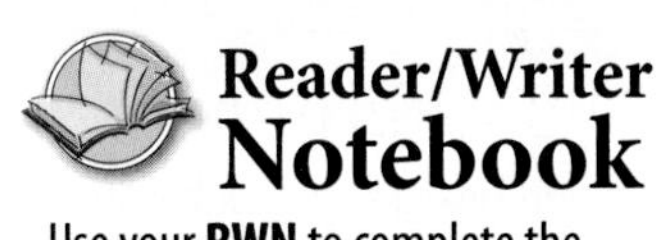

Use your **RWN** to complete the activities for this selection.

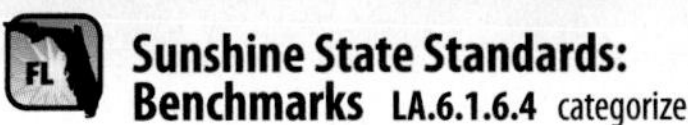

Sunshine State Standards: Benchmarks **LA.6.1.6.4** categorize key vocabulary and identify salient features; **LA.6.1.7.1** use background knowledge of subject and related content areas, prereading strategies, graphic representations, and knowledge of text structure to make and confirm complex predictions of content, purpose, and organization of a reading selection; *Also covered* **LA.6.1.7.8; LA.6.2.1.2**

Literary Focus

Character and Conflict What happens in a story depends on the way the characters respond to the main **conflict.** There are two basic kinds of conflict: **external conflict,** a struggle between a character and an outside force, and **internal conflict,** a struggle within a character's mind or heart. Both kinds of conflict fuel a story and eventually bring it to a resolution.

Literary Perspectives Apply the literary perspective described on page 273 as you read this story.

Reading Focus

Connecting to Characters Reading is more meaningful when you make connections to a text. You may connect the characters and events to your own life, to other literature, or to people and events in the world.

Into Action Use a chart like this one to make connections as you read "Cricket in the Road." Some examples are filled in for you.

I can connect	To myself or my friends	To other stories	To situations in the world
The narrator	He is young like me. He is also a boy, so we're the same gender.	He is tired of rain, like the children in "All Summer in a Day."	I have seen pictures of terrible storms in the Caribbean.

Writing Focus

Think as a Reader/Writer

Find It in Your Reading As you read, jot down words, phrases, and sentences that make the storms seem threatening or scary. Write them in your *Reader/Writer Notebook.*

Vocabulary

torrents (TAWR uhnts) *n.:* rushing streams of water. *The rain was coming down in torrents.*

tumult (TOO muhlt) *n.:* a violent disturbance. *The storm's wind and rains created a tumult that made it hard to hear my friend calling my name.*

downpour (DOWN pawr) *n.:* a large amount of rain that falls in a short time. *Amy got drenched in the downpour.*

depressed (dih PREHST) *adj.:* very sad. *Selo got depressed when the rains came.*

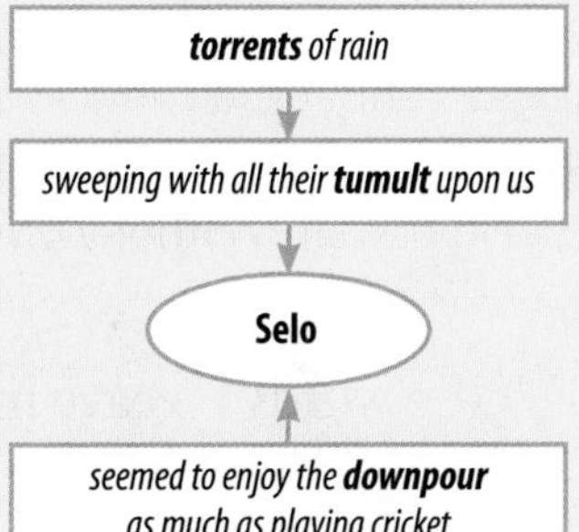

torrents *of rain*
sweeping with all their ***tumult*** *upon us*
Selo
seemed to enjoy the ***downpour*** *as much as playing cricket*
I stood there, ***depressed*** *about the rain, and then I put Vern's bat and ball underneath the house and went indoors.*

Language Coach

Word Families Many words are related—that is, they share a root, or base, word. Which word above is related to the word *torrential*?

Learn It Online

Study words in a new way with Word Watch at:

go.hrw.com L6-271 

MEET THE WRITER

Michael Anthony
(1930–)

From Trinidad to England
Like Selo, the main character in "Cricket in the Road," Michael Anthony grew up in Mayaro, Trinidad. He went to a technical school, after which he worked at a foundry, or metal-casting factory. Wanting to be a journalist, Michael Anthony left Trinidad for England in his early twenties, hoping to improve his chances at a newspaper career. He eventually went to work for the Reuters News Agency. While in England, he married a woman from Trinidad. Anthony moved his family to Brazil for two years before returning to Trinidad in 1970.

A Major Caribbean Writer
Over the course of his career, Michael Anthony has published more than twenty travel books, novels, and books of short stories, and has become a major Caribbean writer. His first novel—*The Games Were Coming*—was published in 1963. The images of his life in Trinidad play an important role in his writing. In the poem "Tree of My Dreams," which recalls his childhood in Mayaro, Anthony observes,

> "The words I weave in memory's name,
> I weave. It is the truth."

Think About the Writer How do you think a writer's childhood home influences what he or she writes about?

Build Background
Trinidad and Tobago The Caribbean island of Trinidad, where "Cricket in the Road" is set, is just off the coast of Venezuela. Together with the island of Tobago, Trinidad forms a country that has been independent since 1962. Before that, Trinidad and Tobago was a British colony.

Cricket The game of cricket is similar to baseball. Its modern form originated in England and spread to many of the British colonies, where it is still popular today.

Preview the Selection
During the rainy season in Trinidad, a boy named **Selo** tries to play cricket with his friends **Vern** and **Amy,** but they are interrupted by a fierce storm.

Read with a Purpose Read this story to find out how three friends in Trinidad deal with a conflict that arises during a game.

CRICKET IN THE ROAD

by **Michael Anthony**

In the rainy season we got few chances to play cricket in the road, for whenever we were at the game, the rains came down, chasing us into the yard again. That was the way it was in Mayaro in the rainy season. The skies were always overcast, and over the sea the rain clouds hung low and gray and scowling, and the winds blew in and whipped angrily through the palms. And when the winds were strongest and raging, the low-hanging clouds would become dense and black, and the sea would roar, and the torrents of rain would come sweeping with all their tumult upon us. (A)

We had just run in from the rain. Amy and Vern from next door were in good spirits and laughing, for oddly enough they seemed to enjoy the downpour as much as playing cricket in the road. Amy was in our yard, giggling and pretending to drink the falling rain, with her face all wet and her clothes drenched, and Vern, who was sheltering under the eaves,[1] excitedly jumped out to join her. "Rain, rain, go to Spain," they shouted. And presently their mother, who must have heard the noise and knew,

(A) **Literary Perspectives** **Author's Techniques** How does the writer create a vivid sense of place in this opening paragraph? What is most effective about the author's technique?

Vocabulary **torrents** (TAWR uhnts) *n.:* rushing streams of water.
tumult (TOO muhlt) *n.:* a violent disturbance.
downpour (DOWN pawr) *n.:* a large amount of rain that falls in a short time.

1. **eaves:** lower edges of a roof extending beyond the sides of a building.

Literary Perspectives

Analyzing an Author's Techniques The author's-technique perspective considers each literary text—whether it is fiction, nonfiction, poetry, or some other form—to be a work of art. The writer is the artist. We discover the beauty of the writer's art by examining the techniques he or she uses. Writers of fiction use literary tools such as figurative language, imagery, and characterization to help convey the mood, tone, and theme of a work. When you're reading a text from this perspective, you don't need to consider such "ouside the text" factors as the writer's biography or historical or current events. Instead, you focus on exactly what's there in the text: the writer's language. Read closely to keep track of—and appreciate— how the writer uses certain techniques to create literary effects. These effects are what help give the work a theme or meaning. As you read, be sure to notice the notes and questions in the text, which will guide you in using this perspective.

appeared from next door, and Vern and Amy vanished through the hedge.

I stood there, depressed about the rain, and then I put Vern's bat and ball underneath the house and went indoors. "Stupes!" I said to myself. I had been batting when the rains came down. It was only when *I* was batting that the rains came down! I wiped my feet so I wouldn't soil the sheets and went up on the bed. I was sitting, sad, and wishing that the rain would really go away—go to Spain, as Vern said—when my heart seemed to jump out of me. A deafening peal[2] of thunder struck across the sky. **B**

THE RAIN HAMMERED AWFULLY ON THE ROOFTOP, AND I KEPT TENSE FOR THE THUNDER WHICH I KNEW WOULD BREAK AGAIN.

Quickly I closed the window. The rain hammered awfully on the rooftop, and I kept tense for the thunder which I knew would break again and for the unearthly flashes of lightning.

Secretly I was afraid of the violent weather. I was afraid of the rain, and of the thunder and the lightning that came with them, and of the sea beating against the headlands,[3] and of the storm winds, and of everything being so deathlike when the rains were gone. I started again at another flash of lightning, and before I had recovered from this, yet another terrifying peal of thunder hit the air. I screamed. I heard my mother running into the room. Thunder struck again, and I dashed under the bed. **C**

"Selo! Selo! First bat!" Vern shouted from the road. The rains had ceased and the sun had come out, but I was not quite recovered yet. I brought myself reluctantly to look out from the front door, and there was Vern, grinning and impatient and beckoning to me. **D**

"First bat," he said. And as if noting my indifference, he looked toward Amy, who was just coming out to play. "Who second bat?" he said.

"Me!" I said.

"Me!" shouted Amy almost at the same time.

"Amy second bat," Vern said.

"No, I said 'Me' first," I protested.

Vern grew impatient while Amy and I argued. Then an idea seemed to strike him. He took out a penny from his pocket. "Toss for it," he said. "What you want?" **E**

"Heads," I called.

2. **peal:** loud, prolonged sound.
3. **headlands** (HEHD luhndz): points of land extending into a body of water.

B **Literary Focus** **Character and Conflict** What external conflict is Selo struggling with?

C **Reading Focus** **Connecting to Characters** Do you have any secret fears you'd rather your friends didn't know about?

D **Read and Discuss** How do you think the narrator, who was so scared, feels when he sees Vern grinning and ready to play?

E **Literary Perspectives** **Author's Techniques** How does the writer show the tension between Selo and Vern and Amy? Do you think their interactions are presented realistically? Explain.

Vocabulary **depressed** (diH PREST) *adj.:* very sad.

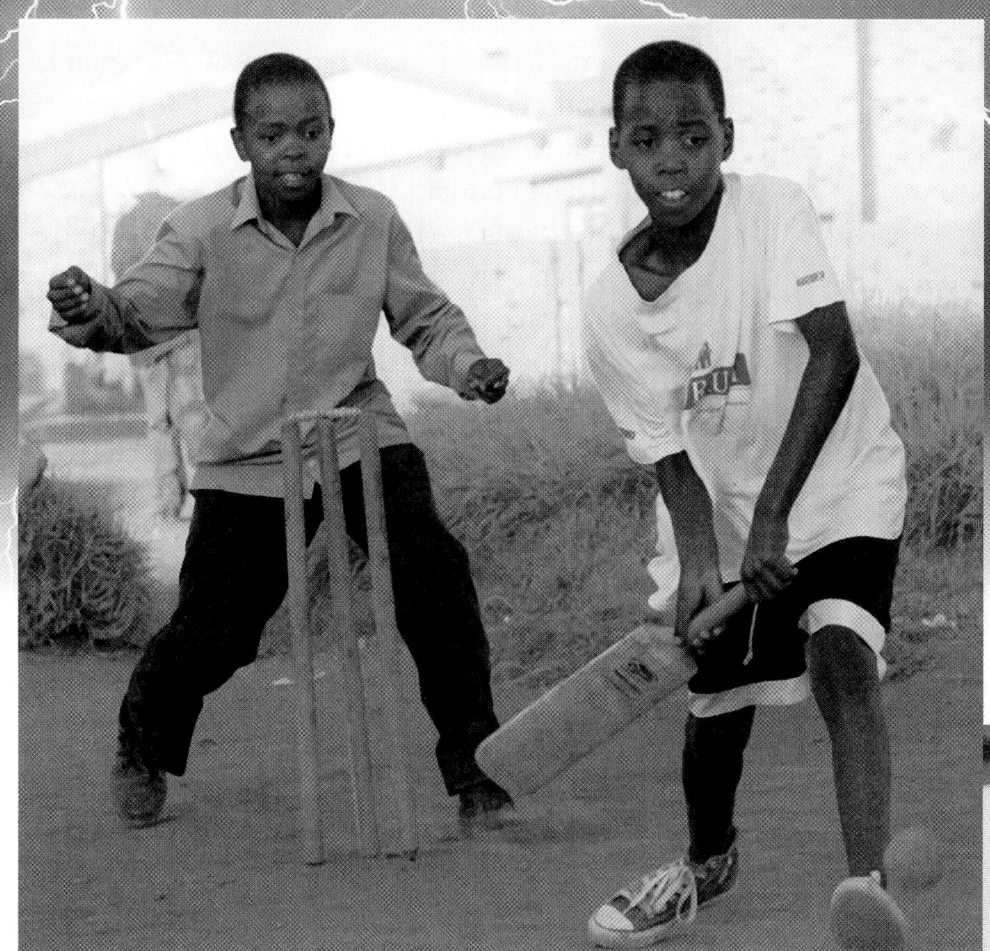

Analyzing Visuals

Viewing and Interpreting How does this picture help you understand what playing cricket is like?

"Tail," cried Amy. "Tail bound to come!" The coin went up in the air, fell down and overturned, showing tail.

"I'm *not* playing!" I cried, stung. And as that did not seem to disturb enough, I ran toward where I had put Vern's bat and ball and disappeared with them behind our house. Then I flung them with all my strength into the bushes. **F**

When I came back to the front of the house, Vern was standing there dumbfounded. "Selo, where's the bat and ball?" he said.

I was fuming. "I don't know about *any* bat and ball!"

"Tell on him," Amy cried. "He throw them away."

Vern's mouth twisted into a forced smile. "What's an old bat and ball," he said.

But as he walked out of the yard, I saw tears glinting from the corners of his eyes. **G**

For the rest of that rainy season, we never played cricket in the road again. Sometimes the rains ceased and the sun came out brightly, and I heard the voices

---

F **Literary Focus** **Character and Conflict** Why do you think Selo throws the bat and ball into the bushes? What does that tell you about him?

G **Read and Discuss** What's going on?

of Amy and Vern on the other side of the fence. At such times I would go out into the road and whistle to myself, hoping they would hear me and come out, but they never did, and I knew they were still very angry and would never forgive me. **H**

And so the rainy season went on. And it was as fearful as ever with the thunder and lightning and waves roaring in the bay, and the strong winds. But the people who talked of all this said that was the way Mayaro was, and they laughed about it. And sometimes when through the rain and even thunder I heard Vern's voice on the other side of the fence, shouting "Rain, rain, go to Spain," it puzzled me how it could be so. For often I had made up my mind I would be brave, but when the thunder cracked I always dashed under the bed. **I**

It was the beginning of the new year when I saw Vern and Amy again. The rainy season was, happily, long past, and the day was hot and bright, and as I walked toward home I saw that I was walking toward Vern and Amy just about to start cricket in the road. My heart thumped violently. They looked strange and new, as if they had gone away, far, and did not want to come back anymore. They did not notice me until I came up quite near, and then I saw Amy start, her face all lit up. **J**

"Vern—" she cried, "Vern look—look Selo!"

Embarrassed, I looked at the ground and at the trees, and at the orange sky, and I was so happy I did not know what to say. Vern stared at me, a strange grin on his face. He was ripping the cellophane paper off a brand new bat. **K**

"Selo, here—*you* first bat," he said gleefully. **L**

And I cried as though it were raining and I was afraid. **M**

H **Reading Focus** **Connecting to Characters** Have you or someone you know ever been in an argument that lasted a long time? How did you feel?

I **Read and Discuss** How is the narrator managing his life now?

J **Read and Discuss** Why do you think Vern and Amy looked "strange and new" to Selo?

K **Reading Focus** **Connecting to Characters** Would you be happy if you were Selo? Why?

L **Literary Focus** **Character and Conflict** When Vern gets a new bat, he lets Selo use it first. Why do you think Vern does this? What does it say about him?

M **Read and Discuss** What does the narrator mean by "And I cried as though it were raining and I was afraid"?

Applying Your Skills

Sunshine State Standards: Benchmarks LA.6.1.7.3 determine the main idea or essential message in grade-level text through inferring, paraphrasing, summarizing, and identifying relevant details; *Also covered* **LA.6.1.7.8; LA.6.2.1.2; LA.6.2.1.5; LA.6.2.1.7**

Cricket in the Road

Respond and Think Critically

Reading Focus

1. How would the story be different if it were told from an **omniscient** point of view by a narrator who could reveal the inner thoughts of every character? FCAT
   - **A** There would be more dialogue.
   - **B** Readers would not be able to understand Selo's point of view.
   - **C** The descriptions would be more vivid.
   - **D** Readers would learn more about Amy and Vern's feelings and ideas.

Read with a Purpose

2. How real did the relationship of these three friends seem to you? What did you think of the way they resolved their conflict?

Reading Skills: Connecting to Characters

3. Review the chart you completed as you read the story. What new connections can you make to the way the conflict is resolved? Add your connections if you haven't already.

I can connect	To myself or my friends	To other stories	To situations in the world
The resolution			

Literary Focus

Literary Analysis

4. **Interpret** Why do you think Selo behaves so badly during the cricket game? Explain.

5. **Literary Perspectives** Which of the author's techniques do you feel MOST helped make this story successful? Consider the imagery that describes the storm, the descriptions of the characters' interactions, the dialogue, and Selo's "voice." Support your answer with details from the story. READ THINK EXPLAIN

Literary Skills: Character and Conflict

6. **Analyze** List all the conflicts you can find in the story, and identify whether each conflict is *external* or *internal*. Explain the circumstance that caused each conflict.

Literary Skills Review: Setting

7. **Evaluate** **Setting** is the time and place of a story. Describe the setting of "Cricket in the Road" and how that setting influences the plot of the story. Support your answer with details from the story. READ THINK EXPLAIN

Writing Focus

Think as a Reader/Writer

Use It in Your Writing Review your notes about the storm in your *Reader/Writer Notebook.* Use vivid imagery to describe a scene in which you are confronted by something you fear.

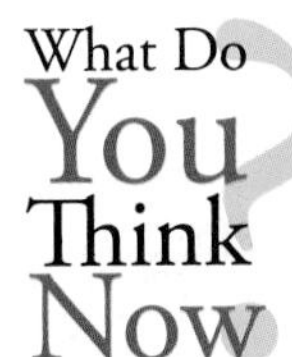

What Do You Think Now?

Do you think you might handle a conflict with a friend differently after reading this story? Why or why not?

Cricket in the Road

Vocabulary Development

Vocabulary Skills: Shades of Meaning

Read these two sentences and discuss the differences between them:

- The rain made Ben feel sad.
- The rain made Ben feel depressed.

Even though both sentences tell you how Ben feels about the rain, the second sentence suggests a deeper emotion than the first.

Recognizing different shades of meaning between words helps you pick the right word when you're writing. It also helps you understand the writer's meaning as you read.

Your Turn

torrents
tumult
depressed
downpour

Read each of the sentences below. Then, choose a word from the pair in parentheses to complete each sentence. Note: You may find that in some sentences either word could be used, depending on what is meant. Be prepared to explain why you chose each word.

1. We sometimes put on our coats and go outside during the (rain/downpour).
2. We got drenched in the (rain/downpour) and had to run for shelter.
3. After the man lost his job, he was (depressed/sad) for a long time.
4. Mia was so (depressed/sad) after she finished the last book in the series that she cried.
5. The rain came down in (drops/torrents), making it impossible to play outside.
6. The (drops/torrents) of rain began to fall, and I saw a woman open her umbrella.

Language Coach

Word Families Some of the Vocabulary words are related to words that share the same base, such as *depress/depressed.* Make a list of all the words you can think of that are related to each of the Vocabulary words. If you can't think of any related words, look the Vocabulary word up in a dictionary to see if you can find any words to add to your list.

Word	Related Words
depressed	pressed
	pressured
	press

Academic Vocabulary

Write About . . .

Write a paragraph explaining which character in the story you think adapts the most to the other characters. How does this help resolve the conflict? What circumstances do you think changed to make the characters come together again? Use the underlined Academic Vocabulary words in your paragraph.

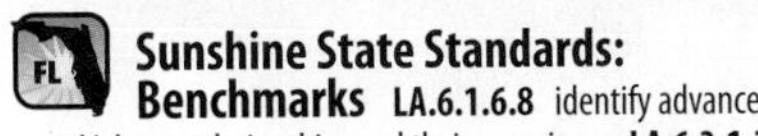

Sunshine State Standards: Benchmarks **LA.6.1.6.8** identify advanced word/phrase relationships and their meanings; **LA.6.3.1.3** using organizational strategies and tools (e.g, technology, outline, chart, table, graph, web, story map); **LA.6.3.4.3** punctuation in simple, compound, and complex sentences, including appositives and appositive phrases, and in cited sources, including quotations for exact words from sources; **LA.6.3.4.5** consistency in verb tense in simple, compound, and complex sentences; **LA.6.4.1.2** write a variety of expressive forms (e.g., short play, song lyrics, historical fiction, limericks) that employ figurative language, rhythm, dialogue, characterization, and/or appropriate format.

Grammar Link

Sentence Structures: Introducing Variety

If writers wrote the same sentence structures over and over, readers would become bored. So, writers use a variety of sentence types, such as these two:

SIMPLE SENTENCES **Simple sentences** are made up of only one independent clause. An **independent clause** is a group of words with a subject and a verb that expresses a complete thought and can stand alone as a complete sentence.

S V

Selo feared storms.

Simple sentences may have more than one subject or more than one verb, or both. For example:

S S V V

Amy and **Vern laughed** and **played** in the rain.

COMPOUND SENTENCES Unlike simple sentences, **compound sentences** always have two or more independent clauses. The clauses are joined by a comma and a connecting word such as *and, but,* or *or*. Each part of a compound sentence could stand alone as a separate sentence.

S V S V

Selo was at bat, *but* it started to rain.

Your Turn

Read each sentence and determine if it is a simple sentence or a compound sentence.

1. Selo was afraid of the thunder and lightning.
2. Vern tossed a coin, and Amy and Selo called it.
3. Selo hid the bat and ball, and Vern cried.
4. Selo wanted to play, but he was afraid.

CHOICES

As you respond to the Choices, use these **Academic Vocabulary** words as appropriate: adapt, circumstance, gender, obvious.

REVIEW

Write a Character Sketch

Timed Writing Selo has strengths and weaknesses like the rest of us. List Selo's traits in a chart like the one below. Then, write a paragraph describing Selo's personality.

CONNECT

Talk About Storms

Role-Playing With a partner, write a script in which an older Selo tries to persuade his younger cousin to adapt to the rainy season and not be so afraid of storms. Role-play the discussion, and alternate characters with your partner.

EXTEND

Take a Different Point of View

Group Discussion With a group of classmates, discuss what you think Vern and Amy were saying, doing, or thinking while they were not playing with Selo. Consider the circumstance that caused them to stop playing with Selo. In your discussion, consider whether gender differences—differences between boys and girls—play any role in the story. Would the story have been different if Selo were a girl, or if the characters were all girls or all boys? Discuss.

Comparing Characters and Their Conflicts

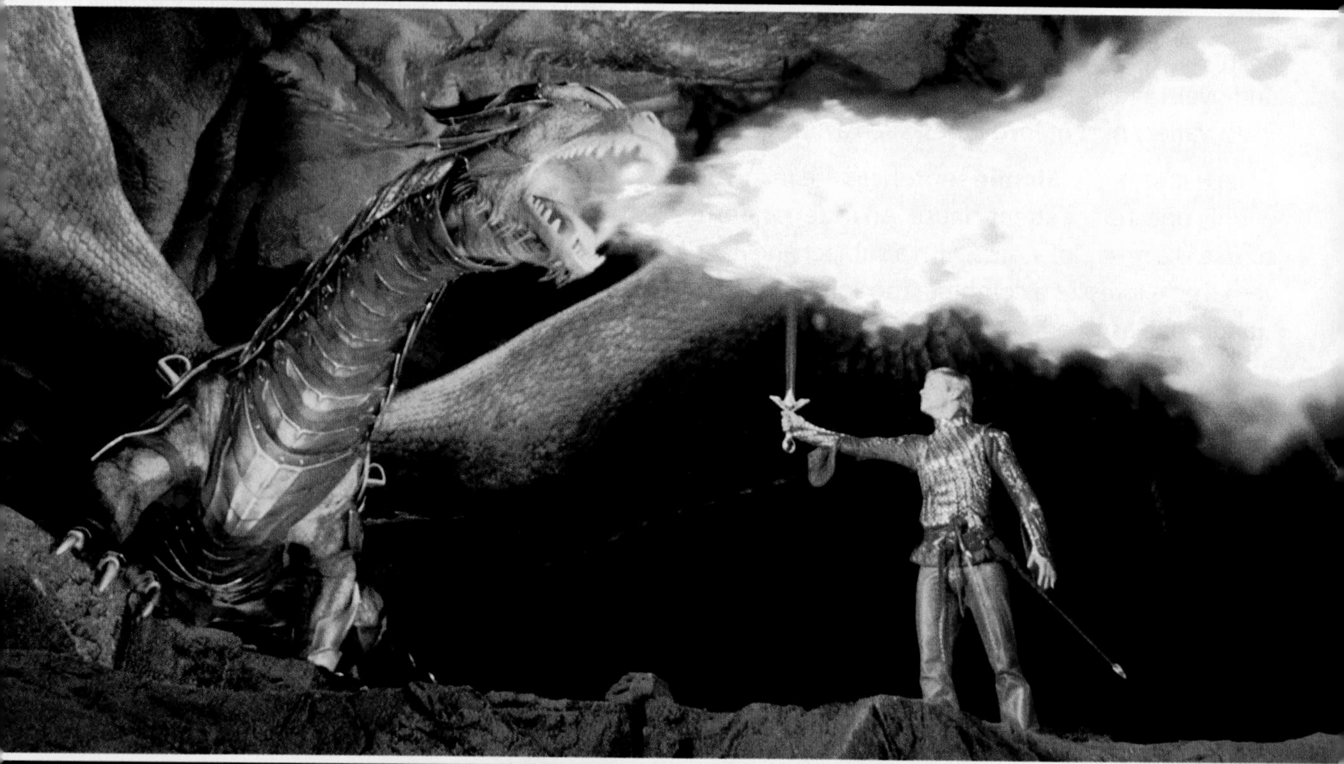

Scene from the movie *Eragon* (2006).

CONTENTS

What Do You Think?

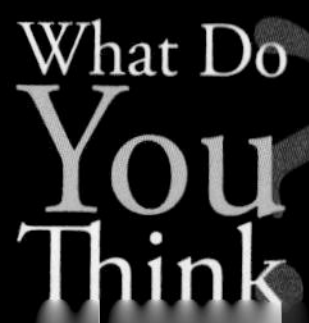

What makes someone a hero? What would you think of a hero who isn't perfect?

QuickWrite

In ancient myths, heroes often slay a monster. What kind of "monster" might a modern hero face? Explain

Preparing to Read

Sunshine State Standards: Benchmarks **LA.6.1.6.1** use new vocabulary that is introduced and taught directly; *Also covered* **LA.6.1.7.7; LA.6.1.7.8; LA.6.2.1.2**

Medusa's Head / Perseus and the Gorgon's Head / Dragon, Dragon

Literary Focus

Character and Conflict Like real people, main characters in most stories have a variety of traits. Characters in myths and folk tales, though, are often defined by a single character trait: the wicked stepmother, the clever trickster, the noble hero. These are **character types,** sometimes called **archetypes** (AHR kuh typs), familiar figures that appear throughout the history of storytelling.

Myths and folk tales usually focus on an obvious **external conflict**—a struggle between the main character and an outside force. The **protagonist,** or hero, has one motivation: to defeat the **antagonist,** who is often a monster.

Reading Focus

Comparing and Contrasting Characters and Conflicts The heroes in these stories have a lot in common, but they have some differences as well. Pay attention to the qualities of each hero that enable him to adapt to the circumstances he faces.

Into Action As you read each selection, fill out a chart that keeps track of your answers to these questions.

	Medusa's Head
Who is the hero? What is the hero like?	Perseus; handsome, strong, a leader, keeps his promises
What conflicts does the hero face? How are they resolved?	

Writing Focus

Think as a Reader/Writer

Find It in Your Reading Myths and folk tales rely on exciting action. In your *Reader/Writer Notebook,* write down your favorite action words, phrases, and passages from each selection.

Reader/Writer Notebook

Use your **RWN** to complete the activities for these selections.

Vocabulary

Medusa's Head

hovered (HUHV uhrd) *v.:* floated; remained still in the air. *Perseus hovered in the air above where the Gorgons slept.*

devour (dih VOWR) *v.:* eat in a greedy way. *The hungry beast was coming to devour Andromeda.*

Perseus and the Gorgon's Head

snatched (snachd) *v.:* grabbed; ran off with. *Perseus snatched Medusa's head.*

Dragon, Dragon

ravaged (RAV ihjd) *v.* damaged greatly. *The dragon ravaged the countryside.*

lunged (luhnjd) *v.* moved suddenly forward. *The dragon lunged at the knight.*

craned (kraynd) *v.* stretched (the neck) in order to see better. *The dragon craned his neck to get a closer look.*

Language Coach

Verb Forms You form the past tense of a regular verb by adding *–d* or *–ed* to its base form: *work* becomes *worked.* Find the Vocabulary word above that is not in the past tense, and make it a past tense verb.

Learn It Online

Hear a professional actor read these stories. Visit the selection online at:

go.hrw.com L6-281 

Olivia Coolidge

(1908–2006)

A Twist of Fate

Olivia Coolidge was enjoying a perfectly normal childhood in London when, one day, she twisted her ankle badly. She was forced to stop playing outdoors for three months. Bored, she started to read the ancient Greek classics that her father had always pestered her to read. So she read—and read. Soon, she was even reading ancient Greek poetry. "I write about history, biography, and ancient legends for teens," she said, "because I am . . . interested in values that have always been of concern to peop

Marcia Williams

(1945–)

Comics Her Way

Marcia Williams developed her distinctive comic book style when she was a child in an English boarding school. Every week she sent illustrated letters to her mother and diplomat stepfather. "My parents didn't let me read comic books," she remembers, "so I decided to create my own."

John Gardner

(1933–1982)

Inspired by Disney and Dickens

When Gardner was young, his favorite storytellers were Walt Disney and Charles Dickens. Gardner kept a bust of Dickens in his study "to keep me honest."

Think About the Writers

Why do you think a writer's experiences as a child can have such a lasting effect on what he or she writes about?

Preview the Selections

In "Medusa's Head," a Greek myth, you'll meet many characters, including the hero **Perseus,** his mother **Danae,** the hideous **Gorgon Medusa,** and the beautiful **Andromeda.**

In "Perseus and the Gorgon's Head," you'll read a very different—and funny—illustrated version of the same **Perseus** story told in "Medusa's Head."

In "Dragon, Dragon," you'll meet a king and queen, a bumbling wizard, and three brothers who take turns fighting a dragon that menaces their kingdom.

The Head of Medusa (1618) by Peter Paul Rubens (1577–1640). Oil on canvas.

Medusa's Head

Retold by **Olivia Coolidge**

Read with a Purpose

Read this Greek myth to see how an ancient hero, Perseus, fulfills his fate.

Build Background

The ancient Greeks believed in fate, circumstances that a person can't escape from and that lead to an unavoidable future outcome.

Use the list below to help you keep track of and learn how to pronounce the names of the various characters and places in this myth.

Characters and Places

Acrisios (uh KREE see ohs): king of **Argos** (AHR gohs), an ancient city and kingdom in southern Greece.

Proitos (proh EE tohs): brother of King Acrisios.

Danae (DAN ay ee): daughter of King Acrisios and mother of Perseus.

Apollo (uh PAHL oh): Greek god of light, medicine, poetry, and prophecy.

Zeus (zoos): king of the Greek gods.

Perseus (PUR see uhs): son of Danae and the god Zeus.

Dictys (DIHK tihs): fisherman, brother of Polydectes.

Polydectes (pahl ee DEHK teez): king of **Seriphos** (suh RY fuhs), an island off the coast of Greece.

Medusa (muh DOO suh): the youngest of the **Gorgons** (GAWR guhns), three monstrous sisters. She has snakes for hair and a face so terrible that it turns anyone who looks at her into stone.

Athene (uh THEE nee): Greek goddess of crafts, war, and wisdom. Her name is also spelled *Athena* (uh THEE nuh).

Phorcides (FAWR suh deez): three sisters who live in a cave and share one eye and one tooth between them.

Hermes (HUR meez): messenger of the gods.

Cepheus (SEE fee uhs) and **Cassiopeia** (kas ee oh PEE uh): king and queen of Ethiopa, in Africa.

Andromeda (an DRAHM uh duh): daughter of the king and queen of Ethiopia.

Nereus (NIHR ee uhs): a minor sea god.

Poseidon (puh SY duhn): god of the sea.

King Acrisios of Argos was a hard, selfish man. He hated his brother, Proitos, who later drove him from his kingdom, and he cared nothing for his daughter, Danae. His whole heart was set on having a son who should succeed him, but since many years went by and still he had only the one daughter, he sent a message to the oracle of Apollo[1] to ask whether he should have more children of his own. The answer of the oracle was terrible. Acrisios should have no son, but his daughter, Danae, would bear him a grandchild who should grow up to kill him. At these words Acrisios was beside himself with fear and rage. Swearing that Danae should never have a child to murder him, he had a room built underground and lined all through with brass. Thither[2] he conducted Danae and shut her up, bidding her spend the rest of her life alone. **A**

It is possible to thwart the plans of mortal men, but never those of the gods. Zeus himself looked with pity on the unfortunate girl, and it is said he descended to her through the tiny hole that gave light and air to her chamber, pouring himself down into her lap in the form of a shower of gold.

When word came to the king from those who brought food and drink to his daughter that the girl was with child, Acrisios was angry and afraid. He would have liked best to murder both Danae and her infant son, Perseus, but he did not dare for fear of the gods' anger at so hideous a crime. He made, therefore, a great chest of wood with bands of brass about it. Shutting up the girl and her baby inside, he cast them into the sea, thinking that they would either drown or starve. **B**

Again the gods came to the help of Danae, for they caused the planks of the chest to swell until they fitted tightly and let no water in.

The chest floated for some days and was cast up at last on an island. There Dictys, a fisherman, found it and took Danae to his brother, Polydectes, who was king of the island. Danae was made a servant in the palace, yet before many years had passed, both Dictys and Polydectes had fallen in love with the silent, golden-haired girl. She in her heart preferred Dictys, yet since his brother was king, she did not dare to make her choice. Therefore she hung always over Perseus, pretending that mother love left her no room for any other, and year after year a silent frown would cross Polydectes' face as he saw her caress the child. **C**

At last, Perseus became a young man, handsome and strong beyond the common and a leader among the youths of the island, though he was but the son of a poor

1. **oracle** (AWR uh kuhl) **of Apollo:** a priest or priestess of the god Apollo who foretold the future.
2. **thither:** an old-fashioned word meaning "over there."

A **Read and Discuss** What have you learned about King Acrisios in this opening paragraph?

B **Literary Focus** **Character and Conflict** What is the first external conflict that Perseus faces? What helps him overcome this conflict?

C **Read and Discuss** What problem does Danae have?

Analyzing Visuals **Viewing and Interpreting** How does this image show the larger-than-life nature of a hero like Perseus?

The Constellation of Perseus with the Head of Medusa by Alexander Mair.

servant. Then it seemed to Polydectes that if he could once get rid of Perseus, he could force Danae to become his wife, whether she would or not. Meanwhile, in order to lull the young man's suspicions, he pretended that he intended to marry a certain noble maiden and would collect a wedding gift for her. Now the custom was that this gift of the bridegroom to the bride was in part his own and in part put together from the marriage presents of his friends and relatives. All the young men, therefore, brought Polydectes a present, excepting Perseus, who was his servant's son and possessed nothing to bring. Then Polydectes said to the others, "This young man owes me more than any of you, since I took him in and brought him up in my own house, and yet he gives me nothing." **D**

Perseus answered in anger at the injustice of the charge, "I have nothing of my own, Polydectes, yet ask me what you will, and I will fetch it, for I owe you my life."

At this Polydectes smiled, for it was what he had intended, and he answered, "Fetch me, if this is your boast, the Gorgon's head." **E**

Now the Gorgons, who lived far off on the shores of the ocean, were three fearful sisters with hands of brass, wings of gold,

---

D **Literary Focus** **Character and Conflict** How did King Polydectes know how Perseus would react when Perseus was criticized for bringing nothing?

E **Read and Discuss** What is Polydectes planning here?

and scales like a serpent. Two of them had scaly heads and tusks like the wild boar, but the third, Medusa, had the face of a beautiful woman with hair of writhing serpents, and so terrible was her expression that all who looked on it were immediately turned to stone. This much Perseus knew of the Gorgons, but of how to find or kill them, he had no idea. Nevertheless, he had given his promise, and though he saw now the satisfaction of King Polydectes, he was bound to keep his word. In his perplexity,[3] he prayed to the wise goddess Athene, who came to him in a vision and promised him her aid. **F**

"First, you must go," she said, "to the sisters Phorcides, who will tell you the way to the nymphs who guard the hat of darkness, the winged sandals, and the knapsack which can hold the Gorgon's head. Then I will give you a shield, and my brother Hermes will give you a sword, which shall be made of adamant, the hardest rock. For nothing else can kill the Gorgon, since so venomous is her blood that a mortal sword, when plunged in it, is eaten away. But when you come to the Gorgons, invisible in your hat of darkness, turn your eyes away from them and look only on their reflection in your gleaming shield. Thus you may kill the monster without yourself being turned to stone. Pass her sisters by, for they are immortal, but smite off the head of Medusa with the hair of writhing[4] snakes. Then put it in your knapsack and return, and I will be with you." **G**

The vision ended, and with the aid of Athene, Perseus set out on the long journey to seek the Phorcides. These live in a dim cavern in the far north, where nights and days are one and where the whole earth is

3. **perplexity** (puhr PLEHK suh tee): puzzlement; confusion.

4. **writhing** (RYTH ihng): wriggling; moving about in a twisting way.

Study for Perseus and the Graiae (1880) by Sir Edward Burne-Jones.

Analyzing Visuals **Viewing and Interpreting** What part of the story does this painting illustrate? Does it match the scene you imagined? Why or why not?

F **Read and Discuss** What gender are the terrifying Gorgons? What else do you learn about them in this section?

G **Reading Focus** **Comparing and Contrasting Characters and Conflicts** Why are the gods and goddesses providing so much help to Perseus? What other stories can you name where heroes are assisted by older or more powerful characters?

light. There sat the three old women mumbling to one another, crouched in a dim heap together, for they had but one eye and one tooth between them, which they passed from hand to hand. Perseus came quietly behind them, and as they fumbled for the eye, he put his strong, brown hand next to one of the long, yellow ones, so that the old crone thought that it was her sister's and put the eye into it. There was a high scream of anger when they discovered the theft, and much clawing and groping in the dim recesses[5] of the cavern. But they were helpless in their blindness and Perseus could laugh at them. At length, for the price of their eye, they told him how to reach the nymphs, and Perseus, laying the eye quickly in the hand of the nearest sister, fled as fast as he could before she could use it.

Again it was a far journey to the garden of the nymphs, where it is always sunshine and the trees bear golden apples. But the nymphs are friends of the wise gods and hate the monsters of darkness and the spirits of anger and despair. Therefore, they received Perseus with rejoicing and put the hat of darkness on his head, while on his feet they bound the golden, winged sandals, which are those Hermes wears when he runs down the slanting sunbeams or races along the pathways of the wind. Next, Perseus put on his back the silver sack with the gleaming tassels of gold, and flung across his shoulder the black-sheathed sword that was the gift of Hermes. On his left arm he fitted the shield that Athene gave, a gleaming silver shield like a mirror, plain without any marking. Then he sprang into the air and ran, invisible like the rushing wind, far out over the white-capped sea, across the yellow sands of the eastern desert, over strange streams and towering mountains, until at last he came to the shores of the distant ocean which flowed round all the world. **H**

Here and there, a man who had looked on the terrible Medusa stood forever with horror on his face.

There was a gray gorge of stone by the ocean's edge, where lay Medusa and her sisters sleeping in the dim depths of the rock. All up and down the cleft, the stones took fantastic shapes of trees, beasts, birds, or serpents. Here and there, a man who had looked on the terrible Medusa stood forever with horror on his face. Far over the twilit gorge Perseus hovered invisible, while he loosened the pale, strange sword from its black sheath. Then, with his face turned away and eyes on the silver shield,

5. **recesses** (REE sehs ehz): inner places.

H **Reading Focus** **Comparing and Contrasting Characters and Conflicts** What other stories do you know of in which a young hero or heroine is given special weapons or powers to help him or her against an enemy?

Vocabulary **hovered** (HUHV uhrd) *v.:* floated; remained still in the air.

he dropped, slow and silent as a falling leaf, down through the rocky cleft, twisting and turning past countless strange gray shapes, down from the bright sunlight into a chill, dim shadow echoing and reechoing with the dashing of waves on the tumbled rocks beneath. There on the heaped stones lay the Gorgons sleeping together in the dimness, and even as he looked on them in the shield, Perseus felt stiff with horror at the sight.

Two of the Gorgons lay sprawled together, shaped like women, yet scaled from head to foot as serpents are. Instead of hands they had gleaming claws like eagles, and their feet were dragons' feet. Skinny metallic wings like bats' wings hung from their shoulders. Their faces were neither snake nor woman, but part both, like faces in a nightmare. These two lay arm in arm and never stirred. Only the blue snakes still hissed and writhed round the pale, set face of Medusa, as though even in sleep she were troubled by an evil dream. She lay by herself, arms outstretched, face upwards, more beautiful and terrible than living man may bear. All the crimes and madnesses of the world rushed into Perseus' mind as he gazed at her image in the shield. Horror stiffened his arm as he hovered over her with his

Analyzing Visuals **Viewing and Interpreting** What are the most obvious characteristics of Medusa in this picture? How does the description of Medusa in the story compare with her appearance in this picture?

Medusa in "Perseus and the Gorgon" from *Jim Henson's the Storyteller: The Greek Myths* (1997).

sword uplifted. Then he shut his eyes to the vision and in the darkness struck. **I**

There was a great cry and a hissing. Perseus groped for the head and seized it by the limp and snaky hair. Somehow he put it in his knapsack and was up and off, for at the dreadful scream the sister Gorgons had awakened. Now they were after him, their sharp claws grating against his silver shield. Perseus strained forward on the pathway of the wind like a runner, and behind him the two sisters came, smelling out the prey they could not see. Snakes darted from their girdles,[6] foam flew from their tusks, and the great wings beat the air. Yet the winged sandals were even swifter than they, and Perseus fled like the hunted deer with the speed of desperation. Presently the horrible noise grew faint behind him, the hissing of snakes and the sound of the bat wings died away. At last the Gorgons could smell him no longer and returned home unavenged. **J**

By now, Perseus was over the Libyan desert, and as the blood from the horrible head touched the sand, it changed to serpents, from which the snakes of Africa are descended.

The storms of the Libyan desert blew against Perseus in clouds of eddying sand, until not even the divine sandals could hold him on his course. Far out to sea he was blown, and then north. Finally, whirled around the heavens like a cloud of mist, he alighted in the distant west, where the giant Atlas held up on his shoulders the heavens from the earth. There the weary giant, crushed under the load of centuries, begged Perseus to show him Medusa's head. Perseus uncovered for him the dreadful thing, and Atlas was changed to the mighty mountain whose rocks rear up to reach the sky near the gateway to the Atlantic. Perseus himself, returning eastwards and still battling with the wind, was driven south to the land of Ethiopia, where King Cepheus reigned with his wife, Cassiopeia. **K**

As Perseus came wheeling in like a gull from the ocean, he saw a strange sight. Far out to sea the water was troubled, seething and boiling as though stirred by a great force moving in its depths. Huge, sullen waves were starting far out and washing inland over sunken trees and flooded houses. Many miles of land were under water, and as he sped over them, he saw the muddy sea lapping around the foot of a black, upstanding rock. Here on a ledge above the water's edge stood a young girl chained by the arms, lips parted, eyes open and staring, face white as her linen garment. She might have been a statue, so still she stood, while the light breeze fluttered her dress and stirred her loosened hair. As Perseus looked at her and looked at the sea, the water began to boil again, and miles out a long gray scaly back of vast length lifted itself above the flood. At that, there was a shriek from a distant knoll where he could dimly see the forms of people, but

6. **girdles:** belts or sashes.

I **Literary Focus** **Character and Conflict** What qualities make Medusa a frightening, powerful foe that only a superhuman hero could defeat?

J **Read and Discuss** What is Perseus doing now?

K **Read and Discuss** What two things have been created from Medusa's head so far?

the girl shrank a little and said nothing. Then Perseus, taking off the hat of darkness, alighted near the maiden to talk to her, and she, though nearly mad with terror, found words at last to tell him her tale. L

Her name was Andromeda, and she was the only child of the king and of his wife, Cassiopeia. Queen Cassiopeia was exceedingly beautiful, so that all people marveled at her. She herself was proud of her dark eyes, her white, slender fingers, and her long black hair, so proud that she had been heard to boast that she was fairer even than the sea nymphs, who are daughters of Nereus. At this, Nereus in wrath stirred up Poseidon, who came flooding in over the land, covering it far and wide. Not content with this, he sent a vast monster from the dark depths of the bottomless sea to ravage the whole coast of Ethiopia. When the unfortunate king and queen had sought the advice of the oracle on how to appease the god, they had been ordered to sacrifice their only daughter to the sea monster Poseidon had sent. Not daring for their people's sake to disobey, they had chained her to this rock, where she now awaited the beast who should devour her. M

Perseus comforted Andromeda as he stood by her on the rock, and she shrank closer against him while the great gray back writhed its half-mile length slowly towards the land. Then, bidding Andromeda hide her face, Perseus sprang once more into the air, unveiling the dreadful head of dead Medusa to the monster, which reared its dripping jaws yards high into the air. The mighty tail stiffened all of a sudden, the boiling of the water ceased, and only the gentle waves of the receding ocean lapped around a long, gray ridge of stone. Then Perseus freed Andromeda and restored her to her father and beautiful mother. Thereafter, with their consent, he married her amid scenes of tremendous rejoicing, and with his bride set sail at last for the kingdom of Polydectes. N

Polydectes had lost no time on the departure of Perseus. First he had begged Danae to become his wife, and then he had threatened her. Undoubtedly, he would have got his way by force if Danae had not fled in terror to Dictys. The two took refuge at the altar of a temple whence Polydectes did not dare drag them away. So matters stood when Perseus returned. Polydectes was enraged to see him, for he had hoped at least that Danae's most powerful protector would never return. But now, seeing him famous and with a king's daughter to wife, he could not contain himself. Openly he laughed at the tale of Perseus, saying that the hero had never killed the Gorgon, only pretended to, and that now he was claiming an honor he did not deserve. At this,

L **Reading Focus** **Comparing and Contrasting Characters and Conflicts** Compare Perseus's actions on his journey home with those on his mission to kill Medusa. Is it obvious why he stops to talk to the girl, or do you have to infer his motivation?

M **Literary Focus** **Character and Conflict** What causes the external conflict between Andromeda and Nereus?

N **Literary Focus** **Character and Conflict** How are Perseus's reasons, or motivations, for challenging the sea monster different from his motivations for going after Medusa? What is the resolution of the conflict with the sea monster?

Vocabulary **devour** (dih VOWR) *v.:* eat in a greedy way.

The Leviathan (1908) by Arthur Rackham.

Analyzing Visuals **Viewing and Interpreting** How is this creature similar to or different from your idea of what the sea monster who comes for Andromeda looks like?

Perseus, enraged by the insult and by reports of his mother's persecution, said to him, "You asked me for the Gorgon's head. Behold it!" And with that he lifted it high, and Polydectes became stone. **O**

Then Perseus left Dictys to be king of that island, but he himself went back to the Grecian mainland to seek out his grandfather, Acrisios, who was once again king of Argos. First, however, he gave back to the gods the gifts they had given him. Hermes took back the golden sandals and the hat of darkness, for both are his. But Athene took Medusa's head, and she hung it on a fleece around her neck as part of her battle equipment, where it may be seen in statues and portraits of the warlike goddess.

> "You asked me for the Gorgon's head. Behold it!"

Perseus took ship for Greece, but his fame had gone before him, and King Acrisios fled secretly from Argos in terror, since he remembered the prophecy and feared that Perseus had come to avenge the wrongs of Danae. The trembling old Acrisios took refuge in Larissa, where it happened the king was holding a great athletic contest in honor of his dead father. **P**

Heroes from all over Greece, among whom was Perseus, came to the games. As Perseus was competing at the discus throwing, he threw high into the air and far beyond the rest. A strong wind caught the discus as it spun, so that it left the course marked out for it and was carried into the stands. People scrambled away to right and left. Only Acrisios was not nimble enough. The heavy weight fell full on his foot and crushed his toes, and at that, the feeble old man, already weakened by his terrors, died from the shock. Thus the prophecy of Apollo was fulfilled at last; Acrisios was killed by his grandson. Then Perseus came into his kingdom, where he reigned with Andromeda long and happily. **Q**

Perseus with the Head of Medusa (1545–1554) by Benvenuto Cellini (1500–1571). Bronze sculpture.

O **Read and Discuss** What happens when Perseus reaches home?

P **Reading Focus** **Comparing and Contrasting Characters and Conflicts** At the end of the story, how is King Acrisios different than he was at the beginning? How is he the same?

Q **Read and Discuss** What's the writer saying at the end?

Read with a Purpose

See how this writer/artist takes a serious heroic myth and turns it into something funny.

Retold by **Marcia Williams**

A Read and Discuss How has the writer/artist set up the story for us?

B **Reading Focus Comparing and Contrasting Characters and Conflicts** How does this version make the conflict developing between Perseus, King Polydectes, and Danaë humorous?

C Read and Discuss Why is it intended to be a "deadly" mission?

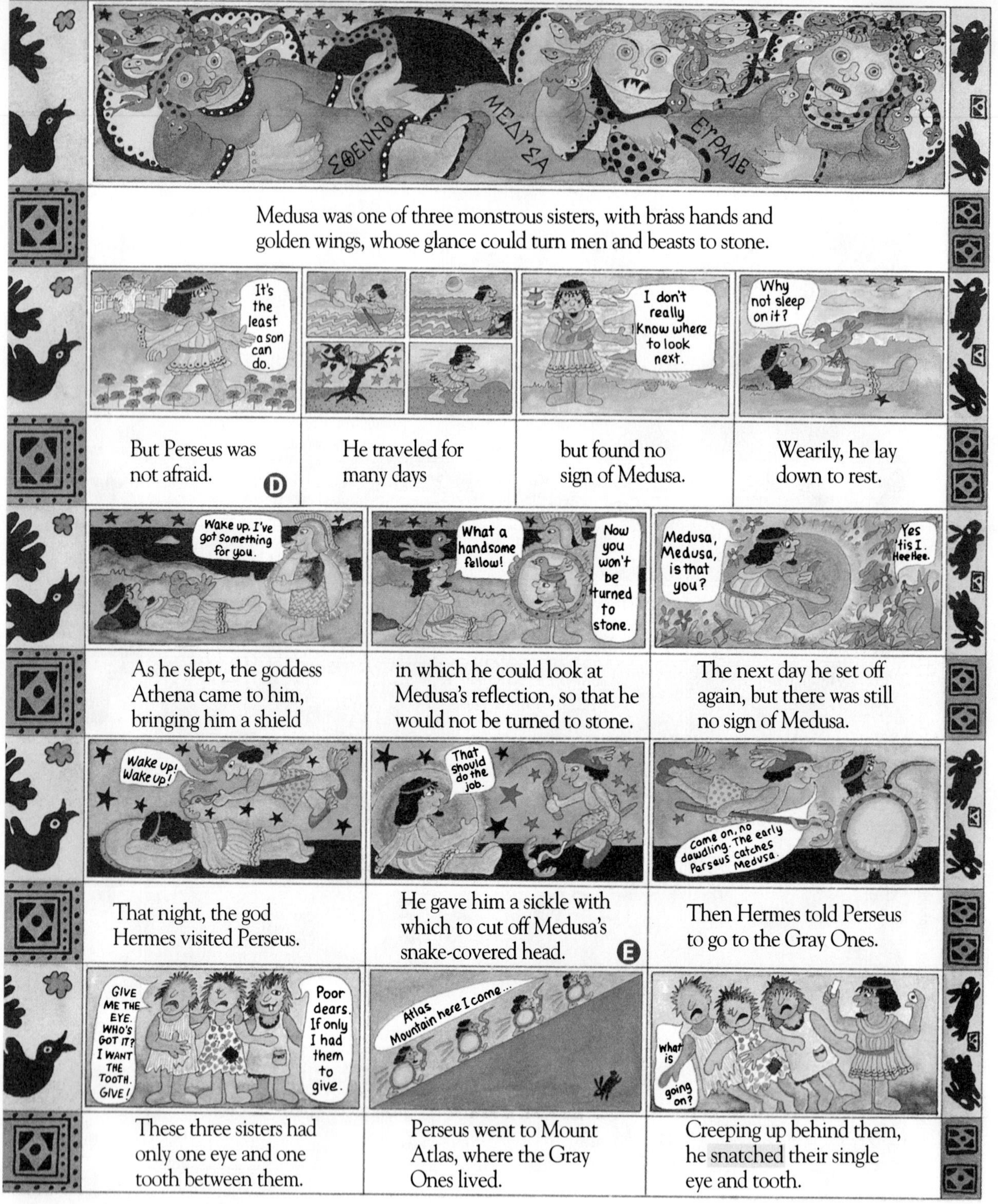

1. **sickle** (SIHK uhl): a tool with a curved blade and a short handle.

D Reading Focus Comparing and Contrasting Characters and Conflicts What is the conflict in the story at this point? What additional information do we get about Perseus?

E Read and Discuss How do the shield and the sickle fit into Perseus's mission?

Vocabulary snatched (snachd) *v.:* grabbed; ran off with.

F **Literary Focus** **Character and Conflict** What character traits does Perseus show in the way he handles the Gray Ones? What do the pictures and word balloons do to the classic image of Perseus as a heroic type?

G **Read and Discuss** What is going on now?

H **Reading Focus** **Comparing and Contrasting Characters and Conflicts** In "Medusa's Head," the scene of Perseus killing Medusa was suspenseful and horrifying. How would you describe the way it's handled here?

I **Read and Discuss** How have things ended up for Perseus and his mother?

Applying Your Skills

Sunshine State Standards: Benchmarks **LA.6.1.7.3** determine the main idea or essential message in grade-level text through inferring, paraphrasing, summarizing, and identifying relevant details; **LA.6.1.7.7** compare and contrast elements in multiple texts; *Also covered* **LA.6.1.7.8; LA.6.2.1.2; LA.6.2.1.4; LA.6.4.2.3**

Medusa's Head / Perseus and the Gorgon's Head

Respond and Think Critically

Reading Focus

FCAT

1. In each version of the story, how does Perseus fulfill his fate?
   - **A** Perseus kills Acrisios.
   - **B** Perseus brings Medusa's head back to the king.
   - **C** Perseus rescues his mother.
   - **D** Perseus marries Andromeda.

Reading Skills: Comparing and Contrasting Characters and Conflicts

2. Update the chart you made to help you keep track of characters and conflicts in these two versions of the Perseus myth.

	Medusa's Head	Perseus and the Gorgon's Head
Who is the hero? What is the hero like?	Perseus; handsome, strong, a leader, keeps his promises	Perseus; the pictures and dialogue make him seem brave but young.
What conflicts does the hero face? How are they resolved?		

Vocabulary Check

Answer the following question.

3. If a person checked a book out of a library, would you say the person **snatched** it? Explain.

Literary Focus

Literary Analysis

4. **Evaluate** In "Medusa's Head," what kind of hero is Perseus? In "Perseus and the Gorgon's Head," how successfully does Marcia Williams adapt this heroic image in order to turn it upside down?
5. **Extend** What books, movies, or TV shows include these elements of the Perseus myth: (a) the hero threatened at birth, (b) dangerous circumstances presented in the form of monsters, (c) the hero's amazing powers or weapons, and (d) good triumphing over evil?

Literary Skills: Character and Conflict

6. **Analyze** In both versions of the story, how does Perseus's character help to set the story's conflicts in motion and keep them in motion?
7. **Infer** Could Perseus have resolved his conflicts without the help of the other characters? Support your answer with details from the selections. 
8. **Make Judgments** How does this myth illustrate the idea that no one can escape fate? What do you think of the ancient Greek belief everything that happens is decided by fate?

Writing Focus

Think as a Reader/Writer

Use It in Your Writing Review the lists of action words that you recorded. Now try using similar action words and descriptions to write your own action-packed scene.

SHORT STORY

Dragon, Dragon

by **John Gardner**

Read with a Purpose

Read "Dragon, Dragon" to learn what problem a king and his kingdom face and discover who ends up fixing the problem.

Preparing to Read for this selection is on page 281.

Build Background

A **parody** is a work that humorously imitates, or spoofs, the content or style of another work. This story is from John Gardner's first collection of stories for young readers, *Dragon, Dragon, and Other Tales* (1975). The book is a collection of fairy tale parodies—new and funny versions of traditional, old-fashioned tales.

There was once a king whose kingdom was plagued by a dragon. The king did not know which way to turn. The king's knights were all cowards who hid under their beds whenever the dragon came in sight, so they were of no use to the king at all. And the king's wizard could not help either because, being old, he had forgotten his magic spells. Nor could the wizard look up the spells that had slipped his mind, for he had unfortunately misplaced his wizard's book many years before. The king was at his wit's end. **A**

Every time there was a full moon, the dragon came out of his lair and ravaged the countryside. He frightened maidens and stopped up chimneys and broke store windows and set people's clocks back and made dogs bark until no one could hear himself think.

He tipped over fences and robbed graves and put frogs in people's drinking water and tore the last chapters out of novels and changed house numbers around.

He stole spark plugs out of people's cars and put firecrackers in people's cigars and stole the clappers from all the church bells and sprung every bear trap for miles around so the bears could wander wherever they pleased.

And to top it all off, he changed around all the roads in the kingdom so that people

A **Read and Discuss** What has the author told us so far?

Vocabulary **ravaged** (RAV ihjd) *v.:* damaged greatly.

could not get anywhere except by starting out in the wrong direction. **B**

"That," said the king in a fury, "is enough!" And he called a meeting of everyone in the kingdom.

Now it happened that there lived in the kingdom a wise old cobbler who had a wife and three sons. The cobbler and his family came to the king's meeting and stood way in back by the door, for the cobbler had a feeling that since he was nobody important, there had probably been some mistake, and no doubt the king had intended the meeting for everyone in the kingdom except his family and him. **C**

"Ladies and gentlemen," said the king when everyone was present, "I've put up with that dragon as long as I can. He has got to be stopped."

All the people whispered amongst themselves, and the king smiled, pleased with the impression he had made. **D**

B **Literary Focus** **Character and Conflict** What kind of character is the dragon? Explain how this dragon's character sets up the story's conflict.

C **Read and Discuss** What do you learn here about the cobbler and his family?

D **Read and Discuss** How has the king changed his approach?

Analyzing Visuals **Viewing and Interpreting** What traits does this dragon seem to share with the dragon in the story?

Scene from the movie *Dragonheart* (1996).

But the wise cobbler said gloomily, "It's all very well to talk about it—but how are you going to do it?"

And now all the people smiled and winked as if to say, "Well, King, he's got you there!"

The king frowned.

"It's not that His Majesty hasn't tried," the queen spoke up loyally.

"Yes," said the king, "I've told my knights again and again that they ought to slay that dragon. But I can't *force* them to go. I'm not a tyrant."

"Why doesn't the wizard say a magic spell?" asked the cobbler.

"He's done the best he can," said the king.

The wizard blushed and everyone looked embarrassed. "I used to do all sorts of spells and chants when I was younger," the wizard explained. "But I've lost my spell book, and I begin to fear I'm losing my memory too. For instance, I've been trying for days to recall one spell I used to do. I forget, just now, what the deuce it was for. It went something like—

Bimble,
Wimble,
Cha, Cha
CHOOMPF!"

Suddenly, to everyone's surprise, the queen turned into a rosebush.

"Oh, dear," said the wizard.

"Now you've done it," groaned the king.

"Poor Mother," said the princess.

"I don't know what can have happened," the wizard said nervously, "but don't worry, I'll have her changed back in a jiffy." He shut his eyes and racked his brain for a spell that would change her back.

But the king said quickly, "You'd better leave well enough alone. If you change her into a rattlesnake, we'll have to chop off her head." **E**

Meanwhile the cobbler stood with his hands in his pockets, sighing at the waste of time. "About the dragon . . . ," he began.

"Oh, yes," said the king. "I'll tell you what I'll do. I'll give the princess's hand in marriage to anyone who can make the dragon stop."

"It's not enough," said the cobbler. "She's a nice enough girl, you understand. But how would an ordinary person support her? Also, what about those of us that are already married?"

"In that case," said the king, "I'll offer the princess's hand or half the kingdom or both—whichever is most convenient."

The cobbler scratched his chin and considered it. "It's not enough," he said at last. "It's a good enough kingdom, you understand, but it's too much responsibility."

"Take it or leave it," the king said.

"I'll leave it," said the cobbler. And he shrugged and went home. **F**

But the cobbler's eldest son thought the bargain was a good one, for the princess was very beautiful, and he liked the idea of having half the kingdom to run as he pleased.

E **Read and Discuss** How are things going? What has happened to the queen?

F **Literary Focus** **Character and Conflict** In what obvious ways are the king and the cobbler different from each other? How do their views affect the conflict?

So he said to the king, "I'll accept those terms, Your Majesty. By tomorrow morning the dragon will be slain." G

"Bless you!" cried the king.

"Hooray, hooray, hooray!" cried all the people, throwing their hats in the air.

The cobbler's eldest son beamed with pride, and the second eldest looked at him enviously. The youngest son said timidly, "Excuse me, Your Majesty, but don't you think the queen looks a little unwell? If I were you, I think I'd water her." H

"Good heavens," cried the king, glancing at the queen, who had been changed into a rosebush, "I'm glad you mentioned it!"

"The old man is not as wise as I thought. If I say something like that to the dragon, he will eat me up in an instant."

Now the cobbler's eldest son was very clever and was known far and wide for how quickly he could multiply fractions in his head. He was perfectly sure he could slay the dragon by somehow or other playing a trick on him, and he didn't feel that he needed his wise old father's advice. But he thought it was only polite to ask, and so he went to his father, who was working as usual at his cobbler's bench, and said, "Well, Father, I'm off to slay the dragon. Have you any advice to give me?"

The cobbler thought a moment and replied, "When and if you come to the dragon's lair, recite the following poem.

Dragon, dragon, how do you do?
I've come from the king to murder you.

Say it very loudly and firmly, and the dragon will fall, God willing, at your feet."

"How curious!" said the eldest son. And he thought to himself, "The old man is not as wise as I thought. If I say something like that to the dragon, he will eat me up in an instant. The way to kill a dragon is to outfox him." And keeping his opinion to himself, the eldest son set forth on his quest. I

When he came at last to the dragon's lair, which was a cave, the eldest son slyly disguised himself as a peddler and knocked on the door and called out, "Hello there!"

"There's nobody home!" roared a voice.

The voice was as loud as an earthquake, and the eldest son's knees knocked together in terror.

"I don't come to trouble you," the eldest son said meekly. "I merely thought you might be interested in looking at some of our brushes. Or if you'd prefer," he added quickly, "I could leave our catalog with you and I could drop by again, say, early next week."

"I don't want any brushes," the voice roared, "and I especially don't want any brushes next week."

G **Read and Discuss** What does the eldest son think of the deal?

H **Read and Discuss** Why is the youngest son the only one not focused on the good news? What do you think he thinks of the deal?

I **Literary Focus Character and Conflict** In what ways is the eldest son like and unlike a familiar character type? What character trait does he plan to rely on to slay the dragon?

Analyzing Visuals

Viewing and Interpreting How does the personality of this dragon seem similar to or different from that of the dragon in the story?

Scene from the movie *Dragonheart* (1996).

"Oh," said the eldest son. By now his knees were knocking together so badly that he had to sit down.

Suddenly a great shadow fell over him, and the eldest son looked up. It was the dragon. The eldest son drew his sword, but the dragon lunged and swallowed him in a single gulp, sword and all, and the eldest son found himself in the dark of the dragon's belly. "What a fool I was not to listen to my wise old father!" thought the eldest son. And he began to weep bitterly. **J**

"Well," sighed the king the next morning, "I see the dragon has not been slain yet."

"I'm just as glad, personally," said the princess, sprinkling the queen. "I would have had to marry that eldest son, and he had warts." **K**

Now the cobbler's middle son decided it was his turn to try. The middle son was very strong and was known far and wide for being able to lift up the corner of a church. He felt perfectly sure he could slay the dragon by simply laying into him, but he thought it would be only polite to ask his father's advice. So he went to his father and said to him, "Well, Father, I'm off to slay the dragon. Have you any advice for me?"

The cobbler told the middle son exactly what he'd told the eldest.

"When and if you come to the dragon's lair, recite the following poem.

J **Read and Discuss** How did things turn out for the cobbler's eldest son?

K **Read and Discuss** How does the princess feel about what happens to the cobbler's eldest son?

Vocabulary **lunged** (luhnjd) *v.:* moved suddenly forward.

Dragon, dragon, how do you do?
I've come from the king to murder you.

Say it very loudly and firmly, and the dragon will fall, God willing, at your feet."

"What an odd thing to say," thought the middle son. "The old man is not as wise as I thought. You have to take these dragons by surprise." But he kept his opinion to himself and set forth. **L**

When he came in sight of the dragon's lair, the middle son spurred his horse to a gallop and thundered into the entrance, swinging his sword with all his might.

But the dragon had seen him while he was still a long way off, and being very clever, the dragon had crawled up on top of the door so that when the son came charging in, he went under the dragon and on to the back of the cave and slammed into the wall. Then the dragon chuckled and got down off the door, taking his time, and strolled back to where the man and the horse lay unconscious from the terrific blow. Opening his mouth as if for a yawn, the dragon swallowed the middle son in a single gulp and put the horse in the freezer to eat another day.

"What a fool I was not to listen to my wise old father," thought the middle son when he came to in the dragon's belly. And he too began to weep bitterly. **M**

That night there was a full moon, and the dragon ravaged the countryside so terribly that several families moved to another kingdom.

"Well," sighed the king in the morning, "still no luck in this dragon business, I see."

"I'm just as glad, myself," said the princess, moving her mother, pot and all, to the window, where the sun could get at her. "The cobbler's middle son was a kind of humpback." **N**

Now the cobbler's youngest son saw that his turn had come. He was very upset and nervous, and he wished he had never been born. He was not clever, like his eldest brother, and he was not strong, like his second-eldest brother. He was a decent, honest boy who always minded his elders.

He borrowed a suit of armor from a friend of his who was a knight, and when the youngest son put the armor on, it was so heavy he could hardly walk. From another knight he borrowed a sword, and that was so heavy that the only way the youngest son could get it to the dragon's lair was to drag it along behind his horse like a plow.

When everything was in readiness, the youngest son went for a last conversation with his father.

"Father, have you any advice to give me?" he asked.

"Only this," said the cobbler. "When and if you come to the dragon's lair, recite the following poem.

Dragon, dragon, how do you do?
I've come from the king to murder you.

L **Literary Focus** **Character and Conflict** How is the middle brother's approach like and unlike his older brother's?

M **Read and Discuss** How did things turn out for the middle son?

N **Read and Discuss** Now how do the princess's feelings about the middle son connect with what we already know about her?

Say it very loudly and firmly, and the dragon will fall, God willing, at your feet."

"Are you certain?" asked the youngest son uneasily.

"As certain as one can ever be in these matters," said the wise old cobbler. **O**

And so the youngest son set forth on his quest. He traveled over hill and dale and at last came to the dragon's cave.

The dragon, who had seen the cobbler's youngest son while he was still a long way off, was seated up above the door, inside the cave, waiting and smiling to himself. But minutes passed and no one came thundering in. The dragon frowned, puzzled, and was tempted to peek out. However, reflecting that patience seldom goes unrewarded, the dragon kept his head up out of sight and went on waiting. At last, when he could stand it no longer, the dragon craned his neck and looked. There at the entrance of the cave stood a trembling young man in a suit of armor twice his size, struggling with a sword so heavy he could lift only one end of it at a time.

At the sight of the dragon, the cobbler's youngest son began to tremble so violently that his armor rattled like a house caving in. He heaved with all his might at the sword and got the handle up level with his chest, but even now the point was down in the dirt. As loudly and firmly as he could manage, the youngest son cried—

Dragon, dragon, how do you do?
I've come from the king to murder you.

Scene from the movie *Dragonslayer* (1981).

"What?" cried the dragon, flabbergasted. "You? *You?* Murder *Me???*" All at once he began to laugh, pointing at the little cobbler's son. "*He he he ho ha!*" he roared, shaking all over, and tears filled his eyes. "*He he he ho ho ho ha ha!*" laughed the dragon. He was laughing so hard he had to hang onto his sides, and he fell off the door and landed on his back, still laughing, kicking his legs helplessly, rolling from side to side, laughing and laughing and laughing. **P**

The cobbler's son was annoyed. "I *do* come from the king to murder you," he said. "A person doesn't like to be laughed at for a thing like that."

O **Reading Focus** **Comparing and Contrasting Characters and Conflicts** The cobbler has given the same advice to all three sons. What's different about the conversation this time? What does that tell you about the youngest son?

P **Read and Discuss** What picture has the author created for us here?

Vocabulary **craned** (kraynd) *v.:* stretched (the neck) in order to see better.

"*He he he!*" wailed the dragon, almost sobbing, gasping for breath. "Of course not, poor dear boy! But really, *he he,* the *idea* of it, *ha ha ha!* And that simply *ridiculous poem!*" Tears streamed from the dragon's eyes, and he lay on his back perfectly helpless with laughter.

"It's a good poem," said the cobbler's youngest son loyally. "My father made it up." And growing angrier he shouted, "I want you to stop that laughing, or I'll—I'll—" But the dragon could not stop for the life of him. And suddenly, in a terrific rage, the cobbler's son began flopping the sword end over end in the direction of the dragon. Sweat ran off the youngest son's forehead, but he labored on, blistering mad, and at last, with one supreme heave, he had the sword standing on its handle a foot from the dragon's throat. Of its own weight the sword fell, slicing the dragon's head off.

"*He he ho huk,*" went the dragon—and then he lay dead. **Q**

The two older brothers crawled out and thanked their younger brother for saving their lives. "We have learned our lesson," they said.

Then the three brothers gathered all the treasures from the dragon's cave and tied them to the back end of the youngest brother's horse and tied the dragon's head on behind the treasures and started home. "I'm glad I listened to my father," the youngest son thought. "Now I'll be the richest man in the kingdom." **R**

There were hand-carved picture frames and silver spoons and boxes of jewels and chests of money and silver compasses and maps telling where there were more treasures buried when these ran out. There was also a curious old book with a picture of an owl on the cover, and inside, poems and odd sentences and recipes that seemed to make no sense.

When they reached the king's castle, the people all leaped for joy to see that the dragon was dead, and the princess ran out and kissed the youngest brother on the forehead, for secretly she had hoped it would be him.

"Well," said the king, "which half of the kingdom do you want?"

"My wizard's book!" exclaimed the wizard. "He's found my wizard's book!" He opened the book and ran his finger along under the words and then said in a loud voice, "Glmuzk, shkzmlp, blam!"

Instantly the queen stood before them in her natural shape, except she was soaking wet from being sprinkled too often. She glared at the king.

"Oh dear," said the king, hurrying toward the door. **S**

Q **Read and Discuss** How did things turn out for the youngest son? What did the cobbler's poem have to do with the youngest son's conquest?

R **Literary Focus** **Character and Conflict** What character trait enabled the youngest son to adapt to the situation and slay the dragon?

S **Read and Discuss** How did things turn out for the people of the kingdom?

Applying Your Skills

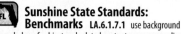

Sunshine State Standards: Benchmarks LA.6.1.7.1 use background knowledge of subject and related content areas, prereading strategies, graphic representations, and knowledge of text structure to make and confirm complex predictions of content, purpose, and organization of a reading selection; *Also covered* LA.6.1.7.8; LA.6.2.1.2; LA.6.2.1.4; LA.6.2.1.5; LA.6.4.1.1

Dragon, Dragon

Respond and Think Critically

Reading Focus

1. Which word BEST describes the tone of "Dragon, Dragon"? FCAT
   - **A** informative
   - **B** disrespectful
   - **C** suspenseful
   - **D** humorous

Read with a Purpose

2. Use this story starter: *A kingdom is plagued by a dragon. The king offers the princess's hand in marriage to anyone who can defeat the dragon. The first volunteer is_________. He_________.* Retell the main events to the end of the story.

Reading Skills: Compare and Contrast Characters and Conflicts

3. Complete the chart you filled out to help you keep track of character and conflict.

	Dragon, Dragon
Who is the hero? What is the hero like?	The cobbler's youngest son; he is nervous and not clever or strong, but he obeys his father.
What conflicts does the hero face? How are they resolved?	

Vocabulary Check

Answer the following questions.

4. What time of day was it when the dragon **ravaged** the countryside?
5. Who **lunged** at the cobbler's eldest son?
6. What would a **craned** neck look like?

Literary Focus

Literary Analysis

7. **Interpret** The poem the cobbler tells his sons to use works only when the youngest son uses it. Why do you think this is so?
8. **Analyze** What features of the plot make this story like old-fashioned fairy tales? What story elements would never appear in a "real" fairy tale? Explain how these elements make the story funny. Support your answer with details from the story. READ THINK EXPLAIN

Literary Skills: Character and Conflict

9. **Compare** The characters in this story are classic character types: a clever eldest brother, a youngest brother who seems least likely to succeed, and a beautiful princess. How are they like and unlike similar characters in traditional fairy tales? How do their traits help to move the story's conflict along?

Writing Focus

Think as a Reader/Writer

Use It in Your Writing Review your *Reader/Writer Notebook* for descriptions of actions in this story that seemed especially vivid to you. Now write an action scene from a familiar fairy tale. Use strong descriptions of actions as well as the kind of exaggeration and humor that John Gardner used in this story.

Sunshine State Standards: Benchmarks LA.6.1.7.5 analyze a variety of text structures (e.g., comparison/contrast, cause/effect, chronological order, argument/support, lists) and text features (main headings with subheadings) and explain their impact on meaning in text; **LA.6.4.1.1** write narrative accounts with an engaging plot (including rising action, conflict, climax, falling action, and resolution) include a clearly described setting with figurative language and descriptive words or phrases to enhance style and tone; *Also covered* **LA.6.4.2.3**

Medusa's Head / Perseus and the Gorgon's Head / Dragon, Dragon

Writing Focus

Write a Comparison-Contrast Essay

In an essay, compare and contrast the characters and conflicts in *two* of these stories. Review the character-conflict charts that you created and updated during and after reading the stories. Then, decide how to organize your essay.

- You can organize the essay by character and conflict, using the **point-by-point method.** In the first paragraph, compare and contrast the main characters—the heroes—of the two stories. Then, write a paragraph comparing and contrasting the central conflicts in the stories and the ways those conflicts are resolved.
- You can use the **block method** to organize your essay. Write all about one story in the first paragraph and all about the other story in the second paragraph. In each paragraph, describe the main character in the story, the conflict, and the way in which the hero resolves the conflict.

At the end of your essay, explain what you thought of each writer's treatment of his or her story. Which story did you prefer? Why?

Use the workshop on writing a Comparison-Contrast Essay, pages 106–113, for help with this assignment.

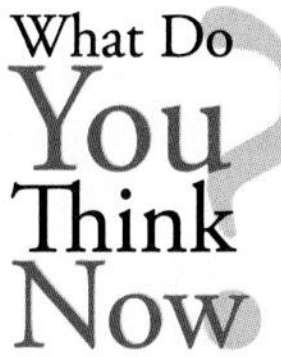

What Do You Think Now?

How do imperfect heroes achieve their goals? In what ways can an imperfect hero be just as heroic as a "perfect" heroic type?

CHOICES

As you respond to the Choices, use these **Academic Vocabulary** words as appropriate: adapt, circumstance, gender, obvious.

REVIEW

Describe a Hero

Timed Writing Heroes in real life can be of either gender; they can be young or old; they can be of any race or nation; they can be famous or unknown. Think of a real-life hero, and in a short essay, describe this person and the obvious—and not-so-obvious—qualities that make him or her heroic.

CONNECT

Create a Graphic Story

Marcia Williams uses plain language to tell the story of Perseus, but she adds illustrations and dialogue to make the story humorous. Adapt her technique to your own retelling of a myth or fairy tale. First, write the story. Then, draw it in a cartoon style and add humorous dialogue.

EXTEND

Continue a Story

At the end of "Dragon, Dragon," the queen glares at the king, who hurries toward the door. What do you suppose happens when the queen catches up with the king? Write the scene that takes place *after* the end of the story. Use what you've learned about the king and queen to keep them both "in character."

Learn It Online
Investigate these Internet links to learn more about these stories:
go.hrw.com L6-307 Go

INFORMATIONAL TEXT FOCUS

Comparison-Contrast Text Structure

CONTENTS

What Do You Think?

What's the difference between winning and doing the right thing?

QuickWrite

In what competitions—sports, games, or other contests—have you participated? Choose your favorite, and then describe its rules in a paragraph or two.

MAGAZINE ARTICLE

Preparing to Read

Sunshine State Standards: Benchmarks **LA.6.1.6.1** use new vocabulary that is introduced and taught directly; *Also covered* **LA.6.1.6.7; LA.6.1.7.5; LA.6.1.7.8**

Olympic Glory: Victories in History

Reader/Writer Notebook

Use your **RWN** to complete the activities for this selection.

Informational Text Focus

Comparison and Contrast

"Allison's pool party was like spending a day at the beach."

"Yes, but Travis's birthday party was twice as fun."

Notice how often your friends use a comparison or a contrast when they're trying to get their ideas and opinions across. We all make sense of the world by noting ways in which people, places, and ideas are similar **(comparing)** and different **(contrasting).** In the following article, you'll read about the Olympic Games. Through the **comparison–contrast text structure,** the writer helps you to see how the modern Olympics are similar to the ancient Olympics in some ways and very different in others.

Into Action A **Venn diagram** is a graphic organizer in which you can record and show similarities and differences between two things. As you read "Olympic Glory: Victories in History," use a Venn diagram like the one below to track the writer's comparison and contrast of the ancient and modern games.

Ancient	Similarities	Modern
Games only in summer	athletes want to achieve victory	Games both summer and winter

Writing Focus

Preparing for **Extended Response**

Writers use words and phrases to signal relationships between ideas. Words such as *similarly* and *likewise* indicate comparisons; phrases such as *instead of* and *on the other hand* indicate contrasts. In your *Reader/Writer Notebook,* list the signal words and phrases you find in this article.

Vocabulary

victorious (vihk TAWR ee uhs) *adj.:* having won. *Sara Hughes was victorious in the 2002 Winter Olympics.*

contemporary (kuhn TEHM puh rehr ee) *adj.:* relating to the present time; modern. *Contemporary Olympic fans can watch the Games on television.*

amateurs (AM uh churz) *n.:* people who participate in sports or other activities for fun rather than money; not professionals. *Since ancient Olympians earned money and prizes, they can't be considered amateurs.*

Language Coach

Latin Roots Many English words and word parts originally came from ancient Latin. For example, the root of *contemporary* comes from the Latin word *tempus,* meaning "time." *Amateur* comes from the Latin verb *amare,* meaning "to love." *Victorious* is built on the Latin root *vict,* "to conquer." Explain how knowing the meanings of these Latin roots can help you recognize and understand related words.

Learn It Online

Need help understanding comparison and contrast? Check out the interactive Reading Workshop:

go.hrw.com L6-309 

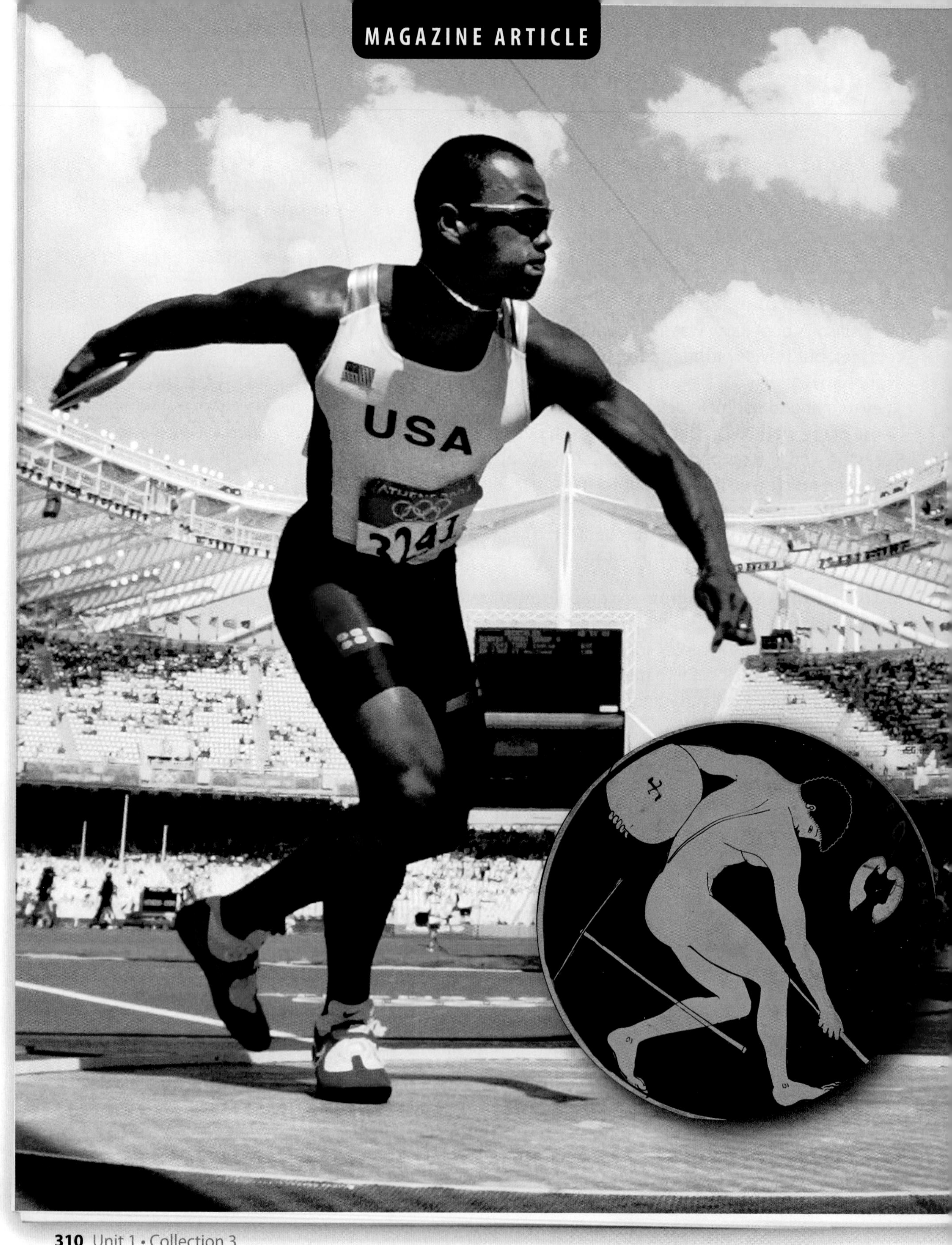
USA
3241

OLYMPIC GLORY: Victories in History

by THE WORLD ALMANAC®

Read with a Purpose

Read this article to learn how times have both changed and stayed the same for the Olympic Games.

In Greece in 1896, a shepherd named Spyridon Louis ran a footrace from Marathon to Athens and became the first "marathon" champion of the modern Olympics. He ran the race in borrowed shoes. In the Olympic Games today and in the future, one would be hard-pressed to find athletes who have trouble finding footwear. Hoping to give their brands important public exposure, makers of specialized athletic shoes can't wait to give expensive shoes to Olympians for free.

However, modern Olympic athletes will always be like Louis in some important ways. Victorious runners will be asked how it feels to triumph, and they will sound like he did: "That hour was something unimaginable, and it still appears in my memory like a dream," Louis said forty years after his moment of glory. "Everybody was calling out my name and throwing their hats in the air." Crowds will always gather. Flags will unfurl. Athletes will triumph. Some elements of the Games change with time; others are eternal. **A**

Exported from Greece

The very first Games were part of a Greek religious festival honoring Zeus, the "father" of Greek gods and goddesses. "They were a celebration of Hellenic culture,"[1] says David Potter, professor of Greek and Latin at the University of Michigan. Now, those gods and goddesses

1. **Hellenic** (heh LEHN ihk) **culture:** culture of the ancient Greeks during the period 776 B.C. to 323 B.C. Hellen was a mythological king believed to be the ancestor of all true Greeks.

A **Informational Focus** **Comparison-Contrast** The writer begins this article by mentioning that even the modern Olympics have changed through time. What is the writer's point here? What features of the Olympics remain the same across time?

Vocabulary **victorious** (vihk TAWR ee uhs) *adj.:* having won.

are ancient myth, and the Games include athletes from all around the world, not just the Greek city-states of ancient times.

The ancient Olympics were held every four years in Olympia from 776 B.C. through A.D. 393—over one thousand years! The Games were revived in 1896 as international competitions. Today's Olympics are run by international committees rather than by Greek officials, and athletes gather in different host cities each time, not just in Olympia. Now, as in ancient times, says Potter, "The point in part is for people to come and represent who they are and where they're from."

Games for All Seasons

The ancient Games were summertime events. In the modern world, however, there are Winter Games as well. Like the ancient Games, the modern Summer and Winter Olympics are each held every four years, with the two alternating on even-numbered years. **B**

When the Olympics began in 776 B.C., they consisted of one footrace—covering a distance of 600 feet. In contrast, twenty-eight summer sports were set for the year 2008, and seven sports are scheduled for the 2010 Winter Games. "The range of sports has expanded enormously," says Potter. "The Olympians established a very small canon[2] of sports initially. Now it appears to be an Olympian sport in itself to see what can be added each time." **C**

Ancient Olympians battled the Mediterranean heat, so to toughen up, they practiced in the sun. At the events, according to historians, they wore little or no clothing. Such a dress code would be shocking to modern sensibilities and a blow to manufacturers of sportswear and accessories—who, like shoemakers, make certain to place their products in the public eye during the Olympic Games. **D**

2. **canon** (KAN uhn): accepted body of rules, principles, or other norms. Here, the word refers to sports approved for the ancient Olympics.

B Informational Focus Comparison and Contrast In terms of when they are held, how are the modern Olympics like the ancient ones? How are they different?

C Informational Focus Comparison and Contrast What point of contrast is Potter making here?

D Read and Discuss What has changed since the ancient Greek games?

Analyzing Visuals **Viewing and Interpreting** How do the athletes in this illustration seem to reflect the attitudes of all Olympic athletes?

Timeless Traditions

What has stayed the same in the Olympic Games between ancient and contemporary times? The motivation of the athletes is one enduring value. The hope of victory and the chance for fame propel an athlete's future, and there is "enormous economic benefit" for winning, says Potter. (In fact, the Greek word *athlete* means "one who competes for a prize.") In 516 B.C., Milo of Kroton wrestled his way into history and became the most famous Olympian of ancient times and the subject of legends. In 2002, Sarah Hughes figure-skated her way to a Gold Medal. One was a man from an ancient world; the other, a woman from our time. However, both stand in a long line of athletes who established Olympian fame and then fortune. Although contemporary athletes may not become the subjects of legends that last for centuries, they can end up temporarily "immortalized" on cereal boxes, in magazine and TV ads, on billboards, and on product labels. **E**

Amateurs and Other Myths

"A myth was promulgated[3] that these guys were amateurs," says Potter of the original Olympians. "But these guys were professionals. The people who go to the Games want to see the best possible performance." Now,

3. **promulgated** (PRAHM uhl gayt ihd): spread; made known.

E **Informational Focus** **Comparison-Contrast** According to the article, what do ancient and modern athletes have in common?

Vocabulary **contemporary** (kuhn TEHM puh rehr ee) *adj.:* relating to the present time; modern.
amateurs (AM uh churz) *n.:* people who participate in sports or other activities for fun rather than money; not professionals.

Analyzing Visuals **Viewing and Interpreting** In what way does the design of this poster for the 1928 Olympics reinforce the author's claim that the Olympics are timeless?

as in ancient times, people expect to witness the highest levels of athletic achievement at the Olympics. The athletes may not be *professionals* in the strict sense of the term—people of outstanding qualifications and experience hired and paid to perform—but they are true professionals in their level of achievement and commitment to their sport.

Another myth is that female Olympians like Hughes are something new. Ancient Olympia had a festival to honor Hera, the wife of Zeus, and in that festival unmarried girls ran footrace competitions. So women, too, have been holding the Olympic torch from the start. **F**

Carrying a Torch for the Olympics

In reality, though, no one has held the torch from the "start" of the Olympics in ancient times. The symbol of the Olympic torch wasn't introduced until 1928. Although the Greeks used torches in many of their religious festivals and kept a fire burning in honor of the god Prometheus during the ancient Olympic Games, there was no opening ceremony involving an Olympic torch. The Olympic torch ceremony—like the Olympic symbol of five interconnected rings—is actually a modern touch, a bit of dramatic staging. **G**

The main constant in the Olympics, says Potter, is the sense that the Games stand apart in time. "That weekend, for that weekend, the world would stop," he says. "You wanted to be there." Judging by the interest in today's Olympics, that old feeling remains. It's just that the audience has widened from those hundreds or thousands in attendance at the ancient Greek Olympic Games to the many millions of fascinated TV and Internet viewers around the world today.

Read with a Purpose In what main ways are the Olympics today still like the Games that were held in ancient Greece?

F **Read and Discuss** What is the writer letting us know here about Olympic athletes?

G **Read and Discuss** What is this paragraph telling us about the Olympic torch?

Applying Your Skills

Sunshine State Standards: Benchmarks LA.6.1.7.5 analyze a variety of text structures (e.g, comparison/contrast, cause/effect, chronological order, argument/support, lists) and text features (main headings with subheadings) and explain their impact on meaning in text ; *Also covered* **LA.6.4.2.3**

Olympic Glory: Victories in History

Practicing for FCAT

Informational Text and Vocabulary

1. Which element was an addition to the Olympic Games in modern times?
   A crowds
   B the Olympic torch
   C footraces
   D competition

2. Which is NOT a difference between the ancient Olympics and the modern Olympics?
   F winter sports
   G sportswear and accessories
   H fame and fortune
   I Olympic rings symbol

3. What does the section of the article titled "Timeless Tradition" mostly discuss?
   A rules of the original Olympic games
   B times when the Olympics were less popular
   C ways in which the Olympics are unchanged
   D the Olympic torch

4. In which situation would reading a comparison/contrast article be MOST helpful?
   F You need to find out how life in China differs from life in the United States.
   G You need to do research on Milo of Kroton.
   H You need to find out why Jack London is considered a great American writer.
   I You need to learn how a sport becomes an Olympic event.

5. Read the sentence from the passage.
   Victorious runners will be asked how it feels to triumph, and they will sound like he did: "That hour was something unimaginable, and it still appears in my memory like a dream," Louis said forty years after his moment of glory.
   What does the word *victorious* mean?
   A winning
   B unsuccessful
   C uninteresting
   D cheating

6. Read the sentence from the passage.
   What has stayed the same in the Olympic Games between ancient and contemporary times?
   What does the word *contemporary* mean?
   F athletic
   G separate
   H exciting
   I current

Writing Focus Extended Response

Compare and contrast the Olympic Games with a game that you play. Include phrases that signal comparisons and contrasts. Support your answer with details from the text.

What Do You Think Now?

Is it possible to be a "winner" and yet not have done the right thing? How might this happen in the Olympics?

Preparing to Read

Sunshine State Standards: Benchmarks
LA.6.1.6.7 identify and understand the meaning of conceptually advanced prefixes, suffixes, and root words; *Also covered* **LA.6.1.7.5**

Going to Bat for Baseball and Cricket

Informational Text Focus

Comparison-Contrast: Point-by-Point and Block Patterns When writers **compare** things, they look for similarities. When they **contrast** things, they look for differences. A writer who wants to explore two subjects that have important similarities and differences will choose a comparison-contrast pattern that makes his or her points obvious to readers.

Writers generally arrange their ideas according to one of two comparison-contrast organizational patterns: the point-by-point pattern and the block pattern. A writer using the **point-by-point pattern** moves back and forth between the subjects being compared, exploring each point for both subjects before moving to the next point. A writer using the **block pattern** covers all the points of comparison for the first subject, then all the points of comparison for the second subject, and so on. (See the charts below.)

Point-by-Point Pattern	
Point 1: teams	Baseball: two teams of nine players Cricket: two teams of eleven players
Point 2: field	Baseball: infield and outfield Cricket: the pitch and wickets

Block Pattern	
Subject 1: baseball	Feature 1: teams; Feature 2: field . . .
Subject 2: cricket	Feature 1: teams; Feature 2: field . . .

Writing Focus

Preparing for **Extended Response**

The following article explains how baseball and cricket have much in common and yet have many differences. Pay attention to the features of each sport and where and how the features are presented in the article.

Reader/Writer Notebook

Use your **RWN** to complete the activities for this selection.

Vocabulary

competition (kahm puh TIHSH uhn) *n.:* contest; struggle to see who is better. *Baseball and cricket are games of competition, with clear winners and losers.*

protective (pruh TEHK tihv) *adj.:* preventing injury. *Different protective gear is used in baseball and cricket.*

aggressive (uh GREHS ihv) *adj.:* ready to attack. *Baseball players are aggressive when they are batting.*

Language Coach

Prefixes A **prefix** is a letter or group of letters added to the beginning of a word to create a new word. Each prefix has a specific meaning—sometimes even more than one meaning. The first two Vocabulary words above have common prefixes: *com–*, meaning "together," and *pro–*, meaning "before," "moving forward," or "in support of." What other words do you know that begin with *com–* or *pro–*? What is the meaning of these words?

Learn It Online

Use Word Watch to dig deeper into your understanding of words:

go.hrw.com L6-316 

ALMANAC ARTICLE

GOING TO BAT for Baseball and Cricket

by

Read with a Purpose

Read this article to discover the ways baseball and cricket are alike—and how they are different.

Although there are other hugely popular American sports, such as football and basketball, baseball has a special place in Americans' hearts. In fact, baseball—which has been part of U.S. culture since the first recorded professional game in 1846—is often called "America's pastime." Not only Americans love the game: Baseball has proven to be a big hit from Canada to Latin America and from Japan to South Korea and Taiwan. Today it's played in more than one hundred countries.

Another famous sport played with bats and balls is a game from England called cricket—and it has nothing to do with the insect! Cricket is so near and dear to British culture that there's even a saying—"It's just not cricket"—to describe something that's unfair, wrong, or just not exactly what it should be. Cricket is a lot older than baseball—some say that a version of cricket started hundreds of years ago, in the Middle Ages. Cricket is especially popular in the Commonwealth nations once ruled by Great Britain: Australia, India, parts of the Caribbean, Kenya, South Africa, and Zimbabwe. In all, cricket is played and enjoyed in over one hundred nations throughout the world. **A**

Both baseball and cricket involve a team that is fielding and another that is batting. Beyond that basic similarity, though, there is a world of difference between the two games. **B**

A Informational Focus **Comparison-Contrast** What pattern of organization does the writer seem to be setting up in these first two paragraphs: block pattern or point-by-point pattern? What makes you think this?

B Read and Discuss What is the writer setting up for the reader in this paragraph?

The In(ning)s and Outs of Baseball

Baseball is a competition between two teams of nine players each (not including reserves).[1] Nine periods called *innings* make up a regular game. The game is played on an infield and an outfield. The *infield* is outlined by four flat *bases* laid out in a diamond shape, with the fourth base, known as *home plate*, at the bottom. Inside the diamond is a *pitcher's mound.* Beyond the diamond top is the *outfield.*

The person throwing the fist-sized ball from the mound is the *pitcher.* An opposing player, known as the *batter,* stands next to home plate and attempts to hit the ball with a rounded, narrow wooden bat. Behind the batter is the *catcher.* The pitcher aims for the *strike zone,* the area over home plate between the batter's shoulders and knees. If the ball goes through the strike zone without bouncing and the batter misses, the pitch is a *strike.*

One batter is up at a time. If the pitcher accidentally hits the batter with the ball, the batter gets to advance to first base. Pitchers try to avoid that, so batters do not need to wear protective pads, as some sports players do. They do, however, wear helmets. After all, some of those baseballs come at them pretty fast—sometimes over a hundred miles per hour in professional games! **C**

A batter's goal is to run the bases, so he or she tries to hit the ball toward an area of the field that is not well guarded. Generally, batters hit the ball in a forceful, aggressive way, using all their might. After hitting the ball, the batter has to immediately drop the bat and run for the bases. Players move around the bases counterclockwise, scoring for each runner who reaches home plate. If the batter has hit the ball forcefully *and* far—maybe even "hitting it out of the ballpark"—he or she may have scored a *home run,* meaning that the batter will be able to make it all the way around the bases without getting tagged "out." (An *out* occurs when a runner is tagged while not on base, though an out can also be called when three strikes are thrown or when a fielder catches a batted ball.) **D**

Because each team gets three outs per inning and those outs can take a while to pile up, the pace of a baseball game can be slow. Most professional games are over in three to three and a half hours, but sometimes a game will go into extra innings. The longest such game in the more-modern history of baseball lasted twenty-five innings—a little over eight hours! Even a nine-inning game can last four and a half hours or more. Still, time spent playing doesn't necessarily equal points. Scores in baseball games tend to be low—often in the single digits. The highest number of runs ever scored in a single baseball game

1. **reserves** (rih ZURVZ): players on a team who back up the starters or come into the game for special situations.

C **Read and Discuss** You've been given a lot of information. What does the writer want you to learn from it?

D **Informational Focus** **Comparison-Contrast** So far in this section, the writer has been telling you only about the rules of baseball and nothing about cricket. Why?

Vocabulary **competition** (kahm puh TIHSH uhn) *n.:* contest; struggle to see who is better.
protective (pruh TEHK tihv) *adj.:* preventing injury.
aggressive (uh GREHS ihv) *adj.:* ready to attack.

Analyzing Visuals

Viewing and Interpreting What similarities and differences between the batter and the batsman described in the article do you see in these photographs?

was 49, way back in 1922, when the Chicago Cubs defeated the Philadelphia Phillies with a final score of 26–23. **E**

What's a Wicket in Cricket?

Cricket is played by two teams of eleven players each on an elliptical, or oval-shaped, field. The center of the field is the *pitch,* a rectangle marked at each end by white lines called *popping creases,* or just *creases.* Beyond each crease is a *wicket:* three wooden stumps topped by two cross pieces. The *bowler* (not pitcher) stands behind a wicket. He or she runs up to the crease from behind the wicket and then releases the ball—which most often bounces at least once—toward an opposing player known as the *batsman.* **F**

Teams are divided into bowling and batting sides. The bowling team has all eleven of its players on the field—one is the bowler, another is the *wicket keeper,* and the rest play various fielding positions. A cricket match is very long, and it is divided up into *overs.* Each *over* consists of the bowler delivering the ball to a batsman six times in a row. After the sixth bowl, the bowler rotates to take a fielding position, and another member of the team takes his or her place.

E **Informational Focus** **Comparison-Contrast**
What was the topic of the section you just read? Is this article organized mostly in a point-by-point pattern or a block pattern?

F **Informational Focus** **Comparison-Contrast**
How many players are on each team in cricket? in baseball? Where in the article did you find each of these facts?

Analyzing Visuals

Viewing and Interpreting What similarities and differences between baseball and cricket described in the article do you see in this photograph?

The batting team has only two batsmen on the field at a time, each standing on opposite ends of the field near a wicket. The batsman who is chosen to receive the ball from the bowler is called the *striker;* the other batsman is the *nonstriker,* who stands near the bowler's end of the field. The bats used in cricket are wide and flat, and a batsman's goal is to keep the ball away from the wicket. When the striker hits the ball into the field, he or she may run across the pitch still holding the bat and change places with the nonstriker. A *run* is scored each time a batsman reaches the opposite crease. Batsmen have to watch out, though. Bowlers are allowed to hit batsmen, so batsmen cover up with protective pads. It can get dangerous on the cricket field! **G**

There are at least ten ways that an *out,* also called a *dismissal,* can be declared against a batsman in cricket. (One way is to break the wicket!) When all ten batsmen from each side have been declared "out" once, an *innings* (the *s* is no mistake) has been completed. Generally, a cricket match of one innings takes place in one day and lasts up to six or even eight hours! (Some cricket matches can take place over three to five days.) In a typical cricket match, the two teams can make hundreds of runs, and scores can be in the triple digits. **H**

The differences between baseball and cricket could fill a book. In fact, both games have very detailed rule books that you can find online. These rule books point to what is perhaps the biggest similarity the games share: their emphasis on good sportsmanship, on playing fairly and "by the rules." Just don't let the presence of a bat and a ball in both sports fool you. It's just not cricket to confuse the two games! **I**

Read with a Purpose What did you learn about either baseball or cricket that you didn't know before?

G **Informational Focus** **Comparison-Contrast** How do cricket bats differ from baseball bats?

H **Read and Discuss** Now what is the author talking about? What do the high scores tell you about the game?

I **Read and Discuss** What is the main point the author is trying to make about baseball and cricket? If you have never played either cricket or baseball, what's to be gained from reading this article?

Applying Your Skills

Going to Bat for Baseball and Cricket

Sunshine State Standards: Benchmarks LA.6.1.7.2 analyze the author's purpose (e.g., to persuade, inform, entertain, or explain) and perspective in a variety of texts and understand how they affect meaning; **LA.6.1.7.5** analyze a variety of text structures (e.g., comparison/contrast, cause/effect, chronological order, argument/support, lists) and text features (main headings with subheadings) and explain their impact on meaning in text; *Also covered* **LA.6.4.2.3**

Practicing for FCAT

Informational Text and Vocabulary

1. Which statement is true of baseball?
   - **A** Each team gets nine outs per game.
   - **B** Batters wear only protective pads, not helmets.
   - **C** The pitcher stands on a mound.
   - **D** Scores tend to be high, often more than one hundred runs.

2. What is the main reason this article was written?
   - **F** to name different sports around the world
   - **G** to persuade people to play baseball more often
   - **H** to prove that cricket is the best sport
   - **I** to explain the differences between baseball and cricket

3. Where do the two batsmen stand in cricket?
   - **A** on top of each wicket
   - **B** on opposite ends of the field
   - **C** next to the bowler
   - **D** outside the pitch

4. Which organizational pattern does this writer mainly use to compare and contrast baseball and cricket?
   - **F** chronological pattern
   - **G** point-by-point pattern
   - **H** block pattern
   - **I** cause-and-effect pattern

5. Read the sentence from the passage.

   Baseball is a competition between two teams of nine players each (not including reserves).

   What does the word *competition* mean?
   - **A** a rivalry between two teams
   - **B** a pitch to the pitcher's mound
   - **C** a fielding position in cricket
   - **D** a fight between baseball and cricket players

6. Read the sentence from the passage.

   Generally, batters hit the ball in a forceful, aggressive way, using all their might.

   What does the word *aggressive* mean?
   - **F** talented
   - **G** attacking
   - **H** professional
   - **I** quick

Writing Focus Extended Response

Compare and contrast baseball and cricket. Present the similarities and differences using either a block or point-by-point pattern. Support your answer with details from the article.

What Do You Think Now

Why do competitive sports like baseball and cricket have strict rules? What would organized sports be like without such rules?

Writing Workshop

"How-to" Explanation FCAT Writing+

Write with a Purpose

Write a "how-to" explanation that teaches readers how to do something or make something. Your **audience** is other students your age. Your **purpose** is to explain each step so clearly that your audience can easily follow your directions.

A Good "How-to" Explanation

- explains why someone would want to complete the task
- lists necessary materials, if any
- is organized in clear chronological order, with steps listed in the correct order they should be completed
- includes specific details and precise language that help readers follow the steps
- concludes by summarizing the steps and/or restating the reason for making the product or completing the process

Reader/Writer Notebook

Use your **RWN** to complete the activities for this workshop.

Think as a Reader/Writer

Before you write your "how-to" explanation, read this excerpt from Paula Morrow's "Making a Flying Fish," published in *FACES* magazine. The article explains how to make a *koinobori,* a fish that is made of cloth or strong paper. The *koinobori* is attached to a pole in the gardens of many Japanese families to honor their children.

You can make your own *koinobori* and fly it from a pole or hang it from your window on May 5. In that way, you can share Children's Day with the boys and girls of Japan.

← The introduction states **why** you would want to make a *koinobori.*

You need an 18- by 30-inch piece of lightweight cloth (cotton, rayon, or nylon), fabric paints or felt-tip markers, a needle and thread, scissors, a narrow plastic headband, and string.

← All the necessary **materials** are listed.

First, choose a piece of cloth with a bright, colorful pattern or decorate it yourself with felt-tip markers. Fold the fabric in half lengthwise, with the bright side on the inside. Sew a seam 1/2 inch from the long (30-inch) edge, making a sleeve.

← Words like *First* help readers know the **order** of steps to follow.

On one end of the sleeve, make a 1-inch-wide hem by turning the right side of the fabric over the wrong side. Then, sew the hem, leaving three 1-inch-wide openings about 5 inches apart.

← The writer is very **precise** about the size and placement of the openings.

Think About the Professional Model

With a partner, discuss the following questions about the model.

1. Which specific details in the list of materials are most helpful?
2. Which step can you picture most clearly in your mind? Why?
3. The magazine article included an illustration of the step described in the last paragraph. Is the step clear without the illustration? Why or why not?

Sunshine State Standards: Benchmarks **LA.6.3.1.1** generating ideas from multiple sources (e.g., prior knowledge, discussion with others, writer's notebook, research materials, or other reliable sources), based upon teacher-directed topics and personal interests; **LA.6.3.1.2** making a plan for writing that prioritizes ideas, addresses purpose, audience, main idea, and logical sequence; **LA.6.3.1.3** using organizational strategies and tools (e.g., technology, outline, chart, table, graph, web, story map); **LA.6.3.2.2** organizing information into a logical sequence and combining or deleting sentences to enhance clarity; **LA.6.3.3.1** evaluating the draft for development of ideas and content, logical organization, voice, point of view, word choice, and sentence variation; *Also covered* **LA.6.3.3.2; LA.6.3.3.4; LA.6.3.4.3; LA.6.3.5.1; LA.6.3.5.2; LA.6.3.5.3; LA.6.4.2.1; LA.6.4.2.3; LA.6.5.2.2**

Prewriting

Choose a Topic

To choose a topic for your "how-to" explanation, follow the rule successful writers live by: Write about what you know. Brainstorm a list of products that you have made or processes that you know how to complete. The Idea Starters in the margin at right might be helpful.

As you narrow your list of ideas, make a chart like the one below to help you evaluate the topics. You can see which topic would be best for this student by examining his answers to the questions.

Topic	Have I made this or done this before, and do I know the process well?	Does this process have a manageable number of steps (between three and five)?
How to make a paper swan	yes	No—it has more than five steps.
How to instant message	yes	Yes—it has about four steps.
How to build a soapbox car	Not really—I helped my older brother make it.	No—this probably takes more than five steps.
How to remove a bicycle wheel with quick-release hubs	yes	No—there are really only two steps.

Present the Steps in Order

One of the most important parts of writing a "how-to" explanation is presenting the steps in the proper order. This structure gives the explanation coherence—that is, the parts fit together in a way that makes sense to the reader. When a "how-to" explanation lacks coherence, readers can become very frustrated. Most "how-to" explanations are written in **chronological order,** or the order in which steps should be carried out.

To think of the steps in chronological order, imagine making the product or completing the process. What do you do first, next, and last? As you picture each step, write it down. Then, look over your steps and add anything you left out.

Idea Starters

- something you have built or made at home
- a school project
- your favorite recipe
- handicrafts you can make
- tasks that relate to your favorite hobby or pastime

Your Turn

Get Started In your **RWN,** list the steps required to make your product or complete your process. Be sure to number the steps in correct **chronological order.** Your explanation should follow this chronological order.

Learn It Online

See how one writer develops a how-to essay at:

go.hrw.com L6-323 

Writing Tip

Think about specific details you can use to describe your steps and materials list. Ask questions such as *when? where? what kind? which one? how?* and *how much?* Write down these specific details in your **RWN** so you will remember to be precise as you write your draft.

List the Materials

Once you have decided on the steps and their correct order, look them over to see what **materials** are required. List the materials, thinking carefully about everything needed to make the product or complete the process. Be **precise** in how you describe materials. For example, "a two-inch length of black yarn" is more precise than merely "yarn." Double-check the list when you complete it. If you leave something out of your materials list, your readers will not be able to follow your directions successfully.

Now decide where you want to place the list of materials within your explanation. Most "how-to" explanations include the materials list at the beginning, separate from the steps. However, as you saw in "Making a Flying Fish," the materials can also be presented in paragraph form.

Consider Purpose and Audience

Since your **purpose** is to teach someone how to do or make something, make sure you can successfully complete this process yourself. You are acting as an expert on the process, so you need to be confident that your instructions are accurate and complete. As you select your final topic, also remember that your **audience** is other students your age. Try to choose something they will *want* to do or make, and think about how specific you'll need to be in describing the steps and materials.

Organize Your Ideas

Use a planning chart like the one below to organize your ideas. This chart has been completed for the Student Draft on pages 327–328.

Planning Chart for "How to Instant Message"	
Purpose statement	Explain how to use instant messaging
Materials list	None (understood that computer or other IM device will be needed)
Steps in order	1. Get registered. 2. Sign on. 3. Fill the buddy list. 4. Select a buddy, type a message, and click "send."
Restatement of purpose	You are instantly connected with buddies.

Your Turn

Create a Planning Chart Use a planning chart to organize your ideas for your own "how-to" explanation. Be sure to include all the **materials** that will be needed and to use **precise language** to describe materials and steps.

Drafting

Get Your Readers' Attention

As you start to write your draft, think of a way to draw the reader into your "how-to" explanation. One way is to begin with a question. For example, if you were going to explain how to make a spicy soup, you could begin with a question like "Do you want to beat the winter blahs?" Then you could state your purpose: "This recipe will show you how to make a chill-chasing soup with ingredients found in most kitchens." You can refer to the **Writer's Framework** at right as you write your draft.

A Writer's Framework

Introduction
- Attention-grabbing opener and purpose statement

Body
- Materials list, if any
- Step 1 (with precise language)
- Step 2 (with precise language) and so on . . .

Conclusion
- Summary of steps and restatement of purpose

Writing Tip

Remember that your conclusion should **restate the reason** for making the product or completing the process.

Present Steps Clearly and Use Transitions

When you present the steps of your process, the best idea is to describe one step per paragraph. That way, the reader has a visual cue that you're presenting a new step.

Another way to make your steps clear is to connect them with transitions. "How-to" explanations most often use chronological transitions and spatial transitions.

- **Chronological transitions,** such as *first, second, after, next, then, finally,* and *last,* answer the question "In what order?"
- **Spatial transitions,** such as *inside, outside, above, below, into,* and *out of,* answer the question "Where?"

Grammar Link Punctuating Words in a Series

When you write a "how-to" explanation, you may present steps or list materials in a series. A **series** consists of three or more items written one after another. Study the following example from "Making a Flying Fish," and be sure to follow the rules for punctuating a series when you write your draft.

> "You need an 18- by 30-inch piece of lightweight cloth (cotton, rayon, or nylon), fabric paints or felt-tip markers, a needle and thread, scissors, a narrow plastic headband, and string."

Use commas to separate three or more items in a series.

Your Turn

Write Your Draft Follow your plan and the framework to write a draft of your "how-to" explanation. Remember to think about the following:

- How will you get your readers' attention?
- What **transitions** can you use to make your steps clear?

Peer Review

Have a partner read your explanation to see how confident he or she feels about being able to complete the process. Take notes about his or her questions. Then, serve as your partner's reviewer. Use this chart to locate where and how your drafts can be improved.

Evaluating and Revising

Once you've written your draft, you'll want to go back through and look for ways to improve your "how-to" explanation. The chart below will help you identify ways to revise your draft.

"How-to" Explanation: Guidelines for Content and Organization

Evaluation Question	Tip	Revision Technique
1. Does the introduction grab the readers' attention and state why they would want to complete this process? Does it state a clear purpose?	**Put an asterisk** next to the statement of the reason readers would want to complete the process. **Put brackets** around the statement of purpose.	If needed, **add** a more powerful statement of the reason. **Add** a statement of purpose.
2. Are all of the required materials listed?	**Circle** all the materials needed, if any.	**Add** any materials that have been left out.
3. Are the steps of the process in the correct chronological order?	**Write a number** next to each step in the margin of the paper.	To improve coherence, **rearrange** the steps so they are in the correct order. To make the order clear, think about putting each step in its own paragraph.
4. Is each step described with precise language?	**Underline** precise verbs, nouns, and adjectives.	If necessary, **elaborate** on the steps by adding precise words.
5. Does the conclusion restate the reason for completing the process?	**Put a star** beside the sentence that restates the reason.	**Add** a sentence that restates the reason.

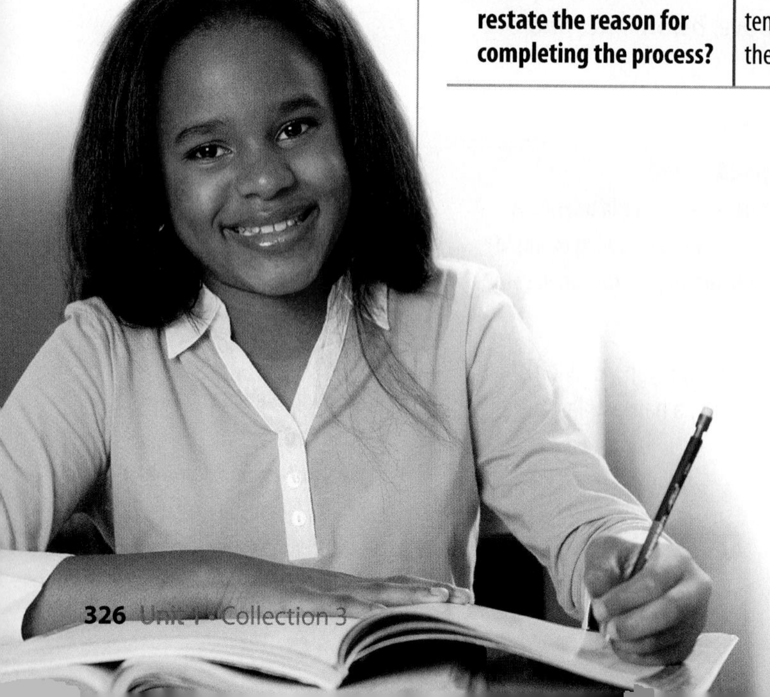

Read this student draft, and notice the comments on its strengths as well as suggestions on how the draft could be improved.

Student Draft

How to Instant Message

by Christopher Cultrara, Queen of Peace Elementary School

Today, people use many different forms of communication, from letters to e-mail. Instant messaging is quickly becoming a favorite of people of all ages. In this essay I'll explain how to get started on instant messaging.

← **The introduction makes general comments about instant messaging.**

The first thing you need to do is get registered and get a screen name. Most people use a common instant messaging engine, so that's where you should start. Go to the instant messaging Web site and click on the "get a new screen name" link. Next, fill in all of the information that's requested. Then, enter the screen name you want to use, and enter a password. Your screen name and password can be anything you want. I always write my password and screen name in a safe place in case I forget them. Finally, click on "submit" to submit all of the information. You should then have your screen name and be able to sign on.

← Steps of the process are in **chronological order,** and Christopher uses clear **time-order transition** words.

← Christopher adds a personal note of advice.

MINI-LESSON How to Introduce a "How-to" Essay

The introduction of a "how-to" essay should explain the writer's personal interest in the topic and connect the **audience** to the task. Your introduction should help a reader answer, "Why do I need to know this?"

Christopher begins his essay with general comments and says that he will explain how to use instant messaging. A clear explanation of *why* readers might want to use instant messaging would make his introduction more effective.

Christopher's Revision of Paragraph One

Today, people use many different forms of communication, from letters to e-mail. ~~In this essay, I'll explain how to get started on instant messaging.~~ If you are looking for a simple and fun way to stay in immediate contact with your family and friends, instant messaging is fun and simple. I stay in contact with everyone and never miss important events or parties anymore. Get ready for flying fingers and instant messaging.

Your Turn

Introduce Your "How-to" Essay Read your draft to make sure your introduction connects with the reader. Ask yourself these questions:

- Have I explained my interest in the topic?
- Have I suggested a possible connection for the reader?

Student Draft *continues*

Specific details and precise examples help readers "see" the steps. →

Now you need to fill your buddy list. To get your buddy list, you must sign on using your screen name. Once you are signed on and your buddy list comes up, you can begin to enter your friends' screen names. Insert them into your buddy list by typing them in under "new buddy."

Once you get some specific names in your list, you can arrange them into groups, such as "friends" or "family." You can also make up new groups and call them anything you want.

The conclusion **restates why** readers would want to complete this process. →

Now that you are set up, instant messaging itself is very simple. Just click on the buddy you want to instant message. That will display the instant message window. Type in your message and hit "send." That's all there is to it. You and your "buddies" are connected in an instant! Enjoy!

MINI-LESSON How to Add Personal Advice

A "how-to" essay can be dry and impersonal if the writer does not include advice or tips throughout. When Christopher revised his paper, he decided to add some personal advice based on his own experience.

Christopher's Draft of Paragraph Three

Now you need to fill your buddy list. To get your buddy list, you must sign on using your screen name. Once you are signed on and your buddy list comes up, you can begin to enter your friends' screen names. Insert them into your buddy list by typing them in under "new buddy."

Christopher's Revision of Paragraph Three

Now you need to fill your buddy list. To get your buddy list, you must sign on using your screen name. Once you are signed on and your buddy list comes up, you can begin to enter your friends' screen names. Insert them into your buddy list by typing them in under "new buddy." When you're sending a message, be careful to select your intended buddy. I once sent a message to an entire group of friends, and I meant to send it only to my brother—extremely embarrassing!

Your Turn

Add Personal Advice Re-read your "how-to" explanation, looking for places where you can add personal advice or experience that is specific and helpful. Add at least one tip or experience that could help your reader be more successful with the task.

Proofreading and Publishing

Proofreading

You have revised your "how-to" explanation and feel confident that readers can follow the steps to make the product or complete the process. Now it's time to make sure your explanation is free from errors, which could confuse or distract your readers. Read your "how-to" explanation carefully, editing to correct any misspellings, punctuation errors, or problems in sentence structure.

Grammar Link Avoiding Overused Adverbs

Be careful to avoid overused adverbs, such as *very* and *really.* Precise adverbs will help readers understand details about your steps, such as *how, when,* and *to what extent.* Overused adverbs won't add much meaning to what you write. For example, Christopher has used *very* in his final paragraph. When he changes *very* to a more descriptive adverb, his sentence becomes much more powerful and convincing.

> Now that you are set up, instant messaging itself is ~~very~~ surprisingly simple.

Publishing

Now it's time to publish your "how-to" explanation to a wider audience. Here are some ways to share your explanation:

- Make copies of your explanation for all of your classmates, and ask your teacher if you can demonstrate the process in class.
- Collect the class's "how-to" explanations, and divide them into categories, such as recipes or crafts. Publish each explanation in an online "how-to" library that is organized by category.

Reflect on the Process Thinking about how you wrote your "how-to" explanation will help you with other types of writing. In your **RWN,** write a short response to each of the following questions:

1. Which step in the process was hardest for you to explain? How did you think through this problem?
2. How did creating a materials list cause you to think differently about using descriptions and explanations in your writing?
3. What writing skill that you learned in this workshop could you use in other types of writing?

Proofreading Tip

Ask two classmates to help you proofread your explanation. This way, each person can focus on a single area that needs attention during the editing process. Ask a peer to look specifically for overused adverbs in your explanation.

Your Turn

Proofread and Publish

As you proofread, look carefully for overused adverbs. Try to replace any overused adverbs with more descriptive words. Share your "how-to" essay with your classmates or others interested in the process.

Scoring Rubric for FCAT Writing+

You can use the six-point rubric below to evaluate your on-demand expository essay.

6-Point Scale

Score 6 ***is focused, purposeful, and reflects insight into the writing situation***

- conveys a sense of completeness and wholeness with adherence to the main idea
- uses an effective organizational pattern with a logical progression of ideas
- provides substantial, specific, relevant, concrete, or illustrative support
- demonstrates a commitment to and an involvement with the subject
- presents ideas with clarity
- may use creative writing strategies appropriate to the purpose of the paper
- demonstrates mature command of language with freshness of expression
- shows variation in sentence structure
- employs complete sentences except when fragments are used purposefully
- contains few, if any, convention errors in mechanics, usage, and punctuation

Score 5 ***is focused on the topic***

- conveys a sense of completeness and wholeness
- uses an organization pattern with a progression of ideas, although some lapses may occur
- provides ample support
- demonstrates a mature command of language with precise word choice
- shows variation in sentence structure
- with rare exceptions, employs complete sentences except when fragments are used purposefully
- generally follows the conventions of mechanics, usage, and spelling

Score 4 ***is generally focused on the topic but may include extraneous or loosely related material***

- exhibits some sense of completeness and wholeness
- uses an apparent organization pattern, although some lapses may occur
- provides adequate support, although development may be uneven
- demonstrates adequate word choice
- shows little variation in sentence structure
- employs complete sentences most of the time
- generally follows the conventions of mechanics, usage, and spelling

Score 3 ***is generally focused on the topic but may include extraneous or loosely related material***

- attempts to use an organization pattern but may lack a sense of completeness or wholeness
- provides some support but development is erratic
- demonstrates adequate word choice but word choice may be limited, predictable, or occasionally vague
- shows little, if any, variation in sentence structure
- usually demonstrates knowledge of the conventions of mechanics and usage
- usually employs correct spelling of commonly used words

Score 2 ***is related to the topic but includes extraneous or loosely related material***

- demonstrates little evidence of an organizational pattern and may lack a sense of completeness or wholeness
- provides inadequate or illogical development of support
- demonstrates limited, inappropriate, or vague word choice
- shows little, if any, variation in sentence structure and may contain gross errors in sentence structure
- contains errors in basic conventions of mechanics and usage
- contains misspellings of commonly used words

Score 1 ***may minimally address the topic and is a fragmentary or incoherent listing of related ideas or sentences or both***

- demonstrates little, if any, evidence of an organizational pattern
- provides little, if any, development of support
- demonstrates limited or inappropriate word choice, which may obscure meaning
- may contain gross errors in sentence structure and usage, which may impede communication
- contains frequent and blatant errors in basic conventions of mechanics and usage
- contains misspellings of commonly used words

Preparing for **FCAT Writing+**

Expository Essay

Sunshine State Standards: Benchmarks LA.6.3.3.1; LA.6.3.3.2; LA.6.3.4.1; LA.6.3.4.3; LA.6.3.5.3; LA.6.4.2.1; LA.6.4.2.3; LA.6.5.1.1

When responding to an on-demand prompt for an expository essay, use the models you have read, what you've learned from writing your own expository essay, the rubric on page 330, and the steps below.

Writing Situation:
Your teacher asks you to explain which school subject you enjoy most.

Directions for Writing:
Think of a school subject that you enjoy. Identify a few reasons why you enjoy that subject.

Now write an expository essay that explains what your favorite school subject is and why that subject is your favorite.

Study the Prompt
Begin by reading the prompt carefully. Notice that the **writing situation** identifies the subject of the prompt. You are being asked to discuss your favorite school subject. Now, notice that the **directions for writing** tell you to identify reasons why you enjoy that subject. This information can be used as support for writing your essay.

Plan Your Response
Reasons Expository essays explain a topic using facts. To plan your essay, **Ask** "What school subject do I enjoy most?" Or "What might my audience want to know about my favorite subject?" Your answers will determine the content of your essay. Brainstorm topics that you can write about easily.

Evidence Next, write down several important facts about your favorite school subject. To develop your **thesis statement**, think of an overall conclusion that you want your audience to understand. Your facts, or evidence, should support this thesis statement.

Organization Once you have decided on a subject, a **thesis statement**, and supporting evidence, plan the order in your essay. Use an outline to organize your notes into paragraphs for your essay. **Tip:** Spend about ten minutes planning your response.

Respond to the Prompt
One way to begin an expository essay is to grab your audience's attention with an interesting anecdote, question, or statement. Then, clearly state why you enjoy this school subject. The rest of your essay should discuss the main facts about the subject, each in a separate paragraph. In the conclusion, summarize the information that you want your audience to understand. Use your outline as a guide to write your essay. **Tip:** Spend about twenty minutes writing your draft.

Improve Your Response
Revising Go back over the key aspects of your essay. Add any missing information.

- Did you explain why you enjoy this particular school subject?
- Did you provide clear details to support your explanation?

Proofreading Take a few minutes to proofread your essay to correct errors in grammar, spelling, punctuation, and capitalization. Make sure all your edits are neat, and erase any stray marks.

Checking Your Final Copy Before you turn in your essay, read it again to catch errors you may have missed. **Tip:** Save five minutes to improve your essay.

Following Oral Instructions and Directions

Listen with a Purpose

Work in a small group to practice giving and following simple instructions and geographic directions.

Think as a Reader/Writer The ability to write clear instructions is a very important skill. Likewise, being able to follow oral instructions is a skill that will be important in many different parts of your life.

Do you sometimes find it hard to follow spoken instructions? Maybe you "tune out" for a moment, only to realize later that you have missed something important. Perhaps the speaker uses terms that are not familiar to you, making the instructions difficult to understand.

Listen to Instructions

Listen for Cues

Good listeners do much more than *hear* a speaker; they really *listen.* Listening is an active process. It involves trying to interpret the main points. The best listeners pick up on cues from the speaker that help them follow the speaker's ideas. These cues include

- **Verbal cues** These cues are spoken hints, including *how* the words are said. Words such as *first, next,* and *last* help you follow the speaker. Also, when you notice ideas or phrases repeated or stressed, you should know that those are key points.
- **Nonverbal cues** These cues are unspoken hints, such as movements, facial expressions, and gestures. Speakers may use nonverbal cues to demonstrate an activity or stress the importance of a point.

Focus and Take Notes

Good listeners also **focus** on the speaker and avoid distractions. One way to maintain your focus is to **take notes** on what the speaker is saying. Jot down key words and phrases, and note any questions that occur to you. Later, when the speaker calls for questions, look at your notes to recall any points of confusion.

If possible, check with the speaker to make sure you have understood the instructions properly. Use your notes to **restate** the instructions in your own words. Then, read the restatement back to the speaker, and ask him or her if your understanding is accurate.

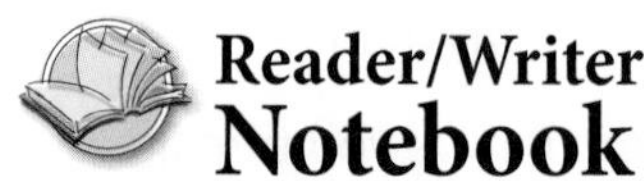

Use your **RWN** to complete the activities for this workshop.

Sunshine State Standards: Benchmarks **LA.6.4.2.2** record information (e.g., observations, notes, lists, charts, legends) related to a topic, including visual aids to organize and record information and include a list of sources used; **LA.6.4.2.5** write directions to unfamiliar locations using cardinal and ordinal directions, landmarks, and distances, and create an accompanying map; **LA.6.5.2.1** listen and gain information for a variety of purposes, (e.g., clarifying, elaborating, summarizing main ideas and supporting details); **LA.6.6.1.3** create a technical manual or solve a problem.

Listen to a Process

Be sure that each member of your small group has several sheets of paper and a pen or pencil. Begin by having each group member draw simple pictures of a four- or five-step process, such as making a sandwich. Next, one by one, each group member should describe his or her picture. Remember what you learned about good "how-to" instructions.

- The directions are given in chronological order, using clear time-order transitions.
- The directions include specific details describing the steps.
- The directions use precise and consistent language.

The listeners in the group should listen, take notes, ask questions, and then try to draw the picture that has been explained. Group members should share their pictures when finished and discuss the similarities and differences between the pictures.

Continue this process until each member of the group has given his or her oral instructions. Then, discuss what you have learned about giving and listening to instructions.

A Good Listener

- looks directly at the speaker and stays focused on what the speaker is saying
- takes notes that include the key ideas and that pose questions
- uses restatement to check his or her understanding

Listen to Geographic Directions

Your group will need a map of your town or city. Have one member select a location, such as a public library or a park, without naming the place. Then, he or she should give oral directions on how to get from your school to that place. The speaker should remember the importance of using spatial and chronological transitions. **Spatial transitions** include directional words, such as *to the right*. **Chronological transitions** are time-order words, such as *next*.

While listening, the other group members should take notes, ask questions, and restate the directions. Then, the listeners should trace the directions along the map exactly as the directions were given and identify the final location. If the place identified by the group is incorrect, discuss where the breakdown in oral communication happened. Group members should take turns giving directions until everyone has had a turn.

Listening Tip

Taking notes is especially important when you are listening to geographic directions. After all, you don't want to get lost! Sketching a map to represent what you hear can be helpful. Show the map to the speaker to make sure your understanding is accurate.

PRACTICING FOR FCAT

Standards Review Literary Text

Character **Directions:** Read the following excerpt from a novel. Then, read and respond to the questions that follow.

from Julie of the Wolves by **Jean Craighead George**

Miyax stared hard at the regal black wolf, hoping to catch his eye. She must somehow tell him that she was starving and ask him for food. This could be done, she knew, for her father, an Eskimo[1] hunter, had done so. One year he had camped near a wolf den while on a hunt. When a month had passed and her father had seen no game, he told the leader of the wolves that he was hungry and needed food. The next night the wolf called him from far away and her father went to him and found a freshly killed caribou. Unfortunately, Miyax's father never explained to her how he had told the wolf of his needs. And not long afterward he paddled his kayak into the Bering Sea to hunt for seal, and he never returned.

She had been watching the wolves for two days, trying to discern which of their sounds and movements expressed good will and friendship. Most animals had such signals. The little Arctic ground squirrels flicked their tails sideways to notify others of their kind that they were friendly. By imitating this signal with her forefinger, Miyax had lured many a squirrel to her hand. If she could discover such a gesture for the wolves, she would be able to make friends with them and share their food, like a bird or a fox.

Propped on her elbows with her chin in her fists, she stared at the black wolf, trying to catch his eye. She had chosen him because he was much larger than the others, and because he walked like her father, Kapugen, with his head high and his chest out. The black wolf also possessed wisdom, she had observed. The pack looked to him when the wind carried strange scents or the birds cried nervously. If he was alarmed, they were alarmed. If he was calm, they were calm.

Long minutes passed, and the black wolf did not look at her. He had ignored her since she first came upon them, two sleeps ago. True, she moved slowly and quietly, so as not to alarm him; yet she did wish he would see the kindness in her eyes. Many animals could tell the difference between hostile hunters and friendly people by merely looking at them. But the big black wolf would not even glance her way.

A bird stretched in the grass. The wolf looked at it. A flower twisted in

1. **Eskimo** (EHS kuh moh): outdated term for the various groups of native peoples of Arctic Circle regions such as Canada, Alaska, and Greenland. Many native peoples, such as the Inuit, find the term offensive.

Sunshine State Standards: Benchmarks LA.6.2.1.2 locate and analyze the elements of plot structure, including exposition, setting, character development, rising/falling action, conflict/resolution, and theme in a variety of fiction.

the wind. He glanced at that. Then the breeze rippled the wolverine ruff on Miyax's parka and it glistened in the light. He did not look at that. She waited. Patience with the ways of nature had been instilled in her by her father. And so she knew better than to move or shout. Yet she must get food or die. Her hands shook slightly and she swallowed hard to keep calm.

1. Which adjective BEST describes Miyax?
   - **A** careless
   - **B** patient
   - **C** timid
   - **D** funny

2. Which adjectives BEST describe Miyax's actions in the selection?
   - **F** hurried and scared
   - **G** graceful and smooth
   - **H** calm and steady
   - **I** hesitant and fumbling

3. Which method of characterization is NOT used in this excerpt from *Julie of the Wolves?*
   - **A** revealing characters thoughts
   - **B** quoting speeches
   - **C** directly naming character traits
   - **D** describing actions

4. Which one is NOT a character trait of the big black wolf?
   - **F** being leader of the pack
   - **G** being quick to attack
   - **H** being wise
   - **I** being larger than other animals

5. Which sentence from the excerpt reveals how Miyax feels about her situation?
   - **A** "Propped on her elbows with her chin in her fists, she stared at the black wolf, trying to catch his eye."
   - **B** "The black wolf also possessed wisdom, she had observed."
   - **C** "Patience with the ways of nature had been instilled in her by her father."
   - **D** "Her hands shook slightly and she swallowed hard to keep calm."

Extended Response

6. Do you think Miyax will succeed in befriending the wolves? Why? Which of her traits lead you to believe this? Support your answer with details from the story. READ THINK EXPLAIN

Standards Review Informational Text

Comparison / Contrast **Directions:** Read the following selection. Then, read and respond to the questions that follow.

from All I Really Need to Know I Learned in Kindergarten by Robert Fulghum

This is my neighbor. Nice lady. Coming out her front door, on her way to work and in her "looking good" mode. She's locking the door now and picking up her daily luggage: purse, lunch bag, gym bag for aerobics, and the garbage bucket to take out. She turns, sees me, gives me the big, smiling Hello, and takes three steps across her front porch. And goes "AAAAAAAAGGGGGGGG-HHHHHHHHH!!!!" *(That's a direct quote.)* At about the level of a fire engine at full cry. Spider web! She has walked full force into a spider web. And the pressing question, of course: Just where is the spider *now?*

She flings her baggage in all directions. And at the same time does a high-kick, jitter-bug sort of dance—like a mating stork in crazed heat. Clutches at her face and hair and goes "AAAAAAAGGGGG-GGHHHHHHHHH!!!!!" at a new level of intensity. Tries opening the front door without unlocking it. Tries again. Breaks key in the lock. Runs around the house headed for the back door. Doppler effect[1] of "AAAAAGGGHHHaaggh . . ."

Now a different view of this scene. Here is the spider. Rather ordinary, medium gray, middle-aged lady spider. She's been up since before dawn working on her web, and all is well. Nice day, no wind, dew point just right to keep things sticky. She's out checking the moorings and thinking about the little gnats she'd like for breakfast. Feeling good. Ready for action. All of a sudden everything breaks loose—earthquake, tornado, volcano. The web is torn loose and is wrapped around a frenzied moving haystack, and a huge piece of raw-but-painted meat is making a sound the spider never heard before: "AAAAAAAG-GGGGGGGHHHHHHHHH!!!!!!" It's too big to wrap up and eat later, and it's moving too much to hold down. Jump for it? Hang on and hope? Dig in?

Human being. She has caught a human being. And the pressing question is, of course: Where is it going, and what will it do when it gets there?

The neighbor lady thinks the spider is about the size of a lobster and has big rubber lips and poisonous fangs. The neighbor lady will probably strip to the skin and

Sunshine State Standards: Benchmarks **LA.6.1.7.5** analyze a variety of text structures (e.g., comparison/contrast, cause/effect, chronological order, argument/support, lists) and text features (main headings with subheadings) and explain their impact on meaning in text; *Also covered* **LA.6.2.2.2**

take a full shower and shampoo just to make sure it's gone—and then put on a whole new outfit to make certain she is not inhabited.

The spider? Well, if she survives all this, she will really have something to talk about—the one that got away that was THIS BIG. "And you should have seen the JAWS on the thing!"

1. **Doppler effect:** change in the pitch of a sound, produced when the source of the sound moves toward or away from the listener.

---

1 What does the writer compare and contrast in this essay?

- **A** a jitterbug and a stork
- **B** people and spiders
- **C** a spider web and a front porch
- **D** breakfast foods

2 What pattern does the writer use to organize his essay?

- **F** block method
- **G** point-by-point method
- **H** chronological order
- **I** cause-and-effect pattern

3 At the beginning of the day, how do both the spider and the human feel?

- **A** They both feel scared.
- **B** They both feel hungry.
- **C** They both feel good.
- **D** They both feel sleepy.

4 Which character trait do both the human and the spider have in common?

- **F** They are both very old.
- **G** They are both male.
- **H** They are both very young.
- **I** They are both female.

5 What is true about the spider?

- **A** The spider thinks of the human as meat.
- **B** The spider thinks of the human as a friend.
- **C** The spider wants to go in and shower.
- **D** The spider wants to bite the human.

6 What is true about the human?

- **F** The human thinks of the spider as meat.
- **G** The human thinks the spider is as big as a lobster.
- **H** The human doesn't think of the spider at all.
- **I** The human thinks the spider is cute.

Extended Response

7 According to the writer, what will the human do after the encounter with the spider? What will the spider do? Support your response with details from the text. READ THINK EXPLAIN

Sunshine State Standards: Benchmarks LA.6.1.6.1 use new vocabulary that is introduced and taught directly.

Standards Review Vocabulary

Synonyms

Directions: Choose the word or group of words that is closest in meaning to the italicized word.

Practicing For FCAT

1. Read the sentence from the story "The King of Mazy May."

Walt was worried, however; the claim was liable to be jumped at any moment because of this delay, and a fresh stampede had started in on the Mazy May.

What does the word *stampede* mean?

A a dance

B a mark

C a rush

D a wind

2. Read this passage from the story "Eleven."

This is when I wish I wasn't eleven, because all the years inside of me–ten, nine, eight, seven, six, five, four, three, two, and one–are pushing at the back of my eyes when I put one arm through one sleeve of the sweater that smells like cottage cheese, and then the other arm through the other and stand there with my arms apart like the sweater hurts me and it does, all itchy and full of germs that aren't even mine.

What does the word *itchy* mean?

F scrawny

G numb

H irritated

I soothed

3. Read the sentence from the story "Cricket in the Road."

I stood there, depressed about the rain, and then I put Vern's bat and ball underneath the house and went indoors.

What does the word *depressed* mean?

A small

B sad

C nervous

D smart

4. Read the sentence from the story "The King of Mazy May."

Not only did he look after his father's claim, but he had agreed to keep an eye on the adjoining one of Loren Hall, who had started for Dawson to record it.

What does the word *adjoining* mean?

F being side by side

G being across from each other

H being separate

I being half the size of each other

Academic Vocabulary

Directions: Choose the word that is closest in meaning to the italicized Academic Vocabulary word.

5. What is an *obvious* mistake?

A a big mistake

B an unimportant mistake

C a noticeable mistake

D an intentional mistake

Writing Skills Review

Sunshine State Standards: Benchmarks **LA.6.3.3.1** evaluating the draft for development of ideas and content, logical organization, voice, point of view, word choice, and sentence variation; *Also covered* **LA.6.3.3.2; LA.6.4.2.1**

"How-to" Explanation

Directions: Read the following paragraph from a draft of a student's "how-to" paper. Then, answer each question.

Easy and Fun Zesty Bagels

[1] Evenly spread 1 tablespoon of spaghetti sauce over the face of each bagel. [2] First, you will need to cut the six plain bagels in half and place the halves on a cookie sheet. [3] Then, sprinkle ¼ cup chopped black olives, 6 finely chopped mushrooms, and 1 cup grated Parmesan cheese evenly over the sauce. [4] Place the cookie sheet in a preheated oven and bake for 15–20 minutes. [5] When the bagels are done, remove them from the oven and let them cool for 5 minutes.

1. Which sentence would you move if you were revising the paragraph above to put the instruction in chronological order?
   - **A** sentence 2
   - **B** sentence 3
   - **C** sentence 4
   - **D** sentence 5

2. Which sentence would be appropriate if the writer wanted to add precise language to the paragraph?
   - **F** You may add other toppings.
   - **G** Your family will enjoy them.
   - **H** The oven should be set at 350 degrees.
   - **I** Prepare the bagels.

3. Which would make the MOST sense if the writer wanted to add transitional words to the beginning of sentence 5?
   - **A** However,
   - **B** Meanwhile,
   - **C** Since,
   - **D** Finally,

4. Which would you suggest the writer add to the recipe to make the instructions more helpful?
   - **F** a list of ingredients to have ready
   - **G** the number of times he or she has made these bagels
   - **H** a definition of *zesty*
   - **I** a quotation from someone who enjoys eating these bagels

Read On For Independent Reading

Fiction

Julie of the Wolves

In Jean Craighead George's Newbery Award–winning novel *Julie of the Wolves,* a thirteen-year-old Inuit girl named Miyax runs away from home and gets lost on the frozen, treeless wilderness of the vast Alaskan tundra. Miyax is menaced by a host of dangers until a pack of wolves gradually accepts her as one of their own.

Perseus

In acclaimed author Geraldine McCaughrean's *Perseus,* you'll follow the teenage Perseus as he struggles with his fate that the oracles foretold. His seemingly impossible and deadly task is to kill the hideous, snake-haired Medusa to save his mother from marriage to an evil king. In McCaughrean's retelling of the classic myth, Perseus becomes a coming-of-age story about an adventurous and lovesick young man.

Dealing with Dragons

When people were polite, they called her "strong-minded." When angry, they said she was "as stubborn as a pig." Cimorene, the hard-headed princess, runs away from her family's boring castle and is taken in by a powerful and good-hearted dragon. Throughout Patricia C. Wrede's *Dealing with Dragons,* you'll find contemporary dialogue woven into several familiar fairy tales that have been tweaked to create laugh-out-loud humor.

PaperQuake

San Francisco isn't the place to be if you're terrified of earthquakes, as Violet Jackstone is. Besides being frightened by the ground's tremors and teased mercilessly by her two popular sisters, she is frail and sickly and still called Baby. As her family renovates an old house, Violet finds mysterious letters and diaries that describe a girl very much like her. The girl, named V, lived nearly one hundred years ago, just before the deadly 1906 earthquake in San Francisco. *PaperQuake* is a popular time-travel mystery novel from author Kathryn Reiss.

Sunshine State Standards: Benchmarks **LA.6.2.1.10** use interest and recommendation of others to select a balance of age and ability appropriate fiction materials to read (e.g., novels, historical fiction, mythology, poetry) to expand the core foundation of knowledge necessary to function as a fully literate member of a shared culture; *Also covered* **LA.6.2.2.5**

Nonfiction

Changing Places

Homelessness is a problem that some people are uncomfortable discussing. In *Changing Places: A Kid's View of Shelter Living,* Margie Chalofsky, Glen Finland, and Judy Wallace give voice to eight homeless children. One of them, Roberto, bursts with pride when his mother finds a job. Another child, Anthony, is troubled with self-doubt and sadness. All tell stories from their own experience—stories you will not soon forget.

Jesse Owens: Champion Athlete

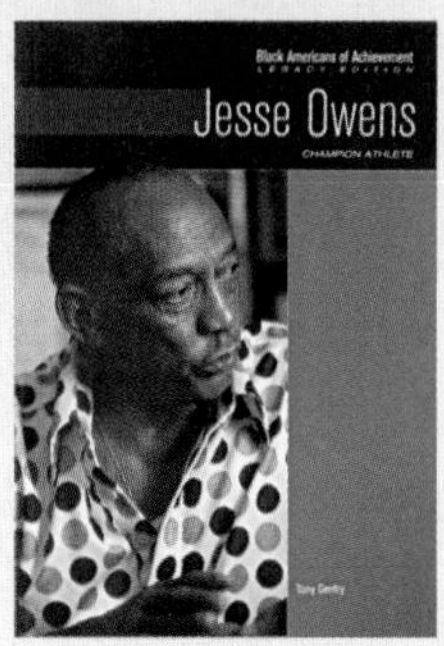

At the 1936 Olympic Games in Berlin, Jesse Owens, an African American athlete, undermined dictator Adolf Hitler's claim of German superiority. In *Jesse Owens: Champion Athlete,* Tony Gentry presents Owens from his youth in segregated Alabama, to his numerous athletic achievements, and to his death in 1980. High-quality black-and-white photographs help chronicle the career of this track-and-field great.

You Wouldn't Want to Be a Greek Athlete! Races You'd Rather Not Run

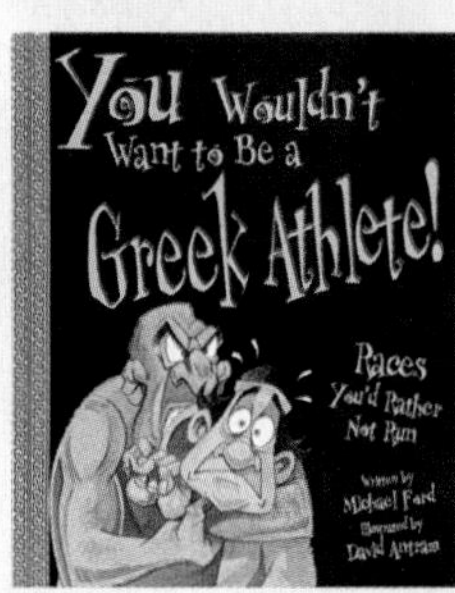

Imagine that you're living near Athens around 650 B.C. Your father sends you to a boarding school for athletes so that you can train for the Olympics. As you learn to compete in the pentathlon—racing and wrestling—you discover that life as an athlete in ancient Greece is not much fun. Michael Ford gives a humorous description, with well-researched facts, about why *You Wouldn't Want to Be a Greek Athlete!*

Gold Rush Dogs: And Other Favorite Dogs of the Last Frontier

Walt Frazier's life-and-death adventures and survival would have been impossible without the dogs of the Yukon. In *Gold Rush Dogs,* authors Claire Rudolf Murphy and Jane G. Haigh share action-filled stories of dogs who provided transportation, security, and companionship to the men, women, and children of the Alaska Gold Rush.

Learn It Online
Explore other novels—and learn how to study them using *NovelWise* at:

go.hrw.com L6-341 

It Takes the Village by Sami Bentil.

COLLECTION 4

Short Story: Theme

INFORMATIONAL TEXT FOCUS

Following Instructions

"In every conceivable manner, the family is link to our past, bridge to our future."

—Alex Haley

What Do You Think? How do the people you consider family help you find your place in the world?

Learn It Online

Listen to the selections in this collection online:

go.hrw.com L6-343 Go

Literary Focus

by **Linda Rief**

What Is Theme?

Do you have posters tacked to the walls of your room? If so, some of them may make statements about life—about friendship, or adventure, or goals. You probably put them on your walls to make a statement about your beliefs or values. Writers make similar statements in their stories' themes. As you read the stories in this collection, think of their themes as posters that each author decided to put on his or her walls.

Theme

"What does it all mean?" When we ask that question about a story, we're asking about its **theme**—an idea about life that the story's characters, events, and images suggest. A theme usually expresses an important truth about one of life's "big issues," such as love, revenge, or power.

Theme or Subject? The theme is not the same as the subject of a story. The **subject** is what the story is *about*; it can usually be stated in one or two words. The theme of a story is an idea, and it's best expressed as a complete sentence. This chart shows the difference between subject and theme.

Subject	Theme
growing up	Growing up means taking responsibility.
nature	Nature can be beautiful but deadly.
love	People will sometimes risk everything, even their lives, for love.

Theme and Character Writers usually don't state themes directly. You won't find a sentence that begins, "This is the theme." Instead, you have to read through the entire story, paying careful attention to all of its elements. One of the best places to look for the theme is in the thoughts or dialogue of the main character, especially if the character makes a sudden discovery near the end of a story. In "The All-American Slurp," the main character has such a moment when she realizes that her non-Chinese friends are as confused by her culture as she is by theirs:

> Then I caught my mother's eyes on me. She frowned and shook her head slightly, and I understood the message: The Gleasons were not used to Chinese ways, and they were just coping the best they could.
>
> from "The All-American Slurp" by Lensey Namioka

Theme and Plot A theme develops side-by-side with the events of a story, but don't confuse a story's theme with its plot. Use what you already know about plot to help you identify the theme. For example, one of the most important elements of plot is conflict**.** When characters face a conflict, they are forced to make a decision based on their beliefs or values. In "Ta-Na-E-Ka," the main character, Mary, doesn't want to take part in an important ritual that's part of her heritage.

Sunshine State Standards: Benchmarks **LA.6.1.7.6** analyze and evaluate similar themes or topics by different authors across a variety of fiction and nonfiction selections; **LA.6.2.1.2** locate and analyze the elements of plot structure, including exposition, setting, character development, rising/falling action, conflict/resolution, and theme in a variety of fiction; **LA.6.2.1.4** identify and explain recurring themes across a variety of works (e.g., bravery, friendship, loyalty, good vs. evil); **LA.6.2.1.7** locate and analyze an author's use of allusions and descriptive, idiomatic, and figurative language in a variety of literary text, identifying how word choice sets the author's tone and advances the work's theme.

> As my birthday drew closer, I had awful nightmares about it. I was reaching the age at which all Kaw Indians had to participate in Ta-Na-E-Ka. Well, not all Kaws. Many of the younger families on the reservation were beginning to give up the old customs. But my grandfather, Amos Deer Leg, was devoted to tradition.
>
> from "Ta-Na-E-Ka"
> by Mary Whitebird

Throughout the story, Mary fights against her desire to abandon her culture. She also fights against her family, who insist that their culture remain a part of her life. The story shows us how Mary gains a deeper understanding of her heritage. The outcome suggests a powerful theme about how people balance their individual needs with the needs of others.

Theme and Images The events of a story are not the only place to look for information about the theme. The writer's **descriptive language**—the images he or she focuses on—creates pictures that support the theme. A writer may include images of violent weather to support a theme having to do with conflict or anger. By paying attention to the descriptive images writers use, you can get valuable clues to the theme. The following image of a bird in flight suggests that the theme of "Aaron's Gift" relates to freedom and to a respect for all living things.

> But suddenly Pidge beat his wings in rhythm, and rose up, up over the roof of the nearest tenement, up over Second Avenue toward the park.
>
> from "Aaron's Gift"
> by Myron Levoy

Recurring Themes

Similar themes often show up in different stories. You've probably read more than one story that makes a statement about the horrors of war or the value of friendship, for example. Ideas that occur in stories from different times and cultures are called **recurring** or **universal themes.** Recurring themes are based on ideas that have been important to human beings in all times and places: love, death, family, loyalty, sacrifice.

Your Turn Analyze Theme

1. Use a chart like the one below to determine the theme of two of your favorite movies or stories.

Work 1	Work 2
Subject:	Subject:
Theme:	Theme:

2. Look at the chart on the previous page. It lists three examples of subjects and themes. Without thinking about any particular story, come up with three additional sets of possible subjects and themes.

3. Pair up with a partner and think of some themes you have encountered more than once in books, movies, plays, and comics. What are the three most common recurring themes that you can think of? What's an example of each?

Learn It Online
Learn more about theme through *PowerNotes:*
go.hrw.com L6-345 Go

Analyzing Visuals

How Can Visual Art Help You Understand Theme?

Stories aren't the only creative works that express themes. Paintings, drawings, sculptures, and other works of art also convey themes, or broad ideas about life. In a literary work, theme develops from a combination of the subject, the plot, the characters' conflicts, and other literary elements. In a work of art, a theme forms from a combination of subject matter, the artist's point of view toward the subject, and visual elements such as color, line, shape, and composition. Like literary works, visual artworks from different times and places may share recurring themes on similar subjects: love, war, death, friendship. These are the themes that express universal human concerns.

Analyzing Theme in Visual Art

Use these guidelines to help you find the theme of an artwork.

1. Identify the subject of the work.
2. Try to determine the main focus of the work. If there are human (or other) figures, what are they doing? Which figures seem most important?
3. What seems to be the artist's view of the subject? Is it serious, playful, admiring, mocking?
4. What clues to the theme does the title of the work give you?
5. What are the most important elements in the work: color? line and shape? the arrangement, or composition? mood? symbolism?
6. Add up all the clues you see in the work, and determine what theme emerges. What are some other examples of this theme you can think of?

Sunshine State Standards: **Benchmarks** LA.6.2.1.4 identify and explain recurring themes across a variety of works (e.g., bravery, friendship, loyalty, good vs. evil).

Vive la Paix (July 1954) by Pablo Picasso (1881–1973). Pen and ink drawing.

1. Describe what's going on in this pen and ink drawing. What seems to be the artist's attitude toward the subject? What makes you think so?

2. In English, this drawing's title means "Lively Peace." What makes it lively? What signs of peace do you see? What do you guess is the reason for this celebration?

3. Add together all the clues you've noted in the details of this drawing. What is the **theme**? Explain whether it is a **universal** (or **recurring**) **theme.**

Your Turn Write About Theme

Explain why you think this work is or is not successful in presenting the theme you identified. What qualities most contribute to its theme?

Reading Focus

by **Kylene Beers**

What Skills Can Help You Find the Theme of a Story?

A story's theme is the truth about life that the story expresses through its characters and events. Many reading skills can help you find a story's theme, including making generalizations and tracing cause-and-effect relationships.

Finding the Theme

Think about a story you read when you were younger. Even if you don't remember the title or the characters' names, you probably remember what the story was about. You probably also remember a message you got from the story. The message or idea that stays with you long after you've read a story is the story's theme.

What the Theme Is—and Isn't To find the theme, you need to understand how it differs from other elements in the story. Suppose a teacher asks three students to state the theme of "The Three Little Pigs." Consider these responses:

- The first student says, "There are three pigs. Each builds a house. A wolf blows two houses down." Is that the theme? No, that's the **plot.**
- The second student says, "There are three pigs. One is really lazy, one is a little lazy, and one isn't lazy at all." Is that the theme? No, that is a description of the **characters.**
- The third student says, "Doing things the easy way often isn't the best way." Is that the theme? Yes! It explains a truth about life.

Looking for Clues to Theme Here are two ways to find clues to the theme.

1. Pay attention to what the characters and narrator say and think.

> "All of us have rituals of one kind or another," Mrs. Richardson said. "And look at it this way: How many girls have the opportunity to compete on equal terms with boys? Don't look down on your heritage."
>
> from "Ta-Na-E-Ka"
> by Mary Whitebird

2. Think about how a character changes.

> "Pretty silly thing to do to a kid," he muttered.
>
> That was just what I'd been thinking for months, but when Ernie said it, I became angry. "No, it isn't silly. It's a custom of the Kaw. We've been doing this for hundreds of years. . . . It's why the Kaw are great warriors."
>
> from "Ta-Na-E-Ka"
> by Mary Whitebird

Making Generalizations

A **generalization** is a broad, general conclusion that you draw from several examples or pieces of evidence. When you state a story's theme, you're actually making a kind of generalization about life and human experience. Here are tips that can help you use generalizations to make statements about a story's theme:

- Consider the story's main events and conflicts.
- Observe what the characters have learned by the end.
- State the idea in a general way so that it applies not just to the story but also to situations in real life.

Let's look at "The Three Little Pigs" again.

Main Characters	Conflict/Story Events	Observations
The three pigs	The wolf wants to eat the pigs. Each pig builds a house, and the wolf blows the two weaker houses down.	**In the story:** Building a strong house keeps pigs safer than building a weak house. **In life:** Doing things the easy way isn't always best.

Notice that the *generalization* is based on what the pigs learn about their *specific* situation. Building weak houses is easier than building strong ones, but, in this story, building weak houses turns out to be a bad idea. From this, you can reason that there are many situations in life when the easy way is not the best way.

Analyzing Cause and Effect

A story is made up of many different events. The first event is the **cause;** it makes something happen. What happens is called the **effect.** A story often follows a chain of causes and effects to its conclusion.

A flow chart can help you see how a main character changes, giving you a clue to the theme.

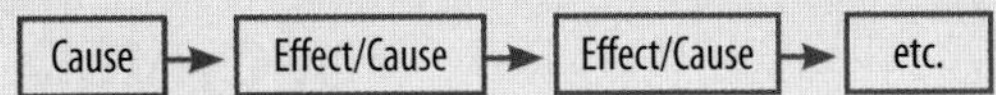

Your Turn Apply Reading Skills

1. Re-read a favorite story from an earlier collection. Look for clues to the theme by jotting down characters' comments and statements. Write your idea of the theme in a sentence.
2. Recall an important experience that you've had recently. Then, use it to make a generalization about life.
3. Think of one of your favorite folk tales or fairy tales from when you were a child. Make a cause-and-effect flow chart of the tale's events. Then, state the theme of the tale.

Now go to the Skills in Action: Reading Model

Learn It Online
Find tips on literature themes using NovelWise:
go.hrw.com L6-349 Go

Reading Model

SHORT STORY

Build Background

Every year in the United States, millions of dogs are abandoned or born in the wild, without homes. This is a fictional account of one such puppy.

Read with a Purpose Read this short story to find out what happens in a family when a stray dog appears one day.

by **Cynthia Rylant**

In January, a puppy wandered onto the property of Mr. Amos Lacey and his wife, Mamie, and their daughter, Doris. Icicles hung three feet or more from the eaves of houses, snowdrifts swallowed up automobiles, and the birds were so fluffed up they looked comic.

The puppy had been abandoned, and it made its way down the road toward the Laceys' small house, its ears tucked, its tail between its legs, shivering.

Literary Focus

Theme The **theme** is the message about life that the author wants you to take from the story. Authors rarely state the theme directly. However, this sentence provides clues to help you start figuring out what the theme might be.

Doris, whose school had been called off because of the snow, was out shoveling the cinder-block front steps when she spotted the pup on the road. She set down the shovel.

"Hey! Come on!" she called.

The puppy stopped in the road, wagging its tail timidly, trembling with shyness and cold.

Doris trudged through the yard, went up the shoveled drive and met the dog.

"Come on, pooch."

"Where did *that* come from?" Mrs. Lacey asked as soon as Doris put the dog down in the kitchen.

Mr. Lacey was at the table, cleaning his fingernails with his pocketknife. The snow was keeping him home from his job at the warehouse.

"I don't know where it came from," he said mildly, "but I know for sure where it's going."

Reading Focus

Finding the Theme As you read, look for clues that can help you identify the theme. Jot down statements that seem important, including characters' dialogue. In this sentence, you can see that Mr. Lacey does not plan to keep the dog.

Analyzing Visuals **Viewing and Interpreting** How does this photograph reflect Doris's feelings for the puppy?

Doris hugged the puppy hard against her. She said nothing.

Because the roads would be too bad for travel for many days, Mr. Lacey couldn't get out to take the puppy to the pound in the city right away. He agreed to let it sleep in the basement, while Mrs. Lacey grudgingly let Doris feed it table scraps. The woman was sensitive about throwing out food.

By the looks of it, Doris figured the puppy was about six months old and on its way to being a big dog. She thought it might have some shepherd in it.

Four days passed and the puppy did not complain. It never cried in the night or howled at the wind. It didn't tear up everything in the basement. It wouldn't even follow Doris up the basement steps unless it was invited.

It was a good dog.

Several times Doris had opened the door in the kitchen that led to the basement, and the puppy had been there, all stretched out, on the top step. Doris knew it had wanted some company and that it had lain against the door, listening to the talk in the kitchen, smelling the food, being a part of things. It always wagged its tail, eyes all sleepy, when she found it there.

Reading Focus

Finding the Theme As you look for clues to theme, also pay attention to statements by the narrator of a story. This description is about the dog, but notice that the dog is being described as though it were a person.

Even after a week had gone by, Doris didn't name the dog. She knew her parents wouldn't let her keep it, that her father made so little money any pets were out of the question, and that the pup would definitely go to the pound when the weather cleared.

Still, she tried talking to them about the dog at dinner one night.

"She's a good dog, isn't she?" Doris said, hoping one of them would agree with her.

Her parents glanced at each other and went on eating.

"She's not much trouble," Doris added. "I like her." She smiled at them, but they continued to ignore her.

"I figure she's real smart," Doris said to her mother. "I could teach her things."

Mrs. Lacey just shook her head and stuffed a forkful of sweet potato in her mouth. Doris fell silent, praying the weather would never clear.

Reading Focus

Cause and Effect A **cause** makes something happen; what happens is called an **effect.** The effect can in turn lead to the cause of something else that happens. The dog's arrival at the Lacey's house is the cause of a chain of events in the story. Notice the effect the dog has on Doris and her parents. There will be more cases of cause and effect that point to the theme of the story.

But on Saturday, nine days after the dog had arrived, the sun was shining and the roads were plowed. Mr. Lacey opened up the trunk of his car and came into the house.

Doris was sitting alone in the living room, hugging a pillow and rocking back and forth on the edge of a chair. She was trying not to cry but she was not strong enough. Her face was wet and red, her eyes full of distress.

Mrs. Lacey looked into the room from the doorway.

"Mama," Doris said in a small voice. "Please."

Mrs. Lacey shook her head.

"You know we can't afford a dog, Doris. You try to act more grown-up about this."

Doris pressed her face into the pillow.

Outside, she heard the trunk of the car slam shut, one of the doors open and close, the old engine cough and choke and finally start up.

"Daddy," she whispered. "Please."

She heard the car travel down the road, and though it was early afternoon, she could do nothing but go to her bed. She cried herself to sleep, and her dreams were full of searching and searching for things lost.

It was nearly night when she finally woke up. Lying there, like stone, still exhausted, she wondered if she would ever in her life have anything. She stared at the wall for a while.

But she started feeling hungry, and she knew she'd have to make herself get out of bed and eat some dinner. She wanted not to go into the kitchen, past the basement door. She wanted not to face her parents.

But she rose up heavily.

Her parents were sitting at the table, dinner over, drinking coffee. They looked at her when she came in, but she kept her head down. No one spoke.

Doris made herself a glass of powdered milk and drank it all down. Then she picked up a cold biscuit and started out of the room.

"You'd better feed that mutt before it dies of starvation," Mr. Lacey said.

Doris turned around.

"What?"

"I said, you'd better feed your dog. I figure it's looking for you."

Doris put her hand to her mouth.

"You didn't take her?" she asked.

"Oh, I took her all right," her father answered. "Worst-looking place I've ever seen. Ten dogs to a cage. Smell was enough to knock you down. And they give an animal six days to live. Then they kill it with some kind of a shot."

Reading Focus

Finding the Theme Pay attention to related ideas and images that keep appearing in a story; they can be important clues to the theme. Consider how this statement echoes the earlier statement about how the dog wanted something, too.

Analyzing Visuals **Viewing and Interpreting** How do details of this photograph relate to the story's setting and conclusion?

Doris stared at her father.

"I wouldn't leave an *ant* in that place," he said. "So I brought the dog back."

Mrs. Lacey was smiling at him and shaking her head as if she would never, ever, understand him.

Mr. Lacey sipped his coffee.

"Well," he said, "are you going to feed it or not?"

Reading Focus

Making Generalizations From the way Mr. Lacey changes his mind, you might make a generalization about how even people who think they don't want a pet can end up caring about an animal. This generalization can help you understand the story's theme.

Read with a Purpose How does the dog affect the relationship between Doris and her parents? How does the dog bring out the best in everyone?

MEET THE WRITER

Cynthia Rylant

(1954–)

The Possibilities of Childhood

Cynthia Rylant spent part of her childhood with her grandparents in West Virginia. Remembering them fondly, she says:

> "They lived life with strength . . . and a real sense of what it means to be devoted to and responsible for other people. The tone of my work reflects the way they spoke, the simplicity of their language, and, I hope, the depth of their own hearts."

Why does Rylant—winner of the Newbery medal and other awards—like to write?

> "I like to show the way our lives are beautiful, breathtaking, in the smallest things. . . . I prefer writing about child characters because they have more possibilities. They can get away with more love, more anger, more fear than adult characters."

Think About the Writer Based on "Stray," how do you think Cynthia Rylant feels about children and pets?

SKILLS IN ACTION Wrap Up

Sunshine State Standards: Benchmarks **LA.6.1.6.1** use new vocabulary that is introduced and taught directly; **LA.6.2.1.2** locate and analyze the elements of plot structure, including exposition, setting, character development, rising/falling action, conflict/resolution, and theme in a variety of fiction.

Into Action: Making a Generalization to State the Theme

Use a table like the one below to make an observation about "Stray." (*Hint:* Try to decide what the main characters might have learned.) Restate your observation as a generalization that applies to life.

Main Characters	Conflict/ Story Events	Observations
Amos, Mamie, and Doris Lacey		In the story: In life:

Talk About . . .

1. Explain to a partner your idea of the theme of "Stray." Remember that readers may state a theme in different ways. Try to use each Academic Vocabulary word listed on the right at least once in your discussion.

Write About . . .

Answer the following questions about "Stray." For definitions of the underlined Academic Vocabulary words, see the column on the right.

2. How does the author illustrate the cruelty of abandoning pets?
3. How does the dog communicate that it wants to belong to the family? How does Doris communicate her pain over losing the dog?
4. How does Mr. Lacey's attitude toward the stray change after he visits the pound? Contrast Mr. Lacey's attitude before he visits the pound with his attitude after he visits the pound.

Writing Focus

Think as a Reader/Writer

In Collection 4, you will read more stories with powerful themes. The Writing Focus activities will give you practice in developing characters and events that communicate truths about life.

Academic Vocabulary for Collection 4

Talking and Writing About Theme

Academic Vocabulary is the language you use to write and talk about literature. Use these words to discuss the stories you read in this collection. The words are underlined throughout the collection.

attitude (AT uh tood) *n.:* opinions and feelings you usually have about someone or something. *A character's attitude may change and be a clue to theme.*

communicate (kuh MYOO nuh kayt) *v.:* express your thoughts or feelings clearly so that other people understand them. *Writers communicate lessons about life.*

contrast (KAHN trast) *v.:* note the differences between two people, situations, ideas, and so on that are being compared. *You can contrast the different themes you find in stories.*

illustrate (IHL uh strayt) *v.:* explain or make something clear by giving examples. *Use details from a story to illustrate your idea of its theme.*

Your Turn

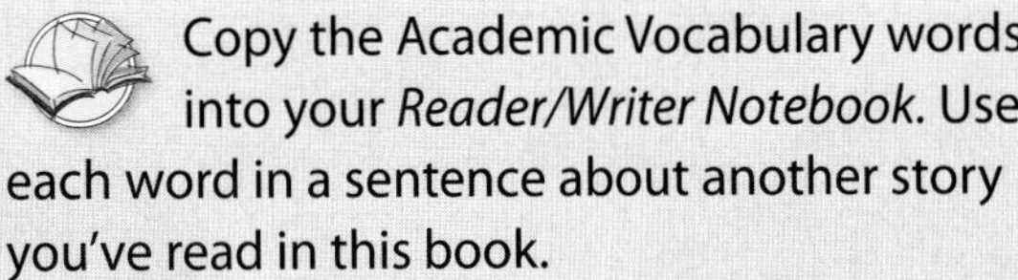

Copy the Academic Vocabulary words into your *Reader/Writer Notebook*. Use each word in a sentence about another story you've read in this book.

SHORT STORY

Preparing to Read

Ta-Na-E-Ka

by **Mary Whitebird**

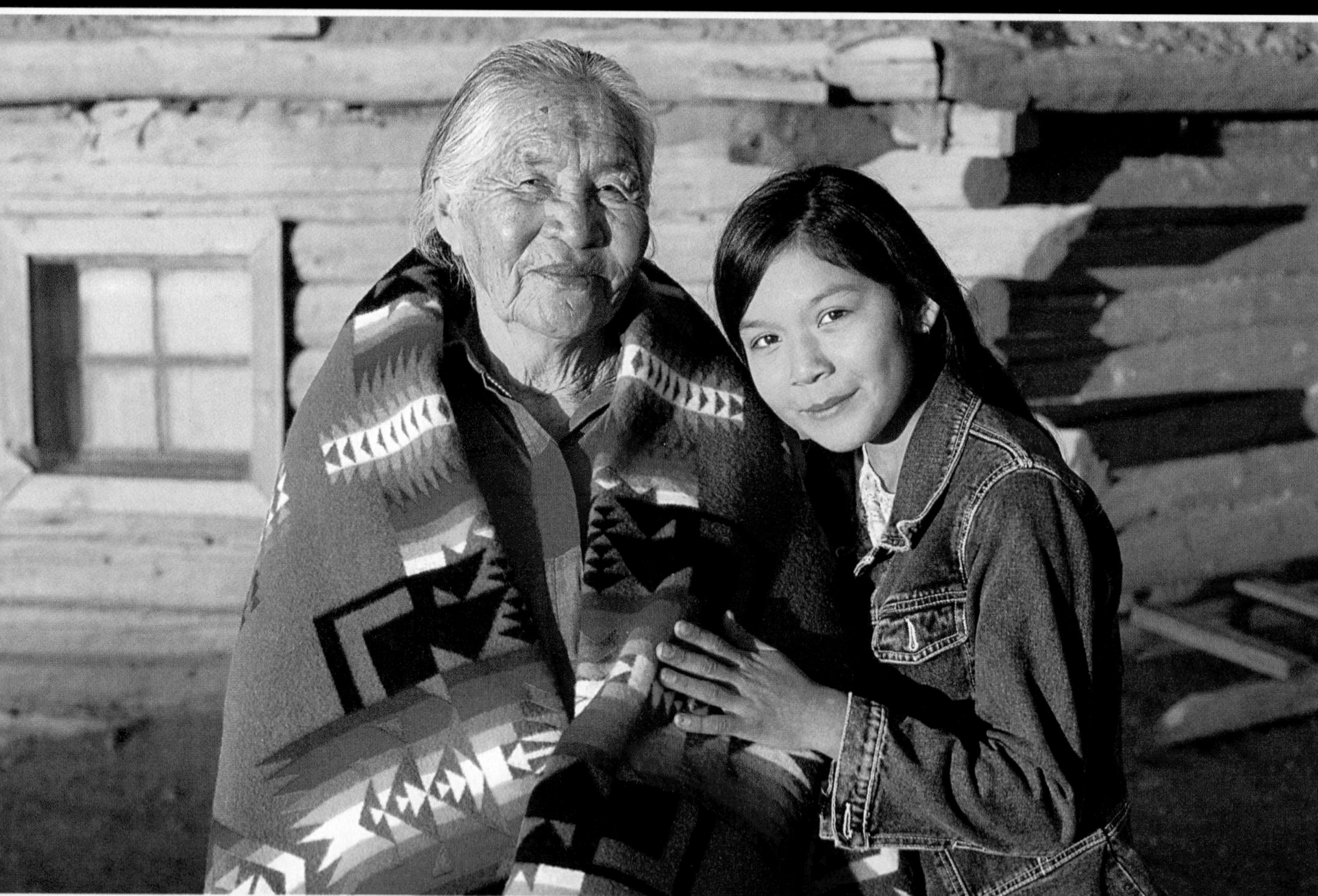

What Do You Think? Why is it important for elders to pass down traditions to the young?

QuickWrite

What kinds of traditions can families have? What can happen when a family member dislikes a tradition and chooses not to follow it?

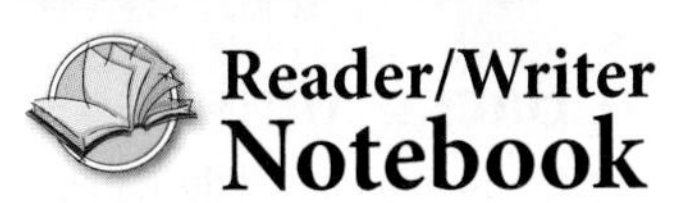

Reader/Writer Notebook

Use your **RWN** to complete the activities for this selection.

Sunshine State Standards: Benchmarks LA.6.1.7.3 determine the main idea or essential message in grade-level text through inferring, paraphrasing, summarizing, and identifying relevant details; *Also covered* **LA.6.1.7.8; LA.6.2.1.2; LA.6.2.1.4; LA.6.3.2.3**

Literary Focus

Theme Writers try to communicate a message through their stories. This message, or **theme,** usually reveals something about people or life in general. You can infer the theme from the story's events, but the theme goes beyond the details of the story—it is what the story *means*. Think about the message in "Ta-Na-E-Ka."

Reading Focus

Finding the Theme In most stories, you must infer the theme from clues in the story—what the characters say, the main events and conflicts, how characters change, and what they learn.

Into Action A helpful strategy is to write and organize brief notes in a chart like this one. Here are notes to get you started.

"Ta-Na-E-Ka"	Notes for Finding the Theme
Comments by Character	Mrs. Richardson says, "All of us have rituals of one kind or another."
Main Events and Conflicts	Mary does not want to participate in Ta-Na-E-Ka.
How Characters Change	

TechFocus As you read, think about this: If Mary, the main character, had had a laptop computer, how could she have recorded her feelings and attitudes about Ta-Na-E-Ka?

Writing Focus

Think as a Reader/Writer

Find It in Your Reading In this story, notice how the writer varies sentence structure, sometimes using extremely short sentences to create a suddenness and directness that longer sentences lack. Record examples of this in your *Reader/Writer Notebook*.

Vocabulary

loftiest (LAWF tee ehst) *adj.:* noblest; highest. *Endurance was the loftiest virtue.*

shrewdest (SHROOD ihst) *adj.:* sharpest; most clever. *The shrewdest survive the test.*

grimaced (GRIHM ihsd) *v.:* twisted the face to express pain, anger, or disgust. *Roger grimaced at the idea of eating bugs.*

gorging (GAWRJ ihng) *v.:* filling up; stuffing. *He was gorging himself on peaches.*

audacity (aw DAS uh tee) *n.:* boldness; daring. *They were shocked at Mary's audacity.*

Language Coach

Comparatives and Superlatives
Comparatives are adjectives that compare two things: *better, faster.* **Superlatives** are adjectives that compare three or more things: *best, fastest.*

In the Vocabulary box above, *loftiest* is a superlative. Which other word is, too?

Positive	lofty
Comparative	loftier
Superlative	loftiest

Learn It Online
Watch a video introduction to this story at:
go.hrw.com L6-357 Go

MEET THE WRITER

Mary Whitebird

Writing with a "Pen Name"

Some authors choose to write under a "pen name," or made-up name, rather than their real name. That seems to be the case with the author of "Ta-Na-E-Ka." Little is known about Mary Whitebird, who may actually have been a male writer.

The author of "Ta-Na-E-Ka" is said to have based the pen name "Mary Whitebird"—as well as the first name of the main character of this story—on a Navajo girl he met. Like the main character in this story, the Navajo girl was trying to balance her place in the wider world with the Navajo customs of her family.

You've probably read other works by authors who use pen names, also known as pseudonyms (SOO duh nihmz). Two of the best-known pen names are Dr. Seuss, the name Theodor Seuss Geisel wrote under, and Lemony Snicket, the pen name of Daniel Handler. Writers who use a pen name of the opposite gender are actually following a literary tradition. The nineteenth-century English novelist Mary Anne Evans wrote under the famous pen name George Eliot.

Think About the Writer

Why do you think the author of "Ta-Na-E-Ka" chose to use the name "Mary Whitebird"?

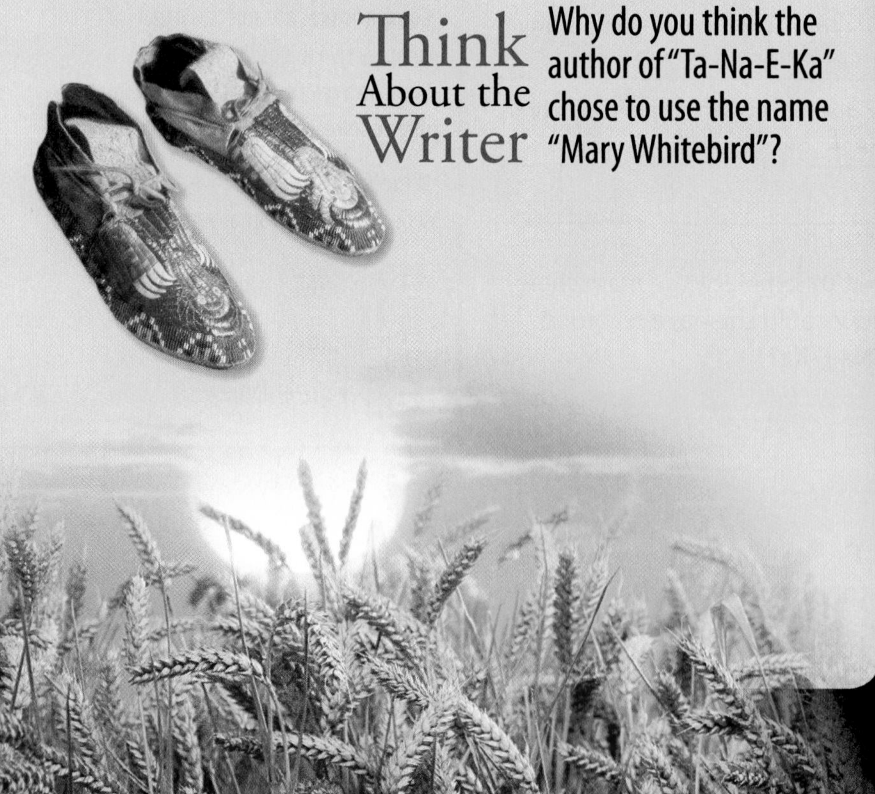

Build Background

This story refers to traditions of the Native American group known as Kaw or Kansa. Both names are forms of a word that means "People of the South Wind." The Kaw originally lived along the river now known as the Kansas River.

Ta-Na-E-Ka is a rite of passage, which is a ritual or ceremony marking an important life transition—in this case, the transition from childhood to adulthood. Rites of passage exist in virtually every culture, marking such important events as birth, marriage, and other changes of social status—including death.

Preview the Selection

Mary and her cousin **Roger,** young Kaw Indians who live on a reservation, are both about to turn the important age of eleven. At this age, Kaw youth traditionally undergo a right of passage into adulthood, a survival test called Ta-Na-E-Ka.

Read with a Purpose Read this story to discover how two eleven-year-olds survive a test involving a rite of passage.

Ta-Na-E-Ka

by **Mary Whitebird**

As my birthday drew closer, I had awful nightmares about it. I was reaching the age at which all Kaw Indians had to participate in Ta-Na-E-Ka. Well, not all Kaws. Many of the younger families on the reservation were beginning to give up the old customs. But my grandfather, Amos Deer Leg, was devoted to tradition. He still wore handmade beaded moccasins instead of shoes and kept his iron-gray hair in tight braids. He could speak English, but he spoke it only with white men. With his family he used a Sioux dialect.[1]

Grandfather was one of the last living Indians (he died in 1953, when he was eighty-one) who actually fought against the U.S. Cavalry. Not only did he fight, he was wounded in a skirmish at Rose Creek—a famous encounter in which the celebrated Kaw chief Flat Nose lost his life. At the time, my grandfather was only eleven years old. **A**

1. **Sioux** (soo) **dialect:** a branch of the Sioux language, spoken by many Plains Indians.

Eleven was a magic word among the Kaws. It was the time of Ta-Na-E-Ka, the "flowering of adulthood." It was the age, my grandfather informed us hundreds of times, "when a boy could prove himself to be a warrior and a girl took the first steps to womanhood."

"I don't want to be a warrior," my cousin, Roger Deer Leg, confided to me. "I'm going to become an accountant."

"None of the other tribes make girls go through the endurance ritual," I complained to my mother.

"It won't be as bad as you think, Mary," my mother said, ignoring my protests. "Once you've gone through it, you'll certainly never forget it. You'll be proud." **B**

I even complained to my teacher, Mrs. Richardson, feeling that, as a white woman, she would side with me.

She didn't. "All of us have rituals of one kind or another," Mrs. Richardson said. "And look at it this way: How many girls have the opportunity to compete on equal terms with boys? Don't look down on your heritage."

A **Read and Discuss** What's the narrator's attitude toward her approaching birthday? How does the information about Amos Deer Leg and the idea of tradition relate to Mary's birthday?

B **Literary Focus** **Theme** What is Mary's mother saying here that might be important to the story's theme? How does her attitude toward the ritual contrast with Mary's?

Heritage, indeed! I had no intention of living on a reservation for the rest of my life. I was a good student. I loved school. My fantasies were about knights in armor and fair ladies in flowing gowns being saved from dragons. It never once occurred to me that being an Indian was exciting. **C**

But I've always thought that the Kaw were the originators of the women's liberation movement. No other Indian tribe—and I've spent half a lifetime researching the subject—treated women more "equally" than the Kaw. Unlike most of the subtribes of the Sioux Nation, the Kaw allowed men and women to eat together. And hundreds of years before we were "acculturated,"[2] a Kaw woman had the right to refuse a prospective husband even if her father arranged the match.

The wisest women (generally wisdom was equated with age) often sat in tribal councils. Furthermore, most Kaw legends revolve around "Good Woman," a kind of supersquaw, a Joan of Arc[3] of the high plains. Good Woman led Kaw warriors into battle after battle, from which they always seemed to emerge victorious.

And girls as well as boys were required to undergo Ta-Na-E-Ka.

2. **acculturated** (uh KUHL chuh rayt ihd): adapted to a new or different culture.
3. **Joan of Arc** (1412–1431): French heroine who led her country's army to victory over the English in 1429.

The actual ceremony varied from tribe to tribe, but since the Indians' life on the plains was dedicated to survival, Ta-Na-E-Ka was a test of survival. **D**

"Endurance is the loftiest virtue of the Indian," my grandfather explained. "To survive, we must endure. When I was a boy, Ta-Na-E-Ka was more than the mere symbol it is now. We were painted white with the juice of a sacred herb and sent naked into the wilderness without so much as a knife. We couldn't return until the white had worn off. It wouldn't wash off. It took almost eighteen days, and during that time we had to stay alive, trapping food, eating insects and roots and berries, and watching out for enemies. And we did have enemies—both the white soldiers and the Omaha warriors, who were always trying to capture Kaw boys and girls undergoing their endurance test. It was an exciting time."

"What happened if you couldn't make it?" Roger asked. He was born only three days after I was, and we were being trained for Ta-Na-E-Ka together. I was happy to know he was frightened, too.

"Many didn't return," Grandfather said. "Only the strongest and shrewdest. Mothers were not allowed to weep over those who didn't return. If a Kaw couldn't survive, he or she wasn't worth weeping over. It was our way."

C **Reading Focus** **Finding the Theme** Pay attention to what a character learns in the course of the story as a clue to the theme. What conflict does Mary express here?

D **Read and Discuss** How does women's liberation connect to Kaw history and traditions? What does Mary think of this?

Vocabulary **loftiest** (LAWF tee ehst) *adj.:* noblest; highest.
shrewdest (SHROOD ihst) *adj.:* sharpest; most clever.

"What a lot of hooey," Roger whispered. "I'd give anything to get out of it."

"I don't see how we have any choice," I replied.

Roger gave my arm a little squeeze. "Well, it's only five days."

Five days! Maybe it was better than being painted white and sent out naked for eighteen days. But not much better.

We were to be sent, barefoot and in bathing suits, into the woods. Even our very traditional parents put their foot down when Grandfather suggested we go naked. For five days we'd have to live off the land, keeping warm as best we could, getting food where we could. It was May, but on the northernmost reaches of the Missouri River, the days were still chilly and the nights were fiercely cold. **E**

Grandfather was in charge of the month's training for Ta-Na-E-Ka. One day he caught a grasshopper and demonstrated how to pull its legs and wings off in one flick of the fingers and how to swallow it.

I felt sick, and Roger turned green. "It's a darn good thing it's 1947," I told Roger teasingly. "You'd make a terrible warrior." Roger just grimaced.

I knew one thing. This particular Kaw Indian girl wasn't going to swallow a grasshopper no matter how hungry she got. And then I had an idea. Why hadn't I thought of it before? It would have saved nights of bad dreams about squooshy grasshoppers.

I headed straight for my teacher's house. "Mrs. Richardson," I said, "would you lend me five dollars?" **F**

"Five dollars!" she exclaimed. "What for?"

"You remember the ceremony I talked about?"

"Ta-Na-E-Ka. Of course. Your parents have written me and asked me to excuse you from school so you can participate in it."

"Well, I need some things for the ceremony," I replied, in a half-truth. "I don't want to ask my parents for the money."

"It's not a crime to borrow money, Mary. But how can you pay it back?"

"I'll baby-sit for you ten times.

E **Read and Discuss** How is Ta-Na-E-Ka of Grandfather's time connected to Ta-Na-E-Ka that Roger and Mary will experience? What does Ta-Na-E-Ka show the elders about the children?

F **Read and Discuss** What do you think Mary is planning to do?

Vocabulary **grimaced** (GRIHM ihsd) *v.:* twisted the face to express pain, anger, or disgust.

"That's more than fair," she said, going to her purse and handing me a crisp, new five-dollar bill. I'd never had that much money at once.

"I'm happy to know the money's going to be put to a good use," Mrs. Richardson said.

A few days later the ritual began with a long speech from my grandfather about how we had reached the age of decision, how we now had to fend for ourselves and prove that we could survive the most horrendous of ordeals. All the friends and relatives who had gathered at our house for dinner made jokes about their own Ta-Na-E-Ka experiences. They all advised us to fill up now, since for the next five days we'd be gorging ourselves on crickets. Neither Roger nor I was very hungry. "I'll probably laugh about this when I'm an accountant," Roger said, trembling.

"Are you trembling?" I asked.

"What do you think?"

"I'm happy to know boys tremble, too," I said. G

At six the next morning, we kissed our parents and went off to the woods. "Which side do you want?" Roger asked. According to the rules, Roger and I would stake out "territories" in separate areas of the woods, and we weren't to communicate during the entire ordeal.

"I'll go toward the river, if it's OK with you," I said.

"Sure," Roger answered. "What difference does it make?"

To me, it made a lot of difference. There was a marina a few miles up the river, and there were boats moored there. At least, I hoped so. I figured that a boat was a better place to sleep than under a pile of leaves.

"Why do you keep holding your head?" Roger asked.

"Oh, nothing. Just nervous," I told him. Actually, I was afraid I'd lose the five-dollar bill, which I had tucked into my hair with a bobby pin. As we came to a fork in the trail, Roger shook my hand. "Good luck, Mary."

"N'ko-n'ta," I said. It was the Kaw word for "courage."

The sun was shining and it was warm, but my bare feet began to hurt immediately. I spied one of the berry bushes Grandfather had told us about. "You're lucky," he had said. "The berries are ripe in the spring, and they are delicious and nourishing." They were orange and fat, and I popped one into my mouth.

Argh! I spat it out. It was awful and bitter, and even grasshoppers were probably better tasting, although I never intended to find out.

G **Read and Discuss** How are Roger and Mary dealing with all the Ta-Na-E-Ka stories?

Vocabulary **gorging** (GAWRJ ihng) *v.:* filling up; stuffing.

SOCIAL STUDIES LINK

Remembering the Wind People

The Kaw people had a rich and proud history. They were known as the Wind People or the People of the South Wind. The Kaw Nation originally covered more than twenty million acres, from what is now Kansas into Missouri, Iowa, and Nebraska. Some familiar place names have their origin in Kaw words: *Wi-Tsi-Ta* became *Wichita* (Kansas), and *U-Moln-Holn* became *Omaha* (Nebraska).

The Kaw, like many other Native American groups, began to decline when Europeans arrived, bringing new diseases like smallpox and influenza with them. These illnesses were especially dangerous to Native Americans, who had no immunity to the diseases. The Kaw's shrinking population grew even smaller after it was moved to a reservation in Oklahoma in 1872. The last member of the Kaw Nation, William Mehojah (shown here), died in 2000.

Ask Yourself

How does knowing what ultimately happened to the Kaw make this story of Kaw traditions more meaningful?

I sat down to rest my feet. A rabbit hopped out from under the berry bush. He nuzzled the berry I'd spat out and ate it. He picked another one and ate that, too. He liked them. He looked at me, twitching his nose. I watched a redheaded woodpecker bore into an elm tree, and I caught a glimpse of a civet cat[4] waddling through some twigs. All of a sudden I realized I was no longer frightened. Ta-Na-E-Ka might be more fun than I'd anticipated. I got up and headed toward the marina. **H**

4. **civet** (SIHV iht) **cat:** furry, spotted catlike mammal.

"Not one boat," I said to myself dejectedly. But the restaurant on the shore, Ernie's Riverside, was open. I walked in, feeling silly in my bathing suit. The man at the counter was big and tough-looking. He wore a sweat shirt with the words "Fort Sheridan, 1944," and he had only three fingers on one of his hands. He asked me what I wanted.

"A hamburger and a milkshake," I said, holding the five-dollar bill in my hand so he'd know I had money.

"That's a pretty heavy breakfast, honey," he murmured.

H **Read and Discuss** What is happening with Mary?

"That's what I always have for breakfast," I lied.

"Forty-five cents," he said, bringing me the food. (Back in 1947, hamburgers were twenty-five cents and milkshakes were twenty cents.)

"Delicious," I thought. "Better 'n grass-hoppers—and Grandfather never once mentioned that I couldn't eat hamburgers."

While I was eating, I had a grand idea. Why not sleep in the restaurant? I went to the ladies' room and made sure the window was unlocked. Then I went back outside and played along the riverbank, watching the water birds and trying to identify each one. I planned to look for a beaver dam the next day.

The restaurant closed at sunset, and I watched the three-fingered man drive away. Then I climbed in the unlocked window. There was a night light on, so I didn't turn on any lights. But there was a radio on the counter. I turned it on to a music program. It was warm in the restaurant, and I was hungry. I helped myself to a glass of milk and a piece of pie, intending to keep a list of what I'd eaten so I could leave money. I also planned to get up early, sneak out through the window, and head for the woods before the three-fingered man returned. I turned off the radio, wrapped myself in the man's apron, and in spite of the hardness of the floor, fell asleep. **I**

"What the heck are you doing here, kid?"

It was the man's voice.

It was morning. I'd overslept. I was scared.

"Hold it, kid. I just wanna know what you're doing here. You lost? You must be from the reservation. Your folks must be worried sick about you. Do they have a phone?"

"Yes, yes," I answered. "But don't call them."

I was shivering. The man, who told me his name was Ernie, made me a cup of hot chocolate while I explained about Ta-Na-E-Ka.

"Darnedest thing I ever heard," he said, when I was through. "Lived next to the reservation all my life and this is the first I've heard of Ta-Na-whatever-you-call-it." He looked at me, all goose bumps in my bathing suit. "Pretty silly thing to do to a kid," he muttered.

That was just what I'd been thinking for months, but when Ernie said it, I became angry. "No, it isn't silly. It's a custom of the Kaw. We've been doing this for hundreds of years. My mother and my grandfather and everybody in my family went through this ceremony. It's why the Kaw are great warriors." **J**

"OK, great warrior," Ernie chuckled, "suit yourself. And, if you want to stick around, it's OK with me." Ernie went to the broom closet and tossed me a bundle. "That's the lost-and-found closet," he said. "Stuff people left on boats. Maybe there's something to keep you warm."

The sweater fitted loosely, but it felt good. I felt good. And I'd found a new friend. Most important, I was surviving Ta-Na-E-Ka.

My grandfather had said the experience would be filled with adventure, and I was having my fill. And Grandfather had never said we couldn't accept hospitality.

I **Read and Discuss** Based on what we know about Grandfather, what might he think of Mary's plan?

J **Read and Discuss** What are we learning about Mary here?

I stayed at Ernie's Riverside for the entire period. In the mornings I went into the woods and watched the animals and picked flowers for each of the tables in Ernie's. I had never felt better. I was up early enough to watch the sun rise on the Missouri, and I went to bed after it set. I ate everything I wanted—insisting that Ernie take all my money for the food. "I'll keep this in trust for you, Mary," Ernie promised, "in case you are ever desperate for five dollars." (He did, too, but that's another story.)

I was sorry when the five days were over. I'd enjoyed every minute with Ernie. He taught me how to make western omelets and to make Chili Ernie Style (still one of my favorite dishes). And I told Ernie all about the legends of the Kaw. I hadn't realized I knew so much about my people. **K**

Malt Shop in Sequim by Pam Ingalis.

Analyzing Visuals **Viewing and Interpreting** What does Mary learn in a restaurant like this one?

But Ta-Na-E-Ka was over, and as I approached my house at about nine-thirty in the evening, I became nervous all over again. What if Grandfather asked me about the berries and the grasshoppers? And my feet were hardly cut. I hadn't lost a pound and my hair was combed.

"They'll be so happy to see me," I told myself hopefully, "that they won't ask too many questions." **L**

I opened the door. My grandfather was in the front room. He was wearing the ceremonial beaded deerskin shirt which had belonged to *his* grandfather. "N'g'da'ma," he said. "Welcome back."

I embraced my parents warmly, letting go only when I saw my cousin Roger sprawled on the couch. His eyes were red

K **Reading Focus** **Finding the Theme** How does Mary's knowledge of the Kaw illustrate another way that she is changing?

L **Read and Discuss** How does Mary's situation look here? How do you think Roger is getting along?

and swollen. He'd lost weight. His feet were an unsightly mass of blood and blisters, and he was moaning: "I made it, see. I made it. I'm a warrior. A warrior."

My grandfather looked at me strangely. I was clean, obviously well fed, and radiantly healthy. My parents got the message. My uncle and aunt gazed at me with hostility.

Finally my grandfather asked, "What did you eat to keep you so well?"

I sucked in my breath and blurted out the truth: "Hamburgers and milkshakes."

"Hamburgers!" my grandfather growled.

"Milkshakes!" Roger moaned.

"You didn't say we had to eat grasshoppers," I said sheepishly.

"Tell us all about your Ta-Na-E-Ka," my grandfather commanded.

I told them everything, from borrowing the five dollars, to Ernie's kindness, to observing the beaver.

"That's not what I trained you for," my grandfather said sadly.

I stood up. "Grandfather, I learned that Ta-Na-E-Ka is important. I didn't think so during training. I was scared stiff of it. I handled it my way. And I learned I had nothing to be afraid of. There's no reason in 1947 to eat grasshoppers when you can eat a hamburger."

I was inwardly shocked at my own audacity. But I liked it. "Grandfather, I'll bet you never ate one of those rotten berries yourself."

Grandfather laughed! He laughed aloud! My mother and father and aunt and uncle were all dumbfounded. Grandfather never laughed. Never.

"Those berries—they are terrible," Grandfather admitted. "I could never swallow them. I found a dead deer on the first day of my Ta-Na-E-Ka—shot by a soldier, probably—and he kept my belly full for the entire period of the test!" **M**

Grandfather stopped laughing. "We should send you out again," he said.

I looked at Roger. "You're pretty smart, Mary," Roger groaned. "I'd never have thought of what you did."

"Accountants just have to be good at arithmetic," I said comfortingly. "I'm terrible at arithmetic."

Roger tried to smile but couldn't. My grandfather called me to him. "You should have done what your cousin did. But I think you are more alert to what is happening to our people today than we are. I think you would have passed the test under any circumstances, in any time. Somehow, you know how to exist in a world that wasn't made for Indians. I don't think you're going to have any trouble surviving." **N**

Grandfather wasn't entirely right. But I'll tell about that another time. **O**

M **Read and Discuss** How does Grandfather react to Mary's recounting of her Ta-Na-E-Ka? What is his attitude?

N **Reading Focus** **Finding the Theme** What is Grandfather saying that might be a clue to the theme?

O **Literary Focus** **Theme** What message from this story could have meaning in your own life?

Vocabulary **audacity** (aw DAS uh tee) *n.:* boldness; daring.

Applying Your Skills

Ta-Na-E-Ka

Sunshine State Standards: Benchmarks **LA.6.1.7.8** use strategies to repair comprehension of grade-appropriate text when self-monitoring indicates confusion, including but not limited to rereading, checking context clues, predicting, note-making, summarizing, using graphic and semantic organizers, questioning, and clarifying by checking other sources; *Also covered* **LA.6.2.1.2; LA.6.3.2.2**

Respond and Think Critically

Reading Focus

1. Which statement BEST describes what the grandfather learns from Mary's Ta-Na-E-Ka?
   A He thinks that his rules should always be followed.
   B He feels guilty that he did not prepare Mary better.
   C He sees that Mary has learned to survive in a different world.
   D He wishes he was smart enough to eat burgers and milkshakes.

Read with a Purpose

2. How do Roger's methods of survival differ from Mary's? Support your answer with examples from the story.

Reading Skills: Finding the Theme

3. Use the chart of notes you completed while reading "Ta-Na-E-Ka" to help identify the story's theme. Add the theme to your chart.

"Ta-Na-E-Ka"	Notes for Finding the Theme
Comments by Character	Mrs. Richarsdon: "All of us have rituals . . . ."
Main Events and Conflicts	Mary does not want to participate in Ta-Na-E-Ka.
How Characters Change	
Story's Theme	

Literary Focus

Literary Analysis

4. **Infer** In addition to what Mary tells us about the Kaw, what Kaw values can you infer from what you learn about the Ta-Na-E-Ka?

Literary Skills: Theme

5. **Analyze** What is the theme of "Ta-Na-E-Ka"? What truth about life does this theme address? Support your answer with details from the story.

Literary Skills Review: Character and Conflict

6. **Analyze/Evaluate** Which of Mary's character traits most affect the resolution of the story's conflicts? Explain which of Mary's conflicts are external and which are internal. Which kind of conflict is most important in the story?

Writing Focus

Think as a Reader/Writer

Use It in Your Writing Review the short sentences you recorded. How do they contrast with longer sentences in their effect? Revise your QuickWrite, varying your sentence structure and using short sentences to emphasize key points.

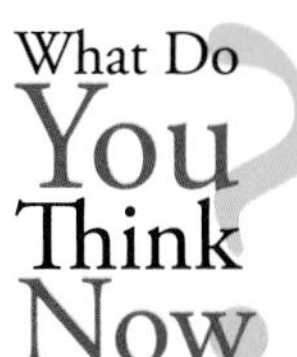

How has this story affected your attitude toward the value of knowledge and traditions that are passed down?

Applying Your Skills

Ta-Na-E-Ka

Vocabulary Development

Developing Fluency in Word Usage

You discover new words by reading. You develop **fluency,** or ease of use, by using those words as often as you can. Understanding the meaning of new words is the first step toward developing fluency with them.

Your Turn

loftiest
shrewdest
grimaced
gorging
audacity

How fluent are you with the Vocabulary words from this story? See if you can answer these questions. Look back at the definitions on page 357 if you need help.

1. In your opinion, what is the *loftiest* goal a person can reach for? What is the opposite of a *lofty* goal?
2. What is the *shrewdest* way to deal with a problem? What adjective is the opposite of *shrewd*?
3. What would you do if someone *grimaced* at you? How is a *grimace* different from a smile?
4. Is *gorging* yourself acceptable or rude behavior? Explain.
5. Name three deeds that would require *audacity* to carry out.

Language Coach

Comparatives and Superlatives

hungry
clean
lucky
healthy
silly

Adjectives that compare two people, places, things, or ideas are called **comparatives**. Adjectives that compare three or more are called **superlatives.** Comparatives of most short words (one or two syllables) are formed by adding *–er* to the base word. Superlatives of most short words are formed by adding *–est*. If the word ends in *y*, change the *y* to *i* before adding *–er or –est*.

Write the comparative and superlative forms of the words from "Ta-Na-E-Ka" in the box above.

Academic Vocabulary

Talk About . . .

If you were part of a family or group that had an unusual tradition, what do you think would be the best way for the elders to communicate the importance of the tradition? How could the elders help young people develop a positive attitude toward the tradition?

Learn It Online
Use Word Watch to increase your word knowledge at:
go.hrw.com
L6-368
Go

Sunshine State Standards: Benchmarks **LA.6.1.6.1** use new vocabulary that is introduced and taught directly; **LA.6.2.1.2** locate and analyze the elements of plot structure, including exposition, setting, character development, rising/falling action, conflict/resolution, and theme in a variety of fiction; **LA.6.3.4.4** the eight parts of speech (noun, pronoun, verb, adverb, adjective, conjunction, preposition, interjection); **LA.6.4.1.1** write narrative accounts with an engaging plot (including rising action, conflict, climax, falling action, and resolution) include a clearly described setting with figurative language and descriptive words or phrases to enhance style and tone; **LA.6.4.1.2** write a variety of expressive forms (e.g., short play, song lyrics, historical fiction, limericks) that employ figurative language, rhythm, dialogue, characterization, and/or appropriate format; **LA.6.4.2.3** write informational/expository essays (e.g., process, description, explanation, comparison/ contrast, problem/solution) that include a thesis statement, supporting details, and introductory, body, and concluding paragraphs.

Grammar Link

Direct and Indirect Objects

A **direct object** is a noun or pronoun that receives the action of the verb or that shows the result of the action. A direct object tells *what* or *whom* after a transitive (action) verb.

Every sentence has a subject and verb. The subject tells you *who* did something, and the verb tells you *about* the action—*what* he, she, or it did. The direct object tells *who* or *what* receives the action of the verb. The example tells *what* Ernie made.

S V DO

EXAMPLE Ernie made a *hamburger*.

An **indirect object** is a noun or pronoun that comes between the verb and the direct object. An indirect object tells *to whom* or *to what* or *for whom* or *for what* the action of the verb is done.

S V IO DO

EXAMPLE Ernie made *Mary* a hamburger.

The example tells *for whom* Ernie made a hamburger—Mary.

Your Turn

Identify the direct objects and the indirect objects in the following sentences. Write *DO* above the direct objects and *IO* above the indirect objects. Remember that a sentence can have more than one direct object and indirect object.

1. Grandfather caught a grasshopper.
2. Mary borrowed five dollars.
3. Mary gave Ernie her five-dollar bill.
4. Roger gave Mary the river territory.
5. Grandfather showed Mary and Roger a grasshopper and pulled off its wings and legs.

CHOICES

As you respond to the Choices, use these **Academic Vocabulary** words as appropriate: communicate, attitude, illustrate, contrast.

REVIEW

Write Mary's Blog

TechFocus Imagine that you are Mary and that you've taken your laptop along on your Ta-Na-E-Ka ritual to keep a blog and write about how you feel about what you are doing. Are you pleased? Do you feel guilty? Are you worried about what Roger thinks of you now? In the final entry, describe what happened when you arrived home, and explain what you learned.

CONNECT

Compare Arguments

Timed Writing This story deals with a conflict between an older generation and a younger one. What arguments do Mary's mother, grandfather, and teacher give in support of Ta-Na-E-Ka? What arguments do Mary and Roger give against it? Compare and contrast their arguments, and explain which side you agree with.

EXTEND

Continue Mary's Story

Grandfather says he thinks Mary will do well "in a world that wasn't made for Indians." Mary hints that he wasn't entirely right. Write a story or play script that shows a scene from Mary's life a few years later. In your scene, show how Mary continues to deal with the conflict between her heritage and the non-Indian world. Your approach can be humorous or serious.

Learn It Online
Enhance your understanding of this story at:
go.hrw.com
L6-369
Go

SHORT STORY

Preparing to Read

The All-American SLURP

by **Lensey Namioka**

What Do You Think? What common ground can people find in their different cultural customs?

QuickWrite

Have you ever been embarrassed because you didn't know how you were supposed to behave in a new situation—at a party, at a new friend's house, in a foreign country? Write a few sentences about your experience.

Reader/Writer Notebook

Use your **RWN** to complete the activities for this selection.

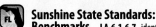

Sunshine State Standards: Benchmarks **LA.6.1.6.7** identify and understand the meaning of conceptually advanced prefixes, suffixes, and root words; **LA.6.1.7.3** determine the main idea or essential message in grade-level text through inferring, paraphrasing, summarizing, and identifying relevant details; **LA.6.1.7.8** use strategies to repair comphrension of grade-appropriate text when self-monitoring indicates confusion, including but not limited to rereading, checking context clues, predicting, note-making, summarizing, using graphic and semantic organizers, questioning, and clarifying by checking other sources; *Also covered* **LA.6.2.1.2; LA.6.2.1.3**

Literary Focus

Theme and Subject A story's theme is different from a story's subject. The **subject** of a story is what the story is about, and you can usually name it in a word or two. **Theme** is the meaning of the story, an idea about life that the story's characters, actions, and images communicate to you. If the subject of the story is "nature," the theme might be, "Nature can be beautiful but deadly."

Reading Focus

Making Generalizations A generalization is a broad conclusion that is drawn from several examples or pieces of evidence. A statement of a story's theme is a kind of generalization. From specific evidence in a story, you can make a universal statement about life: "One person can make a difference," or, "There are no winners in war." As you read "The All-American Slurp," do the following:

- Think about the key events and conflicts in the story.
- Make generalizations about how they apply to life.

Into Action As you read, fill in a chart like the one below:

Key Events	Generalizations
The Lins aren't sure how to act during dinner at the Gleasons'. (1) They pull strings out of celery. (2) They set chairs at the buffet.	When you're not sure about another culture's customs, you may end up doing things that appear strange.

Writing Focus

Think as a Reader/Writer

Find It in Your Reading *Onomatopoeia* (ahn uh maht uh PEE uh) refers to words that sound like what they mean: *buzz, zip, clang.* Look for the writer's use of onomatopoeia in this story. (There's one in the title!) Keep a list of these "sound words" in your *Reader/Writer Notebook.*

Vocabulary

lavishly (LAV ihsh lee) *adv.:* abundantly; plentifully. *The table was lavishly decorated.*

mortified (MAWR tuh fyd) *v.:* ashamed; embarrassed. *I was mortified by my family's mistakes.*

spectacle (SPEHK tuh kuhl) *n.:* strange or impressive sight. *The narrator fears that her brother is making a spectacle of himself with his noisy eating.*

acquainted (uh KWAYNT ihd) *adj.:* to know someone but not know him or her well. *Meg was acquainted with many students in school.*

etiquette (EHT uh keht) *n.:* acceptable manners and behavior. *Slurping is not proper etiquette in a fancy restaurant.*

Language Coach

Word Forms You can change adjectives like *lavish* by adding endings to make adverbs. When adding the suffix *–ly* to most words, you don't change the spelling of the word itself. However, for words that end in *–y*, you usually need to change the *y* to *i* before adding *–ly*. Try adding *–ly* to these story words: *careful, helpful, pretty.*

Learn It Online

Reinforce your learning of terms with Word Watch:

go.hrw.com L6-371 

MEET THE WRITER

Lensey Namioka

(1929–)

A Life on the Move

It's only natural for **Lensey Namioka** to write about young people trying to cope with the strange ways of a new culture, because she's spent so much of her own life adjusting to new people and places. Namioka was born in China, where her family moved around a lot when she was young.

When she was a teenager, Namioka and her family immigrated to the United States, where they continued to move from place to place.

Namioka's Career

Before she began writing for young people, Lensey Namioka was a math teacher. Her realistic stories about teenagers today draw on her Chinese heritage and her experience as a teacher. Namioka has also written adventure and mystery novels about samurai warriors that are set in long-ago Japan. These stories draw on her husband's Japanese heritage.

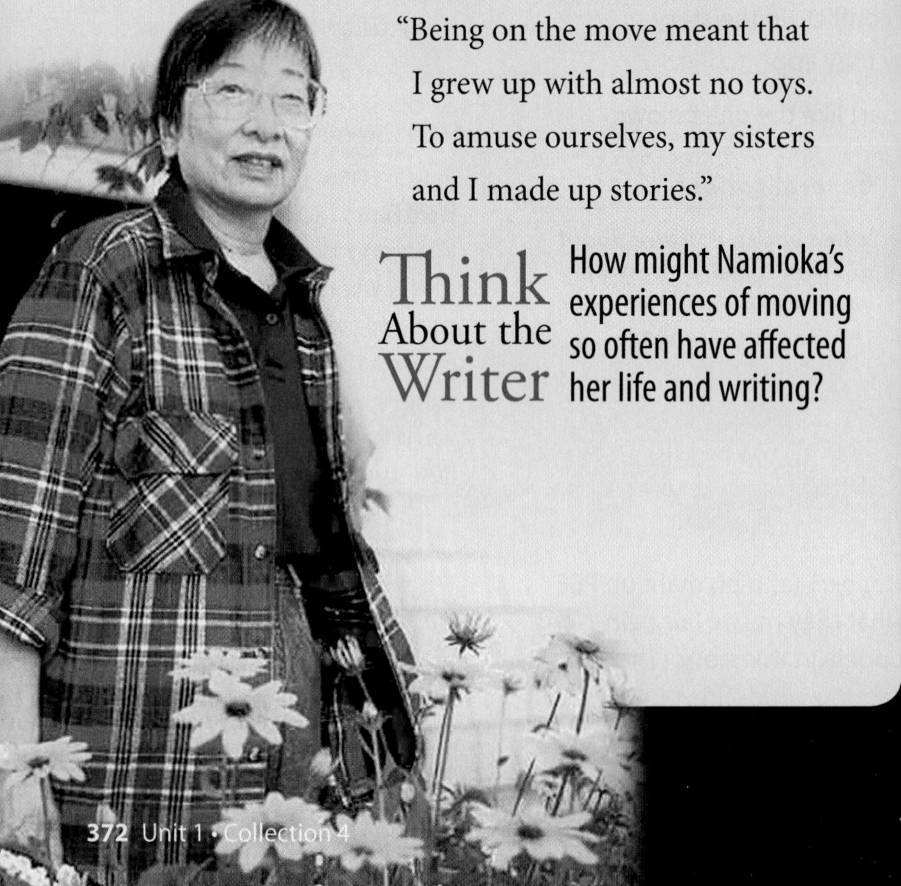

"Being on the move meant that I grew up with almost no toys. To amuse ourselves, my sisters and I made up stories."

Think About the Writer How might Namioka's experiences of moving so often have affected her life and writing?

Preview the Selection

This humorous story is told by a young Chinese girl, who, along with her family, has recently emigrated from China. The **narrator** and her family, the **Lins**, have some trouble adjusting to American food and table manners. However, the narrator learns an important lesson when the tables are turned.

Read with a Purpose Read this story to discover what sort of embarrassing—but funny—situations can develop when families encounter unfamiliar customs.

The All-American Slurp

by **Lensey Namioka**

The first time our family was invited out to dinner in America, we disgraced ourselves while eating celery. We had immigrated to this country from China, and during our early days here we had a hard time with American table manners. **A**

In China we never ate celery raw, or any other kind of vegetable raw. We always had to disinfect the vegetables in boiling water first. When we were presented with our first relish tray, the raw celery caught us unprepared. **B**

We had been invited to dinner by our neighbors, the Gleasons. After arriving at the house, we shook hands with our hosts and packed ourselves into a sofa. As our family of four sat stiffly in a row, my younger brother and I stole glances at our parents for a clue as to what to do next.

Mrs. Gleason offered the relish tray to Mother. The tray looked pretty, with its tiny red radishes, curly sticks of carrots, and long, slender stalks of pale-green celery. "Do try some of the celery, Mrs. Lin," she said. "It's from a local farmer, and it's sweet."

Mother picked up one of the green stalks, and Father followed suit. Then I picked up a stalk, and my brother did too. So there we sat, each with a stalk of celery in our right hand.

Mrs. Gleason kept smiling. "Would you like to try some of the dip, Mrs. Lin? It's my own recipe: sour cream and onion flakes, with a dash of Tabasco sauce."

Most Chinese don't care for dairy products, and in those days I wasn't even ready to drink fresh milk. Sour cream sounded perfectly revolting. Our family shook our heads in unison.

Mrs. Gleason went off with the relish tray to the other guests, and we carefully

---

A **Literary Focus** **Theme and Subject** Based on what you've read in the first paragraph, what do you think the subject of this story might be?

B **Read and Discuss** What has the author told us so far? What does the narrator mean about the family disgracing themselves?

watched to see what they did. Everyone seemed to eat the raw vegetables quite happily.

Mother took a bite of her celery. *Crunch.* "It's not bad!" she whispered.

Father took a bite of his celery. *Crunch.* "Yes, it is good," he said, looking surprised.

I took a bite, and then my brother. *Crunch, crunch.* It was more than good; it was delicious. Raw celery has a slight sparkle, a zingy taste that you don't get in cooked celery. When Mrs. Gleason came around with the relish tray, we each took another stalk of celery, except my brother. He took two.

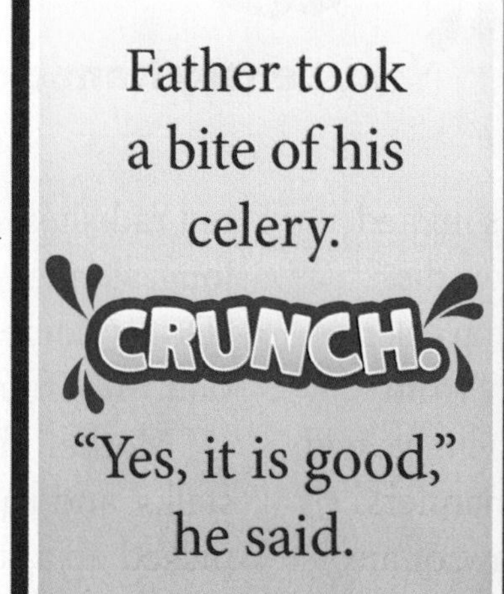
Father took a bite of his celery.
CRUNCH.
"Yes, it is good," he said.

There was only one problem: Long strings ran through the length of the stalk, and they got caught in my teeth. When I help my mother in the kitchen, I always pull the strings out before slicing celery.

I pulled the strings out of my stalk. *Z-z-zip, z-z-zip.* My brother followed suit. *Z-z-zip, z-z-zip, z-z-zip.* To my left, my parents were taking care of their own stalks. *Z-z-zip, z-z-zip, z-z-zip.*

Suddenly I realized that there was dead silence except for our zipping. Looking up, I saw that the eyes of everyone in the room were on our family. Mr. and Mrs. Gleason, their daughter Meg, who was my friend, and their neighbors the Badels—they were all staring at us as we busily pulled the strings of our celery. **C**

That wasn't the end of it. Mrs. Gleason announced that dinner was served and invited us to the dining table. It was **lavishly** covered with platters of food, but we couldn't see any chairs around the table. So we helpfully carried over some dining chairs and sat down. All the other guests just stood there.

Mrs. Gleason bent down and whispered to us, "This is a buffet dinner. You help yourselves to some food and eat it in the living room."

Our family beat a retreat back to the sofa as if chased by enemy soldiers. For the rest of the evening, too **mortified** to go back to the dining table, I nursed a bit of potato salad on my plate. **D**

Next day, Meg and I got on the school bus together. I wasn't sure how she would feel about me after the **spectacle** our family made at the party. But she was just the same as usual, and the only reference she made to the party was, "Hope you and your folks got enough to eat last night. You certainly didn't take very much. Mom never tries to figure out how much food to prepare. She just puts everything on the table and hopes for the best."

I began to relax. The Gleasons' dinner party wasn't so different from a Chinese meal after all. My mother also puts everything on the table and hopes for the best.

C **Read and Discuss** What is the problem with the celery now?

D **Read and Discuss** What is going on at this dinner party? What picture does the line about the family beating "a retreat to the sofa as if chased by enemy soldiers" create in your mind?

Vocabulary **lavishly** (LAV ihsh lee) *adv.:* abundantly; plentifully.
mortified (MAWR tuh fyd) *v.:* ashamed; embarrassed.
spectacle (SPEHK tuh kuhl) *n.:* strange or impressive sight.

Meg was the first friend I had made after we came to America. I eventually got acquainted with a few other kids in school, but Meg was still the only real friend I had.

My brother didn't have any problems making friends. He spent all his time with some boys who were teaching him baseball, and in no time he could speak English much faster than I could—not better, but faster.

I worried more about making mistakes, and I spoke carefully, making sure I could say everything right before opening my mouth. At least I had a better accent than my parents, who never really got rid of their Chinese accent, even years later. My parents had both studied English in school before coming to America, but what they had studied was mostly written English, not spoken.

Father's approach to English was a scientific one. Since Chinese verbs have no tense, he was fascinated by the way English verbs changed form according to whether they were in the present, past, perfect, pluperfect, future, or future perfect tense. He was always making diagrams of verbs and their inflections, and he looked for opportunities to show off his mastery of the pluperfect and future perfect tenses, his two favorites. "I shall have finished my project by Monday," he would say smugly.

Mother's approach was to memorize lists of polite phrases that would cover all possible social situations. She was constantly muttering things like "I'm fine, thank you. And you?" Once she accidentally stepped on someone's foot and hurriedly blurted, "Oh, that's quite all right!" Embarrassed by her slip, she resolved to do better next time. So when someone stepped on *her* foot, she cried, "You're welcome!" **E**

In our own different ways, we made progress in learning English. But I had another worry, and that was my appearance. My brother didn't have to worry, since Mother bought him blue jeans for school, and he dressed like all the other boys. But she insisted that girls had to wear skirts. By the time she saw that Meg and the other girls were wearing jeans, it was too late. My school clothes were bought already, and we didn't have money left to buy new outfits for me. We had too many other things to buy first, like furniture, pots, and pans.

The first time I visited Meg's house, she took me upstairs to her room, and I wound up trying on her clothes. We were pretty much the same size since Meg was shorter and thinner than average. Maybe that's how we became friends in the first place. Wearing Meg's jeans and T-shirt, I looked at myself in the mirror. I could almost pass for an American—from the back, anyway. At least the kids in school wouldn't stop and stare at me in the hallways, which was what they did when they saw me in my white

E **Read and Discuss** The author is giving us a lot of detail here. What is the significance of all of this information?

Vocabulary **acquainted** (uh KWAYNT ihd) *adj.:* to know someone but not know him or her well.

Analyzing Visuals **Viewing and Interpreting** What scene in the story does this photograph illustrate?

blouse and navy-blue skirt that went a couple of inches below the knees.

When Meg came to my house, I invited her to try on my Chinese dresses, the ones with a high collar and slits up the sides. Meg's eyes were bright as she looked at herself in the mirror. She struck several sultry poses, and we nearly fell over laughing. **F**

The dinner party at the Gleasons' didn't stop my growing friendship with Meg. Things were getting better for me in other ways too. Mother finally bought me some jeans at the end of the month, when Father got his paycheck. She wasn't in any hurry about buying them at first, until I worked on her. This is what I did. Since we didn't have a car in those days, I often ran down to the neighborhood store to pick up things for her. The groceries cost less at a big supermarket, but the closest one was many blocks away. One day, when she ran out of flour, I offered to borrow a bike from our neighbor's son and buy a ten-pound bag of flour at the big supermarket. I mounted the boy's bike and waved to Mother. "I'll be back in five minutes!"

Before I started pedaling, I heard her voice behind me. "You can't go out in public like that! People can see all the way up to your thighs!"

"I'm sorry," I said innocently. "I thought you were in a hurry to get the flour." For dinner we were going to have pot stickers (fried Chinese dumplings), and we needed a lot of flour.

"Couldn't you borrow a girl's bicycle?" complained Mother. "That way your skirt won't be pushed up."

"There aren't too many of those around," I said. "Almost all the girls wear jeans while

---

F **Read and Discuss** Now what problem is the narrator facing?

riding a bike, so they don't see any point buying a girl's bike." **G**

We didn't eat pot stickers that evening, and Mother was thoughtful. Next day we took the bus downtown and she bought me a pair of jeans. In the same week, my brother made the baseball team of his junior high school, Father started taking driving lessons, and Mother discovered rummage sales. We soon got all the furniture we needed, plus a dartboard and a 1,000-piece jigsaw puzzle. (Fourteen hours later, we discovered that it was a 999-piece jigsaw puzzle.) There was hope that the Lins might become a normal American family after all.

Then came our dinner at the Lakeview restaurant. The Lakeview was an expensive restaurant, one of those places where a headwaiter dressed in tails conducted you to your seat, and the only light came from candles and flaming desserts. In one corner of the room a lady harpist played tinkling melodies.

Father wanted to celebrate because he had just been promoted. He worked for an electronics company, and after his English started improving, his superiors decided to appoint him to a position more suited to his training. The promotion not only brought a higher salary but was also a tremendous boost to his pride.

Up to then we had eaten only in Chinese restaurants. Although my brother and I were becoming fond of hamburgers, my parents didn't care much for Western food, other than chow mein.

But this was a special occasion, and Father asked his co-workers to recommend a really elegant restaurant. So there we were at the Lakeview, stumbling after the headwaiter in the murky dining room.

At our table we were handed our menus, and they were so big that to read mine, I almost had to stand up again. But why bother? It was mostly in French, anyway.

Father, being an engineer, was always systematic. He took out a pocket French dictionary. "They told me that most of the items would be in French, so I came prepared." He even had a pocket flashlight the size of a marking pen. While Mother held the flashlight over the menu, he looked up the items that were in French.

"Pâté en croûte," he muttered. "Let's see . . . *pâté* is paste . . . *croûte* is crust . . . hmmm . . . a paste in crust." **H**

The waiter stood looking patient. I squirmed and died at least fifty times.

At long last Father gave up. "Why don't we just order four complete dinners at random?" he suggested.

"Isn't that risky?" asked Mother. "The French eat some rather peculiar things, I've heard."

"A Chinese can eat anything a Frenchman can eat," Father declared.

The soup arrived in a plate. How do you get soup up from a plate? I glanced at the other diners, but the ones at the nearby tables were not on their soup course, while the more distant ones were invisible in the darkness.

G **Read and Discuss** What is the narrator trying to do now? What does this tell you about her?

H **Reading Focus** **Generalizations** What generalization can you make about Mr. Lin's approach to life in the United States?

Fortunately my parents had studied books on Western etiquette before they came to America. "Tilt your plate," whispered my mother. "It's easier to spoon the soup up that way."

She was right. Tilting the plate did the trick. But the etiquette book didn't say anything about what you did after the soup reached your lips. As any respectable Chinese knows, the correct way to eat your soup is to slurp. This helps to cool the liquid and prevent you from burning your lips. It also shows your appreciation.

We showed our appreciation. *Shloop,* went my father. *Shloop,* went my mother. *Shloop, shloop,* went my brother, who was the hungriest.

> **SHLOOP, SHLOOP**
> went my brother, who was the hungriest.

The lady harpist stopped playing to take a rest. And in the silence, our family's consumption of soup suddenly seemed unnaturally loud. You know how it sounds on a rocky beach when the tide goes out and the water drains from all those little pools? They go *shloop, shloop, shloop.* That was the Lin family eating soup.

At the next table a waiter was pouring wine. When a large *shloop* reached him, he froze. The bottle continued to pour, and red wine flooded the table top and into the lap of a customer. Even the customer didn't notice anything at first, being also hypnotized by the *shloop, shloop, shloop.*

It was too much. "I need to go to the toilet," I mumbled, jumping to my feet. A waiter, sensing my urgency, quickly directed me to the ladies' room. **I**

I splashed cold water on my burning face, and as I dried myself with a paper towel, I stared into the mirror. In this perfumed ladies' room, with its pink-and-silver wallpaper and marbled sinks, I looked completely out of place. What was I doing here? What was our family doing in the Lakeview restaurant? In America?

The door to the ladies' room opened. A woman came in and glanced curiously at me. I retreated into one of the toilet cubicles and latched the door.

Time passed—maybe half an hour, maybe an hour. Then I heard the door open again, and my mother's voice. "Are you in there? You're not sick, are you?"

There was real concern in her voice. A girl can't leave her family just because they slurp their soup. Besides, the toilet cubicle had a few drawbacks as a permanent residence. "I'm all right," I said, undoing the latch.

Mother didn't tell me how the rest of the dinner went, and I didn't want to know. In the weeks following, I managed to push the whole thing into the back of my mind, where it jumped out at me only a few times

---

I **Read and Discuss** What's the connection between all the slurping and the narrator's need to go to the bathroom?

Vocabulary **etiquette** (EHT uh keht) *n.:* acceptable manners and behavior.

Analyzing Visuals

Viewing and Interpreting What attitude or feeling does the girl in this photograph communicate? How is it similar to the narrator's feelings in the restaurant?

a day. Even now, I turn hot all over when I think of the Lakeview restaurant.

But by the time we had been in this country for three months, our family was definitely making progress toward becoming Americanized. I remember my parents' first PTA meeting. Father wore a neat suit and tie, and Mother put on her first pair of high heels. She stumbled only once. They met my homeroom teacher and beamed as she told them that I would make honor roll soon at the rate I was going. Of course Chinese etiquette forced Father to say that I was a very stupid girl and Mother to protest that the teacher was showing favoritism toward me. But I could tell they were both very proud. **J**

The day came when my parents announced that they wanted to give a dinner party. We had invited Chinese friends to eat with us before, but this dinner was going to be different. In addition to a Chinese American family, we were going to invite the Gleasons.

"Gee, I can hardly wait to have dinner at your house," Meg said to me. "I just *love* Chinese food."

That was a relief. Mother was a good cook, but I wasn't sure if people who ate sour cream would also eat chicken gizzards stewed in soy sauce.

Mother decided not to take a chance with chicken gizzards. Since we had Western guests, she set the table with large dinner plates, which we never used in Chinese meals. In fact we didn't use individual plates at all, but picked up food

---

J **Read and Discuss** What have you learned about Chinese etiquette from this story, and how does it connect to what the narrator has been talking about?

from the platters in the middle of the table and brought it directly to our rice bowls. Following the practice of Chinese American restaurants, Mother also placed large serving spoons on the platters.

The dinner started well. Mrs. Gleason exclaimed at the beautifully arranged dishes of food: the colorful candied fruit in the sweet-and-sour pork dish, the noodle-thin shreds of chicken meat stir-fried with tiny peas, and the glistening pink prawns[1] in a ginger sauce.

At first I was too busy enjoying my food to notice how the guests were doing. But soon I remembered my duties. Sometimes guests were too polite to help themselves and you had to serve them with more food.

I glanced at Meg to see if she needed more food, and my eyes nearly popped out at the sight of her plate. It was piled with food: The sweet-and-sour meat pushed right against the chicken shreds, and the chicken sauce ran into the prawns. She had been taking food from a second dish before she finished eating her helping from the first!

Horrified, I turned to look at Mrs. Gleason. She was dumping rice out of her bowl and putting it on her dinner plate. Then she ladled prawns and gravy on top of the rice and mixed everything together, the way you mix sand, gravel, and cement to make concrete. **K**

I couldn't bear to look any longer, and I turned to Mr. Gleason. He was chasing a pea around his plate. Several times he got it to the edge, but when he tried to pick it up with his chopsticks, it rolled back toward the center of the plate again. Finally he put down his chopsticks and picked up the pea with his fingers. He really did! A grown man!

All of us, our family and the Chinese guests, stopped eating to watch the activities of the Gleasons. I wanted to giggle. Then I caught my mother's eyes on me. She frowned and shook her head slightly, and I understood the message: The Gleasons were not used to Chinese ways, and they were just coping the best they could. For some reason I thought of celery strings.

When the main courses were finished, Mother brought out a platter of fruit. "I hope you weren't expecting a sweet dessert," she said. "Since the Chinese don't eat dessert, I didn't think to prepare any."

"Oh, I couldn't possibly eat dessert!" cried Mrs. Gleason. "I'm simply stuffed!"

Meg had different ideas. When the table was cleared, she announced that she and I were going for a walk. "I don't know about you, but I feel like dessert," she told me, when we were outside. "Come on, there's a Dairy Queen down the street. I could use a big chocolate milkshake!"

Although I didn't really want anything more to eat, I insisted on paying for the milkshakes. After all, I was still hostess.

Meg got her large chocolate milkshake and I had a small one. Even so, she was finishing hers while I was only half done. Toward the end she pulled hard on her straws and went *shloop, shloop.*

"Do you always slurp when you eat a milkshake?" I asked, before I could stop myself.

Meg grinned. "Sure. All Americans slurp." **L**

---

1. **prawns:** large shrimps.

K **Literary Focus** **Theme and Subject** How does the narrator's surprise relate to the subject of the story? to the theme?

L **Read and Discuss** What is the significance of this last line? What point does it illustrate?

Applying Your Skills

Sunshine State Standards: Benchmarks LA.6.1.7.3 determine the main idea or essential message in grade-level text through inferring, paraphrasing, summarizing, and identifying relevant details; *Also covered* LA.6.1.7.8; LA.6.2.1.2; LA.6.2.1.3

The All-American Slurp

Respond and Think Critically

Reading Focus

1. Why is it important that Meg slurps her milkshake? **FCAT**
   - **A** It makes the narrator feel better about her family slurping their soup.
   - **B** It shows that Meg does not respect the narrator's own customs.
   - **C** It shows that the narrator is still uncomfortable with American customs.
   - **D** It makes Meg and the narrator better friends.

Read with a Purpose

2. How does the Lin family adapt to customs in the United States? Support your answer with examples from the story.

Reading Skills: Making Generalizations

3. Review the chart of notes you made while reading the story. Then add two new rows: one for what the narrator discovers through the key events of the story and one for a final generalization about life—the story's theme.

Key Events	Generalizations
The Lins aren't sure how to act during dinner at the Gleasons'. (1) They pull strings out of celery. (2) They set chairs at the buffet.	When you're not sure about another culture's customs, you may end up doing things that appear strange.
What Narrator Discovers	
Final Generalization (Theme)	

Literary Focus

Literary Analysis

4. **Connect** Do you think the author makes the immigrant experience sound too easy, or is she on target? How did the story remind you of your own experiences in a new situation?

Literary Skills: Theme and Subject

5. **Analyze** What is the main subject of this story? How does it relate to the theme?

Literary Skills Review: Point of View

6. **Analyze** This story is told from the first-person point of view. How would the story change if it were told from the third-person point of view? Support your answer with examples from the story. READ THINK EXPLAIN

Writing Focus

Think as a Reader/Writer

Use It in Your Writing Some of the onomatopoeia in the story describes sounds people make while eating. Using at least three examples of onomatopoeia, write a paragraph describing a noisy activity, such as a party, game, or zoo visit.

What Do You Think Now?

How did this story affect your ideas about the things people have in common in spite of their different cultural customs?

Applying Your Skills

The All-American Slurp

Vocabulary Development

Vocabulary Skills: Using Context Clues to Clarify Meaning

When you're reading, you can often figure out the meaning of a word by using what you know about word parts and related words. You can also use the **context,** or all of the information surrounding the word, to help you figure out what the word means.

Unfamiliar Word	Using Context Clues
"The Lakeview was an expensive restaurant, one of those places where a headwaiter *conducted* you to your seat . . . ."	*conducted* I think this means the waiter took people to their seats. A conductor is someone who *leads* an orchestra. *Conducted* probably means *led*.

Your Turn

lavishly
mortified
spectacle
acquainted
etiquette

Using Context Clues to Clarify Meaning Complete each sentence, providing context clues to clarify the meaning of the word in italics.

1. I noticed that the table was *lavishly* set with ________________.
2. I was so *mortified* by my brother's behavior that I ________________.
3. We were afraid that we created a *spectacle* because ________________.
4. Meg was *acquainted* with the new girl but ________________.
5. When you use proper *etiquette*, you ________________.

Language Coach

ready
real
polite
tremendous

Word Forms Make adverbs by adding *–ly* to the words from the story shown in the box at right. Remember that when you add the suffix *–ly* to most words to form adverbs, you don't change the spelling of the word itself. However, for words that end in *–y*, you usually need to change the *y* to *i* before adding *–ly*. Use a dictionary to check your spelling.

Academic Vocabulary

Talk About . . .

The author uses humor to illustrate that people from different cultures feel very similar when they face new situations. The story's events communicate a positive view of the immigrant experience. What types of situations might the writer describe to provide a contrast to that view?

Learn It Online
Use WordSharp to bolster language skills at:
go.hrw.com
L6-382
Go

Sunshine State Standards: Benchmarks **LA.6.1.6.3** use context clues to determine meanings of unfamiliar words; **LA.6.1.6.7** identify and understand the meaning of conceptually advanced prefixes, suffixes, and root words; **LA.6.3.4.4** the eight parts of speech (noun, pronoun, verb, adverb, adjective, conjunction, preposition, interjection); **LA.6.3.5.1** prepare writing using technology in a format appropriate to audience and purpose (e.g., manuscript, multimedia); **LA.6.3.5.3** share the writing with the intended audience; **LA.6.4.2.3** write informational/expository essays (e.g., process, description, explanation, comparison/ contrast, problem/ solution) that include a thesis statement, supporting details, and introductory, body, and concluding paragraphs; **LA.6.6.3.1** analyze ways that production elements (e.g., graphics, color, motion, sound, digital technology) affect communication across the media; **LA.6.6.3.2** demonstrate the ability to select and ethically use media appropriate for the purpose, occasion, and audience; **LA.6.6.4.1** use appropriate available technologies to enhance communication and achieve a purpose (e.g., video, online).

Grammar Link

Predicate Nominatives

A **predicate nominative** is a word or word group that is in the predicate and that identifies or refers to the subject. It may be a noun, a pronoun, or a word group functioning as a noun.

EXAMPLE That was the day we became *Americans.* [*Americans* is the predicate nominative completing the meaning of the linking verb *became.*]

EXAMPLE The Gleasons were gracious *hosts.* [*Hosts* is the predicate nominative completing the meaning of the linking verb *were.*]

It's important to remember that a predicate nominative always completes the meaning of a linking *be* verb.

EXAMPLE My mother was a good *cook.* [*Cook* completes the meaning of the linking verb *was.*]

If two words are connected by an *action* verb, that complement is usually a direct object and *not* a predicate nominative.

Your Turn

Identify the predicate nominative in each of the sentences below.

1. Sour cream is a dairy product.
2. Meg and the narrator were friends.
3. This is a buffet dinner.
4. After all, I was still hostess.
5. Was the Lakeview a restaurant?

CHOICES

As you respond to the Choices, use these **Academic Vocabulary** words as appropriate: communicate, attitude, illustrate, contrast.

REVIEW

Perform a Dramatic Reading

Group Activity With a team, prepare a dramatic reading of a scene from this story. First, prepare a script. Decide how many readers you will need. Consider using props—and make your own sound effects! Rehearse your reading and perform it for the class.

CONNECT

Write an Essay on Friendship

Timed Writing In this story, the friendship with Meg helps the narrator discover new things and helps her change her attitude about making mistakes. Think of a time when you made a new friend. What drew the two of you together? What made the friendship grow? What did you learn from your friend? Write a short essay that illustrates how important the friendship was.

EXTEND

Design a Helpful Web Site

TechFocus To help a newcomer from another culture feel more comfortable in your school, design a Web site of information, including a list of slang expressions, a description of currently popular things (foods, movies, music, TV shows, clothes), a map of your school, and tips on fun things to do in your town.

Learn It Online
Bring your essay to life with digital storytelling at:
go.hrw.com
L6-383
Go

SHORT STORY

Preparing to Read

Aaron's Gift

by **Myron Levoy**

What Do You Think?

What's special about the gifts we receive from or give to the people who are important to us?

QuickWrite

Think about the best gift that you have ever received from someone who means a lot to you. What made it such a good gift? Write down your thoughts.

Reader/Writer Notebook

Use your **RWN** to complete the activities for this selection.

Sunshine State Standards: Benchmarks **LA.6.1.6.7** identify and understand the meaning of conceptually advanced prefixes, suffixes, and root words; **LA.6.1.6.10** determine meanings of words, pronunciation, parts of speech, etymologies, and alternate word choices by using a dictionary, thesaurus, and digital tools; **LA.6.1.7.4** identify cause-and-effect relationships in text; **LA.6.2.1.2** locate and analyze the elements of plot structure, including exposition, setting, character development, rising/falling action, conflict/resolution, and theme in a variety of fiction.

Literary Focus

Theme and Plot Writers are concerned with more than just the events in a story. They are also concerned with the story's message—the important idea it expresses about life. The *events* in a story are the story's **plot;** the *message* is the story's **theme.**

Literary Perspectives Use the Analyzing Archetypes perspective described on page 387 as you read this story.

Reading Focus

Using Cause and Effect to Determine Theme A story's **plot** consists of a series of related events. The first event in a plot **causes** something else to happen—an **effect.** That effect, in turn, becomes the cause of other events.

Understanding the chain of causes and effects in a story can help you discover the story's theme. Be alert for events that happen more than once, or that seem to echo or repeat other events. Pay special attention to events that strongly affect the way the plot unfolds, especially events that occur at the **climax** of a story—the moment when we know how the conflict will be resolved. Such events often communicate the story's theme, or message.

Into Action Use a graphic organizer like the flow chart below to record the chain of causes and effects in this story. You'll use thisinformation later to determine the story's theme.

Cause 1 → Effect 1 → Cause 2

Writing Focus

Think as a Reader/Writer

Find It in Your Reading The pigeon is an important image in this story. As you read, use your *Reader/Writer Notebook* to record descriptions of how Aaron feels about the pigeon.

Vocabulary

plunged (pluhnjd) *v.:* dived down suddenly. *Aaron plunged and caught the bird.*

thrashing (THRASH ihng) *v.:* moving from side to side in an uncontrolled way. *The bird was tired because it was thrashing.*

contented (kuhn TEHNT ihd) *adj.:* happy or satisfied. *The bird was contented when it was living with Aaron.*

consoled (kuhn SOHLD) *v.:* comforted when sad or disappointed. *She couldn't be consoled after losing her goat.*

Language Coach

Base Words All of the Vocabulary words above consist of a base word to which an ending, or suffix, has been added. Identify the base word for each of the words. To which three base words can both *–ed* and *–ing* be added to make new words? What parts of speech are the new words? You may wish to use a dictionary.

Learn It Online
Elevate your vocabulary skills with Word Watch:

go.hrw.com L6-385 

MEET THE WRITER

Myron Levoy

(1930–)

Inspired by an Author's Manuscript

When Myron Levoy was a teenager, he worked at the New York Public Library, and there he came across the original manuscript of the poem "Miniver Cheevy" by Edward Arlington Robinson. Levoy had just read the poem in school, and seeing it written in the author's own hand amazed him. He was inspired to become a writer himself.

Award-Winning Books

After deciding on his career, Myron Levoy wrote a popular book of short stories called *The Witch of Fourth Street,* along with many other books for children. He also wrote *Alan and Naomi*, a novel about two young people whose lives are changed by the effects of World War II. *Alan and Naomi* was named one of the "1969–1992 Best of the Best Books for Young Adults," and eventually a movie was based on it.

> "Seeing the poem before me in 'living' ink and paper, in that neat, tiny hand, was for me an epiphany. Such power, an entire world, on that one small sheet! It was absolute and final: yes, I would be a writer above all else!"

Think About the Writer Why was seeing a famous poem in the author's own handwriting so inspiring to Levoy?

Build Background

This story takes place in an immigrant neighborhood of New York City in the early 1900s. Aaron's grandmother is from Ukraine in Eastern Europe, a territory that was under the rule of Imperial Russia during the 1800s. Many Jewish people, like Aaron's grandmother, lived in Ukraine at the time.

When Czar Alexander II died in 1881, the Jewish people were wrongly accused of his murder, and much violence was aimed at them. The Cossacks, a part of the Russian army famous for military skills and horsemanship, carried out the new Czar's orders. As a result of state-sponsored violence against the Jewish people in Ukraine, many Jews moved to the United States, leaving their homeland behind.

Preview the Selection

In this selection, you will read about a young boy named **Aaron** who finds a pigeon with a broken wing.

Read with a Purpose Read to find out what Aaron's gift is.

Aaron's Gift

by **Myron Levoy**

Aaron Kandel had come to Tompkins Square Park to roller-skate, for the streets near Second Avenue were always too crowded with children and peddlers and old ladies and baby buggies. Though few children had bicycles in those days, almost every child owned a pair of roller skates. And Aaron was, it must be said, a Class A, triple-fantastic roller skater.

Aaron skated back and forth on the wide walkway of the park, pretending he was an aviator in an air race zooming around pylons, which were actually two lampposts. During his third lap around the racecourse, he noticed a pigeon on the grass, behaving very strangely. Aaron skated to the line of benches, then climbed over onto the lawn.

The pigeon was trying to fly, but all it could manage was to flutter and turn round and round in a large circle, as if it were performing a frenzied dance. The left wing was only half open and was beating in a clumsy, jerking fashion; it was clearly broken. **A**

Luckily, Aaron hadn't eaten the cookies he'd stuffed into his pocket before he'd gone clacking down the three flights

A **Reading Focus** **Cause and Effect** What is the first important event in the story? What do you think might happen as a result of this event?

Literary Perspectives

Analyzing Archetypes In literary criticism, the word *archetype* (AHR kuh typ) refers to a pattern or "type" that we find again and again in literature. Certain plots, characters, symbols, and even themes that occur in a variety of literary works may be considered *archetypal*. Examples of archetypal plots include the heroic quest story and the story of the "underdog" hero who defeats a more powerful enemy. Archetypal themes include the search for identity and the struggle for justice. Characters like the heroic youth, the wise elder, and the evil villain are also archetypal. These common story elements reflect ideas, concerns, and values that human beings from all times and places share. As you read, be sure to notice the notes and questions in the text, which will guide you in using this perspective.

of stairs from his apartment, his skates already on. He broke a cookie into small crumbs and tossed some toward the pigeon. "Here pidge, here pidge," he called. The pigeon spotted the cookie crumbs and, after a moment, stopped thrashing about. It folded its wings as best it could, but the broken wing still stuck half out. Then it strutted over to the crumbs, its head bobbing forth-back, forth-back, as if it were marching a little in front of the rest of the body—perfectly normal, except for that half-open wing which seemed to make the bird stagger sideways every so often.

The pigeon began eating the crumbs as Aaron quickly unbuttoned his shirt and pulled it off. Very slowly, he edged toward the bird, making little kissing sounds like the ones he heard his grandmother make when she fed the sparrows on the back fire escape.

Then suddenly Aaron plunged. The shirt, in both hands, came down like a torn parachute. The pigeon beat its wings, but Aaron held the shirt to the ground, and the bird couldn't escape. Aaron felt under the shirt, gently, and gently took hold of the wounded pigeon.

"Yes, yes, pidge," he said, very softly. "There's a good boy. Good pigeon, good."

The pigeon struggled in his hands, but little by little Aaron managed to soothe it. "Good boy, pidge. That's your new name. Pidge. I'm gonna take you home, Pidge. Yes, yes, *ssh*. Good boy. I'm gonna fix you up. Easy, Pidge, easy does it. Easy, boy." **B**

Aaron squeezed through an opening between the row of benches and skated slowly out of the park, while holding the pigeon carefully with both hands as if it were one of his mother's rare, precious cups from the old country. How fast the pigeon's

B **Read and Discuss** What is Aaron planning to do now?

Vocabulary **plunged** (pluhnjd) *v.*: dived down suddenly.

heart was beating! Was he afraid? Or did all pigeons' hearts beat fast?

It was fortunate that Aaron was an excellent skater, for he had to skate six blocks to his apartment, over broken pavement and sudden gratings and curbs and cobblestones. But when he reached home, he asked Noreen Callahan, who was playing on the stoop, to take off his skates for him. He would not chance going up three flights on roller skates this time.

"Is he sick?" asked Noreen.

"Broken wing," said Aaron. "I'm gonna fix him up and make him into a carrier pigeon or something."

"Can I watch?" asked Noreen.

"Watch what?"

"The operation. I'm gonna be a nurse when I grow up."

"OK," said Aaron. "You can even help. You can help hold him while I fix him up."

Aaron wasn't quite certain what his mother would say about his new-found pet, but he was pretty sure he knew what his grandmother would think. His grandmother had lived with them ever since his grandfather had died three years ago. And she fed the sparrows and jays and crows and robins on the back fire escape with every spare crumb she could find. In fact, Aaron noticed that she sometimes created crumbs where they didn't exist, by squeezing and tearing pieces of her breakfast roll when his mother wasn't looking.

Aaron didn't really understand his grandmother, for he often saw her by the window having long conversations with the birds, telling them about her days as a little girl in the Ukraine.[1] And once he saw her take her mirror from her handbag and hold it out toward the birds. She told Aaron that she wanted them to see how beautiful they were. Very strange. But Aaron did know that she would love Pidge, because she loved everything.

To his surprise, his mother said he could keep the pigeon, temporarily, because it was sick, and we were all strangers in the land of Egypt, and it might not be bad for Aaron to have a pet. *Temporarily.*

The wing was surprisingly easy to fix, for the break showed clearly and Pidge was remarkably patient and still, as if he knew he was being helped. Or perhaps he was just exhausted from all the thrashing about he had done. Two Popsicle sticks served as splints, and strips from an old undershirt were used to tie them in place. Another strip held the wing to the bird's body.

Aaron's father arrived home and stared at the pigeon. Aaron waited for the expected storm. But instead, Mr. Kandel asked, "Who *did* this?"

"Me," said Aaron. "And Noreen Callahan."

"Sophie!" he called to his wife. "Did you see this! Ten years and it's better than Dr. Belasco could do. He's a genius!" **C**

As the days passed, Aaron began training Pidge to be a carrier pigeon. He tied a little cardboard tube to Pidge's left leg and stuck tiny rolled-up sheets of paper with secret messages into it: THE ENEMY IS

1. **Ukraine** (yoo KRAYN): a country in Eastern Europe that borders on Russia to the northeast.

C **Read and Discuss** What does Aaron's family think of the pigeon? What is Aaron's father's attitude about the surgery?

Vocabulary **thrashing** (THRASH ihng) *v.*: moving from side to side in an uncontrolled way.

ATTACKING AT DAWN. Or: THE GUNS ARE HIDDEN IN THE TRUNK OF THE CAR. Or: VINCENT DEMARCO IS A BRITISH SPY. Then Aaron would set Pidge down at one end of the living room and put some popcorn at the other end. And Pidge would waddle slowly across the room, cooing softly, while the ends of his bandages trailed along the floor.

At the other end of the room, one of Aaron's friends would take out the message, stick a new one in, turn Pidge around, and aim him at the popcorn that Aaron put down on his side of the room.

And Pidge grew fat and contented on all the popcorn and crumbs and corn and crackers and Aaron's grandmother's breakfast rolls.

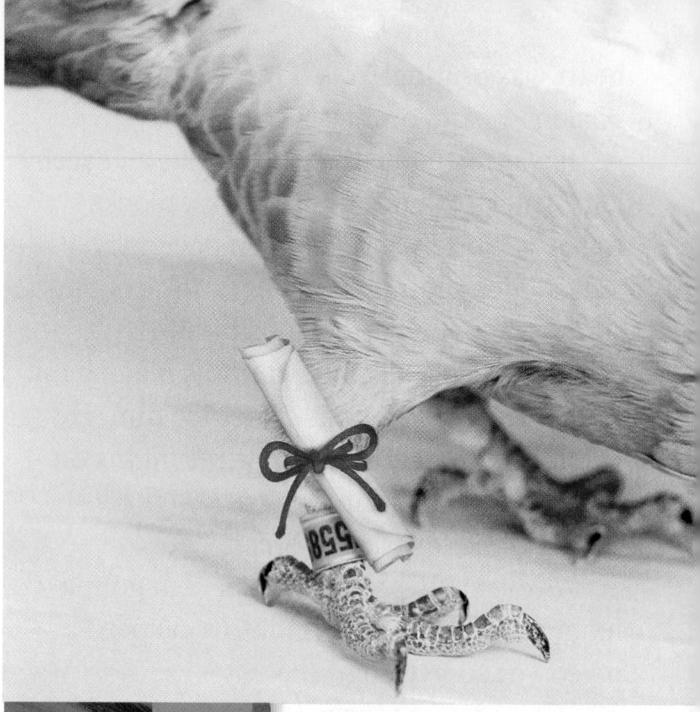

Analyzing Visuals **Viewing and Interpreting**
What idea of Aaron's does this photograph show?

Aaron had told all the children about Pidge, but he only let his very best friends come up and play carrier-pigeon with him. But telling everyone had been a mistake. A group of older boys from down the block had a club—Aaron's mother called it a gang—and Aaron had longed to join as he had never longed for anything else. To be with them and share their secrets, the secrets of older boys. To be able to enter their clubhouse shack on the empty lot on the next street. To know the password and swear the secret oath. To belong. **D**

About a month after Aaron had brought the pigeon home, Carl, the gang leader, walked over to Aaron in the street and told him he could be a member if he'd bring the pigeon down to be the club mascot. Aaron couldn't believe it; he immediately raced home to get Pidge. But his mother told Aaron to stay away from those boys, or else. And Aaron, miserable, argued with his mother and pleaded and cried and coaxed. It was no use. Not with those boys. No.

Aaron's mother tried to change the subject. She told him that it would soon be his grandmother's sixtieth birthday, a very special birthday indeed, and all the family from Brooklyn and the East Side would be coming to their apartment for a dinner and celebration. Would Aaron try to build something or make something for Grandma? A present made with his own hands would be nice. A decorated box for her hairpins or a crayon picture for her room or anything he liked.

In a flash Aaron knew what to give her: Pidge! Pidge would be her present! Pidge

D **Literary Perspectives** **Analyzing Archetypes**
What common human desire is Aaron expressing?

Vocabulary **contented** (kuhn TEHNT ihd) *adj.:* happy or satisfied.

with his wing healed, who might be able to carry messages for her to the doctor or his Aunt Rachel or other people his grandmother seemed to go to a lot. It would be a surprise for everyone. And Pidge would make up for what had happened to Grandma when she'd been a little girl in the Ukraine, wherever that was. **E**

Often, in the evening, Aaron's grandmother would talk about the old days long ago in the Ukraine, in the same way that she talked to the birds on the back fire escape. She had lived in a village near a place called Kishinev with hundreds of other poor peasant families like her own. Things hadn't been too bad under someone called Czar Alexander the Second, whom Aaron always pictured as a tall handsome man in a gold uniform. But Alexander the Second was assassinated, and Alexander the Third, whom Aaron pictured as an ugly man in a black cape, became the Czar.[2] And the Jewish people of the Ukraine had no peace anymore.

One day, a thundering of horses was heard coming toward the village from the direction of Kishinev. *The Cossacks! The Cossacks!* someone had shouted. The czar's horsemen! Quickly, quickly, everyone in Aaron's grandmother's family had climbed down to the cellar through a little trap door hidden under a mat in the big central room of their shack. But his grandmother's pet goat, whom she'd loved as much as Aaron loved Pidge and more, had to be left above, because if it had made a sound in the cellar, they would never have lived to see the next morning. They all hid under the wood in the woodbin and waited, hardly breathing.

Suddenly, from above, they heard shouts and calls and screams at a distance. And then the noise was in their house. Boots pounding on the floor, and everything breaking and crashing overhead. The smell of smoke and the shouts of a dozen men.

The terror went on for an hour and then the sound of horses' hooves faded into the distance. They waited another hour to make sure, and then the father went up out of the cellar and the rest of the family followed. The door to the house had been torn from its hinges and every piece of furniture was broken. Every window, every dish, every stitch of clothing was totally destroyed, and one wall had been completely bashed in. And on the floor was the goat, lying quietly. Aaron's grandmother, who was just a little girl of eight at the time, had wept over the goat all day and all night and could not be consoled.

But they had been lucky. For other houses had been burned to the ground. And everywhere, not goats alone, nor sheep, but men and women and children lay quietly on the ground. The word for this sort of massacre, Aaron had learned, was *pogrom*. It had been a pogrom. And the men on the horses were Cossacks. Hated word. Cossacks.

And so Pidge would replace that goat of long ago. A pigeon on Second Avenue where no one needed trapdoors or secret escape passages or woodpiles to hide under.

2. **Czar** (zahr): a male ruler of Russia before 1917.

E **Literary Focus** **Theme and Plot** Titles often communicate a story's theme. What clues do you have so far to the meaning of the title "Aaron's Gift"—and to the story's theme?

Vocabulary **consoled** (kuhn SOHLD) *v.*: comforted when sad or disappointed.

A pigeon for his grandmother's sixtieth birthday. *Oh wing, heal quickly so my grandmother can send you flying to everywhere she wants!* F

But a few days later, Aaron met Carl in the street again. And Carl told Aaron that there was going to be a meeting that afternoon in which a map was going to be drawn up to show where a secret treasure lay buried on the empty lot. "Bring the pigeon and you can come into the shack. We got a badge for you. A new kinda membership badge with a secret code on the back."

Aaron ran home, his heart pounding almost as fast as the pigeon's. He took Pidge in his hands and carried him out the door while his mother was busy in the kitchen making stuffed cabbage, his father's favorite dish. And by the time he reached the street, Aaron had decided to take the bandages off. Pidge would look like a real pigeon again, and none of the older boys would laugh or call him a bundle of rags. G

Gently, gently he removed the bandages and the splints and put them in his pocket in case he should need them again. But Pidge seemed to hold his wing properly in place.

When he reached the empty lot, Aaron walked up to the shack, then hesitated. Four bigger boys were there. After a moment, Carl came out and commanded Aaron to hand Pidge over.

"Be careful," said Aaron. "I just took the bandages off."

"Oh sure, don't worry," said Carl. By now Pidge was used to people holding him, and he remained calm in Carl's hands.

"OK," said Carl. "Give him the badge." And one of the older boys handed Aaron his badge with the code on the back. "Now light the fire," said Carl.

"What . . . what fire?" asked Aaron.

"The fire. You'll see," Carl answered.

"You didn't say nothing about a fire," said Aaron. "You didn't say nothing to—"

"Hey!" said Carl. "I'm the leader here. And you don't talk unless I tell you that you have p'mission. Light the fire, Al."

The boy named Al went out to the side of the shack, where some wood and cardboard and old newspapers had been piled into a huge mound. He struck a match and held it to the newspapers.

"OK," said Carl. "Let's get 'er good and hot. Blow on it. Everybody blow."

Aaron's eyes stung from the smoke, but he blew alongside the others, going from side to side as the smoke shifted toward them and away.

"Let's fan it," said Al.

In a few minutes, the fire was crackling and glowing with a bright yellow-orange flame.

"Get me the rope," said Carl.

One of the boys brought Carl some cord and Carl, without a word, wound it twice around the pigeon, so that its wings were tight against its body.

"What . . . what are you *doing!*" shouted Aaron. "You're hurting his wing!"

F **Literary Perspectives** **Analyzing Archetypes** Birds are common symbols in literature. What qualities do birds often symbolize? What might be the symbolism of Aaron's intended gift?

G **Read and Discuss** How are things changing for Aaron? What does Aaron think of the gang's offer?

"Don't worry about his wing," said Carl. "We're gonna throw him into the fire. And when we do, we're gonna swear an oath of loyalty to—"

"No! *No!*" shouted Aaron, moving toward Carl. **H**

"Grab him!" called Carl. "Don't let him get the pigeon!"

But Aaron had leaped right across the fire at Carl, taking him completely by surprise. He threw Carl back against the shack and hit out at his face with both fists. Carl slid down to the ground and the pigeon rolled out of his hands. Aaron scooped up the pigeon and ran, pretending he was on roller skates so that he would go faster and faster. And as he ran across the lot he pulled the cord off Pidge and tried to find a place, *any* place, to hide him. But the boys were on top of him, and the pigeon slipped from Aaron's hands.

"Get him!" shouted Carl.

Aaron thought of the worst, the most horrible thing he could shout at the boys. "Cossacks!" he screamed. "You're all Cossacks!"

Two boys held Aaron back while the others tried to catch the pigeon. Pidge flut-

H **Read and Discuss** What have we just found out? What does Aaron think of the gang now?

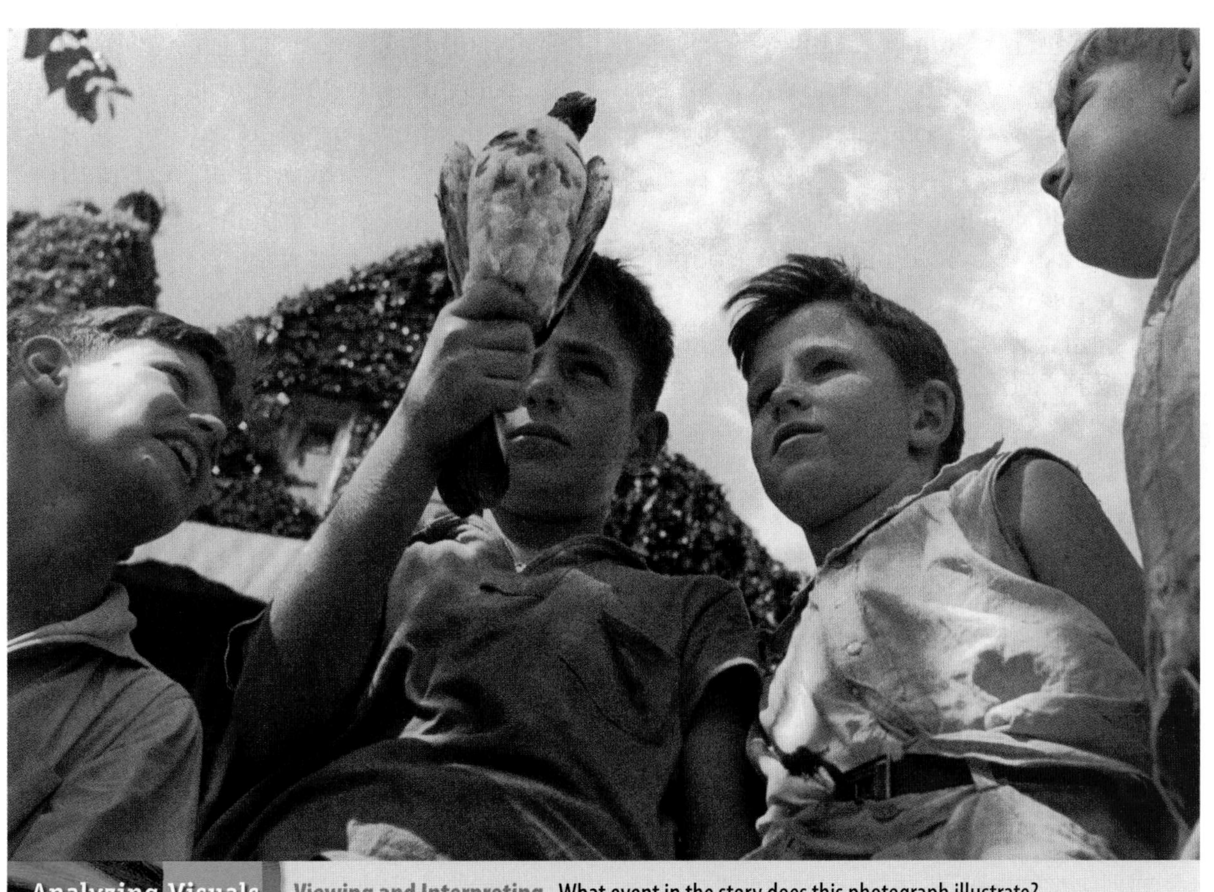

Analyzing Visuals **Viewing and Interpreting** What event in the story does this photograph illustrate?

tered along the ground just out of reach, skittering one way and then the other. Then the boys came at him from two directions. But suddenly Pidge beat his wings in rhythm, and rose up, up over the roof of the nearest tenement, up over Second Avenue toward the park.

With the pigeon gone, the boys turned toward Aaron and tackled him to the ground and punched him and tore his clothes and punched him some more. Aaron twisted and turned and kicked and punched back, shouting "Cossacks! Cossacks!" And somehow the word gave him the strength to tear away from them. **I**

When Aaron reached home, he tried to go past the kitchen quickly so his mother wouldn't see his bloody face and torn clothing. But it was no use; his father was home from work early that night and was seated in the living room. In a moment Aaron was surrounded by his mother, father, and grandmother, and in another moment he had told them everything that had happened, the words tumbling out between his broken sobs. Told them of the present he had planned, of the pigeon for a goat, of the gang, of the badge with the secret code on the back, of the shack, and the fire, and the pigeon's flight over the tenement roof.

And Aaron's grandmother kissed him and thanked him for his present which was even better than the pigeon.

"What present?" asked Aaron, trying to stop the series of sobs.

And his grandmother opened her pocketbook and handed Aaron her mirror and asked him to look. But all Aaron saw was his dirty, bruised face and his torn shirt.

Aaron thought he understood and then, again, he thought he didn't. How could she be so happy when there really was no present? And why pretend that there was? **J**

Later that night, just before he fell asleep, Aaron tried to imagine what his grandmother might have done with the pigeon. She would have fed it, and she certainly would have talked to it, as she did to all the birds, and . . . and then she would have let it go free. Yes, of course. Pidge's flight to freedom must have been the gift that had made his grandmother so happy. Her goat has escaped from the Cossacks at last, Aaron thought, half dreaming. And he fell asleep with a smile.

I **Reading Focus** **Cause and Effect** What caused Aaron to call the boys "Cossacks"? Why is that the worst word he can think of?

J **Literary Focus** **Theme and Plot** What is Aaron's real gift to his grandmother? What theme can you infer from this?

Applying Your Skills

Sunshine State Standards: Benchmarks LA.6.1.7.3 determine the main idea or essential message in grade-level text through inferring, paraphrasing, summarizing, and identifying relevant details; *Also covered* **LA.6.1.7.4; LA6.2.1.2; LA.6.2.1.5**

Aaron's Gift

Respond and Think Critically

Reading Focus

1. Why is Aaron so determined to give Pidge to his grandmother? 
   A He wanted her to set the bird free.
   B He wanted to replace her lost goat.
   C He wanted her to have company.
   D He wanted her to send messages.

Read with a Purpose

2. What does Aaron think was his gift to his grandmother? What gift is she really thankful for? How does she communicate this?

Reading Skills: Using Cause and Effect to Determine Theme

3. Complete your cause-and-effect flow chart. At the bottom of the chart, add a box titled "Theme." Based on the story's events, what do you think is the theme of the story? What final event especially points to the theme?

Grandma thanks Aaron for the present.

↓

Aaron realizes that Grandma is happy that, unlike her goat, Pidge got away.

↓

THEME:

Literary Focus

Literary Analysis

4. **Literary Perspectives** Explain how each of these elements might be considered archetypal: the stories the grandmother tells; Aaron's desire to join a group; Aaron's stand against the gang; the pigeon's escape. How do these elements add to the story's power?

Literary Skills: Theme and Plot

5. **Compare** How does Aaron's experience with the gang echo his grandmother's experiences in the Ukraine? How do both of these experiences connect to the story's theme? Support your answer with details from the story. READ THINK EXPLAIN

Literary Skills Review: Characterization

6. **Analyze** Writers bring characters to life through characterization: by describing how they talk, look, and act; by revealing their inner thoughts; and by showing how other characters react to them. How does the author make Aaron seem like a real person? Support your answer with examples from the story. READ THINK EXPLAIN

Writing Focus

Think as a Reader/Writer

Use It in Your Writing Review your notes about how Aaron views Pidge. Then, write a description of a wild animal as seen through the eyes of someone who cares about it.

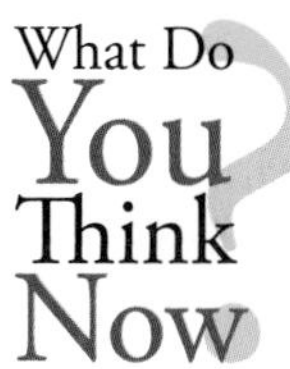

Have your ideas about what makes a gift special changed? How special does Aaron's present seem to you? Explain.

Applying Your Skills

Aaron's Gift

Vocabulary Development

Vocabulary Skills: Words Borrowed from Other Languages

Words from Latin and Old English Many English words that we use today come from other languages, both past and present. Several of the Vocabulary words in "Aaron's Gift" are related to words from Latin or Old English—languages that are no longer spoken today.

Your Turn

plunged
thrashing
contented
consoled

Find the Word Relationships From the Vocabulary list at right, choose the word that correctly completes each sentence.

1. The Latin word *consolari*, meaning "comfort," is related to the word ___________.
2. The Old English word *threscan*, meaning "to thresh," is related to the word ___________.
3. The Latin word *contentus,* meaning "satisfied," is related to the word ___________.
4. The Latin word *plumbum*, meaning "lead," is related to the word ___________.

Words from Russian Other words have come into the English language because of the more recent influence of immigrant cultures in English-speaking countries like the United States. Some words in "Aaron's Gift," like *czar*, *Cossack*, and *pogrom*, came into the English language from Russian. So did the words below:

Use a dictionary to find the meaning of each word below.

parka (PAHR kuh)	babushka (buh BOOSH kuh)
sable (SAY buhl)	steppe (stehp)

Your Turn

Choose the Right Word Complete each sentence below with the correct word from Russian at the bottom of the left-hand column.

5. Put on a ___________ before you go out in this cold weather.
6. The ___________ is a small animal with beautiful dark fur.
7. Grandma always wore a black ___________ on her head when she went out in cold weather.
8. The Russian ___________ is similar to the prairie or the plains.

Language Coach

Base Words What other words can you make from the base words *plunge*, *thrash*, *content*, and *console*? With a partner, brainstorm words that can be formed from these base words. Identify the part of speech of each new word. You may wish to use a dictionary.

Academic Vocabulary

Write About . . .
Write a paragraph explaining how the author communicates the story's theme through the contrast between Aaron and the boys he calls "Cossacks."

Sunshine State Standards: Benchmarks **LA.6.1.6.5** relate new vocabulary to familiar words; **LA.6.1.6.10** determine meanings of words, pronunciation, parts of speech, etymologies, and alternate word choices by using a dictionary, thesaurus, and digital tools; **LA.6.1.6.11** identify the meaning of words and phrases derived from Greek and Latin mythology (e.g., mercurial, Achilles' heel) and identify frequently used words from other languages (e.g., laissez faire, croissant); **LA.6.3.4.4** the eight parts of speech (noun, pronoun, verb, adverb, adjective, conjunction, preposition, interjection); **LA.6.4.2.4** write a variety of informal communications (e.g., friendly letters, thank-you notes, messages) and formal communications (e.g., conventional business letters, invitations) that follow a format and that have a clearly stated purpose and that include the date, proper salutation, body, closing and signature; **LA.6.4.3.1** write persuasive text (e.g., advertisement, speech, essay, public service announcement) that establishes and develops a controlling idea, using appropriate supporting arguments and detailed evidence; **LA.6.5.2.2** deliver narrative and informative presentations, including oral responses to literature, and adjust oral language, body language, eye contact, gestures, technology and supporting graphics appropriate to the situation.

Grammar Link

Add Interest with Predicate Adjectives

A story without adjectives would be colorless and dull, like a black-and-white picture of a rainbow. Adjectives can be used in the subject or the predicate of a sentence. When an adjective in the predicate modifies the subject of a sentence or clause, it is called a **predicate adjective**.

EXAMPLE The pigeon's wing was broken.

The pigeon's wing = subject; *was* = verb; *broken* = predicate adjective

The adjective *broken* completes the verb *was* and modifies, or describes, the subject *wing.*

A predicate adjective is one kind of **subject complement.** It *completes* the meaning of a verb and identifies or modifies the *subject.* A predicate adjective may be compound, which means it contains more than one adjective.

EXAMPLE His clothes were bloody and torn.

The clothes = subject; *were* = verb; *bloody* and *torn* = compound predicate adjective

A predicate adjective may even come *before* the subject and verb.

EXAMPLE How cruel the boys were!

cruel = predicate adjective; *the boys* = subject; *were* = verb

Your Turn

Identify the predicate adjective in each sentence.

1. The messages were secret.
2. Pidge was patient and still.
3. Aaron's mother was worried.
4. How brutal the Cossacks were!

CHOICES

As you respond to the Choices, use these **Academic Vocabulary** words as appropriate: attitude, communicate, contrast, illustrate.

REVIEW

Write a Thank-You Note

Timed Writing Imagine that you are Aaron's grandmother. Write Aaron a thank-you note. Explain how you feel about his actions and tell him what they mean to you. Be sure he understands what his real gift to you was.

CONNECT

Write a Persuasive Essay

One theme of the story might be that people should show compassion to those who have suffered. Research an actual group of people in current times or the recent past who have suffered a devastating loss—perhaps through war, natural disaster, or social injustice. Write a persuasive essay describing how you think this group should be treated. What would be the best way to show compassion in the situation?

EXTEND

Make a Presentation Based on History

Group Project Work with a group to research how the *pogroms* affected Jews in Ukraine, or study how Jewish and Ukrainian immigration affected New York City's East Village in the early 1900s. Either project should help you understand the attitude of Aaron's grandmother. Present what you learn to the class.

Literary Criticism: Evaluating a Story's Credibility

CONTENTS

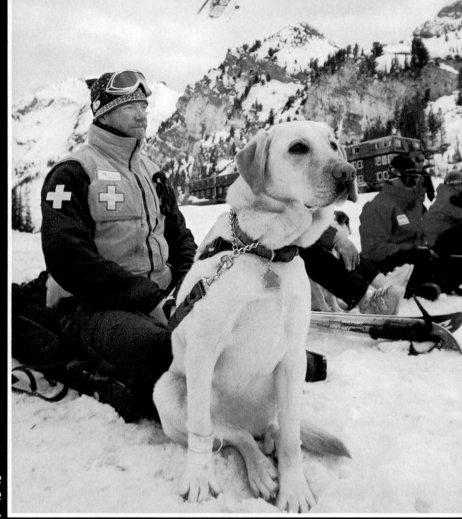

A search-and-rescue dog and his owner in the mountains of Alta, Utah.

How can animals teach people lessons about love and relationships?

QuickWrite

Think about a life lesson you have learned from a pet or other animal you have known or observed. Write a few notes about what you learned about life from this animal.

Preparing to Read

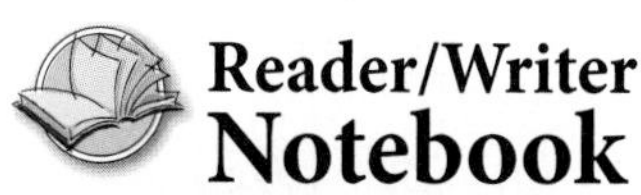

Sunshine State Standards: Benchmarks **LA.6.1.6.1** use new vocabulary that is introduced and taught directly; **LA.6.1.7.3** determine the main idea or essential message in grade-level text through inferring, paraphrasing, summarizing, and identifying relevant details; *Also covered* **LA.6.1.7.8; LA.6.2.1.5**

The Dog of Pompeii / Pompeii / Zlateh the Goat / Trial by Fire

Literary Focus

Literary Criticism: Evaluating a Story's Credibility One of the main tasks of a literary critic is to evaluate whether the characters and plot in a story are **credible,** or believable. Readers expect a story's characters to act the way real people do. Even if the characters are aliens or young wizards, you want the characters' actions to make sense. A plot should also be credible, growing naturally out of the actions of the characters. If a plot has too many coincidences or if the chain of causes and effects is weak, then the plot is *contrived,* or artificial, and it won't hold your interest.

Reading Focus

Making Generalizations A **generalization** is a conclusion drawn from examples or evidence. You combine evidence in the text with prior knowledge to come up with a broad statement that expresses a truth about what you've read—your generalization.

Into Action For each selection, use a chart like this to record details that seem (or don't seem) credible—and explain why. You'll use your charts to make generalizations about the selections.

Title of Story: "The Dog of Pompeii"

Detail about character or plot	Credible or not credible?	Why? (based on my own knowledge)
Bimbo takes total care of Tito.	Credible	Dogs are companions for people who are blind.

Writing Focus

Think as a Reader/Writer

Find It in Your Reading "The Dog of Pompeii" and "Zlateh the Goat" both contain realistic details. As you read, list the details that add to the credibility of the characters and the plot.

Reader/Writer Notebook

Use your **RWN** to complete the activities for these selections.

Vocabulary

The Dog of Pompeii

ambitious (am BIHSH uhs) *adj.:* eager to achieve something. *The ambitious citizens wanted to make their city famous.*

proverb (PRAHV urb) *n.:* short, wise saying that expresses a truth. *"Haste makes waste" is a proverb.*

revived (rih VYVD) *v.:* awakened; brought back to life. *The splash of water revived him, and he opened his eyes.*

Zlateh the Goat

penetrated (PEHN uh tray tihd) *v.:* pierced; made a way through. *Sunlight penetrated the clouds.*

cleft (klehft) *adj.:* split; divided. *Goats have cleft hooves.*

chaos (KAY ahs) *n.:* total confusion or disorder. *The storm created chaos outside Aaron's shelter.*

exuded (ehg ZOO dihd) *v.:* gave off. *The hay exuded warmth.*

Language Coach

Verb Forms What do the words *revived, penetrated,* and *exuded* above have in common?

Learn It Online

For a preview of "The Dog of Pompeii," see the video introduction on:

go.hrw.com L6-399 

Learn It Online
Get more on Singer's life at:
go.hrw.com L6-400 Go

Louis Untermeyer

(1885–1977)

Reviving an Old World

Louis Untermeyer described the writer's job as the "struggle somehow to revive an old world, or create a new one." As a child, he loved to read, but he dropped out of high school to work in his family's jewelry business. He didn't become serious about writing until he met the poet Robert Frost in 1915. They became lifelong friends, and it was Frost who encouraged Untermeyer to write.

Robert Silverberg

(1935–)

The Future and the Past

Robert Silverberg has written hundreds of works in many genres. One of the world's most famous science fiction writers, Silverberg has also written nonfiction about archaeology and history—especially the history of people and places long vanished.

Isaac Bashevis Singer (1904–1991)

"Time Does Not Vanish"

Isaac Bashevis Singer was born in a village like the one in "Zlateh the Goat." As a boy, he read constantly and was curious about everything. Both of his parents were skilled storytellers. Singer watched and listened, carefully storing in his memory scenes, people, and incidents he would write about later in his life. His stories earned him the Nobel Prize for Literature in 1978.

Think About the Writers

Why do you think these writers write about people and places that "used to be"?

Preview the Selections

In the short story "The Dog of Pompeii," you'll meet **Tito,** a boy who is blind, and his faithful dog **Bimbo.** Both characters live in ancient Pompeii, the Roman city that was buried by the eruption of Mount Vesuvius in A.D. 79.

Next, you'll read "Pompeii," a nonfiction historical account of the same event—the eruption of Vesuvius.

In "Zlateh the Goat," you'll read about a boy, **Aaron,** and his adventure when he takes the family goat, **Zlateh,** to market.

Finally, you'll read "Trial by Fire," a nonfiction article that tells the story of a brave mother cat, **Scarlett,** who saves her kittens from a fire.

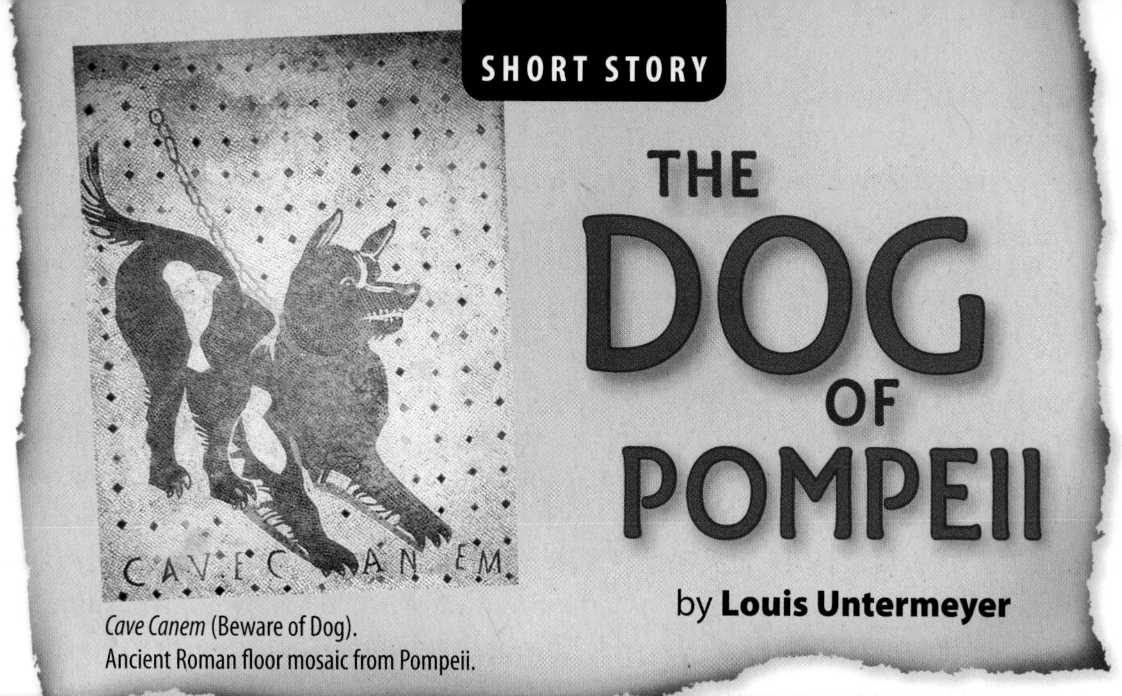

SHORT STORY

THE DOG OF POMPEII

by **Louis Untermeyer**

Cave Canem (Beware of Dog).
Ancient Roman floor mosaic from Pompeii.

Read with a Purpose

Read "The Dog of Pompeii" to find out how the bond between a boy and his dog is tested during one of the greatest natural disasters in history.

Build Background

The setting of this story is Pompeii, an ancient Roman city that was buried by a volcanic eruption in A.D. 79. The story combines the fictional story of Tito and his dog Bimbo with facts about the actual historical event. The volcano that destroyed the city of Pompeii also preserved it. In the eighteenth century, archaeologists began excavating Pompeii. As they uncovered the city captured in time by the ash that buried it, they brought the past to life. Today, you can visit Pompeii and see the city as it was nearly two thousand years ago.

Tito and his dog Bimbo lived (if you could call it living) under the wall where it joined the inner gate. They really didn't live there; they just slept there. They lived anywhere. Pompeii was one of the gayest of the old Latin towns, but although Tito was never an unhappy boy, he was not exactly a merry one. The streets were always lively with shining chariots and bright red trappings; the open-air theaters rocked with laughing crowds; sham[1] battles and athletic sports were free for the asking in the great stadium. Once a year the Caesar[2] visited the pleasure city and the fireworks lasted for days; the sacrifices[3] in the forum were better than a show.

But Tito saw none of these things. He was blind—had been blind from birth. He was known to everyone in the poorer quarters. But no one could say how old he was, no one remembered his parents, no one could tell

1. **sham:** make-believe.

2. **Caesar** (SEE zuhr): Roman emperor. The word *Caesar* comes from the family name of Julius Caesar, a great general who ruled Rome as dictator from 49 to 44 B.C.

3. **sacrifices:** offerings (especially of slaughtered animals) to the gods.

where he came from. Bimbo was another mystery. As long as people could remember seeing Tito—about twelve or thirteen years—they had seen Bimbo. Bimbo had never left his side. He was not only dog but nurse, pillow, playmate, mother, and father to Tito. **A**

Did I say Bimbo never left his master? (Perhaps I had better say comrade, for if anyone was the master, it was Bimbo.) I was wrong. Bimbo did trust Tito alone exactly three times a day. It was a fixed routine, a custom understood between boy and dog since the beginning of their friendship, and the way it worked was this: Early in the morning, shortly after dawn, while Tito was still dreaming, Bimbo would disappear. When Tito awoke, Bimbo would be sitting quietly at his side, his ears cocked, his stump of a tail tapping the ground, and a fresh-baked bread—more like a large round roll—at his feet. Tito would stretch himself; Bimbo would yawn; then they would breakfast. At noon, no matter where they happened to be, Bimbo would put his paw on Tito's knee and the two of them would return to the inner gate. Tito would curl up in the corner (almost like a dog) and go to sleep, while Bimbo, looking quite important (almost like a boy), would disappear again. In half an hour he'd be back with their lunch. Sometimes it would be a piece of fruit or a scrap of meat, often it was nothing but a dry crust. But sometimes there would be one of those flat rich cakes, sprinkled with raisins and sugar, that Tito liked so much. At suppertime the same thing happened, although there was a little less of everything, for things were hard to snatch in the evening, with the streets full of people. Besides, Bimbo didn't approve of too much food before going to sleep. A heavy supper made boys too restless and dogs too stodgy[4]—and it was the business of a dog to sleep lightly with one ear open and muscles ready for action. **B**

But, whether there was much or little, hot or cold, fresh or dry, food was always there. Tito never asked where it came from and Bimbo never told him. There was plenty of rainwater in the hollows of soft stones; the old egg woman at the corner sometimes gave him a cupful of strong goat's milk; in the grape season the fat winemaker let him have drippings of the mild juice. So there was no danger of going hungry or thirsty. There was plenty of everything in Pompeii—if you knew where to find it—and if you had a dog like Bimbo.

As I said before, Tito was not the merriest boy in Pompeii. He could not romp with the other youngsters and play "hare and hounds" and "I spy" and "follow your master" and "ball against the building" and "jackstones" and "kings and robbers" with them. But that did not make him sorry for himself. If he could not see the sights that delighted the lads of Pompeii, he could hear and smell things they never noticed. He could really see more with his ears and nose than they could with their eyes. When he and Bimbo went out walking, he knew just where they were going and exactly what was happening.

4. **stodgy** (STAH jee): heavy and slow in movement.

A **Read and Discuss** What's the author telling you in these opening paragraphs? What's his attitude toward his characters?

B **Literary Focus** **Literary Criticism** Are the characters in this story—Tito and Bimbo—believable so far? Why or why not?

"Ah," he'd sniff and say, as they passed a handsome villa,[5] "Glaucus Pansa is giving a grand dinner tonight. They're going to have three kinds of bread, and roast pigling, and stuffed goose, and a great stew—I think bear stew—and a fig pie." And Bimbo would note that this would be a good place to visit tomorrow. **C**

Or, "H'm," Tito would murmur, half through his lips, half through his nostrils. "The wife of Marcus Lucretius is expecting her mother. She's shaking out every piece of goods in the house; she's going to use the best clothes—the ones she's been keeping in pine needles and camphor[6]—and there's an extra girl in the kitchen. Come, Bimbo, let's get out of the dust!"

Or, as they passed a small but elegant dwelling opposite the public baths, "Too bad! The tragic poet is ill again. It must be a bad fever this time, for they're trying smoke fumes instead of medicine. Whew! I'm glad I'm not a tragic poet!"

Or, as they neared the forum, "Mm-m! What good things they have in the macellum[7] today!" (It really was a sort of butcher-grocer-marketplace, but Tito didn't know any better. He called it the macellum.) "Dates from Africa, and salt oysters from sea caves, and cuttlefish, and new honey, and sweet onions, and—ugh!—water-buffalo steaks. Come, let's see what's what in the forum." And Bimbo, just as curious as his comrade, hurried on. Being a dog, he trusted his ears and nose (like Tito) more than his eyes. And so the two of them entered the center of Pompeii. **D**

The forum was the part of the town to which everybody came at least once during the day. It was the central square, and everything happened here. There were no private houses; all was public—the chief temples, the gold and red bazaars, the silk shops, the town hall, the booths belonging to the weavers and jewel merchants, the wealthy woolen market,

Analyzing Visuals **Viewing and Interpreting**
What does this illustration show about the relationship between Tito and Bimbo?

5. **villa:** large house.
6. **camphor** (KAM fuhr): strong-smelling substance used to keep moths away from clothing. Camphor is still used for this purpose.
7. **macellum** (MUH sehl uhm): market, especially a meat market.

C **Read and Discuss** Why does Bimbo think this villa would be a good place to visit tomorrow?

D **Reading Focus** **Generalizations** From what Tito is describing, what generalizations can you make about life in Pompeii?

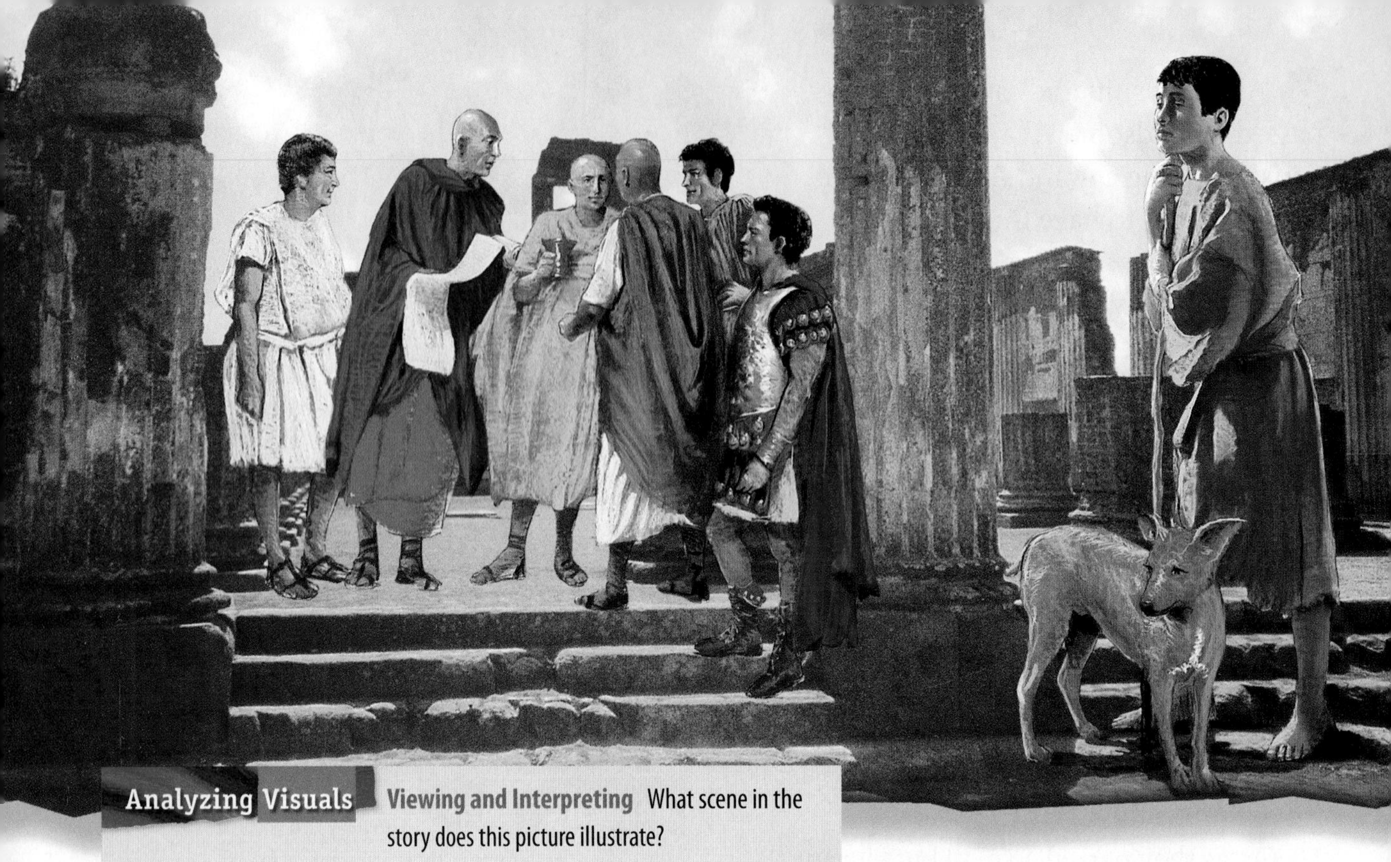

Analyzing Visuals **Viewing and Interpreting** What scene in the story does this picture illustrate?

the shrine of the household gods. Everything glittered here. The buildings looked as if they were new—which, in a sense, they were. The earthquake of twelve years ago had brought down all the old structures and, since the citizens of Pompeii were ambitious to rival Naples and even Rome, they had seized the opportunity to rebuild the whole town. And they had done it all within a dozen years. There was scarcely a building that was older than Tito. **E**

Tito had heard a great deal about the earthquake, though being about a year old at the time, he could scarcely remember it. This particular quake had been a light one—as earthquakes go. The weaker houses had been shaken down, parts of the outworn wall had been wrecked; but there was little loss of life, and the brilliant new Pompeii had taken the place of the old. No one knew what caused these earthquakes. Records showed they had happened in the neighborhood since the beginning of time. Sailors said that it was to teach the lazy city folk a lesson and make them appreciate those who risked the dangers of the sea to bring them luxuries and protect their town from invaders. The priests said that the gods took this way of showing their anger to those who refused to worship properly and who failed to bring enough sacrifices

E **Read and Discuss** What details have you learned about life in ancient Pompeii from this account of Tito and Bimbo's walk through the city?

Vocabulary **ambitious** (am BIHSH uhs) *adj.:* eager to achieve something.

to the altars and (though they didn't say it in so many words) presents to the priests. The tradesmen said that the foreign merchants had corrupted the ground and it was no longer safe to traffic in imported goods that came from strange places and carried a curse with them. Everyone had a different explanation and everyone's explanation was louder and sillier than his neighbor's. **F**

They were talking about it this afternoon as Tito and Bimbo came out of the side street into the public square. The forum was the favorite promenade[8] for rich and poor. What with the priests arguing with the politicians, servants doing the day's shopping, tradesmen crying their wares, women displaying the latest fashions from Greece and Egypt, children playing hide-and-seek among the marble columns, knots of soldiers, sailors, peasants from the provinces[9]—to say nothing of those who merely came to lounge and look on—the square was crowded to its last inch. His ears even more than his nose guided Tito to the place where the talk was loudest. It was in front of the shrine of the household gods that, naturally enough, the householders were arguing.

"I tell you," rumbled a voice which Tito recognized as bath master Rufus's, "there won't be another earthquake in my lifetime or yours. There may be a tremble or two, but earthquakes, like lightnings, never strike twice in the same place."

"Do they not?" asked a thin voice Tito had never heard. It had a high, sharp ring to it and Tito knew it as the accent of a stranger. "How about the two towns of Sicily that have been ruined three times within fifteen years by the eruptions of Mount Etna? And were they not warned? And does that column of smoke above Vesuvius mean nothing?"

"That?" Tito could hear the grunt with which one question answered another. "That's always there. We use it for our weather guide. When the smoke stands up straight, we know we'll have fair weather; when it flattens out, it's sure to be foggy; when it drifts to the east—"

"Yes, yes," cut in the edged voice. "I've heard about your mountain barometer.[10] But the column of smoke seems hundreds of feet higher than usual and it's thickening and spreading like a shadowy tree. They say in Naples—"

"Oh, Naples!" Tito knew this voice by the little squeak that went with it. It was Attilio the cameo cutter.[11] "They talk while we suffer. Little help we got from them last time. Naples commits the crimes and Pompeii pays the price. It's become a proverb with us. Let them mind their own business."

"Yes," grumbled Rufus, "and others', too."

"Very well, my confident friends," responded the thin voice, which now sounded curiously flat. "We also have a proverb—and

---

8. **promenade** (prahm uh NAYD): public place where people stroll.

9. **provinces:** places far from the capital, under Roman control.

10. **barometer** (buh RAHM uh tuhr): instrument for measuring atmospheric pressure. Barometers are used in forecasting changes in the weather.

11. **cameo cutter:** artist who carves small, delicate pictures on gems or shells.

F **Read and Discuss** What is going on at the forum? What didn't people at this time understand about earthquakes?

Vocabulary **proverb** (PRAHV urb) *n.:* short, wise saying that expresses a truth.

it is this: *Those who will not listen to men must be taught by the gods.* I say no more. But I leave a last warning. Remember the holy ones. Look to your temples. And when the smoke tree above Vesuvius grows to the shape of an umbrella pine, look to your lives."

Tito could hear the air whistle as the speaker drew his toga about him, and the quick shuffle of feet told him the stranger had gone. G

"Now what," said the cameo cutter, "did he mean by that?"

"I wonder," grunted Rufus. "I wonder."

Tito wondered, too. And Bimbo, his head at a thoughtful angle, looked as if he had been doing a heavy piece of pondering. By nightfall the argument had been forgotten. If the smoke had increased, no one saw it in the dark. Besides, it was Caesar's birthday and the town was in a holiday mood. Tito and Bimbo were among the merrymakers, dodging the charioteers who shouted at them. A dozen times they almost upset baskets of sweets and jars of Vesuvian wine, said to be as fiery as the streams inside the volcano, and a dozen times they were cursed and cuffed. But Tito never missed his footing. He was thankful for his keen ears and quick instinct—most thankful of all for Bimbo.

They visited the uncovered theater, and though Tito could not see the faces of the actors, he could follow the play better than most of the audience, for their attention wandered—they were distracted by the scenery, the costumes, the byplay,[12] even by themselves—while Tito's whole attention was centered in what he heard. Then to the city walls, where the people of Pompeii watched a mock naval battle in which the city was attacked by the sea and saved after thousands of flaming arrows had been exchanged and countless colored torches had been burned. Though the thrill of flaring ships and lighted skies was lost to Tito, the shouts and cheers excited him as much as any, and he cried out with the loudest of them. H

The next morning there were two of the beloved raisin-and-sugar cakes for his breakfast. Bimbo was unusually active and thumped his bit of a tail until Tito was afraid he would wear it out. The boy could not imagine whether Bimbo was urging him to some sort of game or was trying to tell him something. After a while, he ceased to notice Bimbo. He felt drowsy. Last night's late hours had tired him. Besides, there was a heavy mist in the air—no, a thick fog rather than a mist—a fog that got into his throat and scraped it and made him cough. He walked as far as the marine gate[13] to get a breath of the sea. But the blanket of haze had spread all over the bay and even the salt air seemed smoky.

He went to bed before dusk and slept. But he did not sleep well. He had too many dreams—dreams of ships lurching in the forum, of losing his way in a screaming crowd,

12. **byplay:** action taking place outside the main action of a play.

13. **marine gate:** gate in a city wall leading to the sea.

G Literary Focus Literary Criticism What attitudes among the men does this conversation reveal? How does this scene contribute to the development of the plot?

H Reading Focus Generalizations Based on what you've learned in these last two paragraphs, what generalization can you make about Tito?

of armies marching across his chest, of being pulled over every rough pavement of Pompeii.

He woke early. Or, rather, he was pulled awake. Bimbo was doing the pulling. The dog had dragged Tito to his feet and was urging the boy along. Somewhere. Where, Tito did not know. His feet stumbled uncertainly; he was still half asleep. For a while he noticed nothing except the fact that it was hard to breathe. The air was hot. And heavy. So heavy that he could taste it. The air, it seemed, had turned to powder—a warm powder that stung his nostrils and burned his sightless eyes.

Then he began to hear sounds. Peculiar sounds. Like animals under the earth. Hissings and groanings and muffled cries that a dying creature might make dislodging the stones of his underground cave. There was no doubt of it now. The noises came from underneath. He not only heard them—he could feel them. The earth twitched; the twitching changed to an uneven shrugging of the soil. Then, as Bimbo half pulled, half coaxed him across, the ground jerked away from his feet and he was thrown against a stone fountain. **I**

The water—hot water—splashing in his face revived him. He got to his feet, Bimbo steadying him, helping him on again. The noises grew louder; they came closer. The cries were even more animal-like than before, but now they came from human throats. A few people, quicker of foot and more hurried by fear, began to rush by. A family or two—then a section—then, it seemed, an army broken out of bounds. Tito, bewildered though he was, could recognize Rufus as he bellowed past him, like a water buffalo gone mad. Time was lost in a nightmare.

It was then the crashing began. First a sharp crackling, like a monstrous snapping of twigs; then a roar like the fall of a whole forest of trees; then an explosion that tore earth and sky. The heavens, though Tito could not see them, were shot through with continual flickerings of fire. Lightnings above were answered by thunders beneath. A house fell. Then another. By a miracle the two companions had escaped the dangerous side streets and were in a more open space. It was the forum. They rested here awhile—how long, he did not know. **J**

Tito had no idea of the time of day. He could feel it was black—an unnatural blackness. Something inside—perhaps the lack of breakfast and lunch—told him it was past noon. But it didn't matter. Nothing seemed to matter. He was getting drowsy, too drowsy to walk. But walk he must. He knew it. And Bimbo knew it; the sharp tugs told him so. Nor was it a moment too soon. The sacred ground of the forum was safe no longer. It was beginning to rock, then to pitch, then to split. As they stumbled out of the square, the earth wriggled like a caught snake and all the columns of the temple of Jupiter[14] came down. It was the end of the world—or so it seemed. To walk was not enough now. They must run.

14. **Jupiter:** the supreme god in the religion of the Romans.

I **Read and Discuss** What is causing these peculiar sounds? Why is Bimbo reacting like this?

J **Read and Discuss** What is happening now?

Vocabulary **revived** (rih VYVD) *v.:* awakened; brought back to life.

Tito was too frightened to know what to do or where to go. He had lost all sense of direction. He started to go back to the inner gate; but Bimbo, straining his back to the last inch, almost pulled his clothes from him. What did the creature want? Had the dog gone mad?

Then suddenly he understood. Bimbo was telling him the way out—urging him there. The sea gate, of course. The sea gate—and then the sea. Far from falling buildings, heaving ground. He turned, Bimbo guiding him across open pits and dangerous pools of bubbling mud, away from buildings that had caught fire and were dropping their burning beams. Tito could no longer tell whether the noises were made by the shrieking sky or the agonized people. He and Bimbo ran on—the only silent beings in a howling world.

New dangers threatened. All Pompeii seemed to be thronging toward the marine gate and, squeezing among the crowds, there was the chance of being trampled to death. But the chance had to be taken. It was growing harder and harder to breathe. What air there was choked him. It was all dust now—dust and pebbles, pebbles as large as beans. They fell on his head, his hands—pumice stones from the black heart of Vesuvius. The mountain was turning itself inside out. Tito remembered a phrase that the stranger had said in the forum two days ago: "Those who will not listen to men must be taught by the gods." The people of Pompeii had refused to heed the warnings; they were being taught now—if it was not too late. **K**

Suddenly it seemed too late for Tito. The red-hot ashes blistered his skin, the stinging vapors tore his throat. He could not go on. He staggered toward a small tree at the side of the road and fell. In a moment Bimbo was beside him. He coaxed. But there was no answer. He licked Tito's hands, his feet, his face. The boy did not stir. Then Bimbo did the last thing he could—the last thing he wanted to do. He bit his comrade, bit him deep in the arm. With a cry of pain, Tito jumped to his feet, Bimbo after him. Tito was in despair, but Bimbo was determined. He drove the boy on, snapping at his heels, worrying his way through the crowd, barking, baring his teeth, heedless of kicks or falling stones. Sick with hunger, half dead with fear and sulfur fumes, Tito pounded on, pursued by Bimbo. How long, he never knew. At last he staggered through the marine gate and felt soft sand under him. Then Tito fainted. . . .

Someone was dashing seawater over him. Someone was carrying him toward a boat.

"Bimbo," he called. And then louder, "Bimbo!" But Bimbo had disappeared.

Voices jarred against each other. "Hurry—hurry!" "To the boats!" "Can't you see the child's frightened and starving!" "He keeps calling for someone!" "Poor boy, he's out of his mind." "Here, child—take this!"

They tucked him in among them. The oarlocks creaked; the oars splashed; the boat rode over toppling waves. Tito was safe. But he wept continually.

"Bimbo!" he wailed. "Bimbo! Bimbo!"

He could not be comforted. **L**

K **Read and Discuss** What are you picturing from the words in the last few paragraphs?

L **Literary Focus** **Literary Criticism** Is the story of Tito and Bimbo believable? Explain whether it is possible to believe that such a boy and such a dog really existed at this time in history.

Eighteen hundred years passed. Scientists were restoring the ancient city; excavators[15] were working their way through the stones and trash that had buried the entire town. Much had already been brought to light—statues, bronze instruments, bright mosaics,[16] household articles; even delicate paintings had been preserved by the fall of ashes that had taken over two thousand lives. Columns were dug up, and the forum was beginning to emerge.

It was at a place where the ruins lay deepest that the director paused.

"Come here," he called to his assistant. "I think we've discovered the remains of a building in good shape. Here are four huge millstones that were most likely turned by slaves or mules—and here is a whole wall standing with shelves inside it. Why! It must have been a bakery. And here's a curious thing. What do you think I found under this heap where the ashes were thickest? The skeleton of a dog!"

"Amazing!" gasped his assistant. "You'd think a dog would have had sense enough to run away at the time. And what is that flat thing he's holding between his teeth? It can't be a stone."

15. **excavators** (EHKS kuh vay tuhrz): diggers; here, archaeologists.

16. **mosaics** (moh ZAY ihks): pictures or designs made by inlaying small bits of stone, glass, tile, or other materials in mortar.

Analyzing Visuals **Viewing and Interpreting**
What is happening to Tito here? How does this illustration show the chaos that follows after the volcano's eruption?

"No. It must have come from this bakery. You know it looks to me like some sort of cake hardened with the years. And, bless me, if those little black pebbles aren't raisins. A raisin cake almost two thousand years old! I wonder what made him want it at such a moment." **M**

"I wonder," murmured the assistant. **N**

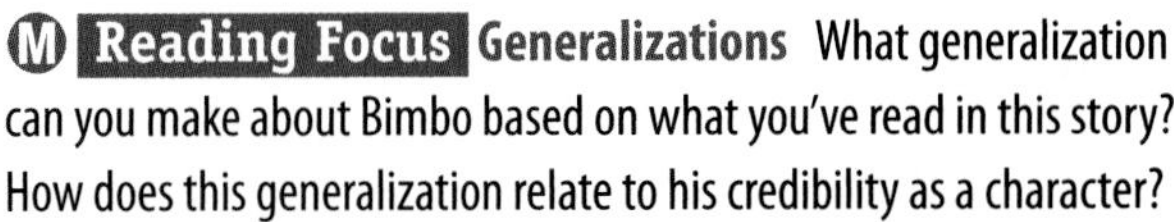

M **Reading Focus** **Generalizations** What generalization can you make about Bimbo based on what you've read in this story? How does this generalization relate to his credibility as a character?

N **Read and Discuss** What is this part about? The scientists are wondering why the dog would want a raisin cake at such a bad time. What strikes you about this?

by **Robert Silverberg**

Read with a Purpose

Read this nonfiction selection to help you evaluate the historical accuracy of "The Dog of Pompeii."

Preparing to Read for the selection is on page 399.

Build Background

In his nonfiction book *Lost Cities and Vanished Civilizations*, Robert Silverberg describes Pompeii in A.D. 79 and tells about the eruption of Mount Vesuvius. In writing his book, Silverberg drew on the findings of archaeologists who conducted excavations of Pompeii and Herculaneum. As you read this excerpt from Silverberg's book, note details that appear both here and in Untermeyer's story.

The people of Pompeii knew that doom was on hand, now. Their fears were doubled when an enormous rain of hot ashes began to fall on them, along with more lapilli.[1] Pelted with stones, half smothered by ashes, the Pompeiians cried to the gods for mercy. The wooden roofs of some of the houses began to catch fire as the heat of the ashes reached them. Other buildings were collapsing under the weight of the pumice stones that had fallen on them.

In those first few hours, only the quick-witted managed to escape. Vesonius Primus,

1. **lapilli** (luh PIHL y): small pieces of hardened lava.

the wealthy wool merchant, called his family together and piled jewelry and money into a sack. Lighting a torch, Vesonius led his little band out into the nightmare of the streets. Overlooked in the confusion was Vesonius' black watchdog, chained in the courtyard. The terrified dog barked wildly as lapilli struck and drifting white ash settled around him. The animal struggled with his chain, battling fiercely to get free, but the chain held, and no one heard the dog's cries. The humans were too busy saving themselves.

Many hundreds of Pompeiians fled in those first few dark hours. Stumbling in the darkness, they made their way to the city gates, then out, down to the harbor. They boarded boats and got away, living to tell the tale of their city's destruction. Others preferred to remain within the city, huddling inside the temples, or in the public baths, or in the cellars of their homes. They still hoped that the nightmare would end—that the tranquility of a few hours ago would return. . . . **A**

It was evening, now. And new woe was in store for Pompeii. The earth trembled and quaked! Roofs that had somehow withstood the rain of lapilli went crashing in ruin, burying hundreds who had hoped to survive the eruption. In the forum, tall columns toppled as they had in 63.[2] Those who remembered that great earthquake screamed in new terror as the entire city seemed to shake in the grip of a giant fist.

Three feet of lapilli now covered the ground. Ash floated in the air. Gusts of poisonous gas came drifting from the belching crater, though people could still breathe. Roofs were collapsing everywhere. Rushing throngs, blinded by the darkness and the smoke, hurtled madly up one street and down the next, trampling the fallen in a crazy, fruitless dash toward safety. Dozens of people plunged into dead-end streets and found themselves trapped by crashing buildings. They waited there, too frightened to run farther, expecting the end. **B**

The rich man Diomedes was another of those who decided not to flee at the first sign of alarm. Rather than risk being crushed by the screaming mobs, Diomedes calmly led the members of his household into the solidly built basement of his villa. Sixteen people altogether, as well as his daughter's dog and her beloved little goat. They took enough food and water to last for several days.

But for all his shrewdness and foresight, Diomedes was undone anyway. Poison gas was creeping slowly into the underground shelter! He watched his daughter begin to cough and struggle for breath. Vesuvius was giving off vast quantities of deadly carbon monoxide that was now settling like a blanket over the dying city.

"We can't stay here!" Diomedes gasped. Better to risk the uncertainties outside than to remain here and suffocate.

2. There had been an earthquake in Pompeii sixteen years before Vesuvius erupted.

A **Read and Discuss** How does this part of the story relate to what you learned earlier about Pompeii?

B **Read and Discuss** How do these events relate to the events in Untermeyer's story?

"I'll open the door," he told them. "Wait for me here."

Accompanied only by an old and faithful servant, who carried a lantern to light Diomedes' way in the inky blackness, the nobleman stumbled toward the door. He held the silver key in his hand. Another few steps and he would have been at the door, he could have opened it, they could have fled into the air—but a shroud of gas swooped down on him. He fell, still clutching the key, dying within minutes. Beneath the porch, fourteen people waited hopefully for him, their lives ticking away with each second. Diomedes did not return. At the last moment, all fourteen embraced each other, servants and masters alike, as death took them. **C**

The poison gas thickened as the terrible night continued. It was possible to hide from the lapilli, but not from the gas, and Pompeiians died by the hundreds. Carbon monoxide gas keeps the body from absorbing oxygen. Victims of carbon monoxide poisoning get sleepier and sleepier, until they lose consciousness, never to regain it. All over Pompeii, people lay down in the beds of lapilli, overwhelmed by the gas, and death came quietly to them. Even those who had made their way outside the city now fell victim to the spreading clouds of gas. It covered the entire countryside.

In a lane near the forum, a hundred people were trapped by a blind-alley wall. Others hid in the stoutly built public bathhouses, protected against collapsing roofs but not against the deadly gas. Near the house of Diomedes, a beggar and his little goat sought shelter. The man fell dead a few feet from Diomedes' door; the faithful goat remained by his side, its silver bell tinkling, until its turn came. **D**

All through the endless night, Pompeiians wandered about the streets or crouched in their ruined homes or clustered in the temples to pray. By morning, few remained alive. Not once had Vesuvius stopped hurling lapilli and ash into the air, and the streets of Pompeii were filling quickly. At midday on August 25, exactly twenty-four hours after the beginning of the holocaust,[3] a second eruption racked the volcano. A second cloud of ashes rose above Vesuvius' summit. The wind blew ash as far as Rome and Egypt. But most of the new ashes descended on Pompeii.

The deadly shower of stone and ashes went unslackening into its second day. But it no longer mattered to Pompeii whether the eruption continued another day or another year. For by midday on August 25, Pompeii was a city of the dead. **E**

3. **holocaust:** great destruction of life.

C **Read and Discuss** From the Diomedes story, how can you picture the Pompeii experience?

D **Reading Focus** **Generalizations** What generalization can you make about how the people of Pompeii felt about their animals? How does this connect with what you read in "The Dog of Pompeii"?

E **Read and Discuss** What does the author mean about the eruption no longer mattering and about Pompeii being "a city of the dead"?

Applying Your Skills

Sunshine State Standards: Benchmarks **LA.6.1.6.1** use new vocabulary that is introduced and taught directly; **LA.6.1.7.3** determine the main idea or essential message in grade-level text through inferring, paraphrasing, summarizing, and identifying relevent details; **LA.6.2.1.5** develop an interpretation of a selection and support through sustained use of examples and contextual evidence; *Also covered* **LA.6.4.1.2**

The Dog of Pompeii / Pompeii

Respond and Think Critically

Reading Focus

FCAT

1. Which event from "The Dog of Pompeii" is MOST realistic based on information from the nonfiction account?
   A Bimbo knew where to find everything in Pompeii.
   B Bimbo fetched Tito flat rich cakes that were sprinkled with raisins and sugar.
   C The night before the eruption, Tito dreamed about losing his way in a screaming crowd.
   D Scientists uncovered the remains of a dog in Pompeii.

Read with a Purpose

2. What does "The Dog of Pompeii" illustrate about the bond between dogs and humans?
3. How did reading "Pompeii" help you evaluate the credibility of "The Dog of Pompeii"?

Reading Skills: Generalizations

READ THINK EXPLAIN

4. What generalization can you make about the credibility of the plot and characters in "The Dog of Pompeii"? How did "Pompeii" help you make your generalization? Support your answer with details from the story

Vocabulary Check

Answer the following questions.

5. How is a proverb different from a riddle?
6. How might a person who is yawning and sleepy be revived?

Literary Focus

Literary Analysis

7. **Analyze/Compare** How does the writer of "The Dog of Pompeii" get us involved in an event from so long ago and far away? From what you've seen in this story, how can fiction communicate ideas about the past in a way that's different from historical accounts?
8. **Make Judgments** What do you learn from the story's final scene that you couldn't have learned any other way? How does this scene add to the story's credibility?

Literary Skills: Literary Criticism

9. **Evaluate** Do you think Tito and Bimbo are credible characters—that is, do they behave like real boys and real dogs you know or have heard about? Discuss details you found believable or hard to believe about the way Tito and Bimbo are portrayed in this story.

Writing Focus

Think as a Reader/Writer

Use It in Your Writing Review the notes about "The Dog of Pompeii" you took in your *Reader/Writer Notebook.* Write a paragraph about one or more people in danger during a natural disaster, such as a flood, earthquake, or fire. (You may wish to research details about the type of disaster before you start writing.) Include details that make the situation—and the characters' reactions—credible.

SHORT STORY

Zlateh the Goat

by **Isaac Bashevis Singer**
pictures by **Maurice Sendak**

Read with a Purpose

Read this story to see how the bond between human and animal is displayed by a boy and the goat he has to take to the butcher's.

Preparing to Read for the selection is on page 399.

Build Background

"Zlateh the Goat" takes place around Hanukkah (HAH nuh kah), a Jewish religious festival usually observed in December. Hanukkah is an eight-day-long celebration of the rededication of the Temple in Jerusalem in 165 B.C., following the victory of Jewish fighters over a huge Syrian army. The Temple, which had been taken over by Antiochus, ruler of the Syrians, had been violated and damaged. While the Jews were purifying and repairing the Temple, a miracle occurred. A tiny bit of oil for the holy lamp—barely enough for one day—lasted eight days.

At Hanukkah time the road from the village to the town is usually covered with snow, but this year the winter had been a mild one. Hanukkah had almost come, yet little snow had fallen. The sun shone most of the time. The peasants complained that because of the dry weather there would be a poor harvest of winter grain. New grass sprouted, and the peasants sent their cattle out to pasture. **A**

For Reuven the furrier[1] it was a bad year, and after long hesitation he decided to sell Zlateh the goat. She was old and gave little milk. Feyvel the town butcher had offered eight gulden[2] for her. Such a sum would buy Hanukkah candles, potatoes and oil for pancakes, gifts for the children, and other holiday necessaries for the house. Reuven told his oldest boy, Aaron, to take the goat to town.

Aaron understood what taking the goat to Feyvel meant, but he had to obey his father. Leah, his mother, wiped the tears from her eyes when she heard the

1. **furrier** (FUR ee uhr): someone who makes and repairs fur garments.

2. **gulden** (GUL duhn): coins formerly used in several European countries.

A **Read and Discuss** What do you learn in this paragraph?

news. Aaron's younger sisters, Anna and Miriam, cried loudly. Aaron put on his quilted jacket and a cap with earmuffs, bound a rope around Zlateh's neck, and took along two slices of bread with cheese to eat on the road. Aaron was supposed to deliver the goat by evening, spend the night at the butcher's, and return the next day with the money. **B**

While the family said goodbye to the goat, and Aaron placed the rope around her neck, Zlateh stood as patiently and good-naturedly as ever. She licked Reuven's hand. She shook her small white beard. Zlateh trusted human beings. She knew that they always fed her and never did her any harm.

When Aaron brought her out on the road to town, she seemed somewhat astonished. She'd never been led in that direction before. She looked back at him questioningly, as if to say, "Where are you taking me?" But after a while she seemed to come to the conclusion that a goat shouldn't ask questions. Still, the road was different. They passed new fields, pastures, and huts with thatched roofs. Here and there a dog barked and came running after them, but Aaron chased it away with his stick. **C**

The sun was shining when Aaron left the village. Suddenly the weather changed. A large black cloud with a bluish center appeared in the east and spread itself rapidly over the sky. A cold wind blew in with it. The crows flew low, croaking. At first it looked as if it would rain, but instead it began to hail as in summer. It was early in the day, but it became dark as dusk. After a while the hail turned to snow.

In his twelve years Aaron had seen all kinds of weather, but he had never experienced a snow like this one. It was so dense it shut out the light of the day. In a short time their path was completely covered. The wind became as cold as ice. The road to town was narrow and winding. Aaron no longer knew where he was. He could not see

B **Read and Discuss** What is on the father's mind, and what is he planning to do? How does his plan affect the family?

C **Literary Focus** **Literary Criticism** Singer suggests that Zlateh can think—that she can question and draw conclusions. Does this make her a more or less believable character? Explain why.

through the snow. The cold soon penetrated his quilted jacket.

At first Zlateh didn't seem to mind the change in weather. She too was twelve years old and knew what winter meant. But when her legs sank deeper and deeper into the snow, she began to turn her head and look at Aaron in wonderment. Her mild eyes seemed to ask, "Why are we out in such a storm?" Aaron hoped that a peasant would come along with his cart, but no one passed by.

The snow grew thicker, falling to the ground in large, whirling flakes. Beneath it Aaron's boots touched the softness of a plowed field. He realized that he was no longer on the road. He had gone astray. He could no longer figure out which was east or west, which way was the village, the town. The wind whistled, howled, whirled the snow about in eddies. It looked as if white imps were playing tag on the fields. A white dust rose above the ground. Zlateh stopped. She could walk no longer. Stubbornly she anchored her cleft hooves in the earth and bleated as if pleading to be taken home. Icicles hung from her white beard, and her horns were glazed with frost. **D**

Aaron did not want to admit the danger, but he knew just the same that if they did not find shelter, they would freeze to death. This was no ordinary storm. It was a mighty blizzard. The snowfall had reached his knees. His hands were numb, and he could no longer feel his toes. He choked when he breathed. His nose felt like wood, and he rubbed it with snow. Zlateh's bleating began to sound like crying. Those humans in whom she had so much confidence had dragged her into a trap. Aaron began to pray to God for himself and for the innocent animal. **E**

Aaron did not want to admit the danger, but he knew just the same that if they did not find shelter, they would freeze to death.

Suddenly he made out the shape of a hill. He wondered what it could be. Who had piled snow into such a huge heap? He moved toward it, dragging Zlateh after him. When he came near it, he realized that it was a large haystack which the snow had blanketed.

D **Literary Focus** **Literary Criticism** What details make this situation seem credible?

E **Read and Discuss** What is happening now? What is the author trying to tell us about Zlateh's and Aaron's thoughts?

Vocabulary **penetrated** (PEHN uh tray tihd) *v.:* pierced; made a way through.
cleft (klehft) *adj.:* split; divided.

Aaron realized immediately that they were saved. With great effort he dug his way through the snow. He was a village boy and knew what to do. When he reached the hay, he hollowed out a nest for himself and the goat. No matter how cold it may be outside, in the hay it is always warm. And hay was food for Zlateh. The moment she smelled it, she became contented and began to eat. Outside, the snow continued to fall. It quickly covered the passageway Aaron had dug. But a boy and an animal need to breathe, and there was hardly any air in their hide-out. Aaron bored a kind of a window through the hay and snow and carefully kept the passage clear.

Zlateh, having eaten her fill, sat down on her hind legs and seemed to have regained her confidence in man. Aaron ate his two slices of bread and cheese, but after the difficult journey he was still hungry. He looked at Zlateh and noticed her udders were full. He lay down next to her, placing himself so that when he milked her, he could squirt the milk into his mouth. It was rich and sweet. Zlateh was not accustomed to being milked that way, but she did not resist. On the contrary, she seemed eager to reward Aaron for bringing her to a shelter whose very walls, floor, and ceiling were made of food. **F**

Analyzing Visuals **Viewing and Interpreting**
What scene in the story does this picture illustrate?

Through the window Aaron could catch a glimpse of the chaos outside. The wind carried before it whole drifts of snow. It was completely dark, and he did not know whether night had already come or whether it was the darkness of the storm. Thank God that in the hay it was not cold. The

F **Read and Discuss** What does it mean that Zlateh "seemed eager to reward Aaron"? How does this fit with what you've already learned about Zlateh?

Vocabulary **chaos** (KAY ahs) *n.:* total confusion or disorder.

Analyzing Visuals **Viewing and Interpreting**
How does this picture compare to the haystack refuge you see in your mind?

dried hay, grass, and field flowers exuded the warmth of the summer sun. Zlateh ate frequently; she nibbled from above, below, from the left and right. Her body gave forth an animal warmth, and Aaron cuddled up to her. He had always loved Zlateh, but now she was like a sister. He was alone, cut off from his family, and wanted to talk. He began to talk to Zlateh. "Zlateh, what do you think about what has happened to us?" he asked.

"Maaaa," Zlateh answered.

"If we hadn't found this stack of hay, we would both be frozen stiff by now," Aaron said.

"Maaaa," was the goat's reply.

"If the snow keeps on falling like this, we may have to stay here for days," Aaron explained.

"Maaaa," Zlateh bleated.

"What does 'Maaaa' mean?" Aaron asked. "You'd better speak up clearly."

"Maaaa. Maaaa," Zlateh tried.

"Well, let it be 'Maaaa' then," Aaron said patiently. "You can't speak, but I know you understand. I need you and you need me. Isn't that right?"

"Maaaa." **G**

Aaron became sleepy. He made a pillow out of some hay, leaned his head on it, and dozed off. Zlateh too fell asleep.

When Aaron opened his eyes, he didn't know whether it was morning or night. The snow had blocked up his window. He tried to clear it, but when he had bored through to the length of his arm, he still hadn't reached the outside. Luckily he had his stick with him and was able to break through to the open

---

G **Reading Focus** **Generalizations** What generalization can you make from the way Aaron and Zlateh communicate? How does their relationship compare with Tito and Bimbo's?

Vocabulary **exuded** (ehg ZOO dihd) *v.:* gave off.

air. It was still dark outside. The snow continued to fall and the wind wailed, first with one voice and then with many. Sometimes it had the sound of devilish laughter. Zlateh too awoke, and when Aaron greeted her, she answered, "Maaaa." Yes, Zlateh's language consisted of only one word, but it meant many things. Now she was saying, "We must accept all that God gives us—heat, cold, hunger, satisfaction, light, and darkness."

Aaron had awakened hungry. He had eaten up his food, but Zlateh had plenty of milk.

For three days Aaron and Zlateh stayed in the haystack. Aaron had always loved Zlateh, but in these three days he loved her more and more. She fed him with her milk and helped him keep warm. She comforted him with her patience. He told her many stories, and she always cocked her ears and listened. When he patted her, she licked his hand and his face. Then she said, "Maaaa," and he knew it meant, I love you too. **H**

The snow fell for three days, though after the first day it was not as thick and the wind quieted down. Sometimes Aaron felt that there could never have been a summer, that the snow had always fallen, ever since he could remember. He, Aaron, never had a father or mother or sisters. He was a snow child, born of the snow, and so was Zlateh. It was so quiet in the hay that his ears rang in the stillness. Aaron and Zlateh slept all night and a good part of the day. As for Aaron's dreams, they were all about warm weather. He dreamed of green fields, trees covered with blossoms, clear brooks, and singing birds. By the third night the snow had stopped, but Aaron did not dare to find his way home in the darkness. The sky became clear and the moon shone, casting silvery nets on the snow. Aaron dug his way out and looked at the world. It was all white, quiet, dreaming dreams of heavenly splendor. The stars were large and close. The moon swam in the sky as in a sea. **I**

Sometimes Aaron felt that there could never have been a summer, that the snow had always fallen, ever since he could remember.

On the morning of the fourth day, Aaron heard the ringing of sleigh bells. The haystack was not far from the road. The

---

H **Literary Focus** **Literary Criticism** How do the characters of Aaron and Zlateh change and develop during the time they are together in the haystack? How do their <u>attitudes</u> change? Explain whether the changes make them more or less credible.

I **Read and Discuss** How do you know that the writer's statement that Aaron "never had a father or mother or sisters" is not literal? What is the writer trying to say here?

peasant who drove the sleigh pointed out the way to him—not to the town and Feyvel the butcher, but home to the village. Aaron had decided in the haystack that he would never part with Zlateh.

Aaron's family and their neighbors had searched for the boy and the goat but had found no trace of them during the storm. They feared they were lost. Aaron's mother and sisters cried for him; his father remained silent and gloomy. Suddenly one of the neighbors came running to their house with the news that Aaron and Zlateh were coming up the road.

There was great joy in the family. Aaron told them how he had found the stack of hay and how Zlateh had fed him with her milk. Aaron's sisters kissed and hugged Zlateh and gave her a special treat of chopped carrots and potato peels, which Zlateh gobbled up hungrily.

Nobody ever again thought of selling Zlateh, and now that the cold weather had finally set in, the villagers needed the services of Reuven the furrier once more. When Hanukkah came, Aaron's mother was able to fry pancakes every evening, and Zlateh got her portion too. Even though Zlateh had her own pen, she often came to the kitchen, knocking on the door with her horns to indicate that she was ready to visit, and she was always admitted. In the evening, Aaron, Miriam, and Anna played dreidel.[3] Zlateh sat near the stove, watching the children and the flickering of the Hanukkah candles. **J**

Even though Zlateh had her own pen, she often came to the kitchen, knocking on the door with her horns to indicate that she was ready to visit.

Once in a while Aaron would ask her, "Zlateh, do you remember the three days we spent together?"

And Zlateh would scratch her neck with a horn, shake her white bearded head, and come out with the single sound which expressed all her thoughts, and all her love. **K**

3. **dreidel** (DRAY duhl): spinning top played with at Hanukkah. Its four sides display Hebrew letters that stand for "A great miracle happened there."

J **Reading Focus** **Generalizations** How have things changed from the way they were at the beginning of the story? What generalization can you make about the bond between humans and animals based on what has happened here?

K **Read and Discuss** How have events turned out for Zlateh, Aaron, and his family?

TRIAL BY FIRE

from ***People Magazine***

Read with a Purpose

Read this true story to learn about the heroic act of a mother cat.

Preparing to Read for the selection is on page 399.

Build Background

This article reports on something that actually occurred in New York City on March 29, 1996. The article appeared in the July 14, 1997, issue of *People Magazine.*

After battling a blaze in an abandoned auto shop on March 29 last year, New York City firefighters were startled to hear meowing. There, amid the smoke, sat three crying kittens; across the street were two more. Within moments, their mother, a badly injured calico,[1] was found nearby. "She had done her job and pulled them out one by one," says firefighter David Giannelli, who placed the animals in a box. "Her eyes were burnt shut, but she touched every one of those babies with the tip of her nose." **A**

Taken to Long Island's North Shore Animal League, the kittens and their mother—named Scarlett at the shelter—were treated for smoke inhalation and burns. "The instinct to save your young is very strong," says Dr. Bonnie Brown, North Shore's medical director. "This was just an extraordinary example." Sifting through 2,000 adoption applications, administrators finally sent Scarlett home with Karen Wellen, a New York City writer, and her parents. (One kitten died from a viral infection; the others were placed in area homes.) Now three times a day, Scarlett—a plump 15 pounds—receives eye cream to counter damage to her lids but otherwise is healthy and loving. Karen can't believe her own luck: "This cat risked her life to save her kittens. To come out of it with such a sweet personality is amazing." **B**

1. **calico** (KAL uh koh): cat with spots and markings of several colors.

A **Read and Discuss** What has the author told you so far? What do the mother cat's actions tell you about her?

B **Read and Discuss** How do things turn out for Scarlett and her kittens? How does the ordeal affect Scarlett?

Applying Your Skills

Sunshine State Standards: Benchmarks LA.6.1.7.3 determine the main idea or essential message in grade-level text through inferring, paraphrasing, summarizing, and identifying relevant details; *Also covered* **LA.6.1.7.8; LA.6.2.1.5**

Zlateh the Goat / Trial by Fire

Respond and Think Critically

Reading Focus

1. Why does Aaron's love of Zlateh grow during the snow storm? FCAT

A She keeps the hay soft and warm.

B She comforts him with her patience.

C She reminds him of Hanukkah.

D She gives him her milk.

Read with a Purpose

2. How does "Zlateh the Goat" illustrate the bonds that can exist between humans and animals?

Reading Skills: Generalizations

3. How credible were the characters and plot of "Zlateh the Goat"? Complete the chart you kept as you read. What generalization can you make about the story?

Title of Story: "Zlateh the Goat"

Character or plot detail	Credible or not credible?	Why? (based on my own knowledge)
Family decides to sell old goat; need money for Hanukkah	Credible	People will sell things they don't need to get money for special occasions.

Vocabulary Check

Answer the following questions.

4. If the cold **penetrated** Aaron's quilted jacket, how did Aaron feel?

5. What kinds of weather can create **chaos**?

Literary Focus

Literary Analysis

6. Compare How is the bond between Aaron and Zlateh like the bond between Bimbo, the dog of Pompeii, and Tito? How is it different?

7. Interpret Isaac Bashevis Singer once said: "I believe men can learn a lot from God's creatures." What does Aaron learn from Zlateh? What does Aaron's family learn from the relationship between the boy and the goat?

8. Make Connections How does the story of Scarlett and her kittens relate to "The Dog of Pompeii" and "Zlateh the Goat"? What do we learn from this nonfiction account that helps us evaluate the credibility of the characters and plots of the two fictional stories?

Literary Skills: Literary Criticism

9. Assess Is the plot of "Zlateh the Goat" credible, or is it contrived and hard to believe? Support your evaluation with details from the story and from "Trial by Fire," using the chart you created as you read. READ THINK EXPLAIN

Writing Focus

Think as a Reader/Writer

Use It in Your Writing Review your notes about "Zlateh the Goat" in your *Reader/Writer Notebook.* Using realistic details from the story, write a one-page article about Zlateh, similar to the article about Scarlett. The article should illustrate Zlateh's efforts to save herself and Aaron and include details about how Zlateh tried to communicate with Aaron.

COMPARING TEXTS
Wrap Up

Sunshine State Standards: Benchmarks **LA.6.1.7.6** analyze and evaluate similar themes or topics by different authors across a variety of fiction and nonfiction selections; **LA.6.4.1.1** write narrative accounts with an engaging plot (including rising action, conflict, climax, falling action, and resolution) include a clearly described setting with figurative language and descriptive words or phrases to enhance style and tone; *Also covered* **LA.6.4.1.2; LA.6.4.2.3**

The Dog of Pompeii / Pompeii / Zlateh the Goat / Trial by Fire

Writing Focus

Write a Literary Criticism

"The Dog of Pompeii" and "Zlateh the Goat" share many similarities, even though their settings and details are different. Write a literary-criticism essay in which you compare and contrast these two stories, evaluating them as credible (or not credible) stories. Focus on the credibility of the stories' plots and characters. When comparing and evaluating the two stories, be specific. Use examples of the language of literary criticism that you see below.

LITERARY CRITICISM: A GLOSSARY

Words and Phrases Used to Describe Plot	
Positive	**Negative**
realistic *or* credible	unrealistic *or* not credible
well-paced	plodding
suspenseful	predictable
satisfying ending	disappointing ending

Words and Phrases Used to Describe Characters	
Positive	**Negative**
original	unoriginal *or* stereotyped
believable *or* credible *or* convincing	unbelievable *or* unconvincing
well-rounded	flat

See the Writing Workshop: Comparison-Contrast Essay, pages 106–113, for additional information.

What Do You Think Now?

What lessons about love and relationships have you learned from the animals in these stories?

CHOICES

As you respond to the Choices, use these **Academic Vocabulary** words as appropriate: attitude, communicate, contrast, illustrate.

REVIEW

Write About Zlateh

Timed Writing In "Zlateh the Goat," Zlateh communicates in different ways to express her thoughts and feelings. What is credible—or not credible—about her methods? What characteristics does she have that make this communication believable?

CONNECT

Pitch a Screenplay Idea

Partner Work With a partner, write an idea for a film based on the stories of Bimbo and Tito, Aaron and Zlateh, or Scarlett and her kittens. First, summarize the story. Then, "pitch" your idea, describing how you imagine the film. Will it be live-action or animated? Will you change the setting or characters? Finally, explain why the film needs to be made. Why is it a story that audiences would pay to see?

EXTEND

Write an Alternate Ending

"Zlateh the Goat" has a happy ending, but "The Dog of Pompeii" does not. Why do you suppose Untermeyer didn't give his story a happier ending? Would the story be as effective it if had one? Write an alternate ending in which Bimbo lives. Based on what you know about Bimbo, how will his story continue?

INFORMATIONAL TEXT FOCUS

Following Instructions

CONTENTS

Animals often seem to be part of the family. What can people do to give animals comfortable homes?

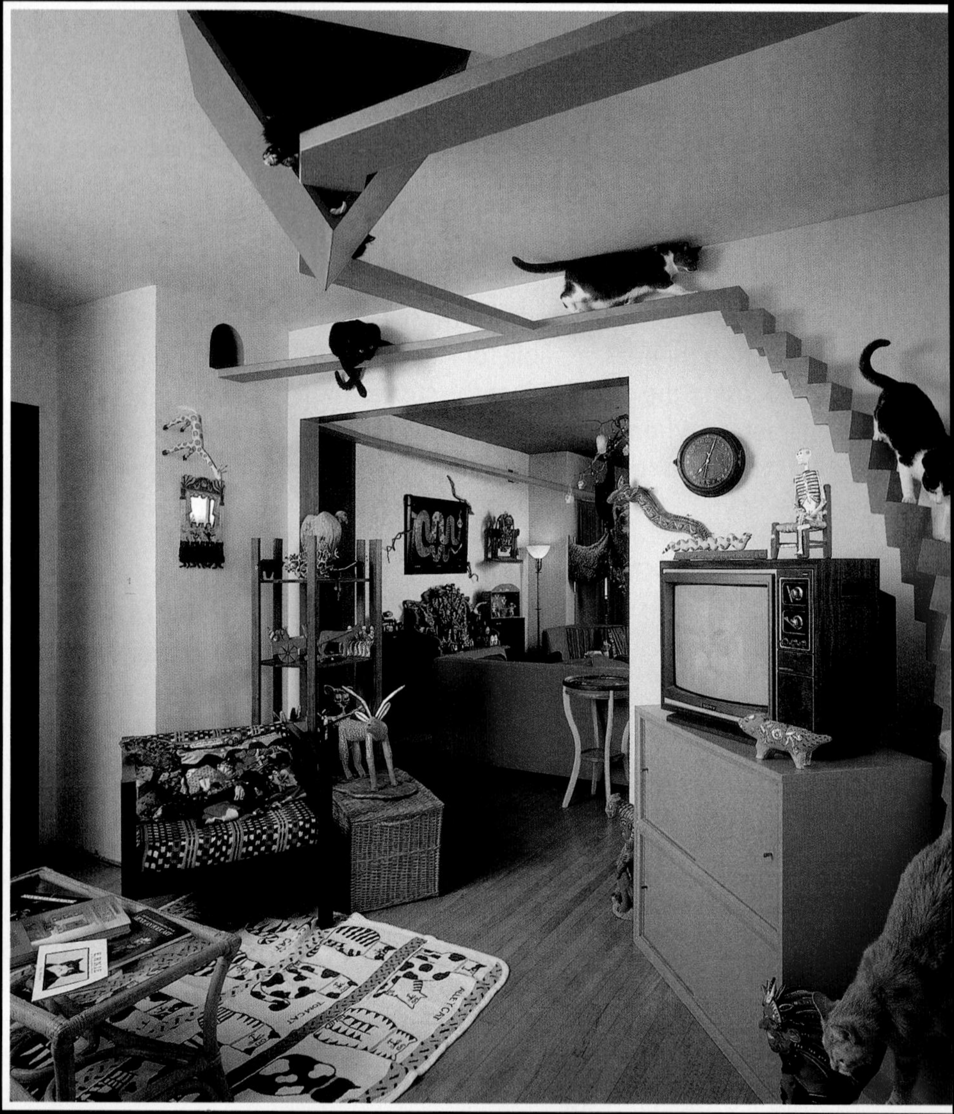

QuickWrite

Think about the responsibilities of caring for an animal. What qualities and attitudes do you think are important in a pet owner? Write a paragraph detailing these qualities.

APPLICATION

Preparing to Read

Sunshine State Standards: Benchmarks
LA.6.1.6.10 determine meanings of words, pronunciation, parts of speech, etymologies, and alternate word choices by using a dictionary, thesaurus, and digital tools; *Also covered* **LA.6.2.2.1; LA.6.2.2.4**

Pet Adoption Application

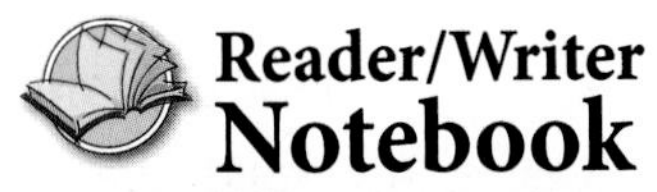

Reader/Writer Notebook

Use your **RWN** to complete the activities for this selection.

Informational Text Focus

Following Instructions: Preparing an Application In the years ahead, you'll be asked to fill out applications for all kinds of things. Right now, if you wanted to get a library card or adopt a pet from a shelter, you'd be asked to fill out an application.

Into Action These are the steps you need to follow when you fill out an application. Write the parts in boldface type on a card or piece of paper that you can keep as a handy reference.

1. **Read the application all the way through** before you do anything. You can often learn a great deal about whatever you're applying for by reading through the application.
2. If there is a question that requires more than a quick answer, **write down or type your response before you write it on the application** itself. Review and, if necessary, revise what you've written. Then, copy your response onto the application.
3. **Answer questions truthfully.**
4. **Print or type the information carefully,** with no cross-outs.
5. **Fill in all the blanks.** Write *n/a* (for "not applicable") in response to questions that don't apply to you.
6. **Check your spelling.**
7. After you fill out the application, read it through carefully to **make sure you didn't miss anything.**
8. **Sign and date your application.**

Some applications require references. A **reference** is the name of someone (possibly a teacher or family friend) who can provide information about your abilities and qualities. You should list only adults as references. Always ask permission first so that your references will have a chance to prepare useful information about you—and so they won't be surprised if they receive a phone call.

Vocabulary

contribution (kahn truh BYOO shuhn) *n.:* payment given for a specific purpose. *I gave the shelter where I found my cat a contribution to help other lost animals.*

occupation (ahk yoo PAY shuhn) *n.:* work a person does regularly. *I had to list my occupation so the shelter could determine the schedule I keep.*

supervisor (SOO puhr vy zuhr) *n.:* person in charge. *Did someone call my supervisor to ask if I was dependable?*

Language Coach

Word Histories Many words commonly used in the business world, like the three Vocabulary words above, are Latinate words—words from ancient Latin roots. Latin was the language of the ancient Romans, who had a rich vocabulary for dealing with ideas connected to business, law, and government. Latinate words are often rather long words, because they are built from two or more word parts consisting of a root and one or more affixes.

In a dictionary or online reference, see how many other words you can find that are related to these Vocabulary words. How many of these words are commonly used in the world of work?

Writing Focus

Preparing for **Extended Response**

Note the main headings, boldface terms, and other features that help guide you through the application.

Learn It Online

Use the interactive Reading Workshop for an example of how to prepare an application:

go.hrw.com L6-425

Read with a Purpose

Read to discover the kinds of information requested on applications.

INSTRUCTIONS: Adopter, print carefully in UNSHADED AREAS ONLY— do not write in shaded areas.

☐ Puppy ☐ Kitten ☐ Dog ☐ Cat

					1		Program	H	T	Adoption Number
Date / /		Single Adoption	Double Adoption	Age				D	O	1
							MTA MID	L	R	
								G	circle one	2
Day	Time	Breed		Color			☐ Mr. ☐ Mrs. ☐ Ms. ☐ Miss			
				Sex			☐ Adopter's Last Name First Name			
Voluntary Contribution		Size: S____ M____ L____		Spay/ Neuter						
Cash	$	☐ Pure	☐ Mix	Vaccine Type			Street Address Apt. #			
Check	$	Pet's Name		Vaccine Date						
D V M A circle one	$	ASC. Int.	No.	Rabies Tag						
Credit A/R	$			Rabies Date			City State Zip Code			
Total Voluntary Contribution	$			Wormed						
X____________				Med. Given			Home Phone ( ) –	Business Phone ( ) –		

Name of Reference	Address	City	State	Telephone	ID Source
				( ) –	☐ Yes ☐ No
				( ) –	

1. WHOM IS THE PET FOR? ☐ Self ☐ Gift For whom?____________ Adopter's age:____

2. IF YOU ARE SINGLE: Do you live alone? ☐ Yes ☐ No Do you live with family? ☐ Yes ☐ No
   Do you work? ☐ Yes ☐ No What are your hours?____________
   IF YOU ARE MARRIED: Do you both work? ☐ Yes ☐ No Husband's hours:____ Wife's hours:____
   How many children do you have at home?____ Ages:____,____,____,____,____,____
   Who will be responsible for the pet? ☐ Husband ☐ Wife ☐ Children ☐ Other

3. DO YOU: ☐ Own ☐ Rent (CHECK ONE) ☐ House ☐ Apt. (CHECK ONE) Floor #____ Elevator in building? ☐ Yes ☐ No
   If renting, does your lease allow pets? ☐ Yes ☐ No Are you moving? ☐ Yes ☐ No When?____
   Do you have use of a private yard? ☐ Yes ☐ No Is it fenced? ☐ Yes ☐ No Fence height:____
   Where will your pet be kept?____________ (DAYTIME) /____________ (NIGHTTIME) Any allergy to pets? ☐ Yes ☐ No

4. DO YOU HAVE OTHER PETS? ☐ Yes ☐ No Breed:____________
   Where did you get the pet?____________ How long have you had it?____________

5. YOUR OCCUPATION:____________ Business Phone: ( )____________
   Company:____________ Supervisor's Name:____________

Vet's Name	City, State	Zip Code
Adopter's Signature		

A Informational Focus Following Instructions What information is required in the upper right-hand area?

B Read and Discuss What did you learn about pet adoption?

Vocabulary **contribution** (kahn truh BYOO shuhn) *n.:* payment given for a specific purpose.
occupation (ahk yoo PAY shuhn) *n.:* work a person does regularly.
supervisor (SOO puhr vy zuhr) *n.:* person in charge.

Applying Your Skills

Sunshine State Standards: Benchmarks LA.6.6.1.2 use information from a variety of consumer (e.g., warranties, instructional manuals), workplace (e.g., applications, contracts) and other documents to explain a situation and justify a decision.

Pet Adoption Application

Practicing for FCAT

Informational Text and Vocabulary

1. Who would NOT be a suitable reference on a pet adoption form?
   A a teacher
   B a parent
   C a classmate
   D an aunt

2. What is the MAIN thing the shelter wants to know about an applicant?
   F whether the applicant will feed the animal the right food
   G whether the applicant plans to let the animal run free through the neighborhood
   H whether the applicant will always keep the pet's best interests in mind
   I what kind of dog or cat the applicant wants

3. The abbreviation *n/a* stands for "not applicable." What does the term *not applicable* mean?
   A none of your business
   B does not apply to me
   C not again
   D no answer

4. Why would the agency care if the pets were to be given as gifts?
   F The agency might charge an extra fee.
   G The agency would want to send a card.
   H The agency wants to know who the actual owner is.
   I The agency disapproves of giving pets as gifts.

5. Who can you list as a reference?
   A your pet
   B your little brother
   C your teacher
   D your classmate

6. What word has the same meaning as *occupation*?
   F application
   G pet
   H volunteer
   I job

7. What word has the same meaning as *supervisor*?
   A boss
   B veterinarian
   C reference
   D clergyman

Writing Focus — Extended Response

READ THINK EXPLAIN

Write a paragraph explaining the most important things a person should do when filling it out. Support your response with details from the text.

What Do You Think Now?

What information is the shelter *really* looking for when it asks what pets you have and whether you rent or own your home?

INSTRUCTIONS
Preparing to Read

Sunshine State Standards: Benchmarks
LA.6.2.2.1 locate, use, and analyze specific information from organizational text features (e.g., table of contents, headings, captions, bold print, italics, glossaries, indices, key/guide words); *Also covered* **LA.6.2.2.4; LA.6.6.1.2**

Going Batty! How to Build a Bat House

Reader/Writer Notebook

Use your **RWN** to complete the activities for this selection.

Informational Text Focus

Following Instructions: Analyzing Directions **Directions** are step-by-step instructions that explain how to complete a task, put something together, or repair something. You've probably followed directions when working on projects in art class or setting up a new computer. Good directions communicate a great deal of information in very few words.

Into Action To make the best use of directions, follow these strategies in order. Summarize these strategies on a card or piece of paper that you can keep as handy reference.

- Preview the task by reading all the **directions** carefully so that you know the scope of the project, including how long it will take. If there are any safety precautions or hazardous-materials warnings, ask for permission and work with adult supervision.
- Study any **diagrams** that show the materials you'll need, recommended methods of working, or examples of the finished product. If there's a list or illustration of needed tools and **materials,** make sure you have everything you need *before* you begin. Look at examples of what the finished product should look like. Study diagrams that illustrate recommended positions of materials or ways of working with tools.
- Set up your work space by gathering all the tools and materials you'll need. Be sure you have them all in one place so that you won't have to stop in the middle of your project to go to the store or to search your garage or workshop.
- Start following the directions from the beginning. If the directions have **steps,** follow them in order. Always work with safety in mind: Carefully follow any safety cautions or warnings about hazardous materials.

Vocabulary

literally (LIHT uhr uh lee) *adv.:* actually; in truth. *Bats literally hang from the ceilings of their homes.*

structure (STRUHK chuhr) *n.:* something built or constructed. *This wooden structure would make a good home for a bat colony.*

exterior (ehk STIHR ee uhr) *adj.:* outdoor. *Exterior-grade wood is specially treated so it can withstand harsh weather.*

Language Coach

Usage The word *literally* means "true to the exact meaning of the words." Many people use *literally* incorrectly, though. For example, someone might say, "My headache was so bad, my head was literally splitting." Unless the speaker was actually rushed to the hospital because his or her head had really split open, the use of the word *literally* here can't be taken—well—literally!

Writing Focus

Preparing for **Extended Response**

As you read the directions that follow on the next few pages, notice the way they are organized in a sequence.

Learn It Online
Become vocabulary-savvy with Word Watch at:
go.hrw.com L6-428 Go

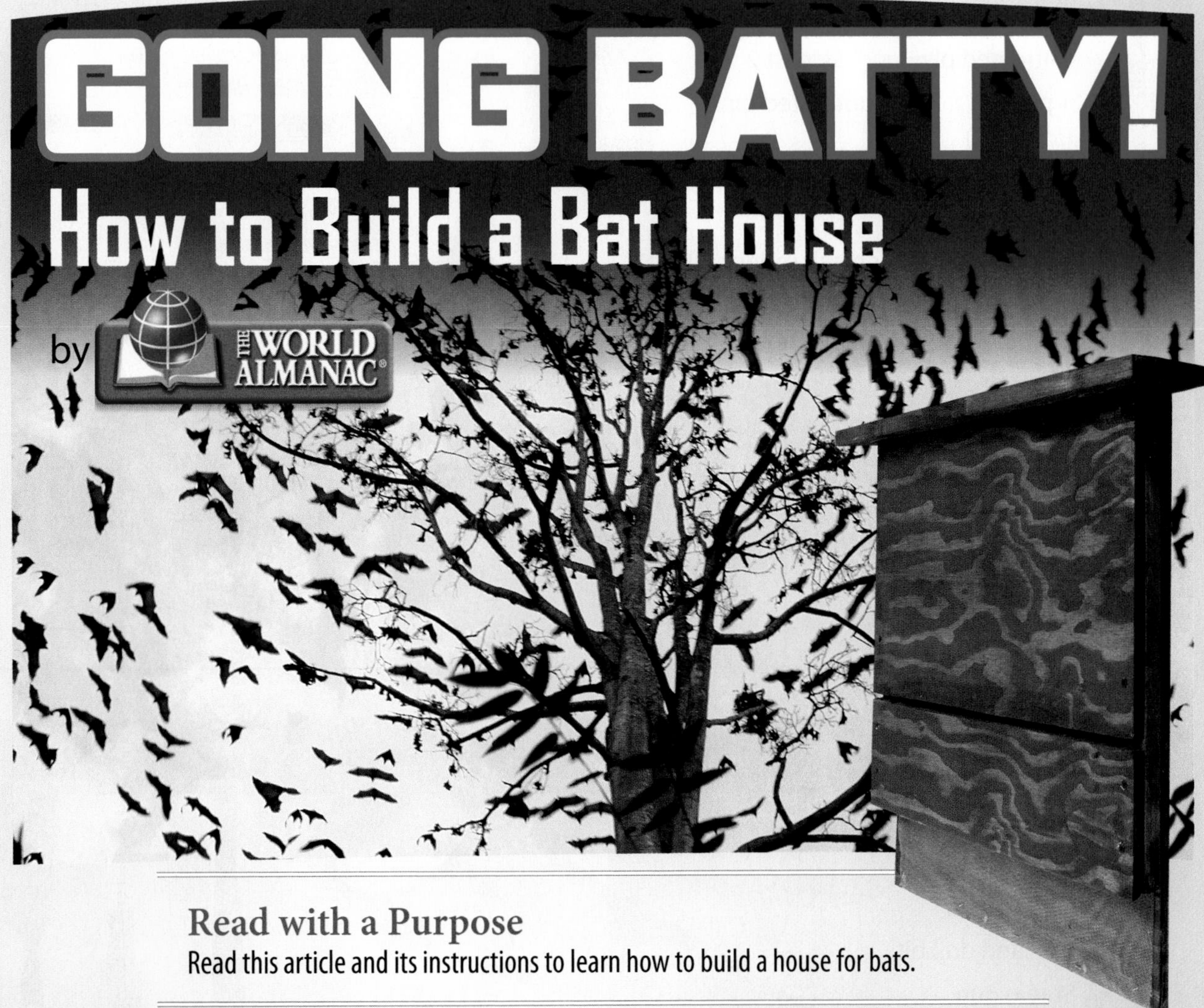

GOING BATTY!

How to Build a Bat House

by THE WORLD ALMANAC®

Read with a Purpose

Read this article and its instructions to learn how to build a house for bats.

Bats have gotten a bad name from horror stories and movies. That's too bad, because bats can be great little guys to have around. Give a bat a place to live, and it will help you cut down on mosquitoes and other insect nuisances.

These tiny creatures, the world's only flying mammals, don't ask for much. They want a warm, enclosed space where they can hang out—literally! Bats climb the walls when home, and yes, they do sleep upside down. So they need a surface to grip with their tiny claws. They also like a place that stays dark at night and is near water. (Bug-eating makes a bat thirsty!)

This easy-to-build structure will welcome a small colony of helpful bats. (Caution: Never touch a bat, however, in case the bat is sick.) Ⓐ

Ⓐ **Read and Discuss** What point about bats is the author making here?

Vocabulary **literally** (LIHT uhr uh lee) *adv.:* actually; in truth.
structure (STRUHK chuhr) *n.:* something built or constructed.

Materials

- 1 sheet ½″ exterior-grade untreated plywood, at least 2′ x 4′
- 1 piece 1″ x 2″ x 8′ untreated pine (for sides)
- 1″ x 4″ x 28″ untreated board (for roof)
- Window screen or mesh (optional), 5 sq. ft.
- 20 to 30 exterior-grade 1-inch screws
- Small box 1-inch nails
- Dark-colored, water-based paint or stain
- Heavy-duty hanging hooks and wire (optional)

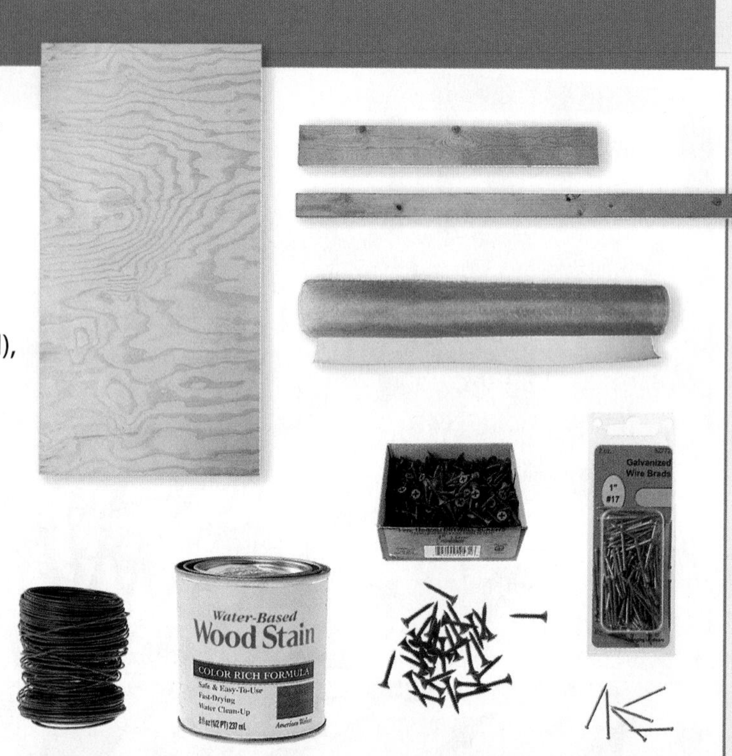

Tools (Caution: Always wear safety goggles when using tools, and get an adult to help!)

- Table saw or handsaw
- Hammer
- Screwdriver
- Drill and drill bits
- Staple gun
- Paintbrush
- Caulk gun

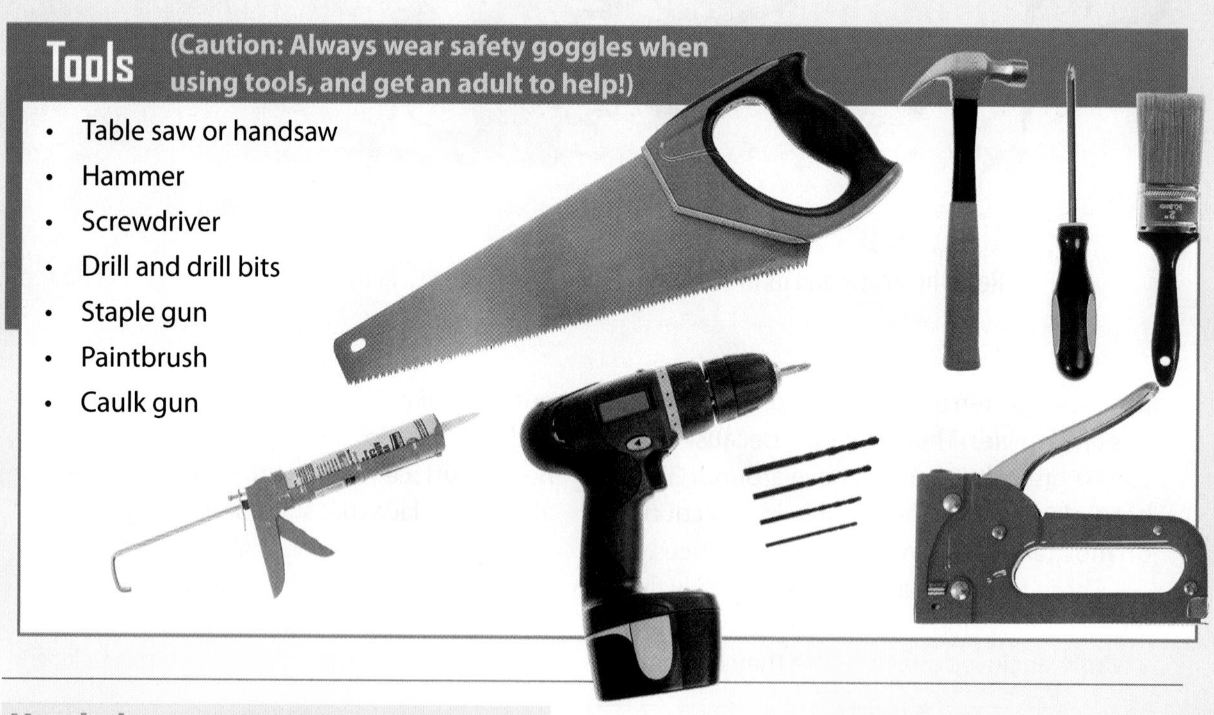

Vocabulary **exterior** (ehk STIHR ee uhr) *adj.:* outdoor.

Let's Get Started: Steps to Building a Bat House

1 Cut the plywood into three pieces as follows if you live in a warm climate. (See step 7 for measurements if you live in a cold climate.)

a) 26½" x 24" (1 back)

b) 26" x 24" (1 top front)

c) 5" x 24" (1 bottom front)

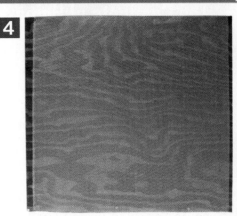

2 Cut the pine into three pieces as follows:

a) 24" (1 ceiling)

b) 20½" (2 side walls)

3 Paint or stain the wood. The dark color absorbs sunlight and keeps the bat house warm.

4 Using the staple gun, cover one side of the back panel with the screen so that bats can grab onto it. (If you don't want to use a screen, you can rough up the surface of the board with a file.)

5 Line up the side walls with the longer sides of the back panel. Screw into place. There will be ½-inch extra back panel at the bottom for bats to land on.

6 Place the ceiling at the top of the back panel, between the side walls. Screw into place.

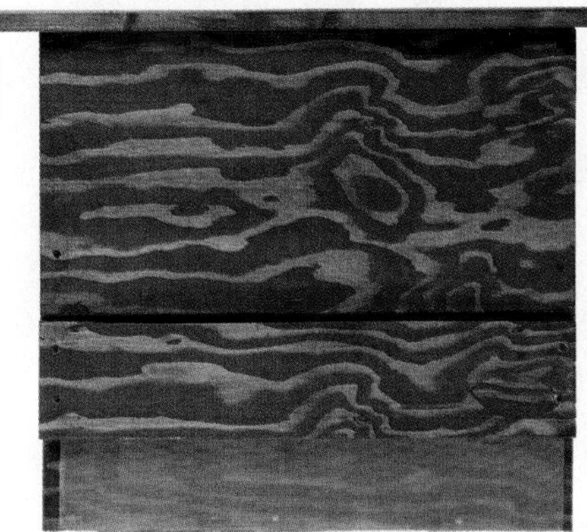

7 Place the top front panel on the house. Line it up with the ceiling, and screw into place. Place the bottom front panel on the house, leaving a ½-inch vent space between the top and bottom front panels. If you live in a cold climate, you can eliminate this vent. Simply cut a single front piece that's 23 inches long.

8 Carefully nail the roof over the top.

9 For best results, apply caulk to the joints.

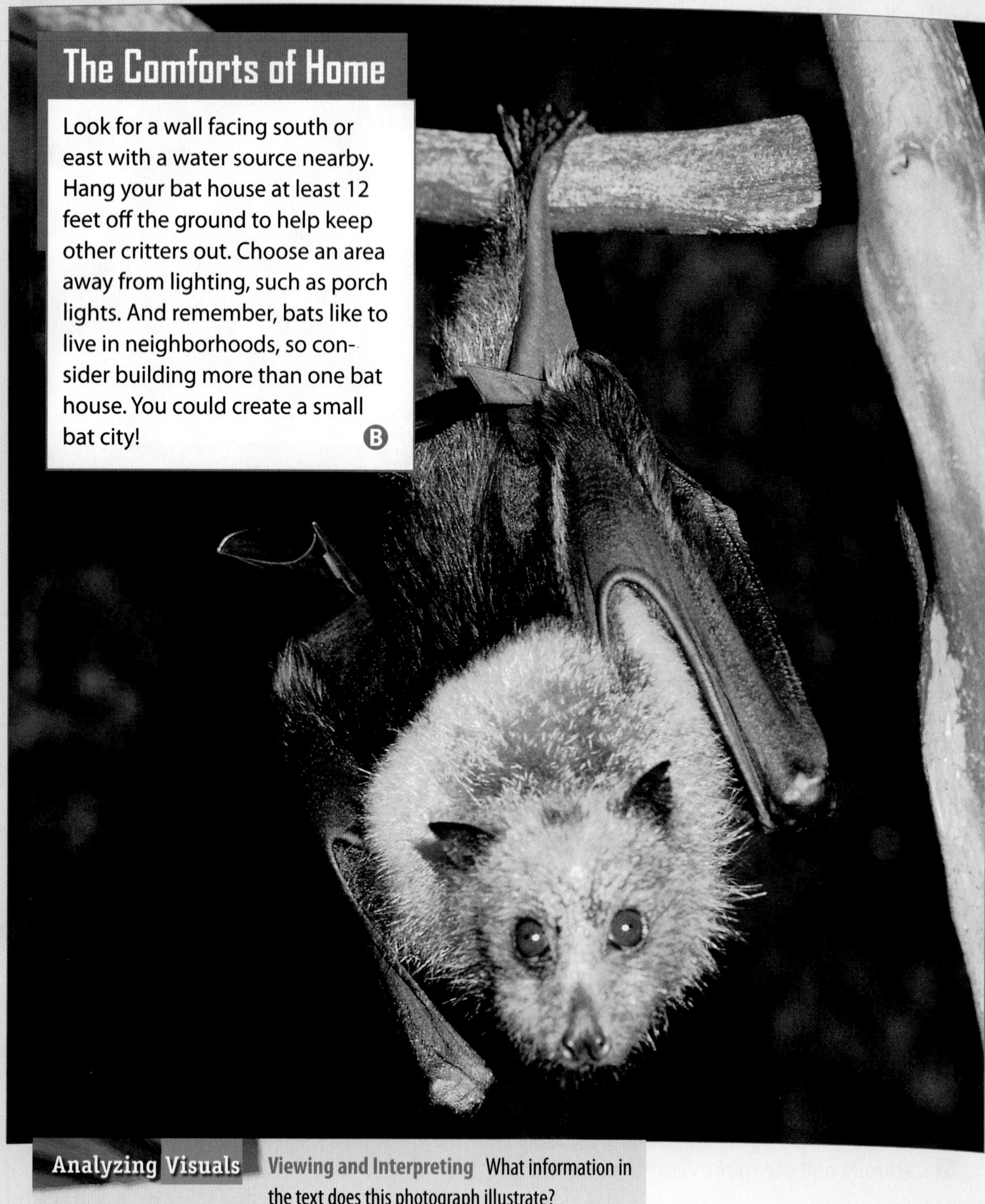

The Comforts of Home
Look for a wall facing south or east with a water source nearby. Hang your bat house at least 12 feet off the ground to help keep other critters out. Choose an area away from lighting, such as porch lights. And remember, bats like to live in neighborhoods, so consider building more than one bat house. You could create a small bat city! B

Analyzing Visuals **Viewing and Interpreting** What information in the text does this photograph illustrate?

B Informational Focus **Following Instructions** What have you learned about building a bat house?

Applying Your Skills

Sunshine State Standards: Benchmarks LA.6.2.2.2 use information from the text to answer questions related to the main idea or relevant details, maintaining chronological or logical order; *Also covered* LA.6.4.2.1; LA.6.6.1.2; LA.6.6.1.3

Going Batty! How to Build a Bat House

Practicing for FCAT

Informational Text and Vocabulary

1. Which is NOT required for building a bat house?
   A plywood
   B hanging hooks
   C exterior-grade screws
   D hammer

2. What should you do if you find a bat near your house?
   F Feed it mosquitoes.
   G Find the rest of its colony.
   H Put it in a wooden box.
   I Do not touch it.

3. Why should the roof be installed over the ceiling?
   A so bats can land more easily
   B so it uses less plywood
   C so rain won't get inside the house
   D so the caulking will fill the joints

4. Why should you create an air vent in the house if you live in a warm climate?
   F so the bats can drink water
   G so the house can get some light
   H so there is something for bats to hold onto
   I so air can flow through the house

5. Read this sentence from "Going Batty!"
   They want a warm, enclosed space where they can hang out – literally!
   What is another word for *literally*?
   A spookily
   B greedily
   C sleepily
   D actually

6. Read this sentence from "Going Batty!"
   This easy-to-build structure will welcome a small colony of helpful bats.
   What is a *structure*?
   F a plywood sheet
   G an enclosed space
   H a bat colony
   I a building

7. What should you do to keep the bat house warm?
   A close the door
   B paint the wood
   C light a fire
   D turn on the heater

Writing Focus Extended Response

Write a paragraph on how to build a Bat House. Support your answer with details from the instructions.

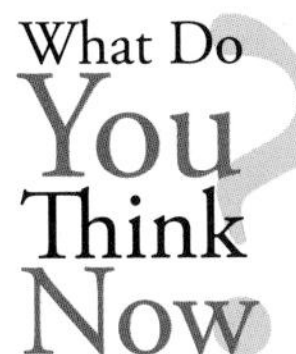

How might you and your family benefit from having bats live near your home?

Writing Workshop

Response to Literature

Write with a Purpose

Analyze an aspect of a literary work by writing a response to literature. Use evidence from the text to support your thesis. Your **audience** includes your classmates and your teacher, and your **purpose** is to persuade them that your interpretation of the work is well-reasoned.

A Good Response to Literature

- identifies the work by title and author
- clearly states the thesis
- supports the thesis with evidence from the text, such as details, examples, and quotations.
- is organized clearly
- restates or reinforces the thesis in a strong conclusion

Think as a Reader/Writer

Whether you realize it or not, when you read a literary work, you are also interpreting it—developing your own understanding of its meaning. Writing a response to literature gives you the chance to explain your interpretation of a literary work and to persuade others that your interpretation is valid. You choose an element of the work that is central to your interpretation, make a statement about that element (called a thesis), and support your interpretation with details, examples, and quotations from the text.

Before you write your own response to literature, read the following excerpt from an essay by Louise Sherman. In this excerpt, Sherman discusses the main character in a Lois Lowry novel called *Number the Stars*. Notice how Sherman uses evidence from the text to support the idea that the character Annemarie is central to the story's meaning.

When an important packet must be taken to the captain of one of the ships smuggling Jews to neutral Sweden, Annemarie finds the courage needed to deliver it despite grave danger to herself. Later her Uncle Hendrick tells her that *brave* means "not thinking about the dangers. Just thinking about what you must do." Lowry's story is not just of Annemarie; it is also of Denmark and the Danish people, whose Resistance was so effective in saving their Jews. Annemarie is not just a symbol, however. She is a very real child who is equally involved in playing with a new kitten and running races at school as in the danger of the occupation.

← Important **background** information is provided.

← A direct **quotation** is used as supporting evidence.

← **Details** provide further evidence that Annemarie is a believable character.

Think About the Professional Model

With a partner, discuss the following questions about the model.

1. Based on this excerpt, how would you state the writer's thesis?
2. Which piece of evidence do you feel is the strongest? Why?
3. How does Sherman let readers know that she thinks the character Annemarie is realistic?

Reader/Writer Notebook

Use your **RWN** to complete the activities for this workshop.

Sunshine State Standards: Benchmarks **LA.6.2.1.2** locate and analyze the elements of plot structure, including exposition, setting, character development, rising/falling action, conflict/resolution, and theme in a variety of fiction; **LA.6.2.1.5** develop an interpretation of a selection around several clear ideas, premises, or images, and justify the interpretation through sustained used of examples and contextual evidence; **LA.6.3.1.2** making a plan for writing that prioritizes ideas, addresses purpose, audience, main idea, and logical sequence; **LA.6.3.1.3** using organizational strategies and tools (e.g., technology, outline, chart, table, graph, web, story map); **LA.6.3.2.2** organizing information into a logical sequence and combining or deleting sentences to enhance clarity; **LA.6.3.3.1** evaluating the draft for development of ideas and content, logical organization, voice, point of view, word choice, and sentence variation; **LA.6.3.3.4** applying appropriate tools or strategies to evaluate and refine the draft (e.g., peer review, checklists, rubrics); *Also covered* **LA.6.3.4.2; LA.6.3.5.3**

Prewriting

Choose a Topic

First, choose a literary work—one that interests you and that you remember well. You will want to re-read the work, studying it closely for details. Try to choose a work with at least one literary element that is important to your understanding of the work as a whole. The Idea Starters at right list different literary elements you could consider.

Develop a Thesis

Once you have chosen a literary work, you will need to draft a **thesis statement,** or **opinion statement,** which sums up the main point that you will make in your response. Your thesis statement should clearly identify your purpose for writing and explain the importance of one element of the literary work, such as character or theme. To help you decide on a thesis statement, consider the following questions about the work.

- **Main Character:** Who or what is the main character? How does that character affect the events of the story? How does the author bring that character to life? Does the author use that character to illustrate a main idea?
- **Plot:** What are the main events in the literary work? What is the main conflict, and is it mainly internal or external? What complications arise? How is the conflict resolved? Does the resolution express a theme?
- **Setting:** Where and when does the story take place? Does the setting affect the characters and the plot? Could the work take place elsewhere?
- **Theme:** What is the theme of the literary work? How do the characters' actions and the chain of events in the work illustrate the theme?

Decide which element of the literary work stands out more than others. Then, determine what your main point is about that element. Here is a sample thesis statement to guide you:

Selection: "All Summer in a Day" (page 155)

> **Thesis:** Although the setting of this short story is otherworldly, the interactions between the characters are something every reader has seen and experienced.

Notice how this thesis states the literary element (setting) and the writer's point about it.

Idea Starters

- setting
- characters
- plot events
- conflict
- theme

Writing Tip

Your **thesis statement** should clearly signal to your readers what you are going to say about your topic. Get together with a partner and exchange thesis statements. Can your partner tell by reading your thesis statement what your literary response is going to be about? If not, keep revising your statement until it is clear.

Your Turn

Get Started Making notes in your **RWN,** decide on the literary work and literary element you'll write about in your essay. Then, write a thesis statement that indicates the element and your main point about it.

Learn It Online
An interactive graphic organizer can help you generate and organize ideas. Try one at:

go.hrw.com L6-435 

Writing Tip

If your thesis is about the importance of character in a literary wrok, your main points of **evidence** may be things like a character's words, a character's actions, and how other characters relate to him or her. Your evidence will include specific details, examples, and quotations from the work.

Gather Evidence

In order to persuade your readers that your interpretation of the literary work is well reasoned, you must use **evidence** from the selection to support your insights and ideas. After you have decided on your thesis statement, re-read any notes you took while reading the literary work, and identify two to four strong points from the text that support your thesis.

To gather evidence, look more closely at the text to identify details, examples, and quotations that you can use to **support** your thesis statement. Your interpretation will be more persuasive if you include various kinds of support. Here are the kinds of support you may include:

- direct quotations
- paraphrased lines or short passages
- details, such as images and dialogue
- examples, such as actions

Choose the evidence that best supports your thesis. For each piece of evidence, include a brief explanation to show how the evidence supports your thesis.

You can use a simple chart like the one below to organize and analyze the evidence you gather. Keeping track of where you find evidence will help you write your draft. This example is a partially completed evidence chart for the model on page 434.

Thesis: The character Annemarie is central to Number the Stars.

Evidence	What it shows	Page numbers
Annemarie takes the packet to the ship's captain.	Annemarie is brave.	

Think About Purpose and Audience

Keeping your purpose and audience in mind will help you write an effective response to literature. Your **purpose** is to explain your interpretation of a literary work by discussing an important element of the work. Additionally, you want to help your **audience**—your teacher and classmates—understand the literary work and to persuade them that your interpretation is a good one. Since your readers may not have read the work that you are interpreting, it is important to provide any background information that might help them better understand your interpretation.

Your Turn

Gather Evidence To help plan your response to literature, create a graphic organizer like the one at right. As you find more **evidence** to support your thesis, you can fill in the blanks of your chart. Keep your audience and purpose in mind, as you plan.

Drafting

Follow the Writer's Framework

The **Writer's Framework** at right outlines how to plan your draft to create an effective response to literature. Remember to include the complete **title** of the literary work and the **author's name** in your introduction.

A Writer's Framework

Introduction
- Complete title and author of the work
- Clear thesis and necessary background

Body
- First piece of evidence from the text and what it shows
- Second piece of evidence from the text and what it shows
- Other evidence from the text and what it shows

Conclusion
- Restatement of thesis
- Brief summary of supporting evidence
- Overall impression or insight into the work

Organize Evidence

The main organizational pattern for your essay will be **order of importance.** Follow these steps to organize the evidence in your response to literature.

- Number your evidence in order of importance. What is the strongest evidence in support of your thesis?
- Decide how many and what kinds of details, examples, paraphrases, or quotations to include as your supporting evidence.
- Decide where to present your most important evidence. If you place your strongest evidence first, readers will easily be able to follow the rest of your essay. If you place your strongest evidence last, readers will be left with a strong, memorable impression.

Grammar Link Capitalizing Proper Nouns

When you write a response to literature, you include the title of a literary work, the author of the work, and other proper nouns such as characters' names and place names. Study the example below from the model on page 434, and remember to follow the rules for capitalizing proper nouns as you write your essay.

> When an important packet must be taken to the captain of one of the ships smuggling **Jews** to neutral **Sweden**, **Annemarie** finds the courage needed to deliver it despite grave danger to herself.

- Proper nouns name a particular person, place, thing, or idea, such as *Jews, Sweden,* and *Annemarie.* Proper nouns always begin with a captial letter.

For more on capitalizing proper nouns, see the Language Handbook.

Writing Tip

Your **thesis** is the most important part of your introduction, so you want the thesis to be easy for readers to identify. Writers often build toward the thesis and then state it in the last sentence of the introduction.

Your Turn

Write Your Draft Follow your plan to write a draft of your essay. Be sure to think about these points:

- What is the most effective way to arrange your evidence?
- What proper nouns do you need to capitalize?

Peer Review

Sometimes an idea seems clear in your head when it is not clear on your paper. Work with one or more of your classmates to review each other's drafts and the guidelines at right. If your partner has difficulty identifying the main idea of a paragraph, the idea might not be clearly stated. Take notes about your partner's suggestions to help you improve your essay, and check the chart for revision suggestions.

Evaluating and Revising

Now that you've written your draft, re-read it carefully and use the chart below to help identify areas that can be improved.

Response to Literature: Guidelines for Content and Organization

Evaluation Question	Tip	Revision Technique
1. Are the author and title of the literary work **included in your introduction?**	**Highlight** the author and title.	**Add** a sentence or phrase naming the author and the title.
2. Does your introduction have a clear thesis that states the literary element and your main point about it?	**Underline** the thesis, the main point you are making. **Circle** the literary element and your main point about it.	**Add** a sentence that clearly states the thesis.
3. Is the main idea of each paragraph clear, and does each main idea support the thesis?	**Bracket** the main idea discussed in each paragraph of the body.	**Revise** the body paragraphs so that each one has a clearly stated main idea.
4. Is the main idea of each body paragraph supported by evidence?	**Draw a box** around each supporting detail, examples, or quotation. **Draw a wavy** line under elaborations, or explanations.	**Add** details, examples, or quotations to support your thesis. **Elaborate** on details, examples, or quotations with commentary.
5. Does the essay end with a restatement of the thesis?	**Put a star** above the restatement.	**Add** a restatement of the thesis, if necessary.

Read this student's draft with comments on its structure and suggestions for how the response could be made even stronger.

Student Draft

Literary Review of the Novel *Iqbal*

by Reid Cline, Murchison Middle School

When children are abused, the only way their lives can be saved is if someone intervenes and fights for their rights. *Iqbal,* a novel by Francesco D'Adamo, is based on the true story of a young boy living in Pakistan.

← The work is identified by **title** and **author.**

Iqbal Masih was forced to work twelve hours a day at a carpet factory, chained to his loom in unimaginable conditions. His parents bonded him into child labor to pay off a debt they owed to moneylenders, a fate shared by more than 700,000 children at that time in Pakistan.

← **Details** and **examples** are used as **evidence.**

Courageous and unwilling to accept his situation, Iqbal once took a knife and sliced down the middle of a beautiful carpet he had just completed. For his defiance, he was imprisoned in the "tomb," an underground cistern filled with snakes, scorpions, and suffocating heat. The other children were also brutally punished for Iqbal's rebellion. Iqbal's bravery, however, showed the other children that they could fight back.

← An **example** supports the idea that Iqbal was courageous.

MINI-LESSON How to Create a Thesis Statement

In the draft of his essay, Reid has identified the title and author of the work he is writing about, but he has not stated his thesis. Without a thesis statement, the essay lacks focus. Readers will not fully understand the purpose of the evidence that Reid presents. Reid revised his introduction by answering these questions and then rewriting the first paragraph:

What does this novel show about how a person can affect others? It shows that one person can help improve other people's lives. *How can I support this idea in my interpretation?* I can use evidence of Iqbal's acts of courage.

Reid's Revision of Paragraph One

One person's act of courage can improve the lives of many other people. Iqbal, the main character in Francesco D'Adamo's novel of the same name, is a perfect example of this. As a young boy living in Pakistan, Iqbal showed selfless courage that helped free thousands of children from slavery.

Your Turn

Create a Thesis Statement

Read your draft. Have you clearly stated your thesis? To write a draft of a thesis statement, complete the following sentence: *In my essay, I will show that the (character, plot, setting, or conflict) of (title of work) by (author's name) is (believable or unbelievable).*

Student Draft *continues*

Here is another **example** of how Iqbal's courage affects the other children.

Reid uses historical **facts** to support his thesis.

A strong **conclusion** restates the **thesis** in a fresh way.

The narrator of the novel is Fatima, a ten-year-old girl imprisoned with Iqbal and hundreds of other children by their cruel master, Hussain Khan. It is through her voice that we learn how Iqbal's courage affected the other children. They learned the master was tricking them with lies. Iqbal convinced the children that the master was cheating them by changing the marks counting their debt payment.

Iqbal vowed never to give up the fight for the children of Pakistan. He eventually escaped from the carpet factory and returned with the Bonded Liberation Front of Pakistan to rescue his friends. He continued to work with the Bonded Liberation Front to free children from slave labor. He became the voice and face for the liberation of bonded child laborers working in the factories, fields, kilns, and mines of Pakistan. Iqbal was gunned down by the "carpet mafia" on April 16, 1995.

Iqbal's example encouraged other oppressed children to stand up against the wrong done to them. He showed them that if they stood together, they could influence change in the society, they could bring this terrible injustice to the attention of the world.

MINI-LESSON How to Add Evidence from the Text

Direct quotations can provide strong and specific evidence to support your thesis. Reid decides to add a direct quotation to the fourth paragraph of his essay to show, rather than tell about, Iqbal's effect on Fatima and the other children.

Reid's Revision to Paragraph Four

The narrator of the novel is Fatima, a ten-year-old girl imprisoned with Iqbal and hundreds of other children by their cruel master, Hussain Khan. It is through her voice that we learn how Iqbal's courage affected the other children. They learned the master was tricking them with lies. ^ *Fatima remembers, "It wasn't true. I never saw a clean slate, neither mine nor one of my companions'. . . . Not enough work done, no rupee, no line erased from our slates; we knew it well."* Iqbal convinced the children that the master was cheating them by changing the marks counting their debt payment.

Your Turn

Add Evidence from the Text

Have you provided your readers with enough evidence to support your thesis? Review the literary work, and make a list of three more pieces of evidence that you could include. Choose the strongest, and add it to your draft.

Proofreading and Publishing

Proofreading

Re-read your essay for errors in punctuation, spelling, grammar, and usage. Make sure you have followed the rules of capitalization for proper nouns and that you do not have any run-on sentences. Trade papers with a partner to proofread each other's work. Then, prepare your final copy to share with your audience.

Grammar Link **Correcting Run-on Sentences**

Sometimes when you write, your pencil or typing cannot keep up with your thoughts. When this happens, you may write run-on sentences. A **run-on sentence** is really two or more sentences incorrectly written as one. As Reid was proofreading his draft, he noticed a run-on sentence in the last paragraph. To correct it, he broke the run-on sentence into two sentences.

He showed them that if they stood together, they could influence change in the society, they could bring this terrible injustice to the attention of the world.

Another way to revise a run-on sentence is to make it into a **compound sentence** by adding a comma and a conjunction, such as *and, but,* or *or*: ". . . they could influence change in the society, ***and*** they could bring this terrible injustice to the attention of the world."

Publishing

Now it's time to publish your response to literature to a wider audience. Think about where you have seen essays about literature or reviews of movies or plays.

- Ask the school librarian if you may post a copy of your essay on a bulletin board in the library.
- If your class has a Web page, see if you can post it there.
- Submit your essay to your school newspaper.

Reflect on the Process In your **RWN,** write a short response to each of these questions:

1. What process did you use to develop a thesis statement?
2. How did you decide which evidence to include? How did you decide how to organize your evidence?
3. What did you learn about the work of literature by writing the essay?

Proofreading Tip

As you proofread your draft, circle every proper noun. Have you followed the rules of capitalization? Draw three lines under any lowercase letter that should be capitalized. This will remind you to correct the capitalization when you prepare your final copy.

Your Turn

Proofread and Publish

As you proofread, look for run-on sentences. Before you publish your response to literature, remember to **revise run-ons** by breaking them into two or more separate sentences. You can also use a comma and conjunction—such as *and, but,* or *or*—to make them compound sentences.

Scoring Rubric

Use one of these rubrics to evaluate your response to literature from the Writing Workshop. Your teacher will tell you which rubric to use.

6-Point Scale

Score 6 ***Demonstrates advanced success***
- focuses consistently on a clear thesis
- shows effective organization throughout, with smooth transitions
- offers thoughtful, creative ideas
- develops ideas thoroughly, using examples, details, and fully elaborated explanations
- exhibits mature control of written language

Score 5 ***Demonstrates proficient success***
- focuses on a clear thesis
- shows effective organization, with transitions
- offers thoughtful ideas
- develops ideas competently, using examples, details, and well-elaborated explanations
- exhibits sufficient control of written language

Score 4 ***Demonstrates competent success***
- focuses on a clear thesis, with minor distractions
- shows effective organization, with minor lapses
- offers mostly thoughtful ideas
- develops ideas adequately, with a mixture of general and specific elaboration
- exhibits general control of written language

Score 3 ***Demonstrates limited success***
- includes some loosely related ideas that distract from the writer's focus
- shows some organization, with noticeable gaps in the logical flow of ideas
- offers routine, predictable ideas
- develops ideas with uneven elaboration
- exhibits limited control of written language

Score 2 ***Demonstrates basic success***
- includes loosely related ideas that seriously distract from the writer's focus
- shows minimal organization, with major gaps in the logical flow of ideas
- offers ideas that merely skim the surface
- develops ideas with inadequate elaboration
- exhibits significant problems with control of written language

Score 1 ***Demonstrates emerging effort***
- shows little awareness of the topic and purpose for writing
- lacks organization
- offers unclear and confusing ideas
- develops ideas in only a minimal way, if at all
- exhibits major problems with control of written language

4-Point Scale

Score 4 ***Demonstrates advanced success***
- focuses consistently on a clear thesis
- shows effective organization throughout, with smooth transitions
- offers thoughtful, creative ideas
- develops ideas thoroughly, using examples, details, and fully elaborated explanations
- exhibits mature control of written language

Score 3 ***Demonstrates competent success***
- focuses on a clear thesis, with minor distractions
- shows effective organization, with minor lapses
- offers mostly thoughtful ideas
- develops ideas adequately, with a mixture of general and specific elaboration
- exhibits general control of written language

Score 2 ***Demonstrates limited success***
- includes some loosely related ideas that distract from the writer's focus
- shows some organization, with noticeable gaps in the logical flow of ideas
- offers routine, predictable ideas
- develops ideas with uneven elaboration
- exhibits limited control of written language

Score 1 ***Demonstrates emerging effort***
- shows little awareness of the topic and purpose for writing
- lacks organization
- offers unclear and confusing ideas
- develops ideas in only a minimal way, if at all
- exhibits major problems with control of written language

Preparing for **FCAT Writing+**

Sunshine State Standards: Benchmarks **LA.6.2.1.5** develop an interpretation of a selection around several clear ideas, premises, or images, and justify the interpretation through sustained use of examples and contextual evidence; *Also covered* **LA.6.3.2.2; LA.6.3.3.1**

The response to literature below is a first draft that Dawn wrote for school. The response to literature contains errors. Read the response to literature to answer questions 1-3.

Mary's Ta-Na-E-Ka

→ [1] In the short story "Ta-Na-E-Ka" by Mary Whitebird, the main character, Mary, turns 11 and must take part in a Kaw Indian tradition called Ta-Na-E-Ka. [2] Instead of living in the woods on her own for 5 days like her cousin does, Mary lives in a restaurant. [3] Even though Mary does not do what she was expected to, she is not a cheater. [4] She takes responsibility for everything she does.

→ [5] Mary insists on earning everything she gets from other people. [6] For example, she pays for the food she eats at the restaurant. [7] She tries eating a wild berry, but she thinks it tastes bitter.

→ [8] She gets the money for the food from her teacher, but she promises to pay it back by helping her.

→ [9] The big test of Mary's honesty comes when she returns home at the end of Ta-Na-E-Ka. [10] She tells her parents and grandfather the truth about how she survived. [11] A cheater would try to hide what she did.

→ [12] Mary was not doing what people expected, but she was not trying to be dishonest about it. [13] She told the truth, and she earned what she got from other people. [14] That's why her parents and grandfather decided she had passed the test of Ta-Na-E-Ka.

1 Which sentence should be deleted because it presents a detail that is unimportant to the response to literature?

A sentence [6]
B sentence [10]
C sentence [7]
D sentence [11]

2 Dawn wants to add the sentence below to her response to literature:

She also helps the restaurant owner by picking fresh flowers for his tables.

Where should this sentence be added to keep the details in a logical order?

F after sentence [6]
G after sentence [8]
H after sentence [11]
I after sentence [13]

3 Which word or phrase should replace "helping her" in sentence [8] to make the wording more specific?

A assisting her
B working for her
C doing jobs for her
D babysitting for her

Giving an Oral Response to Literature

Speak with a Purpose

Present your response to literature as a speech. Practice the speech, and then present it to your class.

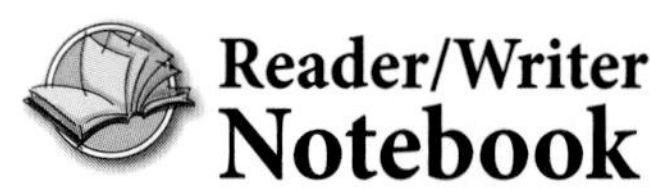

Reader/Writer Notebook

Use your **RWN** to complete the activities for this workshop.

Think as a Reader/Writer You believe that your thesis is solid and that you have supported it well in your written response to literature. Can you make it equally clear to a listening audience that your ideas are valid? To be an effective speaker, you will probably need to adapt your written response to literature instead of just reading it aloud. Listeners cannot re-read spoken words as they can written words. Therefore, it is especially important that you present the key points of your response clearly so your audience can follow and understand them.

Adapt Your Essay

Read with New Eyes

The first step in organizing an oral response to literature is to find the most important points in your written response. Read over your essay. As you read, highlight the most important ideas in every paragraph. Remember to include enough **evidence** to support each main idea. Then, using a note card for each paragraph in your essay, write the points you will include in your speech.

Once you have your ideas on the note cards, you can organize them in a logical order. Remember that **order of importance** works well. In this type of organization, you either start or end with the most important idea. Also remember that you should begin and end your speech with a clear statement of your **thesis.**

Consider Audience and Purpose

Since the occasion, or the situation that prompts you to speak, is a class assignment, your **audience** will be your teacher and classmates. They are probably familiar with the literary work that is the subject of your speech, so that is helpful. You will not have to provide much **background information** to make sure they know the basics.

Remember that the **purpose** of your speech is to share information (your response to the literary work) and to persuade the audience that your **thesis** is valid. Remembering your purpose will help you maintain the right **tone** and include the right information.

Sunshine State Standards: Benchmarks LA.6.5.2.2 deliver narrative and informative presentations, including oral responses to literature, and adjust oral language, body language, eye contact, gestures, technology and supporting graphics appropriate to the situation.

Deliver Your Oral Response

Use Nonverbal Elements

To become a good public speaker, you must use more than just words. **Nonverbal** communication, or body language, adds to your message. Here are some ways to include nonverbal elements in your oral response:

Eye Contact Look audience members in the eyes to keep their attention.

Facial Expression Smile, frown, or raise an eyebrow to show your feelings or to emphasize parts of your message.

Gestures Give a thumbs up, shrug, nod, or shake your head to emphasize a point or to add meaning to your speech.

Use Verbal Elements

How you use your voice can also affect the message you send. Consider these **verbal elements** as you practice and deliver your speech.

Feeling Don't speak in a **monotone**, a dull voice with no change in expression. Instead, show enthusiasm through your voice so your audience will become enthusiastic about your response.

Pitch Your voice rises and falls naturally when you speak. If you are nervous, your voice may get higher. Control your pitch by taking deep breaths. Stay calm as you give your speech. Grab the audience's attention by using the pitch of your voice to emphasize key points.

Rate In conversations you may speak at a fast rate, or speed. When you deliver a speech, speak more slowly to help listeners understand you. Pause now and then so that important points can sink in.

Tone Strive to maintain a reasonable and informed tone. You should sound as if you know what you're talking about. That will go a long way toward supporting your point of view about the story.

Volume Even if you normally speak quietly, you will need to speak loudly when giving your oral response. You shouldn't yell, but the listeners at the back of the room should be able to hear you clearly.

Take Note

On your note cards, you can write cues about the verbal and the nonverbal elements you plan to use in presenting your main ideas.

A Good Oral Response to Literature

- includes a clear thesis statement
- provides background information
- provides a variety of evidence to support the thesis
- uses convincing nonverbal support
- ends by restating the thesis

Make sure the nonverbal elements you use make sense with the verbal elements you use. For example, if you are explaining how a character is always doing something crazy or unexpected in a story, you might raise your eyebrows or shake your head (nonverbal element) and speak with humor in your voice (verbal element) at the same time.

Learn It Online
Find out how you can get and keep your audience's attention. Visit *MediaScope* at:

go.hrw.com L6-445 

Standards Review Literary Text

Theme **Directions:** Read this story and respond to the questions that follow.

A vat is a very large container. Milk vats are often filled with milk that has just come from the cow, so the milk contains a lot of fat. When milk is churned, the fat turns to butter. This story was told to the writer Claude Brown by a teacher who was trying to encourage him to stay out of trouble.

Two Frogs and the Milk Vat

by **Claude Brown**

There were two frogs sitting on a milk vat one time. The frogs fell into the milk vat. It was very deep. They kept swimming and swimming around, and they couldn't get out. They couldn't climb out because they were too far down. One frog said, "Oh, I can't make it, and I'm going to give up."

And the other frog kept swimming and swimming. His arms became more and more tired, and it was harder and harder and harder for him to swim. Then he couldn't do another stroke. He couldn't throw one more arm into the milk. He kept trying and trying; it seemed as if the milk was getting hard and heavy. He kept trying; he knows that he's going to die, but as long as he's got this little bit of life in him, he's going to keep on swimming. On his last stroke, it seemed as though he had to pull a whole ocean back, but he did it and found himself sitting on top of a vat of butter.

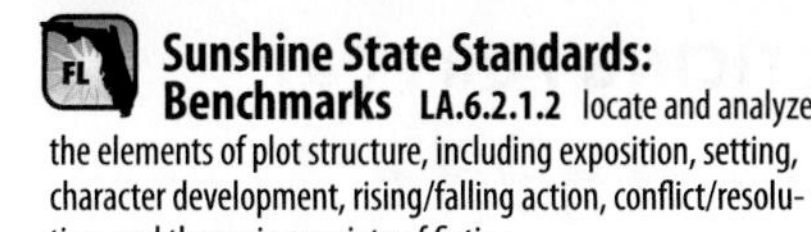

Sunshine State Standards: Benchmarks LA.6.2.1.2 locate and analyze the elements of plot structure, including exposition, setting, character development, rising/falling action, conflict/resolution, and theme in a variety of fiction.

1. Where is this brief story set?
   - **A** on a lily pad
   - **B** in a milk vat
   - **C** underneath a staircase
   - **D** in the distant future

2. Why does the first frog decide to stop swimming?
   - **F** He does not want to get into trouble.
   - **G** The other frog told him to.
   - **H** He does not like to swim.
   - **I** He thinks it is impossible to survive.

3. Which word BEST describes the frog that keeps swimming?
   - **A** determined
   - **B** tricky
   - **C** humorous
   - **D** cowardly

4. Which sentence states this story's theme?
   - **F** Two frogs fall into a vat of milk and live happily ever after.
   - **G** Two frogs cannot figure out how to get out of a vat of milk.
   - **H** One frog gives up, but the other one keeps trying to get out of the vat.
   - **I** Even when things seem hopeless, if you keep trying, you can triumph.

5. Which statement about the second frog is MOST helpful in understanding the story's theme?
   - **A** He was a strong swimmer.
   - **B** He never stopped trying.
   - **C** He got very tired.
   - **D** He did not try to help the first frog.

Extended Response

6. Explain whether knowing why the teacher told this story to Claude Brown helps you determine the story's theme. Support your answer with details from the story.

READ THINK EXPLAIN

Standards Review Informational Text

Following Instructions

Directions: Read the following application form. Then, read and respond to the questions that follow.

Natural History Museum Volunteer Application

1. Name: ____________________

Address: ____________________ City, State, Zip code: ____________________

Home telephone: ____________________ E-mail: ____________________

Social Security number: ____________________ Age: ☐ Under 18 ☐ Over 18

2. Education School most recently attended: ____________________

3. Employment If a résumé is available, please submit it along with your application. (Please check *Past* or *Present*.)

☐ Past ☐ Present Volunteer work: ____________________

Special skills or training: ____________________

Computer skills: ____________________

Fluency in other languages (please specify): ____________________

4. Is there a specific department or program at the museum in which you would like to work if a volunteer job is available? ____________________

5. Availability Please check the times you are available to volunteer.

	Mon.	Tues.	Wed.	Thurs.	Fri.	Sat.	Sun.
9:00 A.M.–1:00 P.M.							
1:00 P.M.–5:00 P.M.							
5:00 P.M.–8:30 P.M.	■	■	■	■			■

When can you start? ____________________

A minimum commitment of one year is required. Can you meet this requirement? ☐ Yes ☐ No

I HAVE READ AND AM IN POSSESSION OF A COPY OF THE "VOLUNTEER REGULATIONS AND PROCEDURES."

Signature: ____________________ Date: ____________________

Sunshine State Standards: Benchmarks **LA.6.2.2.2** use information from the text to answer questions related to the main idea or relevant details, maintaining chronological or logical order; **LA.6.2.2.4** identify the characteristics of a variety of types of nonfiction text (e.g., reference works, newspapers, biographies, procedures, instructions, practical/functional texts).

1 In what section should you indicate that you speak more than one language?

A 1
B 2
C 3
D 4

2 What is the purpose of section 5?

F to find out what hours you're available to work
G to find out what work experience you have
H to find out where you currently live
I to find out your educational background

3 For what department is the museum accepting volunteers?

A tours
B research
C sales
D the application doesn't say

4 Which statement belongs in section 4?

F I can design Web sites.
G I've always been interested in dinosaurs.
H I can start work immediately.
I I am a skilled scuba diver.

5 For how long must you agree to work if you are accepted to be a volunteer?

A six months
B one year
C two years
D three months

Extended Response

6 Explain the purpose of section 3. Support your answer with details from the application.

Sunshine State Standards: Benchmarks LA.6.1.6.9 determine the correct meaning of words with multiple meanings in context.

Standards Review Vocabulary

Multiple-Meaning Words

Directions: The sentences in quotation marks are from the story "Ta-Na-E-Ka." Read each sentence. Then, choose the answer in which the italicized word is used in the same way.

Practicing For FCAT

1. Read the sentence from the story "Ta-Na-E-Ka".

   As my birthday drew closer, I had awful nightmares about it.

   Which sentence uses the word *drew* in the same way?

   A My grandfather drew the blinds to stop the afternoon sun from beating through the window.

   B The year drew to a close with the usual shouts and hugs at midnight.

   C In art class I drew self-portraits using only pen and ink.

   D I reached into the can and drew the name of the raffle winner.

2. Read the sentence from the story "Ta-Na-E-Ka".

   I was reaching the age at which all Kaw Indians had to participate in Ta-Na-E-Ka.

   Which sentence uses the word *age* in the same way?

   F A person's age does not have to be filled in on the entry form.

   G Sometimes my mom says that we age her every time we do something risky.

   H My grandparents say that stress makes us age sooner.

   I My uncle taught me to age avocados more quickly by putting them in a brown paper sack.

3. Read the sentence from the story "Ta-Na-E-Ka".

   Many of the younger families on the reservation were beginning to give up the old customs.

   Which sentence uses the word *reservation* in the same way?

   A I accept your offer to help with my chores without reservation.

   B We made a reservation at the restaurant so we would be sure to get a table.

   C He grew up on a Hopi reservation in Arizona.

   D My aunt is a reservation agent for a major airline.

Academic Vocabulary

Directions: Choose the lettered sentence in which the word in italics is used in the same way as it is used in sentence 4.

4. Read the sentence.

   Please illustrate your point so I can understand it.

   Which sentence uses the word *illustrate* in the same way?

   F Please illustrate the poem with a sketch.

   G He wants to illustrate books for a living.

   H You might want to use some examples to illustrate your idea.

   I The story would be more appealing if it had drawings to illustrate it.

Standards Review Writing

Sunshine State Standards: Benchmarks **LA.6.2.2.2** use information from the text to answer questions related to the main idea or relevant details, maintaining chronological or logical order; *Also covered* **LA.6.3.3.2**

Expository Essay

Directions: Read the following paragraph from an essay that discusses the ways an author makes her main character compelling and believable. Then, answer each question that follows.

[1] In Cynthia Rylant's short story "Boar Out There," she uses her main character, Jenny, to help readers see how the power of sympathy and understanding can overcome fear. [2] In the story the character Jenny shows these emotions in a very believable way. [3] Jenny is a pretty average girl in terms of looks and intelligence. [4] When she hears the boar rushing toward her, Jenny is truly afraid. [5] She forgets to breathe, she chokes and coughs, and she even cries. [6] However, she is brave enough to fight her fear. [7] In fact, she seems to want to test her courage. [8] She does not run or scream. [9] Instead, she stands silently, looking at the boar's scars and "ragged ears, caked with blood." [10] All at once, Jenny is not afraid. [11] Her fear is replaced with sympathy when she realizes that the boar is afraid and alone. [12] Jenny's emotions are unfolded clearly through this sequence of events. [13] Through the use of details and descriptive language, Rylant makes sure readers know how Jenny feels and can relate to those feelings.

1. Which sentence contains the thesis, or main idea, of the essay?
   - **A** sentence 1
   - **B** sentence 3
   - **C** sentence 4
   - **D** sentence 7

2. Which sentence contains direct evidence in the form of a quotation from the short story?
   - **F** sentence 5
   - **G** sentence 9
   - **H** sentence 11
   - **I** sentence 13

3. Which sentence does NOT contain a transitional word or phrase?
   - **A** sentence 2
   - **B** sentence 6
   - **C** sentence 9
   - **D** sentence 10

4. If you were revising this paragraph, which sentence would you delete because it does NOT provide evidence to support the thesis?
   - **F** sentence 3
   - **G** sentence 6
   - **H** sentence 7
   - **I** sentence 10

Read On For Independent Reading

Fiction

The Heart of a Chief

By mixing dialogue and first-person narration, the award-winning author Joseph Bruchac presents the compelling story of an eleven-year-old Pennacock boy, Chris Nicola, in *The Heart of a Chief*. You'll come to understand his harsh life on a reservation and the trials he goes through at his school and in his community. Despite the conditions Chris must deal with, his inner qualities and family traditions help him to recognize his potential.

Bat 6

A fifty-year-old tradition of softball rivalry between sixth-graders from two different towns stands on the edge of disaster. It is 1949, and the shadow of World War II still looms over this year's game. The conflict between two girls from completely different backgrounds explodes in Virginia Euwer Wolff's *Bat 6* as the novel takes a brave look at prejudice, responsibility, and growing up.

The Pigman

In Paul Zindel's novel *The Pigman*, John and Lorraine befriend Mr. Pignati, a lonely widower with a weakness for bad jokes and miniature pigs. He also has a passion for life. This unlikely hero becomes a model of joy, freedom, and courage for John and Lorraine. Read along with these three characters and find yourself learning from their situations.

A Dog's Life: Autobiography of a Stray

Have you ever wondered what a dog is thinking? This diary by a dog named Squirrel lets you in on her puppyhood, from life with her mother and brother in a warm and secure shed to her later life without her family or home. She tells you of her brutal life as a stray, with its constant and dangerous hunt for food and shelter. "Translated" by the well-loved author Ann Martin, *A Dog's Life: Autobiography of a Stray* will change how you think and feel about lost and abandoned dogs.

Sunshine State Standards: Benchmarks **LA.6.2.1.10** use interest and recommendation of others to select a balance of age and ability appropriate fiction materials to read (e.g., novels, historical fiction, mythology, poetry) to expand the core foundation of knowledge necessary to function as a fully literate member of a shared culture; *Also covered* **LA.6.2.2.5**

Nonfiction

Heroic Stories

Anthony Masters looks at the lives of twenty-four exceptional people in *Heroic Stories.* Some are people you've heard of, like Martin Luther King, Jr., and Anne Frank. Others, though, are lesser known people, like Christy Brown, who succeeded despite a devastating lifelong disability, and Pauline Cutting, who worked tirelessly under the conditions of war in Beirut's hospitals. Read *Heroic Stories* to learn more about these people and twenty others who have lived heroic lives.

Endangered Bats

The bat is a misunderstood little mammal. Around the world, humans disturb bat colonies when they enter caves or other places where bats roost. People make up terrifying stories about bats, and some even attempt to exterminate them. *Endangered Bats* gives you a close-up view of these magnificent animals and teaches you about how they live so you will understand why bats should be protected. Perhaps you'll be inspired to build a bat house to protect the bats, the world's only flying mammals.

Pompeii: City of Ashes

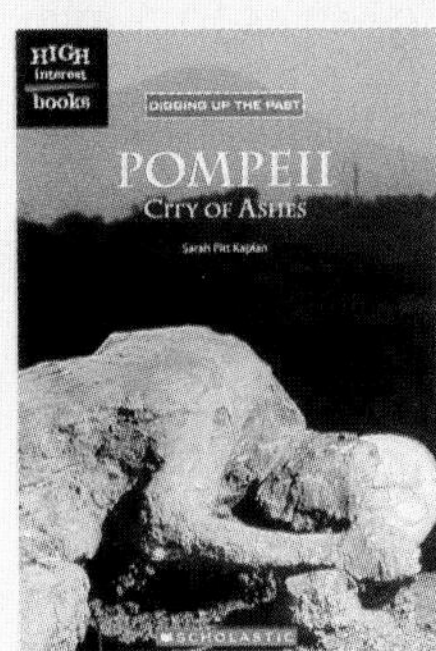

Read along with Sarah Pitt Kaplan as she describes the destruction of Pompeii in A.D. 79 by an eruption of Mount Vesuvius. Then learn how the rediscovery and excavation of this buried city have helped us unlock the mysteries of ancient Roman life. Filled with illustrations, photos, and maps, *Pompeii: City of Ashes* gives you a clear look at the past and present of the lost city.

Orphan Train Rider

Many children were sent west to new families during the late 1800s and early 1900s. Lee Nailling was one such child. Author Andrea Warren recounts Nailling's experiences and eventual happiness in *Orphan Train Rider*. She also presents the history of those train rides and describes the difficulties the children often faced with their new families.

Learn It Online

Find tips for choosing, reading, and studying works with *NovelWise* at:

go.hrw.com L6-453

UNIT 2

Nonfiction
Writers on Writing

Russell Freedman on Nonfiction

Russell Freedman grew up in San Francisco and began his writing career as a reporter. He has gone on to write more than forty nonfiction books for young adults, including award-winning biographies of Abraham Lincoln and Eleanor Roosevelt.

"I still own a copy of a book my father gave me many years ago. That book was packed with incredible tales of great men and women, of battles fought, daring adventures, and heroic deeds. But the best thing—the very best thing—was that every

story in that book was true. *The Story of Mankind* by Hendrik van Loon was a history book! It was a book of nonfiction. Yet I read it not to fulfill a school assignment, not to write a report, but because I was swept along by the stories it told. I read it for the thrill of discovery.History, according to van Loon, wasn't just a bunch of facts and dates. It was the exciting stories of real people leading meaningful lives.

A book of history or biography is like a magic carpet to another time and place. These nonfiction books allow us to glimpse worlds different from our own, yet much the same. They help us recognize the humanity we share with all those who have come before. You might say that history is the story of our parents, our grandparents, and our ancestors going all the way back in time. In that sense, history is the story of ourselves.

If you could stand at one end of a city block and hold the hand of someone from the previous generation, who in turn is holding the hand of someone from the generation before that, and so on, Alexander the Great might be standing at the end of the block. You could yell to him down there: 'Hey, Al! I've been meaning to ask you, how did you manage to win so many battles? How does it feel to conquer the world?'

That's what historians do—ask questions. Doing research is a lot like being a snooping detective who follows one clue after another. You find those clues by reading books and articles about your subject, by going to museums, by interviewing people, and by visiting the places where the events you're writing about took place. I'll never forget walking into the boardinghouse across the street from Ford's Theater in Washington, D.C., and seeing the bed in which Abraham Lincoln died. They had to lay him out diagonally across the corn-husk mattress, which wasn't long enough for his six-foot, four-inch frame.

Several years ago, I won the Newbery Medal for my biography of Lincoln. One of the first things I did was to take my copy of *The Story of Mankind* down from the shelf. It so happens that *The Story of Mankind* was the very first book to win the Newbery when the award was introduced way back in 1922. As I thumbed through the pages, I remembered my excitement while reading that treasured book so long ago. I felt thrilled and honored to be in such great company."

Think as a Writer

Russell Freedman is known for writing biographies of people who made a difference in history. If you were going to write a biography of someone from the past, who would it be? Why?

COLLECTION 5

Elements of Nonfiction

INFORMATIONAL TEXT FOCUS

Connecting Main Ideas Across Texts

"The biggest adventure you can ever take is to live the life of your dreams."

—Oprah Winfrey

What Do You Think

In what ways is life an adventure? How can you make your dreams come true in life?

Walking to the Sky by Jonathan Borofsky.

Learn It Online

Explore more nonfiction with the interactive Reading Workshops online:

go.hrw.com L6-457 

Literary Focus

by **Linda Rief**

What Are the Elements of Nonfiction?

It might seem as if true stories—nonfiction—would be easy to tell, but because they are true it takes skill to make them interesting. Will I tell my story or someone else's? What did I (or my subject) see? hear? think? feel? Nonfiction authors make decisions like these—and make the ordinary seem extraordinary.

Types of Nonfiction

Nonfiction is just what it sounds like—"not fiction." It is writing based on fact, not imagination. Nonfiction deals with real people, events, and places, not the mostly made-up characters, plots, and settings of fictional stories. The subjects of nonfiction are as varied as the world itself. The chart below lists the characteristics of some common types of nonfiction. Two popular types that you will read in this collection are **biography** and **autobiography.**

Nonfiction	Characteristics
Autobiography	Informs about a person's own life
Biography	Informs about another person's life
Reference materials	Present factual information on specific subjects
Newspaper articles	Inform, explain, or persuade (through editorials) about current events
Magazine articles	Inform, explain, or entertain on a variety of subjects
Instructional materials	Explain procedures or provide how-to information

Autobiography

The most personal kind of nonfiction writing is **autobiography**—a writer's account of his or her own life. The word *autobiography* is made up of three parts that explain its meaning. The prefix *auto–* means "self," the root word *–bio–* means "life," and the suffix *–graphy* means "writing."

First-Person Narration Since the narrator is telling his or her own story, an autobiography is written from the **first-person point of view.** That means the writer uses first-person pronouns—*I, me, we, us, our, my, mine*. You learn the writer's thoughts and feelings because the writer can directly tell you what is going on inside his or her own head and heart. Here is an example of the first-person point of view in an autobiography:

> Bailey was the greatest person in my world. And the fact that he was my brother, my only brother, and I had no sisters to share him with, was such good fortune that it made me want to live a Christian life just to show God that I was grateful.
>
> from "Brother" by Maya Angelou

practical/functional texts).

FL
Sunshine State Standards:
Benchmarks LA.6.2.2.4 identify the characteristics of a variety of types of nonfiction text (e.g., reference works, newspapers, biographies, procedures, instructions,

Biography

A **biography** is a person's life story written by another person. Biographers spend a lot of time—sometimes many years—finding out as much as they can about their subject. They read firsthand accounts, such as interviews, letters, and diaries, as well as secondhand accounts, like newspaper and magazine articles. If a biographer is writing about a person who lived long ago, he or she reads historical accounts of the time in order to understand the world in which the subject lived.

Third-Person Narration Biographers do not write as "I" because they are not the subject of the life story. Instead, they write about their subject from the **third-person point of view,** using third-person pronouns like *his, her, their, he, she, they,* and *them*. Below is an example from a biography of Harriet Tubman that you will read. Compare it to the excerpt you just read by Maya Angelou.

> When Harriet heard of the sale of her sisters, she knew that the time had finally come when she must leave the plantation.
>
> from "A Glory over Everything"
> by Ann Petry

What a writer chooses to leave out of a biography is as important as what he or she puts in it. No book is large enough to tell everything about a person's life. The biographer chooses events that reveal something important about the person. When you read a biography, think about the specific details that are included and what they tell you about the subject.

Shifting Points of View

In both autobiographies and biographies, writers may sometimes change the point of view from which they record events. Here, the writer of the autobiography *The Land I Lost* describes his own life, using the **first-person point of view:**

> I was born on the central highlands of Vietnam in a small hamlet on a riverbank that had a deep jungle on one side and a chain of high mountains on the other.
>
> from *The Land I Lost*
> by Huynh Quang Nhuong

In the same autobiography, the author decides to tell a story he heard about a young couple, so he switches to the **third-person point of view:**

> Trung was happiest when Lan was helping his mother. They did not talk to each other but they could look at each other when his mother was busy with her work.
>
> from *The Land I Lost*
> by Huynh Quang Nhuong

Your Turn Analyze Elements of Nonfiction

1. Explain the difference between an autobiography and a biography.
2. Write a short first-person account of an important event from your life. Then, write a third-person account of the same event.

Learn It Online
For more on this lesson, see PowerNotes:
go.hrw.com
L6-459
Go

Analyzing Visuals

How Can a Visual Image Suggest Point of View?

All images have a *visual* point of view. Photographers, for instance, photograph a subject from a certain angle and distance when they could have framed their shot differently. Often, pictures that tell a story also suggest a *literary* point of view. The photographer either is close to the action and seemingly involved in it or is more distant. Also—much like the narrator of an autobiography or biography—a photographer chooses which details are most important to him or her and "composes" the picture accordingly.

Analyzing Point of View in a Photograph

Use these guidelines to help you analyze point of view in a photograph.

1. Identify the subject of the photograph. If a scene is pictured, what's happening in it?
2. Is the subject distant from the photographer, or is the image a close-up? If there are people in the picture, do they seem aware of the photographer's presence?
3. How would the "story" of the photograph be different if the picture were taken from another location?

Look at the details of the photograph below to help you answer the questions on page 461.

Sunshine State Standards: Benchmarks **LA.6.1.7.2** analyze the author's purpose (e.g., to persuade, inform, entertain, or explain) and perspective in a variety of texts and understand how they affect meaning; **LA.6.4.1.1** write narrative accounts with an engaging plot (including rising action, conflict, climax, falling action, and resolution) include a clearly described setting with figurative language and descriptive words or phrases to enhance style and tone.

McLean, Virginia, December 1978 by Joel Sternfeld.

Courtesy of the artist and Luhring Augustine, New York.

1. What two things are happening in this photograph? Which is more dramatic, or exciting?

2. What is the photographer's **point of view** in relation to the drama? Did he take the picture from near or far? What does this tell you?

3. Why is the scene in the foreground (the closer scene) included? What does it contribute to the story of this photograph?

Your Turn Write About Point of View

Write a brief narrative about the photograph above. What is happening in the image? What happened just before this moment was captured, and what happened after? Before you begin writing, decide whether you'll tell the story from the first-person point of view, like an autobiography, or the third-person point of view, like a biography.

Reading Focus

by **Kylene Beers**

What Skills Help You Read Nonfiction?

You're standing in a hallway of your school and you overhear some classmates talking about you. You probably want to know *what* they're saying about you—the main idea of the conversation. You might also want to know if what they're saying is true or just their opinion. You may also want to know *why* they're talking about you—their purpose. It's important to make similar determinations when you read nonfiction.

Main Idea

The topic and the main idea of a nonfiction text are not the same. The **topic** is what the text is all about: *movies*, for example. The **main idea** is the most important point the writer is making about that topic: *This year's top-grossing movies were all low-budget comedies*.

Finding the Main Idea In most texts, the main idea is not stated directly. You have to infer it, or figure it out from clues. This chart shows you the key steps to follow when you want to find the main idea:

1. Identify the topic.
Tip: The topic can usually be stated in one or two words. Sometimes it's in the title.
2. Look for important details.
Tip: Keep the topic in mind. What are the most important details the writer gives you about the topic?
3. Write a statement that expresses the main idea.
Tip: Ask yourself, "What is the writer saying about the topic?" Try to write the answer in one sentence.

More Than One Main Idea There will often be more than one main idea in a nonfiction text. It takes practice to uncover all the main ideas. As you read, use a chart to organize your thinking about possible main ideas. Here is a chart you might develop for a nonfiction selection about a person's relationship with an animal:

Possible Main Ideas	
Main Idea 1 Humans and animals have a special bond.	**Main Idea 2** There are many things about animals that humans can't explain.
Main Idea 3 Animals may understand humans better than humans understand animals.	**Main Idea 4** Humans can learn from their animal friends.

Comparing Selections for Main Idea When you read two or more selections about the same topic, you can compare the main ideas to see how they're connected and how they are different. Collecting main ideas for each selection in a chart like the one above can help you with your comparisons.

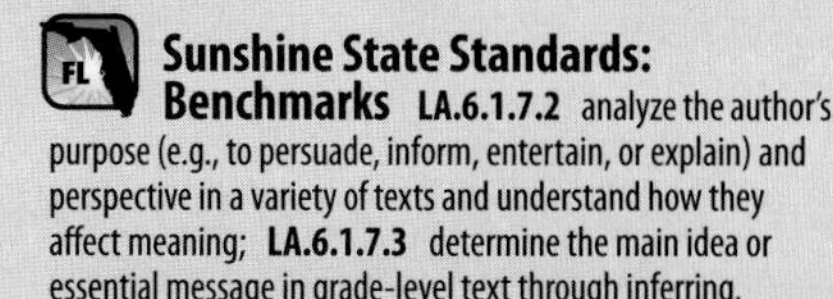

Sunshine State Standards: Benchmarks **LA.6.1.7.2** analyze the author's purpose (e.g., to persuade, inform, entertain, or explain) and perspective in a variety of texts and understand how they affect meaning; **LA.6.1.7.3** determine the main idea or essential message in grade-level text through inferring, paraphrasing, summarizing, and identifying relevant details.

Facts and Opinions

Nonfiction is based on **facts**—information that can be proved true. However, even fact-filled nonfiction may contain a writer's **opinions,** or personal beliefs, feelings, and attitudes. When you read nonfiction, it is important to be able to tell facts from opinions. Compare these statements about Maya Angelou's brother, Bailey, from her autobiography *I Know Why the Caged Bird Sings*.

Term	Definition	Example
Fact	Information that can be proved true	*Bailey is the author's only brother.*
Opinion	A personal belief or attitude	*Bailey is the greatest brother in the world.*

As a reader, you need to watch for opinions stated as facts. Always ask yourself, "Can this statement be proved true?" Look for words that signal opinions, such as these: *believe, seem, may, think, probably, possibly*. Also look for strongly emotional language, like *greatest*, *best*, *finest*, and *worst*.

Supported and Unsupported Opinions In nonfiction writing, some opinions are supported by facts, while others are not. When you identify opinions in a nonfiction text, ask yourself whether the facts in the text support them. Determining whether opinions are supported is especially important when you are deciding whether to agree or disagree with a writer's position on something. You want to identify examples of **bias**—personal ideas and values the writer holds that may lead to conclusions the text does not support. Always suspect bias when you see that only one side of an issue is being addressed.

Author's Purpose

There are many different reasons, or **purposes,** why an author might write nonfiction. The following are common examples of **author's purpose:**

- to inform
- to persuade
- to express feelings
- to entertain

An author may have several purposes for writing, but one usually stands out as the most important. The author's purpose helps determine why and how you read a text. For example, if an author writes a text mainly to share facts and information, you'll need to read slowly and carefully. If an author's purpose is mainly to entertain, you can read the text at whatever pace you like.

Your Turn Apply Reading Skills

1. Write an explanation for how to find the main idea in a nonfiction selection.
2. What would you expect the author's purpose to be for writing an autobiography? a biography? Explain.
3. Write one fact and one opinion about a subject of your choice, such as a sport you enjoy.

Now go to the Skills in Action: Reading Model

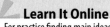

Learn It Online
For practice finding main ideas, visit the interactive Reading Workshops at:

go.hrw.com L6-463 

SKILLS IN ACTION

Reading Model

AUTOBIOGRAPHY

Read with a Purpose Read this true story to see how one piece of ugly clothing affected a famous writer's youth.

by **Gary Soto**

Literary Focus

Autobiography An **autobiography** is a writer's account of his or her own life. You can tell that this is an autobiography, rather than a biography, because Soto is discussing *his* experiences.

Literary Focus

Point of View Autobiographies are written from the first-person point of view. Notice how Soto narrates his story with pronouns like *I*, *me*, and *my*.

My clothes have failed me. I remember the green coat that I wore in fifth and sixth grades, when you either danced like a champ or pressed yourself against a greasy wall, bitter as a penny toward the happy couples.

When I needed a new jacket and my mother asked what kind I wanted, I described something like bikers wear: black leather and silver studs with enough belts to hold down a small town. We were in the kitchen, steam on the windows from her cooking. She listened so long while stirring dinner that I thought she understood for sure the kind I wanted. The next day when I got home from school, I discovered draped on my bedpost a jacket the color of day-old guacamole.[1] I threw my books on the bed and approached the jacket slowly, as if it were a stranger whose hand I had to shake. I touched the vinyl sleeve, the collar, and peeked at the mustard-colored lining.

From the kitchen Mother yelled that my jacket was in the closet. I closed the door to her voice and pulled at the rack of clothes in the closet, hoping the jacket on the bedpost wasn't for me but my mean brother. No luck. I gave up. From my bed, I stared at the jacket. I wanted to cry because it was so ugly and so big that I knew I'd have to wear it a long time. I was a small kid,

1. **guacamole** (gwah kuh MOH lay): a thick green spread made from avocados.

thin as a young tree, and it would be years before I'd have a new one. I stared at the jacket, like an enemy, thinking bad things before I took off my old jacket whose sleeves climbed halfway to my elbow.

I put the big jacket on. I zipped it up and down several times, and rolled the cuffs up so they didn't cover my hands. I put my hands in the pockets and flapped the jacket like a bird's wings. I stood in front of the mirror, full face, then profile, and then looked over my shoulder as if someone had called me. I sat on the bed, stood against the bed, and combed my hair to see what I would look like doing something natural. I looked ugly. I threw it on my brother's bed and looked at it for a long time before I slipped it on and went out to the backyard, smiling a "thank you" to my mom as I passed her in the kitchen. With my hands in my pockets I kicked a ball against the fence, and then climbed it to sit looking into the alley. I hurled orange peels at the mouth of an open garbage can, and when the peels were gone, I watched the white puffs of my breath thin to nothing.

I jumped down, hands in my pockets, and in the backyard on my knees I teased my dog, Brownie, by swooping my arms while making bird calls. He jumped at me and missed. He jumped again and again, until a tooth sunk deep, ripping an L-shaped tear on my left sleeve. I pushed Brownie away to study the tear as I would a cut on my arm. There was no blood, only a few loose pieces of fuzz. Darn dog, I thought, and pushed him away hard when he tried to bite again. I got up from my knees and went to my bedroom to sit with my jacket on my lap, with the lights out.

That was the first afternoon with my new jacket. The next day I wore it to fifth grade and got a *D* on a math quiz. During the morning recess, Frankie T., the playground terrorist, pushed me to the

Reading Focus

Main Idea The topic of this autobiography is the narrator's jacket. To find the main idea, look for important details about what the narrator once thought about the jacket—and about himself.

ground and told me to stay there until recess was over. My best friend, Steve Negrete, ate an apple while looking at me, and the girls turned away to whisper on the monkey bars. The teachers were no help: they looked my way and talked about how foolish I looked in my new jacket. I saw their heads bob with laughter, their hands half covering their mouths.

Even though it was cold, I took off the jacket during lunch and played kickball in a thin shirt, my arms feeling like Braille from goose bumps. But when I returned to class, I slipped the jacket on and shivered until I was warm. I sat on my hands, heating them up, while my teeth chattered like a cup of crooked dice. Finally warm, I slid out of the jacket but a few minutes later put it back on when the fire bell rang. We paraded out into the yard where we, the fifth-graders, walked past all the other grades to stand against the back fence. Everybody saw me. Although they didn't say out loud, "Man, that's ugly," I heard the buzz-buzz of gossip and even laughter that I knew was meant for me.

And so I went, in my guacamole jacket. So embarrassed, so hurt, I couldn't even do my homework. I received *C*'s on quizzes, and forgot the state capitals and the rivers of South America, our friendly neighbor. Even the girls who had been friendly blew away like loose flowers to follow the boys in neat jackets.

I wore that thing for three years until the sleeves grew short and my forearms stuck out like the necks of turtles. All during that time no love came to me—no little dark girl in a Sunday dress she wore on Monday. At lunchtime I stayed with the ugly boys who leaned against the chain-link fence and looked around with propellers of grass spinning in our mouths. We saw girls walk by alone, saw couples, hand in hand, their heads like bookends pressing air together. We saw them and spun our propellers so fast our faces were blurs.

I blame that jacket for those bad years. I blame my mother for her bad taste and her cheap ways. It was a sad time for the heart. With a friend I spent my sixth-grade year in a tree in the alley, waiting for something good to happen to me in that jacket, which had become the ugly brother who tagged along wherever I went. And it was about that time that I began to grow. My

Reading Focus

Fact and Opinion Be aware that some information presented as fact may not be factual. The narrator says that the teachers were laughing at his jacket, but that is his interpretation. It is unlikely that they were actually doing so.

Reading Focus

Author's Purpose Writers of nonfiction write with a purpose. This writer's main purpose is to express feelings he had as a child. As you continue reading, keep in mind other purposes he may have.

Reading Focus

Fact and Opinion "The Jacket" contains many opinions, beginning with what the narrator thinks about his new jacket. Here, he states his opinions about this time in his life and his mother's taste.

chest puffed up with muscle and, strangely, a few more ribs. Even my hands, those fleshy hammers, showed bravely through the cuffs, the fingers already hardening for the coming fights. But that L-shaped rip on the left sleeve got bigger; bits of stuffing coughed out from its wound after a hard day of play. I finally Scotch-taped it closed, but in rain or cold weather the tape peeled off like a scab and more stuffing fell out until that sleeve shriveled into a palsied arm.[2] That winter the elbows began to crack and whole chunks of green began to fall off. I showed the cracks to my mother, who always seemed to be at the stove with steamed-up glasses, and she said that there were children in Mexico who would love that jacket. I told her that this was America and yelled that Debbie, my sister, didn't have a jacket like mine. I ran outside, ready to cry, and climbed the tree by the alley to think bad thoughts and watch my breath puff white and disappear.

Analyzing Visuals **Viewing and Interpreting** From whose point of view in "The Jacket" might this image be seen? Explain.

Literary Focus

Autobiography Throughout "The Jacket," Soto openly shares the private thoughts and emotions of his childhood. Autobiographical writing is often very personal and revealing.

But whole pieces still casually flew off my jacket when I played hard, read quietly, or took vicious spelling tests at school. When it became so spotted that my brother began to call me "camouflage," I flung it over the fence into the alley. Later, however, I swiped the jacket off the ground and went inside to drape it across my lap and mope.

I was called to dinner: Steam silvered my mother's glasses as she said grace; my brother and sister, with their heads bowed,

---

2. **palsied** (PAWL zeed) **arm:** Palsy is a condition that leaves muscles weak. A palsied arm would look limp and thinner than a healthy arm.

made ugly faces at their glasses of powdered milk. I gagged too, but eagerly ate big rips of buttered tortilla that held scooped up beans. Finished, I went outside with my jacket across my arm. It was a cold sky. The faces of clouds were piled up, hurting. I climbed the fence, jumping down with a grunt. I started up the alley and soon slipped into my jacket, that green ugly brother who breathed over my shoulder that day and ever since.

Reading Focus

Main Idea Pay special attention to the last paragraph for clues to the main idea. From this ending, you can infer that the main idea relates not only to the jacket, but to the narrator himself and how he remembers his childhood.

Read with a Purpose How did the jacket affect the narrator in his youth? How might these years have been the same or different if he'd had a different jacket?

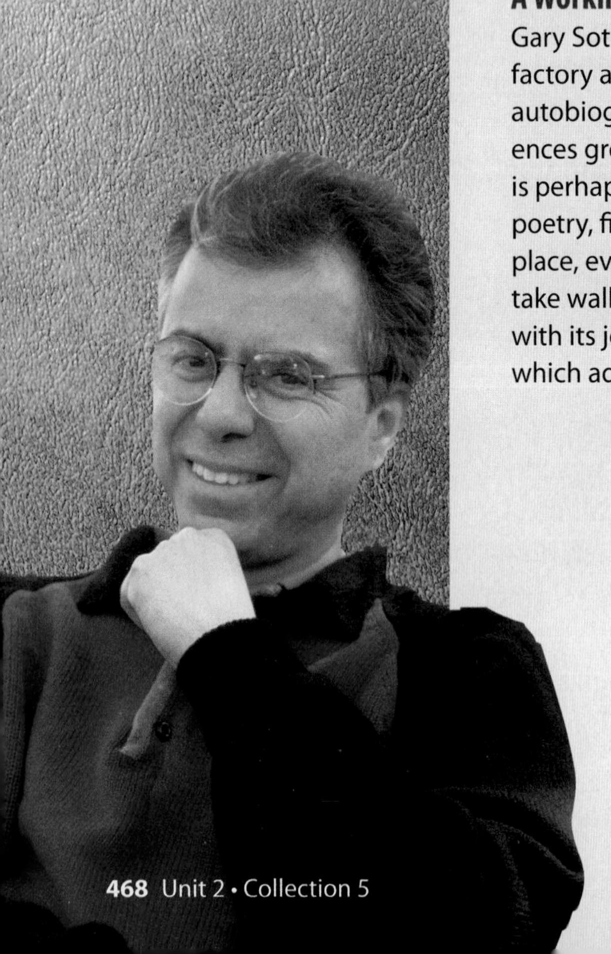

MEET THE WRITER

Gary Soto
(1952–)

A Working Life

Gary Soto was born in Fresno, California. His father worked at a raisin factory and his mother at a potato-processing plant. Soto has written autobiographical works—like "The Jacket"—that describe his experiences growing up in a working-class Mexican American family, but he is perhaps best known as a fiction writer and poet. Whether writing poetry, fiction, or nonfiction, Soto continues to celebrate "commonplace, everyday things," the joys and sorrows of average people who take walks, play games, experience love, and muddle through life with its joys and sorrows. His writing focuses on "the small moments which add up to a large moment—life itself."

"In short, not all my work is autobiographical, but it could be."

Think About the Writer What might Soto mean in saying that all of his work "could be" autobiographical?

SKILLS IN ACTION

Wrap Up

Sunshine State Standards: Benchmarks **LA.6.1.6.1** use new vocabulary that is introduced and taught directly; **LA.6.1.7.2** analyze the author's purpose (e.g., to persuade, inform, entertain, or explain) and perspective in a variety of texts and understand how they affect meaning; **LA.6.1.7.3** determine the main idea or essential message in grade-level text through inferring, paraphrasing, summarizing, and identifying relevant details; **LA.6.2.2.3** organize information to show understanding (e.g., representing main ideas within text through charting, mapping, paraphrasing, summarizing, or comparing/contrasting); **LA.6.2.2.4** identify the characteristics of a variety of types of nonfiction text (e.g., reference works, newspapers, biographies, procedures, instructions, practical/functional texts.

Into Action: Finding the Main Idea of an Autobiography

On a separate sheet of paper, complete this chart to identify the main idea of "The Jacket."

Step 1 Identify the topic of "The Jacket."	Topic: The narrator's jacket
Step 2 Look for important details. List details and make inferences about the topic to help you identify the most important message.	
Step 3 Write a one-sentence statement that answers "What about the topic?" and expresses the main idea.	

Talk About . . .

1. With a partner, discuss the author's purpose for writing "The Jacket" and the main idea he was expressing in the selection. Try to use each of the Academic Vocabulary words listed on the right at least once in your discussion.

Write About . . .

Answer the following questions about "The Jacket." For definitions of the underlined Academic Vocabulary words, see the column on the right.

2. What is the narrator's perspective on his jacket? (For example, is he critical, praising, indifferent, or something else?)
3. How is this autobiography distinct from a fictional story?
4. How does this autobiography contribute to your understanding of Gary Soto?

Writing Focus

Think as a Reader/Writer

In Collection 5, you'll read more nonfiction selections, both autobiographies and biographies. You'll learn more about how writers use point of view and other elements of nonfiction, and you'll write about and practice these methods yourself.

Academic Vocabulary for Collection 5

Talking and Writing About Nonfiction

Academic Vocabulary is the language you use to write and talk about literature. Use these words to discuss the nonfiction you read in this collection. The words are underlined throughout the collection.

contribute (kuhn TRIHB yoot) *v.:* give or add something, such as resources or ideas. *Writers contribute important ideas through their books.*

perspective (puhr SPEHK tihv) *n.:* mental view or outlook; way of thinking. *Biographies and autobiographies can change your perspective on people.*

distinct (dihs TIHNGKT) *adj.:* distinguishable; clearly different or of a different type. *Autobiographies are distinct from biographies.*

uniform (YOO nuh fawrm) *adj.:* having the same shape, size, quality, or other characteristics. *Biographies are uniform in certain characteristics, such as the third-person point of view.*

Your Turn

Copy the Academic Vocabulary words into your *Reader/Writer Notebook*. Think of an easy-to-remember synonym for each term, and write it next to the Academic Vocabulary word.

AUTOBIOGRAPHY

Preparing to Read

Brother

from *I Know Why the Caged Bird Sings*
by **Maya Angelou**

What Do You Think? How can the people closest to you inspire you to live life to the fullest?

QuickWrite
Which family member, or other person you are close to, do you look up to, and why? How does this person bring out the best in you?

Fruit Vendor II (1996)
by Hyacinth Manning.

Reader/Writer Notebook

Use your **RWN** to complete the activities for this selection.

Sunshine State Standards: Benchmarks **LA.6.1.6.4** categorize key vocabulary and identify salient features; **LA.6.2.1.3** locate and analyze the effects of sound, meter, figurative and descriptive language, graphics (illustrations), and structure (e.g., line length, fonts, word placement) to communicate mood and meaning; **LA.6.2.2.3** organize information to show understanding (e.g., representing main ideas within text through charting, mapping, paraphrasing, summarizing, or comparing/contrasting); **LA.6.2.2.4** identify the characteristics of a variety of types of nonfiction text (e.g., reference works, newspapers, biographies, procedures, instructions, practical/functional texts); **LA.6.3.2.3** analyzing language techniques of professional authors (e.g., point of view, establishing mood) to enhance the use of descriptive language and word choices.

Literary Focus

Autobiography / First-Person Point of View An **autobiography** is the true story of a person's life written by that person. Autobiographies are written from the **first-person point of view;** the writer tells his or her own story using pronouns like *I, we, me, us, mine,* and *our*. Reading an autobiography lets you see the world through another person's eyes and gain a different perspective.

Reading Focus

Distinguishing Fact from Opinion A **fact** is information that can be proved true with evidence: *I have only one brother*. An **opinion** is a personal belief: *I have the greatest brother in the world.* In "Brother," Maya Angelou presents a portrait of her brother, Bailey. Because she knew her brother personally, she is able to contribute many facts about him. Someone else who knew Bailey could confirm these facts. Angelou's account is also filled with her opinions. Others who knew Bailey might not share her opinions of him.

Into Action Be on the lookout for facts and opinions in "Brother." Keep track of facts and opinions in a chart like this one.

Fact	Opinion
Bailey was her only brother.	Bailey was "the greatest person in my world."
Bailey was small.	Bailey was "graceful and smooth."

Writing Focus

Think as a Reader/Writer

Find It in Your Reading Angelou uses many sensory details, such as "velvet-black skin," to make her brother come alive for the reader. As you read, use your *Reader/Writer Notebook* to record examples of her descriptive words and phrases.

Vocabulary

outrageous (owt RAY juhs) *adj.:* extreme; shocking. *Somehow, Bailey always got away with his outrageous actions.*

acquaintance (uh KWAYN tuhns) *n.:* friend; someone known casually. *Bailey described the way an acquaintance moved.*

precision (prih SIHZH uhn) *n.:* exactness; accuracy. *Bailey moved with precision.*

apt (apt) *adj.:* skilled; capable. *Among other skills, Bailey was apt at stealing pickles.*

sift (sihft) *v.:* strain or filter through something. *Bailey and his sister used a strainer to sift the flour.*

Language Coach

Word Families *Outrageous* is an adjective formed from *outrage*, a word that can be either a noun or a verb. (The noun *outrage* refers to a kind of extreme annoyance or anger. The verb *outrage* means "to offend, insult, or anger.") Think of some other words that end in *–ous*. How many of them are adjectives? How many of them are formed from words that can be either nouns or verbs?

Learn It Online
Delve into vocabulary using Word Watch at:

go.hrw.com L6-471 

MEET THE WRITER

Learn It Online
Get more on the author's life at:
go.hrw.com L6-472 Go

Maya Angelou
(1928–)

"All Things Are Possible"

The remarkable career of Maya Angelou (AN juh loh) has taken her far from the days when she was Bailey's lonely, awkward sister. Angelou has held many jobs in her long life: streetcar conductor, waitress, singer, dancer, actress, civil rights worker, professor, TV producer, and, above all, writer. In an interview, Angelou talked about how she has triumphed, both as a person and a writer, over life's obstacles. She has said, "I believe all things are possible for a human being, and I don't think there's anything in the world I can't do. Of course, I can't be five feet four because I'm six feet tall. I can't be a man because I'm a woman. The physical gifts are given to me, just like having two arms is a gift. In my creative source, wherever that is, I don't see why I can't sculpt. Why shouldn't I? Human beings sculpt. I'm a human being." Her strength and determination have made her one of America's most admired and respected writers.

"All my work is meant to say, 'You may encounter many defeats, but you must not be defeated.'"

Think About the Writer Do you agree that "all things are possible"? How would you describe Angelou's view of life?

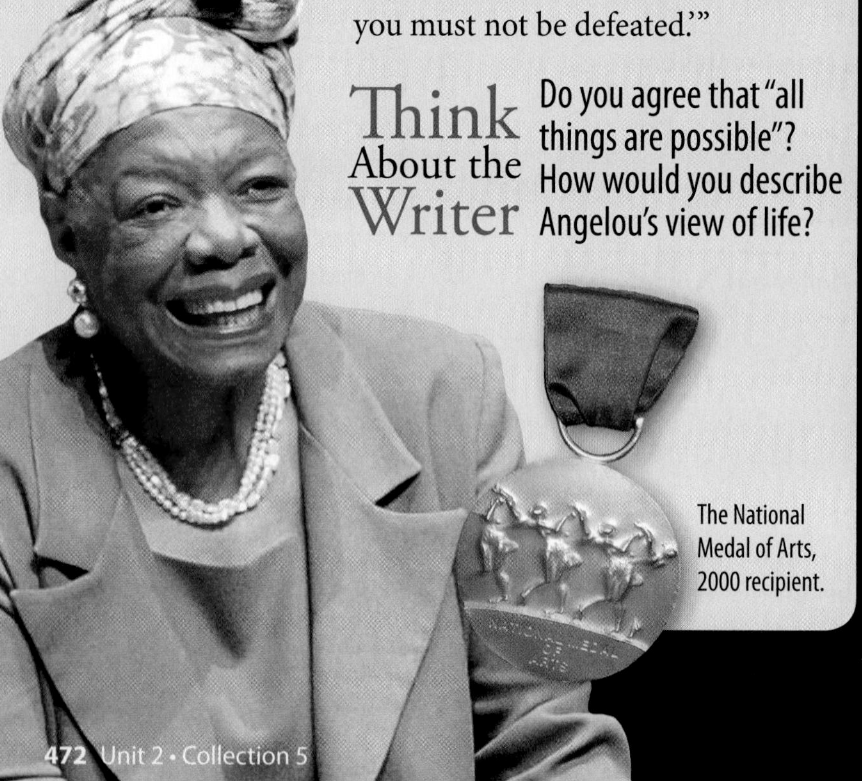

The National Medal of Arts, 2000 recipient.

Build Background

In the following story, which takes place in the 1930s, one of the characters figures out a way to sneak some pickles out of the barrel at his family's store. Pickle barrels were a common sight in stores in both the North and South until recent times. The barrels, as tall as a young child, would sit in the aisle of the corner store or deli, and customers or the store owner would use slotted spoons or tongs to pick out the pickles to purchase. Biting into a big, juicy pickle fresh from the barrel was seen as a treat by most kids.

Preview the Selection

"Brother" is an excerpt from the autobiography of writer **Maya Angelou.** She describes herself and her only brother, **Bailey,** as children and tells why their relationship was so important to her.

Read with a Purpose Read to understand how Maya Angelou feels about her brother, and why.

Brother

from I Know Why the Caged Bird Sings by **Maya Angelou**

Bailey was the greatest person in my world. And the fact that he was my brother, my only brother, and I had no sisters to share him with, was such good fortune that it made me want to live a Christian life just to show God that I was grateful. Where I was big, elbowy, and grating,[1] he was small, graceful, and smooth. . . . He was lauded[2] for his velvet-black skin. His hair fell down in black curls, and my head was covered with black steel wool. And yet he loved me. **A**

When our elders said unkind things about my features (my family was handsome to a point of pain for me), Bailey would wink at me from across the room, and I knew that it was a matter of time before he would take revenge. He would allow the old ladies to finish wondering how on earth I came about, then he would ask, in a voice like cooling bacon grease, "Oh Mizeriz[3] Coleman, how is your son? I saw him the other day, and he looked sick enough to die." **B**

Aghast,[4] the ladies would ask, "Die? From what? He ain't sick."

And in a voice oilier than the one before, he'd answer with a straight face, "From the Uglies." **C**

I would hold my laugh, bite my tongue, grit my teeth, and very seriously erase even the touch of a smile from my face. Later, behind the house by the black-walnut tree, we'd laugh and laugh and howl.

1. **grating** (GRAY tihng): irritating; annoying.
2. **lauded** (LAWD ihd): praised highly.
3. **Mizeriz:** dialect term for "Mrs."
4. **aghast** (uh GAST) **:** shocked; horrified.

A **Reading Focus** **Fact and Opinion** State the facts you learn about Bailey in this opening paragraph. Where do Angelou's opinions come out? How can you tell the difference between fact and opinion here?

B **Literary Focus** **First-Person Point of View** Which pronouns signal that the selection is written from the first-person point of view? Who is the speaker? Who is speaking the words in quotation marks?

C **Read and Discuss** So far, what has Angelou told you about her brother? What do these details contribute to her portrait of him?

Bailey could count on very few punishments for his consistently outrageous behavior, for he was the pride of the Henderson/Johnson family.

His movements, as he was later to describe those of an acquaintance, were activated with oiled precision. He was also able to find more hours in the day than I thought existed. He finished chores, homework, read more books than I, and played the group games on the side of the hill with the best of them. He could even pray out loud in church and was apt at stealing pickles from the barrel that sat under the fruit counter and Uncle Willie's nose.

Once when the Store was full of lunchtime customers, he dipped the strainer, which we also used to sift weevils[5] from meal and flour, into the barrel and fished for two fat pickles. He caught them and hooked the strainer onto the side of the barrel, where they dripped until he was ready for them. When the last school bell rang, he picked the nearly dry pickles out of the strainer, jammed them into his pockets, and threw the strainer behind the oranges. We ran out of the Store. It was summer and his pants were short, so the pickle juice made clean streams down his ashy legs, and he jumped with his pockets full of loot and his eyes laughing a "How about that?" He smelled like a vinegar barrel or a sour angel. **D**

After our early chores were done, while Uncle Willie or Momma minded the Store, we were free to play the children's games as long as we stayed within yelling distance. Playing hide-and-seek, his voice was easily identified, singing, "Last night, night before, twenty-four robbers at my door. Who all is hid? Ask me to let them in, hit 'em in the head with a rolling pin. Who all is hid?" In follow the leader, naturally he was the one who created the most daring and interesting things to do. And when he was on the tail of the pop the whip, he would twirl off the end like a top, spinning, falling, laughing, finally stopping just before my heart beat its last, and then he was back in the game, still laughing.

Of all the needs (there are none imaginary) a lonely child has, the one that must be satisfied, if there is going to be hope and a hope of wholeness, is the unshaking need for an unshakable God. My pretty black brother was my Kingdom Come. **E F**

5. **weevils:** small beetles that feed on grains, cotton, and other crops.

D **Read and Discuss** How does this information about Bailey connect with what you already know?

E **Read and Discuss** What does the author mean when she says, "My pretty black brother was my Kingdom Come"?

F **Reading Focus** **Fact and Opinion** What is Angelou's most important message about her brother? Is this message a fact or an opinion? Explain how this final paragraph is like the first paragraph in this autobiography.

Vocabulary **outrageous** (owt RAY juhs) *adj.:* extreme; shocking.

acquaintance (uh KWAYN tuhns) *n.:* friend; someone known casually.

precision (prih SIHZH uhn) *n.:* exactness; accuracy.

apt (apt) *adj.:* skilled; capable.

sift (sihft) *v.:* strain or filter through something.

Applying Your Skills

Sunshine State Standards: Benchmarks LA.6.2.2.2 use information from the text to answer questions related to the main idea or relevant details, maintaining chronological or logical order; *Also covered* LA.6.2.2.3; LA.6.3.2.3; LA.6.4.1.2; LA.6.4.2.3

Brother

Respond and Think Critically

Reading Focus

FCAT

1. Which statement BEST describes Maya's relationship with Bailey?
   A She is envious of him.
   B She dislikes him.
   C She does not understand him.
   D She likes to pick on him.

Read with a Purpose

2. Why was Bailey so important to Angelou?

Reading Skills: Fact and Opinion

3. Compare your Fact/Opinion chart to the charts others made. Where was it hard to separate facts from opinions? Was this account mostly fact or opinion? Explain.

Fact	Opinion	Difficult to Separate?
Bailey was her only brother.	Bailey was "the greatest person in my world."	

Literary Focus

Literary Analysis

4. **Infer** What qualities in a person did Angelou value as a child? What kind of person do you think she wanted to be?

Literary Skills: Autobiography/ First-Person Point of View

5. **Evaluate** What do we learn about Angelou as she compares and contrasts herself with Bailey? Are her comparisons mostly fact or opinion? Explain what these comparisons contribute to the portrait of Bailey. Support your answer with details from the story. READ THINK EXPLAIN

Literary Skills Review: Characterization

6. **Analyze** A writer reveals **character** by describing characters' appearances, showing how they speak and act, revealing their thoughts and feelings, showing what others say or think about them, and directly telling what they are like. Which methods of **characterization** does Angelou rely on to reveal Bailey's character? Which does she *not* use? Why? Support your answer with examples from the story. READ THINK EXPLAIN

Writing Focus

Think as a Reader/Writer

Use It in Your Writing Use sensory words and images to create your own vivid description of a family member or friend who is important to you.

What Do You Think Now?

How has this selection affected your ideas about what we can gain from close relationships?

Applying Your Skills

Brother

Vocabulary Development

Identifying and Explaining Synonyms and Antonyms

Synonyms are words with the same or nearly the same meaning. *Awkward* and *clumsy* are synonyms. **Antonyms** are words that are opposite in meaning. *Graceful* and *clumsy* are antonyms.

You can use a **thesaurus** (from a Greek word meaning "treasure") to find synonyms for many words. A thesaurus also lists antonyms for some words.

Your Turn

outrageous
acquaintance
precision
apt
sift

In the box to the right, find the Vocabulary word that is an **antonym** of the word in italics in each sentence below. Rewrite the sentence using the word. You may have to change other words so that the new sentence makes sense.

1. The guard's *sloppiness* lost the game for us.
2. Troy's behavior was totally *acceptable*.
3. Melanie saw a *stranger* waving at her.
4. We tried to *combine* the flour and the lumps.
5. My cat is *unskilled* at catching mice.

Look up each Vocabulary word above in a thesaurus. List three or four synonyms you find for each word. Then go back to the text and substitute some of the synonyms for Angelou's original vocabulary choices. Decide which synonyms work best and place a star next to each one.

Language Coach

Word Families Some adjectives are made from words that can be both verbs and nouns, like the vocabulary word *outrageous*.

grating personality
yelling distance
daring things
interesting things

Identify the verb and noun forms of each of these adjectives from "Brother." Write the meanings of all four words. Then, describe how the meaning of the adjective is related to the meanings of the verb and the noun forms.

Academic Vocabulary

Write About . . .

People seldom share a uniform view of things. You may see someone in a way that's different from the way others see that person. Bailey's family let him get away with things because, from their perspective, he was wonderful and could do no wrong. Do you think others saw him this way? Explain.

Learn It Online
For more on synonyms and antonyms, see WordSharp:
go.hrw.com
L6-476
Go

Sunshine State Standards: Benchmarks **LA.6.1.6.4** categorize key vocabulary and identify salient features; **LA.6.1.6.8** identify advanced word/phrase relationships and their meanings; **LA.6.1.6.10** determine meanings of words, pronunciation, parts of speech, etymologies, and alternate word choices by using a dictionary, thesaurus, and digital tools; **LA.6.2.2.4** identify the characteristics of a variety of types of nonfiction text (e.g., reference works, newspapers, biographies, procedures, instructions, practical/functional texts); **LA.6.3.4.5** consistency in verb tense in simple, compound, and complex sentences; **LA.6.4.2.3** write informational/expository essays (e.g., process, description, explanation, comparison/contrast, problem/solution) that include a thesis statement, supporting details, and introductory, body and concluding paragraphs.

Grammar Link

Subject-Verb Agreement

It's easy for a sentence to go astray when its subject and verb don't agree: *The pickles is nearly dry now*. A verb should agree in number with its subject: *The pickles are nearly dry now*. Singular subjects need singular verbs, and plural subjects need plural verbs.

EXAMPLES

> **I knew** that it was a matter of time before he would take revenge. [The singular subject ***I*** agrees with the singular verb ***knew***.]
>
> The **pickles drip** until he is ready for them. [The plural subject ***pickles*** agrees with the plural verb ***drip***.]

When a sentence contains a verb phrase like *had been given,* make sure the first helping verb in the phrase agrees with the subject.

EXAMPLES

> **Bailey has** been stealing pickles.
> **We have** been stealing pickles.

Your Turn

Writing Applications Rewrite each sentence, changing the subject and verb from singular to plural or from plural to singular.

EXAMPLE

> The **elders talk** unkindly about my features.
> The **elder talks** unkindly about my features.

1. The pickle juice runs in streams down his legs.
2. He could count on very few punishments.
3. We ran out of the store.

CHOICES

As you respond to the Choices, use these **Academic Vocabulary** words as appropriate: contribute, perspective, distinct, uniform.

REVIEW

Create a Movie About "Brother"

Imagine you were making a movie based on "Brother." Whom would you cast as Maya and as Bailey? What scenes from the selection would you include in the movie, and how would you expand these scenes to make an entire plot for a full-length film? How would the movie end? Write a summary of the movie in a paragraph.

CONNECT

Write an Autobiography

Timed Writing Think about major events that have happened in your life. Then, pick one of the events and write a paragraph about it from the first-person point of view.

EXTEND

Write a Character Sketch

Who is the "greatest person" in *your* world? Your choice may be someone you know or a public figure you admire. Write a character sketch identifying the person and describing why he or she is the greatest. What does he or she contribute to your world? Write from the first-person point of view, and be sure to make your perspective clear by identifying both the facts about the person and your opinions.

Learn It Online
To make a digital story, go to:
go.hrw.com
L6-477
Go

AUTOBIOGRAPHY

Preparing to Read

from The Land I Lost

by **Huynh Quang Nhuong**

What Do You Think?

How can true stories inspire you to reach for your dreams?

QuickWrite

What lessons have you learned from reading or listening to other people's true stories? Write about a true story that inspired you.

Reader/Writer Notebook

Use your **RWN** to complete the activities for this selection.

Sunshine State Standards: Benchmarks **LA.6.1.6.1** use new vocabulary that is introduced and taught directly; **LA.6.1.6.10** determine meanings of words, pronunciation, parts of speech, etymologies, and alternate word choices by using a dictionary, thesaurus, and digital tools; **LA.6.1.7.2** analyze the author's purpose (e.g., to persuade, inform, entertain, or explain) and perspective in a variety of texts and understand how they affect meaning; **LA.6.2.2.3** organize information to show understanding (e.g., representing main ideas within text through charting, mapping, paraphrasing, summarizing, or comparing/contrasting); **LA.6.3.2.3** analyzing language techniques of professional authors (e.g., point of view, establishing mood) to enhance the use of descriptive language and word choices.

Literary Focus

First-Person and Third-Person Point of View An **autobiography** is the story of a person's life told from the **first-person point of view.** The writer tells you about events that he or she experienced directly, using pronouns such as *I, me,* and *my*.

In this autobiography, the author changes his point of view when he describes events—a story about two other people—that he did *not* directly experience. He uses the **third-person point of view** to describe the thoughts and feelings of other people, using pronouns such as *he, she, they, his, hers,* and *their*.

Reading Focus

Author's Purpose Authors typically write with a **purpose,** such as to **inform,** to **persuade,** to **express feelings,** or to **entertain.**

Into Action As you read this excerpt, try to determine the writer's main purpose in different parts of the autobiography by writing your ideas in a chart like this.

Inform	Persuade	Express Feelings	Entertain
He tells what Vietnam was like before the war.			He tells a story about his neighbors.

TechFocus Think about a story from your own past that you enjoy telling people. How would it look as a movie?

Writing Focus

Find It in Your Reading Writers describe actions to reveal what characters are like. As you read, use your *Reader/Writer Notebook* to note at least three ways the actions of Lan and Trung help you understand the two characters.

Vocabulary

infested (ihn FEHST ihd) *v.:* inhabited in large numbers (said of something harmful). *Crocodiles infested the river.*

wily (WY lee) *adj.:* sly; clever in a sneaky way. *A crocodile becomes more wily with age.*

hallucination (huh loo suh NAY shuhn) *n.:* sight or sound of something that isn't really there. *Trung's relatives think that the voice he hears is a hallucination.*

desperate (DEHS puhr iht) *adj.:* having a great and urgent need. *Trung is desperate to save Lan.*

avenge (uh VEHNJ) *v.:* get even for; get revenge for. *Trung vows to avenge Lan's death.*

Language Coach

Synonyms Synonyms are words that are similar in meaning. You can find synonyms in a thesaurus or, for some words, at the ends of dictionary entries. With a partner, brainstorm synonyms for each of the Vocabulary words above. You can use a thesaurus or dictionary for extra help, if necessary.

Learn It Online
For a preview of this autobiography, see the video introduction on:

go.hrw.com L6-479 

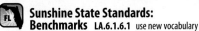

MEET THE WRITER

Huynh Quang Nhuong

(1946–)

To Make People Happy

Huynh Quang Nhuong (hoong KWAHN nyoong) was born in a small village in Vietnam between a deep jungle and a chain of high mountains. At age six, Huynh learned to tend his family's herd of water buffaloes. Tank, his favorite water buffalo, takes part in many of the adventures described in *The Land I Lost*.

Nhuong left his village to study chemistry at the University of Saigon. When war broke out, he recalls, "the land I love was lost to me forever." Nhuong was drafted into the army of South Vietnam. On the battlefield he was shot and paralyzed.

In 1969, Nhuong left Vietnam to receive special medical treatment in the United States. He stayed, earned degrees in literature and French, and settled in Columbia, Missouri. His writing helps form a link between his two countries. He says:

> "I hope that my books will make people from different countries happy, regardless of their political adherences, creeds, and ages."

Think About the Writer Nhuong wants his books to make people happy. What does that tell you about what he values?

Build Background

One place where you're likely to meet up with a crocodile is Vietnam, a tropical country in Southeast Asia with many warm, muddy rivers and swamps. Vietnam is about the size of New Mexico, and as the period map shows, it extends south from China in a long, narrow S-curve.

Most Americans probably still associate Vietnam with war. In this excerpt from his autobiography, Huynh Quang Nhuong recalls a peaceful time in his beautiful country. His story helps you picture the people of Vietnam and gives you a perspective on their relationship with the land and with the animals that live in it.

Preview the Selection

Huynh Quang Nhuong, the author, describes his life as a child in a South Vietnamese village. Then, he tells the story of two neighbors. **Lan** is a young woman who becomes engaged to **Trung,** a fisherman.

Read with a Purpose Read to find out what happens when a crocodile shows up on a happy couple's wedding night.

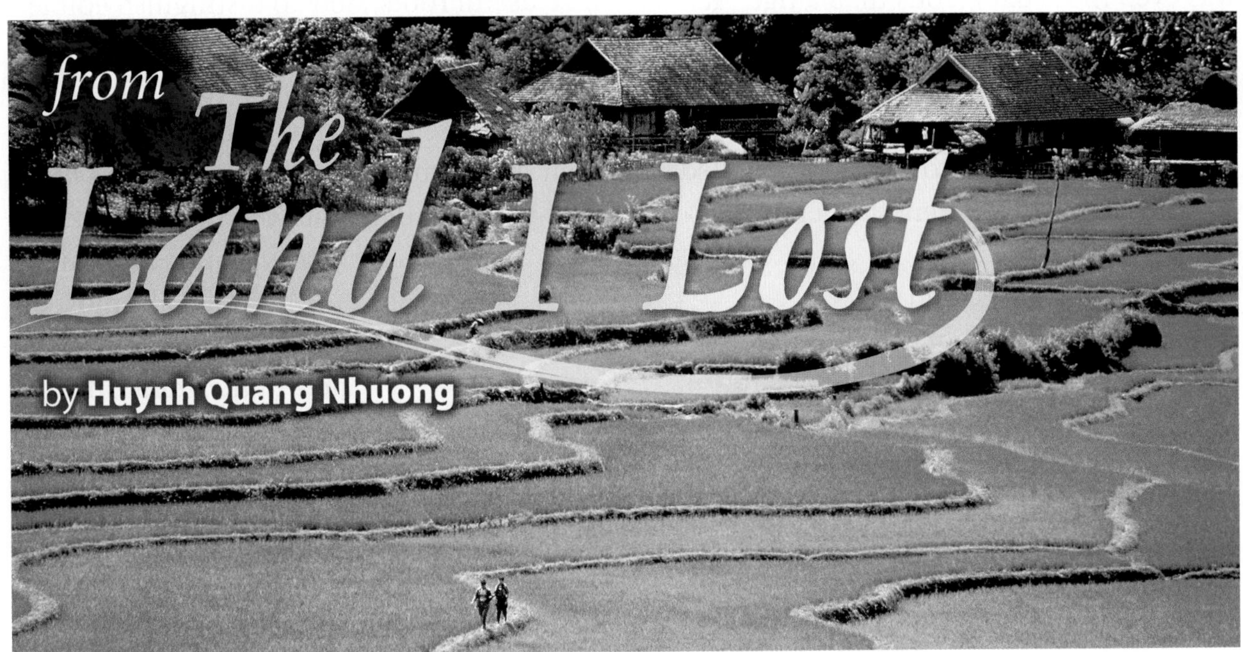

from The Land I Lost

by **Huynh Quang Nhuong**

I was born on the central highlands of Vietnam in a small hamlet on a riverbank that had a deep jungle on one side and a chain of high mountains on the other. Across the river, rice fields stretched to the slopes of another chain of mountains. **A**

There were fifty houses in our hamlet, scattered along the river or propped against the mountainsides. The houses were made of bamboo and covered with coconut leaves, and each was surrounded by a deep trench to protect it from wild animals or thieves. The only way to enter a house was to walk across a "monkey bridge"—a single bamboo stick that spanned the trench. At night we pulled the bridges into our houses and were safe.

There were no shops or marketplaces in our hamlet. If we needed supplies—medicine, cloth, soaps, or candles—we had to cross over the mountains and travel to a town nearby. We used the river mainly for traveling to distant hamlets, but it also provided us with plenty of fish. **B**

During the six-month rainy season, nearly all of us helped plant and cultivate fields of rice, sweet potatoes, Indian mustard, eggplant, tomatoes, hot peppers, and corn. But during the dry season, we became hunters and turned to the jungle.

Wild animals played a very large part in our lives. There were four animals we feared the most: the tiger, the lone wild hog, the crocodile, and the horse snake. Tigers were

A **Literary Focus** **First- and Third-Person Point of View** From what point of view is this paragraph told?

B **Read and Discuss** Can you imagine living in this village? How do you think you would do in these conditions?

always trying to steal cattle. Sometimes, however, when a tiger became old and slow it became a man-eater. But a lone wild hog was even more dangerous than a tiger. It attacked every creature in sight, even when it had no need for food. Or it did crazy things, such as charging into the hamlet in broad daylight, ready to kill or to be killed.

The river had different dangers: crocodiles. But of all the animals, the most hated and feared was the huge horse snake. It was sneaky and attacked people and cattle just for the joy of killing. It would either crush its victim to death or poison it with a bite.

But a lone wild hog was even more dangerous than a tiger. It attacked every creature in sight, even when it had no need for food.

Like all farmers' children in the hamlet, I started working at the age of six. My seven sisters helped by working in the kitchen, weeding the garden, gathering eggs, or taking water to the cattle. I looked after the family herd of water buffaloes. Someone always had to be with the herd because no matter how carefully a water buffalo was trained, it always was ready to nibble young rice plants when no one was looking. Sometimes, too, I fished for the family while I guarded the herd, for there were plenty of fish in the flooded rice fields during the rainy season. **C**

I was twelve years old when I made my first trip to the jungle with my father. I learned how to track game, how to recognize useful roots, how to distinguish edible mushrooms from poisonous ones. I learned that if birds, raccoons, squirrels, or monkeys had eaten the fruits of certain trees, then those fruits were not poisonous. Often they were not delicious, but they could calm a man's hunger and thirst.

My father, like most of the villagers, was a farmer and a hunter, depending upon the season. But he also had a college education, so in the evenings he helped to teach other children in our hamlet, for it was too small to afford a professional schoolteacher.

My mother managed the house, but during the harvest season she could be found in the fields, helping my father get the crops home; and as the wife of a hunter, she knew how to dress and nurse a wound and took good care of her husband and his hunting dogs.

I went to the lowlands to study for a while because I wanted to follow my father as a teacher when I grew up. I always planned to return to my hamlet to live the rest of my life there. But war disrupted my dreams. The land I love was lost to me forever. **D**

These stories are my memories. . . .

C **Read and Discuss** What have you learned about the author and his life so far?

D **Read and Discuss** What does this paragraph show about the author?

Analyzing Visuals **Viewing and Interpreting** What does this image tell you about life in Nhuong's village?

So Close

My grandmother was very fond of cookies made of banana, egg, and coconut, so my mother and I always stopped at Mrs. Hong's house to buy these cookies for her on our way back from the marketplace. My mother also liked to see Mrs. Hong because they had been very good friends since grade-school days. While my mother talked with her friend, I talked with Mrs. Hong's daughter, Lan. Most of the time Lan asked me about my older sister, who was married to a teacher and lived in a nearby town. Lan, too, was going to get married—to a young man living next door, Trung. **E**

Trung and Lan had been inseparable playmates until the day tradition did not allow them to be alone together anymore. Besides, I think they felt a little shy with each other after realizing that they were man and woman. **F**

Lan was a lively, pretty girl, who attracted the attention of all the young men of our hamlet. Trung was a skillful fisherman who successfully plied[1] his trade on the river in front of their houses. Whenever Lan's mother found a big fish on the kitchen windowsill, she would smile to herself. Finally, she decided that Trung was a fine

1. **plied:** worked at.

E **Read and Discuss** How does the retelling of Lan and Trung's story begin?

F **Literary Focus** **First- and Third-Person Point of View** What is the point of view now? Why has it shifted?

young man and would make a good husband for her daughter. **G**

Trung's mother did not like the idea of her son giving good fish away, but she liked the cookies Lan brought her from time to time. Besides, the girl was very helpful; whenever she was not busy at her house, Lan would come over in the evening and help Trung's mother repair her son's fishing net.

Trung was happiest when Lan was helping his mother. They did not talk to each other, but they could look at each other when his mother was busy with her work. Each time Lan went home, Trung looked at the chair Lan had just left and secretly wished that nobody would move it.

> Each time Lan went home, Trung looked at the chair Lan had just left and secretly wished that nobody would move it.

One day when Trung's mother heard her son call Lan's name in his sleep, she decided it was time to speak to the girl's mother about marriage. Lan's mother agreed they should be married and even waived[2] the custom whereby the bridegroom had to give the bride's family a fat hog, six chickens, six ducks, three bottles of wine, and thirty kilos[3] of fine rice, for the two families had known each other for a long time and were good neighbors.

The two widowed mothers quickly set the dates for the engagement announcement and for the wedding ceremony. Since their decision was immediately made known to relatives and friends, Trung and Lan could now see each other often. . . . **H**

At last it was the day of their wedding. Friends and relatives arrived early in the morning to help them celebrate. They brought gifts of ducks, chickens, baskets filled with fruits, rice wine, and colorful fabrics. Even though the two houses were next to each other, the two mothers observed all the proper wedding day traditions.

First, Trung and his friends and relatives came to Lan's house. Lan and he prayed at her ancestors' altars and asked for their blessing. Then they joined everyone for a luncheon. **I**

After lunch there was a farewell ceremony for the bride. Lan stepped out of her house and joined the greeting party that was to accompany her to Trung's home. Tradition called for her to cry and to express her sorrow at leaving her parents behind and forever becoming the daughter of her husband's family. In some villages the bride was even supposed to cling so tightly to her mother that it would take several friends to pull her away from her

2. **waived:** gave up voluntarily.
3. **kilos:** kilograms, about 2.2 pounds each.

G **Read and Discuss** What is Trung up to with the fish?

H **Read and Discuss** What are the two mothers thinking and planning?

I **Reading Focus** **Author's Purpose** The author is telling a story here. What might his purpose be?

home. But instead of crying, Lan smiled. She asked herself, why should she cry? The two houses were separated by only a garden; she could run home and see her mother anytime she wanted to. So Lan willingly followed Trung and prayed at his ancestors' altars before joining everyone in the big welcome dinner at Trung's house that ended the day's celebrations. **J**

Later in the evening of the wedding night, Lan went to the river to take a bath. Because crocodiles infested the river, people of our hamlet who lived along the riverbank chopped down trees and put them in the river to form barriers and protect places where they washed their clothes, did their dishes, or took a bath. This evening, a wily crocodile had avoided the barrier by crawling up the riverbank and sneaked up behind Lan. The crocodile grabbed her and went back to the river by the same route that it had come. **K**

Trung became worried when Lan did not return. He went to the place where she was supposed to bathe, only to find that her clothes were there, but she had disappeared. Panic-stricken, he yelled for his relatives. They all rushed to the riverbank with lighted torches. In the flickering light they found traces of water and crocodile claw-prints on the wet soil. Now they knew that a

---

J **Read and Discuss** What's good about the houses' location?

K **Read and Discuss** Now what's happening at the river?

Vocabulary **infested** (ihn FEHST ihd) *v.:* inhabited in large numbers (said of something harmful).
wily (WY lee) *adj.:* sly; clever in a sneaky way.

SOCIAL STUDIES LINK

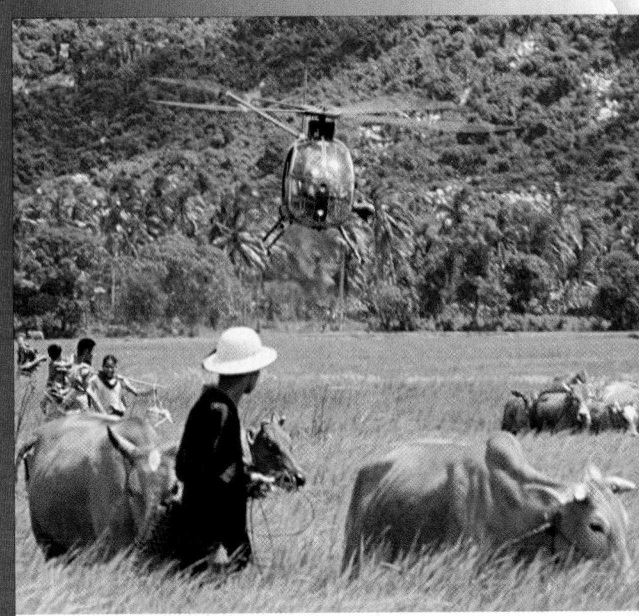

The Vietnam War

The Vietnamese had struggled against domination by China for centuries, but by the early 1880s, it was France that ruled Vietnam. Starting in 1941, a large group of Vietnamese, led by Ho Chi Minh, worked toward a communist revolution they believed could free Vietnam from French rule. The United States, concerned that a communist victory would contribute to the rest of Southeast Asia falling to communism, supported France with military aid.

When the French left in the early 1950s, Vietnam was divided into North Vietnam, which had a communist government, and South Vietnam, which had a Western-style government. Yet many Vietnamese longed to reunite the country under communism, and the American anti-communist military effort grew into all-out war: the Vietnam War, which lasted from 1959 to 1975.

Ask Yourself

How can living through war change a person's perspective on life?

crocodile had grabbed the young bride and dragged her into the river.

Since no one could do anything for the girl, all of Trung's relatives returned to the house, urging the bridegroom to do the same. But the young man refused to leave the place; he just stood there, crying and staring at the clothes of his bride.

Suddenly the wind brought him the sound of Lan calling his name. He was very frightened, for according to an old belief, a crocodile's victim must lure a new victim to his master; if not, the first victim's soul must stay with the beast forever. **L**

Trung rushed back to the house and woke all his relatives. Nobody doubted he thought he had heard her call, but they all believed that he was the victim of a hallucination. Everyone pleaded with him and tried to convince him that nobody could survive when snapped up by a crocodile and dragged into the river to be drowned and eaten by the animal.

The young man brushed aside all their arguments and rushed back to the river. Once again, he heard the voice of his bride in the wind, calling his name. Again he rushed back and woke his relatives. Again they tried to persuade him that it was a hallucination, although some of the old folks suggested that maybe the ghost of the young girl was having to dance and sing to placate[4] the angry crocodile because she failed to bring it a new victim.

4. **placate:** calm or soothe (someone who is angry).

L **Read and Discuss** What is going on with Trung here?

Vocabulary **hallucination** (huh loo suh NAY shuhn) *n.:* sight or sound of something that isn't really there.

No one could persuade Trung to stay inside. His friends wanted to go back to the river with him, but he said no. He resented them for not believing him that there were desperate cries in the wind.

Trung stood in front of the deep river alone in the darkness. He listened to the sound of the wind and clutched the clothes Lan had left behind. The wind became stronger and stronger and often changed direction as the night progressed, but he did not hear any more calls. Still he had no doubt that the voice he had heard earlier was absolutely real. Then at dawn, when the wind died down, he again heard, very clearly, Lan call him for help. **M**

Her voice came from an island about six hundred meters away. Trung wept and prayed: "You were a good girl when you were still alive, now be a good soul. Please protect me so that I can find a way to kill the beast in order to free you from its spell and avenge your tragic death." Suddenly, while wiping away his tears, he saw a little tree moving on the island. The tree was jumping up and down. He squinted to see better. The tree had two hands that were waving at him. And it was calling his name. **N**

Trung became hysterical and yelled for help. He woke all his relatives and they all rushed to his side again. At first they thought that Trung had become stark mad. They tried to lead him back to his house, but he fiercely resisted their attempt. He talked to them incoherently[5] and pointed his finger at the strange tree on the island. Finally his relatives saw the waving tree. They quickly put a small boat into the river,

5. **incoherently:** not clearly.

M **Reading Focus** **Author's Purpose** What is the author's purpose in describing these scenes of Trung listening for Lan? What other stories does *The Land I Lost* remind you of so far?

N **Read and Discuss** What is the narrator describing here?

Vocabulary **desperate** (DEHS puhr iht) *adj.:* having a great and urgent need.
avenge (uh VEHNJ) *v.:* get even for; get revenge for.

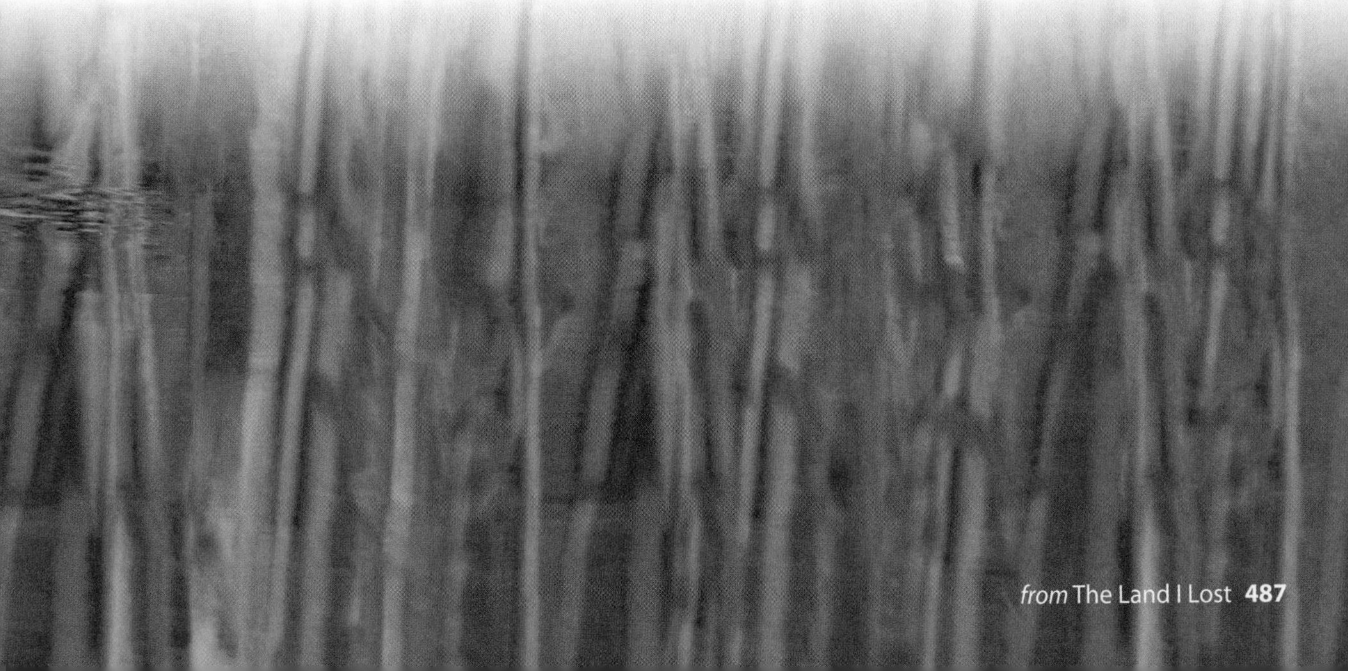

and Trung got into the boat along with two other men. They paddled to the island and discovered that the moving tree was, in fact, Lan. She had covered herself with leaves because she had no clothes on.

At first nobody knew what had really happened because Lan clung to Trung and cried and cried. Finally, when Lan could talk, they pieced together her story.

Lan had fainted when the crocodile snapped her up. Had she not fainted, the crocodile surely would have drowned her before carrying her off to the island. Lan did not know how many times the crocodile had tossed her in the air and smashed her against the ground, but at one point, while being tossed in the air and falling back onto the crocodile's jaw, she regained consciousness. The crocodile smashed her against the ground a few more times, but Lan played dead. Luckily the crocodile became thirsty and returned to the river to drink. At that moment Lan got up and ran to a nearby tree and climbed up it. The tree was very small.

Lan stayed very still for fear that the snorting, angry crocodile, roaming around trying to catch her again, would find her and shake her out of the tree. Lan stayed in this frozen position for a long time until the crocodile gave up searching for her and went back to the river. Then she started calling Trung to come rescue her. **O**

Lan stayed very still for fear that the snorting, angry crocodile, roaming around trying to catch her again, would find her and shake her out of the tree.

Lan's body was covered with bruises, for crocodiles soften up big prey before swallowing it. They will smash it against the ground or against a tree, or keep tossing it into the air. But fortunately Lan had no broken bones or serious cuts. It was possible that this crocodile was very old and had lost most of its teeth. Nevertheless, the older the crocodile, the more intelligent it usually was. That was how it knew to avoid the log barrier in the river and to snap up the girl from behind.

Trung carried his exhausted bride into the boat and paddled home. Lan slept for hours and hours. At times she would sit up with a start and cry out for help, but within three days she was almost completely recovered.

Lan's mother and Trung's mother decided to celebrate their children's wedding a second time because Lan had come back from the dead. **P**

O **Read and Discuss** What is Lan explaining about her plan to get home?

P **Read and Discuss** How does the story conclude? How does the near tragedy contribute to the joy?

Applying Your Skills

Sunshine State Standards: Benchmarks LA.6.1.7.2 analyze the author's purpose (e.g., to persuade, inform, entertain, or explain) and perspective in a variety of texts and understand how they affect meaning; *Also covered* LA.6.1.7.3; LA.6.1.7.8; LA.6.2.1.2; LA.6.2.1.5; LA.6.3.2.3

from The Land I Lost

Respond and Think Critically

Reading Focus

1. Read the sentence from the story. FCAT

   Each time Lan went home, Trung looked at the chair Lan had just left and secretly wished that nobody would move it.

   What does the chair represent for Trung?

   A his love for Lan
   B his need for consistency
   C his admiration for his mother
   D his desire to have luxurious furniture

Read with a Purpose

2. What was most surprising about Lan and Trung's story? Why?

Reading Skills: Author's Purpose

3. Review your chart. Which do you think is the author's *main* purpose?

Inform	Persuade	Express Feelings	Entertain
tells what Vietnam was like before the war		sad because he could not go home	tells a story about his neighbors
Main purpose:			

Literary Focus

Literary Analysis

4. **Analyze** How did the author lose the land he loved? How does his story of Lan and Trung fit with this idea of the loss of a homeland? Support your answer with examples from the text.

Literary Skills: First-Person and Third-Person Point of View

5. **Analyze/Connect** Why does the author's viewpoint shift from first person to third person? What distinct qualities of each point of view most help to reveal the perspectives of the people he is writing about?

Literary Skills Review: Characterization

6. **Interpret** A writer reveals character through **characterization.** Think of what you learned about Lan before the crocodile attack. How did the author prepare you for the story's outcome through his characterization of Lan? Support your answer with examples from the text. READ THINK EXPLAIN

Writing Focus

Think as a Reader/Writer

Use It in Your Writing Look at your notes on how the author uses characters' actions to reveal their traits. Write a paragraph about a real or imagined person, using the character's actions to help your reader "see" and understand the character.

What lessons did you learn from Nhuong's story? What does that make you think about things we learn from other people's stories?

Applying Your Skills

from The Land I Lost

Vocabulary Development

Context Clues

Locate the passage in the story where each Vocabulary word on page 479 is used. Try to find clues in the passage that help explain the word's meaning. Put the context clues for the Vocabulary words in cluster diagrams like this one, which contains clues for the word *infested.*

Crocodiles infested the river—the word must refer to something dangerous.

infested
overrun or infected
Could a synonym be used?
Overrun could be used, but infected could not.

People had to put up barriers to keep them out.

Your Turn

Answer these questions about other words and context clues in the selection.

1. Find the word *hamlet* in the first paragraph. Which words in the first three paragraphs provide clues to the meaning of *hamlet*? How would you define the word?
2. Find the term *monkey bridge* in the second paragraph. Where does the writer provide a definition of this term?
3. Find the passage where the word *edible* is used (page 482). What context clues tell you that this word means "fit to be eaten"?
4. Find the word *disrupted* at the very end of the first section (page 482). Use context clues to find the meaning of *disrupted.*

Language Coach

Synonyms Synonyms are words with the same or nearly the same meaning. For example, *stone* and *rock* are synonyms. Synonyms are not always interchangeable, though. Fill out a chart like the one below for the following Vocabulary words: *wily, hallucination, desperate,* and *avenge.*

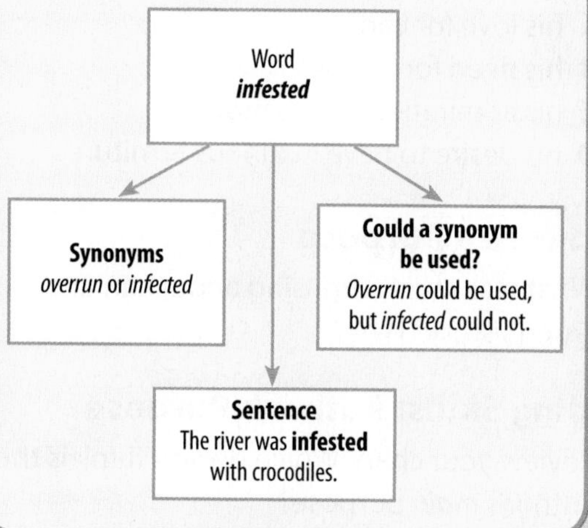

The river was infested with crocodiles.

Academic Vocabulary

Talk About . . .

Huynh Quang Nhuong writes from the unique perspective of a Vietnamese villager. How does his perspective influence your opinion of whether the story is true or fictional? What else does his perspective contribute?

Learn It Online
Learn about context clues with WordSharp on:
go.hrw.com
L6-490
Go

Sunshine State Standards: Benchmarks **LA.6.1.6.3** use context clues to determine meanings of unfamiliar words; **LA.6.1.6.4** categorize key vocabulary and identify salient features; **LA.6.3.4.3** punctuation in simple, compound, and complex sentences, including appositives and appositive phrases, and in cited sources, including quotations for exact words from sources; **LA.6.4.1.2** write a variety of expressive forms (e.g., short play, song lyrics, historical fiction, limericks) that employ figurative language, rhythm, dialogue, characterization, and/or appropriate format; **LA.6.5.2.2** deliver narrative and informative presentations, including oral responses to literature, and adjust oral language, body language, eye contact, gestures, technology and supporting graphics appropriate to the situation; **LA.6.6.4.2** determine and apply digital tools (e.g., word processing, multimedia authoring, web tools, graphic organizers) to publications and presentations.

Grammar Link

Run-on Sentences and Fragments

It is very easy to mistakenly write run-on sentences and fragments, but a few simple rules will help you avoid those mistakes. A **run-on sentence** is two complete sentences run together or combined with just a comma. To revise a run-on, either make two separate sentences or use a comma and a conjunction such as *and, but,* or *or.*

RUN-ON SENTENCE

Lan bakes cookies, Trung fishes.

REVISED

Lan bakes cookies**.** Trung fishes.
Lan bakes cookies**, and** Trung fishes.

A **fragment** is missing a part of the sentence, but it is capitalized and punctuated as if it were a complete sentence. (Remember that a complete sentence must have a subject and a predicate.)

FRAGMENT

The snake the villagers.

REVISED

The snake **frightened** the villagers.

Your Turn

Revise each of the following items to eliminate run-on sentences and fragments.

1. Allowed to go into the jungle alone.
2. Trung and Lan are having a luncheon after the wedding everyone will come.
3. The animals frighten us all the time, we must be very careful.
4. Mrs. Hong's house to take those cookies to her.

CHOICES

As you respond to the Choices, use these **Academic Vocabulary** words as appropriate: contribute, perspective, distinct, uniform.

REVIEW

Go Digital: Screen Your Story

TechFocus What kinds of stories do you like to tell about yourself? Choose a story to "screen" for your classmates. First, write your story in an autobiographical narrative of one or two paragraphs, choosing details that contribute to making your story interesting. Then, use the *Digital Storytelling* instructions on Learn It Online to create a short movie of your story.

CONNECT

Write and Perform a Play

Group Activity Work with a group to turn "So Close" into a play. Include Lan, Trung, their mothers, and a few villagers to serve as onlookers and guests at the wedding. Write dialogue and stage directions for the characters. Once you have created the play, perform it for your class.

EXTEND

Write a Memoir

Timed Writing Imagine that you have to leave home today and can never return. Write a short essay from your own perspective, using first-person point of view, that describes what you would miss most. Include details that contribute to the sense of sadness that you wouldfeel.

Learn It Online
Tell your story in a whole new way. Try digital storytelling. We'll show you how at:

go.hrw.com L6-491 

BIOGRAPHY

Preparing to Read

A GLORY OVER Everything

by **Ann Petry**

What Do You Think?

How can the desire for freedom inspire an entire life?

QuickWrite

Is following a dream for a better future ever worth risking everything—even your life? How brave would you be if you had to risk your life to gain something as essential as your freedom?

Harriet Tubman by Stephen Alcorn.

Reader/Writer Notebook

Use your **RWN** to complete the activities for this selection.

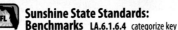

Sunshine State Standards: Benchmarks **LA.6.1.6.4** categorize key vocabulary and identify salient features; **LA.6.1.7.3** determine the main idea or essential message in grade-level text through inferring, paraphrasing, summarizing, and identifying relevant details; **LA.6.2.2.3** organize information to show understanding (e.g., representing main ideas within text through charting, mapping, paraphrasing, summarizing, or comparing/contrasting); **LA.6.2.2.4** identify the characteristics of a variety of types of nonfiction text (e.g., reference works, newspapers, biographies, procedures, instructions, practical/functional texts); *Also covered* **LA.6.3.2.3**

Literary Focus

Biography and Third-Person Point of View This selection is from a **biography,** the true story of a person's life written by another person. Using the **third-person point of view**—the perspective of someone *outside* the narrative—Petry presents what she imagines her real-life subjects must have felt and experienced.

Literary Perspectives Use the Analyzing Responses to Literature perspective on page 495 as you read this biography.

Reading Focus

Finding the Main Idea The **main idea** is the most important point made in a nonfiction text. Although first and last paragraphs often give clues to the main idea, you must infer, or make an educated guess about, the main idea from details the writer provides throughout the text.

Into Action To figure out the main idea in "A Glory over Everything," use a chart like the one below to take notes as you read the selection. List key details and important passages.

Notes for Finding the Main Idea in "A Glory over Everything"

Details in the First Paragraph	A white woman asks about Harriet's scar.
Important Passages/Other Key Details	Dr. Thompson starts selling slaves.
Details in the Last Paragraph	

Writing Focus

Think as a Reader/Writer

Find It in Your Reading As you read this selection, use your *Reader/Writer Notebook* to record dialogue that contributes to your understanding of the main character, Harriet Tubman.

Vocabulary

elude (ih LOOD) *v.:* escape the notice of; avoid detection by. *A runaway must elude the patrol.*

legitimate (luh JIHT uh miht) *adj.:* reasonable; justified. *Runaways had a legitimate reason to fear captors.*

defiant (dih FY uhnt) *adj.:* disobedient; boldly resistant. *Harriet's defiant manner disturbed Dr. Thompson.*

cautiously (KAW shuhs lee) *adv.:* safely; very carefully. *Harriet had to behave cautiously to avoid capture.*

befriended (bih FREHND ihd) *v.:* helped out or encouraged. *The white woman befriended Harriet Tubman.*

Language Coach

Words That Describe Two of the five Vocabulary words are adjectives, words used to modify, or describe, a noun or pronoun by telling what kind, which one, how many, or how much. Match each adjective from the Vocabulary list with one of the following words it can describe:

rebels arguments

Learn It Online

Use Word Watch to explore the meaning of terms at:

go.hrw.com L6-493 

MEET THE WRITER

Learn It Online
Read up on the author's life at:
go.hrw.com L6-494 Go

Ann Petry
(1908–1997)

A Writer at Work
Ann Petry worked as a certified pharmacist in her family's drugstore in Old Saybrook, Connecticut. Later, while living in New York City, she was a journalist and teacher, as well as an actor in the American Negro Theatre.

Petry is best known for presenting the tragedy of slavery in two biographies for young readers: one about Harriet Tubman and the other about Tituba, a young woman from Barbados who was held in slavery by a family in Salem, Massachusetts, and accused of witchcraft in 1692.

Making History Speak
Speaking about her two celebrated subjects, Harriet Tubman and Tituba, Petry said the following:

> "These women were slaves. I hoped that I had made them into real people. I tried to make history speak across the centuries in the voices of people—young, old, good, evil, beautiful, ugly."

Think About the Writer Why do you think Petry chose to write about two women who were enslaved?

Build Background
The Underground Railroad wasn't a railroad, and it didn't run underground. It was made up of people from both the North and the South who offered food, shelter, and protection to African Americans escaping from slavery to freedom in the North. To keep the route secret, the organization used railroad terms, such as *stations* for the houses along the way and *conductors* for the people who offered help.

Harriet Tubman, who escaped from slavery, became one of the most famous "conductors" on the railroad. She helped more than three hundred men, women, and children along the road to freedom.

Slavery was outlawed in the United States after the Civil War, and African American men won voting rights in 1870. African American women won the vote in 1920. However, unfair voting restrictions enacted by state and local governments prevented many African Americans from voting until the Voting Rights Act passed in 1965.

Preview the Selection
In this part of Petry's biography of **Harriet Tubman,** you will meet Tubman in 1849, when she was working as a field hand on the Brodas plantation in Maryland. Tubman knew that as a slave she could be sold at any time, so she had to plan her escape quickly.

Read with a Purpose Read this biography to find out how one determined, courageous woman escaped from slavery.

A GLORY OVER Everything

by **Ann Petry**

One day in 1849, when Harriet was working in the fields near the edge of the road, a white woman wearing a faded sunbonnet went past, driving a wagon. She stopped the wagon and watched Harriet for a few minutes. Then she spoke to her, asked her what her name was, and how she had acquired the deep scar on her forehead. **A**

Harriet told her the story of the blow she had received when she was a girl. After that, whenever the woman saw her in the fields, she stopped to talk to her. She told Harriet that she lived on a farm near Bucktown. Then one day she said, not looking at Harriet but looking instead at the overseer far off at the edge of the fields, "If you ever need any help, Harriet, ever need any help, why, you let me know."

That same year the young heir to the Brodas estate[1] died. Harriet mentioned the fact of his death to the white woman in the faded sunbonnet the next time she saw her. She told her of the panic-stricken talk in the quarter, told her that the slaves were afraid

1. **Brodas estate:** Edward Brodas, the previous owner of the plantation, died in 1849 and left his property to his heir, who was not yet old enough to manage it. In the meantime the plantation was placed in the hands of the boy's guardian, Dr. Thompson.

Literary Perspectives

Analyzing Responses to Literature When you read a text, you view it through the lens of your own perspective—your values, ideas, and experiences. Because we all have different ideas and experiences, we may respond to texts in different ways.

When you use the Analyzing Responses to Literature perspective, you consider not only how the literary elements in the text (such as plot, character, setting, and theme) affect your response but also how your *own* background—what *you* contribute to the reading experience—affects your response. This view suggests that a literary work has no uniform "correct" meaning, but instead inspires different responses from different readers.

Active readers bring their own thoughts, moods, and experiences to what they read. The meaning they get out of a text depends upon their own expectations and ideas. For example, if you read a story about a kid who feels overlooked in her enormous family, and you are the middle child in a large family, the story will have meaning for you that it wouldn't have for, say, an only child.

As you read, be sure to notice and use the Literary Perspective notes at the bottom of the selection's pages.

A **Literary Focus** **Third-Person Point of View** From whose point of view is this first paragraph told?

that the master, Dr. Thompson, would start selling them. She said that Doc Thompson no longer permitted any of them to hire their time.[2] The woman nodded her head, clucked to the horse, and drove off, murmuring, "If you ever need any help—"

The slaves were right about Dr. Thompson's intention. He began selling slaves almost immediately. Among the first ones sold were two of Harriet Tubman's sisters. They went south with the chain gang on a Saturday. **B**

When Harriet heard of the sale of her sisters, she knew that the time had finally come when she must leave the plantation. She was reluctant to attempt the long trip north alone, not because of John Tubman's threat to betray her[3] but because she was afraid she might fall asleep somewhere along the way and so would be caught immediately.

She persuaded three of her brothers to go with her. Having made certain that John was asleep, she left the cabin quietly and met her brothers at the edge of the plantation. They agreed that she was to lead the way, for she was more familiar with the woods than the others.

2. **hire their time:** Some slaveholders allowed the people they held in slavery to hire themselves out for pay to other plantation owners who needed extra help. In such cases, the workers were permitted to keep their earnings.
3. **threat to betray her:** Harriet's husband, John Tubman, was a free man who was content with his life. He violently disapproved of his wife's plan to escape and threatened to tell the master if she carried it out.

The three men followed her, crashing through the underbrush, frightening themselves, stopping constantly to say, "What was that?" or "Someone's coming."

She thought of Ben[4] and how he had said, "Any old body can go through a woods crashing and mashing things down like a cow." She said sharply, "Can't you boys go quieter? Watch where you're going!" **C**

One of them grumbled, "Can't see in the dark. Ain't got cat's eyes like you."

"You don't need cat's eyes," she retorted. "On a night like this, with all the stars out, it's not black dark. Use your own eyes."

She supposed they were doing the best they could, but they moved very slowly. She kept getting so far ahead of them that she had to stop and wait for them to catch up with her, lest they lose their way. Their progress was slow, uncertain. Their feet got tangled in every vine. They tripped over fallen logs, and once one of them fell flat on his face. They jumped, startled, at the most ordinary sounds: the murmur of the wind in the branches of the trees, the twittering of a bird. They kept turning around, looking back.

They had not gone more than a mile when she became aware that they had stopped. She turned and went back to them. She could hear them whispering. One of them called out, "Hat!"

"What's the matter? We haven't got time to keep stopping like this."

4. **Ben:** Harriet Tubman's father. Her mother is called Old Rit.

B **Literary Perspectives** **Responses to Literature** How might someone who has experienced a family separation read this differently than someone who has not?

C **Read and Discuss** What does Harriet's behavior during their escape tell you about her?

Analyzing Visuals

Viewing and Interpreting
How does this image illustrate Harriet Tubman's yearning for freedom?

Under the Midnight Blues (2003) by Colin Bootman.

"We're going back."

"No," she said firmly. "We've got a good start. If we move fast and move quiet—"

Then all three spoke at once. They said the same thing, over and over, in frantic hurried whispers, all talking at once:

They told her that they had changed their minds. Running away was too dangerous. Someone would surely see them and recognize them. By morning the master would know they had "took off." Then the handbills advertising them would be posted all over Dorchester County. The patterollers[5] would search for them. Even if they were lucky enough to elude the patrol, they could not possibly hide from the bloodhounds. The hounds would be baying after them, snuffing through the swamps and the underbrush, zigzagging through the deepest woods. The bloodhounds would surely find them. And everyone knew what happened to a runaway who was caught and brought back alive.

She argued with them. Didn't they know that if they went back they would be sold, if not tomorrow, then the next day, or the next? Sold south. They had seen the chain gangs. Was that what they wanted? Were they going to be slaves for the rest of their lives? Didn't freedom mean anything to them? **D**

5. **patterollers:** patrollers.

D **Reading Focus** **Main Idea** How do Harriet's words here relate to finding the main idea of the story?

Vocabulary **elude** (ih LOOD) *v.:* escape the notice of; avoid detection by.

"You're afraid," she said, trying to shame them into action. "Go on back. I'm going north alone."

Instead of being ashamed, they became angry. They shouted at her, telling her that she was a fool and they would make her go back to the plantation with them. Suddenly they surrounded her, three men, her own brothers, jostling her, pushing her along, pinioning[6] her arms behind her. She fought against them, wasting her strength, exhausting herself in a furious struggle.

They shouted at her, telling her that she was a fool and they would make her go back to the plantation with them.

She was no match for three strong men. She said, panting, "All right. We'll go back. I'll go with you."

She led the way, moving slowly. Her thoughts were bitter. Not one of them was willing to take a small risk in order to be free. It had all seemed so perfect, so simple, to have her brothers go with her, sharing the dangers of the trip together, just as a family should. Now if she ever went north, she would have to go alone. **E**

Two days later, a slave working beside Harriet in the fields motioned to her. She bent toward him, listening. He said the water boy had just brought news to the field hands, and it had been passed from one to the other until it reached him. The news was that Harriet and her brothers had been sold to the Georgia trader and that they were to be sent south with the chain gang that very night. **F**

Harriet went on working but she knew a moment of panic. She would have to go north alone. She would have to start as soon as it was dark. She could not go with the chain gang. She might die on the way because of those inexplicable sleeping seizures. But then she—how could she run away? She might fall asleep in plain view along the road. **G**

But even if she fell asleep, she thought, the Lord would take care of her. She murmured a prayer, "Lord, I'm going to hold steady on to You, and You've got to see me through."

Afterward, she explained her decision to run the risk of going north alone in these words: "I had reasoned this out in my mind; there was one of two things I had a *right* to, liberty or death; if I could not have one, I would have the other; for no man should take me alive; I should fight for my liberty as long as my strength lasted, and when the time came for me to go, the Lord would let them take me." **H**

6. **pinioning** (PIHN yuhn ihng): pinning.

E **Literary Perspectives** **Responses to Literature** How might the experience of having a brother or sister affect the way a reader understands this passage?

F **Read and Discuss** What has Harriet just learned?

G **Literary Focus** **Third-Person Point of View** In this paragraph, Petry shows Harriet's thoughts and fears almost as if they are her own. Why do you think she writes this way?

H **Read and Discuss** What is Harriet up to? How does Harriet's decision fit in with what you already know about her?

At dusk, when the work in the fields was over, she started toward the Big House.[7] She had to let someone know that she was going north, someone she could trust. She no longer trusted John Tubman and it gave her a lost, lonesome feeling. Her sister Mary worked in the Big House, and she planned to tell Mary that she was going to run away, so someone would know.

As she went toward the house, she saw the master, Doc Thompson, riding up the drive on his horse. She turned aside and went toward the quarter. A field hand had no legitimate reason for entering the kitchen of the Big House—and yet—there must be some way she could leave word so that afterward someone would think about it and know that she had left a message.

As she went toward the quarter, she began to sing. Dr. Thompson reined in his horse, turned around, and looked at her. It was not the beauty of her voice that made him turn and watch her, frowning; it was the words of the song that she was singing and something defiant in her manner that disturbed and puzzled him.

When that old chariot comes,
I'm going to leave you,
I'm bound for the promised land,
Friends, I'm going to leave you.
I'm sorry, friends, to leave you,
Farewell! Oh, farewell!
But I'll meet you in the morning,
Farewell! Oh, farewell!
I'll meet you in the morning,
When I reach the promised land;
On the other side of Jordan,
For I'm bound for the promised land. **I**

That night when John Tubman was asleep and the fire had died down in the cabin, she took the ash cake that had been baked for their breakfast and a good-sized piece of salt herring and tied them together in an old bandanna. By hoarding this small stock of food, she could make it last a long time, and with the berries and edible roots she could find in the woods, she wouldn't starve.

She decided that she would take the quilt[8] with her, too. Her hands lingered over it. It felt soft and warm to her touch. Even in the dark, she thought she could tell one color from another because she knew its pattern and design so well.

Then John stirred in his sleep, and she left the cabin quickly, carrying the quilt carefully folded under her arm.

Once she was off the plantation, she took to the woods, not following the North Star, not even looking for it, going instead toward Bucktown. She needed help. She was going to ask the white woman who had stopped to talk to her so often if she would help her. Perhaps she wouldn't. But she would soon find out.

7. **Big House:** plantation owner's house.

8. **the quilt:** Tubman had painstakingly stitched together a quilt before her wedding.

I **Read and Discuss** What is the point of Harriet's singing?

Vocabulary **legitimate** (luh JIHT uh miht) *adj.:* reasonable; justified.
defiant (dih FY uhnt) *adj.:* disobedient; boldly resistant.

When she came to the farmhouse where the woman lived, she approached it cautiously, circling around it. It was so quiet. There was no sound at all, not even a dog barking or the sound of voices. Nothing.

She tapped on the door, gently. A voice said, "Who's there?" She answered, "Harriet, from Dr. Thompson's place."

When the woman opened the door, she did not seem at all surprised to see her. She glanced at the little bundle that Harriet was carrying, at the quilt, and invited her in. Then she sat down at the kitchen table and wrote two names on a slip of paper and handed the paper to Harriet.

She said that those were the next places where it was safe for Harriet to stop. The first place was a farm where there was a gate with big white posts and round knobs on top of them. The people there would feed her, and when they thought it was safe for her to go on, they would tell her how to get to the next house or take her there.

For these were the first two stops on the Underground Railroad—going north, from the eastern shore of Maryland.

Thus Harriet learned that the Underground Railroad that ran straight to the North was not a railroad at all. Neither did it run underground. It was composed of a loosely organized group of people who offered food and shelter, or a place of concealment, to fugitives who had set out on the long road to the North and freedom. J

Harriet wanted to pay this woman who had befriended her. But she had no money. She gave her the patchwork quilt, the only beautiful object she had ever owned.

That night she made her way through the woods, crouching in the underbrush whenever she heard the sound of horses' hoofs, staying there until the riders passed. Each time, she wondered if they were already hunting for her. It would be so easy to describe her, the deep scar on her forehead like a dent, the old scars on the back of her neck, the husky speaking voice, the lack of height, scarcely five feet tall. The master would say she was wearing rough clothes when she ran away, that she had a bandanna on her head, that she was muscular and strong. K

She knew how accurately he would describe her. One of the slaves who could read used to tell the others what it said on those handbills that were nailed up on the trees along the edge of the roads. It was easy to recognize the handbills that advertised runaways because there was always a picture in one corner, a picture of a black man, a little running figure with a stick over his shoulder and a bundle tied on the end of the stick.

Whenever she thought of the handbills, she walked faster. Sometimes she stumbled over old grapevines, gnarled and twisted, thick as a man's wrist, or became entangled in the tough sinewy vine of the honeysuckle. But she kept going.

In the morning she came to the house where her friend had said she was to stop.

J **Read and Discuss** How do things turn out for Harriet? What information does she learn about the Underground Railroad?

K **Literary Focus** **Biography** What does the author reveal about Harriet here? How does the author know this?

Vocabulary **cautiously** (KAW shuhs lee) *adv.:* safely; very carefully.
befriended (bih FREHND ihd) *v.:* helped out or encouraged.

She showed the slip of paper that she carried to the woman who answered her knock at the back door of the farmhouse. The woman fed her and then handed her a broom and told her to sweep the yard.

Harriet hesitated, suddenly suspicious. Then she decided that with a broom in her hand, working in the yard, she would look as though she belonged on the place; certainly no one would suspect that she was a runaway.

That night the woman's husband, a farmer, loaded a wagon with produce. Harriet climbed in. He threw some blankets over her, and the wagon started.

It was dark under the blankets and not exactly comfortable. But Harriet decided that riding was better than walking. She was surprised at her own lack of fear, wondered how it was that she so readily trusted these strangers who might betray her. For all she knew, the man driving the wagon might be taking her straight back to the master.

She thought of those other rides in wagons, when she was a child, the same clop-clop of the horses' feet, creak of

Analyzing Visuals **Viewing and Interpreting** What do you learn about Harriet Tubman from her room and her physical appearance? What distinct details suggest her personal qualities?

the wagon, and the feeling of being lost because she did not know where she was going. She did not know her destination this time either, but she was not alarmed. She thought of John Tubman. By this time he must have told the master that she was gone. Then she thought of the plantation and how the land rolled gently down toward the river, thought of Ben and Old Rit, and that Old Rit would be inconsolable because her favorite daughter was missing. “Lord,” she prayed, “I’m going to hold steady onto You. You’ve got to see me through.” Then she went to sleep.

The next morning, when the stars were still visible in the sky, the farmer stopped the wagon. Harriet was instantly awake.

He told her to follow the river, to keep following it to reach the next place where people would take her in and feed her. He said that she must travel only at night and she must stay off the roads because the patrol would be hunting for her. Harriet climbed out of the wagon. “Thank you,” she said simply, thinking how amazing it was that there should be white people who were willing to go to such lengths to help a slave get to the North.

“Thank you,” she said simply, thinking how amazing it was that there should be white people who were willing to go to such lengths to help a slave get to the North.

When she finally arrived in Pennsylvania, she had traveled roughly ninety miles from Dorchester County. She had slept on the ground outdoors at night. She had been rowed for miles up the Choptank River by a man she had never seen before. She had been concealed in a haycock[9] and had, at one point, spent a week hidden in a potato hole in a cabin which belonged to a family of free Negroes. She had been hidden in the attic of the home of a Quaker. She had been befriended by stout German farmers, whose guttural[10] speech surprised her and whose well-kept farms astonished her. She had never before seen barns and fences, farmhouses and outbuildings, so carefully painted. The cattle and horses were so clean they looked as though they had been scrubbed. **L**

When she crossed the line into the free state of Pennsylvania, the sun was coming up. She said, “I looked at my hands to see if I was the same person now I was free. There was such a glory over everything, the sun came like gold through the trees and over the fields, and I felt like I was in heaven.” **M**

---

9. **haycock:** pile of hay in a field.
10. **guttural:** harsh; rasping.

L **Read and Discuss** The author has presented a lot of detail about Harriet’s journey. What point is the author trying to make?

M **Reading Focus** **Main Idea** What thoughts do you have now about the main idea of this selection? What clues does this final paragraph hold?

Applying Your Skills

Sunshine State Standards: Benchmarks LA.6.1.7.3 determine the main idea or essential message in grade-level text through inferring, paraphrasing, summarizing, and identifying relevant details; *Also covered* **LA.6.2.2.3; LA.6.2.2.4; LA.6.3.2.3; LA.6.4.2.3**

A Glory over Everything

Respond and Think Critically

Reading Focus

1. Why does Harriet become suspicious when the woman at the farm hands her a broom? **FCAT**
   - **A** because Harriet is worried that she will be forced to work as a farm slave
   - **B** because the broom belongs to Dr. Thompson, her old master
   - **C** because Harriet expects to stitch a quilt on the farm
   - **D** because the woman is known for sending slaves to the South

Read with a Purpose

2. How did Harriet Tubman escape from slavery?

Reading Skills: Finding the Main Idea

3. Review your notes from "A Glory over Everything." Use details to make inferences about the main idea. State the main idea.

Notes for Finding the Main Idea in "A Glory over Everything"

Details in the First Paragraph	A white woman asks about Harriet's scar.
Important Passages/ Other Key Details	Dr. Thompson starts selling slaves.
Details in the Last Paragraph	
State the Main Idea:	

Literary Focus

Literary Analysis

4. **Interpret** Slaves often used songs to communicate secretly. When Tubman sings about leaving on a chariot, what message is she sending to her sister? Support your answer with details from the story. READ THINK EXPLAIN

Literary Skills: Biography and Third-Person Point of View

5. **Analyze** Re-read the paragraph on page 499 that begins, "As she went toward..." Why could this passage appear in a biography but not in an autobiography? Choose another paragraph and rewrite it as an autobiography.

Literary Skills Review: Character Traits

6. **Infer** **Character Traits** are the qualities a character has. What are Harriet's traits? How are they revealed? Support your answer with details from the story.

Writing Focus

Think as a Reader/Writer

Use It in Your Writing Look at your notes on how dialogue helped you gain a perspective of Harriet Tubman's character. Write a biographical sketch of someone you know in which the only dialogue is spoken by other characters.

What Do You Think Now?

How did this text affect your thoughts about the value of freedom? Would you be willing to do what Tubman did? Explain.

Applying Your Skills

A Glory over Everything

Vocabulary Development

Vocabulary Skills: Clarifying Word Meanings

One useful way to gain fluency with unfamiliar words is to ask yourself a question that includes the word. Your answer can help you clarify the word's meaning. Here's an example using one of the Vocabulary words from this selection:

Question: How did Tubman manage to *elude* her pursuers?

Answer: She *ran away* at night, and people helped her *hide* and *leave the area*.

Your Turn

elude
legitimate
defiant
cautiously
befriended

Show your mastery of the remaining four Vocabulary words from the box at right by answering the following questions:

1. Explain why Tubman had a *legitimate* reason to fear being sold.
2. In what way was Tubman's song about leaving on a chariot *defiant*?
3. Why did Tubman have to proceed *cautiously* through the woods?
4. Why was Tubman *befriended* by so many people throughout her journey?

Language Coach

Words That Describe In the box to the right are some other descriptive words from the selection you just read. Use a dictionary to find the meaning of each word. Then, write a descriptive paragraph about Harriet Tubman, using at least three of the words.

faded
murmuring
tangled
zigzagging
jostling

Academic Vocabulary

Talk About . . .

With a partner, discuss the meaning of *freedom* from Tubman's perspective. How did the selling of Tubman's sisters contribute to Tubman's decision to seek freedom? What would her future have been like if she had not risked her life to gain her freedom? Use the underlined Academic Vocabulary words in your discussion.

Sunshine State Standards: Benchmarks **LA.6.1.6.3** use context clues to determine meanings of unfamiliar words; **LA.6.1.6.10** determine meanings of words, pronunciation, parts of speech, etymologies, and alternate word choices by using a dictionary, thesaurus, and digital tools; **LA.6.3.4.5** consistency in verb tense in simple, compound, and complex sentences; **LA.6.4.1.1** write narrative accounts with an engaging plot (including rising action, conflict, climax, falling action, and resolution) include a clearly described setting with figurative language and descriptive words or phrases to enhance style and tone; **LA.6.4.2.3** write informational/expository essays (e.g., process, description, explanation, comparison/contrast, problem/solution) that include a thesis statement, supporting details, and introductory, body, and concluding paragraphs; **LA.6.5.2.2** deliver narrative and informative presentations, including oral responses to literature, and adjust oral language, body language, eye contact, gestures, technology and supporting graphics appropriate to the situation.

Grammar Link

Troublesome Verbs

The **past tense** and **past participle** of most verbs are formed by adding *–d* or *–ed,* but **irregular verbs** change in sneaky ways. You just have to memorize them. The past participle is the form you use with the helping verbs *has, have,* and *had.*

Here are some irregular verbs from "A Glory over Everything."

Base Form	Past Tense	Past Participle
sell	sold	(have) sold
wear	wore	(have) worn
see	saw	(have) seen
run	ran	(have) run

Your Turn

Fill in the chart of irregular verbs below.

Base Form	Past Tense	Past Participle
take		
think		
awake		
begin		

Writing Applications Write a brief summary of "A Glory over Everything." In your summary, include past tense and past participle forms of these irregular verbs: *tell, sell, wear, see, run, think, begin.*

CHOICES

As you respond to the Choices, use these **Academic Vocabulary** words as appropriate: contribute, perspective, distinct, uniform.

REVIEW

Paint a Mural

Group Work With a group of classmates, design and paint a mural showing Tubman's escape. Use a long strip of paper that you can post on the wall. Before starting, make sketches and decide on the materials and colors you'll use. Decide together on three or four distinct incidents that you want to depict. Present your mural to the class.

CONNECT

Be a Character in the Story

Timed Writing Imagine that you are one of the people mentioned in "A Glory over Everything," such as one of Harriet's brothers, someone in the Underground Railroad, or Harriet herself. Tell the story from your own perspective, using the first-person point of view. What are your feelings and motivations?

EXTEND

Write an Obituary

Read part of a biography or an encyclopedia article to find out how Harriet Tubman lived the rest of her life after she gained her freedom. What did she contribute to society? Then, write an obituary for Tubman that summarizes the highlights of her life.

Learn It Online
Discover more about the story using Internet links:
go.hrw.com
L6-505
Go

COMPARING TEXTS

Comparing Literary Devices in Fiction and Nonfiction

CONTENTS

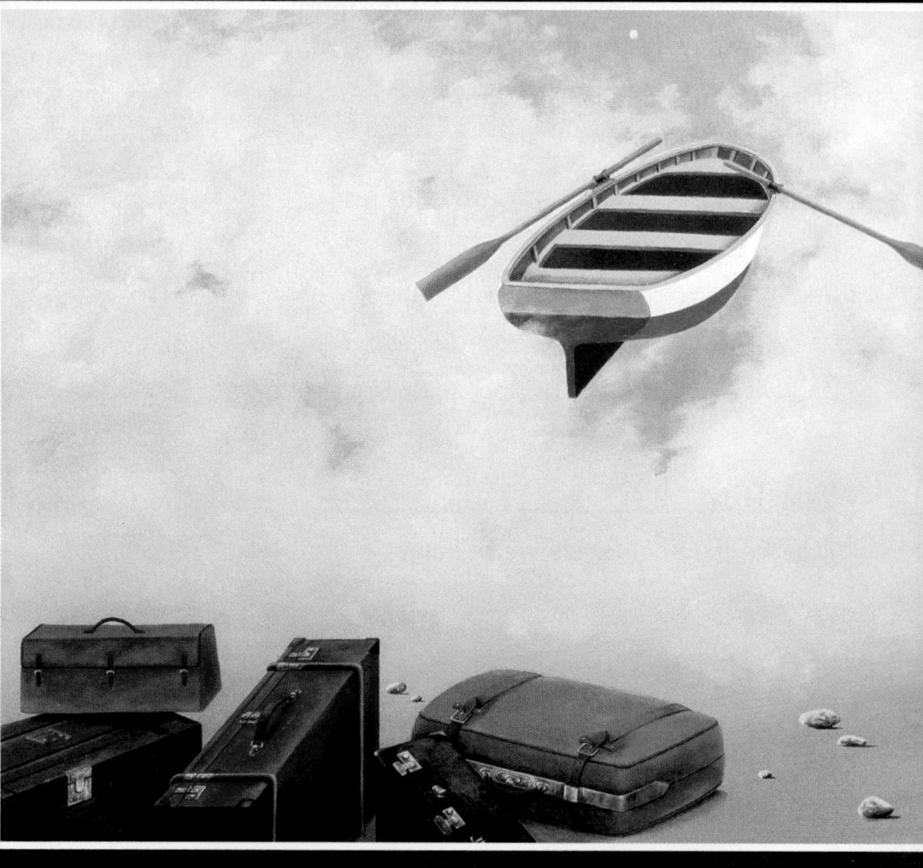

Utopie (1999) by Bob Lescaux.

What lessons do you have to learn before you can achieve your dreams?

QuickWrite

Think about a life lesson you've learned that helped you accomplish something or solve a problem. In a few sentences, describe the lesson and how you learned it.

Preparing to Read

Sunshine State Standards: Benchmarks **LA.6.1.6.1** use new vocabulary that is introduced and taught directly; **LA.6.1.6.4** categorize key vocabulary and identify salient features; *Also covered* **LA.6.1.7.2; LA.6.1.7.8; LA.6.2.1.3; LA.6.2.1.7**

Storm / The Mysterious Mr. Lincoln / What Do Fish Have to Do with Anything?

Literary Focus

Literary Devices One important way writers awaken our feelings and imaginations is through the use of "word tools" or **literary devices** like these:

- **Imagery** consists of "word pictures" that appeal to our senses.
- **Figurative language** refers to imaginative comparisons made between seemingly unlike things. A **metaphor** makes a comparison by saying something *is* something else: *You're a fish out of water*. A **simile** makes a comparison using *like* or *as*: *The moon is like a silver platter.* **Personification** gives human qualities to something that is not human: *The wind slapped us.*
- **Symbols** are concrete images that stand for something beyond themselves: Doves symbolize peace; acorns symbolize growth. The use of symbols by a writer is called **symbolism**.

Reading Focus

Comparing Authors' Purposes A writer's purpose may be to **inform,** to **persuade,** to **express feelings,** or simply to **entertain.** There may be more than one purpose, but usually one is more important than the others.

Into Action For each selection, make a pie chart that you divide into four sections, one for each purpose. Jot down literary devices and other details that support each purpose.

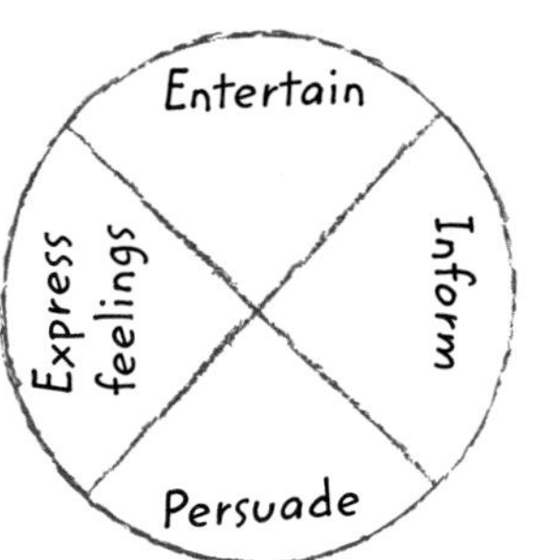

Writing Focus

Think as a Reader/Writer

Find It in Your Reading Look for especially surprising or memorable figurative language in these selections, and write down your favorites in your *Reader/Writer Notebook*.

Reader/Writer Notebook

Use your **RWN** to complete the activities for these selections.

Vocabulary

Storm

resembled (rih ZEHM buhld) *v.:* was similar to. *The dog resembled a bear.*

The Mysterious Mr. Lincoln

defy (dih FY) *v.:* resist. *The problems defy solution.*

ambitious (am BIHSH uhs) *adj.:* very much wanting success. *He and his plans were ambitious.*

cautious (KAW shuhs) *adj.:* careful. *Lincoln's approach to the war was cautious.*

What Do Fish Have to Do with Anything?

urgency (UR juhn see) *n.:* pressure; insistence. *"Go!" the boy said with urgency.*

ashamed (uh SHAYMD) *adj.:* embarrassed. *She was ashamed of being alone.*

Language Coach

Synonyms and Antonyms For each word above, think of one synonym (a word that means nearly the same) and one antonym (a word that means the opposite).

Learn It Online
For previews of these stories, see the video introductions on:

go.hrw.com L6-507 

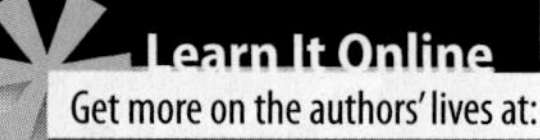

Learn It Online
Get more on the authors' lives at:
go.hrw.com L6-508 Go

Gary Paulsen

(1939–)

A Passion for Writing

An army officer's son, Gary Paulsen lived all over the country when he was a boy. Because he was always moving, he had trouble making friends. He developed a passion for reading, which led to a passion for writing. Paulsen says of his craft, "I have not done anything else in life that gives me the personal satisfaction that writing does."

Russell Freedman

(1929–)

Studying Mr. Lincoln

Russell Freedman has written over three dozen books on historical topics. He says of Abraham Lincoln, "The Lincoln I grew up with was a cardboard figure, too good to believe. . . . When I had some inkling he was a complicated person in his own right, I decided I wanted to know more about him."

Avi

(1937–)

Writing out of Sheer Stubbornness

Determined to prove he could become a writer, Avi says he succeeded out of "sheer stubbornness." He discovered his true audience when he became a father and started writing for children and young adults. "Writing for kids has been at the center of my life ever since."

Think About the Writers

In what sense is each of these writers motivated by trying to prove something?

Preview the Selections

In "Storm," you'll meet **Storm,** a dog with a sense of humor, and his owner, **Gary Paulsen.**

In "The Mysterious Mr. Lincoln," you'll discover the complex personality of **Abraham Lincoln,** one of our nation's greatest presidents.

In "What Do Fish Have to Do with Anything?" you'll meet a thoughtful boy named **Willie;** his mother, **Mrs. Markham;** and a **homeless man** whom they each see from a very different perspective.

AUTOBIOGRAPHY

Storm

from Woodsong by **Gary Paulsen**

Siberian Husky by Scott Kennedy.

Read with a Purpose

Read to find out what qualities make a dog named Storm very special to Gary Paulsen.

Build Background

"Storm" is taken from *Woodsong*, Gary Paulsen's account of his adventures in northern Minnesota. There he ran a team of sled dogs. Paulsen later ran the Iditarod (y DIHT uh rahd), the famous—and dangerous—dog sled race between Anchorage and Nome, Alaska.

It is always possible to learn from dogs, and in fact the longer I'm with them, the more I understand how little I know. But there was one dog who taught me the most. Just one dog. Storm. First dog. . . .

Joy, loyalty, toughness, peacefulness—all of these were part of Storm. Lessons about life and, finally, lessons about death came from him. **A**

He had a bear's ears. He was brindle colored[1] and built like a truck, and his ears were rounded when we got him, so that

1. **brindle colored:** gray or brown and streaked or spotted with a dark color.

A **Read and Discuss** What has Paulsen told us so far?

they looked like bear cub ears. They gave him a comical look when he was young that somehow hung on to him even when he grew old. He had a sense of humor to match his ears, and when he grew truly old, he somehow resembled George Burns.[2]

At peak, he was a mighty dog. He pulled like a machine. Until we retired him and used him only for training puppies, until we let him loose to enjoy his age, he pulled, his back over in the power curve, so that nothing could stop the sled. **B**

In his fourth or fifth year as a puller, he started doing tricks. First he would play jokes on the dog pulling next to him. On long runs he would become bored, and when we least expected it, he would reach across the gang line and snort wind into the ear of the dog next to him. I ran him with many different dogs and he did it to all of them—chuckling when the dog jumped and shook his or her head—but I never saw a single dog get mad at him for it. Oh, there was once a dog named Fonzie who nearly took his head off, but Fonzie wasn't really mad at him so much as surprised. Fonzie once nailed me through the wrist for waking him up too suddenly when he was sleeping. I'd reached down and touched him before whispering his name. **C**

Small jokes. Gentle jokes, Storm played. He took to hiding things from me. At first I couldn't understand where things were going. I would put a bootie down while working on a dog, and it would disappear. I lost a small ladle[3] I used for watering each dog, a cloth glove liner I took off while working on a dog's feet, a roll of tape, and finally, a hat.

He was so clever.

2. **George Burns** (1896–1996): American comedian and actor with large ears.

3. **ladle:** cup-shaped spoon with a long handle for dipping out liquids.

B **Literary Focus** **Figurative Language** What two similes has Paulsen used to describe Storm? How do the similes help you understand what Storm was like?

C **Read and Discuss** What have you learned about Storm?

Vocabulary **resembled** (rih ZEHM buhld) *v.:* was similar to.

Eager to Run by Scott Kennedy.

Analyzing Visuals **Viewing and Interpreting** What does this image suggest about the bond between Paulsen and Storm?

When I lost the hat, it was a hot day and I had taken the hat off while I worked on a dog's harness. The dog was just ahead of Storm, and when I knelt to work on the harness—he'd chewed almost through the side of it while running—I put the hat down on the snow near Storm.

Or thought I had. When I had changed the dog's harness, I turned and the hat was gone. I looked around, moved the dogs, looked under them, then shrugged. At first I was sure I'd put the hat down; then, when I couldn't find it, I became less sure, and at last I thought perhaps I had left it at home or dropped it somewhere on the run.

Storm sat quietly, looking ahead down the trail, not showing anything at all. **D**

I went back to the sled, reached down to disengage the hook, and when I did, the dogs exploded forward. I was not quite on the sled when they took off, so I was knocked slightly off balance. I leaned over to the right to regain myself, and when I did, I accidentally dragged the hook through the snow.

And pulled up my hat.

It had been buried off to the side of the trail in the snow, buried neatly with the snow smoothed over the top, so that it was completely hidden. Had the snow hook not scraped down four or five inches, I never would have found it.

I stopped the sled and set the hook once more. While knocking the snow out of the hat and putting it back on my head, I studied where it had happened.

Right next to Storm.

He had taken the hat, quickly dug a hole, buried the hat and smoothed the snow over it, then gone back to sitting, staring ahead, looking completely innocent.

D **Read and Discuss** What new information about Storm has Paulsen given us?

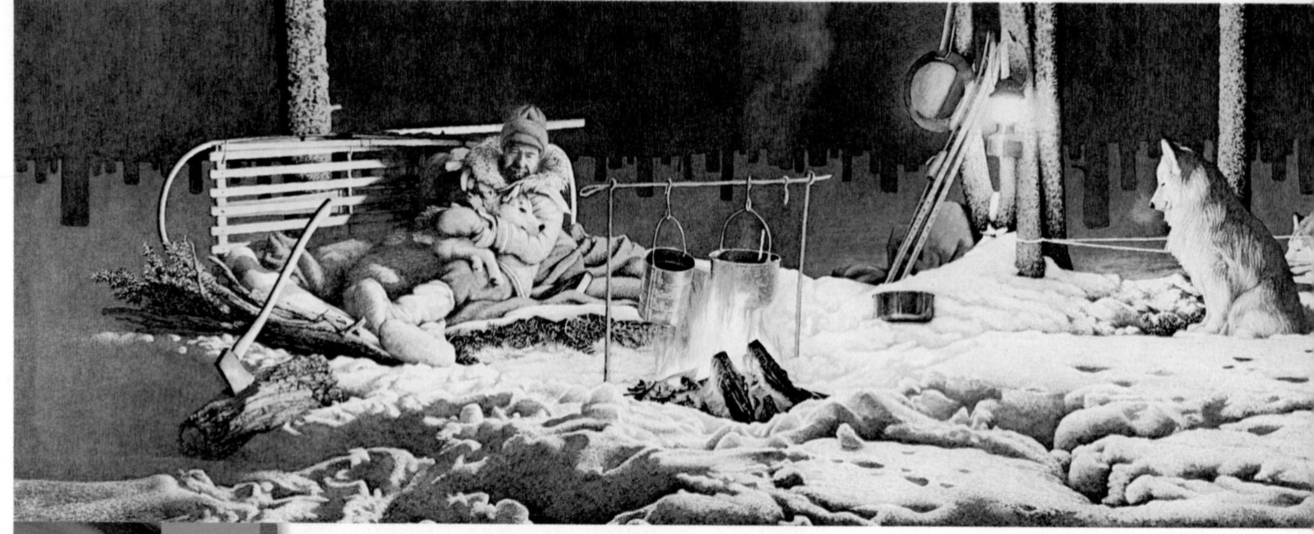

Never Alone by Scott Kennedy.

Analyzing Visuals **Viewing and Interpreting** How accurately does this painting show the relationship between Paulsen, Storm, and the rest of the dogs?

When I stopped the sled and picked up the hat, he looked back, saw me put the hat on my head, and—I swear—smiled. Then he shook his head once and went back to work pulling. **E**

Along with the jokes, Storm had scale eyes. He watched as the sled was loaded, carefully calculated the weight of each item, and let his disapproval be known if it went too far.

One winter a friend gave us a parlor stove with nickel trim. It was not an enormous stove, but it had some weight to it and some bulk. This friend lived twelve miles away—twelve miles over two fair hills followed by about eight miles on an old, abandoned railroad grade.[4] We needed the stove badly (our old barrel stove had started to burn through), so I took off with the team to pick it up. I left early in the morning because I wanted to get back that same day. It had snowed four or five inches, so the dogs would have to break trail. By the time we had done the hills and the railroad grade, pushing in new snow all the time, they were ready for a rest. I ran them the last two miles to where the stove was and unhooked their tugs so they could rest while I had coffee.

We stopped for an hour at least, the dogs sleeping quietly. When it was time to go, my friend and I carried the stove outside and put it in the sled. The dogs didn't move.

Except for Storm.

He raised his head, opened one eye, did a perfect double take—both eyes opening wide—and sat up. He had been facing the front. Now he turned around to face the sled—so he was facing away from the direction we had to travel when we left—and watched us load the sled. **F**

It took some time, as the stove barely fit on the sled and had to be jiggled and shuffled around to get it down between the side rails.

4. **railroad grade:** rise or elevation in a railroad track.

E **Reading Focus** **Author's Purpose** How does this detail help you determine the author's purpose in telling this story?

F **Read and Discuss** What's going on with Storm?

Through it all, Storm sat and watched us, his face a study in interest. He did not get up but sat on his back end, and when I was done and ready to go, I hooked all the dogs back in harness—which involved hooking the tugs to the rear ties on their harnesses. The dogs knew this meant we were going to head home, so they got up and started slamming against the tugs, trying to get the sled to move.

All of them, that is, but Storm. **G**

Storm sat backward, the tug hooked up but hanging down. The other dogs were screaming to run, but Storm sat and stared at the stove.

Not at me, not at the sled, but at the stove itself. Then he raised his lips, bared his teeth, and growled at the stove.

When he was finished growling, he snorted twice, stood, turned away from the stove, and started to pull. But each time we stopped at the tops of the hills to let the dogs catch their breath after pulling the sled and stove up the steep incline, Storm turned and growled at the stove.

The enemy.

The weight on the sled. **H**

I do not know how many miles Storm and I ran together. Eight, ten, perhaps twelve thousand miles. He was one of the first dogs and taught me the most, and as we worked together, he came to know me better than perhaps even my own family. He could look once at my shoulders and tell how I was feeling, tell how far we were to run, how fast we had to run—knew it all. **I**

When I started to run long, moved from running a work team, a trap line team, to training for the Iditarod, Storm took it in stride, changed the pace down to the long trot, matched what was needed, and settled in for the long haul.

He did get bored, however, and one day while we were running a long run, he started

---

G **Reading Focus** **Author's Purpose** How is Paulsen letting you know that you're about to get another amusing example of Storm's personality?

H **Literary Focus** **Imagery** Describe the scene here. How do Paulsen's images make you see the stove as Storm sees it?

I **Read and Discuss** What point about Storm is the author trying to make?

doing a thing that would stay with him—with us—until the end. We had gone forty or fifty miles on a calm, even day with no bad wind. The temperature was a perfect ten below zero. The sun was bright, everything was moving well, and the dogs had settled into the rhythm that could take them a hundred or a thousand miles.

And Storm got bored.

At a curve in the trail, a small branch came out over the path we were running, and as Storm passed beneath the limb, he jumped up and grabbed it, broke a short piece off—about a foot long—and kept it in his mouth.

All day.

And into the night. He ran, carrying the stick like a toy, and when we stopped to feed or rest, he would put the stick down, eat, then pick it up again. He would put the stick down carefully in front of him, or across his paws, and sleep, and when he awakened, he would pick up the stick, and it soon became a thing between us, the stick.

He would show it to me, making a contact, a connection between us, each time we stopped. I would pet him on top of the head and take the stick from him—he would emit a low, gentle growl when I took the stick. I'd "examine" it closely, nod and seem to approve of it, and hand it back to him.

Each day we ran, he would pick a different stick. And each time I would have to approve of it, and after a time, after weeks and months, I realized that he was using the sticks as a way to communicate with me, to tell me that everything was all right, that I was doing the right thing. **J**

I realized that he was using the sticks as a way to communicate with me, to tell me that everything was all right.

Once, when I pushed them too hard during a pre-Iditarod race—when I thought it was important to compete and win (a feeling that didn't last long)—I walked up to Storm, and as I came close to him, he pointedly dropped the stick. I picked it up and held it out, but he wouldn't take it. He turned his face away. I put the stick against his lips and tried to make him take it, but he let it fall to the ground. When I realized what he was doing, I stopped and fed and rested the team, sat on the sled, and thought about what I was doing wrong. After four hours or so of sitting—watching other teams pass me—I fed them another snack, got ready to go, and was gratified to see Storm pick up the stick. From that time forward I looked for the stick always, knew when I saw it out to the sides of his head that I was doing the right thing. And it was always there. **K**

Through storms and cold weather, on the long runs, the long, long runs where there isn't an end to it, where only the sled and the winter around the sled and the wind are there, Storm had the stick to tell me it was right, all things were right.

J Literary Focus Symbol The stick became a symbol for Storm and Paulsen. What did the stick represent?

K Read and Discuss How does this information connect with what you've learned about the stick?

Applying Your Skills

Sunshine State Standards: Benchmarks **LA.6.1.6.1** use new vocabulary that is introduced and taught directly; **LA.6.1.7.2** analyze the author's purpose (e.g., to persuade, inform, entertain, or explain) and perspective in a variety of texts and understand how they affect meaning; *Also covered* **LA.6.1.7.8; LA.6.2.1.5; LA.6.2.1.7; LA.6.3.2.3; LA.6.4.2.3**

Storm

Respond and Think Critically

Reading Focus

1. Which action BEST causes Storm to appear human-like? **FCAT**
   A the way his ears looked as a puppy
   B the way he hid the hat in the snow
   C the way he held the branch in his mouth
   D the way he growled at the stove

Read with a Purpose

2. What qualities make Storm special?

Reading Skills: Author's Purpose

3. "Storm" is just a small part of Paulsen's autobiography. Writers often have more than one purpose for writing their autobiographies. What purposes can you see in "Storm"? Use the pie chart to analyze Paulsen's purpose. Beneath the chart, complete this sentence: *The author's main purpose is to . . .*

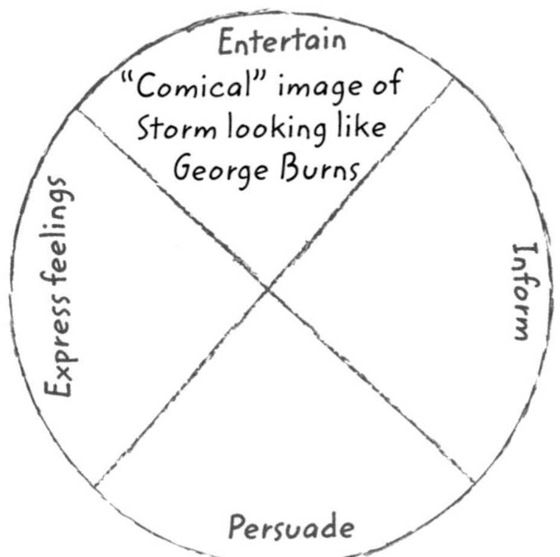

Vocabulary Check

Answer the following question.

4. What animal might a dog **resemble** if he is covered in snow?

Literary Focus

Literary Analysis

5. **Interpret** Explain why Paulsen values Storm as "the dog who taught me the most."
6. **Analyze** Paulsen's descriptions of Storm give clues to his own character. What kind of person do you think Paulsen is? Why?

Literary Skills: Imagery and Figurative Language

7. **Evaluate** Which imagery in the text MOST helped you form a mental picture of Storm? Support your answer with details from the text.

8. **Evaluate** Find three examples of figurative language used to describe Storm's actions. How do they bring Storm to life on the page?

Writing Focus

Think as a Reader/Writer

Use It in Your Writing Write your own description of an animal interacting with a person. Use at least two kinds of figurative language.

BIOGRAPHY

The Mysterious Mr. Lincoln

by **Russell Freedman**

Read with a Purpose

Read this selection to find out why Russell Freedman considers Abraham Lincoln "mysterious."

Preparing to Read for this selection is on page 507.

Build Background

This selection, "The Mysterious Mr. Lincoln," comes from Russell Freedman's book *Lincoln: A Photobiography*. Freedman's biography of Lincoln won the Newbery Medal for the most distinguished contribution to children's literature in 1988.

Abraham Lincoln wasn't the sort of man who could lose himself in a crowd. After all, he stood six feet four inches tall, and to top it off, he wore a high silk hat.

His height was mostly in his long, bony legs. When he sat in a chair, he seemed no taller than anyone else. It was only when he stood up that he towered above other men.

At first glance most people thought he was homely. Lincoln thought so too, referring once to his "poor, lean, lank face." As a young man he was sensitive about his gawky[1] looks, but in time, he learned to laugh at himself. When a rival called him "two-faced" during a political debate, Lincoln replied: "I leave it to my audience. If I had another face, do you think I'd wear this one?" **A**

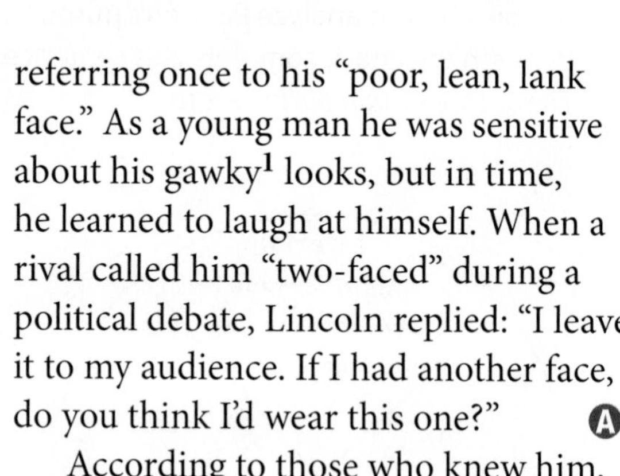

The Granger Collection, New York.

According to those who knew him, Lincoln was a man of many faces. In repose[2] he often seemed sad and

1. **gawky:** clumsy; awkward.
2. **repose** (rih POHZ): state of rest or inactivity.

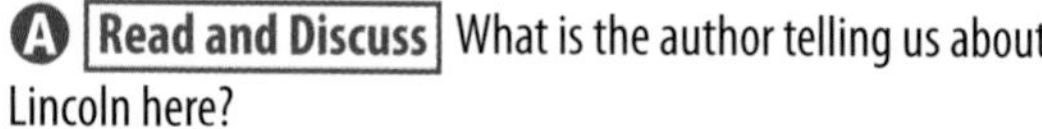

A **Read and Discuss** What is the author telling us about Lincoln here?

Analyzing Visuals **Viewing and Interpreting** In what ways do these images—the photograph of the house Lincoln grew up in and the portrait of him—reveal the "real" man?

Abraham Lincoln (1860) by George Peter Alexander Healy.

gloomy. But when he began to speak, his expression changed. "The dull, listless[3] features dropped like a mask," said a Chicago newspaperman. "The eyes began to sparkle, the mouth to smile; the whole countenance[4] was wreathed in animation, so that a stranger would have said, 'Why, this man, so angular and solemn a moment ago, is really handsome!' " **B**

Lincoln was the most photographed man of his time, but his friends insisted that no photo ever did him justice. It's no wonder. Back then, cameras required long exposures. The person being photographed had to "freeze" as the seconds ticked by. If he blinked an eye, the picture would be blurred. That's why Lincoln looks so stiff and formal in his photos. We never see him laughing or joking.

Artists and writers tried to capture the "real" Lincoln that the camera missed, but something about the man always escaped them. His changeable features, his tones, gestures, and expressions, seemed to defy description.

Today it's hard to imagine Lincoln as he really was. And he never cared to reveal

3. **listless** (LIHST lihs): too tired to care; not interested in anything.
4. **countenance** (KOWN tuh nuhns): face.

B **Literary Focus** **Figurative Language** What examples of figurative language do you find in this description of Lincoln?

Vocabulary **defy** (dih FY) *v.:* resist.

much about himself. In company he was witty and talkative, but he rarely betrayed his inner feelings. According to William Herndon, his law partner, he was "the most secretive—reticent[5]—shut-mouthed man that ever lived." **C**

In his own time, Lincoln was never fully understood even by his closest friends. Since then, his life story has been told and retold so many times he has become as much a legend as a flesh-and-blood human being. While the legend is based on truth, it is only partly true. And it hides the man behind it like a disguise.

> Today it's hard to imagine Lincoln as he really was.

The legendary Lincoln is known as Honest Abe, a humble man of the people who rose from a log cabin to the White House. There's no doubt that Lincoln was a poor boy who made good. And it's true that he carried his folksy manners and homespun speech to the White House with him. He said "howdy" to visitors and invited them to "stay a spell." He greeted diplomats while wearing carpet slippers, called his wife "mother" at receptions, and told bawdy[6] jokes at cabinet meetings.

Lincoln may have seemed like a common man, but he wasn't. His friends agreed that he was one of the most ambitious people they had ever known. Lincoln struggled hard to rise above his log-cabin origins, and he was proud of his achievements. By the time he ran for president he was a wealthy man, earning a large income from his law practice and his many investments. As for the nickname Abe, he hated it. No one who knew him well ever called him Abe to his face. They addressed him as Lincoln or Mr. Lincoln.

Lincoln is often described as a sloppy dresser, careless about his appearance. In fact, he patronized the best tailor in Springfield, Illinois, buying two suits a year. That was at a time when many men lived, died, and were buried in the same suit.

It's true that Lincoln had little formal "eddication," as he would have pronounced it. Almost everything he "larned" he taught himself. All his life he said "thar" for *there,* "git" for *get,* "kin" for *can.* Even so, he became an eloquent public speaker who could hold a vast audience spellbound and a great writer whose finest phrases still ring in our ears. He was known to sit up late into the night, discussing Shakespeare's plays with White House visitors.

He was certainly a humorous man, famous for his rollicking stories. But he was also moody and melancholy,[7] tormented by long and frequent bouts of depression. Humor was his therapy. He relied on his yarns,[8] a friend observed, to "whistle down sadness."

5. **reticent** (REHT uh suhnt): reserved; tending to speak little.
6. **bawdy:** not considered decent; crude.
7. **melancholy** (MEHL uhn kahl ee): sad; gloomy.
8. **yarns:** entertaining stories filled with exaggeration. Storytellers like Lincoln could be said to "spin" yarns.

C **Read and Discuss** From what you've read so far, what is your sense of Lincoln now?

Vocabulary **ambitious** (am BIHSH uhs) *adj.:* very much wanting success.

Analyzing Visuals

Viewing and Interpreting What qualities of this photograph can be explained by what you learned about early photography on page 517?

He had a cool, logical mind, trained in the courtroom, and a practical, commonsense approach to problems. Yet he was deeply superstitious, a believer in dreams, omens, and visions. **D**

We admire Lincoln today as an American folk hero. During the Civil War, however, he was the most unpopular president the nation had ever known. His critics called him a tyrant, a hick, a stupid baboon who was unfit for his office. As commander in chief of the armed forces, he was denounced as a bungling amateur who meddled in military affairs he knew nothing about. But he also had his supporters. They praised him as a farsighted statesman, a military mastermind who engineered the Union victory. **E**

Lincoln is best known as the Great Emancipator, the man who freed the slaves. Yet he did not enter the war with that idea in mind. "My paramount[9] object in this struggle *is* to save the Union," he said in 1862, "and is *not* either to save or destroy slavery." As the war continued, Lincoln's attitude changed. Eventually he came to regard the conflict as a moral crusade[10] to wipe out the sin of slavery.

9. **paramount:** main; most important.

10. **crusade:** struggle for a cause or belief.

D **Reading Focus** **Author's Purpose** Why do you think Freedman points out these contrasts in Lincoln's character?

E **Read and Discuss** What does all this say about Lincoln?

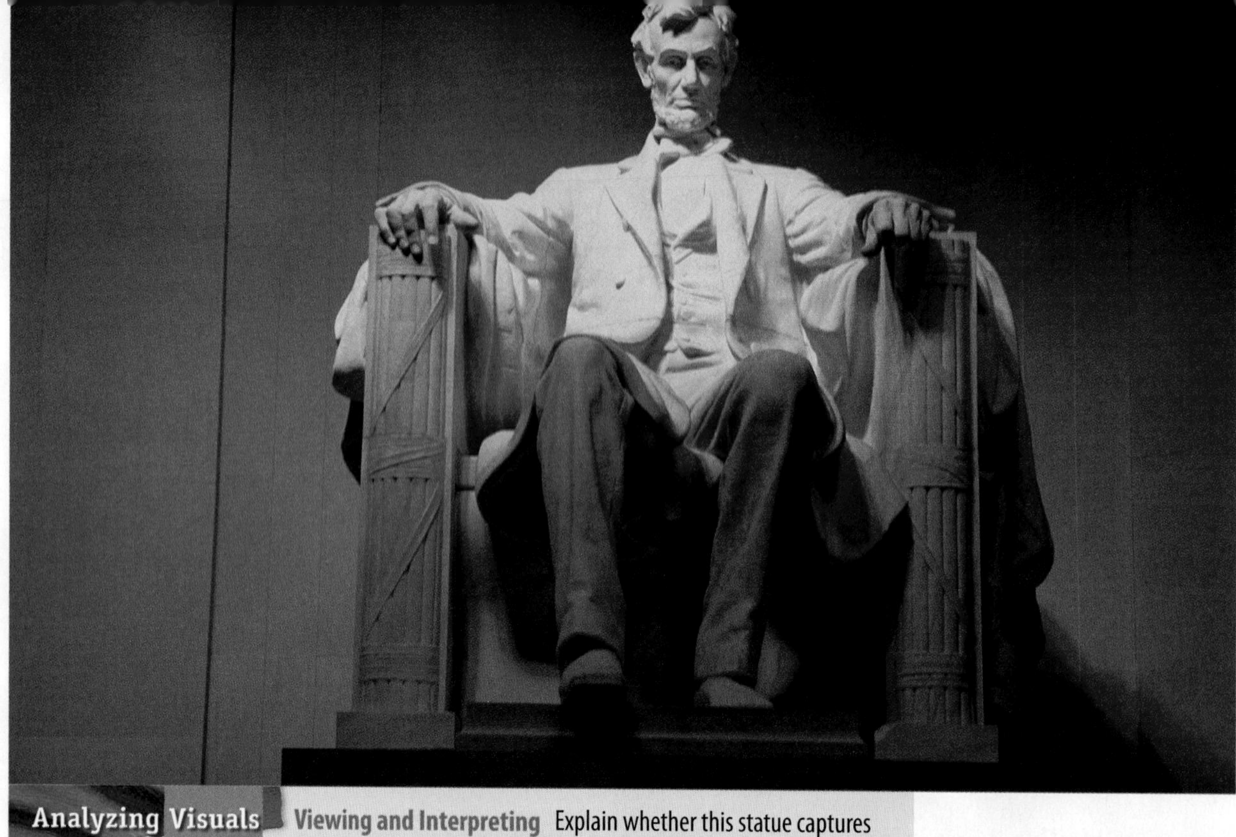

Analyzing Visuals **Viewing and Interpreting** Explain whether this statue captures the qualities of Lincoln described in this autobiography.

No black leader was more critical of Lincoln than the fiery abolitionist[11] writer and editor Frederick Douglass. Douglass had grown up as a slave. He had won his freedom by escaping to the North. Early in the war, impatient with Lincoln's cautious leadership, Douglass called him "preeminently the white man's president, entirely devoted to the welfare of white men." Later, Douglass changed his mind and came to (F) admire Lincoln. Several years after the war, he said this about the sixteenth president:

"His greatest mission was to accomplish two things: first, to save his country from dismemberment[12] and ruin; and second, to free his country from the great crime of slavery. . . . Taking him for all in all, measuring the tremendous magnitude of the work before him, considering the necessary means to ends, and surveying the end from the beginning, infinite wisdom has seldom sent any man into the world better fitted for his mission than Abraham Lincoln." (G)

11. **abolitionist:** person who supported abolishing, or ending, slavery in the United States.

12. **dismemberment:** separation into parts; division.

(F) **Reading Focus** **Author's Purpose** Freedman has revealed many contradictions about Lincoln. What do you think is his purpose for doing this?

(G) **Read and Discuss** How do Douglass's opinions of Lincoln in this part connect to the selection as a whole?

Vocabulary **cautious** (KAW shuhs) *adj.:* careful.

Applying Your Skills

Sunshine State Standards: Benchmarks **LA.6.1.6.1** use new vocabulary that is introduced and taught directly; **LA.6.1.7.2** analyze the author's purpose (e.g., to persuade, inform, entertain, or explain) and perspective in a variety of texts and understand how they affect meaning; *Also covered* **LA.6.1.7.3; LA.6.1.7.8; LA.6.2.1.2; LA.6.2.1.7; LA.4.2.3**

The Mysterious Mr. Lincoln

Respond and Think Critically

Reading Focus

1. Which phrase BEST describes Lincoln? FCAT
   A a furious and opinionated man
   B a man of tradition
   C a selfish but happy man
   D a man of many faces

Read with a Purpose

2. How accurate is the word *mysterious* in describing Lincoln?

Reading Skills: Author's Purpose

3. Review the details in your chart. Now, decide what Freedman's primary purpose is, and note it at the bottom of the chart: *The author's main purpose is to . . .*

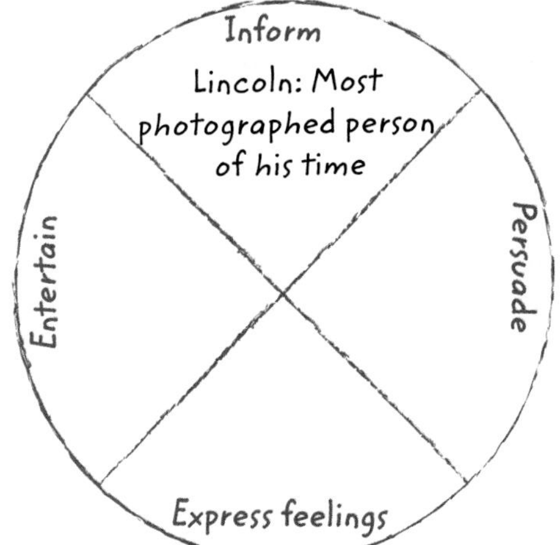

Vocabulary Check

Answer the following questions.

4. Why did Lincoln's face **defy** description?
5. How would an **ambitious** person act if someone asked for volunteers?
6. Why was Lincoln **cautious** about the war?

Literary Focus

Literary Analysis

7. **Analyze** Freedman describes Lincoln in terms of contrasts: *He seemed like . . . but he was really . . . .* Choose three of Lincoln's contrasting qualities, and explain what these contrasts reveal about his character. Do you think it would be possible to create a uniform characterization of Lincoln? Why or why not? Support your answer with details from the text. READ THINK EXPLAIN

Literary Skills: Figurative Language

8. **Analyze** Freedman uses a metaphor when he says that Lincoln "towered above other men." Explain this figure of speech. What distinct point does it make about Lincoln?
9. **Analyze** Douglass uses personification when he says that Lincoln's mission was to "save his country from dismemberment." What point is Douglass making through this comparison?

Writing Focus

Think as a Reader/Writer

Use It in Your Writing Think about the picture you formed of Lincoln as you read this selection. Then, write a description of Abraham Lincoln. Use at least two examples of figurative language that contribute to your image of him.

SHORT STORY

What Do FISH Have to Do with Anything?

by **Avi**

Read with a Purpose

Read this story to find out what its unusual title means.

Preparing to Read for this selection is on page 507.

Build Background

The "fish" of the title are a strange kind of creature called "cave fish." In the United States, these fish are found mostly in eastern and southern states, but they are also found all over the world. In fact, dozens of different species have been identified so far. The uniform traits they all share are a whitish or colorless appearance (some of the fish seem nearly transparent) and a lack of eyes!

Every day Mrs. Markham waited for her son, Willie, to come out of school when it was over. They walked home together. If asked why, Mrs. Markham would say, "Parents need to protect their children."

One Monday afternoon as they approached their apartment building, she suddenly tugged at Willie. "Don't look that way," she said.

"Where?"

"At that man over there."

As they walked, Willie stole a look back over his shoulder. A man Willie had never seen before was sitting on a red plastic milk crate near the curb. His matted, streaky gray hair hung like a ragged curtain over a dirty face. His shoes were torn. Rough hands lay upon his knees. One hand was palm up.

"What's the matter with him?" Willie asked.

Keeping her eyes straight ahead, Mrs. Markham said, "He's sick." She pulled Willie around. "Don't stare. It's rude." **A**

"What kind of sick?"

Mrs. Markham searched for an answer. "He's unhappy," she said.

"What's he doing?"

"Come on, Willie; you know. He's begging."

"Did anyone give him anything?"

"I don't know. Now come on, don't look."

"Why don't you give him anything?"

A Read and Discuss What are you learning about Mrs. Markham?

"We have nothing to spare." **B**

When they got home, Mrs. Markham removed a white cardboard box from the refrigerator. It contained poundcake. Using her thumb as a measure, she carefully cut a half-inch-thick piece of cake and gave it to Willie on a clean plate. The plate lay on a plastic mat decorated by images of roses with diamondlike dewdrops. She also gave him a glass of milk and a folded napkin.

Willie said, "Can I have a bigger piece of cake?"

Mrs. Markham picked up the cake box and ran a manicured pink fingernail along the nutrition information panel. "A half-inch piece is a portion, and a portion contains the following nutrients. Do you want to hear them?"

"No."

"It's on the box, so you can accept what it says. Scientists study people and then write these things. If you're smart enough, you could become a scientist. Like this." Mrs. Markham tapped the box. "It pays well." **C**

Willie ate his cake and drank the milk. When he was done, he took care to wipe the crumbs off his face as well as to blot the milk moustache with the napkin.

His mother said, "Now go on and do your homework. You're in fifth grade. It's important."

Willie gathered up his books that lay on the empty third chair. At the kitchen entrance he paused. "What *kind* of unhappiness does he have?"

"Who's that?"

"That man."

Mrs. Markham looked puzzled.

"The begging man. The one on the street."

"Could be anything," his mother said, vaguely. "A person can be unhappy for many reasons."

"Like what?"

"Willie . . ."

"Is it a doctor kind of sickness? A sickness you can cure?"

"I wish you wouldn't ask such questions."

"Why?"

"Questions that have no answers shouldn't be asked."

"Can I go out?"

"Homework first."

Willie turned to go.

"Money," Mrs. Markham suddenly said. "Money will cure a lot of unhappiness. That's why that man was begging. A salesperson once said to me, 'Maybe you can't buy happiness, but you can rent a lot of it.' You should remember that."

B **Read and Discuss** What's the author letting us know about Mrs. Markham and Willie?

C **Reading Focus** **Author's Purpose** What point might the author be making by showing us how Mrs. Markham reacts to Willie's request for more cake?

A cave fish.

The apartment had three rooms. The walls were painted mint green. Willie walked down the hallway to his room, which was at the front of the building. By climbing up on the windowsill and pressing against the glass, he could see the sidewalk five stories below. The man was still there.

It was almost five when he went to tell his mother he had finished his school assignments. She was not there. He found her in her bedroom, sleeping. Since she had begun working the night shift at a convenience store—two weeks now—she took naps in the late afternoon.

For a while Willie stood on the threshold,[1] hoping his mother would wake up. When she didn't, he went to the front room and looked down on the street again. The begging man had not moved.

Willie returned to his mother's room.

"I'm going out," he announced softly.

Willie waited a decent interval[2] for his mother to waken. When she did not, Willie made sure his keys were in his pocket. Then he left the apartment.

Standing just outside his door, he could keep his eyes on the man. It appeared as if he had still not moved. Willie wondered how anyone could go on without moving for so long in the chilly October air. Was staying in one place part of the man's sickness?

During the twenty minutes that Willie watched, no one who passed looked in the beggar's direction. Willie wondered if they even saw the man. Certainly no one put any money into his open hand.

A lady leading a dog by a leash went by. The dog strained in the direction of the man sitting on the crate. The dog's tail wagged. The lady pulled the dog away. "Heel!" she commanded.

The dog—tail between its legs—scampered to the lady's side. Even so, the dog twisted around to look back at the beggar.

Willie grinned. The dog had done exactly what he had done when his mother told him not to stare.

Pressing deep into his pocket, Willie found a nickel. It was warm and slippery. He wondered how much happiness you could rent for a nickel. **D**

Squeezing the nickel between his fingers, Willie walked slowly toward the man. When he came before him, he stopped, suddenly nervous. The man, who appeared to be looking at the ground, did not move his eyes. He smelled bad.

"Here." Willie stretched forward and dropped the coin into the man's open right hand.

"Bless you," the man said hoarsely, as he folded his fingers over the coin. His eyes, like high beams on a car, flashed up at Willie, then dropped.

Willie waited for a moment, then went back up to his room. From his front room he looked down on the street. He thought he saw the coin in the man's hand but was not sure.

After supper Mrs. Markham got ready to go to work. She kissed Willie good night. Then, as she did every night, she said,

1. **threshold** (THRESH ohld): doorway; entrance.
2. **interval:** period of time between events.

D **Read and Discuss** What is Willie up to here?

Analyzing Visuals **Viewing and Interpreting**
What scene in the story does this photograph show?

"If you have regular problems, call Mrs. Murphy downstairs. What's her number?"

"274–8676," Willie said.

"Extra bad problems, call Grandma."

"369–6754."

"Super-special problems, you can call me."

"962–6743."

"Emergency, the police."

"911."

"Don't let anyone in the door."

"I won't."

"No television past nine."

"I know."

"But you can read late."

"You're the one who's going to be late," Willie said.

"I'm leaving," Mrs. Markham said.

After she went, Willie stood for a long while in the hallway. The empty apartment felt like a cave that lay deep below the earth. That day in school Willie's teacher had told them about a kind of fish that lived in caves. These fish could not see. They had no eyes. The teacher had said it was living in the dark cave that made them like that. **E**

Before he went to bed, Willie took another look out the window. In the pool of light cast by the street lamp, Willie saw the man.

On Tuesday morning when Willie went to school, the man was gone. But when he came home from school with his mother, he was there again.

"*Please* don't look at him," his mother whispered with some urgency.

During his snack Willie said, "Why shouldn't I look?"

"What are you talking about?"

"That man. On the street. Begging." **F**

E **Literary Focus** **Symbol** Think about the symbol of the cave fish introduced by the author. In what ways is Willie's situation similar to that of an eyeless fish in a dark cave? Who or what else in the story might be compared to a fish that cannot see?

F **Read and Discuss** What does it say about Willie that he keeps thinking about the homeless man?

Vocabulary **urgency** (UR juhn see) *n.:* pressure; insistence.

"I told you. He's sick. It's better to act as if you never saw them. When people are that way, they don't wish to be looked at."

"Why not?"

Mrs. Markham thought for a while. "People are ashamed of being unhappy."

"Are you sure he's unhappy?"

"You don't have to ask if people are unhappy. They tell you all the time."

"Is that part of the sickness?"

"Oh, Willie, I don't know. It's just the way they are."

Willie contemplated the half-inch slice of cake his mother had just given him. He said, "Ever since Dad left, you've been unhappy. Are you ashamed?"

Mrs. Markham closed her eyes. "I wish you wouldn't ask that."

Willie said, "Are you?"

"Willie . . ."

"Think he might come back?"

"It's more than likely," Mrs. Markham said, but Willie wondered if that was what she really thought. He did not think so. "Do you think Dad is unhappy?"

"Where do you get such questions?"

"They're in my mind."

"There's much in the mind that need not be paid attention to."

"Fish that live in caves have no eyes."

"What are you talking about?"

"My teacher said it's all that darkness. The fish forget to see. So they lose their eyes."

"I doubt she said that."

"She did."

"Willie, you have too much imagination." **G**

After his mother went to work, Willie gazed down onto the street. The man was there. Willie thought of going down, but he knew he was not supposed to leave the building when his mother worked at night. He decided to speak to the man tomorrow.

Next afternoon—Wednesday—Willie said to the man, "I don't have any money. Can I still talk to you?"

The man's eyes focused on Willie. They were gray eyes with folds of dirty skin beneath them. He needed a shave.

"My mother said you were unhappy. Is that true?"

"Could be," the man said.

"What are you unhappy about?"

The man's eyes narrowed as he studied Willie intently. He said, "How come you want to know?"

Willie shrugged.

"I think you should go home, kid."

"I am home." Willie gestured toward the apartment. "I live right here. Fifth floor. Where do you live?"

"Around."

"*Are* you unhappy?" Willie persisted.

The man ran a tongue over his lips. His Adam's apple bobbed.

Willie said, "I'm trying to learn about unhappiness."

"Why?"

"I don't think I want to say."

"A man has the right to remain silent," the man said and closed his eyes.

Willie remained standing on the pavement for a while before walking back to his apartment. Once inside his own room, he

---

G **Read and Discuss** How do these conversations add to what we've already been thinking about Willie and his mother?

Vocabulary **ashamed** (uh SHAYMD) *adj.:* embarrassed.

looked down from the window. The man was still there. At one moment Willie was certain he was looking at the apartment building and the floor on which Willie lived.

The next day—Thursday—after dropping a nickel in the man's palm, Willie said, "I've decided to tell you why I want to learn about unhappiness."

The man gave a grunt.

"See, I've never seen anyone look so unhappy as you do. So I figure you must know a lot about it."

The man took a deep breath. "Well, yeah, maybe."

Willie said, "And I need to find a cure for it."

"A *what*?"

"A cure for unhappiness."

The man pursed his lips and blew a silent whistle. Then he said, "Why?"

"My mother is unhappy."

"Why's that?"

"My dad left."

"How come?"

"I don't know. But she's unhappy all the time. So if I found a cure for unhappiness, it would be a good thing, wouldn't it?"

"I suppose."

Willie said, "Would you like some cake?"

"What kind?"

"I don't know. Cake."

"Depends on the cake." **H**

On Friday Willie said to the man, "I found out what kind of cake it is."

"Yeah?"

"Poundcake. But I don't know why it's called that."

"Probably doesn't matter."

For a moment neither said anything. Then Willie said, "In school my teacher said there are fish that live in caves and the caves are dark, so the fish don't have eyes. What do you think? Do you believe that?"

"Sure."

"You do? How come?"

"Because you said so."

"You mean, just because someone *said* it you believe it?"

"Not someone. You."

Willie said, "But, well, maybe it *isn't* true."

The man grunted. "Hey, do you believe it?"

Willie nodded.

"Well, you're not just anyone. You got eyes. You see. You ain't no fish." **I**

"Oh."

"What's your name?"

"Willie."

"That's a boy's name. What's your grownup name?"

Willie thought for a moment. "William, I guess."

"And that means another thing."

"What?"

"I'll take some of that cake."

Willie smiled. "You will?"

"Just said it, didn't I?"

"I'll get it."

Willie ran to the apartment. He took the box from the refrigerator as well as a knife, then hurried back down to the street. "I'll

"I've decided to tell you why I want to learn about unhappiness."

H **Read and Discuss** What's going on between Willie and the homeless man?

I **Literary Focus** **Symbol** What does the homeless man mean here? In what ways is Willie "not a fish"?

cut you a piece," he said.

As the man looked on, Willie opened the box, then held his thumb against the cake to make sure the portion was the right size. With a poke of the knife he made a small mark for the proper width.

Just as he was about to cut, the man said, "Hold it!"

Willie looked up. "What?"

"What were you doing with your thumb there?"

"I was measuring the right size. The right portion. One portion is what a person is supposed to get."

"Where'd you learn that?"

"It says so on the box. You can see for yourself." He held out the box.

The man studied the box, then handed it back to Willie. "That's just lies," he said.

"How do you know?"

"William, how can a box say how much a person needs?"

"But it does. The scientists say so. They measured, so they know. Then they put it there."

"Lies," the man repeated.

Willie studied the man. His eyes seemed bleary.[3] "Then how much should I cut?" he asked.

The man said, "You have to look at me, then at the cake, and then you're going to have to decide for yourself." **J**

"Oh." Willie looked at the cake. The piece was about three inches wide. Willie looked up at the man. After a moment he cut the cake into two pieces, each an inch and a half wide. He gave one piece to the man and kept the other.

"Bless you," the man said, as he took the piece and laid it in his left hand. He began to break off pieces with his right hand and one by one put them into his mouth. Each piece was chewed thoughtfully. Willie watched him piece by piece. **K**

When the man was done, he dusted his hands of crumbs.

"Now I'll give you something," the man said.

"What?" Willie said, surprised.

3. **bleary** (BLIHR ee): blurred; misty; dim.

J **Reading Focus** **Author's Purpose** How does the author use the cake to communicate a message? How would you state this message?

K **Read and Discuss** What just happened between Willie and the man?

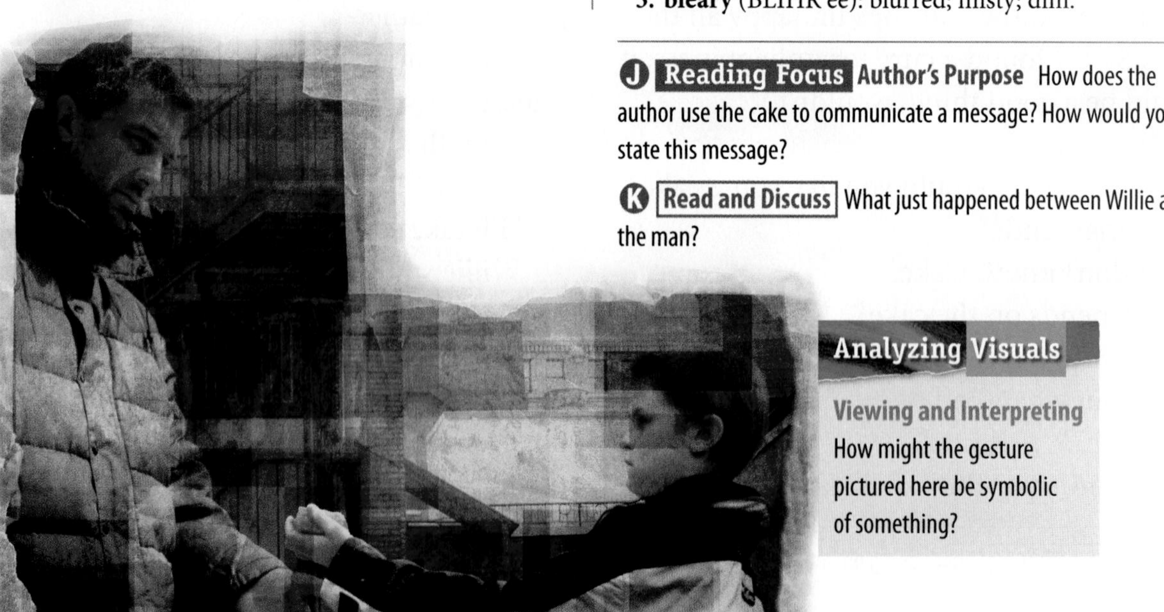

Analyzing Visuals

Viewing and Interpreting How might the gesture pictured here be symbolic of something?

"The cure for unhappiness."

"You know it?" Willie asked, eyes wide.

The man nodded.

"What is it?"

"It's this: What a person needs is always more than they say."

Willie thought for a while. "Who's *they*?" he asked.

The man pointed to the cake box. "The people on the box," he said.

Willie thought for a moment; then he gave the man the other piece of cake.

The man took it, saying, "Good man," and then ate it. **L**

The next day was Saturday. Willie did not go to school. All morning he kept looking down from his window for the man, but it was raining and he did not appear. Willie wondered where he was but could not imagine it.

Willie's mother woke about noon. Willie sat with her while she ate the breakfast he had made. "I found the cure for unhappiness," he announced.

"Did you?" his mother said. She was reading a memo from the convenience store's owner.

"It's, 'What a person needs is always more than they say.'"

His mother put her papers down. "That's nonsense. Where did you hear that?"

"That man."

"What man?"

"On the street. The one who was begging. You said he was unhappy. So I asked him."

"Willie, I told you I didn't want you to even look at that man."

"He's a nice man . . ."

"How do you know?"

"I've talked to him."

"When? How much?"

Willie shrank down. "I did, that's all."

"Willie, I forbid you to talk to him. Do you understand me? Do you? Answer me!"

"Yes," Willie said, but in his mind he decided he would talk to the man one more time. He needed to explain why he could not talk to him anymore.

On Sunday, however, the man was not there. Nor was he there on Monday.

"That man is gone," Willie said to his mother as they walked home from school.

"I saw. I'm not blind."

"Where do you think he went?"

"I couldn't care less. And you might as well know, I arranged for him to be gone."

Willie stopped short. "What do you mean?"

"I called the police. We don't need a nuisance like that around here. Pestering kids."

"He wasn't pestering me."

"Of course he was."

"How do you know?"

"Willie, I have eyes. I can see."

Willie stared at his mother. "No, you can't. You're a fish. You live in a cave."

"Willie, don't talk nonsense."

"My name isn't Willie. It's William." Turning, he walked back to the school playground. **M**

Mrs. Markham watched him go. "Fish," she wondered to herself; "what do fish have to do with anything?" **N**

L **Read and Discuss** What did you learn here?

M **Read and Discuss** What are Willie and his mother trying to say to each other?

N **Literary Focus** **Symbol** Who is the blind cave fish in the story? Explain.

Applying Your Skills

Sunshine State Standards: Benchmarks **LA.6.1.6.1** use new vocabulary that is introduced and taught directly; **LA.6.1.7.2** analyze the author's purpose (e.g., to persuade, inform, entertain, or explain) and perspective in a variety of texts and understand how they affect meaning; *Also covered* **LA.6.1.7.3; LA.6.1.7.8; LA.6.2.1.5; LA.6.2.1.7; LA.6.4.2.3**

What Do Fish Have to Do with Anything?

Respond and Think Critically

Reading Focus

FCAT

1. Which word BEST describes the boy in the story?
   A insensitive
   B lucky
   C curious
   D immature

Read with a Purpose

2. What does the story's title mean? Can you answer the question the title asks?

Reading Skills: Author's Purpose

3. Use your completed pie chart to analyze Avi's purpose. Beneath the chart, complete this sentence: *The author's main purpose is to . . . .*

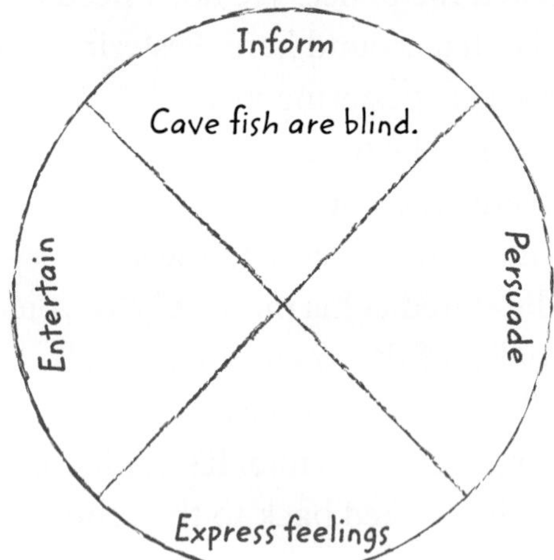

Vocabulary Check

Answer the following questions.

4. What are you feeling when you speak with **urgency**?
5. If someone were **ashamed** of something, would he or she talk about it a lot? Explain.

Literary Focus

Literary Analysis

6. **Interpret** What was the homeless man trying to say to Willie about the amount of cake? What idea might the cake symbolize here?
7. **Analyze** Why do you think Willie wants to be called "William" at the end of the story? What does this show about how his character has grown? Support your answer with details from the text. READ THINK EXPLAIN

Literary Skills: Symbol

8. **Analyze** Think about what Willie's teacher says about why the cave fish have no eyes. What do you think these eyeless fish symbolize? What does the symbol contribute to the story's message?

Writing Focus

Think as a Reader/Writer

Use It in Your Writing Choose something that you could clearly imagine as you read. Write a description of that character, setting, or scene, using two examples of figurative language.

COMPARING TEXTS

Wrap Up

Sunshine State Standards: Benchmarks **LA.6.4.1.1** write narrative accounts with an engaging plot (including rising action, conflict, climax, falling action, and resolution) include a clearly described setting with figurative language and descriptive words or phrases to enhance style and tone; **LA.6.4.2.3** write informational/expository essays (e.g., process, description, explanation, comparison/ contrast, problem/solution) that include a thesis statement, supporting details, and introductory, body, and concluding paragraphs; **LA.6.4.2.4** write a variety of informal communications (e.g., friendly letters, thank-you notes, messages) and formal communications (e.g., conventional business letters, invitations) that follow a format and that have a clearly stated purpose and that include the date, proper salutation, body, closing, and signature; *Also covered* **LA.6.4.3.1; LA.6.5.2.2**

Storm / The Mysterious Mr. Lincoln / What Do Fish Have to Do with Anything?

Writing Focus

Write a Comparison-Contrast Essay

Choose *two* of the selections you've just read, and write an essay in which you compare how each writer uses literary devices—imagery, figurative language, symbolism—to support his purpose. You can organize your essay in one of these ways:

1. **Organize by selection.** In the first paragraph, describe one writer's use of literary devices in his selection. Also discuss how the literary devices support the author's purpose and message. In the second paragraph, do the same for the second selection.
2. **Organize by literary device and author's purpose.** In the first paragraph, discuss how the two writers' purposes are similar and different. In the second paragraph, discuss how both writers use literary devices to get their messages across.

No matter which organization you use, write a conclusion in which you explain which selection uses literary devices more effectively to get the author's purpose and message across.

Use the workshop on writing a Comparison-Contrast Essay, pages 106–113, for help with this assignment.

What lessons did you learn from these three selections? How could you apply these lessons to your own life?

CHOICES

As you respond to the Choices, use these **Academic Vocabulary** words as appropriate: contribute, perspective, distinct, uniform.

REVIEW

Describe a Character

Use three literary devices to bring a favorite real or fictional character to life. Your description should use imagery, figurative language, and a distinct symbol that stands for the character.

CONNECT

Record a Learning Experience

TechFocus Some radio programs combine interviews, narration, and music to tell real-life stories. With a partner, create a five-to-ten-minute radio show–style recording that describes an interesting "learning experience" from your own or someone else's life. Decide on your purpose first. Play the recording for the class.

EXTEND

Write a Letter to the Author

Timed Writing Avi advises young writers: "Don't be satisfied with answers others give you. Don't assume that because everyone believes a thing, it is right or wrong. Reason things out for yourself." Write a letter to Avi, explaining what you think of this perspective. Use examples from "What Do Fish Have to Do with Anything?" to support your opinion.

Learn It Online

There's more to these stories than meets the eye. Expand your view at:

go.hrw.com L6-531 Go

INFORMATIONAL TEXT FOCUS

Connecting Main Ideas Across Texts

CONTENTS

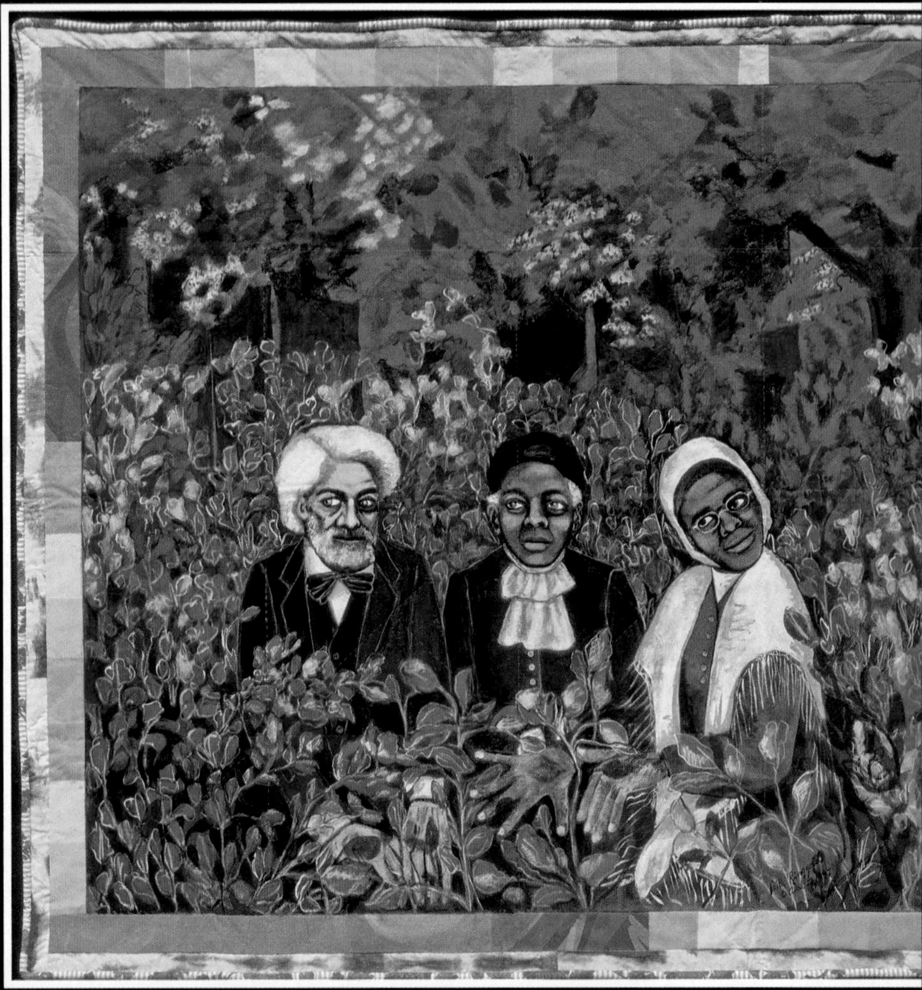

Wanted: Douglas, Tubman, Truth (1997)
American Collection #10
by Faith Ringgold.
Acrylic on canvas with fabric borders,
77 x 82 1/4".

How can the dreams of individual people make a difference in the lives of others?

QuickWrite

Think about someone you believe is a hero—someone who has made a difference. Explain what this person did and how those actions changed others' lives.

Preparing to Read

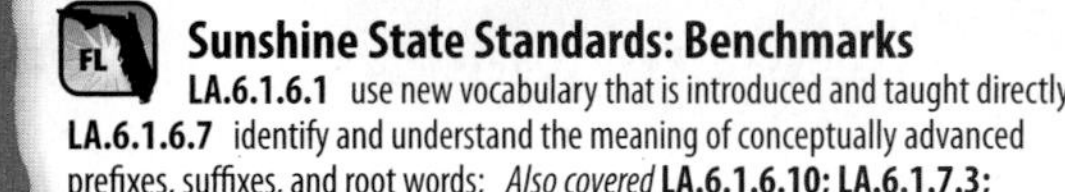

Sunshine State Standards: Benchmarks
LA.6.1.6.1 use new vocabulary that is introduced and taught directly;
LA.6.1.6.7 identify and understand the meaning of conceptually advanced prefixes, suffixes, and root words; Also covered LA.6.1.6.10; LA.6.1.7.3; LA.6.2.2.3

All Aboard with Thomas Garrett / *from* Harriet Tubman: The Moses of Her People / *from* The Life of Harriet Tubman

Informational Text Focus

Connecting Main Ideas Across Texts If you read "A Glory over Everything," you already know a lot about Harriet Tubman. Here are three more texts related to Tubman:

- an article on Thomas Garrett, who sheltered more than 2,700 people fleeing slavery and was a lifelong friend of Tubman's (page 536)
- an excerpt from an 1886 biography of Tubman (page 542)
- four paintings from Jacob Lawrence's *The Life of Harriet Tubman*, accompanied by captions telling about Tubman's life (page 544)

Copy the chart of main ideas on the next page into your *Reader/Writer Notebook,* and keep it handy as you read the selections that follow. Fill in the chart by writing down evidence and support from the three sources.

Look for more main ideas to add to the chart as you read. (Remember, there is often more than one main idea in a work of nonfiction.) Add boxes to your chart if you need them. You don't have to fill in every idea box for each selection; some main ideas will apply to only one of the pieces.

Writing Focus Preparing for **Extended Response**

The following selections all deal with the same subject, but not in the same way. Pay attention to how each writer presents the same facts. Consider the perspective each writer has on the subject. Think about the audience each writer is trying to reach. What distinct message is each trying to send?

Use your **RWN** to complete the activities for these selections.

Vocabulary

prudent (PROO duhnt) *adj.:* wise; sensible. *The runaways stayed until Garrett felt it was prudent to send them on.*

hazardous (HAZ uhr duhs) *adj.:* dangerous; risky. *Runaways were helped to make the hazardous journey north.*

diligence (DIHL uh juhns) *n.:* steady effort. *Garrett promised to double his diligence in helping people escape.*

jubilant (JOO buh luhnt) *adj.:* joyful. *Crowds of jubilant people celebrated.*

resolution (REHZ uh LOO shuhn) *n.:* a decison one is determined to carry out. *Tubman's resolution was to help others be free.*

Language Coach

Related Words Each of the Vocabulary words above is part of a "family tree" of related words. *Jubilant*, for example, comes from the Latin root *jubilare*, "to rejoice." In your dictionary you can find the related words *jubilee*, *jubilation*, and *jubilance*. You can increase your vocabulary by checking a dictionary for words related to each new word you learn. Do a dictionary search on the remaining Vocabulary words, and see how many family trees you can make with your discoveries.

Learn It Online
Increase your word comprehension with Word Watch:

Connecting Main Ideas Across Texts

Main Ideas	Evidence and Support from Readings		
	All Aboard with Thomas Garrett	Harriet Tubman: The Moses of Her People	The Life of Harriet Tubman
Idea 1: It was important for free people to help those who were enslaved.	1. No runaway was ever turned away from his door. 2.	1. "I was free, and they should be free. . . ." 2.	1. Here, she and the fugitives were fed and clothed and sent on their way. 2.
Idea 2: People fleeing slavery were in constant danger.	1."Slave catchers" searched the streets of Wilmington for runaways. 2.	1."I was a stranger in a strange land. . . ." 2.	1. A reward of forty thousand dollars was offered for her [Tubman's] head 2.
Idea 3: Freeing people from slavery required hard work and sacrifice.	1. He fed them hearty meals and dressed their wounds. 2.	1."I would make a home for them in the North, and, the Lord helping me, I would bring them all there." 2.	1. She traveled at night and hid during the day. She climbed mountains and crossed rivers. 2.
Idea 4:			

Harriet Tubman

Thomas Garrett

MAGAZINE ARTICLE

All Aboard *with* Thomas Garrett

by Alice P. Miller

All Aboard *with* Thomas Garrett

by Alice P. Miller

Read with a Purpose

Read this account to learn how one heroic man stood by his anti-slavery principles.

The elderly couple walked sedately down the stairs of the red brick house, every detail of their costumes proclaiming their respectability. The small lady was wearing an ankle-length gray gown, a snowy-white lawn kerchief, and a pleated gray silk bonnet, draped with a veil. The tall white-haired gentleman wore the wide-brimmed beaver hat and the long black waistcoat that was customary among Quakers.

When they reached the sidewalk, he assisted her into the four-wheeled barouche[1] that stood at the curb. Then he climbed into the barouche himself. The driver drove the horses away at a leisurely pace. Not until they were beyond the city limits did he allow the horses to prance along at a brisk pace across the few miles that separated Wilmington, Delaware, from the free state of Pennsylvania.

That tall white-haired gentleman was Thomas Garrett, a white man who had for many years been breaking the law by sheltering runaway slaves. And the little lady at his side was runaway slave Harriet Tubman, clad in clothes donated by his wife. On the preceding night Harriet had slept in a small room secreted behind one wall of Garrett's shoe store, a room that never remained unoccupied for very long. It was Harriet's first visit to Garrett, but she would be returning many times in the future. **A**

Runaway slaves remained with Garrett for one night or two or three until such time as Garrett considered it prudent to send them along to the next station on the Underground Railroad. He provided them with clothing and outfitted them with new shoes from his shoe store. He fed them hearty meals and dressed their wounds. He also forged passes for them so that any slave stopped by a slave catcher would have evidence that he or she was on a legitimate errand.

Some of the money he needed to cover the cost of his hospitality came out of his own pocket, but he was not a rich

1. **barouche** (buh ROOSH): type of horse-drawn carriage.

A **Read and Discuss** What is the author showing you with Harriet Tubman's and Thomas Garrett's actions?

Vocabulary **prudent** (PROO duhnt) *adj.:* wise; sensible.

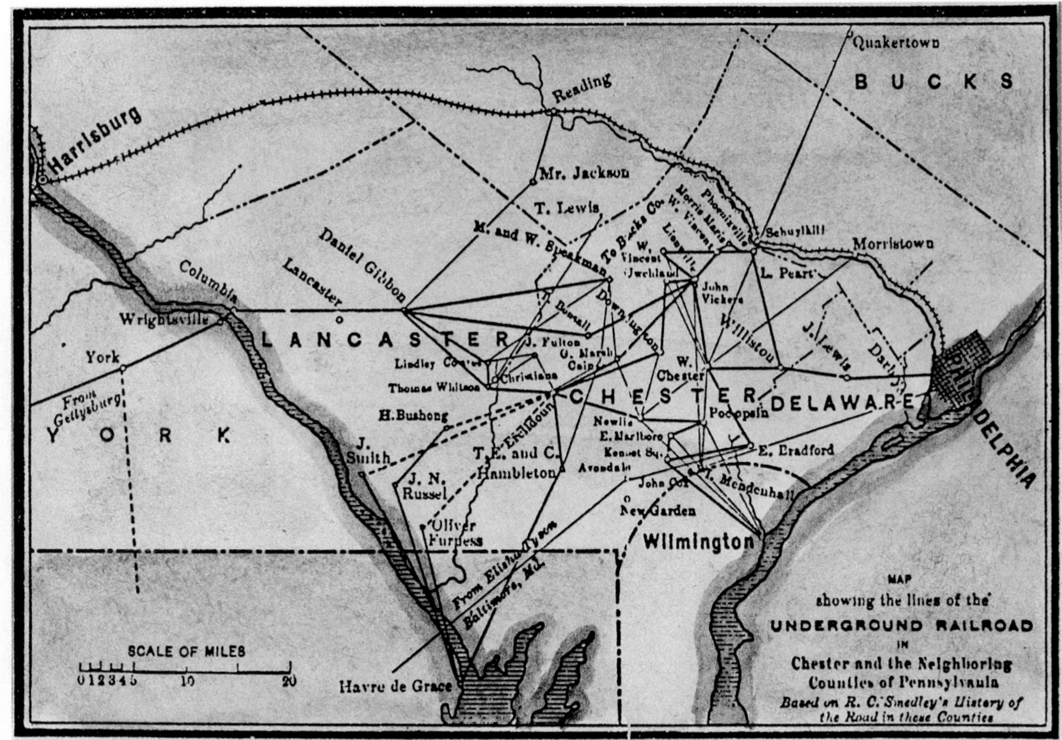

Map of the Underground Railroad. The Granger Collection, New York.

man. He could not have taken care of so many fugitives were it not for donations made by fellow abolitionists in the North as well as from supporters in foreign countries. There was never quite enough money, but no fugitive was ever turned away from his door. He would have gone without food himself before he would have refused food to a hungry slave.

Garrett, who was born in Upper Darby, Pennsylvania, in 1789, had been helping runaway slaves ever since 1822, when he rescued a young black woman who was trying to escape from her master. At that time he vowed to devote the rest of his life to helping fugitives, and he remained faithful to that vow. **B**

Of all the stations on the Underground Railroad his was probably the most efficiently run and the one most frequently used. The fact that Wilmington was so close to Pennsylvania made it the most hazardous stop on the route. Slave catchers prowled the streets of Wilmington, on the alert for any indication that a black person might be a runaway. They kept a sharp eye on all roads leading north from Wilmington. **C**

For many years Garrett managed to get away with his illegal activities

---

B **Informational Focus** **Connect and Clarify Main Ideas** Recall that Tubman first escaped to freedom in 1849. What can you conclude from the fact that Garrett first began helping runaways in 1822?

C **Read and Discuss** What does Thomas Garrett's life's work tell us about him?

Vocabulary **hazardous** (HAZ uhr duhs) *adj.:* dangerous; risky.

Analyzing Visuals **Viewing and Interpreting** Is this how you imagine enslaved people escaping through the Underground Railroad? Why or why not?

On to Liberty (1867) by Theodor Kaufmann. Oil on canvas, 36 x 56 in. (91.4 x 142.2cm)

because he was a clever man and knew ways to avoid detection by the slave catchers. Sometimes he disguised a slave, as he had done with Harriet. Sometimes he dressed a man in a woman's clothing or a woman in a man's clothing or showed a young person how to appear like one bent over with age. Another reason for his success was that he had many friends who admired what he was doing and who could be trusted to help him. They might, for example, conceal slaves under a wagonload of vegetables or in a secret compartment in a wagon.

The slave catchers were aware of what he was doing, but they had a hard time finding the kind of evidence that would stand up in court. At last, in 1848, he was sued by two Maryland slave owners who hoped to bring a stop to his activities by ruining him financially. (D)

The suit was brought into the federal circuit court of New Castle under a 1793 federal law that allowed slave owners to recover penalties from any person who harbored a runaway slave. The case was heard by Willard Hall, United States District Judge, and by Roger B. Taney, Chief Justice of the United States Supreme Court. Bringing in a verdict in favor of the slave owners, the jurors decided that the slave owners were entitled to $5,400 in fines.

Garrett didn't have anywhere near that much money, but he stood up and addressed the court and the spectators in these words:

"I have assisted fourteen hundred slaves in the past twenty-five years on their way to the North. I now consider this penalty imposed upon me as a license for the remainder of my life. I am now past sixty and have not a dollar to my name, but be that as it may, if anyone knows of a poor slave who needs shelter and a breakfast, send him to me, as I now publicly pledge myself to double my diligence and never neglect an opportunity to assist a slave to obtain freedom, so help me God!"

As he continued to speak for more than an hour, some of the spectators hissed while others cheered. When he finished, one juror leaped across the benches and pumped Garrett's hand. With tears in his eyes, he said, "I beg your forgiveness, Mr. Garrett." (E)

After the trial Garrett's furniture was auctioned off to help pay the heavy fine. But he managed to borrow money from friends and eventually repaid those loans, rebuilt his business, and became prosperous. Meanwhile he went on sheltering slaves for many more years. By the time President Lincoln issued the Emancipation Proclamation[2] in 1863, Garrett's records showed that he had sheltered more than 2,700 runaways. (F)

During those years he had many encounters with Harriet Tubman, as she kept returning to the South and coming back north with bands of slaves. Much of what we know about Harriet today is based on letters that he sent to her or wrote about her. A portion of one of those letters reads thus:

"I may begin by saying, living as I have in a slave State, and the laws being

2. **Emancipation Proclamation:** presidential order freeing slaves in states still at war with the Union.

(D) **Informational Focus** **Connect and Clarify Main Ideas** Considering the slaveholders' actions here and those described in "A Glory over Everything," what can you conclude about their determination to keep slaves from escaping?

(E) **Read and Discuss** How do things turn out in court for Garrett?

(F) **Informational Focus** **Connect and Clarify Main Ideas** What personal sacrifice does Garrett make because of his convictions?

Vocabulary **diligence** (DIHL uh juhns) *n.:* steady effort.

Analyzing Visuals

Viewing and Interpreting What does this image show about the reality of sheltering runaway slaves?

very severe where any proof could be made of anyone aiding slaves on their way to freedom, I have not felt at liberty to keep any written word of Harriet's labors as I otherwise could, and now would be glad to do; for in truth I never met with any person, of any color, who had more confidence in the voice of God, as spoken direct to her soul. . . . She felt no more fear of being arrested by her former master, or any other person, when in his immediate neighborhood, than she did in the State of New York or Canada, for she said she ventured only where God sent her, and her faith in the Supreme Power truly was great." **G**

In April, 1870, the black people of Wilmington held a huge celebration upon the passage of the fifteenth amendment to the Constitution of the United States. That amendment provided that the right of citizens to vote should not be denied or abridged by the United States or by any state on account of race, color, or previous condition of servitude.[3]

Jubilant blacks drew Garrett through the streets in an open carriage on one side of which were inscribed the words "Our Moses." **H**

Read with a Purpose

How did Thomas Garrett stand by his principles? What were the effects of his stand—both on himself and on others?

3. **servitude** (SUR vuh tood): condition of being under another person's control.

G **Informational Focus** **Connect and Clarify Main Ideas** How is this description of Tubman consistent with the one in "A Glory over Everything"?

H **Read and Discuss** What do Garrett's words about Tubman show? What does this celebration show you?

Vocabulary **jubilant** (JOO buh luhnt) *adj.:* joyful.

Applying Your Skills

Sunshine State Standards: Benchmarks **LA.6.1.6.1** use new vocabulary that is introduced and taught directly; **LA.6.1.7.3** determine the main idea or essential message in grade-level text through inferring, paraphrasing, summarizing, and identifying relevant details.

All Aboard with Thomas Garrett

Practicing for FCAT

Informational Text and Vocabulary

1. Which did Thomas Garrett NOT do to help people flee from slavery?
   - **A** give them shoes to wear
   - **B** hide them in his store
   - **C** feed them meals
   - **D** drive them to Canada

2. What did the African Americans in Wilmington celebrate in April 1870?
   - **F** the creation of the Underground Railroad
   - **G** the issuing of the Emancipation Proclamation
   - **H** the passage of the Fifteenth Amendment
   - **I** the verdict in Thomas Garrett's trial

3. What does the speech Garrett delivered in court tell you about him?
   - **A** He was angry that he was found guilty.
   - **B** He was eager to turn in the fugitive slaves.
   - **C** He wanted to close his shoe store.
   - **D** He was still devoted to his cause.

4. Read the sentence from the selection.

   Runaway slaves remained with Garrett for one night or two or three until such time as Garrett considered it prudent to send them along to the next station on the Underground Railroad.

   What is the meaning of the word *prudent* in this sentence?
   - **F** cautious
   - **G** warlike
   - **H** modest
   - **I** generous

5. Read the sentence from the selection.

   The fact that Wilmington was so close to Pennsylvania made it the most hazardous stop on the route.

   What does the word *hazardous* mean?
   - **A** difficult
   - **B** reliable
   - **C** risky
   - **D** unbeatable

6. Read the sentence from the selection.

   "I now publicly pledge myself to double my diligence and never neglect an opportunity to assist a slave to obtain freedom, so help me God!"

   What does the word *diligence* mean?
   - **F** complexity
   - **G** confidence
   - **H** risk
   - **I** perseverance

Writing Focus Extended Response

Consider the methods Tubman used to avoid detection as described in this article and in "A Glory over Everything." What main idea about the great difficulty of escaping from slavery do both selections present? Support your answer with examples from the texts.

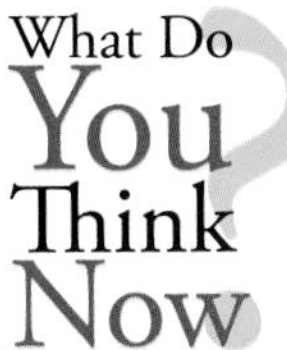

How did Thomas Garrett's vow to help fugitives affect the lives of the runaways who sought his help?

BIOGRAPHY

from Harriet Tubman: The Moses of Her People

by Sarah Bradford

Read with a Purpose

Read this account to learn why Harriet Tubman became the famous guide who led so many slaves to freedom.

Preparing to Read for this selection is on page 533.

Build Background

During the Civil War, Harriet Tubman worked for the Union Army as a spy, scout, and nurse. She refused payment for her services because she wanted to set an example of self-sufficiency and independence. When she returned to her home in New York after the war, she found that she was about to lose her house because she couldn't pay for it. To help Tubman, the abolitionist Sarah Bradford wrote a biography of her in 1869; she revised it in 1886. Bradford turned over to Tubman the earnings from both editions. This part of Bradford's biography starts where Petry's "A Glory over Everything" ends.

After many long and weary days of travel, she[1] found that she had passed the magic line, which then divided the land of bondage from the land of freedom. But where were the lovely white ladies whom in her visions she had seen, who, with arms outstretched, welcomed her to their hearts and homes. All these visions proved deceitful: She was more alone than ever; but she had crossed the line; no one could take her now, and she would never call her man "Master" more.

"I looked at my hands;" she said, "to see if I was the same person now I was free. There was such a glory over everything, the sun came like gold through the trees and over the fields, and I felt like I was in heaven." **A**

But then came the bitter drop in the cup of joy. She was alone, and her kindred were in slavery, and not one of them had the courage to dare what she had dared. Unless she made the effort to liberate them, she would never see them more, or even know their fate. **B**

"I knew of a man;" she said, "who was sent to the State Prison for twenty-five years. All these years he was always thinking of his home, and counting by years, months, and days, the time till he should be free, and

1. **she:** Harriet Tubman.

A **Informational Focus** **Connect and Clarify Main Ideas** This quotation was also used in "A Glory over Everything." What main idea does it suggest?

B **Read and Discuss** How does Harriet view her new freedom? What realization then changes her mood? Why?

Step on Board by Fern Cunningham honors Harriet Tubman, Underground Railroad "conductor." South End. Boston, Massachusetts.

Analyzing Visuals **Viewing and Interpreting** How does this statue of Tubman reflect the resolution she made?

see his family and friends once more. The years roll on, the time of imprisonment is over, the man is free. He leaves the prison gates, he makes his way to his old home, but his old home is not there. The house in which he had dwelt in his childhood had been torn down, and a new one had been put up in its place; his family were gone, their very name was forgotten, there was no one to take him by the hand to welcome him back to life."

"So it was with me;" said Harriet; "I had crossed the line of which I had so long been dreaming. I was free; but there was no one there to welcome me to the land of freedom, I was a stranger in a strange land, and my home after all was down in the old cabin quarter, with the old folks and my brothers and sisters. But to this solemn resolution I came: I was free, and they should be free also; I would make a home for them in the North, and, the Lord helping me, I would bring them all there. Oh, how I prayed then, lying all alone on the cold, damp ground. "Oh, dear Lord," I said, "I haven't got a friend but you. Come to my help, Lord, for I'm in trouble!" **C**

Read with a Purpose

Why did Harriet Tubman decide to help other enslaved people escape?

C **Read and Discuss** What relationship does Harriet's story of the jailed man have with her decision to help free her relatives? What does this thought process show you about Harriet?

Vocabulary **resolution** (REHZ uh LOO shuhn) *n.:* a decison one is determined to carry out.

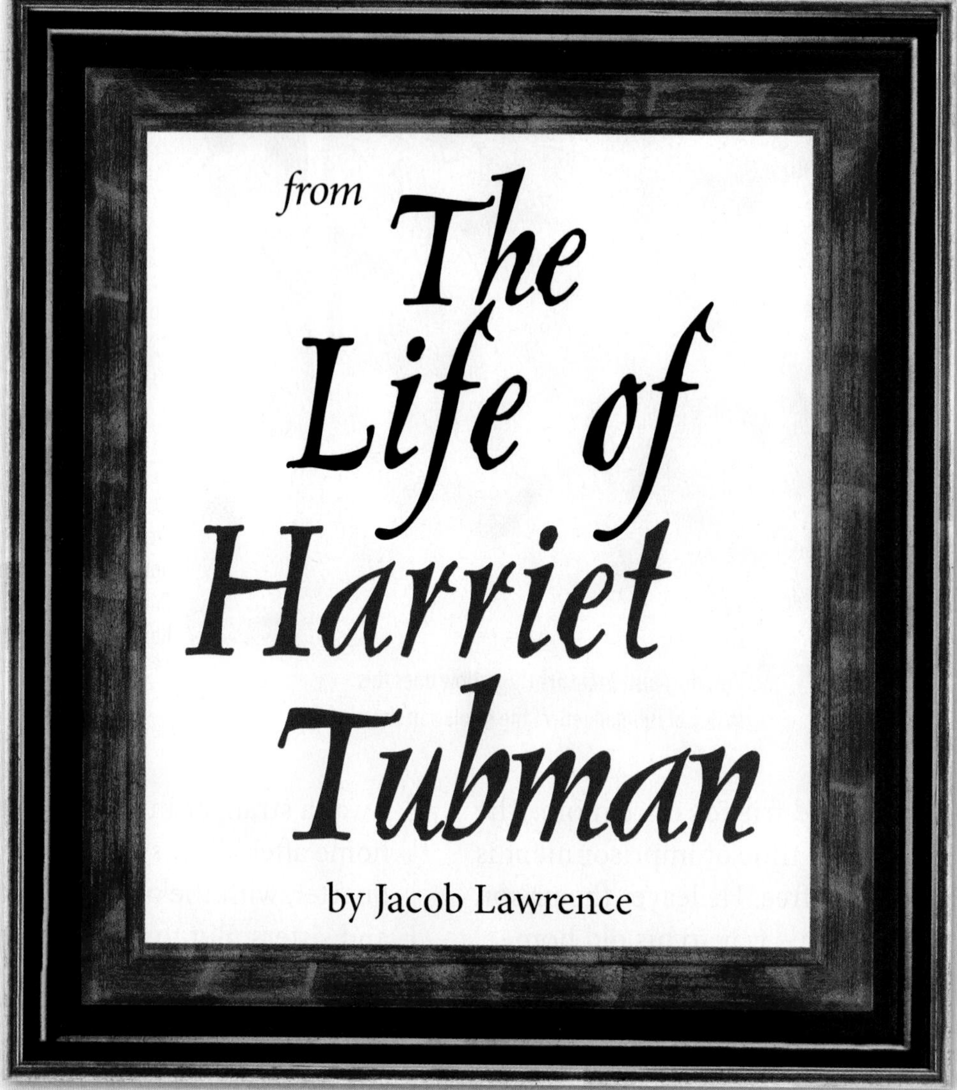

from *The Life of Harriet Tubman*

by Jacob Lawrence

Read with a Purpose

As you look at these paintings and read the captions, notice how the text and the images work together to tell Harriet Tubman's story.

Build Background

Jacob Lawrence (1917–2000) created *The Life of Harriet Tubman,* a series of thirty-one paintings, between 1939 and 1940. The series is a visual biography that depicts Tubman's work with the Underground Railroad and her service in the Civil War. The series is one of Lawrence's most famous works.

Lawrence wrote long captions to go with the paintings because at the time he created the series, most people knew little about Tubman's life. He used the combination of words and images to contribute to the viewers' understanding.

Analyzing Visuals **Viewing and Interpreting** Who are the small figures, and why are they staring at a star? What effect does Jacob Lawrence achieve by making the people seem so small against an enormous sky?

***The Life of Harriet Tubman* (1939–1940), No. 15, by Jacob Lawrence.**

In the North, Harriet Tubman worked hard. All her wages she laid away for the one purpose of liberating her people, and as soon as a sufficient amount was secured, she disappeared from her Northern home, and as mysteriously appeared one dark night at the door of one of the cabins on the plantation, where a group of trembling fugitives was waiting. Then she piloted them North, traveling by night, hiding by day, scaling the mountains, wading the rivers, threading the forests—she, carrying the babies, drugged with paregoric. So she went, nineteen times liberating over three hundred pieces of living, breathing "property." **A**

A **Read and Discuss** What do Tubman's actions show you about the Underground Railroad and her own character?

***The Life of Harriet Tubman* (1939–1940), No. 19, by Jacob Lawrence.**
Such a terror did she become to the slaveholders that a reward of forty thousand dollars was offered for her head, she was so bold, daring, and elusive. **B**

Analyzing Visuals

Viewing and Interpreting Who are the figures in the foreground? What are they doing?

B Informational Focus Connect and Clarify Main Ideas Describe the main idea that this painting and its caption share with the information presented in "All Aboard with Thomas Garrett" and the excerpt from *Harriet Tubman: The Moses of Her People*, as well as Ann Petry's "A Glory over Everything."

The Life of Harriet Tubman (1939–1940), No. 22, by Jacob Lawrence.

Harriet Tubman, after a very trying trip North in which she had hidden her cargo by day and had traveled by boat, wagon, and foot at night, reached Wilmington, where she met Thomas Garrett, a Quaker who operated an Underground Railroad station. Here, she and the fugitives were fed and clothed and sent on their way. Ⓒ

Ⓒ **Read and Discuss** How do this painting and its caption add to what you already know about the Underground Railroad?

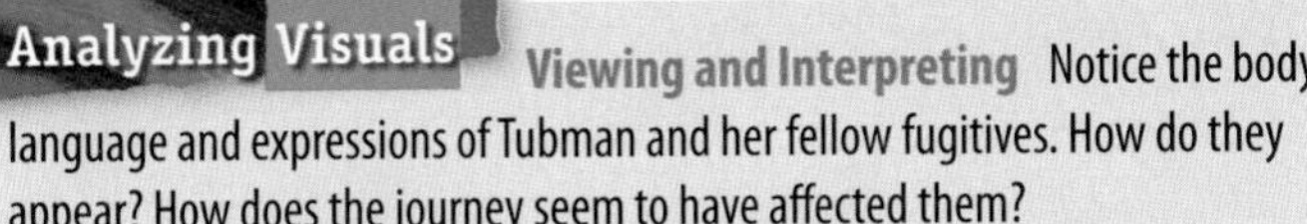

Analyzing Visuals **Viewing and Interpreting** Notice the body language and expressions of Tubman and her fellow fugitives. How do they appear? How does the journey seem to have affected them?

The Life of Harriet Tubman (1939–1940), No. 20, by Jacob Lawrence.

In 1850, the Fugitive Slave Law was passed, which bound the people north of the Mason and Dixon Line to return to bondage any fugitives found in their territories—forcing Harriet Tubman to lead her escaped slaves into Canada. **D**

Read with a Purpose

How does this fine art essay tell the story of Harriet Tubman in a way that's different from the other readings?

Analyzing Visuals

Viewing and Interpreting What feeling do you get from this painting? What does it say about Tubman's life in the North?

D **Read and Discuss** How did Tubman's journeys north connect to laws concerning escaped slaves?

Applying Your Skills

Sunshine State Standards: Benchmarks LA.6.1.6.1 use new vocabulary that is introduced and taught directly; LA.6.1.7.3 determine the main idea or essential message in grade-level text through inferring, paraphrasing, summarizing, and identifying relevant details; LA.6.2.2.2 use information from the text to answer questions related to the main idea or relevant details, maintaining chronological or logical order.

All Aboard with Thomas Garrett / *from* Harriet Tubman: The Moses of Her People / *from* The Life of Harriet Tubman

Practicing for FCAT

Informational Text and Vocabulary

1. Which main idea is presented in all three of the Tubman selections?
   - **A** Runaways were always in danger of being returned to slaveholders.
   - **B** Thomas Garrett spent most of his money sheltering runaways.
   - **C** African Americans celebrated the passage of the Fifteenth Amendment.
   - **D** A reward was offered for Tubman's capture.

2. Read the statement from "All Aboard with Thomas Garrett."

   I now consider this penalty imposed upon me as a license for the remainder of my life.

   Which main idea connects with this statement?
   - **F** Thomas Garrett gave runaways large sums of money.
   - **G** Runaways often faced harsh conditions when they headed north.
   - **H** Thomas Garrett would not allow a fine to stop him from sheltering runaways.
   - **I** Harriet Tubman feared being returned to a slaveholder.

3. Which statement do you think the authors of the three selections would MOST likely agree with?
   - **A** Runaways felt no obligation toward the people they left behind.
   - **B** African Americans enjoyed a comfortable life as soon as they reached the North.
   - **C** Freeing people from slavery required hard work on the part of many people.
   - **D** Everyone Harriet Tubman met was eager to help her

4. Read the statement from "from Harriet Tubman: The Moses of Her People."

   But to this solemn resolution I came:

   What is the meaning of the word *resolution* in this sentence?
   - **F** a decision
   - **G** a beginning
   - **H** an act of bravery
   - **I** an answer

Writing Focus Extended Response

Use the chart you made while reading the three selections to write a paragraph on the main ideas about Harriet Tubman and the Underground Railroad in these texts. Support your answer with details from the selections.

What Do You Think Now?

Based on Tubman's and Garrett's actions, what can you conclude about the value of an individual's efforts in fighting injustice?

Writing Workshop

Research Report FCAT Writing+

Write with a Purpose

Write a research report about a topic that interests you, and support your thesis with evidence from several sources. The **audience** for your report will include your classmates and your teacher. Your **purpose** is to share information about a subject you care about and that might interest your readers.

A Good Research Report

- focuses on a thesis, or central idea, that is supported by details, facts, and explanations
- includes accurately documented information from several sources
- uses clear organization to present information
- ends by summarizing ideas or drawing an overall conclusion

Think as a Reader/Writer

In this collection, you have learned about the techniques writers use in nonfiction. Some of the nonfiction texts were based on the authors' personal experiences. Others, such as the biographies, required research. Now it's time for you to research a topic and write a report that draws on information from several sources. Before you begin, take a few minutes to read this excerpt from an article on the California gold rush, written by Kathy Wilmore and published in *Junior Scholastic* magazine:

Thousands of Forty-Niners made the trek to California with the idea of striking it rich, then returning home to spend their wealth. But for every Forty-Niner whose labor paid off handsomely, countless others had to find other ways of making a living.

← The report opens with **background information,** followed immediately by the **thesis statement.**

Among those were thousands of Chinese. Word of "Gold Mountain"—the Chinese name for California—lit new hope among poverty-stricken peasants in China. In 1849, only 54 Chinese lived in California; by 1852, the number had risen to 14,000.

← **Facts** are used as **evidence** to develop and support the thesis.

Chinese miners faced the resentment of many white Forty-Niners who saw them as unfair competition.... Looking for less risky ways of earning a living, many Chinese turned to service work: cooking meals, toting heavy loads, and washing clothes. Miners happily plunked down money for such service.

← **Details** further support the thesis.

Think About the Professional Model

With a partner, discuss the following questions about the model:

1. Why might the writer have placed the thesis at the very end of the first paragraph?
2. How does the organization of this excerpt affect its clarity?
3. Which piece of evidence most directly supports the thesis? Why?

Use your **RWN** to complete the activities for this workshop.

Sunshine State Standards: Benchmarks **LA.6.3.1.1** generating ideas from multiple sources (e.g., prior knowledge, discussion with others, writer's notebook, research materials, or other reliable sources), based upon teacher-directed topics and personal interests; **LA.6.3.1.2** making a plan for writing that prioritizes ideas, addresses purpose, audience, main idea, and logical sequence; **LA.6.3.1.3** using organizational strategies and tools (e.g., technology, outline, chart, table, graph, web, story map); **LA.6.3.2.1** developing main ideas from the prewriting plan using primary and secondary sources appropriate to purpose and audience; **LA.6.3.2.2** organizing information into a logical sequence and combining or deleting sentences to enhance clarity; *Also covered* **LA.6.3.3.1; LA.6.3.3.2; LA.6.3.3.3; LA.6.3.3.4; LA.6.3.4.1; LA.6.3.4.2; LA.6.3.4.3; LA.6.3.5.1; LA.6.3.5.3; LA.6.4.2.1; LA.6.4.2.2; LA.6.4.2.3; LA.6.6.2.1; LA.6.6.2.2; LA.6.6.2.3; LA.6.6.2.4**

Prewriting

Choose and Narrow a Topic

Begin by brainstorming about broad subjects that interest you, such as sports, nature, animals, or art. The Idea Starters in the margin may help you brainstorm subjects.

With a broad subject in mind, you can narrow it to a manageable topic for your report. Narrow your focus by using an inverted triangle like those shown below. This process involves repeatedly narrowing the subject until you have a focused topic. A focused topic will enable you to write a strong thesis statement, or main idea statement, and to cover the topic in a single paper. Then, select your favorite subject, and answer these questions about it:

- What about the subject do you find especially interesting?
- What do you already know about the subject?
- Where can you find reliable information about the subject?
- Will your audience be interested in the subject? How can you interest them? What will they want to know?

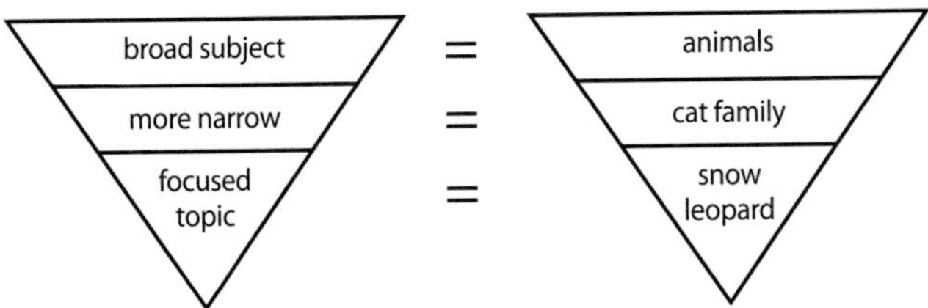

Ask Questions

Make a list of things you already know about your topic. Put a question mark next to information that you will want to verify, or double-check, when doing your research. Then, make a list of questions you would like to answer about your topic. As you research your topic, carefully record the answers to your questions, along with information about the source. Always record the source information, and keep all of your information together where you can find it. For help in recording source information, see the Communications Handbook in the Resource Center.

Idea Starters

- an explanation (Why do cats purr? How do helicopters fly?)
- interesting subjects like those you find in magazine articles (people in the news, new discoveries, medical marvels)
- topics you have discussed in other classes (ancient civilizations, historical events, great adventurers, famous artists)

Your Turn

Get Started Do some brainstorming to choose a few subjects that interest you, and select one for your report. Narrow this subject to a focused topic, and make a list of questions you would like to answer about your topic.

Writing Tip

For more information on evaluating and taking notes on sources, see the Communications Handbook in the resource Center.

Learn It Online
See an online example of a full research report at:
go.hrw.com
L6-551
Go

Peer Review

Learning to schedule your time on a research project is an important skill. Get together with a partner to work out realistic deadlines for your project. For each of these tasks:

- find information
- take notes from sources
- organize notes
- write first draft
- revise draft
- proofread and publish

To fill in dates for each task, work backward from the final due date your teacher gives you to a good starting date for each task. Check in with your partner regularly to see if you're both keeping to your schedules.

Writing Tip

For more information on evaluating and taking notes on sources, see the Communications Handbook in the Resource Center.

Your Turn

Gather Information and Write a Thesis Statement Using your questions as a guide, gather information about your topic. Write a **thesis statement** that expresses your **main idea** about the topic. Make an informal plan to organize your information. As you plan, keep your **audience** and **purpose** in mind.

Gather Facts and Evaluate Sources

Plan to use at least three **sources** of information for your report, such as books, magazines, encyclopedias, newspapers, and the Internet. Be sure to evaluate the reliability of each source—how truthful and accurate its information is. Look for nonfiction sources created by experts and respected organizations. Be especially careful when evaluating Web sites. Make sure the Web site was created by an authoritative source, not just someone interested in the subject. Ask yourself the following questions about each source:

- Is the creator of the source an expert? How do I know?
- How can I tell if the information is up to date and accurate?
- Is the information fact or opinion? How do I know?

Use note cards to write down important facts and to record the source of the information.

Write your Thesis Statement

Thinking about the information you have gathered about your topic, write a **thesis statement** for your report. The thesis states your topic and your **main idea** about it. Here's an example from the Student Draft on page 555:

topic: the microbe
main idea: helpful in unlocking doors to science
thesis: A bug known as a microbe has been the key to unlocking many doors to science.

Make a Plan To make an informal plan, sort your notes into categories, and divide each category into subtopics. The informal plan below was completed for the Student Draft on pages 555–556.

Informal Plan for "Nature's Recyclers"

Thesis: A bug known as a microbe has been the key to unlocking many doors to science.

Category 1: Facts about microbes	Category 2: Effects of microbes	Category 3: Uses of microbes
Subtopic: microscopic organisms, bacteria	Subtopics:	Subtopics: create fertilizer, clean oil spills

Think About Purpose and Audience

You have two **purposes** for writing a research report: to discover information for yourself and to share it with your **audience.** Consider what your audience will *need* to know as well as what they'll *want* to know.

Drafting

Paraphrase Information

Use the **Writer's Framework** at right to help write your draft. Most of your source information can be **paraphrased,** or rewritten in your own words, keeping the essential meaning the same. A paraphrase should be a straightforward summary of the original writer's information, usually shorter than the original text. It should not use any of the original author's style or exact wording. If you need to use exact words from a source, put them in quotation marks, and identify the source.

A Writer's Framework

Introduction:
- Hook to interest readers
- A clear thesis statement

Body:
- Paragraph 1—subtopic and supporting evidence
- Paragraph 2—subtopic and supporting evidence

(Add as many paragraphs/subtopics as needed to support your thesis—usually no fewer than three)

Conclusion:
- Summary of main points
- Reflection on the topic

Cite Your Sources

At the end of your paper, provide a **Works Cited** list that credits all the sources used in your research report. This list enables your readers to find the information in your report. Include the following information for each book you cite: author (last name first), title (underlined or in italics), place of publication, publisher, and date published.

Grammar Link **Using Italics and Quotation Marks in Titles**

When you write your Works Cited list, be sure to follow the rules for using italics and quotation marks with titles.

- **Use italics for the titles of major works.** Major works include books, encyclopedias, magazines, newspapers, databases, Web sites, movies, and television series.
  Example: *Encyclopaedia Britannica*
- **Use quotation marks for the titles of short works.** Short works include chapters of books; articles from encyclopedias, magazines, and newspapers; individual pages from Web sites; and individual television episodes.
  Example: "The California Gold Rush," *Junior Scholastic*

Here is an example of how to cite a book in a Works Cited List:

Farell, Jeanette. Invisible Allies: Microbes That Shape Our Lives. New York: Farrar, Straus, and Giroux, 2005.

Writing Tip

Copying exact words from a source and presenting them as your own is called **plagiarism.** Plagiarizing is the same as stealing another writer's work.

Writing Tip

For more examples of formats for citing sources, see the Communications Handbook in the Resource Center.

Your Turn

Write Your Draft Following the plan you've developed, write a draft of your research report. Remember to think about the following:

- What information is important enough to be quoted word for word? What should you paraphrase?
- What source information will you include in your Works Cited list?

Peer Review

Work with a partner to review your draft. Answer each question in the chart at the right to find out how your draft can be improved. Take notes on what you and your partner discuss so that you can refer to them when you revise your draft.

Evaluating and Revising

You may think your work is over once you've written your draft, but you've really just begun the writing process. Now it's time to review your draft carefully, looking for areas that can be improved. This chart will help you evaluate and revise your draft.

Research Report: Guidelines for Content and Organization

Evaluation Question	Tip	Revision Technique
1. Does your introduction contain a clear thesis statement?	**Underline** your thesis statement.	**Add** a thesis statement, including your topic and main point, if necessary.
2. Does each paragraph in the body of your paper develop one subtopic?	In the margin, **label** each paragraph with the subtopic it develops.	Where necessary, **rearrange** information into separate paragraphs that each discuss one subtopic. **Delete** unrelated ideas.
3. Does each body paragraph contain supporting evidence?	**Highlight** the facts, examples, and quotations that support each subtopic.	**Add** facts and examples from your notes, if necessary.
4. Does your conclusion summarize your findings?	**Put a check mark** next to your final statement or summary.	**Summarize** your research. **Revise** your final statement to clarify your point, if necessary.
5. Have you included at least three sources in your Works Cited list?	**Number** the sources listed.	**Add** information from other sources, if needed. **Add** those sources to your list.
6. Does the Works Cited list use the correct format?	**Check** the format and punctuation by referring to page 553.	**Add** correct format and punctuation as needed.

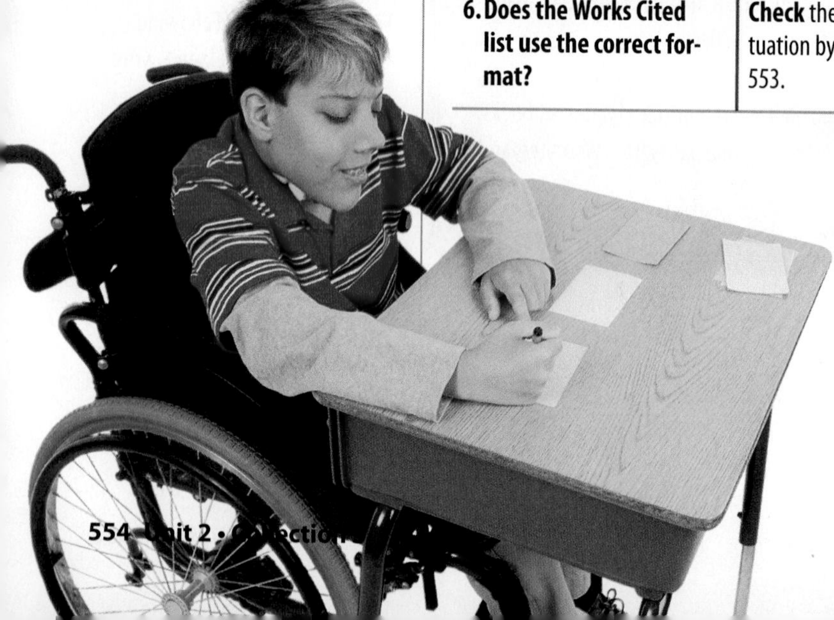

Read this student's draft and the comments about it as a model for revising your own research report.

Student Draft

Nature's Recyclers

by Allison Hamilton, Hillsboro Middle School

A bug known as a microbe has been the key to unlocking many doors to science.

← Allison clearly states her **thesis** in the first sentence.

Microbe is the name for any of millions of microscopic organisms. Microbes are tiny cells. They are so small you can't see them without a microscope. Some of the most common are the ones called bacteria. Bacteria are some of the oldest life forms, and some of the simplest, not having the cell nucleus found in most other microbes.

← Allison **defines** an important term and provides background information.

Most bacteria are harmless to plants and animals. Only a small fraction cause disease. Some attack living things after they're dead. If it weren't for bacteria, animal wastes and dead organisms would build up. Bacteria also make the soil rich. . . .

← Allison narrows her **focus.**

MINI-LESSON How to Create an Interesting Introduction

Allison's draft begins with a clear thesis statement, but she could use a "hook" to make her introduction more interesting. Just as a fishhook dangling in the water catches a fish, an interesting hook catches the attention of a reader. A fact, an unusual image, a striking quote, an unexpected comparison, or a question addressed to the reader may be used as a hook. Allison might use a combination of techniques. She could begin with a question and lead to a memorable image.

Allison's Draft of Paragraph One

A bug known as a microbe has been the key to unlocking many doors to science.

Allison's Revision of Paragraph One

If there were an oil spill off the coast of Alaska, how would you clean it up? You may think this is a machine's job, but scientists have proven that a tiny bug, usually invisible to the naked eye, could take on the work of a one-hundred-ton piece of steel. A bug known as a microbe has been the key to unlocking many doors to science.

Writing Tip

Comparisons make facts interesting and vivid to your readers. Imagine starting out with a fact like this: "If you think public restrooms are the favorite gathering places for germs, think again: the typical desk of an office worker holds an astounding population of ten million germs." To clarify, you add a comparison: "That's about four hundred times more germs than a toilet in a public restroom!"

Your Turn

Create a Hook Try one of these ways of "hooking" your audience:

- State a surprising fact.
- Open with a question.
- Begin with a memorable quote.
- Create an image for the reader.

Student Draft *continues*

...They take nitrogen gas from the air and convert it to a form that green plants use for growth. Bacteria create fertilizer, too. They break down compost made of soil and dead plants.

Allison's report is **organized** clearly. Each paragraph discusses a new subtopic and provides supporting **evidence.** →

Scientists have discovered how to use microbes to clean up oil spills. The scientists found a type of bacteria that feeds on oil and breaks it down into hydrogen, carbon, and oxygen. Microbial decomposition of petroleum by hydrocarbon-oxidizing bacteria and fungi is of considerable ecological importance.

The conclusion includes a **summary** of Allison's findings. →

The microbe is very important to us. I guess you could look at it as nature's recycler. Life as we know it would not exist without these powerful bugs. Scientists have explored only a fraction of these amazing creatures' potential. Discovering the benefits and uses of microbes is an important step into the future.

MINI-LESSON How to Avoid Plagiarism

Allison has used the exact words from a source and has forgotten to use quotation marks. She can either add quotation marks and keep the exact words, or she can paraphrase the information in her own words and leave out quotation marks.

Allison's Draft of Paragraph Four, Sentence Three

Microbial decomposition of petroleum by hydrocarbon-oxidizing bacteria and fungi is of considerable ecological importance.

Allison decided the language of the original was too technical for her audience, so she paraphrased the information to make it easier to understand and ended with a shorter direct quotation from her authoritative source.

Allison's Revision of Paragraph Four, Sentence Three

~~Microbial decomposition of petroleum by hydrocarbon-oxidizing bacte-~~ According to the Encyclopaedia Britannica, using microbes to decompose oil

~~ria and fungi~~ "is of considerable ecological importance."

Your Turn

Check for Plagiarism Review your draft to make sure you haven't presented a source's ideas or exact words as your own. Look for sentences that don't sound like your writing. Then, check to see if you've used the exact words of your source and insert quotation marks if you have. Giving proper credit to your sources helps you avoid plagiarism, and it also lends credibility to your report.

Proofreading and Publishing

Proofreading

Now that you have evaluated and revised your research report, it is time to give it one last cleanup and prepare it for publication. Edit your report carefully, correcting any errors in spelling, punctuation, or sentence structure.

Grammar Link **Varying Sentence Structure**

Varying your sentence structure will make your report easier and more interesting to read. Analyze the sentences in your draft. Have you used mostly simple sentences?

When she proofread her paper, Allison combined two simple sentences into a compound sentence by adding a comma and the coordinating conjunction *and.*

> Most bacteria are harmless to plants and animals. , and Only a small fraction cause disease.

Allison created a complex sentence by using a subordinating conjunction to more clearly show the relationship between two ideas.

> Bacteria create fertilizer, too. Because They break down compost made of soil and dead plants. ,

Publishing

It is time to share your report with a wider audience. Here are some suggestions for sharing your report:

- If you have written about a historical event, e-mail a copy of your report to a friend or relative who is a history buff.
- Have a "discovery day" in class. You and your classmates can form into small groups and share your research.

Reflect on the Process In your **RWN,** write a short response to each of the following questions to reflect on your writing process:

1. Where did you find the best information about your topic? Are there some types of sources that you will avoid in the future? Why?
2. What part of your report do you think is the strongest? What makes it strong?
3. What is the most surprising fact you learned?

Proofreading Tip

If you have used terms in your report that are not part of your everyday vocabulary, be sure to double-check the spelling in a dictionary. Ask a peer to read your draft and circle any terms that might need to be defined for your audience.

Your Turn

Proofread and Publish

Proofread your report, paying particular attention to sentence structure. If your report contains mostly short, simple sentences, try to vary the sentence structure by combining some of the sentences. Publish your report to share your research findings.

Scoring Rubric for FCAT Writing+

You can use the six-point rubric below to evaluate your on-demand expository essay.

6-Point Scale

Score 6 ***is focused, purposeful, and reflects insight into the writing situation***

- conveys a sense of completeness and wholeness with adherence to the main idea
- uses an effective organizational pattern with a logical progression of ideas
- provides substantial, specific, relevant, concrete, or illustrative support
- demonstrates a commitment to and an involvement with the subject
- presents ideas with clarity
- may use creative writing strategies appropriate to the purpose of the paper
- demonstrates mature command of language with freshness of expression
- shows variation in sentence structure
- employs complete sentences except when fragments are used purposefully
- contains few, if any, convention errors in mechanics, usage, and punctuation

Score 5 ***is focused on the topic***

- conveys a sense of completeness and wholeness
- uses an organization pattern with a progression of ideas, although some lapses may occur
- provides ample support
- demonstrates a mature command of language with precise word choice
- shows variation in sentence structure
- with rare exceptions, employs complete sentences except when fragments are used purposefully
- generally follows the conventions of mechanics, usage, and spelling

Score 4 ***is generally focused on the topic but may include extraneous or loosely related material***

- exhibits some sense of completeness and wholeness
- uses an apparent organization pattern, although some lapses may occur
- provides adequate support, although development may be uneven
- demonstrates adequate word choice
- shows little variation in sentence structure
- employs complete sentences most of the time
- generally follows the conventions of mechanics, usage, and spelling

Score 3 ***is generally focused on the topic but may include extraneous or loosely related material***

- attempts to use an organization pattern but may lack a sense of completeness or wholeness
- provides some support but development is erratic
- demonstrates adequate word choice but word choice may be limited, predictable, or occasionally vague
- shows little, if any, variation in sentence structure
- usually demonstrates knowledge of the conventions of mechanics and usage
- usually employs correct spelling of commonly used words

Score 2 ***is related to the topic but includes extraneous or loosely related material***

- demonstrates little evidence of an organizational pattern and may lack a sense of completeness or wholeness
- provides inadequate or illogical development of support
- demonstrates limited, inappropriate, or vague word choice
- shows little, if any, variation in sentence structure and may contain gross errors in sentence structure
- contains errors in basic conventions of mechanics and usage
- contains misspellings of commonly used words

Score 1 ***may minimally address the topic and is a fragmentary or incoherent listing of related ideas or sentences or both***

- demonstrates little, if any, evidence of an organizational pattern
- provides little, if any, development of support
- demonstrates limited or inappropriate word choice, which may obscure meaning
- may contain gross errors in sentence structure and usage, which may impede communication
- contains frequent and blatant errors in basic conventions of mechanics and usage
- contains misspellings of commonly used words

Preparing for FCAT Writing+

Expository Essay

Sunshine State Standards: Benchmarks LA.6.3.1.2; LA.6.3.2.1; LA.6.3.2.2; LA.6.3.3.1; LA.6.3.4.1; LA.6.3.4.2; LA.6.3.4.3; LA.6.3.4.4; LA.6.3.4.5; LA.6.4.2.1; LA.6.4.2.3; LA.6.5.1.1; LA.6.6.2.3

When responding to a prompt for on-demand expository writing, use the models you have read, what you've learned from writing your research report, the rubric on page 558, and the steps below.

Writing Situation:
The editor of your school paper wants to publish an expository essay about important people in students' lives.

Directions for Writing:
Think about a person who has been important to you.

Now write an expository essay for your school paper in which you provide details about this person and why you chose him or her.

Study the Prompt

Read the prompt carefully. Notice that the **writing situation** identifies the subject of the prompt. The editor of your school paper wants to publish an essay about important people in students' lives. Now, notice that the **directions for writing** identify the audience to whom the writing should be directed. Your audience is readers of the school paper. **Tip:** Spend about five minutes studying the prompt.

Plan Your Response

Reasons Focus your thesis by repeatedly narrowing it from a broad subject to a more specific subject. **Ask ,** "Why would someone want to read about an important person in my life?" Or, "What factual information do I know about the person I chose?" Your answers will help focus your thesis.
Evidence After focusing your **thesis,** quickly write down as many **details, facts,** and **examples** as you can think of to support the thesis.

Organization Once you have decided on a detail, fact, or example, plan where you will place it in your thesis. Use an outline to organize your notes into paragraphs for your essay. **Tip:** Spend about ten minutes planning your response.

Respond to the Prompt

You have your thesis and support, so go ahead and start writing. In each body paragraph, concentrate on one subtopic, making sure to provide supporting details. In your conclusion, summarize the main points and reflect on your topic. **Tip:** Spend about twenty minutes writing your response.

Improve Your Response

Revising Go back to the key aspects of the prompt. Add any missing information.

- Have you provided information about your choice?
- Have you given reasons and details about your choice?

Proofreading Take a few minutes to edit your response to correct errors in grammar, spelling, punctuation, and capitalization. Make sure that your edits are neat and essay is legible.

Checking Your Final Copy Before you turn in your essay, read it one more time to catch any errors you may have missed and to make any finishing touches. A final read is worthwhile to make sure you're presenting your best writing. **Tip:** Save five or ten minutes to read and improve your draft.

Giving a Research Presentation

Speak with a Purpose

Adapt your research report as an oral presentation. Practice your presentation, and then present it to your class.

Use your **RWN** to complete the activities for this workshop.

Think as a Reader/Writer Researchers sometimes present their findings in a formal presentation or speech, in addition to sharing the information in a written report. As in your written report, you'll want to present a clear thesis and support the thesis by sharing the most important points of your research. Here is your chance to share your research findings through an oral presentation.

Adapt Your Report

Even the most interesting report can sound dull if a speaker reads it word for word. To turn your research report into an oral presentation, carefully plan your **content.**

Choose Carefully

You may not want to present exactly the same points in your oral presentation that you used in your written report. Time considerations may limit the number of ideas and explanations you can present. To choose the content for your presentation, follow these suggestions.

- **Narrow your focus.** Choose the research questions that you find most interesting or that your audience will probably find most surprising.
- **Remember your purpose.** Because your **purpose** is to inform your listeners about your topic, your **point of view** should be objective. That is, you should not appear to favor one side of an issue. If your research revealed varied opinions about your subject, share them with your audience.
- **Plan your support.** Look at the plan you created for your report. Identify the information you will use to answer the research questions you have chosen. This information should include facts, details, examples, and explanations from several sources.

Make Note Cards

Create a separate note card for each research question that you'll address in your presentation. On each note card, write words or phrases from your research notes or written report that will help you remember the main ideas you want to share with your audience.

Sunshine State Standards: Benchmarks LA.6.5.2.2 deliver narrative and informative presentations, including oral responses to literature, and adjust oral language, body language, eye contact, gestures, technology and supporting graphics appropriate to the situation; LA.6.6.2.1 select a topic for inquiry, formulate a search plan, and apply evaluative criteria (e.g., relevance, accuracy, organization, validity, currentness) to select and use appropriate resources; LA.6.6.4.1 use appropriate available technologies to enhance communication and achieve a purpose (e.g., video, online); *Also covered* LA.6.6.4.2

Deliver Your Research Presentation

Once you know *what* you will say, you need to practice *how* you will say it. Follow these suggestions.

Use Effective Verbal Strategies

Practice your speech out loud. Because the occasion for giving your speech is fairly formal, use **formal English.** Avoid using slang or clichés. Consider your **volume** and **rate,** speaking loudly and slowly. Everyone in your audience—including people at the back of the room—should be able to understand you.

Practice using your voice to add meaning to your ideas. Slow down your rate of speech or change the **modulation** (pitch) of your voice to emphasize an important point. Make sure your **tone** of voice reflects a neutral **point of view.**

Use Effective Nonverbal Elements

Match your gestures and facial expressions to what you say. Raising your voice while pointing a finger, for example, can cue your audience that you are making an important point.

Practice making eye contact. As you rehearse your speech, make eye contact with a practice audience of friends, or glance from one object in the room to another if you practice alone.

Consider Using a Visual or Media Display

Maps, charts, graphs, slide shows, and video segments can be very effective in helping emphasize important ideas in your speech. The design of any display should be clear and direct. Use the display to support the ideas you explain in your speech. Do not overuse visual displays; include only items that clearly support the important points, the main idea, or the purpose of the speech. Add cues to your note cards to remind you when to use supporting visuals or displays during your speech.

A Good Oral Presentation of Research

- includes a clear thesis statement
- organizes and presents main ideas clearly so that the audience can follow and understand them easily
- adequately supports every main idea with a variety of evidence from different sources
- shows that the speaker fully understands the topic
- effectively communicates ideas both verbally and nonverbally

Speaking Tip

If you choose to use visual displays or technology, practice this part of your speech as well. Be sure you can hold and point to displays easily. Have technology equipment ready to go so that you will not fumble around trying to get a piece of equipment to work.

Learn It Online

A media display can bring your report to life. Take a look at *MediaScope* on:

go.hrw.com L6-561 

Standards Review Literary Text

Nonfiction **Directions:** Read the following two selections. Then, answer each question that follows.

John Brown (1800–1859) was an abolitionist, someone working to end slavery in the United States. In this selection from a biography of John Brown, Gwen Everett writes from the point of view of Brown's daughter Annie. Annie recalls her father's fateful raid on a federal arsenal in Harpers Ferry, Virginia, in 1859.

from John Brown: One Man Against Slavery by Gwen Everett

We listened carefully to Father's reasons for wanting to end slavery.

None of us questioned his sincerity, for we knew he believed God created everyone equal, regardless of skin color. He taught us as his father had taught him: To own another person as property—like furniture or cattle—is a sin. When Father was twelve years old, he witnessed the cruel treatment of black men, women, and children held in bondage and he vowed, then and there, that one day he would put an end to the inhumanity.

"I once considered starting a school where free blacks could learn to read and write, since laws in the South forbid their education," he told us. "And, when we moved to North Elba, New York, we proved that black and white people could live together in peace and brotherhood."

"One person—one family—can make a difference," he said firmly. "Slavery won't end by itself. It is up to us to fight it."

Father called us by name: Mary, John, Jason, Owen, and Annie (me). He asked us to say a prayer and swear an oath that we, too, would work to end slavery forever. Then he told us his plan.

He would lead a small group of experienced fighting men into a state that allowed slavery. They would hide in the mountains and valleys during daylight. And, under the cover of night, members of his "liberation army" would sneak onto nearby plantations and help the slaves escape.

Freed slaves who wished to join Father's army would learn how to use rifles and pikes—spear-shaped weapons. Then, plantation by plantation, Father's liberation army would move deeper south—growing larger and stronger—eventually freeing all the slaves.

Father's idea sounded so simple. Yet my brothers and I knew this was a dangerous idea. It was illegal for black people to handle firearms and for whites to show them how. It was also against the law to steal someone else's property; and, in effect, Father was doing this by encouraging slaves to leave their masters.

The fateful night of Sunday, October 16, 1859, Father and eighteen of his men marched into Harpers Ferry. They succeeded in seizing the arsenal and several buildings without firing a single shot. By morning the townspeople discovered the raiders and began to fight back. Then a company of marines led by Lieutenant Colonel Robert E. Lee arrived to reinforce the local troops.

The fighting lasted almost two days. When it was over, Father was wounded and four townspeople and ten of Father's men were dead. Newspapers across the country reported every detail of the trial, which was held during the last two weeks of October in Charles Town, Virginia. On October 31, the jury took only forty-five minutes to reach its decision. They found Father guilty of treason against the Commonwealth of Virginia, conspiring with slaves to rebel, and murder.

On December 1, my mother visited him in jail, where they talked and prayed together for several hours. I wished I could have been there to tell Father how courageous I thought he was.

He was executed the next morning.

Father's raid did not end slavery. But historians said that it was one of the most important events leading to the Civil War, which began in April 1861. The war destroyed slavery forever in our country, but it also took 619,000 lives and ruined millions of dollars' worth of property. My father must have known this would come to pass, for the day he was hanged, he wrote: "I, John Brown, am now quite certain that the crimes of this guilty land will never be purged away but with Blood."

Years after Father's death, I still had sleepless nights. Sometimes I recalled our conversations. Other times I found comfort in the verse of a song that Union soldiers sang about Father when they marched into battle.

His sacrifice we share! Our sword
will victory crown!
For freedom and the right remember
old John Brown!
His soul is marching on.

Yes indeed, I think to myself, one man against slavery did make a difference.

In 1850, Congress passed the Fugitive Slave Law. This law required federal officials to arrest people fleeing slavery and return them to their "owners." Here, Harriet Tubman comes to the aid of a captured runaway who is in danger of being returned to slavery.

from Harriet Tubman: Conductor on the Underground Railroad

by **Ann Petry**

On April 27, 1860, [Harriet Tubman] was in Troy, New York. She had spent the night there and was going on to Boston to attend an antislavery meeting. That morning she was on her way to the railroad station. She walked along the street slowly. She never bothered to find out when a train was due; she simply sat in the station and waited until a train came which was going in the direction she desired.

It was cold in Troy even though it was the spring of the year. A northeast wind kept blowing the ruffle on her bonnet away from her face. She thought of Maryland and how green the trees would be. Here they were only lightly touched with green, not yet in full leaf. Suddenly she longed for a sight of the Eastern Shore with its coves and creeks, thought of the years that had elapsed since she first ran away from there.

She stopped walking to watch a crowd of people in front of the courthouse, a pushing, shoving, shouting crowd. She wondered what had happened. A fight? An accident? She went nearer, listened to the loud excited voices. "He got away." "He didn't." "They've got him handcuffed." Then there was an eruptive movement, people pushing forward, other people pushing back.

Harriet started working her way through the crowd, elbowing a man, nudging a woman. Now and then she asked a question. She learned that a runaway slave named Charles Nalle had been arrested and was being taken inside the courthouse to be tried.

When she finally got close enough to see the runaway's face, a handsome frightened face, his guards had forced him up the courthouse steps. They were trying to get through the door but people blocked the way.

She knew a kind of fury against the system, against the men who would force this man back into slavery when they themselves were free. The Lord did not intend that people should be slaves, she thought. Then without even thinking, she went up the steps, forced her way through the crowd, until she stood next to Nalle.

There was a small boy standing near her, mouth open, eyes wide with curiosity. She grabbed him by the collar and whispered to him fiercely, "You go out in the street and holler 'Fire, fire' as loud as you can."

The crowd kept increasing and she gave a nod of satisfaction. That little boy must have got out there in the street and must still be hollering that there's a fire. She bent over, making her shoulders droop, bending her back in the posture of an old woman. She pulled her sunbonnet way down, so that it shadowed her face. Just in time, too. One of the policemen said, "Old woman, you'll have to get out of here. You're liable to get knocked down when we take him through the door."

Harriet moved away from Nalle, mumbling to herself. She heard church bells ringing somewhere in the distance, and more and more people came running. The entire street was blocked. She edged back toward Nalle. Suddenly she shouted, "Don't let them take him! Don't let them take him!"

She attacked the nearest policeman so suddenly that she knocked him down. She wanted to laugh at the look of surprise on his face when he realized that the mumbling old woman who had stood so close to him had suddenly turned into a creature of vigor and violence. Grabbing Nalle by the arm, she pulled him along with her, forcing her way down the steps, ignoring the blows she received, not really feeling them, taking pleasure in the fact that in all these months of inactivity she had lost none of her strength.

When they reached the street, they were both knocked down. Harriet snatched off her bonnet and tied it on Nalle's head. When they stood up, it was impossible to pick him out of the crowd. People in the street cleared a path for them, helped hold back the police. As they turned off the main street, they met a man driving a horse and wagon. He reined in the horse. "What goes on here?" he asked.

Harriet, out of breath, hastily explained the situation. The man got out of the wagon. "Here," he said, "use my horse and wagon. I don't care if I ever get it back just so that man gets to safety."

Nalle was rapidly driven to Schenectady and from there he went on to the West—and safety.

Standards Review CONTINUED

Literary Text

Sunshine State Standards: Benchmarks **LA.6.2.2.2** use information from the text to answer questions related to the main idea or relevant details, maintaining chronological or logical order; *Also covered* **LA.6.2.2.4**

1. From what point of view is the account *John Brown: One Man Against Slavery* written?
   A in the third person
   B in the first person
   C by Harriet Tubman
   D by John Brown himself

2. With which statement would John Brown and Harriet Tubman MOST likely agree?
   F One person fighting against slavery could make a difference.
   G The Fugitive Slave Law was fair and just.
   H Slavery could be ended without violence.
   I People should not involve family members in attempts to end slavery.

3. Which sentence is an example of first-person narration?
   A "Harriet started working her way through the crowd."
   B "Years after Father's death, I still had sleepless nights."
   C "She knew a kind of fury against the system."
   D "People in the street cleared a path for them."

4. How is *Harriet Tubman: Conductor on the Underground Railroad* written?
   F as a biography
   G as an autobiography
   H as an essay
   I as a short story

5. Which title seems MOST likely to be the title of an autobiography?
   A *The Civil War: 1861-1865*
   B *How I Gained My Freedom*
   C *Work Songs and Field Hollers*
   D *The History of the Underground Railroad*

Extended Response

6. In one or two sentences, state a difference between Ann Petry's account and Gwen Everett's account. Consider the type of narration (first or third person) used in each selection, as well as its genre (biography or autobiography). Support your answer with details from the texts.

READ THINK EXPLAIN

Standards Review Informational Text

Main Idea **Directions:** Read the following passages. Then, answer each question that follows.

Three Pets

We got Max from a group that traps wild kittens and tames them. When Max came to us, he was scrawny and little. Now he's a broad-shouldered, sun-yellow cat, the biggest cat in the 'hood. Max is my hero because he's a gentle giant with a soft meow. Yet he's kept some of his wild ways. He runs from everybody except me and my parents. He insists on his freedom to roam outside, especially on moonlit nights. He won't eat cat food unless he's really, really hungry. He prefers the mice and rats he catches on his own. Max knows we don't want him to catch birds, so he just watches them. He's kind to other cats—as long as they show him respect. He hates being pounced on. He loves curling up next to the sweet-smelling lavender plants in our yard, jumping from high places, cuddling at night, and getting stroked and scratched while giving me a cat massage with his big paws. I used to worry when he took off for a few days, but he always comes back. Max is my golden boy. He has a little voice but a big heart.

—Lynn

Rita is a small, shaggy, sandy-brown fluff ball. She's what some people call a mix—some poodle, some terrier, and a bit of something else. Rita is my hero because she's my hearing-ear dog. A woman from a place that trains dogs for deaf people found Rita in an animal shelter. Rita had been there for weeks, and nobody had claimed her. She went through five months of training. Then I got lucky. I was chosen to be the one who got to take her home.

I get along well by using American Sign Language, but having Rita tell me when she hears sounds like the ringing of an alarm clock or a telephone makes me feel even more independent. I love Rita. She is my special friend.

—Alex and Rita

Before I got Mopsy, I didn't know a bunny could be so much fun. Mopsy likes to play jokes on our cat. She creeps up behind him and nibbles his tail. She follows me around like a hopping shadow. Sometimes, to get attention, she jumps straight up in the air. Then, when she gets tired, she flops down and

Standards Review CONTINUED

Informational Text

Sunshine State Standards: Benchmarks LA.6.1.7.3 determine the main idea or essential message in grade-level text through inferring paraphrasing, summarizing, and identifying relevant details; *Also covered* LA.6.2.2.2; LA.6.2.2.4

takes a power nap. Mopsy loves to play, and she's never mean. My mom says that Mopsy must have learned her playful ways from her mother, who was a classroom rabbit.

Once a week we take Mopsy to visit my great-grandfather at his nursing home. He and his friends love to see her. Mopsy gets to sit on their laps and on their beds. She is quiet and never bites. That's why she's my hero.

—Michael

1. Which title fits all three selections?
   - **A** "Giving Humans a Helping Hand"
   - **B** "My Pet Is My Hero"
   - **C** "Cuddly Critters"
   - **D** "Keeping Animals Safe"

2. Which main idea is found in all three selections?
   - **F** To be considered a hero, an animal must show great courage.
   - **G** Animals make better use of their time than humans do.
   - **H** Pets can surprise and delight us in many ways.
   - **I** People should spend more time with their pets.

3. Which title does NOT describe articles that probably deal with topics related to these readings?
   - **A** "Tips on Caring for Your Dog"
   - **B** "Can Pets Make People Happy?"
   - **C** "My Iguana is a Good Friend"
   - **D** "When Rover Made My Day"

4. Which statement about pets is NOT a fact?
   - **F** Cats make better pets than dogs.
   - **G** Dogs can be trained to help people who are deaf.
   - **H** Some cats like to hunt for their own food.
   - **I** Mopsy visits a nursing home every week.

Extended Response

5. In what ways are the three pets in these selections alike? Support your response with details and examples from the text.

Sunshine State Standards: Benchmarks LA.6.1.6.3 use context clues to determine meanings of unfamiliar words.

Standards Review Vocabulary

Context Clues

Directions: Use **context clues** to help you figure out what the italicized words mean. Then, choose the best answer.

Practicing For FCAT

1. Read the sentence from "Brother."

Bailey could count on very few punishments for his consistently outrageous behavior, for he was the pride of the Henderson/Johnson family.

What does *outrageous* mean in this sentence?

A inspiring
B praised
C shocking
D predictable

2. Read the sentence from "Brother."

He could even pray out loud in church and was apt at stealing pickles from the barrel that sat under the fruit counter.

What is another word for *apt*?

F skilled
G bored
H careful
I interested

3. Read the sentence from "Brother."

His movements, as he was later to describe those of an acquaintance, were activated with oiled precision.

What does *precision* mean in this sentence?

A jerky motions
B little warning
C exactness
D silence

4. Read the sentence from "The Land I Lost."

This evening, a wily crocodile had avoided the barrier by crawling up the riverbank and sneaked up behind Lan.

What is another word for *wily*?

F stubborn
G crazy
H ugly
I clever

5. Read the sentence from "The Land I lost."

Please protect me so that I can find a way to kill the beast in order to free you from its spell and avenge your tragic death.

What does *avenge* mean in this sentence?

A properly mourn
B show his fear of
C get even for
D release

6. Read the sentence from "A Glory Over Everything."

Even if they were lucky enough to elude the patrol, they could not possibly hide from the bloodhounds.

What does *elude* mean in this sentence?

F confront
G betray
H escape the notice of
I fool by tricks

Standards Review CONTINUED

Sunshine State Standards: Benchmarks LA.6.1.6.3 use context clues to determine meanings of unfamiliar words.

Vocabulary

Practicing For FCAT

7. Read the sentence from "A Glory Over Everything."
   It was the words of the song that she was singing and something in her manner that disturbed and puzzled him.
   What does *defiant* mean in this sentence?
   A happy
   B relieved
   C in agreement
   D resistant

8. Read the sentence from "A Glory Over Everything."
   When she came to the farmhouse where the woman lived, she approached it cautiously, circling around it.
   What does *cautiously* mean in this sentence?
   F without fear
   G like a cat
   H carefully
   I slowly

9. Read the sentence from "A Glory Over Everything."
   A field hand had no legitimate reason for entering the kitchen of the Big House.
   What is another word for *legitimate*?
   A foolish
   B justified
   C practical
   D unhealthy

Academic Vocabulary

Directions: Use context clues to help you figure out what the Academic Vocabulary words in italics mean. Then, choose the best answer.

10. Read the sentence.
    A white woman wanted to contribute to Harriet's escape by hiding her and helping her along the Underground Railroad.
    What does *contribute* mean in this sentence?
    F help provide for
    G try to stop
    H cause problems for
    I encourage

11. Read the sentence.
    The people who ran stations along the Underground Railroad had a uniform opinion of slavery.
    What does *uniform* mean in this sentence?
    A identical
    B formal
    C immoral
    D enthusiastic

PRACTICING FOR FCAT

Standards Review **Writing**

Sunshine State Standards: Benchmarks **LA.6.2.2.2** use information from the text to answer questions related to the main idea or relevant details, maintaining chronological or logical order; *Also covered* **LA.6.3.3.1; LA.6.3.3.2**

Research Report

Directions: Read the following paragraph from a research report. Then, answer each question that follows.

[1] One of the North American Indian groups who built mounds was the Adena. [2] They built the mounds as burial places in what is now southern Ohio. [3] Mounds made by other groups are found in Indiana, Michigan, Illinois, Wisconsin, Iowa, Missouri, and Canada. [4] The Adena buried most of their dead in simple graves within the mounds, covering the bodies with dirt and stone. [5] Leaders and other important people from the village were buried in log tombs before being covered with dirt and stones. [6] Gifts were often placed in the tombs. [7] A pipe made of clay or stone was a usual gift placed in the tombs. [8] Grave Creek Mound is one of the largest mounds built by the Adena.[9] At about seventy feet high, it is a mysteriously beautiful monument.

1 Which research question does the information in this paragraph BEST answer?

A Why did the Adena build mounds?

B How were the Adena leaders chosen?

C When did the Adena build mounds?

D Who were the other mound builders?

2 Which sentence would be MOST appropriate for a research report if the writer wanted to add a fact to develop this paragraph?

F I would like to go to Hillsboro, Ohio, to see burial mounds.

G The mounds should be protected.

H The Adena began to build mounds around 700 B.C.

I It is amazing to think how the mounds were built.

3 Which sentence might you delete if you were revising this paragraph to improve its focus?

A sentence 1

B sentence 3

C sentence 5

D sentence 8

4 Which transitional word could be added to the beginning of sentence 5 to show how it relates to sentence 4?

F therefore

G finally

H next

I however

Nonfiction

Year of Impossible Goodbyes

After World War II ended, Korea was divided into two sections: the north, controlled by the communist Soviet Union, and the south, controlled by the United States. Many Koreans in the north feared living under communism. *Year of Impossible Goodbyes* is an autobiographical story based on author Sook Nyul Choi's escape to South Korea. Because of a betrayal, ten-year-old Sookan and her brother are separated from their mother and have to continue the dangerous journey on their own.

My Life in Dog Years

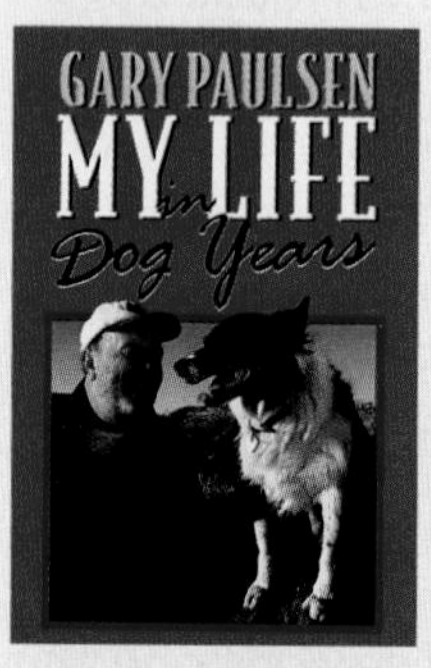

In the story "Storm," Gary Paulsen tells us about one of his favorite dogs. In his autobiography *My Life in Dog Years,* he remembers many of the dogs that have influenced his life, such as Snowball, his first dog, who saved him from being bitten by a poisonous snake; Dirk, who chased bullies away from a school-age Paulsen; and his beloved husky Cookie, who risked her life to save him from drowning after he fell through ice. Paulsen's appreciation of these and other animal companions comes through in these humorous and touching stories.

Shipwreck at the Bottom of the World: The Extraordinary True Story of Shackleton and the Endurance

Imagine that your ship and crew of twenty-seven are trapped by a crushing sea of ice in the coldest place on earth—Antarctica. Your ship breaks up and the only hope for survival is for some of you to trek eight hundred miles for help. You never know what life-or-death challenge is coming next when you read Jennifer Armstrong's *Shipwreck at the Bottom of the World,* the true story of Ernest Shackleton's Antarctic expedition.

Blizzard!

In 1888, weather forecasting was more luck than science. When snow began to fall on the East Coast one day in March of that year, no one expected the storm that would later become known as the Great White Hurricane. Three days of fierce winds and heavy snowfall brought down telegraph lines, stopped all trains, and made getting food and coal almost impossible. Historian Jim Murphy researched newspaper articles and personal stories from 1888 and gathered photographs and drawings in order to retell the harrowing story of this historic blizzard.

Sunshine State Standards: Benchmarks LA.6.2.2.5 use interest and recommendation of others to select a variety of age and ability appropriate nonfiction materials (e.g., biographies and topical areas, such as science, music, art, history, sports, current events) to expand the core knowledge necessary to connect topics and function as a fully literate member of a shared culture.

America's Story from America's Library

The site www.americaslibrary.gov is brought to you by the Library of Congress, our nation's library and the largest one in the world. (It has almost 530 miles of books—that's enough to make a line of books from New Orleans to Oklahoma City!) Designed with you in mind, this students' site is entertaining, interactive, and instructive. Take a look at this site to find out what happened on your birth date; listen to be-bop, a type of music invented long before hip-hop; watch Thomas Edison's favorite movie; and enjoy many more features.

Faces Magazine

This magazine is designed to get you interested in travel with just the turn of a page. In it, you can discover what people are like on the other side of the world or find out what kids in Australia do for fun. *Faces* takes you to different continents and introduces you to people and cultures that are very different from yours, yet very similar too. Stories about daily life, traditions, biographies, activities, and more fill each magazine. Every story is accompanied by beautiful color photographs and drawings that show you faces from all over our planet.

Science News for Kids

Check out www.sciencenewsforkids.org, a site that explores different and surprising zones of science. One zone has games to challenge your logic and memory; another gives exercises for writing science fiction stories. There's an interactive laboratory zone that gives hands-on activities as well as ideas for science projects. *Science News for Kids* will inspire you to let your imagination take off in all directions scientific.

Time for Kids

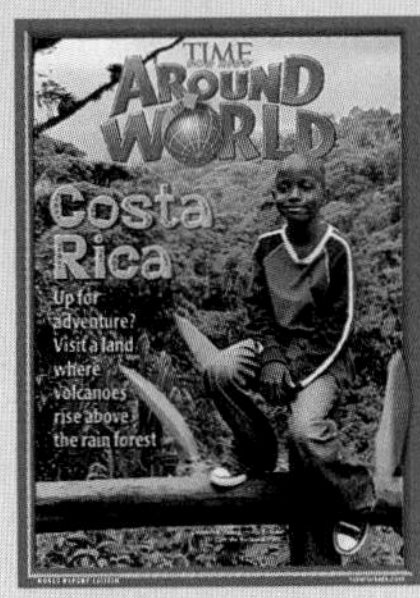

When a news story breaks, the magazine *Time for Kids* is there to report it. For the latest on current events, sports, and culture, pick up the magazine or look at its Web site, www.timeforkids.com. Make your own thoughts count in *Time for Kids* by participating in its polls and writing letters in response to its features and opinions.

Learn It Online

Use *NovelWise* to break down the elements needed to understand and analyze texts:

go.hrw.com L6-573 

COLLECTION 6

Persuasive Texts and Media

INFORMATIONAL TEXT FOCUS

Persuasion and Propaganda

"How wonderful it is that nobody need wait a single moment before starting to improve the world."

—Anne Frank

What Do You Think? What actions can individuals take to improve the world?

Learn It Online

Explore modern methods of persuasion on Media-Scope:

go.hrw.com L6-575 Go 

Informational Text Focus

by **Linda Rief**

How Do Writers Persuade Us?

You want to take guitar lessons, upgrade your computer, or go camping with a friend's family. How do you convince your parents? You state your case clearly, come up with specific reasons to support your cause, and develop some strong arguments to use if they say "No" at first. If you prepare your case well, you might actually persuade them to agree with your point of view!

Persuasion

When a writer's purpose is to influence readers to believe something or do something, the writer is using **persuasion.** First, the writer has a certain **opinion**—a belief or attitude. Then, the writer makes an argument to try to convince, or **persuade,** readers that his or her opinion is one that should be believed and accepted.

A persuasive writer builds a case by using **logic,** or correct reasoning. You're using logic when you put information together and conclude that "if this is true, then that must be true." A logical persuasive argument is built on an opinion that is supported by reasons and evidence. **Reasons** tell *why* writers hold particular opinions. **Evidence** is support or proof that backs up the reasons. This pyramid diagram shows how evidence is the foundation of persuasive writing:

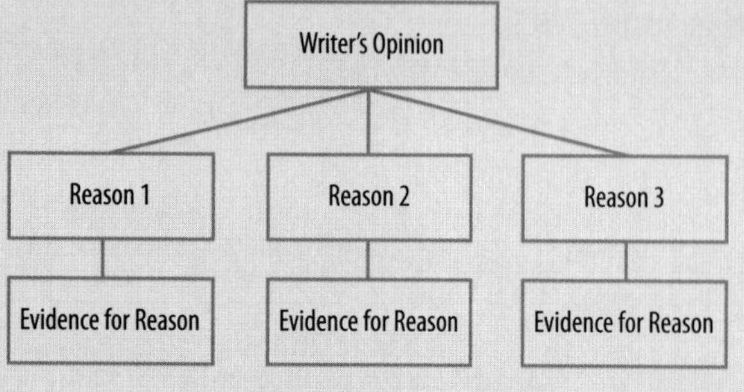

Types of Evidence

It's hard work for writers to get you to believe or do something. Their writing has to present convincing evidence, and they have to draw conclusions that make sense to you. Writers rely on different kinds of evidence to persuade you. Here are some common types and examples of evidence:

- **Facts** are statements that can be proved true. You can find evidence to confirm a fact in reliable sources, such as books and newspapers.

> The first international peace park, Waterton-Glacier International Peace Park, was established between the United States and Canada in 1932. Today there are dozens of peace parks on five continents.
>
> from "Peace Parks Help Environment and Communities"

- **Quotations** are the documented record of people's comments about a topic. **Direct quotations**—people's exact words—are always enclosed in quotation marks. A statement that an expert makes on a topic, such as the quotation from a professor in the following example, is called an **expert opinion.**

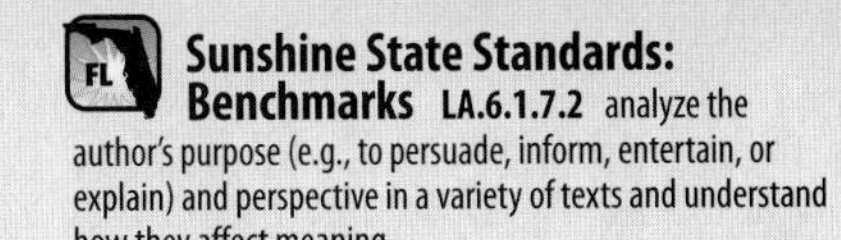

Sunshine State Standards: Benchmarks LA.6.1.7.2 analyze the author's purpose (e.g., to persuade, inform, entertain, or explain) and perspective in a variety of texts and understand how they affect meaning.

> "[The parks] will let animals wander over larger parts of southern Africa, much as they did centuries ago," said Jack Shepherd, a professor of Environmental Studies at Dartmouth College in New Hampshire.
>
> from "Peace Parks Help Environment and Communities"

- **Statistics** are information expressed as numbers. Statistics may be presented in the text, as in this example, or in charts or graphs.

> It turned out that life expectancy at age 35 was extended by as much as one and a half years simply by going to school for one extra year.
>
> from "A Surprising Secret to a Long Life: Stay in School"

- **Examples** are specific instances or illustrations of a general idea. Specific examples are sometimes called **case studies,** especially when they are based on scientific research.

> In one large federal study of middle-aged people, Smith reports, those with less education were less able to think ahead.
>
> from "A Surprising Secret to a Long Life: Stay in School"

- **Anecdotes** are brief personal stories that illustrate a point. In the following example an anecdote about a globe in a classroom suggests how easy and fast technology has made communication today.

> In Jeanne Agnello's sixth-grade classroom in Cold Spring Harbor, N.Y., a globe sits on a cart full of laptop computers. In the time it takes the social studies teacher to spin the globe, her students can connect with classrooms on the other side of the country—or the other side of the world.
>
> from "The Global Classroom"

Logical and Emotional Appeals

When writers use facts and statistics to support an argument, they are using **logical appeals** that target our thinking abilities. When writers use evidence that appeals to emotions, such as fear, pity, jealousy, and love, they are using **emotional appeals.** Since we are most likely to be persuaded by writers who appeal to both our minds *and* our hearts, even the most logical persuasive writing usually makes some appeal to our emotions. Still, don't be swayed by emotional appeals alone. Make sure the writer's position is also supported by hard facts—evidence you can prove.

Your Turn Analyze Persuasion

1. Give an example of a statistic you've heard or read. What conclusion might it support?
2. Describe a television commercial you've seen that included an emotional appeal. To which emotion did it appeal?

Learn It Online
Try the *PowerNotes* version of this lesson on:
go.hrw.com
L6-577
Go

Analyzing Visuals

How Can Visuals Be Persuasive?

On billboards, in magazines, on the sides of buses—you've probably seen many advertisements that include very little text. These ads rely on the power of visual images to make people believe or do something. Whether the suggestion is "Buy our jeans," "Volunteer your time for our charity," or "Stay in school," the actual words aren't always necessary to communicate a persuasive message. As with all persuasion, your job is to identify the message and analyze whether there are good reasons to agree with it.

Analyzing Visual Advertisements

Use these guidelines to help you analyze visual advertisements:

1. Read the fine print. What company or organization is responsible for the ad? What kind of message might that organization be trying to send?
2. Determine the purpose of the ad. Does it want you to buy something, to do something, or simply to be aware of something?
3. Look for clues to the ad's intended audience. Are people or things pictured that might be of particular interest to a specific gender, economic level, age group, ethnic group, or other group with special interests? Are there other clues that suggest an intended audience?
4. What messages does the visual suggest that support the ad's main purpose? The message might not be immediately obvious, but the ad's visuals probably make value judgments, suggesting ideas, such as "Cool, carefree people wear our jeans," that are intended to convince you.
5. Decide for yourself: Does it all *add up*? Think about all the ideas the ad suggests, and ask yourself whether or not they amount to a memorable or persuasive message.

Sunshine State Standards: Benchmarks LA.6.1.7.2 analyze the author's purpose (e.g., to persuade, inform, entertain, or explain) and perspective in a variety of texts and understand how they affect meaning.

Heard of
NICHCY?
For information on children and youth with disabilities, contact:
National Information Center
for Children and Youth
with Disabilities (NICHCY)
P.O. Box 1492
Washington, DC 20013-1492
800·695·0285 Voice/TTY
nichcy@aed.org E-mail
www.nichcy.org Web

Illustration and design by Jeanne Turner.

1. How does this advertisement catch your attention? What makes this such a powerful image?

2. What organization is responsible for this ad? What does the organization want you to do?

3. What idea does the image of the multicolored zebra suggest? What does the zebra probably stand for, or symbolize? How does this image support the ad's **purpose**?

Your Turn Talk About Visual Persuasion

In a small group, think of a popular advertisement or ad campaign. Discuss what makes its images memorable or powerful. What ideas—both obvious and subtle—do the images suggest? Do you agree with these ideas? Why or why not? Share your thoughts with the class.

Reading Focus

by **Kylene Beers**

What Skills Help You Decide If Persuasion Is Convincing?

"How do you know?" you ask your friend, who has just told you some gossip. "I just know" is all your friend can say. That's not good enough. Your friend isn't using evidence to support his or her assertions, or claims. It's important to be able to evaluate evidence that supports someone's claims so that you can evaluate the person's conclusions. Then, you'll know if you should (or should not) be persuaded.

Evaluating Evidence

Read persuasive texts carefully to decide if the evidence is strong enough to support the claims.

Adequate Evidence Decide if there is **adequate,** or enough, evidence to support the writer's points. A direct quotation from a respected expert in the field may be enough evidence all by itself. At other times, the writer may need to provide several facts and statistics.

Appropriate Evidence Make sure the writer uses **appropriate** evidence that relates directly to his or her ideas and supports the claims being made. When something in the text makes you ask, "What does this have to do with anything?" you're dealing with **inappropriate evidence.** Consider what kinds of support would have been stronger.

Accurate Evidence Finally, make sure the writer's evidence is **accurate,** or correct, and comes from a source you trust. Don't assume everything you see in print is accurate! If something doesn't sound right, check the source.

Evaluating the Writer's Conclusions

Evaluating the writer's evidence leads directly to **evaluating the writer's conclusions.** When you read persuasive texts, you expect the writer's evidence to add up to a conclusion that makes sense. Don't be fooled—writers aren't perfect. Just because something looks nice and neat on a printed page doesn't mean it is well thought out.

Summarizing Evidence You can see if a writer's evidence supports his or her conclusions by summarizing the important information. In your own words, sum up the writer's evidence, and then review your summary. Does all the evidence clearly add up to and support the conclusion?

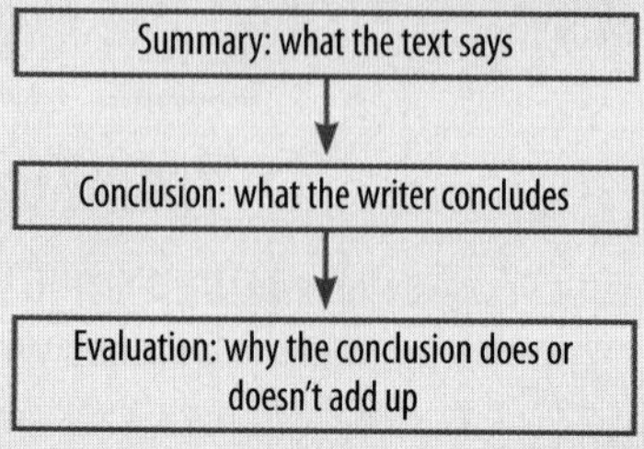
Summary: what the text says
Conclusion: what the writer concludes
Evaluation: why the conclusion does or doesn't add up

Sunshine State Standards: Benchmarks **LA.6.1.7.2** analyze the author's purpose (e.g., to persuade, inform, entertain, or explain) and perspective in a variety of texts and understand how they affect meaning; **LA.6.1.7.3** determine the main idea or essential message in grade-level text through inferring, paraphrasing, summarizing, and identifying relevant details; **LA.6.1.7.8** use strategies to repair comprehension of grade-appropriate text when self-monitoring indicates confusion, including but not limited to rereading, checking context clues, predicting, note-making, summarizing, using graphic and semantic organizers, questioning, and clarifying by checking other sources.

Distinguishing Facts from Opinions

All persuasion tries to convince you to agree with somebody else's opinions. In persuasive writing, if the writer's position is well supported, you'll also find many facts in the text. As a critical reader, though, you need to distinguish between an opinion and the facts that can back it up. Draw on what you have learned about distinguishing between fact and opinion as you read persuasive texts. Remember these key differences:

- **Facts** are pieces of information that can be proved true.
- **Opinions** are personal beliefs or attitudes.
- Some opinions are supported by facts, but others are not.

Facts and supported opinions can provide strong evidence for a writer's conclusions.

Making and Supporting Assertions

You can demonstrate that you understand an author's argument by making and supporting assertions about the text. An **assertion** is a statement or claim. A **citation** is evidence that backs up an assertion. Follow these steps to make an assertion about a text:

- Analyze the facts presented in the text.
- Interpret what the information means.
- Use evidence in the text to make an assertion.
- Evaluate your assertion by asking yourself how well evidence from the text supports it.

You can use a chart like this one to keep track of your assertions and citations:

Assertion (Claim)	Citation (Evidence)
1. The Internet allows U.S. students to communicate with students in other countries.	"Many schools use e-mail and online exchanges that link students throughout the world."
2.	

Your Turn Apply Reading Skills

1. Explain how to determine whether evidence is adequate, appropriate, and accurate in supporting a writer's conclusions.
2. How can you tell the difference between facts and opinions in persuasive writing?
3. Explain how the citation supports the assertion in the chart above.

Now go to the Skills in Action: Reading Model

Learn It Online
Get organized! Find interactive graphic organizers at:
go.hrw.com L6-581 Go

SKILLS IN ACTION
Reading Model

MAGAZINE ARTICLE

Read with a Purpose Read to find out what a "global classroom" is and how much it is like—or not like—your own classroom.

The Global Classroom

by THE WORLD ALMANAC®

In Jeanne Agnello's sixth-grade classroom in Cold Spring Harbor, N.Y., a globe sits on a cart full of laptop computers. In the time it takes the social studies teacher to spin the globe, her students can connect with classrooms on the other side of the country—or the other side of the world.

The Internet has shrunk the planet. People can now send ideas and images across the world in seconds. The Web connects more than a billion users worldwide, providing instant access to a vast amount of information. The walls of the classroom have virtually disappeared—and that's good news for the future of education.

Informational Text Focus

Persuasion When a writer's goal is to get you to believe or do something, the writer is using **persuasion.** This writer is stating her opinion about changes in education. Read on to see what evidence she provides to support her opinion.

Clearing Language Barriers

Many schools recognize that students must be prepared to live as citizens of a global community. The United States government does as well. In 2006, President George W. Bush proposed a plan to increase the number of Americans who speak and teach foreign languages. Stress was placed on "critical-need languages." Those are languages spoken in important or rapidly developing areas of the world. They include Arabic, Chinese, Korean, Japanese, Russian, and Farsi (or Persian, the language of Iran).

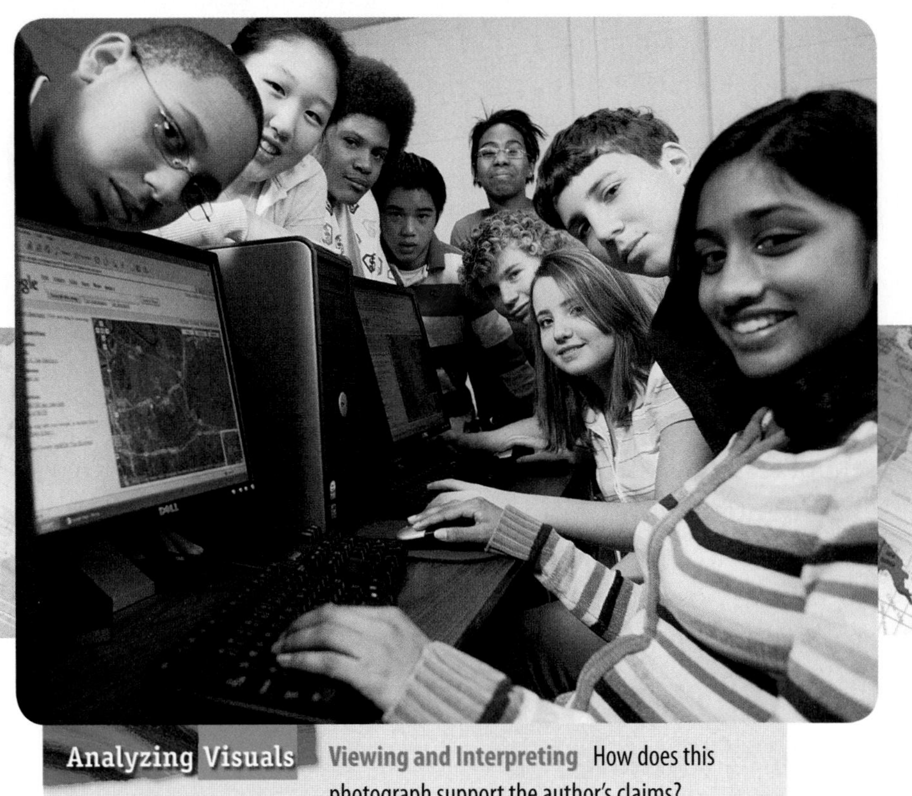

Analyzing Visuals **Viewing and Interpreting** How does this photograph support the author's claims?

"To prepare young Americans to understand the peoples who will help define the 21st century, nothing is more important than our ability to converse in their native languages," said U.S. Secretary of State Condoleezza Rice.

Informational Text Focus

Types of Evidence Writers use different types of evidence to back up statements and conclusions. One type is a **direct quotation**—a person's exact words set within quotation marks. Quotations by experts, such as this one, can be especially persuasive.

East Meets West

With help from the government and nonprofit groups, many more public schools are teaching Chinese and Arabic. China is becoming an economic powerhouse, so Mandarin Chinese is growing in popularity in U.S. schools.

Reading Focus

Evaluating Evidence To support this statement, the writer lists specific schools that have begun teaching these languages. The evidence seems adequate and appropriate to back up the claim. Specific evidence like this can be verified, or checked, so it's possible to prove (or disprove) its accuracy.

At Glenwood Elementary School in Chapel Hill, N.C., some classes are taught in both English and Mandarin. Students at McCormick Elementary School are among 3,000 students in Chicago schools who are learning Chinese. At Brookwood School in Manchester-by-the-Sea, which is a town on Cape Ann, Mass., even preschoolers learn to count and sing in Mandarin. The classes also help students understand the values and traditions of people in other lands, say teachers.

Reading Focus

Distinguishing Facts from Opinions The first highlighted sentence is a **fact—**a statement that can be proved true. The second sentence is an **opinion—**a belief or judgment. This opinion is supported by facts (examples of schools teaching Arabic). Facts and supported opinions can provide strong evidence.

The official language in many Middle Eastern nations is Arabic—a language that, until recently, was rarely taught in American classrooms. In the twenty-first century, however, Arabic is increasingly being seen as a language that's helpful to know in a changing world. At several high schools in Seattle, students are learning to read, write, and speak Arabic in after-school programs. Students at Annandale High School in Virginia are already in their third and fourth years of the language.

New York City planned to open, in fall 2007, its first public school teaching Arabic language and culture. Students at Khalil Gibran International Academy will eventually have half of their lessons in Arabic. "We are . . . looking to attract as many diverse students as possible," said Debbie Almontaser, the school's principal. "We really want to give them the opportunity to expand their horizons and be global citizens."

World of Knowledge

Language classes are just part of a shift to a global outlook in education. The International Baccalaureate Organization (IBO), based in Geneva, Switzerland, has a special program in more than 100 U.S. elementary schools. The program encourages

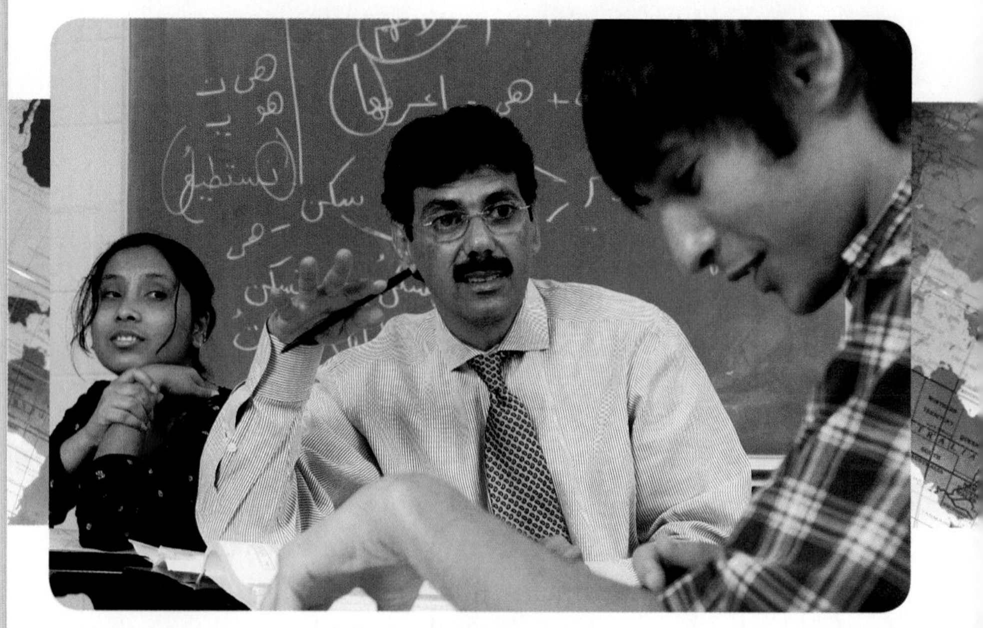

students, beginning with preschoolers, to become multilingual. It aims to help them understand and value other cultures. Every subject takes a world view, from math and science to literature and social studies.

Many schools use e-mail and online exchanges that link students throughout the world. The International Education and Resource Network (iLEARN) is a network of schools teaching students aged 5 to 19 in more than 115 countries. Students and teachers interact in more than 30 languages to carry out online projects with peers worldwide.

One iLEARN project is a newsmagazine, *Backtalk Journal,* in which students from many countries contribute interviews. The stories highlight people "who play some kind of leadership role in service to sustainable development" in their communities. Another ongoing iLEARN project is about endangered great apes in Africa and Asia. The project includes online activities, research projects, and art exchanges.

Another worldwide network is Global Learning and Observations to Benefit the Environment (GLOBE). This is an elementary and a secondary school science program. It connects students, teachers, and scientists in more than 19,000 schools in 109 countries.

The National Aeronautics and Space Administration and the National Science Foundation help GLOBE students carry out studies. Students take air, water, and soil measurements. They use the measurements to create maps and graphs. Teams in Bahrain, Honduras, Sri Lanka, and other nations work together. They share their findings through the GLOBE Web site. In doing so, students "develop awareness, respect, and appreciation for one another's cultures and environmental habitats," according to the American Forum for Global Education.

Informational Text Focus

Types of Evidence Notice the information that the writer gives here and elsewhere in the form of numbers. **Statistics,** or number facts, are another form of evidence that writers use to support their claims.

Going Places

The push to produce graduates who understand the world is increasing opportunities to study abroad. Numerous districts have programs helping U.S. students to be schooled in other

countries. These experiences prepare students to take part in "an increasingly interconnected international community that demands cross-cultural skills and knowledge." That's according to the Strategic Task Force on Education Abroad.

The U.S. Senate even designated 2006 the official Year of Study Abroad. In that year, more than 2,600 American high school students spent a semester or full year studying abroad, according to the Council on Standards for International Education Travel. Nearly 28,000 international students studied in the United States.

By "globalizing" education, schools seek to improve students' knowledge. Educators want students to better understand geography, culture, language, and international viewpoints. Business leaders and government officials agree: A global education helps students understand their role as world citizens. It helps them make connections between local and international communities.

"There's no turning back," says Agnello of her connected classroom. As students look forward to their future in a changing world, they can be pleased that global education is here to stay, helping them to become active, engaged citizens in an exciting new era.

Read with a Purpose What is a "global classroom"? Explain whether or not your classroom is one.

Reading Focus

Making and Supporting Assertions You should be able to make and support reasonable **assertions,** or claims, about a text to show that you understand it. For example, you might assert that studying abroad is a valuable experience for students. You can then list these two sentences as a **citation,** or reference, that supports your assertion.

Reading Focus

Evaluating the Writer's Conclusions Think critically about the conclusions a writer makes. Has the writer convinced you? One way to check a writer's conclusions is to summarize the evidence in your own words and see what conclusions you draw.

Informational Text Focus

Emotional Appeals The writer ends this article with an **emotional appeal**—a statement that will appeal to most people's feelings. This persuasive statement appeals to positive emotions, such as hope and excitement.

SKILLS IN ACTION Wrap Up

Sunshine State Standards: Benchmarks **LA.6.1.6.1** use new vocabulary that is introduced and taught directly; **LA.6.1.7.2** analyze the author's purpose (e.g., to persuade, inform, entertain, or explain) and perspective in a variety of texts and understand how they affect meaning; **LA.6.2.2.3** organize information to show understanding (e.g., representing main ideas within text through charting, mapping, paraphrasing, summarizing, or comparing/contrasting).

Into Action: Evaluating a Writer's Conclusions

Complete the following chart on a separate sheet of paper. Review the article you just read, and summarize the evidence in your own words. Did the writer provide sufficient evidence to support her conclusions? Explain why or why not.

Writer's Conclusions	By "globalizing" education, schools seek to improve students' knowledge.
Your Summary of the Evidence	

Talk About . . .

1. Explain to a partner the assertions you would make about a global classroom. Base them on this article and your experiences. Try to use each of the Academic Vocabulary words listed on the right at least once in your discussion.

Write About . . .

Answer the following questions about "The Global Classroom." For definitions of the underlined Academic Vocabulary words, see the column on the right.

2. What evidence in the article shows that it is crucial for students to have access to the Internet?
3. Consider the following data: 28,000 international students studied in the U.S. in 2006, while 2,600 U.S. students studied abroad that year. What can you conclude?
4. Are you an authority on learning in a global classroom? Explain why or why not.

Writing Focus

Think as a Reader/Writer

In Collection 6, you will read more articles in which writers present evidence and draw conclusions. The Writing Focus activities will give you practice evaluating persuasive texts.

Academic Vocabulary for Collection 6

Talking and Writing About Persuasion

Academic Vocabulary is the language you use to write and talk about texts. Use these words to discuss the informational texts you read in this collection. The words are underlined throughout the collection.

authority (uh THAWR uh tee) *n.:* someone who is respected because of his or her knowledge about a subject. *Writers of persuasion may quote a person who is an authority.*

conclude (kuhn KLOOD) *v.:* decide something after considering all the information you have. *You need to conclude if a writer provides enough evidence.*

crucial (KROO shuhl) *adj.:* very important. *It is crucial that you evaluate a writer's conclusions before accepting them.*

data (DAY tuh) *n.:* facts or figures; information. *Data can be used to back up an opinion.*

Your Turn

Copy the Academic Vocabulary words into your *Reader/Writer Notebook*. Then, use each word in a sentence about an issue or cause that is important to you.

INFORMATIONAL TEXT FOCUS

Persuasion

CONTENTS

What Do You Think?

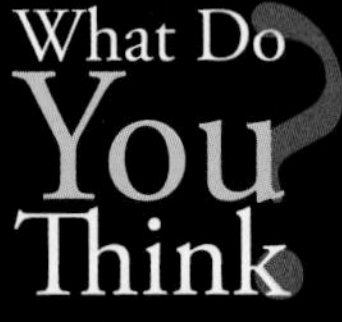

Why is education important in efforts to make the world a better place?

QuickWrite

How has education improved you, your friends and family, or your community? Write a paragraph explaining at least one way education has changed *your* world.

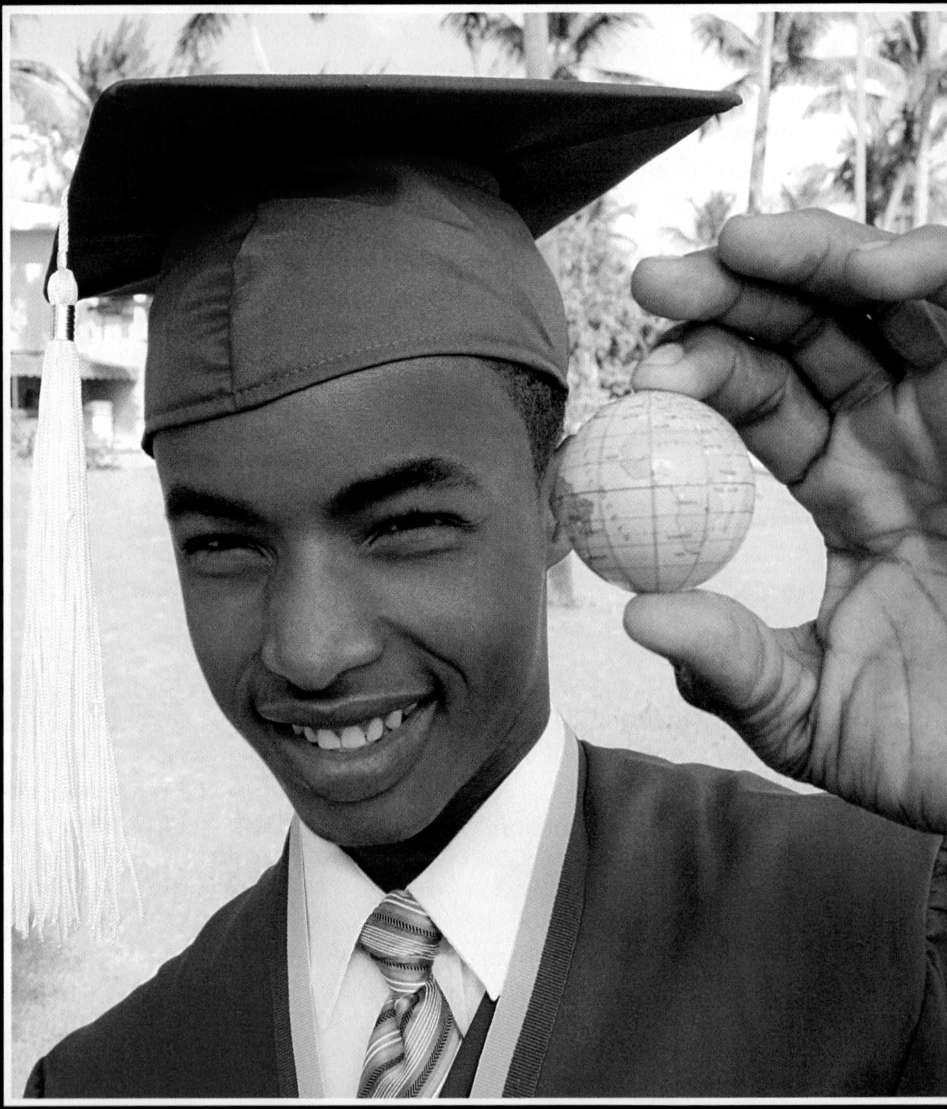

NEWSPAPER ARTICLE

Preparing to Read

Sunshine State Standards: Benchmarks LA.6.1.6.10 determine meanings of words, pronunciation, parts of speech, etymologies, and alternate word choices by using a dictionary, thesaurus, and digital tools; *Also covered* **LA.6.1.7.2; LA.6.2.2.3**

A Surprising Secret to a Long Life: Stay in School

Reader/Writer Notebook

Use your **RWN** to complete the activities for this selection.

Informational Text Focus

Persuasion It's everywhere. Advertisements urge us to buy products, politicians ask for votes, and editorial writers try to influence our thinking on issues. **Persuasion** is the use of language or visual images to get us to *believe* or *do* something. Skillful persuaders use a number of techniques to get us to see things their way.

Reading Focus

Evaluating a Writer's Conclusions Some informative texts are written to present certain **conclusions.** The writer presents crucial **evidence** and then draws a conclusion based on that evidence. For example, a writer might present facts and statistics called data about changing weather conditions and end with the conclusion that we are experiencing the effects of global climate change. Your job, as a reader, is to evaluate the conclusion—to determine if it has been supported well enough to persuade you to agree with it.

Into Action As you read, use a chart like this to help you keep track of how evidence relates to the writer's conclusion. Later, you will be asked to evaluate these conclusions.

Evidence	Conclusion
statement by Michael Grossman, health economist	Education helps determine how long a person lives.

Writing Focus

Preparing for **Extended Response**

The following article explores a connection between staying in school and living a longer life. Pay attention to the way the writer organizes evidence to support her conclusion.

Vocabulary

dispute (dihs PYOOT) *n.:* disagreement; argument. *There's no dispute that education is important.*

isolation (y suh LAY shuhn) *n.:* condition of being apart from others; removed. *Isolation can lead to poor health.*

declined (dih KLYND) *v.:* dropped; went down. *Their income declined when her father was ill.*

Language Coach

Related Words You can figure out the meanings of some new words by recognizing that they resemble other, more familiar words—words they are either formed from or related to. Look at these examples:

Longevity contains the word *long.*

Expectancy contains the word *expect.*

Explanation is built from the word *explain*.

When you come across a new word, see if it is similar to, or has some of the same parts as, another word you know or recognize. Look up the new word in a dictionary. Watch for other words that contain words you recognize. Here are some examples:

gratification *assistance* *financial*

Learn It Online

Explore the use of persuasion in advertisements online at MediaScope:

go.hrw.com L6-589 

A Surprising Secret to a Long Life: STAY IN SCHOOL

by GINA KOLATA

adapted from a *New York Times* article, January 3, 2007

Read with a Purpose

Read this article to find out why education might help you live longer.

James Smith, a health economist at RAND Corporation, has heard many ideas about what it takes to live a long life. The theories include money, lack of stress, a loving family, and lots of friends. It has been Smith's job to question these beliefs. Clearly, some people live longer than others. The rich live longer than the poor in the United States, for instance. But what is cause and what is effect?

In every country, there is an average life span for the nation as a whole, and there are average life spans for groups within, based on race, geography, education, and even churchgoing. Smith and other researchers find that the one factor linked to longer lives in every country studied is education. In study after study, says Richard Hodes, director of the National Institute on Aging, education "keeps coming up."

Education is not the only factor, of course. There is smoking, which curtails life span. There is a connection between having a network of friends and family and living a long and healthy life. But there is little dispute about education's importance. **A**

"If you were to ask me what affects health and longevity,"[1] says Michael Grossman, a health economist at the City University of New York, "I would put education at the top of my list." **B**

Graduate Student Finds Answer

In 1999, Adriana Lleras-Muney was a graduate student at Columbia University. She found a 1969 research paper noting the correlation[2] between education and health. It concluded: You can improve health more by investing in education than by investing in medical care. These findings could be true only if education caused good health, she thought. But there were other possibilities.

Maybe sick children did not go to school or dropped out early. Or maybe education was a part of wealth, and wealth led to health. Perhaps richer parents provided better nutrition, medical care, and education—and their children lived longer.

How, she asked herself, could she sort out causes and effects? Then she read that, about 100 years ago, different states started passing laws forcing children to go to school for longer periods. She knew she had to study those results and see if she could find a difference in life spans.

When she finished, Lleras-Muney says, "I was surprised; I was really surprised." It turned out that life expectancy at age 35 was extended by as much as one and a half years simply by going to school for one extra year.

Lessons Learned

Lleras-Muney has since become an assistant professor at Princeton,[3] and other papers on the subject have appeared in Sweden, Denmark, England, and Wales. In every country studied, forcing children to spend a longer time in school led to better health.

She and others pose this possible reason why education helps people live longer: As a group, less-educated people are less able to plan for the future. They are not as able to delay gratification.[4]

How might that difference in outlook change life spans? Consider smoking. Smokers are at least twice as likely to die as people who never smoked, says Samuel Preston, a researcher at the University of Pennsylvania. And poorly educated people are more likely

1. **longevity** (lahn JEHV uh tee): length of life.
2. **correlation** (kawr uh LAY shuhn): relationship between two ideas, facts, data sets, and so on.
3. **Princeton:** highly respected Ivy League college in New Jersey.
4. **gratification** (grat uh fuh KAY shuhn): satisfaction or pleasure; a source of satisfaction and pleasure.

A Informational Focus **Persuasion** What does the writer want you to believe? How can you tell?

B Reading Focus **Evaluating a Writer's Conclusions** What kind of evidence has the writer used so far?

Vocabulary **dispute** (dihs PYOOT) *n.:* disagreement; argument.

to smoke, he says, even though "everybody [including the poorly educated] knows that smoking can be deadly."

In one large federal study of middle-aged people, Smith reports, those with less education were less able to think ahead. And living for the day, says Smith, can be "the worst thing for your health." **C**

Other Factors at Work

In the late 1970s, Lisa Berkman, now a professor of public policy at the Harvard School of Public Health, worked at a San Francisco health care center. And she noticed something. "In Chinatown and North Beach, there were these tightly bound social networks," Berkman recalls. "You saw old people with young people. In the Tenderloin[5] people were just sort of dumped. People were really isolated."

> In one large federal study of middle-aged people, Smith reports, those with less education were less able to think ahead.

The risks of being socially isolated are "phenomenal,"[6] Berkman says. Isolation was associated with twofold to fivefold increases in mortality rates. These associations emerged in study after study and in country after country.

She asked herself: Does social isolation shorten lives? Or are people isolated when sick and frail? Berkman says, the more she investigated, the more she found that social isolation might lead to poor health and shorter lives. Isolation can, for example, increase stress and make it harder to get assistance. **D**

Researchers at Dartmouth College find that the lowest death rates are in the wealthiest places. An obvious explanation for this is that wealth buys health. Poorer people, at least in the United States, are less likely to have health insurance. But the differences between rich and poor do not shrink in countries where everyone has health care. In fact, says Smith, it is not that lower incomes lead to poor health so much as that poor health leads to lower incomes.

Smith notes that sick people often are unable to work or unable to work full time. He analyzed data from a National Institute on Aging sample of U.S. households with at least one person aged 51 to 61. When someone developed cancer, heart disease, or lung disease, that person's household income declined an average of more than $37,000.

5. **the Tenderloin:** poor area in downtown San Francisco.

6. **phenomenal** (fuh NAHM uh nuhl): out of the ordinary; surprising; rare.

C **Read and Discuss** How does the federal study support Lleras-Muney's findings about education and planning for the future?

D **Reading Focus** **Evaluating a Writer's Conclusions** Why can Berkman be considered an authority? What can you conclude from her research?

Vocabulary **isolation** (y suh LAY shuhn) *n.:* condition of being apart from others; removed.
declined (dih KLYND) *v.:* dropped; went down.

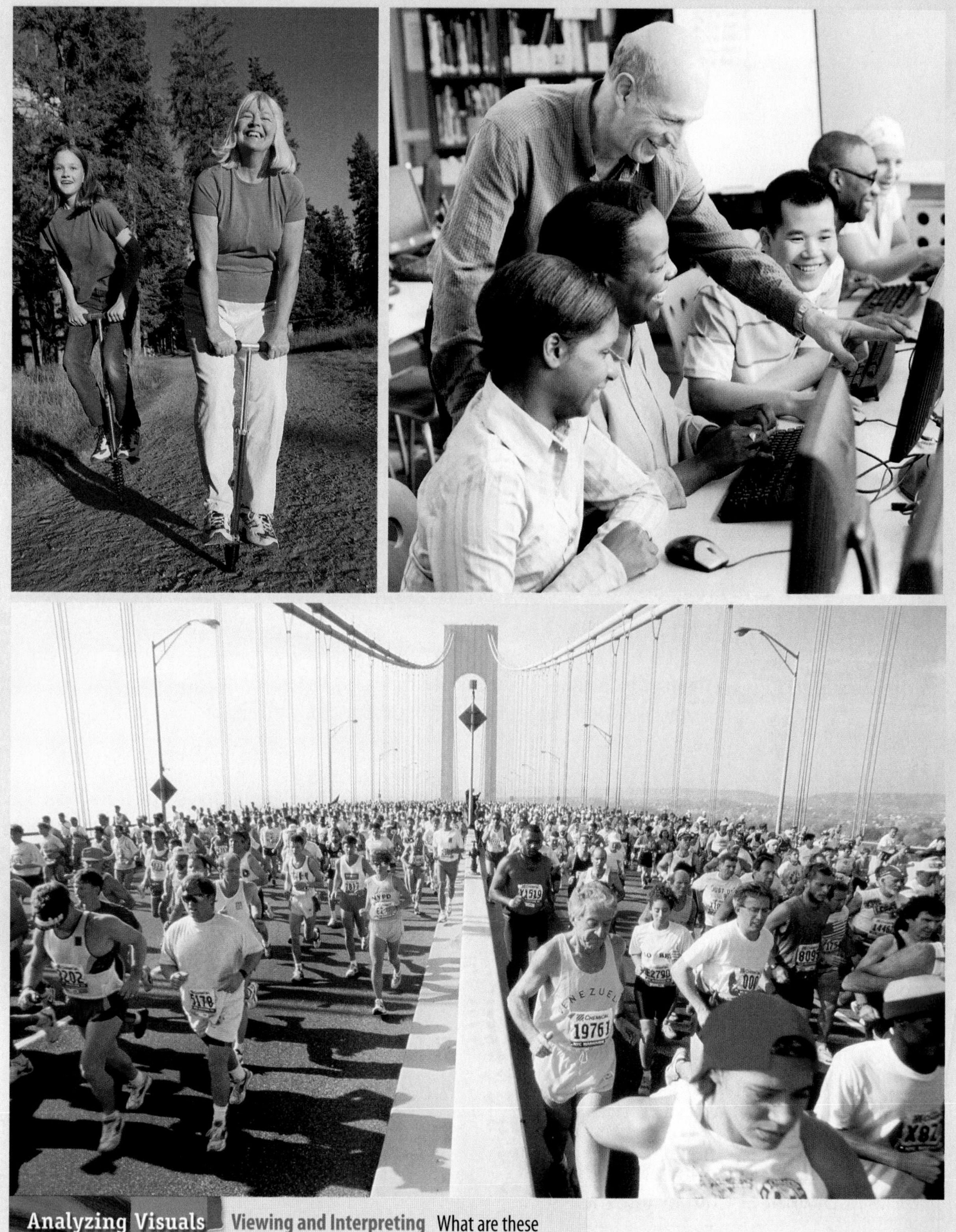

Analyzing Visuals **Viewing and Interpreting** What are these people doing that might increase their life spans?

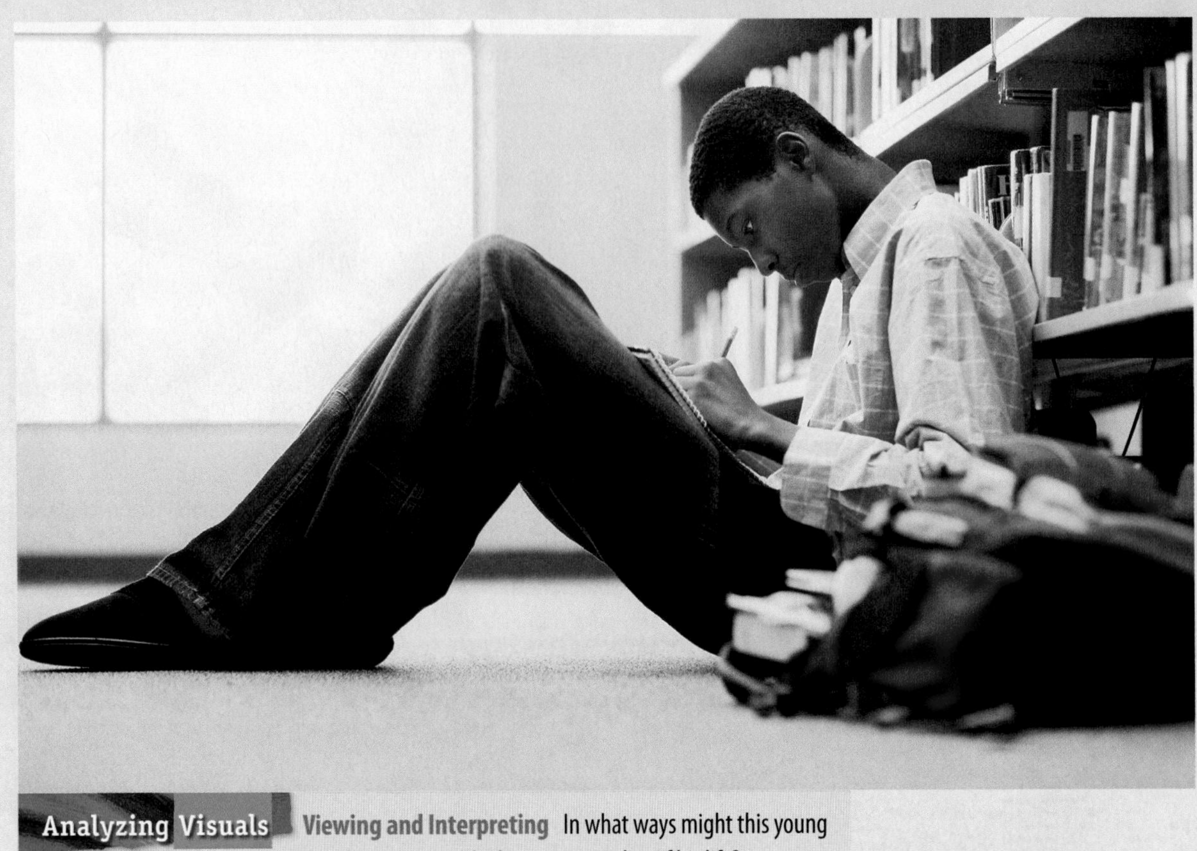

Analyzing Visuals **Viewing and Interpreting** In what ways might this young man be improving the long-term quality of his life?

Smith asked whether getting richer made people healthier, an effect that could lengthen life. It did not, he concluded, after studying increases in income during the stock market surge of the 1990s. "I find almost no role of financial anything in the onset of disease," Smith says.

There are some important findings about factors other than education that make a difference in life span. Health and nutrition in early life can affect adult health and longevity. For the most part, genes have little effect on life spans. But controlling risk factors for heart disease, such as smoking, cholesterol, blood pressure, and diabetes, pays off in a more vigorous old age and a longer life. It seems increasingly likely that education plays a major role in health and life spans. **E** **F**

Read with a Purpose

How can getting a good education help you live longer?

E **Reading Focus** **Evaluating a Writer's Conclusions** How is this conclusion supported by the evidence the writer has provided?

F **Read and Discuss** What else did you learn about lengthening life?

Applying Your Skills

Sunshine State Standards: Benchmarks **LA.6.1.6.1** use new vocabulary that is introduced and taught directly; **LA.6.2.2.2** use information from the text to answer questions related to the main idea or relevant details, maintaining chronological or logical order.

A Surprising Secret to a Long Life: Stay in School

Practicing for FCAT

Informational Text and Vocabulary

1. Which statement BEST expresses the writer's conclusion?

   A Education is the only factor that can accurately determine a person's life span.

   B Education plays a major role in living a long life.

   C It's impossible to figure out why some people live longer than others.

   D People are healthier now than they were a hundred years ago.

2. What form of statistics could be used to support the writer's conclusion?

   F one that shows which countries have healthcare for all citizens

   G one that shows how many doctors and nurses practice in the healthiest countries

   H one that shows the average amount of education people in the healthiest countries have

   I one that shows the number of smokers in the healthiest countries

3. Read this sentence from the selection.

   But there is little dispute about education's importance.

   What is another word for *dispute*?

   A reputation

   B argument

   C correction

   D insult

4. Read this sentence from the selection.

   Isolation was associated with twofold to fivefold increases in mortality rates.

   What is the meaning of the word *isolation*?

   F scattered

   G separation

   H confident

   I social

5. Read this sentence from the selection.

   When someone developed cancer, heart disease, or lung disease, that person's household income declined an average of more than $37,000.

   What is the meaning of the word *declined*?

   A gone up

   C stayed the same

   B gone down

   D doubled

Writing Focus Extended Response

Explain whether or not you were persuaded by the writer's conclusions. Support your response with evidence from the article.

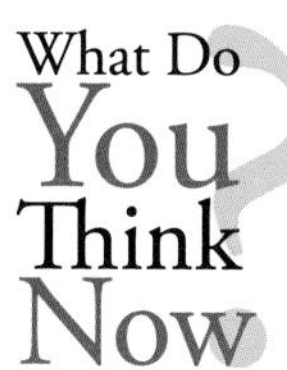

This article discusses one major benefit of education. What other benefits are there?

ARTICLE

Preparing to Read

Sunshine State Standards: Benchmarks
LA.6.1.6.4 categorize key vocabulary and identify salient features; **LA.6.2.2.3** organize information to show understanding (e.g., representing main ideas within text through charting, mapping, paraphrasing, summarizing, or comparing/contrasting).

Oprah Talks About Her South African "Dreamgirls"

Reader/Writer Notebook

Use your **RWN** to complete the activities for this selection.

Informational Text Focus

Recognizing Types of Evidence Writers use many kinds of evidence to support their points. **Quotations** are the direct words of people, often experts or authorities in an area. **Statistics** are information, such as percentages, expressed in the form of numbers. **Case studies** are examples from real life that illustrate a point the writer is making. All these types of evidence help make a piece of writing more convincing, or persuasive.

Reading Focus

Making and Supporting Assertions An **assertion** is a statement or claim you make about a text. **Citations** are the specific pieces of evidence you find in a text to support your assertions.

Into Action As you read, look for claims and supporting evidence the writer provides. After you read, make several assertions about the text. Create a graphic organizer like the one below in which you list each assertion and the citations that support it.

Assertion	Citations
David Levitt was troubled by two big problems.	1. Twenty percent of the food in the United States goes to waste. 2. Millions of Americans go to sleep hungry.

Writing Focus

Preparing for **Extended Response**

As you read, note the kinds of specific evidence both sides—those for and those against the school—use to support their claims. Use your *Reader/Writer Notebook* to record this evidence.

Vocabulary

criticism (KRIHT uh sihz uhm) *n.:* unfavorable remarks about someone or something. *Oprah Winfrey believes in her school, despite the criticism of others.*

circumstance (SUR kuhm stans) *n.:* fact or condition that affects a situation, action, or event. *Sometimes, poverty is a circumstance that people endure.*

yearning (YUR nihng) *n.:* feeling of wanting something badly. *The girls in the school had a yearning to succeed.*

attend school that receives ***criticism***

suffer ***circumstance*** *of poverty*

Dreamgirls

have a ***yearning*** *to become educated*

Language Coach

Word Families The words *criticism* and *circumstance* above are members of word families, or groups of related words. Which word is in the same word family as *criticize*? Which word is in the same word family as *circumstantial*? Name some other words that belong in each word family.

Learn It Online

Check out the *PowerNotes* introduction to this article on:

go.hrw.com L6-596 

Some of the first students at the Oprah Winfrey Leadership Academy for Girls in South Africa.

Oprah Talks About Her South African "Dreamgirls"

ABC News Report

Read with a Purpose

Read the following news story to find out who the South African "dreamgirls" are—and why they have been given that name.

In South Africa on Tuesday, the curtain for the Oprah Winfrey Leadership Academy for Girls parted for 152 girls in ankle socks.

They bring a history of so much suffering and so much hope for the future.

"You want dream girls? Take a look at these," said Oprah Winfrey, who made good on her pledge six years ago to Nelson Mandela to build the school. **A**

Half the population of South Africa lives in poverty, a quarter of the people have HIV, and there is an epidemic of violence among girls. **B**

A **Read and Discuss** What have you learned so far about the Oprah Winfrey Leadership Academy?

B **Informational Focus** **Types of Evidence** What kind of evidence is used here? What position does this evidence support?

Still, for some in the country, Winfrey's school, with its amazing theater, beautiful library and African art everywhere, seems "too much."

Critics inside and outside the country have asked, in a land with this kind of poverty, how can you spend more than $40 million on one school?

"I did love that the minister of education for this entire country stood up and said, 'I'm going to address the criticism. Is it too much? No, it isn't,'" Winfrey said in an exclusive interview with Diane Sawyer for "Good Morning America."

Winfrey said she got resistance from the very beginning, even from the school's architects.

"The resistance was too much," Winfrey said. "'What are you doing? What do they need all that room for? Why does a girl need all that closet space when she has no clothes?' That's what they first said to me."

"And my idea was to understand, yes, you come from nothing, but oh, what a something you will become, if given the opportunity," Winfrey said. **C**

Most of the girls who were admitted to the school have come from very little—no running water, no electricity, many of them studying by candlelight. They are still the best in their class.

At Tuesday's opening ceremony, one irrepressible girl named Losego said, "I went to a lot of effort to come to this school."

Diamonds and Dreams

Winfrey, who will stay very involved with the school and even teach leadership classes, said she believed the future was unimaginably bright for all of the girls.

"Somebody asked me, what do I think will happen or what do I imagine for them. I don't. I don't imagine . . . I can't imagine what it's like to have a miracle like this. It's just a miracle," Winfrey said.

And the girls already have big dreams. Losego had a suggested question for Winfrey: "What did you do with your first million?" **D**

Nelson Mandela and Oprah Winfrey at the groundbreaking for Winfrey's Leadership Academy.

C Reading Focus Making and Supporting Assertions What assertion could you make about what Oprah Winfrey is telling her critics? What citations would you use to support your assertion?

D Read and Discuss What is Losego thinking here?

Vocabulary **criticism** (KRIHT uh sihz uhm) *n.:* unfavorable remarks about someone or something.

Oprah Winfrey and students cut the ribbon at the opening of the Oprah Winfrey Leadership Academy for Girls in South Africa.

Analyzing Visuals **Viewing and Interpreting** What does this photograph tell you about the feelings of those involved with the opening of the school?

Winfrey dressed up for the school's opening ceremony, diamonds and all. The girls had seen them in pictures, and Winfrey said she had worn them as a signal that this was an important celebration.

"One of the things that's very important for me is for the girls to be proud of themselves and to be proud of the way they look and where they come from, and a lot of them in the beginning were very embarrassed about being poor," Winfrey said.

When Winfrey asked some of the girls why they wanted to come to the school, many said they wanted to take care of their families.

"And some of them would say, 'I want to come to this school because I am a poor girl,' and then they would drop their heads," Winfrey said. "I was a poor girl, too. So there's no shame in being a poor girl because being poor is just a circumstance. It's not who you are. It's not what can be possible for you." **E**

The school's curriculum and standards of behavior are high. This is a school for leaders, Winfrey says.

"I said to the girls, 'I'm going to take care of you. I'm going to do everything in my power to make sure you now have a good life and the best opportunity to go to the best schools in the world so when you leave this school you will choose universities all over the world. I cannot now take [sic] of your children,'" she said.

E **Read and Discuss** What did you find out about the girls attending the academy?

Vocabulary **circumstance** (SUR kuhm stans) *n.:* fact or condition that affects a situation, action, or event.

A Responsibility to Her New Daughters

One question that has been asked of Winfrey is why not build a school like this in the United States?

"What is different about this country is that there is this sort of desperate yearning to know better and do better that you just don't have in the United States," she said. "You don't have it because the opportunity's always been there."

The parents of the South African girls are also grateful for the opportunity.

"And I don't know a South African mother or father who didn't understand what a value, what a gift, what an opportunity an education is," Winfrey said. **F**

Winfrey admits that putting such a big stake into this school and these girls is a huge responsibility.

"It's not just about using your money wisely and making the best investment possible by investing in the future of young girls, but now I have a lot of responsibility," she said. "I feel it."

Winfrey has vowed to care for the new students at her school as if they were her own daughters.

"I said to the mothers, the family members, the aunts, the grannies—because most of these girls have lost their families, their parents—I said to them, 'Your daughters are now my daughters and I promise you I'm going to take care of your daughters. I promise you.'"

Read with a Purpose

Why are Oprah's students called "dreamgirls"? Explain why you do or do not think this is a good name for them.

Analyzing Visuals **Viewing and Interpreting**
What does this photograph suggest about the girl's attitude toward the school?

Oprah Winfrey hugs Loyiswa Sibekoat, a future student at Winfrey's Leadership Academy for Girls.

F Reading Focus Making and Supporting Assertions What assertion can you make about Oprah's reasons for building the school in South Africa and not in the United States? What citations can you use to support this assertion?

Vocabulary **yearning** (YUR nihng) *n.:* feeling of wanting something badly.

Applying Your Skills

Sunshine State Standards: Benchmarks **LA.6.1.6.1** use new vocabulary that is introduced and taught directly; **LA.6.2.2.2** use information from the text to answer questions related to the main idea or relevant details, maintaining chronological or logical order.

Oprah Talks About Her South African "Dreamgirls"

Practicing for FCAT

Informational Text and Vocabulary

1. Read this statement from the passage.

   Half the population of South Africa lives in poverty, a quarter of the people have HIV …

   What type of evidence does this statement provide?

   A anecdotal
   B statistical
   C a case study
   D circumstantial

2. Which statement BEST supports the assertion that a school like Oprah's is more necessary in South Africa than in the United States?

   F Educational opportunities have long been available in the United States, but not in South Africa.
   G Forty million dollars is not much money to someone like Oprah Winfrey.
   H Many of the girls in Oprah's school are poor and don't have families.
   I There is an epidemic of violence among girls in South Africa but not among those in the United States.

3. Read this sentence.

   The judge gave a look of criticism to the guilty person.

   What is the meaning of the word *criticism*?

   A praise
   B assignment
   C disapproval
   D report

4. Read this sentence from the selection.

   "What is different about this country is that there is this sort of desperate yearning to know better and do better that you just don't have in the United States," she said.

   What is the meaning of the word *yearning*?

   F to want something badly
   G to feel disgusted by something
   H to have hunger pangs
   I to hold an annual discussion

5. Read this sentence from the selection.

   "So there's no shame in being a poor girl because being poor is just a circumstance."

   What is the meaning of the word *circumstance*?

   A the measurement around a globe
   B the condition that affects the situation
   C evidence that is not fully convincing
   D someone keeping things from others

Writing Focus Extended Response

Choose one assertion made in the article and identify the types of evidence used to support the assertion. Is the evidence effective in supporting the assertion? Support your answer using examples from the article.

In what ways could a school like Oprah Winfrey's Leadership Academy help change the world?

WEB ARTICLE
Preparing to Read

Sunshine State Standards: Benchmarks
LA.6.1.6.7 identify and understand the meaning of conceptually advanced prefixes, suffixes, and root words; **LA.6.1.7.2** analyze the author's purpose (e.g., to persuade, inform, entertain, or explain) and perspective in a variety of texts and understand how they affect meaning.

Peace Parks Help Environment and Communities

Informational Text Focus

Logical and Emotional Appeals When writers make **logical appeals,** they give clear reasons why their opinions should be believed, and they support each reason with evidence. Writers also make **emotional appeals,** which stir feelings and make readers more sympathetic to the writers' arguments. As you read this article, consider whether it appeals to your mind or heart—or both.

Reading Focus

Evaluating Evidence When you read informational materials intended to persuade you, be sure to examine the kind of support the writer has used. Ask yourself:

- Is there *enough* evidence to support the conclusion?
- Has the writer presented the *right kind* of evidence?
- What *other* kinds of support would have worked better?

When you answer questions such as these, you're evaluating whether a writer's evidence is adequate and appropriate.

Distinguishing Between Fact and Opinion Appropriate evidence is based on facts. **Facts** are pieces of information that can be proved true. In contrast, **opinions** are personal beliefs or attitudes. Remember that some opinions can be appropriate evidence, too—as long as they are supported by facts. Look for facts and opinions in the article that follows.

Writing Focus

Preparing for **Extended Response**

As you read, pay attention to the data, examples, and so on that the writer presents. Which types of evidence do you conclude are most persuasive? List this evidence in your *Reader/Writer Notebook.*

Reader/Writer Notebook

Use your **RWN** to complete the activities for this selection.

Vocabulary

cooperation (koh ahp uh RAY shuhn) *n.:* support; working together. *The cooperation between nations needed to create parks may lead to world peace.*

conservation (kahn suhr VAY shuhn) *n.:* protection of natural things, such as animals, plants, and forests. *The society protects wildlife through its efforts in conservation.*

confinement (kuhn FYN muhnt) *n.:* condition of being kept from moving around; lack of freedom. *Confinement to a small area has a bad effect on animals' health.*

pollution (puh LOO shuhn) *n.:* something that makes air, water, and soil dangerously dirty. *Pollution is a major source of danger to the environment.*

Language Coach

Suffixes Three of the vocabulary words above share the suffix *–ion*, which means "state or condition." List five other words that end with this suffix. Use a dictionary if you need help.

Learn It Online
Polish your vocabulary skills with Word Watch at:

go.hrw.com L6-602 

WEB ARTICLE

Read with a Purpose

Read this article to learn what peace parks are and why they have been given this unusual name.

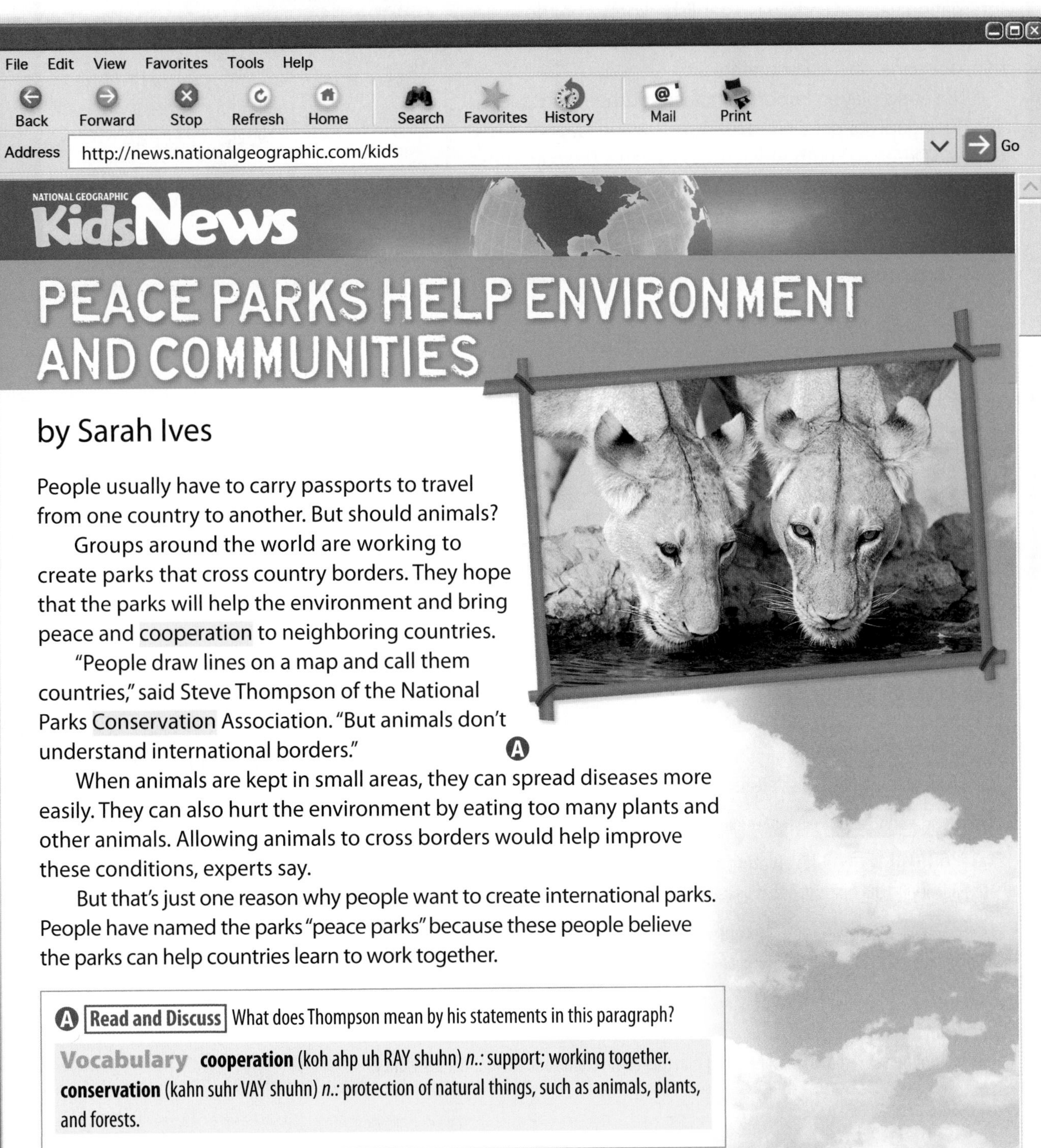

PEACE PARKS HELP ENVIRONMENT AND COMMUNITIES

by Sarah Ives

People usually have to carry passports to travel from one country to another. But should animals?

Groups around the world are working to create parks that cross country borders. They hope that the parks will help the environment and bring peace and cooperation to neighboring countries.

"People draw lines on a map and call them countries," said Steve Thompson of the National Parks Conservation Association. "But animals don't understand international borders." **A**

When animals are kept in small areas, they can spread diseases more easily. They can also hurt the environment by eating too many plants and other animals. Allowing animals to cross borders would help improve these conditions, experts say.

But that's just one reason why people want to create international parks. People have named the parks "peace parks" because these people believe the parks can help countries learn to work together.

A **Read and Discuss** What does Thompson mean by his statements in this paragraph?

Vocabulary **cooperation** (koh ahp uh RAY shuhn) *n.:* support; working together. **conservation** (kahn suhr VAY shuhn) *n.:* protection of natural things, such as animals, plants, and forests.

"[The parks create] a link between communities and a common desire to learn more about one another," said Anushka Bangara of the International Institute for Peace Through Tourism.

According to Steve Thompson, the parks can "help nations resolve international conflict or even war." **B**

The first international peace park, Waterton-Glacier International Peace Park, was established between the United States and Canada in 1932. Today there are dozens of peace parks on five continents.

The parks play an important role in southern Africa. The Kgalagadi (ka-gal-a-GA-dee) Transfrontier Park is in the Kalahari Desert in South Africa and Botswana. The countries work together to manage the land and the animals that live there. Other countries, such as Zimbabwe, Mozambique, Namibia, and Lesotho, are also forming parks. **C**

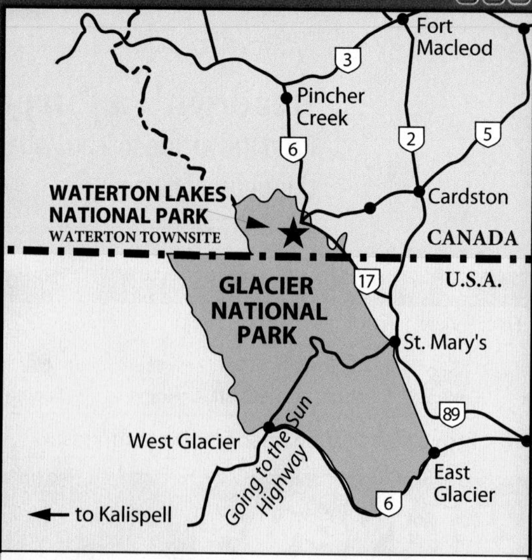

Map of Waterton-Glacier International Peace Park, the world's first international peace park, which crosses the border between Montana and Alberta, Canada.

"[The parks] will let animals wander over larger parts of southern Africa, much as they did centuries ago," said Jack Shepherd, a professor of Environmental Studies at Dartmouth College in New Hampshire. "It should really help expand elephant and lion populations, which are now damaged by confinement in smaller parks." **D**

The parks can also help countries by attracting tourists and creating jobs. But many issues still remain, such as illegal killing of animals, pollution, and population pressure on the land. Plus, some countries have different ideas about how they want to manage their parks and animals.

Countries are trying to solve those problems—and learning to work together in the process. **E**

Read with a Purpose Explain whether you think "peace parks" is a good name for these international parks.

B **Reading Focus** **Distinguishing Between Fact and Opinion** Can Thompson be considered an authority? Is his statement a fact or an opinion? How do you know?

C **Read and Discuss** What have you learned about peace parks so far?

D **Reading Focus** **Evaluating Evidence** Is this quotation appropriate or inappropriate evidence for the conclusion that peace parks can help wildlife? Explain.

E **Informational Focus** **Logical and Emotional Appeals** Which kind of appeal is made in the final sentence—a logical or an emotional one? Explain.

Vocabulary **confinement** (kuhn FYN muhnt) *n.:* condition of being kept from moving around; lack of freedom.
pollution (puh LOO shuhn) *n.:* something that makes air, water, and soil dangerously dirty.

Applying Your Skills

Sunshine State Standards: Benchmarks LA.6.1.6.1 use new vocabulary that is introduced and taught directly; LA.6.2.2.2 use information from the text to answer questions related to the main idea or relevant details, maintaining chronological or logical order.

Peace Parks Help Environment and Communities

Practicing for FCAT

Informational Text and Vocabulary

1. Which statement is an opinion?
   - **A** Animals don't understand international borders.
   - **B** Peace parks "'can help nations resolve international conflict or even war.'"
   - **C** Waterton-Glacier International Peace Park was established in 1932.
   - **D** The Kgalagadi Transfrontier Park is in the Kalahari Desert.

2. Which conclusion is NOT supported by adequate evidence in the article?
   - **F** Peace parks might help nations work together.
   - **G** Peace parks are good for the environment.
   - **H** Peace parks solved the problem of the illegal killing of animals.
   - **I** Peace parks help countries to attract tourists and create jobs.

3. Read this sentence from the selection.

   They hope that the parks will help the environment and bring peace and cooperation to neighboring countries.

   What is the meaning of the word *cooperation*?
   - **A** competition
   - **B** teamwork
   - **C** war
   - **D** education

4. Read these sentences from the selection.

   "People draw lines on a map and call them countries," said Steve Thompson of the National Parks Conservation Association. "But animals don't understand international borders."

   What is the meaning of the word *conservation*?
   - **F** information
   - **G** protection
   - **H** revolution
   - **I** suspension

5. Read this sentence from the selection.

   "It should really help expand elephant and lion populations, which are now damaged by confinement in smaller parks."

   What is the meaning of the word *confinement*?
   - **A** range
   - **B** crime
   - **C** devastation
   - **D** restraint

Writing Focus **Extended Response**

How do peace parks contribute to society? Support your response with details from the article.

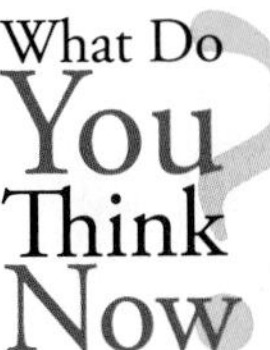

How could educating people and nations about peace parks improve the world in long-lasting ways?

COMPARING TEXTS

Compare Persuasion and Propaganda

CONTENTS

What Do You Think? How does advertising appeal to our desire to improve ourselves and our lives?

QuickWrite
Can you think of an ad, commercial, or poster you've seen lately that was especially clever? Describe it, and explain why you remember it.

Preparing to Read

Start the Day Right!

Sunshine State Standards: Benchmarks **LA.6.1.6.9** determine the correct meaning of words with multiple meanings in context; **LA.6.1.7.2** analyze the author's purpose (e.g., to persuade, inform, entertain, or explain) and perspective in a variety of texts and understand how they affect meaning; *Also covered* **LA.6.2.2.3**

Informational Text Focus

Analyzing Persuasive Techniques **Persuasion** is the use of language or visual images to get you to believe or do something. Audiences can be convinced by **persuasive techniques** that use both **logical appeals** and **emotional appeals.** Logical appeals rely on **reasons** and **evidence** to support an opinion. Emotional appeals stir the feelings of an audience, usually through the use of **loaded words**—words with positive or negative connotations, or suggested meanings.

Into Action Make a chart like this one to keep notes that will help you analyze the persuasive techniques in a media message:

Questions to Ask	Your Response
1. What is the main message, or claim?	
2. Is the claim a fact or opinion? Is it supported by reasons and evidence?	
3. Who made the message? What is his, her, or their purpose?	
4. To whom is the message directed?	
5. Does the message use logical or emotional appeals? If emotional, are they exaggerated or used in moderation?	
6. What does the message ask the audience to do or believe?	

Writing Focus

Preparing for **Extended Response**

As you read this storyboard for a public service announcement, ask yourself, "How are the creators of this announcement trying to persuade me?" In your *Reader/Writer Notebook,* jot down details that strike you as logical appeals—things that can be proven to be true—and those that strike you as emotional appeals.

Reader/Writer Notebook

Use your **RWN** to complete the activities for this selection.

Vocabulary

engaged (ehn GAYJD) *adj.:* busy and interested; absorbed in something. *Most of the students are engaged by the teacher's lecture.*

nutritious (noo TRIHSH uhs) *adj.:* full of nourishment; healthful. *Cereal and fruit can make a nutritious breakfast.*

irritable (IHR uh tuh buhl) *adj.:* in a bad mood; short-tempered. *Tired students are often irritable and unhappy in class.*

Language Coach

Multiple-Meaning Words Some words have multiple—and very different—meanings. The adjective *engaged* can mean "being interested in something," but *engaged* can also refer to the condition or state people enter into before their wedding day, when they have pledged to marry each other. As a class, brainstorm at least four other words that have two or more very different meanings.

Learn It Online

To learn more about analyzing persuasive messages on television, visit MediaScope at:

go.hrw.com L6-607 

CAMPAIGN: START THE DAY RIGHT!

FOR: Health For Kids and Other Important People

TV: 30-second spot

Read with a Purpose

Read this storyboard to decide if the televised public service announcement it represents would convince you that eating breakfast is important.

VIDEO

Camera opens on sunlit classroom with middle school students at desks. Most of them seem engaged, listening to a teacher at the front of the room, out of frame. The camera starts to focus on one boy, who looks like he is about to fall asleep.

AUDIO

Announcer: Every morning, in every classroom in America, students come to school without having eaten a nutritious breakfast. At most, they've eaten empty calories—sugary, fatty junk foods. Maybe they haven't eaten anything at all. The result? They're tired, irritable, unable to concentrate in class. **A**

A Informational Focus Persuasive Techniques Which words here are loaded words? What is their effect?

Vocabulary **engaged** (ehn GAYJD) *adj.:* busy and interested; absorbed in something.

nutritious (noo TRIHSH uhs) *adj.:* full of nourishment; healthful.

irritable (IHR uh tuh buhl) *adj.:* in a bad mood; short-tempered.

VIDEO

Boy puts his head on his desk. His classmate looks over and pokes him in the arm. He looks up, a bit dazed, and realizes he is in class and should be taking notes. He shakes his head as if to wake himself, blinks his eyes a few times, and fights to stay awake. **B**

AUDIO

Announcer: Scientific studies show that the eating habits kids learn when they're young will affect them all their lives. Poor nutrition during the school years can lead to a variety of health problems in adulthood—everything from low energy and obesity to diabetes and heart disease. **C**

VIDEO

Camera shows same boy at kitchen table the next morning with his parents and infant brother. The boy and his parents are eating cereal; a banana is on the table.

AUDIO

Announcer: You wouldn't let them go out the door without their homework—don't let them go out the door without a good breakfast. No matter how rushed you are, there's always a way to fit in a nutritious breakfast—for every member of the family. For some handy tips on how to create healthy on-the-go breakfasts, visit our Web site, Health for Kids and Other Important People, at www.hkoip.org. **D**

Read with a Purpose

How effective was this public service announcement in changing—or supporting—the way you think about eating breakfast in the morning?

B **Read and Discuss** What's going on in this classroom?

C **Informational Focus** **Persuasive Techniques** Facts and evidence can be verified, or checked. Does the information here consist of facts and evidence? Explain.

D **Read and Discuss** How does this new information add to what we know about eating a healthy breakfast?

Applying Your Skills

Sunshine State Standards: Benchmarks **LA.6.1.6.1** use new vocabulary that is introduced and taught directly; **LA.6.2.2.2** use information from the text to answer questions related to the main idea or relevant details, maintaining chronological or logical order.

Start the Day Right!

Practicing for FCAT

Informational Text and Vocabulary

1. Who would MOST likely provide the best supporting evidence in this TV ad?
   - **A** a worried teacher
   - **B** a medical doctor
   - **C** a football coach
   - **D** a student who eats well

2. What can you tell from the announcer's last paragraph about the intended audience?
   - **F** They are tired and irritable students.
   - **G** They are parents of students.
   - **H** They are homeroom teachers.
   - **I** They are classmates of sleepy students.

3. What do the creators of this campaign want you to conclude?
   - **A** that most children skip breakfast
   - **B** that children who eat with their family get good grades
   - **C** that an adult does not need a nutritious breakfast
   - **D** that a healthy breakfast is good for everyone

4. Which statement is NOT an opinion?
   - **F** Maybe they haven't eaten anything at all.
   - **G** If a student is sleepy, she hasn't eaten breakfast.
   - **H** Eating habits of children will affect them as adults.
   - **I** Students can always find time for breakfast.

5. Read this sentence from the selection.

   Most of them seem engaged, listening to a teacher at the front of the room, out of frame.

   What is the meaning of the word *engaged*?
   - **A** attached
   - **B** attentive
   - **C** delightful
   - **D** angry

6. Read this sentence from the selection.

   Every morning, in every classroom in America, students come to school without having eaten a nutritious breakfast.

   What is the meaning of the word *nutritious*?
   - **F** tasty
   - **G** fattening
   - **H** nourishing
   - **I** edible

Writing Focus Extended Response

Find an example of a logical and emotional appeal in the announcement. Explain which appeal you believe is more effective. Support your answer using examples from the announcement.

Preparing to Read

Sunshine State Standards: Benchmarks
LA.6.1.6.6 distinguish denotative and connotative meanings of words; *Also covered* **LA.6.1.7.5**

Shine-n-Grow: Hair Repair That Really Works!

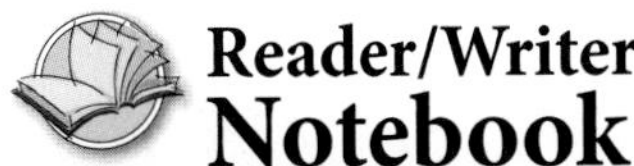

Reader/Writer Notebook

Use your **RWN** to complete the activities for this selection.

Informational Text Focus

Analyzing Fallacious Reasoning **Logic** is correct reasoning. A persuasive message shows **logical reasoning** if it is supported by **facts** and **evidence**—things that can be proven. **Fallacious** (fuh LAY shuhs) **reasoning** is faulty reasoning. (When you see the words *fallacious* or *fallacy*, think of the word *false*.) Fallacious reasoning often seems to make sense on the surface; but if you look closer, you'll find you can easily punch holes in the reasoning. Be alert for these three kinds of fallacies, or fallacious reasoning.

Type of Fallacy	Description	Example
hasty generalization (also called overgeneralization)	broad conclusion based on a limited number of experiences, using all-or-nothing words like *all, always, every,* and *never*	"I ate a bad hamburger at a diner once. Hamburgers at diners are always horrible!"
circular reasoning	reasons that say the same thing over and over, just using different words	"This bicycle is the best on the market because no other bikes are as good. This bike is better than any other bike."
only-cause fallacy	presents a situation or outcome as having only one cause, or the wrong cause	"We started playing better at practices once we got the new uniforms. Those uniforms are going to make us winners!"

Vocabulary

guarantee (gar uhn TEE) *v.:* promise or assure. *We guarantee that you'll be satisfied with this product.*

unique (yoo NEEK) *adj.:* one of a kind; rare or special. *Our hair formula is unique—no one else has it.*

Language Coach

Connotations Words used in advertising are often **loaded words** that carry strong emotional **connotations,** or suggestions. The word *guarantee*, for example, makes us feel a degree of trust. If someone guarantees something, we believe that we will get what we have been promised. The word *unique* appeals to our sense of value. Something that is unique is uncommon, rare—one of a kind. If something is unique, it is special—and who doesn't value and desire something special?

Think about synonyms for the words *guarantee* and *unique*. Do the words *promise*, *pledge*, and *assure* seem stronger or weaker than the word *guarantee*? Why? Explain whether something *special*, *uncommon*, or *rare* sounds as interesting to you as something that is *unique*.

Writing Focus Preparing for Extended Response

Look out for examples of fallacious, or faulty, reasoning in the newspaper advertisement you are about to read. In your *Reader/Writer Notebook,* identify the kinds of fallacious reasoning you discover.

Learn It Online
For a visual approach to learning, try the *PowerNotes* version of this lesson at:

go.hrw.com L6-611 

ADVERTISEMENT

SHINE-N-GROW:

Hair Repair That Really Works!

Read with a Purpose

Read this newspaper advertisement to see if you believe the claims it makes.

Have you ever suffered at the hands of a barber or careless hair stylist who cut your hair much shorter than you wanted? Have you ever envied your friends who have long hair? Now you no longer have to wait for weeks, months, or even years for your hair to grow back the way you want it to. With SHINE-N-GROW shampoo, your hair can grow faster than you ever dreamed possible. We guarantee that in no time at all, you can achieve the look everyone wants: a full head of hair that's long, healthy, and shiny. **A**

SHINE-N-GROW shampoo contains a unique combination of vitamins, minerals, and hair-growth ingredients that

- directly provide nutrients to each strand of hair to help it grow
- wash away dullness and replace it with shine
- bring life back to dry or damaged hair

SHINE-N-GROW research scientists have discovered a combination of natural ingredients that helps hair grow faster. Studies have shown that the average person's hair

A Read and Discuss What is the goal of this advertisement?

Vocabulary **guarantee** (gar uhn TEE) *v.:* promise or assure. **unique** (yoo NEEK) *adj.:* one of a kind; rare or special.

Analyzing Visuals **Viewing and Interpreting** What message does this picture send about Shine-n-Grow?

grows at a rate of one-fourth to one-half inch or less per month. A study was conducted to determine the effects of using the SHINE-N-GROW formula. The results were amazing! Test subjects reported hair growth of up to **five inches in three months!** (See our Web site for results.)

Bacteria and dirty oils slow down hair growth. SHINE-N-GROW**'s** natural ingredients kill bacteria, making it easier for hair to grow through the scalp. Thanks to our secret combination of ingredients, the cleansing value of the shampoo is far superior to that of any other products on the market. Customers who use SHINE-N-GROW just once never go back to their old brands. You'll love SHINE-N-GROW, too. **B**

People who use SHINE-N-GROW shampoo have reported that their hair has grown faster and has been cleaner, shinier, and easier to manage. Happy customers agree that their hair feels better after it's been washed. "I just feel more confident," one customer said, "and I've been getting more dates ever since I started using your shampoo." **C**

SHINE-N-GROW is the only shampoo that actually speeds up hair growth while it makes your hair smooth, shiny, and spectacular! Using SHINE-N-GROW guarantees what no other shampoo can: that you'll always have long, shiny hair. **D**

"My hair has never been so long before in my life. I've tried everything, but nothing has worked as well as Shine-n-Grow to make my hair long and clean."
—Susan Steinberg, actress, Brooklyn, New York

"My boyfriend mentioned the shine in my hair the first time I used Shine-n-Grow. He really noticed how it helped my dry and damaged hair."
—Christine Martinez, nurse, Tucson, Arizona

"My last haircut was way too short, so I tried Shine-n-Grow, and now my hair is long again—and clean! Finally my hair looks the way I like it."
—Roger Canter, accountant, Los Angeles, California

Learn more about SHINE-N-GROW on our Web site at www.shine-n-grow.com, and download a coupon for **15% off** your first purchase! SHINE-N-GROW is available now at better drugstores and supermarkets. **E**

Read with a Purpose Explain why you would—or would not—rush out to buy Shine-n-Grow for your hair.

B **Informational Focus** Fallacious Reasoning What is the fallacy here? Explain.

C **Informational Focus** Fallacious Reasoning What kind of fallacy is this customer using?

D **Informational Focus** Fallacious Reasoning Here's another fallacy. What kind is it?

E **Read and Discuss** How do "secret" formulas and happy customers influence your thinking about this product?

Applying Your Skills

Sunshine State Standards: Benchmarks **LA.6.1.6.1** use new vocabulary that is introduced and taught directly; **LA.6.1.7.5** analyze a variety of text structures (e.g., comparison/contrast, cause/effect, chronological order, argument/support, lists) and text features (main headings with subheadings) and explain their impact on meaning in text.

Shine-n-Grow: Hair Repair That Really Works!

Practicing for FCAT

Informational Text and Vocabulary

1. Read this statement from the ad.

   Customers who use Shine-N-Grow just once never go back to their old brands. You'll love Shine-N-Grow, too.

   What is this statement an example of?

   A reasons and evidence
   B overgeneralization
   C only-cause fallacy
   D circular reasoning

2. Read this statement from the ad.

   I've been getting more dates ever since I started using your shampoo.

   What is this statement an example of?

   F overgeneralization
   G only-cause fallacy
   H reasons and evidence
   I circular reasoning

3. Why is the claim that Shine-N-Grow "brings life back to dry or damaged hair" not supported by reasons and evidence?

   A because the advertisement does not list the kinds of oils in the product
   B because no data are presented as evidence that the shampoo repairs damage
   C because the advertisement does not include pictures of short, damaged hair
   D because no customer mentions dry or damaged hair

4. Read this sentence from the selection.

   We guarantee that in no time at all, you can achieve the look everyone wants: a full head of hair that's long, healthy, and shiny.

   What is another word that nearly means the same as *guarantee*?

   F desire
   G promise
   H gift
   I scheme

5. Read this sentence from the selection.

   Shine-N-Grow shampoo contains a unique combination of vitamins, minerals, and hair growth ingredients.

   Which word means the opposite of *unique*?

   A special
   B expensive
   C common
   D rare

Writing Focus Extended Response

Identify an example of fallacious reasoning in the ad and explain why the reasoning is faulty. Support your answer using details from the ad.

Preparing to Read

Brain Breeze

Sunshine State Standards: Benchmarks
LA.6.1.6.4 categorize key vocabulary and identify salient features; **LA.6.1.7.2** analyze the author's purpose (e.g., to persuade, inform, entertain, or explain) and perspective in a variety of texts and understand how they affect meaning.

Informational Text Focus

Analyzing Propaganda **Propaganda** is an extreme type of persuasion that is usually very one-sided. It relies on appeals to our emotions rather than on logical reasoning. Here are several common techniques used in propaganda.

Technique	How It Works
The **bandwagon appeal** takes advantage of people's desire to be part of a group or to be popular.	You are urged to do something because everyone else is doing it: "Everyone knows what a bargain this cell phone service is. Why not save money like everyone else?"
A **stereotype** presents a narrow, fixed idea about all the members of a certain group.	Stereotyping makes us judge people by their membership in a group instead of by their individual qualities: "No politician can be trusted."
Name-calling is the use of labels and loaded words to create negative feelings about a person, group, or thing.	Instead of giving evidence to support an argument, the name-caller makes fun of the opponent: "Only a granola-eating tree-hugger would think that this rat-infested park should be protected from developers."
Snob appeal sends the message that something is valuable because only "special people" appreciate it.	The advertiser wants you to feel important: "Runway Jeans are designed for people who insist on quality and design—people like you."
A **testimonial** is a recommendation made by someone who is well known but not necessarily an authority.	Famous people recommend a product, cause, or candidate, using their glamour, fame, and talent to persuade you to do or believe something.

Writing Focus

Preparing for **Extended Response**

Advertisers often use propaganda techniques to get you to purchase their products. In your *Reader/Writer Notebook,* list the different propaganda techniques you find in this advertisement.

Reader/Writer Notebook

Use your **RWN** to complete the activities for this selection.

Vocabulary

concentration (kahn suhn TRAY shuhn) *n.:* focused attention. *Effective studying requires concentration.*

enhance (ehn HANS) *v.:* increase; improve. *This feature can enhance the value of the product.*

complexity (kuhm PLEHK suh tee) *n.:* complication; difficulty. *The task took a long time to complete because of its complexity.*

Language Coach

Word Families *Concentration* comes from *concentrate,* and *complexity* comes from *complex*. What other words can you form from *concentrate* and *complex*? What other words can you form from *enhance*? Use a dictionary if you need help.

Learn It Online
Try the PowerNotes version of this lesson at:
go.hrw.com
L6-616
Go

ADVERTISEMENT

Read with a Purpose

Read this magazine ad to find out what "Brain Breeze" is and does—and to see if you're influenced by this advertiser's techniques.

The FIRST and ONLY Mental Power Booster that fits in the palm of your hand!

Uses music and air movement to sharpen your concentration and clear your clouded mind!

- **Study with No Effort!**
- **Finish Big Projects While You Relax!**
- **Feel Smarter and Less Stressed!**

Do you have a big test coming up? a big project to complete? Are you so wound up with stress that you can't think straight? Time to open the windows of your mind and let ***BRAIN BREEZE***® in!

Businesspeople, students, the guy next door—*everyone* is looking for that competitive mental edge. Now, getting that edge is easier than you ever thought possible with ***BRAIN BREEZE***—the Mental Power Booster that uses scientifically researched music and the physics of airflow to make you more productive, less stressed—and smarter! **A**

BRAIN BREEZE is an amazing new technological breakthrough! It increases your concentration and keeps you at the top of your mental game while it soothes and relaxes you with a patented combination of moving air and music—all delivered from a device no larger than the palm of your hand! It's so easy to use that even the laziest couch potato can benefit.

BRAIN BREEZE, the Mental Power Booster, was developed by Professor Gary Fract of the University of Hadleyburg and was tested for effectiveness at Right Idea Labs, a scientific center for the advancement of learning. Researchers found that in a study of one hundred people aged sixteen to sixty-nine, scores were raised an average of five points overall on tests of memory and problem-solving ability among those who used ***BRAIN BREEZE***.

A **Informational Focus** **Propaganda** What propaganda technique do you find in this paragraph?

Vocabulary **concentration** (kahn suhn TRAY shuhn) *n.:* focused attention.

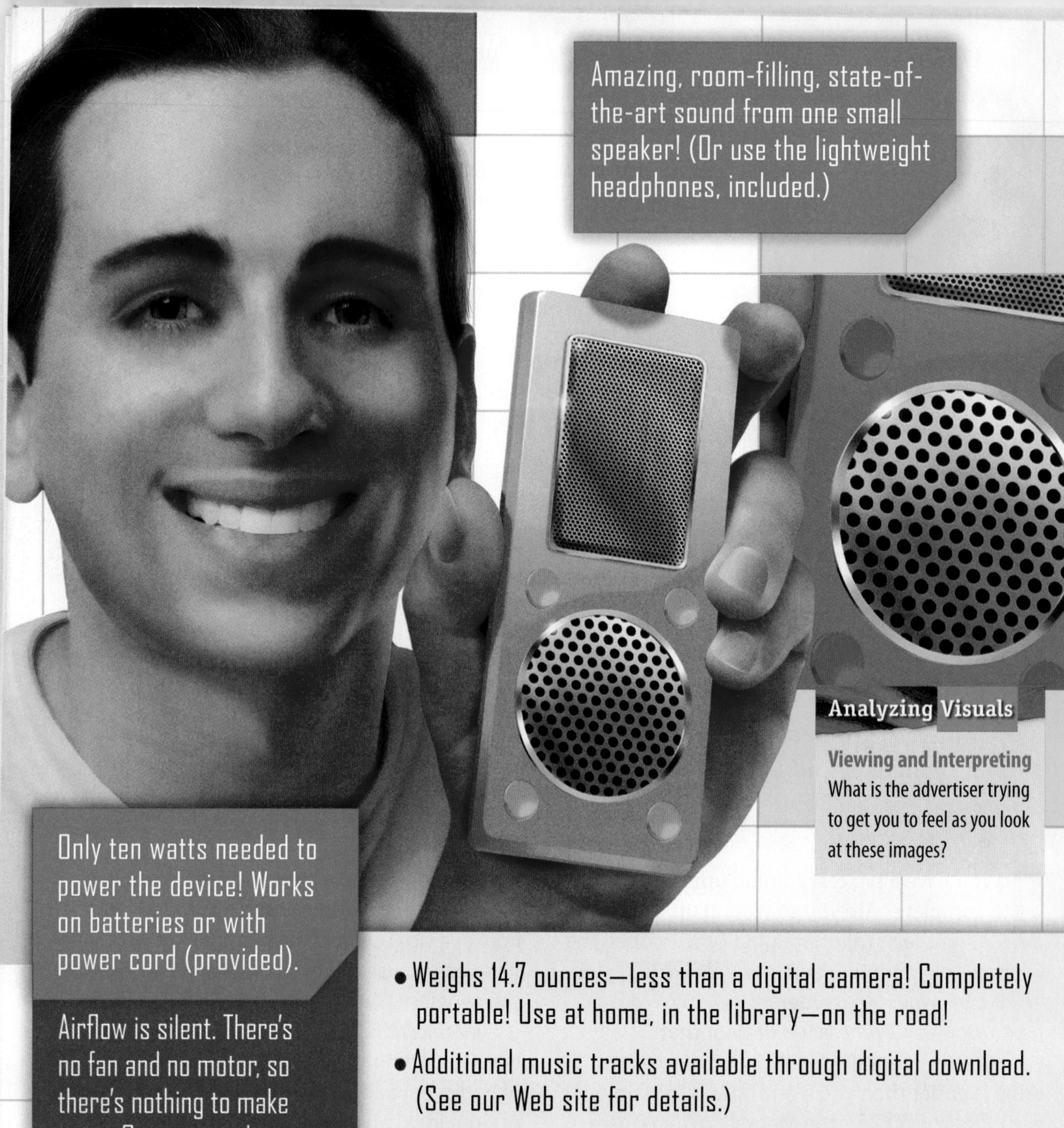

Amazing, room-filling, state-of-the-art sound from one small speaker! (Or use the lightweight headphones, included.)
Only ten watts needed to power the device! Works on batteries or with power cord (provided).
Airflow is silent. There's no fan and no motor, so there's nothing to make noise. Our patented technology moves air molecules electronically.

Analyzing Visuals

Viewing and Interpreting What is the advertiser trying to get you to feel as you look at these images?

- Weighs 14.7 ounces—less than a digital camera! Completely portable! Use at home, in the library—on the road!
- Additional music tracks available through digital download. (See our Web site for details.)
- Available in five fashionable colors to reflect your life-style and personality: Lively Lime, Tranquil Turquoise, Shimmering Silver, Awesome Orange, and Perky Pink.
- Satisfaction guaranteed! You have fourteen days to try ***BRAIN BREEZE***, risk free. Return it for a complete refund if you don't feel smarter and less stressed!
- 90-DAY WARRANTY.

High-achieving, high-income people appreciate the ***BRAIN BREEZE*** advantage. After using ***BRAIN BREEZE*** at his desk for two weeks, financial planner Tony Fine realized he was successfully dealing with two to three more clients per day than he had been able to before. "There's just something about the combination of the music and the airflow. It makes me feel more focused and organized," he says, "and I was already the most organized person I know." **B**

Emery Goodson, a medical student, had been using ***BRAIN BREEZE*** for just a week when she realized that studying no longer felt like a chore. "***BRAIN BREEZE*** is like this little treat I give myself," she says. "Now studying is something I look forward to. It's like a mental vacation, except I'm working!" **C**

Even elderly people can enjoy the benefits of ***BRAIN BREEZE***. Studies have shown that using ***BRAIN BREEZE*** at least once a week can vastly improve people's memories. Imagine—no more forgetting relatives' birthdays! **D**

BRAIN BREEZE comes fully programmed with thirty-nine different music tracks, each carefully selected from a research database of music scientifically proven to enhance concentration and problem-solving abilities. Choose from five different airflow settings, from low to high, based on the complexity of the work you are doing.

For information about scientific research related to ***BRAIN BREEZE***, all you have to do is go to www.gobrainbreeze.com. Find out how you can try ***BRAIN BREEZE*** on a free trial basis—and order one today for overnight delivery. Don't be the last person you know to act on this offer. Get the ***BRAIN BREEZE*** advantage now! **E**

THE DEVELOPMENT TEAM

Professor Gary Fract, *specialist in cognitive advancement, is author of* The Effect of Music on Developing Thought, *a major study of the cognitive changes that individuals undergo when listening to certain types of music. Right Idea Labs pioneered important studies in the effects of indoor airflow on mental focus by testing thousands of participants in the Idea Room, a model controlled environment.*

Find out more about ***BRAIN BREEZE*** at www.gobrainbreeze.com.

Read with a Purpose

How successful has this ad been in convincing you that Brain Breeze is worth a try? What details in the ad helped you reach your conclusion?

B **Read and Discuss** What have we learned about Brain Breeze? What is the purpose of Tony Fine's comment?

C **Read and Discuss** What new information do we have about Brain Breeze? What was the point of Emery Goodson's comment?

D **Informational Focus** **Propaganda** What stereotype is being used here?

E **Informational Focus** **Propaganda** What propaganda technique is being used here?

Vocabulary **enhance** (ehn HANS) *v.:* increase; improve.
complexity (kuhm PLEHK suh tee) *n.:* complication; difficulty.

Applying Your Skills

Sunshine State Standards: Benchmarks **LA.6.1.6.3** use context clues to determine meanings of unfamiliar words; **LA.6.2.2.2** use information from the text to answer questions related to the main idea or relevant details, maintaining chronological or logical order.

Brain Breeze

Practicing for FCAT

Informational Text and Vocabulary

1 What stereotype does this ad support?

A All students would cheat if they could.

B Everyone is looking for an easier way to do things.

C People like music and flowing air.

D Machines can do everything better than people.

2 Who would be the MOST appropriate person to give a testimonial for this product?

F a Super Bowl-winning quarterback

G a doctor who is an authority on brain research

H a famous Hollywood celebrity

I a state governor looking to improve school test scores

3 Which statement is the BEST example of bandwagon appeal?

A It keeps you at the top of your mental game.

B It's like a mental vacation.

C It makes me more focused and organized.

D Everyone is looking for that competitive edge.

4 Read this sentence from the selection.

It increases your concentration and keeps you at the top of your mental game.

What is the meaning of the word *concentration*?

F laziness

G attention

H relaxation

I punishment

5 Read this sentence from the selection.

***Brain Breeze* comes fully programmed with nine different music tracks, each carefully selected from a research database of music scientifically proven to enhance concentration and problem-solving abilities.**

What is the meaning of the word *enhance*?

A to make something smaller

B to make something disappear

C to make something better

D to make something cheaper

6 Read this sentence from the selection.

Choose from five different airflow settings, from low to high, based on the complexity of the work you are doing.

Which word means the opposite of *complexity*?

F similarity

G simplicity

H difficulty

I stupidity

Writing Focus — Extended Response

Explain how the advertisement is an example of propaganda. Support your response using examples from the text.

COMPARING TEXTS

Wrap Up

Sunshine State Standards: Benchmarks LA.6.1.7.5 analyze a variety of text structures (e.g., comparison/contrast, cause/effect, chronological order, argument/support, lists) and text features (main headings with subheadings) and explain their impact on meaning in text; *Also covered* **LA.6.2.2.3; LA.6.4.2.2; LA.6.4.2.3; LA.6.5.2.1; LA.6.6.1.1; LA.6.6.3.2**

Start the Day Right! / Shine-n-Grow /Brain Breeze

Writing Focus

Compare and Contrast Persuasive and Propaganda Techniques

Look back at the notes you took on persuasive and propaganda techniques as you read the public service announcement and advertisements. Which techniques seemed especially effective or powerful to you? Which ones seemed weak or unconvincing? In an essay, compare and contrast the public service announcement and two advertisements. You may wish to go back to the notes you took and assemble them into a chart like the one below. Filling out the chart will help you see at a glance how the ads are alike and different.

	"Start the Day Right!"	"Shine-n-Grow"	"Brain Breeze"
Reasons and evidence			
Fallacious reasoning			
Propaganda techniques			

In your concluding paragraph, state which ad is most successful in sending a convincing persuasive message and why.

What Do You Think Now? How have these examples of persuasive media changed the way you view messages urging you to improve yourself or the world?

CHOICES

As you respond to the Choices, use these **Academic Vocabulary** words as appropriate: authority, conclude, crucial, data.

REVIEW

Identify Fallacious Reasoning

Timed Writing In a paragraph, explain why the reasoning in these sentences is faulty: "Every student should read the Kendra Kaye, Goblin Hunter books because they are great and very popular. My grades have improved because of the new words I have learned from these books."

CONNECT

Analyze Persuasion and Propaganda in Ads

Group Discussion For one week, critically view and listen to advertisements on television, the Internet, and the radio. Take notes on two or three advertisements that you conclude are most effective. Bring your notes to class. With a small group, discuss examples of persuasive techniques and propaganda in each ad.

EXTEND

Create a "Good Propaganda" Campaign

Group Work Not all propaganda is bad. An ad campaign that uses emotional appeals to discourage people from smoking could be considered "good propaganda" because it works toward a positive outcome. Study examples of "good propaganda" about crucial social issues. With a small group, design a "good propaganda" campaign to raise awareness of an issue that you and your classmates believe is important.

Writing Workshop

Problem-Solution Essay FCAT Writing+

Write with a Purpose

Write an essay that describes a problem and provides a persuasive solution to the problem. Your **audience** includes your teacher and classmates. Your **purpose** is to persuade them that your solution is reasonable and practical.

A Good Problem-Solution Essay

- clearly defines the problem
- provides evidence of the effects of the problem and clearly states the proposed solution
- discusses benefits of the solution and answers possible objections
- ends with a convincing call to action

Think as a Reader/Writer

In this collection, you read several persuasive texts. You learned how writers take a position on a topic and persuade readers to agree with the position. Now it's your turn to use these persuasive techniques in a problem-solution essay. A problem-solution essay discusses an important problem, proposes a solution, and persuades readers why the proposed solution is the best one. Take a few minutes to read this excerpt from an essay titled "The U.S. Has a Garbage Crisis," by William Dudley.

We are running out of places to put all the garbage we produce. About 80 percent of it is now buried in landfills. There are 6,000 landfills currently operating, but many of them are becoming full. The Environmental Protection Agency estimates that one-half of remaining landfills will run out of space and close within the next five to ten years . . . .

← The first paragraph states the **problem** and provides **evidence** of the problem.

The only real solution to the garbage crisis is for Americans to reduce the amount of trash they throw away. There are two methods of doing this. One is recycling—reusing garbage . . . . Environmentalist Barry Commoner estimates that we can reduce 70 percent of our garbage by recycling.

← The proposed **solution** is clearly stated at the beginning of the second paragraph.

We must also reduce the amount of garbage we produce in the first place . . . . Consumers should buy foods and goods that use less packaging. We also should buy reusable products rather than things that are used once and thrown away.

← The writer provides more **details** of the solution.

Think About the Professional Model

With a partner, discuss the following questions about the model.

1. How does the writer get your attention with the problem statement?
2. Is the problem statement effective? Why or why not?
3. Is the proposed solution realistic? What information is used to persuade the reader that this is a realistic solution?

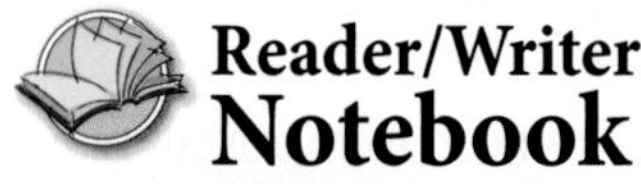

Use your **RWN** to complete the activities for this workshop.

Sunshine State Standards: Benchmarks **LA.6.3.1.1** generating ideas from multiple sources (e.g., prior knowledge, discussion with others, writer's notebook, research materials, or other reliable sources), based upon teacher-directed topics and personal interests; **LA.6.3.1.2** making a plan for writing that prioritizes ideas, addresses purpose, audience, main idea, and logical sequence; **LA.6.3.1.3** using organizational strategies and tools (e.g., technology, outline, chart, table, graph, web, story map); **LA.6.3.2.1** developing main ideas from the prewriting plan using primary and secondary sources appropriate to purpose and audience; **LA.6.3.2.2** organizing information into a logical sequence and combining or deleting sentences to enhance clarity; **LA.6.3.3.1** evaluating the draft for development of ideas and content, logical organization, voice, point of view, word choice, and sentence variation; *Also covered* **LA.6.3.3.2; LA.6.3.3.4; LA.6.3.4.1; LA.6.3.4.3; LA.6.3.4.4; LA.6.3.5.1; LA.6.3.5.3; LA.6.4.2.3; LA.6.4.3.1; LA.6.4.3.2**

Prewriting

Choose a Problem

The first step in writing a problem-solution essay is choosing a problem that is important to you and your audience. Work in a small group to brainstorm a list of problems. The Idea Starters at right may help you generate ideas. Then, on your own, choose two or three problems that are most important to you. Consider some realistic solutions to those problems, and choose the problem that seems to be most promising.

Develop a Thesis

Once you've identified a problem, you must write a **thesis statement,** or opinion statement, that clearly states the problem. (The solution will come later in your essay.) Here is an example of a student's thesis statement: *Sibling rivalry, or competition between brothers and sisters, can seriously harm families.*

Find a Solution

The solution is the heart of the matter, your reason for writing the essay. There's no one "correct" way to go about finding a solution. One person might begin by brainstorming different possibilities, while another might write freely about the problem just to put words on paper. If you take the second approach, you might want to imagine that you're writing a letter to a friend about the problem.

Whatever approach you take, be sure you clearly explain your solution to your readers. You might stress how practical your solution is, how easy it is to accomplish, or the consequences of taking no action at all. Fill in a chart like the one below to keep track of some possible solutions to the problem you've chosen. This chart is partially completed for the model on page 622.

Problem	Possible Solution
Landfills are filling up, and there's no place to put garbage.	Reduce garbage by recycling.
	Reduce garbage by using less packaging in consumer products.

Idea Starters

Think about problems involving

- you and your classmates
- your school or community
- the global community
- a situation you noticed recently

Your Turn

Get Started Record in your **RWN** the **problem** and **solution** you have selected. Then, spend some time thinking about both. Is the problem one your audience will care about? Are there any flaws in your solution to the problem? Can you think of a better solution? Use this information as you plan your draft.

Learn It Online
See how one writer develops a problem-solution essay:

go.hrw.com L6-623 

Peer Review

Getting together with a classmate who can serve as your "practice audience" is a good way to help you think through the objections you might face to your proposed solution. Sit down with a partner and ask him or her to "punch holes" in your argument. Your partner may see weaknesses in your solution that you are unable to see or haven't considered.

Gather Evidence

In order to persuade others that you've identified a real problem and that you've found a good solution, you must support your position with **evidence.** Here are some types of evidence you might use:

- facts (including statistics)
- anecdotes and other examples from personal experience
- expert opinions
- analysis of whether the solution is practical (in terms of cost, time, and difficulty)
- comparisons of solutions (mention other solutions that might be—or have been—tried in order to show they are not as good as yours)

Consider Your Purpose and Audience

Remember that your **purpose** is not only to persuade your **audience** that your problem is valid, but also to convince them that *your* solution is the very best one. However, that doesn't mean you should present your solution as the *only* possible solution. In fact, a powerful persuasive technique is to discuss other reasonable solutions, as well as possible objections to the solution you are offering.

Always take time to consider the point of view, or perspective, of your audience. It's easy to persuade readers who are likely to agree with your ideas from the beginning. People who are already recycling don't need to be convinced to recycle plastic. (This is sometimes called "preaching to the choir.") The real challenge in presenting a solution is to change the minds of people who may not agree with you at first. Imagine yourself in the shoes of a reader who is unlike you—who perhaps sees things very differently than you do. What parts of your solution might seem weak to that person? Openly acknowledge the pros and cons of each solution. Anticipate your audience's objections, and plan a response to each objection. This approach lets your readers know that you've given full consideration to the problem. A flowchart like this one can help you think through the process.

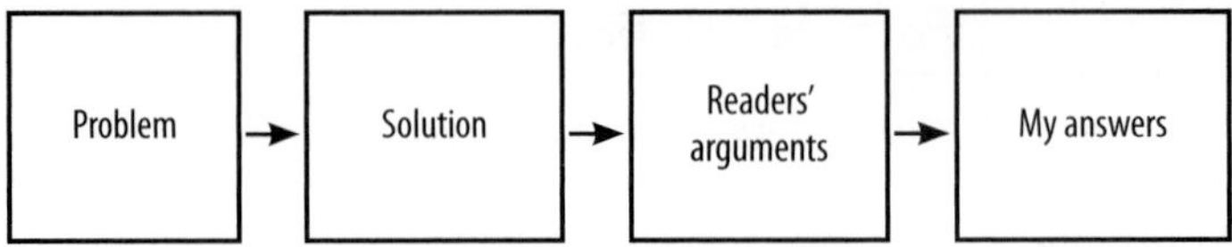

Your Turn

Plan Your Essay Use research and your knowledge of the problem and its solution to plan your essay. Use a flowchart like the one on this page to plan and organize your information.

Drafting

Follow the Writer's Framework

The **Writer's Framework** at right outlines how to plan your draft to create an effective problem-solution essay.

A Writer's Framework

Introduction
- State the problem and why it is important.
- Include evidence that it is a serious problem.

Body
- Present and describe your proposed solution.
- Provide details about the solution.
- Provide evidence that explains the benefits of the solution.
- Answer possible objections to the solution.

Conclusion
- Restate the problem.
- Summarize your proposed solution.
- End with a strong call to action.

Discuss the Pros and Cons

As you write your draft, analyze your proposed solution and evidence as your readers would. Ask yourself questions like these:

- Is my solution adequate and practical?
- Is my evidence persuasive and accurate?
- What are other possible solutions?
- What are the pros and cons of these other possible solutions?
- What are some possible objections to my solution?
- What evidence shows that my solution is best?

Write a Persuasive Conclusion

Persuasive writing, perhaps more than any other kind, requires a concise (not wordy) and clear conclusion. It should restate the problem and your solution, repeating why your solution is best. If you want your readers to do something to help solve the problem, include a call to action—a request urging them to take a specific action. If you end with a call to action, make it reasonable and specific. Tell your readers what you want them to do, and remind them why they should do it.

Grammar Link Using Numbers Correctly

You may need to use numbers to state your problem or its solution or to write a persuasive conclusion. Use the following guidelines and examples if you do.

Use numerals for indicating numbers over ten.	Use a hyphen with compound numbers from twenty-one to ninety-nine	Spell out the numbers *ten* and below.
"There are 6,000 landfills. . . ." "...reduce 70 percent of our garbage..."	"...over seventy-five wells had to be closed . . . ."	"...within the next five to ten years..."

Writing Tip

Try one of the following techniques to draft a strong introduction:

- Tell an anecdote that puts the problem on a personal level.
- Present a startling fact or statistic about the problem.
- Include a quotation by an authority on the topic.

Writing Tip

A call to action is a specific suggestion about something your readers can do about the problem and solution. It is a powerful way for you to end your essay.

Your Turn

Write Your Draft Following your plan, write a draft of your essay. Be sure to think about the following:

- What other possible solutions will you discuss?
- What possible objections will you answer?
- What, if any, call to action will you present?

Peer Review

Get together with a classmate to review your draft. Ask your classmate to answer the questions in the chart at the right as he or she reviews your essay. Be sure to write down your partner's suggestions so you can use them when you revise your draft.

Evaluating and Revising

Your draft is merely the starting point of the writing process. Now it's time to evaluate your essay to look for any weak areas and to improve your essay by revising those weak areas.

Problem-Solution Essay: Guidelines for Content and Organization

Evaluation Question	Tip	Revision Technique
1. Does your introduction get the reader's attention and clearly state the problem in a thesis statement?	**Underline** the attention-getting opening. **Highlight** the thesis, or statement of the problem.	**Add** a strong statement, statistic, or example of the problem. **Clarify** your statement of the problem.
2. Do you provide details that describe the problem?	**Put stars** next to details that describe the problem.	**Add** evidence that reveals the seriousness of the problem.
3. Does your essay propose a solution to the problem? Does it examine the pros and cons of the solution?	**Circle** statements that suggest a solution. **Bracket** the pros and cons discussed.	**Write** a clear statement of the solution, if needed. **Add** pros and cons of the solution.
4. Have you provided strong reasons and convincing evidence to support your proposed solution?	**Put a check mark** next to each reason or piece of evidence.	**Add** facts, statistics, anecdotes, examples, or expert opinions, as needed.
5. Does the conclusion include a convincing argument, a summary, or a call to action?	**Draw a box** around the argument, summary, or call to action.	**Add** a call to action, or **revise** your conclusion to make it more persuasive.

Read this student's draft and the comments about it as a model for revising your own problem-solution essay.

Student Draft

Household Hazardous Wastes

by Michelle Burrows, Paradise Canyon Elementary

In daily life, for work or pleasure, people use products that later become hazardous wastes. Household items such as beauty products, car-care products, cleaning supplies, and gardening products are a few examples. When no longer usable or wanted, these products are thrown in the trash and become hazardous wastes. If they are disposed of improperly, they pose a threat to the health of our environment and the organisms living in it.

Improperly stored and disposed of household products can cause serious problems. Accidental poisonings can occur. It may ignite or explode in the truck, threatening the environment and workers. If they make it to the landfill, waste liquids can go into our surface water or groundwater—our drinking water. Down the drain, these wastes can kill the organisms that make the system work.

← Michelle clearly states the **problem** in the first sentence.

← Michelle provides further **details** of the problem.

← Consequences of ignoring the problem are presented through cause-effect reasoning.

MINI-LESSON How to Use Cause and Effect to Persuade

In her second paragraph, Michelle explained the effects of hazardous wastes. After working with a partner, she realized the some of the cause-effect relationships are unclear. She revised to make the causes clearer and to specify how and why the hazards exist. The revisions make her essay more persuasive.

Michelle's Revision of Paragraph Two

Improperly stored and disposed of household products can cause serious problems. *If hazardous wastes such as bleach and cleaning supplies are left within children's reach,* accidental poisonings can occur. *When you place combustible items such as paint and paint thinner in the trash, the garbage* may ignite or explode in the truck, threatening the environment and workers. If they make it to the landfill, waste liquids can go into our surface water or groundwater—*poisoning* our drinking water. Down the drain, these wastes can kill the organisms that make the system work.

?design/there is no word "it" to delete
it reads "garbage may ignite or explode".

Your Turn

Use Cause and Effect

Read your draft and then ask yourself the following:

- Have I defined the problem and explained why it is serious?
- Have I made sure to explain any cause-effect relationships so my essay is both clear and persuasive?

Student Draft *continues*

Michelle's **solution** includes several specific suggestions.

This problem may seem hopeless, but it is not. Remember this handy mnemonic device the three R's, which stands for Reduce, Reuse, and Recycle. Some household products have labels containing words such as *caustic, corrosive, danger, explosive, flammable, poison, toxic, volatile,* or *warning.* Avoid purchasing these products. You can find books with recipes for safer alternatives in a library or purchase the books in stores. If you need to use a certain product, buy only the amount you need and use the directed amount. Some common products can be reused. Contact your local solid waste officials for recycling locations in your area! When the three R's cannot be used, there is another option: Relocation. Keep the product in its original container, label it clearly, and take it to a hazardous waste collection site.

A less-desirable, but realistic, solution is presented as an alternative.

Household hazardous waste management is a problem, but not one without solutions. Use the three R's or Relocation to protect our health and our environment.

The final paragraph provides a brief **summary** of the problem and proposed solution.

MINI-LESSON How to Write a Call to Action

Michelle proposes realistic solutions to the problem. She concludes with a broad suggestion of action, but she decides to write a more direct call to action by asking her readers to do something specific. The revision gives her conclusion the persuasive power it needs.

Michelle's Draft of the Final Paragraph

Household hazardous waste management is a problem, but not one without solutions. Use the three R's or Relocation to protect our health and our environment.

Michelle's Revision of the Final Paragraph

Household hazardous waste management is a problem, but not one
If every person takes one small action, we will add far less hazardous waste to the environment. Choose just one thing to do. For example, make your own natural cleaner, buy smaller amounts of gardening products, or recycle one reusable item in your garage. Taking action now will help
without solutions. ~~Use the three R's or Relocation~~
for the future
to protect our health and our environment.

Your Turn

Write a Call to Action As you revise your draft, consider the following questions about your conclusion:

- What action have you asked your readers to take?
- Is the action likely to be effective?
- Can you be more specific about what you want your readers to do?

Proofreading and Publishing

Proofreading

You have evaluated and revised your problem-solution essay to improve its content and organization. Now it's time to put the final touches on your essay and prepare it for publication. You do this by reading it with the critical eyes of a proofreader. Edit your essay for misspellings, punctuation errors, grammar errors, and problems in sentence structure.

Grammar Link **Punctuating Appositives**

An **appositive** is a noun or pronoun that identifies or describes more specifically another noun or pronoun beside it. An appositive phrase is an appositive with modifiers. Use commas to separate an appositive from the rest of the sentence.

As she was proofreading, Michelle found an appositive that needed to be set off by a comma.

> Remember this handy mnemonic device, the three R's, which stands for Reduce, Reuse, and Recycle.

Publishing

Now it is time to publish your problem-solution essay to a wider audience. Here are some ways to share your essay:

- Present your essay to your school newspaper as an editorial.
- Publish your essay in your community's newsletter or newspaper.
- Post your essay on a community Internet site to see how readers respond to your ideas.
- Read your essay on a local or school television broadcast that addresses problems in your school or community.

Reflect on the Process In your **RWN,** write a short response to each of the following questions.

1. What was your most persuasive piece of evidence? Where did you find this information?
2. What did you learn about your audience and their possible objections to your solution?
3. What was the most difficult part of writing a problem-solution essay? Why do you think it was difficult?
4. What did you learn by writing persuasively that will be useful in other types of writing?

Proofreading Tip

Get help from at least two of your classmates during the proofreading process. Ask each person to focus on only one area, such as spelling, punctuation, or sentence structure.

Your Turn

Proofread and Publish As you proofread your essay, look closely for appositives that lack punctuation. Corrrect them and any other errors in punctuation, usage, or spelling before you publish your essay.

Scoring Rubric for FCAT Writing+

Use the six-point rubric below to evaluate your response to the prompt on the next page.

6-Point Scale

Score 6 ***is focused, purposeful, and reflects insight into the writing situation***
- conveys a sense of completeness and wholeness with adherence to the main idea
- uses an effective organizational pattern with a logical progression of ideas
- provides substantial, specific, relevant, concrete, or illustrative support
- demonstrates a commitment to and an involvement with the subject
- presents ideas with clarity
- may use creative writing strategies appropriate to the purpose of the paper
- demonstrates mature command of language with freshness of expression
- shows variation in sentence structure
- employs complete sentences except when fragments are used purposefully
- contains few, if any, convention errors in mechanics, usage, and punctuation

Score 5 ***is focused on the topic***
- conveys a sense of completeness and wholeness
- uses an organization pattern with a progression of ideas, although some lapses may occur
- provides ample support
- demonstrates a mature command of language with precise word choice
- shows variation in sentence structure
- with rare exceptions, employs complete sentences except when fragments are used purposefully
- generally follows the conventions of mechanics, usage, and spelling

Score 4 ***is generally focused on the topic but may include extraneous or loosely related material***
- exhibits some sense of completeness and wholeness
- uses an apparent organization pattern, although some lapses may occur
- provides adequate support, although development may be uneven
- demonstrates adequate word choice
- shows little variation in sentence structure
- employs complete sentences most of the time
- generally follows the conventions of mechanics, usage, and spelling

Score 3 ***is generally focused on the topic but may include extraneous or loosely related material***
- attempts to use an organization pattern but may lack a sense of completeness or wholeness
- provides some support but development is erratic
- demonstrates adequate word choice but word choice may be limited, predictable, or occasionally vague
- shows little, if any, variation in sentence structure
- usually demonstrates knowledge of the conventions of mechanics and usage
- usually employs correct spelling of commonly used words

Score 2 ***is related to the topic but includes extraneous or loosely related material***
- demonstrates little evidence of an organizational pattern and may lack a sense of completeness or wholeness
- provides inadequate or illogical development of support
- demonstrates limited, inappropriate, or vague word choice
- shows little, if any, variation in sentence structure and may contain gross errors in sentence structure
- contains errors in basic conventions of mechanics and usage
- contains misspellings of commonly used words

Score 1 ***may minimally address the topic and is a fragmentary or incoherent listing of related ideas or sentences or both***
- demonstrates little, if any, evidence of an organizational pattern
- provides little, if any, development of support
- demonstrates limited or inappropriate word choice, which may obscure meaning
- may contain gross errors in sentence structure and usage, which may impede communication
- contains frequent and blatant errors in basic conventions of mechanics and usage
- contains misspellings of commonly used words

Persuasive Essay

Sunshine State Standards: Benchmarks LA.6.3.1.2; LA.6.3.2.1; LA.6.3.2.2; LA.6.3.3.1; LA.6.3.3.2; LA.6.3.3.4; LA.6.3.4.1; LA.6.3.4.2; LA.6.3.4.3; LA.6.3.4.4; LA.6.3.4.5; LA.6.4.2.3; LA.6.4.3.1; LA.6.4.3.2; LA.6.5.1.1

When responding to an on-demand problem-solution prompt, use the models you have read, what you've learned from writing your own problem-solution essay, the rubric on page 630, and the steps below.

Writing Situation:

School officials have decided that students should not be allowed to eat lunch on the football field because they are leaving too much litter.

Directions for Writing:

Think about a solution that would both eliminate the litter problem and still allow students to eat lunch on the football field.

Now write a persuasive essay in which you propose a solution. Write your essay in the form of a letter to your principal, and provide evidence to persuade him or her to agree with you.

Study the Prompt

Begin by reading the prompt carefully. Notice that the **writing situation** identifies the problem. Now, notice that the **directions for writing** identify the form your essay should take and the audience. The form is a letter, and your audience is your principal. You are required to propose a solution to the litter problem at your school. **Tip:** Spend about five minutes studying the prompt.

Plan Your Response

Reasons After you think about all sides of the problem, write down the solution. Then, write down several reasons why your audience should agree with your solution. **Ask**, "Why will this solution be effective?" Consider any objections your audience might have to your solution, and think about how you'll answer those objections.

Evidence Next, answer the question *How?* Your answer will lead to supporting evidence for each reason. Think about **facts, anecdotes, analyses,** or **comparisons** that will persuade your audience that your solution is the best one.

Organization Once you have decided on a solution, reasons, and supporting evidence, plan the order in your essay. **Tip:** Spend about ten minutes planning your response.

Respond to the Prompt

Using your notes, draft your essay. In the introduction, state the **problem** and tell why it is important. In the body, describe and give details about your solution, provide reasons or **evidence** that explains why your solution is best, and address possible **objections** to your solution. In the conclusion, wrap up your essay with a **summary** of the problem and solution or **call to action.** As you are writing, remember to use persuasive language. **Tip:** Spend about twenty minutes writing your draft.

Improve Your Response

Revising Go back over the key aspects of the essay.

- Did you state your solution clearly?
- Did you provide reasons for all your points?

Proofreading Take a few minutes to proofread your essay to correct errors in grammar, spelling, punctuation, and capitalization. Make sure all your edits are neat and your handwriting is fluent and legible.

Checking Your Final Copy Before you turn in your essay, read it again to catch errors you may have missed. **Tip:** Save ten minutes to improve your paper.

Delivering a Persuasive Speech

Speak with a Purpose

Adapt your problem-solution essay into a persuasive presentation. Practice your presentation, and then present it to your class.

Think as a Reader/Writer You've already written a persuasive problem-solution essay. Now you will try your hand at delivering it as an oral presentation. Adapting your essay into an oral presentation will still require you to think as a writer. However, in your oral presentation, you may need to pay more attention to your audience (the listeners) than you did in your essay.

Adapt Your Essay

Giving a persuasive presentation may seem as simple as reading aloud the problem-solution essay you wrote in the Writing Workshop, but there is much more to it. You need to begin by adapting your essay.

Make It Engaging

Your presentation will address the same problem and propose the same solution as those in your essay. However, you have only one chance to persuade your audience when giving an oral presentation. Listeners cannot go back and re-read your words. Therefore, it is especially important to engage your audience and make them care about the issue as much as you do. Answer the following questions to make sure your presentation will engage your audience. If you answer "no" to any of these questions, make adjustments in the text you will use for your presentation.

- Do you begin by grabbing your listeners' attention?
- Do you address possible objections your audience may have to your solution?
- Does each piece of evidence that you use to support your solution appeal to your listeners' interests and backgrounds?
- Do you use rhetorical devices to emphasize major points and deliver a memorable message? Specifically, do you repeat words or phrases to stress their importance and help your audience remember main ideas?

Check for Clear Transitions

To help listeners follow your presentation, you might need to add words that clarify the connections between ideas. Help your listeners by adding **transitions** such as *however, therefore, for this reason,* and *finally.*

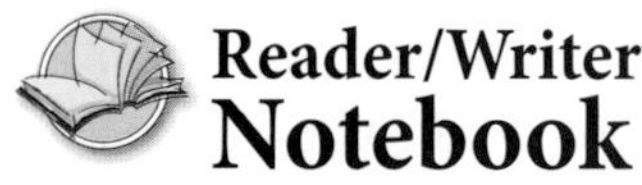

Use your **RWN** to complete the activities for this workshop.

Sunshine State Standards: Benchmarks LA.6.5.2.1 listen and gain information for a variety of purposes (e.g., clarifying, elaborating, summarizing main ideas and supporting details); LA.6.5.2.2 deliver narrative and informative presentations, including oral responses to literature, and adjust oral language, body language, eye contact, gestures, technology and supporting graphics appropriate to the situation.

Deliver Your Persuasive Speech

Even the most persuasive ideas can fall flat if they aren't delivered well. For example, if you get rattled by distractions, mumble, or speak in a dull monotone, your listeners are probably not going to have much confidence in you. Practice your speech to make sure you don't fall into any of these bad speaking habits. As you practice, concentrate on using **verbal elements** (what your voice does as you speak) and **nonverbal elements** (what your face and body do as you speak).

Use Verbal Elements

When you give a persuasive speech, it is important to speak at a slow **rate** so your audience can keep up with what you are saying. You should also speak at a loud enough **volume** so the people in the back of the room can hear you. Varying your **vocal modulation,** or **pitch**—the rise and fall of your speaking voice—can help keep your audience interested. Adjusting the **tone,** or attitude, of your voice to match your message helps the audience understand your feelings about the issue. When giving a persuasive speech, use an enthusiastic and believable tone to help convince your audience to agree with your position.

Use Nonverbal Elements

Your **posture, eye contact** with the audience, **gestures,** and **facial expressions** are examples of nonverbal elements. Standing tall while looking directly at your audience shows that you are confident, and using appropriate gestures and facial expressions can help **emphasize** important ideas. For example, you might raise your eyebrows to show your disapproval of a possible objection to your position.

Deal with Distractions

Try not to let noises or unexpected events distract you. For example, if your presentation is interrupted by continuous or recurring background noise, ignore it and speak louder. If you are interrupted by a more noticeable but temporary noise, pause until the noise stops and then continue. Similarly, if you realize you accidentally skipped a minor point in your speech, go on as if nothing happened. If you skip an important point, explain the point to your listeners and then resume your presentation.

A Good Persuasive Speech

- clearly presents the speaker's position on an important issue
- employs a positive tone
- includes believable, relevant evidence that supports the speaker's position
- uses logical transitions that help listeners follow from one idea to the next
- makes effective use of verbal and nonverbal techniques

Learn It Online

A media display can help persuade your listeners. Check out MediaScope on:

go.hrw.com L6-633 

Standards Review Informational Text

Persuasion **Directions:** Read the article. Then, answer the questions that follow.

Too Much TV Can Equal Too Much Weight

from **Children's Express** by **Jamie Rodgers, 12 years old**

In 1970, only 10 percent of kids in America were overweight. In the 1980s, it was 30 percent, and in the 1990s, it was 60 percent. Studies show that obesity is linked to watching TV and using the Internet.

Children's Express interviewed two professors from Johns Hopkins University School of Medicine about the link. Ross Andersen, M.D., is with the weight management center, and Carlos Crespo, M.D., is an assistant professor of health and fitness.

"Dr. Crespo and I have published a study that appeared in the *Journal of the American Medical Association.* We looked at how fat kids were in relation to the number of hours of television they watch per day," said Andersen. "We found that kids who are low TV watchers were much leaner. The kids who were the fattest were those who watched a lot of TV. We defined a lot as four or more hours per day. Roughly, one in three kids in America is watching four or more hours per day. I would estimate sitting in front of a computer would be just as great a risk factor for being overweight."

Andersen and Crespo say the blame is not just on the parents. Sometimes it's a lack of places to play.

"[It's a] lack of facilities, services for the children to be able to go out and play basketball or go to a swimming pool. The community should have open spaces and safe spaces for girls and boys to be active," said Crespo.

"The thing is not that it's bad to watch TV; it's just that you need to have a balance. There [is] a certain number of hours in the day you're supposed to sleep, do your homework, . . . [and] go to school, and then there is a certain [number] of hours that you're free to do whatever you want. If you spend that time watching TV, then you spend less time doing physical activity." . . .

"Kids and parents need to look for opportunities to remain physically active. So instead of sitting down to watch *Who Wants to Be a Millionaire,* it may be that the whole family could get up and go for a walk." . . .

Sunshine State Standards: Benchmarks LA.6.1.7.2 analyze the author's purpose (e.g., to persuade, inform, entertain, or explain) and perspective in a variety of texts and understand how they affect meaning; **LA.6.1.7.5** analyze a variety of text structures (e.g., comparison/contrast, cause/effect, chronological order, argument/support, lists) and text features (main headings with subheadings) and explain their impact on meaning in text.

1. What evidence supports the conclusion that obesity is linked to watching TV?
   - **A** a study published in the *Journal of the American Medical Association*
   - **B** the opinion that communities should have swimming pools
   - **C** the fact that 30 percent of kids in America were overweight in the 1980s
   - **D** the fact that lean kids watch as much TV as overweight kids

2. Which statement is NOT true?
   - **F** The author uses quotations to support her conclusions.
   - **G** The author uses appropriate evidence to support her conclusions.
   - **H** The author uses expert opinions to support her conclusions.
   - **I** The author does not provide adequate support for her conclusions.

3. Which statement is a FACT?
   - **A** Kids and parents need to exercise together.
   - **B** Lack of places to play is the main reason kids watch too much TV.
   - **C** About one third of kids in America watch TV more than four hours per day.
   - **D** Kids waste their time by spending free time watching TV.

4. When the author states that in 1970, only 10 percent of kids were overweight, but by the 1990s, 60 percent of kids were overweight, what type of evidence is she using?
   - **F** quotations
   - **G** statistics
   - **H** case study
   - **I** inappropriate evidence

5. On what does Anderson and Crespo place part of the blame for obesity in children?
   - **A** lack of playgrounds
   - **B** poor health education
   - **C** lack of medical attention
   - **D** fast foods

6. Which statement BEST expresses the author's conclusion?
   - **F** Watching TV today is more common than ever.
   - **G** Obesity is linked to watching TV and using the Internet.
   - **H** Families need to watch TV and surf the Internet together.
   - **I** Doctors say that parents are the real cause of childhood obesity.

Extended Response

7. What conclusion does the author draw about children and obesity? Based on the evidence provided in this article, what assertion can you make? Support your response with examples from the text.

READ THINK EXPLAIN

Standards Review Vocabulary

Sunshine State Standards: Benchmarks **LA.6.1.6.3** use context clues to determine meanings of unfamiliar words; **LA.6.1.6.9** determine the correct meaning of words with multiple meanings in context.

Context Clues

Directions: Read each item. Then, choose the answer in which the italicized word is used in the same way as in the first sentence.

Practicing For FCAT

1. Read the sentence from the selection "Oprah Talks About Her South African 'Dreamgirls.'"

"I did love that the minister of education for this entire country stood up and said, I'm going to address the criticism."

Which sentence uses the word *criticism* in the same way?

A The criticism of a movie review can be both positive and negative.

B Despite the loud criticism of many citizens, the mayor approved the plan.

C My big brother decided to take a course in literary criticism at the university.

D My coach gave me constructive criticism about improving my grades.

2. Read the sentence from the selection "Start the Day Right!"

Most of them seem engaged, listening to a teacher at the front of the room, out of frame.

Which sentence uses the word *engaged* in the same way?

F My sister is engaged to be married next September.

G The media company engaged him to create public service announcements.

H The two countries were engaged in a long, but intermittent, war.

I The debaters were engaged in a heated discussion about climate change.

3. Read the sentence from the selection "Brain Breeze."

It increases your concentration and keeps you at the top of your mental game.

Which sentence uses the word *concentration* in the same way?

A The substance was a concentration of citrus juices.

B The concentration of delegates from Iowa reflected the high level of interest in the subject in that state.

C The artist's level of concentration was so great that he painted for ten hours.

D The concentration of bald eagles in the nesting area assured scientists of the birds' recovery.

Academic Vocabulary

Directions: Use context clues to determine the meaning of the italicized Academic Vocabulary word below.

4. Read the excerpt from the selection "Shine-n-Grow: Hair Repair That Really Works!"

Shine-N-Grow shampoo contains a unique combination of vitamins, minerals, and hair-growth ingredients

What is the meaning of the word *unique* in this sentence?

F one of a kind

G common

H important

I very difficult

Standards Review Writing

Sunshine State Standards: Benchmarks LA.6.2.2.2 use information from the text to answer questions related to the main idea or relevant details, maintaining chronological or logical order.

Persuasive Text

Directions: Read the following paragraph from a student's persuasive letter. Then, answer each question that follows.

[1] The Helping Hands Community Assistance Program needs our school's help. [2] The supplies of clothing, shoes, and blankets are very low and will not be enough to help everyone who seeks assistance. [3] Only four coats, six blankets, and one pair of shoes are available. [4] Also, winter is coming soon. [5] The cooler winter temperatures always bring a higher demand for warm clothing. [6] Last winter some families left without supplies because the supplies were gone.

1. This paragraph presents the problem. The next paragraph will present a proposed solution. Which sentence would you expect to see in that paragraph?
   - **A** Everyone should call the governor of our state and tell her about the problem.
   - **B** The Helping Hands Community Assistance Program needs help now!
   - **C** Our school should organize a clothing and blanket drive to help the program gather supplies.
   - **D** The people of our community should do something to help.

2. Which would BEST address the concern that helping the program may cost money?
   - **F** Suggest that they donate used clothing instead of buying new ones.
   - **G** Tell them to borrow money from someone to purchase clothing and blankets.
   - **H** Provide them with a list of stores that have nice blankets, boots, and coats.
   - **I** Ignore this concern since not all readers may share it.

3. Which sentence BEST summarizes the writer's opinion about this issue?
   - **A** Last year, some people were not able to get supplies.
   - **B** The school is in a good position to help collect supplies for the Helping Hands Program.
   - **C** During cold weather, many people need coats, shoes, and blankets.
   - **D** The program has four coats, six blankets, and one pair of shoes.

Read On

For Independent Reading

Nonfiction

Media Madness: An Insider's Guide to Media

This humorously illustrated book, written by Dominic Ali, offers you a lesson in how to read media. In *Media Madness,* Ali shares many secrets and influences of television, music, magazines, video games, and the Internet. Ali urges readers to approach media with a critical eye by asking questions like "What is the message, and who is the sender?" "How does it grab your attention?" and "What does it *not* tell you?"

My Life with the Chimpanzees

As a young girl, Jane Goodall spent hours in patient observation of animals all around her. She dreamed of spending her life working with them. At the age of twenty-six, she got her wish: She went to the forests of Tanzania to observe chimpanzees in the wild. She came to know a group of wild chimpanzees—intelligent animals whose lives, in work and play and family relationships, bear a surprising resemblance to our own. Her adventures gained her worldwide recognition, and now she tells her exciting story in her own words.

Oprah Winfrey

Learn details about Oprah Winfrey's childhood, education, and career in this biography by Heather Hudak. The biography also includes self-improvement tools for readers, such as tips on public speaking and suggestions for starting a book club similar to Oprah's. Read *Oprah Winfrey* for an introduction to one of the most influential people in the United States.

At the Controls: Questioning Video and Computer Games

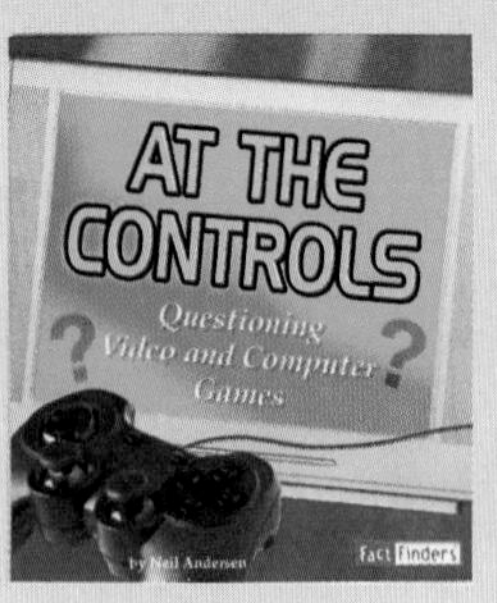

Play smart! Analyze the messages directed at you by the games you're playing. Neil Andersen gives you the information you need to take a critical look at video and computer games. After reading *At the Controls: Questioning Video and Computer Games,* you'll be able to recognize and challenge the content contained in popular games and better understand their effects on you.

Sunshine State Standards: Benchmarks **LA.6.2.2.5** use interest and recommendation of others to select a variety of age and ability appropriate nonfiction materials (e.g., biographies and topical areas, such as science, music, art, history, sports, current events) to expand the core knowledge necessary to connect topics and function as a fully literate member of a shared culture.

Nonfiction

Explorers Wanted! On Safari

Would you like to take an exciting and educational excursion to Africa? Author Simon Chapman tells you how to prepare for the trip and what you'll find once you arrive. You'll track elephants, escape hungry insects, and even speak some Swahili. In *Explorers Wanted! On Safari,* you'll take a fact-filled adventure and learn all about the people and animals of the African savanna.

Advertising

In this book, Bess Milton investigates the effects of advertising on America's past, present, and future. She discusses how advertisements convey the American dream and how they've united us behind patriotic causes. *Advertising* also explores the psychology behind many marketing tactics.

Internet: Electronic Global Village

In this brightly illustrated book by David Jefferis, you'll be introduced to the Internet's history, its workings, and the changes it has brought about in society. *Internet: Electronic Global Village* reveals the many tasks forever altered by the Internet revolution, for example, communicating, researching, shopping, and publishing.

Television and Movies

Television shows and movies shape our lives perhaps more than any other art form does. In *Television and Movies,* Philip Abraham examines the invention of these entertaining technologies and probes how they have affected American pop culture. You'll be a more knowledgeable watcher after reading this informative book.

Learn It Online

Learn to analyze novels. Get tips to help in your study at *NovelWise:*

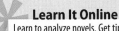

go.hrw.com L6-639 

UNIT 3

Poetry

Writers on Writing

Janet Wong on Poetry Janet Wong was born and raised in California. She has published six collections of poetry and many picture books. Many of her award-winning poems reflect her childhood experiences as an Asian American. Her poems have been read on the radio and presented on television.

"Sometime around fourth grade, I decided I hated poetry. I did not enjoy copying poems in cursive. I was terrible at memorizing poems. And I couldn't stand analyzing poems, picking them apart, trying to find the "hidden meaning."

How did I change from a poetry hater to a poet who preaches about the power of poetry? After a brief career as a lawyer, I decided to become a children's book writer. I went to a one-day seminar where I heard Myra Cohn Livingston read her poem "There Was a Place." Myra's poem, about the loss of a father, made me remember how my grandmother looked when she was in the hospital dying, hooked up to so many machines. I started blinking back tears. *How could such a short poem—thirty seconds long—make me feel so much inside?* The poem had touched a memory I hadn't thought about for years. Poems will do that to you. They'll grab hold of loose memories like a cowboy roping cattle, and the next thing you know, you're all tied up.

I figured that learning about the poetic techniques of rhyme, repetition, and rhythm would help me become a better writer. I started Myra's class in beginning poetry. Myra pushed me to read tons of poems. If I read a hundred poems, I found myself disliking about ten or twenty, feeling neutral about the bulk of them—but really loving at least ten or fifteen poems. I realized that I didn't hate poetry, I just hadn't found the right poems for me.

You'll read a lot of poems in this book. You might hate some of them. But I hope that you find some poems that you love too, poems that rope some forgotten memory or just make you laugh.

Pay attention to the poems you like. If you find yourself liking poems with no punctuation and no capital letters, experiment with that; you might become as famous as E. E. Cummings. Play with made-up words, and you might become the new Lewis Carroll. Which poems stick with you, days after you've read them? Serious poems about history? Poems about injustice? Then write some of those.

Even if you have no intention of becoming a poet, poetry might still become part of your future. If you are good at imagery, you might draft a video game proposal that turns you into a millionaire. If you are good at rhyme and repetition, you might make your mark in advertising, inventing snappy jingles. If your sentences have a rhythm that flows like music, this might help you win grants for your science research.

And maybe you'll become a poet whose work will appear in a book like this. Why not? Why not poetry—and you! ”

Think as a Writer

Janet Wong believes that poems have a power to connect with our feelings and memories. Do you agree or disagree with her? Explain. As you read the poems in this collection, consider Wong's ideas about the power of poetry.

COLLECTION 7

Elements of Poetry

"The best and most beautiful things in the world cannot be seen or even touched—they must be felt with the heart."

—**Helen Keller**

What Do You Think?

How can poetry help us appreciate "the best and most beautiful things in the world"?

Literary Focus

by **Linda Rief**

What Are the Sounds of Poetry?

What is it that makes remembering the hundreds of lyrics to your favorite songs so easy? It's the rhythm, the beat, the way the words flow. It's powerful words arranged in the best order. It's the strongest line—repeated again and again for emphasis. It's the feeling you get as you slip under the spell of poetry!

Rhythm

Rhythm is a musical quality produced by repeated sound patterns. All language has rhythm, but it's especially important in poetry.

Meter The most obvious kind of rhythm is the regular pattern of stressed and unstressed syllables in the words poets put together. This regular pattern, or beat, is called **meter.** When poets decide on a regular beat, they make all the lines about the same length. Lines with an equal number of stressed syllables produce the same beat.

Scanning To find a poem's meter, read the poem aloud. Mark each stressed syllable you hear with the symbol ⁄ and each unstressed syllable with the symbol ◡. Marking this pattern is called **scanning.** Read these marked lines aloud, and listen for the beat:

◡ ◡ ⁄ ◡◡ ⁄ ◡
Now, the Star-Belly Sneetches
◡ ⁄ ◡ ◡ ⁄
Had bellies with stars.
◡ ⁄ ◡◡ ⁄ ◡
The Plain-Belly Sneetches
◡ ⁄ ◡◡ ⁄
Had none upon thars.

from "The Sneetches" by Dr. Seuss

Rhyme

Words **rhyme** when they end with the same vowel or vowel/consonant sound, as in the words *clown* and *noun* (both have an *ow* sound followed by an *n* sound). In poetry, rhymes can be simple *(moth* with *cloth)* or more complicated *(antelope* with *cantaloupe)*. Rhyme adds a musical quality to poetry, making it easier to memorize lines, **stanzas** (groups of lines that express a complete idea), or an entire poem.

End Rhyme Most rhymes are **end rhymes:** The last word in one line is paired with the last word in the next line. In the excerpt from "The Sneetches" on the left, *stars* and *thars* are end rhymes.

Internal Rhyme Sometimes the last word in one line will be echoed by a word placed at the beginning or in the middle of the following line. This is called an **internal rhyme.** Listen for internal rhymes in these lines:

The rumbling, tumbling stones,
And "Bones, bones, bones!"

from "The Sea" by James Reeves

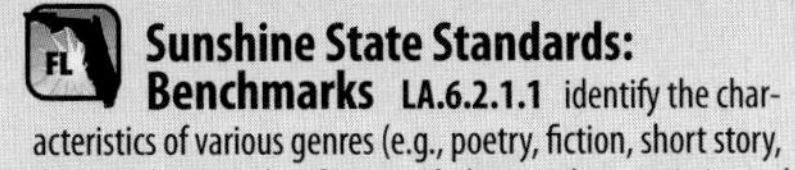

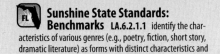

Sunshine State Standards: Benchmarks **LA.6.2.1.1** identify the characteristics of various genres (e.g., poetry, fiction, short story, dramatic literature) as forms with distinct characteristics and purposes; **LA.6.2.1.3** locate and analyze the effects of sound, meter, figurative and descriptive language, graphics (illustrations), and structure (e.g., line length, fonts, word placement) to communicate mood and meaning.

Rhyme Scheme The pattern of rhyming sounds at the ends of lines in a poem is the **rhyme scheme.** In addition to marking the meter in a poem, you can also mark the rhyme scheme. To mark rhyme scheme, identify words that rhyme by labeling them with the same letter. This rhyme scheme from "The Sea" is *a-b-b-b-a*. Listen:

Hour upon hour he gnaws a
The rumbling, tumbling stones, b
And "Bones, bones, bones!" b
The giant sea dog moans, b
Licking his greasy paws. a

Free Verse Not all poems rhyme, nor do all poems have a regular meter. A poet may decide not to use a regular meter and rhyme scheme, writing instead in loose groupings of words and phrases. This style is known as **free verse.** Like a conversation, free verse does not have a regular beat, and it usually does not rhyme. Here's the beginning of a poem written in free verse:

Fifty cents apiece
To eat our lunch
We'd run
Straight from school
Instead of home

from "Good Hot Dogs"
by Sandra Cisneros

Other Sound Effects

Repetition and Refrain Poetry relies on **repetition,** the recurrence or repeating of something. Rhymes are created by ending sounds that repeat. Rhythm is created by beats that repeat. A poet may repeat a word, phrase, line, or group of lines to make a **refrain.** A poem's refrain, like a song's chorus, may be the part that sticks in our minds.

Alliteration The repetition of consonant sounds in words that are close together is called **alliteration.** Alliteration often occurs at the beginning of a word, but sometimes it is within or at the end of a word. Hear the repetition of *wh* sounds in these lines. Can you also hear the *s* sounds?

It laughs a lovely whiteness,
And whitely whirs away.

from "Cynthia in the Snow"
by Gwendolyn Brooks

Onomatopoeia The use of a word whose sound suggests its meaning—such as *buzz* or *sniff*—is called **onomatopoeia** (ahn uh mat uh PEE uh). The word *meow* is another example.

With a meow
Like the rusty latch
On a gate.

from "Ode to Mi Gato" by Gary Soto

Your Turn Analyze Sounds of Poetry

1. Why might a poet want to write in free verse instead of using a regular rhyme and meter?
2. Give an example of the following sounds from a poem or song, or make up your own:

Sound	Example
Rhyme	
Alliteration	
Onomatopoeia	

Learn It Online
Try the *PowerNotes* version of this lesson at:
go.hrw.com L6-645 Go

Literary Focus

by **Linda Rief**

How Does Poetry Make You *See*?

Poets make imaginative comparisons that can help you see things in a different way. They create imagery that not only paints pictures in your mind but appeals to your other senses as well. They convey ideas and emotions with the fewest and best words. Poetry comes alive through the power of strong imagery.

Figurative Language

Poets have a special talent for making imaginative comparisons, often describing one thing in terms of something else, usually something very different. These comparisons are called **figures of speech,** or **figurative language.** Three of the most common figures of speech are metaphor, simile, and personification.

Metaphor A **metaphor** directly compares two unlike things. If you said "My baby sister is a real doll," you would be comparing your sister's appearance and personality to the cuteness of a doll. If you said "My brother is a rat," you'd be comparing him to the nastiest little creature you can think of. Poets use unexpected and original comparisons to create metaphors such as this one:

> The sea is a hungry dog,
> Giant and gray.
>
> from "The Sea" by James Reeves

Often, a poet will see how thoroughly he or she can develop a metaphor. A single comparison that is explored in great depth and detail, sometimes through the entire length of a poem, is called an **extended metaphor.**

Simile Let's return to the sister and brother comparisons. If you said "My sister is *like* a doll" or, with a change of heart, exclaimed "My brother's as good *as* gold!" you would be using similes. A **simile** is a comparison between unlike things that uses specific words of comparison, such as *like* or *as*. Here's a poem that begins with a simile:

> He's white
> As spilled milk,
> My cat who sleeps
> With his belly
> Turned toward
> The summer sky.
>
> from "Ode to Mi Gato" by Gary Soto

Imagine milk spilled on a table. The poet compares the color of his cat to that of the spilled milk to help you picture the cat in your mind.

Personification A common type of figurative language is **personification**—speaking of something that is not human as if it had human abilities, emotions, and reactions. When you **personify** something, you give it human qualities or feelings: "The sky wept bitterly all day." Isn't that a much more imaginative description than a statement of fact, such as "Yesterday it rained for hours"?

Sunshine State Standards: Benchmarks **LA.6.2.1.3** locate and analyze the effects of sound, meter, figurative and descriptive language, graphics (illustrations), and structure (e.g., line length, fonts, word placement) to communicate mood and meaning; **LA.6.2.1.7** locate and analyze an author's use of allusions and descriptive, idiomatic, and figurative language in a variety of literary text, identifying how word choice sets the author's tone and advances the work's theme; **LA.6.3.2.3** analyzing language techniques of professional authors (e.g., point of view, establishing mood) to enhance the use of descriptive language and word choices; **LA.6.4.1.2** write a variety of expressive forms (e.g., short play, song lyrics, historical fiction, limericks) that employ figurative language, rhythm, dialogue, characterization, and/or appropriate format.

What human ability is the locomotive in this example given?

And every locomotive comes a-roaring by
Says, "There lies a steel-driving man,
Lord, Lord!
There lies a steel-driving man."
from "John Henry"

As you read and analyze poems, use a chart like this one to help you identify different figures of speech:

Figure of Speech	Definition
Metaphor	Makes a direct comparison by saying one object *is* the other
Simile	Compares, using *like, as,* and other comparison words
Personification	Gives nonhuman things human qualities

Imagery

Poets often use **descriptive language** to create **imagery** that appeals to our senses. Imagery is also referred to as **sensory details,** because the images that are created in our minds often appeal to more than just our sense of sight—they can also appeal to our senses of hearing, touch, taste, and smell. Notice how this image from a poem appeals to sight, smell, taste, and touch, all at the same time:

Yellow mustard and onions
And french fries piled on top all
Rolled up in a piece of wax
Paper for us to hold hot
In our hands
from "Good Hot Dogs,"
by Sandra Cisneros

Structure and Word Choice

Nothing is left to chance in a poem. Everything from rhyme scheme to punctuation is a poet's deliberate decision. Poets can even choose to use different forms of poetry. Some forms, such as **haiku** and **sonnets,** have a set structure and strict rules of form; other forms, such as the **ode,** offer a poet more freedom. In **free verse,** a poet can create his or her own structure to help convey meaning. In all cases, it is **word choice** that gives a poet the biggest range of expression: choosing just the right words is what poetry is all about.

Tone

All of a poet's choices affect not only the meaning of a poem but also its **tone,** the feeling expressed by the **speaker** (the person talking in the poem). Tone is the speaker's *attitude* toward his or her subject: playful or serious, joyous or sad, mournful or humorous. Figurative language, imagery, word choice, and even structure help to create tone.

Your Turn Analyze Images of Poetry

1. Create a metaphor, a simile, and an example of personification to describe what fire is like.
2. Re-read the lines from "Good Hot Dogs" on the left. What kind of tone would you expect this poem to have? Explain why you think so.

Learn It Online
See this lesson a new way with *PowerNotes:*
go.hrw.com
L6-647
Go

Analyzing Visuals

What Do Poetry and Art Share?

Poetry and works of art express the ideas and feelings of their creators in ways that appeal to our senses. Poets and visual artists have a similar purpose—they try to express a personal idea or vision in a way that is focused and "compact," reduced to its essentials. Poets are "word artists" who use words to create sensory images in our minds. Visual artists use color, line, shape, texture, and form to bring images to life for us. Both poets and visual artists express a specific tone, or attitude toward their subject. Most of all, perhaps, both also create unusual and unexpected comparisons that help us to see even everyday things in new ways.

Comparing Visual Art to Poetry

Use these guidelines to connect visual art and poetry.

1. Identify the subject of the work. What aspect of that subject seems to be the main focus? Explain.
2. To which of your senses does the work appeal? How does the poet or artist create these sensory images?
3. What feelings, ideas, or mood does the imagery suggest? Are the images sad or joyful, humorous or tragic, playful or serious? What elements in the work make you say so?
4. Determine whether any of the images make interesting or unusual comparisons. How does the work make you think about something in a new way?
5. Make inferences about the poet's or artist's tone, or attitude toward the subject. What elements in the poem or the artwork most reveal this tone?

Sunshine State Standards: Benchmarks **LA.6.2.1.1** identify the characteristics of various genres (e.g., poetry, fiction, short story, dramatic literature) as forms with distinct characteristics and purposes; **LA.6.2.1.3** locate and analyze the effects of sound, meter, figurative and descriptive language, graphics (illustrations), and structure (e.g., line length, fonts, word placement) to communicate mood and meaning;

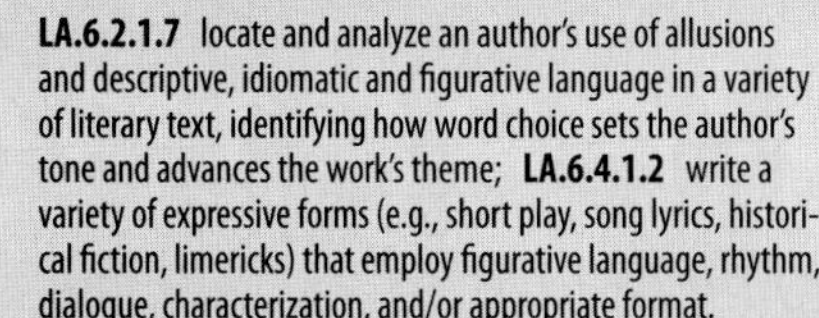

LA.6.2.1.7 locate and analyze an author's use of allusions and descriptive, idiomatic and figurative language in a variety of literary text, identifying how word choice sets the author's tone and advances the work's theme; **LA.6.4.1.2** write a variety of expressive forms (e.g., short play, song lyrics, historical fiction, limericks) that employ figurative language, rhythm, dialogue, characterization, and/or appropriate format.

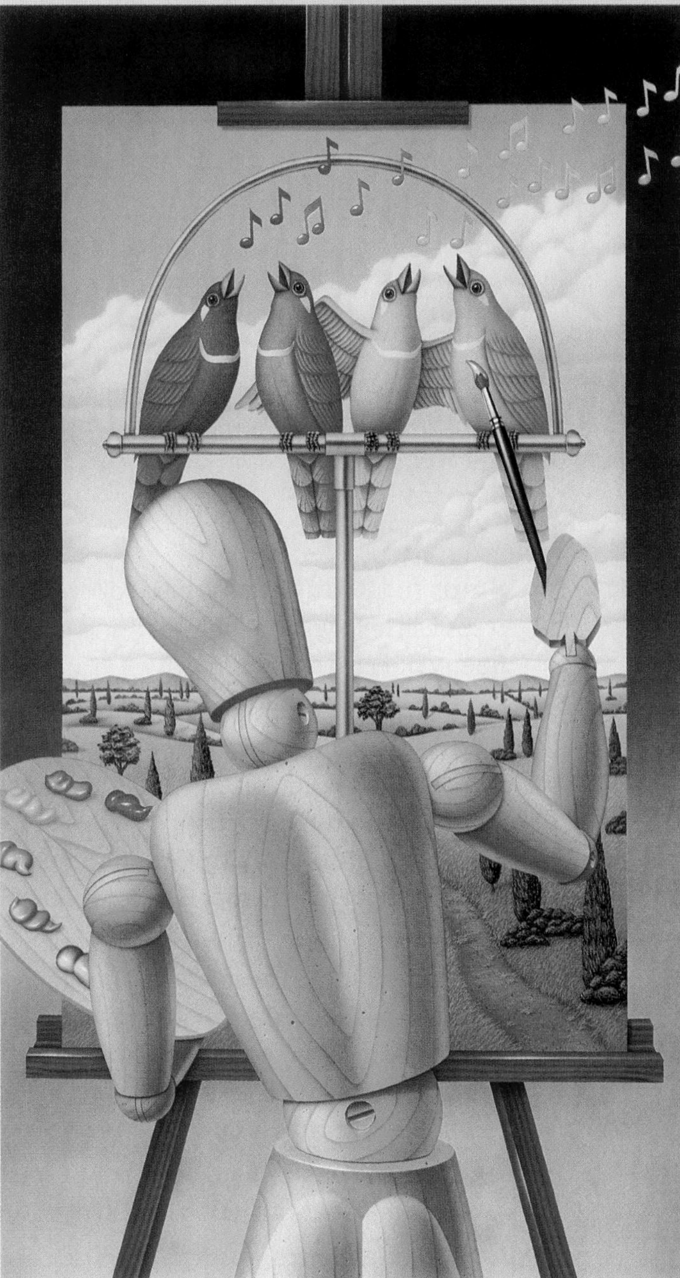

Quartet by Jeff Fitz-Maurice.

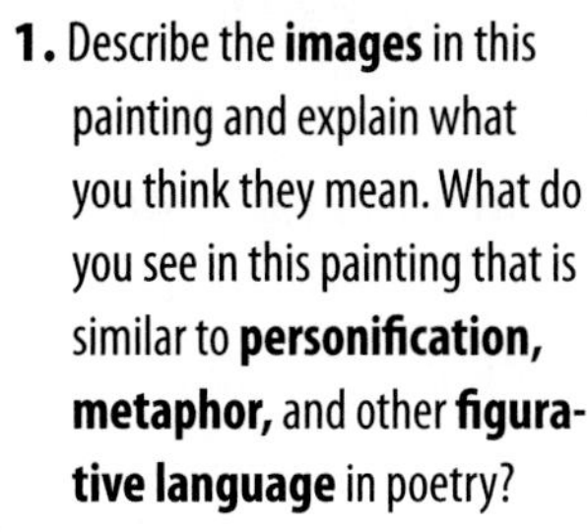

1. Describe the **images** in this painting and explain what you think they mean. What do you see in this painting that is similar to **personification, metaphor,** and other **figurative language** in poetry?

2. In poetry, poets use words to create sound effects. How does the artist, limited to visual cues, suggest sounds in this painting?

3. What **tone,** or attitude toward his subject, does the artist suggest? How does he create that tone?

Your Turn Write a Poem About a Painting

Like most works of art and most poems, this painting can be interpreted in more than one way. Write a poem describing this painting or explaining what you think it means. Your poem should use sound effects, imagery, and figurative language and express a particular tone.

Reading Focus

by **Kylene Beers**

What Helps You Read a Poem?

It's not so hard to read a poem once you know some basic approaches, such as these: *Read from the inside out.* Enjoy the idea the poem offers (the inside) before focusing on things such as imagery (the outside). *Read it aloud* at least twice. *Focus on each word*—because every word counts! Re-read as many times as you need to. Finally, use the questioning strategy to uncover meaning.

Reading a Poem

Reading a poem is not like reading a novel or a note from a friend. You need to go about reading a poem in a different way.

- **Visualize Images** As you read a poem, think about the **images,** or pictures, the poet creates. You know that poets often use **figurative language**—imaginative comparisons—to create images. If a poem you're reading describes snowflakes as if they were insects, let the comparison create a picture in your mind. What does the comparison help you *see*?
- **Identify Personification** Watch for examples of **personification**—human qualities given to something that is not human. ("The leaves danced in the breeze" is an example.)
- **Listen for Onomatopoeia** Once you see the images in a poem, listen for the sounds. Words such as *boom* and *bang* are examples of **onomatopoeia** (ahn uh mat uh PEE uh), words whose sounds imitate their meanings.
- **Listen for Rhyme and Repetition** Listen for other "sound effects" as you read, such as words that **rhyme** or **repetition** of sounds or words. Remember, though, that not all poems use sound effects like rhyme.

Steps for Reading a Poem Following these steps will help you not only read and understand poetry but also enjoy it:

1. Pay attention to the **title.** Think about the images it creates. What images come to mind when you read the titles of these poems in this collection: "Cynthia in the Snow"; "Yes, It Was My Grandmother"; "The Sneetches"; and "Good Hot Dogs"?
2. Read the poem silently. Pay attention to **punctuation.** Pause briefly at commas and semicolons, and pause longer after periods. If you see a dash, expect a sudden shift in thought. If there's no punctuation at the end of a line, don't pause.
3. Read the poem aloud. *Hear* how it sounds. Feel the poem's **rhythm** as you read.
4. Pay attention to **word choice.** Use context clues to figure out the meanings of unfamiliar words. Think about shades of meaning in the words the poet has chosen. Each word was chosen for a reason.
5. Visualize the poem's **images** as you read.
6. Think about the poem's **meaning.** What does it say to you? How does it relate to your experience?

Sunshine State Standards: Benchmarks **LA.6.1.5.1** adjust reading rate based on purpose, text difficulty, form, and style; **LA.6.1.7.8** use strategies to repair comprehension of grade-appropriate text when self-monitoring indicates confusion, including but not limited to rereading, checking context clues, predicting, note-making, summarizing, using graphic and semantic organizers, questioning, and clarifying by checking other sources; **LA.6.2.1.3** locate and analyze the effects of sound, meter, figurative and descriptive language, graphics, (illustrations), and structure (e.g., line length, fonts, word placement) to communicate mood and meaning; **LA.6.3.2.3** analyzing language techniques of professional authors (e.g., point of view, establishing mood) to enhance the use of descriptive language and word choices.

Re-reading a Poem

Often, you won't fully understand a poem's meaning the first time through, and that's nothing to worry about. **Re-reading a poem** is the best way to make sure that you understand what you've read. In fact, you may need to read some poems several times to understand their meaning. For poems that you especially enjoy, you may simply want to re-read and savor them again and again.

Reading Fluency and Reading Rate It's especially helpful to re-read a poem aloud. Re-reading can help you improve your reading fluency and reading rate. **Reading fluency** (how fast and how well you read) and **reading rate** (how fast or slow you read) are related. If you want to improve your fluency, practice re-reading a poem by recording it or by reading it to a friend or family member. Fluent reading has these characteristics:

- You read with expression.
- You know when to pause and when to come to a full stop.
- You correctly read by phrases or thought groups instead of word by word.
- You know when you have made a mistake, so you back up and correct your reading.
- You know how to adjust your rate, reading more quickly during certain passages and more slowly during others, depending on the content of what you are reading.

As you re-read a poem, you can concentrate on different elements each time, such as language one time and sound effects the second or third time. Here's another benefit of re-reading: You may find you're starting to memorize the poem, truly making it your own!

Questioning

Think of the **questioning** strategy as a way of having a conversation with the poet. As you read, ask questions and note your observations about the poem—things you like, things you don't understand, things you agree or disagree with. As you re-read the poem, you can answer your questions, make new observations, and even ask more questions. Use a simple chart like this one (for "The Sneetches") to record your thoughts:

Questions	Observations
What is a Sneetch?	Having stars seems like something that's not very important.
When are the Sneetches going to figure out what McBean is doing?	

Your Turn Apply Reading Skills

1. Summarize tips for reading a poem that you would share with a third-grader.
2. Explain why re-reading is an important strategy for increasing understanding and enjoyment of poetry.
3. How can it be helpful to record observations as well as questions while you read? Explain your ideas.

Now go to the Skills in Action: Reading Model

Learn It Online
Use online graphic organizers as you read:
go.hrw.com
L6-651
Go

POEM

Read with a Purpose Read to discover one poet's unique way of describing the sea.

The Sea

by **James Reeves**

Literary Focus

Figurative Language A **metaphor** is a type of figurative language that makes a direct comparison. The poet extends this dog-sea comparison throughout the poem, creating an extended metaphor in which the stones are seen as the dog's bones.

Reading Focus

Reading a Poem Pay attention to punctuation as you read the poem aloud. Don't stop at the ends of lines that have no punctuation. Here, the poet wants you to keep reading without pause until you reach the comma after *stones*.

The sea is a hungry dog,
Giant and gray.
He rolls on the beach all day.
With his clashing teeth and shaggy jaws
Hour upon hour he gnaws
The rumbling, tumbling stones,
And "Bones, bones, bones!"
The giant sea dog moans,
Licking his greasy paws.

And when the night wind roars
And the moon rocks in the stormy cloud,
He bounds to his feet and snuffs and sniffs,
Shaking his wet sides over the cliffs,
And howls and hollos long and loud.

But on quiet days in May or June,
When even the grasses on the dune
Play no more their reedy tune,
With his head between his paws
He lies on the sandy shores,
So quiet, so quiet, he scarcely snores.

Literary Focus

Rhyme and Sound Effects Notice that the rhyme scheme for this stanza is *a-b-c-c-b*. The poet uses **onomatopoeia** (words that sound like the actions they represent) to create sound effects. *Roars* is one example. Listen for others.

Reading Focus

Re-reading and Questioning When you finish the poem, re-read it. Jot down your observations and questions, such as words or images that you don't completely understand. Finally, re-read the poem a third time—or more—to answer your questions.

Read with a Purpose What characteristics of the sea does Reeves describe? How do these descriptions bring the sea to life?

MEET THE WRITER

James Reeves
(1909–1978)

An Englishman of Letters

James Reeves was born in a suburb of London, but he grew up in the small county of Buckinghamshire, England. As a child, Reeves loved reading, and he started writing poetry when he was only eleven years old.

Reeves attended Cambridge University and then taught for many years before becoming a writer and editor. Reeves wrote poetry and edited books for a series called the Poetry Bookshelf. Even though Reeves is known primarily for his poetry, he also had a particular interest in folk tales and myths. As a result, he wrote various adaptations of traditional tales and classics.

"A Continuing Craving for Poetry"

When he was forty-one years old and already established as a respected author of books for adults, Reeves turned his attention to writing for children. He edited various prose and poetry anthologies for children that proved popular. Critics praised his original poems for children, which had widespread appeal. As Reeves once declared:

> "We must always provide poetry in such a way that it creates and nourishes a continuing craving for poetry and does not kill it by making poetry seem something childish."

The Giant (1923) by N. C. Wyeth (1882–1945). Collection of Westtown School, Westtown, PA. Photography courtesy of Brandywine River Museum.

Think About the Writer Why might Reeves have started writing poetry for children after he had already been writing it for adults?

SKILLS IN ACTION

Wrap Up

Sunshine State Standards: Benchmarks **LA.6.1.6.1** use new vocabulary that is introduced and taught directly; **LA.6.1.7.8** use strategies to repair comprehension of grade-appropriate text when self-monitoring indicates confusion, including but not limited to rereading, checking context clues, predicting, note-making, summarizing, using graphic and semantic organizers, questioning, and clarifying by checking other sources; **LA.6.2.1.3** locate and analyze the effects of sound, meter, figurative and descriptive language, graphics (illustrations), and structure (e.g., line length, fonts, word placement) to communicate mood and meaning; *Also covered* **LA.6.2.1.5; LA.6.2.7.1; LA.6.5.2.1**

Into Action: Re-reading and Questioning

Fill in a chart like this one with your observations and questions about "The Sea." Re-read the poem, and think about what's clearer to you the second time. Continue re-reading until you can answer all your questions, or as many as possible.

Questions	Observations	Answers
How are the sea and a dog similar?	The sea is compared to a large, hungry gray dog.	Both the sea and a dog roll on the beach.

Talk About . . .

1. Discuss with a partner how you could extend the metaphor in "The Sea" even further. In how many other ways could the sea be compared to a dog? For example, what might happen when the napping dog wakes up? What if the dog sees something, such as a ship, that interests him? Try to use each Academic Vocabulary word listed on the right at least once in your discussion.

Write About . . .

Answer the following questions about "The Sea." For definitions of the underlined Academic Vocabulary words, see the column on the right.

2. Which visual images in the poem did you most appreciate, and why?
3. How many examples of onomatopoeia did you detect in the poem? List all the words you found.
4. Which poetic device did you feel most contributed to the poem's meaning: onomatopoeia, extended metaphor, or rhyme? Explain.

Writing Focus

Think as a Reader/Writer

The Writing Focus activities in Collection 7 will draw your attention to each poet's style. You'll then be given the chance to write about and practice the same elements of poetry used by these poets.

Academic Vocabulary for Collection 7

Talking and Writing About Poetry

Academic Vocabulary is the language you use to write and talk about literature. Use these words to discuss the poetry you read in this collection. The words are underlined throughout the collection.

appreciate (uh PREE shee ayt) *v.:* understand and enjoy the good qualities or value of something. *Careful reading can help you appreciate poetry.*

detect (dih TEHKT) *v.:* notice or discover, especially something that is not easy to see, hear, and so on. *Listen to detect how the rhyme scheme changes in a poem.*

device (dih VYS) *n.:* way of achieving a particular purpose. *Figurative language is a device for creating imaginative poetry.*

visual(VIHZH oo uhl) *adj.:* related to seeing or to sight. *Color words are visual and help you imagine an object more clearly.*

Your Turn

Copy the Academic Vocabulary words into your *Reader/Writer Notebook*. Use each word in a sentence about your personal thoughts on poetry.

The Sounds of Poetry

CONTENTS

What is a "beautiful sound"? How can sounds affect our emotions?

QuickWrite

Why do some word combinations sound "just right"? What's it like to read, listen to, or recite words that just sound good to your ears?

POEM

Preparing to Read

Sunshine State Standards: Benchmarks **LA.6.1.6.1** use new vocabulary that is introduced and taught directly; *Also covered* **LA.6.1.7.8; LA.6.2.1.3; LA.6.4.2.1; LA.6.6.2.2; LA.6.6.3.2**

The Sneetches

Literary Focus

Rhyme and Rhyme Scheme Words that have similar ending sounds, such as *nose* and *rose*, are called **rhymes**. In many poems the last word in one line will rhyme with the last word in another line, forming what is called an **end rhyme.** The pattern of end rhymes is the **rhyme scheme.** You can detect the rhyme scheme of a poem by marking the first line and all the lines that rhyme with it *a;* the second line and all the lines that rhyme with it *b;* and so on.

Reading Focus

Reading a Poem The first time you read a poem, just enjoy it for what it says. Then read it again, paying closer attention to its individual parts, such as word choice, punctuation, rhythm, and rhyme.

Into Action In your *Reader/Writer Notebook,* answer each question below to help you appreciate "The Sneetches."

Read to enjoy. How do I see the poets playing with words, sounds, rhymes, rhythms, and punctuation?

Read aloud. How would I read the poem in a normal voice, as if I were speaking to a friend? What do I notice about the poem's music?

Pay attention to each word. Which words do I need to look up in a dictionary to make sure the meanings are clear before I read on?

TechFocus Find and review a Web site that gives you interesting, useful information about poets, poetry, or poetry writing.

Writing Focus

Think as a Reader/Writer

Find It in Your Reading List your favorite rhymes in this poem—especially "real" words that rhyme with made-up words.

Reader/Writer Notebook

Use your **RWN** to complete the activities for this selection.

Vocabulary

keen (keen) *adj.:* eager; enthusiastic. *McBean tells the Sneetches in a keen voice that he can help them.*

guaranteed (gar uhn TEED) *adj.:* condition of being promised or pledged to pay or do something if another fails to do it. *My work is one hundred percent guaranteed.*

peculiar (pih KYOOL yuhr) *adj.:* strange. *McBean puts together a peculiar machine.*

Language Coach

Vowel Sounds Each of the Vocabulary words above can cause spelling and pronunciation problems because of tricky vowels. *Keen* is sometimes misspelled as *kean*. A common misspelling of *guaranteed* is *garenteed*. (How else could it be misspelled?) How might someone who had never encountered the word *peculiar* before pronounce it? The only way to spell and pronounce such words correctly is to memorize them.

Learn It Online
Practice your vocabulary with Word Watch online:
go.hrw.com L6-657 Go

MEET THE WRITER

Learn It Online
Get more on the author's life at:
go.hrw.com L6-658 Go

Theodor Seuss Geisel

(1904–1991)

Wacky Wisdom in Rhythm and Rhyme

Dr. Seuss (soos) is the pen name of Theodor Seuss Geisel, who began drawing fantastic animal cartoons while he was still a child. An art teacher told him that he would never learn to draw, and twenty-seven publishers rejected his first children's book, *And to Think That I Saw It on Mulberry Street* (1937). Even so, Dr. Seuss went on to write and illustrate more than forty children's classics, full of rhymes and wacky creatures. Dr. Seuss often used his zany characters to look at serious issues as if "through the wrong end of a telescope."

Dr. Seuss explained how he decided on his pen name:

"The 'Dr. Seuss' name is a combination of my middle name and the fact that I had been studying for my doctorate when I decided to quit and become a cartoonist. My father had always wanted to see a Dr. in front of my name, so I attached it. I figured by doing that, I saved him about ten thousand dollars."

Think About the Writer What kind of person do you think Geisel was? What makes you think so?

Build Background

Once, when he was asked "What is rhyme?" Dr. Seuss replied, "A rhyme is something without which I would probably be in the dry-cleaning business." To keep his poems galloping along with catchy rhymes, Dr. Seuss often invented words. In "The Sneetches" he rhymes the real word *stars* with the made-up word *thars*—and *Sneetches* with *beaches*. Seuss's playful way with words has delighted generations of children who have grown up with his simple-seeming but masterful rhymes and his wacky characters, like Cat in the Hat and the Grinch.

"The Sneetches" is a **narrative poem**—a long poem that tells a story.

Preview the Selection

In "The Sneetches" we enter a world inhabited by **Star-Belly Sneetches** and **Plain-Belly Sneetches.** See what happens when a "Fix-it-Up Chappie" named **Sylvester McMonkey McBean** comes along. (A "chappie" is a *chap*—a British term for "fellow" or "guy.")

Read with a Purpose Underneath the clever wordplay and lively rhythms of Dr. Seuss's works, there is usually a serious message, or moral. Read to see what point Dr. Seuss is making about people and the way they treat one another.

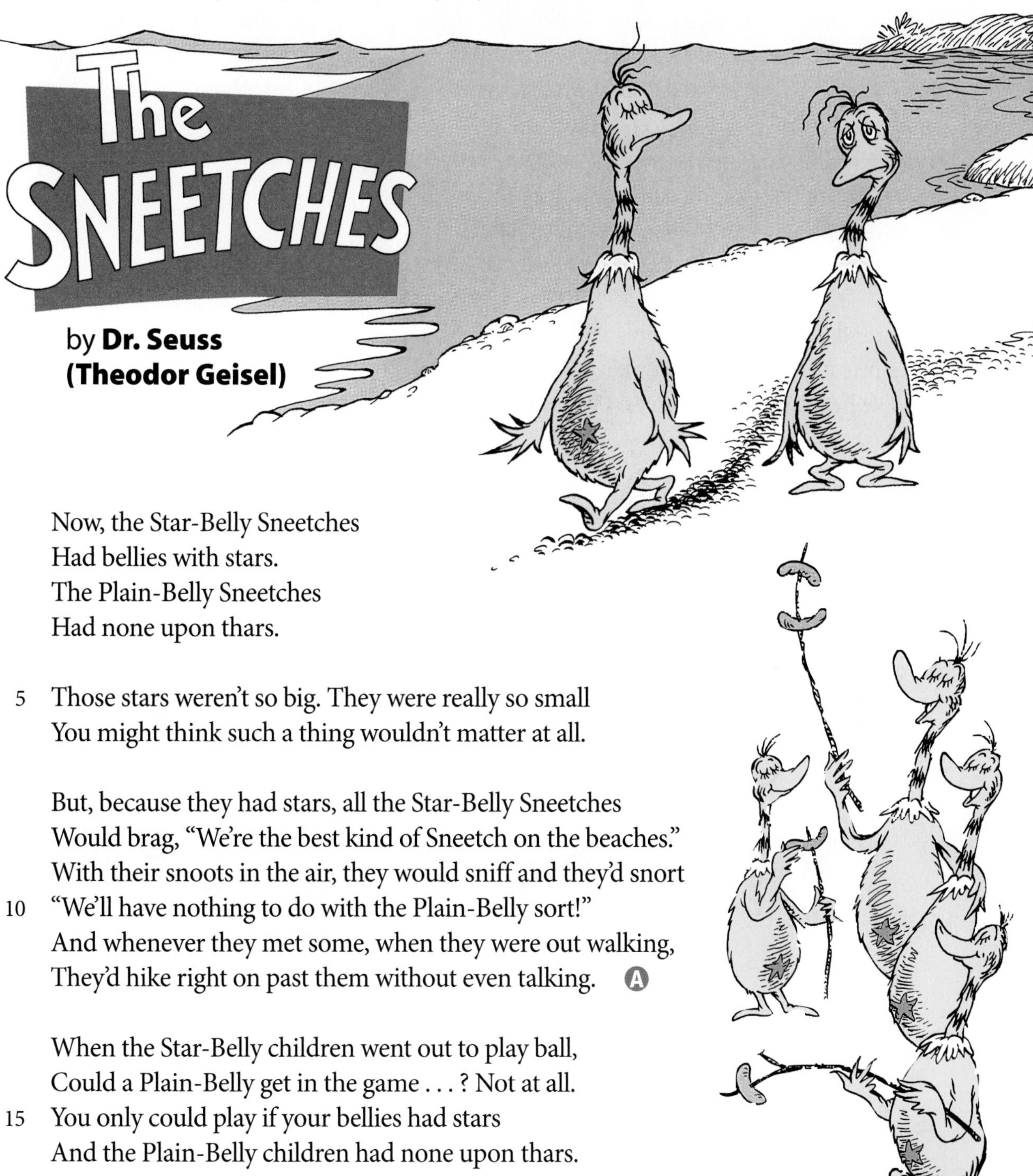

The Sneetches

by **Dr. Seuss (Theodor Geisel)**

Now, the Star-Belly Sneetches
Had bellies with stars.
The Plain-Belly Sneetches
Had none upon thars.

Those stars weren't so big. They were really so small
You might think such a thing wouldn't matter at all.

But, because they had stars, all the Star-Belly Sneetches
Would brag, "We're the best kind of Sneetch on the beaches."
With their snoots in the air, they would sniff and they'd snort
"We'll have nothing to do with the Plain-Belly sort!"
And whenever they met some, when they were out walking,
They'd hike right on past them without even talking. **A**

When the Star-Belly children went out to play ball,
Could a Plain-Belly get in the game . . . ? Not at all.
You only could play if your bellies had stars
And the Plain-Belly children had none upon thars.

A **Literary Focus** **Rhyme** Which words rhyme in this stanza? What is the rhyme scheme?

When the Star-Belly Sneetches had frankfurter roasts
Or picnics or parties or marshmallow toasts,
They never invited the Plain-Belly Sneetches.
They left them out cold, in the dark of the beaches.
They kept them away. Never let them come near.
And that's how they treated them year after year. **B**

Then ONE day, it seems . . . while the Plain-Belly Sneetches
Were moping and doping alone on the beaches,
Just sitting there wishing their bellies had stars . . .
A stranger zipped up in the strangest of cars! **C**

"My friends," he announced in a voice clear and keen,
"My name is Sylvester McMonkey McBean.
And I've heard of your troubles. I've heard you're unhappy.

B **Read and Discuss** What has Dr. Seuss set up here?

C **Literary Focus** **Rhyme** What is the rhyme scheme of this stanza? Identify whether the rhyme scheme is the same in all stanzas.

Vocabulary **keen** (keen) *adj.:* eager; enthusiastic.

CULTURE LINK

Photo courtesy of the Springfield Museum.

The Grinch and his dog, Max.

Seussmania!

How influential is Dr. Seuss? Consider these facts:

- Educators have praised his Beginner Books series for teaching generations of children to become successful readers.
- His books have sold more than 200 million copies, stayed in print for decades, and been translated into more than fifteen languages.
- His works have inspired eleven television specials, several feature films, and a Broadway musical called *Seussical.*
- He earned dozens of awards and medals, including a Pulitzer Prize in 1984 for his contributions to children's literature.
- His hometown (Springfield, Massachusetts) honored him with the Dr. Seuss National Memorial in 2002—a sculpture garden with bronze statues of his characters.

Ask Yourself

Why do you think Dr. Seuss's creations have become a part of our culture?

But I can fix that. I'm the Fix-it-Up Chappie.
And I've come here to help you. I have what you need.
And my prices are low. And I work at great speed.
And my work is one hundred per cent guaranteed!"

Then, quickly, Sylvester McMonkey McBean
Put together a very peculiar machine.
And he said, "You want stars like a Star-Belly Sneetch . . . ?
My friends, you can have them for three dollars each!" **D**

"Just pay me your money and hop right aboard!"
So they clambered inside. Then the big machine roared
And it klonked. And it bonked. And it jerked. And it berked
And it bopped them about. But the thing really worked!
When the Plain-Belly Sneetches popped out, they had stars!
They actually did. They had stars upon thars!

D **Read and Discuss** What is going on now?

Vocabulary **guaranteed** (gar uhn TEED) *adj.:* condition of being promised or pledged to pay or do something if another fails to do it.
peculiar (pih KYOOL yuhr) *adj.:* strange.

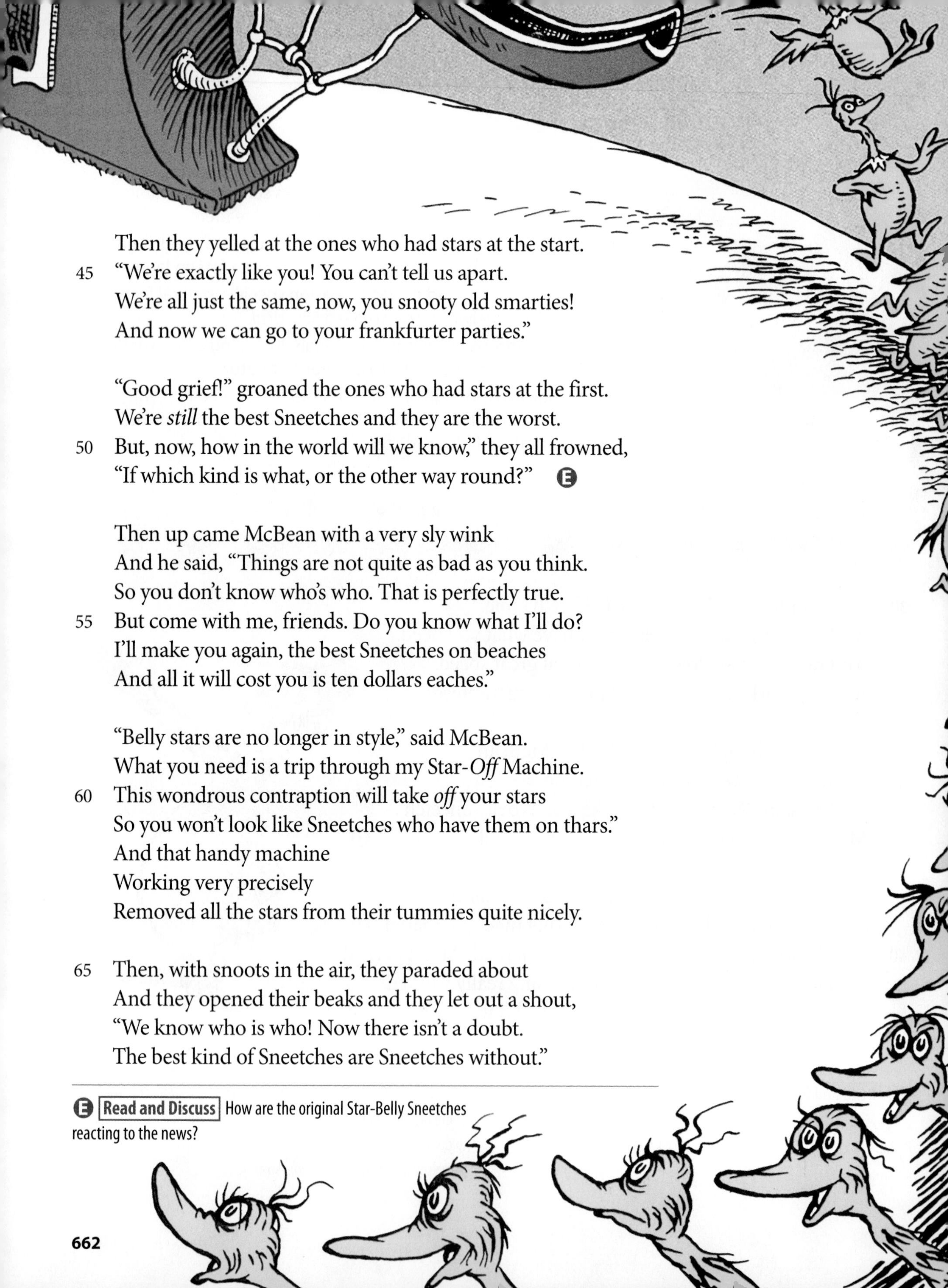

Then they yelled at the ones who had stars at the start.
"We're exactly like you! You can't tell us apart.
We're all just the same, now, you snooty old smarties!
And now we can go to your frankfurter parties."

"Good grief!" groaned the ones who had stars at the first.
We're *still* the best Sneetches and they are the worst.
But, now, how in the world will we know," they all frowned,
"If which kind is what, or the other way round?" **E**

Then up came McBean with a very sly wink
And he said, "Things are not quite as bad as you think.
So you don't know who's who. That is perfectly true.
But come with me, friends. Do you know what I'll do?
I'll make you again, the best Sneetches on beaches
And all it will cost you is ten dollars eaches."

"Belly stars are no longer in style," said McBean.
What you need is a trip through my Star-*Off* Machine.
This wondrous contraption will take *off* your stars
So you won't look like Sneetches who have them on thars."
And that handy machine
Working very precisely
Removed all the stars from their tummies quite nicely.

Then, with snoots in the air, they paraded about
And they opened their beaks and they let out a shout,
"We know who is who! Now there isn't a doubt.
The best kind of Sneetches are Sneetches without."

E **Read and Discuss** How are the original Star-Belly Sneetches reacting to the news?

Then, of course, those with stars all got frightfully mad.
To be wearing a star now was frightfully bad.
Then, of course, old Sylvester McMonkey McBean
Invited *them* into his Star-Off Machine.

Then, of course from THEN on, as you probably guess,
Things really got into a horrible mess.

All the rest of the day, on those wild screaming beaches,
The Fix-it-Up Chappie kept fixing up Sneetches.
Off again! On again!
In again! Out again!
Through the machines they raced round and about again,
Changing their stars every minute or two.
They kept paying money. They kept running through
Until neither the Plain nor the Star-Bellies knew
Whether this one was that one . . . or that one was this one
Or which one was what one . . . or what one was who. **F**

Then, when their last cent
Of their money was spent,
The Fix-it-Up Chappie packed up
And he went.

And he laughed as he drove
In his car up the beach,
"They never will learn.
No. You can't teach a Sneetch!"

But McBean was quite wrong. I'm quite happy to say
That the Sneetches got really quite smart on that day,
The day they decided that Sneetches are Sneetches
And no kind of Sneetch is the best at the beaches.
That day, all the Sneetches forgot about stars
And whether they had one, or not, upon thars. **G**

F **Reading Focus** **Reading a Poem** Read this stanza aloud. How do these lines sound to you? Where did you pause or stop, and why?

G **Read and Discuss** How does McBean influence the behavior of the Sneetches?

Applying Your Skills

Sunshine State Standards: Benchmarks LA.6.1.6.1 use new vocabulary that is introduced and taught directly; *Also covered* LA.6.1.7.3; LA.6.1.7.8; LA.6.2.1.3; LA.6.2.1.4; LA.6.2.1.7; LA.6.2.1.8; LA.6.4.1.2

The Sneetches

Respond and Think Critically

Reading Focus

FCAT

1. What important lesson does this story teach?
   - **A** We are not all equal.
   - **B** We are all alike.
   - **C** Stars make you popular.
   - **D** Sneetches can't be friends.

Read with a Purpose

2. What point does Dr. Seuss make in this poem about the way people treat one another?

Reading Skills: Reading a Poem

3. Complete the chart by writing in the right-hand column what you learned from following each of the tips in the left-hand column.

Read to enjoy.	
Read aloud.	
Pay attention to each word.	

Vocabulary Check

4. Use each Vocabulary word in a sentence about "The Sneetches":
   keen **guaranteed** **peculiar**

Literary Focus

5. **Pair-Share** Discuss with a classmate how the clothes we wear might define for others who we are. What does this poem teach us about thinking in those terms?

6. **Interpret** What is McBean's opinion of the Sneetches in general? Do you agree? Support your answer with details from the poem.

Literary Skills: Rhyme/Rhyme Scheme

7. **Analyze/Compare** Mark the rhyme scheme in at least three different stanzas of "The Sneetches," using the letter code you learned on page 657. Why do you think Dr. Seuss varied the rhyme scheme? Explain.
8. **Analyze** Dr. Seuss sometimes changes a spelling, adds a new ending sound, or even invents a new word. Find an example of each of these, and explain what effect Seuss achieves by playing with words in this way.

Literary Skills Review: Theme

9. **Draw Conclusions** **Theme** is the moral, or lesson about life, that a work presents. What main theme do you detect in this poem? On what evidence do you base your conclusion?

Writing Focus

Think as a Reader/Writer

Use It in Your Writing Write a few rhymed lines that include both real and made-up words. Use your examples from Dr. Seuss for inspiration.

Why might nonsense verse with a strong rhythm be effective in making a serious point about human behavior?

Sunshine State Standards: Benchmarks
LA.6.1.7.8; LA.6.2.1.3; LA.6.2.1.7

POEM
Preparing to Read

John Henry

Literary Focus

Repetition and Refrain In poetry and songs, certain words, phrases, lines, stanzas, and even sounds may be repeated again and again. This poetic device is called **repetition.** Poets use repetition to emphasize important ideas, create a mood, or build suspense. One of the simplest kinds of repetition is the refrain. A **refrain** is a repeated word, phrase, line, or group of lines that reappears regularly throughout a work. Songs and even speeches can have a refrain. For example, Martin Luther King, Jr.'s, most famous speech is built on the refrain "I have a dream."

Reading Focus

Questioning Questioning can help you find the meaning in a poem and experience it in a way that is meaningful to you. As you read, write down your questions and reactions to this poem.

Into Action Use a chart like this one to organize your questions and observations as you read. Some examples are included.

Observations	Questions
A three-day-old boy holding a hammer and singing is pretty unrealistic and exaggerated.	Are we supposed to think that John Henry is superhuman?
The captain says he's going to bring in a steam drill.	Why does John Henry want to die with a hammer in his hand?

Writing Focus

Think as a Reader/Writer

Find It in Your Reading Pay attention to words, phrases, and lines that repeat throughout the poem. In your *Reader/Writer Notebook*, jot down the ones that especially appeal to you.

Reader/Writer Notebook

Use your **RWN** to complete the activities for this selection.

Language Coach

Hyperbole When a friend says, "I just ate a mountain of food," you know that she didn't literally eat a mountain-sized portion of food; she simply means that she ate a *lot* of food. She is using a kind of **figurative language** called **hyperbole** (hy PUR buh lee), language that is exaggerated or overstated for comical effect or to make a strong point. Like many tall tales, "John Henry" uses hyperbole, starting with "John Henry was about three days old / Sittin' on his papa's knee." We're not supposed to believe that John Henry was literally three days old and already working with a hammer; the writer is just trying to tell us that John Henry seemed born to be a "steel-driving man" from the beginning. What other examples of hyperbole can you find in this poem? How do they fit the subject and theme of the poem?

Learn It Online
Hear a professional actor read this ballad. Visit the selection online at:

go.hrw.com L6-665 

ABOUT THE POEM

The Story of John Henry

Working on the Railroad

In the years following the Civil War, laborers toiled long and hard to build America's railroads. African Americans and recent immigrants from China did much of the work. In those days no unions protected the railroad construction crews. The men sweated long hours, cutting down trees, digging tunnels, and laying track. "Steel drivers" used a ten-pound hammer and a drill to crack the rock so that they could carve out a tunnel. Many of these laborers lost their jobs to the newly invented steam drill, which could do their work faster and more cheaply.

Mystery Song, Mystery Man

Nobody knows who wrote this popular song about John Henry. In fact, no one even knows whether John Henry was a real person. According to legend, he was an African American laborer in the crew constructing the Big Bend Tunnel of the Chesapeake and Ohio Railroad. Someone set up a contest between John Henry and a steam drill. This contest between man and machine became the subject of various **tall tales**—exaggerated folk tales about larger-than-life men and women. John Henry joined the ranks of America's tall-tale figures, such as Pecos Bill and Paul Bunyan, and became the subject of stories, poems, and songs in the 1870s. The "steel-driving man" is an enduring part of America's cultural legacy.

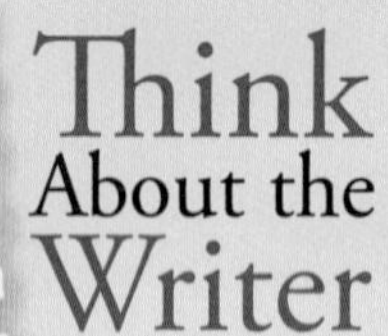

What kind of person do you think wrote the ballad of "John Henry"? Why?

Build Background

"John Henry" is a **ballad**, a type of **narrative poem**, or poem that tells a story. Ballads are often about a hero or an important event. Most ballads are meant to be sung; they have refrains and a regular rhyme scheme. Try to find one of the many recordings of "John Henry" sung by rock, blues, or folk musicians.

Preview the Selection

John Henry is a "steel-driving man" practically born holding a hammer. He's strong and determined to hold his own against a machine that threatens to take his job.

Read with a Purpose

Read to find out why John Henry believes he can outperform a machine.

The Museum of African American Art, Los Angeles, California, Palmer C. Hayden Collection, gift of Miriam A. Hayden.

John Henry on the Right, Steam Drill on the Left (1944–1947) by Palmer C. Hayden.

JOHN HENRY

Anonymous African American

John Henry was about three days old
Sittin' on his papa's knee.
He picked up a hammer and a little piece of steel
Said, "Hammer's gonna be the death of me, Lord, Lord!
Hammer's gonna be the death of me." **A**

A **Literary Focus** **Repetition** What feeling do you get from the repeated words and phrases? Pay attention to whether that feeling changes as you read more of the poem.

The captain said to John Henry,
"Gonna bring that steam drill 'round
Gonna bring that steam drill out on the job
Gonna whop that steel on down, Lord, Lord!
Whop that steel on down."

John Henry told his captain,
"A man ain't nothin' but a man
But before I let your steam drill beat me down
I'd die with a hammer in my hand, Lord, Lord!
I'd die with a hammer in my hand." **B**

John Henry said to his shaker,°
"Shaker, why don't you sing?
I'm throwing thirty pounds from my hips on down
Just listen to that cold steel ring, Lord, Lord!
Listen to that cold steel ring."

John Henry said to his shaker,
"Shaker, you'd better pray
'Cause if I miss that little piece of steel
Tomorrow be your buryin' day, Lord, Lord!
Tomorrow be your buryin' day."

The shaker said to John Henry,
"I think this mountain's cavin' in!"
John Henry said to his shaker, "Man,
That ain't nothin' but my hammer suckin' wind,
  Lord, Lord!
Nothin' but my hammer suckin' wind." **C**

The man that invented the steam drill
Thought he was mighty fine
But John Henry made fifteen feet
The steam drill only made nine, Lord, Lord!
The steam drill only made nine. **D**

16. shaker (SHAY kuhr): the worker who holds the drill.

B Read and Discuss What have you learned about John Henry so far?

C **Reading Focus** **Questioning** What questions do you have about the shaker and about what is happening here? Record your questions and reactions.

D Read and Discuss What has happened?

Analyzing Visuals **Viewing and Interpreting** Does this image convey the same emotions as the ballad? Why or why not?

He Laid Down His Hammer and Cried (1944–1947) by Palmer C. Hayden.

John Henry hammered in the mountain
His hammer was striking fire
But he worked so hard, he broke his poor heart
He laid down his hammer and he died, Lord, Lord!
He laid down his hammer and he died.

John Henry had a little woman
Her name was Polly Ann
John Henry took sick and went to his bed
Polly Ann drove steel like a man, Lord, Lord!
Polly Ann drove steel like a man. **E**

John Henry had a little baby
You could hold him in the palm of your hand
The last words I heard that poor boy say,
"My daddy was a steel-driving man, Lord, Lord!
My daddy was a steel-driving man."

They took John Henry to the graveyard
And they buried him in the sand
And every locomotive comes a-roaring by
Says, "There lies a steel-driving man, Lord, Lord!
There lies a steel-driving man." **F**

Well, every Monday morning
When the bluebirds begin to sing
You can hear John Henry a mile or more
You can hear John Henry's hammer ring, Lord, Lord!
You can hear John Henry's hammer ring. **G**

E **Reading Focus** **Questioning** What questions do you have about Polly Ann? Record your questions and reactions.

F **Read and Discuss** How do things turn out?

G **Literary Focus** **Refrain** What words or phrases have been repeated throughout the poem to create the refrain? What has been their effect?

Applying Your Skills

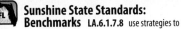

Sunshine State Standards: Benchmarks LA.6.1.7.8 use strategies to repair comprehension of grade-appropriate text when self-monitoring indicates confusion, including but not limited to rereading, checking context clues, predicting, note-making, summarizing, using graphic and semantic organizers, questioning, and clarifying by checking other sources; *Also covered* **LA.6.2.1.5; LA.6.2.1.7; LA.6.3.2.3; LA.6.4.1.2**

John Henry

Respond and Think Critically

Reading Focus

1. What greater significance can be attributed to John Henry's defeat of the machine? FCAT
   - **A** It establishes John Henry's value as an American legend.
   - **B** It shows that machines can never replace humans.
   - **C** It illustrates advances in railroading through hard work.
   - **D** It is a significant event in American history.

Read with a Purpose

2. Was John Henry heroic or foolish in wanting to compete with a machine? Explain.

Reading Skills: Questioning

3. Add a column to your questioning chart. As you think about the poem and re-read it, record the answers you find to your questions.

Observations	Questions	Answers
A three-day-old boy holding a hammer and singing is pretty unrealistic and exaggerated.	Are we supposed to think that John Henry is superhuman?	I think John Henry is like a tall tale hero.
The captain says he's going to bring in a steam drill.	Why does John Henry want to die with a hammer in his hand?	

Literary Focus

Literary Analysis

4. **Interpret** Who ends up winning the contest, and why?
5. **Analyze** Folk heroes such as John Henry have admirable qualities that make them worthy of lasting fame. What heroic qualities does John Henry demonstrate in this poem? Support your answer with details from the poem. READ THINK EXPLAIN

Literary Skills: Repetition and Refrain

6. **Infer** What purpose does repetition serve in "John Henry"?
7. **Analyze** Identify the refrains in this poem.

Literary Skills Review: Tone

8. **Draw Conclusions** The attitude a writer takes toward a subject is **tone.** What is the tone of this ballad—humorous, proud, defiant, angry, or something else? Explain.

Writing Focus

Think as a Reader/Writer

Use It in Your Writing Write an idea for a ballad about someone today who challenges a machine. Write the refrain for your ballad, using examples from "John Henry" for inspiration.

What Do You Think Now

What beautiful qualities did you find in this poem? How did the language of the poem support the message of the poem?

POEMS

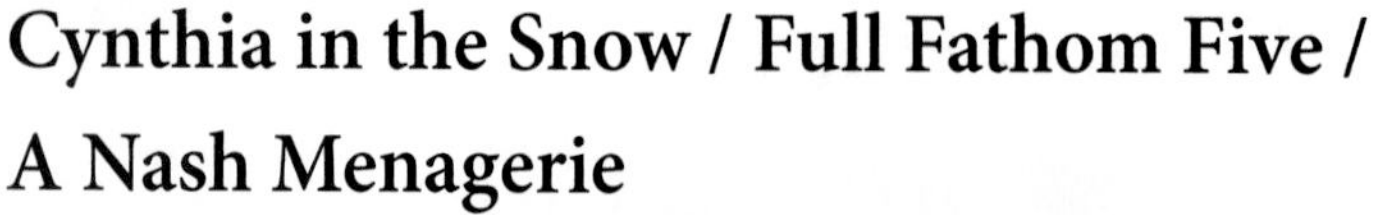

Preparing to Read

Sunshine State Standards: Benchmarks
LA.6.1.5.1 adjust reading rate based on purpose, text difficulty, form, and style; *Also covered* **LA.6.1.6.10; LA.6.2.1.3; LA.6.3.4.3**

Cynthia in the Snow / Full Fathom Five / A Nash Menagerie

Literary Focus

Sound Effects: Alliteration and Onomatopoeia Various "sound effects" can give a poem a musical quality. One of the most common sound effects poets use is **alliteration** (uh liht uh RAY shuhn), the repetition of the same consonant sound in words that are close together. Alliteration usually occurs at the beginning of words, as in "**S**he **s**ells **s**eashells." Alliteration can create a mood, imitate a sound, or simply emphasize certain words.

Another device that helps create the music of poetry is **onomatopoeia** (ahn uh mat uh PEE uh), the use of a word whose sound imitates or suggests its meaning. *Boom, bang, rumble, hush,* and *snort* are all everyday examples of onomatopoeia.

Reading Focus

Reading a Poem If you don't pay attention to **punctuation** when you're reading poetry, you may lose much of the poem's meaning. Pause briefly at commas and semicolons and longer after periods, question marks, and exclamation marks.

Into Action Use this chart to guide you as you read poetry:

If You See This Punctuation...	Do This
Period at end of a sentence	Make a full stop.
Comma, colon, semicolon, dash	Pause briefly.
No punctuation at end of a line	Don't stop; go on to the next line.

Writing Focus

Think as a Reader/Writer

Find It in Your Reading As you read, note the sound effects the poets use. List examples of alliteration and onomatopoeia.

Reader/Writer Notebook

Use your **RWN** to complete the activities for these selections.

Vocabulary

A Nash Menagerie

marvel (MAHR vuhl) *v.:* wonder at. *The speaker can only marvel at the octopus and its many limbs.*

behold (bih HOHLD) *v.:* look at; see. *In his poetry, Nash invites the reader to behold many kinds of animals.*

extinct (ehk STIHNGKT) *adj.:* no longer existing. *The speaker cautions that humans might become extinct if we are not careful.*

Language Coach

Word Roots The adjective *extinct,* like the verb *extinguish,* comes from the Latin verb *extinguere.* How are the meanings of *extinct* and *extinguish* similar? What are some other related words? Use a dictionary if necessary.

Learn It Online
Use Word Watch to improve your vocabulary at:

go.hrw.com L6-672 

MEET THE WRITERS

The Granger Collection, New York.

Gwendolyn Brooks (1917–2000)

Gwendolyn Brooks spent much of her childhood reading and writing. She published her first poem at fourteen. After finishing junior college, Brooks was a domestic worker and a secretary. She went on to write more than twenty books and win a Pulitzer Prize for poetry.

The Granger Collection, New York.

William Shakespeare (1564–1616)

William Shakespeare was born in Stratford-upon-Avon, England, during the Renaissance period. At eighteen, Shakespeare left Stratford for the theater in London. He began to act and to write such famous plays as *Romeo and Juliet.* He also wrote some of the best poetry of his day. Today he is considered the greatest English playwright.

Ogden Nash (1902–1971)

Generations of readers have enjoyed Ogden Nash for his comical poetry and clever rhymes. He taught and worked in advertising and publishing before turning to writing "silly" verse. A master of the English language, Nash admitted having intentionally ignored or mangled every known rule of grammar and spelling.

Think About the Writers

What kinds of poems would you expect each of these writers to write?

Build Background

"Full Fathom Five" is an excerpt from *The Tempest,* one of Shakespeare's most widely read plays and one of the last ones he wrote. The English language has changed a lot since Shakespeare's time, so you'll notice words we no longer use, such as *thy* ("your") and *doth* ("does").

In the Nash Menagerie you'll also notice some odd words, such as *thou* ("you") and the made-up *anther* ("answer")—not because Nash wrote long ago but because he enjoyed playing with language.

Preview the Selections

In "Cynthia in the Snow" the speaker is reflecting on the beauty of snowfall.

In "Full Fathom Five" the sprite **Ariel** is singing to **Ferdinand,** who believes that his father has drowned in a shipwreck.

The Nash Menagerie introduces us to some interesting creatures—and a poet's unique sense of humor. A *menagerie* (muh NAJ uhr ee) is a collection or assortment of animals, usually in a zoo.

Read with a Purpose Read this poem to find out how the speaker feels about snow.

Cynthia in the Snow

by **Gwendolyn Brooks**

It SHUSHES.
It hushes **A**
The loudness in the road.
It flitter-twitters,
And laughs away from me.
It laughs a lovely whiteness,
And whitely whirs away,
To be **B**
Some otherwhere,
Still white as milk or shirts.
So beautiful it hurts. **C**

A **Literary Focus** **Sound Effects** How does onomatopoeia make this setting come alive?

B **Reading Focus** **Reading a Poem** Since there is no punctuation at the end of this line, how should you read it?

C **Read and Discuss** What visual images does this poem create for you?

Read with a Purpose Read this poem to find out how a character in *The Tempest* describes someone who has drowned.

Full Fathom Five

from ***The Tempest***
by **William Shakespeare**

Full Fathom Five from "The Tempest" by Edmund Dulac.

Full fathom° five thy father lies:
Of his bones are coral made; **A**
Those are pearls that were his eyes:
  Nothing of him that doth fade
But doth suffer a sea-change **B**
Into something rich and strange.
Sea-nymphs° hourly ring his knell:°
  Ding-dong.
Hark! now I hear them—ding-dong, bell. **C**

1. **fathom** (FATH uhm): unit of measurement equal to about six feet, used to measure the depth of water.

7. **sea-nymphs** (see nihmfs): goddesses once thought to inhabit the sea. **knell** (nehl): sound of a bell rung after someone has died.

A **Reading Focus** **Reading a Poem** Notice the semicolon at the end of this line. How should you read the line?

B **Read and Discuss** What does "But doth suffer a sea-change" mean?

C **Literary Focus** **Sound Effects** What examples of onomatopoeia can you find in this poem? What do they add to the poem's meaning and effect?

Read with a Purpose Read these poems to discover what Nash thinks of the octopus, the panther, the camel, the duck, an extinct bird—and people.

A Nash Menagerie

by **Ogden Nash**

The Octopus

Tell me, O Octopus, I begs,
Is those things arms, or is they legs? **A**
I marvel at thee, Octopus;
If I were thou, I'd call me Us.

The Panther

The panther is like a leopard,
Except it hasn't been peppered. **B**
Should you behold a panther crouch,
Prepare to say Ouch.
Better yet, if called by a panther,
Don't anther.

A **Literary Focus** **Sound Effects** Notice the alliteration here. What sounds are repeated in this line?

B **Read and Discuss** What is this describing?

Vocabulary **marvel** (MAHR vuhl) *v.:* wonder at.
behold (bih HOHLD) *v.:* look at; see.

The Duck

Behold the duck
It does not cluck.
A cluck it lacks.
It quacks.
It is especially fond
Of a puddle or pond.
When it dines or sups,
It bottoms ups. **C**

The Camel

The camel has a single hump;
The dromedary, two;
Or else the other way around.
I'm never sure. Are you? **D**

C **Read and Discuss** What aspect of duck behavior is this line describing?

D **Reading Focus** **Reading a Poem** Read the last line of this poem aloud. How do the two punctuation marks in this line affect the way you read it?

A Caution to Everybody

Consider the auk;°
Becoming extinct because he forgot
  how to fly, and could only walk.
Consider man, who may well
  become extinct
Because he forgot how to walk and
  learned how to fly before he
  thinked.

1. **auk** (awk): the great auk, a large, flightless bird once common in North Atlantic regions but now extinct.

Analyzing Visuals

Viewing and Interpreting How does this photograph relate to the poem on this page?

Vocabulary **extinct** (ehk STIHNGKT) *adj.:* no longer existing.

Applying Your Skills

Sunshine State Standards: Benchmarks **LA.6.1.5.1** adjust reading rate based on purpose, text difficulty, form and style; **LA.6.1.6.1** use new vocabulary that is introduced and taught directly; *Also covered* **LA.6.1.7.8; LA.6.2.1.3; LA.6.2.1.5; LA.6.2.1.7**

Cynthia in the Snow / Full Fathom Five / A Nash Menagerie

Respond and Think Critically

Reading Focus

1. What does the author mean when he says he "learned how to fly before he / thinked"? **FCAT**
   - **A** He thinks humans push boundaries without regard for consequences.
   - **B** He believes that people should not fly; they should only walk.
   - **C** He supports campaigns to help birds on the brink of extinction.
   - **D** He thinks flying is as dangerous for humans as walking is for birds.

Read with a Purpose

2. In "Cynthia in the Snow," how would you describe the speaker's feelings about snow?
3. According to Ariel in "Full Fathom Five," what has really happened to Ferdinand's father?
4. What do Ogden Nash's observations in the five poems have in common? Support your answer with examples from the text.

Reading Skills: Reading a Poem

5. Choose two of the poems to read aloud. Practice reading them smoothly and clearly, paying attention to punctuation and pausing when appropriate. Once you've practiced reading the poems, record your thoughts about each poem's meaning in a chart:

Poem 1:	My thoughts:
Poem 2:	My thoughts:

Vocabulary Check

Fill in the blank in each sentence with one of the Vocabulary words: **marvel, behold, extinct.**

6. Did you stop and _______________ the beautiful view?
7. We have to _______________ at the incredible abilities of some animals.
8. Every century, there are many animal species that become___________.

Literary Focus

Literary Skills: Sound Effects

9. In "A Nash Menagerie," how does alliteration affect the meaning of the poems and the feelings the poems convey? Support your answer with examples from the poems. READ THINK EXPLAIN

Writing Focus

Think as a Reader/Writer

Use It in Your Writing Review the examples of sound effects you noted. How do you think these sound effects contribute to the **tone** of the poems? Support your response with examples from the poems.

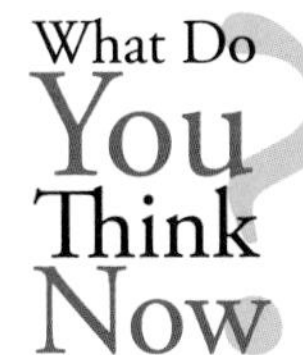

How do the sounds of a poet's words convey the feeling—and the meaning—of a poem?

Sunshine State Standards: Benchmarks LA.6.1.6.1 use new vocabulary that is introduced and taught directly; *Also covered* LA.6.2.1.1; LA.6.2.1.3; LA.6.2.1.7; LA.6.3.5.2; LA.6.5.2.2; LA.6.6.2.2; LA.6.6.4.2

Vocabulary Development

Figurative Language

Figurative language, which is not literally true, compares one thing to another, very different thing. Three common figures of speech are similes, metaphors, and personification.

A **simile** is a comparison of two very different things in which a word of comparison, such as *like, as, as if, resembles,* or *seems* is used.

Her face was *like a blazing fire*.

A **metaphor** is also a comparison of two very different things, but it does not use a word of comparison.

Life *is a flowing river*.

Personification is a figure of speech in which human traits are given to nonhuman things such as animals or forces of nature.

The *river sang* a song of triumph.

Your Turn

Identify the things being compared in the quotation. Explain how they are alike. Identify the figure of speech used: simile, metaphor, personification.

"I hear America singing, the varied carols
I hear . . ." —Walt Whitman

Academic Vocabulary

Write About . . .

What purpose do devices like onomatopoeia and alliteration serve in poetry? Would you still be able to appreciate a poem like "Cynthia in the Snow" if it did not use sound effects? Explain.

CHOICES

As you respond to the Choices, use these **Academic Vocabulary** words as appropriate: appreciate, detect, device, visual.

REVIEW

Evaluate a Narrative Poem

Timed Writing Evaluate either "The Sneetches" (page 659) or "John Henry" (page 667) as a good example of a **narrative poem**—a poem that tells a story. Explain how a story told in the form of a poem is both similar to and different from a story told in prose. What elements of poetry work especially well for storytelling?

CONNECT

Create a Multimedia Presentation

TechFocus Find a poem that uses a variety of strong sound effects, such as rhyme and alliteration. Use presentation software to present and explain the poem to the class, incorporating sound files, images, and drawings to help your audience better appreciate the poem you found.

EXTEND

Recite a Poem

Listening and Speaking Find another Ogden Nash poem from the library, or search for one on the Internet. Introduce your poem first, providing any necessary background. Recite the poem for your class. Afterward, point out poetic devices such as figurative language and rhyme, as well as Nash's playful use of language.

Learn It Online
Use MediaScope to create an attention-grabbing multimedia presentation:
go.hrw.com L6-680 

POEMS

Preparing to Read

Sunshine State Standards: Benchmarks
LA.6.1.6.4 categorize key vocabulary and identify salient features; *Also covered* LA.6.1.7.8; LA.6.2.1.1

Good Hot Dogs / Yes, It Was My Grandmother / In the Blood / That Day / About "That Day"

Literary Focus

Free Verse **Free verse** is poetry that is written to sound the way people speak, "free" of regular meter and rhyme scheme. Poems written in free verse use loose groupings of words and phrases and do not have a regular beat. They do, however, have the natural rhythm of conversation. When you read free verse, pay attention to punctuation and to the meaning of the lines to determine when to pause and when to read straight through to the next line.

Reading Focus

Questioning Pay attention to your reactions to these poems as you read. Ask questions and make comments along the way, and jot down your thoughts. When you finish the poems, look again at your questions and observations. Do you have new questions that did not occur to you as you were reading?

Into Action As you read each poem, write your thoughts and questions on a chart like the one below:

Observations About "Good Hot Dogs"	Questions About "Good Hot Dogs"
Maybe Cisneros is still grateful to Kiki because Kiki shared her money to buy them both lunch.	Why does Cisneros include the price of the hot dogs?

Writing Focus

Find It in Your Reading As you read each poem, use the sense of the lines to decide when to pause and when to keep reading. Make notes about which lines call for a pause at the end and which ones don't.

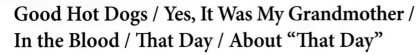

Reader/Writer Notebook

Use your **RWN** to complete the activities for these selections.

Vocabulary

Yes It Was My Grandmother

tangles (TANG guhlz) *v.:* becomes twisted into knots. *Her hair tangles in the wind and is difficult to comb.*

That Day

gesture (JEHS chuhr) *n.:* act performed to show feelings. *The poet thought his father's playing ball with him was a beautiful gesture.*

previously (PREE vee uhs lee) *adv.:* before now. *After his father played ball with him, the son found that he had previously not appreciated his father's love.*

Language Coach

Antonyms Words that are opposite in meaning are called **antonyms**. Can you think of words that mean the opposite of any of the Vocabulary words above?

Learn It Online

Focus on words with Word Watch. Get the whole story at:

go.hrw.com L6-681 

Get more on Cisneros's life at:

go.hrw.com L6-682 Go

MEET THE WRITERS

Sandra Cisneros (1954–)

Sandra Cisneros was born in Chicago and grew up speaking Spanish and English. Her childhood experiences, her family, and her Mexican American heritage all find a place in her writing. For more about Cisneros, see the biography on page 246.

Luci Tapahonso (1953–)

Luci Tapahonso, a member of the Navajo nation, was born and raised in Shiprock, New Mexico. Ever since she was young, Tapahonso and her family have shared stories and songs. This storytelling tradition has been a rich source of material for her.

Pat Mora (1942–)

Pat Mora is a Mexican American who grew up in Texas. Much of her poetry is about the ways Hispanic culture has blended into American society. In addition to poetry, she has written children's books based on her own experiences.

David Kherdian (1931–)

The award-winning author David Kherdian was born in Racine, Wisconsin, to parents from Armenia. Kherdian has written more than sixty books, including novels, memoirs, biographies, and poetry collections.

Think About the Writers How might the importance of ethnic heritage show up in the work of each of these writers?

Build Background

When Sandra Cisneros was a child, she and her family moved around often. As you read "Good Hot Dogs," think about how a lunchtime routine with a friend might be comforting to a girl who had to keep making new friends in new places.

The hard-riding, horse-training grandmother in Luci Tapahonso's poem is not an oddity in Navajo culture. Navajo women have always been respected as leaders and have traditionally been the ones who have passed down cultural identity as well as a family's possessions—even land and livestock.

Pat Mora writes because she believes Hispanics need to take their rightful place in American literature. "In the Blood" appears in both English and Spanish. If you know Spanish, compare the two poems as you read. If you don't, look for words in the Spanish version that remind you of English words.

In "That Day," David Kherdian remembers a time when his Armenian-born father attempted to participate in his American culture—and how that action of his father taught Kherdian about the power of love.

Preview the Selections

In"Good Hot Dogs" the speaker describes a lunchtime routine.

In "Yes, It Was My Grandmother" the speaker talks about her grandmother, a horse trainer.

In "In the Blood" the speaker describes a family relationship.

In "That Day" David Kherdian presents a

Read with a Purpose

Read this poem to find out why the speaker still remembers those good hot dogs.

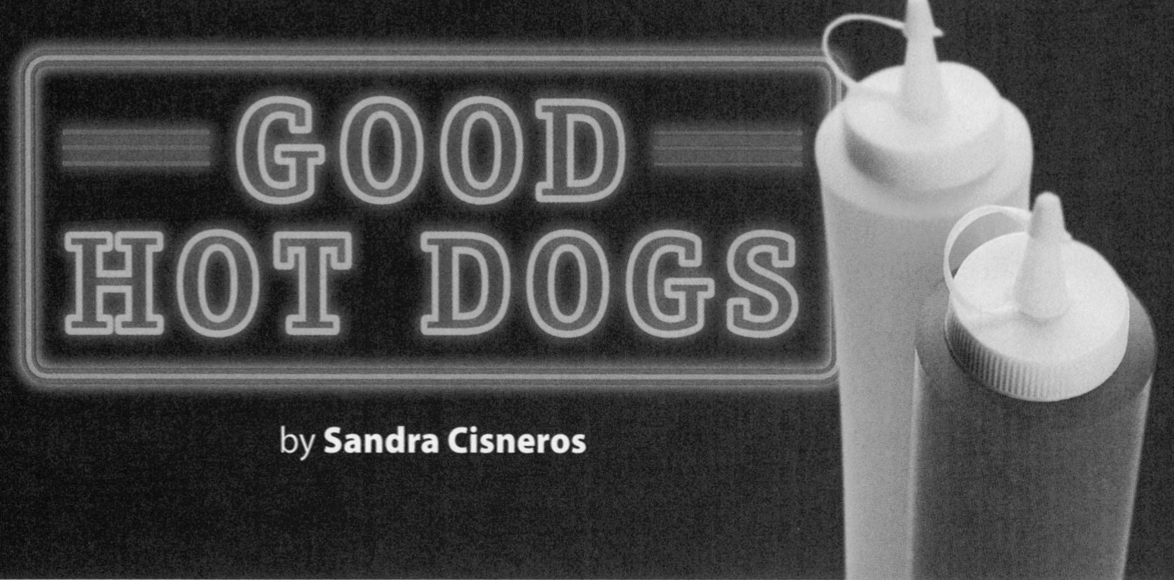

for Kiki

Fifty cents apiece
To eat our lunch
We'd run
Straight from school
Instead of home
Two blocks
Then the store
That smelled like steam
You ordered
Because you had the money
Two hot dogs and two pops
    for here (A)
Everything on the hot dogs
Except pickle lily
Dash those hot dogs (B)
Into buns and splash on
All that good stuff
Yellow mustard and onions
And french fries piled on top all
Rolled up in a piece of wax
Paper for us to hold hot
In our hands
Quarters on the counter
Sit down
Good hot dogs
We'd eat
Fast till there was nothing left
But salt and poppy seeds even
The little burnt tips
Of french fries
We'd eat
You humming
And me swinging my legs (C)

(A) **Read and Discuss** What is going on in the poem?

(B) **Reading Focus Questioning** Who is "dashing" the hot dogs into buns?

(C) **Read and Discuss** How does the narrator feel about her friend?

Read with a Purpose

Read this poem to find out how the narrator's grandmother has influenced her.

Yes, It Was My Grandmother

by **Luci Tapahonso**

Yes, it was my grandmother
who trained wild horses for pleasure and pay.
People knew of her, saying:
She knows how to handle them.
Horses obey that woman. **A**

She worked,
skirts flying, hair tied securely in the wind and dust.
She rode those animals hard and was thrown,
time and time again.
She worked until they were meek
and wanting to please.
She came home at dusk,
tired and dusty,
smelling of sweat and horses.
She couldn't cook,
my father said smiling,
your grandmother hated to cook. **B**
Oh, Grandmother,
who freed me from cooking.
Grandmother, you must have made sure
I met a man who would not share the kitchen.

I am small like you and
do not protect my careless hair
from wind or rain—it tangles often,
Grandma, and it is wild and untrained. **C**

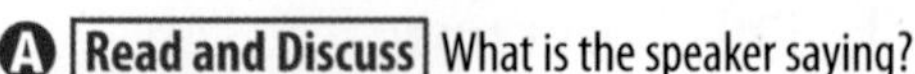

A **Read and Discuss** What is the speaker saying?

B **Reading Focus** **Questioning** Why does the speaker's father smile? How does he feel about his mother?

C **Literary Focus** **Free Verse** What makes this poem an example of free verse?

Vocabulary **tangles** (TANG guhlz) *v.:* becomes twisted into knots.

Analyzing Visuals

Viewing and Interpreting What qualities does the woman shown in this photograph share with the grandmother described in the poem?

Read with a Purpose

Read this poem to learn about the relationship between a child and her grandfather.

In the Blood Ⓐ

by **Pat Mora**

The brown-eyed child
and the white-haired grandfather
dance in the silent afternoon.
They snap their fingers
to a rhythm only those
who love can hear. Ⓑ

En la Sangre

La niña con ojos cafés
y el abuelito con pelo blanco
bailan en la tarde silenciosa.
Castañetean los dedos
a un ritmo oído solamente
por los que aman.

Baile en 1958 (detail)
by Carmen Lomas Garza.
Alkyds and oils, 24 x 32 inches.

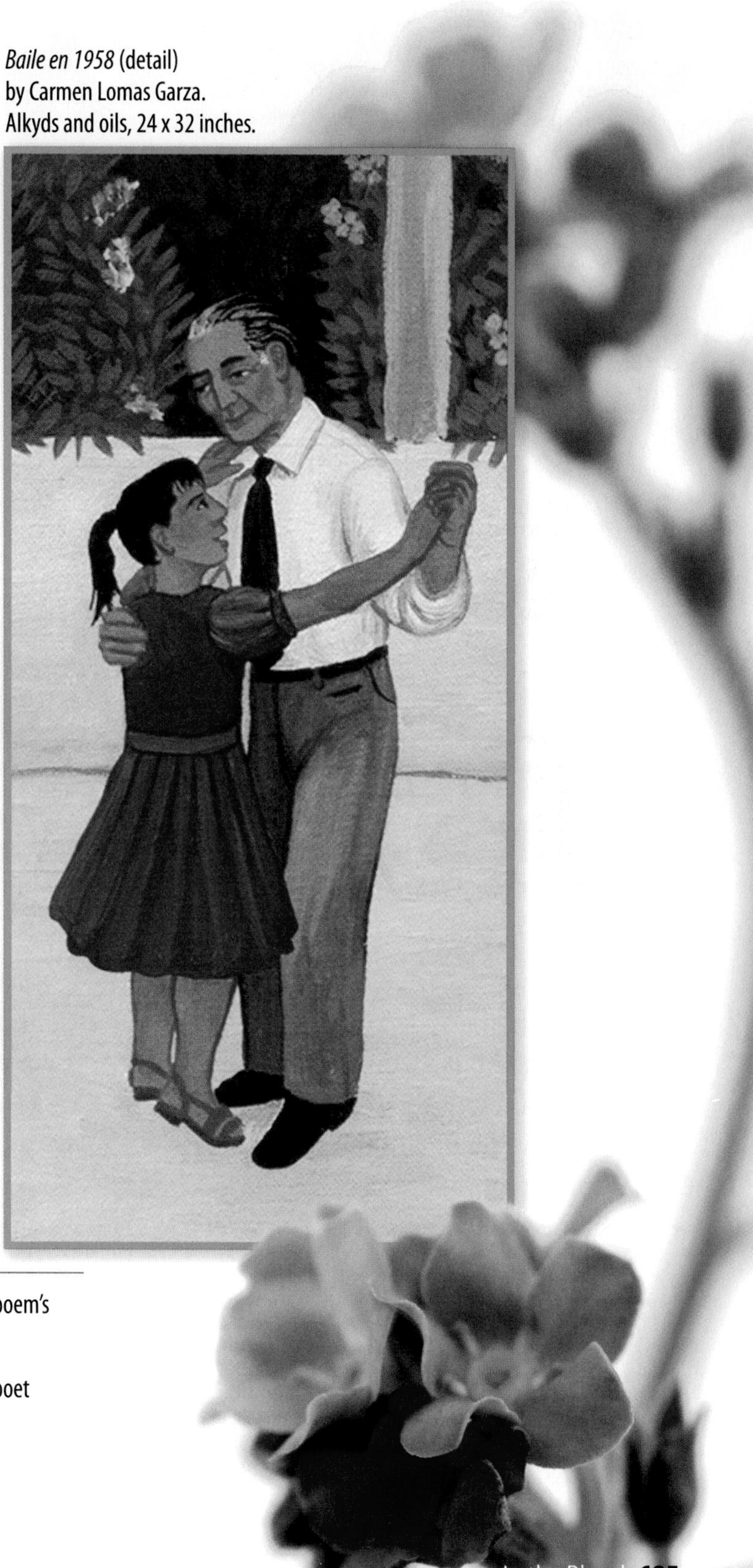

Ⓐ **Reading Focus** **Questioning** What does the poem's title have to do with the rest of the poem?

Ⓑ **Reading Focus** **Questioning** What does the poet mean here?

Read with a Purpose

Read to find out why the speaker is surprised when his father joins in a softball game.

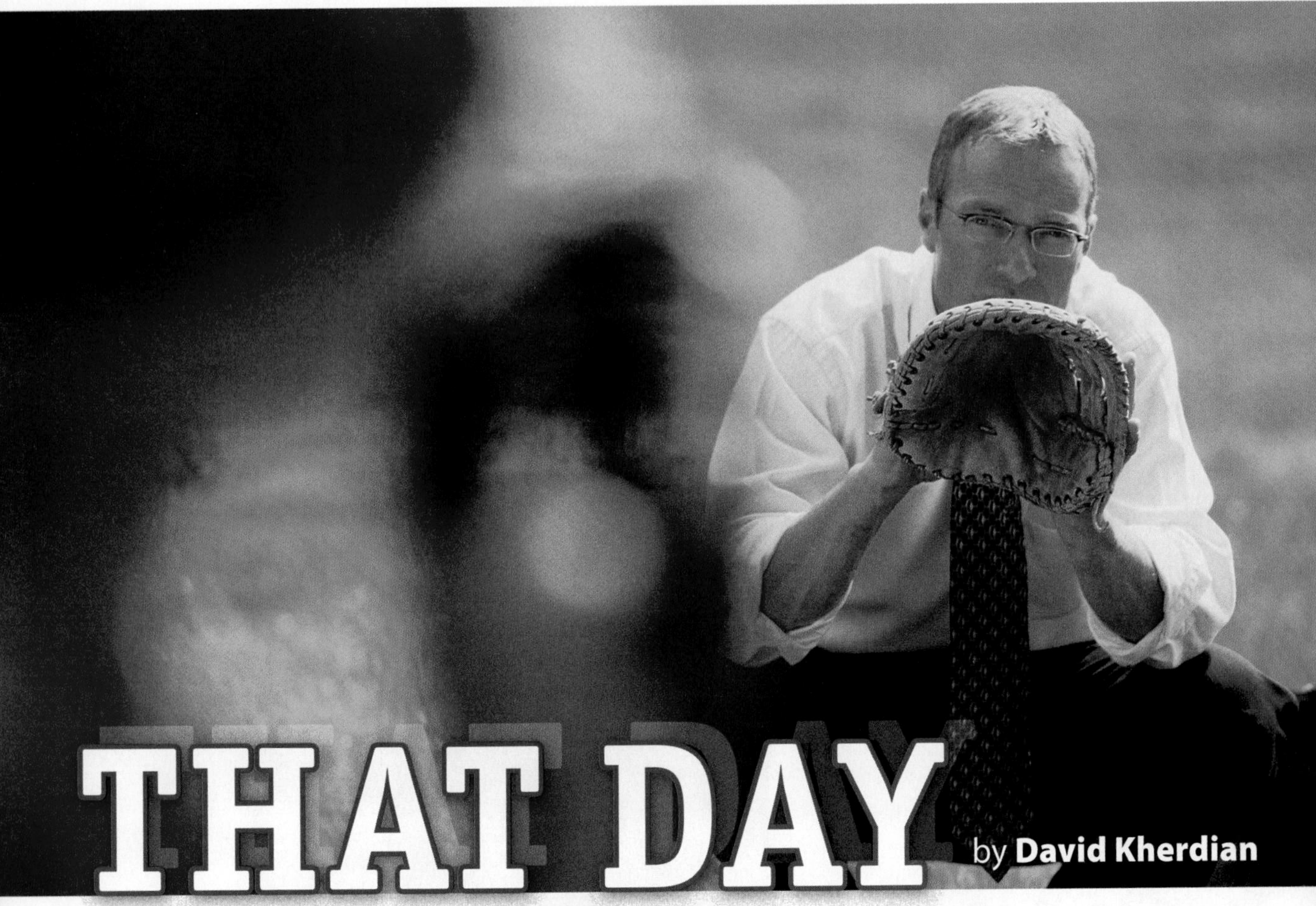

THAT DAY

by **David Kherdian**

Just once
my father stopped on the way
into the house from work
and joined in the softball game
we were having in the street,
and attempted to play in *our*
game that *his* country had never
known. **A**

Just once
and the day stands out forever
in my memory
as a father's living gesture
to his son,
that in playing even the fool
or clown, he would reveal
that the lines of their lives
were sewn from a tougher fabric
than the son had previously known. **B**

A Read and Discuss What is happening in the poem?

B **Reading Focus** **Questioning** What is the "tougher fabric" the speaker is referring to?

Vocabulary **gesture** (JEHS chuhr) *n.:* act performed to show feelings.
previously (PREE vee uhs lee) *adv.:* before now.

About "THAT DAY"

by **David Kherdian**

In many ways my father and I were strangers to each other. At home I was his Armenian son, but in the streets I was an American stranger. I'm putting this a little bluntly. I'm exaggerating. So far as I knew, children did not play games in the Old Country. Therefore I did not believe that he understood any of the games I was involved in. And then, one day, while walking home from work, along the street where we were playing a pick-up game of softball, he stopped and either pitched the ball, or picked up the bat and tried to give the ball a hit. He was *intentionally* participating, he was joining in, and by doing so he was sharing with me something that was of value in my life that I did not believe had any importance in his life. I was deeply touched by this, though why I was touched, or where I was touched, or even how I was touched, was beyond my understanding at the time. Which brings me to poetry and why I write: But that's another story, and has to do with why I wrote *all* of my poems, not just the one you are looking at today. **A**

David Kherdian as a boy.

A **Read and Discuss** David Kherdian did not completely understand his own reaction to his father's gesture. What does that suggest about the reason he writes?

Applying Your Skills

Good Hot Dogs / Yes, It Was My Grandmother / In the Blood / That Day / About "That Day"

Read and Think Critically

Reading Focus

1. What has the speaker of the poem learned from her grandmother's example? FCAT
   - **A** She learned how to make herself happy.
   - **B** She learned how to tame and train wild horses.
   - **C** She learned to cook for her husband and family.
   - **D** She learned to be independent and unconventional.

Read with a Purpose

2. Why do you think the speaker in "Good Hot Dogs" still remembers those hot dogs? What did the grandmother in "Yes, It Was My Grandmother" do for her granddaughter?
3. What can you tell about the child and grandfather's relationship in "In the Blood/En la Sangre"? Support your answer with details from the poem.

Reading Skills: Questioning

4. Review the chart you made. With a partner, discuss the questions you had and work together to answer them. Add a third column to your chart and write your answers.

Observations	Questions	Answers
Maybe Cisneros is still grateful to Kiki because Kiki shared her money to buy them both hot dogs.	Why does Cisneros include the price of the hot dogs?	It helps the reader to guess when the events took place.

Vocabulary Check

5. Use each Vocabulary word in a sentence: **tangles** **gesture** **previously**

Literary Focus

Literary Analysis

6. **Interpret** How does the title "In the Blood" reflect the relationship shared by the child and the grandfather?
7. **Connect** What does the speaker of "That Day" mean by "a father's living gesture"? What "living gestures" might we all find in life?

Literary Skills Review: Tone

8. **Analyze** The speaker's attitude is **tone**—the way the speaker feels about the subject of the poem. You must interpret the speaker's words in order to detect his or her real feelings. How would you describe the tone of each of these poems? Support your answer with details from the poems. READ THINK EXPLAIN

Writing Focus

Think as a Reader/Writer

Use It in Your Writing Use what you learned about when to pause when reading a free-verse poem, and write your own free-verse poem. Use examples of word groupings and punctuation from the poems to create the natural rhythms of everyday speech.

Sunshine State Standards: Benchmarks **LA.6.1.6.1** use new vocabulary that is introduced and taught directly; **LA.6.1.6.3** use context clues to determine meanings of unfamiliar words; **LA.6.1.7.7** compare and contrast elements in multiple texts; **LA.6.1.7.8** use strategies to repair comprehension of grade-appropriate text when self-monitoring indicates confusion, including but not limited to rereading, checking context clues, predicting, note-making, summarizing, using graphic and semantic organizers, questioning, and clarifying by checking other sources; **LA.6.2.1.1** identify the characteristics of various genres (e.g., poetry, fiction, short story, dramatic literature) as forms with distinct characteristics and purpose; **LA.6.2.1.5** develop an interpretation of a selection and support through sustained use of examples and contextual evidence; **LA.6.2.1.7** locate and analyze an author's use of allusions and descriptive, idiomatic, and figurative language in a variety of literary text, identifying how word choice sets the author's tone and advances the work's theme; *Also covered* **LA.6.4.2.3; LA.6.3.5.2**

Vocabulary Development

Context Clues

When you come across an unfamiliar word, try to use the words and sentences around it—its **context**—to make an educated guess about the word's meaning. What clues do you detect in the sentence below that can help you understand the meaning of the word *participating*?

"He was *intentionally* participating; he was joining in, and by doing so he was sharing with me something that was of value."

Your Turn

tangles
gesture
previously

Complete the following sentences with one of the Vocabulary words at right. Circle the context clues that tell you each word's meaning.

1. When it is not packed away neatly, the thread in the sewing kit ____________ and becomes impossible to use.
2. Giving her a present is a ____________ that shows my love for her.
3. I had ____________ thought that I would be able to go to the party, but now, after getting this cold, I cannot.

Academic Vocabulary

Talk About . . .

Discuss with your classmates the poetic devices used by the poets in this section that help create strong visual images for you. What qualities do you most appreciate in these poems that you've just read?

CHOICES

As you respond to the Choices, use these **Academic Vocabulary** words as appropriate: appreciate, detect, device, visual.

REVIEW

Write a Comparison-Contrast Essay

Write an essay in which you compare and contrast the four poems from this section (pages 683–687). Organize your essay this way: **Paragraphs 1 to 4:** Present a key detail from each poem, and discuss what the poem might reveal about the importance of relationships. **Paragraph 5:** Explain which poem you think expresses the most powerful feelings about relationships. Cite examples from the poem.

CONNECT

Write About the Speaker

Timed Writing From the four poems you have just read, choose one you especially appreciate and relate to. Write a paragraph about what you learned about the speaker of the poem. Is the speaker the same as the writer? Use evidence from the poem to support your views.

EXTEND

Make a Poetic Collage

Create a collage that describes, in visual form, a point you want to make about human relationships. The collage can be made up of various items you have collected, not just pictures. Arrange the different items together in an interesting way. How is your collage like a poem?

Learn It Online
For more on context clues, try *WordSharp:*
go.hrw.com
L6-689
Go

Images in Poetry

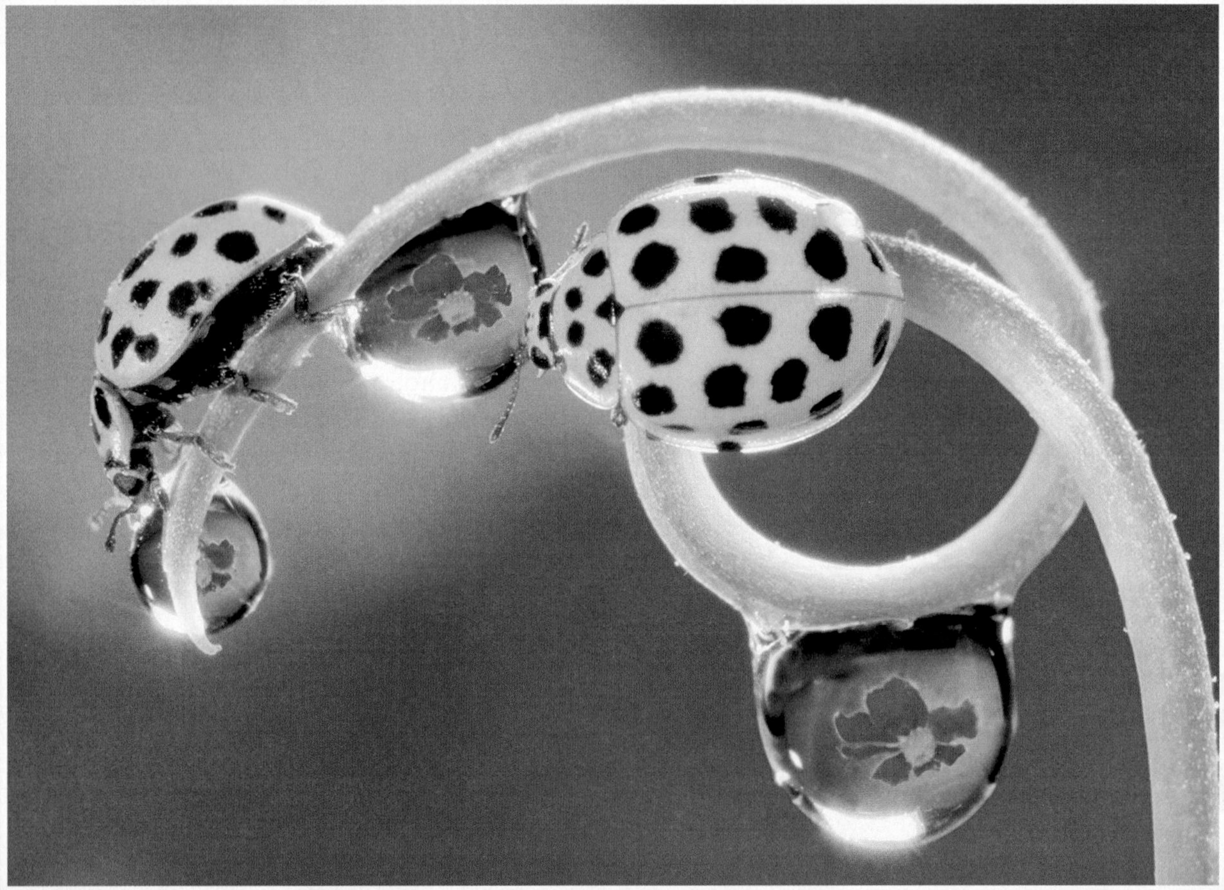

CONTENTS

What Do You Think?

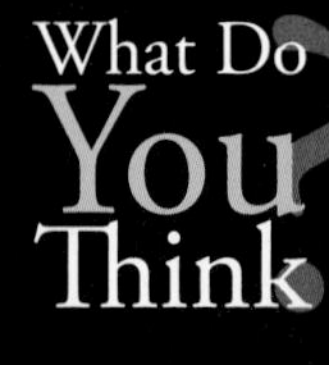

How can the simple details of everyday life make good subjects for poems?

QuickWrite

Write down three things you saw or did on the way to school today—no matter how simple or unimportant they may seem to you. Choose one of the three, and describe it using two or more images.

Sunshine State Standards: Benchmarks
LA.6.1.6.9 determine the correct meaning of words with multiple meanings in context; *Also covered* **LA.6.1.7.8; LA.6.2.1.3; LA.6.2.1.7**

POEMS

Preparing to Read

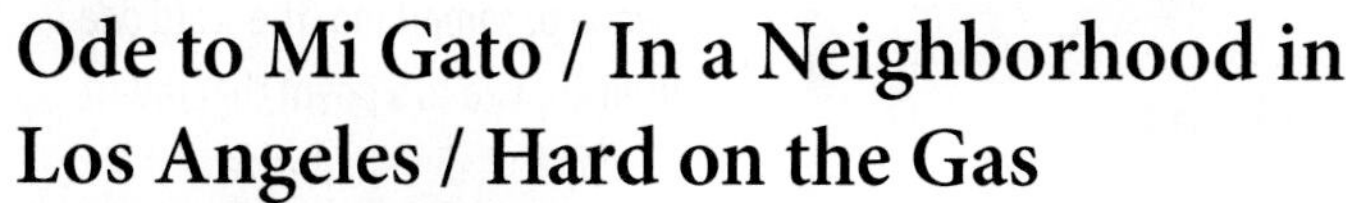

Reader/Writer Notebook

Use your **RWN** to complete the activities for these selections.

Ode to Mi Gato / In a Neighborhood in Los Angeles / Hard on the Gas

Literary Focus

Figurative Language Language that describes one thing in terms of something else is called **figurative language.** When Gary Soto describes his white cat leaping from a tree "Like a splash of / Milk," he is using a kind of figurative language called a **simile.** Look for other examples of figurative language, such as **personification** and **metaphors,** in these poems. (See Figurative Language, p. 646.)

Tone **Tone** refers to the way the speaker (the voice talking to you in the poem) seems to feel about his or her subject. When you read a poem, pay special attention to words that may hint at the tone.

Literary Perspectives Apply the literary perspective described on page 693 as you read "Ode to Mi Gato."

Vocabulary

Ode to Mi Gato

dribble (DRIHB uhl) *n.:* irregular drops that flow slowly. *The cat loved to lick the dribble of milk that came out of old milk cartons.*

dangled (DANG guhld) *v.:* held something or swung it loosely. *The speaker dangled a sock in front of his cat.*

abandoned (uh BAN duhnd) *adj.:* not used or taken care of any longer. *The speaker of the poem found the cat on an abandoned car.*

Hard on the Gas

clutch (kluhch) *v.:* hold something tightly. *When she would clutch the rail in fear, her grandfather knew she needed encouragement.*

Reading Focus

Re-reading Read each poem straight through to get the sense of it. Then, re-read the poem to clarify your understanding.

Into Action Set up a chart like the one below. As you read each poem, keep track of words, lines, or sections you want to re-read.

"Ode to Mi Gato"	"In a Neighborhood in Los Angeles"	"Hard on the Gas"
Line 13	Fish canneries?	"bar above your right shoulder"?
Line 27, "Porque"	lines 28-30	

Language Coach

Multiple-Meaning Words Two of the words above can be used as both a verb and a noun. Can you find them? Use a dictionary if necessary.

Writing Focus

Find It in Your Reading Look for words the speaker uses to express emotions toward the subject. What can you infer about the speaker's feelings? In your *Reader/Writer Notebook,* jot down notes.

Learn It Online
For a preview of "Ode to Mi Gato," see the introductory video at:

go.hrw.com L6-691 

MEET THE WRITERS

Learn It Online
Get more on Soto's life at:
go.hrw.com L6-692 Go

Gary Soto
(1952–)

Gary Soto grew up in a Mexican American family in California's San Joaquin Valley. He dreamed of being a hobo, a geographer, a priest, and a paleontologist. He was not a very good student until he discovered poetry in college. Soon afterward, he yearned to become a writer—to recapture the world of his childhood in words. Soto has won awards and widespread recognition for his poems, short stories, and novels.

Francisco X. Alarcón
(1954–)

Francisco X. Alarcón, who grew up in the United States and in Mexico, says that his family has belonged to two countries for four generations. Alarcón's roots are important to him. He regularly visits the Mexican village where his ancestors lived. Alarcón was brought up mainly in Los Angeles by his grandmother, the woman he celebrates in his poem "In a Neighborhood in Los Angeles."

Janet S. Wong
(1962–)

Janet S. Wong bases many of her poems on her experiences growing up as an Asian American. Wong decided to become a poet after working as a lawyer for several years. For Wong, "Poetry is, in a way, like shouting. Since you can't yell at the top of your lungs for a long time, you have to decide what you really need to say, and say it quickly."

Think About the Writers

Why do you think these poets use childhood experiences as subject matter?

Build Background

Gary Soto's poem "Ode to Mi Gato" is a special form of poetry called an **ode**—a poem written to honor or celebrate someone or something. The word *ode* is often applied to a poem that is written in a grand, dignified style and is dedicated to an important subject, such as a famous person. Soto, though, takes a playful approach with his ode, using ordinary language and the rhythms of everyday speech to celebrate an ordinary but much-loved cat.

Preview the Selections

The speaker of "Ode to Mi Gato" describes his relationship with his cat over time.

The speaker of "In a Neighborhood in Los Angeles" fondly recalls the Mexican grandmother who raised him.

"Hard on the Gas" describes a young girl's reaction to her grandfather's driving and how it taught her a lesson about life.

Read with a Purpose Read this poem to discover why a white cat is special to the speaker.

Ode to Mi Gato

by **Gary Soto**

He's white
As spilled milk,
My cat who sleeps
With his belly
Turned toward
The summer sky.
He loves the sun,
Its warmth like a hand.
He loves tuna cans
And milk cartons
With their dribble
Of milk. He loves
Mom when she rattles
The bag of cat food,
The brown nuggets
Raining into his bowl. **A**
And my cat loves
Me, because I saved
Him from a dog,
Because I dressed him
In a hat and a cape
For Halloween, **B**

Literary Perspectives

Analyzing Responses to Literature A literary work isn't like a locked box that a reader needs a special key to unlock; it's more like a door that any reader's key can open. What lies behind the door differs a bit for every reader and depends on what the reader brings along. One thing that all readers bring to their reading is their own experience, which will cause them to see or feel different things in a text. Let's say you have a pet. As you read this poem, you might compare your relationship with your pet to Soto's relationship with his cat. Your interpretation of the poem will be influenced by how you appreciate pets. As you read, pay attention to the notes and questions in the text, which will guide you in using this perspective.

A **Read and Discuss** What is the speaker telling you?

B **Literary Perspectives** **Analyzing Responses to Literature** What helps you understand the speaker's feelings?

Vocabulary **dribble** (DRIHB uhl) *n.:* irregular drops that flow slowly.

Analyzing Visuals

Viewing and Interpreting How is the cat in this painting similar to or different from Soto's cat in the poem?

Cat Lying on Yellow Cushion by Franz Marc.

Because I dangled
A sock of chicken skin
As he stood on his
Hind legs. I love mi gato,
Porque I found
Him on the fender
Of an abandoned car.
He was a kitten,
With a meow
Like the rusty latch
On a gate. I carried
Him home in the loop
Of my arms.
I poured milk
Into him, let him
Lick chunks of
Cheese from my palms,
And cooked huevo
After huevo
Until his purring
Engine kicked in
And he cuddled
Up to my father's slippers. **C**
That was last year.
This spring,
He's excellent at sleeping
And no good
At hunting. At night
All the other cats
In the neighborhood
Can see him slink
Around the corner,
Or jump from the tree
Like a splash of
Milk. We lap up
His love and
He laps up his welcome. **D**

C **Read and Discuss** So far, what have you learned about the speaker and his cat?

D **Literary Focus** **Figurative Language** How has the comparison between the white cat and milk been developed?

Vocabulary **dangled** (DANG guhld) *v.:* held something or swung it loosely.
abandoned (uh BAN duhnd) *adj.:* not used or taken care of any longer.

Read with a Purpose Read this poem to experience the speaker's fond memories of his grandmother.

In a Neighborhood in Los Angeles

by **Francisco X. Alarcón**

I learned
Spanish
from my grandma

mijito°
don't cry
she'd tell me

on the mornings
my parents
would leave

to work
at the fish
canneries

---

4. ***mijito*** (mee HEE toh): contraction of *mi hijito,* Spanish for "my little child."

my grandma
would chat
with chairs

sing them
old
songs
dance
waltzes with them
in the kitchen **A**

when she'd say
niño barrigón°
she'd laugh

with my grandma
I learned
to count clouds

to point out
in flowerpots
mint leaves

my grandma
wore moons
on her dress

Mexico's mountains
deserts
ocean
in her eyes
I'd see them
in her braids

I'd touch them
in her voice
smell them

one day
I was told:
she went far away

but still
I feel her
with me **B**

whispering
in my ear
mijito **C**

---

23. ***niño barrigón*** (NEEN yo bah ree GOHN): Spanish for "potbellied boy."

A **Reading Focus** **Re-reading** Look at this section again. Why do you think the grandmother chats, sings, and dances with chairs?

B **Read and Discuss** What is the speaker letting you know?

C **Literary Focus** **Tone** What is the tone of the poem's ending?

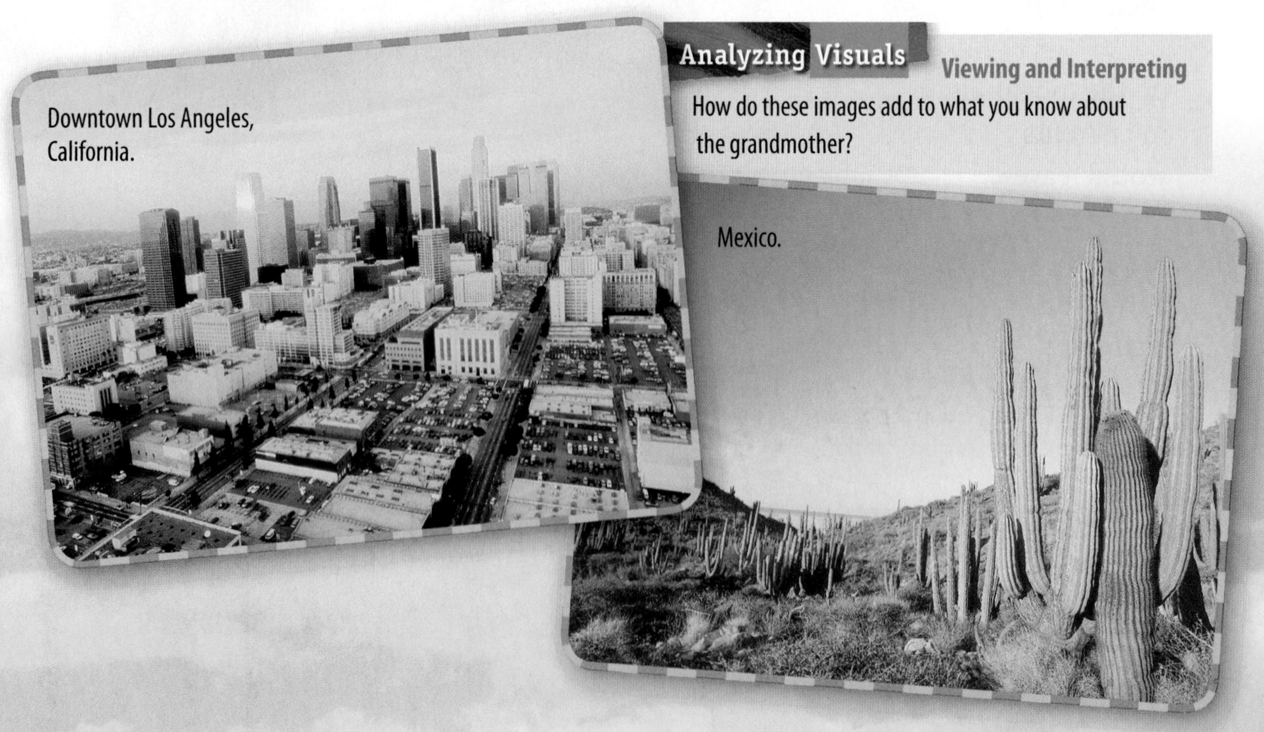

Downtown Los Angeles, California.

Mexico.

Analyzing Visuals **Viewing and Interpreting**

How do these images add to what you know about the grandmother?

Read with a Purpose Read this poem to find out what the speaker learns from her grandfather's driving.

HARD ON THE GAS

by **Janet S. Wong**

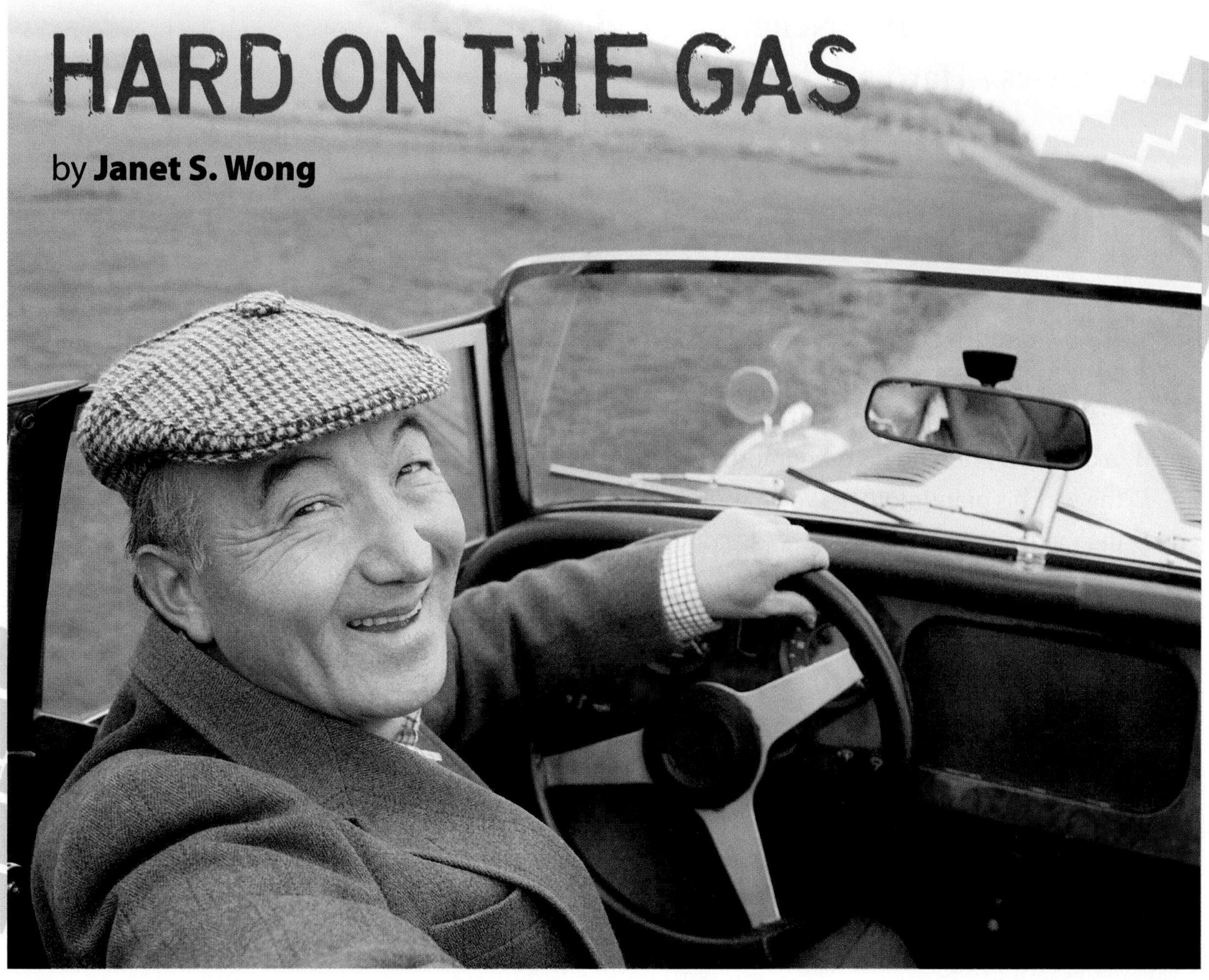

My grandfather taught himself
    to drive **A**
rough, the way he learned to live,

push the pedal, hard on the gas,
rush up to 50,
coast a bit,
rush, rest, rush, rest— **B**

When you clutch the bar above your
    right shoulder
he shoots you a look that asks,
Who said the ride would
    be smooth? **C**

A Reading Focus Re-reading Why do you think the poet broke this line after "drive"? How does pausing at the end of this line change the meaning of the section?

B Literary Focus Tone What do you learn from the way the speaker describes her grandfather's driving?

C Read and Discuss Now what has happened? What does the speaker's grandfather think of her actions?

Vocabulary **clutch** (kluhch) *v.:* hold something tightly.

Applying Your Skills

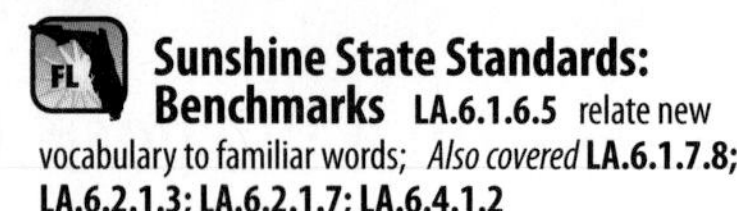

Sunshine State Standards: Benchmarks LA.6.1.6.5 relate new vocabulary to familiar words; *Also covered* **LA.6.1.7.8; LA.6.2.1.3; LA.6.2.1.7; LA.6.4.1.2**

Ode to Mi Gato / In a Neighborhood in Los Angeles / Hard on the Gas

Respond and Think Critically

Reading Focus

1. What is the speaker describing when he says, "I'd touch them in her voice"?
   A the heritage his grandmother shared
   B a geography lesson his grandmother gave
   C the way his grandmother's voice sounds
   D the family's homesickness for Mexico

Read with a Purpose

2. What do you learn about each poem's speaker from the way he or she describes the subject of the poem?

Reading Skills: Re-reading

3. Review the notes you took while reading the poems. Now make notes about what you learned after re-reading them.

"Ode to Mi Gato"	"In a Neighborhood in Los Angeles"	"Hard on the Gas"
Line 13: The speaker might be a child, since he talks about Mom.	Fish canneries? A place where fish are processed and canned	"bar above your right shoulder?" bar for hangers

✓ Vocabulary Check

Match each of the numbered words below with a synonym on the right:

4. **dribble** — **a.** grab
5. **dangled** — **b.** deserted
6. **abandoned** — **c.** trickle
7. **clutch** — **d.** swung

Literary Focus

Literary Analysis

8. **Literary Perspectives** How did personal experience help you appreciate the feelings expressed in "Ode to Mi Gato"?

Literary Skills: Figurative Language and Tone

READ THINK EXPLAIN

9. **Analyze** How is personification—making something that is not human seem human—used in "In a Neighborhood in Los Angeles"? Support your answer with details from the poem.
10. **Analyze** An extended metaphor can carry a comparison through an entire poem. Explain the extended metaphor in "Hard on the Gas."
11. **Analyze** For each poem, think of a word or two that describe the speaker's tone, or the way he or she feels about the subject.

Writing Focus

Think as a Reader/Writer

Use It in Your Writing In each poem, the author describes his or her feelings about a person or thing. Write your own poem expressing a speaker's feelings about a person or thing.

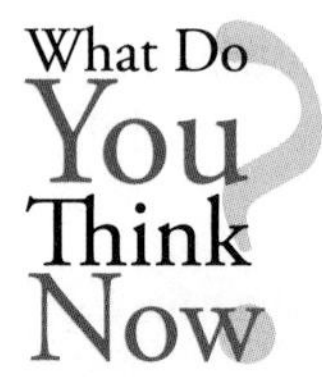

What important things do poets celebrate by describing everyday events?

POEMS

Preparing to Read

Sunshine State Standards: Benchmarks **LA.6.1.5.1** adjust reading rate based on purpose, text difficulty, form, and style; **LA.6.1.6.4** categorize key vocabulary and identify salient features; *Also covered* **LA.6.2.1.7**

Poem / Motto

Use your **RWN** to complete the activities for these selections.

Literary Focus

Tone **Tone** is the attitude a speaker takes toward a subject. On the page, poets can't use their voices, facial expressions, or body language to express their attitudes. Instead, they create tone through rhythm and meter, figurative language, line length, word choice, punctuation, capital letters—even the way lines break.

Reading Focus

Reading Fluency and Reading Rate **Reading fluency** is how easily and well you read. It means that you are able to read with expression, pausing and stopping appropriately. It means that you know how to adjust your **reading rate**—how quickly or slowly you read something.

Into Action With a partner, take turns reading this sentence aloud: "I *won*!" Use your voice to express the joyfulness in the words. Notice how italics, which indicate emphasis, and punctuation suggest the tone. Now try saying the same words with doubt: "*I* won?" Now try saying them with sarcasm: "I *won*?"

Refer to the list of tones below as you read "Poem" and "Motto" aloud to one or more listeners. Which tones would you match with "Poem"? with "Motto"? Which do not apply to either poem?

sad	bitter	defiant
upbeat	desperate	boastful
sarcastic	wistful	joyful
	sorrowful	

Writing Focus

Find It in Your Reading How are the tones of "Poem" and "Motto" alike or different? In your *Reader/Writer Notebook*, list the words and lines that most contribute to each poem's tone.

Vocabulary

motto (MAHT oh) *n.:* short statement that expresses the aims or beliefs of a person or institution. *The boy had a catchy motto for his philosophy of living.*

Language Coach

Slang Slang is informal, nonstandard language, usually spoken by members of a group who share some common bond. Slang usually changes frequently; a term popular in one time period may seem dated or may even be forgotten in a few years. In "Motto," Langston Hughes uses slang words popular with jazz musicians of his time, including *cool* and *dig.* (In fact, one word he uses—*jive*—is another word for *slang*.) Which of these slang words survive today? What slang words used today do you think will still be around years from now?

Learn It Online

Listen for the tone in these poems through the audio versions online:

go.hrw.com L6-699 

Get more on the author's life and work at:
go.hrw.com L6-700 Go

Langston Hughes

(1902–1967)

Langston Hughes was a lonely child until he found a home in the world of books. Hughes wrote his first poem in elementary school—but only *after* his classmates had elected him class poet:

"[My class] had elected all the class officers, but there was no one in our class who looked like a poet, or had ever written a poem. . . . The day I was elected, I went home and wondered what I should write. Since we had eight teachers in our school, I thought there should be one verse for each teacher, with an especially good one for my favorite teacher. I felt the class should have eight, too. So my first poem was about the longest poem I ever wrote—sixteen verses, which were later cut down. In the first half of the poem, I said that our school had the finest teachers there ever were. And in the latter half, I said our class was the greatest class ever graduated. So at graduation, when I read the poem, naturally everybody applauded loudly. That was the way I began to write poetry."

Hughes grew up in the Midwest, but he eventually moved to New York City, where he became a leading figure in the cultural movement known as the Harlem Renaissance. His poems often echo the rhythms of blues and jazz.

Think About the Writer

Why might a poet such as Hughes be drawn to the rhythms of blues and jazz?

The Granger Collection, New York.

Read with a Purpose Read this poem to learn how the speaker feels about a friend who is no longer around.

Poem

by **Langston Hughes**

I loved my friend.
He went away from me.
There's nothing more to say.
The poem ends,
Soft as it began—
I loved my friend. Ⓐ Ⓑ

Ⓐ **Literary Focus** **Tone** How would you describe the speaker's attitude in this poem?

Ⓑ **Read and Discuss** Sometimes we learn not by what is said, but by what is *not* said. How does the speaker convey his feelings more powerfully by *not* telling us everything?

Analyzing Visuals

Viewing and Interpreting Does this image convey the same tone, or mood, as Hughes's poem? Explain.

Witness (1987) by Hughie Lee-Smith. Courtesy, June Kelly Gallery, New York. Art © Estate of Hughie Lee-Smith/Licensed by VAGA, New York, NY.

Read with a Purpose Read this poem to discover the speaker's motto—the idea he lives by.

Motto

by **Langston Hughes**

I play it cool
And dig all jive.
That's the reason
I stay alive. **A**

My motto,
As I live and learn,
is:
Dig And Be Dug
In Return. **B**

A **Literary Focus** **Tone** How would you describe the speaker's attitude here?

B **Reading Focus** **Reading Fluency and Reading Rate** How would you say these lines?

Vocabulary **motto** (MAHT oh) *n.:* short statement that expresses the aims or beliefs of a person or institution.

Analyzing Visuals

Viewing and Interpreting How does this painting match the tone of the poem?

Cool Hand by Gil Mayers.

Applying Your Skills

Sunshine State Standards: Benchmarks **LA.6.1.5.1** adjust reading rate based on purpose, text difficulty, form, and style; **LA.6.1.6.1** use new vocabulary that is introduced and taught directly; *Also covered* **LA.6.1.6.10; LA.6.2.1.3; LA.6.2.1.7; LA.6.4.1.2**

Poem / Motto

Respond and Think Critically

Reading Focus

1. How does the repeated line in "Poem" affect the poem's tone? FCAT
   - **A** It emphasizes the speaker's longing for his friend.
   - **B** It emphasizes the speaker's anger.
   - **C** It emphasizes the friend's happiness.
   - **D** It emphasizes the friend's feelings for the speaker.

Read with a Purpose

2. In "Poem," how does the speaker feel about the friend? In "Motto," what is the speaker's motto, or the idea he lives by?

Reading Focus: Reading Fluency and Reading Rate

3. What tone, or tones, from the list on page 699 did you identify for "Poem"? for "Motto"? When you read each poem aloud, how did you express the tone?

Vocabulary Check

4. Is the Boy Scout saying "Be prepared" a **motto**? Why or why not?
5. What kinds of institutions might have a **motto**?

Literary Focus

Literary Analysis

6. **Connect** In "Motto," what does "playing it cool" allow the speaker to do? What benefits could come from this attitude? What might be a negative aspect of such an attitude?

Literary Skills: Tone

7. **Analyze** In "Poem," Hughes repeats a line twice. How does this affect the poem's tone?
8. **Analyze** You may know what the speaker in "Motto" means when he says, "I play it cool." What do *dig* and *jive* mean? (Use a dictionary if you need to.) Try rephrasing "Motto," substituting different words for *cool, dig,* and *jive.* What happens to the tone of the poem?

Literary Skills Review: Speaker

9. **Analyze** Think about the "I" in "Motto." What do you know about this speaker? Support your answer with details from the poem.

Writing Focus

Think as a Reader/Writer

Use It in Your Writing Review your notes on these poems. Use what you learned to write a short poem with a strong and consistent tone. You may want to write about your own motto.

What Do You Think Now? How do these short poems convey strong feelings with few words?

Sunshine State Standards: Benchmarks
LA.6.1.6.9 determine the correct meaning of words with multiple meanings in context; Also covered LA.6.1.7.8; LA.6.2.1.1; LA.6.2.1.7

POEMS Preparing to Read

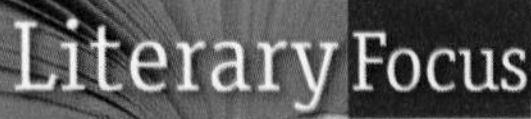

Haiku

Reader/Writer Notebook

Use your **RWN** to complete the activities for these selections.

Literary Focus

Haiku and Imagery **Haiku** (HY koo) is a Japanese poetry form with a strict traditional structure. Each haiku consists of three lines and seventeen syllables: five syllables each in lines 1 and 3 and seven syllables in line 2. Haiku relies on precise **imagery**—word pictures, or **sensory details,** that appeal to all our senses.

Word Choice In haiku, poets must pack meaning into just a few phrases, so choosing just the right word is essential.

Reading Focus

Questioning Asking questions as you read will help you get the most out of each haiku.

Into Action For each haiku, make a chart like the one below. The questions refer to the traditional content that haiku poets generally put in their poems. (See Build Background, p. 705.)

Title: "An old silent pond"

What specific things does the haiku deal with?	pond; frog
What are the sensory images?	Sight—pond; frog jumps Sound—silence; splash; silence
What are the contrasting images?	
What season is being described?	
What feeling or discovery about life is made?	

Writing Focus

Find It in Your Reading In your *Reader/Writer Notebook*, note words in these haiku that suggest what season is being described.

Vocabulary

balmy (BAH mee) *adj.:* weather or air that is warm and pleasant. *The balmy wind felt good as the man sat outdoors, thinking.*

recall (rih KAWL) *v.:* remember; bring to mind. *The speaker could not recall the memory the wind stirred up.*

Language Coach

Shades of Meaning **Synonyms** are words with the same or nearly the same meaning. For example, *stone* and *rock* are synonyms. Synonyms are not always interchangeable, though; there are usually shades of meaning that make them a bit different from each other. For example, the vocabulary word *balmy* above refers to warm and pleasant weather, often involving a mild breeze. The words *calm* and *mild* have similar meanings, but only *balmy* suggests a pleasant breeze. Be aware of such shades of meaning when you choose synonyms.

Learn It Online

Build vocabulary skills and increase learning comprehension at:

go.hrw.com L6-704 

MEET THE WRITERS

Matsuo Bashō and Nozawa Bonchō

(1644–1694) (16??–1714)

Matsuo Bashō is one of Japan's most famous poets. He took his pen name from a banana tree (*bashō* in Japanese) that he planted in his yard. Bashō was born into a wealthy family and grew up in a village in western Japan. He began writing verse when he was nine. By the time Bashō was thirty, he was traveling around Japan as a professional poetry teacher.

Nozawa Bonchō was one of Bashō's students. Many of the haiku written by Bashō and his students were inspired by the natural world. Bashō encouraged students like Bonchō to look for the "true nature of things," insisting that haiku should be written in simple language and deal with everyday life.

Ōshima Ryōta

(1707–1787)

Ōshima Ryōta wrote haiku and created paintings inspired by Zen, a form of Buddhism that emphasizes meditation and oneness with nature.

Richard Wright

(1908–1960)

Modern poets in many countries have written haiku, finding beauty and discipline in the form. **Richard Wright,** an African American writer famous for his autobiography *Black Boy,* composed more than four thousand haiku in the two years before his death.

Think About the Writers

Why do you think these writers wanted to write haiku? What is special about the form?

Build Background

Haiku follows strict rules, not just in form but in content. Here are some rules that haiku poets generally follow when crafting their poems:

1. A haiku is about a simple moment in daily life.
2. A haiku describes particular things, often two contrasting things.
3. A haiku records a moment of enlightenment—a sudden discovery of a truth about life.
4. A haiku is usually about a particular season of the year. Often a haiku contains a *kigo*, or "season word," like *frog* for summer or *willow* for spring.

Preview the Selections

In "An old silent pond," the sudden splash of a frog disturbs the peaceful silence of a pond. "Winter rain" presents an image of a warmly lighted farmhouse as seen from the outside through winter rain. "Bad-tempered, I got back" suggests that the poet's mood improves when he sees the willow tree in his yard. In "A balmy spring wind," a memory is brought back to the poet by the caress of a warm spring breeze.

Read with a Purpose Read these haiku to see how skilled poets can convey powerful sensory images in just three lines.

Night Rain at Oyama by Utagawa Toyokuni.

Haiku

An old silent pond . . .
A frog jumps into the pond,
splash! Silence again. **A**
—Matsuo Bashō

Winter rain:
A farmhouse piled with firewood,
A light in the window. **B**
—Nozawa Bonchō

Bad-tempered, I got back:
Then, in the garden,
The willow tree. **C**
—Ōshima Ryōta

A **Read and Discuss** What visual images do you see when you read this?

B **Literary Focus** **Haiku and Imagery** Think about the author's use of three separate images. How do these images combine to create one picture in your mind?

C **Reading Focus** **Questioning** What questions do you have after reading this poem?

Analyzing Visuals **Viewing and Interpreting** Which haiku captures the moment in time shown in this picture?

A balmy spring wind
Reminding me of something
I cannot recall **D**
—Richard Wright

D **Literary Focus** **Word Choice** The author uses the words *reminding* and *recall.* What state of mind do these words suggest?

Vocabulary **balmy** (BAH mee) *adj.:* weather or air that is warm and pleasant.
recall (rih KAWL) *v.:* remember; bring to mind.

Applying Your Skills

Haiku

Respond and Think Critically

Reading Focus

1. What is the significance of the willow tree in "Bad-tempered, I got back"? **FCAT**
   - **A** The willow tree has bloomed unexpectedly.
   - **B** The willow tree has died, and this makes the speaker upset.
   - **C** The willow tree is the reason for the speaker's bad mood.
   - **D** The willow tree is so beautiful that it changes the speaker's mood.

Read with a Purpose

2. What images formed in your mind as you read these haiku? Were you surprised by how much information short poems can convey?

Reading Skills: Questioning

3. Look at the chart you made. Try to answer any questions. Then, compare your chart with a friend's and discuss your ideas.

Title: "An old silent pond"

What specific things does the haiku deal with?	pond; frog
What are the sensory images?	Sight—pond; frog jumps Sound—silence; splash; silence
What are the contrasting images?	splash and silence
What season is being described?	probably summer "Frog" is a season word for summer.
What feeling or discovery about life is made?	A little thing can seem big when you focus on it.

Vocabulary Check

Write a sentence using each of these Vocabulary words in context:

4. **balmy**
5. **recall**

Literary Focus

Literary Analysis

6. **Analyze** Which haiku contain contrasting images? What do these contrasts reveal? Support your answer with details from the poems. 

Literary Skills: Word Choice and Haiku

7. **Interpret** Describe the tone of one haiku. Which words in the haiku suggest this tone?
8. **Draw Conclusions** In each haiku, what discovery does the speaker make? What role does nature play in each discovery? Support your answer with details from the poems. READ THINK EXPLAIN

Writing Focus

Think as a Reader/Writer

Use It in Your Writing Look at the examples of *kigo*, or "season words," that you wrote. Write your own haiku about a season, using a *kigo*.

What did these haiku teach you about what makes a good subject for poetry?

Sunshine State Standards: Benchmarks **LA.6.1.6.1** use new vocabulary that is introduced and taught directly; **LA.6.1.6.6** distinguish denotative and connotative meanings of words; **LA.6.1.7.8** use strategies to repair comprehension of grade-appropriate text when self-monitoring indicates confusion, including but not limited to rereading, checking context clues, predicting, note-making, summarizing, using graphic and semantic organizers, questioning, and clarifying by checking other sources; **LA.6.2.1.7** locate and analyze an author's use of allusions and descriptive, idiomatic, and figurative language in a variety of literary text, identifying how word choice sets the author's tone and advances the work's theme; **LA.6.4.1.2** write a variety of expressive forms (e.g., short play, song lyrics, historical fiction, limericks) that employ figurative language, rhythm, dialogue, characterization, and/or appropriate format; **LA.6.4.2.1** write in a variety of informational/expository forms (e.g., summaries, procedures, instructions, experiments, rubrics, how-to manuals, assembly instructions); **LA.6.5.2.2** deliver narrative and informative presentations, including oral responses to literature, and adjust oral language, body language, eye contact, gestures, technology, and supporting graphics appropriate to the situation.

Vocabulary Development

Connotations and Denotations

Why do we call the president's wife the *First Lady* instead of the *First Woman*? *Woman* and *lady* have similar **denotations,** or dictionary meanings, but different connotations. **Connotations** are the feelings and ideas that have become attached to certain words. Can you detect the difference between the connotations of *woman* and *lady? Woman* refers to any adult female, but *lady* suggests a woman who is cultured and sophisticated.

A word's connotations can be positive or negative. A word with positive connotations calls up good associations; a word with negative connotations calls up bad associations.

"I am careful; you are thrifty; he is stingy": This old saying shows how words with related meanings can have very different connotations.

Your Turn

You may use a dictionary to answer the following questions.

1. Would you rather be considered *clever* or *cunning*? Why?
2. Would people laugh more at a *hilarious* joke than at an *amusing* one? Why or why not?

Academic Vocabulary

Write About . . .

Which poem in this section did you most appreciate? Was there a particular literary device that made the poem stand out for you? What was the strongest visual image in the poem? Write your thoughts.

CHOICES

As you respond to the Choices, use these **Academic Vocabulary** words as appropriate: appreciate, detect, device, visual.

REVIEW

Prepare a Poetry Reading

Listening and Speaking Prepare one of the poems you have just read in this section for oral presentation. Make a script for the poem. Check punctuation, and mark the points where you'll pause. Underline the words or lines you'll emphasize. Decide what tone, or attitude, you want to convey. Read your poem to an audience.

CONNECT

Write About Poetry

Timed Writing Write a paragraph or two in response to this statement: "Good poetry can be about anything, from old socks to an ordinary person no one ever heard of. Poetry can make even the most common, everyday things seem beautiful and important." In your response, use examples from the poems you have read.

EXTEND

Organize a Poetry Collection

Group Work Start a class poetry collection. Ask each person to bring to class at least one poem that he or she especially likes. Build the poetry collection until there is enough for a classroom booklet. Decide how to organize the collection and how to present it. Make a special section for original poems written by students.

Learn It Online
There's more to these poems than meets the eye. Expand your view at:
go.hrw.com L6-709 Go

Comparing Extended Metaphors

CONTENTS

How do comparisons help us better understand or <u>appreciate</u> the qualities of things we're comparing?

QuickWrite

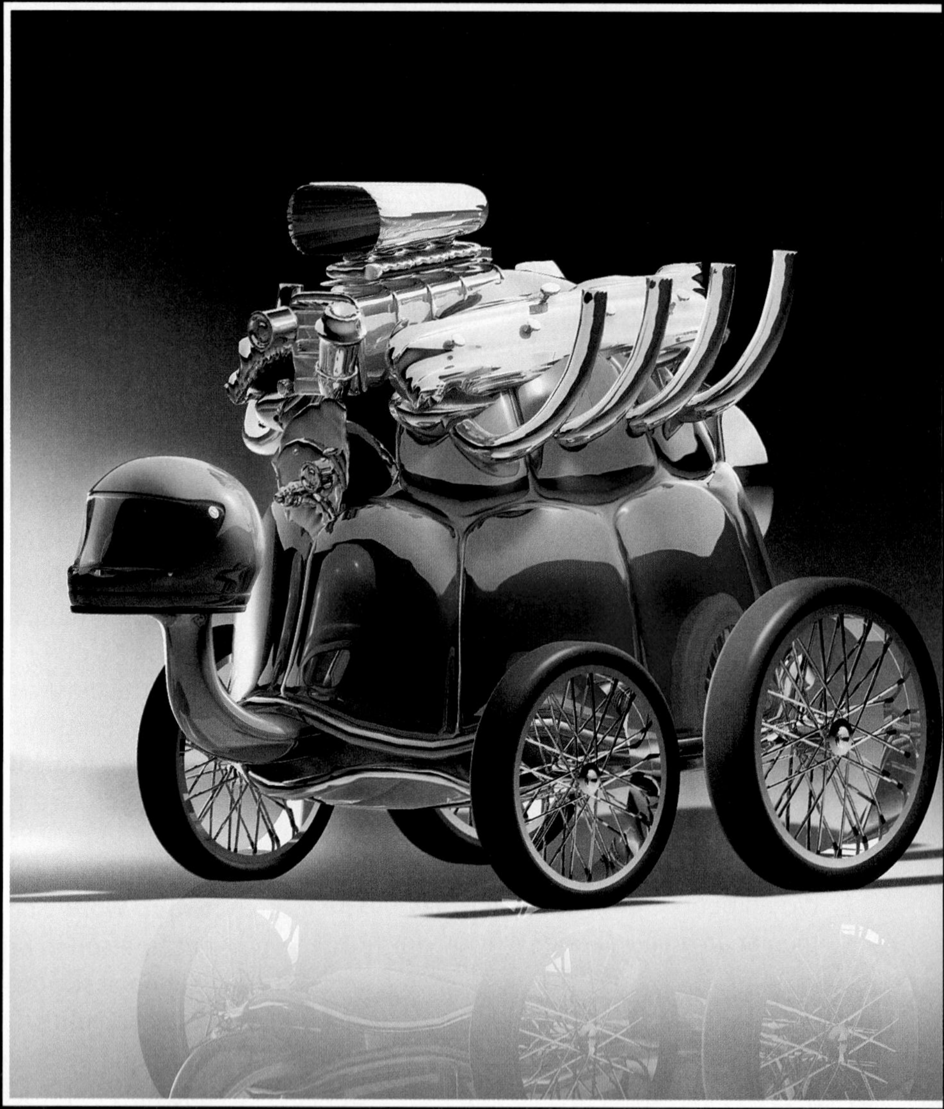

We often refer to nonliving objects as if they were alive: A car engine "purrs," for instance. Think of other, similar comparisons. Why do we make such comparisons?

Preparing to Read

Sunshine State Standards: Benchmarks
LA.6.1.6.9 determine the correct meaning of words with multiple meanings in context; **LA.6.1.6.10** determine meanings of words, pronunciation, parts of speech, etymologies, and alternate word choices by using a dictionary, thesaurus, and digital tools; *Also covered* **LA.6.1.7.7; LA.6.2.1.3**

The Toaster / Steam Shovel / The Sidewalk Racer / Things to Do If You Are a Subway

Literary Focus

Extended Metaphor A **metaphor** is a figure of speech, a direct comparison of two unlike things, as in the statement "You are my sunshine." Metaphors say that something *is* something else. An **extended metaphor** carries the comparison through several lines or even through an entire work: "You are my sunshine. Your smile fills my day with light . . ." and so on.

Reading Focus

Comparing and Contrasting Poems When you **compare** and **contrast** poems, you explain how they are alike and how they are different. To do this, list what you know about each poem.

Into Action For each of the two sets of poems that follow, use a chart like this one to record details about the poems.

Comparing Poems	"The Toaster"	"Steam Shovel"
What is the poem about?	a toaster	
To what is it compared?		
How does it look/sound?	metal; red coils	
What does it do?		raises head; watches

Writing Focus

Think as a Reader/Writer

Find It in Your Reading In your *Reader/Writer Notebook,* list the words that refer to how machines sound, move, and look.

Reader/Writer Notebook

Use your **RWN** to complete the activities for these selections.

Vocabulary

Steam Shovel

cropped (krahpt) *v.:* bit or cut off the top. *The dinosaur cropped the grass with its teeth and then chewed it.*

amiably (AY mee uh blee) *adv.:* in a friendly way. *The dinosaur smiled amiably at the man walking by.*

Things to Do If You Are a Subway

express (ehk SPREHS) *n.:* train that travels from one point to another without making stops. *The A train is an express that gets people to their destinations quickly.*

Language Coach

Multiple-Meaning Words Many words have more than one meaning. Sometimes these various meanings are also different parts of speech. The noun *express,* for instance, can also be a verb meaning "to put into words." What are some other meanings of *express?* Use a dictionary to list three additional meanings and their parts of speech.

Learn It Online
Go beyond the definitions with Word Watch at:

go.hrw.com L6-711 

MEET THE WRITERS

William Jay Smith

(1918–)

William Jay Smith started writing poems in high school. He decided to write poems for children after listening to his four-year-old son recite a verse he made up as he was marching around the room. Smith completed that poem, and it became the first poem in a collection called *Laughing Time*. Published in 1955, the book has never gone out of print.

Charles Malam

(1906–1981)

Charles Malam graduated in 1928 from Middlebury College in Vermont. Throughout the 1930s, his award-winning work appeared regularly in poetry magazines. He also wrote stories that appeared in the widely read *Saturday Evening Post*. Today, Malam is best known for the poem you are about to read.

Lillian Morrison

(1917–)

Lillian Morrison worked in the New York Public Library for forty years. She wrote books of her own poems and is especially known for her sports poems. "There is an affinity between sports and poetry. Each is a form of play. . . . Each has the power to take us out of ourselves and at times to lift us above ourselves. They go together naturally."

Bobbi Katz

(1933–)

Bobbi Katz has been an art historian, fashion editor, social worker, and host of a radio talk show, as well as a poet. She delights in using rhythms and rhymes. "I love the very taste of words. . . . There's nothing better than finding just the right words to make a new connection between ideas and images."

Preview the Selections

"The Toaster" will help you see a common household appliance in a new light.

"Steam Shovel" gives you a new way of looking at heavy equipment on a construction site.

"The Sidewalk Racer" lets you imagine what it's like to be in command of a skateboard.

"Things to Do If You Are a Subway" makes you think about what it's like to be a subway train.

POEM

The Toaster

by **William Jay Smith**

Read with a Purpose

Read this poem to discover how the speaker imaginatively views an ordinary toaster.

Build Background

In the 1950s, when William Jay Smith wrote this poem, toasters were typically chrome-plated and shiny.

A silver-scaled Dragon with jaws flaming red
Sits at my elbow and toasts my bread.
I hand him fat slices, and then, one by one,
He hands them back when he sees they are done. Ⓐ Ⓑ

Ⓐ **Read and Discuss** What is the speaker describing for you?

Ⓑ **Literary Focus** **Extended Metaphor** What parts of the toaster are the dragon's flaming red jaws?

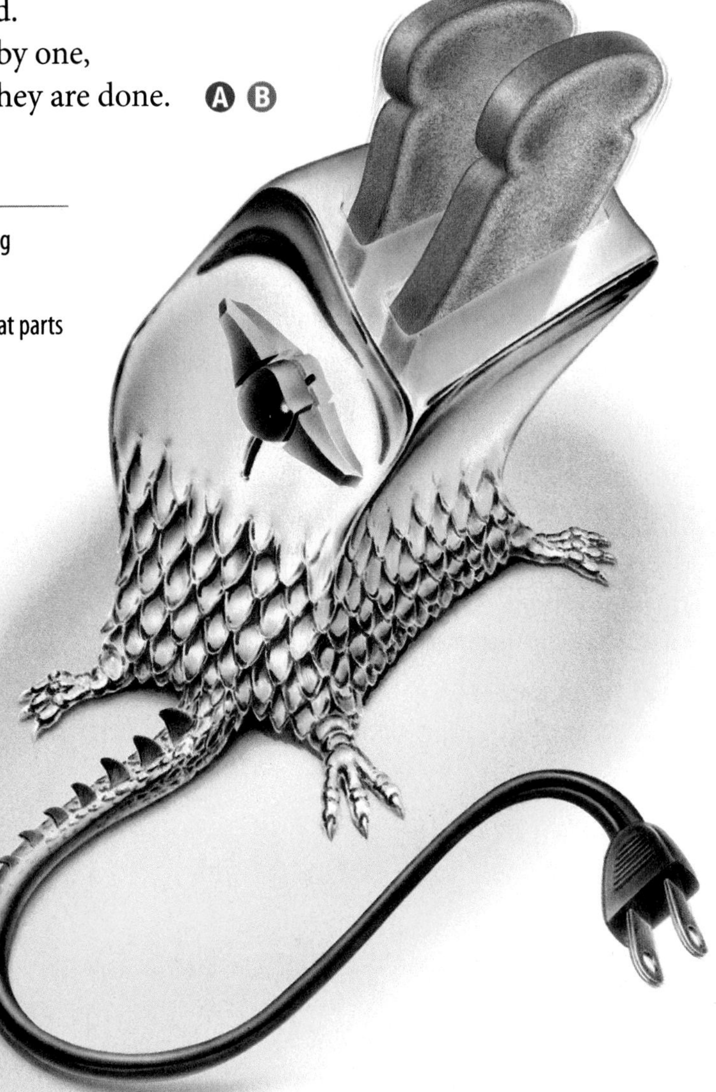

Analyzing Visuals

Viewing and Interpreting
Which parts of this toaster remind you of the dragon described in the poem?

POEM

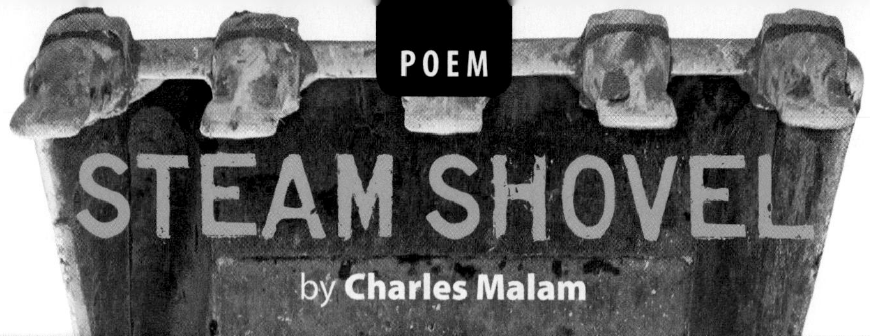

STEAM SHOVEL

by **Charles Malam**

Read with a Purpose

Read this poem to find out how the speaker describes a steam shovel.

Preparing to Read for this selection is on page 711.

Build Background

Steam shovels don't exist anymore, but they were once used for digging and moving large amounts of earth. Today, the machine that is most like the steam shovel is the backhoe. Backhoes are powered by diesel engines rather than steam engines but are used for the same purpose as old steam shovels.

The dinosaurs are not all dead.
I saw one raise its iron head
To watch me walking down the road
Beyond our house today.
Its jaws were dripping with a load
Of earth and grass that it had cropped. **A**
It must have heard me where I stopped,
Snorted white steam my way,
And stretched its long neck out to see,
And chewed, and grinned quite amiably! **B**

Analyzing Visuals

Viewing and Interpreting How is this machine similar to and different from the one described in the poem?

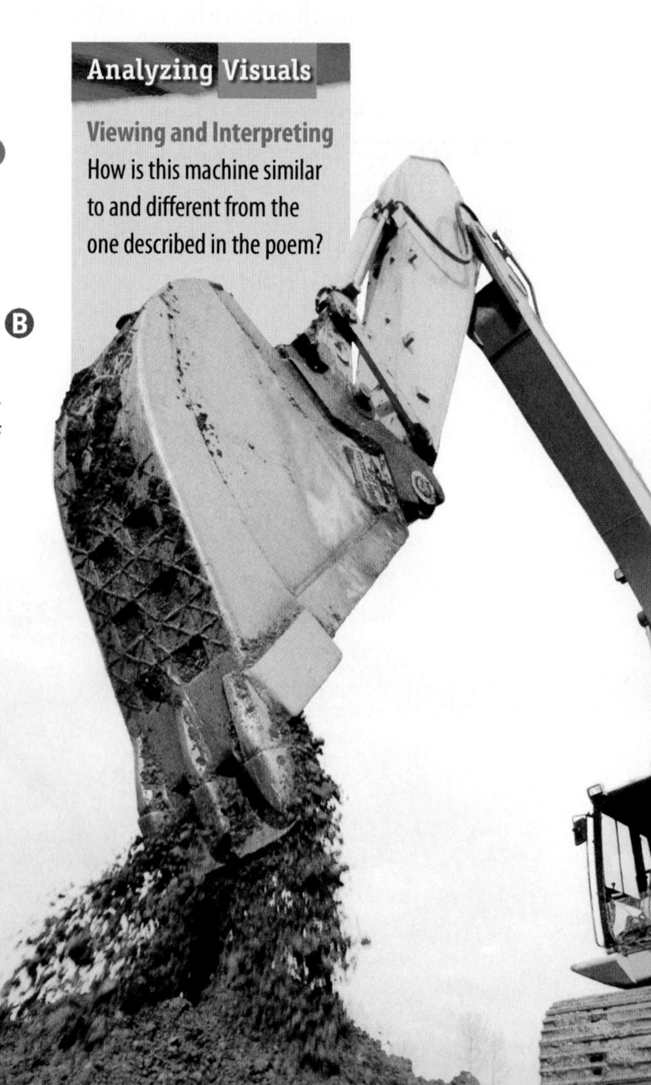

A **Literary Focus** **Extended Metaphor** What visual image of the steam shovel's actions do you form from the description in lines 2-6?

B **Read and Discuss** Think about the way this poet views the world. What might you learn from his unique perspective?

Vocabulary **cropped** (krahpt) *v.:* bit or cut off the top.
amiably (AY mee uh blee) *adv.:* in a friendly way.

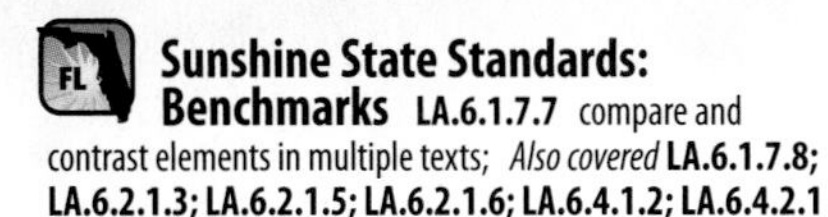

Sunshine State Standards: Benchmarks LA.6.1.7.7 compare and contrast elements in multiple texts; *Also covered* LA.6.1.7.8; LA.6.2.1.3; LA.6.2.1.5; LA.6.2.1.6; LA.6.4.1.2; LA.6.4.2.1

The Toaster / Steam Shovel

Respond and Think Critically

Reading Focus

1. What is the tone of "Steam Shovel"? FCAT
   - **A** light-hearted
   - **B** indifferent
   - **C** fearful
   - **D** sad

Read with a Purpose

2. What metaphor is used to describe a toaster? What metaphor is used to describe a steam shovel?

Reading Skills: Comparing and Contrasting Poems

3. Review the chart you filled out while you read "The Toaster" and "Steam Shovel." Then, use the chart below to analyze the ways the two poems are alike and different.

"The Toaster" and "Steam Shovel"

Similarities	Differences
Both compare a common machine to a giant monster.	

Vocabulary Check

Answer the following questions.

4. What kind of animal might have **cropped** the grass?
5. What experience with a machine would cause you to smile **amiably**?

Literary Focus

Literary Analysis

6. **Interpret** How would you describe the character of the dragon to which the toaster is being compared? To what kind of dinosaur is the steam shovel being compared?
7. **Analyze** Suppose that neither of these poems had a title or a picture. What clues in each poem would help you determine what mechanical object the poet is describing? Support your answer with details from the poems. READ THINK EXPLAIN
8. **Analyze** How can reading the imaginative comparisons in poems like these help you appreciate your everyday world more?

Literary Skills: Extended Metaphor

9. **Extend** Continue to develop the extended metaphor of either "The Toaster" or "Steam Shovel." Explain what the dragon is doing when the toast burns or gets stuck, or what the dinosaur is doing when the steam shovel moves to dig in another spot.

Writing Focus

Think as a Reader/Writer

Use It in Your Writing Review your list of words and phrases that refer to machines. Think of another appliance or machine that reminds you of an animal or a monster. Write some ideas for an extended metaphor you could use to describe your machine.

POEM

THE SIDEWALK RACER
or On the Skateboard

by **Lillian Morrison**

Read with a Purpose

Read this poem to discover how the speaker feels about skateboarding.

Preparing to Read for this selection is on page 711.

Build Background

A **concrete poem,** like this one by Dorthi Charles, is shaped like the subject it describes. How is "The Sidewalk Racer" like a concrete poem?

Concrete Cat

A e r   e A r
eYe   eYe   stripestripestripestripe
whisker   whisker   stripestripestripe   tail/tail
whisker m   h whisker   stripestripestripestripes
o   t   stripestripestripe
U   stripestripestripestripe
paw paw   paw paw   ǝsnoɯ
dishdish   litterbox
litterbox

Skimming
an asphalt sea
I swerve, I curve, I
sway; I speed to whirring
sound an inch above the
ground; I'm the sailor
and the sail, I'm the
driver and the wheel
I'm the one and only
single engine
human auto
mobile. **A**

A **Literary Focus** **Extended Metaphor** How does the poet convey the idea of a skateboarder being one with the board?

POEM

THINGS TO DO IF YOU ARE A SUBWAY

by **Bobbi Katz**

Read with a Purpose

Read this poem to discover a new way of seeing a subway train.

Preparing to Read for this selection is on page 711.

Build Background

A subway is an underground railway system, a form of public transportation in very large cities. Subways exist in several American cities, such as Chicago, Boston, Philadelphia, and Washington, D.C. To Americans, however, the word *subway* very often specifically means the rapid transit system in New York City.

Pretend you are a dragon.
Live in underground caves.
Roar about underneath the city.
Swallow piles of people.
Spit them out at the next station. **A**
Zoom through the darkness.
Be an express.
Go fast.
Make as much noise as you please. **B** **C**

A **Reading Focus** **Comparing and Contrasting Poems** Which of the other poems you've just read compares an object to a dragon? How is this "dragon" different from that one?

B **Read and Discuss** What is the speaker's point here?

C **Reading Focus** **Comparing and Contrasting Poems** Compare the personality of the subject in this poem with that of "The Sidewalk Racer." What differences can you detect in their attitudes?

Vocabulary **express** (ehk SPREHS) *n.:* train that travels from one point to another without making stops.

Applying Your Skills

FL
Sunshine State Standards: Benchmarks LA.6.1.7.7 compare and contrast elements in multiple texts; Also covered LA.6.1.7.8; LA.6.2.1.3; LA.6.2.1.5; LA.6.2.1.6; LA.6.4.1.2

The Sidewalk Racer / Things to Do If You Are a Subway

Respond and Think Critically

Reading Focus

1. How do the words *city, station,* and *express* influence the extended metaphor in "Things to Do If You Are a Subway"? 
   A They help the reader imagine a dragon in a city.
   B They help the reader understand what a subway is.
   C They remind the reader that the subject is a subway.
   D They maintain the portrayal of the subway as a dragon.
2. In what ways is the subway in "Things to Do If You Are a Subway" like a dragon?

Read with a Purpose

3. What do the comparisons in the first poem tell you about how the speaker feels about skateboarding? What metaphor is used to describe the subway in the second poem?

Reading Skills: Comparing and Contrasting Poems

4. Review the chart you filled out. Use the chart below to compare and contrast the poems.

"The Sidewalk Racer" and "Things to Do If You Are a Subway"

Similarities	Differences
Both have a lot of motion and speed.	One compares a subway to a dragon; the other compares skateboarding to sailing and driving.

Vocabulary Check

Answer the following question.

5. Why would you want to take the **express** if you were in a hurry to get somewhere?

Literary Focus

Literary Analysis

6. How do the rhythm, rhymes, and sound effects create a feeling of movement and speed in "The Sidewalk Racer"? Support your answer with examples from the poem. READ THINK EXPLAIN
7. **Analyze** A **concrete poem** is a poem whose visual shape suggests its subject matter. Explain whether "The Sidewalk Racer" could be considered a concrete poem.

Literary Skills: Extended Metaphor

8. **Evaluate** Which of the two poems do you think provides the better example of an extended metaphor? Support your answer with details from the poems. READ THINK EXPLAIN

Writing Focus

Think as a Reader/Writer

Use It in Your Writing Review the words you jotted down that refer to how machines sound, move, and look. Add a line or two to one of the poems to continue the extended metaphor.

COMPARING TEXTS

Wrap Up

Sunshine State Standards: Benchmarks **LA.6.1.7.7** compare and contrast elements in multiple texts; **LA.6.2.1.6** write a book report, review, or critique that compares two or more works by the same author; **LA.6.4.1.2** write a variety of expressive forms (e.g., short play, song lyrics, historical fiction, limericks) that employ figurative language, rhythm, dialogue, characterization, and/or appropriate format; *Also covered* **LA.6.4.2.1; LA.6.4.2.3; LA.6.6.1.1**

The Toaster / Steam Shovel / The Sidewalk Racer / Things to Do If You Are a Subway

Writing Focus

Write a Comparison-Contrast Essay

Compare and contrast two of the four poems you have just read. Choose the two poems you enjoyed the most. Refer to the charts you filled in (see pages 715 and 718) for details to use in your essay. You can organize your essay according to these guidelines.

1. Name the poems you chose, and identify the extended metaphor in each poem.
2. Discuss the first poem by explaining the extended metaphor and how the poet carries it through the poem. Explain whether the metaphor did or did not help you see the subject in a new way. Use details from the poem in your explanation.
3. Do the same for the second poem.
4. In a concluding paragraph, state which poem you think used extended metaphor more effectively and explain your answer.

Use the workshop on writing a Comparison-Contrast Essay, pages 106–113, for help with this assignment.

What Do You Think Now?

How did the comparisons in these poems make you see ordinary things differently? What made the metaphors so effective?

CHOICES

As you respond to the Choices, use these **Academic Vocabulary** words as appropriate: appreciate, detect, device, visual.

REVIEW

Explain a Metaphor

Timed Writing In a paragraph or two, explain the appeal of an imaginative, well-thought-out metaphor. How can a metaphor surprise you and inspire you to look at things in a new way? What do you most appreciate about the imaginative qualities of metaphors like the ones you've just read? In what ways are they simply fun? Use examples from any or all of these four poems in your response.

CONNECT

Create a Poetic Work of Art

William Jay Smith's favorite illustration of his poem "The Toaster" was done by a student like you. Try creating your own illustration or three-dimensional version of "The Toaster" or another one of the poems you just read. Be sure your artwork captures as many of the visual details of the extended metaphor in the poem as possible. Draw, paint, use collage techniques, put objects together, or make a sculpture of your poem.

EXTEND

Create a Concrete Poem

A **concrete poem** takes the shape of the object it describes. In "The Sidewalk Racer," the lines are arranged so that the shape of the poem recalls the shape of a skateboard. Select an object that inspires you, and write a concrete poem that describes it. Display your poem in the classroom for your classmates to appreciate.

Writing Workshop

Descriptive Essay

Write with a Purpose

Choose a subject that you would enjoy observing and describing: a place, a person, an object, an animal, or an event. Write a descriptive essay about this subject for an **audience** of students your age. Your **purpose** is to bring the subject to life through detailed description.

A Good Descriptive Essay

- clearly identifies the subject being described
- uses sensory details and figures of speech to help the reader hear, see, smell, taste, or feel the subject
- organizes details in a clear way
- reveals the writer's thoughts and feelings about the subject
- states why the subject is important to the writer

Use your **RWN** to complete the activities for this workshop.

Think as a Reader/Writer In this collection you've seen how poets bring **images** to life. In addition, you've learned how **figures of speech,** such as similes and metaphors, can be used to create vivid and memorable descriptions. These same techniques are used in descriptive writing. In a descriptive essay, you use words to paint a vivid picture of an object, place, animal, person, or event. You choose words that will help your readers to see, hear, smell, taste, and feel the qualities of the subject you're describing. As part of your descriptive essay, you may also choose to include your thoughts, memories, and feelings about your subject, sharing your views and perspective with your readers.

Before you begin your own descriptive essay, read this excerpt from *Two in the Far North,* by Margaret E. Murie. This book is about life in the Alaskan backcountry during the early 1920s. The paragraph excerpted here describes the arctic plain after nightfall.

> The sky is midnight blue and fully spangled with stars, and the moon is rising brighter and brighter behind the pointed trees. In the north a flicker of green and yellow; then an unfurled bolt of rainbow ribbon shivering and shimmering across the stars—the Aurora. The dogs begin to speed up; we must be nearing a cabin; yes, there it is, a little black blotch on the creek bank. The air is cold and tingling, fingers are numb. A great dark form flops slowly across the trail—a great horned owl, the speaking spirit of the wilderness.

← The writer creates a vivid image by describing specific colors and objects in the night sky.

← **Sensory details** that appeal to sight and touch draw the reader into the scene.

Think About the Professional Model

With a partner, discuss the following questions about the model.

1. Which sentence draws you into the scene most strongly? Why does that sentence affect you more powerfully than the others?
2. How does the writer seem to feel about the subject?
3. No sounds or smells are included in this description. How might the writer have described the sounds and smells of this scene?

Sunshine State Standards: Benchmarks **LA.6.3.1.1** generating ideas from multiple sources (e.g., prior knowledge, discussion with others, writer's notebook, research materials, or other reliable sources), based upon teacher-directed topics and personal int erests; **LA.6.3.1.2** making a plan for writing that prioritizes ideas, addresses purpose, audience, main idea, and logical sequence; **LA.6.3.1.3** using organizational strategies and tools (e.g., technology, outline, chart, table, graph, web, story map); **LA.6.3.2.1** developing main ideas from the prewriting plan using primary and secondary sources appropriate to purpose and audience; **LA.6.3.2.2** organizing information into a logical sequence and combining or deleting sentences to enhance clarity; *Also covered* **LA.6.3.2.3; LA.6.3.3.1; LA.6.3.3.2; LA.6.3.3.3; LA.6.3.3.4; LA.6.3.4.1; LA.6.3.4.3; LA.6.3.4.5; LA.6.3.5.1; LA.6.4.2.3**

Prewriting

Choose a Subject

A good subject for a descriptive essay must meet these criteria.

- You can observe it directly or picture it clearly in your mind.
- You can describe it with a variety of sensory details.
- You can fully decribe it in a short essay; its "scope" is manageable.
- You have a strong reaction to it because it is important or meaningful to you.

As you think of an idea for a subject, try freewriting about it for a few minutes. Then, using what you've written, try to fill in all the bubbles of an idea web like the one below. List the sensory details that apply to each bubble heading. The Idea Starters in the margin might help you think of some subject ideas.

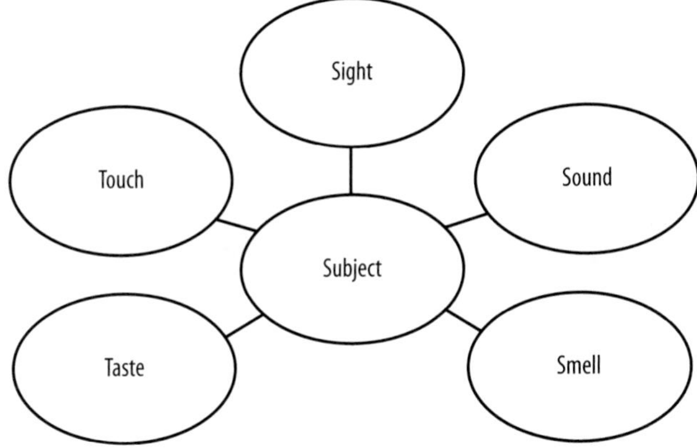

Gather Details

Gather details about your subject by observing it directly or by using your memory. Try to include both **sensory details** and **factual details** (details that can be proved true). Ask yourself:

- What does the subject look like? (What color, size, and shape is it?)
- What does the subject sound like? (What sounds can you hear?)
- What does the subject smell like? (Is there a particular scent?)
- What does the subject taste like? (Is it sweet, sour, salty?)
- What does the subject feel like? (Is it silky, rough, gritty, moist?)
- How do I feel about the subject? Why is it meaningful to me?
- What does the subject make me think of?

Idea Starters

- an interesting person
- an animal
- a fascinating, beautiful, or weird place
- a strange or useful object
- a spectacular event
- something you see every day that has unexpected interesting qualities

Sensory details tell what something looks, sounds, smells, tastes, or feels like. **Factual details** tell what something *is,* rather than what it looks, sounds, smells, tastes, or feels like.

Your Turn

Get Started Record your subject in your **RWN,** and write down why you have chosen the subject. Record details about your subject that appeal to each of the five senses. Also list factual details, such as measurements, numbers, and names.

Learn It Online
Plan and organize your essay with an interactive graphic organizer:

go.hrw.com L6-721 

Focus on Your Dominant Impression

As you think about the sensory details you'll use to describe your subject, you should also consider your **thoughts** and **feelings** about the subject. Together, these form the **dominant impression** about the subject that you'll leave with your readers.

Thinking about the impression you want to leave with readers will help you decide which details to keep and which to leave out. For example, if you wanted to describe the peace and beauty of a mountain lake, you might want to leave out details about a crowded lodge on its shores.

Writing Tip

Use transition words to keep your organization clear. Here are some transition words that match each organizational method.

- **Spatial:** *across from, near, far, by, around, inside, outside, between, down, next to, beside, up, under*
- **Chronological:** *first, next, last, after, now, before, eventually, finally, then, later*
- **Order of Importance:** *to begin with, mainly, then*

Organize Ideas

There are three common ways to organize descriptive essays. Choose the method that works best for your topic.

- **Spatial Order:** Tell where details are located, moving from right to left , top to bottom, or near to far, for example.
- **Chronological Order:** Put details in the order that they occur.
- **Order of Importance:** Present details from most to least important or least to most important.

Once you decide on your organization, you can create a simple chart to list your details in correct order. This chart shows the combination of spatial and chronological order used in the Student Draft on pages 725–726.

Order of Details for "The Smoky Mountains"
1. I follow the mountain path.
2. The path snakes upward in the distance.
3. The brook runs downhill, mirroring the trail's ascent.
4. I make my way to a rock by the bank.
5. I step back to the mossy ground.
6. I return to the path.

Your Turn

Plan Your Description To help you plan your descriptive essay, use your **RWN** to record your **dominant impression** and a list of **details** you'll use. Then, decide how you'll **organize** your details, and make a chart that shows the **order** in which you'll present them. Share your plan with a classmate, and revise your plan as needed. Keep in mind your **purpose** and **audience.**

Think About Purpose and Audience

Your **purpose** is to inform and entertain your audience with a description of a place, person, object, animal, or event. As you choose your subject and consider the details you'll include, think about what will appeal to your **audience.** How can you make something as common and ordinary as a dog or a park interesting to them? Select details to which your audience can easily relate, but point out unexpected details as well.

Drafting

Use Precise Language

Precise language makes details come alive. Use specific nouns, verbs, adjectives, and adverbs rather than more general words. The description "the lake was *cold* and *beautiful*" is vague and weak; it doesn't help the reader form a mental image. Compare that description with one that uses precise language: "The *icy* waters *shimmered* in the morning sun, as if the *sleepy* mountain lake was slowly *awakening* and still *shivering* from the *clear* and *frigid* night."

A Writer's Framework

Introduction

- identifies the subject, time, and place, and provides background

Body

- presents details in clear order
- includes sensory and factual details as well as figures of speech

Conclusion

- includes a main impression
- expresses thoughts and feelings
- tells why the subject is important

Use Figurative Language

Figurative language—descriptive language that compares one thing to another—adds color to your writing. In the description above, a mountain lake is described as having human characteristics (*sleepy*, *awakening*, *shivering*). There are three types of figurative language:

- **Similes** compare two unlike things using *like* or *as.*
  My *cat is like a race car,* slender and built for speed.
- **Metaphors** compare two unlike things by saying one *is* the other.
  My cat's *claws are sharpened daggers.*
- **Personification** uses human characteristics to describe something nonhuman.
  My *cat scowls* at me when I accidentally step on his tail.

Grammar Link Using Present Participles

An effective way to draw the reader into your description is to use present participles to add movement and action to your descriptions. Present participles are made from verbs but are used as adjectives. Murie uses participles as a part of her description of Alaska.

"...rainbow ribbon**, shivering** and **shimmering** across the stars..."

When used at the end of a sentence, the participial phrase is separated from the main clause by a comma.

"...a great horned owl, the **speaking** spirit of the wilderness."

When used as a simple adjective, the participle is not separated by a comma.

Writing Tip

Vivid Verbs

Vivid verbs increase the action, movement, and interest in your description. Instead of weak, overused verbs like *appear, take, move, give, hold, seem, look, has, had, was*, *going*, and *went,* try to use vivid, action-oriented verbs that paint a picture. For example, use *grabbed* instead of *took*; *swayed* instead of *moved*; *shuffled away* instead of *went away*.

Your Turn

Write Your Draft Following your plan, write a draft of your essay. Remember to think about the following:

- What precise words can you use?
- What kind of figurative language can you use?

Peer Review

Working with a peer, review your draft. Answer each question in this chart to decide where and how your drafts can be improved. As you discuss your essays, be sure to take notes about each other's suggestions.

Evaluating and Revising

Read the questions in the left column of the chart and then use the tips in the middle column to help you make revisions to your essay. The right column suggests techniques you can use to revise your draft.

Descriptive Essay: Guidelines for Content and Organization

Evaluation Question	Tip	Revision Technique
1. Does your introduction catch the reader's attention? Does it identify the subject?	**Bracket** interesting or surprising statements. **Circle** the subject of the essay.	**Add** an attention-getting statement or a quotation. **Add** a sentence that identifies the subject.
2. Does your description include a variety of details and figures of speech?	**Highlight** sensory details and imaginative comparisons. **Put an *S*** above sensory details. **Put an *F*** above sentences that employ figures of speech.	**Add** sensory details and figures of speech. **Delete** irrelevant details.
3. Are the details arranged in a clear order?	In the margin, **write** the method of organization used—spatial, chronological, or order of importance.	**Rearrange** details if necessary. **Add** transitions for greater coherence.
4. Does your description include your thoughts and feelings?	**Put a check mark** next to any statement of your thoughts or feelings.	**Add** specific details about your thoughts and feelings.
5. Does your conclusion state why the subject is important to you? Does it convey a clear impression of the subject?	**Underline** the statement that tells why the experience is important. **Put parentheses** around statements that hint at the main impression.	**Add** a statement explaining why the experience is important. **Add** a statement that conveys the main impression of the subject.

Read this student's draft and the comments about it as a model for revising your own descriptive essay.

Student Draft

The Smoky Mountains

by Melissa Jones, Murchison Middle School

The summer sun tickles my face as a calming breeze swirls my hair. The rolling foothills envelop me with their blue, smoky mist as I follow the dirt mountain path. In the distance, the path snakes up the mountain, mirroring the brook's journey downward.

← Melissa uses **spatial organization** to describe her walk up a mountain path.

I draw the warm air into my lungs and admire the natural beauty around me. I stare into a sky so blue that the clouds floating in it appear to be puffs of cotton. I carefully make my way over to a large rock by the bank of the brook. The running water makes a gurgling, babbling noise that calms me. All around me, majestic pines shade me from the sun, except for random sunbeams filtering like spider webs through the lush greenery.

← Notice Melissa's use of **vivid action verbs.**

← **Sensory details** describe how the scene feels, looks, and sounds.

MINI-LESSON How to Include Thoughts and Feelings

Melissa could share her thoughts and feelings to help draw readers into the setting. This will also give the readers a dominant impression of the place she is describing and its effect on her.

Melissa's Draft of the First Paragraph

The summer sun tickles my face, as a calming breeze swirls my hair. The rolling foothills envelop me with their blue, smoky mist as I follow the dirt mountain path. In the distance, the path snakes up the mountain, mirroring the brook's journey downward.

Melissa's Revision of the First Paragraph

I smile with anticipation. I breathe deeply. Nothing makes me feel quite as free and complete as spending time in the mountains.

The summer sun tickles my face, as a calming breeze swirls my hair.^ The rolling foothills envelop me with their blue, smoky mist as I eagerly follow the dirt mountain path. In the distance, the path snakes up the mountain, mirroring the brook's journey downward.

Your Turn

Include Your Thoughts and Feelings Read your draft and ask yourself the following:

- Are my thoughts and feelings coming through?
- What main impression about the subject am I leaving with the reader?

Melissa provides specific details that appeal to the senses of **sound, sight,** and **touch.**

A combination of **spatial** and **chronological organization** guides the reader along the trail, and Melissa ends by stating how the experience makes her feel.

Student Draft *continues*

As birds chirp in the distance, I absorb the beauty of the brook. There's a fog that's hovering over the water. It hugs the surface like a winter blanket. As the water dips over a tiny waterfall, it swirls in foamy rapids at the base. The sun seems to cast a spell on the water, making it sparkle in the light. I dip my fingers into the bone-chilling, crystal-clear water. Its chill runs up my arm and down my spine. The breeze whirls through the trees and makes me shiver. The beauty and mystery of the mountains make me feel so alive.

I step back onto the mossy ground and return to the sunny dirt path. I faintly smell jasmine as I make my way through the trees up the mountain. Today is the perfect day for hiking in the Smokies.

MINI-LESSON How to Add Figurative Language

In her draft, Melissa uses a variety of vivid sensory details. Her description is clear, but Melissa can make it even more appealing by adding figurative language. When she evaluates her essay, she looks for descriptions that can be revised to include a simile, a metaphor, or personification.

Melissa's Draft of Paragraph Three

. . . The sun seems to cast a spell on the water, making it sparkle in the light. I dip my fingers into the bone-chilling, crystal-clear water. Its chill runs up my arm and down my spine. The breeze whirls through the trees and makes me shiver. The beauty and mystery of the mountains make me feel so alive.

In her revision, Melissa focuses on "cast a spell" as the basis for a simile.

Melissa's Revision of Paragraph Three

Like a wizard waving a golden wand, transforming it into a pool

The sun seems to cast a spell on the water, ~~making it sparkle in the light.~~

of sparkling gemstones.

I dip my fingers into the bone-chilling, crystal-clear water. Its chill runs up my arm and down my spine. The breeze whirls through the trees and makes me shiver. The beauty and mystery of the mountains make me feel so alive. It is magic.

Your Turn

Add Figurative Language With a partner, look for descriptions in your essay that can be revised to include figurative language. Remember that figurative language is used to compare two unlike things. Share your revisions with your partner.

Proofreading and Publishing

Proofreading

Now that you have revised your descriptive essay, it is time to edit it and eliminate any errors that might confuse or distract your readers. Proofread your essay carefully, looking for misspellings, punctuation errors, or problems with sentence structure.

Grammar Link Using Consistent Verb Tense

Be careful to use a consistent verb tense throughout your essay. You can use past tense to describe something as if it has already happened, or you can use present tense to make the reader feel more a part of the description. When she first proofread her description, Melissa noticed that she had used present tense in all but two sentences. She revised those sentences, changing them from past tense to present tense for consistency.

The running water ~~made~~ makes a gurgling, babbling noise that calms me. All around me majestic pines ~~shaded~~ shade me from the sun, except for random sunbeams filtering like spider webs through the lush greenery.

Publishing

Now it is time to publish your descriptive essay to a wider audience. Here are some ways to share your essay:

- Add illustrations or photos, and publish your essay as a small booklet.
- Create a multimedia presentation to enhance the sensory details you have included in your essay.

Reflect on the Process In your **RWN,** write a short response to each of the following questions.

1. How did you organize your ideas during the brainstorming part of the assignment?
2. How did you think of figurative language to include in your essay?
3. What did you learn from writing a descriptive essay that you can use in other types of writing?

Proofreading Tip

There are three main areas to focus on when editing, so it makes sense to involve three people in proofreading. Ask two classmates to help you. Have each person focus on just one area: spelling, punctuation, or sentence structure.

Your Turn

Proofread and Publish Proofread to make sure you have used a consistent verb tense throughout your essay. Then, publish your description to a wider audience.

Scoring Rubric

You can use one of these rubrics to evaluate your descriptive essay from the Writing Workshop. Your teacher will tell you which rubric to use.

6-Point Scale

Score 6 *Demonstrates advanced success*
- focuses consistently on describing a single subject
- shows effective organization throughout, with smooth transitions
- offers thoughtful, creative descriptions
- develops the descriptions thoroughly, using precise and vivid sensory details
- exhibits mature control of written language

Score 5 *Demonstrates proficient success*
- focuses on describing a single subject
- shows effective organization, with transitions
- offers thoughtful descriptions
- develops the descriptions competently, using sensory details and images
- exhibits sufficient control of written language

Score 4 *Demonstrates competent success*
- focuses on a single subject, with minor digressions
- shows effective organization, with minor lapses
- offers mostly thoughtful descriptions
- develops the descriptions adequately, with some sensory details and images
- exhibits general control of written language

Score 3 *Demonstrates limited success*
- includes some loosely related material that distracts from the writer's descriptive focus
- shows some organization, with noticeable flaws
- offers routine, predictable descriptions
- develops the descriptions with uneven use of sensory details
- exhibits limited control of written language

Score 2 *Demonstrates basic success*
- includes loosely related material that seriously distracts from the writer's focus
- shows minimal organization, with major flaws
- offers descriptions that merely skim the surface
- develops the descriptions with inadequate sensory details
- exhibits significant problems with control of written language

Score 1 *Demonstrates emerging effort*
- shows little awareness of the topic and the descriptive purpose
- lacks organization
- offers unclear and confusing descriptions
- uses sensory details in only a minimal way, if at all
- exhibits major problems with control of written language

4-Point Scale

Score 4 *Demonstrates advanced success*
- focuses consistently on describing a single subject
- shows effective organization throughout, with smooth transitions
- offers thoughtful, creative descriptions
- develops the descriptions thoroughly, using precise and vivid sensory details
- exhibits mature control of written language

Score 3 *Demonstrates competent success*
- focuses on a single subject, with minor digressions
- shows effective organization, with minor lapses
- offers mostly thoughtful descriptions
- develops the descriptions adequately, with some sensory details and images
- exhibits general control of written language

Score 2 *Demonstrates limited success*
- includes some loosely related material that distracts from the writer's descriptive focus
- shows some organization, with noticeable flaws
- offers routine, predictable descriptions
- develops the descriptions with uneven use of sensory details
- exhibits limited control of written language

Score 1 *Demonstrates emerging effort*
- shows little awareness of the topic and the descriptive purpose
- lacks organization
- offers unclear and confusing descriptions
- uses sensory details in only a minimal way, if at all
- exhibits major problems with control of written language

Preparing for **FCAT Writing+**

Sunshine State Standards: Benchmarks **LA.6.3.4.1** spelling, using spelling rules, orthographic patterns, generalizations, knowledge of root words, prefixes, suffixes, and knowledge of Greek and Latin root words and using a dictionary, thesaurus, or other resources as necessary; *Also covered* **LA.6.3.4.2; LA.6.3.4.4; LA.6.3.4.5**

Read the article "The Cafeteria." Choose the word that correctly completes questions 1–4.

The Cafeteria

A __(1)__ cafeteria is where students come to eat their lunch. Students can bring their own lunch to school. They can also buy __(2)__ lunch in the cafeteria. The cafeteria has many types of food, such as fruits, vegetables, pizza, and milk. The pizza smells cheesy and delicious. The fruit and vegetables taste crisp and fresh. Students look over the food and choose the kind of meal that they want.

After they buy a meal, students choose a seat at one of the tables. Students sit with their friends and eat their lunches. The cafeteria can get loud and busy! So it's important to __(3)__ in a low voice and use proper table manners. Eating their lunches gives students time to get to know their __(4)__. Eating lunch also energizes students and helps them complete the rest of their day.

1. Which answer should go in blank (1)?
   A school's
   B schools'
   C schools

2. Which answer should go in blank (2)?
   F there
   G they're
   H their

3. Which answer should go in blank (3)?
   A speaks
   B speak
   C spoke

4. Which answer should go in blank (4)?
   F Class Mates
   G Classmates
   H classmates

Presenting a Description

Speak with a Purpose

Present your descriptive essay orally. Your goal is to engage and entertain your fellow students as you describe the details of a person, place, object, animal, or event. Practice your presentation, and then present it to the class.

Think as a Reader/Writer

As a writer, you carefully plan the organization of your description and decide exactly which details to use. This kind of purposeful planning is equally important when giving an oral description.

Now is your chance to give an oral presentation and describe something that is special to you. You will carefully plan what to say, practice saying it, and then impress your audience with an interesting and entertaining description.

Adapt Your Essay

Consider Your Purpose and Audience

For this speech, your **purpose** is to entertain your fellow students. Make sure you are clear about your specific purpose—what you hope to achieve through speaking. Ask yourself, "What is the main impression I want to give my audience?" Then, write a sentence that answers your question. For example, you might state your purpose this way: "I want my audience to understand how truly amazing my pet snake is."

As you plan your presentation, remember that different people rely on their senses in different ways. If you include **sensory details** that appeal to all of the senses, you will capture everyone's attention. Read your essay to see if you should add details to meet this goal.

Organize Your Ideas

Re-read your essay to see how easy it is to follow. Listeners need more frequent clues than readers do. You might need to add more transitional words and phrases, for example, to help listeners follow your description of the subject. Use transitions that work best with your organizational pattern.

Also, make sure the introduction and conclusion function very clearly to meet the goals of the presentation.

- **Introduction** In just a few sentences, grab your listeners' attention and give your thesis statement, which should reflect the specific purpose of your speech.
- **Conclusion** Remind your readers why you wanted to present this description. Tell them why your subject matters to you.

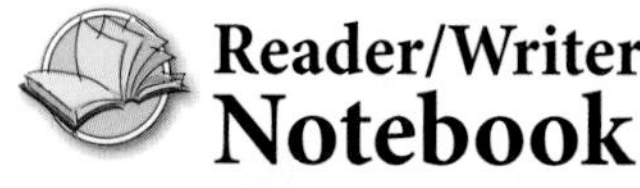

Reader/Writer Notebook

Use your **RWN** to complete the activities for this workshop.

Sunshine State Standards: Benchmarks **LA.6.1.5.1** adjust reading rate based on purpose, text difficulty, form, and style; **LA.6.3.3.1** evaluating the draft for development of ideas and content, logical organization, voice, point of view, word choice, and sentence variation; **LA.6.3.3.3** creating precision and interest by expressing ideas vividly through multiple language techniques (e.g., foreshadowing, imagery, simile, metaphor, sensory language, connotation, denotation) and modifying word choices using resources and reference materials (e.g., dictionary, thesaurus); *Also covered* **LA.6.4.2.3; LA.6.5.2.2**

Deliver Your Description

Practice your presentation until you are sure you know it well. Ask friends or family members to listen to your presentation and suggest ways to make it better. Also, use these tips to help you deliver your presentation effectively.

Stay calm and confident. Before you begin speaking, take a deep breath. Stand up straight, look alert, and pay attention to what you are saying.

Use body language. The chart below lists nonverbal signals, or body language, that will add to your message.

Nonverbal Signals	Purpose
Eye contact: Look into the eyes of your audience members.	shows that you are honest or sincere; keeps audience's attention
Facial expressions: Smile, frown, or raise an eyebrow.	shows your feelings; emphasizes parts of your message
Gestures: Give a thumbs up, shrug, nod, or shake your head.	emphasizes your point; adds meaning to the speech
Posture: Stand tall and straight.	shows that you are sure of yourself

Use your voice effectively. Here are verbal elements to consider as you practice and deliver your speech.

Verbal Elements	
Diction	Pronounce words clearly. Speak carefully so that your listeners can understand you.
Pitch	Let your voice rise and fall naturally as you speak. If you are nervous, take deep breaths to keep your pitch from going too high.
Rate	Talk more slowly than you would during a conversation.
Volume	Be sure listeners at the back of the room can hear you clearly.

An Effective Oral Description

- grabs the audience's attention and gives a clear thesis statement
- uses a variety of sensory details to help all types of listeners picture the subject
- organizes information in a way that is easy for listeners to follow
- uses effective verbal and nonverbal techniques
- ends in a memorable way

Speaking Tip

Your description will include many details. Don't be afraid to include brief pauses throughout your speech. These pauses will give your listeners time to process the details. Restating important ideas is also helpful.

PRACTICING FOR FCAT

Standards Review Literary Text

Poetry **Directions:** Read the following poem. Then, read and respond to the questions that follow.

This poem describes a moment in the 1998 National Basketball Association Finals game between the Chicago Bulls and the Utah Jazz. Bulls superstar Michael Jordan scored the winning shot with just 5.2 seconds left in the game. This victory brought the team their sixth NBA title. The game, which took place on June 14, 1998, in Salt Lake City, Utah, was Jordan's last with the Chicago Bulls.

Forty-one Seconds on a Sunday in June, in Salt Lake City, Utah

for Michael Jordan by **Quincy Troupe**

rising up in time, michael jordan hangs like an icon,° suspended in space,
cocks his right arm, fires a jump shot for two, the title game on the line,
his eyes two radar screens screwed like nails into the mask of his face

bore in on the basket, gaze focused, a thing of beauty, no shadow, or trace,
no hint of fear, in this, his showplace, his ultimate place to shine,
rising up in time michael jordan hangs like an icon, suspended in space,

after he has moved from baseline to baseline, sideline to sideline, his coal-face
shining, wagging his tongue, he dribbles through chaos, snaking serpentine,°
his eyes two radar screens screwed like nails into the mask of his face,

he bolts a flash up the court, takes off, floats in for two more in this race
for glory, it is his time, what he was put on earth for, he can see the headline,
rising up in time, michael jordan hangs like an icon, suspended in space,

inside his imagination, he feels the moment he will embrace, knows his place
is written here, inside this quickening pace of nerves, he will define,
his eyes two radar screens screwed like nails into the mask of his face,

---

1. **icon** (Y kahn): image; also, person or thing regarded with great respect and admiration.
8. **serpentine** (SUR puhn teen): in a snakelike way.

Sunshine State Standards: Benchmarks **LA.6.2.1.1** identify the characteristics of various genres (e.g., poetry, fiction, short story, dramatic literature) as forms with distinct characteristics and purposes; *Also covered* **LA.6.2.1.3; LA.6.5.1.1**

inside this moment he will rule on his own terms, quick as a cat he interfaces°
time, victory & glory, as he crosses over his dribble he is king of this shrine,°
rising up in time, michael jordan hangs like an icon, suspended in space,
his eyes two radar screens screwed like nails into the mask of his face

16. **interfaces** (IHN tuhr fays ihz): brings together; joins.

17. **shrine** (shryn): place held in high honor because of its association with an event, a person, or a holy figure.

1 Which phrase from the poem contains a simile?

- **A** "he bolts a flash up the court"
- **B** "fires a jump shot for two, the title game on the line"
- **C** "he feels the moment he will embrace"
- **D** "rising up in time, michael jordan hangs like an icon"

2 Of what is "quick as a cat" (line 16) an example?

- **F** metaphor
- **G** simile
- **H** personification
- **I** refrain

3 Which statement describes the poem's structure?

- **A** The first and third lines of each stanza rhyme.
- **B** Each stanza begins with the same line.
- **C** Each line has the same number of words.
- **D** The first and second lines of each stanza rhyme.

4 Which phrase shows the effectiveness of repetition?

- **F** "his eyes two radar screens screwed like nails into the mask of his face"
- **G** "he bolts a flash up the court, takes off, floats in for two more in this race"
- **H** "for glory, it is his time, what he was put on earth for, he can see the headline"
- **I** "time, victory & glory, as he crosses over his dribble he is king of this shrine"

5 Which word best describes the speaker's tone in this poem?

- **A** dazed
- **B** admiring
- **C** critical
- **D** envious

Extended Response

6 Identify examples of alliteration in the poem. How does the alliteration contribute to the poem's purpose? Support your response with details from the poem.

Standards Review Vocabulary

Sunshine State Standards: Benchmarks **LA.6.1.6.1** use new vocabulary that is introduced and taught directly; **LA.6.1.6.3** use context clues to determine meanings of unfamiliar words; **LA.6.1.6.5** relate new vocabulary to familiar words.

Synonyms

Directions: Identify the word or group of words that is closest in meaning to the italicized word in each item.

Practicing For FCAT

1. Read this sentence.

   "My friends," he announced in a voice clear and keen / "My name is Sylvester McMonkey McBean."

   Which word has the same meaning as *keen*?

   A nervous
   B bored
   C eager
   D offended

2. Read this sentence.

   I marvel at thee, Octopus; / If I were thou, I'd call me Us.

   Which word has the same meaning as *marvel*?

   F stare
   G frown
   H wonder
   I laugh

3. Read this sentence.

   I am small like you and / do not protect my careless hair / from wind or rain—it tangles often, / Grandma, and it is wild and/ untrained.

   Which word has the same meaning as *tangles*?

   A falls over
   B unravels
   C wraps up
   D twists

4. Read this sentence.

   I love mi gato, / Porque I found / Him on the fender / Of an abandoned car.

   Which word has the same meaning as *abandoned*?

   F left
   G turned over
   H large
   I fixed

Academic Vocabulary

Directions: Use context clues to determine the meaning of the italicized Academic Vocabulary words below.

5. Read this sentence.

   Figurative language is a device for creating imaginative poetry.

   Which word has the same meaning as *device*?

   A idea
   B choice
   C method
   D machine

Standards Review Writing

Sunshine State Standards: Benchmarks LA.6.3.3.2

Descriptive Writing

Directions: Read the following paragraph from a descriptive essay. Then, answer the questions that follow.

[1] My favorite time to be on the beach is at the end of the day in late summer, after the crowds have packed up and gone home. [2] I love walking along the edge of the beach, looking for seashells. [3] I collect various seashells that I put in glass vases. [4] I use them to decorate my room. [5] The sky is streaked with rays of color from the setting sun—purple, orange, and gold. [6] Sunrise at the beach is also beautiful. [7] My toes sink into the soothing sand. [8] I enjoy wading in the water, which has absorbed the sun's rays all summer and is now warm. [9] The scent of spicy, grilled food from someone's backyard barbecue comes on a light breeze. [10] In the distance I hear the gentle music of wind chimes tinkling when blown by the wind.

1 Which correctly matches a sensory detail with the sentence in which it appears?

A sentence [5]: smell
B sentence [7]: touch
C sentence [9]: sound
D sentence [10]: sight

2 What is the BEST way to combine sentences [2], [3], and [4]?

F I love walking along the edge of the beach, and I decorate my room and put the seashells I collect in glass vases.
G I love walking along the edge of the beach, collecting various seashells to put in glass vases to decorate my room.
H I love collecting various seashells along the edge of the beach that I use to decorate my room in glass vases.
I To collect various seashells to use in decorating my room, I love walking along the edge of the beach.

3 Which is the BEST way to revise sentence [9]?

A A light breeze brings the scent of spicy, grilled food from someone's backyard barbecue.
B Someone is cooking spicy, grilled food, and a light breeze brings the scent in a backyard barbecue.
C There is the scent of spicy, grilled food on a light breeze from someone's backyard barbecue.
D On a light breeze from someone's backyard barbecue is brought the scent of spicy, grilled food.

Read On

For Independent Reading

Poetry

Rimshots: Basketball Pix, Rolls, and Rhythms

Charles R. Smith, Jr., combines his love for basketball, photography, and reading into *Rimshots,* a Parents' Choice Silver Award–winning title. His poems are like basketball: quick and energetic, with sounds of scuffling feet and swishing baskets. Also included in *Rimshots* are short prose selections written with the same passion for the game.

The Tree Is Older Than You Are: A Bilingual Gathering of Poems & Stories from Mexico

Author and poet Naomi Shihab Nye has collected poems and folk tales from all over Mexico, including some by well-known writers such as Octavio Paz and Rosario Castellanos. Most of the poems are written in Spanish, but some are in Tzotzi and Tzeltal, two Mayan languages. In *The Tree Is Older Than You Are,* you'll find an English translation next to each selection as well as artwork by various Mexican artists.

Rainbows Are Made

The winner of two of the most acclaimed book awards in the United States—the Pulitzer Prize and the National Book Award—Carl Sandburg left his mark on poetry in the twentieth century. Chosen with young people in mind, the selections in *Rainbows Are Made* include seventy poems, both humorous and serious, dealing with people, wordplay, nature, night, and other aspects of life. The quality of the writing is matched by strong, dramatic wood engravings.

Langston Hughes—Young Black Poet

The famous poet Langston Hughes was one of the first African American writers to win worldwide favor. This biography focuses on Hughes's early life, when he developed a love of storytelling and an appreciation for hard work from his grandmother. Read Montrew Dunham's *Langston Hughes—Young Black Poet* to imagine yourself in Hughes's childhood. Then, see what poetry might come from you.

Sunshine State Standards: Benchmarks LA.6.2.1.10 use interest and recommendation of others to select a balance of age and ability appropriate fiction materials to read (e.g., novels, historical fiction, mythology, poetry) to expand the core foundation of knowledge necessary to function as a fully literate member of a shared culture.

Poetry

Whisked Away—Poems for More Than One Voice

This collection of new poems was written to be read aloud, preferably by more than one voice. When read aloud, the poems in *Whisked Away* become conversations, chants, demands, and spoken thoughts. Notes at the back of the book give practical guidance on volume, pace, actions, and sound effects to ensure that you get the most out of every poem . . . and every poem gets the most out of you.

Poetry Matters—Writing a Poem from the Inside Out

Have you ever been asked to write a poem? Have you ever struggled to start or to even come up with ideas? Ralph Fletcher's *Poetry Matters* gives you a nuts-and-bolts approach to creating poetry. It includes chapters on generating ideas, dealing with images, and creating music within your poem. You'll also find interviews with published poets, such as Janet S. Wong, discussing how they write. The interviews are followed by examples of poems that prove the techniques work.

Home: A Journey Through America

In this collection by Thomas Locker, famous American writers from different regions of the United States—such as Willa Cather, Henry David Thoreau, and Eloise Greenfield—give voice to the region that each calls home. Lavish oil paintings that accompany each passage take you from the crashing waves of the Pacific Coast to the vast expanse of the Great Plains to the bluebonnet prairie of Texas. Come along on a spectacular literary journey through America.

The Yearling

Have you ever dreamed of finding a wild baby animal that you could raise? That dream comes true for Jody Baxter in *The Yearling*. Besides being an adventure story, the book is interwoven with imagery, rural dialogue, and the rhythms of nature. Marjorie Kinnan Rawlings was awarded the 1939 Pulitzer Prize for this novel, which is set near her home in the wilds of central Florida.

Learn It Online

Use *NovelWise* to go further in your exploration of novels at:

go.hrw.com L6-737 Go

UNIT 4

Drama

Writers on Writing

Willie Reale on Drama

Willie Reale has written plays, musicals, song lyrics, and television shows. He wrote the spoken script and song lyrics for the musical *A Year with Frog and Toad,* which won the Tony Award for Best Musical. He also founded the 52nd Street Project, where students and professional actors and directors produce plays together.

"Okay, this is going to sound a little odd, but when you read plays, read with your ears. I tell you this because I think most playwrights or screenwriters or people who write TV shows or cartoons *write* with their

ears. I don't think I've ever written a line of dialogue that I didn't hear in my head first. In fact for me, when I'm writing well, I have characters talking in my head and I simply write down what they say. Sure, I make an outline and I have a theme in mind, because in the end, I'm telling a story in scenes and I want to make sure that story gets told in a crisp way. But when I'm actually writing at the keyboard or operating a pencil, I'm merely taking dictation.

The trick for you, the reader, is to hear what the writer heard as your eyes are running over the words. By the way, when actors read a script they do the same thing. They try and listen to characters' voices in order to figure out who the characters are and how to become them.

Many of you already have experienced reading with your ears. If you communicate through texting or instant messaging, you are receiving a line from a friend (who is like a character in the play that is your life). As you read, you can hear your friend's voice. If you read back over several lines of texting or IM-ing, you are actually reading a scene. There it is on the screen in dialogue form. It is a very short play. Obviously, it would be hard to get people to pay money to see someone's instant messaging performed, but you get the idea. The playwright is trying to write in a way that mirrors how people sound and act so that the audience will be drawn in and believe what they are watching.

And that is what the writers who work in the dramatic form strive to do. They try to see and hear a world that an audience will accept and believe in and then to tell a story in that world. They create characters and choose the moments of the characters' lives that best tell the story. Those of us that do this kind of work like to say that we write life with the boring parts left out. ”

Think as a Writer

What does Willie Reale mean when he suggests that you read plays "with your ears"?

Lord of the Rings musical

June 19, 2007- London, England, UK - Front three characters L to R: Sam (PETER HOWE), Frodo (JAMES LOYE) and Arwen (ROSALIE CRAIG). Background L to R: Gollum (MICHAEL THERRIAULT), Legolas (MICHAEL ROUSE), Ent (DAVID GRANT), Gandalf (MALCOLM STORRY), Black Rider (Adam SALTER), Gimli (SEVAN STEPHAN). *Lord of the Rings* musical at Drury Lane Theatre Royal.

COLLECTION 8

Elements of Drama

INFORMATIONAL TEXT FOCUS

Text Structures: Chronological Order and Cause/Effect

"Imagination is more important than knowledge. For knowledge is limited, whereas imagination embraces the entire world."

—**Albert Einstein**

What Do You Think? How can your imagination help you enter the fictional world of a play?

Learn It Online

Explore drama through *PowerNotes* online:

go.hrw.com L6-741 

Literary Focus

by **Linda Rief**

What Are the Elements of Drama?

When a play is performed, characters spring to life. Audiences can hear and see all of the action. When you're reading a play, your imagination can help you hear and see the characters as you step into their shoes and enter their world.

The Structure of a Play

A **drama,** or **play,** is a story written to be performed. Dramas have the same basic parts as other forms of fiction. The **introduction,** or **exposition,** provides the **basic situation:** who the main characters are and what the **conflict,** or struggle, is. Then **complications,** or new problems, arise as events unfold. Recall the plot of a story:

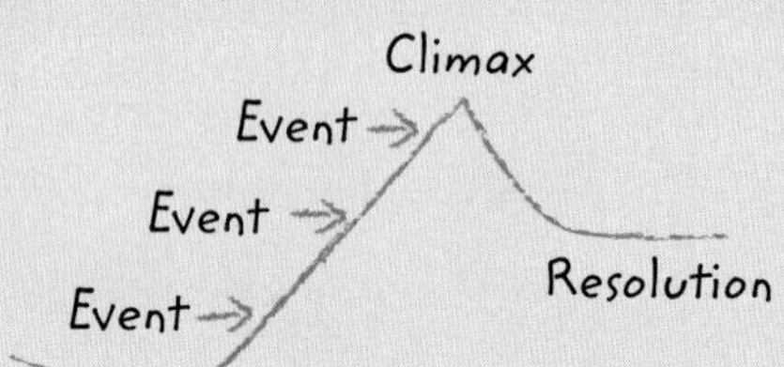

Plays have the same basic plot structure, but the action of a play is organized in a unique way. Long plays are broken up into smaller parts, called **acts.** Each act may contain many shorter sections, or **scenes.** Toward the end of a play is a scene that provides the **climax**—the most emotional and intense part of the play. The character we're rooting for either gets what he or she wants or loses it. In the **resolution,** all the problems are resolved, or worked out—happily or unhappily.

Conflict In drama, as in other forms of fiction, there are two main types of conflict. **External conflict** occurs between a character and an outside force, such as nature or another character. **Internal conflict,** on the other hand, takes place inside a character's mind. Playwrights (the authors of plays) use many of the same tools as other writers to move plots along and keep audiences—and readers—interested in the conflict.

Suspense Have you ever noticed your heart begin to beat a little faster as you wondered what was about to happen in a book or movie? Did you grip the book tightly or lean forward in your seat? If so, you've felt **suspense,** the anxious curiosity about what will happen next in a story. Some common characteristics of suspenseful stories and plays are listed below.

- plot twists and surprise endings
- a dark night
- a deserted road
- fog
- knocks on the door
- foreshadowing
- thunder or lightning
- strange footprints
- mysterious characters or events
- a creaky door
- a howling dog or wolf
- a shot in the dark
- strong winds or violent rains

Sunshine State Standards: Benchmarks **LA.6.2.1.1** identify the characteristics of various genres (e.g., poetry, fiction, short story, dramatic literature) as forms with distinct characteristics and purposes; **LA.6.2.1.2** locate and analyze the elements of plot structure, including exposition, setting, character development, rising/falling action, conflict/resolution, and theme in a variety of fiction; **LA.6.3.3.3** creating precision and interest by expressing ideas vividly through multiple language techniques (e.g., foreshadowing, imagery, simile, metaphor, sensory language, connotation, denotation) and modifying word choices using resources and reference materials (e.g., dictionary, thesaurus).

Foreshadowing Playwrights, as well as other writers, often employ foreshadowing to build suspense. **Foreshadowing** is the use of clues or hints to suggest what will happen later in a story. The following example from a play suggests that trouble is ahead, creating suspense in the process.

Zeke (*mildly*). What's your trade, mister?
Doctor. I . . . I'm a doctor. Why?
Zeke (*to* EBEN). Doctor.
Eben (*nods; then to* DOCTOR). Yer the man we want.
Zeke. Ye'll do proper, we're thinkin'.
Eben. So ye'd better come along, mister.

from *In the Fog*
by Milton Geiger

What might the fact that Zeke and Eben want a doctor to come with them foreshadow?

Flashback In addition to giving readers clues about what might happen later, writers sometimes relate events that happened *before* the main action of the story. A scene that breaks the normal time order of the plot to show a past event is called a **flashback.** Notice the shift in time between the first and second of these three lines:

Adams. Six days ago I left Brooklyn, to drive to California. . . .
Mother. Goodbye, Son. Good luck to you, my boy. . . .
Adams. Goodbye, Mother. Here—give me a kiss, and then I'll go. . . .

from *The Hitchhiker*
by Lucille Fletcher

Dialogue and Stage Directions

Dialogue **Dialogue** is conversation between characters in any kind of story, but it is especially important in drama. Most plays consist mainly of dialogue. When a new character begins speaking in a play, the character's name is set off from the rest of the text in some way—often in **boldface** at the beginning of the line.

Stage Directions In a play, you'll notice that some lines have words and phrases printed in italics and set in parentheses or brackets. These are called **stage directions** and are not meant to be read aloud. They tell the actors how to act out certain parts and let the reader know what characters are doing, thinking, or feeling, as in this example:

Don Ricardo (*addressing* JUANITO). Why are you here! Didn't she tell you to leave!
Blanca Flor (*scared*). Don't hurt him.

from *Blanca Flor* by Angel Vigil

Your Turn Analyze Elements of Drama

1. How are plays similar to other kinds of stories? How are they different?
2. Think of a suspenseful book or movie you liked. What in the story created suspense?
3. Add stage directions to the lines from *The Hitchhiker* on the left. Indicate what you think Mother and Adams are doing and feeling.

Learn It Online
Try the *PowerNotes* version of this lesson on:
go.hrw.com L6-743 Go

Analyzing Visuals

What Can Visuals Tell You About Drama?

By the time a play is performed, the playwright and director have made many decisions about the characters, the setting, and the conflict—and how they want to reveal these decisions to an audience. Looking closely at an image from a live performance can help you analyze the elements of drama "in action." Compare the two images that follow: an old illustration from a book of fables and a photograph from a present-day dramatized version of a similar fable. By comparing the illustration to the photograph, you see how plays can take a story from the printed page to the stage, appealing to our imaginations in new and different ways.

1. How does this illustration suggest a story? What narrative, or storytelling, elements do you see in it?

2. What can you tell about the characters and their interactions? What details of the **setting** stand out?

3. What clues are there that the characters have a conflict? What do you think this story is about, and why?

An illustration based on the fable "The Wolf, the Nanny Goat, and the Kids" by Jean de La Fontaine.

Sunshine State Standards: Benchmarks **LA.6.1.7.1** use background knowledge of subject and related content areas, prereading strategies, graphic representations, and knowledge of text structure to make and confirm complex predictions of content, purpose, and organization of a reading selection; **LA.6.2.1.1** identify the characteristics of various genres (e.g., poetry, fiction, short story, dramatic literature) as forms with distinct characteristics and purposes.

4. Describe the costumes the actors in this photograph are wearing. How do these **characters** seem similar to and different from those in the other image?

5. How are the actors positioned on the stage? Why might there be so little scenery to suggest the **setting**?

Fables de La Fontaine, presented as part of the Lincoln Center Festival 2007.

Analyzing an Image from a Play

Use these guidelines to help you analyze an image from a play:

1. What costumes are the actors wearing? What are the actors' facial expressions? What do the actors' appearances tell you about character and conflict in the play?
2. Notice the set design (the onstage scenery) and the blocking (how the characters are arranged physically on the stage). What can you determine about setting and conflict in the play from these visual clues?

Your Turn Write About the Elements of Drama

Think of a scene from a story that you'd like to see performed as a play. Write a description of how you would costume the actors and design the set for the scene. Then, explain how and why your choices are faithful to or different from the original story.

Reading Focus

by **Kylene Beers**

What Are the Best Ways to Read a Drama?

Watching a play is one thing, but *reading* a play requires different skills. A good way to read and understand a play is to create a mental map of events by visualizing the scenes. You'll also want to use your prior knowledge and pay attention to the sequence of events in a play to better follow what's happening.

Visualizing a Drama

To **visualize** is to form images in your mind based on details in a story. When you watch a drama, the setting, the characters, and the action are presented for you. When you *read* a drama, though, you have to use dialogue and the notes provided by the playwright or screenwriter (the author of a movie or television script) to visualize the places, people, and events. Details about the setting are often included in stage directions. Here's an example ("Sets" refers to the scenery on the stage):

> ***Sets:*** *A signpost on Pennsylvania Route 30. A rock or stump in the fog. A gas station pump.*
>
> *Night. At first we can only see fog drifting across a dark scene devoid of detail. Then, out of the fog, there emerges toward us a white roadside signpost with a number of white painted signboards pointing to right and to left. The marker is a Pennsylvania State Route—marked characteristically* "PENNA-30." *Now a light as from a far headlight sweeps the signs.*
>
> from *In the Fog* by Milton Geiger

Tips for Visualizing

- Pay attention to sensory details that describe how something looks, sounds, smells, feels, and tastes.
- As you read, draw a sketch of the setting or characters as you imagine them to be.
- Take notes as you read. You can use a chart to identify details that help with visualizing. Here is the start of a chart for *In the Fog:*

Visualizing	Details
Setting	foggy night on a Pennsylvania highway; white signpost; headlight in the distance
Action	car approaches
Characters	

Also, be aware that everyone visualizes differently. Although you are given some descriptive details, you'll also have to use your imagination to fill in the gaps. In the example on the left, you are told that there is a gas pump in the scene. What color is it? Is it old-fashioned, or is it newer? You can decide for yourself when you read this play later.

Sunshine State Standards: Benchmarks **LA.6.1.7.1** use background knowledge of subject and related content areas, prereading strategies, graphic representations, and knowledge of text structure to make and confirm complex predictions of content, purpose, and organization of a reading selection; **LA.6.1.7.5** analyze a variety of text structures (e.g., comparison/contrast, cause/effect, chronological order, argument/support, lists) and text features (main headings with subheadings) and explain their impact on meaning in text; **LA.6.1.7.8** use strategies to repair comprehension of grade-appropriate text when self-monitoring indicates confusion, including but not limited to rereading, checking context clues, predicting, note-making, summarizing, using graphic and semantic organizers, questioning, and clarifying by checking other sources; **LA.6.2.1.1** identify the characteristics of various genres (e.g., poetry, fiction, short story, dramatic literature) as forms with distinct characteristics and purposes.

Sequencing in Drama

When writers indicate the **sequence,** or order, of events in a story, they give you time cues such as *later, the day before, last year,* or *just after sunset* that tell you exactly when events occur. The same time cues can be found in dramas, but it helps to look for them in certain places. Sometimes a narrator tells you what happens when—just as in a short story or novel. Whether there is a narrator or not, however, you can often find sequencing information in the scene descriptions or stage directions of a play.

A Model for Understanding Sequence

Note where the underlined time cues in the following passage from a play appear, and pay attention to what they tell you:

Scene 4.
The Next Morning. ← This scene takes place the morning after the previous scene.

As THE NARRATOR *speaks,* JUANITO *and* BLANCA FLOR *enter and act out the scene as it is described.* ← If this play were being performed, Juanito and Blanca Flor would be acting *while* the narrator is talking.

The Narrator. Immediately upon waking the next morning, Juanito tried to move the rocks in the field, but they were impossible to move because of their great size. ← Juanito wakes up and *then* begins moving rocks.

from *Blanca Flor*
by Angel Vigil

Using Prior Knowledge

When you are reading a play, you can put your **prior knowledge**—what you've already learned and experienced—to good use in these ways:

To Help You Visualize If you've ever been on a foggy road at night, it will be easier for you to imagine such a scene in a play—and feel its eeriness. If a play is set in another time, knowing something about the historical period will help you picture the characters and setting.

To Help You Make Inferences and Predictions Writers sometimes **foreshadow,** or give you clues about, what might happen later. Combining these clues with what you already know makes it easier to **predict** what's likely to happen as the play unfolds. You can also use text details and your prior knowledge to make **inferences**—educated guesses—about things the writer does not state directly, such as certain aspects of a character's personality.

Your Turn Apply Reading Skills

1. Look back at the set description from *In the Fog* on the previous page. Draw a sketch of how you visualize this setting.
2. How do you think the writer of a play might signal a flashback to a previous event?

Now go to the Skills in Action: Reading Model

Learn It Online
Use the graphic organizers online to help you as you read:
go.hrw.com L6-747 Go

SKILLS IN ACTION

Reading Model

PLAY

Build Background

This play is a dramatized version of an old Vietnamese folk tale. For more than a thousand years, beginning around the last century B.C., the Vietnamese people lived under Chinese rule. *The Fly* likely takes place during (or not long after) this era in Vietnamese history.

Read with a Purpose Read this short play to see how a young boy uses some clever tricks to help his parents.

The Fly

retold by **Penni L. Ericson**
from **Plays Magazine**

Characters

Wealthy Banker
Small Boy
Boy's Mother
Boy's Father
The Mandarin (judge)

SCENE 1

Setting: *Small yard. Backdrop shows a little hut.*

At Rise: BOY *is playing with sticks and stones in front of hut.* BANKER *enters, carrying a large and ornate walking stick.*

Banker. Child, are your parents home?

Boy. No sir. *(Keeps playing)*

Banker. Then where are they? *(*BOY *doesn't answer.* BANKER *is irritated.)* I asked you a question, child—where are your parents?

Boy. Well, sir, my father has gone to cut living trees and plant dead ones. My mother is at the marketplace selling the wind and buying the moon.

Literary Focus

Dialogue and Stage Directions The **stage directions** here (the words in italics in parentheses) tell what the characters are doing while they deliver their lines. The lines of speech that follow are the **dialogue.** The name of each new **speaker**—the character talking—is boldface at the beginning of the line.

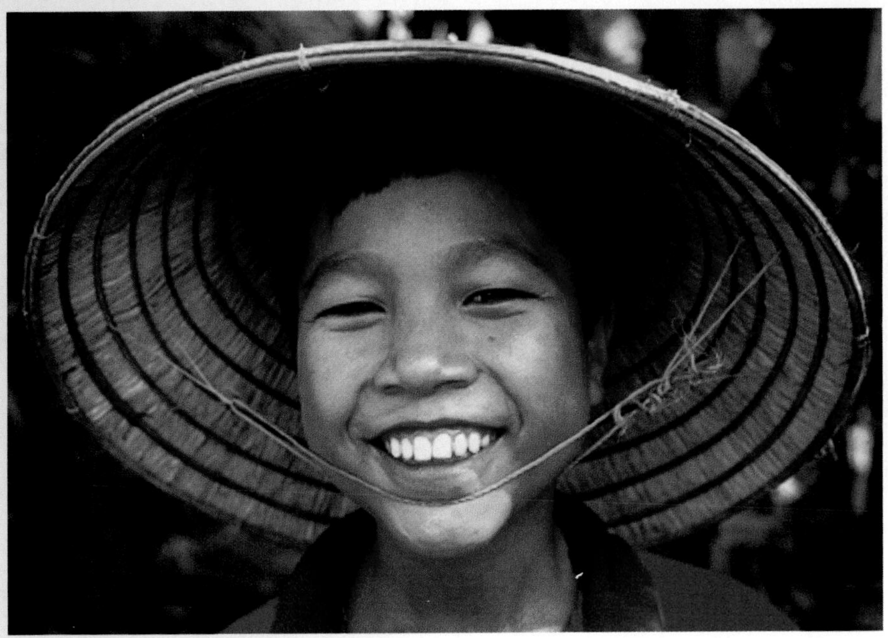

Banker *(Exasperated)*. Listen, boy, you had better tell me where your parents are, or you will see just what this stick *(Raises stick)* will do to you!

Boy. Sir, my father has gone to cut living trees and plant dead ones, and my mother is at the marketplace selling the wind and buying the moon.

Banker *(Nearly yelling)*. All right, now you listen to me! I came here today to collect the money your parents owe me. But if you will tell me where they really are and what they are really doing, I will forget all about their debt. Now, where are they?

Boy. Oh, sir, what you say cannot be true. How can I believe you?

Banker *(Pointing up and down)*. There is heaven and earth to be my witness that I tell the truth.

Boy *(Laughing)*. Sir, heaven and earth cannot talk and so cannot testify. I want a living thing to be our witness.

Banker. Look, boy, over on the pole *(Pointing)*. There is a fly to be our witness. Now tell me what you mean!

Boy. Hm-m-m. A fly is a good enough witness for me.

Banker. Then tell me immediately!

Boy. Are you sure you will keep your promise?

Banker. Yes!

Literary Focus

Structure of a Play This play has one act, divided into three short scenes. The first scene reveals the basic situation of the story: The boy is the main character and is in an external conflict with the banker, who wants to collect a debt.

Boy. Well, here is the truth. My father has gone to cut bamboo and build a fence with it. He is cutting living trees to plant dead ones. And my mother . . . *(Pauses)* you promise?

Banker. Yes, yes, I swear with this fly as my witness. Now tell me!

Boy. My mother has gone to the market to sell fans so she can buy oil for our lamps. Isn't that like selling the wind to buy the moon?

Banker. Thank you, boy, I will return soon to make good on my promise. *(Walking away)* This little boy may be clever, but he has a lot to learn. A fly for a witness. Ha! (*Curtain*)

SCENE 2

Setting: *Same.*

At Rise*:* BOY, MOTHER, *and* FATHER *sit in front of their hut.* BANKER *strides in with his fancy walking stick in hand.*

Banker. Hello! I am glad to find you at home. You owe me a great deal of money, and I'm here to collect it.

Father. Oh, sir, please give me a little more time and I am sure I will be able to pay you back. Times are very hard.

Banker. No! I am tired of your begging. You must pay me now.

Mother. But we cannot pay!

Boy. Wait, Father! You don't have to pay him. He promised to forgive all the money you owe him.

Banker *(Shaking his stick).* Nonsense! You cannot believe the lies of a child. I have never seen this boy. Now, are you going to pay me or not?

Father *(Holding up his hand).* Wait! What do you say, son?

Boy. This man promised to forgive all the money you owe him.

Banker. You little liar!

Mother. Why don't we let the Mandarin[1] judge for us?

Banker. The Mandarin will judge in my favor. He will not believe the story this child has spun.

Father. But I agree with my wife that the Mandarin must judge, for I know my son is truthful.

Banker. As you wish. I only want what is owed to me. *(Curtain)*

1. **Mandarin:** high official in the old Chinese empires.

Literary Focus

Foreshadowing The Banker's last statement in this scene is an example of **foreshadowing**—it strongly hints that he might not do what he says he will.

Reading Focus

Sequencing The playwright presents events in **chronological order**—the sequence in which they occur. We don't know precisely when these three scenes take place, but we do know that they happen one after the other.

Reading Focus

Using Prior Knowledge Based on what you know about the banker and people who behave like him—your prior knowledge—you shouldn't be surprised by his actions here. You may even be able to predict whether the boy's father will believe the boy or the banker.

The Granger Collection, New York.

Analyzing Visuals

Viewing and Interpreting Which character in the play probably looks most like this? Explain.

SCENE 3

Setting: *Judge's chamber. Desk and ornate chair are center. On a table next to him are stacks of important-looking books and papers.*

At Rise: MANDARIN *sits at desk.* BOY, MOTHER, *and* FATHER *stand to one side,* BANKER *to the other.*

Reading Focus

Visualizing When you read a play, use the description of the setting and stage directions to help you visualize the time, the place, the characters, and their actions. Also, draw upon any prior knowledge you have of similar people and places.

Mandarin. Young man, the banker says your parents owe him a great deal of money and that you are telling tales only to postpone their payment. What do you have to say?

Boy. I am telling the truth, your honor.

Mandarin. Well, if the banker had made such a wild promise, I have only your word. How do I know you have not made up this whole story? *(Kindly)* You need a witness, son, and you have none.

Boy. But I do have a witness, your honor.

Banker. Ha, ha! Another story.

Mandarin. Who is that, child?

Boy. A fly.

Mandarin *(Sternly)*. A fly? Young man, I do not tolerate fantasy. You are wasting my time!

Boy. Yes, your honor, a fly! A fly, which lit[2] on his nose *(Points to* BANKER*)* as we spoke!

---

2. **lit:** Here, *lit* means "landed."

Banker *(Yelling)*. Another lie! The fly was not on my nose, it was on the pole—*(Gasps and claps his hands over his mouth)*

Mandarin *(Laughing)*. It seems that promises were made to you, young man. (*To* BANKER) This court finds that you must keep your promises and forgive the debts of this family. (*As the curtain closes,* BOY, MOTHER, *and* FATHER *hug one another,* MANDARIN *returns to his paperwork, and* BANKER *stamps his feet in anger.)*

The End

Read with a Purpose How does the boy use trickery to get his parents' debts forgiven? How does his trickery show cleverness—and imagination?

MEET THE WRITER

Penni L. Ericson

Plays: The Drama Magazine for Young People

Penni L. Ericson is a contributor to *Plays,* a magazine for students that publishes short dramas in seven issues throughout the year. *Plays* magazine often includes dramatized folk tales such as *The Fly.*

Vietnamese Folk Theater

Vietnamese folk tales emphasize traditional cultural values, especially the importance of relying on cleverness to survive. Because Vietnam is a small country next to China—a rich and mighty giant—it has had two thousand years of practice in outwitting a more powerful neighbor.

Even today, in twenty-first-century Vietnam, groups of traveling actors specialize in a style of traditional folk theater known as Cheo (pronounced CHEE ow). The actors perform stories that are set hundreds of years ago but often have timeless themes. Like *The Fly,* many Cheo performances involve tales of clever triumph.

Think About the Writer Why do you think Ericson chose to dramatize *The Fly*?

SKILLS IN ACTION
Wrap Up

Sunshine State Standards: Benchmarks **LA.6.1.6.1** use new vocabulary that is introduced and taught directly; **LA.6.1.7.8** use strategies to repair comprehension of grade-appropriate text when self-monitoring indicates confusion, including but not limited to rereading, checking context clues, predicting, note-making, summarizing, using graphic and semantic organizers, questioning, and clarifying by checking other sources; **LA.6.2.1.1** identify the characteristics of various genres (e.g., poetry, fiction, short story, dramatic literature) as forms with distinct characteristics and purposes; *Also covered* **LA.6.2.1.2**

Into Action: Diagramming the Structure of the Play

On a separate sheet of paper, draw a plot diagram like this one to show the structure of *The Fly*. Explain the basic situation of the play, and then identify events that lead to the climax. Describe the climax in your own words, and then explain the resolution.

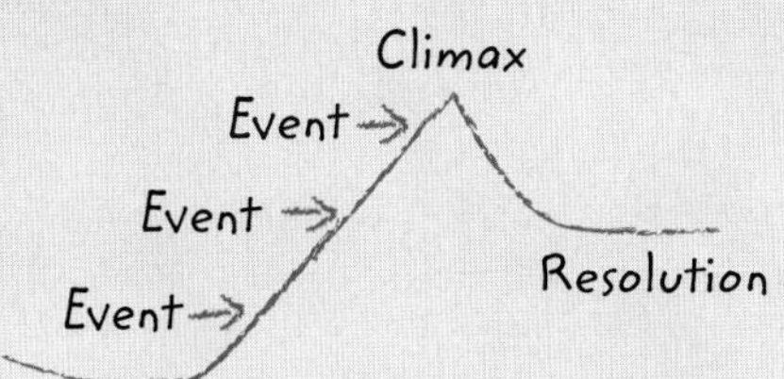

Talk About . . .

1. Discuss with a partner what you liked or didn't like about this play. For example, do you think it was realistic? Does that matter to you? Were the boy's tricks the right thing to do? Jot down your ideas to share with the class. Try to use each Academic Vocabulary word listed at the right at least once in your discussion.

Write About . . .

Answer the following questions about *The Fly*. For definitions of the underlined Academic Vocabulary words, see the column on the right.

2. Who is the principal character in the play? Explain whether you think he or she is dynamic.
3. What character qualities does the banker display?
4. Do you think this would be a complex play to perform? Why or why not?

Writing Focus

Think as a Reader/Writer

The plays in this collection have many of the same elements as other types of stories, but they also have some features that are unique to drama. You'll identify examples as you read, and then you'll write about these examples later.

Academic Vocabulary for Collection 8

Talking and Writing About Elements of Drama

Academic Vocabulary is the language you use to write and talk about literature. Use these words, which are underlined throughout the collection, to discuss the plays you read.

complex (kahm PLEHKS) *adj.:* complicated; not simple. *Complications in the plot make a play more complex.*

display (dihs PLAY) *v.:* show clearly; reveal. *Actors display a range of emotions when they play a character.*

dynamic (dy NAM ihk) *adj.:* characterized by action; energetic changing. *Drama is a dynamic art form.*

principal (PRIHN suh puhl) *adj.:* most important. *The principal character in a play is usually the one the audience cares about the most.*

Your Turn

Copy the Academic Vocabulary words into your *Reader/Writer Notebook*. Use each word in a sentence about your favorite movie, television show, or video game.

DRAMA

Preparing to Read

BLANCA FLOR

by **Angel Vigil**

What Do You Think?

What role does your imagination play when you stop to consider the possibilities for your life?

QuickWrite

You've probably thought about plans for your future or adventures you'd like to have. Do you think they'll turn out just as you imagine them? Why or why not?

Reader/Writer Notebook

Use your **RWN** to complete the activities for this selection.

Sunshine State Standards: Benchmarks **LA.6.1.6.1** use new vocabulary that is introduced and taught directly; **LA.6.1.6.11** identify the meaning of words and phrases derived from Greek and Latin mythology (e.g., mercurial, Achilles' heel) and identify frequently used words from other languages (e.g., laissez faire, croissant); **LA.6.1.7.8** use strategies to repair comprehension of grade-appropriate text when self-monitoring indicates confusion, including but not limited to rereading, checking context clues, predicting, note-making, summarizing, using graphic and semantic organizers, questioning, and clarifying by checking other sources; **LA.6.2.1.1** identify the characteristics of various genres (e.g., poetry, fiction, short story, dramatic literature) as forms with distinct characteristics and purposes.

Literary Focus

Dialogue and Stage Directions Like all plays, or dramas, *Blanca Flor* is written in the form of **dialogue**—conversations between characters. **Stage directions**—notes within parentheses or brackets—give instructions that aren't read aloud in a performance. They enable readers to imagine the setting and the characters' actions. The writer of this play also uses a **narrator,** a speaker who is not a character in the story, to describe actions and events.

Literary Perspectives Apply the literary perspective described on page 757 as you read this play.

Reading Focus

Visualizing When you read a drama, you have to **visualize,** or picture in your mind, what is happening. You'll need to read all of the dialogue, stage directions, and narrator's parts to get the full experience of this play.

Into Action Use details from dialogue, stage directions, and the narrator's descriptions to help you visualize the setting and principal characters. You may want to use a chart like this one as you read *Blanca Flor.*

Setting	"river," "middle of the forest," "came to a house"
Juanito	
Blanca Flor	"young woman," "took out her brush and began to brush his hair," "cradled Juanito in her arms"

Writing Focus

Think as a Reader/Writer

Find It in Your Reading Because *Blanca Flor* is a drama, the story is told almost entirely through dialogue. As you read, note lines of dialogue that particularly reveal what characters are like.

Vocabulary

valiant (VAL yuhnt) *adj.:* determined; brave. *Juanito made a valiant effort to help Blanca Flor.*

barren (BAR uhn) *adj.:* unable to bear crops or fruit. *Don Ricardo had a barren field.*

flourish (FLUR ihsh) *n.:* sweeping movement. *Don Ricardo left with a flourish.*

apprehensively (ap rih HEHN sihv lee) *adv.:* fearfully; uneasily. *Blanca Flor looked around apprehensively.*

Language Coach

Spanish Words in English American English has been borrowing words from Spanish for a long time. Many of these words relate to foods, places, and animals. A *tortilla* (tawr TEE yuh), for example, is a flat Mexican bread made from cornmeal or flour. Look for other words in this play that come from Mexican culture.

Learn It Online
Preview this play by watching the video introduction at:

go.hrw.com L6-755 

MEET THE WRITER

Angel Vigil

(1947–)

A Family of Storytellers

Angel Vigil was born in New Mexico and was raised "in a large, traditional Hispanic extended family, with loving grandparents and plenty of aunts and cousins." Storytelling was an important part of his family life. In his book *The Corn Woman: Stories and Legends of the Hispanic Southwest,* Vigil explains how he was influenced by family stories:

> "I was amazed to discover that my living relatives were sources of folklore. . . . I felt it was my calling to do what I could to make sure that the rich oral tradition of my childhood would continue through my generation."

Vigil is an award-winning educator, author, and storyteller. Most of the legends and folk tales he retells—sometimes in the form of plays such as *Blanca Flor*—come from the Hispanic oral tradition. Vigil is also a performer and stage director and serves as chairman of the Fine and Performing Arts Department and director of drama at Colorado Academy in Denver.

Think About the Writer How do you think Vigil's childhood influenced his life as an author and educator?

Build Background

Although *Blanca Flor* is based on a traditional European tale, the play also draws on Hispanic folklore. The mischievous little trickster known as a *duende* (DWEHN day) makes trouble for people in stories told throughout the Hispanic Southwest.

Preview the Selection

Blanca Flor tells the story of **Juanito,** a young man who leaves his parents, **Doña Arlette** and **Don Ramon,** to seek his fortune. After crossing paths with a mischievous creature called a **Duende,** Juanito meets a beautiful young woman named **Blanca Flor** and a man named **Don Ricardo.**

Read with a Purpose Read this drama to discover what happens to a young man named Juanito when he leaves home to seek his fortune.

BLANCA FLOR

by **Angel Vigil**

Characters (in order of appearance)

The Narrator
Juanito, a young man
The Duende, a gnomelike, mischievous creature who lives in the forest
Blanca Flor, a young woman
Don[1] Ricardo, an evil man
Don Ramon, the father of Juanito
Doña[2] Arlette, the mother of Juanito
Two Doves, actors in costume

Scene 1.
In the Forest.

The Narrator. *Blanca Flor,* "White Flower." There never was a story with such a beautiful name as this story of Blanca Flor. At the beginning of our story, a young man named Juanito has left home to seek his fortune in the world. With the blessing of his parents to aid and protect him, he has begun what will be a fantastic adventure. At the beginning of his journey, he wanders into a forest and stops by a stream to rest and eat some of the tortillas his mother had packed for his journey. **A**

1. **Don** (dahn): Spanish for "Sir" or "Mr."
2. **Doña** (DOH nyah): Spanish for "Lady" or "Madam."

A Literary Perspectives **Archetypes** What literary archetype is presented by the narrator in the first paragraph? What other stories have you read that begin in a similar way?

Literary Perspectives

The following perspective will help you think about the characters and events in *Blanca Flor*.

Analyzing Archetypes No matter what culture or time period they are from, many stories share similar themes and characteristics. You're certain to recognize some familiar story elements in this play. These familiar features are called **archetypes** (AHR kuh typs) or **motifs** (moh TEEFS): patterns that appear again and again in literature. Why do so many stories share common elements? Perhaps it's because human beings everywhere share the same basic emotions and find satisfaction in the familiar but powerful ways certain stories play out.

Look for these archetypes: a son who is seeking his fortune; an enchanted forest; characters with magical powers; an evil curse; a powerful villain; transformations; events occurring in threes; magical objects. As you read, be sure to answer the Literary Perspectives questions at the bottom of this selection's pages.

[JUANITO *enters and walks around the stage as if looking for a comfortable place to rest. He finally decides upon a spot and sits down. He takes out a tortilla from his traveling bag and he begins to talk to himself.*] **B**

Juanito. Whew! I'm hot. This river looks like a good spot to rest for a while. I'm so tired. Maybe this journey wasn't such a good idea. Right now I could be home with *la familia* eating a good supper that *mamacita* cooked for us. But no, I'm out in the world seeking my fortune. So far I haven't found very much, and all I have to show for my efforts are two worn-out feet and a tired body . . . oh, and don't forget (*holding up a dried tortilla*) a dried-out tortilla . . . (*He quickly looks around as if startled.*) What was that? (*He listens intently and hears a sound again.*) There it is again. I know I heard something . . .

[*As* JUANITO *is talking,* THE DUENDE *enters, sneaking up behind him.*]

Juanito. Must be my imagination. I've been out in the woods too long. You know, if you're alone too long, your mind starts to play tricks on you. Just look at me. I'm talking to my tortilla and hearing things . . .
The Duende (*in a crackly voice*). Hello.
Juanito. Yikes! Who said that! (*He turns around quickly and is startled to see* THE DUENDE *behind him.*) Who are you?
The Duende (*with a mischievous twinkle in his eye*). Hello.
Juanito. Hello . . . who, who are you? And where did you come from?

[THE DUENDE *grabs the tortilla out of* Juanito's *hand and begins to eat it. During the rest of the scene* THE DUENDE *continues to eat tortillas.*]

Juanito. Hey, that's my tortilla.
The Duende (*in a playful manner*). Thank you very much. Thank you very much.
Juanito (*to the audience*). He must be a forest Duende. I've heard of them. They're spirits who live in the wood and play tricks on humans. I better go along with him or he might hurt me. (*He offers* THE DUENDE *another tortilla.* THE DUENDE *takes the tortilla and begins to eat it, too.*) I hope he's not too hungry. If he eats all my tortillas, I won't have any left, and it'll be days before I get food again. I'll have to eat wild berries like an animal. (*He reaches for the tortilla and* THE DUENDE *hits his hand.*) Ouch, that hurt!
The Duende. Looking for work, eh?
Juanito. Now I know he's a Duende. He can read minds. **C**
The Duende. No work here. Lost in the forest. No work here.
Juanito. I know that. We're in the middle of the forest. But I know there'll be work in the next town.
The Duende. Maybe work right here. Maybe.
Juanito. Really. Where?

[THE DUENDE *points to a path in the forest.* Juanito *stands up and looks down the path.*]

B **Literary Focus** **Dialogue and Stage Directions** How do you know these are stage directions? Who are they for, and what information do they provide?

C **Read and Discuss** Why do you think the author has Juanito talk directly to the audience here?

Juanito. There's nothing down that path. I've been down that path and there is nothing there.
The Duende. Look again. Look again. Be careful. Be careful. (*He begins to walk off, carrying the bag of tortillas with him.*)
Juanito. Hey, don't leave yet. What type of work? And where? Who do I see? Hey, don't leave yet!
The Duende (THE DUENDE *stops and turns*). Be careful. Danger. Danger. (*He exits.*)
Juanito. Hey! That's my bag of tortillas. Oh, this is great. This is really going to sound good when I get back home. My tortillas? . . . Oh, they were stolen by a forest Duende. Not to worry . . . (*He yells in the direction of the departed* DUENDE.) And I'm not lost! . . . This is great. Lost and hungry and no work. I guess I'm never going to find my fortune in the world. But what did he mean about work . . . and be careful . . . and danger. I've been down that path and there was nothing there . . . I don't think there was anything there. Oh well, there is only one way to find out. It certainly can't get much worse than things are now, and maybe there is work there.

[JUANITO *exits, in the direction of the path* THE DUENDE *indicated.*] **D**

Scene 2.
Farther in the Forest.

The Narrator. In spite of the Duende's warning, Juanito continued on the path of danger. As he came into a clearing, he came to a house and saw a young woman coming out of it. **E**

[JUANITO *enters,* BLANCA FLOR *enters from the opposite side of the stage and stops, remaining at the opposite side of the stage.*]

Juanito. Where did this house come from? I was here just yesterday and there was no house here. I must really be lost and turned around. (*He sees the young woman and waves to her.*) Hey! Come here. Over here!

[BLANCA FLOR *runs to* JUANITO.]

Analyzing Visuals **Viewing and Interpreting** What does the expression on this forest creature's face suggest?

D **Read and Discuss** What have we learned so far?

E **Reading Focus** **Visualizing** How does the playwright's use of a narrator help you visualize the setting?

Blanca Flor (*with fear in her voice*). How did you find this place? You must leave right away. The owner of this place is gone, but he will return soon. He leaves to do his work in the world, but he will return unexpectedly. If he finds you here, you'll never be able to leave. You must leave right away.

Juanito. Why? I haven't done anything.

Blanca Flor. Please, just leave. And hurry!

Juanito. Who are you? And why are you here?

Blanca Flor. I am Blanca Flor. My parents died long ago, and I am kept by this man to pay off their debts to him. I have to work day and night on his farm until I can be free. But he is mean, and he has kept prisoner others who have tried to free me. He makes them work until they die from exhaustion.

Juanito. Who would be so mean?

Blanca Flor. His name is Don Ricardo.

[DON RICARDO *enters, suddenly and with great force.*] **F**

Don Ricardo (*addressing* JUANITO). Why are you here! Didn't she tell you to leave!

Blanca Flor (*scared*). Don't hurt him. He is lost in the forest and got here by mistake. He was just leaving.

Don Ricardo. Let him answer for himself. Then I will decide what to do with him.

Juanito (*gathering all his courage*). Yes, she did tell me to leave. But . . . but I am in the world seeking my fortune and I am looking for work. Is there any work for me to do here?

Don Ricardo. Seeking your fortune! They always say that, don't they, Blanca Flor. Well, I will give you the same chance I have given others. For each of three days, I will give you a job. If in three days you have completed the jobs, then you may leave. If not, then you will work here with me until you are dead. What do you say, fortune-seeker?

Blanca Flor (*pulling* JUANITO *aside*). Do not say yes. You will never leave here alive. Run and try to escape.

Juanito. But what about you? You are more trapped than anybody.

Blanca Flor. That is not your worry. Just run and try to escape.

Juanito (*suddenly turning back to* DON RICARDO). I will do the work you ask.

Don Ricardo (*laughing*). Blanca Flor, it is always your fault they stay. They all think they will be able to set you free. Well, let's give this one his "fair" chance. (*To* JUANITO) Here is your first job. See that lake over there? Take this thimble (*he gives a thimble to* JUANITO) and use it to carry all the water in the lake to that field over there. **G**

Juanito. You want me to move a lake with a thimble?!

Don Ricardo. You wanted work, fortune-seeker. Well, this is your job. Have it finished by morning or your fate will be the same as all the others who tried to save poor Blanca Flor. (*He exits.*)

Juanito. What type of man is he? I have heard legends of evil men who keep people captive, and in my travels I heard many stories of young men seeking their fortunes who were never seen again, but I always thought they were just stories.

F **Literary Perspective** **Archetypes** What has happened so far in this scene that is familiar from other stories? Do you see more than one kind of archetype presented here? Explain.

G **Read and Discuss** Why is Don Ricardo laughing? Does this action make his character more complex? Why or why not?

Blanca Flor. You have had the misfortune to get lost in a terrible part of the forest. Didn't anyone warn you to stay away from here?

Juanito. Yes . . . one person did. But I thought he was a forest Duende, and I didn't really believe him.

Blanca Flor. It was a forest Duende. In this part of the forest there are many creatures with magic. But my keeper, his magic is stronger than any of ours.

Juanito. Ours? . . . What do you mean, ours? Are you part of the magic of this forest?

Blanca Flor. Do not ask so many questions. The day is passing by, and soon it will be morning.

Juanito. Morning. I'm supposed to have moved the lake by then. I know this job is impossible, but while God is in his heaven there is a way. I will do this job. And when I am done, I will help you escape from here.

[JUANITO *and* BLANCA FLOR *exit.*] (H)

Scene 3.
The Next Morning.

JUANITO *and* BLANCA FLOR *enter. As* THE NARRATOR *speaks,* JUANITO *and* BLANCA FLOR *act out the scene as it is described.*

The Narrator. Juanito took the thimble and started to carry the water from the lake. He worked as hard as he could, but soon he began to realize that the job really was an impossible one, and he knew he was doomed. He sat down and began to cry because his luck had abandoned him and because his parents' blessings offered no protection in that evil place. Blanca Flor watched Juanito's valiant effort to move the water. As she watched him crying, her heart was touched, and she decided to use her powers to help him. She knew that it was very dangerous to use her powers to help Juanito and to cross Don Ricardo, but she felt it was finally time to end her own torment. As Juanito cried, Blanca Flor took out her brush and began to brush his hair. She cradled Juanito in her arms and her soothing comfort soon put him to sleep . . .

You want me to move a lake with a thimble?!

[*As soon as* JUANITO *is asleep,* BLANCA FLOR *gently puts his head down and leaves, taking the thimble with her.*]

The Narrator. When Juanito awoke, he frantically looked for the thimble and, not finding it, ran to the lake. When he reached the lake, he stood at its banks in amazement. All the water was gone. He looked over to the other part of the field, and there stood a lake where before there was nothing. He turned to look for Blanca Flor, but instead there was Don Ricardo.

[DON RICARDO *enters.*]

Don Ricardo (*in full force and very angry*). This must be the work of Blanca Flor, or else you have more power than I thought. I know Blanca Flor is too scared to ever use her powers against me, so as a test of your powers, tomorrow your next job will not be so easy.

(H) **Read and Discuss** What is going on with Juanito now?

Vocabulary **valiant** (VAL yuhnt) *adj.:* determined; brave.

See that barren ground over on the side of the mountain? You are to clear that ground, plant seeds, grow wheat, harvest it, grind it, cook it, and have bread for me to eat before I return. You still have your life now, but I better have bread tomorrow. (*He exits, with a flourish.*)

[JUANITO *exits.*]

Scene 4.
The Next Morning.

As THE NARRATOR *speaks,* JUANITO *and* BLANCA FLOR *enter and act out the scene as it is described.*

The Narrator. Immediately upon waking the next morning, Juanito tried to move the rocks in the field, but they were impossible to move because of their great size. Once again, Juanito knew that his efforts were useless. He went over to the new lake and fell down in exhaustion. As he lay in the grass by the lake, Blanca Flor came to him once more and began to brush his hair. Soon, Juanito was asleep. ❶

[BLANCA FLOR *exits.*]

The Narrator. As before, when he awoke, Juanito dashed to the field to make one last attempt to do his work. When he got there, he again stopped in amazement. The field was clear of rocks, and the land had been planted and harvested. As he turned around, there stood Blanca Flor.

[BLANCA FLOR *enters.*]

Blanca Flor (*She hands a loaf of bread to* JUANITO.) Give this to Don Ricardo.

Juanito. How did you do this?

[DON RICARDO *enters, quickly.*]

---

❶ **Literary Focus** **Dialogue and Stage Directions** Most of the drama is presented in the form of dialogue. How does the narrator's description help move the story along?

Vocabulary **barren** (BAR uhn) *adj.:* unable to bear crops or fruit.
flourish (FLUR ihsh) *n.:* sweeping movement.

Don Ricardo. What do you have?

Juanito (*shaking with fear*). Just . . . just this loaf of bread. (*Giving the bread to* DON RICARDO) Here is the bread you asked for.

Don Ricardo (*very angry*). This is the work of Blanca Flor. This will not happen again. Tomorrow, your third job will be your final job, and even the powers of Blanca Flor will not help you this time! (*He exits.*)

Blanca Flor. Believe me, the third job will be impossible to do. It will be too difficult even for my powers. We must run from here if there is to be any chance of escaping his anger. He will kill you because I have helped you. Tonight I will come for you. Be ready to leave quickly as soon as I call for you.

[JUANITO *and* BLANCA FLOR *exit.*] J

Scene 5.
Later That Night.

On one side of the stage, JUANITO *sits waiting. On the other side,* BLANCA FLOR *is in her room grabbing her traveling bag. As she leaves her room, she turns and mimes spitting three times as* THE NARRATOR *describes the action.*

The Narrator. Late that night, as Juanito waited for her, Blanca Flor packed her belongings into a bag. Before she left the house, she went to the fireplace and spat three times into it.

[BLANCA FLOR *joins* JUANITO.]

Blanca Flor (*quietly calling*). Juanito . . . Juanito.

Juanito. Blanca Flor, is it time?

Blanca Flor. Yes. We must leave quickly, before he finds out I am gone, or it will be too late.

Juanito. Won't he know you are gone as soon as he calls for you?

Blanca Flor. Not right away. I've used my powers to fool him. But it won't last long. Let's go!

[JUANITO *and* BLANCA FLOR *exit.*]

The Narrator. When Don Ricardo heard the noise of Juanito and Blanca Flor leaving, he called out . . .

Don Ricardo (*from offstage*). Blanca Flor, are you there?

The Narrator. The spit she had left in the fireplace answered.

Blanca Flor (*from offstage*). Yes, I am here.

The Narrator. Later, Don Ricardo called out again.

Don Ricardo (*from offstage*). Blanca Flor, are you there?

The Narrator. For a second time, the spit she had left in the fireplace answered.

Blanca Flor (*from offstage*). Yes, I am here.

The Narrator. Still later, Don Ricardo called out again, a third time.

Don Ricardo (*from offstage*). Blanca Flor, are you there?

The Narrator. By this time, the fire had evaporated Blanca Flor's spit, and there was no answer. Don Ricardo knew that Blanca Flor was gone, and that she had run away with Juanito. He saddled his horse and galloped up the path to catch them before they escaped from his land. K

J **Read and Discuss** What has happened during the last two days?

K **Read and Discuss** What is this part about?

Scene 6.
In the Forest.

JUANITO and BLANCA FLOR enter, running and out of breath.

Juanito. Blanca Flor, we can rest now. We are free.
Blanca Flor. No, Juanito, we will not be free until we are beyond the borders of Don Ricardo's land. As long as we are on his land, his powers will work on us.
Juanito. How much farther?
Blanca Flor. Remember the river where you met The Duende? That river is the border. Across it we are free.
Juanito. That river is still really far. Let's rest here for a while.
Blanca Flor. No, he is already after us. We must keep going. I can hear the hooves of his horse.
Juanito (*he looks around desperately*). Where? How can that be?
Blanca Flor. He is really close. Juanito, come stand by me. Quickly!
Juanito (*still looking around*). I don't hear anything.
Blanca Flor (*grabbing him and pulling him to her*). Juanito! Now!

[*As THE NARRATOR describes the action, JUANITO and BLANCA FLOR act out the scene. BLANCA FLOR does not actually throw a brush. She mimes throwing the brush and the action.*]

The Narrator. Blanca Flor looked behind them and saw that Don Ricardo was getting closer. She reached into her bag, took her brush, and threw it behind her. The brush turned into a church by the side of the road. She then cast a spell on Juanito and turned him into a little old bell ringer. She turned herself into a statue outside the church. **L**

[*DON RICARDO enters, as if riding a horse.*]

Don Ricardo (*addressing the bell ringer* [JUANITO]). Bell ringer, have you seen two young people come this way recently? They would have been in a great hurry and out of breath.
Juanito (*in an old man's voice*). No . . . I don't think so. But maybe last week, two young boys came by. They stopped to pray in the church . . . Or was it two girls. I don't know. I am just an old bell ringer. Not many people actually come by this way at all. You're the first in a long time.
Don Ricardo. Bell ringer, if you are lying to me you will be sorry. (*He goes over to the statue* [BLANCA FLOR], *who is standing very still, as a statue. He examines the statue very closely and then addresses the bell ringer* [JUANITO].) Bell ringer, what saint is this a statue of? The face looks very familiar.
Juanito. I am an old bell ringer. I don't remember the names of all the saints. But I do know that the statue is very old and has been here a long time. Maybe Saint Theresa or Saint Bernadette.
Don Ricardo. Bell ringer, if you are lying, I will be back! (*He exits.*)
Juanito. Adiós, Señor!

L **Reading Focus** **Visualizing** Can you imagine the action occurring here? What details help you visualize the scene?

[BLANCA FLOR *breaks her pose as a statue and goes to* JUANITO.]

Blanca Flor. Juanito, Juanito. The spell is over.
Juanito. What happened? I did hear the angry hooves of a horse being ridden hard.
Blanca Flor. We are safe for a while. But he will not give up, and we are not free yet.

[JUANITO *and* BLANCA FLOR *exit.*] **M**

Scene 7.
Farther into the Forest.

The Narrator. Blanca Flor and Juanito desperately continued their escape. As they finally stopped for a rest, they had their closest call yet.

[BLANCA FLOR *and* JUANITO *enter.*]

Juanito. Blanca Flor, please, let's rest just for a minute.
Blanca Flor. OK. We can rest here. I have not heard the hooves of his horse for a while now.
Juanito. What will he do if he catches us?
Blanca Flor. He will take us back. I will be watched more closely than ever, and you will—
Juanito (*sadly*). I know. Was there ever a time when you were free? Do you even remember your parents?
Blanca Flor. Yes. I have the most beautiful memories of my mother, our house, and our animals. Every day, my father would saddle the horses and together we would— **N**
Juanito. Blanca Flor . . . I hear something.
Blanca Flor (*alarmed*). He's close. Very close.

[As THE NARRATOR *describes the action,* JUANITO *and* BLANCA FLOR *act out the scene.* BLANCA FLOR *does not actually throw a comb. She mimes throwing the comb and the action.*]

Analyzing Visuals **Viewing and Interpreting**
What object in this picture holds Blanca Flor's power?

M **Read and Discuss** What did you just find out, and what does this say about Blanca Flor?

N **Literary Focus** **Dialogue and Stage Directions** Take a close look at this dialogue between Juanito and Blanca Flor. What does it tell you about what they think of each other?

The Narrator. Blanca Flor quickly opened her bag and threw her comb behind her. Immediately the comb turned into a field of corn. This time she turned Juanito into a scarecrow, and she turned herself into a stalk of corn beside him.

[DON RICARDO *enters, as if riding a horse.*]

Don Ricardo. Where did they go? I still think that the bell ringer knew more than he was saying. They were just here. I could hear their scared little voices. Juanito will pay for this, and Blanca Flor will never have the chance to escape again . . . Now where did they go? Perhaps they are in this field of corn. It is strange to see a stalk of corn grow so close to a scarecrow. But this is a day for strange things. (*He exits.*)

Blanca Flor. Juanito, it is over again. Let's go. The river is not far. We are almost free.

[JUANITO *breaks his pose as a scarecrow and stretches and rubs his legs as* BLANCA FLOR *looks around apprehensively.*]

Juanito. Blanca Flor, that was close. We have to hurry now. The river is just through these trees. We can make it now for sure if we hurry.

The Narrator. But they spoke too soon. Don Ricardo had gotten suspicious about the field of corn and returned to it. When he saw Juanito and Blanca Flor he raced to catch them.

[DON RICARDO *enters suddenly and sees them.*]

Don Ricardo. There you are. I knew something was wrong with that field of corn. Now you are mine.

[*As* THE NARRATOR *describes the action,* JUANITO *and* BLANCA FLOR *act out the scene.* BLANCA FLOR *does not actually throw a mirror. She mimes throwing the mirror and the action.*]

The Narrator. When Blanca Flor saw Don Ricardo, she reached into her bag and took out a mirror, the final object in the bag. She threw the mirror into the middle of the road. Instantly, the mirror became a large lake, its waters so smooth and still that it looked like a mirror as it reflected the sky and clouds. When Don Ricardo got to the lake, all he saw was two ducks, a male and a female, swimming peacefully in the middle of the lake. Suddenly, the ducks lifted off the lake and flew away. As they flew away, Don Ricardo knew that the ducks were Juanito and Blanca Flor, and that they were beyond his grasp. As they disappeared, he shouted one last curse.

[JUANITO *and* BLANCA FLOR *exit.*]

Don Ricardo. You may have escaped, Blanca Flor, but you will never have his love. I place a curse on both of you. The first person to embrace him will cause him to forget you forever! (*He exits.*) O

O **Read and Discuss** How is the escape going now?

Vocabulary **apprehensively** (ap rih HEHN sihv lee) *adv.:* fearfully; uneasily.

Scene 8.

Near Juanito's Home.

BLANCA FLOR *and* JUANITO *enter.*

The Narrator. Disguised as ducks, Blanca Flor and Juanito flew safely away from that evil land and escaped from Don Ricardo. They finally arrived at Juanito's home, and using Blanca Flor's magical powers, they returned to their human selves.

Juanito. Blanca Flor, we are close to my home. Soon we will be finally safe forever. I will introduce you to my family, and we will begin our new life together . . . Blanca Flor, why do you look so sad? We have escaped the evil Don Ricardo, and soon we will be happy forever.

Blanca Flor. We have not escaped. His final curse will forever be over us.

Juanito. Remember, that curse will work only in his own land. You yourself told me that once we were beyond the borders of his land, his powers would have no hold on us.

Blanca Flor. His powers are very great, Juanito.

Juanito. Blanca Flor, you have never explained to me the source of your own powers. Are your powers also gone?

Blanca Flor. The powers have always been in the women of my family. That is why Don Ricardo would not let me leave. He was afraid that I would use my powers against him. I have never been away from that land, so I do not know about my powers in this new land.

Juanito. You will have no need for your powers here. Soon we will be with my family. Wait outside while I go and tell my family that I have returned from seeking my fortune, safe at last. Then I will tell them that the fortune I found was you.

Blanca Flor. Juanito, remember the curse.

Juanito. I am not afraid of any curse. Not with you here with me. All my dreams have come true. Come, let's go meet my family. P

[JUANITO *and* BLANCA FLOR *exit.*]

P Literary Focus **Dialogue and Stage Directions**
What does this dialogue tell you about what Juanito thinks of his adventure now?

Analyzing Visuals

Viewing and Interpreting
What scene in the play does this picture illustrate?

Scene 9.

At Juanito's Home.

DON RAMON *and* DOÑA ARLETTE *are sitting at home passing the time with idle talk.*

The Narrator. Juanito's parents had waited patiently for their son to return from seeking his fortune in the world. They did not know that his return home was only the beginning of another chapter of his great adventure.

Doña Arlette. Do you ever think we will hear from Juanito? It has been months since he left to seek his fortune in the world.

Don Ramon. We will hear word soon. I remember when I left home to seek my fortune in the world. Eventually, I found that the best thing to do was return home and make my fortune right here, with my *familia* at my side. Soon he will discover the same thing and you will have your son back.

Doña Arlette. It is easier for a father to know those things. A mother will never stop worrying about her children.

Don Ramon. I worry about the children just as much as you do. But there is no stopping children who want to grow up. He has our blessing and permission to go, and that will be what brings him back safe to us. Soon. You just wait.

[JUANITO *enters. His parents are overjoyed to see him.*]

Juanito. Mama! Papa! I am home.

Doña Arlette. *¡Mi 'jito!*[3]

Don Ramon. Juanito!

[*Overjoyed with seeing* JUANITO, *his parents rush and embrace him.*] **Q**

Doña Arlette. God has answered my prayers. *Mi 'jito* has returned home safe.

Don Ramon. Juanito, come sit close to us and tell us all about your adventures in the world. What great adventures did you have?

Juanito. I had the greatest adventures. For the longest time I was unlucky and unable to find work but finally I . . . I . . .

Doña Arlette. What is it? Are you OK? Do you need some food?

Juanito. No, I'm OK. It's just that I was going to say something and I forgot what I was going to say.

Don Ramon. Don't worry. If it is truly important, it'll come back.

Juanito. No, I've definitely forgotten what I was going to say. Oh well, it probably wasn't important anyway.

Doña Arlette. Did you meet someone special? Did you bring a young woman back for us to meet?

Juanito. No, I didn't have those kind of adventures. Pretty much nothing happened, and then I finally decided that it was just best to come home. **R**

Don Ramon (*to* DOÑA ARLETTE). See what I told you? That is exactly what I said would happen.

---

3. **mi 'jito** (mee HEE toh): contraction of *mi hijito,* Spanish for "my little son."

Q Literary Focus **Dialogue and Stage Directions**
When reading a drama, you must pay close attention to stage directions. Why are these directions especially meaningful?

R Read and Discuss What does the conversation between Juanito and his mother tell you about Don Ricardo's curse?

Doña Arlette. Now that you are home, it is time to settle down and start your own family. You know our neighbor Don Emilio has a younger daughter who would make a very good wife. Perhaps we should go visit her family this Sunday.
Juanito. You know, that would probably be a good idea. I must admit that I was hoping I would find love on my adventures, but I have come home with no memories of love at all. Perhaps it is best to make my fortune right here, close to home.
Don Ramon (*to* DOÑA ARLETTE). See? That is exactly what I said would happen.

[*All exit.*] Ⓢ

SCENE 10.

Months Later at Juanito's Home.

The Narrator. Blanca Flor had seen the embrace and knew that the evil curse had been fulfilled. Brokenhearted, she traveled to a nearby village and lived there in hopes that one day the curse could be broken. The people of the village soon got to know Blanca Flor and came to respect her for the good person she was. One day, Blanca Flor heard news that a celebration was being held in honor of Juanito's return home. She immediately knew that this might be her one chance to break the curse. From the times when she had brushed Juanito's hair, she had kept a lock of his hair. She took one strand of his hair and made it into a dove. She then took one strand of her own hair and turned it into another dove. She took these two doves to Juanito's celebration as a present.

[JUANITO *and* DON RAMON *are sitting talking.*]

Don Ramon. Juanito, what was the most fantastic thing that happened on your adventures?
Juanito. Really, Father, nothing much at all happened. Sometimes I begin to have a memory of something, but it never becomes really clear. At night I have these dreams, but when I awake in the morning I cannot remember them. It must be some dream I keep trying to remember . . . or forget.
Don Ramon. I remember when I went into the world to seek my fortune. I was a young man like you . . .

[DOÑA ARLETTE *enters.*]

Doña Arlette. Juanito, there's a young woman here with a present for you.
Juanito. Who is it?
Doña Arlette. I don't really know her. She is the new young woman who just recently came to the village. The women of the church say she is constantly doing good works for the church and that she is a very good person. She has brought you a present to help celebrate your coming home safe.
Juanito. Sure. Let her come in.

[BLANCA FLOR *enters with the* TWO DOVES. *The* DOVES *are actors in costume.*]

Blanca Flor (*speaking to* JUANITO). Thank you for giving me the honor of presenting these doves as gifts to you.
Juanito. No. No. The honor is mine. Thank you. They are very beautiful.

Ⓢ **Read and Discuss** What is this conversation showing you?

Blanca Flor. They are special doves. They are singing doves.

Doña Arlette. I have never heard of singing doves before. Where did you get them?

Blanca Flor. They came from a special place. A place where all things have a magic power. There are no other doves like these in the world.

Don Ramon. Juanito, what a gift! Let's hear them sing!

Doña Arlette. Yes, let's hear them sing.

Blanca Flor. (*to* JUANITO). May they sing to you?

Juanito. Yes, of course. Let's hear their song.

[*Everyone sits to listen to the* DOVES' *song. As the* DOVES *begin to chant, their words begin to have a powerful effect on* JUANITO. *His memory of* BLANCA FLOR *returns to him.*]

Doves. Once there was a faraway land
A land of both good and evil powers.
A river flowed at the edge like a
steady hand
And it was guarded by a Duende for
all the hours.
Of all the beautiful things the land
did hold
The most beautiful with the purest power
Was a young maiden, true and bold
Named Blanca Flor, the White Flower. **T**

Juanito. I remember! The doves' song has made me remember. (*Going to* BLANCA FLOR) Blanca Flor, your love has broken the curse. Now I remember all that was struggling to come out. Mama, Papa, here is Blanca Flor, the love I found when I was seeking my fortune.

[JUANITO *and* BLANCA FLOR *embrace.*]

Don Ramon. This is going to be a really good story!

[*All exit, with* JUANITO *stopping to give* BLANCA FLOR *a big hug.*] **U**

T **Reading Focus** **Visualizing** What images do you visualize when you read the song of the doves?

U **Read and Discuss** What was Blanca Flor's plan? How has it worked out?

Applying Your Skills

Sunshine State Standards: Benchmarks **LA.6.1.7.3** determine the main idea or essential message in grade-level text through inferring, paraphrasing, summarizing, and identifying relevant details; *Also covered* **LA.6.2.1.2; LA.6.2.1.5**

Blanca Flor

Respond and Think Critically

Reading Focus

1. Which BEST describes the main theme from *Blanca Flor*?

A Important events happen in threes.

B There is no magic stronger than love.

C Be sure to always listen to your parents.

D Be courageous, but know your own limits.

Read with a Purpose

2. Do you think Juanito was successful in finding his fortune? Why or why not? Support your answer with details from the play.

Reading Skills: Visualizing

3. Review the notes from your visualizing chart for *Blanca Flor*. Add details from the drama that helped you visualize <u>dynamic</u> action scenes.

Setting	
Juanito	
Blanca Flor	
Action	

Literary Focus

Literary Analysis

4. Interpret Why didn't Blanca Flor escape from her captor before Juanito came to the forest?

5. Literary Perspective: Archetypes The play's bare-bones plot could be summed up as "boy meets girl; boy loses girl; boy wins girl." Why can this plot be described as an archetype? Name one or more stories with a similar plot. Why is this plot so popular?

Literary Skills: Dialogue and Stage Directions

6. Evaluate How were the stage directions necessary to your understanding of the plot? What was the <u>principal</u> means the playwright used to present the events of the story: dialogue or stage directions? Explain.

Literary Skills Review: Character

READ THINK EXPLAIN

7. Analyze Choose two <u>principal</u> characters from the play, and list two or three character traits that each of those characters <u>displays</u>. Which character had the greatest effect on the plot and the resolution of the conflict? Support your answer with details from the play.

Writing Focus

Think as a Reader/Writer

Use It in Your Writing Review the dialogue you noted as you read *Blanca Flor*. How well did the dialogue capture the characters' qualities? Write a dialogue between two characters you invent. Be sure your dialogue conveys a strong sense of the personalities of both characters.

How has *Blanca Flor* affected your ideas about how things you imagine doing in the future might turn out?

Applying Your Skills

Blanca Flor

Vocabulary Development

Vocabulary Skills: Synonyms and Antonyms

Many words have **synonyms,** or words that are similar in meaning. The words *clumsy* and *awkward* mean about the same thing, for example. Many words also have **antonyms,** or words that are opposite in meaning, like the words *graceful* and *clumsy*. A **thesaurus** is a reference book containing lists of synonyms that can help you find just the right word.

Your Turn

valiant
barren
flourish
apprehensively

Answer the following questions about the words in the Vocabulary list at right. Use a dictionary or thesaurus if you need help.

1. What are two synonyms for *flourish*? (Hint: Be sure you choose synonyms that are nouns.)
2. What is an antonym for *barren*?
3. What are two synonyms for *apprehensively*?
4. How many synonyms and antonyms can you find for *valiant*?

Academic Vocabulary

Talk About . . .

Discuss the personalities of the principal characters in this play. Are they simple or complex? Are they dynamic characters, or do they stay the same? What personality traits do they display?

Language Coach

Spanish Words in English You can sometimes figure out the meaning of a Spanish word you don't know by thinking of English words that resemble it. (If Spanish is your first language, you can figure out the meanings of some English words in a similar way.)

Make a chart like the one below. Then, use an English dictionary that includes word origins to complete the chart with information about each word. Some information is given to help you begin.

Word	Spanish Origin/ Meaning	English Meaning	Sample Sentence
tortilla	*torta,* "a cake"	a thin, round cake of flour or cornmeal	Juanito ate the dried-out tortilla.
tornado	*tornar,* "to turn"	rapidly rotating column of air	
alligator			
armadillo			
bonanza			
cafeteria			
canyon			
chocolate			
mascara			
patio			

Learn It Online
Focus on synonyms and antonyms with *WordSharp* at:
go.hrw.com L6-772 Go

Sunshine State Standards: Benchmarks **LA.6.1.6.4** categorize key vocabulary and identify salient features; **LA.6.1.6.10** determine meanings of words, pronunciation, parts of speech, etymologies, and alternate word choices by using a dictionary, thesaurus, and digital tools; **LA.6.1.6.11** identify the meaning of words and phrases derived from Greek and Latin mythology (e.g., mercurial, Achilles' heel) and identify frequently used words from other languages (e.g., laissez faire, croissant); **LA.6.1.7.4** identify cause-and-effect relationships in text; **LA.6.3.4.4** the eight parts of speech (noun, pronoun, verb, adverb, adjective, conjunction, preposition, interjection); **LA.6.3.5.1** prepare writing using technology in a format appropriate to audience and purpose (e.g., manuscript, multimedia); **LA.6.3.5.3** share the writing with the intended audience; **LA.6.4.1.2** write a variety of expressive forms (e.g., short play, song lyrics, historical fiction, limericks) that employ figurative language, rhythm, dialogue, characterization, and/or appropriate format; **LA.6.5.2.2** deliver narrative and informative presentations, including oral responses to literature, and adjust oral language, body language, eye contact, gestures, technology and supporting graphics appropriate to the situation; *Also covered* **LA.6.6.4.1**

Grammar Link

Choosing the Correct Forms of Pronouns

The **case** of a pronoun shows how it is used in a sentence. A pronoun that is the subject of a verb is in the **nominative case**:

She was still at home.

A pronoun that is a direct object, indirect object, or object of a preposition is in the **objective case:**

The new movie amazed *us.* (direct object)
I asked *him* a question. (indirect object)
They live near *us.* (object of a preposition)

If you know whether a pronoun is acting as the subject or the object of the verb, you can choose the correct form of the pronoun. Most personal pronouns have different forms for the nominative and objective cases, as shown below.

SINGULAR PERSONAL PRONOUNS	
Nominative Case	**Objective Case**
I	me
you	you
he, she, it	him, her, it

PLURAL PERSONAL PRONOUNS	
Nominative Case	**Objective Case**
we	us
you	you
they	them

Your Turn

Identify the correct pronoun in parentheses.

1. He sat beside (*she, her*) on the rock.
2. (*They, Them*) avoided Don Ricardo.
3. Blanca gave (*he, him*) a unique present.
4. Juanito's story fascinated (*they, them*).

CHOICES

As you respond to the Choices, use these **Academic Vocabulary** words as appropriate: complex, display, principal, dynamic.

REVIEW

Write About a Character

Timed Writing If Blanca Flor had had a different, less complex personality, how would the outcome of the play have been different? In a paragraph or two, explain how the chain of causes and effects in the story would have been changed if Blanca Flor had been less dynamic, shyer, and more accepting of her fate.

CONNECT

Write a New Version

Retell the story of Blanca Flor in one of the following ways: as a short story with a contemporary setting and characters; as a spoof, or parody, in play form; or as a graphic story with panels and word balloons. What parts of the story can you safely change and still keep the same basic plot? Share your version with the class.

EXTEND

Present the Play

TechFocus Record a class performance of *Blanca Flor.* You will need a director and a stage manager, people to make costumes, and people to design and create scenery. Select actors for each role, and rehearse the play. Then, as you display your talents onstage, videotape the performance.

Learn It Online
Learn more about this play from these Internet links:
go.hrw.com
L6-773
Go

PLAY

Preparing to Read

IN THE FOG

by **Milton Geiger**

How do mysterious, unknown, or unexplained things affect your imagination?

QuickTalk

You're driving down a dark, foggy road. Lost, you get out of the car to read a sign. A voice calls from out of the fog. What happens next?

Reader/Writer Notebook

Use your **RWN** to complete the activities for this selection.

Sunshine State Standards: Benchmarks **LA.6.1.6.1** use new vocabulary that is introduced and taught directly; **LA.6.1.6.7** identify and understand the meaning of conceptually advanced prefixes, suffixes, and root words; **LA.6.1.7.1** use background knowledge of subject and related content areas, prereading strategies, graphic representations, and knowledge of text structure to make and confirm complex predictions of content, purpose, and organization of a reading selection; **LA.6.1.7.8** use strategies to repair comprehension of grade-appropriate text when self-monitoring indicates confusion, including but not limited to rereading, checking context clues, predicting, note-making, summarizing, using graphic and semantic organizers, questioning, and clarifying by checking other sources; *Also covered* **LA.6.2.1.1; LA.6.2.1.2**

Literary Focus

Structure of a Play *In the Fog* uses the traditional **structure of a play** to tell its story. The most exciting part of any story is its **climax.** Some stories, though, introduce a "twist" during the **resolution** (when the conflict is resolved). The twist can be a new event or some information that changes our view of earlier events.

Suspense When you feel an anxious curiosity about what might happen next in a story, you are experiencing **suspense.** Writers create suspense with mysterious settings or characters and with **foreshadowing**—the use of hints that suggest what is to come.

Reading Focus

Visualizing / Using Prior Knowledge When you read or listen to a story, you form pictures in your mind. Applying knowledge from your own life can help you better **visualize** a story—especially the action of a play—and feel its suspense more strongly.

Into Action As you read this play, fill in a chart with the stage directions and dialogue to help you visualize the action.

Stage Directions Help Me See	Dialogue Helps Me See
It's night and foggy. A driver gets out of his car to read a sign. His flashlight goes out.	A strange voice comes out of the fog and startles the doctor, making him turn around.

TechFocus *In the Fog* was written in the late 1940s, long before there were cell phones and GPS devices. Think about how the events of this play might change if it took place today.

Writing Focus

Think as a Reader/Writer

Find It in Your Reading As you read, note instances of foreshadowing that create suspense in the play.

Vocabulary

perplexed (puhr PLEHKST) *adj.:* puzzled. *When the doctor sees the two men, he is perplexed by their condition.*

indignant (ihn DIHG nuhnt) *adj.:* offended; angry. *The doctor was indignant that the men came to him.*

arrogant (AR uh guhnt) *adj.:* unpleasantly proud; thinking oneself is more important than other people. *The men seem arrogant because they're not afraid of the police.*

finality (fy NAL uh tee) *n.:* feeling that something is finished and can't be changed. *The men objected with finality.*

Language Coach

Using Word Parts: Suffixes Many English words are made up of word parts. A **suffix** is a word part added to the end of a word to create a new word. *Final* is an adjective that means "last" or "not to be changed." How does adding *–ity* change its meaning? What do you think the suffix *–ity* might mean? Can you think of other words with this suffix?

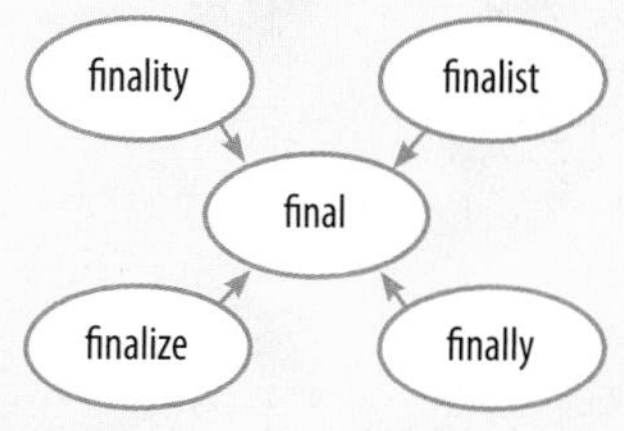

Learn It Online

There's more to words than just definitions. Get the whole story at:

go.hrw.com L6-775 

MEET THE WRITER

Milton Geiger

(1907–1971)

Scripting for Stage and Screen

Milton Geiger was born in New York City but grew up in Cleveland, Ohio. He developed a love for live performances when he was introduced to plays at the Cleveland Playhouse. As an adult, he moved back to New York to make his living as a script writer for radio, television, and theater. He later moved to Southern California to work in the entertainment industry.

Small-Town Heroes

Trained as a pharmacist, Geiger used his specialized knowledge about medicine when writing his first successful script, which was about a small-town pharmacist. In fact, many of his scripts involve similar kinds of small-town characters: middle-aged medical professionals with quiet, wise personalities.

One of Geiger's most successful works was the 1958 Broadway play *Edwin Booth,* about the acclaimed Shakespearean actor who happened to be the brother of John Wilkes Booth, the man who killed Abraham Lincoln. Geiger also wrote scripts for several popular television series, including *Perry Mason, Dragnet,* and *Night Gallery.*

Think About the Writer Why do you think Geiger's first successful script was about a pharmacist?

Preview the Selection

In this suspenseful play, you will read about a **doctor** who is lost on a Pennsylvania highway. As he stops to check a road sign in the fog, two strange men named **Eben** and **Zeke** arrive and ask for his help.

Read with a Purpose Read to find out what happens when a doctor meets two strange men on a lonely highway.

IN THE FOG

by **Milton Geiger**

CHARACTERS

A Doctor **A Wounded Man** **Eben**
Zeke **A Gas Station Attendant**

Sets: *A signpost on Pennsylvania Route 30. A rock or stump in the fog. A gas station pump.*

Night. At first we can only see fog drifting across a dark scene devoid of[1] *detail. Then, out of the fog, there emerges toward us a white roadside signpost with a number of white painted signboards pointing to right and to left. The marker is a Pennsylvania State Route—marked characteristically* "PENNA-30." *Now a light as from a far headlight sweeps the signs.*

An automobile approaches. The car pulls up close. We hear the car door open and slam and a man's footsteps approaching on

1. **devoid** (dih VOYD) **of:** without.

the concrete. Now the signs are lit up again by a more localized, smaller source of light. The light grows stronger as the man, offstage, approaches. The DOCTOR *enters, holding a flashlight before him. He scrutinizes*[2] *the road marker. He flashes his light up at the arrows. We see the legends on the markers. Pointing off right there are markers that read: York, Columbia, Lancaster; pointing left the signs read: Fayetteville, McConnellsburg, Pennsylvania Turnpike.*

The DOCTOR'S *face is perplexed and annoyed as he turns his flashlight on a folded road map. He is a bit lost in the fog. Then his flashlight fails him. It goes out!* **A**

Doctor. Darn! (*He fumbles with the flashlight in the gloom. Then a voice is raised to him from offstage.*)
Eben (*offstage, strangely*). Turn around, mister. . . .

[*The* DOCTOR *turns sharply to stare offstage.*]

Zeke (*offstage*). You don't have to be afraid, mister. . . .

[*The* DOCTOR *sees two men slowly approaching out of the fog. One carries a lantern below his knees. The other holds a heavy rifle. Their features are utterly indistinct as they approach, and the rifleman holds up his gun with quiet threat.*] **B**

Eben. You don't have to be afraid.
Doctor (*more indignant than afraid*). So you say! Who are you, man?
Eben. We don't aim to hurt you none.
Doctor. That's reassuring. I'd like to know just what you mean by this? This gun business! Who *are* you?
Zeke (*mildly*). What's your trade, mister?
Doctor. I . . . I'm a doctor. Why?
Zeke (*to* EBEN). Doctor.
Eben (*nods; then to* DOCTOR). Yer the man we want.
Zeke. Ye'll do proper, we're thinkin'.
Eben. So ye'd better come along, mister.
Zeke. Aye.
Doctor. Why? Has—anyone been hurt?
Eben. It's for you to say if he's been hurt nigh to the finish.
Zeke. So we're askin' ye to come along, doctor. **C**

[*The* DOCTOR *looks from one to another in indecision and puzzlement.*]

Eben. In the name o' mercy.

2. **scrutinizes** (SKROO tuh nyz ihz): examines carefully.

A **Reading Focus** **Visualizing** Consider the stage directions you just read. Which details form pictures in your mind? How do these details create a sense of mystery and suspense?

B **Literary Focus** **Suspense** How does the fact that the men are not clearly visible add to the suspense?

C **Literary Focus** **Suspense and Foreshadowing** What details in this scene might foreshadow danger ahead?

Vocabulary **perplexed** (puhr PLEHKST) *adj.:* puzzled.
indignant (ihn DIHG nuhnt) *adj.:* offended; angry.

Zeke. Aye.

Doctor. I want you to understand—I'm not afraid of your gun! I'll go to your man all right. Naturally, I'm a doctor. But I demand to know who you are.

Zeke (*patiently*). Why not? Raise yer lantern, Eben. . . .

Eben (*tiredly*). Aye.

[EBEN *lifts his lantern. Its light falls on their faces now, and we see that they are terrifying. Matted beards, clotted with blood; crude head bandages, crusty with dirt and dry blood. Their hair, stringy and disheveled. Their faces are lean and hollow cheeked; their eyes sunken and tragic. The* DOCTOR *is shocked for a moment—then bursts out—*]

Doctor. Good heavens!— **D**

Zeke. That's Eben; I'm Zeke.

Doctor. What's happened? Has there been an accident or . . . what? **E**

Zeke. Mischief's happened, stranger.

Eben. Mischief enough.

Doctor (*looks at rifle at his chest*). There's been gunplay—hasn't there?

Zeke (*mildly ironic*). Yer tellin' us there's been gunplay!

Doctor. And I'm telling you that I'm not at all frightened! It's my duty to report this, and report it I will!

Zeke. Aye, mister. You do that.

Doctor. You're arrogant about it now! You don't think you'll be caught and dealt with. But people are losing patience with you men. . . . You . . . you moonshiners![3] Running wild . . . a law unto yourselves . . . shooting up the countryside!

MISCHIEF'S HAPPENED, MISTER, WE'LL WARRANT THAT.

Zeke. Hear that, Eben? Moonshiners.

Eben. Mischief's happened, mister, we'll warrant[4] that. . . .

Doctor. And I don't like it!

Zeke. Can't say we like it better'n you do, mister. . . .

Eben (*strangely sad and remote*). What must be, must.

Zeke. There's no changin' or goin' back, and all 'at's left is the wishin' things were different. **F**

Eben. Aye.

Doctor. And while we talk, your wounded man lies bleeding, I suppose—worthless

---

3. **moonshiners:** people who distill liquor illegally.

4. **warrant** (WAWR uhnt): declare positively.

D **Read and Discuss** What has the author shown you about the doctor?

E **Read and Discuss** What do you think happened to Zeke and Eben? What makes you think so?

F **Literary Focus** **Suspense** Mystery helps create suspense. What mysterious, unexplained things do Zeke and Eben do and say?

Vocabulary **arrogant** (AR uh guhnt) *adj.:* unpleasantly proud; thinking one is more important than other people.

though he may be. Well? I'll have to get my instrument bag, you know. It's in the car.

[EBEN *and* ZEKE *part to let* DOCTOR *pass between them. The* DOCTOR *reenters, carrying his medical bag.*]

Doctor. I'm ready. Lead the way.

[EBEN *lifts his lantern a bit and goes first.* ZEKE *prods the* DOCTOR *ever so gently and apologetically but firmly with the rifle muzzle. The* DOCTOR *leaves.* ZEKE *strides off slowly after them.* **G**

A wounded man is lying against a section of stone fence. He, too, is bearded, though very young, and his shirt is dark with blood. He breathes but never stirs otherwise. EBEN *enters, followed by the* DOCTOR *and* ZEKE.] **H**

Zeke. Ain't stirred a mite since we left 'im.
Doctor. Let's have that lantern here! (*The* DOCTOR *tears the man's shirt for better access to the wound. Softly*) Dreadful! Dreadful . . . !
Zeke's voice (*off scene*). Reckon it's bad in the chest like that, hey?
Doctor (*taking pulse*). His pulse is positively racing . . . ! How long has he been this way?
Zeke. A long time, mister. A long time. . . .
Doctor (*to* EBEN). You! Hand me my bag.

[EBEN *puts down lantern and hands bag to the* DOCTOR. *The* DOCTOR *opens bag and takes out a couple of retractors.*[5] ZEKE *holds lantern close now.*]

Doctor. Lend me a hand with these retractors. (*He works on the man.*) All right . . . when I tell you to draw back on the retractors—draw back.
Eben. Aye.
Zeke. How is 'e, mister?
Doctor (*preoccupied*). More retraction. Pull them a bit more. Hold it. . . .
Eben. Bad, ain't he?
Doctor. Bad enough. The bullet didn't touch any lung tissue far as I can see right now. There's some pneumothorax[6] though. All I can do now is plug the wound. There's some cotton and gauze wadding in my bag. Find it. . . .

[ZEKE *probes about silently in the bag and comes up with a small dark box of gauze.*]

Doctor. That's it. (*Works a moment in silence*) I've never seen anything quite like it.
Eben. Yer young, doctor. Lots o' things you've never seen.
Doctor. Adhesive tape!

5. **retractors** (rih TRAK tuhrz): surgical instruments for holding back the flesh at the edge of a wound.
6. **pneumothorax** (noo moh THAWR aks): air or gas in the chest cavity.

G **Literary Focus** **Structure of a Play: Conflict** Who has been introduced so far? Describe in your own words the doctor's situation. What conflict does he face?

H **Read and Discuss** Who do you think the injured person is? What do you think will happen to the doctor?

[ZEKE *finds a roll of three-inch tape and hands it to the* DOCTOR, *who tears off long strips and slaps them on the dressing and pats and smooths them to the man's chest.* EBEN *replaces equipment in* DOCTOR's *bag and closes it with a hint of the finality to come. A preview of dismissal, so to speak.*]

Doctor (*at length*). There. So much for that. Now then—(*takes man's shoulders*) give me a hand here.
Zeke (*quiet suspicion*). What fer?
Doctor. We've got to move this man.
Zeke. What fer?
Doctor (*stands; indignantly*). We've got to get him to a hospital for treatment; a thorough cleansing of the wound; irrigation.[7] I've done all I can for him here.
Zeke. I reckon he'll be all right 'thout no hospital.
Doctor. Do you realize how badly this man's hurt!
Eben. He won't bleed to death, will he?
Doctor. I don't think so—not with that plug and pressure dressing. But bleeding isn't the only danger we've got to—
Zeke (*interrupts*). All right, then. Much obliged to you. **I**
Doctor. This man's dangerously hurt!
Zeke. Reckon he'll pull through now, thanks to you.
Doctor. I'm glad you feel that way about it! But I'm going to report this to the Pennsylvania State Police at the first telephone I reach!
Zeke. We ain't stoppin' ye, mister. **J**
Eben. Fog is liftin', Zeke. Better be done with this, I say.
Zeke (*nods, sadly*). Aye. Ye can go now, mister . . . and thanks. (*Continues*) We never meant a mite o' harm, I can tell ye. If we killed, it was no wish of ours.
Eben. What's done is done. Aye.
Zeke. Ye can go now, stranger. . . . **K**

WE NEVER MEANT A MITE O' HARM, I CAN TELL YE. IF WE KILLED, IT WAS NO WISH OF OURS.

[EBEN *hands* ZEKE *the* DOCTOR's *bag.* ZEKE *hands it gently to the* DOCTOR.]

Doctor. Very well. You haven't heard the last of this, though!

7. **irrigation:** here, flushing out a wound with water or other fluid.

I **Literary Focus** **Structure of a Play: Complications** What complication occurs when the doctor tries to take the wounded man to the hospital?

J **Read and Discuss** How does the doctor's attitude toward the wounded man differ from Zeke and Eben's? Why do you think Zeke and Eben do not want to take the man to the hospital?

K **Literary Focus** **Structure of a Play: Climax** Has the doctor's conflict been resolved? Do Zeke and Eben feel that their problem has been resolved?

Vocabulary **finality** (fy NAL uh tee) *adj.:* feeling that something is finished and can't be changed.

Zeke. That's the truth, mister. We've killed, aye; and we've been hurt for it. . . .
Eben. Hurt bad.

[*The* DOCTOR*'s face is puckered with doubt and strange apprehension.*[8]]

Zeke. We're not alone, mister. We ain't the only ones. (*Sighs*) Ye can go now, doctor . . . and our thanks to ye. . . .

[*The* DOCTOR *leaves the other two, still gazing at them in strange enchantment and wonder and a touch of indignation.*] **L**

THAT'S THE TRUTH, MISTER. WE'VE KILLED, AYE; AND WE'VE BEEN HURT FOR IT.

Eben's voice. Thanks, mister. . . .
Zeke's voice. In the name o' mercy. . . . We thank you. . . .
Eben. In the name o' mercy.
Zeke. Thanks, mister. . . .
Eben. In the name o' kindness. . . .

[*The two men stand with their wounded comrade at their feet—like a group statue in the park. The fog thickens across the scene. Far off the long, sad wail of a locomotive whimpers in the dark.* **M**

The scene now shifts to a young ATTENDANT *standing in front of a gasoline pump taking a reading and recording it in a book as he prepares to close up. He turns as he hears the car approach on the gravel drive. The* DOCTOR *enters.*] **N**

Attendant (*pleasantly*). Good evening, sir. (*Nods off at car*) Care to pull 'er up to this pump, sir? Closing up.
Doctor (*impatiently*). No. Where's your telephone, please? I've just been held up!
Attendant. Pay station[9] inside, sir. . . .
Doctor. Thank you! (*The* DOCTOR *starts to go past the* ATTENDANT.)
Attendant. Excuse me, sir. . . .
Doctor (*stops*). Eh, what is it, what is it?
Attendant. Uh . . . what sort of looking fellows were they?
Doctor. Oh—two big fellows with a rifle;

8. **apprehension** (ap rih HEHN shuhn): uneasiness; fearfulness.

9. **pay station:** pay telephone.

L Read and Discuss Has the doctor's attitude toward Zeke and Eben changed? Do you think he has more sympathy for them than he did at first? Explain.

M **Reading Focus** **Visualizing** How does this stage direction help you picture Zeke and Eben? How does it help create a mood of suspense?

N Read and Discuss The doctor says he is going to report Zeke and Eben to the police. Do you think he will now? Why do you think Zeke and Eben seemed unconcerned about being reported?

faces and heads bandaged and smeared with dirt and blood. Friend of theirs with a gaping hole in his chest. I'm a doctor, so they forced me to attend him. Why?

Attendant. *Those* fellers, huh?

Doctor. Then you know about them!

Attendant. I guess so.

Doctor. They're armed and they're desperate!

Attendant. That was about two or three miles back, would you say? O

Doctor (*fumbling in pocket*). Just about—I don't seem to have the change. I wonder if you'd spare me change for a quarter . . . ?

Attendant (*makes change from metal coin canister at his belt*). Certainly, sir. . . .

Doctor. What town was that back there, now?

Attendant (*dumps coins in other's hand*). There you are, sir.

Doctor (*impatient*). Yes, thank you. I say—what town was that back there, so I can tell the police?

Attendant. That was . . . Gettysburg, mister. . . .

Doctor. Gettysburg . . . ?

Attendant. Gettysburg and Gettysburg

O **Literary Focus** **Suspense** How does the attendant react to the doctor's story? Does his reaction surprise you? Why or why not?

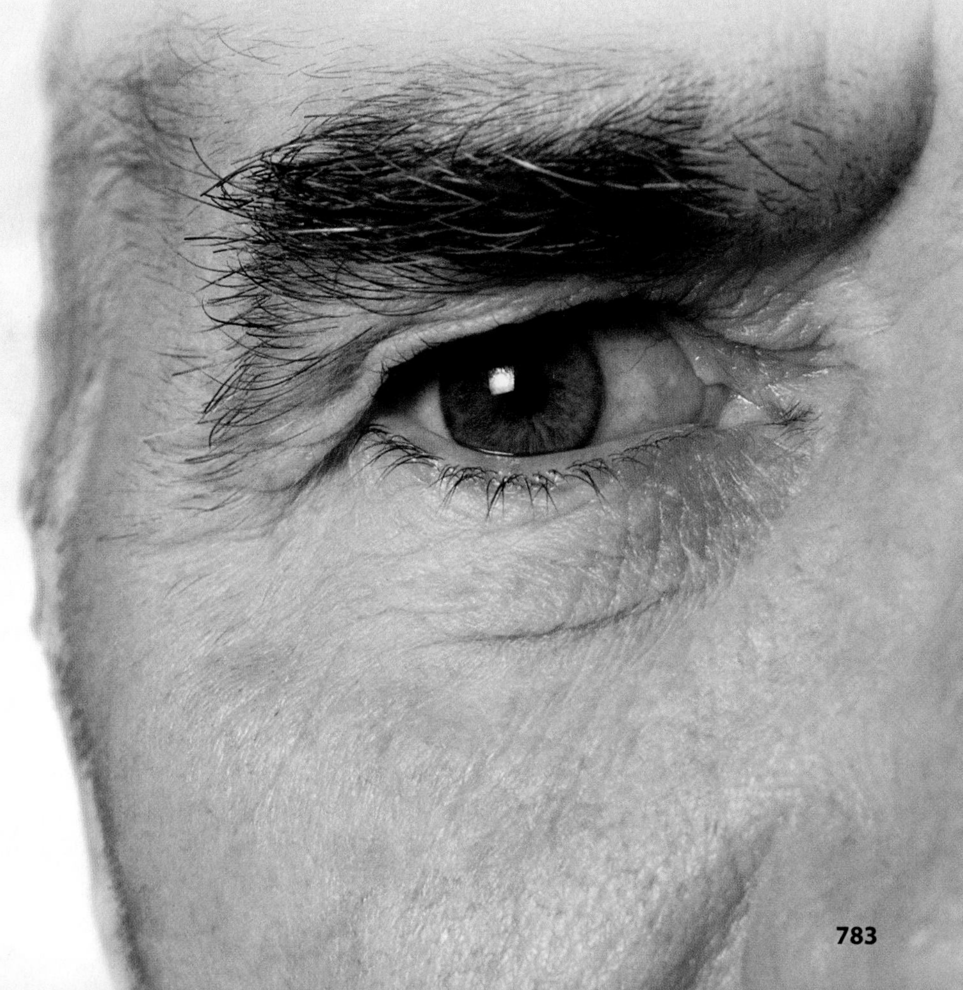

Analyzing Visuals

Viewing and Interpreting What feelings and thoughts might be going through the doctor's mind at the end of this play?

battlefield. . . . (*Looks off*) When it's light and the fog's gone, you can see the gravestones. Meade's men . . . Pickett's men, Robert E. Lee's. . . .[10] **P**

10. **Meade's men . . . Lee's:** The Battle of Gettysburg was a turning point in the American Civil War. On July 1–3, 1863, the Confederate forces, under Robert E. Lee, met the Union forces, under George Gordon Meade. The climax of the battle came when 15,000 Confederate soldiers, led by George Pickett, charged Cemetery Ridge and were repelled. The North suffered about 23,000 casualties; the South, about 20,000.

[*The* DOCTOR *is looking off with the* ATTENDANT; *now he turns his head slowly to stare at the other man.*]

Attendant (*continues*). On nights like this—well—you're not the first those men've stopped . . . or the last. (*Nods off*) Fill 'er up, mister? **Q**

Doctor. Yes, fill 'er up. . . .

P **Read and Discuss** How does the information about Gettysburg connect with what the doctor experiences?

Q **Literary Focus** **Structure of a Play: Resolution** What important information does the attendant give the doctor?

Applying Your Skills

FL **Sunshine State Standards: Benchmarks** LA.6.2.1.2 locate and analyze the elements of plot structure, including exposition, setting, character development, rising/falling action, conflict/resolution, and theme in a variety of fiction; *Also covered* LA.6.2.1.5; LA.6.4.1.2

In the Fog

Respond and Think Critically

Reading Focus

1. What might the doctor learn from his interaction with Eben and Zeke? **FCAT**
   - **A** There are many kinds of criminals.
   - **B** History often repeats itself.
   - **C** People can survive terrible injuries.
   - **D** He should not make assumptions about people.

Read with a Purpose

2. What can you can guess about the identity of the two strange men the doctor meets?

Reading Skills: Visualizing

3. Review the visualizing chart you filled out as you read. Now, add a final column in which you explain how what you are visualizing affects you. Does it fill you with suspense or make you anxious or curious?

Stage Directions Help Me See	Dialogue Helps Me See	What I'm "Seeing" Makes Me Feel
It's night and foggy. A driver gets out of his car to see a sign. His flash-light goes out.	A strange voice comes out of the fog and startles the doctor, making him turn around.	It's dangerous to be out on a foggy night. I'd be scared to hear a voice come out of nowhere.

Literary Focus

Literary Analysis

4. **Infer** What might have happened if the doctor had refused to go with the men? Support your answer with details from the play.

Literary Skills: Structure of a Play/ Suspense

5. **Interpret** How do fog and darkness add to the play's suspense? Support your answer with details from the play.

Literary Skills Review: Characterization

6. **Describe** Use the doctor's words, appearance, actions, and the way others respond to him to describe his character. Then, describe the other principal characters, Zeke and Eben. READ THINK EXPLAIN

Writing Focus

Think as a Reader/Writer

Use It in Your Writing Review your notes on the stage directions and how they helped you visualize the play. Think of a suspenseful story you know, and write stage directions for a dramatic version of it. The directions might be for the opening of the play—setting the stage for the action.

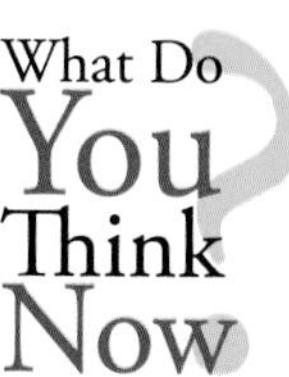

Now that you've read this play, what do you think about the idea that the unknown is more frightening than the known?

In the Fog

Vocabulary Development

Vocabulary Skills: Context Clues

If you are not sure what a word means, you can sometimes use the words nearby to help you clarify its meaning. Read this sentence from the play:

> *The* DOCTOR *leaves the other two, still gazing at them in strange* enchantment *and wonder and a touch of indignation.*

Enchantment means "condition of acting as if a spell has been placed on you." What word or words near *enchantment* help clarify its meaning?

Your Turn

perplexed
indignant
arrogant
finality

Choose the Vocabulary word from the box at right that best fits in each blank below. Remember to look at nearby words for context clues.

1. The doctor thought Zeke and Eben were ____________ and overconfident in their attitude to getting caught by the police.
2. The doctor, getting angry, is more __________ than fearful when the man with the gun tells him not to be afraid.
3. The doctor was _____________ and bewildered by Zeke and Eben's refusal to take the wounded man to the hospital.
4. Zeke and Eben allowed no argument. Making it clear that they had what they wanted, they said goodbye to the doctor with an air of ____________.

Language Coach

Using Word Parts: Suffixes Sometimes, you can figure out the meaning of an unfamiliar word if you analyze the meaning of its parts. A word part added to the end of a word is a **suffix.** The more suffixes you know, the more words you'll be able to figure out. Two commonly used suffixes are *–ment* and *–ion.* The chart explains their meanings and lists words from *In the Fog* that have these suffixes.

Suffix	Meaning	Example
–ment	result, means, process or place of action	puzzlement, equipment
–ion	act or condition of	retraction, indignation

Think of three more words that end with the suffix *–ment* and three with *–ion,* and use each in a sentence.

Academic Vocabulary

Talk About . . .

The principal characters in *In the Fog* seem to act out a very simple situation until the doctor arrives at the gas station. How does what the doctor learns from the gas station attendant suddenly make the story more complex?

Learn It Online
Learn about context clues with *WordSharp*:
go.hrw.com L6-786 Go

Sunshine State Standards: Benchmarks **LA.6.1.6.3** use context clues to determine meanings of unfamiliar words; **LA.6.1.6.7** identify and understand the meaning of conceptually advanced prefixes, suffixes, and root words; **LA.6.3.4.4** the eight parts of speech (noun, pronoun, verb, adverb, adjective, conjunction, preposition, interjection); **LA.6.4.2.4** write a variety of informal communications (e.g., friendly letters, thank-you notes, messages) and formal communications (e.g., conventional business letters, invitations) that follow a format and that have a clearly stated purpose and that include the date, proper salutation, body, closing and signature; **LA.6.5.2.2** deliver narrative and informative presentations, including oral responses to literature, and adjust oral language, body language, eye contact, gestures, technology and supporting graphics appropriate to the situation; **LA.6.6.2.1** select a topic for inquiry, formulate a search plan, and apply evaluative criteria (e.g., relevance, accuracy, organization, validity, currentness) to select and use appropriate resource; **LA.6.6.2.3** write an informational report that includes a focused topic, appropriate facts and relevant details, a logical sequence, a concluding statement, and list of sources used.

Grammar Link

Possessive Pronoun and Contraction Mix-Ups

It's easy to mix up possessive pronouns and contractions because they sound the same in speech. Study the chart and rules below to make sure you use the right word in your writing.

Contraction	Possessive Pronoun
it's (it is/has)	its
they're (they are)	their
you're (you are)	your
who's (who is/has)	whose

1. Use an apostrophe to show where letters are missing in a **contraction** (a shortened form of a word or group of words):

   Who's [Who is] approaching the doctor?

   It's [It is] Zeke and Eben.

2. Do *not* use an apostrophe with a **possessive personal pronoun.**

   The flashlight, *its* battery dead, was of no use to the doctor.

Your Turn

Writing Applications Write a short dialogue between the doctor and the gas station attendant that takes place after the doctor learns more about Zeke and Eben. Use *it's* and *its, they're* and *their, you're* and *your,* and *who's* and *whose* in your dialogue.

CHOICES

As you respond to the Choices, use these **Academic Vocabulary** words as appropriate: complex, display, principal, dynamic.

REVIEW

Write a Review

Timed Writing Write a short review of an imaginary production of *In the Fog.* Describe the plot as either complex or simple (don't give away the ending!). Rate the quality of the acting by the principal characters, as well as the effectiveness of the staging. Convince your audience that the play is (or is not) worth attending.

CONNECT

Write Text Messages

TechFocus Imagine that the play takes place today and the doctor has a cell phone. Eben and Zeke have already arrived, so the doctor has to be careful. He figures out a way to sneak in some text messages to a friend he hopes can help him. Write the text messages that travel back and forth between the doctor and his friend.

EXTEND

Prepare an Oral Report

Listening and Speaking Research an aspect of the Battle of Gettysburg for an oral report. You could focus on the fighting, the men who led the battle, the effect on those living nearby, or Lincoln's address commemorating the battle. Write an outline, and make notes for your report. Then, practice giving the report orally.

RADIO PLAY

Preparing to Read

THE HITCHHIKER

by **Lucille Fletcher**

How can our imaginations make stories we listen to more eerie or frightening than stories we watch?

QuickWrite

What stories have made your heart beat faster? Think about what those stories have in common. Write a list of elements you expect to find in a suspenseful story.

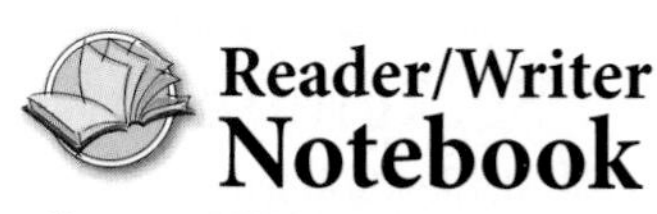

Reader/Writer Notebook

Use your **RWN** to complete the activities for this selection.

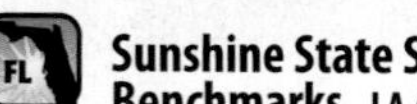

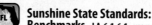

Sunshine State Standards: Benchmarks **LA.6.1.6.1** use new vocabulary that is introduced and taught directly; **LA.6.1.6.5** relate new vocabulary to familiar words; **LA.6.1.7.5** analyze a variety of text structures (e.g., comparison/contrast, cause/effect, chronological order, argument/support, lists) and text features (main headings with subheadings) and explain their impact on meaning in text; **LA.6.2.1.2** locate and analyze the elements of plot structure, including exposition, setting, character development, rising/falling action, conflict/resolution, and theme in a variety of fiction; *Also covered* **LA.6.2.1.3**

Literary Focus

Suspense / Foreshadowing The stage directions at the beginning of this play indicate that the music should be "weird and shuddery." The main character says he might be going insane. Right away, the playwright establishes a mood of **suspense,** or anxious curiosity about what will happen next. Sometimes a playwright will use **foreshadowing**—giving hints about what is to come—to help build suspense. Look for such hints as you read *The Hitchhiker.*

Reading Focus

Sequencing Most plays are written in **chronological order**—the playwright presents events in the sequence in which they happen. Sometimes, however, a playwright will include a **flashback** to an earlier time to give the audience background information on what is happening in the present.

Into Action As you read *The Hitchhiker,* answer the following questions to help clarify the sequence of events. Write your answers in your *Reader/Writer Notebook.*

What are the play's key events?

When did each event happen?

What happened before that event?

What happened afterward?

Did one event cause another event to happen?

Writing Focus

Think as a Reader/Writer

Find It in Your Reading In this radio play, music and sound effects help create a suspenseful mood. Note the kind of music and sound effects you think would help set the mood, and explain why.

Vocabulary

coincidence (koh IHN suh duhns) *n.:* accidental happening of events that seem to be connected. *Adams wonders whether it is only a coincidence that he sees the same man he saw before.*

sinister (SIHN uh stuhr) *adj.:* creepy; threatening. *Why did the hitchhiker seem so sinister?*

menacing (MEHN uh sihng) *adj.:* threatening. *The man didn't seem menacing as he stood by the side of the road.*

indifference (ihn DIHF uhr uhns) *n.:* state of being unconcerned about something. *He drove past the landscape with indifference, focusing instead on the road ahead.*

Language Coach

Compound Words One way the English language grows is through the invention of **compound words**—new words formed from two separate words. The word *hitchhiker* is one example of a compound word. It is formed from the words *hitch*—"to catch"—and *hiker*—"a walker." The word refers to someone who is traveling on foot but "catches" rides on vehicles.

Learn It Online
Broaden your word power with Word Watch at:

go.hrw.com L6-789 

MEET THE WRITER

Lucille Fletcher

(1912–2000)

Creating Suspense

Lucille Fletcher, best known for writing the classic suspense film *Sorry, Wrong Number,* once shared her secret to writing convincing suspense stories:

> "Writing suspense stories is like working on a puzzle. You bury the secret, lead the reader down the path, put in false leads, and throughout the story remain completely logical. Each word must have meaning and be written in a fine literary style."

The Hitchhiker contains all of these elements, as well as a kernel of truth. The idea for the play originated during a drive to California. As Fletcher, a Brooklyn native, was leaving New York, she saw a strange man on the Brooklyn Bridge. The same stranger later appeared on the Pulaski Skyway in New Jersey. It's no accident, then, that the gray man who haunts Ronald Adams in *The Hitchhiker* appears on both of these bridges.

Fletcher had wanted to become a writer since her childhood, but it was only when she was typing radio plays at CBS that she realized she could write radio plays of her own.

Think About the Writer What might Fletcher have learned when typing radio plays at CBS?

BARBARA
STANWYCK
BURT
LANCASTER
The prize-winning radio suspense drama that thrilled 40,000,000 people ... now electrifies the screen!
"SORRY, WRONG NUMBER"
HAL WALLIS
Directed by ANATOLE LITVAK · Produced by HAL WALLIS and ANATOLE LITVAK

Build Background

In the 1930s and 1940s, Americans gathered around the radio the way we now gather around the television. Like television shows, radio shows came in many varieties: adventure series, detective stories, Westerns, comedies, and even soap operas (in fact, soap operas began on the radio). However, radio was different from television in important ways. Without pictures that showed what was happening, *dialogue* and *sound effects* had to tell the story and create mood. The rest was left to the listener's imagination.

The Hitchhiker is a popular and suspenseful radio play from the golden age of radio. As you read *The Hitchhiker,* use your imagination to "watch" the hair-raising events unfold.

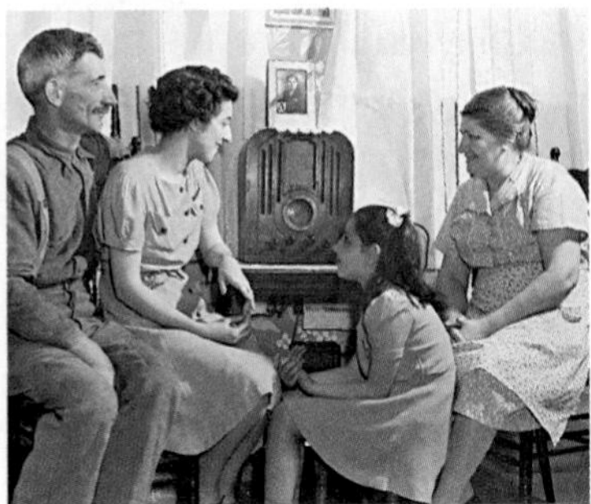

Preview the Selection

In this play, you will meet **Ronald Adams,** a man driving alone from New York to California, and the mysterious stranger he encounters: **the hitchhiker.**

Read with a Purpose Read this radio play to find out why a hitchhiker becomes such a frightening figure to Ronald Adams as he drives across the country on his own.

THE HITCHHIKER

by **Lucille Fletcher**

CHARACTERS

Ronald Adams	Henry	A Long-Distance Operator
His Mother	Henry's Wife	An Albuquerque Operator
The Gray Man	A Girl	A New York Operator
A Mechanic	A Telephone Operator	Mrs. Whitney

The time of the play is the early 1940s.

[Sound: *Automobile wheels humming over concrete road.* Music: *Something weird and shuddery.*]

Adams. I am in an auto camp[1] on Route Sixty-six just west of Gallup, New Mexico. If I tell it, perhaps it will help me. It will keep me from going mad. But I must tell this quickly. I am not mad now. I feel perfectly well, except that I am running a slight temperature. My name is Ronald Adams. I am thirty-six years of age, unmarried, tall, dark, with a black moustache. I drive a 1940 Ford V-8, license number 6V-7989. I was born in Brooklyn. All this I know. I know that I am at this moment perfectly sane. That it is not I who have gone mad—but something else—

1. **auto camp:** campground with places for drivers to park their cars.

something utterly beyond my control. But I must speak quickly. At any moment the link with life may break. This may be the last thing I ever tell on earth . . . the last night I ever see the stars. . . . **A**

[Music: *In.*]

Adams. Six days ago I left Brooklyn, to drive to California. . . .
Mother. Goodbye, Son. Good luck to you, my boy. . . .
Adams. Goodbye, Mother. Here—give me a kiss, and then I'll go. . . .
Mother. I'll come out with you to the car.
Adams. No. It's raining. Stay here at the door. Hey—what is this? Tears? I thought you promised me you wouldn't cry.
Mother. I know, dear. I'm sorry. But I—do hate to see you go.
Adams. I'll be back. I'll only be on the Coast three months. **B**
Mother. Oh, it isn't that. It's just—the trip. Ronald—I wish you weren't driving.
Adams. Oh—Mother. There you go again. People do it every day.
Mother. I know. But you'll be careful, won't you? Promise me you'll be extra careful. Don't fall asleep—or drive fast—or pick up any strangers on the road. . . .
Adams. Lord, no. You'd think I was still seventeen to hear you talk—
Mother. And wire me as soon as you get to Hollywood, won't you, Son?
Adams. Of course I will. Now don't you worry. There isn't anything going to happen. It's just eight days of perfectly simple driving on smooth, decent, civilized roads, with a hot dog or a hamburger stand every ten miles. . . . (*Fade*)

[Sound: *Auto hum.* Music: *In.*]

Adams. I was in excellent spirits. The drive ahead of me, even the loneliness, seemed like a lark.[2] But I reckoned without *him.* **C**

[Music: *Changes to something weird and empty.*] **D**

Adams. Crossing Brooklyn Bridge that morning in the rain, I saw a man leaning against the cables. He seemed to be waiting for a lift. There were spots of fresh rain on his shoulders. He was carrying a cheap overnight bag in one hand. He was thin, nondescript,[3] with a cap pulled down over his eyes. He stepped off the walk and if I hadn't swerved, I'd have hit him.

2. **lark:** good time; spree.
3. **nondescript** (NAHN duh skrihpt): without distinguishing characteristics; not memorable.

A Read and Discuss What have we learned about Ronald Adams so far?

B Reading Focus **Sequencing** When does this scene take place? How do you know? Read carefully, and see if you can figure out how much of this play is told in flashback.

C Read and Discuss What is Ronald up to? Ronald mentions "him," and the author puts the word in italics. What does that let us know about the character we haven't even met?

D Literary Focus **Suspense** How do the music directions hint that something is strange about the hitchhiker?

Analyzing Visuals **Viewing and Interpreting** How does this image reflect the play's eerie mood?

Tunnel on Pennsylvania Turnpike.

[Sound: *Terrific skidding.* Music: *In.*]

Adams. I would have forgotten him completely, except that just an hour later, while crossing the Pulaski Skyway[4] over the Jersey flats, I saw him again. At least, he looked like the same person. He was standing now, with one thumb pointing west. I couldn't figure out how he' d got there, but I thought probably one of those fast trucks had picked him up, beaten me to the Skyway, and let him off. I didn't stop for him. Then—late that night, I saw him again.

4. **Pulaski Skyway:** long-span bridge connecting the cities of Newark and Jersey City, New Jersey.

[Music: *Changing.*]

Adams. It was on the new Pennsylvania Turnpike between Harrisburg and Pittsburgh. It's two hundred and sixty-five miles long, with a very high speed limit. I was just slowing down for one of the tunnels—when I saw him—standing under an arc light by the side of the road. I could see him quite distinctly. The bag, the cap, even the spots of fresh rain spattered over his shoulders. He hailed me this time. . . .

Voice (*very spooky and faint*). Hall-ooo. . . . (*Echo as through tunnel*) Hall-ooo . . . !

Adams. I stepped on the gas like a shot. That's lonely country through the Alleghenies,[5] and I had no intention of stopping. Besides, the coincidence, or whatever it was, gave me the willies.[6] I stopped at the next gas station. **E**

[Sound: *Auto tires screeching to stop . . . horn honk.*]

Mechanic. Yes, sir.
Adams. Fill her up.
Mechanic. Certainly, sir. Check your oil, sir?
Adams. No, thanks.

[Sound: *Gas being put into car . . . bell tinkle, etc.*]

Mechanic. Nice night, isn't it?
Adams. Yes. It—hasn't been raining here recently, has it?
Mechanic. Not a drop of rain all week.
Adams. Hm. I suppose that hasn't done your business any harm.
Mechanic. Oh—people drive through here all kinds of weather. Mostly business, you know. There aren't many pleasure cars out on the Turnpike this season of the year.
Adams. I suppose not. (*Casually*) What about hitchhikers?
Mechanic (*half laughing*). Hitchhikers *here*?
Adams. What's the matter? Don't you ever see any?
Mechanic. Not much. If we did, it'd be a sight for sore eyes.
Adams. Why?
Mechanic. A guy'd be a fool who started out to hitch rides on this road. Look at it. It's two hundred and sixty-five miles long, there's practically no speed limit, and it's a straightaway. Now what car is going to stop to pick up a guy under those conditions? Would you stop?
Adams. No. (*Slowly, with puzzled emphasis*) Then you've never seen anybody?
Mechanic. Nope. Mebbe they get the lift before the Turnpike starts—I mean, you know just before the tollhouse—but then it' d be a mighty long ride. Most cars wouldn't want to pick up a guy for that long a ride. And you know—this is pretty lonesome country here—mountains, and woods. . . . You ain't seen anybody like that, have you? **F**
Adams. No. (*Quickly*) Oh no, not at all. It was—just a—technical question.
Mechanic. I see. Well—that'll be just a dollar forty-nine—with the tax. . . .

(*Fade*) **G**

5. **Alleghenies** (al uh GAY neez): the Allegheny mountain range, a part of the Appalachian Mountains that runs through Pennsylvania, Maryland, West Virginia, and Virginia.
6. **willies:** feeling of nervousness; jitters.

E Read and Discuss How is Ronald's trip going?

F Literary Focus **Suspense** What does the mechanic tell Adams that adds to the mystery of the hitchhiker?

G Read and Discuss What mood has been created by the conversation between Adams and the mechanic?

Vocabulary **coincidence** (koh IHN suh duhns) *n.:* accidental happening of events that seem to be connected.

[Sound: *Auto hum up.* Music: *Changing.*]

Adams. The thing gradually passed from my mind, as sheer coincidence. I had a good night's sleep in Pittsburgh. I did not think about the man all next day—until just outside Zanesville, Ohio, I saw him again.

[Music: *Dark, ominous note.*]

Adams. It was a bright sunshiny afternoon. The peaceful Ohio fields, brown with the autumn stubble, lay dreaming in the golden light. I was driving slowly, drinking it in, when the road suddenly ended in a detour. In front of the barrier, *he* was standing.

[Music: *In.*]

Adams. Let me explain about his appearance before I go on. I repeat. There was nothing sinister about him. He was as drab as a mud fence. Nor was his attitude menacing. He merely stood there, waiting, almost drooping a little, the cheap overnight bag in his hand. He looked as though he had been waiting there for hours. Then he looked up. He hailed me. He started to walk forward.

Voice (*far-off*). Hall-ooo . . . Hall-ooo. . . .

Vocabulary **sinister** (SIHN uh stuhr) *adj.:* creepy; threatening.
menacing (MEHN uh sihng) *adj.:* threatening.

CULTURE LINK

Urban legends united: Bigfoot meets an alien from a visting UFO.

Urban Legends—Today's Scary Stories

The ancient Greeks were fascinated by tales about heroes and the frightening creatures they fought; people in medieval times looked out for dragons and vampires. These myths and legends, along with folk and fairy tales, are part of narrative folklore. Some of the tales reflect history; others teach moral lessons. Many exist simply to entertain—often by scaring us silly.

"Urban legends" are modern folk tales. Some of them, such as stories about alligators in sewers, seem almost believable. Some may be based on a small grain of truth. These word-of-mouth stories about everything from Bigfoot and crop circles to hauntings and hoaxes fly around today's world at the speed of the Internet.

Ask Yourself

How does this story about a mysterious hitchhiker resemble an urban legend?

Adams. I had stopped the car, of course, for the detour. And for a few moments, I couldn't seem to find the new road. I knew he must be thinking that I had stopped for him.
Voice (*closer*). Hall-ooo . . . Hallll . . . ooo. . . .

[Sound: *Gears jamming . . . sound of motor turning over hard . . . nervous accelerator.*]

Voice (*closer*). Halll . . . oooo. . . .
Adams (*panicky*). No. Not just now. Sorry. . . .
Voice (*closer*). Going to California?

[Sound: *Starter starting . . . gears jamming.*]

Adams (*as though sweating blood*). No. Not today. The other way. Going to New York. Sorry . . . sorry. . . .

[Sound: *Car starts with squeal of wheels on dirt . . . into auto hum.* Music: *In.*]

Adams. After I got the car back onto the road again, I felt like a fool. Yet the thought of picking him up, of having him sit beside me, was somehow unbearable. Yet, at the same time, I felt, more than ever, unspeakably alone. **H**

[Sound: *Auto hum up.*]

Adams. Hour after hour went by. The fields, the towns ticked off, one by one. The lights changed. I knew now that I was going to see him again. And though I dreaded the sight, I caught myself searching the side of the road, waiting for him to appear.

[Sound: *Auto hum up . . . car screeches to a halt . . . impatient honk two or three times . . . door being unbolted.*]

Sleepy Man's Voice. Yep? What is it? What do you want?
Adams (*breathless*). You sell sandwiches and pop here, don't you?
Voice (*cranky*). Yep. We do. In the daytime. But we're closed up now for the night.
Adams. I know. But—I was wondering if you could possibly let me have a cup of coffee—black coffee.
Voice. Not at this time of night, mister. My wife's the cook and she's in bed. Mebbe further down the road—at the Honeysuckle Rest. . . .

[Sound: *Door squeaking on hinges as though being closed.*]

Adams. No—no. Don't shut the door. (*Shakily*) Listen—just a minute ago, there was a man standing here—right beside this stand—a suspicious-looking man. . . .
Woman's Voice (*from distance*). Hen-ry? Who is it, Hen-ry?
Henry. It's nobuddy, Mother. Just a feller thinks he wants a cup of coffee. Go back to bed.

H **Read and Discuss** What does Ronald's encounter with the hitchhiker let us know about his thoughts?

Analyzing Visuals **Viewing and Interpreting** How would you describe the mood of this image? How well does it fit the atmosphere of the play?

Adams. I don't mean to disturb you. But you see, I was driving along—when I just happened to look—and there he was. . . .

Henry. What was he doing?

Adams. Nothing. He ran off—when I stopped the car.

Henry. Then what of it? That's nothing to wake a man in the middle of his sleep about. (*Sternly*) Young man, I've got a good mind to turn you over to the sheriff.

Adams. But—I—

Henry. You've been taking a nip, that's what you've been doing. And you haven't got anything better to do than to wake decent folk out of their hard-earned sleep. Get going. Go on.

Adams. But—he looked as though he were going to rob you.

Henry. I ain't got nothin' in this stand to lose. Now—on your way before I call out Sheriff Oakes. **I**

I **Literary Focus** **Suspense** How has the playwright increased the suspense here?

(*Fade*)

[Sound: *Auto hum up.*]

Adams. I got into the car again, and drove on slowly. I was beginning to hate the car. If I could have found a place to stop . . . to rest a little. But I was in the Ozark Mountains of Missouri now. The few resort places there were closed. Only an occasional log cabin, seemingly deserted, broke the monotony[7] of the wild wooded landscape. I *had* seen him at that roadside stand: I knew I would see him again—perhaps at the next turn of the road. I knew that when I saw him next, I would run him down. . . . **J**

[Sound: *Auto hum up.*]

Adams. But I did not see him again until late next afternoon. . . .

[Sound: *Of railroad warning signal at crossroads.*]

Adams. I had stopped the car at a sleepy little junction[8] just across the border into Oklahoma—to let a train pass by—when he appeared, across the tracks, leaning against a telephone pole.

7. **monotony** (muh NAHT uhn ee): tiresome sameness.

8. **junction** (JUHNGK shuhn): point where two sets of railroad tracks join.

[Sound: *Distant sound of train chugging . . . bell ringing steadily.*]

Adams (*very tense*). It was a perfectly airless, dry day. The red clay of Oklahoma was baking under the southwestern sun. Yet there were spots of fresh rain on his shoulders. I couldn't stand that. Without thinking, blindly, I started the car across the tracks.

[Sound: *Train chugging closer.*]

Adams. He didn't even look up at me. He was staring at the ground. I stepped on the gas hard, veering the wheel sharply toward him. I could hear the train in the distance now, but didn't care. Then something went wrong with the car. It stalled right on the tracks.

[Sound: *Train chugging closer. Above this, sound of car stalling.*]

Adams. The train was coming closer. I could hear its bell ringing, and the cry of its whistle. Still he stood there. And now—I knew that he was beckoning—beckoning me to my death.

[Sound: *Train chugging close. Whistle blows wildly. Then train rushes up and by with pistons going, etc.*]

J **Read and Discuss** What do Ronald's thoughts and actions reveal to us?

Adams. Well—I frustrated him that time. The starter had worked at last. I managed to back up. But when the train passed, he was gone. I was all alone in the hot, dry afternoon. (K)

[Sound: *Train retreating. Crickets begin to sing.* Music: *In.*]

Adams. After that, I knew I had to do something. I didn't know who this man was or what he wanted of me. I only knew that from now on, I must not let myself be alone on the road for one moment.

Still he stood there. And now—I knew that he was beckoning—beckoning me to my death.

[Sound: *Auto hum up. Slow down. Stop. Door opening.*]

Adams. Hello, there. Like a ride?
Girl. What do you think? How far you going?
Adams. Amarillo . . . I'll take you to Amarillo.
Girl. Amarillo, Texas?
Adams. I'll drive you there.
Girl. Gee!

[Sound: *Door closed—car starts.* Music: *In.*]

Girl. Mind if I take off my shoes? My dogs[9] are killing me.
Adams. Go right ahead.
Girl. Gee, what a break this is. A swell car, a decent guy, and driving all the way to Amarillo. All I been getting so far is trucks.
Adams. Hitchhike much?
Girl. Sure. Only it's tough sometimes, in these great open spaces, to get the breaks.
Adams. I should think it would be. Though I'll bet if you get a good pickup in a fast car, you can get to places faster than—say, another person, in another car.
Girl. I don't get you.
Adams. Well, take me, for instance. Suppose I'm driving across the country, say, at a nice steady clip of about forty-five miles an hour. Couldn't a girl like you, just standing beside the road, waiting for lifts, beat me to town after town—provided she got picked up every time in a car doing from sixty-five to seventy miles an hour?
Girl. I dunno. Maybe she could and maybe she couldn't. What difference does it make?
Adams. Oh—no difference. It's just a—crazy idea I had sitting here in the car.
Girl (*laughing*). Imagine spending your time in a swell car thinking of things like that!

---

9. **dogs:** slang word for feet.

(K) **Literary Focus** **Foreshadowing** What do you think will happen to Adams? What clues foreshadow his future?

Adams. What would you do instead?
Girl (*admiringly*). What would I do? If I was a good-looking fellow like yourself? Why—I'd just *enjoy* myself—every minute of the time. I'd sit back, and relax, and if I saw a good-looking girl along the side of the road . . . (*Sharply*) Hey! Look out!
Adams (*breathlessly*). Did you see him too?
Girl. See who?
Adams. That man. Standing beside the barbed-wire fence.
Girl. I didn't see—anybody. There wasn't nothing but a bunch of steers—and the barbed-wire fence. What did you think you was doing? Trying to run into the barbed-wire fence?
Adams. There was a man there, I tell you . . . a thin, gray man, with an overnight bag in his hand. And I was trying to—run him down.
Girl. Run him down? You mean—kill him?
Adams. He's a sort of—phantom. I'm trying to get rid of him—or else prove that he's real. But (*desperately*) you say you didn't see him back there? You're sure?
Girl (*queerly*). I didn't see a soul. And as far as that's concerned, mister . . .
Adams. Watch for him the next time, then. Keep watching. Keep your eyes peeled on the road. He'll turn up again—maybe any minute now. (*Excitedly*) There. Look there—

[Sound: *Auto sharply veering and skidding.* GIRL *screams.* Sound: *Crash of car going into barbed-wire fence. Frightened lowing of steer.*]

Girl. How does this door work? I—I'm gettin' outta here.
Adams. Did you see him that time?
Girl (*sharply*). No. I didn't see him that time. And personally, mister, I don't expect never to see him. All I want to do is to go on living—and I don't see how I will very long driving with you—
Adams. I'm sorry. I—I don't know what came over me. (*Frightened*) Please—don't go. . . .

He's a sort of—phantom. I'm trying to get rid of him—or else prove that he's real.

Girl. So if you'll excuse me, mister—
Adams. You can't go. Listen, how would you like to go to California? I'll drive you to California.
Girl. Seeing pink elephants[10] all the way? No thanks.
Adams (*desperately*). I could get you a job there. You wouldn't have to be a waitress. I have friends there—my name is Ronald Adams—you can check up.

[Sound: *Door opening.*]

Girl. Uhn-hunh. Thanks just the same.

---

10. **pink elephants:** imaginary objects seen by someone who is drunk or delirious.

Adams. Listen. Please. For just one minute. Maybe you think I am half cracked. But this man. You see, I've been seeing this man all the way across the country. He's been following me. And if you could only help me—stay with me—until I reach the Coast—
Girl. You know what I think you need, big boy? Not a girlfriend. Just a good dose of sleep. . . . There, I got it now.

[Sound: *Door opens . . . slams.*]

Adams. No. You can't go.
Girl (*screams*). Leave your hands offa me, do you hear! Leave your—
Adams. Come back here, please, come back.

[Sound: *Struggle . . . slap . . . footsteps running away on gravel . . . lowing of steer.*]

Adams. She ran from me, as though I were a monster. A few minutes later, I saw a passing truck pick her up. I knew then that I was utterly alone. (L)

[Sound: *Lowing of steer up.*]

Adams. I was in the heart of the great Texas prairies. There wasn't a car on the road after the truck went by. I tried to figure out what to do, how to get hold of myself. If I could find a place to rest. Or even, if I could sleep right here in the car for a few hours, along the side of the road. . . . I was getting my winter overcoat out of the back seat to use as a blanket (*Hall-ooo*) when I saw him coming toward me (*Hall-ooo*), emerging from the herd of moving steers. . . .
Voice. Hall-ooo . . . Hall-ooo. . . .

[Sound: *Auto starting violently . . . up to steady hum.* Music: *In.*]

Adams. I didn't wait for him to come any closer. Perhaps I should have spoken to him then, fought it out then and there. For now he began to be everywhere. Whenever I stopped, even for a moment—for gas, or oil, for a drink of pop, a cup of coffee, a sandwich—he was there.

[Music: *Faster.*] (M)

Adams. I saw him standing outside the auto camp in Amarillo that night, when I dared to slow down. He was sitting near the drinking fountain in a little camping spot just inside the border of New Mexico.

[Music: *Faster.*]

Adams. He was waiting for me outside the Navajo reservation, where I stopped to check my tires. I saw him in Albuquerque, where I bought twelve gallons of gas. . . . I was afraid now, afraid to stop. I began to drive faster and faster. I was in lunar landscape now—the great arid mesa[11]

11. **mesa** (MAY suh): elevated flat-topped land formation with steep sides.

(L) **Read and Discuss** Ronald says that his passenger ran from him as though he were a monster. Why did she run?

(M) **Literary Focus** **Suspense** Why is the music getting faster now? What effect would this create?

country of New Mexico. I drove through it with the indifference of a fly crawling over the face of the moon.

[Music: *Faster.*]

Adams. But now he didn't even wait for me to stop. Unless I drove at eighty-five miles an hour over those endless roads—he waited for me at every other mile. I would see his figure, shadowless, flitting before me, still in its same attitude, over the cold and lifeless ground, flitting over dried-up rivers, over broken stones cast up by old glacial upheavals, flitting in the pure and cloudless air. . . . N

[Music: *Strikes sinister note of finality.*] O

Adams. I was beside myself when I finally reached Gallup, New Mexico, this morning. There is an auto camp here—cold, almost deserted at this time of year. I went inside, and asked if there was a telephone. I had the feeling that if only I could speak to someone familiar, someone that I loved, I could pull myself together.

[Sound: *Nickel put in slot.*]

Operator. Number, please?
Adams. Long distance.
Operator. Thank you.

[Sound: *Return of nickel; buzz.*]

Long Distance. This is long distance.
Adams. I'd like to put in a call to my home in Brooklyn, New York. I'm Ronald Adams. The number is Beechwood 2-0828.[12]
Long Distance. Thank you. What is your number?
Adams. 312.
Albuquerque Operator. Albuquerque.
Long Distance. New York for Gallup. (*Pause*)
New York Operator. New York.
Long Distance. Gallup, New Mexico, calling Beechwood 2-0828.

(*Fade*)

Adams. I had read somewhere that love could banish demons. It was the middle of the morning. I knew Mother would be home. I pictured her, tall, white-haired, in her crisp housedress, going about her tasks. It would be enough, I thought,

12. **Beechwood 2-0828:** phone number. At the time of this story, phone numbers in the United States began with two letters (called an exchange), followed by five numbers. Names (called exchange names) like Beechwood were used to tell callers which two letters to dial—usually the first two letters of the name (e.g., *BE* for *Beechwood*).

N **Literary Focus** **Suspense** Why do you think the man appears unless Adams drives at 85 miles per hour? What is the author setting up?

O **Read and Discuss** What mood is the author creating for us?

Vocabulary **indifference** (ihn DIHF uhr uhns) *n.:* state of being unconcerned about something.

Analyzing Visuals **Viewing and Interpreting** How does this painting help convey Adams's isolation?

Gas (1940) by Edward Hopper. Oil on canvas (26¼" x 40¼" Digital Image © The Museum of Modern Art / Licensed by SCALA.

merely to hear the even calmness of her voice. . . . Ⓟ

Long Distance. Will you please deposit three dollars and eighty-five cents for the first three minutes? When you have deposited a dollar and a half, will you wait until I have collected the money?

[Sound: *Clunk of six coins.*]

Long Distance. All right, deposit another dollar and a half.

[Sound: *Clunk of six coins.*]

Long Distance. Will you please deposit the remaining eighty-five cents?

[Sound: *Clunk of four coins.*]

Ⓟ **Literary Focus** **Foreshadowing** Do you think Adams will reach his mother? Will the phone call really help him feel calmer? Explain your predictions.

Long Distance. Ready with Brooklyn—go ahead, please.

Adams. Hello.

Mrs. Whitney. Mrs. Adams's residence.

Adams. Hello. Hello—Mother?

Mrs. Whitney (*very flat and rather proper*). This is Mrs. Adams's residence. Who is it you wished to speak to, please?

Adams. Why—who's this?

Mrs. Whitney. This is Mrs. Whitney.

Adams. Mrs. Whitney? I don't know any Mrs. Whitney. Is this Beechwood 2-0828?

Mrs. Whitney. Yes.

Adams. Where's my mother? Where's Mrs. Adams?

Mrs. Whitney. Mrs. Adams is not at home. She is still in the hospital.

Adams. The hospital!

Mrs. Whitney. Yes. Who is this calling, please? Is it a member of the family?

Adams. What's she in the hospital for?

Mrs. Whitney. She's been prostrated[13] for five days. Nervous breakdown. But who is this calling?

Adams. Nervous breakdown? But—my mother was never nervous.

Mrs. Whitney. It's all taken place since the death of her oldest son, Ronald.

Adams. Death of her oldest son, Ronald . . . ? Hey—what is this? What number is this?

Mrs. Whitney. This is Beechwood 2-0828. It's all been very sudden. He was killed just six days ago in an automobile accident on the Brooklyn Bridge.

Operator (*breaking in*). Your three minutes are up, sir. (*Pause*) Your three minutes are up, sir. (*Pause*) Your three minutes are up, sir. (*Fade*) Sir, your three minutes are up. Your three minutes are up, sir.

Adams (*in a strange voice*). And so, I am sitting here in this deserted auto camp in Gallup, New Mexico. I am trying to think. I am trying to get hold of myself. Otherwise, I shall go mad. . . . Outside it is night—the vast, soulless night of New Mexico. A million stars are in the sky. Ahead of me stretch a thousand miles of empty mesa, mountains, prairies—desert. Somewhere among them, he is waiting for me. Somewhere I shall know who he is, and who . . . I . . . am. . . . Q

[Music: *Up.*]

13. **prostrated** (PRAHS tray tihd): overcome by exhaustion or grief; weak.

Q **Reading Focus** **Sequencing** What really happened at the beginning of the story on the Brooklyn Bridge? Read that section again, if necessary.

Applying Your Skills

The Hitchhiker

Sunshine State Standards: Benchmarks **LA.6.1.6.1** use new vocabulary that is introduced and taught directly; **LA.6.1.7.5** analyze a variety of text structures (e.g., comparison/contrast, cause/effect, chronological order, argument/support, lists) and text features (main headings with subheadings) and explain their impact on meaning in text; *Also covered* **LA.6.2.1.2; LA.6.4.2.1**

Respond and Think Critically

Reading Focus

1. Which does the hitchhiker MOST likely represent? **FCAT**

A an old acquaintance from Adams's past

B his guilt for leaving his mother

C the spirit of death

D Adams's destiny in California

Read with a Purpose

2. What does Adams eventually discover about himself on his cross-country drive? What finally triggers his discovery?

Reading Skills: Identifying Sequence

3. Review your responses to the sequencing questions you answered while reading the play. Then, make a sequence chart like the one below, listing the main events in chronological order.

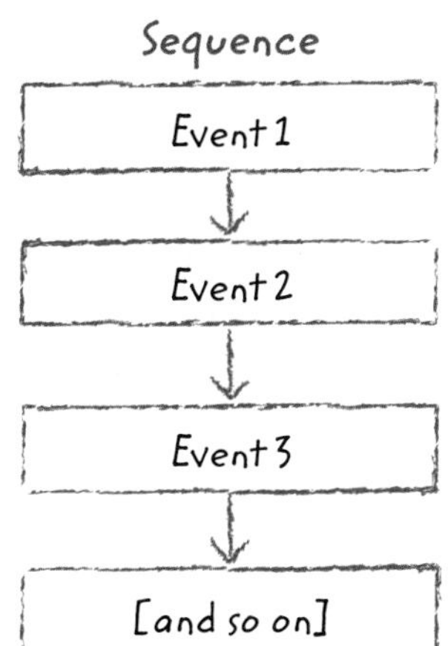

Literary Focus

Literary Analysis

4. Extend In a way, this play doesn't end at all—Adams and the reader are kept in suspense. What do you think Adams will do after the end of the play? Support your answer with details from the play.

Literary Skills: Suspense and Foreshadowing

5. Identify What characteristics does the mysterious man display that suggest he is no ordinary hitchhiker?

Literary Skills Review: Setting

6. Analyze Describe the settings in *The Hitchhiker* where the principal events take place. How do these settings affect the plot of the story? Support your answer with details from the play.

Writing Focus

Think as a Reader/Writer

Use It in Your Writing Review your notes about how music and sound effects help set the play's mood. Write instructions for music and sound effects that would help set the mood for a dramatized version of a story you like.

If you heard this story read aloud in person or on the radio, would it be as suspenseful as seeing it acted out on film? Explain.

Applying Your Skills

The Hitchhiker

Vocabulary Development

Vocabulary Skills: Related Words

You can easily add to your vocabulary by finding words related to each new word you learn. Look at the word *coincidence.* What related words can you think of? How about *coincide*? Look up *coincide* in a dictionary. You'll find that it comes from the Latin prefix *co–* plus the word *incidere.* Together, these Latin words mean "to fall into."

Here's the beginning of a word family tree for *incidere:*

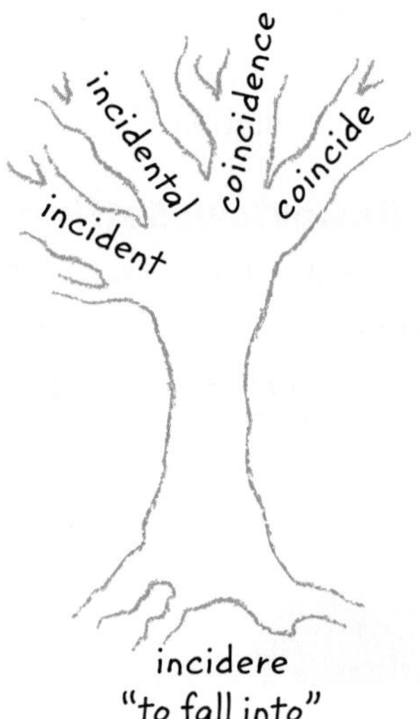

Your Turn

coincidence
sinister
menacing
indifference

1. Complete the family tree for *incidere* by defining each of the four words shown in the tree's branches.
2. Create a family tree for each of the other Vocabulary words. Remember that related words may have prefixes or suffixes, but the root word is what makes the words related.

Language Coach

Compound Words **Compound words** are formed from two or more separate words that can stand on their own. Compound words may be "closed," meaning that the words fit together to make a single word: *hitch* and *hiker* can be joined to make *hitchhiker.* They may also be "open," written as two words (*middle school*), or hyphenated (*good-looking*). Look in a dictionary to see how to write a compound word.

Find the word in column A that forms a compound with the word in column B. Write the new compound word.

A	B
car	shine
sign	side
road	wash
sun	post

Academic Vocabulary

Talk About . . .
Ronald Adams is a caught in a very complex situation. Is he a dynamic character? That is, does his character change or grow as the story progresses? Explain. Use the underlined Academic Vocabulary words in your discussion.

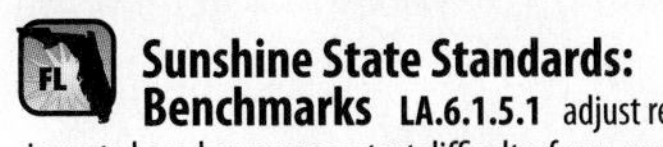
Sunshine State Standards: Benchmarks **LA.6.1.5.1** adjust reading rate based on purpose, text difficulty, form, and style; **LA.6.1.6.5** relate new vocabulary to familiar words; **LA.6.1.7.7** compare and contrast elements in multiple texts; **LA.6.3.4.4** the eight parts of speech (noun, pronoun, verb, adverb, adjective, conjunction, preposition, interjection); **LA.6.4.1.1** write narrative accounts with an engaging plot (including rising action, conflict, climax, falling action, and resolution) include a clearly described setting with figurative language and descriptive words or phrases to enhance style and tone; **LA.6.5.2.2** deliver narrative and informative presentations, including oral responses to literature, and adjust oral language, body language, eye contact, gestures, technology and supporting graphics appropriate to the situation; **LA.6.6.4.1** use appropriate available technologies to enhance communication and achieve a purpose (e.g., video, online).

Grammar Link

Misplaced Modifiers

To work well, modifiers have to be in the right place. A modifier that seems to modify the wrong word in a sentence is called a **misplaced modifier.** Here's an example of a misplaced modifier:

I read a play about a man who is pursued by a hitchhiker *in my literature book*.

Was the hitchhiker who pursued the man inside a literature book? No, so the phrase *in my literature book* is misplaced. To fix the sentence, place the modifier as close as possible to the word it modifies—*read.*

In my literature book, I read a play about a man who is pursued by a hitchhiker.

Your Turn

Move the misplaced modifiers in these sentences to the correct place.

1. The conversation at the gas station is a key scene in this play between the man and the mechanic.
2. Sitting on a curb near the drinking fountain, the driver of the car dared to slow down enough to see the hitchhiker.
3. The unexplained raindrops contributed to the story on the hitchhiker's jacket.
4. The man's mother was lying in the hospital with her white hair in New York.
5. There's a play about a man who is followed by a hitchhiking stranger in this book.

CHOICES

As you respond to the Choices, use these **Academic Vocabulary** words as appropriate: complex, display, principal, dynamic.

REVIEW

Record a Radio Play

TechFocus With a group, record a reading of *The Hitchhiker.* Decide what sound effects and music to use. Be creative with the sounds, and remember that they should contribute to the suspenseful mood of the play. Practice reading the play several times while following the cues for music and sound. Then, record the reading and play it for your class.

CONNECT

Update the Story

Suppose you wanted to retell *The Hitchhiker,* setting it in the present rather than the 1940s. What details would you have to change to reflect life today? Go through the play, and note each detail you would need to update. Be specific about how you would change the details.

EXTEND

Compare and Contrast Plays

Timed Writing *The Hitchhiker* and *In the Fog* (page 777) share several similarities. In an essay, compare and contrast these plays. What do the mysterious situations that the Doctor and Ronald Adams face have in common? Is the role of ghostly characters similar or different in each play? End your essay with an explanation of which play you preferred, and why.

COMPARING TEXTS

Comparing Versions of a Text

CONTENTS

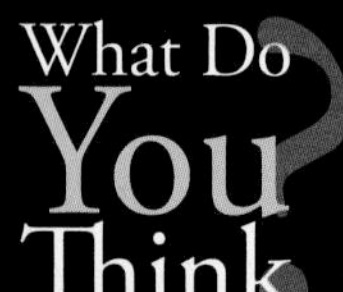

What Do You Think?

How can the same story be imaginatively presented in more than one form?

QuickTalk

Think of a story you've encountered in more than one form, such as a book and a film version. How did the versions differ from each other? What did you think of the differences?

Preparing to Read

Sunshine State Standards: Benchmarks
LA.6.1.5.1 adjust reading rate based on purpose, text difficulty, form, and style; *Also covered* **LA.6.1.6.1; LA.6.1.7.6; LA.6.1.7.7; LA.6.1.7.8; LA.6.2.1.1; LA.6.2.1.8**

from The Adventures of Tom Sawyer: The Novel, the Play, and the Graphic Novel

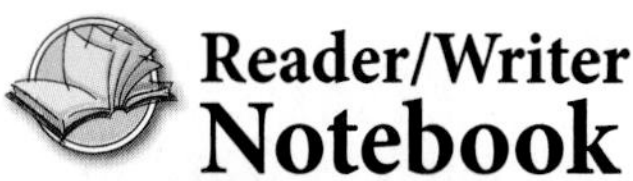

Reader/Writer Notebook

Use your **RWN** to complete the activities for these selections.

Literary Focus

Versions of a Text When a story is "translated" from one form to another, we say that it has been **adapted.** Popular books, for example, are often adapted into films. An adaptation usually keeps the same **main characters, conflict, resolution,** and **theme** as the original. Some characters may be added or removed, and the setting or other details may be changed. The biggest change, though, is the *way* the story is told. For example, short stories and novels rely mostly on narration and description; plays and films use mostly visual scenes and dialogue. Graphic stories, another form, are told through illustrations, dialogue, and some narration.

Reading Focus

Adjusting Reading Rate Your **reading rate,** how fast you read, often depends on what you're reading. When you read a novel, you may read more slowly because there are many details and descriptions. When you read a play, you may read the dialogue quickly but slow down for the stage directions. You may read a graphic story quickly and then go back and linger over the pictures.

Into Action Use a chart like this one to track your reading rate. Add a new row for each version of the *Tom Sawyer* excerpt that follows, and explain when and why you sped up or slowed down.

	What I Read Easily	What I Read Slowly	Why
Novel			

Writing Focus

Think as a Reader/Writer

Find It in Your Reading As you read, list in your *Reader/Writer Notebook* the ways the three versions are similar and different.

Vocabulary

from The Adventures of Tom Sawyer: The Novel

surveyed (suhr VAYD) *v.:* looked over and examined closely. *Tom surveyed his work proudly.*

vigor (VIHG uhr) *n.:* energy; physical or mental strength. *Tom's vigor at the start soon vanished when he saw how much he had to do.*

resumed (rih ZOOMD) *v.:* began again; went back to. *He resumed his work after the interruption.*

privilege (PRIHV uh lihj) *n.:* special right or benefit. *Tom made whitewashing the fence seem like a privilege.*

Language Coach

Dialect People from different regions and social groups have their own **dialect**, or way of speaking, that includes the words they use and how they pronounce them. Tom Sawyer and his friends talk the way kids in a small Missouri town in 1876 would have talked. Notice how their dialect is handled in the three versions of the story.

Learn It Online

Use Word Watch to focus on building your vocabulary. Visit:

go.hrw.com L6-809 

MEET THE WRITERS

Mark Twain

(1835–1910)

The Great Humorist

Mark Twain's real name was Samuel Langhorne Clemens, but he took his famous pen name from the cry "Mark twain!" shouted by Mississippi River boatmen measuring water depth. Twain's two famous novels about growing up, *The Adventures of Tom Sawyer* and *The Adventures of Huckleberry Finn,* are among the most beloved books in American literature. For more about Twain's remarkable life, read the informational article on page 828.

Cheryl Capshaw

(1964–)

Plays for Students

Cheryl Capshaw writes and adapts plays for school performance. She is a regular contributor to *Plays: The Drama Magazine for Young People.*

Michael Ploog

(1942–)

Comics and Beyond

Michael Ploog started his career by doing layout work on animated TV series. He learned the comic-art trade from master artist Will Eisner and gained attention for his work on Marvel Comics titles such as *Ghost Rider* and *Man-Thing.* In the 1980s, Ploog began working as a designer and storyboard artist in the film industry. He produces both original and adapted graphic stories.

Think About the Writers

What do you think a writer needs to keep in mind when he or she adapts another writer's work?

Preview the Selections

In these excerpts from three versions of the same classic story, you'll meet **Tom Sawyer**. Tom, who is about twelve, lives with his aunt, half brother, and cousin. **Aunt Polly,** who is not married, loves Tom dearly—but she doesn't really understand his lively nature and craving for fun and freedom. Tom has a number of young friends and neighbors, including **Jim,** an African American boy, and **Ben Rogers.**

NOVEL

from

THE ADVENTURES OF Tom Sawyer

by **Mark Twain**

Read with a Purpose

Read this novel excerpt carefully so that you will recognize the similarities and differences in the two adaptations that follow—a scene from a play and an excerpt from a graphic novel.

Build Background

The Adventures of Tom Sawyer, written by Mark Twain in 1876, is still the most famous American story about a boy growing up. The novel takes place in the small Mississippi River town of St. Petersburg, Missouri. In this episode from the novel, Tom has once again gotten into trouble with Aunt Polly—this time for sneaking away from home and fighting another boy. For his punishment, Tom has to spend his precious Saturday whitewashing a large fence. Whitewash is a kind of cheap paint made from lime and chalk. It protects wood, so it was an important part of building and fence maintenance in rural areas in the past.

CHAPTER 2

Saturday morning was come, and all the summer world was bright and fresh, and brimming with life. There was a song in every heart; and if the heart was young the music issued at the lips. There was cheer in every face and a spring in every step. The locust-trees were in bloom and the fragrance of the blossoms filled the air. Cardiff Hill, beyond the village and above it, was green with vegetation and it lay just far enough

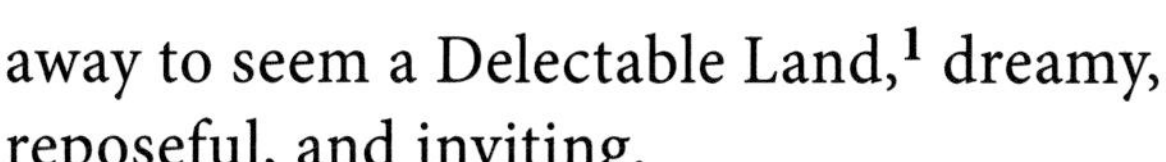

away to seem a Delectable Land,[1] dreamy, reposeful, and inviting.

Tom appeared on the sidewalk with a bucket of whitewash and a long-handled brush. He surveyed the fence, and all gladness left him and a deep melancholy

1. **Delectable Land:** a reference to the Delectable Mountains in John Bunyan's allegory *Pilgrim's Progress,* which was written in 1678. The allegory was intended to teach Christian moral values, and readers during Twain's time would have been familiar with the work and its moral lessons.

Vocabulary **surveyed** (suhr VAYD) *v.:* looked over and examined closely.

settled down upon his spirit. Thirty yards of board fence nine feet high. Life to him seemed hollow, and existence but a burden. Sighing, he dipped his brush and passed it along the topmost plank; repeated the operation; did it again; compared the insignificant whitewashed streak with the far-reaching continent of unwhitewashed fence, and sat down on a tree-box discouraged. Jim came skipping out at the gate with a tin pail, and singing "Buffalo Gals." Bringing water from the town pump had always been hateful work in Tom's eyes, before, but now it did not strike him so. He remembered that there was company at the pump. White, mulatto, and negro boys and girls were always there waiting their turns, resting, trading playthings, quarrelling, fighting, skylarking. And he remembered that although the pump was only a hundred and fifty yards off, Jim never got back with a bucket of water under an hour—and even then somebody generally had to go after him. Tom said: **A**

"Say, Jim, I'll fetch the water if you'll whitewash some."

Jim shook his head. . . .

"Jim, I'll give you a marvel. I'll give you a white alley!"[2]

Jim began to waver. **B**

"White alley, Jim! And it's a bully taw. . . .[3] And besides, if you will I'll show you my sore toe."

Jim was only human—this attraction was too much for him. He put down his pail, took the white alley, and bent over the toe with absorbing interest while the bandage was being unwound. In another moment he was flying down the street with his pail and a tingling rear, Tom was whitewashing with vigor, and Aunt Polly was retiring from the field with a slipper in her hand and triumph in her eye.

But Tom's energy did not last. He began to think of the fun he had planned for this day, and his sorrows multiplied. Soon the free boys would come tripping along on all sorts of delicious expeditions, and they would make a world of fun of him for having to work—the very thought of it burnt him like fire. He got out his worldly wealth and examined it—bits of toys, marbles, and trash; enough to buy an exchange of *work,* maybe, but not half enough to buy so much as half an hour of pure freedom. So he returned his straitened means to his pocket, and gave up the idea of trying to buy the boys. At this dark and hopeless moment an inspiration burst upon him! Nothing less than a great, magnificent inspiration. **C**

2. **marvel . . . white alley:** *Marvel* is an old word for *marble.* A "white alley" is a type of marble made of a white mineral called alabaster.

3. **bully taw:** A *taw* is a marble used to shoot with when playing marbles; *bully* means "excellent" or "fancy."

A **Read and Discuss** What situation has the author set up for the principal character?

B **Reading Focus** **Reading Rate** How do you have to adjust your reading rate while reading these opening paragraphs?

C **Literary Focus** **Versions of a Text** What character traits does Tom display? Why doesn't Twain just come out and reveal what Tom's "inspiration" is?

Vocabulary **vigor** (VIHG uhr) *n.:* energy; physical or mental strength.

He took up his brush and went tranquilly to work. Ben Rogers hove in sight presently—the very boy, of all boys, whose ridicule he had been dreading. Ben's gait[4] was the hop-skip-and-jump—proof enough that his heart was light and his anticipations high. He was eating an apple, and giving a long, melodious whoop, at intervals, followed by a deep-toned ding-dong-dong, ding-dong-dong, for he was personating[5] a steamboat. As he drew near, he slackened speed, took the middle of the street, leaned far over to starboard and rounded to ponderously and with laborious pomp and circumstance[6]—for he was personating the *Big Missouri*, and considered himself to be drawing nine feet of water. He was boat and captain and engine-bells combined, so he had to imagine himself standing on his own hurricane-deck giving the orders and executing them: **D**

"Stop her, sir! Ting-a-ling-ling!" The headway ran almost out, and he drew up slowly toward the sidewalk.

At this dark and hopeless moment an inspiration burst upon him! Nothing less than a great, magnificent inspiration.

"Ship up to back! Ting-a-ling-ling!" His arms straightened and stiffened down his sides.

"Set her back on the stabboard! Ting-a-ling-ling! Chow! ch-chow-wow! Chow!" His right hand, meantime, describing stately circles—for it was representing a forty-foot wheel.

"Let her go back on the labboard! Ting-a-ling-ling! Chow-ch-chow-chow!" The left hand began to describe circles.

"Stop the stabboard! Ting-a-ling-ling! Stop the labboard! Come ahead on the stabboard! Stop her! Let your outside turn over slow! Ting-a-ling-ling! Chow-ow-ow! Get out that head-line! *Lively* now! Come—out with your spring-line—what're you about there! Take a turn round that stump with the bight of it! Stand by that stage, now—let her go! Done with the engines, sir! Ting-a-ling-ling! . . . **E**

Tom went on whitewashing—paid no attention to the steamboat. Ben stared a moment and then said: "Hi-*yi*! *You're* up a stump, ain't you!"

No answer. Tom surveyed his last touch with the eye of an artist, then he gave his brush another gentle sweep and surveyed

4. **gait:** a way of walking.
5. **personating:** impersonating, or pretending to be something.
6. **pomp and circumstance:** dignified and showy display of formality in an important ceremony.

D Reading Focus Reading Rate Read the next three paragraphs aloud. How does your reading rate change here? Why?

E Literary Focus Versions of a Text What is Ben doing? Why do you think Twain spends so much time describing Ben's actions?

Illustration by Worth Brehm (1910).

Analyzing Visuals **Viewing and Interpreting**
What details in this painting tell you which characters it portrays?

the result, as before. Ben ranged up alongside of him. Tom's mouth watered for the apple, but he stuck to his work. Ben said:

"Hello, old chap, you got to work, hey?"

Tom wheeled suddenly and said:

"Why, it's you, Ben! I warn't noticing."

"Say—I'm going in a-swimming, I am. Don't you wish you could? But of course you'd druther *work*—wouldn't you? Course you would!"

Tom contemplated the boy a bit, and said:

"What do you call work?"

"Why, ain't *that* work?"

Tom resumed his whitewashing, and answered carelessly:

"Well, maybe it is, and maybe it ain't. All I know, is, it suits Tom Sawyer."

"Oh come, now, you don't mean to let on that you *like* it?"

The brush continued to move.

"Like it? Well, I don't see why I oughtn't to like it. Does a boy get a chance to whitewash a fence every day?"

That put the thing in a new light. Ben stopped nibbling his apple. Tom swept his brush daintily back and forth—stepped back to note the effect—added a touch here and there—criticized the effect again—Ben watching every move and getting more and more interested, more and more absorbed. Presently he said: **F**

"Say, Tom, let *me* whitewash a little."

Tom considered, was about to consent; but he altered his mind:

"No—no—I reckon it wouldn't hardly do, Ben. You see, Aunt Polly's awful particular about this fence—right here on the street, you know—but if it was the back fence I wouldn't mind and *she* wouldn't. Yes, she's awful particular about this fence; it's got to be done very careful; I reckon there ain't one boy in a thousand, maybe two thousand, that can do it the way it's got to be done."

F **Literary Focus** **Versions of a Text** How does Twain show that Tom is carefully manipulating Ben? Why is Tom succeeding?

Vocabulary **resumed** (rih ZOOMD) *v.:* began again; went back to.

"No—is that so? Oh come, now—lemme just try. Only just a little—I'd let *you,* if you was me, Tom."

"Ben, I'd like to . . . but Aunt Polly—well, Jim wanted to do it, but she wouldn't let him; Sid wanted to do it, and she wouldn't let Sid. Now don't you see how I'm fixed? If you was to tackle this fence and anything was to happen to it—"

"Oh, shucks, I'll be just as careful. Now lemme try. Say—I'll give you the core of my apple."

"Well, here—No, Ben, now don't. I'm afeard—"

"I'll give you *all* of it!" **G**

Tom gave up the brush with reluctance in his face, but alacrity[7] in his heart. And while the late steamer *Big Missouri* worked and sweated in the sun, the retired artist sat on a barrel in the shade close by, dangled his legs, munched his apple, and planned the slaughter of more innocents. There was no lack of material; boys happened along every little while; they came to jeer, but remained to whitewash. By the time Ben was tired out, Tom had traded the next chance to Billy Fisher for a kite, in good repair; and when he played out, Johnny Miller bought in for a dead rat and a string to swing it with—and so on, and so on, hour after hour. And when the middle of the afternoon came, from being a poor poverty-stricken boy in the morning, Tom was literally rolling in wealth. He had, besides the things before mentioned, twelve marbles, part of a jews-harp,[8] a piece of blue bottle-glass to look through, a spool cannon, a key that wouldn't unlock anything, a fragment of chalk, a glass stopper of a decanter, a tin soldier, a couple of tadpoles, six fire-crackers, a kitten with only one eye, a brass door-knob, a dog-collar—but no dog—the handle of a knife, four pieces of orange-peel, and a dilapidated[9] old window sash. **H**

7. **alacrity:** eager willingness.

8. **jews-harp:** a small musical instrument shaped like a lyre or harp that is held between the teeth and played with one finger, making a twanging sound.

9. **dilapidated:** shabby and run-down; worn-out.

G **Read and Discuss** What did Tom's "magnificent inspiration" turn out to be?

H **Reading Focus** **Reading Rate** How do you have to adjust your reading rate here? Why?

Illustration by Scott McKowen.

He had had a nice, good, idle time all the while—plenty of company—and the fence had three coats of whitewash on it! If he hadn't run out of whitewash he would have bankrupted every boy in the village. **I**

Tom said to himself that it was not such a hollow world, after all. He had discovered a great law of human action, without knowing it—namely, that in order to make a man or a boy covet[10] a thing, it is only necessary to make the thing difficult to attain. If he had been a great and wise philosopher, like the writer of this book, he would now have comprehended that Work consists of whatever a body is *obliged*[11] to do, and that Play consists of whatever a body is not obliged to do. And this would help him to understand why constructing artificial flowers or performing on a tread-mill is work, while rolling ten-pins[12] or climbing Mont Blanc is only amusement. There are wealthy gentlemen in England who drive four-horse passenger-coaches twenty or thirty miles on a daily line, in the summer, because the privilege costs them considerable money; but if they were offered wages for the service, that would turn it into work and then they would resign. **J**

The boy mused awhile over the substantial change which had taken place in his worldly circumstances, and then wended toward headquarters to report.

10. **covet:** yearn for; greedily desire; enviously long for.
11. **obliged:** required; obligated; forced.
12. **ten-pins:** the game of bowling.

from Chapter 3

Tom presented himself before Aunt Polly, who was sitting by an open window in a pleasant rearward apartment, which was bedroom, breakfast-room, dining-room, and library, combined. The balmy summer air, the restful quiet, the odor of the flowers, and the drowsing murmur of the bees had had their effect, and she was nodding over her knitting—for she had no company but the cat, and it was asleep in her lap. Her spectacles were propped up on her gray head for safety. She had thought that of course Tom had deserted long ago, and she wondered at seeing him place himself in her power again in this intrepid way. He said: "Mayn't I go and play now, aunt?"

"What, a'ready? How much have you done?"

"It's all done, aunt."

"Tom, don't lie to me—I can't bear it."

"I ain't, aunt; it *is* all done."

Aunt Polly placed small trust in such evidence. She went out to see for herself; and she would have been content to find twenty per cent of Tom's statement true. When she found the entire fence whitewashed, and not only whitewashed but elaborately coated and recoated, and even a streak added to the ground, her astonishment was almost unspeakable. She said:

I **Read and Discuss** In what way is Tom "rolling in wealth"?

J **Read and Discuss** What "law of human action" has Tom discovered? Explain it in your own words.

Vocabulary **privilege** (PRIHV uh lihj) *n.:* special right or benefit.

Analyzing Visuals **Viewing and Interpreting** Which of Tom Sawyer's character traits that you've seen in this excerpt does this painting display?

Illustration by Mike Wimmer.

"Well, I never! There's no getting round it, you can work when you're a mind to, Tom." And then she diluted the compliment by adding, "But it's powerful seldom you're a mind to, I'm bound to say. Well, go 'long and play; but mind you get back some time in a week, or I'll tan you."

She was so overcome by the splendor of his achievement that she took him into the closet and selected a choice apple and delivered it to him, along with an improving lecture upon the added value and flavor a treat took to itself when it came without sin through virtuous effort. And while she closed with a happy Scriptural flourish, he "hooked" a doughnut. **K**

K **Literary Focus** **Versions of a Text** How does Tom manage to con even Aunt Polly? Keep this scene in mind when you read the graphic novel version.

PLAY

from The Adventures of Tom Sawyer

by **Mark Twain**

adapted by **Cheryl Capshaw**

Read with a Purpose

Read this excerpt from a dramatized version of the novel to see how the playwright adapts the "white-washing the fence" scene for live performance.

Preparing To Read for this selection is on page 809.

Build Background

This excerpt is Scene 2 of the play. The opening stage direction "At Rise" is a term that comes from the theatrical tradition of a curtain rising to reveal the stage as the lights come on. "At Rise" simply means that a new scene or act is beginning. In modern plays, the setting of the scene or the opening stage directions are usually described in the At Rise.

TIME: *Saturday morning.*

SETTING: *A fence (real or imagined) set across stage.*

AT RISE: TOM *is sitting in front of fence, holding a paintbrush and bucket. He is grumbling as he half-heartedly slops on some imaginary paint.*

Tom: Look at this perfect spring day! Sun shining, a slight little breeze—oh, I had so much fun planned for this here day. Aunt Polly said I could play after I paint this old fence (*He kicks at it.*), but she knows that will take 47 years or more! It must be at least a hundred miles long! (*Working up a panic*) I might be an old man with a beard by the time I get finished here! I have to figure something out. My friends will be coming along soon, and they will laugh me all the way up to Indiana when they find out. (*He checks his pockets.*) Let's see what I've got to trade for work; maybe I can buy a half hour or so of freedom, anyway. Two pennies, a button and a marble—I don't think that will even get me ten minutes. (*Looks off right*) Oh, gosh, here comes Ben! (*He gets back to painting, but much more slowly and carefully now.* BEN ROGERS *enters, munching on an apple.*) **A**

A **Reading Focus** **Reading Rate** How did you adjust your reading rate to understand the stage directions? Now re-read Tom's lines aloud without speaking the stage directions.

Ben: Look at you, Tom. You're in a fix, ain't you? (TOM *doesn't answer. He stands back and looks at his work with the eye of an artist and dips his brush again. He is very focused.*) You've got to work today, huh?

Tom: (*Turning suddenly, as if he didn't notice* BEN *before now*): Why, hello, Ben! I didn't notice you at first.

Ben: I'm going swimming. Do you want to come with me? Oh, but you have to work, don't you? (TOM *stops and stares at him, offended.*) **B**

Tom: Now just what is it that you are calling work, Ben Rogers?

Ben: Well, ain't that work? That painting that you are doing?

Tom (*Resuming his painting*): Maybe it is and maybe it ain't. All I know is I sure do like it. It suits me just fine.

Ben: Oh, come on, now, Tom. You don't really mean to say that you like it!

Tom: Why shouldn't I like it? It's not every day that a fellow gets a chance to whitewash a fence! Matter of fact, I don't think I've ever gotten the chance before today. It's a new and exciting challenge for me. **C**

Ben (*Thinking for a second*): Here, Tom, let me try.

Tom: No way. I'm afraid I can't, Ben. Aunt Polly is very particular about this fence. It has to be done very carefully. It's right here on the street where everyone can see it, so it needs to be done in nice, even strokes. Why, I'll bet there isn't a boy in a thousand—or maybe even two thousand—that can do it the way it's got to be done.

Ben (*Coaxing*):[1] Tom, come on. Let me whitewash just a little. I can do a good job—(*Insisting*) I can.

Tom (*Dubious*):[2] I don't know. There is a certain satisfaction in seeing this dingy old gray

1. **coaxing:** talking into doing something; gently urging; sweet talking.
2. **dubious:** doubtful; uncertain.

B **Literary Focus** **Versions of a Text** Ben's appearance in the novel is treated at much greater length. Do you think the playwright has lost anything by just having him show up eating an apple? Explain.

C **Read and Discuss** How is Tom leading Ben to believe that painting the fence is a privilege? How is his approach in the play similar to and different from his approach in the novel?

Analyzing Visuals

Viewing and Interpreting This image is from the staging of a different dramatic adaptation of the story. What makes this image appear dynamic?

fence turn all shiny and clean and white. It's very refreshing. I may not want to give it up, even for a little while.

Ben: Let me try. I'd let you if you were me.

Tom (*Slowly*): Gee, Ben, I just don't know . . . I sure do like it a lot— **D**

Ben (*Suddenly*): Hey, I know! I'll let you have the rest of my apple if you'll let me whitewash!

Tom (*Relenting*): Well, O.K., maybe for a minute or two. (TOM *sits cross-legged on the floor and munches the apple while* BEN *takes the brush and dips it. He begins to paint with slow careful strokes and does a very nice job.*)

Ben: Hey, you were right, this is really fun! (TOM *nods in agreement and winks at the audience. Soon* BILLY FISHER *enters, carrying a kite.*) **E**

Billy: Hey, Tom, want to go to the park and fly my kite with me?

Tom: No, thanks, Billy. Ben and I are having too much fun whitewashing Aunt Polly's fence.

Ben: Yeah, it's great. You ought to try it. But it will cost you something.

Billy: Cost me? Are you kidding?

Ben: No. It cost me an apple, and I barely talked Tom into it. This isn't work at all. It is like a wonderful game, and you have to be very skilled. You probably can't do it right, Billy. Only one in two thousand boys can do this right.

Billy (*In challenging tone*): Well, I bet I'm one of them that can do it right. You have to give me a chance.

Ben: Don't ask me, ask the boss man.

Billy: What do you say, Tom? Can I?

Tom: I don't know, Billy. Aunt Polly will get mad if we mess it up and turn it into a party or something.

Ben: Yeah, you'd better just leave it to Tom and me.

Billy (*Protesting*): That's not fair. Let me show you how good I can do it. I'll bet I'm better than both of you. **F**

Ben: Do you have something to pay the boss for letting you try?

Billy: Sure I do. He can have my new kite.

Tom: Let me take a look at that kite, Billy. (TOM *stands up, takes the kite, inspects it carefully.*) It's not a bad kite.

Billy: It's a really fine kite, Tom!

Tom (*After thinking a moment*): O.K., Ben, give him the brush.

Ben (*Upset*): Hey, no fair!

Billy: That's O.K.! My pappy has an extra brush! I'll go get it and be back to paint.

Tom: O.K., that will make things go much faster. (*After a pause*) Not that you want them to go faster, seeing as how this is so much fun—(BILLY *runs off,* BEN *gets back to work, and* TOM *gives the audience a smile and a "thumbs up" sign as curtain closes.*) **G**

D **Literary Focus** **Versions of a Text** How has the playwright modernized the language so that the boys don't have the same dialect they had in the novel? Why do you think she did this?

E **Read and Discuss** Why does the playwright have Tom wink at the audience?

F **Literary Focus** **Versions of a Text** In the novel, Billy and his kite were just mentioned briefly. What's the effect of expanding Billy's role here? Why do you think the writer did this?

G **Read and Discuss** How do things turn out for Tom in this version?

from The Adventures of Tom Saw

by **Mark Twain** adapted by **Michael Ploog**

Read with a Purpose

Read this excerpt from a graphic novel to discover what a visual version of the "whitewashing the fence" episode adds to your understanding of the scene.

Preparing To Read for this selection is on page 809.

B

A **Literary Focus** **Versions of a Text** This part isn't in the novel excerpt. What does it add to your understanding of Tom?

B **Literary Focus** **Versions of a Text** How is this scene different from the novel's version of the interaction with Jim?

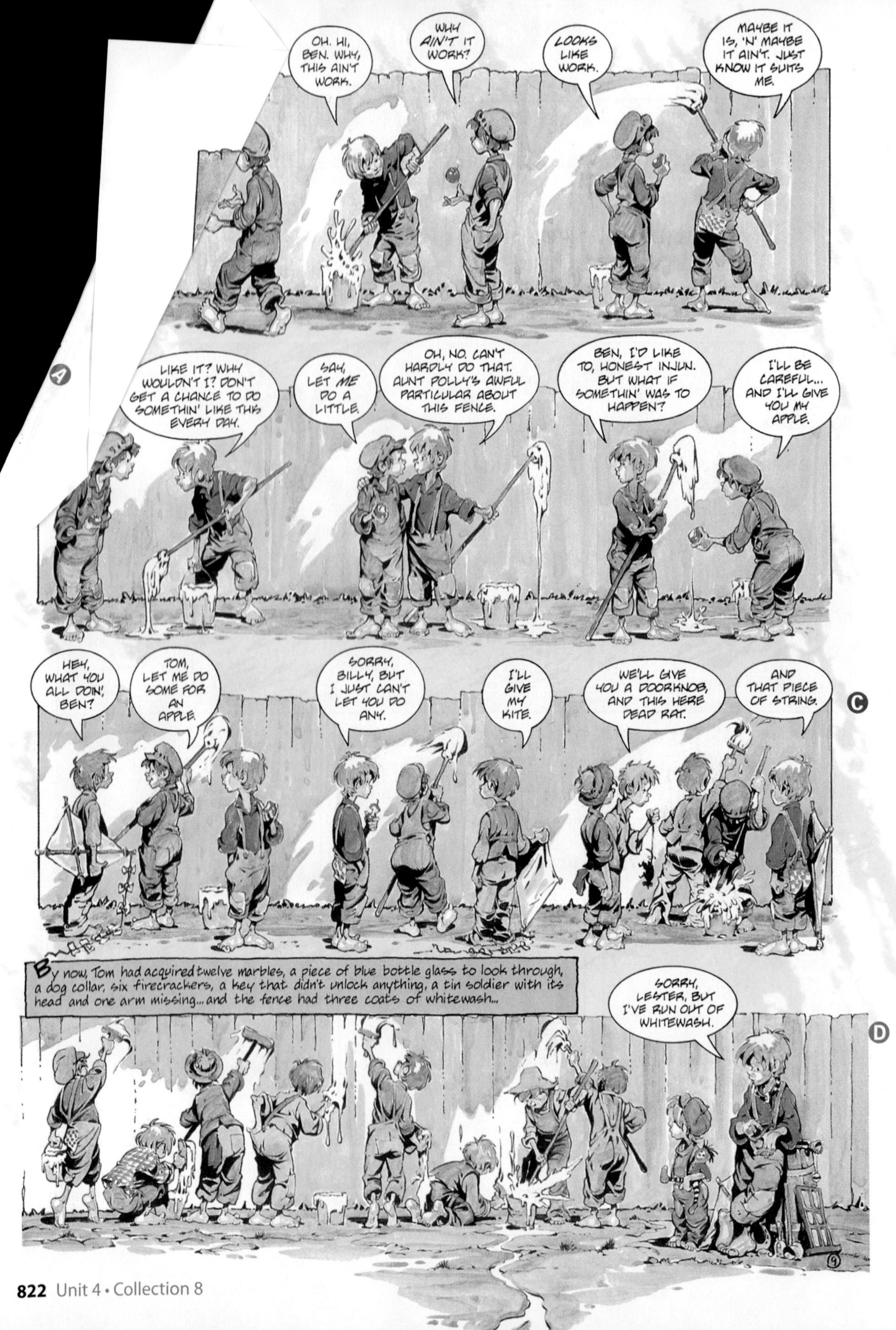
OH. HI, BEN. WHY, THIS AIN'T WORK.
WHY AIN'T IT WORK?
LOOKS LIKE WORK.
MAYBE IT IS, 'N' MAYBE IT AIN'T. JUST KNOW IT SUITS ME.
A
LIKE IT? WHY WOULDN'T I? DON'T GET A CHANCE TO DO SOMETHIN' LIKE THIS EVERY DAY.
SAY, LET ME DO A LITTLE.
OH, NO. CAN'T HARDLY DO THAT. AUNT POLLY'S AWFUL PARTICULAR ABOUT THIS FENCE.
BEN, I'D LIKE TO, HONEST INJUN. BUT WHAT IF SOMETHIN' WAS TO HAPPEN?
I'LL BE CAREFUL... AND I'LL GIVE YOU MY APPLE.
HEY, WHAT YOU ALL DOIN', BEN?
TOM, LET ME DO SOME FOR AN APPLE.
SORRY, BILLY, BUT I JUST CAN'T LET YOU DO ANY.
I'LL GIVE MY KITE.
WE'LL GIVE YOU A DOORKNOB, AND THIS HERE DEAD RAT.
AND THAT PIECE OF STRING.
C
By now, Tom had acquired twelve marbles, a piece of blue bottle glass to look through, a dog collar, six firecrackers, a key that didn't unlock anything, a tin soldier with its head and one arm missing... and the fence had three coats of whitewash...
SORRY, LESTER, BUT I'VE RUN OUT OF WHITEWASH.
D
9

C **Read and Discuss** How does Ploog show us what's happening between Tom and his friends?

D **Literary Focus** **Versions of a Text** How does Ploog compress the events in the novel into one page here and make the action dynamic? What carries the story's events more here: the illustrations or the dialogue? Why?

E **Read and Discuss** What does Aunt Polly's questioning about Tom's work show us about her?

F **Literary Focus** **Versions of a Text** Is this how you pictured Aunt Polly when you read the novel excerpt? How does Ploog show the relationship between Tom and Aunt Polly? How did Twain show it?

Your Skills

Ap…es of Tom Sawyer: The Novel, …Graphic Novel

fro…

th…

Sunshine State Standards: Benchmarks LA.6.1.5.1 adjust reading rate based on purpose, text difficulty, and style; **LA.6.1.7.3** determine the main idea or essential message in grade-level or higher text through inferring, paraphrasing, summarizing, and identifying relevant details; *Also covered* **LA.6.1.7.7; LA.6.2.1.1; LA.6.2.1.2**

Respond and Think Critically

…cus

FCAT

…h characterized in all …sions of this episode?

…behaved

…y clever

…nean-spirited

… very timid

Read with a Purpose

2. Which version of this episode from *Tom Sawyer* seemed most "modern" to you? Why?

Reading Skills: Adjusting Reading Rate

3. Review the chart you kept while reading the three versions. When did you read quickly? When did you slow down in order to better understand the text? What conclusions about reading rate can you draw from this?

Vocabulary Check

Answer the following questions.

4. If you **surveyed** your surroundings, would you look at them briefly or take time to really look?
5. Why would you approach an activity you liked with more **vigor** than one you disliked?
6. If the rain has **resumed** after the skies cleared, would you need an umbrella?
7. How might someone your age earn a **privilege**?

Literary Focus

Literary Analysis

8. **Analyze** What are the principal techniques each writer uses to get across the character of Tom Sawyer? Support your answer with details from the texts. READ THINK EXPLAIN
9. **Make Judgments** One common **archetype,** or recurring character type, is the trickster. A **trickster** is a clever, mischievous, and often selfish character who gets what he or she wants by tricking others. In what ways does Tom Sawyer fit the trickster archetype? Which version of the story makes him seem more like a trickster than the others?

Literary Skills: Versions of a Text

10. Which characters and parts of the novel, the play, and the graphic novel are identical? What are the biggest differences? What effect do they have on the storytelling?
11. **Analyze** The graphic novel adaptation is the only version that illustrates the action. In what other ways is it unique among the three versions?

Writing Focus

Think as a Reader/Writer

Use It in Your Writing Review your lists of similarities and differences you found among the three versions. Which version do you think is closer to the original novel: the play or the graphic novel? Explain.

Sunshine State Standards: Benchmarks **LA.6.1.7.7** compare and contrast elements in multiple texts; **LA.6.3.5.2** use elements of spacing and design for graphic (e.g., tables, drawings, charts, graphs) when applicable to enhance the appearance of the document; **LA.6.** essays (e.g., process, de contrast, problem/solutio supporting details, and int paragraphs; *Also covered* **LA**

from The Adventures of Tom Sawyer: The Novel, the Play, and the Graphic Novel

Writing Focus

Write a Comparison-Contrast Essay

Write an essay in which you compare the three versions of the "whitewashing the fence" scene from *The Adventures of Tom Sawyer.* You may want to organize your essay in this way:

- Begin by summarizing the scene in the novel—the original version of the story.
- Then, identify the ways in which the two adaptations—the play and the graphic novel—are the same as the original novel.
- Next, identify the ways in which the novel, play, and graphic novel are different. Mention story events, characters, dialogue, descriptions, and the writers' use of language.
- Draw conclusions about why the writers of the adaptations either added details not found in the original or took out details that were in the original.
- Conclude your essay by explaining how you responded to the versions. Which one was most memorable? Which was easiest to relate to and understand?

Use the workshop on writing a Comparison-Contrast Essay, pages 106–113, for help with this assignment.

What Do You Think Now?

How can different versions of the same story add to our appreciation and enjoyment of the work?

CHOICES

As you respond to the Choices, use these **Academic Voca** words as appropriate: complex, display, principal, dynamic.

REVIEW

Write a Character Study

Timed Writing Consider what you've learned about Tom Sawyer. Is he a complex character or a simple one? Why does he behave the way he does? What values does he display? What can you determine by the way other characters react to him? Write a short essay sharing your impressions of Tom Sawyer's personality. Support your ideas with details from the story.

CONNECT

Write a Review

Think of a movie that is based on a book you've read, or think of a novelization of a movie you've seen. Write a review in which you compare the movie and book. Focus on principal differences. Did the differences improve the original work? End by explaining which version you preferred.

EXTEND

Create a Graphic Scene

Create a storyboard or graphic story based on a scene from one of the selections you enjoyed in this textbook. Illustrate your scene in several dynamic panels, and provide word balloons with dialogue and boxes for narration. (Use the graphic story you just read as a model.)

XT FOCUS

INFOR

ructures:

T gical Order and Cause/Effect

(S

y:

Krull
of the Writers

ARTICLE

"War of the Worlds": Behind the 1938 Radio Show Panic
by Stefan Lovgen
from National Geographic News
page 834

What Do You Think?

How do nonfiction writers show imagination in their work?

QuickTalk

Why do people enjoy "behind the scenes" stories about real people's lives or stories about actual events? How do such stories prove that "truth is stranger than fiction"?

BIOGRAPHY

Preparing to Read

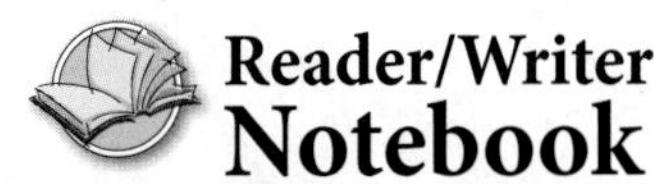

Sunshine State Standards: Benchmarks **LA.6.1.6.1** use new vocabulary that is introduced and taught directly; **LA.6.1.6.4** categorize key vocabulary and identify salient features; *Also covered* **LA.6.1.7.3; LA.6.1.7.5; LA.6.1.7.8**

Killingly Funny: Mark Twain

Reader/Writer Notebook

Use your **RWN** to complete the activities for this selection.

Informational Text Focus

Chronological Order Writers use different patterns of organization—or **text structures**—to arrange the information in a text. They choose a text structure that best fits their material. One of the most common text structures is **chronological order,** also called **time order** or **sequence.**

Chronological order is a structure most often used in biographies, autobiographies, and reports of historical or current events. The structure helps organize large amounts of complex information. A text arranged in chronological order relates events in the order in which they happened: *first, next, last.* A writer rarely organizes the *entire* text in this way, however, and may interrupt the time sequence at certain points. Much of the information about Mark Twain's dynamic life in "Killingly Funny" is in chronological order, as you might expect from a biography.

Into Action You can keep track of and display chronological sequences in a chart like this one.

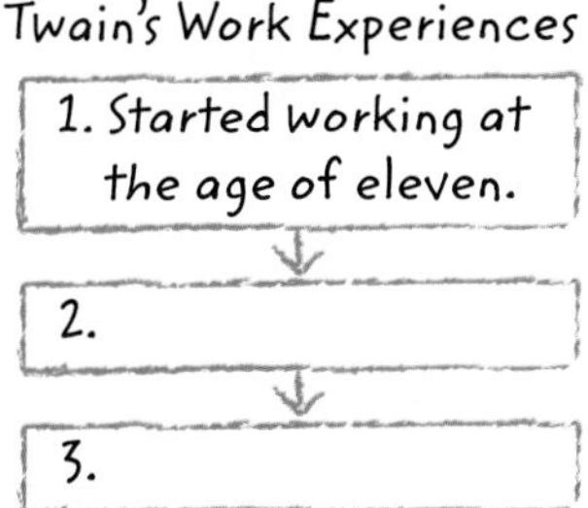

Twain's Work Experiences
1. Started working at the age of eleven.
2.
3.

Vocabulary

fascinated (FAS uh nayt ihd) *v.:* charmed by something. *Listeners were often fascinated by Twain's lectures.*

eccentric (ehk SEHN trihk) *adj.:* peculiar; unusual. *Twain's eccentric habits were part of his unique personality.*

conspicuous (kuhn SPIHK yoo uhs) *adj.:* attracting attention. *Twain's conspicuous house amazed his neighbors.*

persistent (puhr SIHS tuhnt) *adj.:* repeated or continuing. *Persistent bad investments cost Twain large sums of money.*

Language Coach

Idioms An **idiom** is an expression that means something different from what the words actually say. Try to identify and explain the idiom in the following sentence from "Killingly Funny":

Luckily, people hung on his every word.

You can't *literally* hang on a word, so what might this expression mean?

Writing Focus

Preparing for **Extended Response**

As you read this biography, note places where sequences of events told in chronological order begin and end. Jot down these notes in your *Reader/Writer Notebook.*

BIOGRAPHY

KILLINGLY FUNNY MARK TWAIN

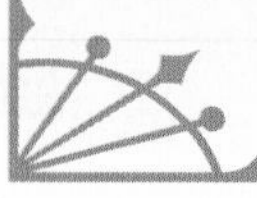

by **Kathleen Krull**

Read with a Purpose

Read this biography of Mark Twain to see what facts about the famous author's life are "stranger than fiction."

Born in Florida, Missouri, 1835

Died near Redding, Connecticut, 1910

Considered the greatest American humorist, creator of Tom Sawyer, Huckleberry Finn, The Prince and the Pauper, *and other influential works*

The Granger Collection, New York.

"SAMUEL LANGHORNE CLEMENS!" yelled the teacher, her patience gone.

The boy whose name she called knew that when a teacher uses your whole name it means trouble. And he always was in some kind of trouble—for putting snakes in his aunt's sewing basket, hiding bats in his pockets for his mother to find, or perhaps faking death to get out of going to school. Once, from a height of three stories, he dropped a watermelon shell onto his brother's head. "I was born excited," he admitted. **A**

A **Read and Discuss** What is the author telling you here about Samuel Clemens?

Later, perhaps wanting to turn over a new leaf, he took a new name. Growing up on the Mississippi River in Hannibal, Missouri, he was fascinated by the steamboats that brought tourists and entertainers. His boyhood dream, which he fulfilled at age twenty-three, was to become a licensed riverboat pilot. *Mark twain* is a Mississippi River expression that means "safe water—twelve feet deep," and by age twenty-eight, he was using this phrase as his pen name.

Twain first went to work at age eleven when his father died, always taking a book along for companionship. He worked in print shops and newspaper offices, prospected for gold and silver out West, and traveled to Hawaii and came back to lecture about it. **B**

His first appearance in a magazine was as Mike Swain (the editor couldn't read Twain's handwriting), author of "Forty-Three Days in an Open Boat." A thrilling account of the survivors of a disaster at sea, this was a big story Twain almost didn't get to write. Much to his embarrassment, on the day he was to interview the survivors, he was suffering so badly from saddle sores that he had to be carried to the meeting on a stretcher and take his notes lying down.

The first time he ever told a funny story, he discovered that he loved, above all else, being "killingly" funny. His sense of humor became his trademark. With his humorous short story "The Celebrated Jumping Frog of Calaveras County," Mark Twain fell into writing and stayed. **C**

On their first date, Twain took Olivia Langdon, whom he later married, to hear Charles Dickens speak. Olivia called her husband Youth or Little Man. All during their marriage, she acted as his first reader, using a pencil to cross out any part of his writing she didn't like. They had four children.

The best compliment Twain ever got was when his daughter Susy praised the "perfectly delightful" stories he would tell her and her sister, Clara, as they perched on the arms of his chair. He had total recall of his own childhood, things both happy and sad—"A boy's life is not all comedy"—and used the material throughout his books. **D**

Wealthy from his writing, Twain amazed the neighbors by building the most elaborate and eccentric house in Hartford, Connecticut—it had nineteen

---

B **Informational Focus** **Chronological Order** Which words act as time clues in these opening paragraphs?

C **Read and Discuss** What did you learn about the author and his early years?

D **Read and Discuss** What do you think of this quotation? How does it match what you've learned about Twain's childhood?

Vocabulary **fascinated** (FAS uh nayt ihd) *v.:* charmed by something.
eccentric (ehk SEHN trihk) *adj.:* peculiar; unusual.

luxurious rooms, plus five bathrooms. (The neighbors included Harriet Beecher Stowe, famous as the author of *Uncle Tom's Cabin.*) He slept in a black bed with carved angels on it that was large enough to hold a whole family. He spent summers at Quarry Farm, near Elmira, New York, where he wrote in a small, eight-sided room lined with windows. He had the travel bug and would live in Europe for years at a time.

As much money as Twain made, he would often lose it by investing in the wrong gadgets. Once he lost $200,000 on a failed typesetting machine. When he was offered a chance to invest in Alexander Graham Bell's new telephone, he turned it down as too risky. (Later, however, he owned the first telephone ever installed in a private house . . . where he got calls day and night.) **E**

Whenever he went bankrupt, he would do another lecture tour to make his money back. Twain's tours were world famous. He enjoyed performing. He simply liked to hear himself talk, and indeed, he wasn't happy unless he was dominating a conversation. Luckily, people hung on his every word. Hardly a day passed without a reporter seeking his opinion on something, and he was thought to be the most photographed man in the world—so famous that there was even a Mark Twain impersonator working in Australia. He felt like the "most conspicuous person on the planet"—but on most days he liked the attention.

Twain took a day off now and then to go skating or play with his children, but most often he worked, frequently in bed. When rheumatism[1] affected his writing arm, he became the first professional writer to use a typewriter. Protective of his good reputation, he would burn whole manuscripts if he felt they weren't up to his usual standards. **F**

Twain's favorite escape was to play pool. Sometimes he stayed up and played all night. He also liked to watch baseball, and he loved to read his writings aloud to his family. For exercise he took ten-mile walks in the country. He carried cats around on his shoulders and gave them names like Lazy, Satan, Sin, Cleveland, Pestilence,[2] and Famine. **G**

Twain was not known as a fighter.

1. **rheumatism** (ROO muh tihz uhm): disease that causes stiffness in the joints.
2. **Pestilence** (PEHS tuh luhns): humorous name meaning any rapidly spreading, fatal disease.

E **Informational Focus** **Chronological Order** Why did the author add the information in parentheses?

F **Read and Discuss** How does this detail about Twain's habits add to what you already know about him?

G **Read and Discuss** What side of Twain's personality do the details in this paragraph reveal?

Vocabulary **conspicuous** (kuhn SPIHK yoo uhs) *adj.:* attracting attention.

He had left the Civil War after just two weeks, weary (as he joked) from "persistent retreating." He would leave town rather than fight a duel. He even avoided touching other people—he was not a back-slapper. But he did have a temper. Once, when a button was missing from the third shirt he tried on in a row (he designed his own shirts; they buttoned in back), he threw all the shirts out the window and screamed swear words loud enough to wake up the neighborhood.

Twain wore white clothes, winter and summer. He said they made him feel "clean in a dirty world." He ordered his trademark white linen suits from his tailor six at a time. Around the house he lounged about in slippers, and he wore a long nightgown to bed. He kept his bushy hair shiny by washing it every day and rubbing the shampoo lather off with a coarse towel....

As funny as he was, Twain always looked serious and older than his age. When he was sad, he played hymns on the piano.

Photograph of Mark Twain, taken about 1908, standing at the pool table in his house in Hartford.

Three of Twain's children died before he did, as did his beloved wife. Shortly after his youngest daughter died, when Twain was seventy-four, he found her Christmas present to him: a large globe, something he had always wanted. Overcome by sadness, he stopped writing, and four months later, he slipped into a coma and died of heart disease. His last words were about Robert Louis Stevenson's *The Strange Case of Dr. Jekyll and Mr. Hyde.* **H**

Twain might not have liked this book. He thought that a person's real life

H **Read and Discuss** What do these details about Twain's last days reveal about his complex personality?

Vocabulary **persistent** (puhr SIHS tuhnt) *adj.:* repeated or continuing.

Analyzing Visuals

Viewing and Interpreting How does this historical photo reflect what Twain appreciated most of all?

Mark Twain and his family on the porch of their house in Hartford.
The Granger Collection, New York.

story is lived inside that person's head: "And *that* you can never know." **I**

BOOKMARKS

- The most famous fence in American literature is the one Tom Sawyer tricked his friends into painting for him. Twain created this scene while he was living in London. He wrote much of *Tom Sawyer* quickly, completing as many as fifty pages a day—but as with almost all his books, he ran out of steam in the middle and set the story aside for two years before completing it. Most of the adventures in *Tom Sawyer* really happened, according to Twain. The book sold two million copies while he was alive and continues to be his most popular work.
- American writer Ernest Hemingway once said that "all modern American literature comes from. . . *Huckleberry Finn.*" Many consider this sequel to *Tom Sawyer* to be America's greatest novel—but it is also controversial. Banned upon publication as "trash" because of its nonstandard grammar and Huck's "casual morals," it is sometimes banned now because of Huck's acceptance of racial stereotypes.

Twain did not think of himself as a racist; he thought *Huck Finn* was about equality and the universal dreams of all people. He hated slavery, was ashamed of the way whites treated blacks, and paid the expenses of the first black students at Yale Law School and various colleges. **J**

Read with a Purpose What details of Twain's life did you find "stranger than fiction"?

I **Read and Discuss** What insight into Twain's personality can you get from this last section?

J **Read and Discuss** What's the point of this section called "Bookmarks"? What do you learn from it?

Applying Your Skills

Sunshine State Standards: Benchmarks LA.6.1.6.1 use new vocabulary that is introduced and taught directly; *Also covered* LA.6.1.7.3; LA.6.1.7.5; LA.6.2.1.2

Killingly Funny: Mark Twain

Practicing for FCAT

Informational Text and Vocabulary

1 Based on this selection, which statement MOST accurately summarizes Clemens's childhood?

A Clemens got into trouble often.

B Clemens sailed steamboats on the Mississippi River.

C Clemens worked hard after his father died.

D Clemens was always reading books.

2 Which event happened first?

F The first phone installed in a private house was put in Twain's home.

G Twain commented on a Robert Louis Stevenson novel.

H Twain built a large house in Connecticut.

I Twain published "The Celebrated Jumping Frog of Calaveras County."

3 Which event happened last?

A Samuel Clemens took the name Mark Twain.

B Twain published "Forty-Three Days in an Open Boat."

C Twain's youngest daughter died.

D Twain threw all his shirts out the window.

4 Read this sentence.

He felt like the "most conspicuous person on the planet"—but on most days he liked the attention.

Which word has nearly the opposite meaning of *conspicuous*?

F notorious

G unnoticeable

H clumsy

I alarming

Writing Focus Extended Response

When does the author break from chronological order? *Why* does she do so? Support your answer with details from the story.

What have you learned about Mark Twain's complex personality? What information most surprised you? Explain.

WEB ARTICLE

Preparing to Read

"War of the Worlds": Behind the 1938 Radio Show Panic

Informational Text Focus

Cause and Effect When your best friend comes to school with her arm in a cast, what is the first thing you ask? The natural question is, "What happened?" You're looking at the **effect,** or result, of an event, and you want to know what **caused** this effect. If your friend fell while practicing a bike trick, a bike crash was the cause, and a broken arm is the effect.

One way to analyze informational text is to look for causes and effects. Ask yourself questions such as "What caused this to happen?" and "What happened as a result of this event?"

Into Action Although some events start a chain reaction of cause-effect, cause-effect, and so on, other events simply cause a series of related effects. As you read this selection about the "War of the Worlds" broadcast, you can use a chart like this one to note and display the many related effects.

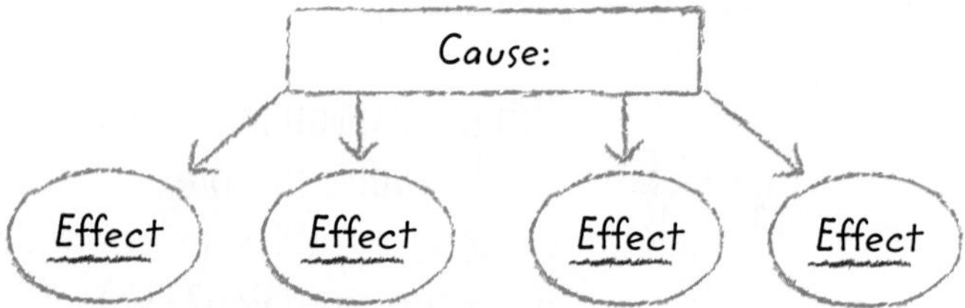

Writing Focus

Preparing for **Extended Response**

Skillful writers often use transitions such as *then, because, therefore,* and *since* to show how ideas are connected in cause-and-effect organization. Equally important are common transitions such as *however* and *but.* Although this Web article is written in a journalistic style that uses few transitions, make note in your *Reader/Writer Notebook* of any transitions you notice as you read.

Sunshine State Standards: Benchmarks
LA.6.1.6.1 use new vocabulary that is introduced and taught directly; **LA.6.1.6.4** categorize key vocabulary and identify salient features; **LA.6.1.7.4** identify cause-and-effect relationships in text; *Also covered* **LA.6.1.7.5; LA.6.1.7.8; LA.6.2.2.4**

Reader/Writer Notebook

Use your **RWN** to complete the activities for this selection.

Vocabulary

rival (RY vuhl) *adj.:* competing. *People listening to a rival network missed the introduction of the broadcast.*

duplicate (DOO pluh kayt) *v.:* copy. *The show tried to duplicate live radio news.*

primary (PRY mehr ee) *adj.:* main; first in importance. *In 1938, radio was the primary news source for some people.*

manipulate (muh NIHP yuh layt) *v.:* manage or control, often in an unfair way. *The broadcast showed how mass communication could be used to manipulate the public.*

improbable (ihm PRAHB uh buhl) *adj.:* unlikely to be true. *Welles thought listeners might be bored with such an improbable story.*

Language Coach

Jargon Words that have special meanings among a group of people are called **jargon.** Journalism is a profession that uses a lot of jargon. Words such as *breaking news, newscaster,* and *scoop* are good examples. Unlike the scoop used for ice cream, a journalistic scoop means "getting the story first."

Learn It Online

Take an in-depth look at terms using Word Watch:

WEB ARTICLE

Read with a Purpose

Read this Web article to see why, in 1938, many people mistook a radio play for a horrifying "breaking news" story.

Build Background

Before televisions became widespread in the 1940s and 1950s, radios were a popular means of entertainment. Families gathered around the radio in the evening to listen to sporting events, variety shows, or dramatic presentations by actors. This article recounts the broadcast—and results—of a science fiction adaptation by actor Orson Welles and his theater group.

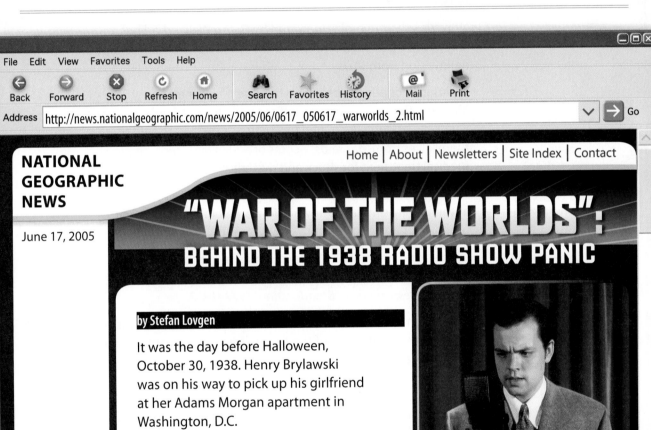

File Edit View Favorites Tools Help

Back Forward Stop Refresh Home Search Favorites History Mail Print

Address http://news.nationalgeographic.com/news/2005/06/0617_050617_warworlds_2.html Go

Home | About | Newsletters | Site Index | Contact

NATIONAL GEOGRAPHIC NEWS

June 17, 2005

"WAR OF THE WORLDS": BEHIND THE 1938 RADIO SHOW PANIC

by Stefan Lovgen

It was the day before Halloween, October 30, 1938. Henry Brylawski was on his way to pick up his girlfriend at her Adams Morgan apartment in Washington, D.C.

As he turned on his car radio, the 25-year-old law student heard some startling news. A huge meteorite had smashed into a New Jersey farm. New York was under attack by Martians.

"I knew it was a hoax," said Brylawski, now 92. **A**

Orson Welles performing live for a radio broadcast.

A **Read and Discuss** Why does the author begin with these details?

Others were not so sure. When he reached the apartment, Brylawski found his girlfriend's sister, who was living there, "quaking in her boots," as he puts it. "She thought the news was real," he said.

It was not. What radio listeners heard that night was an adaptation, by Orson Welles's Mercury Theater group, of a science fiction novel written 40 years earlier: *The War of the Worlds,* by H. G. Wells.

However, the radio play, narrated by Orson Welles, had been written and performed to sound like a real news broadcast about an invasion from Mars.

Thousands of people, believing they were under attack by Martians, flooded newspaper offices and radio and police stations with calls, asking how to flee their city or how they should protect themselves from "gas raids." Scores of adults reportedly required medical treatment for shock and hysteria.[1] **B**

The hoax worked, historians say, because the broadcast authentically simulated how radio worked in an emergency.

"Audiences heard their regularly scheduled broadcast interrupted by breaking news," said Michele Hilmes, a communications professor at University of Wisconsin in Madison and author of *Radio Voices: American Broadcasting, 1922–1952.*

FACTOID

By the end of the first half of the program, the radio studios themselves were under attack.

Stations then cut to a live reporter on the scene of the invasion in New Jersey. "By the end of the first half of the program, the radio studios themselves were under attack," Hilmes said. **C**

Tuning In Late

Orson Welles and his team had previously dramatized novels such as *The Count of Monte Cristo* and *Dracula.* The introduction to *War of the Worlds* broadcast on CBS Radio emphasized that it was based on the H. G. Wells novel.

1. **hysteria** (his TIHR ee uh): feelings of extreme anxiety; uncontrolled excitement.

B **Informational Focus** **Cause and Effect** What caused people to panic?

C **Read and Discuss** What has been set up for you about this story so far?

Analyzing Visuals **Viewing and Interpreting** How does this scene relate to what people must have imagined as they listened to Welles's broadcast?

Movie still from *War of the Worlds* (2005).

But many people didn't hear that introduction. They were tuned in to a rival network airing the popular *Chase and Sanborn Hour* program featuring the ventriloquist Edgar Bergen and his dummy Charlie McCarthy.[2] D

Ten minutes into that show, at a time when its star took a break, many listeners dialed into *War of the Worlds* instead. Having missed the introduction, they found themselves listening to "the music of Ramon Raquello and his Orchestra," live from New York's Hotel Park Plaza.

2. **Charlie McCarthy:** a wooden puppet, or "dummy," made famous by comedian Edgar Bergen on radio shows in the 1930s through 1950s. Bergen moved the puppet's head and mouth with his concealed arm, while "throwing" his voice to make it sound as if the puppet were speaking.

D **Informational Focus** **Cause and Effect** Why did so many people fail to understand that the broadcast was a dramatic presentation?

Vocabulary **rival** (RY vuhl) *adj.:* competing.

In reality, the orchestra was playing in a CBS studio. The dance music was soon interrupted by a series of increasingly alarming news bulletins. An astronomer, played by Welles, commented on reports that several explosions of "incandescent[3] gas" had been observed on the planet Mars.

Then a news bulletin reported that a "huge flaming object" had struck a farm near Grovers Mill, New Jersey. A "newscaster" described seeing an alien crawl out of a spacecraft. "Good heavens —something's wriggling out of the shadow," he reported. "It glistens like wet leather. But that face—it . . . it is indescribable." **E**

Newspapers vs. Radio

In 1938, with the world on the brink of World War II, audiences were already on razor's edge. The format used in *War of the Worlds,* with its shrill news bulletins and breathless commentary, echoed the way in which radio had covered the "Munich crisis"—a meeting of European powers that became the prelude to World War II—a month before.

FACTOID
There are estimates that about 20 percent of those listening believed it was real.

"Welles and his company managed to closely duplicate the style and the feel of those broadcasts in their own program," said Elizabeth McLeod, a journalist and broadcast historian in Rockland, Maine, who specializes in 1930s radio. "Some [listeners] heard only that 'shells were falling' and assumed they were coming from Hitler." **F**

It was also the time during which science fiction developed as a popular genre. "We were on the brink of scientific discoveries about space," Hilmes said. "Dangers lurked abroad—why not in outer space?"

Panicked listeners packed roads, hid in cellars, and loaded their guns. In one block of Newark, New Jersey, 20 families rushed out of their houses with wet towels over their faces as protection from Martian poison gas, according to a front-page article in the *New York Times* the next day.

---

3. **incandescent** (ihn kuhn DEHS uhnt): glowing caused by heat; very bright.

E **Read and Discuss** How did other radio programs affect the unfolding drama?

F **Informational Focus** **Cause and Effect** What effect did recent news and world events have on some people's understanding of the broadcast?

Vocabulary **duplicate** (DOO pluh kayt) *v.:* copy.

But historians also claim that newspaper accounts over the following week greatly exaggerated the hysteria. There are estimates that about 20 percent of those listening believed it was real. That translates to less than a million people.

At the time, newspapers considered radio an upstart rival. Some in the print press, resentful of the superior radio coverage during the Munich crisis, may have sought to prove a point about the irresponsibility of the radio broadcast. G

"The exaggeration of the *War of the Worlds* story can be interpreted as the print media's revenge for being badly scooped[4] during the previous month," McLeod said.

Movie still from *War of the Worlds* (2005).

4. **scooped:** in a journalistic sense, being beaten to a news story by another news organization.

G **Read and Discuss** How did newspapers make the "War of the Worlds" situation even more complex?

Power of Imagination

There is no doubt that radio held a unique power over its audience. For rural audiences, in particular, it was the primary point of contact with the outside world, providing news, entertainment, and companionship, McLeod noted.

Orson Welles knew how to use radio's imaginative possibilities, and he was a master at blurring the lines between fiction and reality.

"No movie special effects . . . could have conjured up enormous aliens striding across the Hudson River toward the CBS studios 'as if it were a child's wading pool' [in Welles's words] as convincingly as the listeners' imaginations could," Hilmes said.

War of the Worlds also revealed how the power of mass communications could be used to create theatrical illusions and manipulate the public. Some people say the broadcast contributed to diminishing the trustworthiness of the media. **H**

According to the *New York Times*, Welles expressed profound regret that his dramatic efforts could cause consternation.[5] "I don't think we will choose anything like this again," he said. He hesitated about presenting it, Welles said, because "it was our thought that perhaps people might be bored or annoyed at hearing a tale so improbable." **I**

The War of the Worlds, The First Martian Emerges from the Cylinder (1906) by Henrique Alvim Corrêa.

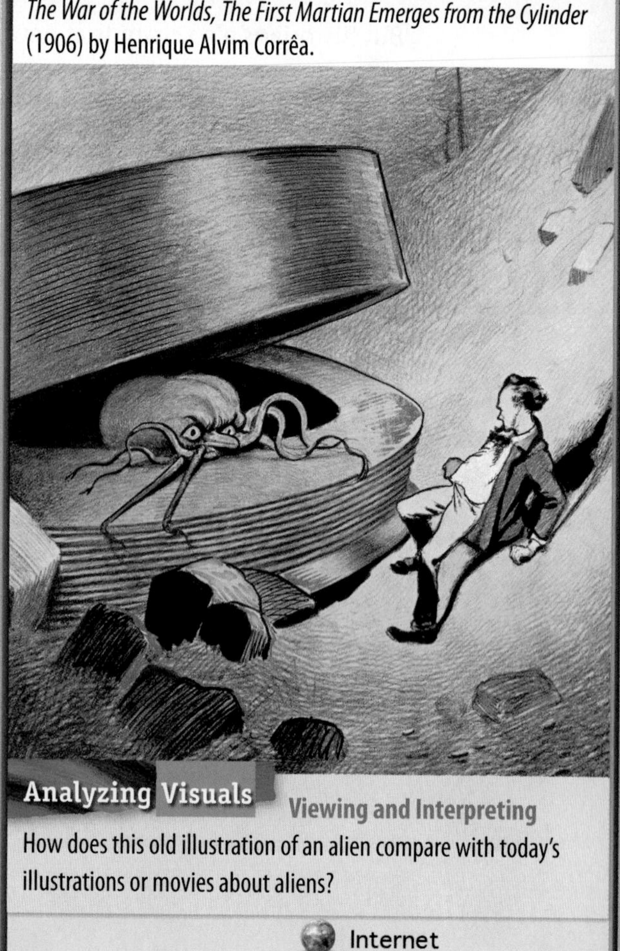

Analyzing Visuals Viewing and Interpreting
How does this old illustration of an alien compare with today's illustrations or movies about aliens?

Internet

Read with a Purpose

What were some of the causes for people thinking "War of the Worlds" was "breaking news"?

5. **consternation** (kahn stuhr NAY shuhn): concern that makes you feel helpless.

H **Read and Discuss** What lesson did the world learn from the "War of the Worlds" panic?

I **Informational Focus** **Cause and Effect** What effect did Orson Welles expect his dramatic adaptation to have on listeners?

Vocabulary **primary** (PRY mehr ee) *adj.:* main; first in importance.
manipulate (muh NIHP yuh layt) *v.:* manage or control, often in an unfair way.
improbable (ihm PRAHB uh buhl) *adj.:* unlikely to be true.

Internet

Applying Your Skills

Sunshine State Standards: Benchmarks **LA.6.1.6.1** use new vocabulary that is introduced and taught directly; **LA.6.1.7.4** identify cause-and-effect relationships in text.

"War of the Worlds"

Practicing for FCAT

Informational Text and Vocabulary

1. Which was NOT caused by the "War of the Worlds" broadcast?
   - **A** People flooded police stations with calls.
   - **B** People hid in their cellars.
   - **C** The *Chase and Sanborn Hour* was canceled.
   - **D** Some people thought Hitler was attacking.

2. Why did people misunderstand the broadcast?
   - **F** because Orson Welles was a famous actor
   - **G** because it sounded like a real news report
   - **H** because alien sightings were commonly reported
   - **I** because it was the only show on the radio that night

3. What did the radio broadcast do?
   - **A** It may have caused news organizations to stop live reports.
   - **B** It may have decreased newspaper sales.
   - **C** It may have decreased people's trust in the media.
   - **D** It may have been intended to cause panic.

4. Read this sentence.

   ***War of the Worlds* also revealed how the power of mass communications could be used to create theatrical illusions and manipulate the public.**

   What does the word *manipulate* mean?
   - **F** to take care of something
   - **G** to compete against someone
   - **H** to respect something
   - **I** to control something

2. Read this sentence.

   He hesitated about presenting it, Welles said, because "it was our thought that perhaps people might be bored or annoyed at hearing a tale so improbable."

   Which word has nearly the OPPOSITE meaning of *improbable*?
   - **A** likely
   - **B** impossible
   - **C** practical
   - **D** foolish

Writing Focus Extended Response

Write a paragraph explaining one cause and one effect described by the writer. Use transition words to connect your ideas. Support your response with details from the text.

What Do You Think Now?

How did this Web article help you imagine the "War of the Worlds" panic and what listeners of the 1938 broadcast feared?

Media Workshop

Adapting Literature for Performance

Write with a Purpose

Work with other students to adapt a literary work for performance onstage. Use as many forms of media as possible to present your drama. Your **audience** may be fellow students or even relatives and friends. Your **purpose** is to entertain while being true to the literary work you've adapted.

A Good Adaptation

- communicates the overall concept of the literary work
- includes dialogue and stage directions
- includes directions about props, costumes, and scenery
- involves different media, such as lighting, visual projections, sound effects, and recorded sounds and music

Think as a Reader/Writer As you read the plays in this collection, you learned how dialogue, stage directions, and a play's structure help the audience to understand the action of a play. Now it's your turn to work with other students to adapt a literary work for the stage. Begin by reviewing how a drama should look on paper. Study this excerpt from the play *Blanca Flor,* by Angel Vigil (page 757).

The Narrator. In spite of the Duende's warning, Juanito continued on the path of danger. As he came into a clearing, he came to a house and saw a young woman coming out of it.

← A **narrator** helps to "fill in the gaps," describing actions that are not seen onstage.

[JUANITO *enters,* BLANCA FLOR *enters from the opposite side of the stage and stops, remaining at the opposite side of the stage.*]

← **Stage directions** tell how the actors move around the stage.

Juanito. Where did this house come from? I was here just yesterday and there was no house here. I must really be lost and turned around. (*He sees the young woman and waves to her.*) Hey! Come here. Over here!

← Stage directions may also reveal a character's feelings.

[BLANCA FLOR *runs to* JUANITO.]

Blanca Flor (*with fear in her voice*). How did you find this place? You must leave right away. The owner of this place is gone, but he will return soon. He leaves to do his work in the world, but he will return unexpectedly. If he finds you here, you'll never be able to leave. You must leave right away.

← **Dialogue** helps develop the plot and conflict.

Think About the Professional Model

With a partner, discuss the following questions about the model.

1. How do you know which words are spoken and which ones are stage directions?
2. Which stage directions tell you about the characters and how they are feeling? Explain.
3. What media, such as lighting, sound effects, and visuals, would you add to the stage directions?

Use your **RWN** to complete the activities for this workshop.

Sunshine State Standards: Benchmarks **LA.6.3.1.1** generating ideas from multiple sources (e.g., prior knowledge, discussion with others, writer's notebook, research materials, or other reliable sources), based upon teacher-directed topics and personal interests; **LA.6.3.1.2** making a plan for writing that prioritizes ideas, addresses purpose, audience, main idea, and logical sequence; **LA.6.3.1.3** using organizational strategies and tools (e.g., technology, outline, chart, table, graph, web, story map); **LA.6.3.2.2** organizing information into a logical sequence and combining or deleting sentences to enhance clarity; **LA.6.3.2.3** analyzing language techniques of professional authors (e.g., point of view, establishing mood) to enhance the use of descriptive language and word choices; **LA.6.3.3.1** evaluating the draft for development of ideas and content, logical organization, voice, point of view, word choice, and sentence variation; *Also covered* **LA.6.3.3.2; LA.6.3.3.4; LA.6.3.4.1; LA.6.3.4.3; LA.6.3.5.1; LA.6.3.5.3; LA.6.4.1.2; LA.6.5.2.2**

Prewriting

Choose a Literary Work

Remember that you are adapting a literary work so that it can be performed for an audience. To hold your audience's attention, you should choose a story that will make a strong and interesting play. As you consider different stories, review the questions in the Idea Starters in the margin at right. If you can only answer "yes" to one question, you might want to consider another work.

As you narrow your choices, discuss with your group the overall impression each work creates. Is it a funny story with a serious message? Is it a story that explores a particular event or period in history? Be sure the entire group agrees on these ideas. Your interpretation of the work will affect the way you adapt it for the stage.

Make Key Decisions

Once you choose a literary work, you need to re-read it carefully and consider how best to adapt the narrative to the stage. Consider the questions below, and write notes as you plan your presentation.

- How many actors will be needed?
- Will a narrator be needed?
- Should we adapt the whole story, or just part of it? Which part?
- How many scenes will be needed?
- Should we pick up dialogue directly from the story, or adapt it?

Think About Purpose and Audience

Your **purpose** in adapting a literary work is to take the author's original story and present it in a new and fresh way for the stage. When you adapt a story into a play, you need to look at ways to make the characters come alive through the actors' dialogue and movements. You can be creative in adapting the story, especially when it comes to setting, props, costumes, and effects, but be careful to preserve the author's original meaning.

Take some time to consider your **audience** for the play. Who will be invited to watch your performance? Will they be your classmates, or will your audience include a larger group, such as the school or even the community? Knowing your audience can help you make decisions about dialogue and what kinds of media to use.

Idea Starters

Does the literary work have

- interesting characters?
- suspense, action, or humor?
- plenty of dialogue?
- opportunities to use different kinds of media?

Your Turn

Get Started Making notes in your **RWN,** think of different stories and books you've read. Narrow your choices until you have decided on one that is best suited to the stage. Then, make key decisions about how to adapt the story.

Get help with script writing and learn how to use story boards on the Digital Storytelling mini-site at:

go.hrw.com L6-843 

Writing Tip

Since you are working with a group to adapt the literary work, assign each member some aspect of the work. For example, one person may be in charge of rounding up the props. Another person may be in charge of the audio work. Share the responsibility and work as a team. As much as possible, try to assign people tasks that suit their talents or interests.

Think Like a Director

Before drafting your script, your group will need to make a few more decisions that will affect your stage directions. Consider the following issues as you plan your production.

- How many sets will you need, and what will they look like? How detailed do they need to be?
- What kinds of costumes and props will you need? How will you find or make them?
- What kinds of lighting and sound effects will you use, and how will you produce them? What equipment will you need?

Be creative as you think about the types of media to use for your play. You could paint your own sets, or you might create settings by projecting photos or video onto a screen. Will music add drama to the play? If so, what kind of music? Where will you find it? Think about adding sound effects. For example, if you have a street scene, you might play a recording of traffic sounds to add authenticity.

Map Out the Action

Before you begin working on the script, use a story map or a set of panels to map out the main action of the play, scene by scene. Look carefully at the work you are adapting, and decide what the main event is going to be for each scene. You can revise your plan as you work on your draft. The important thing is to have a plan to start with.

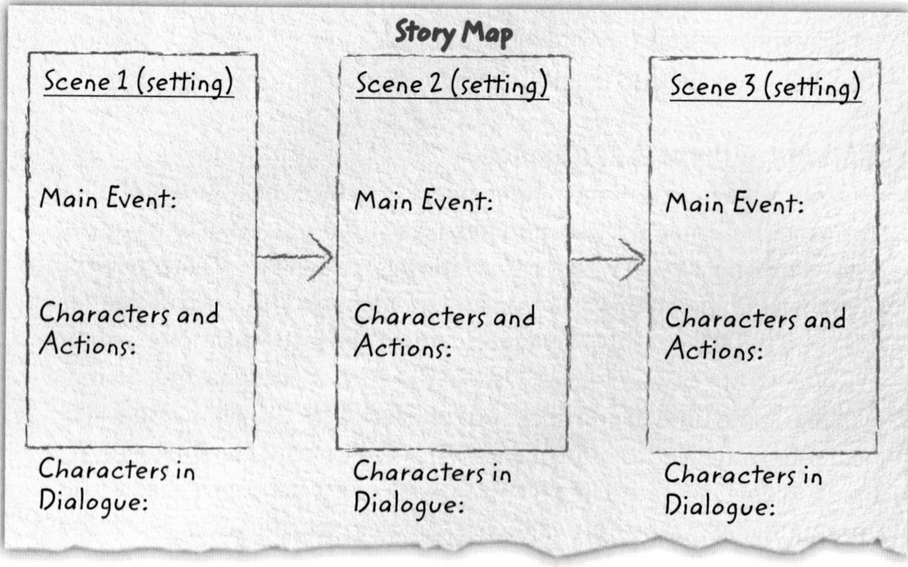

Your Turn

Plan Your Performance Make notes in your **RWN** as you make decisions and plan your performance. You may want to have one group member be in charge of recording and managing the plan.

Drafting

Write Dialogue

Dialogue in a play can be formal or informal. Formal language contains few contractions, no slang, and few sentence fragments or interrupted sentences. Informal dialogue sounds more like everyday speech and will probably be more useful for your adaptation. Choose the style that matches the tone of your play and characters. Consider the following as you adapt dialogue for your play.

- The dialogue needs to be understood by the audience.
- The dialogue should move the action forward and help the audience understand what the characters are like.
- The dialogue and action should communicate the main point of the original literary work.

Write Stage Directions

To write stage directions, imagine each scene being played onstage. How should the characters look and move? How should they react to other characters' lines or to props on the stage? Should special sounds or music be heard coming from offstage? Consider the following as you write stage directions for your play.

- Use the stage directions to show what the actors should do and any special gestures or expressions they should use.
- Note special instructions for sound, lighting, visuals, props, and scene changes in the stage directions.

Grammar Link **Writing Dialogue in Scripts**

In a literary work, a character's dialogue is usually set off by quotation marks. When writing dialogue in a play, however, you don't need to use quotation marks to show the character's exact words. Instead, write the character's name in boldface, followed by a period. Then, write the dialogue (or *monologue* if the character is talking to himself or the audience) in regular type.

> **Juanito.** Where did this house come from? I was here just yesterday and there was no house here. I must really be lost and turned around.

Writing Tip

As you're working on your draft, stop occasionally for informal readings. Have team members read the different parts to see if the dialogue sounds believable. Make revisions as necessary, and use the readings to make notes about stage directions.

Your Turn

Write Your Draft Following your plan, write a draft of your literary adaptation. As you write your draft, remember to think about the following:

- How does the **dialogue** help your audience understand the characters?
- Do your **stage directions** help stage the play and seem appropriate for the dialogue?

Peer Review

Working with your team, review the draft of your script. Answer each question in this chart to locate where and how your draft can be improved. As you discuss your draft, be sure to note each team member's suggestions. You can refer to the notes as you revise your draft.

Evaluating and Revising

Read the questions in the left column of the chart. Then, use the tips in the middle column to help you make revisions to your script. The right column suggests techniques you can use to revise your draft.

Literary Adaptation: Guidelines for Content and Organization

Evaluation Question	Tip	Revision Technique
1. Does your adaptation stick closely to the original story line?	**Bracket** any elements that don't tie to the original work.	**Delete** any elaborations that stray too far from the original work.
2. Does your script include all of the important characters in the story?	**Put a check mark** beside each character's name. Compare these characters to those in the original work.	**Add** any missing characters to the script, and write lines of dialogue for them.
3. Does the dialogue sound natural?	**Highlight** any lines of dialogue that seem awkward.	**Rewrite** lines to sound more natural.
4. Do the stage directions include ideas about how lines should be delivered?	**Underline** all suggestions about facial expressions, gestures, and feelings.	**Add** specific directions about how actors should look, move, and sound.
5. Do the stage directions include instructions about props, costumes, scenery, and sound effects?	**Draw a wavy line** under all suggestions about props, costumes, scenery, and sound effects.	**Add** specific directions about props and sound effects, as needed. **Add** details about costumes and scenery.

Read this draft and the comments about it as a model for revising your own literary adaptation. The script is based on Thomas J. Dygard's short story "Just Once" (page 143).

Student Model

Script Based on "Just Once"

Coach Williams (*to the Moose*). It was your great blocking that did it.
The Moose. I want to carry the ball.
Coach Williams. What did you say?
The Moose (*a little louder, with more conviction*). I want to carry the ball.
Coach Williams [smiling in a tolerant way and giving a little nod]. You keep right on blocking, son.

← The writer uses **dialogue** to develop the central characters and their relationship.

← **Stage directions** provide instructions on how the actor should look and move.

MINI-LESSON How to Turn Description into Stage Directions

As you adapt your literary work, look for descriptions of settings and actions that you can turn into stage directions. The writer could improve this adaptation of "Just Once" by including stage directions based on descriptions from the story.

Revision

[Scene: The locker room at Bedford City High. COACH WILLIAMS is making the rounds among the players, who are celebrating their victory. He stops in front of THE MOOSE.]

Coach Williams (*to the Moose*). It was your great blocking that did it.

The Moose. I want to carry the ball.

[COACH WILLIAMS turns away and moves toward the next player, but then freezes, as if an idea has just struck him. He turns back to THE MOOSE, a look of disbelief on his face.]

Coach Williams. What did you say?

The Moose. (*a little louder, with more conviction*). I want to carry the ball.

Coach Williams [smiling in a tolerant way and giving a little nod]. You keep right on blocking, son.

Your Turn

Write Clear Stage Directions Read your draft and ask yourself the following:

- Have I described the setting and the characters' actions through stage directions?
- What can I add to the script to make the setting and actions clearer?

The writer uses an on-stage **narrator** to fill in time gaps for the audience.

Student Model *continues*

[*All action in the background freezes as the Narrator walks on stage.*]

Narrator. Coach Williams and the Moose both went on with life as usual, as if the Moose had never said anything about carrying the ball. The next week's practice and game passed without further incident. Of course, that game was an away game. What the Moose wanted was to carry the ball at home, in front of Bedford City fans. So it was a good week and a half later before the Moose spoke up again.

MINI-LESSON How to Include Sound Effects and Other Media

Your stage directions should indicate the use of any special media, such as sound effects, music, and video. After evaluating the script for "Just Once," the writer revised the stage directions to include sound effects, music, and lighting effects.

Revision

Soft instrumental music begins to play, lights dim in the background, and a blue spotlight focuses on the NARRATOR at the side of the stage.

[*All action in the background freezes as the Narrator walks on stage.*] ^

Narrator. Coach Williams and the Moose both went on with life as usual, as if the Moose had never said anything about carrying the ball. The next week's practice and game passed without further incident. Of course, that game was an away game. What the Moose wanted was to carry the ball at home, in front of Bedford City fans. So it was a good week and a half later before the Moose spoke up again.
[As the NARRATOR exits, the blue spotlight goes off, the background lighting comes back up, and the locker room comes back to life. The sound of players cheering and lockers slamming returns.]

Your Turn

Use a Variety of Media As a group, review your script. Have you used media effectively? Is there any way you could make your stage presentation more appealing through the use of audio or visual effects? Do you need to add anything to make the presentation more exciting for your audience?

Proofreading and Publishing

Proofreading

Edit your script one last time to make sure it is free of errors in spelling, punctuation, and sentence structure. You don't want errors to get in the way of a good presentation. Proofread your writing carefully, using proofreading marks to make the necessary corrections.

Grammar Link **Scriptwriting Conventions**

Stage directions should always be in italic type so they stand out from the dialogue. Stage directions that apply to a single character should follow the character's name and be set in parentheses. Stage directions that apply to more than a single character should be set apart from the dialogue (on a line of their own) and set in brackets, with the characters' names in capital letters. While proofreading the script for "Just Once," the writer revised the stage directions to conform to these conventions.

(italics)

Coach Williams [smiling in a tolerant way and giving a little nod].

NARRATOR

[*All action in the background freezes as the ~~Narrator~~ walks on stage.*]

Publishing

Now it is time to present your literary adaptation. Here are some ideas for sharing your adaptation.

- Stage it for your class or for the whole school.
- Videotape your performance and put it in the class library for future classes.

Reflect on the Process In your **RWN,** write a short response to the following questions.

1. What was most difficult about adapting a story?
2. What did you enjoy the most about adapting a literary work? Why?
3. Do you think your adaptation preserved the message of the original literary work? Why or why not?

Proofreading Tip

Proofread your script as a group, assigning different proofreading tasks to different members. Although your adaptation is for a stage performance, you want your script to be equally useful for reading. The three main areas to look at carefully are spelling, punctuation, and sentence structure.

Your Turn

Proofread and Publish As you proofread your script, make sure you have used scriptwriting conventions correctly and consistently. Revise any errors to keep from confusing actors or readers. Then, share your adaptation with an audience.

Standards Review Literary Text

Elements of Drama

Directions: Read the following play. Then, read and respond to the questions that follow.

Crocodile Gives Monkey a Ride

an African folk tale
from **Rainforest Trio**
adapted by **Barbara Winther**

Setting: By the Congo River, deep in the tropical rainforest of central Africa.

At Rise: CROCODILE sleeps on riverbank; MONKEY comes swinging through the trees.

Monkey (*Chattering excitedly*): Wonderful, wonderful—a big mango tree beside the river, and the fruit is ripe, and oh, oh, how I love to eat mangoes.
Crocodile (*Interrupting in an evil voice*): Hello, Friend Monkey.
Monkey: My goodness. I thought you were a log on the riverbank.
Crocodile: Sometimes I feel like a log. It's nice to see you, Friend Monkey. I've missed your company.
Monkey: I didn't know I was your friend.
Crocodile: Of course you are. Come down here and talk to me.
Monkey: No! I prefer to stay in this tree. I'll talk to you from up here.

Crocodile: But I can't hear you very well. It rained hard last night, and the river flows fast. It makes a loud, churning noise.

Monkey: You must have water in your ears. I can hear you fine. Why don't you come closer to this tree?

Crocodile (*Yelling*): What did you say?

Monkey (*Yelling back*): I said, "Come closer to this tree."

Crocodile (*Resigned*): Oh, all right. (*Crawls over to tree*)

Monkey: Now, what do you want to talk about, Friend Crocodile?

Crocodile (*Slyly*): About the party I'm giving this afternoon.

Monkey: Oh, I love parties. Where is this one going to be?

Crocodile: At my house across the river. Some of your best friends will be there.

Monkey: Such as?

Crocodile: Um, ah—(*Thinking fast*) well, there's Elephant and, um, oh, yes, Warthog. He's offered to play the drums.

Monkey: I didn't know Warthog could play the drums, and I had no idea you knew Elephant and Warthog.

Crocodile: I consider them my closest friends.

Monkey: Is that so? Well, I've always heard that nobody likes you.

Crocodile: Gossip, that's what it is. Many animals like me.

Monkey: Mm-m-m. (*Suspicious*) What kind of food will you have at your party?

Crocodile: Lots and lots of what you like more than anything else—plantains.

Monkey (*Jumping around with excitement*): Plantains? I love plantains. They're like bananas, and you know how much I like bananas.

Crocodile (*Slyly*): I know that very well. That's why you should come to the party: friends, drums, plantains.

Monkey: Sounds wonderful. (*Sadly*) I can't come, though.

Crocodile: Why not?

Monkey: The river is too wide, and I don't swim very well.

Crocodile: No problem. I'm a strong swimmer. You can ride over on my back.

Monkey: Plantains, you say? And Elephant will be there. And Warthog will play the drums?

Crocodile: Yes, yes, all of that. Hop on my back. Let's go to the party.

Monkey (*Forgetting all caution*): Off to the party. Here I come. (*Leaps on* CROCODILE*'s back*)

Crocodile (*Swimming into river*): I'm glad you made that decision.

Monkey: This will be great fun. I can hardly wait.

Crocodile (*Stopping*): Now we are in the middle of the river.

Standards Review CONTINUED

Literary Text

Monkey: Why are you stopping?
Crocodile: I'm not going to take you to the party.
Monkey (*Nervously*): What did you say?
Crocodile (*Louder*): I said, "I'm not going to take you to the party." Instead, I'm going to eat you.
Monkey (*Horrified*): Eat me! Oh, no!
Crocodile: First I will sink into the river and drown you. Then, I will have you for my dinner. (*Starts to sink*)
Monkey: Wait a minute. Wait a minute. You can't eat me yet.
Crocodile: Why not?
Monkey (*Sputtering*): Because—because I left my heart on a limb in the mango tree.
Crocodile: So what?
Monkey: So, you can't eat an animal without a heart.
Crocodile: What's wrong with eating a heartless animal?
Monkey: An animal without a heart has no flavor. You might as well eat a rock or a log. Everyone knows that.
Crocodile: Well, I didn't know that.
Monkey: Well, now you do. Take me back to the mango tree. I'll get my heart. Then, you can eat me.
Crocodile (*Snorting*): You stupid animal. (*Turning around and swimming back, grumbling*) You're the dumbest creature in the rainforest. Imagine going to a party without a heart.
Monkey: I'm terribly sorry. Swim faster.
Crocodile (*Climbing out of water*): All right, here we are on the riverbank. Go get your heart.
Monkey (*Leaping ashore and jumping into tree*): Thank goodness, I've made it back to the mango tree.
Crocodile: Hurry up. I'm hungry.
Monkey (*Thoughtfully*): I've decided not to go to your party. (*Starts eating a mango*)
Crocodile: What? Come on down here right now.
Monkey: No!
Crocodile (*After a pause*): Hey, you've played a trick on me.
Monkey (*Yelling*): What? I can't hear anything you say. It rained hard last night and the river flows fast. It makes a loud, churning noise.
Crocodile (*Bellowing*): I said, "You've played a trick on me."
Monkey: Oh, no, I'm too dumb to do that. But, just to show you we're still friends, I'll give you my heart. (*Hurls mango seed at* CROCODILE*'s head*)
Crocodile (*Holding head*): Ouch! You have a hard heart.
Monkey: So do you, Friend Crocodile. So do you. (*Swings off through the trees. Curtains close.*)

Sunshine State Standards: Benchmarks **LA.6.2.1.1** identify the characteristics of various genres (e.g., poetry, fiction, short story, dramatic literature) as forms with distinct characteristics and purposes; **LA.6.2.1.2** locate and analyze the elements of plot structure, including exposition, setting, character development, rising/falling action, conflict/resolution, and theme in a variety of fiction.

1. When does the major conflict in this play occur?
   - **A** when Monkey is deciding whether or not to go to Crocodile's party
   - **B** when Crocodile is deciding whether or not to take Monkey back to the tree to get his heart
   - **C** when Crocodile wants to eat Monkey, and Monkey doesn't want to be eaten
   - **D** There is no conflict.

2. Which type of information is NOT provided in the stage directions of the play?
   - **F** the motivation of the characters
   - **G** the gestures made by the characters
   - **H** the actions of the characters
   - **I** the way the characters speak

3. When does the play's climax occur?
   - **A** when Monkey decides to go to the party
   - **B** when Crocodile tells Monkey he plans to eat him
   - **C** when Monkey jumps back onto the mango tree
   - **D** There is no climax.

4. What happens at the play's resolution?
   - **F** Monkey goes to the party.
   - **G** Crocodile outwits Monkey.
   - **H** Monkey outwits Crocodile.
   - **I** Monkey finds out that Warthog doesn't actually play the drums.

5. At what point in the play do you feel the MOST suspense?
   - **A** when Crocodile and Monkey first meet
   - **B** when Monkey decides to go to the party
   - **C** when Crocodile tells Monkey he's not going to take him to the party
   - **D** There is no suspense. The reader knows all along what will happen.

Extended Response

6. If you were directing this play, what would you do to create a realistic set—one that accurately reflects the setting? Based on the stage directions, what kinds of props and costumes would you need? How would you ask your characters to speak to each other? Consider these questions, and write your recommendations. Support your response with details from the text.

READ THINK EXPLAIN

Standards Review **Informational Text**

Text Structures: Chronological Order / Cause and Effect

Directions: Read the following selection. Then, read and respond to the questions that follow.

An Important Lesson for Stage and Life by **Joann Leonard**

Minor emergencies—forgotten lines, ripped costumes, missed light cues—constantly arise in the theater. Dealing with the unexpected onstage is an important part of working in the theater—and is also excellent practice for the dramas of real life.

A young actor named Robby fractured his leg just one day before a performance. He returned the following day wearing a cast that went from his toes to his thigh. His stiff peg leg would have been great if he were playing Long John Silver in *Treasure Island,* but it posed a real challenge for him in the role he was playing: He was part of a group of kids racing around as they time-warped through cyberspace back to pioneer days.

Theater is about using your imagination, so we quickly found a solution to Robby's problem: a wheelchair. After silencing an annoying squeak in the wheels with lubricating oil provided by a helpful janitor, we were set. The other cast members adjusted their positions onstage, and each time the characters "reeled through time," one of the actors would zoom the wheelchair around the stage. The show went on looking as if it were just the way it had been planned.

We all kidded Robby, telling him that he shouldn't take it literally when people said "break a leg" to wish him good luck. (After the show, he had a real "cast" party.)

Sometimes a production kit comes to the rescue. Moments before going onstage, an actress named Sara discovered a rip in her pants. No problem. An inside patch was quickly made from a roll of duct tape in the production kit, and the curtain went up only a few seconds late. Simple items like safety pins, a needle and thread, scissors, a hot-glue gun, a hammer and nails, pliers, and bandages—along with quick thinking—can be backstage lifesavers.

Sunshine State Standards: Benchmarks **LA.6.1.7.4** identify cause-and-effect relationships in text; **LA.6.1.7.5** analyze a variety of text structures (e.g., comparison/contrast, cause/effect, chronological order, argument/support, lists) and text features (main headings with subheadings) and explain their impact on meaning in text; **LA.6.4.2.3** write informational/expository essays (e.g., process, description, explanation, comparison/contrast, problem/solution) that include a thesis statement, supporting details, and introductory, body, and concluding paragraphs.

1. Choose the answer that BEST describes the chronological order of Robby breaking his leg and performing in a play.
   - **A** Robby runs around the stage; he breaks his leg; the janitor fixes the wheelchair; the wheelchair squeaks.
   - **B** Robby runs around the stage; he rides in a wheelchair; the chair squeaks; he breaks his leg.
   - **C** Robby breaks his leg; he rides in a wheelchair; he is pushed around the stage; the janitor fixes the wheelchair.
   - **D** Robby breaks his leg; the wheelchair squeaks; the janitor fixes the wheelchair; Robby is pushed around the stage.

2. Which set of words contain words that ALL signal a change or step in chronological order?
   - **F** after, first, next, when
   - **G** because, if, instead of, since
   - **H** above, below, next to, onto
   - **I** about, past, until, upon

3. Choose the answer that BEST describes the cause and effect of the janitor's involvement with the cast of the play.
   - **A** Robby needed a wheelchair; the chair squeaked.
   - **B** The wheelchair squeaked; the janitor had oil to fix the squeak.
   - **C** Robby needed a wheelchair; the janitor had oil to fix the squeak.
   - **D** Robby needed to zoom around the stage; the wheelchair squeaked.

Extended Response

4. Discuss the author's use of chronological order. Support your response with details from the text.

Standards Review Vocabulary

Sunshine State Standards: Benchmarks **LA.6.1.6.3** use context clues to determine meanings of unfamiliar words; **LA.6.1.6.5** relate new vocabulary to familiar words.

Synonyms

Directions: Write the letter of the word or group of words that is closest in meaning to the italicized word.

Practicing For FCAT

1. Read this sentence.

   There was nothing sinister about him.

   Which word has nearly the same meaning as *sinister*?

   A friendly
   B evil
   C drab
   D quiet

2. Read this sentence.

   You're arrogant about it now!

   What does the word *arrogant* mean?

   F kind
   G eager
   H considerate
   I rude

3. Read this sentence.

   Blanca Flor watched Juanito's valiant effort to move the water.

   What does the word *valiant* mean?

   A brave
   B cowardly
   C sinful
   D obvious

4. Read this sentence.

   The doctor's face is perplexed and annoyed as he turns his flashlight on a folded road map.

   Which word has nearly the same meaning as *perplexed*?

   F confused
   G excited
   H relieved
   I calm

5. Read this sentence.

   Besides, the coincidence, or whatever it was, gave me the willies.

   What does the word *coincidence* mean?

   A an ordinary meeting time
   B an ugly occurrence
   C a sales transaction
   D an unlikely event

6. Read this sentence.

   See that barren ground over on the other side of the mountain?

   Which word or phrase has nearly the same meaning as *barren*?

   F bursting with new growth
   G growing rapidly
   H having no growth
   I sprouting from a seedling

Academic Vocabulary

Directions: Write the letter of the word or group of words that is closest in meaning to the italicized Academic Vocabulary word.

7. Read this sentence.

   The complex mystery novel took me three days to read.

   Which word or phrase has nearly the same meaning as *complex*?

   A simple
   B made up
   C complicated
   D unbelievable

Standards Review **Writing**

Sunshine State Standards: Benchmarks LA.6.1.6.3 use context clues to determine meanings of unfamiliar words; *Also covered* LA.6.1.7.2; LA.6.3.3.2

Paragraphs

Directions: Read the following paragraph. Then, read and respond to the questions that follow.

[1] Literary works may be adapted in many ways. [2] One common way involves adapting a work into a different literary genre, such as a novel or short story made into a play. [3] Another kind of adaptation involves presenting a work in a different medium, such as a movie based on a book. [4] I think the film version of a book is usually so different from the original that people should never see a movie version without reading the book first. [5] Another kind of adaptation involves musical interpretation, as making a literary work into a stage musical or an opera. [6] Another kind of adaptation involves interpreting a literary work through the medium of dance. [7] Many classic novels now appear in comic-book versions; some have become popular as animated cartoons.

1. Which would BEST improve this paragraph?
   - **A** deleting sentence [2]
   - **B** adding a discussion about how movies are filmed
   - **C** adding comments about why books are better than movies
   - **D** giving examples of each type of adaptation

2. What is the PRIMARY purpose of this paragraph?
   - **F** to classify types of media
   - **G** to identify different kinds of adaptations
   - **H** to explain the purpose of adaptations
   - **I** to show how easy it is to adapt literary works

3. Which sentence does NOT belong in the paragraph?
   - **A** sentence [2]
   - **B** sentence [4]
   - **C** sentence [6]
   - **D** sentence [7]

4. Which word or word group could replace the word *another* in sentences [3], [5], and [6]?
   - **F** any other
   - **G** the same
   - **H** each
   - **I** one more

Read On For Independent Reading

Fiction

Theater Shoes

Set in England during World War II, *Theater Shoes* is the story of three motherless children who go to live with their grandmother after their father is reported missing in action. Their grandmother, a famous actress, enrolls them in a school that trains children for the stage. Out of place and terribly unhappy, the children are ready to run away—until they discover their hidden talents. Noel Streatfeild presents the war as a quiet but ever-present background, making this an exceptional introduction to what everyday life was like for some English families during World War II.

The Shakespeare Stealer

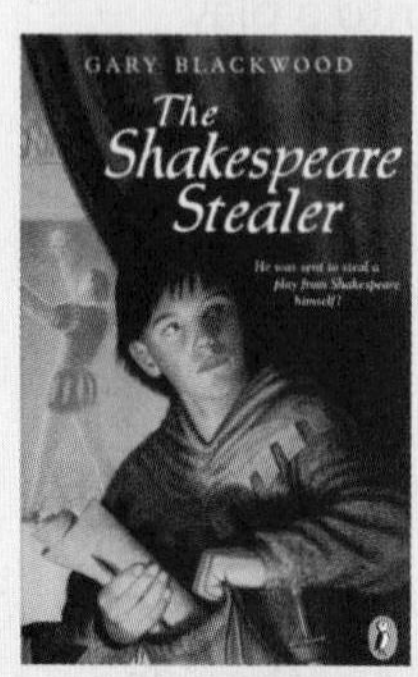

Raised in a Yorkshire orphanage, fourteen-year-old Widge is hired by a mysterious traveler and sent off to London to copy the script of a new play called *Hamlet*. Earlier, he had been apprenticed to an unprincipled clergyman who, in order to pirate others' sermons, taught Widge a cryptic shorthand. All does not go smoothly in London, and Widge ends up working at the Globe Theatre, the home of Shakespeare's company. Author Gary Blackwood puts Widge in a sink-or-swim situation that keeps readers guessing what will become of him.

The True Confessions of Charlotte Doyle

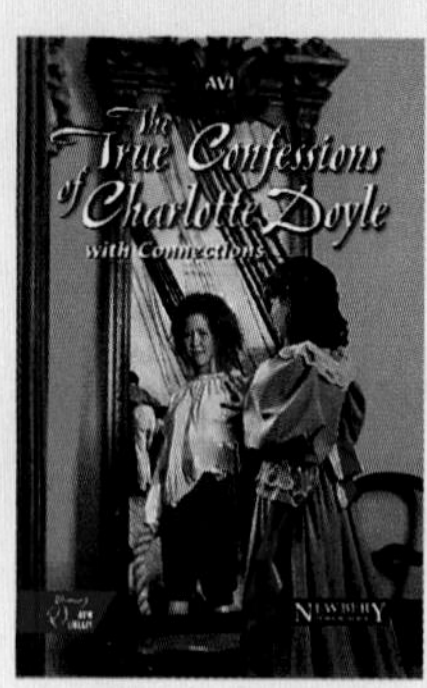

When she boards an English ship bound for Rhode Island, Charlotte Doyle has no idea that she'll be the only female passenger on board. She soon finds herself caught up in a conflict between a power-mad captain and his bitter, rebellious crew. When Charlotte is given an unusual gift, events take a shocking turn in Avi's *The True Confessions of Charlotte Doyle.*

The Watsons Go to Birmingham—1963

In Christopher Paul Curtis's novel *The Watsons Go to Birmingham—1963,* ten-year-old Kenny's big brother Byron keeps getting into trouble. Kenny's parents decide to head south from their home in Flint, Michigan, to visit Grandma Sands in Alabama, hoping she'll bring Byron into line. However, the trip takes a terrifying turn when the family experiences racial tensions firsthand.

Sunshine State Standards: Benchmarks LA.6.2.1.10 use interest and recommendation of others to select a balance of age and ability appropriate fiction materials to read (e.g., novels, historical fiction, mythology, poetry) to expand the core foundation of knowledge necessary to function as a fully literate member of a shared culture; *Also covered* **LA.6.2.2.5**

Nonfiction

Backstage at a Movie Set

Have you ever read the credits that come after a movie and asked yourself: "What is a 'grip' or a 'gaffer' or a 'Foley artist,' and what does a second assistant director actually do?" In *Backstage at a Movie Set,* you'll get a behind-the-scenes look at movie making, along with historical background and information about the industry's technological advances, from silent movies to today's extensive special effects. Katherine Wessling delivers a fresh look at the business of film, describing careers that you never guessed existed.

Acting & Theatre

The theatrical world is covered from all angles in this exciting introduction to acting and theater. Authors Cheryl Evans and Lucy Smith have done a remarkable job explaining the complex subject of theater. You'll be introduced to the basics of acting, learn theater terms, and read brief histories of theater in Europe, America, and Asia.

Short Scenes and Monologues for Middle School Actors

This book is a practical resource that will help you understand acting from the inside out. It provides short monologues (some less than a minute), as well as scenes with two, three, or four characters. Chosen especially with students your age in mind, the selections are balanced between boys' and girls' roles.

Under the Greenwood Tree: Shakespeare for Young People

Every page of this book offers a song, a sonnet, or a story from a play by Shakespeare. Lively portrayals will draw you into the world of Shakespeare's characters. In *Under the Greenwood Tree,* Editor Barbara Holdridge and illustrators Robin and Pat Dewitt provide an attractive introduction to Shakespeare's world-famous poems and plays.

Learn It Online

For tips on understanding fiction, visit *NovelWise* at:

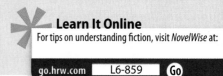

Resource Center

Handbook of Literary Terms

For more information about a topic, turn to the page(s) in this book indicated on a separate line at the end of the entries.

On another line are cross-references to entries in this Handbook that provide closely related information. For instance, *Autobiography* contains a cross-reference to *Biography*.

ALLITERATION **The repetition of the same or very similar consonant sounds in words that are close together.** Alliteration usually occurs at the beginning of words, as in the phrase "*busy* as *a bee*." It can also occur within or at the end of words.

Alliteration can establish a mood and emphasize words. If you've ever twisted your tongue around a line like "She sells seashells by the seashore" or "How much wood could a woodchuck chuck if a woodchuck could chuck wood?" you have already had some fun with alliteration.

See pages 645, 672

ALLUSION **A reference to a statement, a person, a place, or an event from literature, history, religion, mythology, politics, sports, or science.** Writers expect readers to recognize an allusion and to think, almost at the same time, about the literary work, person, place, or event that it refers to. The cartoon at the right makes an allusion you will recognize right away.

"Someone's been sleeping in my bed, too, and there she is on Screen Nine!"

AUTOBIOGRAPHY **The story of a person's life, written or told by that person.** Maya Angelou's account of her childhood experiences, called "Brother" (page 473), is taken from her autobiography *I Know Why the Caged Bird Sings*.

See pages 458, 464, 471, 479.
See also *Biography*.

BIOGRAPHY **The story of a real person's life, written or told by another person.** A classic American biography is Carl Sandburg's life of Abraham Lincoln. A biography popular with young adults is Russell Freedman's *Lincoln: A Photobiography* (see excerpt on page 516). Frequent subjects of biographies are movie stars, television personalities, politicians, sports figures, self-made millionaires, and artists. Today biographies are among the most popular forms of literature.

See pages 458, 459
See also *Autobiography*.

CHARACTER A person or an animal in a story, play, or other literary work. In some works, such as folk tales, animals are characters (see "He Lion, Bruh Bear, and Bruh Rabbit" on page 49). In other works, such as fairy tales, fantastic creatures, like dragons, are characters. In still other works, characters are gods or heroes (see "Medusa's Head" on page 283). Most often characters are ordinary human beings, as in "The All-American Slurp" (page 373).

The way in which a writer reveals the personality of a character is called **characterization.** A writer can reveal character in six ways:

1. by describing how the character looks and dresses
2. by letting the reader hear the character speak
3. by showing the reader how the character acts
4. by letting the reader know the character's inner thoughts and feelings
5. by revealing what other people in the story think or say about the character
6. by telling the reader directly what the character's personality is like (cruel, kind, sneaky, brave, and so on)

See page 232

CONFLICT A struggle or clash between opposing characters or opposing forces. An **external conflict** is a struggle between a character and some outside force. This outside force may be another character, a society as a whole, or a natural force, like bitter-cold weather or a ferocious shark. An **internal conflict,** on the other hand, is a struggle between opposing desires or emotions within a person. A character with an internal conflict may be struggling against fear or loneliness or even being a sore loser.

See pages 75, 128, 165, 233,240, 255, 271,742

CONNOTATIONS The feelings and associations that have come to be attached to a word. For example, the words *inexpensive* and *cheap* are used to describe something that is not costly. The dictionary definitions, or **denotations,** of these words are roughly the same. A manufacturer of DVD players, however, would not use *cheap* in advertising its latest model, since the word *cheap* is associated with something that is not made well. *Inexpensive* would be a better choice. Connotations can be especially important in poetry.

See pages 252, 611

DESCRIPTION The kind of writing that creates a clear image of something, usually by using details that appeal to one or more of the senses: sight, hearing, smell, taste, and touch. Description works through images, words that appeal to the five senses. Writers use description in all forms of writing—in fiction, nonfiction, and poetry. Here is a description of a famous character who has found a place in the hearts of readers everywhere. The writer's description appeals to the sense of sight, but it also gives a hint of the girl's character. Viewing this lone figure in a deserted train station, an "ordinary observer" would see

> a child of about eleven, garbed in a very short, very tight, very ugly dress of yellowish gray wincey. She wore a faded brown sailor hat and beneath the hat, extending down her back, were two braids of very thick, decidedly red hair. Her face was small, white, and thin, also much freckled; her mouth was large and so were her eyes, that looked green in some lights and moods and gray in others.
>
> —L. M. Montgomery,
> *from* Anne of Green Gables

See page 647

DIALECT A way of speaking that is characteristic of a particular region or of a particular group of people. A dialect may have a distinct vocabulary, pronunciation system, and grammar. In a sense, we all speak dialects. The dialect that is dominant in a country or culture becomes accepted as the standard way of speaking. Writers often reproduce regional dialects or dialects that reveal a person's economic or social class. For example, the animal characters in "He Lion, Bruh Bear, and Bruh Rabbit" (page 49) use an African American dialect spoken in the rural South. In the passage below, a spunky young girl gets up the courage to ask her uncle a hard question (she is speaking an African American urban dialect).

> So there I am in the navigator seat. And I turn to him and just plain ole ax him. I mean I come right on out with it. . . . And like my mama say, Hazel—which is my real name and what she remembers to call me when she bein serious—when you got somethin on your mind, speak up and let the chips fall where they may. And if anybody don't like it, tell em to come see your mama. And Daddy look up from the paper and say, You hear your mama good, Hazel. And tell em to come see me first. Like that. That's how I was raised. So I turn clear round in the navigator seat and say, "Look here, . . . you gonna marry this girl?"
>
> —Toni Cade Bambara,
> *from* "Gorilla, My Love"

DIALOGUE Conversation between two or more characters. Most plays consist entirely of dialogue. Dialogue is also an important element in most stories and novels. It is very effective in revealing character and can add realism and humor to a story.

In the written form of a play, such as *Blanca Flor* (page 757), dialogue appears without quotation marks. In prose or poetry, however, dialogue is usually enclosed in quotation marks.

See pages 743, 755

DRAMA A story written to be acted in front of an audience. A drama, such as *Blanca Flor* (page 757), can also be appreciated and enjoyed in written form. The related events that take place within a drama are often separated into **acts.** Each act is often made up of shorter sections, or **scenes.** Many plays have two or three acts, but there are many variations. The elements of drama are often described as **introduction** or **exposition, complications, conflict, climax,** and **resolution.**

See pages 4, 746-747
See also *Dialogue*.

ESSAY A short piece of nonfiction prose. An essay usually examines a subject from a personal point of view. The French writer Michel de Montaigne (1533–1592) is credited with creating the essay. Robert Fulghum, a popular essayist, is represented in this book (page 336).

FABLE A very brief story in prose or verse that teaches a moral, a practical lesson about how to succeed in life. The characters of most fables are animals who behave and speak like human beings. Some of the most popular fables are those thought to have been told by Aesop, who was a slave in ancient Greece. You may be familiar with his fable about the sly fox who praises the crow for her beautiful voice and begs her to sing for him. When the crow opens her mouth to sing, she lets fall from her beak the piece of cheese that the fox had been after the whole time.

See also *Folk Tale*, *Myth*.

FANTASY Imaginative writing that carries the reader into an invented world where the laws of nature as we know them do not operate. In fantasy worlds, fantastic forces are often at play. Characters wave magic wands, cast spells, or appear and disappear at will. These characters may be ordinary human beings—or they may be Martians, elves, giants, or fairies. Some of the oldest fantasy stories are called **fairy tales.** A newer type of fantasy, one that deals with a future world changed by science, is called **science fiction.** "All Summer in a Day" (page 155) is Ray Bradbury's science fiction story about life as he imagines it on the planet Venus.

FICTION **A prose account that is made up rather than true.** The term *fiction* usually refers to novels and short stories.

See pages 4-5, 47
See also *Fantasy*, *Nonfiction*.

FIGURATIVE LANGUAGE **Language that describes one thing in terms of something else and is not literally true.** Figures of speech always involve some sort of imaginative comparison between seemingly unlike things. The most common forms are **simile** ("My heart is like a singing bird"), **metaphor** ("The road was a ribbon of moonlight"), and **personification** ("The leaves were whispering to the night").

See pages 507, 646, 650, 680, 691
See also *Metaphor*, *Personification*, *Simile*.

FLASHBACK **A scene that breaks the normal time order of the plot to show a past event.** A flashback can be placed anywhere in a story, even at the beginning. There, it usually gives background information. Most of the play *The Diary of Anne Frank* is a flashback.

See pages 743, 789

FOLK TALE **A story with no known author, originally passed on from one generation to another by word of mouth.** Folk tales generally differ from myths in that they are not about gods and they were never connected with religion. The folk tales in this book include "Little Mangy One" (page 118) and "He Lion, Bruh Bear, and Bruh Rabbit" (page 49). Sometimes similar folk tales appear in many cultures. For example, stories similar to the old European folk tale of Cinderella have turned up in hundreds of cultures.

See pages 4, 10, 13, 47
See also *Fable*, *Myth*, *Oral Tradition*.

FORESHADOWING **The use of clues or hints to suggest events that will occur later in the plot.** Foreshadowing builds suspense or anxiety in the reader or viewer. In a movie, for example, strange, alien creatures glimpsed among the trees may foreshadow danger for the exploring astronauts.

See page 747
See also *Suspense*.

FREE VERSE **Poetry that is "free" of a regular meter and rhyme scheme.** Poets writing in free verse try to capture the natural rhythms of ordinary speech. The following poem is written in free verse:

The City
If flowers want to grow
right out of the concrete sidewalk cracks
I'm going to bend down to smell them.
—David Ignatow

See pages 647, 681
See also *Poetry*, *Rhyme*, *Rhythm*.

IMAGERY **Language that appeals to the senses—sight, hearing, touch, taste, and smell.** Most images are visual—that is, they create pictures in the mind by appealing to the sense of sight. Images can also appeal to the senses of hearing, touch, taste, and smell. They can appeal to several senses at once. Though imagery is an element in all types of writing, it is especially important in poetry. The following poem is full of images about rain:

The Storm
In fury and terror
the tempest broke,
it tore up the pine
and shattered the oak,
yet the hummingbird hovered
within the hour
sipping clear rain
from a trumpet flower.
—Elizabeth Coatsworth

See pages 507, 647, 704

IRONY A contrast between what is expected and what really happens. Irony can create powerful effects, from humor to horror. Here are some examples of situations that would make us feel a sense of irony:

- A shoemaker wears shoes with holes in them.
- The children of a famous dancer trip over their own feet.
- It rains on the day a group of weather forecasters have scheduled a picnic.
- Someone asks, "How's my driving?" after going through a stop sign.
- A Great Dane runs away from a mouse.
- Someone living in the desert keeps a boat in her yard.
- The child of a police officer robs a bank.
- Someone walks out in the midst of a hurricane and says, "Nice day."

LEGEND A story, usually based on some historical fact, that has been handed down from one generation to the next. Legends often grow up around famous figures or events. For example, legend has it that Abraham Lincoln was a simple, ordinary man. In reality, Lincoln was a complicated man of unusual ability and ambition. The stories about King Arthur and his knights are legends based on the exploits of an actual warrior-king who probably lived in Wales in the 500s. Legends often make use of fantastic details.

See page 4

LIMERICK A humorous five-line verse that has a regular meter and the rhyme scheme *aabba*. Limericks often have place names in their rhymes. The following limerick was published in Edward Lear's *Book of Nonsense* in 1846, when limericks were at the height of their popularity:

> There was an old man of Peru
> Who dreamt he was eating a shoe.
> He awoke in the night
> With a terrible fright
> And found it was perfectly true!

MAIN IDEA The most important idea expressed in a piece of writing. Sometimes the main idea is stated directly by the writer; at other times the reader must infer it.

See pages 462, 465, 468, 493

METAPHOR A comparison between two unlike things in which one thing becomes another thing. An **extended metaphor** carries the comparison through an entire work. A metaphor is an important type of figure of speech. Metaphors are used in all forms of writing and are common in ordinary speech. When you say about your grumpy friend, "He's such a bear today," you do not mean that he is growing bushy black fur. You mean that he is in a bad mood and is ready to attack, just the way a bear might be.

Metaphors differ from **similes,** which use specific words, such as *like*, *as*, *than*, and *resembles*, to make their comparisons. "He is behaving like a bear" is a simile.

The following famous poem compares fame to an insect:

> Fame is a bee.
> It has a song—
> It has a sting—
> Ah, too, it has a wing.
>
> —Emily Dickinson

See pages 252, 507, 646, 647, 652, 680, 691, 711
See also *Figurative Language*, *Personification*, *Simile*.

MOOD The overall emotion created by a work of literature. Mood can often be described in one or two adjectives, such as *eerie*, *dreamy*, *mysterious*, *depressing*. The mood created by the poem below is sad and lonely:

Since Hanna Moved Away
The tires on my bike are flat.
The sky is grouchy gray.
At least it sure feels like that
Since Hanna moved away.

Chocolate ice cream tastes like prunes.
December's come to stay.
They've taken back the Mays and Junes
Since Hanna moved away.

Flowers smell like halibut.
Velvet feels like hay.
Every handsome dog's a mutt
Since Hanna moved away.

Nothing's fun to laugh about.
Nothing's fun to play.
They call me, but I won't come out
Since Hanna moved away.

—Judith Viorst

MYTH A story that usually explains something about the world and involves gods and superheroes. Myths are deeply connected to the traditions and religious beliefs of the cultures that produced them. Myths often explain certain aspects of life, such as what thunder is or where sunlight comes from or why people die. **Origin myths,** or **creation myths,** explain how something in the world began or was created. Most myths are very old and were handed down orally for many centuries before being put in writing. The story of the hero Perseus (page 293) is a famous Greek myth.

See pages 4, 61
See also *Fable*, *Folk Tale*, *Oral Tradition*.

NARRATION The kind of writing that relates a series of connected events to tell "what happened." Narration (also called **narrative**) is the form of writing storytellers use to tell stories. Narration can be used to relate both fictional and true-life events.

See pages 458, 459, 464

NONFICTION Prose writing that deals with real people, events, and places without changing any facts. Popular forms of nonfiction are the autobiography, the biography, and the essay. Other examples of nonfiction are newspaper stories, magazine articles, historical writing, travel writing, science reports, and personal diaries and letters.

See pages 458-459
See also *Fiction*.

NOVEL A long fictional story that is usually more than one hundred book pages in length. A novel includes all the elements of storytelling—**plot, character, setting, theme,** and **point of view.** Because of its length, a novel usually has a more complex plot, subplots, and more characters, settings, and themes than a short story.

See page 4

ONOMATOPOEIA The use of a word whose sound imitates or suggests its meaning. Onomatopoeia (ahn uh mat uh PEE uh) is so natural to us that we begin to use it at a very early age. *Boom*, *bang*, *sniffle*, *rumble*, *hush*, *ding*, and *snort* are all examples of onomatopoeia. Onomatopoeia helps create the music of poetry. The following poem uses onomatopoeia:

Our Washing Machine
Our washing machine went whisity whirr
Whisity whisity whisity whirr
One day at noon it went whisity click
Whisity whisity whisity click
click grr click grr click grr click
Call the repairman
Fix it . . . quick.

—Patricia Hubbell

See pages 645, 650, 678
See also *Alliteration*.

ORAL TRADITION A collection of folk tales, songs, and poems that have been passed on orally from generation to generation.

See pages 4, 10
See also *Folk Tale*.

PARAPHRASE A restatement of a written work in which the meaning is expressed in other words. A paraphrase of a poem should tell what the poem says, line by line, but in the paraphraser's own words. A paraphrase of a work of prose should briefly summarize the major events or ideas. Here is the first stanza of a famous poem, followed by a paraphrase:

> Once upon a midnight dreary, while I pondered, weak and weary,
> Over many a quaint and curious volume of forgotten lore—
> While I nodded, nearly napping, suddenly there came a tapping,
> As of someone gently rapping, rapping at my chamber door.
> "'Tis some visitor," I muttered, "tapping at my chamber door—
> Only this, and nothing more."
>
> —Edgar Allan Poe, from "The Raven"
>
> **Paraphrase:** One midnight, when I was tired, I was reading some interesting old books that contain information no one learns anymore. As I was dozing off, I suddenly heard what sounded like someone tapping at the door to the room. "It is someone coming to see me," I said to myself, "knocking at the door. That's all it is."

Notice that the paraphrase is neither as eerie nor as elegant as the poem.

See page 553

PERSONIFICATION A special kind of metaphor in which a nonhuman or nonliving thing or quality is talked about as if it were human or alive. You would be using personification if you said, "The leaves danced along the sidewalk." Of course, leaves don't dance—only people do. The following poem personifies the night wind:

> **Rags**
> The night wind
> rips a cloud sheet
> into rags,
> then rubs, rubs
> the October moon
> until it shines
> like a brass doorknob.
>
> —Judith Thurman

In the cartoon below, history and fame are talked about as though they were human.

"While you were out for lunch, History passed by and Fame came knocking."

See pages 507, 646, 647, 680, 691
See also *Figurative Language, Metaphor, Simile*.

PLOT The series of related events that make up a story. Plot tells "what happens" in a short story, novel, play, or narrative poem. Most plots are built on these bare bones: An **introduction** tells who the characters are and what their **conflict,** or problem, is. **Complications** arise as the characters take steps to resolve the conflict. When the outcome of the conflict is decided one way or another, the plot reaches a **climax,** the most exciting moment in the story. The final part of the story is the **resolution,** when the characters' problems are solved and the story ends.

See pages 128-129, 130, 132, 153
See also *Conflict*.

POETRY **A kind of rhythmic, compressed language that uses figures of speech and imagery to appeal to emotion and imagination.** Poetry often has a regular pattern of rhythm, and it may have a regular pattern of rhyme. **Free verse** is poetry that has no regular pattern of rhythm or rhyme.

See pages 644, 645, 646, 647, 732
See also *Free Verse*, *Imagery*, *Refrain*, *Rhyme*, *Rhythm*, *Speaker*, *Stanza*.

POINT OF VIEW **The vantage point from which a story is told.** Two common points of view are the omniscient (ahm NIHSH uhnt) and the first person.

1. In the **omniscient,** or all-knowing, **third-person point of view,** the narrator knows everything about the characters and their problems. This all-knowing narrator can tell us about the past, the present, and the future. Below is part of a familiar story told from the omniscient point of view:

> Once upon a time in a small village, there were three houses built by three brother pigs. One house was made of straw, one was made of twigs, and one was made of brick. Each pig thought his house was the best and the strongest. A wolf—a very hungry wolf just outside the town—was practicing house-destroying techniques and was trying to decide which pig's house was the weakest.

2. In the **first-person point of view,** one of the characters, using the personal pronoun ***I***, is telling the story. The reader becomes familiar with this narrator and can know only what he or she knows and can observe only what he or she observes. All information about the story must come from this one narrator. In some cases, as in the following example, the information this narrator gives may not be correct:

> As soon as I found out some new pigs had moved into the neighborhood, I started to practice my house-destroying techniques. I like to blow down houses and eat whoever is inside. The little pigs have built their houses of different materials—but I know I can blow 'em down in no time. That brick house looks especially weak.

See pages 458, 459, 460, 464, 471, 479, 493

PROSE **Any writing that is not poetry.** Essays, short stories, novels, news articles, and letters are written in prose.

REFRAIN **A repeated word, phrase, line, or group of lines in a poem or song or even in a speech.** Refrains are usually associated with songs and poems, but they are also used in speeches and some other forms of literature. Refrains are often used to create rhythm. They are also used for emphasis and emotional effects.

See pages 645, 665

RHYME **The repetition of accented vowel sounds and all sounds following them.** *Trouble* and *bubble* are rhymes, as are *clown* and *noun*. Rhymes in poetry help create rhythm and lend a songlike quality to a poem. They can also emphasize ideas and provide humor or delight.

End rhymes are rhymes at the ends of lines. **Internal rhymes** are rhymes within lines. Here is an example of a poem with both kinds of rhymes:

> In days of *old* when knights caught *cold*,
> They were not quickly *cured*;
> No aspirin *pill* would check the *ill*,
> Which had to be *endured*.
>
> —David Daiches,
> from "Thoughts on Progress,"
> from *The New Yorker*

Rhyme scheme is the pattern of rhyming sounds at the ends of lines in a poem. Notice the pattern of end rhymes in the poem in the following cartoon.

See pages 644-645, 650, 657

RHYTHM A musical quality produced by the repetition of stressed and unstressed syllables or by the repetition of other sound patterns. Rhythm occurs in all language—written and spoken—but is particularly important in poetry. The most obvious kind of rhythm is the repeated pattern of stressed and unstressed syllables, called **meter.** Finding this pattern is called **scanning.** If you scan or say the following lines aloud, you'll hear a strong, regular rhythm. (Crowns, pounds, and guineas are British currency.)

> When I was one-and-twenty
>   I heard a wise man say,
> "Give crowns and pounds and guineas
>   But not your heart away."
>
> —A. E. Housman, from
> "When I Was One-and-Twenty"

See pages 644, 650
See also *Free Verse*, *Poetry*.

SETTING The time and place of a story, a poem, or a play. The setting can help create mood or atmosphere. The setting can also affect the events of the plot. In some stories the conflict is provided by the setting. This happens in "The Dog of Pompeii" (page 401) when the characters' lives are threatened by a volcano. Some examples of vivid settings are the gloomy planet where it rains for seven years in "All Summer in a Day" (page 155), the snow-covered countryside in "Zlateh the Goat" (page 414), and Ernie's Riverside restaurant in "Ta-Na-E-Ka" (page 359).

See pages 71, 128-129, 130, 153, 165

SHORT STORY A fictional prose narrative that is about five to twenty book pages long. Short stories are usually built on a plot that consists of these elements: **introduction, conflict, complications, climax,** and **resolution.** Short stories are more limited than novels. They usually have only one or two major characters and one setting.

See pages 4, 17
See also *Conflict*, *Fiction*, *Novel*, *Plot*.

SIMILE A comparison between two unlike things using a word such as *like, as, than,* or *resembles*. The simile (SIHM uh lee) is an important figure of speech. "His voice is as loud as a trumpet" and "Her eyes are like the blue sky" are similes. In the following poem the poet uses a simile to help us see a winter scene in a new way:

> **Scene**
> Little trees like pencil strokes
> black and still
> etched forever in my mind
> on that snowy hill.
>
> —Charlotte Zolotow

See pages 252, 647, 680, 691, 698
See also *Figurative Language*, *Metaphor*.

Calvin and Hobbes **by Bill Watterson**

SPEAKER **The voice talking to us in a poem.** Sometimes the speaker is identical to the poet, but often the speaker and the poet are not the same. A poet may speak as a child, a woman, a man, an animal, or even an object. The speaker of "Things to Do If You Are a Subway" (page 717) asks the reader to imagine that he or she is a subway train and to act like one.

See page 647

STANZA **In a poem, a group of lines that form a unit.** A stanza in a poem is something like a paragraph in prose; it often expresses a unit of thought.

See pages 644

SUSPENSE **The anxious curiosity the reader feels about what will happen next in a story.** Any kind of writing that has a plot evokes some degree of suspense. Our sense of suspense is awakened in "The Gold Cadillac" (page 31), for example, when the narrator and her family begin their trip to Mississippi. The anxious and fearful warnings of the family's friends and relatives make us eager to read on to see if the journey will prove dangerous.

See pages 128, 742, 789
See also *Foreshadowing*, *Plot*.

SYMBOL **A person, a place, a thing, or an event that has its own meaning and stands for something beyond itself as well.** Examples of symbols are all around us—in music, on television, and in everyday conversation. The skull and crossbones, for example, is a symbol of danger; the dove is a symbol of peace; and the red rose stands for true love. In literature, symbols are often more personal. For example, in "The Gold Cadillac," the Cadillac stands for success in the eyes of Wilbert.

See pages 507

TALL TALE **An exaggerated, fanciful story that gets "taller and taller," or more and more far-fetched, the more it is told and retold.** The tall tale is an American story form. John Henry (page 667) is a famous tall-tale character. Here is a short tall tale:

> When the temperature reached 118 degrees, a whole field of corn popped. White flakes filled the air and covered the ground six inches deep and drifted across roads and collected on tree limbs.
> A mule that saw all this thought it was snowing and lay down and quietly froze to death.

See page 4

THEME **A truth about life revealed in a work of literature.** A theme is not the same as a subject. A subject can usually be expressed in a word or two—*love*, *childhood*, *death*. A theme is the idea the writer wishes to reveal about that subject. A theme has to be expressed in a full sentence. A work can have more than one theme. A theme is usually not stated directly in the work. Instead, the reader has to think about the elements of the work and then make an inference, or educated guess, about what they all mean.

See pages 350, 351, 357, 809

TONE **The attitude a writer takes toward an audience, a subject, or a character.** Tone is conveyed through the writer's choice of words and details. The tone can be light and humorous, serious and sad, friendly or hostile toward a character, and so forth. The poem "The Sneetches" (page 659) is light and humorous in tone. In contrast, Francisco X. Alarcón's "In a Neighborhood in Los Angeles" (page 695) has a loving and respectful tone.

See pages 647, 671, 688, 691, 699

Handbook of Reading and Informational Terms

For more information about a topic, turn to the page(s) in this book indicated on a separate line at the end of the entry.

On another line there are cross-references to entries in this Handbook that provide closely related information. For instance, *Chronological Order* contains a cross-reference to *Text Structures*.

AUTHOR'S PURPOSE The author's purpose may be to **inform,** to **persuade,** to **express feelings,** or to **entertain.** An author may create a **text,** which is any written work, with more than one purpose in mind. One of the purposes is usually more important than the others. Once you've identified the author's purpose, you'll have a pretty good idea of how to read the text. If you're reading an **informational text,** you may need to read slowly and carefully. You may also want to complete a question sheet like the one below or take notes. If you're reading a text that the author wrote mostly for you to enjoy, you can read at your own pace—any way you want.

Question Sheet for Informational Texts

1. What is the topic? ________
2. Do I understand what I'm reading? ______
3. What parts should I re-read? ________

   ____
4. What are the main ideas and details?

Main idea: ________ Details: ________
Main idea: ________ Details: ________
Main idea: ________ Details: ________
Main idea: ________ Details: ________

5. Summary of what I learned:

____

____

See pages 463, 466, 479
See also *Note Taking*; *Reading Rate*.

CAUSE AND EFFECT A **cause** is the reason something happens. An **effect** is *what happens* as a result of the cause. The cause happens first in time. The *later* event is the effect. In most stories, events in the plot are connected by cause and effect. Look for a **cause-and-effect text structure** in informational materials. Watch out! Sometimes writers put the effect first even though that event happened as a result of (and after) the cause. For instance, consider the following sentence:

> Bears come out of their dens when the winter snow melts.

The *cause* is the melting snow. The *effect* is that bears come out of their dens. Some of the clue words that signal cause-and-effect relationships are *because*, *since*, *so that*, *therefore*, and *as a result*.

See page 352
See also *Text Structures*.

CHRONOLOGICAL ORDER Most narratives are written in **chronological** or **time order,** the order in which events happen in time. When you read a story, look for time clues— words and phrases like *next*, *then*, *finally*, and the *following night*. Writers use time clues as signals to help you follow the **sequence,** or order, of events. Sometimes writers break into the sequence with a **flashback,** an event that happened earlier. Look for chronological order in any kind of text where the order of events is important. For instance, in an article explaining how to make something, the steps are usually listed in chronological order.

See pages 750, 789, 827
See also *Text Structures*.

COMPARISON AND CONTRAST When you **compare,** you look for **similarities,** ways in which things are alike. When you **contrast,** you look for **differences.** In a comparison-contrast text, the features looked at are called **points of comparison.** The points of comparison are usually organized in either a **block pattern** or a **point-by-point pattern.** When you read a comparison organized in a block pattern, you find the points of comparison about each subject presented separately, first one, then the other. Here is a **block-pattern** paragraph comparing Mary's and Roger's ways of surviving Ta-Na-E-Ka (page 359):

> Mary survived by getting help from other people. She borrowed money from a teacher and used it to pay for food at Ernie's restaurant. Ernie gave her warm clothes to wear and a place to stay at night. In contrast, Roger survived on his own in the traditional Kaw way. He ate berries and maybe even grasshoppers. He lost weight during Ta-Na-E-Ka and was never warm and comfortable.

A writer who uses the **point-by-point pattern** goes back and forth between the two subjects being compared, like this:

> Mary ate well, but Roger lost weight. Mary ate good food at a restaurant while Roger lived on berries. Mary got help from others, but Roger survived by himself.
> Both passed the test; however, Roger survived in the traditional way. Mary found a new way of surviving.

Some of the clue words that signal comparison and contrast are *although, but, either . . . or, however,* and *yet.*

See pages 281, 309, 711, 825
See also *Text Structures.*

CONTEXT CLUES You can often find clues to the meaning of a word you don't know by looking at its **context,** the words and sentences around it. Here is the beginning of a paragraph from "The Dog of Pompeii"(page 401):

> The water—hot water—splashing in his face *revived* him. He got to his feet, Bimbo steadying him, helping him on again.

If you don't know the meaning of *revived* in the first sentence, look at the context. The beginning of the second sentence, "He got to his feet," helps you figure out that *revived* means "brought back to life."

EVALUATING EVIDENCE When you read informational and persuasive texts, you need to weigh the **evidence** that writers use to support their ideas. That means you need to read carefully and decide whether the writer has presented evidence that's **adequate, appropriate,** and **accurate.** *Adequate* means "sufficient" or "enough." You make sure there's enough evidence to prove the writer's points. Sometimes one example or one fact may be adequate. Other times the writer may need to provide several facts and maybe even statistics. A direct quotation from a well-respected expert in the field can often be convincing. Make sure that the writer chooses *appropriate* evidence that relates directly to the writer's idea. To be sure that evidence is *accurate,* or correct, make sure it comes from a source you can trust. Don't assume that everything you see in print is accurate. If a fact, example, or quotation doesn't sound right, check out the magazine or book that it came from. Is the magazine or book a trustworthy and reliable source? What is the author's background?

See pages 580, 583, 602
See also *Fact and Opinion.*

EVIDENCE **Evidence** is the support or proof that backs up an idea, conclusion, or opinion. When you're reading an informational or persuasive text, you look for evidence in the form of examples, quotations from experts, statistics (information expressed as numbers), and personal experiences.

See pages 576, 580, 585 589

FACT AND OPINION A **fact** is something that can be proved true.

> **Fact:** Abraham Lincoln was the sixteenth president of the United States.

An **opinion** expresses a personal belief or feeling. An opinion cannot be proved true or false.

> **Opinion:** Abraham Lincoln was the best president the United States has ever had.

A **valid opinion** is a personal belief that is strongly supported by facts. When you read "The Mysterious Mr. Lincoln" (page 516), look for the facts that Russell Freedman uses to back up his opinions.

See pages 463, 471, 576, 581, 584, 602, 611
See also *Evidence*.

GENERALIZATION A **generalization** is a broad statement based on several particular situations. When you make a generalization, you combine evidence in a text with what you already know to make a broad, universal statement about some topic. For example, after reading "Wartime Mistakes, Peacetime Apologies" (page 198), you might want to make a generalization about the treatment of Japanese Americans during World War II.

See page 355
See also *Evidence*.

GRAPHIC FEATURES Headings, design features, maps, charts, tables, diagrams, and illustrations are all **graphic features.** They present information visually. Shapes, lines, and colors combine with words to help you understand a text.

A **heading** is a kind of title for the information that follows it. Size and color set off the heading from the rest of the text. A repeated heading like "Question" in this textbook is always followed by the same type of material.

Some of the **design features** you may find in a text are colors, borders, boldface and italic type, type in different styles (fonts) and sizes, bullets (the dots that set off items in a list), and logos (like computer icons). The "Quickwrite" heading always appears with the pencil logo, for instance. Design features make a text look more attractive. They steer your eyes to different types of information and make the text easier to read.

Graphic features such as **maps, charts, diagrams, graphs,** and **tables** communicate complex information with lines, drawings, and symbols. The following elements help to make them effective:

1. A **title** identifies the subject or main idea of the graphic.
2. **Labels** identify specific information.
3. A **caption** is the text (usually under a photo or another kind of illustration) that explains what you're looking at.
4. A **legend** or **key** helps you interpret symbols and colors. Look for a **scale,** which helps you relate the size or distance of something on the graphic to real-life sizes and distances.
5. The **source** tells where the information in the graphic came from. Knowing the source helps you evaluate the graphic's accuracy.

Charts and **diagrams** use symbols, lines, and numbers to explain or to display information. They are used to compare ideas, show steps in a process, illustrate the way something is made, or show how the parts of something relate to the whole thing. A **pie graph,** for instance, shows proportions. It's a circle divided into different-sized sections, like slices of pie.

Pie Graph

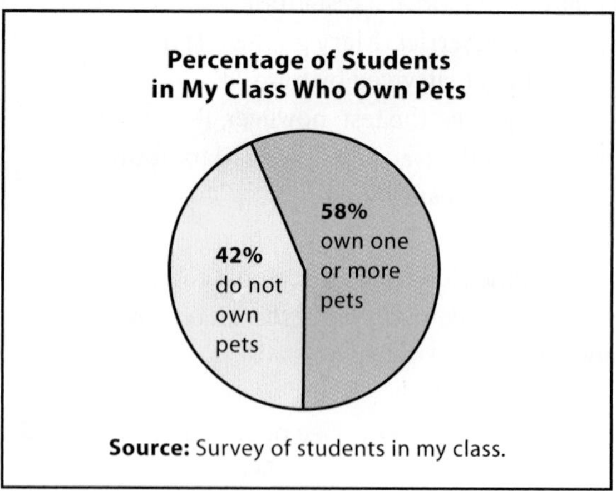

A **flowchart** shows you the steps in a process, a sequence of events, or cause-and-effect relationships.

Graphs, including bar graphs and line graphs, show changes or trends over time. Notice that the same information is presented in the following bar graph and line graph:

Bar Graph

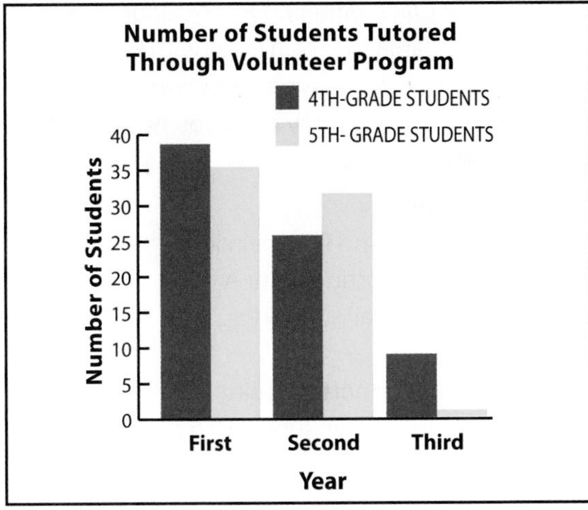

Line Graph

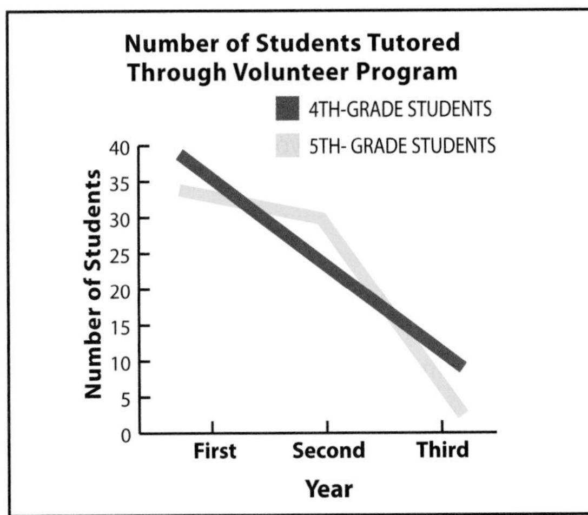

A **table** presents facts and details arranged in rows and columns. It simplifies information to make it easy to understand.

Table

Number of Volunteers in the Peer-Tutoring Program	
First year	15
Second year	10
Third year	8

Viewing Tips: When you come across graphic features, use the tips below:

1. Read the title, labels, and legend before you try to analyze the information.
2. Read numbers carefully. Note increases or decreases. Look for the direction or order of events and for trends and relationships.
3. Draw your own conclusions from the graphic, and compare them with the conclusions the writer makes.

INFERENCE An **inference** is an educated guess. You make inferences all the time in real life. For instance, if you see pawprints crossing the snow, you can **infer** that an animal walked there. The pawprints are the **evidence.** On the basis of your experience with animal tracks, you might be able to infer that the animal was a rabbit, a cat, a dog, or a raccoon.

Readers **make inferences** on the basis of clues writers give them and experiences from their own lives. When you make inferences, you read between the lines to figure out what the writer suggests but does not state directly.

Read this passage from Avi's story "What Do Fish Have to Do with Anything?"(page 522).

> During the twenty minutes that Willie watched, no one who passed looked in the beggar's direction. Willie wondered if they even saw the man. Certainly no one put any money into his open hand.
>
> A lady leading a dog by a leash went by. The dog strained in the direction of the man sitting on the crate. The dog's tail wagged. The lady pulled the dog away. "Heel!" she commanded.

Here are some **inferences** you might draw from the passage: People don't want to look at the man who is begging. It's as if he doesn't exist for them. The dog is friendlier than the people.

See pages 234-235, 245, 7477

MAIN IDEA The most important idea in a piece of nonfiction writing is the **main idea.** There may be more than one main idea in a nonfiction story or article. Sometimes the writer states a main idea directly; at other times the writer only **implies,** or suggests, the main idea. Then the reader must **infer** or guess what it is.

To infer the main idea, look at the **key details** or **important events** in the text. See whether you can create a statement that expresses the idea that these details or events develop or support. In a nonfiction text the writer may state the main idea more than once and use different words for each statement. Look especially for a **key passage** near the end of the piece. That's where the writer often emphasizes or sums up a main idea.

See pages 462, 493
See also *Outlining*.

NOTE TAKING Taking notes is important for readers who want to remember ideas and facts. It's especially useful when you read **informational texts.** You can jot down notes in a notebook or on note cards. Notes don't have to be written in complete sentences. Put them in your own words; use phrases that will help you recall the text. You may want to put each important idea at the top of its own page or note card. As you read, add details that relate to that idea. Put related ideas on the same page or card as the main idea they support.

Whenever you copy a writer's exact words, put quotation marks around them. Write down the number of the page that was the source of each note. Even though no one but you may see your notes, try to write clearly so that you'll be able to read them later. When you finish taking notes, review them to make sure they make sense to you.

See also *Author's Purpose*.

OUTLINING **Outlining** an informational text helps you identify important ideas and understand how they are connected or related to each other. Once you've made an outline, you have a quick visual summary of the information. Start with the notes you've taken on an article. (See *Note Taking.*) You should have each **main idea** with **supporting details** in one place, either on a page or on a card. Many outlines label the main ideas with Roman numerals. You need to have at least two headings at each level. Three levels may be all you need. A four-level outline is arranged like this:

I. First main idea
  A. Detail supporting first main idea
    1. Detail supporting point A
    2. Another detail supporting point A
      a. Detail supporting point 2
      b. Another detail supporting point 2
    3. Another detail supporting point A
  B. Another detail supporting first main idea
II. Second main idea

See also *Main Idea*.

PARAPHRASING When you **paraphrase** a text, you put it into your own words. You can check how well you understand a poem, for instance, by paraphrasing it, line by line. When you paraphrase, you follow the author's sequence of ideas. You carefully reword each line or sentence without changing the author's meaning or leaving anything out.

See page 553

PERSUASION **Persuasion** is the use of language or visual images to get you to *believe* or *do* something. Writers who want to change your mind about an issue use **persuasive techniques.** Learning about these techniques will help you evaluate persuasion.

Emotional appeals get the reader's feelings involved in the argument. Some writers use vivid language and give reasons, examples, and anecdotes (personal-experience stories) that appeal to basic feelings such as fear, pity, jealousy, and love.

Logical appeals make sense because they're based on correct reasoning. They appeal to your brain with reasons and evidence. (See *Evidence*.) When you're reading a persuasive text, make sure that the writer has good reasons to support each opinion or conclusion. Evidence such as facts, personal experiences, examples, statistics, and statements by experts on the issue should back up each reason.

Logical fallacies are mistakes in reasoning. If you're reading a text quickly, an argument based on **fallacious reasoning** may look as if it makes sense. Watch out for these fallacies:

1. **Hasty generalizations.** Valid generalizations are based on solid evidence. (See *Generalization*.) Not all generalizations are valid. Here's an example of a hasty generalization, one made on the basis of too little evidence.

> "The Sneetches" is a poem that rhymes.
> "John Henry" is a poem that rhymes.
> **Hasty generalization:** All poems rhyme.

Sometimes hasty generalizations can be corrected by the use of **qualifying words,** such as *most, usually, some, many,* and *often*. After you've read all the poems in this textbook and considered all the evidence, you could make this generalization:

> **Valid generalization:** Some poems rhyme.

2. **Circular reasoning.** This example illustrates circular reasoning, another kind of logical fallacy:

> We have the greatest football team because no other school has a team that's as fantastic as ours.

Someone using circular reasoning simply repeats an argument instead of backing it up with reasons and evidence.

3. **Only-cause fallacy.** This fallacy assumes that a problem has only one cause. It conveniently ignores the fact that most situations are the result of many causes. The **either-or fallacy** is related to the only-cause fallacy. The either-or fallacy assumes that there are only two sides to an issue.

> **Only-cause fallacy:** I didn't do well on the test because it wasn't fair.
> **Either-or fallacy:** If your parents don't buy this set of encyclopedias for you, they don't care about your education.

Persuasion tends to be most interesting—and effective—when it appeals to both head and heart. However, it's important to be able to recognize logical fallacies and emotional appeals—and to be aware of how they can mislead you.

See pages 479, 507, 576-577, 582, 589, 607

PREDICTING Making **predictions** as you read helps you think about and understand what you're reading. To make predictions, look for clues that the writer gives you. Connect those clues with other things you've read, as well as your own experience. You'll probably find yourself **adjusting predictions** as you read.

See pages 9, 11, 17, 29, 747

PRIOR KNOWLEDGE *Prior* means "earlier" or "previous." **Prior knowledge** is what you know about a subject when you're at the starting line—before you read a selection. **Using prior knowledge** is a reading skill that starts with recalling experiences you've had, as well as what you've learned about the subject of the text. Glancing through the text, looking at the pictures, and reading subtitles and captions will help you recall what you already know. As you focus on the subject, you'll come up with questions that the text may answer. Making a **KWL chart** is one way to record your reading process. Here is part of a KWL chart for Mildred D. Taylor's "The Gold Cadillac" (page 31).

K	W	L
What I **Know**	What I **Want** to Know	What I **Learned**
A Cadillac is an expensive car.	How would someone feel in a gold Cadillac?	

See pages 747, 750

PROPAGANDA **Propaganda is an organized attempt to persuade people to accept certain ideas or to take certain actions.** Writers sometimes use propaganda to advance a good cause. However, most writers of propaganda use emotional appeals to confuse readers and convince them that the writers' opinions are the only ones worth considering. Propaganda relies on emotional appeals rather than on logical reasons and evidence.

Here are some common propaganda techniques:

1. The **bandwagon** appeal suggests that you need something or should believe something because everyone else already has it or believes it. It's an appeal to "join the crowd, climb on the bandwagon, and join the parade."
2. A **testimonial** uses a famous person, such as an actor or an athlete, to promote an idea or a product. People who use snob appeal associate the product or idea they're promoting with power, wealth, or membership in a special group.
3. Writers who use **stereotypes** refer to members of a group as if they were all the same. For instance, an article stating that all professional wrestlers have limited intelligence unfairly stereotypes wrestlers. Stereotyping often leads to prejudice, or forming unfavorable opinions with complete disregard for the facts.
4. People who engage in **name-calling** offer no reasons or evidence to support their position. Instead, they attack opponents by calling them names, such as "busy bodies," "nitpickers," or "rumormongers."

See page 616

READING RATE **Readers adjust the rate at which they read depending on their purpose for reading and the difficulty of the material.** The following chart shows how you can adjust your reading rate for different purposes.

Reading Rates According to Purpose

Reading Rate	Purpose	Example
Scanning	Reading quickly for specific details	Finding the age of a character
Skimming	Reading quickly for main points	Previewing a science chapter by reading the headings
Reading slowly and carefully	Reading for mastery (reading to learn)	Reading and taking notes from an article for a research report
Reading at a comfortable speed	Reading for enjoyment	Reading a novel by your favorite writer

See pages 651, 809
See also *Author's Purpose*.

RETELLING **Retelling** is a reading strategy that helps you recall and understand the major events in a story. From time to time in your reading—for instance, after something important has happened—stop for a few moments. Review what has just taken place before you go ahead. Focus on the major events. Think about them, and retell them briefly in your own words.

See pages 132, 136, 141

SUMMARIZING When you **summarize** a text, you restate the author's main points in your own words. You include only the important ideas and details. A **summary** of a text is much shorter than the original, while a paraphrase may be the same length as, or even longer than, the original text.

When you're summarizing, stop after each paragraph you read. Try to restate in one sentence what the author wrote. If you're summarizing a story, look for the major events in the **plot,** the ones that lead to the **climax.** If you're summarizing an **essay,** look for the important ideas. Here is a summary of Maya Angelou's "Brother" (page 473):

> Bailey was the person who was most important to the writer when she was a child. She loved Bailey because he was smart, generous, kind, and full of life. He always defended her whenever anyone insulted her. He always came up with ideas to have fun. The author says that Bailey was someone she trusted and loved with all her heart.

See pages 133, 137, 165

TEXT STRUCTURES Understanding the way a text is structured, or organized, can help you follow the writer's ideas. **Analyzing text structures** will help you understand the information you're reading. The five patterns of organization that writers use most often are **cause and effect, chronological order, comparison and contrast, listing,** and **problem solution.** Some texts contain just one pattern; others combine two or more patterns. The following guidelines can help you analyze text structure:

1. Look for words that hint at a specific pattern of organization. (See *Cause and Effect*, *Chronological Order*, and *Comparison* and *Contrast*.)
2. Look for important ideas. See whether these ideas are connected in an obvious pattern.
3. Draw a graphic organizer that shows how the text is structured. Compare your graphic organizer with the following five diagrams, which illustrate the most common text structures.

A **cause-and-effect pattern** focuses on the relationship between causes and effects. The **causal chain** below shows how the city of Pompeii was destroyed.

Causal Chain

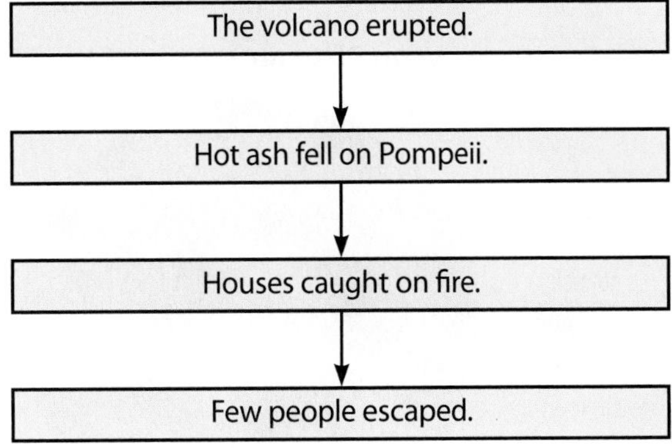

Chronological order shows events in the order in which they happen. The **sequence chain** below is a list of steps for making salsa.

Sequence Chain

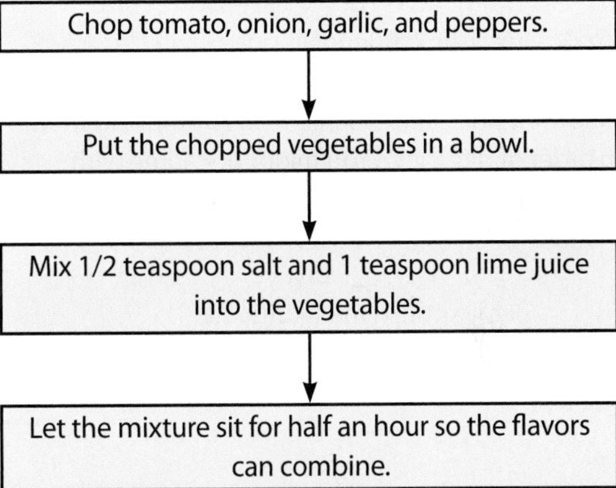

A **comparison-and-contrast** pattern focuses on similarities and differences between things. The Venn diagram below compares and contrasts Mary's and Roger's experiences during Ta-Na-E-Ka (page 359).

Venn Diagram

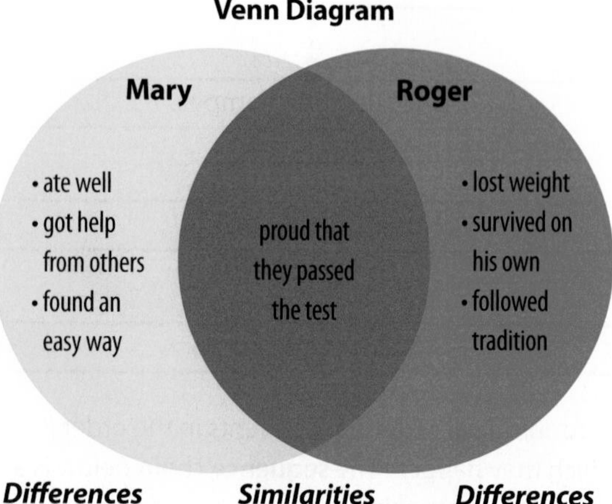

An **enumeration** or **list pattern** organizes information in a list by order of importance, size, or location or by another order that makes sense. The list below organizes after-school jobs by ranking them in order of difficulty. (You might not agree with this order!)

List

1. Baby-sitting (most difficult)
2. Walking dogs
3. Lawn and garden work

A **problem-solution pattern** focuses on a problem and solutions to the problem. The cluster below shows a problem and some possible solutions:

Cluster

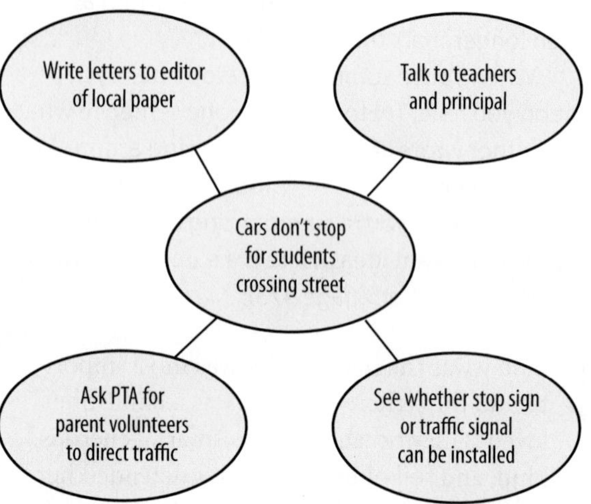

See page 827

See also *Cause and Effect, Chronological Order, Comparison and Contrast.*

Spelling Handbook

COMMONLY MISSPELLED WORDS

Some words that cause spelling problems need to be memorized. The list of fifty "demons" below contains words that you should be able to spell automatically, without pause. Note the letters that are underlined. These letters are the ones that students most often miss when attempting to spell each word correctly.

Fifty Spelling Demons				
ache	cough	guess	ready	though
again	could	half	said	through
always	country	hour	says	tired
answer	doctor	instead	seems	tonight
blue	does	knew	shoes	trouble
built	don't	know	since	wear
busy	early	laid	straight	where
buy	easy	minute	sugar	women
can't	every	often	sure	won't
color	friend	once	tear	write

ONE HUNDRED SPELLING WORDS

The list that follows includes words that you should know. They are grouped by tens so that you may study them group by group. Again, the underlining points out places in the words that may give you the most trouble.

One Hundred Spelling Words				
absence	century	explanation	myth	rumor
achieve	choice	fantasy	nuclear	safe
adjective	communicate	faucet	occurrence	seize
advertisement	conservation	fiction	ounce	separate
against	constitution	fourth	passage	similar
aisles	courteous	gasoline	pesticide	solar
angle	criticism	gene	physical	solemn
apology	curiosity	genuine	pieces	species
arithmetic	decimal	grammar	poisonous	surface
assignment	delicate	height	popularity	temporary
autobiography	disguise	heir	population	theme
average	divide	humorous	practice	tragedy
bacteria	early	imitation	preferred	treasure
ballad	ecology	interview	prejudice	trial
benefit	eighth	legislature	pyramid	tropical
brief	environment	liter	recipe	vegetable
brilliant	equipment	magazine	remainder	veil
career	exact	medicine	rescue	weapon
careless	excellent	message	resources	wonder
ceased	experience	musician	review	wrestle

The Reference Section

Every library has materials you can use only in the library. Some examples are listed below. (Some reference works are available in both print and electronic form.)

Encyclopedias
- *Collier's Encyclopedia*
- *The World Book Encyclopedia*

General Biographical References
- *Current Biography Yearbook*
- *The International Who's Who*
- *Webster's New Biographical Dictionary*

Special Biographical References
- *American Men & Women of Science*
- *Biographical Dictionary of American Sports*
- *Mexican American Biographies*

Atlases
- *Atlas of World Cultures*
- *National Geographic Atlas of the World*

Almanacs
- *Information Please Almanac*
- *The World Almanac and Book of Facts*

Books of Quotations
- *Bartlett's Familiar Quotations*

Books of Synonyms
- *Roget's International Thesaurus*
- *Webster's New Dictionary of Synonyms*

Research Strategies

Using a Media Center or Library

To find a book, audiotape, film, or video in a library, start by looking in the **catalog.** Most libraries use an **online,** or computer, **catalog.**

Online catalogs vary from library to library. With some you begin searching for resources by **title, author,** or **subject.** With others you simply enter **keywords** for the subject you're researching. With either system, you enter information into the computer and a new screen will show you a list of materials or subject headings relating to your request. When you find an item you want, write down the title, author, and **call number,** the code of numbers and letters that shows you where to find the item on the library's shelves.

Some libraries still use card catalogs. A **card catalog** is a collection of index cards arranged in alphabetical order by title and author. Nonfiction is also cataloged by subject.

ELECTRONIC DATABASES.

Electronic databases are collections of information you can access by computer. You can use these databases to find such resources as encyclopedias, almanacs, and museum art collections.

There are two kinds of electronic databases: **Online databases** are accessed at a computer terminal connected to a modem. The modem allows the computer to communicate with other computers over telephone lines. **Portable databases** are available on CD-ROM.

A **CD-ROM** (compact disc-read only memory) is played on a computer equipped with a CD-ROM player. If you were to look up *Maya Angelou* on a CD-ROM guide to literature, for example, you could see and hear her reading passages from her books and also read critical analyses of her work.

- **Periodicals.** Most libraries have a collection of magazines and newspapers. To find up-to-date magazine or newspaper articles on a topic, use a computerized index, such as *InfoTrac* or *EBSCO.* Some of these indices provide a summary of each article. Others provide the entire text, which you can read on-screen or print out. *The Readers' Guide to Periodical Literature* is a print index of articles that have appeared in hundreds of magazines.

Using the Internet

The **Internet** is a huge network of computers. Libraries, news services, government agencies, researchers, and organizations communicate and share information on the Net. The Net also lets you chat online with students around the world. For help in using the Internet to do research or to communicate with someone by computer, explore the options on the following page.

The World Wide Web

The easiest way to do research on the Internet is on the World Wide Web. On the Web, information is stored in colorful, easy-to-access files called **Web pages.** Web pages usually have text, graphics, photographs, sound, and even video clips.

USING A WEB BROWSER.

You look at Web pages with a **Web browser,** a program for accessing information on the Web. Every page on the Web has its own address, called a **URL,** or Uniform Resource Locator. If you know the address of a Web page you want to go to, just enter it in the location field on your browser.

Hundreds of millions of Web pages are connected by **hyperlinks,** which let you jump from one page to another. These links usually appear as underlined or colored words or images, or both, on your computer screen. With hundreds of millions of linked Web pages, how can you find the information you want?

USING A WEB DIRECTORY.

If you're just beginning to look for a research topic, click on a **Web directory,** a list of topics and subtopics created by experts to help users find Web sites. Think of the directory as a giant index. Start by choosing a broad category, such as Literature. Then, work your way down through the subtopics, perhaps from Poetry to Poets. Under Poets, choose a Web page that looks interesting, perhaps one on Robert Frost.

USING A SEARCH ENGINE.

If you already have a topic and need information about it, try using a **search engine,** a software tool that finds information on the Web. To use a search engine, just go to an online search form and enter a **search term,** or keyword. The search engine will return a list of Web pages containing your search term. The list will also show you the first few lines of each page.

You've Got Mail!

E-mail is an electronic message sent over a computer network. On the Internet you can use e-mail to reach institutions, businesses, and individuals. When you e-mail places like museums, you may be able to ask **experts** about a topic you're researching. You can also use e-mail to chat with students around the country and around the world.

Internet forums, or newsgroups, let you discuss and debate lots of subjects with other computer users. You can write and send a question to a forum and get an answer from someone who may (or may not) know something about your topic.

Techno Tip

- If you get too few hits, use a more general word or phrase as your search term.
- If you get too many hits, use a more specific word or phrase as your search term.

Common Top-level Domains and What They Stand For	
.edu	Educational institution. Site may publish scholarly work or the work of elementary or high school students.
.gov	Government body. Information should be reliable.

Common Top-level Domains and What They Stand For	
.org	Usually a nonprofit organization. If the organization promotes culture (as a museum does), information is generally reliable; if it advocates a cause, information may be biased.
.com	Commercial enterprise. Information should be evaluated carefully.
.net	Organization offering Internet services.

Common Search Operators and What They Do	
AND	Demands that both terms appear on the page; narrows search
+	Demands that both terms appear on the page; narrows search
OR	Yields pages that contain either term; widens search
NOT	Excludes a word from consideration; narrows search
–	Excludes a word from consideration; narrows search
NEAR	Demands that two words be close together; narrows search
ADJ	Demands that two words be close together; narrows search
" "	Demands an exact phrase; narrows search

A search term such as *Frost* may produce thousands of results, or **hits,** including weather data on frost. If you're doing a search on the poet Robert Frost, most of these thousands of hits will be of no use. To find useful material, you have to narrow your search.

REFINING A KEYWORD SEARCH.
To focus your research, use **search operators,** such as the words AND or NOT, to create a string of keywords. If you're looking for material on Robert Frost and his life in Vermont, for example, you might enter the following search terms:

Frost AND Vermont NOT weather

The more focused search term yields pages that contain both *Frost* and *Vermont* and nothing about weather. The chart at the bottom left explains how several search operators work.

Evaluating Web Sources

Since anyone—you, for example—can publish a Web page, it's important to evaluate your sources. Use these criteria to evaluate a source:

AUTHORITY.
Who is the author? What is his or her knowledge or experience? Trust respected sources, such as the Smithsonian Institution, not a person's newsletter or home page.

ACCURACY.
How trustworthy is the information? Does the author give his or her sources? Check information from one site against information from at least two other sites or print sources.

OBJECTIVITY.
What is the author's **perspective,** or point of view? Find out whether the information provider has a bias or a hidden purpose.

CURRENCY.
Is the information up-to-date? For a print source, check the copyright date. For a Web source, look for the date on which the page was created or revised. (This date appears at the bottom of the site's home page.)

COVERAGE.
How well does the source cover the topic? Could you find better information in a book? Compare the source with several others.

Listing Sources and Taking Notes

When you write a research paper, you must **document,** or identify, your sources so that readers will know where you found your material. You must avoid **plagiarism,** or presenting another writer's words or ideas as if they were your own.

Listing Sources

List each source, and give it a number. (You'll use these source numbers later, when you take notes.) Here's where to find the publication information (such as the name of the publisher and the copyright date) you'll need for different types of sources:

- **Print sources.** Look at the title and copyright pages of the book or periodical.
- **Online sources.** Look at the beginning or end of the document or in a separate electronic file. For a Web page, look for a link containing the word *About.*
- **Portable electronic databases.** Look at the start-up screen, the packaging, or the disk itself.

There are several ways to list sources. The chart on page 887 shows the style created by the Modern Language Association.

Taking Notes

Here are some tips for taking notes:

- Put notes from different sources on separate index cards or sheets of paper or in separate computer files.
- At the top of each card, sheet of paper, or file, write a label that briefly gives the subject of the note.
- At the bottom, write the numbers of the pages on which you found the information.
- Use short phrases, and make lists of details and ideas. You don't have to write full sentences.
- Use your own words unless you find material you want to quote. If you quote an author's exact words, put quotation marks around them.
- Include in your notes opinions from experts and analogies (or comparisons to more familiar topics or situations).
- Take notes from a variety of sources, including those with different perspectives, or opinions, on your topic.

Techno Tip

To evaluate a Web source, look at the top-level domain in the URL. Here is a sample URL with the top-level domain—a government agency—labeled.

top-level domain

http://www.loc.gov

Sample Note Card

Bradbury on Education 3

—Teach "tools" of reading & writing at gr. K–2; no Internet till gr. 3

—"Teach students to be in love with life, to love their work, to create at the top of their lungs." p. F1

The sample note card above shows how to take notes.

Preparing a List of Sources

Use your source cards to make a **works cited** list at the end of your report. List your sources in alphabetical order, following the MLA guidelines for citing sources (see the chart on the next page). Note the sample that follows:

Works Cited

"Bradbury, Ray." The World Book Encyclopedia. 2003 ed.

Geirland, John. "Interview with Ray Bradbury." The Fresno Bee 3 Jan. 1999: F1.

Mogen, David. Ray Bradbury. New York: Macmillan, 1986.

The chart on the next page shows citations of print, audiovisual, and electronic sources.

MLA Guidelines for Citing Sources	
Books	Give the author, title, city of publication, publisher, and copyright year. Mogen, David. Ray Bradbury. New York: Macmillan, 1986.
Magazine and newspaper articles	Give the author, title of the article, name of the magazine or newspaper, date, and page numbers. Geirland, John. "Interview with Ray Bradbury." The Fresno Bee 3 Jan. 1999: F1.
Encyclopedia articles	Give the author (if named), title of the article, name of the encyclopedia, and edition (year). "Bradbury, Ray." The World Book Encyclopedia. 2003 ed.
Films, videotapes, and audiotapes	Give the title, producer or director, or medium, distributor, and year of release. Ray Bradbury: Tales of Fantasy. Listening. Library Productions. Audiocassette. Filmic Archives, 1992.
CD-ROMs and DVDs	In many cases, not all the information is available. Fill in what you can. Give the author, title of document or article; database title; publication medium (use the term *CD-ROM* or *DVD*); city of publication; publisher; date. "Science Fiction." Britannica Student Encyclopedia 2004. DVD. Chicago: Encyclopaedia Britannica, 2004.
Online sources	In many cases, not all the information is available. Fill in what you can. Give the author, title of document or article; title of complete work or database; name of editor; publication date or date last revised; name of sponsoring organization; date you accessed the site; the full URL in angle brackets. Jepsen, Chris. *Ray Bradbury Online.* 2001. 20 Dec. 2003. <http://www.spacecity.com/bradbury/bradbury/>.

Proofreaders' Marks		
Symbol	**Example**	**Meaning**
≡	New mexico	Capitalize lowercase letter.
/	next Spring	Lowercase capital letter.
^	a book ^of quotations	Insert.
ℓ	A good good idea	Delete.
⁀‿	a grape fruit tree	Close up space.
∿	doesn't	Change order (of letters or words).
¶	¶ "Who's there?" she asked.	Begin a new paragraph.
⊙	Please don't forget ⊙	Add a period.
^,	Maya, did you call me?	Add a comma.
^:	Dear Mrs. Mills :	Add a colon.
^;	Columbus, Ohio; Dallas, Texas	Add a semicolon.
" "	"Are you OK?" he asked.	Add quotation marks.

Media Handbook

Analyzing Propaganda on TV

Persuasive messages are everywhere—in essays, letters, and speeches. You also find them in television, radio, and movies. The persuasive messages you listen to and view usually contain *persuasive techniques* or *propaganda techniques.* **Persuasive techniques** convince an audience by providing sound reasons. These reasons persuade through strong, relevant supporting evidence. **Propaganda techniques,** though, appeal primarily to an audience's emotions and may contain false or misleading information. When you unquestioningly listen to or view messages that contain propaganda techniques, you may make poor decisions. The information presented here will help you identify persuasive and propaganda techniques, including false and misleading information. These skills will help you make well-informed decisions when watching TV.

Persuasive Techniques

To be persuasive, you must make sense. Signs of persuasive techniques include

- a clearly stated opinion, or claim
- logical reasons for the opinion supported by relevant evidence
- an appeal to the interests and backgrounds of a particular audience

Watch for these signs as you view, but don't automatically accept a message that includes them. First, check for propaganda techniques.

Propaganda Techniques

Propaganda techniques appeal more to your emotions than to common sense or logic. Like persuasive techniques, they are used to convince you to think, feel, or act a certain way. The difference is that a **propagandist,** a person who uses propaganda techniques, does not want you to think critically about the message.

For example, when you hear the name of a product or see its logo associated with your favorite football team, your excitement about that team is being used to sell that product. If you connect your excitement about the team with the product enough times, this propaganda technique, known as **transfer,** may eventually persuade you to buy the product. Your decision would be based not on logical reasons for buying the product but on your emotional response to the propaganda technique.

A persuasive message that includes propaganda techniques may be sound—as long as it also provides strong and accurate supporting evidence. The term *propaganda* describes a message that relies too heavily on any particular idea. Propaganda may also contain false or misleading information. (See pages 616–619.)

The chart on the next page gives definitions and examples of other common propaganda techniques found in television ads and programs. As you watch TV, look for the given clues to identify these techniques in every kind of programming you watch.

False and Misleading Information

As you know, a propagandist counts on you to be led by your emotions and not by your intelligence. Even if you wanted to think critically about a propagandist's message, you would not have much to go on because propaganda is so strongly **biased.** That is, it favors one point of view and ignores information that supports another point of view. Here are some signals that a persuasive message contains misleading information:

PRESENTING OPINIONS AS FACTS **Opinions** are beliefs, judgments, or claims that cannot be tested and proved true. Watch out for opinions presented as if they were facts. For example, a news report may quote an expert who says, "Space exploration is necessary for the future of human survival." How could such a statement be proved? Opinions presented as facts and not supported with evidence

Propaganda Techniques Used on Television		
Techniques	**Clues**	**Examples**
Bandwagon tries to convince you to do something or believe something because everyone else does.	Listen for slogans that use the words *everyone, everybody, all,* or in some cases, *nobody*.	While being interviewed on a talk show, an author might encourage viewers to join the thousands of other people who have benefited from his new diet book.
Loaded language uses words with strongly positive or negative meanings.	Listen for strongly positive or negative words, such as *perfect* or *terrible*.	*Wake-up Juice is a fantastic way to start your day!*
Product placement uses brand-name products as part of the scenery. The products' companies may pay producers for this seemingly unintended advertising.	As you watch TV, keep your eyes peeled for clearly visible brand names. Ask yourself if the brand names have anything to do with the plot of the show.	In the middle of a TV movie, an actor may drink a bottle of juice. The juice is not an important part of the plot, but the brand name of the juice is clearly visible.
Snob appeal suggests that a viewer can be special or part of a special group if he or she agrees with an idea or buys a product.	Listen for words such as *exclusive, best*, or *quality*. Look for images of wealth, such as big houses, expensive cars, and fancy boats.	*Treat your cat like a queen; give her the cat food preferred exclusively by discriminating cats.*
Symbols associate the power and meaning of a cultural symbol with a product or idea.	Look for flags, team mascots, state flowers, or any other symbol that people view with pride.	A political candidate might use a national flag as a backdrop for a speech on TV.
Testimonials use knowledgeable or famous people to endorse a product or idea.	Look for famous actors, athletes, politicians, and experts. Listen for their names or titles as well.	*TV star Zen Williams actively supports alternative-energy research—shouldn't you?*

can be misleading.

MISSING INFORMATION A persuasive message may downplay or leave out negative information. For example, car commercials often downplay the high price of the car. Instead, the commercials focus on the comfort, design, speed, and other positive features of the car.

To avoid believing false information, consider the source of any fact or statistic. An authoritative source such as a respected research institution—for example, the Smithsonian Institution—probably provides accurate facts. If the information comes from a source you suspect may be strongly biased—for example, an oil company providing information that "proves" environmental regulations don't work—look for a more reliable source that can confirm the facts before you accept them.

Analyzing False and Misleading Information

The following steps will help you identify and analyze examples of false and misleading information on TV:

Step 1 Focus on a specific program or advertisement. Briefly describe the message you have chosen and how it makes you feel. You might pick an interview on a talk show, a segment of a newscast, a sports broadcast, or a commercial shown during your favorite TV program.

Step 2 Identify the main message or claim of the program or ad.

Step 3 Ask yourself, "Is the claim a fact, which can be proved true, or is it someone's opinion?" Remember that scientific-sounding words do not necessarily point to factual information.

Step 4 Ask yourself, "What is missing from the message?" Is there any information you still do not know after watching the program or advertisement? Are there other parts of the event, product, service, or idea that were not presented?

Step 5 Using your answers from the previous questions, decide whether or not you think the TV program or advertisement is misleading. Explain your answer.

Using Electronic Texts to Locate Information

Types of Electronic Texts

When you think of electronic sources of information, your first thought may be the Internet, but do not limit your searches to the Web alone. Explore the other electronic options at your library—the online library catalog, library databases, encyclopedias on CD-ROM, even e-mail. To choose the best source for your search, consider the purposes and limitations of each type of electronic text listed at right.

ONLINE LIBRARY CATALOG

Purpose: The online catalog will tell you whether a book is available for checkout and where in the library the book is located.

Limitation: If your library's collection is small, you may not find much information in the catalog.

CD-ROM ENCYCLOPEDIA

Purpose: Use a CD-ROM encyclopedia for the same purpose as a printed encyclopedia. The only difference is that, using a CD-ROM, you can more easily move from one entry to another than you might with a large set of printed encyclopedias.

Limitation: Like a printed encyclopedia, a CD-ROM encyclopedia may not include the most up-to-date information, depending on the date of the edition you are using.

LIBRARY DATABASES

Purpose: A periodical index is a good place to start (and narrow) your search. It can direct you to the specific issue of a periodical that contains the information you need.

Limitation: A database may include listings for a large pool of books or periodicals; you might find a listing for an interesting book but not find a copy of the book in your library.

WEB SITES

Purpose: The variety of sites available can help you find many different perspectives on your topic.

Limitation: Web sites are not checked for accuracy. Try to stick with sites sponsored by trustworthy organizations, which often have addresses ending in *edu*, *gov*, or *org*.

E-MAIL

Purpose: You can use e-mail to ask experts directly for information.

Limitation: Like Web sites, e-mail does not necessarily provide accurate information. Make sure anyone you consult really does know about your topic.

Features of Electronic Texts

When you search most types of electronic text for information, you need to think of a *keyword*. A **keyword** is a word or phrase, such as *giant panda*, that identifies your specific topic. You may need to experiment with keywords in order to find the information you need. Any time you use an electronic source, be prepared to think of all the ways your topic might be listed in order to get the most useful information.

Each type of electronic text is organized in a slightly different manner. To use electronic texts effectively, you need to understand the features of each type of text and the methods for using each type. Here are examples of four different types of electronic texts along with descriptions, explanations, and search tips:

ELECTRONIC ENCYCLOPEDIA You might find this record by typing the keyword *panda* in the encyclopedia's search box:

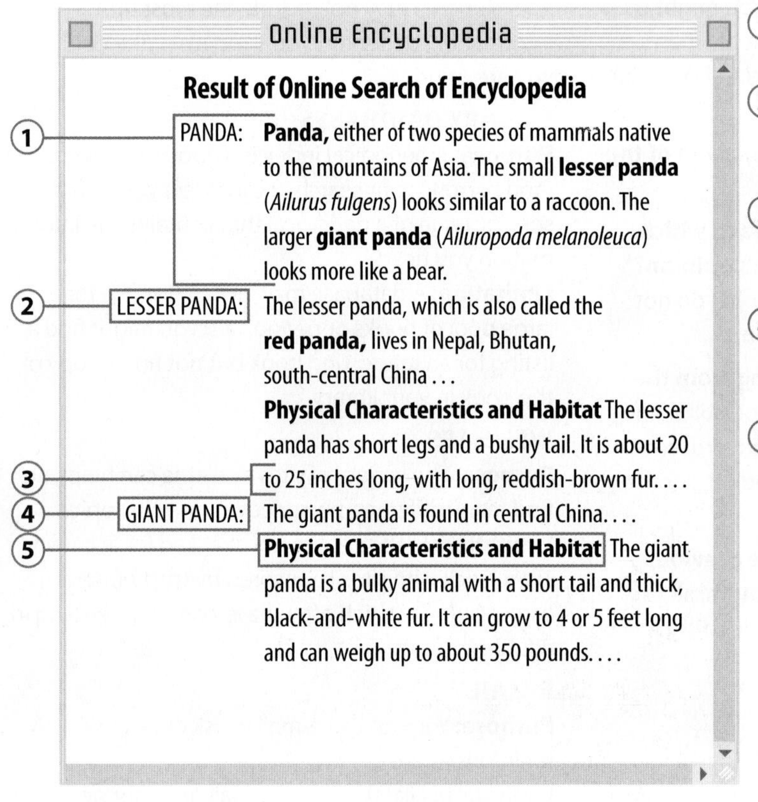

Online Encyclopedia
Result of Online Search of Encyclopedia
1
PANDA: Panda, either of two species of mammals native to the mountains of Asia. The small lesser panda (Ailurus fulgens) looks similar to a raccoon. The larger giant panda (Ailuropoda melanoleuca) looks more like a bear.
2
LESSER PANDA: The lesser panda, which is also called the red panda, lives in Nepal, Bhutan, south-central China . . .
Physical Characteristics and Habitat The lesser panda has short legs and a bushy tail. It is about 20
3
to 25 inches long, with long, reddish-brown fur. . . .
4
GIANT PANDA: The giant panda is found in central China. . . .
5
Physical Characteristics and Habitat The giant panda is a bulky animal with a short tail and thick, black-and-white fur. It can grow to 4 or 5 feet long and can weigh up to about 350 pounds. . . .

1. **First search result** finds two different entries about pandas.
2. **Heading** for the entry about the first type of panda, the lesser panda
3. Since you are interested in pandas with black-and-white fur, skip to the next entry.
4. **Heading** for the entry about the second type of panda, the giant panda
5. **Subheadings** introduce smaller sections of the entry. As you read, take notes. You can search for additional information by using details, such as names of places pandas inhabit, as keywords.

WEB SITE You can use a *directory* or a *search engine* to find Web sites relevant to your search. A **directory** organizes sites into categories, such as Sports. Each category is then broken down into smaller and smaller categories to help you narrow your search. A **search engine** allows you to type in your keyword and then provides you with a list of Web sites that include your keyword. In searching for information on giant pandas, you can eliminate irrelevant listings in most search engines by

- putting the words *giant panda* in quotation marks to find sites that include those words, next to each other and in that order
- using *AND* to find sites that include two terms (though not necessarily right next to each other), such as *computer AND games*
- using *NOT* to rule out irrelevant sites that commonly come up using your keyword. For example, in searching for sites on the human heart, you can eliminate the sites on romance by searching for *heart NOT love.*

Here is an example of a Web page in a browser frame:

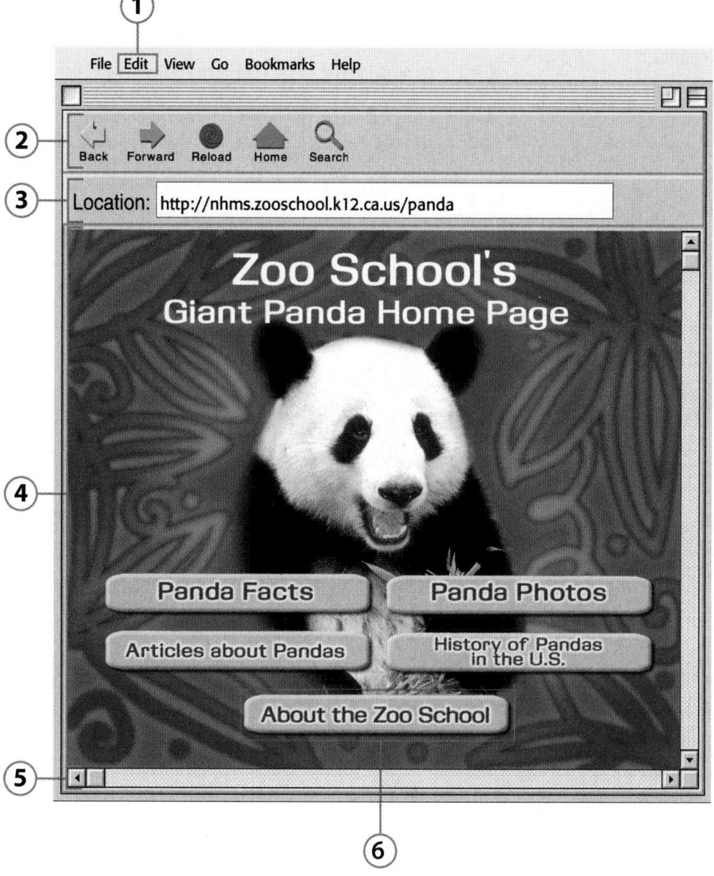

1. **Pull-down menu buttons** allow you to perform a variety of functions. Use the Find command on the pull-down Edit menu to locate quickly individual uses of a word in a text-heavy Web page.
2. **Toolbar buttons** help you navigate the Web.
3. The **Uniform Resource Locator** (URL) is the address of the Web page.
4. **Content area** of the Web page contains text, photos, and sometimes audio or video clips.
5. The horizontal and vertical **scroll bars** allow you to move side-to-side or up and down on a Web page.
6. When you click on underlined text or **hyperlink** buttons, your browser jumps to another part of the current page, a different page on the same Web site, or a page on a different Web site.

ONLINE LIBRARY CATALOG Like a traditional card catalog, an online catalog allows you to search for books and other information in a library by author, title, or subject. In most cases, when you are doing research, you will search by subject. Look at the example of a subject entry below:

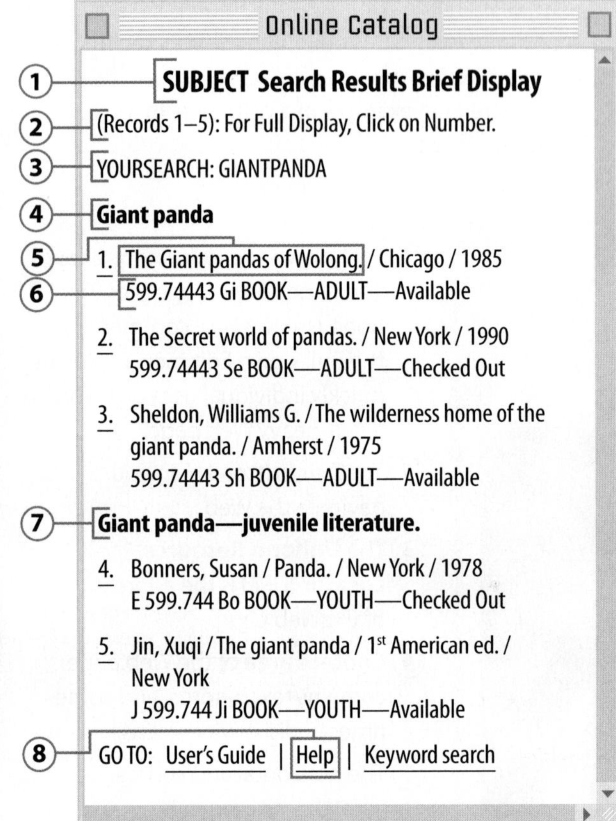

1. This line shows what kind of search (title, author, or subject) you performed. "Brief Display" means that just the basic information about each book is listed here.
2. Click on the number next to a listing to bring up a record containing more detailed information about the book.
3. The keyword you entered is noted here.
4. This is the first subject heading that matches your search request. (Compare it with item 7 below.)
5. This is the title of the first book on the subject of giant pandas.
6. This line notes the book's **call number,** which indicates where in the library the book is located and tells whether the book is available for checkout.
7. This next subject heading starts a section of children's books about giant pandas.
8. Click on the Help button for instructions on using the library catalog. If on-screen help or an instruction sheet is not available, ask a librarian for help.

DATABASE RECORD FROM A PERIODICAL INDEX Your library may carry hundreds of periodicals containing articles on every subject you can imagine. To search efficiently for articles about a particular topic in magazines, newspapers, or journals, refer to an online periodical index. You can search a periodical index, such as the *Readers' Guide to Periodical Literature,* to find a listing of magazine articles that fit your subject keyword. An example of a search result appears below.

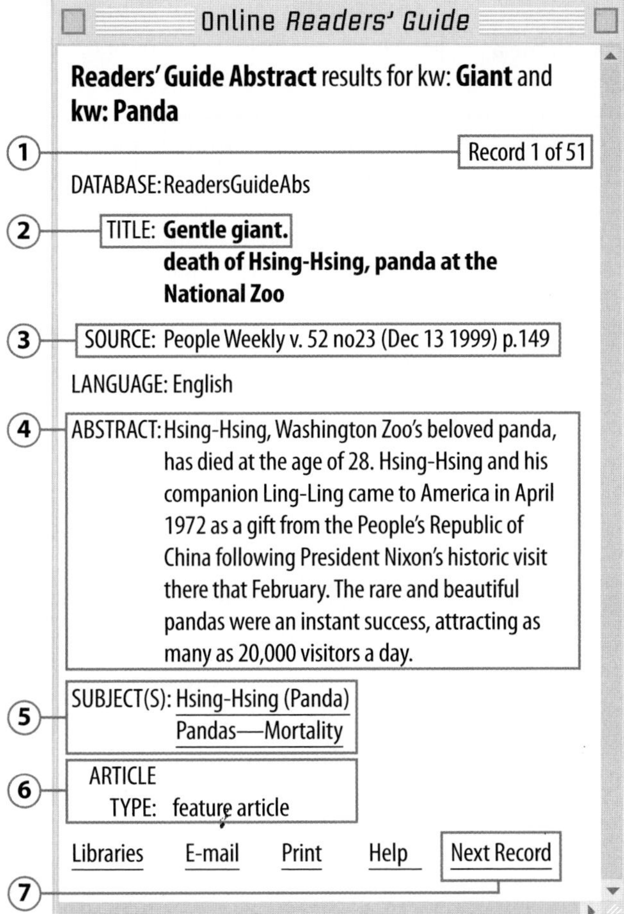

1. Your search for the keywords ("kw") *Giant* and *Panda* produced 51 records. This is the first record in the database.
2. Each line in a database is called a *field.* The **title field** contains the title of an article about giant pandas.
3. The **source field** indicates the name, issue number, and page number of the magazine in which the article was published.
4. An **abstract** gives you a summary of the article's contents.
5. The database shows **additional subject** headings related to your search.
6. Examining the **type of article** will also help you decide if the article will be useful for your research.
7. To see information about the next article that fits your search, click on the words *Next Record.*

Language Handbook

1. The Parts of Speech

Part of Speech	Definition	Examples
NOUN	**1a. A noun is a word used to name a person, a place, a thing, or an idea.**	
common noun	a general name for a person, place, thing, or idea	grandmother [person], home [place], tree [thing], courage [idea]
proper noun	names a particular person, place, thing, or idea, and always begins with a capital letter	Maya Angelou, Cascade Range, Tuesday, "The Fun They Had"
collective noun	names a group	team, band, crew
compound noun	two or more words combined and used together as a single noun	matchstick (match+ stick) [one word] flea collar [separate words] two-thirds [hyphenated word]
PRONOUN	**1b. A pronoun is a word used in place of one or more nouns or pronouns.**	When Bailey heard the elders' unkind words, **he** spoke up.
personal pronoun	• refers to the one speaking (first person), the one spoken to (second person), or the one spoken about (third person) • either singular (one) or plural (more than one)	**First Person:** • Singular: I, me, my, mine • Plural: we, us, our, ours **Second Person:** • Singular: you, your, yours • Plural: you, your, yours **Third Person:** • Singular: he, she, it, him, her, hers, its • Plural: they, them, their, theirs
reflexive pronoun	• refers to the subject and directs the action of the verb back to the subject • either singular or plural	**First Person:** myself, ourselves **Second Person:** yourself, yourselves **Third Person:** himself, herself, itself, themselves Frances Hodgson Burnett made **herself** a promise when her son died.

Part of Speech	Definition	Examples
intensive pronoun	• emphasizes a noun or another pronoun • either singular or plural • has the same form as a reflexive pronoun	**First Person:** myself, ourselves **Second Person:** yourself, yourselves **Third Person:** himself, herself, itself, themselves The artist carved the frame **himself.** [emphasizes that he alone did it]
indefinite pronoun	refers to a person, a place, or a thing that is not specifically named	All, any, both, each, either, everything, few, many, none, no one, nobody, one, several, some, somebody
relative pronoun	introduces a subordinate clause: *that, what, which, who, whom, whose*	Edgar Allan Poe wrote of thoughts and feelings **that** he had. She is the actress **who** won the award.
demonstrative pronoun	points out a person, a place, a thing, or an idea: *this, that, these, those*	**This** is a scrapbook of her clippings and reviews.
interrogative pronoun	introduces a question: *what, which, who, whom, whose*	**What** were Poe's thoughts and feel-
ADJECTIVE	**1c. An adjective is a word used to modify a noun or a pronoun. An adjective tells *what kind, which one, how many,* or *how much.***	*what kind:* **tired** dog, **pretty** girl *which one:* **first** one, **that** year *how many or:* **few** others, **fifty** people, *how much:* **only** half
definite article	refers to someone or something in particular: *the*	**The** story "Storm" is on **the** summer reading list.
indefinite article	• refers to someone or something in general: *a, an* • *a* before words that begin with consonants; *an* before words that begin with vowels (*a, e, i, o, u*)	**a** cat; **an** umbrella; **an** early sunrise
proper adjective	• formed from a proper noun • begins with a capital letter	**Alaskan** king crab [from the proper noun *Alaska*] ancient **Greek** myths[from the proper noun *Greece*]
demonstrative adjective	• modifies a noun or pronoun: *this, that, these, those* • called a **demonstrative pronoun** when used alone [see *Pronouns*]	Is **this** dog Storm? **Those** dogs are strong. **That** is the way to bake a pie. **These** are common foods in Vietnam.
nouns used as adjectives	refers to a noun that modifies another noun	**wood** stove; **jury** room; **New York** minute

Part of Speech	Definition	Examples
VERB	**1d.** **A verb is a word used to express action or state of being.**	
ACTION VERB	**1e.** **An action verb expresses physical or mental action. There are two types of action verbs:** *transitive* **and** *intransitive.*	PHYSICAL ACTION build, climb, yell, speak, wash MENTAL ACTION plan, think, feel, imagine, remember
transitive verb	• expresses an action directed toward a person or thing • The action passes from the doer (the subject) to the receiver of the action. Words that receive the action are called **objects.**	She **climbed** the tree. [The action of *climbed* is directed toward *tree.*] She **wrote** "The Tree House." [*"The Tree House"* is the object of the verb *wrote.*]
intransitive verb	expresses action (or tells something about the subject) without passing the action to a receiver	She **climbed** carefully. [The action of *climbed* has no object; *carefully* tells how she climbed.]
LINKING VERB	**1f.** **A linking verb links, or connects, the subject with a noun, a pronoun, or an adjective in the predicate.**	
	• common linking verbs formed from the verb *be: am, are, being, is, was, been, may be, would be, should have been, will have been, has been, will be, was being, can be, must be* • other linking verbs: *appear, grow, seem, stay, become, look, smell, taste, feel, remain, sound, turn*	One of her best friends **was** Leah. [The linking verb *was* links *friends* and *Leah.*] The writer **was** he. [writer = he] That day, she **became** an enemy. [The linking verb *became* links *she* and *enemy.*] The actor **looks** amused. [actor = amused] The room **smells** fresh. [room = fresh]
HELPING VERB	**1g.** **A helping verb (auxiliary verb) helps the main verb to express an action or a state of being.**	
	A helping verb joins with a main verb to form a **verb phrase.** • forms of *be: am, is, being, was, are, been, is, were* • forms of *do: do, does, did* • forms of *have: have, has, had* • other helping verbs: *can, may, must, should, would, could, might, shall, will*	She **is** crying. [*is* = helping verb; *crying* = main verb; *is crying* = verb phrase.] He **did** sing the song. [*did* = helping verb; *sing* = main verb; *did sing* = verb phrase] She **has** gone to the theater. [*has* = helping verb; *gone* = main verb; *has gone* = verb phrase] He **might** train the horse to race. [*might* = helping verb; *train* = main verb; *might train* = verb phrase]

Part of Speech	Definition	Examples
ADVERB	**1h. An adverb is a word used to modify a verb, an adjective, or another adverb.**	
	• Adverbs tell *where, when, how,* or *to what extent (how much* or *how long).*	**WHERE?** The outlaws took them **away.** [*away* modifies the verb *took*] **WHEN? Then** they released their arrows. [*then* modifies the verb *released*] **HOW?** The crowd become **intensely** quiet. [*intensely* modifies the adjective *quiet*] **TO WHAT EXTENT? Very** soon, there would be war. [*very* modifies the adverb *soon*]
	• Adverbs may come before, after, or between the words they modify.	**BEFORE** **Slowly**, the sun was sinking in the sky. **AFTER** The sun was sinking **slowly** in the sky. **BETWEEN** The sun was **slowly** sinking in the sky.
	• The word *not* is an adverb. When *not* is part of a contraction like *hadn't, the –n't* is an adverb.	The sun had **not** risen yet. The sun had**n't** risen yet.
PREPOSITION	**1i. A preposition is a word used to show the relationship of a noun or pronoun to another word in the sentence.**	
	• commonly used prepositions: *about, above, across, against, around, before, below, beside, between, from, in, in front of, in spite of, into, out of, over, past, since, with* • A **prepositional phrase** begins with a preposition and ends with a noun or pronoun, called the **object of the preposition.** A preposition may have more than one object.	Notice how a change in the preposition changes the relationship between the snake and the chair in each sentence. A snake is **on** your chair. A snake is **under** your chair. A snake is **next to** your chair. A snake is **near** your chair.
	• The prepositional phrase includes any modifiers of the object of the preposition.	Rattlesnakes can be found **in the desert.** Rattlesnakes can be found **in the desert or on the forest floor.**

Part of Speech	Definition	Examples
CONJUNCTION	**1j. A conjunction is a word used to join words or groups of words.**	
coordinating conjunction	connects words or groups of words used in the same way: *and, but, or, nor, for, so, yet*	Have you ever heard of Buck Jones, Tom Tyler, **or** Hoot Gibson? Did you buy the cards **and** get a present for Papi?
correlative conjunction	pairs of conjunctions that connect words or groups of words used in the same way: *both . . . and, either . . . or, neither . . . nor, not only . . . but also, whether . . . or*	**Both** the trumpet **and** the trombone are brass instruments. [*both . . . and* joins two nouns] John **both** plays keyboards **and** writes songs. [*both . . . and* joins two verbs, *plays* and *writes*] **Either** John would play the piano, **or** he would be out of work. [*either . . . or* joins two complete ideas] I, on the other hand, sing **neither** strongly **nor well.** [*neither . . . nor* joins two adverbs]
INTERJECTION	**1k. An interjection is a word used to express emotion.**	
	• An interjection is usually followed by an exclamation point or set off by a comma. • Common interjections: *aw, hooray, oh, oops, ouch, well, whew, wow, yippee*	**Oh!** Is that a President Cleveland card? **Wow!** This must be your lucky day! **Well,** at least one good thing happened today.

Your Turn Using Parts of Speech

Rewrite the following paragraph. Replace vague nouns and adjectives with concrete ones. Replacethe verb be or dull action verbs with vivid action verbs. Reword sentences to eliminate the adverb *very* without losing descriptive meaning.

Hot and tired from playing a game, the boy was very thirsty. He went into the house and was very surprised to find a wild animal sitting on an item of furniture and eating a piece of fruit. The boy was still for a minute or two. Then he got a drink and went next to the animal..

2. Agreement

Number

Number is the form of a word that indicates whether the word is singular or plural.

2a. A *singular* word refers to one person, place, thing, or idea. A *plural* word refers to more than one.

SINGULAR	road	goat	child	he	each
PLURAL	roads	goats	children	they	all

AGREEMENT OF SUBJECT AND VERB

2b. A verb agrees with its subject in number. Singular subjects take singular verbs. Plural subjects take plural verbs. The first helping verb in a verb phrase must agree with its subject.

SINGULAR **Hanukkah comes** once a year.

PLURAL Isaac Bashevis Singer's **stories celebrate** ordinary life.

PROBLEMS IN AGREEMENT

Prepositional Phrases Between Subjects and Verbs

2c. The number of a subject is not changed by a prepositional phrase following the subject.

Drifts of snow **cover** the roads.

Indefinite Pronouns

Some pronouns do not refer to a definite person, place, thing, or idea and are therefore called ***indefinite pronouns.***

2d. The following indefinite pronouns are singular: *anybody, anyone, each, either, everybody, everyone, neither, nobody, no one, one, somebody, someone.*

No one knows where the boy and the goat are.

2e. The following indefinite pronouns are plural: *both, few, many, several.*

Both of them **were** safe.

2f. The following indefinite pronouns may be either singular or plural: *all, any, most, none, some.*

If the subject *all, any, most, none,* or *some* refers to a singular object, the subject is singular. If the subject refers to a plural object, the subject is plural.

Some of the hay **has been eaten.** [*Some* refers to *hay.*]

Some of his dreams **were** of warm days. [*Some* refers to *dreams.*]

Compound Subjects

2g. Subjects joined by *and* usually take a plural verb.

Aaron and Zlateh are sleeping in the haystack.

2h. When subjects are joined by *or* or *nor,* the verb agrees with the subject nearer the verb.

Neither **Aaron nor his sisters want** to sell Zlateh.

Neither **Aaron's sisters nor he wants** to sell Zlateh.

2i. When the subject follows the verb, find the subject and make sure the verb agrees with it. The subject usually follows the verb in sentences beginning with *here* or *there* and in questions.

There **is food** for Zlateh in the haystack. [food is]

Does Aaron dream of flowers? [Aaron does dream]

The contractions *here's, there's, and where's* contain the verb *is* and should be used only with singular subjects.

Here **are** the **books.**

Here**'s** the **book.**

2j. Collective nouns may be either singular or plural.

A collective noun takes a singular verb when the noun refers to the group as a unit. A collective noun takes a plural verb when the noun refers to the individual parts or members of the group.

An oxen **herd goes** with Hercules. [The herd as a unit goes.]

The **herd call** to the stolen cattle. [The members of the herd individually call.]

2k. **Words stating a weight, a measure, or an amount of money or time are usually singular.**

Five **dollars is** too much for a movie ticket.

2l. **The title of an artistic work or the name of an organization or country, even when plural in form, usually takes a singular verb.**

Aesop's Fables is on our reading list.
Has the **United States** signed the treaty?

2m. **A few nouns that end in *s* are singular and take singular verbs.**

news, measles, mathematics, civics, mumps, physics

Your Turn Correcting Agreement Errors

Revise the following sentences to correct any errors in subject-verb agreement. If a sentence is already correct, write *C.*

1. A sudden storm cover the road with snow.
2. Icicles forms on the goat's beard.
3. Has Aaron and the goat gotten lost?
4. Aaron see a haystack in the snow.
5. Aaron and Zlateh burrows into the haystack and huddles together for warmth.

3. Using Verbs

The Principal Parts of a Verb

The four basic forms of a verb are called the ***principal parts*** of the verb.

3a. **The principal parts of a verb are the *base form,* the *present participle,* the *past,* and the *past participle.***

BASE FORM	work, sing
PRESENT PARTICIPLE	(is) working, (is) singing
PAST	worked, sang
PAST PARTICIPLE	(have) worked, (have) sung

The principal parts of a verb express the time when an action occurs.

PRESENT	Ray Bradbury **writes** science fiction.
	I **am writing** a report on "The Rocket
PAST	I **wrote** the first paragraph last night.
	I finally **had written** an introduction.
FUTURE	I **will write** the rest of it this weekend.
	By Monday, I **will have finished.**

REGULAR VERBS

3b. **A *regular verb* forms its past and past participle by adding *-d* or *-ed* to the base form.**

Base Form	Present Participle	Past Participle
use	(is) using	used
suppose	(is) supposing	supposed
attack	(is) attacking	attacked

IRREGULAR VERBS

3c. **An *irregular verb* does not form its past and past participles by adding *-d* or *-ed* to the base form.**

An irregular verb forms its past and past participle by:

- changing vowels *or* consonants

Base Form	Past	Past Participle
ring	rang	(have) rung
make	made	(have) made
hold	held	(have) held

- changing vowels *and* consonants

Base Form	Past	Past Participle
eat	ate	(have) eaten
go	went	(have) gone
be	was/were	(have) been

- by making no changes

Base Form	Past	Past Participle
spread	spread	(have) spread
burst	burst	(have) burst
cost	cost	(have) cost

Common Irregular Verbs		
BASE FORM	**PAST**	**PAST PARTICIPLE**
begin	began	(have) begun
break	broke	(have) broken
catch	caught	(have) caught
choose	chose	(have) chosen
come	came	(have) come
do	did	(have) done
drink	drank	(have) drunk
know	knew	(have) known
run	ran	(have) run
see	saw	(have) seen
set	set	(have) set
sink	sank	(have) sunk
swim	swam	(have) swum
win	won	(have)won
write	wrote	(have) written

VERB TENSE

3d. The *tense* of a verb indicates the time of the action or state of being that is expressed by the verb.

Every verb has six tenses: *present, past, future, present perfect, past perfect, and future perfect.* This list shows how the six tenses are related to one another.

PAST PERFECT	existing or happening before a specific time in the past
PAST	existing or happening in the past
PRESENT PERFECT	existing or happening before now or starting in the past and continuing now
PRESENT	existing or happening now
FUTURE PERFECT	existing or happening before a specific time in the future
FUTURE	existing or happening in the future

PRESENT PERFECT PRESENT
She **has read** "Petals" and **has** a topic for her paper.

PAST PERFECT PAST
She **had chosen** another poem but **decided** against it.

FUTURE PERFECT FUTURE
She **will have written** it by Friday and **will proofread** it on Monday.

Listing all forms of a verb in the six tenses is called ***conjugating*** a verb.

Conjugation of the Verb Sing	
SINGULAR	**PLURAL**
Present Tense	
I sang	we sing
you sing	you sing
he, she, or it sings	they sing
Past Tense	
I sang	we sang
you sang	you sang
he, she, or it sang	they sang
Future Tense	
I will sing	we will sing
you will sing	you will sing
he, she, or it will sing	they will sing

Conjugation of the Verb Sing	
SINGULAR	**PLURAL**
Present Perfect Tense	
I have sung	we have sung
you have sung	you have sung
he, she, or it has sung	they have sung
Past Perfect Tense	
I had sung	we had sung
you had sung	you had sung
he, she, or it had sung	they had sung
Future Perfect Tense	
I will have sung	we will have sung
you will have sung	you will have sung
he, she, or it will have sung	they will have sung

Six Confusing Verbs

3e. **English contains three commonly confused verb pairs.**

SIT AND *SET*

(1) The verb *sit* means "to rest in an upright, seated position." *Sit* seldom takes an object.

(2) The verb set means "to put (something) in place." *Set* often takes an object.
She **sits** in the market. [no object]
Sellers **set** their goods on the tables. [*Goods* is the object.]

Base Form	Present Participle	Past	Past Participle
sit (to rest)	(is) sitting	sat	(have) sat
set (to put)	(is) setting	set	(have) set

LIE AND *LAY*

(1) The verb *lie* means "to rest," "to recline," or "to be in a place." *Lie* never takes an object.

(2) The verb *lay* means "to put (something) in place." *Lay* usually takes an object.
Puppets **are lying** under the table. [no object]
A girl **is laying** a puppet down. [*Puppet* is the object.]

lie (to recline)	(is) lying	lay	(have) lain
lay (to put)	(is) laying	laid	(have) laid

RISE AND *RAISE*

She **rises** very early on market days. [no object]
She **raises** her eyes to face me. [*Eyes* is the object.]

(1) The verb *rise* means "to go up " or "to get up." *Rise* seldom takes an object.

(2) The verb *raise* means "to lift up" or "to cause (something) to rise." *Raise* usually takes an object.

rise (to go up)	(is) rising	rose	(have) risen
raise (to lift up)	(is) raising	raised	(have) raised

Your Turn Using Tense Correctly

Read the following paragraph and rewrite it in either the present or past tense. Keep the verb tense consistent.

We frequently go to the flea market just outside town. The sellers had some unique merchandise. At lunch, we stop and get a sandwich there. Usually, someone like the woman in Pat Mora's "Petals" was there. I enjoyed talking with these interesting people.

4. Using Pronouns

The Forms of Personal Pronouns

The form of a personal pronoun shows its use in a sentence.

Pronoun Form	Use
Suject	• subject • predicate nominative
SINGULAR PLURAL	I, you, he, she, it we, you, they
Object	• direct object of a verb • indirect object of a verb • object of a prepositionp
SINGULAR PLURAL	me, you, him, her, it us, you, them
Possessive	• shows ownership or relationship
SINGULAR PLURAL	my, mine, your, yours, his, her, hers, its our, ours, your, yours, their, theirs

THE SUBJECT FORM

4a. Use the subject form for a pronoun that is the subject of a verb.

They set out on their journey. [*They* is the subject of *set.*]

4b. Use the subject form for a pronoun that is a predicate nominative.

Her husband was **he.** [*He* identifies the subject *husband.*]

To choose the correct pronoun in a compound subject, try each form of the pronoun separately.

Liza or (*me, I*) will play Harriet Tubman.
Me will play Harriet Tubman.
I will play Harriet Tubman.
Liza or **I** will play Harriety Tubman.

THE OBJECT FORM

4c. Use the object form for a pronoun that is the direct object of a verb.

Her story amazed **us.** [*Us* tells *who* was amazed.]

4d. Use the object form for a pronoun that is the indirect object of a verb.

Harriet gave **her** a quilt. [*Her* tells *to whom* Harriet gave a quilt.]

4e. Use the object form for a pronoun that is the object of a preposition.

to **them**   in front of **me**   according to **her**

To choose the correct pronoun in a compound object, try each form of the pronoun separately.

Did anyone help (*she, her*) and the others?
Did anyone help *she*?
Did anyone help *her*?
Did anyone help **her** and the others?

Special Pronoun Problems

Who and *Whom*

The pronoun *who* has different forms. *Whom* is the object form. When deciding whether to use *who* or *whom* in a question, follow these steps:

(*Who, Whom*) did Harriet tell?

STEP 1: Rephrase the question as a statement. Harriet did tell (who, whom).

STEP 2: Decide how the pronoun is used—as subject, predicate nominative, or object of a verb or preposition. (direct object)

STEP 3: Determine whether the subject form or the object form is correct according to the rules of standard English. (object form)

STEP 4: Select the correct form of the pronoun. **Whom** did Harried tell?

PRONOUNS WITH APPOSITIVES

Sometimes a pronoun is followed directly by an appositive. To decide which pronoun to use before an appositive, omit the appositive, and try each form of the pronoun separately.

(*We, Us*) boys will read for the parts. [Boys is the appositive identifying the pronoun.]

We will read for the parts.

Us will read for the parts.

We boys will read for the parts.

Your Turn Using Pronoums Correctly

Choose the correct form of the pronoun in parentheses.

1. In the fields, (them, they) sang songs with hidden meanings.
2. Tubman disagreed with (he, him) about whether to leave.
3. (Her, She) and many others helped slaves escape on the Underground Railroad.
4. Tell (I, me) another story about Harriet Tubma .
5. The next reader will be Tarik or (him, he).

5. Using Modifiers

Comparison of Modifiers

A ***modifier*** describes or limits the meaning of a word. Two kinds of modifiers—*adjectives* and *adverbs*—may be used to compare things. In making comparison, adjectives and adverbs take different forms depending on how many syllables the modifier has and how many things are being compared.

5a. **The three degrees of comparison of modifiers are *positive, comparative,* and *superlative.***

The ***positive degree*** is used when only one thing is being described.

The diver sank **deep** under the waves.

The ***comparative degree*** is used when two things are being compared.

The diver sank **deeper** than his companion.

The ***superlative degree*** is used when three or more things are being compared.

Which diver sank **deepest** of all?

REGULAR COMPARISON

- Most one-syllable modifiers form their comparative and superlative degrees by adding *–er* and *–est.*

Positive	dark	warm
Comparative	darker	warmer
Superlative	darkest	warmest

- Some two-syllable modifiers form their comparative and superlative degrees by adding *–er* and *–est.* Others form their comparative and superlative degress by using *more* and *most.*

Positive	angry	helpful
Comparative	angrier	more helpful
Superlative	angriest	most helpful

- Modifiers that have three or more syllables form their comparative and superlative degress by using *more* and *most.*

Positive	beautiful	fearfully
Comparative	more beautiful	more fearfully
Superlative	most beautiful	most fearfully

To show decreasing comparisons, all modifiers form their comprative and superative degrees with *less* and *least*.

less angry **least** beautiful

IRREGULAR MODIFIERS

Some modifiers do not form their comparative and superlative degrees by using the regular methods. Here are six common irregular modifiers:

Positive	bad	far
Comparative	worse	farther
Superlative	worst	farthest

Positive	good	well
Comparative	better	better
Superlative	best	best

Positive	many	much
Comparative	more	more
Superlative	most	most

Special Problems With Modifiers

5b. **The modifier *well* has different meanings and different uses.**

(1) *Well* is an adverb meaning "in a good way." Use this meaning of *well* to modify a verb. When you wish to modify a noun or pronoun with this meaning, use the adjective *good.*

ADVERB John listened **well** to Althea's advice.
ADJECTIVE The three women had only one **good** eye among them.

(2) *Well* is an adjective meaning "in good health." Use this meaning of *well* to modify a noun or a pronoun.

In spite of their ordeal, Rebecca and her son were **well.**

5c. **Avoid using double comparisons.**

A ***double comparison*** is the use of both *–er* and *more* (*less*) or *–est* and *most* (*least*) to form a comparison. Form a comparison in only one of these two ways, not both.

INCORRECT No one was more lovelier than Samantha's daughters.
CORRECT No one was **lovelier** than Samantha's daughters.

DOUBLE NEGATIVES

5d. **Avoid the use of double negatives.**

A ***double negative*** is the use of two negative words to express one negative idea.

Common Negative Words			
barely	never	none	nothing
hardly	no	no one	nowhere
neither	nobody	no 9(-n't)	scarcely

INCORRECT Polly shouldn't never have laughed.
CORRECT Polly **should never** have laughed.
CORRECT Polly should**n't** have laughed.

Your Turn Using Modifiers Correctly

The following sentences contain incorrect forms of comparison. Revise each sentence, using the correct form.

1. Who could have been more braver than Perseus?
2. He did good on his quest.
3. Medusa's head was the most horriblest sight in the world.
4. Perseus became more angrier at the king's insult.

6. Phrases

6a. A *phrase* is a group of related words that is used as a single part of speech. A phrase does not contain a verb and its subject.

Phrases cannot stand alone. They must always be used with other words as part of a sentence.

PHRASE from the Persian culture.

SENTENCE "Ali Baba and the Forty Thieves" is a tale **from the Persian culture.**

The Prepositional Phrase

6b. A *prepositional phrase* includes a preposition, a noun or a pronoun called the *object of the preposition*, and any modifiers of that object.

In the distant past, great things happened **to him.** [The noun *past* is the object of the preposition *in*. The pronoun *him* is the object of the preposition *to*.]

A preposition may have more than one object.

The tale is the story **of a man and a treasure.**

THE ADJECTIVE PHRASE

6c. An *adjective phrase* is a prepositional phrase that modifies a noun or a pronoun.

Adjective phrases answer the same questions that single-word adjectives answer: *What kind? Which one? How many?* or *How much?* More than one adjective phrase may modify the same noun or pronoun.

Huynh Quang Nhuong's journey **from Vietnam to the United States** makes an interesting read.

An adjective phrase may modify the object of another adjective phrase.

The name **of the hero in this myth** is Jason.

THE ADVERB PHRASE

6d. An *adverb phrase* is a prepositional phrase that modifies a verb, an adjective, or an adverb.

An adverb phrase tells *how, when, where, why,* or *to what extent* (that is, *how long, how many,* or *how far*).

Ali Baba stared **in amazement.** [How?]

In front of him was a heap of gold, silver, and fine silks. [Where?]

His life changed **on that morning.** [When?]

For years, Ali Baba kept his secret. [How long?]

The gold pieces he found numbered **in the thousands.** [How many?]

The thieves traveled together **over many miles.** [How far?]

An adverb phrase may come before or after the word it modifies.

In the story "All Summer in a Day," children on Venus experience sunshine for the first time.

Children on Venus experience sunshine for the first time **in the story "All Summer in a Day."**

More than one adverb phrase may modify the same word or words.

Without any guidance, Richard's Shetland pony can lead him **to the apple orchard.** [Both adverb phrases modify *can lead*.]

An adverb phrase may be followed by an adjective phrase that modifies the object of the preposition in the adverb phrase.

In their rush to the door, the other children forget Margot. [The adverb phrase *in their rush* modifies the verb *forget*. The adjective phrase *to the door* modifies *rush*, which is the object in the adverb phrase.]

Your Turn Combining Sentences

Use prepositional phrases to combine each of the following pairs of choppy sentences into one smooth sentence.

1. The Lins immigrated to the United States. China had been their homeland.
2. Mrs. Gleason offered the Lins celery. The celery was on a relish tray.
3. The celery strings got caught. The strings got caught in the Lins' teeth.
4. The Lins dined out. The restaurant served French food.
5. Mr. Gleason chased a pea on his plate. He chased it with his chopsticks.

7. Sentences

Sentence or Sentence Fragment?

7a. A *sentence* is a group of words that has a subject and a verb and expresses a complete thought.

A sentence begins with a capital letter and ends with a period, a question mark, or an exclamation point.

Did the ending surprise you**?**
What a clever boy he was**!**

A ***sentence fragment*** is a group of words that either does not have a subject and verb or does not express a complete thought.

The boy's mother and father. [no verb]
With its twist at the end. [no subject or verb]

The Subject and the Predicate

A sentence consists of two parts: a *subject* and a *predicate.*

THE SUBJECT

7b. A *subject* tells whom or what the sentence is about. A *complete subject* may be one word or more than one word.

The fly in the story has only a small part.
It has only a small part.

Finding the Subject

The subject does not always come at the beginning of a sentence. The subject may be in the middle or even at the end. To find the subject of a sentence, ask *Who?* or *What?* before the predicate.

The **boy** saw the stick. [Who saw the stick? The boy saw it.]
In his hand was a stick. [What was in his hand? A stick.]
Did **you** read this story? [Who did read it? You did.]

THE SIMPLE SUBJECT

7c. A *simple subject* is the main word or words in the complete subject.

The **boy** did not become upset. [The complete subject is *the boy*.]
"Dragon, Dragon" by John Gardner is in this book. [The complete subject is the *"Dragon, Dragon" by John Gardner*.]
What a clever boy was **he!** [*He* is both the simple and complete subject.]

The simple subject is *never* part of a prepositional phrase.

Many of the students laughed at the ending. [Who laughed? You might be tempted to say *students*, but *students* is part of the prepositional phrase *of the students*. Many laughed. *Many* is the subject.]

THE PREDICATE

7d. The *predicate* of a sentence is the part that says something about the subject. A *complete predicate* consists of a verb and all the words that describe the verb and complete its meaning.

In the following examples, the vertical line separates the complete subject from the complete predicate.

The boy's mother and father | **owed a debt.**
From a traditional story comes | this surprising tale.

Finding the Predicate

The predicate usually comes after the subject. Sometimes, however, the predicate comes before the subject. Part of the predicate may even appear on one side of the subject and the rest on the other side.

On a bamboo pole near them was a fly.
In a few sentences, the boy **solved the riddle.**
Could a fly **be a witness**?

7e. **A *simple predicate*, or *verb*, is the main word or group of words in the complete predicate.**

A simple predicate may be a one-word verb, or it may be a verb phrase. A ***verb phrase*** consists of a main verb and its helping verbs.

The moneylender **is** angry at the boy.

He **should** not **have made** such a promise to the boy.

Notice in the second example that the word *not* is not part of the verb phrase. The words *not* and *never* and the contraction *-n't* are adverbs, not verbs.

The Compound Subject

7f. **A *compound subject* consists of two or more connected subjects that have the same verb.**

The usual connecting word between the subjects is the conjunction *and, or,* or *nor.*

Neither the **boy** nor the **moneylender** had been honest.

Among the people at court were the **boy**, his **parents**, and the **lender**.

The Compound Verb

7g. **A *compound verb* consists of two or more verbs that have the same subject.**

A connecting word—usually the conjunction *and, or,* or *but*—is used between the verbs.

The mandarin **listened, asked** questions, and **made** a decision.

Both the subject and the verb of a sentence may be compound.

S S V V
The **mother** and **father laughed** and **went** home.

V S S V V
Did José or **Klara make** dinner and **set** the table?

Your Turn Combining Sentences

Use a compound subject or verb to combine each pair of sentences.

1. A metaphor is a figure of speech. A simile is a figure of speech.
2. Compare the modern world with the ancient world. Contrast the modern world with the ancient world.
3. Saddles can express the personality of the rider. Bridles can do so, too.

8. Complements

Recognizing Complements

8a. **A *complement* is a word or a group of words that completes the meaning of a verb.**

Every sentence has a subject and a verb. Sometimes the subject and the verb can express a complete thought without a complement.

Fish swim.

Each evening my grandfather walks with his neighbor.

Linking verbs and transitive verbs need complements to complete their meaning and create a complete sentence.

A complement may be a noun, a pronoun, or an adjective.

S V C
John Gardner became a **writer**.

S V C
His stories are **wonderful**.

S V C C
Rachel will tell **us** the story.

A complement is never in a prepositional phrase.

COMPLEMENT	A dragon was **loose.**
OBJECT OF A PREPOSITION	A dragon was on the **loose.**

Direct Objects

8b. **A *direct object* is a noun or a pronoun that receives the action of the verb or that shows the result of the action. A direct object tells *what* or *whom* after a transitive verb.**

A fierce dragon threatens **them.** [The pronoun *them* receives the action of the transitive verb *threaten* and tells *whom.*]

The king made a **bargain.** [The noun *bargain* shows the results of the action verb *made* and tells *what.*]

A direct object may be compound.

The dragon stole **jewels, treasure,** and the wizard's **book**. [The nouns *jewels, treasure* and *book* receive the action of the transitive verb *stole* and tells *what.*]

A direct object never follows a linking verb.

The king **seems** cowardly. [The verb *seems* does not express action; therefore, it has no direct object.] A direct object is never part of a prepositional phrase.

DIRECT OBJECT	He needs **volunteers**.
OBJECT OF A PREPOSITION	He calls for **volunteers.**

Indirect Objects

8c. **An *indirect object* comes between the verb and the direct object. It tells *to* or *for what* or *whom* the action of the verb is done.**

The king gave the young **man** a chance. [The noun *man* tells *to whom* the king gave the chance.]

Linking verbs do not have indirect objects. Also, an indirect object is never in a prepositional phrase.

LINKING VERB	A dragon **is** a fearsome beast.
INDIRECT OBJECT	It causes **people** trouble.
OBJECT OF A PREPOSITION	It causes trouble for many **people.**

An indirect object may be compound.

The dragon caused the **king** and his **subjects** a great deal of trouble.

Subject Complements

A ***subject complement*** completes the meaning of a linking verb and identifies or describes the subject.

The youngest **son** became a **hero**.
His **task** was **difficult**.

The two kinds of subject complements are the *predicate nominative* and the *predicate adjective*.

PREDICATE NOMINATIVES

8d. **A *predicate nominative* is a noun or pronoun that follows a linking verb and identifies the subject or refers to it.**

The queen became a **rosebush.** [The noun *rosebush* is a predicate nominative that identifies the subject *queen.*]

Predicate nominatives may be compound.

The troublesome dragon was a **thief**, a **vandal**, and a **mischief-maker**.

Predicate nominatives never appear in prepositional phrases.

His father's advice was only two **lines** of poetry. [*Lines* is a predicate nominative that identifies the subject *advice. Poetry* is the object of the preposition *of.*]

PREDICATE ADJECTIVES

8e. **A *predicate adjective* is an adjective that follows a linking verb and describes the subject.**

The dragon felt **confident.** [*Confident* is a predicate adjective that describes the subject *dragon.*]

Predicate adjectives may be compound.

The youngest son was neither **clever** nor **strong**.

Your Turn

Identify the predicate nominative(s) in each sentence.

1. Did the oldest son and the middle son become the dragon's lunch?
2. The wizard was not a young man.
3. A sense of humor can be a weakness.
4. This cobbler was a shoemaker and wise teacher.
5. It was they in the dragon's belly.

9. Kinds of Sentences

Simple and Compound Sentences

9a. A simple sentence has only one subject and one verb. Both the subject and verb may be compound; (two or more nouns or verbs joined by a word such as ***and***). See the chart below.

9b. A compound sentence consists of two or more simple sentence usually joined by a connecting words. The sentences may also be joined by a semicolon. See the chart below.

	Subject(s)	Verb(s)	Connecting Word?	Examples
SIMPLE SENTENCE	one (may be compound)	one (may be compound)	none needed	"Baucis and Philemon" is an ancient tale. Zeus and Hermes ate heartily.
COMPOUND SENTENCE	two or more	two or more	*and, but, for, nor, so, yet* or a semi-colon (;)	Paula wrote the book *Greek Myths*, and Ali illustrated it. It had been a good season; they had a good harvest.

Sentences Classified by Purpose

9c. A sentence can also be classified according to its purpose: *declarative, interrogative, imperative,* or *exclamatory.*

Sentence Type	Description	End Punctuation	Example
DECLARATIVE	Makes a statement	.	Their home became a temple**.**
INTERROGATIVE	Asks a question	?	How did the gods reward them**?**
IMPERATIVE	• Gives a command • Makes a request	. or !	Please light the candles**.** Don't go in there**!**
EXCLAMATORY	• Shows excitement • Expresses strong feeling	!	How fortunate they are**!**

Your Turn

Combine each pair of simple sentences into one sentence.

1. Olives lay on the table. Baked eggs lay on the table.
2. The goose cackled. The goose ran away.
3. The guests were hungry. Patricia fed them.
4. Patricia and David loved each other. They would never part.

10. Writing Effective Sentences

Writing Clear Sentences

A ***complete sentence*** has both a subject and a verb and expresses a complete thought.

I often dream of a secret garden.
Do you dream about a garden, too?

Sentence fragments and *run-ons* are not clear because they do not show the boundaries between complete sentences.

SENTENCE FRAGMENTS

10a. Avoid using sentence fragments.

A ***sentence fragment*** is part of a sentence that has been capitalized and punctuated like a complete sentence.

Traveled far away to England. [no subject]
As soon as she arrived in England. [does not express a complete thought]

RUN-ON SENTENCES

10b. Avoid using run-on sentences.

You create a ***run-on sentence*** by running together two complete sentences, or by putting a comma between two complete sentences.

Mr. Craven will be Mary's guardian the girl has no other relatives.
Mrs. Medlock offers Mary sandwiches, Mary refuses them.

Here are two ways to revise run-on sentences:

(1) Make two sentences.
(2) Use a comma and a coordinating conjunction (*and, but, or*).

Mr. Craven will be Mary's guardian**.** The girl has no other relatives.
Mrs. Medlock offers Mary sandwiches**, but** Mary refuses them.

Combining Sentences

10c. Combine choppy sentences into longer, smoother sentences.

Too many short sentences make writing look and sound choppy.

INSERTING WORDS

Try inserting a key word or group of words from one sentence into the other. You may need to change the form of the key word, or add or change a word to make the ideas fit smoothly.

A wind blows across the moors. The wind is mournful.
A wind blows **mournfully** across the moors.

The garden has a wall. The wall goes all the way around it.
The wall goes all the way **around the garden.**

If the group of words renames or explains a noun or pronoun in the sentence, set off the word group with commas.

Martha is kind to Mary. Martha is a maid at the manor.
Martha, **a maid at the manor,** is kind to Mary.

USING CONNECTING WORDS

Conjunctions such as *and, but,* and *or* can join related sentences and sentence parts.

Dead leaves litter the ground. Dead branches do, too.
Dead **leaves and branches** litter the ground.

AFTER TRANSPOSED TEXT

The roses are ugly now. They must have been lovely once.

The roses are ugly now**, but** they must have been lovely once

When you connect two sentences by using *and, but,* or *or*, place a comma before the conjunction.

COMBINING SENTENCES

One sentence may help explain another by telling *how, where, why,* or *when*. Combine these sentences by adding a connecting word such as *after, although, as, because, before, if, since, so that, until, when, whether,* or *while.*

The door was shut. No one could see it.
When the door was shut, no one could see it.

REVISING WORDY SENTENCES

As you revise your writing, read each sentence aloud to check for wordiness. If you run out of breath before the end of a sentence, chances are the sentence is wordy. You can revise wordy sentences by

(1) replacing a group of words with one word

WORDY With great happiness, she began her work.

REVISED **Happily**, she began her work.

(2) replacing a clause with a phrase

WORDY She always felt happier when she was in the garden.

REVISED She always felt happier **in the garden**.

(3) taking out unnecessary words or phrases

WORDY What I mean to say is that *The Secret Garden* was suspenseful.

REVISED *The Secret Garden* was suspenseful.

Your Turn Correcting Sentence Fragments

Correct each item by connecting the word groups to create a complete sentence.

1. The woman was Mrs. Medlock. A tall, thin housekeeper more than sixty years old.
2. According to Mrs. Crawford. Mary's mother did not care for the girl. Because Mary was not beautiful.
3. Because they were strange and unfamiliar to her. Mary apparently disliked everyone and everything in England.
4. With her attitude of cold, rude, and rejecting silence. Mary offends just about everyone.

11. Capital Letters

11a. Capitalize the first word in every sentence.

Have you ever heard this song?

(1) Capitalize the first word of a direct quotation even iwithin a sentence.

Eva whispered, "**S**he's mad at you."

(2) Traditionally the first word of a line of poetry is capitalized. However, some modern poets do not follow this style. When you are quoting, use capital letters exactly as in the source for the quotation.

Desolate and lost
All night long on the lake
Where fog trails and mist creeps....
—Carl Sandburg, "Lost"

11b. Capitalize the pronoun *I*.

Mark and **I** made a music video.

11c. Capitalize proper nouns.

A ***common noun*** is a general name for a person, place, thing, or idea. A ***proper noun*** names a particular person, place, thing, or idea and is always captialized. A common noun is capitalized only when it begins a sentence or is part of a title. In proper nouns of more than one word, short prepositions (fewer than five letters) and articles (*a, an, the*) are not capitalized.

(1) Capitalize the names of persons and animals.

Cindy **C**hang, **N**ick de **V**ries, **B**lack **B**eauty

(2) Capitalize geographical names.

Type of Name	Example
Towns, Cities	**C**airo, **N**ew **Y**ork **C**ity
Counties, States	**P**olk **C**ounty, **W**yoming
Countries	**N**igeria, **F**rance
Islands	**E**llis **I**sland, **I**sle of **H**ispaniola
Bodies of Water	**D**ead **S**ea, **S**an **F**rancisco **B**ay
Forests, Parks	**B**lack **F**orest, **A**rches **N**ational **P**ark
Streets, Highways	**R**oute 41, **K**eltner **S**treet
Mountains	**C**amelback **M**ountain, **M**ount **S**t. **H**elens,
Continents, Regions	**S**outh **A**merica, the **N**orthwest

In a hyphenated street number, the second part of the number is not capitalized.

West Fifth-fourth Street

Words such as *north*, *east*, and *southwest* are not capitalized when they indicate direction.

flying **n**orth, southeast of Boise

(3) Capitalize the names of planets, stars, and other heavenly bodies.

Mercury, **A**ntares, **S**agitarius, the **C**rab **N**ebula

The word *earth* should not be capitalized unless it is used along with the names of other heavenly bodies. The words *sun* and *moon* are not capitalized.

In an eclipse, the **m**oon comes between the **E**arth and the **s**un.

(4) Capitalize the names of teams, organizations, businesses, institutions, and government bodies.

Type of Name	Example
Teams	**B**altimore **O**rioles, **I**ndiana **P**acers
Organizations, Businesses	**G**lee **C**lub, **W**allpaper **W**orld
Countries	**N**igeria, **F**rance
Institutions, Government Bodies	**B**ay **M**emorial **H**ospital, **D**epartment of **H**ealth

(5) Capitalize the names of historical events and periods, special events, holidays, and calendar items.

Type of Name	Example
Historical Events, Historical Periods	**B**attle of **B**ritain, **C**old **W**ar
Special Events, Holidays	**O**hio **S**tate **F**air, **M**emorial **D**ay
Calendar Items	**S**aturday, **D**ecember, **F**ourth of **J**uly

(6) Capitalize the names of nationalities, races, and peoples.

Italian, **S**udanese, **C**aucasian, **H**ispanic, **C**herokee

(7) Capitalize the names of religions and their followers, holy days, sacred writings, and specific deities.

Type of Name	Example
Religions and Followers	**S**hintoism, **R**oman **C**atholic
Holy Days	**C**hristmas, **D**iwali
Sacred Writings	**K**oran, **T**orah
Specific Deities	**V**ishnu, **Y**ahweh

(8) Capitalize the names of buildings and other structures.

Sears **T**ower, **G**olden **G**ate **B**ridge, the **P**yramids

(9) Capitalize the names of monuments and awards.

Tomb of the **U**nknowns, **C**aldecott **M**edal

(10) Capitalize the names of trains, ships, airplanes, and spacecraft.

Type of Name	Example
Trains	***M**idnight **S**pecial, **O**rient **E**xpress*
Ships	***Y**armouth **C**astle, **USS S**aratoga*
Aircraft	***G**lamorous **G**lennis **S**pirit of **C**olumbus*
Spacecraft	***E**agle, **C**handra **X**-ray **O**bservatory*

(11) Capitalize the brand names of business products.

Pilot pens, **C**orvette convertible, **L**ee jeans

Notice that the names of the types of products are not capitalized.

11d. **Capitalize proper adjectives.**

A *proper adjective* is formed from a proper noun and is almost always capitalized.

PROPER NOUNS	China	Pawnee
PROPER ADJECTIVES	Chinese art	Pawnee customs.

11e. **Capitalize titles.**

(1) Capitalize the title of a person when it comes before a name.
Dr. Washington, Governor Hill just called.

(2) Capitalize a title used alone or following a person's name only when you want to emphasize the position of someone holding a high office. A title used alone is direct address is usually capitalized.
Everyone was waiting for the Rabbi's decision.
How long have you wanted to become a rabbi?
May I speak with you for a moment, Doctor?

(3) Capitalize a word showing a family relationship when the word is used before or in place of a person's name.
Hey, Mom, Aunt Lisa and Uncle John are here!

Do not capitalize a word showing a family relationship when a possessive comes before the word.
Bill's mother and my grandfather lived in Chad.

(4) Capitalize the first and last words and all important words in titles.
Unimportant words in titles include prepositions of fewer than five letters (such as *to, for, with*), coordinating conjunctions (such as *and, or*), and articles (*a, an, the*).

Type of Name	Example
Books	*The Land I Lost, Science in Ancient Japan*
Magazines	*Time, Horse and Pony*
Newspapers	*Milwaukee Journal*
Poems	*"The Sneetches," "Jimmy Jet and His TV Set"*
Short Stories	*"Hansel and Gretel," "The Golden Serpent"*
Historical Documents	*Magna Carta, Articles of Confederation*
Movies	*Apollo 13, The Lion King*
Television Programs	*The Amazing Race, Mythbusters*
Works of Art	*Black Painting*
Musical Compositions	*West Side Story, "America the Beautiful"*

11f. **Do not capitalize the name of school subjects, except language courses and course names followed by a number.**

I am planning to take Spanish, math, and Music II.

Your Turn Capitalizing Words Correctly

Correct errors in capitalization.

1. I read in the television listing that tonight *Ancient warriors* is about the romans.
2. I am calling the poem that I wrote about dickon in *the secret garden* "nature's magic."
3. For my project in English class, I wrote an essay about "The fox and the crow."
4. Wasn't there a photo in *Newsweek* of *Ducks in a stream* and some other paintings of hokusai's?
5. How about reading the *book of changes* for your report on confucianism?

12. Punctuation

End Marks

An ***end mark*** is a mark of punctuation placed at the end of a sentence. The three kinds of end marks are the *period*, the *question mark*, and the *exclamation point.*

12a. **Use a period at the end of a statement.**

Huynh Quang Nhuong is a writer**.**

12b. **Use a question mark at the end of a question.**

Didn't he write *The Land I Lost***?**

12c. **Use an exclamation point at the end of an exclamation.**

What a life he has led**!**

12d. **Use a period or an exclamation point at the end of a request or a command.**

Please tell us about it**.** [request]
Give me a chance**!** [command]

12e. **Use a period after most abbreviations.**

Types of Abbreviations	Examples		
Personal Names	J.R.R. Tolkein Herbert S. Zim		
Titles Used with Names	Mr. Sr.	Ms. Dr.	Jr.
States	Fla. Calif.	Tenn. Ill.	
Addresses	St. Blvd.	Rd. Apt.	
Organizations and Companies	Co. Corp.	Inc. Assn.	
Times	A.M. B.C.	P.M. A.D.	

Place A.D. before the number and B.C. after the number. For centuries expressed in words, place both A.D. and B.C. after the century.

A.D. 540 sixth century B.C.

When an abbreviation with a period ends a sentence, another period is not needed. However, a question mark or an exclamation point is used as needed.

Have you been introduced to Yoshiko, P.J.**?**

Commas

12f. **Use commas to separate items in a series.**

Make sure that there are three or more items in a series; two items do not need a comma.

Joey has been to Hawaii, Venezuela, and Panama. [words in a series]

We looked for our cat under the bed, in the closet, and under the porch. [phrases in a series]

If all items in a series are joined by *and* or *or*, do not use commas to separate them.

I miss Andrea **and** our talks **and** our walks.

12g. **Use a comma to separate two or more adjectives that come before a noun.**

Andrea was a good, true friend.

Do not place a comma between an adjective and the noun immediately following it.

Her new house [*not* new, house] is far from here.

Sometimes the last adjective in a series is closely connected to the noun. In that case, do not use a comma before the last adjective.

Andrea was my only best [*not* only, best] friend.

12h. **Use a comma before and, but, or, nor, for, so, or yet when it joins the parts of a compound sentence.**

I liked *Owls*, **but** I did my report on *Volcano*.

You may omit the comma before *and, but, or,* or *nor* if the clauses are very short and there is no risk of misunderstanding.

Interrupters

12i. **Use commas to set off an expression that interrupts a sentence.**

Two commas are needed if the interrupter is in the middle of a sentence. One comma is needed if the expression comes first or last.

The author of this story, **Ray Bradbury,** sometimes appears on television.

Yes, he's a science fiction writer.

Isn't one of his stories in our book, **Jess**?

(1) Use commas to set off appositives and appositive phrases that are not needed to understand the meaning of a sentence.

His drawing, **a sketch of a swan,** is very detailed.

Do not use commas when an appositive is necessary for the meaning of the sentence.

My brother **Tyrone** drew it. [I have more than one brother and am identifying which brother I mean.]

My brother, **Tyrone,** drew it. [I have only one brother and am identifying him simply as extra information.]

(2) Use commas to set off words in direct address.

Mona, tell us about yourself.

(3) Use commas after such words as well, yes, no, and why when they begin a sentence.

Well, they did say that they would meet us here.

Conventional Situations

12j. **Use commas in certain conventional situations.**

(1) Use commas to separate items in dates and addresses.

On November 14, 2010, please celebrate with us at 110 Oak Drive, Minneapolis, MN 55424. [Notice that no comma is used between the state abbreviation and the ZIP Code.]

(2) Use commas after the salutation of a friendly letter and after the closing of any letter.

Dear Grandma, Best wishes, Sincerely,

Semicolons

12g. **Use a semicolon between parts of a compound sentence if they are not joined by *and, but, or, nor, for, so,* or *yet*.**

The Rum Tum Tugger is quite a character**;** he, not his owners, is the boss.

Colons

12h. **Use a colon before a list of items, especially after expressions like *as follows* or *the following.***

Poets may use the following**:** rhyme, metaphor, and imagery.

12i. **Use a colon in certain conventional situations.**

(1) Use a colon between the hour and the minute.

1**:**15 P.M. 4**:**32 A.M.

(2) Use a colon after the salutation of a business letter.

Dear Ms. Cruz**:** Dear Sir or Madam**:**

(3) Use a colon between a title and a subtitle.

"Snakes**:** Facts and Folklore"

Your Turn Using Commas and Semicolons

The following items contain errors in the use of commas and semicolons. Rewrite each item, correcting the errors.

1. Soto's cat loves the crunchy rattle of dry cat food equally appetizing are pieces of soft, cold, aromatic cheese taken from the writer's own hand.
2. Some cats hunt mice and small birds we have a cat.
3. For this skinny kitten Soto unlike many cat owners cooked eggs eggs rich in nutrients helped the kitten back to health.
4. Some cats enjoy a nap on an article of their owner's clothing in this case slippers other cats prefer the privacy and darkness of a closet.
5. Soto's family protected fed and cuddled the kitten in turn the kitten responded with love and happiness.

13. Punctuation

Underlining (Italics)

13a. Use underlining (italics) for titles of publications and literary and artistic works, and for the names of trains, ships, aircraft, and spacecraft.

Type of Title	Examples
Books	*Hank the Cowdog.*
Plays	*The Secret Garden*
Periodicals	*TV Guide, Car and Driver.*
Works of Art	*The Pietà, View of Toledo*
Films	*Casablanca, Toy Story*
Television Programs	*Ancient Warriors, The Magic School Bus*
Recordings	*Unforgettable*
Long Musical Compositions	*The Mikado, Water Music, Also Sprach Zarathustra*
Ships and Trains	*Calypso, Empire Builder*
Aircraft and Spacecraft	*Spruce Goose, Friendship 7*

13b. Place quotation marks before and after a *direct* quotation—a person's exact words.

"I read it last night," said Carlos.

Do not use quotation marks for an ***indirect quotation***—a rewording of a direct quotation.

Carlos said that he had read it last night.

13c. A direct quotation begins with a capital letter.

Nicole added, "**I**t's based on an Indian folk tale."

13d. When the expression identifying the speaker interrupts a quoted sentence, each part of the quotation is enclosed in quotation marks.

"This story by Rudyard Kipling," said Tanya, "is my favorite so far."

When the second part of a divided quotation is a new sentence, it begins with a capital letter.

"Rudyard Kipling is famous for this type of story," said Mrs. Perkins. "**H**ave any of you read *The Jungle Book*?"

13e. A direct quotation is set off from the rest of the sentence by a comma, a question mark, or an exclamation point, but not by a period.

If a quotation comes at the beginning of a sentence, a comma follows it. If a quotation comes at the end of a sentence, a comma comes before it. If a quoted sentence is interrupted, a comma follows the first part and comes before the second part.

Mark said**,** "Didn't somebody already write a story like that?"

"Maybe**,**" Alyssa argued**,** "but we can, too."

When a quotation ends with a question mark or an exclamation point, no comma is needed.

"Didn't he write *Just So Stories***?**" asked Delia.

13f. A period or a comma is always placed inside the closing quotation marks.

"I'll get started right away**,"** said Chip.

13g. A quotation mark or an exclamation point is placed inside the closing quotation marks when the quotation itself is a question or an exclamation. Otherwise, it is placed outside.

"Why does the camel have such a bad attitude**?"** asked Mario. [The quotation is a question.]

Did Ms. Johnson say, "All reports are due on Friday"**?** [The sentence, not the quotation, is a question.].

13h. Use single quotation marks to enclose a quotation within a question.

"What happened to the **'**steel-driving man**'** John Henry?" Mr. Zinn asked.

13i. When you write dialogue (conversation), begin a new paragraph each time you change speakers.

"He says 'Humph!'" said the Dog, "and he won't fetch and carry."

"Does he say anything else?"

—Rudyard Kipling, "How the Camel Got His Hump"

13j. **Use quotation marks to enclose titles of short literary and artistic works.**

Type of Title	Examples
Short Stories	"All Summer in a Day," "The Fun They Had"
Poems	"Excitement," "The Sidewalk Racer"
Articles	"Looking Ahead"
Songs	"Amazing Grace," "Listen to Your Heart"
Television Program Episodes	"Boys and Girls," "Objects in Space"
Chapters and Other Book Parts	"Parts of Speech," "Chapter Summary"

Your Turn Using Punctuation Correctly

Revise the following sentences by adding commas, end marks, and quotation marks where necessary.

1. Read the next chapter, Food for Health, by Monday, said Mr. Carl.
2. I'm calling my poem Wind at Morning.
3. She and my sister are like the girls in that story The Tree House.
4. I'll be playing So Rare at my recital; it's an old tune.
5. Wow! Read this review titled Too Little, Too Late exclaimed Paul.

14. Punctuation

Apostrophes

POSSESSIVE CASE

The ***possessive case*** of a noun or a pronoun shows ownership or relationship.

14a. **To form the possessive case of a singular noun, add an apostrophe and an *s*.**

a person**'s** best friend a day**'s** time

A proper name ending in *s* usually takes only an apostrophe, not an additional *s*.

Hercules**'** feats Rawlings**'** novels

14b. **To form the possessive case of a plural noun ending in *s*, add only the apostrophe.**

dreams**'** meanings wolves**'** dens

14c. **To form the possessive case of a plural noun that does not end in *s*, add an apostrophe and an *s*.**

people**'s** habits mice**'s** holes

14d. **Do *not* use an apostrophe with possessive personal pronouns.**

The cat was **hers**. That dog is **theirs**.

14e. **To form the possessive case of some indefinite pronouns, add an apostrophe and an *s*.**

anyone**'s** guess no one**'s** report

CONTRACTIONS

14f. **To form a contraction, use an apostrophe to show where letters have been left out.**

A ***contraction*** is a shortened form of a word, a number, or a group of words. The apostrophe in a contraction shows where letters, numerals, or words have been left out.

I am ⟶ I**'**m 1997 ⟶ **'**97
where is ⟶ where**'**s of the clock ⟶ o**'**clock

The word *not* can be shortened to *-n't* and added to a verb, usually without changing the spelling of the verb.

has not = has**n't** do not = do**n't**
EXCEPTIONS will not = wo**n't** cannot = ca**n't**

Do not confuse contractions with possessive pronouns.

Contractions	Possessive Pronouns
It's an African fable. [*It is*]	**Its** explanation of dogs and cats amuses me.
Who's Eve's favorite? [*Who is*]	**Whose** home was the cave?
There's not much food. [*There is*]	This home was **theirs**.

14g. Use an apostrophe and an s to form the plurals of letters, numerals, and signs, and of words referred to as words.

Your *T*'**s** look like *F*'**s**.
Don't use so many *!*'**s** and *oh*'**s**.

Hyphens

14g. Use a hyphen to divide a word at the end of a line.

When dividing a word at the end of a line, remember the following rules:

(1) Divide a word only between syllables.
(2) Do not divide a one-syllable word.
(3) Do not divide a word so that one letter stands alone.

14h. Use a hyphen with compound numbers from *twenty-one* to *ninety-nine* and with fractions used as adjectives.

twenty-two verbs
fifty-first state
one-half pint

Your Turn Using Apostrophes Correctly

Correct errors in apostrophe usage.

1. Were reading "The Fun They Had" next.
2. Its not right to break a promise.
3. Does the # symbol mean "pound's"?
4. Lets ask him if hes going there, too.
5. "Whos it's owner?" I asked.

15. Spelling

Using Word Parts

Many English words are made up of various word parts. Learning to spell the most frequently used parts can help you spell many words correctly.

Word Parts			
PART	DEFINITION	EXAMPLES	WORDS
Root	word part that carries the word's core meaning	–ped– = foot –port– = carry –vid–, –vis– = sight	pedal, biped portable, export video, invisible
Prefix	one or more letters added to the beginning of a word or root to change its meaning	dis– = away il–, im–, in–, ir– = not semi– = half	disarm, disagree illegal, incomplete semicircle
Suffix	one or more letters added to the end of a word or root to change its meaning	–en = made of, become –ful = full of –ness = quality, state of	wooden, broaden joyful, hopeful sadness, falseness

Spelling Rules

IE AND *EI*

15a. **Except after *c*, write *ie* when the sound is long *e*.**

pi**e**ce bel**ie**ve c**ei**ling rec**ei**ve
EXCEPTIONS **ei**ther, sh**ei**k, prot**ei**n, s**ei**ze, w**ei**rd

15b. **Write *ei* when the sound is not long *e*, especially when the sound is long *a*.**

eight sl**ei**gh v**ei**n th**ei**r
EXCEPTIONS anc**ie**nt, misch**ie**f, p**ie**, fr**ie**nd, consc**ie**nce

-CEDE, -CEED, AND *-SEDE*

15c. **The only English word ending in *-sede* is *supersede.* The only words ending in *-ceed* are *exceed, proceed,* and *succeed.* Most other words with this sound end in *-cede.***

con**cede** inter**cede** pre**cede** re**cede**

ADDING PREFIXES

15d. **When adding a prefix to a word, do not change the spelling of the word itself.**

pre + view = **pre**view
mis + spell = **mis**spell

ADDING SUFFIXES

15e. **When adding the suffix *-ly* or *-ness* to a word, do not change the spelling of the word itself.**

quick + ly = quick**ly**
near + ness = near**ness**

For words that end in *y* and have more than one syllable, change the *y* to *i* before adding *-ly* or *-ness*.

tardy + ly = tard**ily**
ready + ness = read**iness**

15f. **Drop the final silent *e* before a suffix beginning with a vowel.**

strange + er = strang**er** close + ing = clos**ing**

Keep the final silent *e* in a word ending in *ce* or *ge* before a suffix beginning with *a* or *o*.

change + able = change**able**
service + able = service**able**

15g. **Keep the final silent *e* before a suffix beginning with a consonant.**

pride + ful = pride**ful** wide + ness = wide**ness**

EXCEPTIONS nine + th = ninth; argue + ment = argument

15h. **For words ending in *y* preceded by a consonant, change the *y* to *i* before any suffix that does not begin with *i*.**

empty + ness = empt**iness**
dry + ed = dr**ied**

15i. **For words ending in *y* preceded by a vowel, keep the *y* when adding a suffix.**

stay + ing = stay**ing** pay + ment = pay**ment**

EXCEPTIONS day—daily; lay—laid; pay—paid; say—said

15j. **Double the final consonant before a suffix beginning with a vowel if the word**

(1) has only one syllable or has the accent on the last syllable ***and***
(2) ends in a single consonant preceded by a single vowel.

wed + ing = we**dd**ing
begin + er = begi**nn**er

Do not double the final consonant in words ending in *w* or *x*.

bow + ing = bo**w**ing
tax + ed = ta**x**ed

The final consonant is usually not doubled before a suffix beginning with a vowel.

send + er = sen**d**er
final + ist = fina**l**ist

FORMING THE PLURALS OF NOUNS

15k. **For most nouns, add *-s*.**

logs	thoughts	pens
hoes	sodas	Bakers

15l. **For nouns ending in *s, x, z, ch,* or *sh*, add *-es*.**

lass**es**	box**es**	waltz**es**
pinch**es**	blush**es**	Ruíz**es**

15m. For nouns ending in y preceded by a consonant, change the *y* to *i* and add *-es*. If the noun is a proper noun, then do not change *y* to *i*.

fly—fl**ies** Kelly—Kelly**s**

For nouns ending in *y* preceded by a vowel, add *-s*.

joy—joys key—key**s** Wiley—Wiley**s**

15n. For some nouns ending in *f* or *fe*, add *-s*. For others, change the *f* or *fe* to *v* and add *-es*.

belief—beliefs giraffe—giraffes
wife—wives life—lives

15o. For nouns ending in *o* preceded by a vowel, add *-s*.

radio—radios patio—patios

15p. For nouns ending in *o* preceded by a consonant, add *-es*. For musical terms and proper nouns ending this way, just add *-s*.

potato—potato**es** tomato—tomato**es**
soprano—sopranos Soto—Sotos

15q. A few nouns form their plurals in irregular ways.

ox—oxen mouse—mice
woman—women child—children
goose—geese tooth—teeth

15r. For some nouns, the singular and the plural forms are the same.

Sioux Japanese salmon
deer moose sheep

WRITING NUMBERS

15s. Spell out a number that begins a sentence.

Thirteen people helped stage *The Secret Garden.*

Within a sentence, spell out numbers that can be written in one or two words.

More than **sixty-five** people came for the opening performance.

15t. If you use several numbers, some short and some long, write them all the same way. Usually, it is better to write them all as numerals.

In all, we spent **23** days rehearsing and sold **250** tickets.

15u. Spell out numbers used to indicate order.

This was our **third** stage play of the year.

Your Turn

Spell each of the following words, adding the prefix or suffix given.

1. im + mobile
2. re + set
3. un + lucky
4. happy + ly
5. semi + precious
6. force + able
7. shop + er
8. dirty + ness
9. hurry + ed
10. outrage + ous

16. Glossary of Usage

The Glossary of Usage is an alphabetical list of words and expressions with definitions, explanations, and examples. Some examples are labeled Standard or Formal. These labels identify language that is appropriate in serious writing or speaking, such as in compositions for school or in speeches. Expressions labeled Informal are acceptable in conversation and in everyday writing. *Nonstandard* expressions do not follow the guidelines of standard English.

a, an Use *a* before words or expressions that begin with consonant sounds. Use *an* before words or expressions that begin with vowel sounds.

Tom Sawyer was **a** friend of Huckleberry Finn.
The two boys had quite **an** adventure.

accept, except *Accept* is a verb that means "receive." *Except* may be either a verb or a preposition. As a verb, *except* means "leave out" or "exclude." As a preposition, *except* means "other than" or "excluding."

The Lins **accept** a dinner invitation from the Gleasons.

No guest was **excepted** from the Gleasons' hospitality. [verb]

No one **except** the Lins zipped the strings from the celery. [preposition]

affect, effect *Affect* is a verb meaning "influence." As a noun, *effect* means "the result of some action."

One error will not greatly **affect** your score on the test.

What **effect** did Rosa Parks's action have on the civil rights movement?

ain't Avoid this word in speaking and writing. It is nonstandard English.

all ready, already *All ready* means "completely prepared." *Already* means "before a certain point in time.

Mary was **all ready** for the test of endurance.

Her grandfather had **already** passed the test.

all right Used as an adjective, *all right* means "unhurt" or "satisfactory." Used as an adverb, *all right* means "well enough." *All right* should always be written as two words.

Mary wondered if she would be **all right.** [adjective]

She did **all right** during her time away from home. [adverb]

a lot *A lot* should always be written as two words.

She certainly learned **a lot** during those few days.

among *See* **between, among**.

anywheres, everywheres, nowheres, somewheres Use these words without the final *s*.

She didn't want to go **anywhere** [*not* anywheres].

at Do not use *at* after *where.*

Where was Roger? [*not* Where was Roger at?]

bad, badly *Bad* is an adjective. *Badly* is an adverb.

The berries taste **bad**. [*Bad* modifies the noun berries.]

Roger's eyes had swollen **badly**. [*Badly* modifies the verb had swollen.]

between, among Use *between* when referring to two things at a time, even though they may be part of a group containing more than two.

A deal was made **between** Ernie and Mary.

Use *among* when referring to a group rather than to the separate individuals in the group.

She walked **among** the many flowers.

bring, take *Bring* means "come carrying something." *Take* means "go carrying something." Think of *bring* as related to *come*. Think of *take* as related to *go*.

Please **bring** your new puzzle when you come over.

Take your bathing suit when you go to the beach.

bust, busted Avoid using these words as verbs. Use a form of either *burst* or *break*.

The dam **burst** [*not* busted], causing a flood.

Did you **break** [*not* bust] that window!

If you **break** [*not* bust] anything, you have to pay for it.

choose, chose *Choose* is the present tense form of the verb *choose*. It rhymes with *whose* and means "select." *Chose* is the past tense form of *choose*. It rhymes with *grows* and means "selected."

What story did you **choose** for your report?

I **chose** a Greek myth.

could of Do not write *of* with the helping verb *could*. Write *could have*. Also avoid using *ought to of, should of, would of, might of,* and *must of.*

Roger **could have** [*not* could of] done as Mary did.

Of is also unnecessary with *had*.

If he **had** [*not* had of] done so, he would have had a better time.

doesn't, don't *Doesn't* is the contraction of *does not. Don't* is the contraction of *do not*. Use *doesn't* with most singular subjects and *don't* with plural subjects and with *I* and *you*.

He **doesn't** look well.

I **don't** think so. They **don't** either.

double subject See **he, she, they**.

effect See **affect, effect**.

everywheres See **anywheres,** etc.

except See **accept, except.**

fewer, less *Fewer* is used with plural words. *Less* is used with singular words. *Fewer* tells "how many"; *less* tells "how much."

My family has **fewer** traditions than Mary's family.

Next time, use **less** chili powder.

good, well *Good* is always an adjective. Never use *good* as an adverb. Instead, use *well*.

Mary did **well** [*not* good] after her endurance ritual.

Although *well* is usually an adverb, *well* may also be used as an adjective to mean "healthy."

She looked **well** after her test.

had ought, hadn't ought *Had* should not be used with *ought*.

Eric **ought** [*not* had ought] to help us; he **oughtn't** [*not* hadn't ought] to have missed our meeting yesterday.

had of See **could of**.

had ought, hadn't ought Unlike other verbs, *ought* is not used with *had*.

Mary **ought to** [*not* had ought to] tell the truth.

hardly, scarcely The words *hardly* and *scarcely* are negative words. They should never be used with other negative words.

Grandfather **could** [*not* couldn't] **hardly** believe it.

He **had** [*not* hadn't] **scarcely** begun his Ta-Na-E-Ka when he found a dead deer.

he, she, they Avoid using a pronoun along with its antecedent as the subject of a verb. This error is called the ***double subject.***

NONSTANDARD	Ray Bradbury he wrote "All Summer in a Day."
STANDARD	Ray Bradbury wrote "All Summer in a Day."

hisself *Hisself* is nonstandard English. Use *himself.*

He fed **himself** [*not* hisself] on that deer the whole time.

how come In informal situations, *how come* is often used instead of *why.* In formal situations, *why* should always be used.

I don't know **why** [*not* how come]Roger left.

its, it's *Its* is a personal pronoun in the possessive form. *It's* is a contraction of *it is* or *it has.*.

Its purpose is to build confidence [possessive pronoun]

It's been practiced for many years. [contraction of *it has*]

kind of, sort of In informal situations, *kind of* and *sort of* are often used to mean "somewhat" or "rather." In formal English, *somewhat* or *rather* is preferred.

Mary seemed **somewhat** upset about the ritual.

learn, teach *Learn* means "gain knowledge." *Teach* means "instruct" or "show how."

The young people **learned** how to survive in the wilderness.

Their parents **taught** them what foods to eat.

less See **fewer, less**.

might of, must of See **could of**.

of Do not use *of* with other prepositions such as *inside, off,* and *outside.*

She waited **outside** [*not* outside of] the restaurant.

Jesse dared me to jump **off** [*not* off of] the dock.

ought to of See **could of.**

should of See **could of.**

sort of See **kind of, sort of.**

take See **bring, take.**

than, then *Than* is a conjunction used in making comparisons. *Then* is an adverb that means "at that time."

Are dogs friendlier **than** cats?

Back **then**, Dog and Cat were best friends.

their, there, they're *Their* is used to show ownership. *There* is used to mean "at that place" or to begin a sentence. *"They're* is a contraction of *they* are.

Won't **their** parents be pleased?

They will go into the woods over **there**.

There are many ways to gain self-confidence.

They're leaving today for their Ta-Na-E-Ka.

your, you're *Your* shows possession. *You're* is the contraction of *you are*.

Your story was very interesting.

You're part of a long tradition.

Your Turn Correcting Usage Errors

Revise each of the following sentences to correct any errors in usage. A sentence may contain more than one error.

1. The Kaw people treated one another good.
2. Take the time to research you're own culture's past.
3. Perhaps your a member of more then one culture.
4. Your family's traditions can learn you about yourself.

Glossary

The glossary that follows is an alphabetical list of words found in the selections in this book. Use this glossary just as you would use a dictionary—to find out the meaning of unfamiliar words. (Some technical, foreign, and more obscure words in this book are defined for you in the footnotes that accompany many of the selections.)

This glossary gives the meanings that apply to the words as they are used in the selections in this book.

The following abbreviations are used:

adj.	adjective
adv.	adverb
n.	noun
v.	verb

Each word's pronunciation is in parentheses. For more information about the words in this glossary or for information about words not listed here, consult a dictionary.

A

abandoned (uh BAN duhnd) *adj.* not used or taken care of any longer.

acquaintance (uh KWAYN tuhns) *n.* friend; someone known casually.

acquainted (uh KWAYNT ihd) *adj.* to know someone but not know him or her well.

adjoining (uh JOY nihng) *adj.* next to.

aggressive (uh GREHS ihv) *adj.* ready to attack.

amateurs (AM uh churz) *n.* people who participate in sports or other activities for fun rather than money; not professionals.

ambitious (am BIHSH uhs) *adj.* eager to achieve something; very much wanting success.

amiably (AY mee uh blee) *adv.* in a friendly way.

anonymous (uh NAHN uh muhs) *adj.* unknown; unidentified.

apprehensively (ap rih HEHN sihv lee) *adv.* fearfully; uneasily.

apprentice (uh PREHN tihs) *n.* beginner; someone who is just starting to learn a craft or job.

apt (apt) *adj.* skilled; capable.

arrogant (AR uh guhnt) *adj.* unpleasantly proud; thinking oneself is more important than others.

ashamed (uh SHAYMD) *adj.* embarrassed.

audacity (aw DAS uh tee) *n.* boldness; daring.

authorities (uh THAWR uh teez) *n.* people with the official responsibility for something.

avenge (uh VEHNJ) *v.* get even for; get revenge for.

B

balmy (BAH mee) *adj.* warm, pleasant; used especially for weather.

barren (BAR uhn) *adj.* unable to bear crops or fruit.

befriended (bih FREHND ihd) *v.* helped out or encouraged.

behold (bih HOHLD) *v.* to look at; to see.

C

cast (kast) *n.* group of performers in a play or event.

cautious (KAW shuhs) *adj.* careful.

cautiously (KAW shuhs lee) *adv.* safely; carefully.

chaos (KAY ahs) *n.* total confusion or disorder.

circumstance (SUR kuhm stans) *n.* fact or condition that affects a situation, action, or event.

civilizations (sihv uh luh ZAY shuhnz) *n.* advanced cultures characteristic of particular times and places.

claim (klaym) *n.* piece of land a prospector takes as his or her own.

cleft (klehft) *adj.* split; divided.

clenched (klehnchd) *v.* closed tightly.

clutch (kluhch) *v.* hold something tightly.

coincidence (koh IHN suh duhns) *n.* accidental happening of events that seem connected.

compensation (kahm puhn SAY shuhn) *n.* payment given to make up for a loss or injury.

competition (kahm puh TIHSH uhn) *n.* contest; struggle to see who is better.

complexity (kuhm PLEHK suh tee) *n.* complication; difficulty.

concentration (kahn suhn TRAY shuhn) *n.* focused attention.

confinement (kuhn FYN muhnt) *n.* condition of being kept from moving around; lack of freedom.
consequence (KAHN suh kwehns) *n.* importance.
conservation (kahn suhr VAY shuhn) *n.* protection of natural things such as animals, plants, and forests.
consoled (kuhn SOHLD) *v.* comforted when sad or disappointed.
conspicuous (kuhn SPIHK yoo uhs) *adj.* attracting attention.
contemporary (kuhn TEHM puh rehr ee) *adj.* relating to the present time; modern.
contented (kuhn TEHN tihd) *adj.* happy or satisfied.
contribution (kahn truh BYOO shuhn) *n.* payment given for a specific purpose.
cooperation (koh ahp uh RAY shuhn) *n.* support; working together.
craned (kraynd) *v.* stretched (the neck) in order to see better.
criticism (KRIHT uh sihz uhm) *n.* unfavorable remarks.
cropped (krahpt) *v.* bit or cut off the top.

D

dangled (DANG guhld) *v.* held something or swung it loosely.
declined (dih KLYND) *v.* dropped; went down.
defense (dih FEHNS) *n.* team acting to keep the opposing team from scoring points.
defiant (dih FY uhnt) *adj.* disobedient; boldly resistant.
defy (dih FY) *v.* resist.
depressed (dih PREHST) *adj.* very sad.
desperate (DEHS puhr iht) *adj.* having a great and urgent need.
devastating (DEHV uh STAY tihng) *adj.* causing great damage.
devour (dih VOWR) *v.* eat in a greedy way.
diligence (DIHL uh juhns) *n.* steady effort.
discretion (dihs KREHSH uhn) *n.* authority to make decisions.
dismal (DIHZ muhl) *adj.* cheerless; depressing.
dispute (dihs PYOOT) *n.* disagreement; argument.
downpour (DOWN pawr) *n.* a large amount of rain that falls in a short time.
dribble (DRIHB uhl) *n.* irregular drops that flow slowly.
duplicate (DOO pluh kayt) *v.* to copy.
dusk (duhsk) *n.* the period of time when the sky darkens as the sun goes down.

E

eccentric (ehk SEHN trihk) *adj.* peculiar; unusual.
elude (ih LOOD) *v.* escape the notice of; avoid detection by.
endured (ehn DURD) *v.* withstood or held out.
engaged (ehn GAYJD) *adj.* busy and interested; absorbed in something.
enhance (ehn HANS) *v.* increase; improve.
erupt (ih RUHPT) *v.* release suddenly or violently.
etiquette (EHT uh keht) *n.* acceptable manners and behavior.
evacuated (ih VAK yoo ayt uhd) *v.* removed from an area.
evident (EHV uh duhnt) *adj.* easily seen or understood; obvious.
express (ehk SPREHS) *n.* train that travels from one point to another without making stops.
exterior (ehk STIHR ee uhr) *adj.* outdoor.
extinct (ehk STIHNGKT) *adj.* no longer existing.
exuded (ehg ZOO dihd) *v.* gave off.

F

fascinated (FAS uh nayt ihd) *v.* charmed by something.
feat (feet) *n.* accomplishment; daring act.
finality (fy NAL uh tee) *n.* feeling that something is finished and can't be changed.
flattery (FLAT uhr ee) *n.* praise that is false or pretended.
flourish (FLUR ihsh) *n.* sweeping movement.
forsaken (fawr SAY kuhn) *adj.* abandoned.
frail (frayl) *adj.* not very strong; easily broken.
fraud (frawd) *n.* someone who pretends to be what he or she is not.

G

gesture (JEHS chuhr) *n.* act performed to show feelings.
gorging (GAWHRJ ihng) *v.* filling up; stuffing.
grimaced (GRIHM ihsd) *v.* to twist the face to express pain, anger, or disgust.
groove (groov) *n.* state of being comfortable.
guarantee (gar uhn TEE) *v.* promise or assure.

guaranteed (gair uhn TEED) *adj.* condition of being promised or pledged to pay or do something if another fails to do it.

H

hallucination (huh loo suh NAY shuhn) *n.* sight or sound of something that isn't really there.
hazardous (HAZ uhr duhs) *adj.* dangerous; risky.
hovered (HUHV uhrd) *v.* floated; remained still in the air.

I

ignorance (IHG nuhr uhns) *n.* lack of knowledge.
impressing (ihm PREHS ihng) *v.* making someone feel admiration.
improbable (ihm PRAHB uh buhl) *adj.* unlikely to be true.
indifference (ihn DIHF uhr uhns) *n.* state of being unconcerned about something.
indignant (ihn DIHG nuhnt) *adj.* offended; angry.
infested (ihn FEHST ihd) *v.* inhabited in large numbers (said of something harmful).
instrumental (ihn struh MEHN tuhl) *adj.* helping to make something happen.
interned (ihn TURND) *v.* imprisoned or confined.
intriguing (ihn TREE gihng) *adj.* causing great interest.
investigate (ihn VEHS tuh gayt) *v.* look into; examine.
invincible (ihn VIHN suh buhl) *adj.* unable to be defeated.
invisible (ihn VIHZ uh buhl) *adj.* not able to be seen.
irritable (IHR uh tuh buhl) *adj.* in a bad mood; short-tempered.
isolation (y suh LAY shun) *n.* condition of being apart from others; removed.
itchy (IHCH ee) *adj.* causing a feeling on the skin that makes you want to rub or scratch.

J

jammed (jamd) *v.* got stuck and became unworkable.
jubilant (JOO buh luhnt) *adj.* joyful.

K

keen (keen) *adj.* eager; enthusiastic.

L

lair (lair) *n.* the home of a wild animal; den.
lavishly (LAV ihsh lee) *adv.* abundantly; plentifully.
legacy (LEHG uh see) *n.* something handed down or left for others.
legitimate (luh JIHT uh miht) *adj.* reasonable; justified.
linen (LIHN uhn) *n.* fine-quality writing paper.
literally (LIHT uhr uh lee) *adv.* actually; in truth.
loftiest (LAWF tee uhst) *adj.* noblest; highest.
lunged (luhnjd) *v.* moved suddenly forward.

M

maneuvered (muh NOO vuhrd) *v.* moved, as a group, into position.
manipulate (muh NIHP yuh layt) *v.* to manage or control, often in an unfair way.
marvel (MAHR vuhl) *v.* to wonder at.
menacing (MEHN uh sihng) *adj.* threatening.
montage (mahn TAHZH) *n.* combination of pictures.
mortified (MAWR tuh fyd) *v.* used as *adj.* ashamed; embarrassed.
motto (MAHT oh) *n.* short statement that expresses the aims or beliefs of a person or institution.

N

nurturing (NUR chuhr ihng) *v.* keeping alive.
nutritious (noo TRIHSH uhs) *adj.* full of nourishment; healthful.

O

occupation (ahk yuh PAY shuhn) *n.* work a person does regularly.
outrageous (owt RAY juhs) *adj.* extreme; shocking.

P-Q

peculiar (pih KYOOL yuhr) *adj.* strange.
penetrated (PEHN uh tray tihd) *v.* pierced; made a way through.
permanent (PUR muh nuhnt) *adj.* lasting; unchanging.
perplexed (puhr PLEHKST) *adj.* puzzled.
persistent (puhr SIHS tuhnt) *adj.* repeated or continuing.

plunged (pluhnjd) *v.* dived down suddenly.
pollution (puh LOO shuhn) *n.* something that makes air, water, and soil dangerously dirty.
ponder (PAHN duhr) *v.* think over carefully.
precision (prih SIHZH uhn) *n.* exactness; accuracy.
prehistoric (pree hihs TAWR ihk) *adj.* relating to the time before written history.
prescribe (prih SKRYB) *v.* define officially.
previously (PREE vee uhs lee) *adv.* before now.
primary (PRY mehr ee) *adj.* first in importance.
privilege (PRIHV uh lihj) *n.* special right or benefit.
projection (pruh JEHKT shuhn) *n.* display of an image made by shining light through a small version of the image.
protective (pruh TEHK tihv) *adj.* preventing injury.
proverb (PRAHV urb) *n.* short wise saying.
prudent (PROO duhnt) *adj.* wise; sensible.

R

raggedy (RAG uh dee) *adj.* torn; in bad condition.
rash (rash) *adj.* impatient; reacting quickly.
rattling (RAT lihng) *v.* shaking and hitting together.
ravaged (RAV ihjd) *v.* damaged greatly.
recall (rih KAWL) *v.* remember; bring to mind.
recovered (rih KUHV uhrd) *v.* got back something lost.
rectify (REHK tuh fy) *v.* correct.
remedy (REHM uh dee) *n.* cure; solution.
resembled (rih ZEHM buhld) *v.* was similar to.
resumed (rih ZOOMD) *v.* began again.
revived (rih VYVD) *v.* awakened; brought back to life.
rival (RY vul) *adj.* competing.
rural (RUR uhl) *adj.* having to do with country life.

S

savored (SAY vuhrd) *v.* delighted in.
shrewdest (SHROOD uhst) *adj.* sharpest; most clever.
sift (sihft) *v.* strain or filter through something.
sinister (SIHN uh stuhr) *adj.* creepy; threatening.
snatched (snachd) *v.* grabbed; ran off with.
spectacle (SPEHK tuh kuhl) *n.* strange or impressive sight.
splendor (SPLEHN duhr) *n.* brightness; glory.
stampede (stam PEED) *n.* sudden rush.
structure (STRUHK chuhr) *n.* something built or constructed.
supervisor (SOO puhr vy zuhr) *n.* person in charge.
surged (surjd) *v.* moved forward, as if in a wave.
surveyed (suhr VAYD) *v.* looked over and examined closely.
suspicion (suh SPIHSH uhn) *n.* a feeling that someone is guilty of something.

T

tangles (TANG guhlz) *v.* becomes twisted into knots.
techniques (tehk NEEKS) *n.* ways of doing complex activities.
thrashing (THRASH ihng) *v.* moving from side to side in an uncontrolled way.
thrust (thruhst) *v.* shoved; pushed.
timid (TIHM ihd) *adj.* shy; lacking self-confidence.
tolerant (TAHL uhr uhnt) *adj.* patient; accepting of others.
torrents (TAWR ruhnts) *n.* rushing streams of water.
treacherous (TREHCH uhr uhs) *adj.* dangerous.
tumult (TOO muhlt) *n.* a violent disturbance.

U

unique (yoo NEEK) *adj.* one of a kind; rare or special.
urgency (UR juhn see) *n.* pressure; insistence.

V

valiant (VAL yuhnt) *adj.* determined; brave.
victorious (vihk TAWR ee uhs) *adj.* having won.
vigor (VIHG uhr) *n.* energy; physical or mental strength.
vital (VY tuhl) *adj.* necessary for life; very important.
vivid (VIHV ihd) *adj.* producing strong, clear images.

W-Z

wily (WY lee) *adj.* sly; clever in a sneaky way.
yearning (YUR nihng) *n.* feeling of wanting something badly.

Spanish Glossary

A-B

ademán *sust.* gesto que demuestra lo que uno siente.

adulación *sust.* alabanza o elogio que es falso o fingido.

afablemente *v.* de manera amigable; amablemente.

aferrar *v.* agarrar algo con firmeza.

aficionado *sust.* persona que participa en deportes u otras actividades por diversión y no por dinero; persona que no es un profesional.

agresivo *adj.* listo para atacar.

aguacero *sust.* lluvia abundante y repentina de poca duración.

aislamiento *sust.* estado de incomunicación con otras personas; soledad.

alucinación *sust.* percepción de un sonido o una imagen que en realidad no existe.

ambicioso *adj.* que tiene deseos y entusiasmo por lograr algo.

ambicioso *adj.* que tiene deseos y entusiasmo por lograr algo.

anhelo *sust.* sensación de desear mucho algo.

anónimo *adj.* desconocido; que no está identificado con un nombre.

apremio *sust.* urgencia; insistencia.

aprendiz *sust.* principiante; alguien que empieza a aprender un arte o un oficio.

aprensivamente *adv.* temerosamente; con preocupación.

apto *adj.* capaz.

arrastrar *v.* mover hacia adelante.

arrebatar *v.* agarrar de un manotazo.

arriesgado *adj.* peligroso.

arrogante *adj.* orgulloso de un modo desagradable.

artero *adj.* astuto; inteligente y engañoso.

asemejarse *v.* ser parecido a alguien o a algo.

asomarse *v.* estirar (el cuello) para ver mejor.

aspaviento *sust.* movimiento amplio.

atardecer *sust.* momento del día en el que se oscurece el cielo a medida que el sol se pone.

atascar *v.* atorar y hacer que algo ya no funcione.

atiborrar *v.* llenar; atestar.

audacia *sust.* atrevimiento.

autoridad *sust.* persona que tiene la responsabilidad oficial para hacer algo.

auxiliar *v.* ayudar.

bienestar *sust.* sensación de comodidad y agrado.

C-E

caos *sust.* desorden o confusión total.

cautelosamente *adv.* con cuidado.

cauteloso *adj.* cuidadoso.

cavilar *v.* pensar detenidamente en algo.

cercenar *v.* cortar la punta de algo.

cimbrar *v.* hacer vibrar algo.

circunstancia *sust.* hecho o condición que afecta a una situación, una acción o un suceso.

civilización *sust.* cultura avanzada característica de un tiempo y un lugar determinados.

cohibido *adj.* tímido; que no tiene seguridad en sí mismo.

coincidencia *sust.* hechos que suceden de forma accidental y parecen estar relacionados.

competencia *sust.* concurso; lucha por ver quién es mejor en algo.

complacido *adj.* feliz o satisfecho.

complejidad *sust.* complicación; dificultad.

comprometido *adj.* interesado por algo y ocupado en eso.

concentración *sust.* atención profunda en algo.

confinamiento *sust.* condición de estar retenido en un lugar; falta de libertad.

conocido *adj.* persona que se conoce pero con quien no hay mucha confianza.

conocido *sust.* persona que se conoce pero con quien no hay mucha confianza.

conservación *sust.* protección de la naturaleza, como los animales, las plantas y los bosques.

consolar *v.* confortar o aliviar cuando uno está triste o desilusionado.

contemplar *v.* mirar algo detenidamente.

contemporáneo *adj.* relativo al tiempo presente; moderno.

contribución *sust.* pago que se hace con un propósito determinado.
cooperación *sust.* apoyo; trabajo en conjunto.
criterio *sust.* capacidad para tomar decisiones con responsabilidad.
crítica *sust.* comentario desfavorable.
decrecer *v.* disminuir; descender.
defensa *sust.* acción de equipo para evitar que el equipo contrario anote puntos.
deprimido *adj.* muy triste.
desafiante *adj.* desobediente; que se resiste.
desafiar *v.* resistir.
desatendido *adj.* que ya no se usa o no se cuida.
desesperado *adj.* que tiene una necesidad grande y urgente.
desolado *adj.* abandonado.
devastador *adj.* que causa mucho daño.
devastar *v.* causar destrucción, daño.
devorar *v.* comer con glotonería.
dictar *v.* establecer oficialmente.
diligencia *sust.* cuidado y empeño al hacer algo.
disputa *sust.* desacuerdo; discusión.

duplicar *v.* hacer una copia.
elenco *sust.* grupo de actores de una obra de teatro o espectáculo.
eludir *v.* evitar; esquivar.
embestir *v.* empujar de repente hacia adelante.
enmarañar *v.* enredar.
entusiasta *adj.* que tiene mucho interés en algo o muchas ganas de hacer algo.
escandaloso *adj.* vergonzoso.
espectáculo *sust.* algo que se ve y produce extrañeza o asombro.
esplendor *sust.* brillo; gloria.
estampida *sust.* huida repentina.
estéril *adj.* que no da frutos o no produce cosecha.
estructura *sust.* algo construido.
estrujar *v.* apretar con fuerza.
etiqueta *sust.* comportamiento y modales aceptables.
evacuar *v.* desocupar un área.
evidente *adj.* fácil de ver o entender; claro.
evocar *v.* recordar; traer a la memoria.
excéntrico *adj.* raro; extravagante.
exclusivo *adj.* único; raro o especial.
expreso *sust.* tren que viaja de u punto a otro sin hacer paradas.
expulsar *v.* liberar de repente o violentamente.
exterior *adj.* al aire libre.
extinto *adj.* que ya no existe.
exultante *adj.* lleno de alegría.

F-K

fascinar *v.* provocar atracción.

flotar *v.* mantenerse quieto en el aire.
frágil *adj.* débil; que se rompe fácilmente.
garantizado *adj.* que se prometió hacer o se aseguró que se haría si otra persona no lo hacía.
garantizar *v.* prometer o asegurar.
generosamente *adv.* mucho; en abundancia.
gesticular *v.* retorcer la cara para expresar algo, como dolor, enojo o disgusto.
goteo *sust.* cantidades pequeñas de un líquido que caen lentamente.
guarida *sust.* lugar donde vive un animal salvaje; refugio.

harapiento *adj.* roto y en malas condiciones.

ignorancia *sust.* falta de conocimiento.
impeler *v.* empujar; impulsar.
impostor *sust.* alguien que finge ser lo que no es.
impresionar *v.* hacer que alguien sienta admiración.
improbable *adj.* que no parece que pueda ser cierto.
indemnización *sust.* pago que se da como compensación por una pérdida o un daño.
indiferencia *sust.* estado de ánimo en que no se siente interés por algo.
indignado *adj.* ofendido; enojado.
inspeccionar *v.* investigar; examinar.
inspeccionar *v.* observar o examinar de cerca.
instrumental *adj.* que sirve como medio para que algo suceda.
intimidante *adj.* amenazante.
intrigante *adj.* que causa gran curiosidad o interés.
invencible *adj.* que no puede ser derrotado.
invisible *adj.* que no se puede ver.
irascible *adj.* de mal humor; irritable.
irrevocabilidad *sust.* sensación de que algo es definitivo y no se puede cambiar.

L-Q

legado *sust.* algo que se deja o se transmite a otros.
legítimo *adj.* razonable; conforme a las leyes.
lema *sust.* frase breve que expresa los objetivos o las creencias de una persona, una escuela o una institución.
lindante *adj.* que está próximo a algo.
literalmente *adv.* realmente; en verdad.
llamativo *adj.* que atrae la atención.
lúgubre *adj.* sombrío; deprimente.
maniobrar *v.* mover algo.
manipular *v.* manejar o controlar, a menudo de manera injusta.
montaje sust. combinación de imágenes.
nutrir *v.* alimentar.
nutritivo *adj.* que tiene las sustancias alimenticias necesarias; saludable.
ocupación *sust.* trabajo que realiza una persona de forma regular.
paladear *v.* saborear.
papel tela *sust.* papel para escribir de muy buena calidad que antiguamente se hacía con trapos de lino.
parcela *sust.* porción de tierra.
partido *adj.* dividido; separado.
pasmar *v.* asombrar; maravillar.
peculiar *adj.* extraño.
pender *v.* estar algo colgado o suspendido.
perforar *v.* agujerear; atravesar.
permanente *adj.* definitivo; duradero.
perplejo *adj.* desconcertado.
persistente *adj.* que se repite o continúa.
picor *sust.* sensación en la piel que provoca ganas de frotarse o rascarse.
plagar *v.* habitar en gran número (algo dañino).
polución *sust.* algo que hace que el aire, el agua y el suelo se ensucien de manera peligrosa.
precipitado *adj.* impaciente..
precisión *sust.* exactitud.
prehistórico *adj.* relacionado con la época anterior a la historia escrita.
previamente *adv.* antes de ahora.
primordial *adj.* principal; primero en importancia.
privilegio *sust.* derecho o beneficio especial.
proeza *sust.* logro; acción valerosa.
protector *adj.* que impide que se produzcan lesiones.
proverbio *sust.* dicho corto y sabio
proyección *sust.* imagen que, por medio de un foco luminoso, se fija temporalmente sobre una superficie plana.
prudente *adj.* sensato.

R-Z

realzar *v.* mejorar.
reanimar *v.* despertar; revivir.
reanudar *v.* comenzar de nuevo; continuar.
recluir *v.* encarcelar o encerrar.
recobrar *v.* recuperar algo perdido.
rectificar *v.* corregir.
remedio *sust.* cura; solución.
rezumar *v.* liberar, despedir algo.
riesgoso *adj.* peligroso; arriesgado.
rival *adj.* que compite; que trata de igualar o sobrepasar a otro.
rural *adj.* del campo o relacionado con él.
sagaz *adj.* astuto; inteligente.
siniestro *adj.* escalofriante; amenazante.
soportar *v.* resistir o aguantar.
sospecha *sust.* sensación de que alguien es culpable de algo.
sublime *adj.* noble; muy elevado.
supervisor *sust.* persona a cargo.
tamizar *v.* pasar por un filtro.
técnica *sust.* modo de llevar a cado actividades complejas.
templado *adj.* relativo al clima o al aire, cálido y agradable.
tolerante *adj.* paciente; que acepta a los demás.
torrente *sust.* corriente brusca de agua.
trascendencia *sust.* importancia.
tumulto *sust.* alboroto o agitaciÛn violenta.
turbado *adj.* avergonzado.
turbar *v.* avergonzar; abochornar.
valeroso *adj.* valiente; decidido.
vengar *v.* hacer un mal a alguien que le hizo mal a uno; tomar represalias.
victorioso *adj.* que obtuvo un triunfo.
vigor *sust.* energía; fuerza física o mental.
vital *adj.* necesario para la vida; muy importante.
vívido *adj.* que produce imágenes claras y fuertes.
zambullirse *v.* sumergirse de repente.
zarandear *v.* mover de un lado a otro de manera incontrolada.

Academic Vocabulary Glossary

The Academic Vocabulary Glossary is an alphabetical list of the Academic Vocabulary words found in this textbook. Use this glossary just as you would use a dictionary—to find out the meanings of words used in your literature class. For each word, the glossary includes the pronunciation, part of speech, and meaning. A Spanish version of the glossary immediately follows the English version. For more information about the words in the Academic Vocabulary Glossary, please consult a dictionary.

ENGLISH

A-C

achieve (uh CHEEV) *v.* succeed in getting a good result or in doing something you want.

adapt (uh DAPT) *v.* to change ideas or behavior to fit a new situation.

appreciate (uh PREE shee ayt) *v.* understand and enjoy the good qualities or value of something.

attitude (AT uh tood) *n.* the opinions and feelings you usually have about someone or something.

authority (uh THAWR uh tee) *n.* someone who is respected because of his or her knowledge about a subject.

circumstance (SUR kuhm stans) *n.* event or condition that affects a person.

communicate (kuh MYOO nuh kayt) *v.* to express your thoughts or feelings clearly so that other people understand them.

complex (kahm PLEHKS) *adj.* complicated; not simple.

concept (KAHN sehpt) *n.* idea of how something is or could be.

conclude (kuhn KLOOD) *v.* to decide something after considering all the information you have.

contrast (KAHN trast) *n.* a difference between two people, situations, ideas, and so on, that are being compared.

contribute (kuhn TRIHB yoot) *v.* to give or add something, such as resources or ideas.

create (kree AYT) *v.* to make something new exist or happen.

crucial (KROO shuhl) *adj.* very important.

D-G

data (DAY tuh) *n.* facts or figures; information.

detect (dih TEHKT) *v.* notice or discover, especially something that is not easy to see, hear, and so on.

device (dih VYS) *n.* way of achieving a particular purpose.

display (dihs PLAY) *v.* show clearly; reveal.

distinct (dihs TIHNGKT) *adj.* distinguishable; clearly different or of a different type.

dynamic (dy NAM ihk) *adj.* characterized by action; energetic; changing.

features (FEE chuhrz) *n.* important, typical parts.

gender (JEHN duhr) *n.* the fact of being male or female.

H-O

illustrate (IHL uh strayt) *v.* to explain or make something clear by giving examples.

indicate (IHN duh kayt) *v.* show; express; suggest.

interact (ihn tuhr AKT) *v.* talk to and deal with others.

interpret (ihn TUR priht) *v.* decide on the meaning of something.

major (MAY juhr) *adj.* very large and important, especially compared with other things of a similar kind.

obvious (AHB vee uhs) *adj.* easy to notice or understand.

P-Z

perspective (puhr SPEHK tihv) *n.* mental view or outlook; way of thinking.

principal (PRIHN suh puhl) *adj.* most important.

uniform (YOO nuh fawrm) *adj.* having the same shape, size, quality, or other characteristics.

visual (VIHZH oo uhl) *adj.* related to seeing or to sight.

SPANISH

A-C

actitud *sust.* opiniones que uno toma y sentimientos que uno tiene con respecto a alguien o a algo.

adaptarse *v.* cambiar las ideas o la conducta para amoldarse a una situación nueva.

apreciar *v.* comprender y disfrutar de la calidad o el valor de algo.

autoridad *sust.* alguien que es respetado por su conocimiento acerca de un tema.

característica *sust.* rasgo importante, típico.

circunstancia *sust.* suceso o situación que rodea a una persona y la afecta.

complejo *adj.* que no es sencillo; complicado, difícil.

comunicar *v.* expresar los pensamientos o sentimientos claramente para que otras personas los entiendan.

concepto *sust.* idea de cómo es o cómo podría ser algo.

concluir *v.* decidir algo después de considerar toda la información disponible.

contraste *sust.* diferencia entre dos personas, situaciones, ideas, etc. al compararlas.

contribuir *v.* dar o agregar algo, como recursos o ideas.

crear *v.* hacer que suceda o que exista algo nuevo.

crucial *adj.* muy importante.

D-G

dato *sust.* hecho o cifra; información.

detectar *v.* notar o descubrir, especialmente algo que no es fácil de ver, oír, etc.

dinámico *adj.* que se caracteriza por la acción; enérgico.

distinto *adj.* diferente; claramente diferenciado o de otro tipo.

estrategia *sust.* modo de alcanzar un objetivo determinado.

exteriorizar *v.* mostrar claramente los sentimientos o cualidades.

fundamental *adj.* muy importante, especialmente en comparación con otras cosas del mismo tipo.

fundamental *adj.* muy importante.

género *sust.* hecho de que algo o alguien sea femenino o masculino.

H-O

ilustrar *v.* demostrar o explicar algo mediante ejemplos.

indicar *v.* mostrar; expresar; sugerir.

interactuar *v.* hablar con otras personas y trabajar con ellas.

interpretar *v.* decidir sobre el significado de algo.

lograr *v.* tener éxito en algo que uno quiere.

obvio *adj.* fácil de notar o entender.

P-Z

perspectiva *sust.* punto de vista; modo de pensar.

uniforme *adj.* que tiene la misma forma, tamaño, calidad u otras características.

visual *adj.* de la vista o relacionado con ella.

ACKNOWLEDGMENTS

Grateful acknowledgment is made to the following sources for permission to reproduce copyrighted material:

"Oprah Talks About Her South African 'Dreamgirls'" *from ABC News* Web site, accessed October 1, 2007, at http://abcnews.go.com/GMA/story?id=2767103&page=1&CMP=OTC-RSSFeeds0312. Copyright © 2007 by **ABC News.** Reproduced by permission of the copyright holder.

From *Two in the Far North* by Margaret E. Murie. Copyright © 1978 by Margaret E. Murie. Reproduced by permission of **Alaska Northwest Books®, an imprint of Graphic Arts Center Publishing Company.**

From "Letters to Rev. Phillips Brooks" from *The Story of My Life* by Helen Keller. Copyright © 2005 by **The American Foundation for the Blind.** Reproduced by permission of the copyright holder.

"A Balmy Spring Wind" from *Haiku: This Other World* by Richard Wright. Copyright © 1998 by Ellen Wright. Reproduced by permission of **Arcade Publishing, New York, New York. [No web allowed]**

"In the Blood" from *Chants* by Pat Mora, www.patmora.com. Copyright © 1985 by Pat Mora. Reproduced by permission of **Arte Público Press/University of Houston.**

"En la Sangre" from *Chants* by Pat Mora, www.patmora.com. Copyright © 1985 by Pat Mora. Reproduced by permission of **Arte Público Press/University of Houston.**

"The Bracelet" by Yoshiko Uchida from *The Scribner Anthology for Young People,* edited by Anne Diven. Copyright © 1976 by Yoshiko Uchida. Reproduced by permission of **Atheneum Books for Young Readers, an imprint of Simon & Schuster Children's Publishing Division.**

"Stray" from *Every Living Thing* by Cynthia Rylant. Copyright © 1985 by Cynthia Rylant. Reproduced by permission of **Atheneum Books for Young Readers, an imprint of Simon & Schuster Children's Publishing Division.**

From *Desert Exile: The Uprooting of a Japanese American Family* by Yoshiko Uchida. Copyright © 1982 by Yoshiko Uchida. Reproduced by permission of **Bancroft Library, University of California, Berkeley.**

"Eleven" from *Woman Hollering Creek* by Sandra Cisneros. Copyright © 1991 by Sandra Cisneros. Published by Vintage Books, a division of Random House, Inc., New York, and originally in hardcover by Random House, Inc. All rights reserved. Reproduced by permission of **Susan Bergholz Literary Services, New York.**

"Good Hot Dogs" from *My Wicked, Wicked Ways* by Sandra Cisneros. Copyright © 1987 by Sandra Cisneros. Published by Third Woman Press and in hardcover by Alfred A. Knopf. All rights reserved. Reproduced by permission of **Susan Bergholz Literary Services, New York.**

"Straw into Gold" by Sandra Cisneros from *The Texas Observer,* September 1987. Copyright © 1987 by Sandra Cisneros. Reproduced by permission of **Susan Bergholz Literary Services, Inc., New York.**

"Dragon, Dragon" from *Dragon, Dragon and Other Tales* by John Gardner. Copyright © 1975 by Boskydell Artists Ltd. Reproduced by permission of **Georges Borchardt, Inc., for The Estate of John Gardner.**

"Winter Rain" by Nozawa Bonchō from *The Penguin Book of Japanese Verse,* translated by Geoffrey Bownas and Anthony Thwaite, Penguin Books, 1964. Translation copyright © 1964 by **Geoffrey Bownas and Anthony Thwaite.** Reproduced by permission of the translators.

"Bad-tempered, I got back" by Ōshima Ryōta from *The Penguin Book of Japanese Verse,* translated by Geoffrey Bownas and Anthony Thwaite, Penguin Books, 1964. Translation copyright © 1964 by **Geoffrey Bownas and Anthony Thwaite.** Reproduced by permission of the translators.

"Cynthia in the Snow" from *Bronzeville Boys and Girls* by Gwendolyn Brooks. Copyright © 1956 by Gwendolyn Brooks. Reproduced by permission of **Brooks Permissions.**

"A Caution to Everybody," "The Camel," "The Duck," "The Octopus," and "The Panther" from *Verses From 1929 On* by Ogden Nash. Copyright © 1953, 1935, 1940, 1942, 1940 by Ogden Nash. Reproduced by permission of **Curtis Brown, Ltd.**

Quote by Ogden Nash. Reproduced by permission of **Curtis Brown, Ltd.**

From *What Do Fish Have to Do With Anything?* by Avi, illustrated by Tracy Mitchell. Copyright © 1997 by Avi. Reproduced by permission of **Candlewick Press, Inc., Cambridge, MA.**

"Perseus and the Gorgon's Head" from *Greek Myths for Young Children* by Marcia Williams. Copyright © 1991 by Marcia Williams. Reproduced by permission of **Candlewick Press, Inc., Cambridge, MA, on behalf of Walker Books Ltd., London.**

Quote about comic books by Marcia Williams from *Candlewick Press* Web site, accessed October 1, 2007, at http://www.candlewick.com/authill.asp?b=Author&m=bio&id=1779&pix=y. Reproduced by permission of **Candlewick Press, Inc., Cambridge, MA.**

"Wartime Mistakes, Peacetime Apologies" by Nancy Day from *Cobblestone: Japanese Americans,* April 1996. Copyright © 1996 by Cobblestone Publishing, 30 Grove Street, Suite C, Peterborough, NH 03458. All rights reserved. Reproduced by permission of **Carus Publishing Company.**

"Making a Flying Fish" by Paula Morrow, adapted from *FACES: Happy Holidays,* vol. 7, no. 4, December 1990. Copyright © 1990 by Cobblestone Publishing, 30 Grove Street, Suite C, Peterborough, NH 03458. All rights reserved. Reproduced by permission of **Carus Publishing Company.**

"The Storytelling Stone" by John Cech from *Parabola, The Magazine of Myth and Traditions,* vol. IV, no. 4, 1979. Copyright © 1979 by **John Cech.** Reproduced by permission of the author.

From "Too Much TV Can Equal Too Much Weight" by Jamie Rodgers from *Children's Express* Web site, accessed September 22, 2000 at http://www.cenews.org/news/200007obesetv.htm. Copyright © 2000 by **Children's Express Foundation.** Reproduced by permission of the copyright holder. **[No Web allowed]**

"In a Neighborhood in Los Angeles" from *Body in Flames/Cuerpo en Llamas* by Francisco X. Alarcón. Copyright © 1990 by Francisco X. Alarcón. Reproduced by permission of **Chronicle Books LLC, San Francisco.**

"Forty-One Seconds on a Sunday in June, in Salt Lake City, Utah" from *Choruses: Poems* by Quincy Troupe. Copyright © 1999 by Quincy Troupe. Reproduced by permission of **Coffee House Press.**

"The All-American Slurp" by Lensey Namioka from *Visions,* edited by Donald R. Gallo. Copyright © 1987 by Lensey Namioka. All rights reserved by the author. Reproduced by permission of **Ruth Cohen for Lensey Namioka.**

Quote by Lensey Namioka. Reproduced by permission of **Ruth Cohen for Lensey Namioka.**

"All Summer in a Day" by Ray Bradbury. Copyright © 1954 and renewed © 1982 by Ray Bradbury. Reproduced by permission of **Don Congdon Associates, Inc. [No web allowed]**

Quote by Ray Bradbury from *Something About the Author,* vol. 40. Reproduced by permission of **Don Congdon Associates, Inc. [No web allowed]**

From *Cricket in the Road* by **Michael Anthony.** Copyright © 1973 by Michael Anthony. Reproduced by permission of **Andre Deutsch Limited, an imprint of Carlton Publishing Group** and electronic format by permission of the author.

From *The Gold Cadillac* by Mildred D. Taylor. Copyright © 1987 by Mildred D. Taylor. Reproduced by permission of **Dial Books for Young Readers, a Division of Penguin Books for Young Readers, a Division of Penguin Group (USA) Inc., 345 Hudson Street, New York, NY 10014, www.penguin.com.**

"Author's Note" from *The Gold Cadillac* by Mildred D. Taylor. Copyright © 1987 by Mildred D. Taylor. All rights reserved. Reproduced by permission of **Dial Books for Young Readers, A Division of Penguin Young Readers Group, A Member of Penguin Group (USA) Inc., 345 Hudson Street, New York, NY 10014, www.penguin.com.**

From *John Brown: One Man Against Slavery* by Gwen Everett. Copyright © 1993 by **Gwen Everett.** Reproduced by permission of the author.

"The Toaster" from *Laughing Time: Collected Nonsense* by William Jay Smith. Copyright © 1990 by William Jay Smith. Reproduced by permission of **Farrar, Straus and Giroux, LLC.**

Essay by Russell Freedman. Copyright @ 2007 by **Russell Freedman.** Reproduced by permission of the author.

In the Fog by Milton Geiger. Reproduced by permission of **Katie Gerard, Trustee for Dorothy Geiger.**

"The Path Through The Cemetery" by Leonard Q. Ross from *The Saturday Review of Literature,* November 29, 1941. Copyright © 1941 by **General Media International, Inc.** Reproduced by permission of the copyright holder.

From "The U.S. has a garbage crisis" from *The Environment: Distinguishing Between Fact and Opinion* by William Dudley. Copyright © 1990 by **Greenhaven Press, Inc., a division of Thomson Learning.** Reproduced by permission of the publisher.

Adapted from "Blanca Flor/White Flower" from *¡Teatro! Hispanic Plays for Young People* by Angel Vigil. Copyright © 1996 by Teacher Ideas Press. Reproduced by permission of **Greenwood Publishing Group, Inc., Westport, CT.**

Quote by Pearl Bailey from *The Raw Pearl.* Copyright © 1968 by Pearl Bailey and copyright renewed © 1996 by Louis P. Bellson. Reproduced by permission of Harcourt, Inc. and electronic format by permission of **The William Morris Agency.**

"Killingly Funny: Mark Twain" by Kathleen Krull from *Lives of the Writers: Comedies, Tragedies (and What the Neighbors Thought).* Copyright © 1994 by Kathleen Krull. Reproduced by permission of **Harcourt, Inc.**

"La Bamba" from *Baseball in April and Other Stories* by Gary Soto. Copyright © 1990 by Gary Soto. Reproduced by permission of **Harcourt, Inc.**

"Ode to Mi Gato" from *Neighborhood Odes* by Gary Soto. Copyright © 1992 by Gary Soto. Reproduced by permission of **Harcourt, Inc.**

Excerpt from "Amaroq, the wolf" (retitled "Lost on the Tundra") from *Julie of the Wolves* by Jean Craighead George. Copyright © 1972 by Jean Craighead George. Reproduced by permission of **HarperCollins Publishers, Inc.**

"Aaron's Gift" from *The Witch of Fourth Street and Other Stories* by Myron Levoy. Copyright © 1972 by Myron Levoy. Reproduced by permission of **HarperCollins Publishers, Inc.**

"Love that Boy" from *Brown Angels: An Album of Pictures and Verse* by Walter Dean Myers. Copyright © 1993 by Walter Dean Myers. Reproduced by permission of **HarperCollins Publishers, Inc.**

Introduction to poem "Love that Boy" from *Brown Angels: An Album of Pictures and Verse* by Walter Dean Myers. Copyright © 1993 by **HarperCollins Publishers, Inc.**

From *The Land I Lost* by Huynh Quang Nhuong. Copyright © 1982 by Huynh Quang Nhuong. Reproduced by permission of **HarperCollins Publishers, Inc.**

Zlateh the Goat and Other Stories by Isaac Bashevis Singer, illustrated by Maurice Sendak. Text copyright © 1966 by Isaac Bashevis Singer. Reproduced by permission of **HarperCollins Publishers, Inc.**

Quote by Oprah Winfrey from *O Magazine,* July 2002, accessed November 16, 2007 at http://www.oprah.com/omagazine/200207/omag_200207_mission.jhtml. Copyright © 2002 by Oprah Winfrey. Reproduced by permission of **The Hearst Corporation.**

"Steam Shovel" from *Upper Pasture: Poems* by Charles Malam. Copyright 1930, © 1958 by Charles Malam. Reproduced by permission of **Henry Holt and Company, LLC.**

Quote by Ann Petry from *Horn Book Magazine,* April 1965. Copyright © 1965. Reproduced by permission of **The Horn Book, Inc.**

"Medusa's Head" from *Greek Myths* by Olivia Coolidge. Copyright © 1949 and renewed © 1977 by Olivia E. Coolidge. All rights reserved. Reproduced by permission of **Houghton Mifflin Company.**

"The Mysterious Mr. Lincoln" from *Lincoln: A Photobiography* by Russell Freedman. Copyright © 1987 by Russell Freedman. All rights reserved. Reproduced by permission of **Houghton Mifflin Company.**

Essay by **Cynthia Kadohata.** Copyright © 2007 by Cynthia Kadohata. Reproduced by permission of the author.

"Things to Do If You Are a Subway" by Bobbi Katz from *Upside Down and Inside Out: Poems for All Your Pockets.* Copyright © 1971 by **Bobbi Katz.** Reproduced by permission of the author, www.bobbikatz.com.

Quote by Bobbi Katz from *Bobbi Katz* Web site, accessed November 19, 2007 at http://www.bobbikatz.com/bio.htm. Reproduced by permission of **Bobbi Katz.**

"About 'That Day'" by **David Kherdian.** Copyright © 1991 by **David Kherdian.** Reproduced by permission of the author.

Text from "He Lion, Bruh Bear, and Bruh Rabbit" from *The People Could Fly: American Black Folktales* by Virginia Hamilton, illustrated by Leo and Diane Dillon. Copyright © 1985 by Virginia Hamilton; illustrations copyright © 1985 by Leo and Diane Dillon. Reproduced by permission of **Alfred A. Knopf, a division of Random House, Inc. [NO web allowed]**

"Motto" from *The Collected Poems of Langston Hughes.* Copyright © 1994 by The Estate of Langston Hughes. Reproduced by permission of **Alfred A. Knopf, a division of Random House, Inc.** and electronic format by permission of **Harold Ober Associates Incorporated.**

"Poem" from *The Collected Poems of Langston Hughes.* Copyright © 1994 by The Estate of Langston Hughes. Reproduced by permission of **Alfred A. Knopf, a division of Random House, Inc.** and electronic format by permission of **Harold Ober Associates Incorporated.**

From "The Southpaw" by Judith Viorst from *Free to Be ... You and Me* by Marlo Thomas and Associates. Copyright © 1974 by Judith Viorst. All rights reserved. Reproduced by permission of **Lescher & Lescher, Ltd.**

"Hard on the Gas" from *Behind the Wheel: Poems About Driving* by Janet S. Wong. Copyright © 1999 by Janet S. Wong. Reproduced by permission of **Margaret K. McElderry Books, an imprint of Simon & Schuster Children's Publishing.**

"All Aboard with Thomas Garrett" by Alice P. Miller from *Cobblestone,* vol. 2, no. 2, February 1981. Copyright © 1981 by **The Estate of Alice P. Miller.** Reproduced by permission of the author.

The Hitchhiker by Lucille Fletcher. Copyright © 1947, 1952 and renewed © 1980 by Lucille Fletcher. Reproduced by permission of **William Morris Agency, LLC on behalf of the author.**

"The Golden Serpent" by Walter Dean Myers. Copyright © 1980 by Walter Dean Myers. Reproduced by permission of **Miriam Altshuler Literary Agency on behalf of the author.**

"Peace Parks Help Environment and Communities" by Sarah Ives from *National Geographic Kids News,* September 10, 2004. Copyright © 2004 by Sarah Ives. Reproduced by permission of **National Geographic Society.**

"'War of the Worlds': Behind the 1938 Radio Show Panic" by Stefan Lovgen from *National Geographic News,* June 17, 2005. Reproduced by permission of **National Geographic Society.**

"'Monster Writer' - Walter Dean Myers Knocks Out His 80th" from The *New York Post,* New York Pulse section, page 26. Copyright © 2004 by **NYP Holdings, Inc., www.nypost.com.** Reproduced by permission of the copyright holder.

"A Surprising Secret to a Long Life: Stay in School" (adapted), by Gina Kolata from *The New York Times,* January 3, 2007. Copyright © 2007 by **The New York Times Company.** Reproduced by permission of the copyright holder.

North Shore Animal League Pet Adoption Application. Copyright © 2000 by North Shore Animal League. Reproduced by permission of **North Shore Animal League, Port Washington, New York.**

"That Day" from *I Remember Root River* by David Kherdian. Copyright © 1978 by David Kherdian. Reproduced by permission of **The Overlook Press.**

"Do or Die" from *Gilgamesh the Hero* by Geraldine McCaughrean. Copyright © 2002 by Geraldine McCaughrean. Reproduced by permission of **Oxford University Press.**

"Little Mangy One" from *Arab Follktales* by Inea Bushnaq. Copyright © 1986 by Inea Bushnaq. Reproduced by pemission of **Pantheon Books, a division of Random House, Inc., www.randomhouse.com.**

Essay by Willie Reale. Copyright © 2007 by Willie Reale. Reproduced by permission of **Paradigm, Office of William Craver.**

From "Brave Hearts" (retitled "Trial by Fire") by Dan Jewel and Sophronia Scott Gregory from *People Weekly,* July 14, 1997. Copyright © 1997 by Time Inc. All rights reserved. Reproduced by permission of **People Weekly** and **Sophronia Scott Gregory.**

"The Jacket" from *The Effects of Knut Hamsun on a Fresno Boy: Recollections and Short Essays* by Gary Soto. Copyright © 1983, 2001 by Gary Soto. Reproduced by permission of **Persea Books, Inc., New York.**

"The Fly" by Penni L. Ericson from *PLAYS, The Drama Magazine for Young People,* vol. 66, issue 4, pp. 44-46, Jan/Feb 2007. Copyright © 2007 by Penni L. Ericson. Separate performance rights are required from the publisher. Reproduced by permission of **PLAYS/Sterling Partners, Inc., PO Box 600160, Newton, MA 02460.**

"Crocodile Gives Monkey a Ride" from *Rainforest Trio* adapted by Barbara Winther, from *PLAYS, The Drama Magazine for Young People,* vol. 66, issue 5, March 2007. Copyright © 2007 by Barbara Winther. Separate performance rights are required from the publisher. Reproduced by permission of **PLAYS/Sterling Partners, Inc., PO Box 600160, Newton, MA 02460.**

Scene 2 from "The Adventures of Tom Sawyer" by Mark Twain, adapted by Cheryl Capshaw from *PLAYS, The Drama Magazine for Young People,* vol. 63, issue 7, May 2004. Copyright © 2004 by Cheryl Capshaw. Separate performance rights are required from the publisher. Reproduced by permission of **PLAYS/Sterling Partners, Inc., PO Box 600160, Newton, MA 02460.**

Graphic: The Adventures of Tom Sawyer by **Michael Ploog.** Copyright © 1990 by The Berkley Publishing Group and First Publishing, Inc. Reproduced by permission of the author.

"Concha" by **Mary Helen Ponce,** the author of *Hoyt Street: An Autobiography.* Copyright © 2007 by the University of New Mexico Press. Reproduced by permission of the author.

Quote by Lillian Morrison from *Prentice Hall* Web site, accessed August 29, 2007, at http://phschool.com/atschool/literature/author_biographies/morrison_l.html. Copyright © 2007 by Lillian Morrison. Reproduced by permission of **Prentice Hall, Inc.**

Quote by Albert Einstein from *The New Quotable Einstein,* collected and edited by Alice Calaprice. Copyright © 2005 by Princeton University Press and the Hebrew University of Jerusalem. Reproduced by permission of **Princeton University Press.**

From *Bud, Not Buddy* by Christopher Paul Curtis. Copyright © 1999 by Christopher Paul Curtis. Reproduced by permission of **Random House Children's Books, a division of Random House, Inc., www.randomhouse.com** and CD-ROM format by permission of **Charlotte Sheedy Literary Agency.**

"Just Once" by Thomas Dygard from *Ultimate Sports,* edited by Donald R. Gallo. Copyright © 1995 by Thomas Dygard. Reproduced by permission of **Random House Children's Books, a division of Random House, Inc., www.randomhouse.com.**

"Priscilla and the Wimps" by Richard Peck from *Sixteen: Short Stories by Outstanding Writers for Young Adults,* edited by Donald R. Gallo. Copyright © 1984 by Richard Peck. Reproduced by permission of **Random House Children's Books, a division of Random House, Inc., www.randomhouse.com.**

"The Sneetches" from *The Sneetches and Other Stories* by Dr. Seuss. Copyright © 1953, 1954, 1961 and renewed © 1989 by Dr. Seuss Enterprises, L.P. Reproduced by permission of **Random House Children's Books, a division of Random House, Inc., www.randomhouse.com** and electronic format by permission of **Dr. Seuss Enterprises, L.P.**

Excerpt (retitled "Brother") from *I Know Why the Caged Bird Sings* by Maya Angelou. Copyright © 1969 and renewed © 1997 by Maya Angelou. Reproduced by permission of **Random House, Inc., www.randomhouse.com.**

Quote from "The Last Safe Place on Earth" by Richard Peck. Copyright © 2004 by Richard Peck. Reproduced by permission of **Random House, Inc., www.randomhouse.com.**

"The Sea" from *Complete Poems for Children* by James Reeves. Copyright © 1950 by James Reeves. Reproduced by permission of the **The James Reeves Estate.**

"An Old Silent Pond" by Bashō from *Cricket Songs: Japanese Haiku,* translated by Harry Behn. Copyright © 1964 by Harry Behn; copyright renewed © 1992 by Prescott Behn, Pamela Behn Adam, and Peter Behn. Reproduced by permission of **Marian Reiner, Literary Agent.**

"The Sidewalk Racer or On the Skateboard" from *The Sidewalk Racer and Other Poems of Sports and Motion* by Lillian Morrison. Copyright © 1965, 1967, 1968, 1977 by Lillian Morrison. Reproduced by permission of **Marian Reiner for Lillian Morrison.**

"A Glory over Everything" from *Harriet Tubman: Conductor on the Underground Railroad* by Ann Petry. Copyright © 1955, renewed © 1983 by Ann Petry. Reproduced by permission of **Russell & Volkening as agents for Ann Petry.**

"With the Union Army" (retitled from "Harriet Tubman: Conductor on the Underground Railroad") by Ann Petry. Copyright © 1955 by Ann Petry and renewed © 1983 by Ann Petry. Reproduced by permission of **Russell & Volkening as agents for Ann Petry.**

Quote by Gary Soto from *Scholastic* Web site, accessed August 29, 2007, at http://content.scholastic.com/browse/contributor.jsp?id=3642&printable=true. Copyright © 2007 by **Scholastic Inc.** Reproduced by permission of the publisher.

"Ta-Na-E-Ka" by Mary Whitebird from *Scholastic Voice,* December 13, 1973. Copyright © 1973 by **Scholastic Inc.** Reproduced by permission of the publisher.

"The California Gold Rush" by Kathy Wilmore from *Junior Scholastic,* December 1, 1997, vol. 100, no. 8. Copyright © 1997 by **Scholastic Inc.** Reproduced by permission of the publisher.

From a book review of Lois Lowry's *Number the Stars in School Library Journal,* vol. 35, no. 7, March 1989. Copyright © 1989 by Reed Business Information, a division of Reed Elsevier, Inc. Reproduced by permission of **School Library Journal.**

Excerpt (retitled "Two Frogs and the Milk Vat") from *Manchild in the Promised Land* by Claude Brown. Copyright © 1965 by Claude Brown. Reproduced by permission of **Scribner, an imprint of Simon & Schuster Adult Publishing Group.**

From "Pompeii" from *Lost Cities and Vanished Civilizations* by **Robert Silverberg.** Copyright © 1962 and renewed © 1990 by Agberg, Ltd. Reproduced by permission of the author.

Excerpt (retitled "Storm") from *Woodsong* by Gary Paulsen. Copyright © 1990 by Gary Paulsen. Reproduced by permission of **Simon & Schuster Books for Young Readers, an imprint of Simon & Schuster Children's Publishing Division** and electronic format by permission of Flannery Literary Agency.

Comment on "Summer School" by **Gary Soto.** Copyright © 1993 by Gary Soto. Reproduced by permission of the author.

Quote by Maya Angelou from *Black Women Writers at Work,* edited by **Claudia Tate.** Copyright © 1983 by Claudia Tate. Reproduced by permission of the copyright holder.

"The Dog of Pompeii" from *The Donkey of God* by Louis Untermeyer. Copyright © 1932 by Harcourt, Inc. Reproduced by permission of **Laurence S. Untermeyer on behalf of the Estate of Louis Untermeyer, Norma Anchin Untermeyer, c/o Professional Publishing Services Company.**

From "The Game" by Walter Dean Myers from *fast sam, cool clyde, and stuff.* Copyright © 1975 by Walter Dean Myers. Reproduced by permission of **Viking Penguin, division of Penguin Group (USA) Inc., www.penguin.com.**

From *All I Really Need to Know I Learned in Kindergarten* by Robert L. Fulghum. Copyright © 1986, 1988 by **Robert L. Fulghum.** Reproduced by permission of **Villard Books, a division of Random House, Inc.** and electronic format by permission of the author.

"Yes, It Was My Grandmother" from *A Breeze Swept Through* by Luci Tapahonso. Copyright © 1987 by Luci Tapahonso. Reproduced by permission of **West End Press.**

Essay by **Janet Wong.** Copyright © 2007 by Janet Wong. Reproduced by permission of the author.

From "Cynthia Rylant" from *Something About the Author,* vol. 50, edited by Anne Commire. Published by Gale Research, Inc., MI, 1988.

Quote by Marcia Williams from *Walker Books* Web site Copyright © 2005 by Marcia Williams.

PICTURE CREDITS

The illustrations and photographs on the Contents pages are picked up from pages in the textbook. Credits for those can be found either on the textbook page on which they appear or in the listing below.

Photo Credits: Page iii (all), Sam Dudgeon/HRW Photo; **iv** (bl, bc, br), Sam Dudgeon/HRW Photo; (tl), Courtesy of Hector Rivera; (tr), Courtesy of Eric Cooper; **v** (l, cl,), Sam Dudgeon/HRW Photo; (cr), Courtesy of Margaret McKeown; (r), Courtesy of Mabel Rivera; **vi** (all), Sam Dudgeon/HRW Photo; **vii** (tl), Reed Saxon/AP Photo; (tr), ©Randy Duchaine; (bl), ©Anne Lindsay Photography; (br), Courtesy of Willie Reale; **A4,** Courtesy of Agra-Art S. A.; **A5** (br), National Motor Museum, Beaulieu; **A6,** HRW photo by Nathan Keay, SMINK, Inc.; **A7** (bl), ©LeRoy Neiman; (bc, br), ©Everett Collection, Inc.; **A8,** © Jim Shores; **A9** (bl), ©Leonard de Selva/CORBIS; (br), ©Chad Baker/Getty Images; **A10–A11** (b), ©VisionsofAmerica/Joe Sohm/Getty Images; **A10** (tl), Courtesy of Sami Bentil; **A11** (bl), ©Westend 61/Alamy; **A12,** ©Stephen Chernin/Getty Images; **A13** (bl), ©Randy Olson/Getty Images; (br), Courtesy of Scott Kennedy; **A14,** ©Todd Gipstein/CORBIS; **A15** (br), ©Denis Farell/AP Photo; **A16,** ©Greg Pease/Getty Images; **A18,** ©Graeme Robertson/eyevine/ZUMA Press; **A19,** ©Hallmark Institute/Index Stock Imagery; **A30** (t inset), ©Group 9/Image Source Black/Alamy; (c), ©Peter Dazeley/Photodisc/Getty Images; (br), ©VEER Renee DeMartin/Getty Images; **A30–A31** (bkgd), ©Peter Dazeley/Photodisc/Getty Images; **A31** (br inset), ©Steve Satushek/Photographer's Choice/Getty Images; (bl inset), HRW Photo; (ribbons), ©Photodisc/Alamy; **0** (inset), Reed Saxon/AP Photo; (bkgd), ©Yagi Studio/SuperStock; **2–3,** Courtesy of Agra-Art S. A.; **3,** ©Gerard Fritz/Getty Images; **6,** ©Art Resource, NY; **11,** ©Hans Strand/CORBIS; **12–13,** ©Catherine Karnow/CORBIS; **14** (t), ©Jim Cooper/Getty Images; (b), Courtesy of John Cech; **16,** ©Stuart Cohen/The Image Works; **18** (l), Courtesy of Gary Soto; (r), ©Royalty-Free/CORBIS; **21,** ©Bettmann/CORBIS; **22,** ©Royalty-Free/CORBIS; **24,** ©Randy Faris/CORBIS; **28** (bkgd), ©Map Resources; (inset), National Motor Museum, Beaulieu; **30** (r), ©Michael Nelson/Getty Images; **33,** ©Connie Hayes; **35** (bkgd), ©Map Resources; **39,** ©Lake County Museum/CORBIS; **42** (bkgd), ©Map Resources; **46,** Courtesy of William Wegman; **48** (t), ©Arnold Adoff, used by permission; (b), ©Bettmann/CORBIS; **50,** ©Steve Maslowski/Getty Images; **51,** ©David Cole/Alamy; **52,** ©age fotostock/SuperStock; **53** (l), ©Royalty-Free/CORBIS; (r), ©Phyllis Greenberg/Animals Animals; **62,** The Daily Telegraph, London; **67** (t, b), ©Araldo de Luca/CORBIS; **74,** ©Awilli/Zefa/CORBIS; **76** (t), Milton Viorst; (b), Courtesy Mary Helen Ponce; **77** (t), ©Siede Preis/Royalty-free/Getty Images; (bl), ©Radius Images/Alamy; (bkgd), ©Brand X Pictures/Alamy; **78–79** (bkgd), ©Brand X Pictures/Alamy; **78** (l), ©Image Source/Getty Images; **79** (tr), ©Barry Bland/Alamy; **80** (l, bkgd), ©Brand X Pictures/Alamy; **82,** ©Hans Neleman/Getty Images; **83,** ©Ant Strack/CORBIS; **84,** ©Hans Neleman/Getty Images; **85,** ©Michael Newman/PhotoEdit, Inc.; **90,** ©Richard Hutchings/PhotoEdit, Inc.; **91,** (r) ©Private Collection/©Look and Learn/The Bridgeman Art Library; **93,** (r) ©Catherine Karnow/CORBIS; **102,** ©Gianni Dagli Orti/CORBIS; **103,** ©Petit Philippe/Paris-Match/GAMMA/Newscom; **104,** ©Sisse Brimberg/National Geographic Images/Getty Images; **110,** HRW Photo; **124** (tr), Cover image from Regarding the Sink by Kate Klise. Copyright ©2004 by Kate Klise. Reproduced by permission of Harcourt, Inc.; **125** (bl), Cover image from Ancient Mesopotamia: The Sumerians, Babylonians, and Assyrians by Virginia Schomp. Copyright ©2004 by Scholastic, Inc. Reproduced by permission of the publisher; (br), Cover image from But That's Another Story: Famous Authors Introduce Popular Genres, edited by Sandy Asher. Copyright ©1996 by Sandy Asher. Reproduced by permission of Walker and Company, Inc.; **126–127,** HRW photo by Nathan Keay, SMINK, Inc.; **134,** ©Bob Rowan/Progressive Image/CORBIS; **137,** ©Photodisc/Fotosearch Stock Photography; **138** (t), ©Christopher Stevenson/zefa/CORBIS; (b), ©Stuart Ramson/Associated Press; **140,** ©LeRoy Neiman; **142** (l), University of Arkansas; (r), ©Comstock Images/Alamy; **145,** ©Stockbyte Silver/Alamy; **152,** ©Digital Art/CORBIS; **154,** ©Associated Press; **155, 157,** ©Anthony Redpath/CORBIS; **158,** ©Antonio Rosario/The Image Bank/Getty Images; **159,** ©Private Collection/The Bridgeman Art Library; **166** (l), Courtesy of The Brancroft Library. University of California, Berkeley, 4/80 Banc pic1986.059:268; (r), Courtesy of The Brancroft Library. University of California, Berkeley, 1986.059:215pic; **167** (r), HRW Photo; **168** (l), Dorothea Lange/National Archives; (r), HRW Photo; **171** (r), Courtesy of The Brancroft Library. University of California, Berkeley, Bancmss86/97 0S 12:4; (bkgd), HRW Photo; **172,** HRW Photo; **176** (tr), Courtesy of the Walter Dean Myers Collection; (tl), ©Nancy Kaszerman/Zuma Press; (cr), Courtesy of the Walter Dean Myers Collection; (c), ©Brian Heath; **178,** ©Hugh Grannum/Knight Ridder/Tribune/Newscom; **179,** ©Brian Heath; **180** (c), Courtesy of the Walter Dean Myers Collection; **181,** Courtesy of Constance Myers; **183,** ©Anne-Marie Weber/Getty Images; **185,** ©Photodisc/Getty Images; **193** (inset), ©Jim Erickson/CORBIS; (border), ©Photodisc/Getty Images; **196,** ©Dorothea Lange/CORBIS; **198,** Dorothea Lange/National Archive; **200** (t), Library of Congress; (c), ©Douglas Kirkland/CORBIS; (b), ©CORBIS; **202,** ©Wally McNamee/CORBIS; (c) ©Douglas Kirkland/CORBIS; (b) ©David Valdez/White House/Sygma/CORBIS; **206,** (tr) ©Everett Collection, Inc.; (c) ©CBS/Photofest; (cr) ©Everett Collection, Inc.; **207,** Courtesy of The Brancroft Library. University of California, Berkeley, 1967.014v. ts,eh-706pic; **214,** HRW Photo; **228** (tr), Cover image from Life As We Knew It by Susan Beth Pfeffer. Copyright ©2006 by Susan Beth Pfeffer. Reproduced by permission of Harcourt, Inc.; (br), Cover image from Roughnecks by Thomas Cochran. Copyright ©1997 by Thomas Cochran. Reproduced by permission of Harcourt, Inc.; (bl), Cover image from Love That Dog by Sharon Creech. Copyright ©2001 by Sharon Creech. Reproduced by permission of HarperCollins Publishers, Inc.; **229** (tr), Cover image from How We Lived: Invasion, War, and Travel, edited by Dr. John Haywood. Copyright ©2001, 2006 by Anness Publishing, Ltd. Reproduced by permission of the publisher; (bl), Cover image from Here's Looking at Me: How Artists See Themselves by Bob Raczka. Copyright ©2006 by Bob Raczka. Reproduced by permission of Millbrook Press; **230–231,** ©Jim Shores; **234–235,** ©Melissa Moseley/Sony Pictures/Bureau L.A./CORBIS; **238,** ©John Vachon/CORBIS; **241,** ©Jeff Greenberg/PhotoEdit. Inc; **242** (t), ©Jim West/The Image Works; (b), ©Miriam Berkley; **244,** ©1989 Carmen Lomas Garza; **246** (bl), ©Ulf Andersen/Getty Images; (br), ©Bryce Harper; **249,** ©Rosa Ibarra/Omni-Photo Communications; **250,** ©Michael Prince/CORBIS; **253,** ©Elyse Lewin/Brand X Pictures/Jupiter Images; **254,** ©Layne Kennedy/CORBIS; **256** (l), ©Bettmann/CORBIS; (r), ©Robert Holmes/CORBIS; **257,** ©Julian Winslow/CORBIS; **259,** ©Colin Hawkins/Getty Images; **262,** ©Karen Su/CORBIS; **264–265,** ©2007 Vladimir Vinitzki/AlaskaStock; **270,** ©Private Collection/The Bridgeman Art Library; **272,** ©Dave Bartruff/

CORBIS; **274** (bkgd), A & J Verkaik/CORBIS; **275** (inset), ©Reuters/ CORBIS; (bkgd), A & J Verkaik/CORBIS; **276,** ©PhotoSpin, Inc/ Alamy; **280,** ©20th Century Fox Film Corp. All rights reserved/ Courtesy Everett Collection; **282** (t), ©Random House; (c), Courtesy Candlewick Press; (b), ©Bettmann/CORBIS; **283** (t), Kunsthistorisches Museum, Vienna, Austria/Erich Lessing/Art Resource, NY; **285,** Bridgeman Art Library/Getty Images; **286,** ©The Makins Collection/Bridgeman Art Library; **288,** ©Henson Associates/Photofest; **291,** ©Bibliotheque des Arts Decoratifs, Paris, France/Archives Charmet/The Bridgeman Art Library; **292,** Loggia dei Lanzi, Florence, Italy/©Glenn Harper/ Alamy; **298,** ©Chad Baker/Getty Images; **299,** ©Everett Collection, Inc.; **301** (bkgd), ©Chad Baker/Getty Images; **302** (inset), ©Everett Collection, Inc.; (bkgd), ©Chad Baker/Getty Images; **304,** ©Paramount Pictures Photographers: Joe Pearce, Laura Ridley/Photofest; **308,** ©Dynamic Graphics Group/Alamy; **310** (bkgd), AP Photo/David J. Phillip; (inset), ©Erich Lessing/Art Resource, NY; **312–313,** ©Pete Saloutos/CORBIS; **314,** ©Leonard de Selva/CORBIS; 317 (tl), ©Jules Frazier/Getty Images; (tr), ©PhotoSpin, Inc./Alamy; (bkgd), ©Peter Dazeley/Getty Images; **318–319** (bkgd) ©Peter Dazeley/Getty Images; **319** (tr), ©Clive Mason/Getty Images; (tl), ©Bill Hickey/The Image Bank/Getty Images; **320** (t), ©Jeff Greenberg/The Image Works; (bkgd), ©Peter Dazeley/Getty Images; **326,** ©CORBIS; **340** (tr), Cover image from Perseus, retold by Geraldine McCaughrean. Copyright ©2003 by Geraldine McCaughrean. Reproduced by permission of Oxford University Press; (br), Cover image from PaperQuake: a Puzzle by Kathryn Reiss. Copyright ©1998 by Kathryn Reiss. Reproduce by permission of Harcourt, Inc.; **341** (tr), Cover image from Jesse Owens: Champion Athlete by Tom Gentry. Copyright ©2005 by Chelsea House Publishers, a subsidiary of Haights Cross Communications. Reproduced by permission of the publisher; (bl), Cover image from You Wouldn't Want to be a Greek Athlete! by Michael Ford. Copyright ©2004 by The Salariya Book Company Ltd. Reproduced by permission of the copyright holder.; (br), Cover image from Gold Rush Dogs by Claire Rudolf Murphy and Jane G. Haigh. Copyright ©2001 by Alaska Northwest Books, an imprint of Graphic Arts Publishing Company. Reproduced by permission of the publisher; **342–343,** Courtesy of Sami Bentil; **343** (r), ©Sylvain Grandadam/Getty Images; **347,** Musee d'Art et d'Histoire, St. Denis, France/Scala/Art Resource, NY; **351,** ©Syracuse Newspapers/Mike Roy/The Image Works; **353,** ©Design Pics Inc./Alamy; **354,** Margaret Miller; **356,** ©Alison Wright/CORBIS; **358** (t), ©Werner Forman/Art Resource, NY; (b), ©Tim Platt/Getty Images; **361,** ©Worldwide Picture Library/Alamy; **362** (t), ©Jonathan Kantor/Getty Images; (b), ©image100/CORBIS; **363,** ©Portraits Now Expressions; **365,** ©Pam Ingalls/CORBIS; **370,** ©Westend 61/Alamy; **372,** Courtesy of Lensey Namioka; **375** (b), ©Royalty-Free/ CORBIS; **376,** ©Kevin Dodge/CORBIS; **379,** ©Sean Justice/Getty Images; **384,** ©Annie Griffiths Belt/CORBIS; **386** (cr), Hulton Archive/Getty Images; (bl), Courtesy of Myron Levoy; (br), ©Rudy Sulgan/CORBIS; **387,** ©Patrick Byrd/Alamy; **388,** ©Robert Brenner/Photo Edit; **390,** ©Neil Snape/Getty Images; **393,** ©Time & Life Pictures/Getty Images; **394,** ©DK Limited/ CORBIS; **398,** Steve C. Wilson/AP Photo; **400** (t), ©Bettmann/ CORBIS; (c), ©Miriam Berkley; (b), ©Robert Maass/CORBIS; **401,** ©Scala/Art Resource, NY; **410,** ©Roger Ressmeyer/CORBIS; **414–419,** (bkgd) ©VisionsofAmerica/Joe Sohm/Getty Images; **420** (t), ©VisionsofAmerica/Joe Sohm/Getty Images; **421** (tl), ©Taro Yamasaki/Time & Life Pictures/Getty Images; **424,** ©The Cats' House; **426,** ©Rena Durham/ZUMA/newscom; **429** (bkgd), ©Co Rentmeester Inc./Getty Images; (inset), HRW Photo; **430, 431** (all), Scott B. Rosen/HRW Photo; **432,** ©Royalty-Free/ CORBIS; **438,** HRW Photo; **452** (tl), Cover image from The Heart of a Chief by Joseph Bruchac. Copyright ©1998 by Joseph Bruchac. Reproduced by permission of Dial Books for Young Readers, a division of Penguin Group (USA) Inc., www.penguin.com; (br), Cover image from A Dog's Life: The Autobiography of a Stray by Ann M. Martin. Copyright ©2005 by Matt Mahurin. Reproduced by permission of Scholastic, Inc.; **453** (tr), Cover image from Endangered Bats by Bobbie Kalman. Copyright ©2006 by Crabtree Publishing Company. Reproduced by permission of the publisher; (bl), Cover image from Pompeii: City of Ashes by Sarah Pitt Kaplan. Copyright ©2005 by Rosen Book Works, Inc. Cover art copyright by Roger Ressmeyer/ Corbis. Reproduced by permission of Children's Press, an imprint of Scholastic Library Publishing; **454** (inset), ©Randy Duchaine; (bkgd), ©Garry Gay/Getty Images; **456–457,** ©Stephen Chernin/ Getty Images; **457** (r), ©Travel Ink/Getty Images; **464,** ©Goodshoot/CORBIS; **465,** ©Mike Greenslade/Alamy; **467,** ©Steve Smith/Getty Images; **468** (t), ©Arthur S Aubry/ Stockbyte/Getty Images; (b), Courtesy of Gary Soto; **470,** ©Hyancinth Manning/SuperStock; **472** (l), ©Syracuse Newspapers/Frank Ordonez/The Image Works; (r), ©David Sanger Photography/Alamy; (br), Photo Courtesy of the National Endowment for the Arts; **473,** ©Michele Salmieri/ Masterfile; **478,** ©John William Banagan/Getty Images; **480,** ©2005 Antonia Deutsch/Getty Images; **481,** ©Owen Franken/Getty Images; **483,** ©Bertrand Gardel/Getty Images; **485,** ©Tim Page/CORBIS; **486–487,** ©Randy Olson/Getty Images; **492,** ©Gulliver Books; Harcourt, Inc.; New York, NY; **494** (l), Jacob Harris/AP/Wide World Photos; (r), ©Bettmann/ CORBIS; **497,** ©Bridgeman Art Library; **501** (r), ©North Wind Picture Archives/Alamy; (bkgd), ©Stanley Walker/Syracuse Newspapers/The Image Works; **506** Private Collection/ Bridgeman Art Library; **508** (t), Random House; (c), Houghton Mifflin Company; (b), ©Jim Shea/AP/Wide World Photos; **509,** Courtesy of Scott Kennedy; **510–513,** Courtesy of Scott Kennedy; **517** (bkgd), ©Morton Beebe/CORBIS; (inset), ©The Corcoran Gallery of Art/CORBIS; **519** (bkgd), ©Hugh Talman/ Smithsonian Images; (inset), ©Bettmann/CORBIS; **520,** ©Alan Schein Photography/CORBIS; **522** (all), Mark Preston/HRW; **523,** ©Dante Fenolio/Photo Researchers, Inc.; **525, 527, 528,** Mark Preston/HRW; **534** (bl), ©Folio Inc/Alamy; (br), Courtesy of the Historical Society of Delaware; (bkgd), ©Jeremy Woodhouse/Getty Images; **535** (bkgd), ©Louie Psihoyos/CORBIS; (inset), Courtesy of the Historical Society of Delaware; **538,** Private Collection, Photo c Christie's Images/The Bridgeman Art Library; **540,** ©Louie Psihoyos/CORBIS; **543** (l), ©age fotostock/SuperStock; (r), ©Folio Inc/Alamy; **544,** ©Stockbyte/Getty Images; **545, 546, 547, 548,** Photo: The Jacob and Gwendolyn Lawrence Foundation/Art Resource, NY; **554,** HRW Photo; **573** (tl), ©Getty Images; (tr), Cover image from Faces: People, Places, and Cultures, April 2007. Cover copyright ©2007 by Thinkstock/Alamy. Reproduced by permission of Cobblestone Publishing, Inc; (bl), ©Getty Images; (br), ©Adriana Zehbrauskas/Polaris Images; **574–575,** ©Todd Gipstein/CORBIS; **575** (br), ©Peter Dazeley/Getty Images; **582–583** (bkgd), ©Artifacts Images/Getty Images; **583,** ©Will & Deni McIntyre/ CORBIS; **584** (bkgd), ©Artifacts Images/Getty Images; (inset), ©Robin Nelson/Zuma/CORBIS; **586** (bkgd), ©Artifacts Images/ Getty Images; (inset), ©blue jean images/Getty Images;

588, ©David Deas/Getty Images; **590,** ©Hans Neleman/Getty Images; **593** (tl), ©Brad Wrobleski/Masterfile; (tr), ©Nick White/ Getty Images; (b), ©Sylvain Grandadam/Getty Images; **594,** ©Tim Pannell/CORBIS; **597** (bkgd), Photos.com; (inset), ©Fani Mahuntsi/Images24; **598,** ©Louise Gubb/CORBIS; **599,** ©Denis Farell/AP Photo; **600,** ©AFP PHOTO/Joe Alexander/Newscom; **603** (bkgd), ©Timothy Hearsum/Getty Images; (inset), ©Steve & Ann Toon/Robert Harding World Imagery/CORBIS; **604** (t), ©Gregor Schuster/Getty Images; (bkgd), ©Timothy Hearsum/ Getty Images; (inset), Courtesy of Parks Canada; **608–609** (bkgd), ©UntitledOne productions inc./Getty Images; **608** (tr), ©David Toase/Getty Images; (c), ©Digital Vision/Getty Images; **609** (tc), ©David Toase/Getty Images; (br), ©David Toase/Getty Images; **612–613,** ©Allana Wesley White/CORBIS; **626,** Victoria Smith/HRW Photo; **638** (tl), Cover image for Media Madness: An Insider's Guide to Media by Dominic Ali. Illustrations copyright ©2005 by Michael Cho. Reproduced by permission of Kids Can Press Ltd.; (bl), Cover image from Oprah Winfrey by Heather Hudak. Copyright ©2006 by Weigl Publishers Inc. Reproduced by permission of the publishers; (tr), Cover image by National Geographic from My Life with the Chimpanzees by Jane Goodall. Copyright 1988, 1996 by Byron Preiss Visual Publications, Inc. Reproduced by permission of National Geographic Society; (br), Cover image for At the Controls: Questioning Video and Computer Games by Neil Anderson. Copyright ©2007 by Capstone Press. Reproduced by permission of the publisher. Cover photos ©David Hsu/Shutterstock; **639** (tl), Cover image from Explorers Wanted! On Safari by Simon Chapman. Copyright ©2003 by Simon Chapman. Reproduced by permission of Little, Brown and Company; (tr), Cover image from Advertising by Bess Milton. Cover copyright ©2004 by Lester Lefkowitz/Corbis. Reproduced by permission of Children's Press, an imprint of Scholastic Library Publishing; (br), Cover image from Television and Movies by Philip Abraham. Copyright ©2004 by Rosen Book Works, Inc. Reproduced by permission of Children's Press, an imprint of Scholastic Library Publishing; (bl), Cover image from Internet: Electronic global village by David Jefferis. Copyright ©2002 by David Jefferis and Alpha Communications. Reproduced by permission of Crabtree Publishing Company; **640** (inset), ©Anne Lindsay Photography; (bkgd), ©Visions of America/Joe Sohm/Getty Images; **642–643,** ©Greg Pease/Getty Images; **643** (br), ©John Foxx/ Getty Images; **649,** Courtesy of Jeff Lavaty; **652–653,** ©Kim Westerskov/Getty Images; **656,** Everett Collection, Inc.; **658** (bl), ©James L. Amos/CORBIS; (br), AFP PHOTOS/USPS/Newscom; **661** (t), ©Randy Duchaine; **666,** John Henry Stamp Design ©1996 United States Postal Service. All Rights Reserved. Used with Permission; **668–669,** ©Martin Diebel/Getty Images; **670,** ©John Kelly/Getty Images; **673** (b), ©Hulton Archive/Getty Images; **674,** ©Geoff Manasse/Getty Images; **675** (inset), ©Christie's Images/CORBIS; (bkgd), ©John Foxx/Getty Images; **676** (t), ©Geoff Brightling/Getty Images; (b), ©Dave King/Getty Images; **677** (t), ©blickwinkel/Meyers/Alamy; (b), ©Christopher Scott/Alamy; **678,** ©Bettmann/CORBIS; **682** (t), ©Ulf Andersen/ Getty Images; (c), ©Cheron Bayna; (b), Courtesy of David Kherdian; **683,** ©Tetra Images/Getty Images; **684,** ©FLILET Patrick/Hemis/Alamy; **685** (l), Collection of Aaron & Marion Borenstein, Miami, Florida. ©1995 Carmen Lomas Garza; (br), ©ZenShui/Michele Constantini/Getty Images; **686,** ©LWA-Dann Tardif/CORBIS; **687** (bkgd), ©LWA-Dann Tardif/CORBIS; (inset), Courtesy of David Kherdian; **690,** ©blickwinkel/Alamy; **692** (t), Courtesy of Gary Soto; (c), ©Neil Michael/Axiom; (b), ©Anne Lindsay Photography; **693,** ©Leana Alagia/Getty Images; **694,** ©SuperStock, Inc.; **695** (bkgd), ©Peter Dazeley/Getty Images; (inset), ©Frank Conaway/Getty Images; **696** (bkgd), ©Peter Dazeley/Getty Images; (l), ©Larry Brownstein/Getty Images; (r), ©Jeff Foott/Getty Images; **697,** ©Dave & Les Jacobs/ Alamy; **700** (bl), Hulton Archive/Getty Images; (br), ©Stewart Smith/Illustration Works/Getty Images; **701,** Veer; **702,** ©Gilbert Mayers/SuperStock; **705** (t), ©Snark/Art Resource, NY; (b), ©Robert Kradin/AP Photos; **706–707,** ©Christie's Images/ SuperStock; **710,** ©CORBIS; **712** (t), ©Oscar White/CORBIS; (bc), photo by Elizabeth Gilliland; (b), Courtesy of Bobbi Katz; **714** (t), ©Steven Puetzer/Getty Images; (b), ©Albert Normandin/ Masterfile; **716** (bkgd), ©John Chard/Getty Images; (t), ©Chris Trotman/CORBIS; **724,** HRW Photo; **732,** ©George Diebold/ Getty Images; **736** (tl), Cover image from Rimshots by Charles R. Smith. Copyright ©1999 by Charles R. Smith Jr. Reproduced by permission of Penguin Books for Young Readers, a division of Penguin Group (USA) Inc., www.penguin.com; (br), Cover image from Langston Hughes: Young Black Poet by Montrew Dunham. Copyright ©1972 by the Bobbs-Merrill Company, Inc. Reproduced by permission of Simon & Schuster Children's Publishing Division.; (tr), Cover image by Leticia Tarrago from The Tree is Older Than You Are by Naomi Shihab Nye. Copyright ©1995 by Naomi Shihab Nye. Reproduced by permission of Simon & Schuster Children's Publishing Division; **737** (tr), Cover image from Poetry Matters: Writing a poem from the Inside Out by Ralph Fletcher. Copyright ©2002 by Ralph Fletcher. Reproduced by permission of HarperCollins Publishers, Inc.; (tl), Cover image from Whisked Away by Richard Brown. Copyright ©1993 by Cambridge University Press. Reproduced by permission of the publisher; (bl), Cover image from Home: A Journey Through America by Thomas Locker. Copyright ©1998 by Thomas Locker. Reproduced by permission of Harcourt, Inc.; **738** (inset), courtesy of Willie Reale; (bc), Courtesy of Arden Theatre Company, Philadelphia, PA; (bl), Courtesy of PLAYBILL; (br), Courtesy of PLAYBILL; (bkgd), Green Shoots Communications/Alamy; **740–741,** ©Graeme Robertson/ eyevine/ZUMA Press; **741** (r), ©Jayme Thornton/Getty Images; **744,** ©Stefano Bianchetti; **745,** ©Richard Termine; **749,** ©Sean Sprague/The Image Works; **752,** Chau Doan/OnAsia; **756** (l), Courtesy of Angel Vigil; (br), ©Alan Hanson/Alamy; **774,** ©Allan Davey/Masterfile; 776 (bl), California State University, Northridge; (br), ©Barney Taxel, 1993, Courtesy of the Cleveland Play House; **777,** ©Photowood Inc./CORBIS; **783,** ©Zac Macaulay/Getty Images; **784,** ©Chris E. Heisey/Place Photography; **788,** ©Douglas Black/Trevillion Images; **790** (cr), ©Bettmann/CORBIS; (bl), Special Collections, Vassar College Libraries; (br), ©Everett Collection, Inc.; **791,** ©Raymond K Gehman/Getty Images; **793,** ©Lake County Museum/CORBIS; **795,** ©Dale O'Dell/Alamy; **797,** ©Hallmark Institute/Index Stock Imagery; **799, 800,** ©Patrick Strattner/Getty Images; **803,** Art Resource, NY; **804,** ©Ingram Publishing (Superstock Limited)/ Alamy; **808** (tl), ©Mary Evans Picture Library/The Image Works; (b), ©Joan Marcus; **810,** (c) Courtesy of Plays Magazine; (b) Courtesy of Michael Ploog; **814,** ©Mary Evans Picture Library/ The Image Works; **815,** From The Adventures of Tom Sawyer ©2004 by Mark Twain, Illustrations by Scott McKowen. Used with permission from Sterling Publishing Co., Inc.; **816–817,** ©Mike Wimmer; **818,** ©Santokh Kochar/Getty Images; **819** (b), ©Joan Marcus; **831,** ©adoc-photos/Art Resource, NY; **835,** ©Photofest; **837,** Dreamworks/Paramount/The Kobal Collection; **839,** Dreamworks/Paramount/The Kobal Collection;

840, ©Bettmann/CORBIS; **846,** HRW Photo; **858** (tl), Cover image from Theater Shoes by Noel Streatfeild. Copyright ©1945 and renewed ©1973 by Noel Streatfeild. Reproduced by permission of Random House Children's Books, www.randomhouse.com; (tr), Cover image from The Shakespeare Stealer by Gary Blackwood. Copyright ©1998 by Gary Blackwood. Reproduced by permission of Penguin Books for Young Readers, a division of Penguin Group (USA) Inc., www.penguin.com; **859** (tl), Cover image from Backstage at a Movie Set by Katherine Wessling. Copyright ©2003 by Rosen Book Works, Inc. Reproduced by permission of Globe Photos, Inc.; (bl), Cover image from Short Scenes and Monologues for Middle School Actors by Mary Hall Surface. Copyright ©1999 by Mary Hall Surface. Reproduced by permission of Smith and Kraus, Inc.; (tr), Cover image from Acting and Theatre by Cheryl Evans and Lucy Smith. Reproduced by permission of EDC Publishing; (br), Cover image from Under the Greenwood Tree: Shakespeare for Young People, edited by Barbara Holdridge. Copyright ©1986 By Stemmer House Publishers, Inc. Reproduced by permission of the publisher; **861,** ColorBlind Images/Getty Images.

INDEX OF SKILLS

The boldface page numbers indicate an extensive treatment of the topic.

The Index of Skills is divided into the following categories:

LITERARY SKILLS

Informational Text Skills

VOCABULARY SKILLS

READING SKILLS

WRITING SKILLS

FCAT PREPARATION

LANGUAGE SKILLS (GRAMMAR, USAGE, AND MECHANICS)

LISTENING AND SPEAKING SKILLS

READ ON

INDEX OF AUTHORS AND TITLES